General History of the Caribbean – V

General History of the Caribbean

Titles in the series

Volume I Autochthonous Societies

Volume II New Societies: The Caribbean in the 'Long' Sixteenth Century

Volume III The Slave Societies of the Caribbean

Volume IV The Long Nineteenth Century: Nineteenth-Century Transformations

Volume V The Caribbean in the Twentieth Century

Volume VI Methodology and Historiography of the Caribbean

General History of the Caribbean

Volume V

The Caribbean in the Twentieth Century

Editor: Bridget Brereton

Co-editors: Teresita Martínez-Vergne, René A. Römer and Blanca G. Silvestrini

palgrave macmillan

UNESCO

UNESCO Publishing

First published in 2003
Published jointly by
UNESCO Publishing, Paris, France, and Macmillan Publishers Ltd, London and Oxford
This edition published in 2007 by
PALGRAVE MACMILLAN ™
175 Fifth Avenue, New York, N.Y. 10010 and
Houndmills, Basingstoke, Hampshire, England RG21 6XS
Companies and representatives throughout the world.

PALGRAVE MACMILLAN is the global academic imprint of the Palgrave Macmillan division of St Martin's Press, LLC and of Palgrave Macmillan Ltd. Macmillan® is a registered trademark in the United States, United Kingdom and other countries. Palgrave is a registered trademark in the European Union and other countries.

ISBN-13: 978-1-4039-7593-5

Library of Congress Cataloging-in-Publication Data is available from the Library of Congress.

A catalogue record for this book is available from the British Library.

10 9 8 7 6 5 4 3 2
2011 2010 2009 2008 2007

Transferred to Digital Printing 2011

Contents

PREFACE

Federico Mayor
Director-General of UNESCO, 1987–99

How should the Caribbean be defined? It is here understood as encompassing not only the islands but also the coastal part of South America, from Colombia to the Guyanas and the riverine zones of Central America, insofar as these parts of the mainland were the homes of people engaged from time to time in activities which linked their lives with those of people in the islands. Despite the varieties of languages and customs resulting from the convergence there – by choice or constraint – of peoples of diverse cultures, the Caribbean has many cultural commonalities deriving from the shared history and experience of its inhabitants. In this region, endowed with exceptionally beautiful landscapes and still undiscovered ocean resources, there grew up from the sixteenth century onwards a completely new society, which has in our own time distinguished itself by producing a relatively large number of internationally recognized personalities in many fields – poets, novelists, painters, dancers, designers, musicians, sportsmen, jurists, historians, politicians.

In seeking to promote the preservation of cultural identities and greater understanding among peoples through the exchange of cultural information, UNESCO has found it important to facilitate the writing of a new history of this region. I call this history 'new' because until quite recently Caribbean histories were more about exploits of European nation states in the Caribbean – histories of war and trade in the islands and the mainland. Such histories of the individual islands as were published before this time tended to be written from the standpoint of resident Europeans. It was the movement for political autonomy, and the broadening of historiography in the European and American universities in the first half of the century, that led initially to changes of emphasis in the study of the history of single islands, and later to histories of topics which linked the islands, notably the sugar industry, slavery, slave laws and Asian immigration.

In the established universities of Havana and Puerto Rico and in new ones such as the University of the West Indies, departments of Caribbean studies were opened with the aim of undertaking teaching and research on Caribbean literature, history, culture and society, the better to understand forces that had shaped the region and to identify the many elements which constitute Caribbean culture. The main findings of the scholars since then are reflected in the six volumes of this history, thereby presenting a more regional account than before of the Caribbean past and of the people who have constituted Caribbean society.

This history traces the development of the region starting with the autochthonous peoples of the Caribbean. This includes the hunters and the gatherers as well as the incipient cultivators associated with the beginnings of village life. Situated as they were at what had become the gateway to the New World, these populations were the first to be enslaved. The inhabitants of the Greater Antilles were decimated by acts of excessive inhumanity and disease. The Caribs survived longer through their well-honed fighting skills, but their numbers dwindled nevertheless and in the eighteenth century those who still resisted were transported to the coast of Belize where they established communities that exist to this day and from where they now return to teach their native language – 'Garifuna' – to the few Caribs who remain in Dominica and in St Vincent. The story of these early societies is told in the first two volumes.

Volume III of this history (The Slave Societies) will constitute a central point of reference. In examining the creation of new societies, full account is taken of slavery, the terrible toll of human life and suffering it exacted and its pervasive impact on the psyche of the Caribbean people, both white and black. Resistance to slavery took many forms, of which marronnage in Haiti, Jamaica and Suriname, where the numbers were large, has received the most attention. Revolts and rebellions persisted throughout the region from the seventeenth century, although the best known is understandably that which led to Haiti's independence at the beginning of the nineteenth century. The abolition of the British slave trade left slavery itself intact, until it gradually succumbed in the decades of the nineteenth century, first to the creed of the French Revolution, then to the combination of slave rebellions in the islands and the determined protestations of humanitarians and free traders in Europe.

By the middle of the nineteenth century the disputes between estate owners and the emancipated field labourers, referred to in Volumes I and IV, opened the way for the influx of people from Asia, predominantly from India, thus adding a new element to the Creole societies which had gradually been formed since the sixteenth century. To avoid this supply of new labour for sugar estates becoming the restoration of slavery in a new guise, the recruitment of the labourers and their condition of work in the islands were regulated by law. Nevertheless, the constraints of indenture and the indignities attendant on being estate labourers affected the way in which Creole societies developed in the twentieth century. Undoubtedly, slavery and indenture have influenced the social and economic relations of societies in the circum-Caribbean in ways productive of ethnic and class conflict. Yet they have not only been the sources of cruelty and injustice, of acts remembered and resented. By persistent resistance to these oppressive regimes, these societies have also endowed themselves with the dignity and self-confidence of free men.

During the latter part of the nineteenth century, the impulse towards autonomy which was felt by some of the propertied and educated elites was frustrated by international, political and economic circumstances outside their control. The production of sugar from cane continued to dominate the Caribbean economies, with oil, minerals and tourism becoming important items in the twentieth century. The influx of American capital and the gradual diminution of European interests in the Caribbean led to the expansion of American influence in the region from the turn of the century onwards, notably in Cuba, Haiti and Santo Domingo. This was the context in which the movements for self-determination worked, complicated everywhere by racial prejudice and disparities in the ownership of property.

In the years following the Second World War, examined in Volume V, the islands and their immediate mainland neighbours have sought a variety of solutions to the problems which arise from societies asserting political autonomy while possessing economies dependent on overseas markets where their goods are protected from competition. Puerto Rico became the 'Estado Libre', a Commonwealth; the French-speaking islands became departments of France; the Dutch-speaking islands, prior to the independence of Suriname, all became part of the Kingdom of the Netherlands; the British islands first flirted with a Federation, then became independent states separately; other states, following periods of military dictatorship, have pursued the path of socialist revolution. Currently, both in the islands and on the continent, there is a growing tendency for policy to be guided by regionalism, by the impulse towards association and co-operation, towards the formation of trading blocs, initially prompted by geographical propinquity.

These subregions have recently begun concerted efforts towards recognizing and confirming that their mutual interests will be served by closer association. It is therefore appropriate that the two UNESCO projects of the *General History of the Caribbean* and the *General History of Latin America* are being undertaken simultaneously. The two histories should be read together as distinct parts of a unified whole, as an element in UNESCO's contribution to regional development through mutual understanding and cultural integration. Every effort will be made for both histories to reach as wide a public as possible in the major languages of the region, through the universities, through the schools by means of specially adapted versions (textbooks and children's books), and eventually through radio and television, plays and films.

I wish, in conclusion, to extend my sincere thanks to the Chairman, Rapporteur and members of the International Scientific Committee and to the editors and authors of the various volumes who have come together to participate in this significant enterprise. My thanks also go to the governments and universities which have supported the project and to the Association of Caribbean Historians, so many of whose members have contributed generously to the creation of this work.

Description of the Project

Professor Sir Roy Augier
Chairman of the Drafting Committee for
the General History of the Caribbean

The decision to commission a UNESCO General History of the Caribbean, taken by the twenty-first session of the General Conference of UNESCO (1980), was an instance of the change in cultural policy which resulted in a shift in emphasis from the 'common heritage of all mankind' to acknowledging the 'diversity of cultures' and commissioning the histories of Africa, Central Asia, Latin America and the Caribbean, as well as a revision of the *History of Mankind*. In all these cases, the brief of the Director-General was for a history observed from inside the region not from the outside, as if from the ports and capitals of European colonizers. Cultural identity, unity in diversity, and therefore the cultural heritages of the regions, were to inform the themes chosen for the history, giving prominence to those groups, persons and cultures hitherto either excluded from historical narratives, or treated more as objects than as actors in the description of events.

By December 1981, when the Working Group for the Preparation of a General History of the Caribbean met in Paris, the ideas and aims expressed by the UNESCO General Conferences of 1978 and 1980 were widely shared by the twenty scholars, Caribbean and European, whom the Director-General had invited in their personal capacity to break ground for the project. The aspirations of the ground-breakers embraced geography, anthropology, archaeology, ethnography, demography, society, religion, politics, ethnicity, culture, rituals, customs, socio-linguistics, music, dance, festivals, oral tradition, historiography, and cartography. One is tempted to conclude *etcetera*, and rightly so, because their successors noticed that, in 1981, the Working Group had overlooked gender and the environment. The inclusiveness of their vision of the history of the Caribbean was, no doubt, due to the desire of the twenty scholars that the history of its people and their habitat should be written as if observed from inside the region.

How was this vision to be made concrete in a few volumes, limited to twenty chapters each? How, within that general framework, to deal adequately with the wide diversity of size, ancestry, religion, language, custom, politics? How to set the chronological limits to volumes without cutting off themes artificially? How to integrate the material into a Caribbean narrative and avoid writing history as merely summary accounts of the larger islands?

The task was given to the Drafting Committee which first met in Kingston in April 1983. Of its nineteen members, twelve were from the Caribbean and seven from Africa, India, Europe and the Americas. At first, the Committee used the text of the Report of the Working Group (1981) to elicit the themes significant for Caribbean history. But in the discussion which followed, the form of organization proposed by the Working Group was abandoned and replaced by five themes which would make for a coherent history of the Caribbean region while being consonant with the UNESCO guidelines.

These were Autochthonous Societies, New Societies: The Long Sixteenth Century, Slave Societies, The Long Nineteenth Century, The Caribbean in the Twentieth Century, and they became, with slight elaboration, the titles for the first five volumes of the history. The Drafting Committee also promised to consider adding an annexe containing maps and statistics, and this in time became the sixth volume, Methodology and Historiography of the Caribbean.

Volume I – Autochthonous Societies
This volume relates the history of the origins of the earliest Caribbean peoples, and analyses their various political, social, cultural and economic organizations over time, in and around the Caribbean region.

Volume II – New Societies: The Caribbean in the 'Long' Sixteenth Century
The subject of this volume is the evolution of Caribbean society through the intrusion of Europeans, and it examines the dramatic changes in politics, society and culture which occurred until 1680. These changes are studied in conjunction with the rapidly dwindling presence of the Amerindians and the increasing numbers of Spanish English, French and Dutch settlers.

Volume III – Slave Societies of the Caribbean
The slave societies were more than societies with enslaved Africans, so this volume examines the demographic and economic as well as social and cultural aspects of all those communities which resulted from the establishment of the Caribbean slave systems.

Volume IV – The 'Long' Nineteenth Century: Nineteenth-Century Transformations
Emphasizing themes rather than chronology, this volume covers the period from the end of slavery (although this varies in time from territory to territory) to the twentieth century. Its major themes are dependent labour groups, especially emigrants from Asia, the development and diversification of local economies, and the emergence throughout the region of varying degrees of national consciousness as well as forms of government.

Volume V – The Caribbean in the Twentieth Century
The prevalence and persistence of the plantation, the ubiquity of underemployment, the vulnerability of dependent Caribbean economies, popular and labour protests, decolonisation and neo-colonialism are all considered in this volume. It also explores the effects of migration, mass communications and modernization on the cultures of local societies.

Volume VI – Methodology and Historiography of the Caribbean
This volume has three sections. The first examines sources of historical evidence and the techniques used to study them for the purpose of writing Caribbean history. In the second, the historiography of the region is treated thematically, tracing the changes in

the interpretation of the past. The third is devoted to the historiography of particular territories and history-writing in all its branches.

At its first meeting, the Drafting Committee also made three decisions which should be noticed here: it appointed editors for the five volumes and the proposed annexe; it decided that since it had provided in some detail the contents of Volumes II and III, the editors could complete work on the contents of their volumes and name the authors by the end of 1983; it acknowledged that the contents of Volume I needed detailed elaboration and agreed that the editor should have the help of a workshop of specialists to provide the details. Nevertheless, the Committee proposed that Volumes I, II and III should be published first and together and set July 1986 as the date for the final submission of manuscripts to UNESCO.

Provisional calendars for producing histories in several volumes and with chapters from scores of authors are not dates that are likely to be met. As has been the case with other multi-volume histories, inviting the most competent historians to be editors and authors has also meant taking the risk that the publication of the work will be long-delayed, since such persons normally have many other commitments. The estimates made in April of 1983 were soon wildly out. The first meeting of the Bureau of the Drafting Committee scheduled for September 1984 was held in May 1985. The new date proposed for the submission of manuscripts of Volumes I, II and III was December 1987. Volume III, which was published in 1997, was submitted in 1992.

When the General History of the Caribbean was first proposed, there were just enough historians who had researched their topics across the barriers of language. Ten years later, the existence of the Association of Caribbean Historians has made possible a substantial increase of our comparative knowledge of the region's past. At its meetings, papers on similar topics and related themes pertaining to different territories, are presented in the languages of the Caribbean, thus giving historians access to the results of research done across the barriers of language. To that extent these six volumes can be said to be a work in progress, a marker towards a fully integrated Caribbean history.

List of Contributors

Anthony T. Bryan, Professor of International Relations, is Director of the Caribbean Studies Program at the North-South Center, University of Miami, and a senior research associate of the Center for Strategic and International Studies in Washington, DC. Previously he was Professor and Director of the Institute of International Relations at the University of the West Indies, St Augustine campus, Trinidad; a senior associate at the Carnegie Endowment for International Peace; and a fellow at the Woodrow Wilson Center in Washington, DC. He is the author or co-author of 10 books and more than 80 scholarly articles in his field.

Patrick Bryan holds the Douglas Hall Chair of History at the Mona, Jamaica, campus of the University of the West Indies, and is a former Head of the Department of History at Mona. Among his major publications are *The Jamaican People 1880–1902* (1991) and *Marcus Garvey: His Work and Impact* (co-edited: 1988). He has published extensively on the history of Jamaica, the Dominican Republic and the Caribbean region.

Carl Campbell is Professor of History at the University of the West Indies, Mona, Jamaica, campus. His main areas of research have been the Caribbean free coloureds and the social history of education in Jamaica and Trinidad & Tobago. He is currently working on a history of education in the Spanish Antilles. His main publications are: *Cedulants and Capitulants: The Politics of the Coloured Opposition in the Slave Society of Trinidad 1783–1838* (1992) and *The Young Colonials: A Social History of Education in Trinidad and Tobago 1834–1939* (1996).

Roberto Cassá is a Professor in the Department of History and Anthropology at the Universidad Autónoma, Santo Domingo, Dominican Republic. He is a member of the Academia Dominicana de la Historia, and Professor and Member of the Council of the Facultad Latinoamericana de Ciencias Sociales, Programa Santo Domingo. He is the author of *Capitalismo y Dictadura* (1982) and other books, articles and book chapters.

Alice Colón is Researcher at the Social Science Research Center of the University of Puerto Rico, Río Piedras campus. She has edited and published books and articles on various issues regarding Puerto Rican women, including women's poverty and employment, their reproductive health and rights, and their participation in Puerto Rican social and historical processes.

Claus Füllberg-Stolberg is Professor of History at the University of Hanover (Germany) and was Visiting Lecturer at the University of the West Indies, Mona, Jamaica, campus (1988–90). His publications on Caribbean history include: *Jamaica 1938 – the Living Conditions of the Urban and Rural Poor: Two Social Surveys* (1990) and *Plantation Economy, Land Reform and the Peasantry in a Historical Perspective:*

Jamaica 1838–1980 (1992), co-edited with Swithin Wilmot. He is currently completing a book on Jamaica during the Great Depression (1925–45).

Antonio Gaztambide-Géigel, is 'Eugenio María de Hostos' Honorary Chair, University of Puerto Rico, 2001–2; and regularly Professor, School of Social Sciences, University of Puerto Rico, Río Piedras campus. He has published in Cuba, Mexico, Puerto Rico, Spain and Venezuela about the contemporary Caribbean and its international relations. He was the founding President of the Puerto Rican Association of Historians, 1993–5.

Fe Iglesias García is a research scholar at the Institute of Social Sciences of the Academy of Sciences, Havana, Cuba. She has published extensively on the social and economic history of Cuba, and is the author of the chapter on Cuban historiography in Volume VI of the *UNESCO General History of the Caribbean* (1999).

Franklin W. Knight is the Leonard and Helen R. Stulman Professor of History at the Johns Hopkins University in Baltimore, Maryland. A Jamaican with academic degrees from the University of the West Indies and the University of Wisconsin in Madison, he has published widely on Latin America and the Caribbean.

Anthony P. Maingot is Professor of Sociology at Florida International University, Miami. Born in Trinidad, he has held positions at Yale University (1966–72) and the University of the West Indies, Trinidad (1972–4). He is a co-author of *A Short History of the West Indies* (1987); and the author of *Small Country Development and International Labor Flows: Experiences in the Caribbean* (1991) and *The United States and the Caribbean: Trends in U.S.-Caribbean Relations* (1994).

Tony Martin is Professor of Africana Studies at Wellesley College, Massachusetts. He is author of *Race First: The Ideological and Organizational Struggles of Marcus Garvey and the Universal Negro Improvement Association* (1976), *Literary Garveyism: Garvey, Black Arts and the Harlem Renaissance* (1983), *The Pan-African Connection* (1983) and many other works.

James Millette was for many years a member of the Department of History, at the University of the West Indies, St Augustine campus, Trinidad & Tobago. He is now Professor and Chair, Department of African American Studies, Oberlin College, Oberlin, Ohio. He has taught and written for more than thirty years on Caribbean history, imperial history, labour movements, Third World politics and economics, and the modern Caribbean. His publications include *The Genesis of Crown Colony Government: Trinidad, 1782–1810* (1970), and *Freedom Road* (1988).

Rex Nettleford is Vice-Chancellor of the University of the West Indies. A Jamaican, he has been associated with the University of the West Indies since he entered its Mona campus as an undergraduate in 1953. He is the founder of the National Dance Theatre Company of Jamaica, was for years its chief choreographer, and has written many books and articles on Jamaican and Caribbean culture, history and identity. He is the recipient of innumerable awards and honours, including his country's highest honour.

Marifeli Pérez-Stable is a Professor in the Department of Sociology and Anthropology at Florida International University in Miami. She is the author of *The Cuban Revolution: Origins, Course, and Legacy* (1993). *Cuba's Long Twentieth Century (1868–2002)* is her work in progress.

Rhoda Reddock is Professor and Head of the Centre for Gender and Development Studies at the University of the West Indies, St Augustine campus, Trinidad & Tobago. Her major publications are *Women, Labour and Politics in Trinidad and Tobago* (1994) and *Elma François: The NWCSA and the Workers' Struggle for Change in the Caribbean in the 1930s* (1988) and she has also edited or authored many other books, book chapters and journal articles. She is a founding member of the Caribbean Association for Feminist Research and Action (CAFRA).

Bonham C. Richardson is Professor of Geography at Virginia Polytechnic Institute and State University, Blacksburg, Virginia. Since 1967 he has conducted field and archival research in Guyana, Trinidad, Carriacou, St Kitts-Nevis and Barbados as well as in London. Among his books, *The Caribbean in the Wider World, 1492–1992* (1992) won the 1993 Gordon K. Lewis award from the Caribbean Studies Association. He is currently finishing a book that deals with the history of fire in the Lesser Antilles.

Joseph L. Scarpaci is a Professor of Urban Affairs and Planning, in the School of Public and International Affairs, College of Architecture and Urban Studies, at Virginia Polytechnic Institute and State University, Blacksburg, Virginia. His research interests include comparative urban social policy, historic preservation and economic development, especially in Cuba and the Southern Cone. He is the recent co-author of *Havana: Two Faces of the Antillean Metropolis* (2002) and author of the forthcoming *Barrios and Plazas: The Transformation of the Latin American Centro Histórico*.

Raymond T. Smith is a social anthropologist who has carried out research in Guyana, Jamaica, Ghana and the United States. Formerly a member of the Institute of Social and Economic Research, and the Department of Sociology, at the University of the West Indies, Mona, Jamaica campus, he moved to the University of Chicago in 1966 where he is now Professor Emeritus in the Department of Anthropology. For further information see http://home.uchicago.edu/~rts1/index.htm

Robert J. Stewart is the author of *Religion and Society in Post-Emancipation Jamaica* (1992). He has a doctorate in history from the University of the West Indies, Mona, Jamaica campus. A former Jesuit, his interest in religion and history in the Caribbean was sparked by his experience of the contradictions in Christian missionary work in the West Indies. Stewart now teaches history at Trinity School in New York City.

Members of the International Scientific Committee for the Drafting of the General History of the Caribbean

Bureau

Professor Sir Roy Augier
(St Lucia)
Chairman of the International Scientific Committee for the Drafting of the General History of the Caribbean

Professor Woodville Marshall
(Barbados)
Rapporteur

Professor Pieter Emmer
(Netherlands)
Editor Volume II

Professor Franklin Knight
(Jamaica/USA)
Editor Volume III

Professor Manuel Moreno Fraginals
(Cuba)
Editor Volume IV
Deceased 2001

Professor Blanca Silvestrini-Pacheco
(Puerto Rico)
Co-Editor Volume V

Members

Professor René Acheen
(France/Martinique)

Professor German Carrera-Damas
(Venezuela)
Co-Editor Volume II

Professor Jean Casimir
(Haiti)

Professor J.E. Inikori
(Nigeria)

Professor J.C. Jha
(India)

Professor Keith Laurence
(Trinidad and Tobago)
Editor Volume IV

Professor Gordon Lewis
(United Kingdom)
Deceased 1991

Professor Leslie F. Manigat
(Haiti)
Resigned

Professor Mary Noel Menezes
(Guyana)

Professor Sidney W. Mintz
(USA)

Professor Francisco Morales Padron
(Spain)

Professor René Romer
(Netherlands Antilles)
Co-Editor Volume V
Deceased 2003

Professor J.P. Siwpersad
(Suriname)

Professor Hugo Tolentino Dipp
(Dominican Republic)

Secretariat

Alwin Bully
Adviser for Culture in the Caribbean/Project Coordinator
UNESCO Culture Sector
25 Dominica Drive
Kingston 5, Jamaica

ABBREVIATIONS

AACC	Anglo-American Caribbean Commission
ACH	Association of Caribbean Historians
ACP	African, Caribbean and Pacific group of countries
ACS	Association of Caribbean States
AFL	American Federation of Labor
AFL-CIO	American Federation of Labor-Congress of Industrial Organizations
AIFLD	American Institute for Free Labor Development
AJR	Asociación de Jóvenes Rebeldes (Association of Rebel Youths)
ALCOA	Aluminium Company of America
APU	African Progress Union
ATLAS	Agrupación de Trabajadores Latinoamericanos Sindicalistas (Group of Latin American Syndicalist Workers)
ATS	Auxiliary Territorial Service
ATSEFWU	All Trinidad Sugar Estates and Factory Workers Trade Union
BA/MA	Bundesarchiv/Militärarchiv der Bundesrepublik Deutschland (National Archives/Military Archives of the Federal Republic of Germany), Freiburg
BBC	British Broadcasting Corporation
B.d.U.	Befehlshaber du Unterseeboote (Commander of Submarines)
BGEIA	British Guiana East Indian Association
BITU	Bustamante Industrial Trade Union
BLP	Barbados Labour Party
BOWAND	Belize Organization for Women and Development
BWIR	British West Indies Regiment
BWU	Barbados Workers Union
C-47	Centrale 47 (Surinamese labour union)
CACM	Central American Common Market
CADEC	Christian Action for Development in the Eastern Caribbean
CADORIT	Caribbean Division of ORIT
CAFRA	Caribbean Association for Feminist Research and Action
CARICOM	Caribbean Community
CARIFORUM	Caribbean Forum (Caribbean members of ACP group)
CARIFTA	Caribbean Free Trade Area
CARISFORM	Caribbean Institute for Social Formation
CARIWA	Caribbean Women's Association
CBERA	Caribbean Basin Economic Recovery Act
CBI	Caribbean Basin Initiative
CBTAG	Caribbean Basin Technical Advisory Group
CC	Central Committee
CCC	Caribbean Conference of Churches
CDB	Caribbean Development Bank

CDCC	Caribbean Development and Co-operation Committee
CDR	Comités de Defensa de la Revolucíon (Committees for the Defence of the Revolution)
CDT	Confederación Dominicana del Trabajo (Dominican Federation of Labour)
CDW	Committee for the Development of Women (St Vincent & the Grenadines)
CEDAW	Convention on the Elimination of all Forms of Discrimination Against Women
Ce-Mujer	Centro de Solidaridád para el Desarrollo de la Mujer (Solidarity Centre for Women's Development)
CERES	Centro de Estudios, Recursos y Servicios a la Mujer (Centre for Research, Resources and Services for Women)
CFW	Curaçaose Federatie van Werknemers (Curaçao Workers Federation)
CGT	Confederación General de Trabajadores (General Federation of Labour)
CIA	Central Intelligence Agency
CIC	Caribbean Investment Corporation
CIM	Comisión Interamericana de Mujeres (Inter-American Commission of Women)
CIPAF	Centro de Investigación para la Acción Femenina (Centre for Women's Research and Action)
CMO	Caribbean Meteorological Organization
CNOC	Confederación Nacional de Obreros Cubanos (National Confederation of Cuban Workers)
CO	Colonial Office, Public Record Office, London
CODECA	Corporación Desarollo del Caribe (Caribbean Economic Development Corporation)
COMECON	Council for Mutual Economic Assistance (East European and Soviet trading bloc)
CPFO	Centre de Promotion des Femmes Ouvrières (Centre for the Promotion of Working Women)
CRESFED	Centre de Recherche et de Formation Economique et Sociale pour le Développement (Centre for Economic and Social Research and Policy Formation for Development)
CSA	Caribbean Studies Association
CSM&E	CARICOM Single Market and Economy
CTAL	Confederación de Trabajadores de America Latina (Confederation of Latin American Trade Unions)
CTC	Confederación de Trabajadores de Cuba (Central Organization of Cuban Trade Unions)
CXC	Caribbean Examinations Council
DEU	Directorio Estudiantil Universitario (Directory of University Students)

DLP	Democratic Labour Party
DOM	Département d'Outre Mer (Overseas department)
DRE	Diurectorio Revolucionario Estudiantil (Revolutionary Student Directorate)
DVF	Democratische Volks Front (Democratic Peoples Front)
EAI	Enterprise of the Americas Initiative
ECCM	East Caribbean Common Market
ECLA(C)	Economic Commission for Latin America (and the Caribbean)
EEC	European Economic Community
EINC	East Indian National Congress
ENFOFANM	Centre National et International de Documentation et d'Information des Femmes en Haïti (National and International Centre for Documentation and Information on Women in Haiti)
EU	European Union
FAR	Fuerzas Armadas Revolucionarias (Armed Revolutionary Forces)
FDIM/WIDF	Federación Democrática Internacional de Mujeres (Women's International Democratic Federation)
FDRL	Franklin D. Roosevelt Library, New York
FES	Frederich Ebert Stiftung (Frederich Ebert Foundation)
FGA	Front for Guadeloupean Autonomy
FLT	Federación Libre de los Trabajadores (Free Federation of Workers)
FMC	Federación de Mujeres Cubanas (Federation of Cuban Women)
FNTA	Federación Nacional de Trabajadores del Azúcar (National Federation of Sugar Workers)
FOL	Frente Obrero de Liberashon (Workers' Liberation Front)
FTAA	Free Trade Area of the Americas
FWTU	Federated Workers Trade Union
G-3	Group of Three
GATT	General Agreement on Tariffs and Trade
GAWU	Guyana Agricultural and Workers Union
GDP	Gross Domestic Product
GMMWU	Grenada Manual and Mental Workers Union
GNP	Gross National Product
GONG	Groupe des Organisations Nationales de la Guadeloupe (Group of National Organisations of Guadeloupe)
GULP	Grenada United Labour Party
HMSO	Her (His) Majesty's Stationery Office
ICFTU	International Confederation of Free Trade Unions
ICTA	Imperial College of Tropical Agriculture
IDRC	Industrial Development Research Council (Canada)
ILO	International Labour Organisation
IMF	International Monetary Fund
INRA	Instituto Nacional de Reforma Agraria (National Institute of Agrarian Reform)

INSTRAW	United Nations International Research and Training Institute for the Advancement of Women
IRA	Industrial Relations Act
ISA	Industrial Stabilization Act
ITAC	Inter-Trades Union Advisory Council
ITS	International Trade Secretariats
JALGO	Jamaica Local Government Organization
JARA	Jamaica Association for the Repeal of Abortion Laws
JLP	Jamaica Labour Party
JTURDC	Joint Trade Union Research Development Council
JUCEPLAN	Junta Central de Planificación (Central Planning Board)
KOPAK	Koperativa di Agrikultornan di Korsou (Farmers' Co-operative of Curaçao)
LDCs	Less-developed countries
LRIDA	Labour Relations and Industrial Disputes Act
MAN	Movemento Antiyas Nobo (Movement for a New Antilles, Curaçao)
MERCOSUR	Mercado Común del Sur (Southern Common Market)
MININT	Ministerio del Interior (Ministry of the Interior)
MDCs	More-developed countries
MPLA	Movimento Popular de Liberação de Angola (Popular Movement for the Liberation of Angola)
MUDE	Mujeres en Desarrollo (Women in Development)
NAFTA	North American Free Trade Agreement
NAR	National Alliance for Reconstruction
NAW	National Archives of the United States, Washington DC
NGOs	Non-governmental organizations
NJAC	National Joint Action Committee
NJM	New Jewel Movement
NPP	New Progressive Party
NPS	Nationale Partij Suriname (National Party of Suriname)
NWCSA	Negro Welfare Cultural and Social Association (better known as the NWA)
NWU	National Workers Union
OAS	Organization of American States
ODECABE	Organización Deportiva Centroamericano y del Caribe (Central American and Caribbean Sports Organization)
OECD	Organization of Economic Cooperation and Development
OECS	Organization of Eastern Caribbean States
OFC	Offshore financial centre
OPEC	Organisation of Petroleum Exporting Countries
OPMT	Organización Puertorriqueña de la Mujer Trabajadora (Puerto Rican Organization of Working Women)
OPP	Órganos del Poder Popular (Organs of Popular Power)
ORI	Organizaciones Revolucionarias Integradas (Integrated Revolutionary Organizations)

ORIT	Organización Regional Interamericana del Trabajo (Inter-american Regional Organization of Labour)
OWTU	Oilfield Workers Trade Union
PAA	Pan-African Association
PALU	Progressieve Arbeiders en Landbouwers Unie (Progressive Union of Workers and Peasants, Suriname)
PCC	Partido Comunista de Cuba (Communist Party of Cuba)
PCF	Parti Communiste Français (French Communist Party)
PCM	Parti Communiste Martiniquais (Communist Party of Martinique)
PCG	Parti Communiste Guadeloupéen (Communist Party of Guadeloupe)
PDP	People's Democratic Party
PIP	Partido Independentista Puertorriqueño (Puerto Rico Independence Party)
PLD	Partido de Liberación Dominicana (Dominican Liberation Party)
PNC	People's National Congress
PNM	People's National Movement
PNP (Curaçao)	Partido Nashonal di Pueblo (People's National Party)
PNP (Jamaica)	People's National Party
PNP (Suriname)	Progressieve Nationale Party (Progressive National Party)
PNR	Partij Nationalistiche Republiek (Nationalist Republican Party)
PPD	Partido Popular Democrático (Popular Democratic Party)
PPP	People's Progressive Party (Guyana)
PRD	Partido Revolucionario Dominicano (Dominican Revolutionary Party)
PRERA	Puerto Rican Emergency Relief Administration
PRRA	Puerto Rican Reconstruction Administration
PSP	Popular Socialist Party
PTTI	Postal, Telegraph and Telephone International
RFO	Société Nationale de Radio-télévision Française d'Outre-mer (National Society of French Overseas Radio and Television)
RG	Record Group
RNM	Regional Negotiating Machinery
SAWO	Surinaamse Algemene Werknemers Organisaite (Surinamese General Labourers' Organization)
SDPE	Sistema de Dirección Planificación de la Economía (Economic Management and Planning System)
SEDA	Sentro di Dama (Women's Centre, Curaçao)
SHADA	Société Haïtiano-Américaine de Développement Agricole (Haitian-American Agricultural Development Society)
SOFA	Solidarité Fanm Aysyén (Solidarity with Haitian Women)
SoS	Secretary of State
SPAN	Society for the Propagation of African Nationalism
SPAO	Society of Peoples of African Origin
SPIC	Society for the Propagation of Indian Culture
SSU	Surinaamse Socialistische Unie (Surinamese Socialist Union)

TLP	Trinidad Labour Party
TUAC	Trades Union Advisory Council
TUC	Trades Union Congress
TWA	Trinidad Workingmen's Association
UAWU	University and Allied Workers Union
UGT	Unión General de Trabajadores (General Union of Workers)
UNC	United National Congress
UN/ECLA(C)	United Nations Economic Commission for Latin America (and the Caribbean)
UNESCO	United Nations Educational, Scientific and Cultural Organization
UNIA	Universal Negro Improvement Association
USAID	United States Agency for International Development
USSR	Union of Soviet Socialist Republics
USWA	United Steel Workers of America
UWI	University of the West Indies
VHP	Verenigde Hindustaanse Partij (United Hindu Party)
VP	Volks Partij (People's Party)
WAND	Women and Development Unit, UWI
WASU	West African Students' Union.
WESCAR	Werkspoor Caribbean
WFTU	World Federation of Trade Unions
WICP	Women in the Caribbean Project
WISCO	West Indies Shipping Corporation
WPA	Working People's Alliance
WPJ	Workers' Party of Jamaica
WTO	World Trade Organization

Maps and Charts

TABLES

Plates

ACKNOWLEDGEMENTS

The authors and publishers would like to thank the following for permission to reproduce the following photographic material:

Cover photo courtesy of the Institute of Puerto Rica Culture Collection

Alamy ©Jon Mitchell/Lightroom Photos, Plate 73; Associated Press, Plate 98; Audio Visual Aids Department, Ministry of Education, Barbados, Plate 38; Leila Augier, Trinidad & Tobago, Plate 20; Cecile Crawford, Barbados, Plate 61; Barbados National Trust, Plate 75; Hilary Beckles, UWI Cave Hill, Plate 55; Dame Hilda Bynoe and Peter Bynoe, Trinidad & Tobago, Plate 27; Camera Press ©Pressens Bild, Plate 85, ©Mark Bever, Plates 89, 93; Canadian Jamaican Chinese 2000, Plate 26; Doreen Chen, Plate 57; Collection Isabel Pico de Hernandez, Puerto Rico, Plate 25; Alice Colón, Puerto Rico, Plate 95; Corbis ©Bettmann, Plates 12, 33, ©Hulton Deutsch Collection, Plate 23, ©Mcpherson Colin/Corbis Sygma, Plate 85, ©Bassouls Sophie/Corbis Sygma, Plate 90; Ellis Island Immigration Museum, National Parks Service Library, Augusta Sherman Collection, Plate 22; ERLENBACH - Zurich Leipzig, Rotaphel-Verlag, 1937, Plate 15; Folklore Group: La Cinta, Coleccio la realidad de un sueño; published by Asamblea del Poder Popular, Ciego de Avila, 1989, Plate 54; Jacqueline Gannie, Jamaica, Plate 96; Rosan Girard Collection, Jean-Pierre Sainton, Guadaloupe, Plate 62; Gleaner Company Limited, Jamaica, Plates 28, 65, 97, 99; Government Information Service, Dominica, Plate 64; Patricia E. Green, Jamaica, Plate 78; the *Guyana Review*, Plates 35, 46, 48, 49; Hulton Archive, Plate 82; Janet Jagan and Nadira Jagan-Brancier, Guyana, Plates 36, 37; Main Library, UWI, St Augustine, Plates 3, 8, 24, 39, 47, 51, 70; Historical Museum of Southern Florida, Miami News Collection, Plates 31, 66, 94; Hulton Archive/Getty, Plate 84; Instituto Dominicano de Folklore, Plate 79; International Relations Department, UAG, Fouillole, Plate 72; Franklin Knight, USA, Plate 71; Lady St. John, Barbados, Plates 50, 60; Lennox Honychurch, Dominica, Plates 52, 59; 'Mancrab' designed by Peter Minshall and portrayed by Peter Samuel Jr, Photo: Norton Studios, Trinidad & Tobago, 1983, Plate 102; Marryshow House, University Centre, Grenada, Plates 7, 13, 63; Mutabaruka, Jamaica, Plate 67; National Archives of Cuba, Plates 68, 87; National Archives, St Kitts: The Basil Henderson Collection, Plates 4, 58; National Gas Company, Trinidad & Tobago, Plate 40; National Library of Jamaica, Plates 10, 11, 19, 74, 76, 81, ©Dennis Valentine, Plate 21; ©The Nobel Foundation, Plate 83; Photo Collection, El Mundo Newspaper, University of Puerto Rico, Digital Archives, Rio Piedras Campus, Plates 16, 32, 34; Popperfoto, Plate 91, ©Sue Ogrocki REUTERS , Plate 92; Meg Price Craig, Belize: ION Media, Belize, Plate 29; Public Relations Office, UWI, Mona,

Plate 80; Ras DaSilva, Photo: Ruth Wilson, Jamaica, Plate 56; Rupert Lewis, Jamaica, Plate 18; Ruth Reynolds Papers, Centros Estudios Puertoriqueños, Hunter College, CUNY, Plate 9; Sandals Resorts International Limited, Plate 77; Gail and Winston Saunders, Artist: Brent Malone, Bahamas, Plate 101; "Side by Side" Estate of Ann Watson Yates, Plate 5; St Christopher Heritage Society, Plates 1, 6, 17; Stoute Collection, Barbados National Trust, Plate 42; St Lucia Archaeological and Historical Society, Plate 100; Topham Picturepoint, Plate 30; UNESCO, Plate 88; University of Puerto Rico-RRP/2202, Photo: J.Perez-Mesa, Plate 69; US Marine Corps Archive, Plate 14; Karl Watson, Barbados, Plate 2; West Indian Welfare Centre, Cuba, Latin America and Caribbean Centre, UWI, Mona, Plates 44, 45.

The publishers have made every effort to trace the copyright holders, but if they have inadvertently overlooked any, they will be pleased to make the necessary arrangements at the first opportunity.

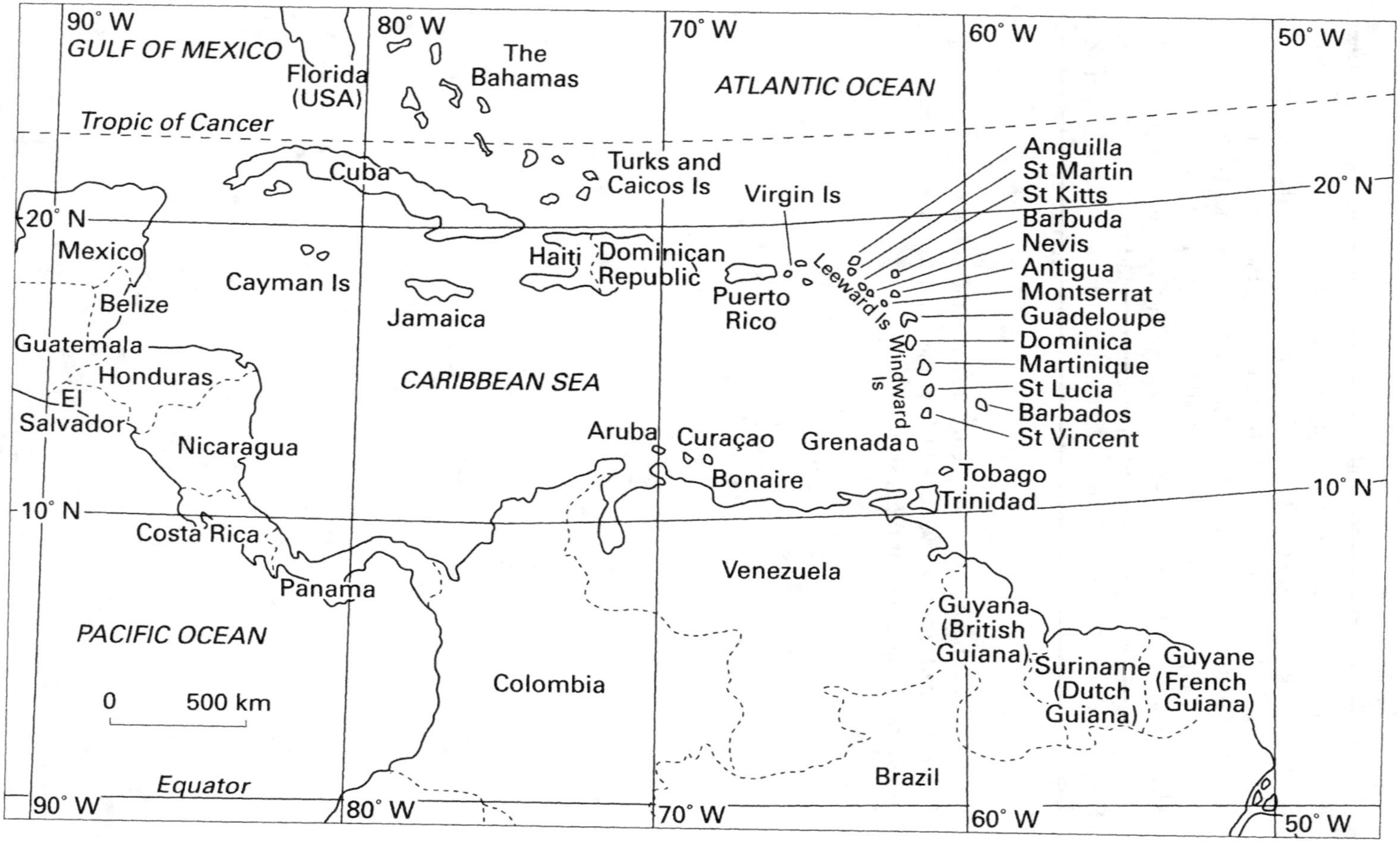

The Caribbean in the Twentieth Century

Introduction

Bridget Brereton

THE major objective of Volume V of the UNESCO *General History of the Caribbean* is to provide an account and interpretation of the historical development of the region from around 1930 to the end of the century. As in the series as a whole, the definition of 'Caribbean' used in this volume encompasses all the islands (including the Bahamas) and the continental enclaves whose history was similar to that of the islands: the three Guianas and Belize. Because Volume IV covers the 'long' nineteenth century, with chapters going chronologically up to the 1920s, this volume speaks to a 'short' twentieth century: from the 1930s to its end. Inevitably there is overlap with chapters in Volume IV, but most of the material in the present volume deals with post-1930 developments. Many chapters – written at varying times during the 1990s – try to take up the analysis to the authorial present.

Though the imperatives of chronology have certainly not been ignored in the volume's structure, a thematic approach dominates. After a first chapter intended to bridge Volumes IV and V by analysing the key economic developments between 1880 and 1930, two chapters consider the region's evolution in the decade of the 1930s, and during the Second World War. A later chapter examines the experience of Cuba between 1959 and the end of the century. All the remaining fourteen chapters are devoted to key themes or movements in the region's history since the 1930s. Political and economic developments have certainly not been neglected, but there is some leaning towards social and cultural history; fittingly, the last chapter considers the 'quality of life' in the Caribbean in the second half of the twentieth century.

*

In Chapter 1, Roberto Cassá analyses the key economic developments which transformed the region between 1880 and 1930, the era of the 'second industrial revolution'. (A parallel chapter on political changes in the same period unfortunately did not materialize, but Volume IV in the series takes events up to the 1920s). Cassá concentrates on the dialectical relationships between the plantation sector – modernizing and consolidating through local and especially US capital – and the 'peasants', of many different types and ethnic backgrounds. He does not neglect the influence of international market developments and of the global revolution in transport and communications. Cassá provides the essential economic background to understand the rest of the volume.

The 'turbulent thirties' form the subject of Franklin Knight's Chapter 2. To understand the proletarian and middle-class upheavals which characterized the era, Knight examines economic and demographic developments – depression, retrenchment in the plantation sector, urban drift, repatriation of migrants, growing populations – and analyses the living conditions of the people. The Cuban revolutionary moment of 1933, the establishment of Trujillo's dictatorship in the Dominican Republic, the consequences of the US occupation of Haiti which ended in 1934, the crises in Puerto Rico culminating in the emergence of Muñoz Marín's PPD in 1938, the labour protests in the British colonies in 1937–9, are all put in their international and regional contexts. Finally, Knight shows how the events of the decade changed the region in significant ways.

If the 1930s have always been considered a watershed era for the region, the war years were no less transforming; and Claus Füllberg-Stolberg provides a comprehensive narrative and interpretation of the region's history during the Second World War (Chapter 3). He gives an incisive account of the region's geo-strategic position in the war and analyses British, French and US actions designed to defend and protect the Caribbean and its trade from German submarines (and Vichy France). But Stolberg also thoroughly examines the social and economic conditions of the people in a time of war and hardships, looking at food production and exports, welfare measures, unemployment, wages and cost of living. Finally, he considers wartime political and constitutional developments, both in the independent states and in the colonies.

Chapters 4, 5 and 8 address political processes and organizations in the region between the 1940s and the end of the century. Patrick Bryan (Chapter 4) examines the development and significance of proletarian movements, considering the impact of the Second World War and of the Cold War on organized labour and carefully analysing the many links between the trade unions and political parties in most Caribbean countries. He concludes by pointing to the setbacks experienced by the labour movement in the last two decades of the twentieth century. In Chapter 5, James Millette looks at decolonization and the formation of new nations in the anglophone Caribbean during the 25 years after the Second World War. He also considers populist and anti-imperialist movements in Puerto Rico, the French Caribbean and Suriname during the same period. It falls to Anthony Maingot (Chapter 8) to analyse political processes in the region between the 1970s and the century's end. He considers the post-1968 mass movements, especially Black Power, in the Anglophone states and the 'turn to the left' in the 1970s and early 1980s, culminating in the Grenada Revolution (1979); then he examines the conservative reaction in the wake of the collapse of the People's Revolutionary Government in Grenada (1983). Separate sections carefully analyse the complexities of political evolution in the French and Dutch Caribbean, in Puerto Rico, the Dominican Republic and finally Haiti, whose political trajectory was very different from that of the rest of the region.

Of course, the single most important event in the history of the Caribbean in the second half of the twentieth century was the Cuban Revolution, the subject of Marifeli Pérez-Stable's Chapter 7. She examines the trajectory of Cuban political development from Fidel Castro's triumph in 1959 to the 'special period' of the 1990s. While Pérez-Stable concentrates on the institutionalization of the Revolution and on the effects of events in the Soviet Union after the mid-1980s, she also considers the impact of the Cuban Revolution on the region as a whole over the forty years since Castro took power in 1959.

While labour, anti-colonial and revolutionary movements have been critical to the region's development in the twentieth century, race consciousness has also played a leading role; ethnicity has been a significant organizing and mobilizing principle. In Chapter 6, Tony Martin examines African-Caribbean race consciousness movements from the early 1900s to century's end, focusing especially on the Anglophone Caribbean. He also considers the parallel development of ethnic consciousness among people in the southern Caribbean descended from immigrants from India. Using Trinidad as his case study, Martin examines the rise of Indian ethnic nationalism, especially in the period between the 1930s and the 1980s, and compares it with its African counterpart. In Trinidad, Guyana and Suriname, ethnic mobilization could, and did, cut across class lines and divide anti-colonial or nationalist movements.

Chapters 9 and 10 take up aspects of the region's international relations. Antonio Gaztambide-Géigel analyses the movements towards regional cooperation from the Anglo-American Caribbean Commission of the wartime period to the Association of Caribbean States of the 1990s. He considers the rise (and in some cases, fall) of regional institutions such as the Caribbean Commission, ECLAC, Carifta and Caricom, but also shows how the global 'cultural revolutions' of the period since 1960 have created multiple, often transnational identities, forging many different unofficial, non-governmental links between people within (and outside) the region. In Chapter 10, Anthony Bryan surveys Caribbean international relations at century's end. He sees a 'new regionalism' emerging which represents, perhaps, a true paradigm shift, from vertical relationships with the metropoles of the North, to horizontal relationships between the states of the wider Caribbean and Latin America, exemplified in the Association of Caribbean States. Examining the urgent security and developmental issues confronting small Caribbean states, Bryan looks to a 'new diplomacy' in which nation-states become less significant players.

The remaining seven chapters address aspects of Caribbean development in the twentieth century which fall under the rubric of social and cultural history. Fe Iglesias García takes up the challenging task, in Chapter 11, of attempting to survey demographic and social structural changes in the region since the 1940s. She examines the ethnic and racial structures of the various populations, noting the fluidity – and changing definitions – of ethnicity especially in the Hispanic Caribbean. Iglesias García then analyses demographic shifts, including migration, urbanization and employment patterns, and considers changes in class structures and race/colour hierarchies. Fittingly, the eminent Cuban historian ends with a study of social structural change in her native country since the 1959 Revolution.

Most of the present-day population of the Caribbean are descended from people who came to the region, whether voluntarily or not, since 1492, and migration has always constituted a crucial aspect of its history. In Chapter 12, Bonham Richardson explores the evolution of a migration tradition, and takes us through the major twentieth-century movements of Caribbean people both outside and within the region. He pays considerable attention to the Caribbean diaspora in Britain, France, Canada and (above all) the United States, but he is especially interested in analysing what Caribbean migration means to the region's people and how it has helped to transform the sending societies, socially, economically and culturally.

Social change has been pervasive and rapid in the Caribbean since the Second World War, and nowhere more so than in the status and role of women, and in the family, areas explored in Chapters 13 and 14. Alice Colón and Rhoda Reddock show how social and economic changes after the war opened up new spaces for women's participation in public life and salaried work (other than the traditional jobs in domestic service and estate agriculture). They examine the impact of 'Second Wave' feminism on the region from the 1960s to the 1990s, looking at the emergence of highly diverse women's movements, at legal and institutional reforms affecting women, at the changing employment and migration patterns from a gendered perspective, at transformations in gender relations, and at the levels and nature of female participation in political life. This chapter is well complemented by R. T. Smith's essay on the Caribbean family (Chapter 14), an erudite survey of theoretical constructs of, and scholarly research on, the region's family and kinship systems in the twentieth century. Smith notes that since around 1970, feminist studies have been increasingly important in research on the

Caribbean family, placing the gender approach in the ascendant; but despite significant changes, he sees older values and traditions of household, family, kin and marriage still retaining considerable force in the last decade of the century.

In Chapter 15, a leading Caribbean humanist, Rex Nettleford, considers ideology, culture and identity as motifs in the region's development. Like so many before him, he notes the dialectical relationships between unity and diversity, between fragmentation and the formation of a shared Caribbean culture and identity, which have been part of the region's history since European conquest. Nettleford examines the ways in which Caribbean identity has been shaped by conflict and marronage, by the creolizing experience, by cultural assertion or resistance, and by appeals to religion, nationalism and ethnicity. The 'African presence' looms large in the region's culture and identity, though less so in the 'Latin' Caribbean; and in the southern territories, the 'Indian presence' has made a successful bid for space and place. Above all, Nettleford argues, culture and all the arts must be harnessed for the crucial task of self-definition; 'many Caribbean people are becoming increasingly weary of being engaged as minstrels or being treated as specimens for anthropological research', he writes.

Religious beliefs and cosmologies are a critical part of Caribbean culture and identity at the end of the twentieth century, and they form the subject of Robert Stewart's Chapter 16. The Caribbean is a place where the world's religions have flowed together, he notes, and where Western distinctions between the sacred and the secular are blurred. Stewart begins by examining African-Caribbean religious world views, in the Afro-Christian forms (Revivalism, Spiritual/Shouter Baptists, Rastafari) and in the neo-African forms (Vodou, Santería, Shangó). He then considers Roman Catholicism in the Francophone and Hispanophone Caribbean, including its unique history in modern Haiti, and the mainstream Protestant churches in the Anglophone territories. The growth of Pentecostalism in the second half of the twentieth century, notably in the Anglophone Caribbean, Puerto Rico and Haiti, is given its proper importance. Finally, Stewart examines the development of Islam and Hinduism in the southern territories and their contribution to religious and cultural pluralism in those countries.

The expansion of formal education has been a striking feature of the region's development since the war, and it is carefully analysed by Carl Campbell in Chapter 17. Though the organization, growth and traditions of the educational systems of the different states or colonial groups were very diverse, Campbell analyses some common developments: American influences, especially but not exclusively in Cuba, Puerto Rico, Haiti and the Dominican Republic; the impact of depression and war between 1930 and 1945; the huge investments made nearly everywhere between 1945 and about

1980 in the secondary and tertiary sectors and in 'technical/vocational' education. In most places, the expansion of the schools, colleges and universities was a key agent of modernization, even if the promise of post-war 'education for economic development' was not altogether fulfilled.

In a volume which leans towards social and cultural history, it seems appropriate that the last chapter, by Bonham Richardson and Joseph Scarpaci, seeks to survey the quality of life in the twentieth-century Caribbean. The authors start with a striking vignette of Barbados in 1950 and in 2000, revealing the dramatic transformations in people's lifestyles and life chances over fifty years. Richardson and Scarpaci go on to analyse systematically a remarkably wide range of topics: the promise and hazards of the regional environment; transport, travel and communications; tourism, drugs, crime and consumerism; politics; the media; carnivals, music and sports; health, life expectancy, housing, AIDS and sexual mores.

*

These 18 chapters were written at different times during the 1990s, and the authors, it should be emphasized, are in no way responsible if their sources or references reflect this fact. Originally 20 chapters were planned; missing from the volume are proposed chapters on political developments between 1880 and 1930 (parallel to Chapter 1) and on problems of economic dependency and models of development between 1945 and the 1990s. Three chapters – 1, 9 and 11 – have been translated into English from the authors' original Spanish.

The original editors of this volume were (in sequence) Leslie Manigat and Blanca G. Silvestrini. Much of the conceptualization and planning of Volume V was done by them and I wish to record my gratitude here. I have also received support and advice from co-editors Teresita Martínez-Vergne and René A. Römer. For devoted and efficient assistance with copy-editing, preparation of the Bibliography, word-processing and correspondence, I am grateful to Maureen Henry, Nalini Deyalsingh, Tara Sookhoo and Verona Kalloo, all of the University of the West Indies, St Augustine campus, Trinidad & Tobago; and to Janey Fisher, Macmillan Caribbean's excellent copy-editor.

René A. Römer died in February 2003. His contribution to this volume, and to the entire UNESCO General History of the Caribbean project, is gratefully acknowledged.

The economic development of the Caribbean from 1880 to 1930

Roberto Cassá

The modernization of exports

During the period from 1880 to 1930, the most striking feature of the economy of the Caribbean, like that of other regions of the periphery,[1] was its expansion into foreign markets, an expansion sustained through the modernization of the export apparatus. Although the various countries in the region moved at different speeds and achieved differing results, in all cases the development of new export goods and products was conditioned by the incorporation of capitalist technological and economic elements. Although the expansion of capitalist relations on the domestic front was limited during this period, its scope did extend beyond the strict sphere of production, influencing activities such as transportation and communication which then helped to make it possible to institute schemes of large-scale agricultural production aimed at the market-place.

The impetus for this growth and development stemmed from an international pattern of division of labour, and this pattern in turn stemmed from a demand, on the part of the countries of the centre, that was a result of the renewed industrialization brought on by the second Industrial Revolution.[2] The changes in schemes of production in the countries of the centre led to a search for increased foreign markets for their manufactured goods. This search led to a systematic opening of the economies of the periphery and also, subsequently, to innovative dynamics of growth.

In most of the countries of the Caribbean, this context allowed internal capital to begin to form and to move to the area of production of goods. Until this time, capital had been limited, with certain very restricted exceptions, to the sphere of circulation. But the new process was not limited to the transfer of local mercantile capital to the area of production; it also finally culminated

1 Osvaldo Sunkel and Pedro Paz, 1970.
2 Eric Hobsbawn, 1987.

in the entrance into the countries of the Caribbean of capital from the countries of the centre, especially the United States and Britain, and this capital became key to the changes that occurred in the relations of production. For the region as a whole, this modernization crowned the decay of economic and social relations grounded in slavery and made possible the transition toward the predominance of modern corporate capitalism.

From the foregoing, one can see that one of the most notable features of the economic scheme that emerged in the last decades of the nineteenth century was a growth centred basically in the export sector, although there were important consequences in other areas as well. Transformations of the systems of production – transformations that stemmed from the modernization of the export sector – manifested themselves on two basic planes. On the one hand, the plantation of earlier years was replaced by units, formed in response to the abolition of slavery and technological parameters, which required wage labour.[3] On the other hand, the peasant unit adopted a generally mercantile outlook.[4] These two variables came, in fact, to be interdependent, given that the renewal of the peasant economy derived from the variable of capitalist growth: to the degree that this growth did not take in all the sectors of the population, the peasant sector, progressively integrated into the market-place, maintained a competitive edge.

The modernization of the export sectors of the Caribbean allowed these economies to regain ground lost in the depressive trend caused in large part by the abolition of slavery and the growing adoption of free trade policies by nations that consumed tropical products, especially Britain. A consequence of this last factor was that the Caribbean had lost importance within international economic relations.[5] The export sector's recovery was slow, however, and accompanied by notable inequalities in the magnitude of its impact; in some countries there was relative success, while in others, the earlier economic patterns tended to persist.[6] This difficult transition was the main factor in the

3 One should not infer from this statement that 'technologization' along capitalist lines is completely incompatible with slavery, although it certainly did favour the expansion of wage labour. Cuban researchers have engaged in a debate over this issue (see María del Carmen Barcia, 1987). A preliminary bibliography can be found in Instituto de Ciencias Históricas, 1986.

4 The concept of a peasantry in the region is used here to signify the independent agricultural producer, with free variables among elements of societal and economic relations, such as antecedents in slavery, the formulas of ownership, eventual planes of extra-economic coercion, the degree and mechanisms of linkage with the market-place, and the payment or non-payment of rents to landlords (Eric Wolf, 1966).

5 Eric Williams, 1970 (1984).

6 Franc Báez Evertsz, 1986.

moderate expansion of production regionally. Although no calculations of national statistics have been carried out for this period in most countries, the figures for Jamaica may serve as an indicator, even though not in every category, given that this island experienced one of the region's most prolonged depressions. On a foundation of average demographic growth of 1.2 per cent per year, the per capita GDP grew 0.2 per cent, 0.5 per cent, and 0.7 per cent per year in the three twenty-year periods between 1870 and 1930.[7] What is significant about this is that one finds a slower rate of growth in the national product than in other areas of the world, though it does begin to rise.

Some conditions specific to the situation in the Caribbean at the time impacted the region relatively uniformly – such as the fall in sugar prices in 1884 and the stimulus lent by the First World War – but other conditions produced very different effects in different countries, for example the occupation of Cuba and Puerto Rico by the United States in 1898.

All in all, the introduction of technological patterns characteristic of the 'second industrial revolution' presented so many difficulties that the transition was left relatively unfinished. The context of a more integrated world increased the need for competitiveness, but countries in the region could not always achieve the level of capital formation necessary to sustain a rate of growth capable of overcoming internal problems and countering outside competition. To the degree to which modernization was concentrated in the export sector, it depended on the fluctuations of international prices for certain goods. The limited internal effects caused by fluctuating prices prolonged the precarious state of the export sector's modernization. Despite the changes occurring in the economy and in technology, it was difficult for individual countries, and the region as a whole, to put together the complex pieces in the puzzle in order to maintain competitiveness in international markets, which placed limits on the boom in exports.[8]

The result was that until 1871–3, the generally positive effects of the economic situation in the Western world – defined as a rising phase in the Kondratieff cycle – were wiped out.[9] The underlying depression, which lasted until the middle of the 1890s, was certainly a factor in the slow pace of the region's transition to capitalism. Another factor was that some of the tropical goods most in demand in the countries of the centre began to be produced in increasing quantities in other regions: sugar in Java and cacao in Cameroon, for example. Of particular importance here, too, was the protectionist policy adopted for the beet-sugar industry in Europe, beets being a

7 Gisela Eisner, 1974, xvi.
8 Schiller Thébaud, 1967.
9 E. Labrousse, 1962; Ciro F. S. Cardoso and B. Héctor Pérez, 1983.

crop which profited more than sugar-cane from the application of innovative technologies.[10]

These difficulties in the modernization process meant that only when a conjunction of factors favourable to a boom at the regional level occurred would the region's competitive ability be able to reach its full potential. Such a conjunction occurred on the eve of the First World War when, with the stimulus of rising prices, the flow of United States capital increased and an accelerated rise in production occurred.

It was for this reason that during the First World War, patterns of economic relations were established that made possible an opening to the outside world. With surplus funds, systems of transportation and communication were created or improved, cities grew in terms of population and employment opportunities, and social groups linked to modernization were formed.[11]

This boom, however, turned out to be a limited one. In late 1920, a depression began in the prices for Caribbean products, especially sugar. Although in 1923 prices partially recovered and conditions were once again favourable for the expansion of export production, that production confronted growing difficulties in maintaining its rate of growth. The crisis of 1920 thus presaged that of 1929, whose intensity and duration led to a restructuring of the patterns of economic reproduction, putting an end to the simple export pattern that had been functioning for about half a century.

The entrance of the peasant class into the mercantile sector in the late nineteenth century

At the turn of the eighteenth century, the beginning of the disintegration of slavery, and the dynamic of slow-paced development of the export sectors, had caused, in virtually every country in the Caribbean, the emergence of a peasant sector that made up the majority of the population.[12] In Haiti and the Dominican Republic, where all forms of the plantation had been discontinued since the 1830s, the peasant class had become synonymous with the working population.[13] Thus, cases such as Barbados, Antigua and St Kitts were exceptional, for in those islands, even as late as the end of the nineteenth century, the sugar plantation still contributed almost all of the exports

10 David Watts, 1987.
11 Franklin W. Knight, 1990.
12 Sidney Mintz, 1974.
13 Gérard Pierre-Charles, 1967; Roberto Cassá, 1978–80.

and employed most of the active population; this obviously had particular effects on the social structure.[14] Even in Cuba, which, after the formation of the Haitian state and the abolition of slavery in the British colonies, had become the region's sugar exporter *par excellence,* the peasant class gradually gained strength, especially in the eastern region of the island and when the crisis of the slave system became clear after the War of Independence began in 1868.[15]

Behind this trend toward the strengthening of a peasant class was the insufficiency of the flow of capital from the centre of imperial power (Britain, Spain and so on) until the last decades of the nineteenth century. The turn to trade taken by small producers meant that they became the fundamental medium by which several countries reinserted themselves into the world market-place and also the mechanism by which profits were generated, and this trend had become apparent sometimes even before 1870.[16] In the British colonies, this process was even clearer since, until a short time before, the slaves freed in 1834, who had access to land in differing degrees, had often avoided becoming actively associated with the market.[17] Such access to land was sometimes general, as in Trinidad, where significant numbers of the freed slaves who left the plantation wound up becoming the owners (or occupiers) of parcels of land that usually ranged from one to ten acres.[18]

In the contributions of the peasant class and the plantation to the process of export modernization, we should note two distinct periods. The first roughly corresponds to the last decades of the nineteenth century and was characterized by an increase in exports mainly because of the peasants' recourse to the market-place. In the second period, beginning in the first decade of the twentieth century, a more widespread trend, the capitalist plantation owned by a large corporation, took shape. In the first stage conditions were created for the second, among which we might note the internal formation of capital in required amounts.

In Trinidad, for example, the immigrants from Venezuela, as well as the free Blacks and the Indians who had completed their indentures, colonized uncultivated lands in the interior in order to plant cacao, the crop that began the export boom. Exports grew from an average of 8 million lbs per year between 1871 and 1880 to 56 million between 1911 and 1921.[19] In the

14 Richard Frucht, 1967, pp.295–301; Otis P. Starkey, 1939.
15 Ramiro Guerra y Sánchez *et al.*, 1952, VII, bk IV, chap. II.
16 Woodville K. Marshall, 1996, pp.99–106.
17 William Green, 1991.
18 Bridget Brereton, 1981.
19 *Ibid.*, p.93.

Dominican Republic, although the capitalist sugar-producing sector made its appearance shortly before 1880, cacao had its highest rate of growth between 1890 and 1910.[20] As in Trinidad, in the Dominican Republic this crop was produced mainly by *campesinos* (peasants) who took advantage of internal colonization, in this case made possible by the opening of the first railway in 1886.[21] In Puerto Rico, coffee offers an example of the connection between the predominance of a rural peasant economy and a partial advance in capitalist relations.[22] The boom in coffee between 1876 and 1898 was followed by a marked retreat in favour of sugar, due to the tariff conditions imposed by the United States' colonial administration which took over in that latter year.

As important as this route to modernization was, it had obvious limits; these limits of course varied from country to country, owing to the absence of consistent policies regarding the encouragement and growth of the peasant economy – or even to resistance on the part of authorities to committing to such policies. For years, British colonial authorities made it hard for freed slaves to acquire property, imposing an artificially elevated price on state-owned land and prohibiting the sale of small plots. Toward the end of the 1890s, when this policy was modified, although the reasonableness of sustained development of peasant agriculture had become obvious, there was still no coherent policy of encouragement. In fact, the expansion of the mercantile element of peasant production to the point where it might sustain an overall process of modernization would have required a whole range of measures and instruments, such as a public banking system, regulation of the mechanisms of exchange, services of technical extension, free distribution of land, and the construction of roads and irrigation canals.

Naturally, some measures along those lines were implemented, although they were almost invariably limited.[23] In Jamaica, for example, the construction of irrigation canals in arid regions was important. In the British colonies, the Norman Commission Report in 1897 led to a reorientation of pro-peasant policies in official spheres.[24] Yet even in the face of the crisis in the sugar industry, that commission found no better way to stimulate the peasant class than creating agricultural offices, constructing settlements, and building up the infrastructure. Before this, some islands had favoured turning labourers into small-scale landowners, as Governor A. H. Gordon had done

20 Patrick Bryan, 1979, pp.29–62.

21 Jaime de Jesús Domínguez, 1986.

22 Pedro San Miguel, 1992. The author accepts Fernando Picó's thesis regarding the primacy of the peasantry in coffee and questions Laird Bergad's disagreement. (See in that line Fernando Picó, 1981; Laird Bergad, 1983.)

23 Patrick Bryan, 1991.

24 Thomas C. Holt, 1992.

in Trinidad. Even before 1870, Gordon had ordered a network of roads to be built to support the cacao producers. In some countries, such as Haiti and the Dominican Republic, and under varying formulas, parcels of land were distributed, free of cost, to peasants who promised to engage in the permanent cultivation of export crops, for which they were exempted from military service. In others, such as Trinidad, Indian immigrants were offered for a time the alternative of grants of land in lieu of repatriation.[25] In some British colonies there was an attempt to create credit mechanisms in support of small-scale production. Overall, however, these were never more than isolated measures, and cannot be given credit for even the limited modernization of the peasant class. Often one measure was not complemented by another necessary measure; an example of this is land distribution, which was not accompanied by systems allowing access to credit. Thus there was a strengthening of the inherent tendency of the peasant economy to incorporate itself into the market-place to a degree exactly corresponding to its needs to reproduce itself, and this, of course, implied the continuity of the preference for self-subsistence.

At any rate, the number of peasant production units did grow, with the exception of a few cases such as Barbados, where the planter class was especially strong. In several islands of the Lesser Antilles, within forty years the number of landowners doubled. Thus, the peasant class was soon responsible for most production, including exports, except in those countries where sugar predominated.

The expansion of the peasant-based economy was especially logical because of the absence of governing-class forces able to create or put in place conditions favourable for the exportation of agricultural goods. The peasant class, albeit in a fundamentally unregulated way, filled a void left by the decline of the old planter class and not yet filled by the still-weak capitalists who would replace the planters. One should also note the weakness of the state apparatus in almost all countries, whether due to the colonies' loss of economic importance or the particular country's internal dynamics of class. The rise of the peasant class therefore was inversely proportional to the weakening of the 'dominant' sectors, which resulted from the peculiarities of political development. Simultaneously, its rise was the result of the resistance on the part of slaves and freedmen to their incorporation into labour patterns that wiped out the freedoms they had gained, as well as of the impossibility of establishing alternative patterns of social dominance which would do away with obstacles to proletarianization. Producers universally desired to attain the status of independent landowners, and to a considerable degree they did so.

25 Eric Williams, 1962 (1993).

Haiti, an extreme example both of the 'peasantization' of a country's economy, and of a state unable to impose itself upon the productive population and undertake development programmes, is also the most illustrative example of a precarious expansion of mercantile surpluses that never managed to generate a dynamics of economic modernization. The only moment at which consistent measures were attempted was during the administration of President Lycius Salomon (1879–88), when parcels of land were distributed, producers of new export crops were exempted from military service, an attempt was made to encourage immigration, a minimal agricultural-extension office and a national banking system were created, and the first plans for a railway were drawn up.[26] Despite the ambition of this president's development plans, his undertaking turned out to be a colossal failure, since he could not manage to divert certain structural tendencies that accompanied independent life, or avoid conflicts confronted by his modernization plans.[27] For precisely the same reason, the United States military intervention, between 1915 and 1934, had very few consequences for effective modernization.

The birth of a widespread rural mercantile class able to assimilate new technological patterns and become the agent of modernization was, thus, a limited phenomenon. In Cuba, where the peasant class of this type was most able to coalesce (around the cultivation of tobacco), it was still limited to pockets located mainly in Pinar del Río and La Habana provinces, and its share of exports never reached as high as 20 per cent.[28] In the Dominican Republic, the tobacco-growing sector, which since the end of the eighteenth century had been located mainly around Santiago, was a kind of paradigm of the advance of modernization,[29] but revealingly, tobacco experienced grave difficulties at the end of the century, concomitant with the rise of the sugar industry.[30]

Between these two extreme cases – the persistence of the autarchic economy and the predominance of production for the market-place – the most common scenario in the movement of the peasant classes toward their incorporation into the world market-place did not always imply a break with former patterns of production.[31] The peasantry did not feel the need to abandon many of its traditional social and technological features: small-scale farm-

26 Spenser St John, 1889; Roche Grellier, 1891; Paul Vibert, 1895.

27 Brenda Gayle Plummer, 1988, chap. IV; Robert Debs Heinl and Nancy Gordon Heinl 1996, pp.314 ff.

28 Julio Le Riverend, 1965.

29 Michiel Baud, 1996, pp.9–40.

30 Michiel Baud, 1995.

31 Pedro San Miguel, 1996.

ing or planting, lax systems of land ownership, the considerable persistence of production for self-consumption, archaic tools, a restricted use of modern agricultural methods, and, in summary, low levels of productivity.

Out of these conditions characteristic of the peasant economy there had emerged the agricultural-export crops that typified economic development during the decades following 1870 and that in part achieved their maximum expansion in the early years of the twentieth century: bananas in Jamaica; cacao in the Dominican Republic, Trinidad, Tobago and Grenada; rice in Suriname and Guyana; cotton in Grenada; coffee in the Dominican Republic, Puerto Rico and Jamaica; arrowroot in St Vincent; coconuts and copra in Grenada and Tobago; pepper in Jamaica; ginger in Jamaica and Grenada; lemons, limes and other citrus fruits in Montserrat and Dominica; nutmeg in Grenada, and so on. In some cases, the emergence of these crops was entirely in the hands of the peasant classes, while in others it was linked to the recomposition of mixed plantation systems, whether in the form of temporary wage labour or various share-cropping mechanisms.

Food crops for domestic consumption, on the other hand, were almost exclusively produced by the peasant class, only the rare product such as arrowroot catching the attention of the planters.[32] With these products it was possible to achieve low prices, which in turn made possible surpluses that contributed to making the economic system better integrated. Because of the growing importance of the mercantile sector, flows of foodstuffs were created from the rural areas to the plantations, such as those between Cibao and the East in the Dominican Republic, the mountainous eastern region and the southern plains in Jamaica, or between Montserrat and Antigua.[33]

The peasants and the capitalist plantation

From the foregoing it can be seen that the coexistence of economic patterns imposed limits on the ability of the peasant population to serve as an agent of expansion in the export sector. Thus, when the plantation gained strength in certain spaces, it tended to displace or uproot the peasant. This process became more widespread from the early twentieth century, giving way to a new stage in the development of the agricultural export industry. This was

32 J. S. Handler, 1971, pp.46–93.

33 There were other variants of spatial division, such as in Guyana, between coastal plantations and forest and mining exploitation in the interior (*cf.* Walter Rodney, 1981).

the case in Puerto Rico, as a result of which a marked process of proletarianization took place.[34] Although a dominant trend in the region as a whole, the shift from peasant exploitation of the land to the new capitalist plantation did not take place in every country. In some countries, in fact, the reverse occurred, when the old plantation system continued to decay yet no modern systems emerged to replace it. At the end of the nineteenth century in Tobago, the sugar-processing plantations disappeared completely, and their lands were parcelled out, sold, or farmed by sharecroppers.

What we see, therefore, is a plane of partial incompatibility between the survival of the peasant class and the development of the plantation. Nevertheless, just as had occurred during earlier decades after the abolition of slavery, the development of the capitalist agricultural export sector and the evolution of the peasant classes were closely interdependent. The backward nature of capitalist relations in the region meant that the expansion of capitalism did not necessarily entail complete proletarianization but rather that, from certain watershed moments onward, the expansion of the plantation was actually achieved on the basis of the peasant sector. Here we should distinguish between the constant interdependence between the peasants and capitalist relations on the one hand, and the uprooting of peasants as a consequence of the dynamism of the plantation on the other.

In both dynamics, what operated was the 'primary accumulation of capital',[35] which tended to lead to formation of capitalist export sectors. In the first instance, capital accumulation occurred in a continuous way, through extraordinary mechanisms of transfer of wealth from pre-capitalist sectors, socially homologous to the peasant class. The other variant implied the expropriation of that class, although not always its full proletarianization. In both cases, the trigger for these processes was the appearance of social agents who, from their businesses and maritime trade, or their governmental positions, were able to manipulate irregular mechanisms of enrichment which, with various types of mediation, resulted in investments in capitalist systems of production.[36]

The emerging leadership groups maintained an ambivalent relationship with the traditional elites: on the one hand, they subjected them to expropriations, but they also merged with them, as can be seen in Barbados, by means of marriage and corporate agreements.[37] Often, they employed public authority as a means toward accumulation. The strengthening of the state apparatus

34 Gervasio García and Angel Quintero Rivera, 1982.
35 Karl Marx, 1973, chap. XXIV.
36 Astrid Cubano, 1981, pp.67–124; Benoit Joachim, n.d.
37 Hilary Beckles, 1990, pp.132–4.

was, in fact, one of the bases for the innovations of the time, since the fiscal pressure that came to be exerted on the mass of producers, and the capacity for violence of modernized apparatuses, became the pillars of the formation of capital.

Even in Haiti – an overpopulated country with acute social conflicts and a weak state apparatus – preparations for the construction of sections of railway line from 1911 to 1913 were accompanied by a cession to the contractors of up to 20 km of land to both sides of the right-of-way, a practice which led to massive expulsions of peasants.[38] Later, the United States invaders forced the expulsion of thousands of inhabitants in order to set up a hemp plantation near Fort Liberté.[39]

However, the importance of extortionate demands on the peasants as a means for the formation of capital gradually declined after reaching its zenith during the final decades of the nineteenth century. The economic conditions of the twentieth century, combined with US expansion, paved the way toward the increase in size of the already established capitalist sectors. This means of accumulation was consolidated as a result of direct foreign investment, which also continued to benefit widely from extra-economic procedures unrelated to expanded production. In general, flows of capital to the region were gradually restricted, and were limited to relatively short periods of time. Such was the case in Cuba, where the capital of most of the United States sugar-processing plants was generated *in situ,* through re-investments, and despite constant and considerable repatriation of profits.[40] The slow and precarious nature of the advance of capitalist relations meant that the parallelism between the two modes continued, giving way to a kind of 'permanent original accumulation', as has been posited for Latin America as a whole.[41] This phenomenon has been observed in the Dominican Republic during the United States military intervention of 1916, when the entrance of fresh capital was accompanied by the dispossession of peasants in the areas where the cultivation of sugar was promoted.[42]

Despite all these factors – the importance of expropriation, the constant transfer of capital from the pre-capitalist sector, and the reproduction of capitalist relations – the peasantry continued, sometimes over long periods of time, to fill the gaps that resulted from the impossibility of modernizing the

38 André-Marcel d'Ans, 1987, p.199.

39 Hans Schmidt, 1971; Georges Michel, 1985.

40 Manuel Moreno Fraginals, 1985, pp.330–40; Eric Williams, 1970 (1984), pp.428–42.

41 Roger Bartra, 1980.

42 Bruce Calder, 1989.

former plantations. What is striking about this period is that this interrelationship extended beyond the boundaries of the political and administrative sector, forming the rudiments of a regional labour market.

Where the capitalist plantation expanded rapidly, the peasantry's struggle to survive caused grave difficulties in the supply of labour, making it essential to employ migrant workers. Peasants tried to escape proletarianization, perpetuating the behaviour that they had already exhibited after the abolition of slavery in the British colonies. At best, in all the colonies, including those which abolished slavery at the latest date, peasants tended to accept only temporary incorporation into the ranks of wage labour, and this made their role in solving the problems of labour demand more and more limited.[43]

These situations combined to make labour migrations increasingly important.[44] When the plantation's demands for labour could not be satisfied by the peasantry, seasonal labourers were introduced. Inversely, where the high population density of the plantation zones tended to exclude the formation of a widespread independent peasantry, flows of emigration occurred to places where wages were higher and there were eventual possibilities of becoming small landowners.

Thanks to this interdependence, the movement of seasonal labourers came to have greater importance than the importation of workers from other regions of the world, as had been characteristic of prior decades,[45] although imported workers continued to have a crucial function in several countries. Thus, Indians continued to enter British Guiana and Trinidad until 1917, Indonesians from Java entered Suriname until 1939, as did small contingents of Chinese. Despite the increase of intra-regional migrations, Indians employed in Trinidad and British Guiana continued to be essential to the existence of the sugar plantation, since they earned lower wages and thus kept wages low in other sectors. Migrants to Trinidad and the three Guianas from Barbados and other islands worked under similar conditions, although since many of them moved for short periods, they were better able to negotiate. In any case, the presence of migrants compensated for what the planters perceived as a lack of regularity or dependability on the part of the peasants for certain tasks.

Other contingents which came from across the ocean had no link with the labour market, but instead helped to form or expand the bourgeoisies and middle classes of the various countries.[46] Arabs from the Middle East settled

43 O. Nigel Bolland, 1996, pp.107–23.
44 Walton Look Lai, 1993.
45 Malcolm Cross, 1972.
46 Some of these contingents were formed in previous decades, such as the case of the Portuguese in Guyana (see Brian Moore, 1987).

in almost all countries, contributing to the formation of commercial circuits.[47] In Cuba, during the first two decades of the twentieth century, Spaniards came to represent almost 10 per cent of the population, although their role in the modernization of the country was much greater, since at least half of all merchants came from this group.[48]

As we have noted, as an expression of the capitalist reconstitution of the plantation, a web of intra-regional migrations occurred; for example: from the Lesser Antilles to Trinidad, the Guianas and the Dominican Republic; from Jamaica to Cuba; and from Haiti and Puerto Rico to Cuba and the Dominican Republic. The first emigrations out of the region also began occurring: from Cuba and the Bahamas to the United States; from Jamaica, Barbados and the Leeward Islands to the Panama Canal and Central America; from Curaçao and Trinidad to Venezuela.

In some cases, these emigrations were of such magnitude that they affected structural trends. In Barbados, for example, there was an emigration of some 45,000 persons (of whom, some 20,000 settled in the Panama Canal Zone), contributing to a net diminution of the population from 172,000 to 156,000 between 1911 and 1921. The labour market experienced great changes, such as women joining the labour force *en masse,* which allowed wages to remain low. In addition, with emigrants' remittances, and upon their eventual return, they were able to acquire land, and this finally contributed to a certain 'peasantification' of the population (as opposed to the proletarianization evidenced in other contexts), which became an element in the promotion of Blacks into craft occupations, small agriculture, business and the professions.[49]

Yet despite the boom in intra-regional migrations, the interaction between the peasantry and the plantation continued to be of greater importance than intra-regional emigrations in most societies, and this fact led to the emergence of various models by which small producers were subordinated to capitalism. Variants of seasonal wage labour and share-cropping and other forms of rent-farming were developed on the plantations and other units that operated on a large scale under capitalist parameters. For those plantations which did not manage to change their technological patterns drastically, as well as for the new landholders even in places that did manage to maintain a quasi-monopoly on land ownership, the way *par excellence* of attracting peasants was to grant them ownership of small parcels of land in exchange for work and cash rents or for a commitment to join the work-force as wage workers at times of maximum demand for labour.[50] The ability to attract

47 David Nicholls, 1981, pp.415–31.

48 Francisco López Segrera, 1979a, pp.165–293.

49 Bonham C. Richardson, 1983.

50 Woodville K. Marshall, 1965, pp.28–55; Howard Johnson, 1996.

peasants was linked to a number of factors which included the quality of the soil, mechanisms of commercialization, nearby roads, or contributions by the landholders of goods needed for the crops. All of this generated an intermediate, transition stage which led toward more defined class forms but which was still not fully capitalist.[51]

These readjustments on the part of large landowners frequently implied a diversification of production. When the economy entered a phase of expansion, the former plantations that had abandoned areas once dedicated to sugar-cane tended to put those lands to use for growing new export or food crops, in agreement with the peasants. The formation of cattle ranches in the larger countries corresponded to the demands of the economy, becoming the counterpoint to the large sugar-cane estate and a means of giving birth to modern landholding sectors.

In Jamaica, this diversification into cattle and miscellaneous articles such as pepper was common.[52] In several countries, such as the Dominican Republic and Puerto Rico, large cattle ranches and coffee plantations were developed with the help of peasants who were granted land for a certain number of years, to be returned planted. Variants of this practice and of sharecropping continued to appear in Haiti, the Bahamas, and some of the Lesser Antilles such as Tobago and St Lucia.[53] Indeed, far from decreasing, these 'semi-feudal' variants tended to gain strength.

As we have noted, despite this symbiosis between the peasantry and the plantation, there continued to be a conflict that restrained the recomposition of the export-oriented plantation, since the peasantry was never available in the numbers needed. This difficulty stemmed, basically, from the slow pace of the transformation of the slave-era plantations, which attempted to sustain themselves on a technological base dating from the first decades of the nineteenth century, at a time when steam engines, steel parts for the mills, and steam evaporators and desiccators came into use. In some countries, principally in the Lesser Antilles, the traditional sugar sector managed to survive for a long time, though in a moribund state that was increasingly isolated from the demands of technological renewal and expansion of capacity.

Because of this complex of factors, the sugar sector, which never ceased to be the decisive element in the region's economic base, developed in very different ways in the different countries. Despite the growing difficulties of the old planter class, in some places this survived as the leading social sector, and its control of the land made any concessions to workers largely

---

51 Roberto Cassá, 1982.
52 Patrick Bryan, 1991.
53 For Haiti, Paul Moral, 1978; for Tobago, Eric Williams, 1962 (1993), p.124.

unnecessary. In Barbados, the most outstanding case in this respect, the sugar plantation, which continued to represent almost the totality of exports, had no difficulty in finding the 30,000 workers it needed. It is interesting that in 1897, only 8,500 freedmen and their descendants were owners of a minuscule 10,000 acres of land.[54] With an average plantation size of approximately 250 acres, only a few plantations would consist of more land than was owned by all the peasants put together. In Barbados, the price of land reached 40 times that of neighbouring Dominica.

In other cases, the plantation simply disappeared, as in Grenada, Dominica and Tobago.[55] Due to the special circumstances of some islands, the antiquated sugar-cane processing mills that produced varieties of muscovado and clayed sugar could survive a long time without reducing the absolute total of their production, as can be seen in St Kitts and Antigua, where the decline of the plantation occurred relatively slowly. But even in Barbados, the transition to modern forms of sugar production confronted severe difficulties. The first modern unit was founded only in 1910, when the slow reduction in the number of sugar-cane processing mills is an indicator of the resistance made by the archaic plantations; at the beginning of the twentieth century, there were 411 sugar-cane processing mills, of which only 265 still survived in 1923.

The most common variant of the transition was the partial modernization of the sugar sector, based on an equilibrium between the obsolete mills and the capitalist-type industrial units, the so-called central factories. Even in countries such as Trinidad, Jamaica and Puerto Rico, the total production might fall or, more frequently, lose its relative share in the overall economy. Jamaica suffered both losses when the sugar sector's percentage of exports dropped from 44 per cent to 10 per cent between 1870 and 1900 at the same time as bananas rose to over 50 per cent. Planters followed in the steps of the peasants in developing this latter crop.

Lastly, Cuba remained a paradigm of the systematic modernization of the sugar sector, even though it experienced difficulties when slavery was abolished and the transition to modern capitalism began.[56] It was, in fact, at the beginning of the twentieth century that the capitalist sugar plantation entered a phase of rapid expansion, a model that was adopted and thus typified modernization in Cuba, Puerto Rico and the Dominican Republic; in other countries such as Haiti, Jamaica, Trinidad and Guyana its advances were not so notable. Although there were always plantations producing other

54 Hilary Beckles, 1990.

55 Michel-Rolph Trouillot, 1988.

56 Rebecca J. Scott, 1985.

crops, sugar continued to be the basis of the region's overall financial evolution, and therefore of the capitalist modernization of the agricultural export sector.

The central factory

In those countries where the sugar sector evolved in a clearly capitalistic direction, there was a tendency to rethink the relationship between the peasantry and the plantation. It would no longer be a question of using the peasants' 'left-over' time by leasing or renting out land, but rather of employing them in wage work or subordinating them to an accessory position for the provisioning of raw materials.

As a consequence of the application of the technological advances of the second industrial revolution, starting around the 1880s, there was a widespread transfer of the work of the former small mill to the central factory, or centralized processing plant. There was a great gap between the size of the two entities. In 1830, the average production of a Cuban mill was about 30 tons per year, while a half-century later it had surpassed 500 tons. During the last decade of the nineteenth century, the largest central factories could produce 20,000 tons or more per year.

The first element that accompanied the emergence of this new type of unit was the concentration of production in an ever-smaller number of facilities. Cuba was, naturally, the country where the process was most dramatic: the number of mills fell from approximately 2,000 in 1860 to 1,190 in 1877, 850 in 1890, 207 in 1899, and 175 in 1927.[57] Clearly, this decrease achieved its greatest intensity in the 1890s, precisely when there was a marked turn toward the construction of central factories. Similar concentrations occurred, although not in such a pronounced way, in all the countries of the region that possessed a large sugar-producing sector. In Jamaica, the number of mills fell from 316 in 1848 to 122 in 1900 and 70 in 1910;[58] in Puerto Rico, it fell from 550 in 1860 to 146 in 1910, of which 41 were considered central factories and were virtually all of recent construction.[59]

This trend was based on the merger of units into larger establishments, given that the smallest mills were forced out of the market by competitive pressures. Often, the mergers entailed a transfer to new owners, who had

57 Francisco López Segrera, 1979a, p.191.

58 Clinton V. Black, 1983.

59 James L. Dietz, 1986.

been taking part in credit or commercialization activities. Likewise, there was direct investment of United States and British capital. There emerged a new concept of ownership, ownership by corporations, whose capital increasingly came from the countries of the centre.[60] These companies would swallow up several mills, with the largest of them achieving a high percentage of the country's total product. Although before 1898 there were Cuban central factories with United States owners, it has been calculated that United States investments in Cuban- or Spanish-owned factories in Cuba reached approximately US$50 million after that date. In the Dominican Republic, during the first decade of the twentieth century the United States company Bartram Brothers, which specialized in credit and machinery sales, took over some of the factories or mills that had been founded by Cuban or local capitalists.[61]

Technological innovations were introduced into the new units, and the mechanized factory became the standard type in the twentieth century. The most noteworthy aspects of these changes, which began to happen very fast, beginning in the 1890s, were the vacuum pan evaporator, the centrifuge, and the three horizontal press rollers. The main result of the use of these innovations was a uniform product, 96-grade sugar, which replaced the variety of qualities of muscovado obtained from the small mills.

To the degree that this technological base required large amounts of capital, it took out of circulation those units which could not meet high standards of efficiency. Thus concentration of property was accompanied by widespread bankruptcy among the Creole sector that had once made up the planter class. A large number of these former large landholders and millowners were reduced to the category of cane-farmers or *colonos* in Cuba, now not processing but merely growing and supplying sugar-cane to the industrial units. This phenomenon entailed a division of labour between industry and agriculture that left behind the old mill's way of functioning.

The first experiments with the *colonato* (cane-farming) system occurred in Martinique in the mid-nineteenth century,[62] but the system gained force following the Cuban model in the 1870s. With the construction of the first units that technologically retooled the production process, the factory began to be the general rule. It was supplied with raw material exclusively or to a large degree from its associated agricultural producers. By 1887, almost 40 per cent of the sugar-cane grown in Cuba was sold by *colonos*. The division of labour between the agricultural and industrial sectors allowed the owners of factories to concentrate their initially scarce resources in the industrial phase of

60 For the case of several well-known planters in this process, see Roland Ely, 1963.
61 Franc Báez Evertsz, 1978.
62 Armand Nicolas, 1996, II, pp.60–4.

sugar production and to profit from the lower costs realized by freeing themselves from the agricultural cycle. Paying the *colonos* by assigning them a percentage of the sugar produced became the usual way of paying for raw materials; a calculation was made of the productivity of the land and the yield from the sugar-cane in the industrial phase.

Around the system of *colonato* there emerged an agricultural bourgeoisie, made up of former planters, modern estate- or plantation-owners, and segments of the peasantry that 'recycled' themselves in sugar-cane. It was the peasants, including even those of a certain affluence, who had the least power to negotiate with the factories. Some of these *colonos* eventually even leased land from the mill, and this is a sign that a transfer of profits occurred from the agricultural to the industrial sector. In these cases, the industrial unit operated as what was known in the Hispanic Caribbean as a *refaccionista,* that is, a supplier of credit, and this, of course, increased the producers' subordination. The magnitude of the *colonato* system in Cuba can be seen in the following figures from 1931: 9.3 per cent of the sugar-cane was supplied by 'independent' *colonos,* 68.7 per cent by 'controlled' *colonos,* and only 22 per cent came from the factory itself.[63]

Toward the end of the nineteenth century, central factories were being formed at a relatively slow rate, although they continued to be responsible for the increase in sugar production. Around 1890, once Cuba emerged from the depression whose epicentre had been the 1884 fall in prices, a growth began that led to the first million-ton harvest in 1894. Later, during the second War of Independence, begun in 1895, the destruction of cane fields ordered by the leadership of the Army of Liberation caused a pronounced fall in production.

Other countries followed Cuba's pattern of founding central factories, although to a notably lesser degree. In Puerto Rico, difficulties with credit and other factors led to an expansion that was initially fairly restricted, to the extent that the fall in production was not at first stemmed; this lack of dynamism led to the bankruptcy of several units.[64] In the Dominican Republic, the experiment was more successful, but its quantitative impact was not at first great, due to the absence of a sugar sector prior to 1875, with the exception of rustic cane presses. At any rate, the founding or expansion of central factories during the 1890s around San Pedro de Macorís consolidated the pre-eminence of the sugar sector in the Dominican economy.

In Trinidad, sugar production began to recover after 1850. Although large new tracts of land had been added, the increase in production was

63 Foreign Policy Association, 1935.
64 Teresita Martínez-Vergne, 1992.

linked especially to technological improvement, which led to the establishment of central factories; and this, combined with the merger of estates, had occurred early on, unlike in other British colonies. In 1872, Usine St Madeleine began production; this factory was founded with an investment of British capital from the Colonial Company totalling about £340,000 in 1897 and some 10,000 acres of plantation proper. This example was followed by other investments of British capital which modernized mills or created new ones. One such case was the Tennant Company, which, with an investment of about £400,000, owned Malgretout and La Fortune. Some English families who lived on the island also joined the modernization trend, although production was concentrated in 11 of the 59 units, almost all founded on metropolitan capital. With these investments, it became feasible to weather lowered prices and phase out the technologies that produced muscovado sugar, which at the beginning of the twentieth century fell to a secondary position.[65]

The sugar corporation

In the early twentieth century, several factors came together to open a new chapter in the production of sugar; this conjunction occurred mainly in the Hispanophone islands and was characterized by the investment of monopolizing United States capital that replaced those of individual investors.[66] The material forerunner of this phenomenon was the central factory, whose large investments explain the presence of Wall Street capital.Secondly, the influx of capital was associated with the United States' political and economic control of these islands. The United States invasion of Cuba and Puerto Rico in 1898 did away with the difficulties presented by Spanish colonial domination and allowed the penetration of United States capital. In the future, not only would the amount of United States capital rise enormously, but these investments would also lead to exclusive ownership of many units. Lastly, the promise of an improvement in prices that began with the twentieth century and the subsequent increase world wide in sugar-cane production attracted direct investment. The moderate boom in the first years of the century turned quickly to a phase of expansion stemming from the conditions created by the First World War: demand for sugar increased; there was difficulty in supplying sugar due to the closing-down of production facilities in the European sugar-beet industry; and there was a subsequent rise in prices.

65 Bridget Brereton, 1981, pp.84ff.
66 Oscar Pino Santos, 1973.

At the beginning of the twentieth century, then, conditions in the international economy, and especially *vis-à-vis* the commercialization of sugar, were ripe to attract investors. Due to agreements reached at the International Sugar Conference in Brussels that came into effect in 1903, the previous decades' trend of increased world sugar-beet production was reversed, and within a few years it began to be clear that sugar prices, low for at least two decades, were beginning to rise.[67]

The former increase in sugar-beet production had been due to technological innovations, subsidies granted to producers by European governments, and the free-trade policy adopted by England, a country which had decided to open its market to imports of foodstuffs in order to lower the cost of feeding its population and favour its industrial sector's competitiveness.

As part of this policy, since 1846 England had opted to sacrifice the interests of its colonies in the Caribbean, eliminating all former tariff advantages. European sugar-beet producers immediately took advantage of the levelling of tariffs in the British market, and in this they were supported by their respective governments, which granted bonuses to exporters. Given this change, planters in the British colonies could barely stave off total extinction.[68] At the end of the century, pressures from the planters, the colonial interests of the British government, and the needs of imperial refiners, who believed that it was better to re-establish a 'special relationship' with the colonies, came together to produce a reaction on the part of the British government to the impending death of the sugar industry in their Caribbean possessions. England at last saw fit to provide grants and loans for the retooling of the mills.[69]

Still more drastic was the position adopted by the United States. In the 1890s, the domination of the United States sugar market by the American Sugar Corporation (the prop that kept the Sugar Trust of the refineries owned by Henry O. Havemeyer standing) had been embodied in mutual preferred-tariff agreements between the United States and several countries in the Caribbean Basin.[70] In exchange for waiving or reducing import duties on sugar into the United States market, Caribbean nations granted tariff advantages to merchandise imported from the United States. But these agreements were applied only briefly, and combined with divergent interests in the domestic market and tariff wars with Spain – a country which attempted to

67 Thomas C. Holt, 1992.
68 R. W. Beachey, 1957.
69 Thomas C. Holt, 1992, pp.365ff.
70 Louis A. Pérez, 1983.

maintain a rigid policy of protection for her manufacturers in the Cuban market – had little effect in opening the United States market.[71]

This situation changed when the United States, as one aspect of its domestic political situation, expressed an interest in making the Caribbean a protected zone for its sugar supply. Parallel to its takeover of Cuba and Puerto Rico in 1898, the United States government levied a tax on European beet sugar which cancelled out the effect of the subsidies granted by the producers' home governments and thereby prevented easy entry into the United States market.

These developments culminated in pressures from the United States and Britain, the two largest consumers, on the European beet producers for the elimination of subsidies, and the effect of this pressure was the Brussels agreement of 1902. These changes in the international commercialization of sugar soon began to have consequences in the region.

Counting on its political control, the United States unveiled a strategy whereby it would encourage expansion of the sugar industry in the Caribbean. This strategy was based on the assumption that a flood of direct capital investment would occur and that Caribbean markets would be opened to United States industrial products. Given its status as a colonial possession, Puerto Rico was integrated into the United States market by means of the elimination of all trade and tariff barriers and the unification of the two monetary and tax systems. As a result of the advantage given by the free entrance of sugar into the US market, a large influx of capital into the island occurred: of the US$176 million that entered (27 per cent of total gross investments), US$140 million came from the United States, and of this, 22 per cent went into sugar. In addition, when the two monetary systems were merged, investors took advantage of the devaluation of the Spanish *peso* and of the difficulties experienced on that account by local planters.

Until the First World War, some local landowners and European investors could take advantage of the tariff exemption – only shared with the Philippines and Hawaii – to increase profits from the plantations under their control.[72] But in the long run, four American companies set up shop on the island (South Porto Rico, Fajardo, Aguirre and United Porto Rico), and, with their 11 central factories, by 1928 they controlled fully half of the sugar-cane harvest. Thanks to their control of the best land, these companies pushed local producers who had managed to survive the vicissitudes so far into a more and more marginal position in the market. This context manifested itself in a dramatic increase in sugar production, which rose almost tenfold, from

71 Ramiro Guerra y Sánchez *et al.*, 1952, VIII, bk IV, chap. V.

72 Humberto García Muñiz, 1996.

100,000 tons in 1900 to 866,000 tons in 1930, with a respective value of US$5.9 and US$53.6 million.[73]

In 1902, the United States forced the government of Cuba to accept a proposed trade agreement, considered the counterpart of the Platt Amendment which had given the United States the power to intervene in the internal affairs of the new government. Cuba was given 'most-favoured nation' status and conceded a 20 per cent reduction in tariffs. In return, dozens of industrial and agricultural products from the United States were exempted or given exclusive tariff reductions when they entered Cuba, thereby fostering the unilateral growth of the sugar industry to the exclusion of the development of agricultural or industrial sectors to supply the domestic market. In Cuba there were better conditions than in Puerto Rico for sugar-industry expansion, because of a more developed tradition in production and the existence of broad tracts of virgin land.

In the first years after the Spanish-American War, United States capital began to take over existing units and construct other even larger ones. Although before the First World War the individual company, not yet tied to monopolistic capital, tended to dominate, this influx of investment was tied to businesses connected with the Sugar Trust. United States companies directed their attention mainly toward the provinces of Camagüey and Oriente, where there was a great deal of virgin land.

Even more intensely than in Puerto Rico, during the first two decades of the twentieth century in Cuba there was a local estate-owning class, mostly of Spanish descent, which had supplanted the original class of Creole slaveholders. Although after Spain's withdrawal from the island there was a connection between sugar investment and US high finance, the formation of consortia began to have notable consequences after 1914, as independent companies began to be left in a secondary position or taken over. A portent of this development could be seen in the establishment of a company named Cuban Cane, in 1914, with US capital totalling US$50 million, a considerable percentage of it contributed by the New York branch of Czarnikow Rionda, a well-known international trading house. Within a short time, Cuban Cane had taken over 12 central factories which together generated 17 per cent of the yearly production.

As a result of the conditions outlined above, Cuban sugar production grew at a rapid pace. By 1902 the 1895 level of a million tons had been met and surpassed. The following years saw dynamic growth, although it would be only after the beginning of the First World War that truly spectacular

73 James L. Dietz, 1986, p.105.

growth occurred, with the harvest reaching more than 5 million tons in 1925.[74]

The growth of the Cuban sugar industry was decisively associated with monopolistic control by United States capital of virtually the entire Cuban economy. During the 1920s, United States investment in Cuba totalled approximately US$1.14 billion, second in Latin America only to investments in Mexico. Logically, the preponderant sector in these investments was sugar, with some US$600 million, 52 per cent of the total.[75] In fact, other areas of United States investment were also connected with the plantation, such as railways and public services, each of which held 10 per cent of total investments.

In 1927, businesses backed with United States capital held the property of 75 estates, with production equivalent to 70 per cent of the harvest. There were, in addition, 14 estates of mixed capital and 10 of Canadian. Cuban capital's share stood at some 25 per cent of the production. At the end of this period, United States central factories controlled five million hectares, 30 per cent of the country's total territory.

More or less the same situation obtained in the Dominican Republic where, at the end of the 1920s, two corporations, the South Porto Rico Sugar Company and the West Indies Sugar Corporation, holding two and four central factories respectively, processed just over 70 per cent of the harvest; an additional 20 per cent was controlled by factories held by independent United States investors, although most of them were linked in various ways to West Indies Sugar, and the rest to two local families, one of which went under after the crash of 1930.

We have already seen that in some British colonies British capital played a key role in the modernization of the sugar industry, also allowing production to boom at the time of the First World War. In Jamaica, sugar temporarily recovered a leading position among exports. Barbados illustrates the consequences of the construction of central factories, causing production to grow from 11,000 tons in 1913 to 70,000 in 1919.[76]

Massive control by monopolistic capital had implications for the characteristics of the sugar central factory which became what has been called an 'enclave', a category denoting foreign ownership of the export apparatus.[77] We have observed above how it became associated with absentee corporate owners, whose only intermediaries were administrators and technicians who were almost entirely foreigners. At the same time, the industry became ever

74 Ramiro Guerra y Sánchez *et al.*, 1952, IX, bk II, chap. III.

75 Leland H. Jenks, 1966.

76 Noel Deerr, 1949–50.

77 Fernando Henrique Cardoso and Enzo Falleto, 1969.

more dependent on the import of seasonal workers; the epicentre of this phenomenon was Cuba, with the highest corporate presence together with a net migratory population of 217,000 Haitians and Jamaicans between 1910 and 1929.[78] Among the countries in which sugar was especially important, Puerto Rico was an anomalous case, since its socio-demographic make-up allowed it to function without the importation of seasonal labourers.

In addition, the enclave entailed a certain isolation *vis-à-vis* the other elements of the overall society, although the importance of the export sector necessarily implied effects on that society. But the eyes of the central factories were turned toward the exterior, to which they were connected by railways and ports that allowed them to import directly most of the goods necessary to their functioning.[79] The magnitude of the large estates, the *latifundios,* led, in addition, to their becoming replicas of the State, even to the extent that central factories normally had their own police forces which replaced public officials. The central factory attempted to control the commercial system and supply the goods consumed by its personnel by installing its own facilities for supplying those needs (bakeries, butcher shops, sawmills, dairies, and the like), thereby keeping the commercial portion of the surplus value on the premises; to help in this, wages were often paid in chits called 'fichas' and 'vales,' which forced labourers to make their purchases of food and other items in the company stores.

United States investment expanded owing to the effect of the inflated profits that followed the First World War. To prevent the trend of rising prices brought on by the destruction of sugar-beet fields in Europe, the government of the United States set a fixed price of US$5.50 per hundredweight on imported sugar. This measure was abandoned in 1919, and the result was that prices skyrocketed – the so-called 'dance of the millions' – because of the time required for the sugar-beet fields to recover. In May of 1920, the price of brown sugar reached a high of US$22.50 per hundredweight.

In the second half of 1920, sugar prices began a slow decline. A collapse in prices occurred in October of that year, by 1922 reaching lows of about US$2.00 per hundredweight. Many owners of mills and cane-farmers were unable to meet the credit payments for which they had contracted when they could expect high profits spurred by the speculation fever. Suddenly a bank panic broke out, which wiped out most of the banks supported by Cuban capital. Branches of United States banks came to have virtually complete control of the Cuban banking system when they took over the paper left by the bankrupt Cuban institutions and proceeded to make indiscriminate

---

78 Juan Pérez de la Riva, 1979, pp.38–43.
79 *United Fruit Co....*, 1976.

foreclosures. In 1921, the National City Bank became, at least temporarily, the owner of some fifty sugar factories.

This massive control by corporations in the major producing countries meant that the 1920 crisis had tangible consequences for the working population. Jobs were restricted, salaries fell, and greater use was made of migrant labourers. Likewise, the features of the enclave system became even more pronounced when many local landowners abandoned their mills and fields.

The crash of 1920 affected all those countries which in previous years had experienced a reactivation of the sugar industry, although only in a few cases was there a dependency as great as Cuba's. Initially, as in other countries, Cuban producers, compelled to adopt a policy of survival by lowering their unit cost, simply increased their harvests, though this, of course, only helped to further depress prices.[80] As the world's principal producer of sugar, in order to prevent prices falling, in 1926 Cuba decided unilaterally to adopt a policy to control harvests, ordering a reduction of 10 per cent from the preceding year's crop. But it proved impossible for all the exporting countries of the region to reach an agreement that would stabilize market functioning. Thus, Cuba's isolated efforts were doomed to failure. Meanwhile, in 1923 the United States imposed the Fordney Tariff on sugar which raised the duty from 1.0 cent to 1.7 cents, eroding producer profits; this restriction became worse in 1930 with the Hawley-Smoot Tariff, which raised the tariff to two cents.[81] In consequence, from about 1923 onwards, most Caribbean producers, with the exception of Puerto Rico and to a lesser degree Cuba, began to sell their sugar to Canada, Britain and other countries. Despite the fact that between 1924 and 1928 prices experienced some recovery and production continued to rise, the events of 1920 were of such great significance that they heralded the limits to sugar production by the agro-exporters of the entire region.

Alternatives to agricultural exports

Although holding secondary positions overall, alternatives to agricultural exports did arise as a mechanism of modernization, whether because of the difficulties faced by agricultural exports or because of hopes for higher profits. Some of these developments were aimed at expanding exports of minerals. They were also the effects of an increase in exports at the beginning of the period of economic diversification.

80 Melvin M. Knight, 1939.
81 Ramiro Guerra y Sánchez, 1970.

The first variant among the alternative exports emerged in response to the world's growing demand for mineral resources, a demand caused by the economic changes occurring in the countries of the centre. These nations required greater and greater amounts of raw materials for their industrial processes. This was what began to happen with Trinidadian oil and Guyana and Suriname's bauxite.[82] This process also impacted on certain traditional mining practices: copper in Cuba and gold in Guyana were the most important products mined in previous periods.

In all cases, mineral exploitation was disconnected from the respective country's domestic markets, even more sharply so than was the case with agricultural exports. In Cuba, no industrial processes for transforming copper were established; the same was true for Guyana and Suriname and their bauxite. Another factor in the isolation lay in the relatively small demand for labour generated by the extractive activities. In Trinidad, to cite but one case, in the late 1920s when oil was becoming the most valuable export product in the country, the industry only employed some 5,000 persons.

The impact of these activities on the economy was variable. While in Trinidad oil and asphalt virtually came to determine the state of the economy, copper in Cuba never achieved an important position in the export picture. In all cases – with the exception of gold – the appearance of mining as a significant element in the economy came late and at a time of growing strengthening of capitalist production. Although mining in Trinidad, for example, had begun with the exploitation of asphalt in 1886, it only came to have any special importance in the economy when oil drilling was attempted in the first decade of the twentieth century. It was the demand brought on by the First World War that encouraged new companies and kept production high. In the following years, Trinidad began its shift to an extractive-based economy; oil rose from 10 per cent of exports in 1919 to 50 per cent in 1932, and represented 44 per cent of production in British possessions world wide.[83]

Interest in mining bauxite began around the same time, the first shipments being made from Guyana in 1917, a few years later from Suriname. Volumes were limited because worldwide demand for aluminum only became important after the start of the Second World War.

In the Guianas, the gold boom was a result of the search for alternatives on the part of coastal settlers, largely Creole Blacks, who were attempting to find a way out of the disadvantageous conditions on the plantation by temporary incursions into the interior. Generally, these were not organized or large-scale activities. Only in French Guyane did gold achieve a dominant

---

82 Vere Daly, 1975.

83 Bridget Brereton, 1981, pp.199–205.

place in the export picture, and this occurred during the last quarter of the nineteenth century, coinciding with the disappearance of the last plantations and their white inhabitants and with the parallel demographic and administrative impact of the penitentiary system.[84]

Another raw material of considerable importance in some countries was lumber. On some of the larger islands, the cutting down of forests for pasture land or cane fields kept the timber industry alive, although it tended to be somewhat marginal. In Jamaica, Haiti and other countries there was a short-lived boom in logwood, or *campeche*, but this activity ended in the 1890s with the development of an artificial dye. Overall, lumber activity was more important in the continental territories, where the forests were virtually intact, but even in the Guianas it did not displace the importance of coastal activities, as it tended to be limited to balata production (similar to latex or gutta-percha) and rosewood essence.

The only country in which the exploitation of the forests became dominant was Belize, and this was due to a population so sparse that logging was unable to cause the irreversible destruction of the forests. Yet for this same reason it was carried on under primitive conditions: there were few roads, so that trees had to be carted to rivers on oxcarts, and this limited exploitation to areas near large rivers. Only in the 1930s did the use of tractors become widespread and the first sawmills were installed.[85]

Despite the opening of export markets, these countries almost always produced only raw materials, or at best developed limited manufacturing processes. Among these, one might mention manufactured goods aimed at a domestic demand spurred by the increase in wealth generated within the economy, and by export industries. Although manufacturing processes aimed at the domestic market only rarely produced goods of better than artisan-grade quality, they did begin to increase as a result of stimulus from the formation of regional markets which grew up around the ports.[86] Among the stimuli to the growth of these particular goods were the availability of raw materials, savings on transportation costs, and the peculiarities of demand due to cultural traditions. Depending on the country, the goods might be cigars, matches, leather goods of various kinds, baskets, shoes, carpentry goods, hats, foodstuffs and candies, etc. Since national markets emerged late, difficulties with transportation, the modest size of the demand for these goods, and the scarcity of capital prevented development of a factory phase.[87]

---

84 Serge Mam-Lam-Fouck, 1996.
85 O. Nigel Bolland, 1997, chaps 3 and 6.
86 H. E. Friedlander, 1944.
87 Angel G. Quintero Rivera, 1988.

These same reasons made the development of modern industries the exception rather than the rule. Even so, small-scale industrial companies became the norm in fields such as brewing, soft drinks, cigarettes, leather goods, rum and the like. The only possibility for the emergence of industrial plants on a large scale came from the diversification of traditional export goods due to changes in demand. This is what happened, for example, in Martinique, which became the world's largest producer of rum, to the extent that sugar fell to second place and molasses had to be imported from Guadeloupe and other nearby islands. The boom in rum production, which rose to 70 per cent of exports in 1918, at a value of 52 million francs, was a result of French tariff strategies and increased consumption during the war.[88]

A similar derivation of traditional exports occurred with the manufacture of cigars and cigarettes, which reached important dimensions especially in the three Hispanophone countries from which tobacco had been exported since the eighteenth century. The establishment of plants for the large-scale manufacture of cigars had begun in Cuba toward the middle of the nineteenth century. As time went on, the quality of Cuban cigars improved and the industrial production of cigarettes also began to expand.[89] The manufacture of cigars entered a new phase with the United States invasion of 1898, which made it possible for new capital from that country to enter Cuba. A handful of businesses came to control most of the prestigious brands; chief among these was the American Cigar Company, which acquired more than twenty manufacturing establishments and soon relegated other United States, British and German investors to second place. United States investments came to control half the cigar factories and in some years as much as 90 per cent of all tobacco exports.

In Puerto Rico the demand generated by the establishment of United States companies, which achieved even greater control of the industry here than in Cuba, stimulated a resurgence in tobacco cultivation. In virtue of this, tobacco exports increased steadily until the late 1920s, when they reached a peak of 16 per cent of total exports, to which might be added another 3.5 per cent for cigars.

Only in exceptional cases did there occur manufacturing activities which were not linked to traditional agricultural-export products. For example, in Puerto Rico, especially the eastern region, the 'needlework industry' took on importance when the island became linked to the United States market. For the clothing-assembly companies of the United States, it was profitable to sub-contract to Puerto Rican suppliers, who would hire female workers to work

88 Armand Nicolas, 1996, I, p.188; Alain-Philippe Blérald, 1986.

89 Jean Stubbs, 1989a.

in their homes.[90] This practice was begun around 1910, and a decade later the clothing industry was booming, with exports of US$15.4 million in 1929, 9.3 per cent of total exports, and 40,000 women employed, though the wages they received were very low, averaging between 25 and 50 cents per day.[91] Oil refining had even greater importance in Curaçao, which processed crude oil for Venezuela as part of the business strategy of Shell Oil starting in 1916, and in Aruba in 1924.

Linked to the need to generate profits, there were similar diversification attempts in the service area. The first decades of the twentieth century saw the beginning of the flow of tourists to the Bahamas, and to a lesser degree Barbados, from Britain and the United States.[92] But one should also note the emergence of services connected to the expansion of the export sector and the formation of urban social sectors. Havana, then the largest city in the Caribbean and one of the largest in the Americas, was the model for feasible achievements in modernization, with systems based on paradigms found at the centre of empire. Foreign investment gave rise to extended systems of trade, finance, educational services and health, as well as transportation, communication and energy.

Transportation systems

Changes in worldwide patterns of transportation provided the technological basis for a more solid integration of the Caribbean into the world market. Industrial centres were obliged to seek strategies for placing their products, while at the same time they demanded raw materials or foodstuffs. Thus, a reduction in transportation costs was one of the key components in the expansion of the productive sector in the region, allowing even goods that had formerly not been profitable to enter the international market-place.

The replacement of sailing ships with steamers in the 1880s, which made it feasible to reduce transportation charges, had the consequent effect of increasing the flow of goods and passengers. This occurrence also aided the seasonal migrations so characteristic of this period. Until this time, shipping between some of these countries was largely limited to relationships with neighbouring islands.

90 Francisco Scarano, 1993.
91 María del Carmen Baerga, 1993; María Angustias Guerrero, 1991.
92 Gail Saunders, 1990.

On that same theme of integration into the outside market and links to regions of larger size, we should mention new systems for communication. In this period almost all the countries under consideration became connected to Europe and the United States by telegraph cables laid under the sea; in time, domestic lines also expanded, and the telegraph service completely covered urban centres.[93] The first telephone lines were installed on a modest scale toward the end of the century, and by the 1920s all the larger cities had an extensive telephone service.

No less important than these developments were advances in domestic systems of transportation. Until late in the nineteenth century, most travel was accomplished on roads traversable only by draft animals; the use of carriages and coaches was limited to short stretches of road in the coastal and plantation areas, and even then the roads tended to be in poor condition. Thus, travel was enormously difficult during the rainy seasons. The general obstacles to overland transportation gave rise to coastal sailing, but this did not help exchanges with the interior. The result was the fragmentation of the region's economies into markets that connected instead to the outside world.

The first modern means of transport were not aimed at altering this pattern of exchange; indeed, they had the paradoxical effect of making it all the more systematic. The networks of railway lines were conceived as an accessory to the export-oriented plantation. The same thing occurred, though to a lesser degree, with the system of vehicular roads in the coastal zones. The relative importance of railways and carriage roads depended on the particular circumstances of each country. Railways were characteristic of large territories in which there was a network of plantations or the possibility for their expansion, which explains why only a few countries, such as Cuba and Jamaica, had railway lines before 1875. Following the lead of Cuba, it became characteristic of the region that sugar-cane plantations would have their own private railway lines. Only between the end of the nineteenth century and the beginning of the twentieth did public railways become relatively important in the larger countries.

In almost all these cases, the systems had serious defects, which naturally led to scandals, protests, and criticism by intellectuals, who saw railways as agents of foreign control in their countries, and who advocated national road-building efforts.[94] In Puerto Rico, the project for a rail line that would circle the island along the coastal plain was never fully implemented, but was limited to unconnected stretches of track with a total length of 159 miles. More serious was the case of Haiti with the McDonnald concession and its fraudulent dealings; in addition to the fact that stretches of track were never

93 H. Hoetink, 1972.

94 Emilio Rodríguez Demorizi, 1964.

interconnected, they covered only the coastal zones, precisely where they were not needed. In the Dominican Republic, the two commercial rail lines not only had technical defects, they could never be completed, and were moreover built to competing ports.[95] In Cuba, railways at the beginning of the twentieth century were almost exclusively limited to the western region of the island; it was only in the early years of the century that the Scottish investor Van Horne developed plans to construct a central rail line that would connect the various regions of the country, although this line was always conceived as being at the service of the agricultural export system.[96] This project was the most relevant in a wave of railway construction that expanded the network to some 6,400 miles of track, counting only those owned by United States interests and investors.

The basic relationship between the rail system and lands traditionally dedicated to export crops prevented new areas from being fully used, since outside the railway lines' zones of influence transportation costs were equal to or greater than those of transatlantic trade. Thus, very early in the century the urgent necessity of road construction became clear.

However, undertaking the construction of integrated systems of transportation required that the administrative services of the state be modernized, since intra-regional communication did not fall within the interests of foreign investors. What happened in the larger British colonies was in that respect exceptional. In Cuba, outside loans were used, and that, too, created a unique situation. In Puerto Rico, the construction of highways was made easier by the relatively smaller expanse of territory that had to be covered, and by the development plans of the United States government. Haiti and the Dominican Republic would have to await the United States invasion of their respective territories in 1915 and 1916 before construction of their national networks of roads began. Americans considered it necessary to employ forced labour in both countries; this practice was behind both the 'cacos' rebellion' in the Central Plateau of Haiti,[97] and informal methods of resistance on the part of Dominican peasants.[98] The network of highways in Haiti remained, as well as dreadful in quality, incomplete, since the occupiers had to give up on the use of the *corvée* (forced labour).

Despite these setbacks, the introduction of railways, and more especially of highways, laid the physical foundation for the formation of integrated national markets. In the larger countries, national markets had barely begun

95 Michiel Baud, 1994.

96 Oscar Zanetti and Alejandro García, 1987.

97 Roger Gaillard, 1981.

98 Pedro San Miguel, 1993, pp.77–100.

to take shape at the end of this period, and this would have serious consequences later. However, the reduction of transportation costs brought about by domestic systems of transportation and communication was a spur to the advance of agricultural production for the domestic markets and laid the groundwork for processes which would take fuller shape in later years. This can be seen in the increased 'inward' growth in all the countries, a development which gave added complexity to the previously overwhelming tendency to grow 'toward the outside.'

The construction of highways and other infrastructure projects aided in bringing about a rational system for producing foodstuffs for the domestic market. Agricultural expansion dovetailed with demands resulting from the appearance of new export goods. Suriname is in this respect a perfect illustration: thanks to traditions brought with them by immigrants from India and Java, in the first decade of the twentieth century rice-growing entered a period of such strong expansion that in only a few years it had surpassed the quantity required for domestic demand and had begun to yield a considerable surplus for export. During the 1920s the beginnings of modernized agriculture for the domestic market laid the foundations of the economic situation which would be characteristic of the following decade throughout the region, in response to the depression in prices subsequent to 1929.

The *mare nostrum*

In the late nineteenth century, with the onset of the Spanish-American War, the United States realized its goal, set a little more than a decade earlier, of achieving hegemony in the region. In withdrawing from their positions, the European powers left the road open for the Americans to combine their political and economic interests in a setting of diplomatic and military control. The establishment of a defensive perimeter around the Panama Canal entailed the need for greater territorial control in the area, especially over those territories which were not colonies. As we have seen clearly in the case of Cuba, this political and diplomatic control had economic implications of vast proportions.[99]

Once the patterns that were to govern its relations with Cuba were set, in 1902 the government of the United States gave signs of intending to reduce the Dominican Republic to a similar quasi-colonial condition. Since the early 1890s, Americans had been the country's largest investors of capital, even surpassing the French in that regard, whilst at the same time (with the tacit

99 In addition, *cf.* Dirección Política de las Fuerzas Armadas Revolucionárias, 1983.

approval of the dictator Ulises Heureaux) administration of the debt-collection agency charged with collecting money for European bond-holders was transferred to the hands of a United States company organized for that purpose – the San Domingo Improvement Company.[100] Although the agreement with the Improvement Company was rescinded in 1901, the government of the United States won compensation for that company and began to intervene actively in the internal affairs of the Dominican Republic. This led to the Dominican-American Convention, which was approved by both parties in 1907. This accord allowed the government of the United States to oversee the collection of foreign debt, for which it took over administration of the Dominican customs office; it was also agreed that the government of the Dominican Republic could neither adjust tariffs nor raise the public debt without the consent of the President of the United States.

In essence, the clauses imposed on the Dominican Republic in the Convention of 1907 were also imposed on Haiti when United States troops occupied that country in 1915. Although there was still a national government, it was completely subject to directives issued in Washington. Months later, United States troops disembarked in the neighbouring Dominican Republic, where they deposed the government and set up a military dictatorship. As preparations for entering the war in Europe began, a ring was closed around the region. In 1917, as the Panama Canal was finished, the colonial subjection of Puerto Rico consolidated, and the two states on the island of Hispaniola occupied, the United States purchased the Danish Virgin Islands for US$25 million.

All this seemed to point toward an irresistible move to transfer the British colonies to the United States. Indeed, the governing class in Jamaica, which placed much confidence in the opening of the United States market, explored this possibility at two separate times. The same thing occurred in the French colonies, as has been documented in Martinique.

Although no other transfer such as that of the Virgin Islands occurred, the overall direction of the economy of the countries of the region was toward the United States. The background of this was that the economy of the United States had become the most important economy in the world in the late nineteenth century, and the proximity of the region gave it distinct advantages in a strictly economic sense. This movement reached its culmination during the First World War years with American military expansion, when the United States took advantage of the inability of their rivals, heavily engaged in the conflict, to maintain normal relations with the territories of the Caribbean, even including their own colonies.

---

100 Cyrus Veeser, 1996.

While formerly almost all the countries of the region had engaged in closer and more friendly relations with Europe, relations with the United States now began to be more and more important, until they were virtually overwhelming during the First World War. In the Hispanophone Caribbean, trade with the United States approximated an average of 90 per cent of total trade, but the most important British colonies were not far behind: in 1902, 63 per cent of Barbados' exports went to the United States market and 27 per cent to Canada; Britain held a very marginal position of 5 per cent. Although the countries of the Caribbean almost always registered a trade surplus in this exchange, it was relatively small, thanks to the interaction of diverse political and economic factors.

The attractiveness of the United States was based on a combination of its demographic growth (on account of immigration from Europe) and the economic dynamics which had made it the world's leading economy. Additionally, the United States adopted a policy of exempting all goods that it did not produce locally – such as coffee, cacao, and bananas – from tariffs, which made it an exceptionally desirable market. For most of these products, the Caribbean enjoyed the advantage derived from lower transportation costs. In other goods, such as sugar, despite the fact that 80 per cent of all sugar consumed came from abroad, the tariff policy was unstable, putting Caribbean countries in a difficult position. But independent of trade benefits in the strictest sense of the word, for strategic reasons it was in the interest of the government of the United States to absorb increasingly large portions of the surplus products of the Caribbean.

Out of this commercial predominance there derived in large part the flow of direct investments from the United States, which surpassed those of Europe from the early twentieth century onwards. The interests of United States capital were linked to free-trade policies that made the movement of goods and capital easy. In the first two decades of the twentieth century, the government of the United States lobbied for tariff reductions in all the countries within its orbit and in other cases applied them directly. These tariffs had such devastating effects that they were the object of important correctives on the part of the governments of Cuba and the Dominican Republic before the crisis broke in 1929.[101]

Although US investment was centred on the sugar industry, it was involved in a variety of activities, as we have seen in the case of Cuba. It should be noted that although British capital continued to flow into the region during the first years of the century, it later lost ground, even in its own colonies. In large measure, British capital, like that of other European coun-

101 Francisco López Segrera, 1979a, pp.127–83.

tries, tended to lag behind in emerging areas of production, preferring to remain in the circulation and services sectors.

The outbreak of the First World War had serious repercussions: it halted the flow of British capital, at the moment when United States capital entered its phase of maximum growth. Although United States capital operated especially in countries with independent governments and Puerto Rico, it had great importance in other countries as well. We have already seen this in the beginnings of bauxite and oil exploitation, but the same thing happened with the banana boom in Jamaica that is associated with the early days of the United Fruit Company.[102] The companies that came before United Fruit not only established some plantations, but also were successful in their attempts to frustrate the intentions of the British government to support the independence of the producers.

The most serious factor in the interaction between economics and politics was the increase in the public debt. The importance of this factor can be seen in the massive concession of loans to the nascent Cuban government, whose foreign debt rose to US$100 million at one point. In the Dominican Republic, the Dominico-American Convention was followed by a renegotiation of the debt for US$20 million, which was later acquired exclusively by Wall Street bankers.[103] In Haiti, in 1910 (before the United States military intervention), Americans managed to restructure the Banque National, allowing them to eliminate French and German control.[104] It was through foreign debt that the financial consortiums' circle of benefits was closed. More important was the fact that it allowed these countries' development to take a particular bias toward modernization programmes.

102 Cyril Hamshere, 1972.

103 César Herrera, 1955.

104 Alain Turnier, 1955; François Chatelain, 1954; Leslie Manigat, 1967, pp.326–55.

2

THE CARIBBEAN IN THE 1930S

Franklin W. Knight

¡West Indies! Nueces de coco, tabaco y aguardiente...
Este es un oscuro pueblo sonriente,
conservador y liberal,
ganadero y azucarero,
donde a veces corre mucho dinero,
pero donde siempre se vive muy mal.

Nicolás Guillén, *West Indies Ltd.*, 1934

(West Indies! Coconuts, tobacco and *aguardiente*...
This is a dark, smiling people,
conservative and liberal,
cattlemen and sugarmen,
Where occasionally money flows,
But where, generally, life is very hard.)[1]

THE decade of the 1930s constituted an exceptionally poignant and clearly defining period in the history of the entire Caribbean region. Serious challenges to the political system occurred everywhere. This crucial turning point in the history of the region provided a transitional phase between the older Caribbean societies dominated by a few and a more open and modern era based on universal adult suffrage. The decade also had some obviously memorable boundaries in the Great Depression which began starkly in the Caribbean in the 1920s and ended – or at least changed direction sharply – with the Second World War which started in 1939. Most of the world, too, experienced a decade of transcendental importance, especially among the great majority of nations in the Atlantic community. The principal political and economic factors that shaped the western world as well as the

1 Nicolás Guillén, 1972, I, 212. All translations, unless otherwise indicated, are by the author. This essay has benefited enormously from the careful reading and the insightful comments of Alain Buffon, Selwyn Carrington, Bridget Brereton, Howard Johnson, Joyce Johnson, Teresita Martínez-Vergne, René Römer and Irene Toro Martínez. All shortcomings, however, remain exclusively those of the author. Note that prevailing pre-independence names are used when dealing with some territories during the period, hence British Honduras (not Belize), British Guiana (not Guyana), and Surinam (not Suriname), but references to the independent states reflect their current names.

Caribbean during that turbulent decade were closely intertwined. Both the wider world and the Caribbean region experienced severe disruptions during the Great Depression.[2] Both suffered prolonged consequences from the Second World War at the end of it. For both, the adjustments to an unprecedented combination of depression and war would be painful and protracted. Yet the principal forces that created the distinctiveness of that important decade were not confined narrowly within a ten-year framework. Forces of serious change manifested themselves long before 1930 – in some cases as early as the eighteenth century – and lasted well beyond 1940. Worker unrest, political ineptitude, expatriation, forced return, economic uncertainty, natural disasters and soil exhaustion were not new issues in the Caribbean of the 1930s. Indeed, they all had a very long antecedence. But in many ways they all reached their apogee during that remarkable decade. That decade represented an important crossroads for the region with some basic changes affecting all aspects of the society – culturally, economically, politically, institutionally, and psychologically. How do we account for the coincidence of change everywhere across the region? And why were the dénouements so different for so many places? The answers to these questions reside in the combination of local and external factors then prevailing across the Caribbean as well as in the character of the individuals who emerged in positions of power at that time.

As the decade unfolded the Caribbean peoples were all buffeted to a greater or lesser degree by actions taken far away in political and economic centres in Washington, London, Paris or Amsterdam. The experience was a quite familiar one in the past and would continue to be so in the future. In the case of the then nominally independent states – Cuba, the Dominican Republic and Haiti – the most pervasive influences came from the United States.[3] The United States had intervened belatedly in the Cuban War of Independence in 1898 and in the post-war years played an inordinate role in Cuban domestic affairs, making and unmaking local governments before 1959. United States domination was also characteristic of Puerto Rico, unfortunately drawn as an afterthought into the American military enterprise in 1898.[4] After 1898 Puerto Rico became virtually an American colony,

2 The Depression may be examined in Charles P. Kindelberger, 1973; John A. Garraty, 1986; Michael Bernstein, 1987; Robert S. McElvaine, 1984; Kim Quaile Hill, 1988; Thomas E. Hall and J. David Ferguson, 1998; Tom H. Watkins, 1993.

3 For an excellent bibliography of the United States and the War of 1898 see Louis A. Pérez, 1998; the two best studies of the War in English are David F. Trask, 1981 and John L. Offner, 1992.

4 See Fernando Picó, 1987; Silvia Alvarez Curbelo *et al.*, 1998; Antonio Gaztambide Géigel and Silvia Alvarez Curbelo, 1996; Pedro A. Cabán, 1999; Luis E. González Vales, 1998; and Charnel Anderson, 1998.

conquered, dominated and dependent but never fully integrated into the American scheme of things. In the case of the Dominican Republic marines from the United States occupied the country and sporadically fought the locals between 1916 and 1924. Their parting legacy was inadvertently to lay the foundation for the long, brutal and bloody dictatorship of Rafael Leonidas Trujillo y Molina between 1930 and 1961.[5] Neighbouring Haiti also endured a violent military occupation by the United States between 1915 and 1934.[6] The other territories of the Caribbean were still, *de facto* and *de jure*, colonies of, and administratively directly subject to, several European powers – Great Britain, France and the Netherlands. But the world was changing rapidly in the twentieth century and the United States had already started to manifest an ubiquitous presence all across the entire Caribbean, a region which it came to regard as its 'American Mediterranean'.[7]

Despite the powerful forces that emanated from the various European metropolitan centres and the United States of America (a sort of self-imposed metropolis to Cuba, Puerto Rico, the Dominican Republic and Haiti), the Caribbean as a whole managed to evolve in distinctive ways during the period. But the going was not easy. Caribbean peoples, whether living in independent states or living under colonial rule, had little impact on territorial political and economic events. Everywhere political power rested in the hands of a tiny, almost self-selected minority. In the British Caribbean colonies the various representative legislatures were anything but representative. In the late 1930s only in the Bahamas and Trinidad & Tobago did the number of voters exceed 6 per cent of the population – and those colonies did indeed have relatively small populations.[8] Colonialism, direct or indirect, sharply differentiated the Caribbean region from the rest of the hemisphere. The islands and mainland enclaves never lost their peculiarly Caribbean ethos despite the barrage of factors that assaulted them during the period. Political and economic domination did not result in cultural annihilation. But life in the region was far from static. An examination of certain facets of regional

5 See Dana G. Munro, 1964; *idem.*, 1974; Sumner Welles, 1928 (1966); Eric P. Roorda, 1998.

6 David Nicholls, 1979; Brenda Gayle Plummer, 1992; Richard Haggerty, 1991.

7 For the impact of the United States of America on the Caribbean in general see the collection of essays in Blanca G. Silvestrini, 1983b.

8 See Richard Hart, 1998, pp.99–134. Barbados and the Bahamas had Representative Assemblies. All the other colonies had Crown Colony governors with a mixed nominated and elected Legislative Council. Jamaica surrendered its status after the Morant Bay Rebellion of 1865. The political process, however, was confined to a relatively small proportion of the population as indicated in Table 2.1 (see page 46). Even as a proportion of adult males – the potential voting bloc – these numbers represented a very small group.

politics, economics, daily life and culture, demonstrates that Caribbeanness was achieved both by borrowing from the wider world and by creative engineering of local customs. Borrowing from the outside invariably had a price but the price was not equal everywhere and for all groups. Besides, there continued to be a distinctive Caribbean regional community closely linked to itself that was evident despite uneven patterns of subordination resulting from the linkages to the wider Atlantic world community.

In the first thirty years of the twentieth century Caribbean populations in general exhibited a buoyant growth spurt. The reasons for this robust growth varied from territory to territory. In some cases such as Cuba substantial immigration, especially from Spain, fuelled the population increase.[9] Cuba had also ended nearly half a century of continuous, demographically hæmorrhaging, civil war. After the war natality rates in Cuba, as elsewhere, increased gradually, facilitated by improvements in general sanitation and public health conditions as well as more effective control of epidemic and endemic diseases.[10] Consequently infant and child mortality declined and life expectancy inevitably lengthened. It was not easy to explain each case of individual increase (or decrease), however. Added to the local natural population increases of the 1930s was the gradual reduction in external employment opportunities that had previously siphoned off a significant proportion of the most fertile age groups. As the West India Royal Commission Report of 1938–9 noted:

> For some ten years or more the emigration outlets that previously existed have been virtually closed ... Thus emigration no longer relieves the growth of population. On the contrary, in some colonies, the return of many of those who had previously emigrated is now an aggravating factor. This is particularly true in Barbados where, over the last eight years, the return of emigrants has contributed more to the growth of population than the excess of births over deaths. Yet almost everywhere the excess of births over deaths is both high and increasing.[11]

The last sentence of the report applied to almost the entire Caribbean region. In Cuba and Puerto Rico populations doubled in the first thirty years

9 See Jordi Maluquer de Motes, 1992; Rolando Alvarez Estévez, 1988; Nicolás Sánchez Albornoz, 1988.

10 See, for example, Sergio Díaz-Briquets, 1983; Blanca G. Silvestrini, 1983a, pp.67–84. Juanita de Barros has studied the situation in British Guiana during the early twentieth century in her doctoral dissertation, 1998.

11 *West India Royal Commission Report*, 1945, pp.10–11. The Commission visited the Caribbean between November 1938 and April 1939. Because of the intervening war the report was not published until June 1945.

TABLE 2.1 Electors in the British West Indies in 1938

Colony	No. of electors	Percentage of the population
Antigua	1 048	3.06
Barbados	6 359	3.30
British Guiana	6 578	2.84
British Honduras	1 156	2.00
Dominica	1 248	2.46
Grenada (1921)	N/A	3.25 (?)
Jamaica	61 621	5.25
Montserrat	260	1.90
St Kitts-Nevis	1 628	2.30
St Lucia	1 509	2.18
St Vincent	1 598	2.78
Trinidad & Tobago	30 911	6.64
The Bahamas	13 146	21.97

Source: Richard Hart, 1998, p.109.

of the twentieth century. The Cuban population increased from slightly more than a million and a half in 1899 to almost five million in 1943. Between the census of 1931 and that of 1943 the Cuban population jumped from 3,962,344 to 4,778,583, an increase of 816,239 – almost equivalent to adding the entire population of Jamaica in 1931.[12] Puerto Rico saw an increase from slightly over 900,000 in 1899 to slightly less than two million in 1940.[13] Growth appeared less remarkable, and occasionally erratic, elsewhere across the region. In British Honduras the inhabitants increased from 46,000 in 1931 to 52,000 in 1938. At the same time in British Guiana they went from 301,000 to 318,000. Trinidad & Tobago's population increased from 366,000 to 425,000, undoubtedly boosted by migrants from the neighbouring smaller Windward Islands. Curaçao more than doubled its population between 1918 and 1946. In Aruba the increase was proportionally even more dramatic, from 9,070 in 1918 to 45,907 in 1946. Increases in both islands resulted from the building of large petroleum refineries. The population of Surinam grew from about 130,000 inhabitants in 1930 to 151,000 in 1940. Barbados added 24,055 to its 1931 population, bringing the total to 180,055. The Jamaica figure went from 863,000 to 1,121,823. In the Bahamas the population moved slightly from 60,000 in 1931 to 61,812 in 1938. The same was true in the Windward Islands where the pop-

12 The census figures for Cuba have been conveniently collected in Table I of Maluquer de Motes, 1992, p.243.

13 The population for Puerto Rico in 1940 is taken from Arturo Morales Carrión, 1983, p.243.

ulation remained virtually constant over the decade, moving from 162,000 in 1931 to 162,254 in 1938. The population of the Leeward Islands, however, declined sharply from 140,000 in 1931 to 132,973 in 1938.[14] So did populations in the smaller Dutch islands of St Martin, Saba and Bonaire. The notable decline in the United States Virgin Islands reversed itself in the 1930s and the population added 2,877 individuals during the decade (see Table 2.2, page 48). In the Bahamas, the Leeward Islands and the Windward Islands, dismal economic conditions acted as a catalyst for emigration.

Throughout the 1930s the Caribbean as a whole was still distinctively rural, as might have been expected from societies that remained predominantly agricultural, and export oriented. Latifundism and plantation export agriculture still predominated in all the larger territories. Sugar production was the dominant crop of Cuba for more than two centuries. In 1940, 57 per cent of all cultivated land, or 2,285,000 acres, were devoted to sugar-cane cultivation.[15] Large international sugar corporations controlled much of this sugar land. Four such corporations controlled approximately 25 per cent of the sugar lands of Cuba in 1940. The Cuban-American Sugar Company owned six central factories with more than 14,867 *caballerías* of land, or 492,989 acres. The Cuba Cane Sugar Company, the General Sugar Company and the United Fruit Company together owned 23 large sugar mills and 28,394 *caballerías* (941,545 acres) of land. The agricultural census of 1946 indicated emphatically the extent to which land in Cuba was concentrated in the hands of a few. In that year 75 per cent of Cuban farmers controlled a mere 11 per cent of all farmland (see Table 2.3). Land concentration went hand in hand with crop specialization. More than 82 per cent of diversified farms contained less than 100 acres each (see Table 2.4). But diversified farms altogether comprised about 20 per cent of all farms in Cuba in 1946.

As in so many places in the Caribbean in the 1930s the overall economy was inordinately dependent on the sugar industry. Despite the vagaries of the international market, sugar dominated the Cuban economy throughout the decade. But the situation was extremely portentous. Owing to the imposition of the Hawley-Smoot Tariff Act in mid-1930, the duty charged on Cuban sugar imports to the United States increased sharply, thereby driving down the volume of Cuban sales on the mainland. Between 1930 and 1933

14 Population figures for the British West Indian colonies are taken from *The Handbook of Jamaica*, 1938, p.8. It is most likely that rounded numbers indicate an estimate rather than the results of an official census and that the figures for 1938 are really for the previous year.

15 Data derived from Lowry Nelson, 1950, pp.95–6. A *caballería* is equal to about 33.16 acres.

TABLE 2.2 Populations of the Caribbean in the decade of the 1930s

Territory	*Population in 1931*	*Population in 1938*
Bahamas	60 000	61 812
Barbados	156 000	180 055
British Guiana	301 000	318 000
Cuba	3 962 344	4 252 959 (1939)
Dominican Republic	1 479 417 (1936)	2 135 872 (1950)
Dutch Antilles: St Eustatius, St Martin, Saba, Curaçao, Aruba, Bonaire	69 000	107 152
Guadeloupe	267 407	278 464 (1946)
Haiti	N/A	N/A
Jamaica	863 000	1 121 823
Leeward Islands: (Antigua, St Kitts, Nevis, Anguilla, Dominica, Montserrat, Virgin Islands)	140 000	132 973
Martinique	N/A	N/A
Puerto Rico	1 543 013	1 869 225
Surinam	130 000	15 100
Trinidad and Tobago	366 000	425 512
Windward Islands: (Grenada, St Lucia, St Vincent)	162 000	162 254
United States Virgin Islands: (St Thomas, St Croix and St John)	22 012	24 889

Sources: For the British Caribbean colonies, *Handbook of Jamaica*, 1938, p.8. For Cuba, José Cantón Navarro, *et al.*, 1998, p.395; Lowry Nelson, 1950, p.24. For Cuba in 1940, Jordi Maluquer de Motes, 1992, p.15. For Puerto Rico, City University of New York, 1979, p.121 and Arturo Morales Carrión, 1983, p.243. For the Virgin Islands, Isaac Dookhan, 1994, pp.271, 289. For the Dominican Republic, Emilio Betances, 1995, p.10, and 1988, pp.9–10. For the Dutch Caribbean, René Römer, 1981; Cornelis Ch. Goslinga, 1990. The figures for Guadeloupe were supplied by Alain Buffon.

TABLE 2.3 Cuban farm sizes, 1946

Approximate acreage	*Number of farms*	*Percentage of all farms*
Under 16.5 acres	76	10.5
16.5–49	174	24.0
50–99	199	27.5
100–164	96	13.3
165–329	77	10.6
330–659	41	5.7
660–1655	28	3.9
More than 1656 acres	33	4.5
Total farms	724	100.0

Source: Lowry Nelson, 1950, p.135.

TABLE 2.4 Cuban farms differentiated by product, 1946

Farm size	*Tobacco*		*Coffee*		*Sugar cane*		*Cattle and dairy*		*Diverse crops*	
	No.	*%*	*No.*	*%*	*No.*	*%*	*No.*	*%*	*No.*	*%*
Less 16.5	25	15.7	10	9.0	22	15.6	2	1.2	17	11.5
16.5–49	51	32.1	27	24.3	15	10.6	13	7.9	68	45.9
50–99	66	41.6	39	35.2	23	16.3	34	20.6	37	25.0
100–64	12	7.5	22	19.8	16	11.4	29	17.6	17	11.5
165–329	4	2.5	8	7.2	10	7.1	14	8.5	5	3.4
330–659	0	0.0	4	3.6	22	15.6	14	8.5	1	0.7
660–1655	1	0.6	0	0.0	6	4.3	20	12.1	1	0.7
1656+	0	0.0	1	0.9	27	19.1	3	1.8	2	1.3
Total	159	100.0	111	100.0	141	100.0	165	100.0	148	100.0

Source: Lowry Nelson, 1950, p.135.

the proportion of Cuban sugar sold on the United States market fell from 49.4 per cent to 25.3 per cent.[16] To make matters worse, both United States domestic and world beet-sugar production were increasing rapidly. In 1930 Cuba accounted for 16.8 per cent of total sugar production and 29.3 per cent of all cane sugar sold on the world market. By 1940 tariff restrictions in the United States of America, market complications in general, and voluntary self-imposed production quotas at home reduced Cuban sugar production by nearly one-half, to 14.4 per cent of world cane sugar and 9.1 per cent of total world sugar production (see Table 2.5).

16 Louis A. Pérez, 1986 (1991), p.279.

TABLE 2.5 World sugar production in the 1930s (tons)

Year	Cane	Beet	Total	Cuban production
1930	15 942 000	11 911 000	27 853 000	4 671 000
1931	16 216 000	8 782 000	24 997 000	3 121 000
1932	14 742 000	7 994 000	22 736 000	2 604 000
1933	15 113 000	9 159 000	24 272 000	1 994 000
1934	14 842 000	9 792 000	24 634 000	2 256 000
1935	16 598 000	10 430 000	27 029 000	2 538 000
1936	18 416 000	10 233 000	28 649 000	2 557 000
1937	18 782 000	11 194 000	29 975 000	2 975 000
1938	18 451 000	10 225 000	28 676 000	2 976 000
1939	19 395 000	11 116 000	30 511 000	2 724 000
1940	19 255 000	11 244 000	30 499 000	2 779 000

Source: Hugh Thomas, 1971, pp.1563–4.

As an integral part of the commercial world of the United States of America, Puerto Rico benefited from the tariff restrictions placed on Cuba. Sugar became Puerto Rico's principal and most valuable export during the 1930s. In 1930 sugar and sugar products accounted for about 56 million dollars of the 108 million dollars Puerto Rican export income. Although concentrated in enclaves around the island, sugar-cane plantations took up more than 40 per cent of the cultivated land and almost 11 per cent of the total land area of the island.[17] Yet the cost of producing sugar in Puerto Rico in 1930 was considerably higher than in Cuba or Hawaii. Transportation costs to mainland markets were also higher. Given that in 1930 Puerto Rico had already utilized all its prime sugar lands and had reached its maximum capacity production of some 750,000 tons, the future for sugar remained extremely unpromising at the end of the decade. Coffee, once the mainstay of the Puerto Rican peasants – and in the nineteenth century of large landowners as well – suffered greatly from two disastrous hurricanes in 1926 and 1928, and would flounder throughout the decade of the 1930s, generally yielding less income than tobacco.[18] With agricultural labour requirements declining, Puerto Rico faced massive unemployment and severe underemployment in the 1930s. Some measure of employment relief, however, came from the hiring of a large number of rural women in the expanding domestic needlework industry.

17 Victor Clark *et al.*, 1930, p.611.

18 See Luis Pumarada O'Neill, 1990, pp.58–64. Pre-1928 production levels were never again attained in Puerto Rico but for this the hurricane bore only partial responsibility.

TABLE 2.6 Cultivation in Jamaica, 1934

Crop	*Acreage*	*Production*	*Value*
Sugar-cane	40 091	54 227 tons sugar	£448 160
		459 798 gallons rum	£135 803
Bananas	72 909	15 974 906 stems	£1 665 081
Coffee	6 265	7 132 563 lbs	£168 091
Coconuts	40 074	37 144 647 nuts	£96 747
Cocoa	964	4 439 480 lbs	£42 708
Citrus	1 245	N/A	N/A
Mixed cultivation	23 122	N/A	N/A
Ground provisions	17 774	N/A	N/A
Guinea Grass	132 731	N/A	N/A
Common pasture	436 943	N/A	N/A

Source: Handbook of Jamaica, 1938, p.410.

In Jamaica commercial agricultural production was more diversified than in either Cuba or Puerto Rico. In 1934 the island had 72,909 acres in banana cultivation, by far its leading crop in quantity and value. Sugar-cane and coconuts had about equal area, and were often inter-cropped. Both products accounted for slightly more than 40,000 acres each. Far down the scale of acreage came coffee, cocoa, citrus and tobacco.[19] Nevertheless, Jamaica devoted more than 17,774 acres to the cultivation of ground provisions and another 23,122 acres to small, diversified crops. This indicated that although the export sector was not dynamic, the internal marketing system and peasant production for domestic self-sufficiency may have been strong. Much of the land area of Jamaica lay fallow in the 1930s. Part of this abandoned land was extremely mountainous and virtually uncultivable. But part of it reflected the ongoing depression in world markets for the principal export products (see Table 2.6). Other factors were also at work. One was the prevalence of disease on many banana plantations in the 1930s. Another was the forced dismantling of the association of banana-growers by the government in an effort to control production, thereby adversely affecting many small producers.[20]

Although agriculture provided the greatest opportunity for employment in the 1930s, it was facing a major crisis. Part of the crisis derived from low wages and increasing costs of living. But part had to do with the international market conditions. With the exception of Cuba (with sugar) and Trinidad (with petroleum), it was obvious that the Caribbean territories did not produce a single export commodity of either sufficient value or in sufficient quantity

19 *Handbook of Jamaica,* 1938, pp.404–5.
20 See Claus Füllberg-Stolberg, 1992, pp.39–69.

to command attention in a depressed international market. Exports represented the overall index of economic health. Nevertheless, agricultural production for domestic consumption also seemed to be declining. Indeed, the comments of the Royal Commission on the agriculture of the British West Indies could be applicable to the region as whole. 'Present production,' it noted, 'is in many places by no means sufficient to satisfy local demand for vegetables, ground provisions, eggs, poultry, plantains, maize, pulses, and other common products'.[21] Economic problems would therefore contribute greatly to political instability and social conflict during the decade, especially given the relatively high population pressure on the land and the increasing demand for modernization of the social structure.

Yet, during the decade the region, like most of the Americas, was becoming more urban. Before the 1930s many had used the small towns as way stations on their outward journeys to seek economic opportunity in foreign lands. This was especially true for seasonal worker emigrants from Jamaica, Barbados, St Kitts, Nevis, St Lucia and Grenada who travelled to Panama, Venezuela, Costa Rica, Cuba, the Dominican Republic and the United States.[22] With those opportunities considerably reduced by the 1930s, local towns became the final destination. Moreover, many of the returnees set up residence in the towns rather than return to the rural areas. People were also expelled from the land by crop diseases affecting the primary peasant and plantation crops such as bananas, cocoa and coconuts. The ejected joined the exodus to the towns, and if they could, continued on to foreign destinations. Towns provided employment opportunities as well as the perception of an improved way of life. There was, however, considerable variety in the degree of urbanization.

Cuba was the most urbanized, with the highest proportion of the population living in cities of more than 100,000. Havana, the prominent, large, extensive, bustling capital of Cuba, was the only genuinely cosmopolitan city throughout the Caribbean, with a population in 1940 of more than 560,000. (The province of that name bounded on the west by Pinar del Río and on the east by Matanzas had a population of more than a million in 1940.) But Vedado was a relatively new suburb, and the imposing Capitol and the ostentatious presidential palace were new architectural additions to the broad tran-

21 *West India Royal Commission Report*, 1945, p.51. Lord Moyne led the Commission and so in much of the literature the report is referred to as the Moyne Report.

22 For an excellent examination of this phenomenon see Bonham C. Richardson, 1983; see also William F. Stinner *et al.*, 1982; Constance R. Sutton and Elsa M. Chaney, 1987; Robert A. Pastor, 1985.

sition belt between Centro Havana and the expanding middle-class areas to the west of the harbour. Unlike Cuba, Puerto Rico and the other islands did not present such concentrated examples of splendid urban architecture. The Brookings Institution Report of 1930 described the Puerto Rican population as 'essentially rural. Many of the so-called towns are little more than village crossroads that owe their petty dignity to the political system introduced by Spain rather than to economic reasons ... 27 per cent of the population is classed as urban.'[23] San Juan had a population of only about 100,000 and Ponce had less than 46,000 persons in 1930.

Metropolitan Kingston, the largest city in the British Caribbean, was rebuilt after the devastating earthquake and fire of 1907 that took more than a thousand lives. It covered an area of only about one and one-half square miles, and its densely packed urban zone hardly extended north of the Parade Grounds – slightly more than a thousand acres. In 1936 Kingston had a population of 76,986, densely packing into its confined area a population equivalent to its much larger surrounding parishes. Port of Spain had slightly less, and was beginning to realize the problems of urban planning – or the lack of it.[24] Bridgetown, in Barbados, retained much of a rural ambience despite its centrality to administration and commerce, as did Pointe-à-Pitre in Guadeloupe and, to a lesser extent, Fort-de-France in Martinique.

The central sections of most Caribbean towns had properly constructed streets laid down in a rectangular pattern, reminiscent of the early grid patterns of Spanish colonial towns. The principal thoroughfares were normally paved with asphalt, but unpaved streets, or streets covered with limestone, were common everywhere, producing prodigious amounts of dust in the dry season. Sewer and drainage received relatively little co-ordinated communal attention (although increasingly more than before), except where the Americans occupied and introduced improvements along with other construction projects. All the major Caribbean cities had begun systems of street illumination. Nevertheless, pictures of the 1930s do not indicate the extensive use of electricity. Motor transport was increasing rapidly and many Caribbean towns had introduced motorized public transportation in the form of buses or electric trams. However, urban transport still included – indeed, depended on – animal-drawn carts and drays, saddle horses, pack horses, pack mules and donkeys, and in Kingston, Jamaica, the earliest models of the ingeniously constructed and colourful handcarts.[25] Also ubiquitous were large numbers of itinerant

23 Victor Clark *et al.*, 1930, p.9.

24 See Michael Anthony, 1978, vol.1, p.1.

25 See B. W. Higman, 1999. Higman claims that this ingenious method of transportation was not found in any other Caribbean island.

vendors skillfully balancing their wares on their colourfully turbaned heads.[26]

The cities of Cuba, the Dominican Republic and Puerto Rico had many substantial, lovely buildings of stone, rubble, brick, wood, or masonry for both public and private purposes. Elsewhere throughout the Caribbean private construction employed various styles of wooden structures, sometimes beautifully painted, as illustrated in the books by Jack Berthelot and Martine Guamé or Carol Jopling.[27] Indeed, the houses of the traditionally rich and professionally upwardly mobile families could be, and in many cases were, architecturally impressive all across the Caribbean, but many of those pre-dated the 1930s.[28] Lord Olivier, a former governor, remarked on the situation in the early 1930s in Kingston, Jamaica. 'The better streets' he wrote,

> had indeed many small white-painted, green-shuttered, shingle-roofed houses of pleasant aspect, with garden frontages, bright with flowering shrubs and creepers and that general distribution of evergreen trees which give the place, as seen from the harbour, a cheerful appearance … But all around Kingston there has sprung up, almost entirely since the [First World] War, a pleasant suburban district now studded with hundreds of well designed and well built houses and bungalows with delightful gardens.[29]

Nevertheless, for most of the Caribbean cities the quality of housing provided for the lower orders of society left much to be desired. The description painted by the Royal Commission in 1938–9 could have been applicable to most towns in the Caribbean:

> In both town and country the present housing of the large majority of the working people in the West Indian Colonies leaves much to be desired; in many places it is deplorable; in some the conditions are such that any human habitation of buildings now occupied by large families must seem impossible to a newcomer from Europe. It is no exaggeration to say that in the poorest parts of most towns and in many of the

26 See John Gilmore, 1995, pp.56–7. See also the reproduced photographs in Sydney Olivier, 1933, between pages 304 and 305, and Bonham C. Richardson, 1983, pp.112–17.

27 Jack Berthelot and Martin Guamé, 1982; Carol F. Jopling, 1988.

28 See, for example, Anghelen A. Phillips and Geoffrey de Sola Pinto, 1982. Note that the lovely Norton house in Oracabessa (Illustration 313) probably dates from the 1930s.

29 Sydney Olivier, 1933, pp.34–5.

> country districts a majority of the houses is largely made of rusty corrugated iron and unsound boarding; quite often the original floor has disappeared and only the earth remains, its surface so trampled that it is impervious to any rain which may penetrate through a leaking roof; sanitation in any form and water supply are unknown in such premises, and in some cases no light can enter when the door is closed. These decrepit homes, more often than not, are seriously overcrowded, and it is not surprising that some of them are dirty and verminous in spite of the praiseworthy efforts of the inhabitants to keep them clean. In short, every condition that tends to produce disease is here found in serious form. The generally insanitary environment gives rise to malaria, worm infection and bowel diseases; leaking roofs, rotten flooring and lack of light encourage the spread of tuberculosis, respiratory diseases, worm infections, jigger lesions and rat-borne diseases; overcrowding, which is usually accompanied by imperfect ventilation, is an important agent in contributing to the high incidence of yaws, tuberculosis, venereal diseases and, to a certain extent, leprosy.[30]

A Brookings Institution study team reported in 1930 that for Puerto Rico 'the condition of the masses of the island remains deplorable.'[31] Historian James Dietz noted that:

> Housing conditions were wretched. The average dwelling accommodated nearly eight persons. More than half the houses had only one or two rooms – and the two-room houses typically were one room with a divider that did not reach to the ceiling. The houses were crudely built and generally lacked furniture. Hammocks served as bedding or people slept on the floor, and cooking facilities were located outside, as were toilet and bathing facilities in most cases. The wooden structures deteriorated rapidly from the effects of rain and sun. Slums had already begun to appear in the cities, but there was also better housing there for professionals, merchants, bankers, and others connected to the U.S. and Puerto Rican capital.[32]

Several factors combined to sharpen the divide between urban and rural existence in the 1930s. Country roads were poorly built, poorly maintained, and subject to frequent erosion from floods and landslides, especially during

---

30 *West India Royal Commission Report,* 1945, p.174.

31 Victor Clark *et al.,* cited in James L. Dietz, 1986, p.127.

32 James L. Dietz, 1986, p.128.

the hurricane season from June to October. As late as 1946 Lowry Nelson noted that for Cuba,

> One can truthfully say that … the absence of passable roads is one of the great tragedies of Cuba. Another is that after they do construct roads, they fail to keep them in repair and they again become impassable. The great Central Highway is a case in point. The pavement was for long stretches pitted and broken, with no apparent effort having been made at repairs nor any warning signals posted to caution the driver.[33]

Lack of proper road maintenance has been a historical Caribbean condition.

The then-new communication technologies of radios, telephones, and television were being introduced, but in any case, depended on the availability of electricity in the rural areas. Electrification was slowly being extended in all the territories, with the priority given to cities and residences of the better classes. Access to electricity was often one clear indication of urban living. Distance, then, constituted only one – and not necessarily the major – consideration in exacerbating the relative isolation of rural life. Most territories had a good system of telegraph communications connecting all the important towns and most of the larger villages.

The deplorable condition of many roads certainly handicapped the economy, especially in the transportation of basic commodities to the urban market. Despite this, several Caribbean islands tried to develop or expand their tourist industries, although with little attention to nature or cultural heritage. The Bahamas, Cuba and Jamaica had all entered the tourist business since the middle of the nineteenth century, and the industry seemed promising before it was overtaken by the First World War.[34] Success, however, was elusive. Prohibition in the United States in the 1920s and the expansion of steamship lines – sometimes to service the new banana trade – provided a fresh boost for Caribbean destinations. In 1934 Cuba enacted a new tourist law. Its definition of a tourist reflects a longstanding Caribbean conception that has plagued the industry through the years, one that implies that a tourist ought be a foreigner, and preferably white. 'A tourist,' the Cuban law stated, 'is a foreigner not resident in Cuba, who may visit locations in the Republic for purposes of diversion, rest, recreation, study or such other legitimate activity that one may deem convenient provided that no work or employment is

33 Lowry Nelson, 1950, p.19.
34 See John Gilmore, 1995; Polly Pattullo, 1996.

involved.'[35] Cuba listed a number of hotels across the island, some of which still exist – for example, the Nacional, Plaza, Royal Palm, Inglaterra, Saratoga, Sevilla-Biltmore and Roma in Havana – and promised that the visitor would find something to match any budget. By 1940 Cuba hosted about 300,000 tourists per year, most from the United States of America.

After Cuba, the most extensively developed tourist industry was probably that of Jamaica. In 1931 the *Handbook of Jamaica* listed more than 111 hotels and boarding houses throughout the island. By 1938 the number of hotels had grown to 122. It is hard, however, to measure the economic health of the industry from the available data, since room capacity, occupancy rates and comparative quality for each establishment were not recorded. In the seven-year interval a number of changes had taken place. Some names disappeared from the list. Other establishments changed names, or locations, or both. The number of listed enterprises increased from 42 to 44 for Kingston and lower St Andrew and from 16 to 20 for Montego Bay. On the other hand, the number for Mandeville declined from ten to seven and that for Port Antonio from eight to five. The important Jamaica travel news of the decade might have been the opening of the luxurious Constant Spring Hotel in lower St Andrew and the going-out-of-business of the venerable Titchfield Hotel in Port Antonio.[36]

The Brookings Institution Report on Puerto Rico in 1930 remarked on the underdevelopment of the tourist industry on that island. 'In fact,' it stated, 'on the basis of our estimates, the amount which Puerto Rican residents spent in travelling outside the Island was about US$110,000 in excess of the income from the tourist trade in the year 1928.'[37] Most tourists in Puerto Rico came from the Virgin Islands and the Dominican Republic. But tourism was spreading across the region. Most islands had at least one large, elegant, first-class hotel (usually in the capital city) such as the Colonial Hotel in Nassau, the Royal, Marine and Crane in Barbados, the Queen's Park and Standard Hotels in Port of Spain, and the Hotel Americano in Curaçao.

It is quite interesting that the Royal Commission Report written at the end of the decade identified tourism as a potential area for efficacious economic development. But it had some strong admonitions on the matter.

> ...The tourist trade is a factor of some importance in the economic life of Jamaica, Barbados and Trinidad, where it has grown materially in

35 *Cuba en la Mano: Encyclopedia Popular Ilustrada*, 1940 (1969), p.1064; also, Rosalie Schwartz, 1997.

36 All data compiled from *Handbook of Jamaica*, 1931, pp.527–9 and *Handbook of Jamaica*, 1938, pp.579–81. On the Jamaica tourist industry see Frank Fonda Taylor, 1993.

37 Victor Clark *et al.*, 1930, p.593.

> recent years. Notwithstanding its susceptibility to changes of fashion and its liability to sudden and sharp fluctuations, it is a trade which should be encouraged. We do not feel able to recommend that any West Indian Colonies should undertake substantial liabilities for this purpose – as was suggested in evidence to us – since we consider that the risks to capital in the tourist trade are such that they cannot in fairness be imposed on the taxpayer and should be borne by private enterprise. The rewards, when success attends efforts to attract tourists, are considerable and, given a reasonable degree of encouragement by Governments, in the form of advertising, the provision of better roads (though not at the expense of agricultural needs) and the improvement of external communications, we see no reason why private capital should not become available for the development of this enterprise. Much will, however, depend on the state of public security. Tourists will not visit, nor will investors risk their money in territories which by repute are subject to disturbances such as those that have characterized West Indian life in recent years.[38]

Tourism, however, did not engage the vast majority of the people of the region and they received scant benefits from its existence. Socially conscious visitors did not examine tourist enclaves to ascertain the real condition of the people and life outside the small foreign enclaves left much to be desired.

The dreadful condition of women in particular and families in general – especially of the humbler classes – attracted attention throughout the Caribbean. Incessant childbearing represented only a part of the heavy responsibilities of women everywhere. The dismally low family incomes and the inconsistency of paternal support made family life more precarious. 'Three out of four of the children born are registered as offspring of parents not formally married. The predominant mode of conjugal life is voluntary cohabitation, without a civil contract or ecclesiastical sacrament.' That was the observation in the early 1930s of Lord Olivier, a past governor of Jamaica.[39] The fluidity of family life placed a more onerous responsibility on women everywhere. Women not only worked the proverbial two shifts; they worked three shifts. They were mothers. They were consorts. And they often increasingly were the principal wage-earners and heads of families. Edith Clarke brilliantly examined the bewildering complexity of the Caribbean family structure

38 *West India Royal Commission Report*, 1945, pp.387–8.

39 Sydney Olivier, 1933, p.372.

in *My Mother Who Fathered Me*.[40] The Brookings Institution Report for Puerto Rico at about the same time painted a similar dismal picture. 'Though the percentage of consensually married has steadily declined since the American occupation,' it noted, 'the number so married, and of technically illegitimate children born to them, is appalling.'[41] Neither the legal status of children nor the size of families would have mattered much had not poverty been so general and so persistent. The Caribbean was not generating sufficient wealth to fuel significant improvement in the material standards of daily life. Women realized this and went to work to support their families in increasing proportions, either by working outside the home or by emigrating. In Puerto Rico, according to historian James Dietz, 'between 1930 and 1940, the number of employed women grew 17.9 percent (from 122,488 to 144,360).'[42] This increase apparently was not generally applicable to the region as a whole, however, since wage-earning females, especially in agriculture, declined in the British West Indies over the decade.[43] Women worked at anything and everything for which they would receive wages – often wages that were far smaller than those paid to men for comparable work.[44] Some types of work attracted a disproportionate number of women. In Puerto Rico women predominated in needlework and as tobacco-leaf strippers. In Cuba, Jamaica, St Lucia and Trinidad they constituted the principal carriers of coal, stones and sand. Another arduous and overwhelmingly female physical activity was the loading of banana boats.[45] Women participated actively in all sorts of field labour as well as domestic service and clerical sales. The remuneration for such work was abominably low. In 1938 when the minimum wage was legally established at 40 cents per hour in the United States, the needlework that attracted the largest proportion of female workers in Puerto Rico paid between two and four cents per hour. In Trinidad and Jamaica, female day labourers earned about two-thirds the wages of their male counterparts, about 25 cents per day – incredibly, much higher than the wages for carrying bananas, sand, coal or stone.

---

40 Edith Clarke, 1957 (1999). Clarke's anthropological research was conducted in the mid-1940s but it is probably safe to say that the conditions she describes would have been applicable in the 1930s as well.

41 Victor Clark *et al.*, 1930, p.571.

42 James Dietz, 1986, p.142.

43 I am grateful to Professor Bridget Brereton for pointing this out.

44 *Handbook of Trinidad and Tobago*, 1924, p.219; *West India Royal Commission Report*, 1945, pp.217–20.

45 James Dietz, 1986, pp.142–3; Blanca G. Silvestrini and María D. Luque de Sánchez, 1987, pp.443–5; *West India Royal Commission Report*, 1945, pp.215–20.

Work apparently did not inhibit procreation and increasing family sizes. A rapidly growing population required an increase of public expenditure on vital social services such as health, education and welfare – all factors that had, in turn, catalytic effects on population growth. The steadily increasing population presented a major challenge for the State – and everywhere the local state was intellectually bankrupt and economically nearly so. In the 1930s the upper orders of society continually bemoaned the situation of expanding penury and unemployment, but there is not much evidence that their observations led to meaningful action. The middle and lower orders acted rather than talked. They rioted and burned and protested against their cruel and increasingly unjust and inhumane conditions. Eventually across the Caribbean the working classes spontaneously erupted, often supported (and led) by the middle classes. The latter sought political transformation which gave power to their group. The working classes sought economic justice and respect.[46] The Caribbean political manifestations of the 1930s had much in common, but individual leadership, time, place and circumstances combined to shape the different outcomes across the region.

The revolution that overthrew Gerardo Machado in Cuba on 12 August 1933 had been building for a long time. Indeed, the republic established in 1902 had several fatal flaws. It was neither sovereign, nor independent, nor stable. With authority divided between Washington and Havana it was impossible to generate sustained political legitimacy. Washington made and unmade local governments to suit their own purposes and Cuban politicians tried to anticipate the political will of Washington in order to take advantage of it. But without a consistent foreign policy, reading the political will in Washington was like catching mercury on a polished concrete floor. As sociologist Marifeli Pérez-Stable noted lucidly, 'During the 1920s, the United States found the terms of its relations with Cuba progressively problematic. Continuous intervention did not bring stable governments capable of maintaining order and defending foreign capital. Presidential successions were almost always moments of turmoil. Actual or threatened military intervention did not bring lasting peace and tranquillity.'[47] Machado was elected in the 1920s when the economy was doing well. But by the 1930s things had begun to fall apart rapidly. It all started with the depression that arrived in Cuba ahead of the

46 O. Nigel Bolland, 1995; the politics of the period may also be followed in José Cantón Navarro, *et al.*, pp.282–333; Jorge I. Domínguez, 1978, pp.54–110; Marifeli Pérez-Stable, 1993, pp.14–60; Oscar Zanetti and Alejandro García, 1998, pp.322–47; Ken Post, 1978; Bridget Brereton, 1981, pp.160–98; Kelvin Singh, 1994, pp.158–85; Michael Craton and Gail Saunders, 1998, vol. 2, pp.270–300.

47 Marifeli Pérez-Stable, 1993, p.39.

rest of the hemisphere. In 1921 a number of banks had collapsed. By 1925 the sugar business was in turmoil, largely the result of overproduction. The imposition of Hawley-Smoot tariff regulations in mid-1930 was virtually a prescription of economic and social disaster. All economic indices in Cuba fell precipitately. National income fell from 571 million *pesos* in 1929 to 294 million in 1933.[48] Wages fell in some cases by 60 per cent. Purchasing power fell by almost 50 per cent. By 1930 Machado had engineered a second extended term of office to the delight of the better-off social classes. They distrusted Machado and his broken promises that he would not seek re-election; but they feared the rising tide of discontent from students and workers even more. Students and workers saw much to upset them. The second Machado administration was as fascistic as it was corrupt. Machado closed the university for two years, and relentlessly murdered student leaders such as the radical, Julio Antonio Mella, a founder of the Communist Party, and Rafael Trejo, the founder of the Directorio Estudiantil Universitario (Directory of University Students: DEU) in 1930. He was equally brutal against labour organizers and those he deemed in opposition to his government. By early 1933 Cuba was a country irreconcilably divided in which violence on the part of the government created a savage counter-violence. On the one hand were the government, some of the merchant groups, some foreigners and some members of the armed forces. Confronting them were their defectors joined by the National Confederation of Cuban Workers (CNOC), the ABC Revolutionary Society, the Communist Party of Cuba (PCC), and the DEU. With chaos and violence the order of the day, the new United States administration of Franklin Delano Roosevelt sent his good friend and old schoolmate, Sumner Welles – who had served in negotiating the withdrawal from the Dominican Republic – to mediate an acceptable political transition in Cuba. Welles failed in the short term. Finally a massive, island-wide general strike and a military revolt terminated the Machado dictatorship.

Unfortunately the overthrow of Machado did not end the basic political problems of Cuba. Nevertheless, during the succeeding years Cuban political life underwent a major transformation. The United States abrogated the Platt Amendment, exchanging the 'Big Stick Policy' for the 'Good Neighbor Policy' – a sort of intervention with kid gloves. It also reduced the punitive tariff on Cuban sugar imports, thereby expanding the market. The State assumed a greater say in economic planning and social protection. Workers and students entered the political equation. Much worker legislation passed Congress and ambitious social programmes were announced. Fulgencio Batista, who started the anti-Machado revolution as a lowly sergeant, rose to be the main

48 José Cantón Navarro, *et al.*, pp.282–6.

political arbiter, aided by the astute Sumner Welles.[49] The Communist Party gained political acceptance and would remain a part of the system until the Cold War. In 1940 Cuba acquired a new liberal constitution and a new, democratically elected president: Fulgencio Batista. The Second World War, however, obscured for a long time the fact that the ideals and aspirations of 1933 produced more rhetoric than reality. Politics and economics were intimately interrelated and true reform would require new measures and new men. In retrospect the Revolution of 1933 turned out to be more tantalizing reform for Cubans than fundamental change.

In the 1930s the Dominican Republic was still recovering from the aftereffects of the eight-year military occupation by the United States. With neither the advanced economic development nor the social complexity of Cuba, the impact of the Great Depression was not as pronounced here. Nevertheless it was extremely important. The timing, too, was significant because of two factors, both related to the military occupation between 1916 and 1924. In the first place, the United States accelerated the pace of modernization of the country, providing the catalyst for industrial development, especially in the sugar industry. With its public-works projects and more careful attention to shoring up the economic infrastructure, the society had just begun to develop an appetite for foreign-made products. The depression brought an abrupt halt to the capacity to import sufficient goods to satisfy internal market demand because of the immediate fall in exports and export earnings. The Dominican Republic, then, had little option but to boost domestic production of foodstuff – and in the 1930s was probably more self-sufficient in domestic food production than any other Caribbean country.[50] In the second place the United States disarmed much of the local population and created a new National Guard to keep the peace. Political instability was bad for business and one important reason for the occupation had been to promote business and generate custom receipts to repay United States loans. When the United States left

49 Fulgencio Batista Zaldivar illustrated the social fluidity of Republican Cuba. Born in northern Oriente in 1900 of mixed ancestry he achieved a modest elementary education at the public school in Banes and as a young man worked as a sugarcane cutter in the *zafra*. He wandered to Holguín, again working as a cane cutter, then apprenticing himself first to a tailor, then to a carpenter, and then to a barber. He joined the army in 1921 and learned stenography and typing. These useful skills brought him promotion under Machado to sergeant when the opportunity of 1933 presented itself to him. See Hugh Thomas, 1971, pp.636–7.

50 The data are not available for a systematic comparison of food production. But Roberto Cassá has examined the economic consequences of the depression on the Dominican local economy and has some impressive figures for the increase in local food production. Of course, much of this increase was offset by the high population growth rate of the country. See Roberto Cassá, 1982.

and the political system collapsed in 1929–30 the Guardsmen controlled the guns and quickly established themselves in power contrary to the wishes of their external creator. The head of the Guard (renamed the National Army in 1927) was Rafael Trujillo, who exploited the occupation to lay the foundation for both his fame and his fortune.

Rafael Leonidas Trujillo (1891–1961), an ambitious former telegraph-operator from San Cristóbal, a small town west of Santo Domingo, was an enthusiastic product of the Guard, which he joined in 1918 at the age of 27; he apparently admired the methods and manner of the United States marines.[51] Later he needed to look no farther for his authoritarian models of total political control. As Bruce Calder observed:

> It is also abundantly clear that the (United States) military government's public works program changed the country politically, though perhaps not the way U.S. officials envisioned. The relatively stable administration of Horacio Vásquez (1924–1930) gave the first indication that now a central government could control the entire republic. But it remained for Rafael Trujillo to demonstrate clearly that the United States had left behind the basis, in form of modernized communications and a modernized military, not only for unity and stability but [also] for the most repressive regime the Dominicans had ever known.[52]

Trujillo took office as President of the Dominican Republic on 16 August 1930 after a bloody election campaign earlier in the spring in which he and his Vice President, Rafael Estrella Ureña, were the only candidates. The presidency provided Trujillo with a more effective platform, using the national army 'to impose his will on a disarmed population, using violence, terror, torture, and assassination.'[53] As head of the army he had used his public office as the basis for creating immense private wealth in urban real estate and commercial enterprise. As head of government he established monopolies in salt, rice, meat, milk and other basic commodities vested in the Trujillo family and its close supporters. Trujillo more effectively erased the boundaries between public and private, personal and national, than any other political leader anywhere in the Americas.

The role of the army in establishing the Trujillo dictatorship was crucial. It provided the muscle for his illegal acts and it blindly supported him. It was a relationship of mutually rewarding convenience as Trujillo sought to forge

51 See Bruce J. Calder, 1984; and Frank Moya Pons, 1995.

52 Bruce J. Calder, 1984, p.53.

53 Frank Moya Pons, 1995, p.358.

a nationalist state along the lines of a fiefdom. As Emelio Betances shows, under the Trujillo presidency army expenditures as a proportion of the national budget increased from 11 per cent in 1930 to 21 per cent in 1940 – and occasionally approached one-third of the budget in the later 1930s.[54] In the expanded military, loyalty and kinship to the dictator took precedence over merit. The army became adept at intimidating unarmed citizens and eliminating the enemies of the President. Their most notorious act came in October 1937 when the army, on orders from Trujillo, callously murdered more than 18,000 Haitian peasants and workers living along the western border of the Dominican Republic. After extended negotiations Trujillo agreed to an indemnity to the surviving relatives of US$750,000 but the final sum paid was probably no more than US$525,000.[55]

Trujillo expanded the administrative apparatus of the Dominican State. He effectively broadened the economy, renegotiating, reducing, and eventually paying off the United States debt (one reason for the invasion of 1916). He built many new roads and set up settlements throughout the country. He established a strong, highly personal, extremely paternal political party that provided the veneer of democratic support for his various actions. He even changed the name of the capital city to aggrandize his family. In the final analysis, however, Trujillo did not modernize the Dominican Republic and the long-term cost of his dictatorship to his people was enormous. Neither during the 1930s nor after would there be freedom of thought, association and expression, much less freedom from fear, in the Dominican Republic. The political vitality and social mobility observed in the rest of the Caribbean were not evident there. But in 1940 conditions did not look all that bad. Worse was yet to come.

Haiti had always been somehow special, and somewhat different, in Caribbean history. As the second independent state in the hemisphere – and the first to have a thorough revolution – it deserved a better fate than its extremely sad and isolated history demonstrates. Persistent poverty did nothing to undermine the pride and devotion of Haitians. Yet Haiti has never been able to reconcile its profound fissures of class and colour. The occupation of the United States between 1915 and 1934 did very little to improve any aspect of Haitian society – although valiant attempts were made. As in the case of the neighbouring Dominican Republic, the United States found it easy to enter but difficult to disengage its military forces. Haiti benefited from the administrative ambivalence in Washington on costly foreign military enterprises, especially those that resulted in the death of American soldiers. 'The end of the occupation,' wrote historian David Nicholls, 'has also to be seen

54 Emilio Betances, 1995, p.97.

55 Frank Moya Pons, 1995, pp.368–9; Emilio Betances, 1995, p.98.

in the context of (Franklin D.) Roosevelt's so-called "Good Neighbor Policy". The threat of European invasion had receded, a superficial stability had been achieved in Haiti, and a climate safe for American investment had been created. Continued military involvement by the United States was therefore unnecessary, costly, and unwise.'[56] The United States military occupation did not really help open Haiti to American capital – at least not in the way it did in Cuba and the Dominican Republic. The National City Bank of New York became the most important bank, but the economy remained in the hands of a disparate group of foreigners and locals. The occupation, however, was more important for cultural and literary production than for economic and political achievements. A dynamic *noiriste* movement developed in the 1920s and increased throughout the 1930s.[57] Writers such as Arthur Holly, Jean Price Mars, Jacques Alexis and Jacques Roumain celebrated the beautiful, intrinsic and authentic aspects of Haitian language, art and culture, publishing much of their material in Haiti. In this way they helped validate and reinforce Haitian nationalism.[58] Pride in Haiti did not translate itself into economic well-being, however; Haiti remained a very poor country throughout the decade. Yet the blame for that deplorable condition did not rest entirely with outsiders. Brenda Gayle Plummer points out:

> The causes of Haitian impoverishment were only partially attributable to the exploits of alien traders. The reason for the near-total absence of industrialization and modern commercial farming also lay in traditional attitudes toward work, landownership and national security. The American occupation failed to alter the status quo and left the island republic with the same slim resource base it had possessed when the marines arrived. The necessary corollary to the absence of capital in Haiti was the exploitation of human capital, the labor force. Migration of labor to the canefields of Cuba and the Dominican Republic began in the early 1900s and has continued into the present, now supplemented by immigration to the metropoles. At home, affluent Haitians and foreigners refused to pay a decent wage and cemented the edifice of material deprivation with immiserization and political repression.[59]

---

56 David Nicholls, 1979.

57 See J. Michael Dash, 1981, pp.43–155. Black consciousness in Haiti in the 1930s has much broader roots than merely anti-US sentiments. Part of it goes back to traditional Haitian atavism, part to the Harlem Renaissance, and part to the developing nationalism of the 1920s. All this was demonstrated in the *Les Griots* journal which came out in Port-au-Prince between 1938 and 1939 (see *ibid.*, p.102) .

58 See Roberto Márquez, 1989, pp.293–340.

59 Brenda Gayle Plummer, 1988, pp.243–4.

When the United States marines left Haiti in 1934 their payroll of US$700,000 was equivalent to 10 per cent of the national budget.[60] Sténio Vincent, a president acceptable to the Americans, was an eloquent speaker, and a strong nationalist. He was also an incompetent administrator and a self-serving politician whose principal achievement was to reform the constitution in 1936 to perpetuate his dictatorship.The Americans did very little in 19 years and their feeble attempt at good deeds did not long survive their departure.

Although Cuba remained politically unsettled and the Dominican Republic and Haiti were sliding into stifling dictatorship, the political winds of change were much more favourable in Puerto Rico and the rest of the Caribbean. The decade of the 1930s represented for them the difficult and contested construction of the foundations of the substantial rejuvenescent reforms implemented in the following period. Reforms came, however, because the common people pressured the authorities – not because the governing classes discovered ways of ameliorating the deteriorating conditions aggravated by the Great Depression.

In Puerto Rico, in common with the agricultural export-oriented British and French Caribbean, the depression hit the rural workers hardest, especially rural sugar workers. The worst years fell before 1933. Two major hurricanes in four years severely reduced basic agricultural food production. Even worse, they savaged coffee production, the most important cash crop of the peasantry. An already increasing dependence on imported food became more pronounced. Increased prices of imports meant that living standards plunged. The price of basic imported commodities like rice, beans, and lard nearly doubled in two years. Milk and bread increased almost threefold.[61] To make matters worse, underemployment and unemployment further constrained the ordinary worker's ability to provide adequately for his or her family. According to a study by the Legislative Assembly in 1930, the average family needed an income of US$1,142 annually to maintain itself but at best the fully employed earned only between US$360 and US$720 per year. In 1932 the per capita income had fallen from US$122 to US$86 over the preceding three years.[62] This perilous economic situation partly explains why Puerto Rico ranked among the first Caribbean countries to experience severe labour problems in the 1930s. The series of contagious labour strikes on sugar estates increased from 10 in 1931–2 to about 40 in 1936–7, and in the peak strike

60 Robert Debs Heinl and Nancy Gordon Heinl, 1978, p.517.
61 James Dietz, 1986, p.139; Blanca G. Silvestrini and Maria D. Luque de Sánchez, 1987, pp.466–71.
62 Blanca G. Silvestrini and Maria D. Luque de Sánchez, 1987, p.468.

years of 1933–4 involved more than 50,000 workers on virtually every sugar estate across the island.[63]

Puerto Rico represented the stark inadequacy of the colonial policy of the United States. As citizens of the United States – although hardly considered equal to those on the mainland – Puerto Rico received much political attention in Washington in the 1930s. Measures designed to alleviate the economic plight on the mainland were extended to the island in the form of federal relief agencies such as the Puerto Rican Emergency Relief Administration (PRERA) and the Puerto Rican Reconstruction Administration (PRRA). At their best both programmes sought not only to bring immediate practical relief to the chronic distress of the population at large but also to engineer new measures for permanently resolving what were perceived as fundamental problems of economic and social retardation in Puerto Rico. Personal conflicts, arrogant paternalism and woeful misunderstanding of the people of Puerto Rico, however, vitiated the high ideals. All these deficiencies came together in the mid-1930s with the assassination in Puerto Rico of the North American police chief, a personal friend of an important United States senator from the state of Maryland. In retaliation, the federal government immediately arrested Pedro Albizu Campos and some of his National Party colleagues, proposed a punitive bill to grant immediate independence to Puerto Rico, and planned to reduce federal support programmes. An eyewitness to the times wrote:

> The period from 1936 to 1940 was one of the most critical in Puerto Rican history. The crisis reached beyond politics and the economy into every aspect of social life and organization. It was a crisis of the whole system of tutelage. For nearly half a century the United States had ruled Puerto Rico as a colony, as a possession, with powers retained in Washington and in its insular appointees. There had been modernization: roads, schools, bridges, and dams were built; business and banking developed; new programs were begun; political institutions associated with democratic republicanism were introduced. But the policy had overlooked the Puerto Rican drive for self-government, and the people's desire to have their own personality, their own sense of belonging respected and understood. Americanization meant more than an affirmative of the worth of the individual and the protection of his freedoms. Americanization meant the supremacy and superiority of everything American, and blind loyalty to the symbols of American cultural and political nationalism. With Americanization had come the rise of absentee ownership, the collapse of the coffee culture, and migration to

63 James Dietz, 1986, pp.164–7.

> the growing slums; the shocking poverty in the rural areas; and, finally, confusion and fatalism settling as a dark psychological fog on the society. To many Americans, with little grasp of the complex and pathetic experience, Puerto Ricans were ungrateful emotional children who must be taught a lesson or cast adrift as [Senator Millard] Tydings wanted. It was difficult for them to understand that the United States had taken the island as war booty and had ruled it with a mixture of paternalism and neglect, with self-righteousness and condescension. Primary responsibility for the crisis thus devolved on those who had asserted primary rights. For absolute power also implies absolute responsibility.[64]

Puerto Rican politics had become violent before the murder of the Police Commissioner. It would become more violent after Albizu was sentenced to jail for ten years and the United States administration sought to destroy the Nationalist Party. Between 1934 and 1938 party politics in Puerto Rico virtually collapsed in turmoil. The Nationalists, the Socialists, and the Liberals were all consumed with suicidal infighting. But the crisis propelled Luis Muñoz Marín into the mainstream of Puerto Rican politics. In 1938 he founded the Partido Popular Democrático (Popular Democratic Party: PPD) in the north-eastern community of Luquillo and the central district of Barranquitas. With an appealing emblem – the *jíbaro* (country folk) – an appealing, though hardly original, slogan – *Pan, Tierra y Libertad* (Bread, Land and Liberty) – and an effective newspaper – *El Batey* (the *Central Square*) – the PPD would revolutionize Puerto Rican politics and society in the next 12 years.[65] Muñoz Marín and his associates at Fomento, the Development Bureau, rescued Puerto Rico from political chaos and depressing poverty and made it a model for ameliorative change in the Caribbean.

This story of political self-directed regeneration had a parallel path in the British Antilles. Again the Great Depression was the catalyst for general discontent. With exports falling and unemployment rising, the living conditions of the lower sectors of society – the great majority of the inhabitants – plummeted everywhere. The response of the authorities seemed to be too little and far too late. The perilous plight of the citizens was compounded by natural disasters with a succession of disastrous hurricanes, floods, droughts and famine. A hurricane hit Belize City on 10 September 1931 killing more than 1,000 inhabitants – 6 per cent of the residents of the city – and destroying 75 per

64 Arturo Morales Carrión, 1983, pp.236–7.

65 In the Antillean world of sugar production the *Batey* was the core manufacturing area. The word is probably of indigenous origins, and connotes a place where social discourse takes place. It is sometimes translated as the sugar mill, but that overlooks the social connotations of the word.

cent of the dwellings. Three years later relief measures were still inadequate and the despair drove the ordinary people into organizing themselves on their own behalf. The discontent eventually exploded into widespread labour unrest. The strikes of Belize in 1934, like those in Puerto Rico in 1931–2, found immediate parallels across the rest of the English-speaking Caribbean, fuelled in part by similar factors of economic suffering, rising political consciousness, and increased inter-regional communication. For the next four years workers in St Kitts, Antigua, British Guiana, Jamaica, Barbados, St Lucia and Trinidad engaged in spontaneous, angry riots, protests, and strikes. The strikers included lumbermen, cane-cutters, longshoremen, government workers, oilfield workers, and even the unemployed in hunger marches in the towns.[66] Neither strikes nor marches were new. But in the 1930s there was a new urgency. Discontented workers and peasants joined forces with repatriated workers from Panama, Cuba and the United States as well as thousands of veterans of the First World War still waiting for the British government to fulfil its promises of economic relief. The growing population of the towns produced larger urban crowds that seemed more desperate and, to the governing classes, more menacing. Radio and cinema newsreels provided information about distant events, and the latter visually displayed the dismal conditions that were common across the dispersed colonies. Articulate groups, such as the followers of Marcus Garvey, blended politics, economics and race, exhorting their followers to improve their conditions through their own efforts rather than those of the local governments; Garveyites joined with radicals, and race and political radicalism went hand in hand in the 1930s. The response of the authorities was the conventional, unimaginative one of reinforcing the police and army and requesting another Commission of Enquiry.

The situation of the 1930s was far more serious than anything previously experienced and required drastically new measures. Everywhere people found new, articulate leaders who formed workers' associations with more than mutual aid in mind. British Honduras had the Labourers and Unemployed Association, the British Honduras Workers and Tradesmen Union, and the General Workers Union. Jamaica produced the Jamaica Tradesmen and Workers Union, the Jamaica United Clerks Association, and the Bustamante Industrial Trades Union. In Trinidad the Oilfield Workers Trade Union and the Federated Workers Trade Union sprang up, along with about a dozen smaller unions. Barbados produced two strong early trade unions, the Barbados Workers Union and the National Union of Public Workers. The British Guiana Labour Union, the Seamen's Union and the Transport Workers Union led the movement in

66 The best study of the labour unrest in the British Caribbean is O. Nigel Bolland, 1995.

British Guiana.[67] Although no permanent trade unions developed in the Bahamas, the transient workers' associations may have had some effect on the institution of new labour legislation. Establishment of political parties and a re-examination of the political status of the colonies followed legal recognition of workers' unions, but the Second World War interrupted any immediate implementation of most of these measures.[68]

The workers' organizations of the 1930s were far more militant than their predecessors. Moreover, the issue of race compounded the reality of working-class concerns, especially in the more segmented colonies of British Guiana and Trinidad. To the usual situation of white (and sometimes European) employer versus local black worker, was added the complicating ingredients of Indian ethnicity, especially among the rural workers. Trinidad provided an excellent example of the changes. The original major labour organization was that of Captain Arthur Andrew Cipriani, a Trinidadian Creole of French (Corsican) ancestry, elected as president of the Trinidad Workingmen's Association in 1923. Influenced by the British Fabian Society, Cipriani championed political reform during the 1920s. By the 1930s he was serving as Mayor of Port of Spain but his influence waned. His trade union leadership encountered strong challenges from a number of rival working-class organizations such as the Trinidad Citizens League and the Negro Welfare Cultural and Social Association – and even from associated unemployed represented by the National Unemployed Movement. The plight of the poor also drew the attention of young radicals such as C. L. R. James, Albert Gomes and Alfred Mendes through interesting but short-lived journals such as *Trinidad*, published between 1929 and 1930, and the *Beacon*, edited by Gomes between 1931 and 1933. Many of the working-class leaders of the 1930s had worked abroad and were attracted by the new communist parties developing in Panama, Costa Rica or Cuba. In any case, socialist rhetoric, international political solidarity, and human-rights sensitivities permeated the language of trade unionism throughout the Caribbean.

Nowhere was this clearer than in the case of Tubal Uriah 'Buzz' Butler, an immigrant from Grenada and former pipefitter in the oilfields of southern

67 Some labour organization preceded the 1930s. The venerable British Guiana Labour Union was formed in 1919 and even before that, Trinidad had the Trinidad Workingmen's Association that dates back to the end of the nineteenth century, as well as the Trinidad and Tobago Trade Union Centre organized in 1929. See W. Arthur Lewis, 1977.

68 The events of the British West Indies are drawn from O. Nigel Bolland, 1995; Bridget Brereton, 1981, pp.170–2; Kelvin Singh, 1994, pp.158–87; Hilary Beckles, 1990, pp.154–74; Ken Post, 1978; Gordon K. Lewis, 1968, pp.179–80; René A. Römer, 1981a, pp.137–49.

Trinidad. Butler served in the West India Regiment during the First World War, and worked in the oilfields until he became disabled in 1929. By 1931 Butler mixed pastoral duties in his own church with organizational activities in Cipriani's Trinidad Workingmen's Association and the Negro Welfare Cultural and Social Association. Increasingly Butler's emphasis on race and poverty strained his relationship with Cipriani, who in 1934 registered his association as the Trinidad Labour Party. Mobilizing his strong black support, especially around Fyzabad where many of the oilfield managers were white South Africans with manifest contempt for their workers, Butler created the British Empire Workers and Citizens Home Rule Party in 1936. Butler remained active, relentlessly organizing demonstrations and strikes which plagued Trinidad between 1935 and June 1937, when he was forced into hiding and later arrested on charges of incitement. He would suffer internment between 1939 and 1945.

Another 'graduate' of the early Cipriani working-class organization was Adrian Cola Rienzi, an Indo-Trinidadian from San Fernando formerly called Krishna Deonarine. Rienzi studied law in Dublin, returning to Trinidad in 1934. He proved himself to be a superb labour organizer, balancing Indian ethnic pride with advocacy of working-class interests. In 1935 he founded the Trinidad Citizens League and along with John Rojas, Clement Payne, MacDonald Moses, E. R. Blades and Ralph Mentor, laid the foundations for the strong unionized working class throughout the colony before the Second World War. 'The rapid rise of trade unionism,' wrote O. Nigel Bolland, 'was the most important result of the labour rebellion and Rienzi played a leading role in the process, creating and consolidating organizations in the vanguard sectors of oil and sugar.'[69]

Although lacking the pronounced East Indian dimension found in Trinidad and British Guiana, race and radicalism strongly energized early Jamaican trade unionism too. Labour organizations were legally recognized in Jamaica since 1919 but, for a number of reasons, few unions had any long-term success before the late 1930s. Economic conditions deteriorated, eventually creating the crisis that culminated in widespread rioting across the island which involved urban and rural workers as well as the unemployed. Many of the leaders of the new demonstrations had spent time abroad. Marcus Garvey created the largest mass movement in the history of the United States before his deportation in 1927. Before he left Jamaica in 1935 his Universal Negro Improvement Association had established a dynamic network of working-class, race-conscious black people across the island and throughout the Atlantic world. Although Garvey left before the popular

69 O. Nigel Bolland, 1995, p.99. See also Kelvin Singh, 1994, pp.158–85.

explosions, others remained. William Alexander Bustamante, formerly William Clark, had lived and worked in Cuba, Spain and the United States. L. W. Rose had laboured in Costa Rica. H. C. Buchanan and Cleveland Antonio King previously worked in Cuba. Lionel Lynch returned from the United States of America. Foreign sojourn sharpened their racial and ethnic identity, while exposing them to socialist and communist rhetoric and organizational methods. During the riots between 1935 and 1938 these men joined with middle-class representatives such as Audley Thomas, Ken Hill, Frank Hill, Richard Hart, Vernon Arnett, and Norman Washington Manley to provide leadership to the discontented masses and to mould them into highly politicized workers' organizations. Colour and class worked well together for a time in Jamaica.

One legacy of the highly politicized workers' organizations of the 1930s throughout the British Caribbean was an inordinately intimate relationship with the political parties that emerged during and after the Second World War. Leading early party politicians such as George Price in British Honduras, Alexander Bustamante and Norman Manley in Jamaica, Vere Bird in Antigua, Eric Gairy in Grenada, Grantley Adams and Errol Barrow in Barbados, and Cheddi Jagan in British Guiana recognized their affiliated trade unions as effective arms of their political parties. Eric Williams' People's National Movement in Trinidad & Tobago was among the very few that bucked the trend.

In the Dutch Antilles the process varied slightly from that elsewhere in the region. There the populations were much smaller, and the intervention of the State much more direct and necessary. The economic recession was shorter; the development of oil refineries in Curaçao and Aruba provided a budgetary surplus and permitted local improvements in roads and water supply. Aruba and Curaçao attracted back those emigrants who had left to work abroad – and whose opportunities for such labour were being increasingly foreclosed.[70] The Great Depression was weathered in the Dutch islands more easily than on the mainland, although it resulted in the expatriation of many foreign labourers. By 1934 the depression was virtually over in Curaçao and Aruba. In Surinam, the population was relatively larger and the problems a lot more complex than on any of the Dutch Caribbean islands.[71] With a variety of potential resources, only sugar, bauxite, timber and balata employed large numbers of people. As in other sugar areas of the Caribbean, local government placed more emphasis on saving the waning and embattled plantation economy than on developing a viable, economically self-sustaining, and just society. One measure employed was the importation of strategic groups

70 See René A. Römer, 1981a, pp.138–50; Cornelis Ch. Goslinga, 1979, pp.142–9.
71 Cornelis Ch. Goslinga, 1990.

of labourers to depress wage rates and provide workers at the crucial harvest time. The colonial government made no serious efforts to build roads, or to develop small farming or to provide a general education for the population. When supplies of labour dried up in one area of the world other supplies were sought and brought in under comparable circumstances. This led to a sharply segmented society with virtually isolated communities of East Indians, Javanese, Chinese, Jews, European Whites, Lebanese, Creoles, Bush Negroes and Amerindians. The segmentation was not only demographic, it was also occupational. This made it extremely difficult to organize collective action, as the failure of Anton De Kom's organization in 1933 illustrated.[72] In Surinam the misery and neglect of the poorer classes were mitigated only by the coming of the Second World War and the wartime measures imposed on the colony. No foundations for improved basic changes, however, emerged from the experience of the pre-war and wartime years.

Inescapably the Second World War brought enormous changes all over the world, not least in the Caribbean. It accelerated the transfer and adaptation of certain new technologies, especially in communication and commerce. It also aggravated local deficiencies, exposing them and making them more intolerable. There was no doubt about it, the post-war Caribbean would be, in many ways, a very different sort of place. Yet any review of the decade of the 1930s produces some obvious observations that support the centrality of that transitional period in the history of the Atlantic world.

The first observation lies in the way in which Caribbean societies were increasingly linked economically, politically, intellectually and culturally to one another and to the wider world. During the 1930s those links were reinforced. The connections between colonies and their respective metropoles formed only one part of their externally dependent relations, however. Caribbean colonies were as dependent on the United States of America as on Great Britain, France or Holland. Independent Caribbean states had their sovereignty and autonomy severely circumscribed and became even more politically and economically dependent on the United States. Both colonies and metropoles were inseparably subordinated to a universal capitalist system that consistently placed profits over people and market considerations over material conditions of life. That was a fundamental part of the failure of colonialism – whether of the old-fashioned atavistic type as in the British, French and Dutch Antilles, or the benevolent, newer type as in the American sphere. The ruling classes under colonialism had great difficulty in separating narrow class interests from emerging broader national interests.

72 Cornelis Ch. Goslinga, 1979, pp.165–6; *idem*, 1990, pp.497–523.

In the second place, the decade represented the crucial transition from the old society to the new, modern Caribbean – although that was not achieved in all cases during the decade. The simultaneous combination of natural disasters, the Great Depression and intellectually incompetent political leadership exposed the precarious existence of the lower orders of society and forced them to take matters into their own hands. Everywhere from Belize to Surinam people spontaneously protested about their conditions and demanded that the authorities urgently address their complaints. Eventually the authorities came to the conclusion that police measures alone constituted an inadequate response. The people had to be heard and their grievances addressed with the required urgency. This took the form of legal recognition for labour organizations, of better working conditions and higher wages, and eventually of basic political reforms with a larger, more open – and therefore more representative – electoral franchise.

In the third place, after the 1930s politics-as-usual was no longer possible – thanks to the autonomous initiative of the lower orders of society. Workers came into their own, but the unemployed also won political recognition. Political legitimacy became democratized – at least in Cuba, Puerto Rico, the British West Indies and the Dutch Antilles. Democracy proved more elusive in Haiti and the Dominican Republic. The awareness that societies could only be improved by the co-ordinated efforts of the State gave the State – colonial or independent – a greater say in non-political affairs. Nevertheless, conditions favouring the growth of the State were not quite the same everywhere. In Surinam the extreme ethnic fragmentation of the working classes inhibited effective worker pressure. The political future of Surinam would therefore be quite different from that of the Dutch Antillean islands. The process was undermined in Haiti and the Dominican Republic because of the nature of the political authority which had been established and was supported by the United States of America after their withdrawal.

In the fourth place, it is possible to observe that individuals as well as groups were important in the way politics played itself out in the 1930s. It is impossible to say why some individuals such as Luis Muñoz Marín in Puerto Rico or Norman Manley of Jamaica supported open, democratic political measures while Fulgencio Batista in Cuba, Rafael Trujillo in the Dominican Republic, and Sténio Vincent in Haiti found dictatorial authoritarianism more acceptable. Yet, where leading individuals were able to overcome the temptation to place personal opportunism above the common good, the result was a manifest improvement of the political culture and the economic foundation of the State. The rising tide of economic well-being lifted all boats. On the other hand, selfish dictators such as Batista, Vincent, and Trujillo preferred to enrich a selected few at the expense of the many.

In the fifth place, the experience of the 1930s made it patently obvious that agriculture alone – especially plantation export agriculture – could not provide the panacea for all economic ills. Given the differential in prices between commodity exports and finished-product imports the countries of the Caribbean found it increasingly difficult to generate sufficient income from exports to alleviate the increasing misery of a rapidly growing population. But prices were only a part of the problem. The example of Cuba demonstrated that open markets were important, although unreliable. Every Caribbean territory found that one consequence of the Great Depression was to reduce dramatically the demand for agricultural products and raw materials. This made the Caribbean countries extremely vulnerable economically. Not surprisingly, therefore, by the end of the decade new voices arose demanding that Caribbean countries be more self-sufficient in the production of foodstuffs and that industrialization be adopted to alleviate the high unemployment of the labour force, especially in urban areas. Development became irrevocably linked to industrialization.

Finally, it is possible to observe that, although challenged and neglected, Caribbean social, educational and cultural institutions appeared impressively resilient. Good schools were producing good students who distinguished themselves locally as well as in the metropoles. Above all, young (and not so young) Caribbean writers were discovering a new, confident self-awareness.[73] Across the region creative writers such as Jean Price Mars, Lorimer Denis, François Duvalier, Léon Laleau, and Jacques Roumain in Haiti, Manuel del Cabral in the Dominican Republic, C. L. R. James in Trinidad, Alejo Carpentier, Nicolás Guillén and Fernando Ortiz in Cuba, Luis Palés Matos in Puerto Rico, Aimé Césaire in Martinique, Léon Damas in French Guiana, and Marcus Garvey in Jamaica were successfully articulating a new type of anti-European, almost atavistically African-Caribbean, literature. Both from inside the region and abroad they published seminal new works that presented a vastly different picture of the people and their view of their Caribbean reality, confronting race and colour in a far more positive way than previously.[74] Authentic Haitian culture seemed to thrive under the

73 J. Michael Dash, 1981; Janis L. Pallister, 1991; Amon Saba Saakana, 1987, pp.63–88; Barbara J. Webb, 1992.

74 The theme is developed in G. R. Coulthard, 1962, pp.40–57. Race and colour have always been aspects of Caribbean literature but in the 1920s and 1930s local writers started to regard them less as social liabilities than as admirable attributes. Of course even in Haiti the attitudes to race and colour varied widely but the change of emphasis from an earlier period was obvious and grew into the later *négritude* movement.

adversity of the North American occupation. In Puerto Rico the people resisted the strenuous efforts of the United States to eliminate the Spanish language and the Roman Catholic religion. The number of later distinguished writers who were born in the decade also indicated that the elementary school system was not beyond the pale of intellectual salvation. Indeed, the primary and secondary school systems of the British Caribbean produced at best as high a quality of education as that of the metropolis. Dr Eric Williams, the first prime minister of Trinidad & Tobago, reflected on his colonial education in the first part of the twentieth century in his autobiographical *Inward Hunger*:

> If there was a difference between the English public schools and its Trinidad imitation, it was this, that the Trinidad school provided a more thorough preparation for the university than the average English school, partly because the students stayed to the age of twenty rather than eighteen and took a higher examination, partly also because it was not even the cream of the crop, but the top individual from Trinidad, who found himself competing with a large number of English students of varying ability.[75]

The trickle of students in the 1930s from the British West Indies who entered British universities would expand greatly after the Second World War. Nevertheless, the transformations of the 1940s and 1950s had their roots in the tumultuous decade of the 1930s. The Caribbean people in the 1930s were poor, in general, in material things. They were not poor in spirit and self-confidence. Of that there can be absolutely no doubt.

75 Eric Williams, 1969 (1971), p.33.

Appendix: Important Caribbean events of the 1930s

1930

- **Puerto Rico:** Pedro Albizu Campos returned from visit to the Dominican Republic, Haiti, Cuba, Mexico, Panama, Peru, and Venezuela and was elected president of the Puerto Rican Nationalist Party
- **Cuba:** Directorio Estudiantil Universitario (DEU) founded in Havana by Rafael Trejo.
- United States Commission recommended reforms for **Haiti** and urged Sténio Vincent to be president.
- **Dominican Republic:** Hurricane killed 1200. Trujillo engineered coup that overthrew the government of Horacio Vásquez. Trujillo elected President in August.
- **Trinidad:** Witchbroom disease affected cocoa plantations.
- **United States:** Hawley-Smoot tariff reduced sugar quota resulting in severe hardship in Cuba.
- **Jamaica:** Lord Olivier headed delegation sent to inquire into the state of the sugar industry. East Indian Association formed in Kingston in August.

1931

- United States began civil government in **Virgin Islands**.
- Luis Muñoz Marín returned with his family to **Puerto Rico**.
- **Cuba:** Revolt in Havana.
- **Jamaica:** Constant Spring Hotel opened in Kingston. Branch of the League of Nations formed in Kingston.
- **Curaçao** set up Labour Exchange.
- **British Honduras:** Belize City seriously damaged by hurricane and tidal wave in September.
- **Trinidad:** Franchise for Electric Company terminated. Pan American Airways initiated passenger air service between Trinidad and the United States of America.
- Léon Laleau published *Musique nègre* in Port-au-Prince, **Haiti**.

1932

- **Cuba:** 2 February earthquake killed 1500 in Santiago.
- **Trinidad:** Divorce legalized. Trade unions legally recognized. First female, Eileen Ramsaran, admitted to the Bar. Dr Lennox Pawan became the first to isolate rabies virus. Fires destroyed several important buildings in Port of Spain.

- **Surinam:** Surinamese General Labourers Organization (SAWO) founded.
- Jamaican Claude McKay published *Gingertown*, a collection of short stories.
- **Cayman Islands** and western end of **Jamaica** hit by hurricane on 8 November with 67 lives lost on Cayman Brac.
- **Puerto Rico** hit by hurricane San Ciprián on 20 September.
- **St Kitts:** Albert Marryshow of Grenada and Arthur Cipriani of Trinidad visited to discuss worker co-operation
- **Dominica:** Cecil Rawle chaired an Unofficial Meeting of West Indian Delegates from Antigua, St Vincent, Dominica, St Lucia, Trinidad & Tobago, Barbados, and St Kitts to discuss a West Indies Federation.

1933

- **Cuba:** Revolution and overthrow of Gerardo Machado. Fulgencio Batista emerged as strongman. Later in year Sumner Welles withdrawn as United States Ambassador to Cuba.
- **Trinidad:** C. L. R. James published *The Life of Captain Cipriani: The Case for West Indian Self Government*. Alfred Mendes published his first novel, *Pitch Lake*.
- Alejo Carpentier published *Ecué-Yamba-O* in Madrid.
- **St Vincent** passed law recognizing labour unions.
- Claude McKay published *Banana Bottom*, a novel.
- Second official tour of a West Indies cricket team to England included Learie Constantine (Trinidad), George Headley (Jamaica) and E. A. Martindale (Barbados).
- **Jamaica:** Hurricane hit the island on 17 July and on 15–16 August with major flooding in Kingston and St Andrew: 53 lives were lost. Second hurricane in October swept across western end of the island. Heavy rains in December caused flooding by Moneague Lake.
- **Trinidad** hit by hurricane 24 June and floods 1 August.
- **Surinam:** Anton De Kom returned from the Netherlands and began to advocate independence.
- J. B. Cinéas published *Le drame de la terre* in Port-au-Prince, **Haiti**.

1934

- **Washington DC:** President F. D. Roosevelt recognized new Cuban government installed by Batista in January.
- Italy invaded Ethiopia and many Caribbean countries, especially **Jamaica** and **Trinidad**, organized support for Haile Selassie.
- **Jamaica:** Trade exhibition opened in February.
- 29 May United States proposed annulment of Platt Amendment.

- **Haiti:** 14 August, end of United States occupation in effect since July 1915.
- **Cuba:** Poet Nicolás Guillén published *West Indies, Ltd.*
- Aimé Césaire, Léon Damas and Léopold Sédar Senghor founded Review in Paris called *L'Etudiant noir* in which Césaire first used word *négritude.*
- Labour unrest in Belize City (**British Honduras**), Nassau (**Bahamas**), Port of Spain (**Trinidad**), Falmouth, Oracabessa and Kingston (**Jamaica**), Puerto Rico, and Demerara (**British Guiana**).
- **Curaçao:** Roman Catholic Labourers Union founded.
- **Barbados:** First radio transmission overseas.

1935

- **Trinidad:** Former Gonzales Estates incorporated into the city of Port of Spain as site for workers' homes.
- **St Vincent and St Kitts** had riots.
- **Jamaica:** Hurricanes occurred in September and October.
- **Haiti:** Devastating flood damage from hurricane drowned 2,000.
- **Puerto Rico** adopted eight-hour labour day and workers' compensation for injuries on the job.
- Antonio Arredondo published *El negro en Cuba* in Havana.
- Manuel del Cabral published *Doce poemas negros* in the Dominican Republic.

1936

- **Cuba** changed government.
- **Puerto Rico:** Muñoz Marín expelled from the Liberal Party.
- **Dominican Republic:** Trujillo changed name of the capital to Ciudad Trujillo.
- **Jamaica** established radio-telephone service with Cuba, Mexico, Canada, the United States and England.
- Constitutional change in **British Honduras**, **British Windward Islands** and **British Leeward Islands** provided elected members to the Legislative Council, with a majority of the Windwards Council elected.
- **Trinidad:** C. L. R. James published *Minty Alley.* Audrey Jeffers became first woman elected to Port of Spain City Council.
- **Cuba:** Fernando Ortíz published 'Más acerca una poesía mulata' in *Revista Bimestre* (Havana).
- **Dutch Antilles:** *Koloniale Raad* replaced by *Staten,* a modification of the colonial status of the Dutch Antilles.
- **Barbados:** Bridgetown Housing Act began redress of urban housing conditions.

1937

- **San Juan, Puerto Rico:** Police fired on nationalists killing seven and injuring 50.
- **Barbados** and **Trinidad** had riots.
- C. L. R. James published *World Revolution*.
- Léon Damas published *Pigments*.
- Luis Palés Matos published first edition of *Tun tun de pasa y grifería* in San Juan.
- Fernando Ortíz published 'Contra los racismos' in *Revista de Estudios Afrocubanos* in Havana.
- McKay published his autobiographical *A Long Way From Home.*
- **Dominican Republic** massacred over 18,000 Haitian cane-cutters along the western frontier provinces.

1938

- **Bahamian** sponge industry destroyed by fungus disease.
- **Dominican Republic:** October – massacre and deportation of Haitian residents.
- **Jamaica:** Labour disturbances in Frome, followed by unrest in Kingston, St Mary and St James. First island-wide labour union formed by Bustamante.
- **Jamaica:** People's National Party formed by Norman W. Manley.
- C. L. R. James published *Black Jacobins.*
- Melville J. Herskovits published *Life in a Haitian Valley.*
- **British West Indies:** Royal (Moyne) Commission investigated economic conditions.
- **Cuba:** Communist Party legally recognized.
- **Puerto Rico:** Luis Muñoz Marín organized Popular Democratic Party in Luquillo and Barranquitas, 28 July 1938.
- **St Lucia:** Landslides and heavy rains resulted in loss of large number of lives.
- **Haiti:** *Les Griots* started publication, giving voice to black self-consciousness.
- **Trinidad:** Port of Spain deep-water pier opened. Government began to oversee Carnival through the Carnival Improvement Committee.

1939

- Batista made successful visit to Mexico.
- World War II began in September.
- Oil industry important in **Trinidad** and **Curaçao**.
- **Jamaica:** All internal towns connected by telephone service.

- **Cuba:** Labour unions reorganized as Confederación de Trabajadores de Cuba (CTC).
- **Haiti:** Sténio Vincent published *En posant les jalons* in Port-au-Prince. *Les Griots* folded.
- Ramón Guirao published *Orbita de la poesía afro-cubana 1928–37* in Havana.
- **Martinique:** Aimé Césaire published 'Cahier d'un retour au pays natal' in journal *Volontés* and returned to teach in Martinique at Lycée Victor Schoelcher where two of his students were Edouard Glissant and Frantz Fanon.
- **Trinidad:** The steel drum (musical instrument), the product of several persons, emerged around this time.

1940

- **Puerto Rico:** Muñoz Marín elected Senate president.
- **Dominica** included in the Windward Islands.
- **British West Indies:** Development and Welfare Organization established for economic relief.
- **Cuba:** New constitution ratified. Batista elected to a four-year term as president.

3

The Caribbean in the Second World War

Claus Füllberg-Stolberg

Introduction

The outbreak of war in September 1939 in Europe had tremendous repercussions in the Caribbean. Germany's invasion of Poland and the declaration of war by France and Britain had an immediate impact on the European colonies in the western hemisphere, which further deepened when the German war machine rapidly occupied Western Europe.

The West India Royal Commission of 1938/9 and other investigations into the social and economic conditions of the British West Indies had increased fears of a new outbreak of the riots that had spread throughout the Caribbean in consequence of the Great Depression.[1] The world-wide economic crisis had not bypassed the French possessions – Martinique, Guadeloupe or French Guiana. Here too, strikes and social unrest had occurred, which had not, however, presented a serious challenge to the colonial power. At the outbreak of war, the French Headquarters of the Western Hemisphere was established in Martinique. Admiral Georges Robert, a retired naval commander, was reactivated as High Commissioner.

Despite the disturbances, the daily papers of the British West Indies of the time give the impression that the colonies had, from the very outset, supported the war effort of the motherland with great solidarity. Michael Anthony reports a spontaneous outbreak of enthusiasm for the war in Port of Spain, Trinidad, where hundreds of young men volunteered for service, and the Legislative Council of the island granted $1,000,000 to help the war effort.[2] Even from Jamaica, the greatest trouble spot of the region, Governor Richards was able to inform the Colonial Office, with some relief, that all fears of new unrest had given way to widespread loyalty.[3] Other European colonies in the

1 Report of the West India Royal Commission, 1945; see also chap.2, this volume.
2 Michael Anthony, 1983, pp.1–2. The sum is in local currency
3 Ken Post, 1981, vol. I, p.54. Even the People's National Party (PNP), which had been formed as an anticolonial and socialist party during the unrest, declared a moratorium of its activities towards self-government.

Caribbean also seemed to be content, for the moment, to follow the course of the metropolis.

The outbreak of war forced the independent republics of America to take their stance in the world-wide battle for regional hegemony. An American security zone under the leadership of the United States was already established when the hegemonic power finally became actively involved in the war at the end of 1941.

The U-boat battle in the Caribbean opened a new theatre of war. Although the real threat of the German submarines was only short-lived, it revealed the great vulnerability of the United States backyard. The extension of the war zone to the coastal waters of the Gulf of Mexico affected the economy of the region and the living conditions of Caribbean societies quite fundamentally. The trade in strategically relevant raw materials (oil and bauxite), in traditional cash crops (sugar and banana) and in commodities vital to the survival of the population was heavily disrupted during the early 1940s. The transatlantic routes were closed for export crops and import capacity was reduced to basic necessities.

The United States developed a military defence scheme for the Caribbean and also took over other responsibilities of the European colonial powers. The work of the Anglo-American Caribbean Commission showed the essential, but contradictory, co-operation of the old and new world powers during the war and after. Military activities went hand in hand with the general interest of the United States in this region and reinforced its dominance, accelerating the process of decolonization and preparing the ground for economic and cultural penetration of the region during the post-war period.

The geo-strategic position of the Caribbean in the Second World War

The Caribbean had already played a crucial role in joint military planning undertaken by the British and American navies during the inter-war period. As Assistant Secretary of the Navy in the First World War Franklin D. Roosevelt had always emphasized the exceptional strategic significance of the Caribbean and the Gulf of Mexico for the safety of the United States. His British counterpart for most of the war, Winston Churchill, who had had a similar career as the First Lord of the British Admiralty, was also naval-minded. He encouraged the American president to give the Caribbean a high ranking in his military-strategic thinking. Churchill had realized from the onset of war that emphasizing the importance of this region could help to change the United States from a neutral state with an allied bias into the active war ally he badly needed. The Anglo-American naval staff talks of 1938/9, though mainly concerned with the Far East, also led to a secret agreement to lease sites in Bermuda, St Lucia and Trinidad to the United States for military bases.[4] On 30 June 1939, Roosevelt officially requested the lease of base facilities in these three British West Indian islands through the British Ambassador, Sir Ronald Lindsay. United States military personnel visited proposed sites for the bases and negotiated leasehold agreements with the colonial authorities. The Foreign Office instructed the Governors to grant only short-term leases revocable at short notice. These first leasehold agreements were already finalized before the outbreak of war and the declaration of American neutrality.[5]

The request for the cession of military bases was connected to preparations for the patrolling of the American neutrality zone formally declared at the Pan-American Conference at Panama in September/October 1939. This first base agreement is part of the prehistory of the 'destroyers for bases deal', which finally made the Caribbean the focus of joint Anglo-American defence strategies. On the American side, military strategic planning and preparations for the protection of the western hemisphere from single as well as combined attacks from Europe and the Far East, which had been drastically stepped up since the European crisis, formed the background to this agreement. In these greatly differing military scenarios – because of the multiple threat posed, dubbed 'rainbow plans' – the Caribbean, with its geo-strategic position and its important resources for the war economy, became exceptionally significant.[6]

The two major resources that were crucial for the war effort were the oil-petrol complexes in Trinidad and Aruba-Curaçao-Venezuela, and the bauxite mines in British and Dutch Guiana. However, the highly frequented sea routes proved to be even more important than these strategic resources. These waterways were not only used for the transportation of important goods by the United States and Britain, but also to provide the West Indies with foodstuffs on which they depended heavily.[7]

It became apparent just how great this dependence was when the German U-boats began operations in the Caribbean in the spring of 1942. The threat to the strategic resources had already become acute after German troops occupied the Netherlands in May 1940. As a consequence the oil-petrol

4 James R. Leutze, 1977, pp.15–28; David Reynolds, 1981, p.60; Fitzroy André Baptiste, 1988, pp.3–4.
5 Fitzroy André Baptiste, 1988, p.12.
6 Donald Allen Yerxa, 1991, p.112.
7 See Gerhard Sandner, 1993.

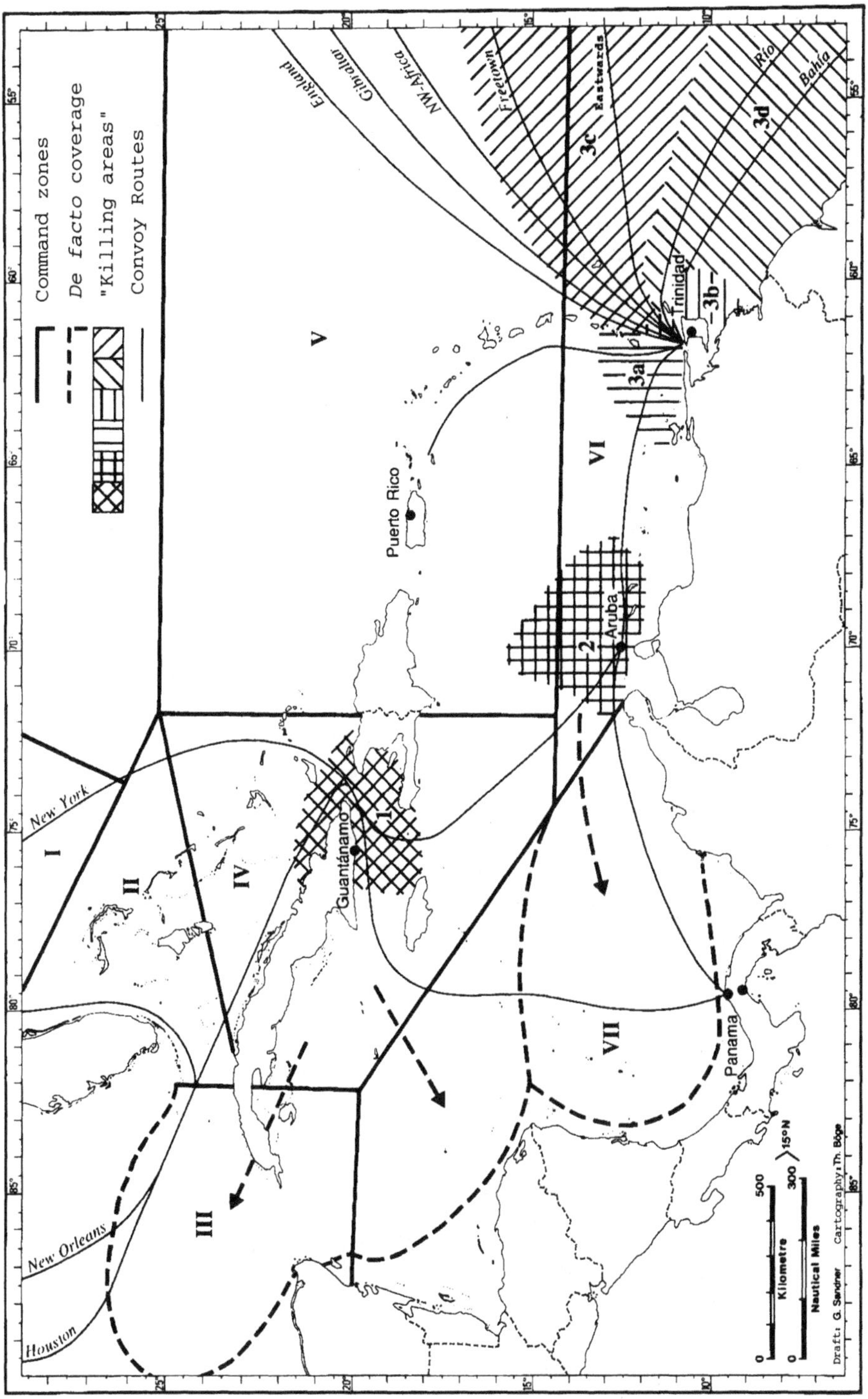

Figure 3.1 Command zones, killing areas and convoy routes in the Caribbean (*Map courtesy Gerhard Sandner, 1993*)

complex of Aruba-Curaçao, the world's largest exporter of this strategic raw material and the major source for Germany and England, was no longer under the control of the Dutch government, which had fled into exile in London.[8] The bauxite mines in Dutch Guiana (Suriname), controlled by a United States-based multinational company (Alcan), were a major supplier of the United States aluminium industry. As aluminium was the most important raw material for the aircraft industry and thus the air force, the single most decisive military unit in the Second World War, its strategic significance clearly cannot be underestimated.[9]

ANGLO-FRENCH MILITARY CO-OPERATION IN THE DUTCH WEST INDIES

Despite the great importance of its resources for the war effort, the Caribbean region played no prominent role in Anglo-French military co-operation. Both allies relied on the direct strategic interest of the United States. This assumption proved to be correct in the long run but created short-term problems when the German 'Blitzkrieg' overran the Dutch and French colonial powers within two months and also threatened the British Empire.

The invasion of the Netherlands by German troops on 10 May 1940 had immediate consequences in the Dutch West Indies. On the morning of 10 May the Dutch Governor of Curaçao declared martial law and arrested all German nationals on land and on board German ships anchoring in Curaçao harbours, including some Jewish refugees who had escaped from Nazi Germany. A second proclamation by the Governor the same day stated that 'the international status of this territory would remain as before: that the government established here had resolved to continue to rule … this part of the Netherlands on land and sea and that any outside help from whatsoever source would be refused and considered unwelcome.'[10]

In the meantime, the Dutch government in exile, on arrival in London, was confronted with a *fait accompli* to invite British and French troops to Aruba and Curaçao for the protection of the oil industry.[11] The British had been concerned about what they deemed to be the insufficient security of the

8 In 1938, the oil-refining zone at Aruba and Curaçao off the Caribbean coast of Venezuela accounted for 44 per cent of the German and 38 per cent of the British oil and petrol imports respectively. See Howard Johnson, 1984a, p.33; Fitzroy André Baptiste, 1988, pp.29–32.

9 See Howard Johnson, 1984a, pp.32–3; Fitzroy André Baptiste, 1988, pp.115–17.

10 National Archives of the United States, Washington DC, RG 856 B. 00/24 American Consul at Curaçao to Secretary of State, 24 May 1940, pp.1–2.

11 Fitzroy André Baptiste, 1988, p.34.

Aruba-Curaçao oil complex for quite some time. They feared surprise attacks by the Germans or from Nazi-sympathizing forces from Latin America, via sea or air. Greatly concerned about the rapid occupation of Denmark and Norway, they had little faith in the resistance of the Dutch army in the event of a German attack. Therefore, at a conference of naval commanders in Kingston, Jamaica, on 4 May the British and French agreed upon a joint landing of their troops on the oil-producing islands of Aruba and Curaçao, in order to be prepared for this eventuality.

The United States was only informed of these plans at the last minute, when rumours had already reached its Department of State.[12] On 10 May Lord Lothian, the British Ambassador, presented a note to the Secretary of State (SoS) Hull, expressing concern about the safety of the Aruba and Curaçao oil refineries and informing him of the decision that 'a small additional British force should be landed in Curaçao.'[13]

The Americans launched a formal protest at this action, but their initial irritation soon gave way to relief that the United States had not been called on to protect the refineries. Through the Department of State, Roosevelt despatched a memorandum to the British Ambassador which acknowledged the status quo on the island as unchanged, and diplomatically accepted the move. Roosevelt also insisted 'that any forces landed must be so landed at the request of the Dutch authorities, subject to the command of the Dutch authorities, acting under the Dutch flag, and merely by way of temporary assistance.'[14] This was agreed to by the British Ambassador in the name of his government. Following an agreement with the local authorities in Curaçao and Aruba, about 500 British and 200 French soldiers landed. In addition, there were some 200 Dutch 'seasoned marines and police and ... about 2,000 raw troops.'[15]

Immediately, Venezuela protested vehemently against this thrust by the colonial powers on foreign terrain. She viewed the landing of British and French troops on the Dutch West Indies as a violation of the Declaration of Panama, which had established a neutral security zone to protect the American continent against involvement in the European war, and expected an appropriate reaction from the United States. In fact, the United States was still hesitant about military intervention. Instead, she launched a new Pan-American initiative, to consult on a solution for trusteeship over European territories in the Caribbean, should the colonial powers suffer further defeats in the war.

---

12 *Ibid.*, p.34.
13 NAW RG 856 B. 00/24 Department of State, Memorandum Berle, 11 May 1940.
14 *Ibid.*, p.2.
15 NAW RG 856 B. 00/24 American Consul at Curaçao to SoS, 24 May 1940, p.5.

The development of the US-Continental defence scheme for the Caribbean

Pan-American conferences

The Good Neighbor Policy of the United States, started under the Coolidge administration, was strengthened by Roosevelt's efforts for a Pan-American security system, and was seen as the best provision against the American continent's involvement in the war.[16] Before the outbreak of open military conflict in Europe, the United States had begun to try to integrate the independent states of the region into a joint security system.[17] Just before the German attack on Poland, Roosevelt pressed for the summoning of a Pan-American conference, at which agreement on a General Declaration of Neutrality and a 300-mile security zone around the American continent up to the Canadian border was expected. At the Panama meeting of foreign ministers (23 September to 3 October 1939), the declarations worked out by the American team of experts were accepted without alterations. This meant that the security patrols already started by the United States navy were sanctioned and put on a mutual Pan-American basis in order to keep the western hemisphere free of belligerent activities. In addition to these two essential declarations, the meeting agreed on a series of further decrees relating to, *inter alia*, economic co-operation, and anticipating the Pan-Americanization of European colonies in case of the German occupation of the European metropoles of the colonial powers.[18]

When war broke out, the independent states of the Americas were united in their determination to avoid becoming involved in the conflict. In the case of the United States, from the very beginning her declaration of neutrality must be understood as 'neutrality with an allied bias'.[19] Since the First World War, military co-operation between Britain and the United States was evident in joint geo-political defence strategies with regard to possible aggression from either Germany or Japan.

The belligerent parties rejected the declaration of Panama, and did not respect the 300-mile offshore security zone resolved at the conference. The first spectacular test of the security zone occurred in December 1939, when British warships severely damaged the German destroyer *Graf Spee* off the coast of Uruguay so that it was forced to call at the port of Montevideo.

16 Irwin F. Gellman, 1979; Edward O. Guerrant, 1950; Robert Dallek, 1979, pp.38–9.
17 J. Lloyd Mecham, 1961, pp.149–80.
18 *Ibid.*, pp.181–4; Fitzroy André Baptiste, 1988, pp.18–21; Irwin F. Gellman, 1979, pp.83–5.
19 Irwin F. Gellman, 1979.

When the Captain realized that he would not be able to make the ship navigable again within the set time limit of 72 hours, he sank it in the shallow waters of the La Plata river. The sinking of the *Graf Spee* presented a spectacular sight to the world press assembled in Montevideo, as well as to the British battleships at the mouth of the La Plata. At the same time it demonstrated that it was unfeasible to keep the European war away from the American coast.

The course of the war in Europe now also became a cause of alarm to the American public, and persuaded the United States military planners to change from 'a watchful wait-and-see stance ... to final preparations for conflict' in areas of strategic concern.[20] Following the Allied landing in the Dutch West Indies, the first diplomatic steps were taken to strengthen Pan-American unity to prepare the ground for the possibility of direct engagement in European colonies in the Caribbean in the future. In general, military preparations began for the assumption of the defence of the western hemisphere in the event of a total defeat of the Allies in the European war.

In June 1940, Germany invaded France and defeated the French army within a matter of weeks. A bewildered American strategic command now also had to face the frightening prospect of Britain's imminent defeat. The German armistice with Vichy France threatened the American Republics with a potential German foothold in the French West Indies, whose military commander expressed his loyalty to Marshal Pétain, the leader of Vichy France.

At the conference of American foreign ministers in Panama, the next inter-American meeting had been scheduled for October 1940. However, events in Europe, and in particular their repercussions in the Caribbean, necessitated an earlier meeting in July. The United States Department of State's special concern at this meeting, taking place in Havana, was to reconfirm collective trusteeship over the European colonies in the Caribbean in the event of a transfer of power, as had already been envisioned at the Panama conference. The American states agreed upon the establishment of a provisional administrative regime for every European possession in the hemisphere that 'may be converted into strategic centres of aggression against nations of the American continent.'[21] Britain, Vichy France, the Dutch government in exile, and their respective colonial administrations, unanimously rejected the Act of Havana and insisted on their unlimited sovereign rights. They did not have to wait long for the first test case.

20 Donald Allen Yerxa, 1991, p.108.

21 Quoted in Fitzroy André Baptiste, 1988, p.43; see also J. Lloyd Mecham, 1961, p.186–8.

The destroyers-bases agreement between Great Britain and the United States

During the weeks of the German 'Blitzkrieg', the invasion and military defeat of Britain seemed possible to her closest friends, and at times even probable, without United States military support. Even Churchill, who had become both prime minister and First War Lord on 10 May 1940, shared his concern about the poor state of the British army in his private correspondence with Roosevelt.

In order to prevent the immediate collapse of the navy, Churchill desperately needed 50 destroyers built from American resources for action in the First World War, in addition to other war material. On the American side, the need to establish the permanent American military bases already selected in the British West Indies, to enable the single-handed defence of the western hemisphere in an emergency, became more and more pressing. From this point, diplomatic negotiations over the exact wording of a destroyers agreement took several months. The deal had to be presented as profitable to the American public while at the same time not appear like horse trading in Britain. On the one hand, the American public needed to understand how crucial the destroyers were for British military survival, while on the other, it was clear that the defeat of the Royal Navy could see American destroyers in the hands of the enemy.[22]

Besides public support, Roosevelt also had to find the legal authority for the transfer of the destroyers, enabling him to make the decision without first consulting Congress. Churchill had to avoid creating the impression that he was giving away important parts of the Empire to the hegemonic power of the USA permanently. Roosevelt was forced to sell the destroyers-bases deal as a measure to prevent or at least delay direct entry into the war by the United States. Churchill, on the other hand, could best champion the establishment of American military bases in the West Indies as the beginning of direct United States military involvement on the British side.

In hindsight, these months of negotiations over sometimes hair-splitting details, in the light of Britain's increasingly desperate situation, as well as the perceived threat that was growing visibly for the United States of America, seem somewhat unrealistic. Be that as it may, both sides placed a high symbolic value on the negotiations, which were about a real threat to Britain's existence, as well as the gradual and tacit entry of the United States into the war alongside Britain, or, as was increasingly projected, alone against fascist Europe and Japan. The course of events in Europe confirmed Roosevelt's

22 See James R. Leutze, 1977, pp.72–113; David Reynolds, 1981, pp.95–144; and Fitzroy André Baptiste, 1988, pp.51–62.

opinion that it would be better to establish military bases on the islands (in principle already agreed to by Britain), as quickly as possible, before the fall of Britain could force the USA into a position of being solely, or with Pan-American collaboration, responsible for the military occupation and provision of these islands.

The Italian entry into the war, the sudden collapse of the French, and the latter's effects on the West Indies, accelerated the will to act in the United States of America. From then on, the United States threw its support behind Britain, as the sole remaining opposition to the fascist powers in Europe, up to the limit of actual entry into the war. Public opinion in the United States, too, showed a definite majority in favour of active support for Britain. Roosevelt had long been convinced of the need for this step, but had hesitated because of his decision to run for the presidency for a third term, which was imminent. The pro-British faction of his party secured the support of influential Republicans, including Wendell Wilkie, the Republican candidate for the presidency. Finally, the formal legalization of the transfer of the destroyers as discarded war material, and its clever connection to the transfer of power at the military bases in the West Indies, was achieved. What was regarded by Britain as a generous gesture had to appear to the American public as an exchange for the security of the United States. The appearance of a *quid pro quo,* on the other hand, had to be avoided in Britain at all costs. Thus, the deal required new packaging for the British public: so Britain ceded some of the sites for military bases as a grant (Bermuda, Newfoundland) and leased the other sites for a period of 99 years to the United States of America in exchange for 50 recommissioned destroyers.[23] Altogether, the conclusion of the agreement took from Churchill's first request on 15 May until late August, when the Roosevelt adminstration finally approved the agreement and released it to the press on 3 September 1940.

The French West Indies under the rule of Admiral Robert

In the meantime, the situation in the Caribbean was further aggravated by Admiral Robert, the High Commissioner of the French West Indies (Martinique, Guadeloupe and French Guiana) who declared his loyalty to Marshal Pétain and Vichy France. A part of the peace treaty with Germany consisted of demobilizing the navy 'except a portion of the fleet designated to represent French interest in the colonial empire.'[24] This paragraph referred to warships stationed at Mers-el-Kébir, Alexandria (North Africa) and

23 Richard M. Ketchum, 1989, pp.477–9.

24 Article VIII of Franco-German Armistice, quoted in Fitzroy André Baptiste, 1988, p.65.

Fort-de-France (Martinique). Fort-de-France regularly hosted a small naval force which was, at the time of the armistice, augmented by an aircraft carrier loaded with 100 planes and 700 men and a modern cruiser with an additional 500 men. Altogether there were about 2,400 French army personnel stationed in France's West Indian colonies. Originally, the cruiser had been on its way to Canada with a cargo of gold from the Bank of France, valued at 12 billion francs (250–300 million US$).[25]

When Admiral Robert expressed his loyalty to Vichy France, British and American naval forces were put on alert to occupy Martinique and Guadeloupe, as well as French Guiana. It soon became obvious, however, that the United States had her own plans with respect to Vichy France, which also affected the French colonies. It was with difficulty that the USA prevented Britain from immediate military intervention; it was only when the British military leaders realized that Admiral Robert would not surrender without a fight, and that the United States navy was sending control warships to Martinique and Guadeloupe, that they rescinded their plans. When Robert had broken internal resistance to his rule, and when coup attempts from the outside by de Gaulle's Free France Movement had failed, the USA put its hopes on more or less neutral conduct by Vichy during the war, and concentrated on the demobilization of ships and troops in the French West Indies. Although the population in the French West Indies now had to live under a totalitarian regime ruling with martial law, the United States was prepared to tolerate the claims to sovereignty made by the French Admiral under the following conditions:

- no movement of the French naval forces with the exception of minor vessels;
- the gold bullion to be kept in Martinique;
- the posting of a representative of the United States of America in Fort-de-France and the daily landing of patrol planes.[26]

If these conditions were respected, the USA was prepared to provide the islands with imports of vital commodities.

For the negotiation of the details of such an agreement, Rear Admiral Greenslade was ordered to Martinique on 5 August 1940. As a member of the commission charged with the build-up of military bases in the British Caribbean, Greenslade was an expert on the defence strategies in the Caribbean. A second round of talks in early November finalized the agreement.

25 National Archives/Military Archives of the Federal Republic of Germany, Freiburg (BA/MA) RM 7/255; Fitzroy André Baptiste, 1988, p.64.

26 For details see BA/MA 7/255 and Fitzroy André Baptiste, 1988, pp. 72–3.

THE UNITED STATES MILITARY DEFENCE OF THE DUTCH WEST INDIES

After the fall of France and her subordination to Vichy, the commander-in-chief of the French naval forces in the western Atlantic and High Commissioner of the French West Indies, Admiral Robert, gave orders to his troops stationed at Aruba to return to Martinique immediately. The British, highly alarmed by the sudden loss of their ally and fearing a potential foothold of the Vichy regime in the Caribbean, moved into Aruba.[27] The British government failed to persuade Canada to join its action,[28] but trusted the Americans to agree to a military division of labour to take over the defence of the Caribbean areas where the crucial war resources of oil and bauxite were located. Bauxite, especially, was in great demand because of a huge aircraft production scheme planned for 1941.[29]

Talks about a British memorandum on an exchange of troops began in June 1941.[30] On 1 September President Roosevelt sent a letter to Queen Wilhelmina of the Netherlands officially asking for her government's approval to send troops to Suriname for the defence of the bauxite mines.[31] The Dutch government-in-exile approved the proposal in principle, but insisted on the recognition of its sovereignty, as had been the case earlier when French and British troops were stationed in Suriname. They were more reserved in their reaction to the participation of Latin American neighbours, in this case Brazil, as had been decided in the Act of Havana. Only after some months of negotiations could the Dutch reservations be resolved and a formulation acceptable to both parties be found. Finally, in mid-October 1941, a joint declaration was passed: 'The United States Government has sent armed contingents to Surinam upon the invitation of the Netherlands Government for the purpose of co-operation with the Armed Forces of the Netherlands in ensuring adequate protection to the bauxite mines.'[32]

At the same time, the Brazilian government was invited 'to participate in this measure.'[33] More weeks passed before the American troops already waiting in Trinidad and Panama were sent to Suriname, whilst there were

27 The British Ambassador informed the American government of these plans, without, however, having gained their approval. NAW RG 59/856 B. 01/44 Memorandum of Conversation, SoS Hull and Ambassador Lord Lothian, 7 August 1940.

28 The Canadian government did not want to risk a conflict with its Franco-Canadian population.

29 Fitzroy André Baptiste, 1988, p.116.

30 NAW RG 59/856 B. 014/16 Memorandum of Conversation, British Minister Butler and Under-SoS Welles, 4 June 1941.

31 Fitzroy André Baptiste, 1988, p.119.

32 Quoted in *Ibid.*, p.121.

33 *Ibid.*

ongoing arguments with the Dutch government-in-exile about Brazil's participation. It was only on 3 December that all 1,000 officers and troops were landed in Paramaribo.

Although one might expect that these long and intensive negotiations had prepared the ground for a quick handling of the immediately following exchange of British for American soldiers in Curaçao and Aruba, this was not the case. On the contrary, the experiences in Suriname had hurt the national pride of the Dutch and increased their distrust of the Americans. The Dutch government-in-exile as well as the local authorities in the Dutch West Indies found it very difficult to accept the now plainly formulated military High Command of the Americans.[34] They were especially stubborn in refusing to allow the participation of Latin American partners, in this case Venezuela. Despite, or perhaps because of, their necessary co-operation in oil production and processing, the relations between these two countries had always been somewhat tense.[35]

After entering the war in December 1941, the Americans left no doubt that the military situation urgently required the increased protection of the Aruba-Curaçao-Venezuela oil complex, because of the direct threat posed to American interests. When, however, the Dutch government continued to oppose the participation of Venezuela, Roosevelt himself interfered and instructed his Under-Secretary of State, Berle, to begin sending troops without even settling the conflict about the participation of Venezuela:

> It took three months of perfectly childish negotiations before we got troops to protect the bauxite mines in Surinam....their absolutely essential high octane gas refineries might be destroyed by a German submarine tomorrow.... Here is a solution. When we get our troops there, the commanding officer can very easily arrange to invite two or three Venezuelans as his personal guests. Venezuela will certainly be kept fully in touch with the entire situation, and this is no time to quibble when a critical phase of conduct of the war is involved.[36]

---

34 A solution that practically transferred the command of all the forces to the American Admiral Ohlendorf, but formally recognized the Dutch Governor as the Commander-in-Chief , was only found in March 1942.

35 NAW RG 59/856 B.20/30 Memorandum of Conversation, Under-SoS Welles and British Ambassador Viscount Halifax, 29 December 1941, RG 59/856 B. 20/42. Memorandum of Conversation, SoS Hull and Dutch Foreign Minister van Kleffens and Netherlands Minister Dr Loudon, 2 February 1942. See also Fitzroy André Baptiste, 1988, pp.137–40.

36 NAW RG 59/856 B. 20/77 Memorandum of President Roosevelt for Under-SoS Berle, 29 January 1942.

Urgent action was needed, because during these negotiations the German navy was preparing submarine attacks on American targets. Three days after the troops landed, German submarines fired at ships and tanks in Aruba and Curaçao. Operation Neuland, the battle of the Caribbean, had begun.

The establishment of United States military bases in the Caribbean

After the conclusion of the destroyers-bases agreement, the American military command sent a team of experts under the leadership of Admiral Greenslade to the British West Indies to inspect the sites for the construction of the military bases. The Greenslade Board worked out suggestions which were to be discussed with the local governments. In some places, this led to considerable conflict with the population and the British colonial administration. Governor Young of Trinidad, who regarded the Americans as invaders of the British Empire,[37] entered into a course of open confrontation with the American team of experts over the site of the planned military bases.

Instead of the five sites the Americans had chosen for the different military divisions, spread over the island, Young suggested draining the Caroni swamp south of the capital city, Port of Spain, and concentrating the whole military complex there. On behalf of the people of Trinidad, he demanded that the daily life of the civilian population should be disrupted as little as possible, and that the site especially favoured by the Americans, the Chaguaramas-Tucker Valley (the most extensive recreation area of Port of Spain and its surroundings), should not be touched.[38] In addition to this, he also opposed the long-term lease of 99 years, an agreement that was to lead to severe post-war conflicts.[39]

On Bermuda there was also strong resistance to the insensitive actions of the Americans, who wanted to establish their military base adjacent to the tourist centre of the island.[40] The Colonial Office acted very reluctantly concerning the question of the sites and voiced severe criticism of the behaviour of the American military. The Secretary of State for the Colonies, Lord Lloyd, 'argued that base leases would be the thin end of an American imperialistic wedge in the Caribbean'.[41] At a Base Lease conference, scheduled for January

37 Philip Goodhart, 1965, p.218.
38 Fitzroy André Baptiste, 1988, pp.87–8; Annette C. Palmer, 1989, pp.84–9.
39 Eric Williams, 1962, pp.272–7; Carl Parris, 1976.
40 Fitzroy André Baptiste, 1988, pp.88–90.
41 Quoted in David Reynolds, 1981, p.169.

1941 in London, further questions were openly discussed. The Americans now made it clear that they were going to implement the agreement, despite the resistance of the Colonial Office and the local administrations. They were not willing to compromise on the important question of military sovereignty and, in the case of Trinidad, insisted on their original sites for the bases, especially for the large navy complex at Chaguaramas.[42] Furthermore, it was decided that the import of supplies to the United States military bases was to be duty free, and that, in the case of 'an offence of a military nature', American jurisdiction would prevail.[43] In order to preserve the formal rights of the Governors, a Local Combined Defence Committee was established, which included representatives from the British and American forces, as well as the Governor. While its official duty was to prepare a local defence scheme, its *de facto* function was no more than as a 'decorative device to meet British sensibility'.[44]

At the conference, the American military leadership, though in some cases only after Churchill's direct intervention, clearly gained the upper hand against the reservations of the British, in particular of the Colonial Office and the Governors. British concessions to the Americans, which opened the region for far-reaching United States penetration, were noticeably greater than vice versa.[45] The conflicts occurring during the construction of the military bases, and the long-lasting social changes caused by the dominant presence of the American military personnel, confirm this.

The Anglo-American Naval and Air Base-Lease Agreement was signed on 27 March 1941. This did not, however, solve the conflicts in Trinidad. During the setting up of the military bases, Governor Young continued to oppose the Americanization of the island, which finally led to his sudden recall from his post in March 1942.[46] The biggest naval operating base and naval air station outside the United States were planned for Chaguaramas Bay. They were to be responsible for the military protection of the most important bauxite and oil transport routes. It was planned that troop contingents of

42 Annette C. Palmer, 1989, p.87. On Bermuda, the Americans accepted an area at the eastern end of the island, far off from the centre of tourism.

43 Great Britain-United States. Agreement for the use and operation of naval and air bases, *American Journal of International Law*, 35, 1941, Suppl., p.136.

44 Fitzroy André Baptiste, 1988, p.112.

45 Eric Williams, 1962, pp.267–71; Annette C. Palmer, 1989, p.73; Fitzroy André Baptiste, 1988, p.100.

46 According to a conversation with Charles Taussig 'he was given 24 hour notice by London to prepare for public announcement of his resignation due to ill health' and blamed 'the U.S. War Department for agitating his removal.' Franklin D. Roosevelt Library, New York, (FDRL), Taussig Papers, Box 46, Note for Under-SoS Welles from Taussig, 28 March 1942. He announced his resignation on 18 March and left the island on 4 April 1942; Michael Anthony, 1983, pp.111–12.

more than 16,000 officers and soldiers, including two anti-aircraft regiments and a composite wing of 100 aircrafts, were to be stationed there for the duration of the war. In Bermuda there were some 4,700 men, in Jamaica, about 1,800. St Lucia, Antigua and British Guiana each received a company of 350 American soldiers.[47]

Attracted by the prospect of well-paid work, a wave of migrants now flooded the islands on which military bases were built, especially Trinidad. Here, consequences first became apparent shortly after building commenced: in many places, unemployment figures dropped and more money came into circulation. On Trinidad, where more than 40,000 labourers were employed in the building works, there was an acute labour shortage in the countryside. With regard to wages, the American employers had agreed with the colonial governments to adjust wages to the average income of each island.[48] This, however, was a constant source of conflict, which sometimes led to sporadic unrest and strikes.[49]

Furthermore, the massive presence of the American soldiers in Trinidad led to socio-cultural disruption, which threatened to undermine the traditional colonial society. The construction of the bases created 'a boom-time atmosphere in which prostitution and vice flourished'.[50] The Trinidadians admired the Americans because of 'their efficiency, their genius for organization ... their latest techniques and the best machinery, more sensible clothes and more informal manners. They would have proved a charming ingredient had they left behind one vice – their racial prejudices', as one contemporary observer put it.[51]

American racism, added to the hypocritical indignation of the colonial administration, created a highly explosive mixture of different levels of prejudice, which threatened to erupt in May 1942 when a regiment of 2,500 black American soldiers, the 99th Coastal Artillery Regiment, was transferred to Trinidad just prior to the arrival of the new Americophile Governor,

47 Annette C. Palmer, 1989, p.193; Fitzroy André Baptiste, 1988, p.103.

48 CO 971/2/1 Leases to USA, 'Employment of Local Labour. Schedule of daily rates for local labour paid of the United States Naval and Air Bases'; FDRL, Taussig Papers, Box 35, 'Regulations and wage rates for employment of local labour for construction U.S. Bases in Jamaica'; Caribbean Commission, 1943, pp.6–9, 41–4; Annette C. Palmer, 1989, pp.191–211; Michael Anthony, 1983, pp.63, 108.

49 CO 971/1/2 Leases to USA, 'Employment of local labour'. Gov. Young/Trinidad to CO 10 June 1941 'strike involving 1,800 labourers ... on United States base'. From Jamaica, too, there were reports of social unrest during the construction of the military facilities. Ken Post, 1981, vol. I, pp.170–1, 245–6.

50 Bridget Brereton, 1981, p.192.

51 Eric Williams, 1942b, p.514.

Sir Bede Clifford. The Americans had been hesitant about moving black soldiers into the Caribbean for several reasons. Firstly, they feared that the comparatively mild racism of the British would bring American race segregation into question and secondly, in the event of a recurrence of the social uprisings of the 1930s in the Caribbean islands, they wanted to prevent discontent spreading among American black soldiers through fraternizing with the local population. At the same time, the American military leadership was blinded by racist assumptions, and considered black troops to be less effective than their white counterparts. Consequently, when the United States of America entered the war, black troops were deployed in non-combat roles, primarily as labourers, including on the construction sites in Trinidad.[52]

At this point, problems in the more subtle British attitude to race issues emerged. A collision of different and distinct forms of racial discrimination within British colonial and American society occurred, giving rise to violent conflicts. The first source of conflict was the demand by white Americans for segregation in, for example, social life (nightclubs, bars and so on). This exclusion would apply to both black American soldiers and the local population. Another example was the refusal by white Americans to recognize the authority of local officials such as black traffic officers. The arrival of black soldiers with greater spending power and consequently higher social prestige threatened the fragile social and cultural fabric of Trinidadian society around the base sites. Written and oral complaints from Trinidadians, accusing black Americans of stealing 'their women', piled up in the offices of the Governor and the commanding General of the army base. There were frequent outbreaks of violence between black American soldiers and local men. In 1942, when the German submarines became a real threat, the colonial administration became temporarily subordinate to the exigencies of the war. Once the direct military threat had subsided, Governor Clifford called for the removal of the 99th regiment, citing the outbreak of serious fights between black American soldiers and locals in the suburbs of Port of Spain as the reason for this request.[53]

> Concern was expressed that too many black Americans were being stationed in the Caribbean, and that this could cause resentment and jealousy among the local population when they saw much better paid black foreigners spending vast sums of money in bars, clubs, and shops

---

52 Annette C. Palmer, 1983, pp.59–60; *idem*, 1985, pp.203–4; *idem*, 1989, pp.235–45.

53 In the Basilon Street incident, 20 people were injured, some of them severely, and several houses and shops were demolished. Annette C. Palmer, 1983, p.60; *idem.*, 1985, pp.211. See also Michael Anthony, 1983, pp.135–6 for other incidents.

on the islands. If Britain felt unable to control the actions of the white Americans, it at least felt confident in exercising some authority over the rights of Blacks.[54]

Although the British authorities had so far been willing to make substantial concessions on American military decisions, Governor Clifford and the Colonial Office proved very stubborn in this matter and demanded the unconditional departure of black soldiers from Trinidad, the only place in the Caribbean where they had been stationed. The American military leadership, which was also well informed on the situation, at first demanded that the 99th regiment should remain in Trinidad and, moreover, planned to replace the white troops with units from Puerto Rico. This did not please the colonial administration at all. They feared a further deterioration of the tense situation because, in the words of Governor Clifford, Puerto Ricans 'consider themselves white, but are not regarded so here.'[55] Instead he suggested exchanging the black soldiers for Puerto Ricans as, 'though neither are wanted here, Puerto Ricans would be preferable to United States Negroes.'[56] The issue was considered 'most explosive' by Under-Secretary of State Sumner Welles, and as a result, both sides agreed not to document the ensuing negotiations to contain the risk of embarrassment.[57] Thus, little more is known about the negotiations that led to the black regiment's recall from the island 'at night on secret order' to be replaced by 'white Puerto Ricans with a knowledge of English and high educational standards.'[58] What is also remarkable is that 'New Deal liberals', such as Taussig or Tugwell, who had been so concerned about social and colonial issues, failed to speak out consistently and strongly about racial discrimination during the war.

The experiment of stationing black American units in the Caribbean was not repeated during the war. Contemporary calypso singers highlighted the basic problems which prevailed – 'both mother and daughter working for the Yankee dollar'. Similar incidents also occurred on other base sites in the Caribbean, but not on the same scale, and without the racial element added by the presence of black troops. Annette Palmer, who is owed thanks for her thorough research on this episode, correctly concluded that:

> The presence of white troops was, however, the ultimate irony, for white soldiers, even more than the blacks, contributed to the undermining of

54 Ben Bousquet and Colin Douglas, 1991, p.68.
55 Quoted in Annette C. Palmer, 1985, p.210.
56 *Ibid.*
57 *Ibid.*, p.212.
58 *Ibid.*, p.213.

> racial ideology which supported the colonial structure in Trinidad. White soldiers were seen performing hard manual labour, something which had never been seen in the island before. White soldiers were seen drunk and disorderly on the streets, brawling and fighting. These sights contributed to a revolution in sentiment and mentality among local blacks during the war, thereby weakening both ideas of white superiority and confidence in colonial control.[59]

The battle of the Caribbean

In 1942, the submarine war in the Caribbean, which had begun with a series of attacks on the oil refineries at Aruba and on oil-tankers entering the harbour of Willemstad in Curaçao, now threatened to cut off the United States of America and Britain from the important supplies of strategic raw materials (oil products and bauxite). It had also affected the local populations, who had already been forced to reduce their export-oriented production drastically, and who were now also cut off from essential imports.

In the first half of 1942, a small force of German U-boats had already sunk a worrying number of Allied ships. Despite its long-planned defence strategy and the practical measures undertaken during the construction of the military bases in the Caribbean region, the American navy was nevertheless not yet ready for effective resistance to the German U-boat force. Admiral Hoover, Commander of the Caribbean Sea Frontier, had to admit that the German U-boats 'had a field day down there':[60]

> In 1942–1943 a 150-mile strip around Trinidad suffered the greatest concentration of shipping losses experienced anywhere during World War II. During 1942 some 43.3 ships were sunk for every U-boat in the circum-Trinidad area, but only 9.2 world-wide. The total number of ships, exclusive of schooners and other small craft … sunk by U-boats in the Trinidad arc by the end of 1942 was 130 or 750,000 tons of shipping. Approximately three-quarters of those ships were cargo vessels. They included bauxite shuttles from The Guianas to Trinidad. Just under one quarter were tankers. … Britain, followed by the United States and Norway, lost the most shipping.[61]

59 *Ibid.*, p.214.
60 Quoted in Fitzroy André Baptiste, 1988, p.143.
61 *Ibid.*

The Germans attacked in waves, during which on average five to ten U-boats were in operation at the 'junctions' of Caribbean traffic, or the 'killing fields', as the Americans called them. From April 1942 onwards they could even be refuelled from U-boat tanks, so-called 'milk cows', already stationed in the operational area. The course of events in the submarine war in the Caribbean has recently been researched and very thoroughly documented.[62] Its main outcomes have been graphically summarized by Gerhard Sandner in the following maps (see pages 102–7).[63]

My research at the German military archives has revealed that Hitler and the navy command, although pleased with the unexpected successes of Operations Paukenschlag and Neuland, had nevertheless anticipated as early as mid-1942 that this trend would be halted once the Americans had developed their defence strategy to U-boat warfare. This rather sceptical, but realistic assessment of the German navy gave way to a temporary euphoria, with the unexpectedly high success rate of the first months of 1942. The U-boat operation was continuously subjected to efficiency controls. 'The B.d.U. [the Commander of Submarines, Dönitz] intends to stay with the U-boat operation in America for as long as this region remains profitable. This is why the effectiveness of the U-boat war is carefully checked by the B.d.U. every month, i.e. the average sinking height of every submarine that is in the sea is noted per sea day.'[64] By September, the U-boat war had reached its peak, and plans were already in place that in future 'single boats at most would be put in this region occasionally.' After the Allies' transition to the convoy system and the increase of air control, only a few chance hits were expected, which would have to be paid for with relatively high losses. The report reached the conclusion that after the termination of individual traffic the Gulf of Mexico and the Caribbean coast were no longer profitable and that there was little point in keeping the boats there for much longer. Only the area east of Trinidad had still proved worthwhile.[65] This pessimistic view of the operation area by the German Naval High Command persisted during the early months of 1943.

---

62 See Anthony Maingot, 1994a, pp.46–69; Gerhard Sandner, 1993; Michael Gannon, 1990; Fitzroy André Baptiste, 1988, pp.141–70; G. T. M. Kelshall, 1988.

63 Gerhard Sandner, 1993, using the data presented by G. T. M. Kelshall, 1988. I wish to thank Gerhard Sandner for his generous permission to reproduce his maps in this publication.

64 BA/MA Freiburg RM 7/186 Report Dönitz to Hitler 14 May 1942.

65 BA/MA Freiburg RM/846 Telex Oberkommando der Marine (High Command of the Navy) 24 September 1942.

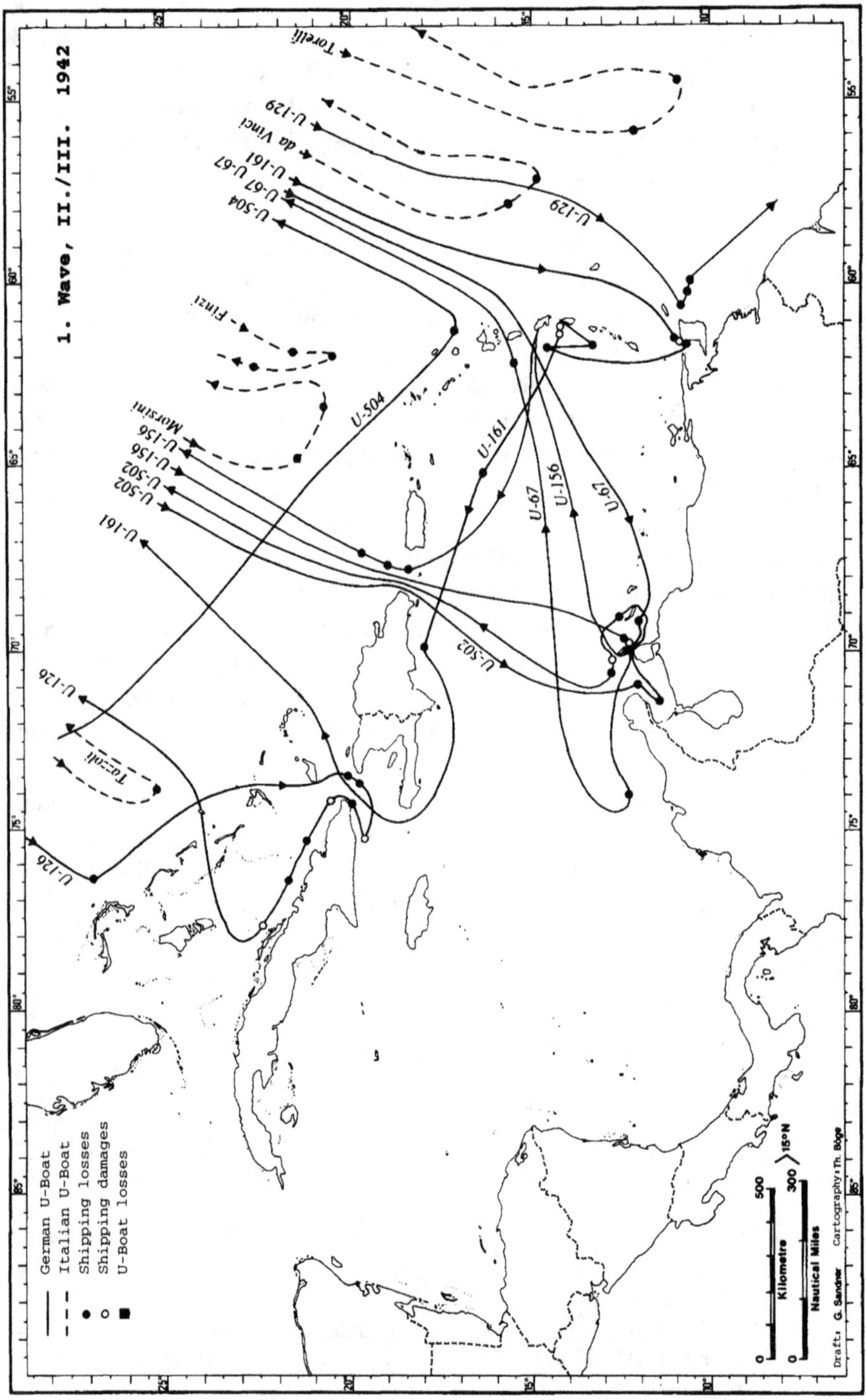

Figure 3.2 U-boat attacks February–March 1942 (*Map courtesy Gerhard Sandner, 1993*)

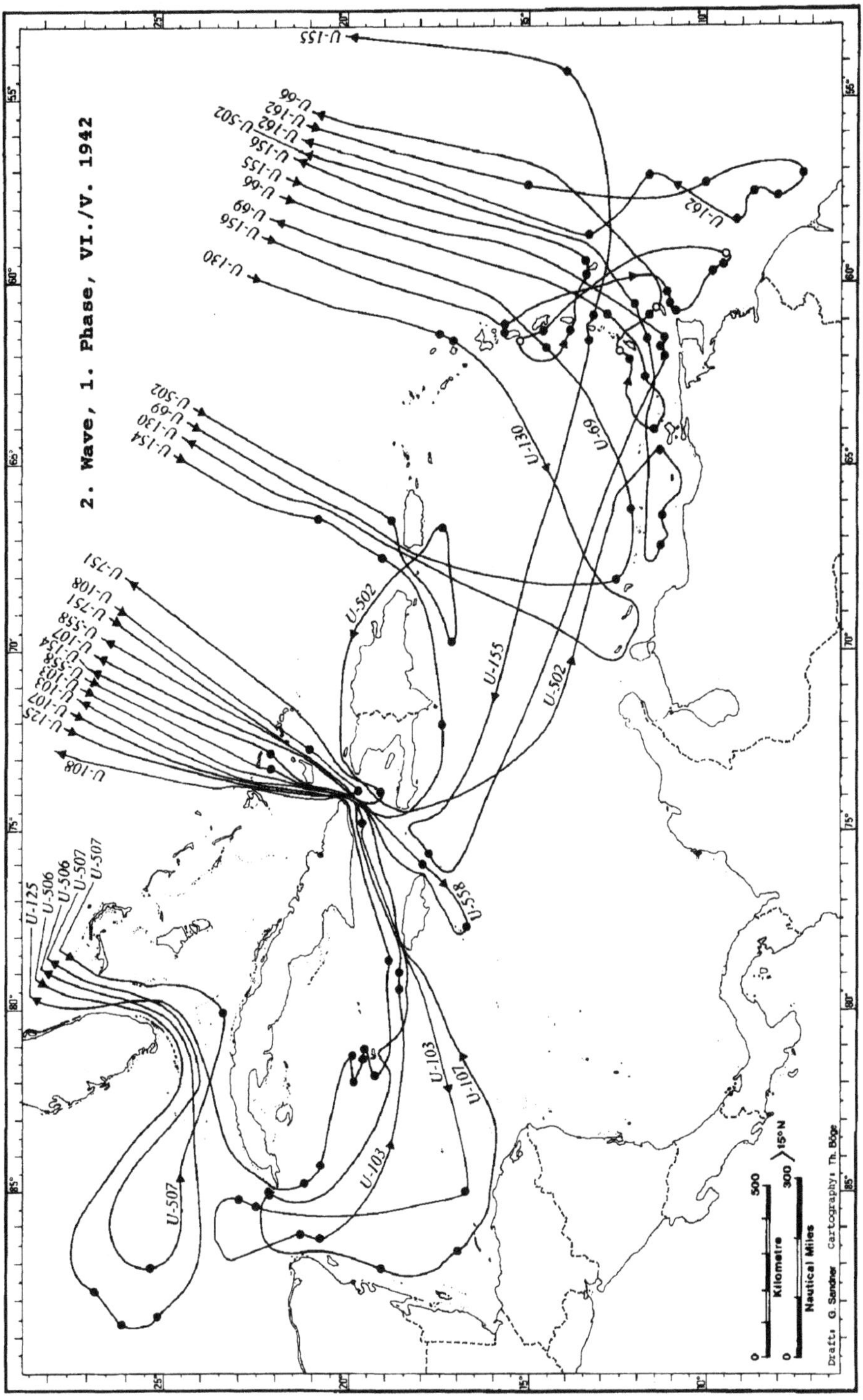

Figure 3.3 U-boat attacks April–May 1942 (*Map courtesy Gerhard Sandner, 1993*)

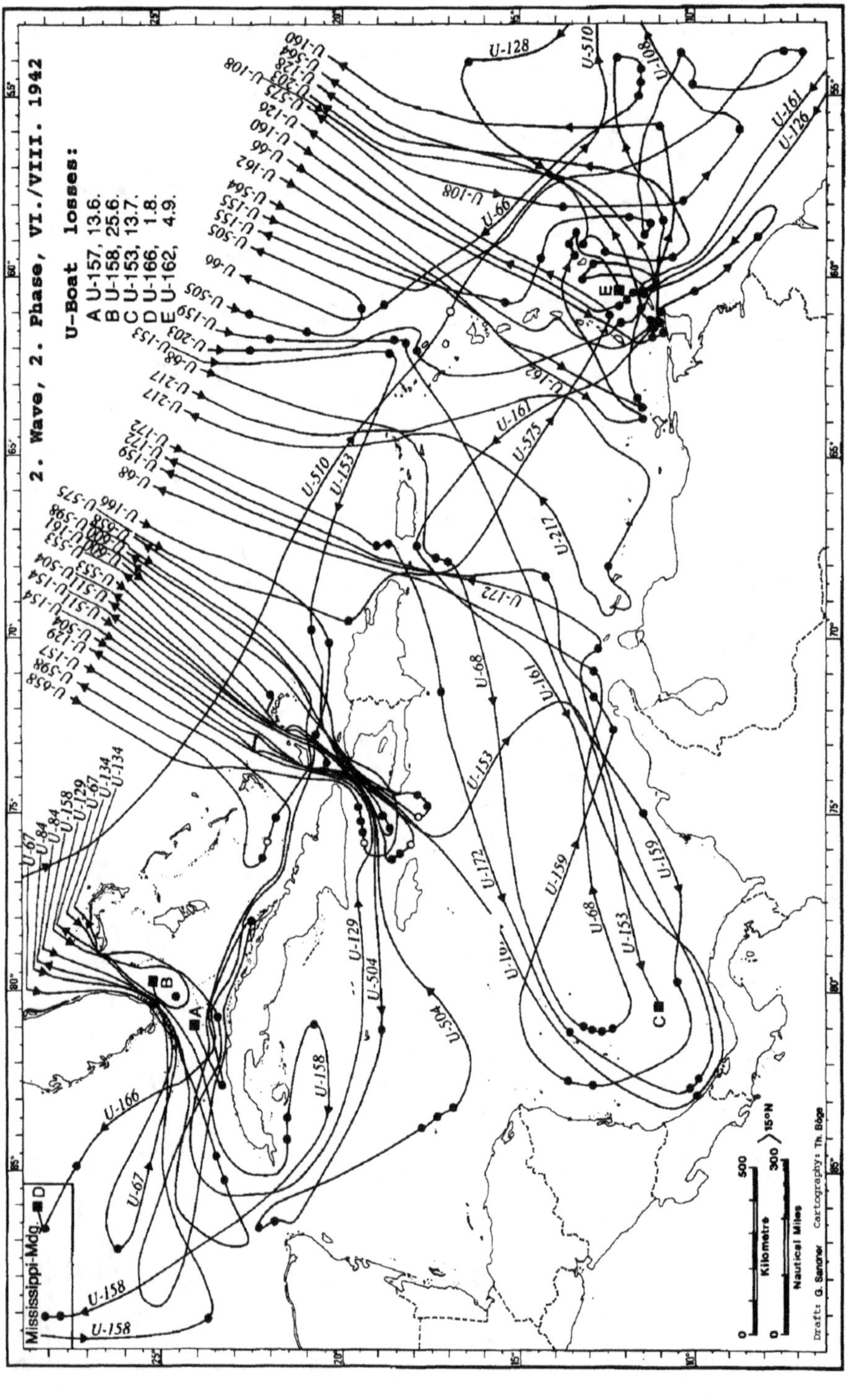

Figure 3.4 U-boat attacks June–August 1942 (*Map courtesy Gerhard Sandner. 1993*)

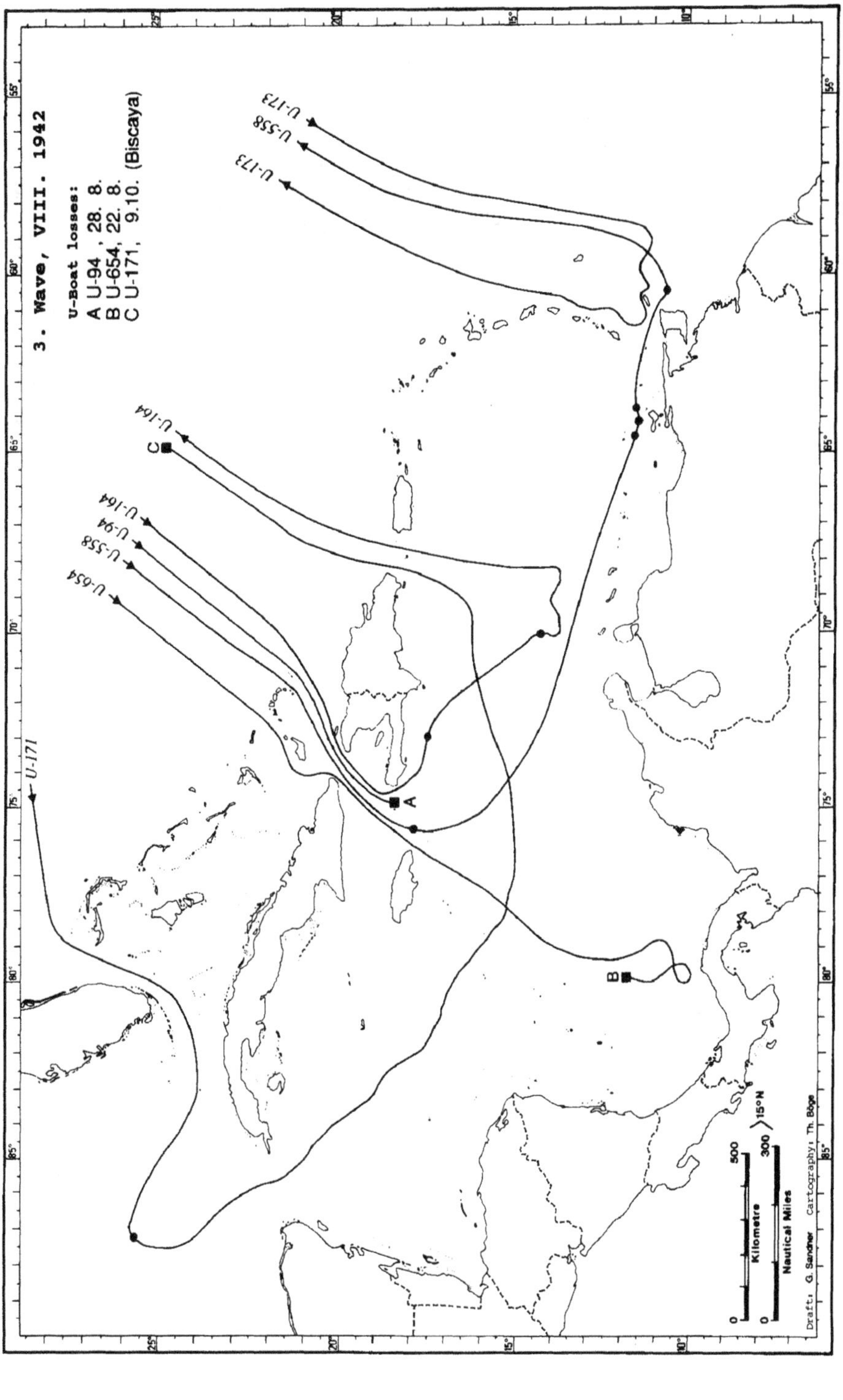

Figure 3.5 U-boat attacks August 1942 (*Map courtesy Gerhard Sandner, 1993*)

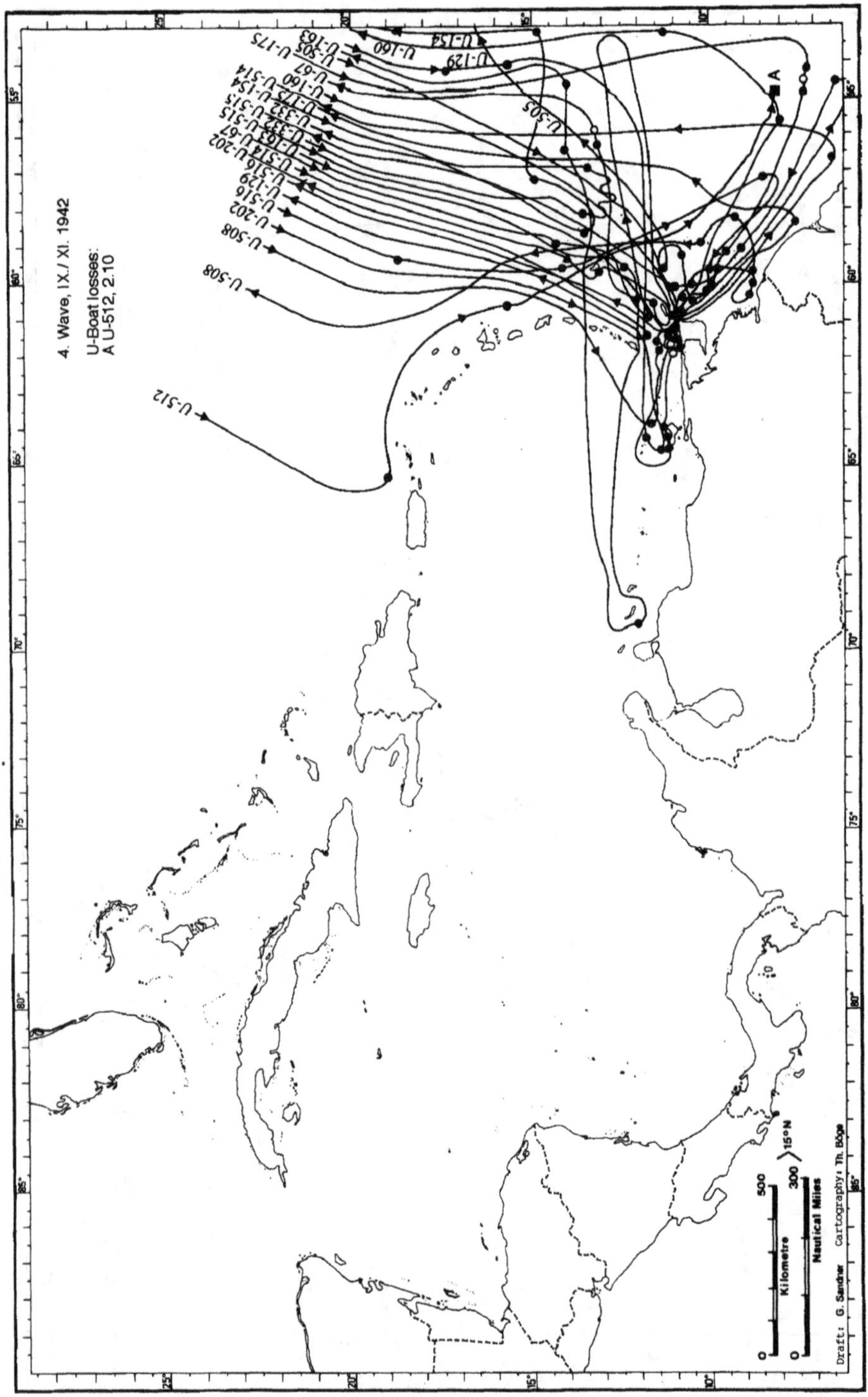

Figure 3.6 U-boat attacks September–November 1942 (*Map courtesy Gerhard Sandner, 1993*)

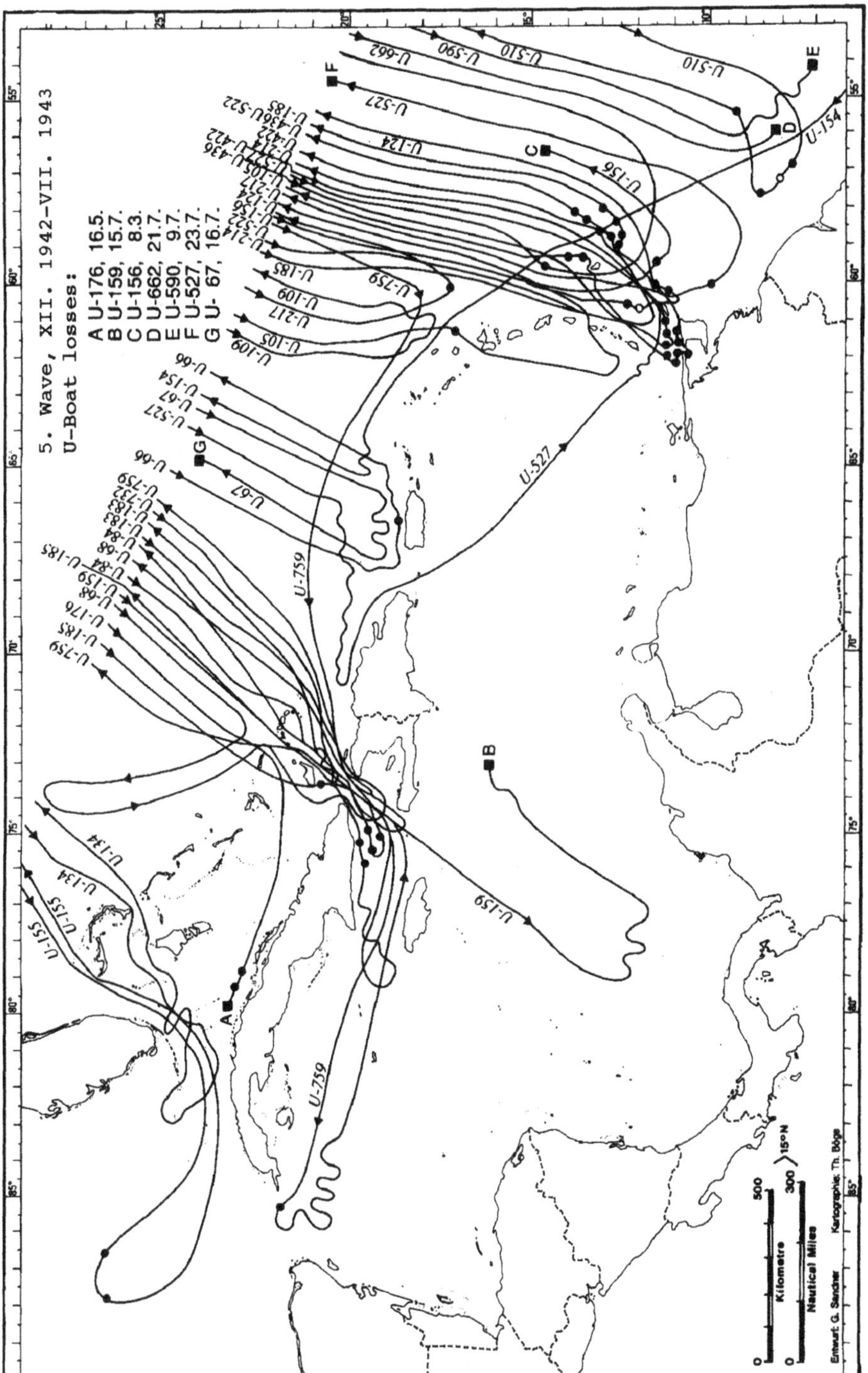

Figure 3.7 U-boat attacks November 1942–July 1943 (*Map courtesy Gerhard Sandner, 1993*)

At a discussion of the military situation with Hitler on 31 May 1943, a 'crisis of the U-boat war' was mentioned. It was reported that losses had increased from 13 per cent to 36–7 per cent and that the Germans were powerless against the superiority of the Allied air force and their new detectors. The report closed on a note of uncertainty: 'but how far the effectiveness of the U-boat war, in view of success, can recover, cannot be predicted.' Despite these gloomy prophecies, Hitler insisted on continuing with the U-boat war, even though German technological inferiority was obvious. 'There is no question of relenting in the U-boat war ... the value of the resources the U-boat war, even without constant successes, would tie down, is so great that we cannot afford to release them to the enemy.'[66] With this key decision of Hitler's, the U-boat war in American waters entered its final, and for the German navy, fatal phase.

According to Kelshall, altogether 97 German and six Italian submarines were in operation in the Caribbean war arena. In 152 operations, they sank about 400 trading vessels and severely damaged 50 more. A total of 24 U-boats were sunk in the war area or on their return journey.[67]

The Anglo-American Caribbean Commission

The military history of the Second World War in the Caribbean is well documented. Its effects on the local population, however, must be drawn together from a variety of primary sources. The most significant reports on the supply of goods to the West Indies in this period are to be found in the records of the Anglo-American Caribbean Commission (AACC). The Commission was set up on 9 March 1942 with the keen support of the Americans and despite much resistance from the British, and began work after the first military action in the area,

> for the purpose of encouraging and strengthening social and economic cooperation between the United States of America and its possessions and bases in the … Caribbean, and the United Kingdom and the British colonies in the same area, and to avoid unnecessary duplication of research in these fields …. Members of the Commission will concern themselves primarily with matters pertaining to labour, agriculture, housing, health, education, social welfare, finance, economics, and related subjects … and will advise their respective Governments.[68]

66 BA/MA, Freiburg RM 7/186.
67 G. T. M. Kelshall, 1988, p.446.
68 CO 318/452/2 West Indies, Collaboration with the US in the Caribbean. See also Bernard C. Poole, 1951, p.186; Herbert Corkran, 1970, pp.12–13.

For the Americans, the origins of the commission lay in the extensive investigatory research into the socio-economic and cultural background of the Caribbean that had underpinned their defence strategy in the region before military operations took place. Majority public opinion and government thinking in the United States were both largely supportive of the need for military and political involvement in the Caribbean. While many also saw this as a mission to rid the area of colonial oppression, the Roosevelt administration, well-informed about the prevalent social and economic problems, avoided assuming any colonial responsibilities.

Roosevelt himself had recognized the key strategic position occupied by the region since the First World War, and had travelled frequently in the Caribbean, most recently just prior to the construction of the military bases. He had also commissioned two experts closely associated with his New Deal brains-trust to monitor the situation in the West Indies. Charles Taussig, a modern entrepreneur with business contacts in the sugar industry in the Caribbean, and Rexford Tugwell, then Professor of Economics at Columbia University and subsequently Governor of Puerto Rico, had witnessed first-hand the devastating effects of the Great Depression during a joint visit to the region in the 1930s, and had subsequently pointed out the danger of social disruption.

With the conclusion of the destroyers-bases deal and at the same time as negotiations on the form of the base-lease agreements were in progress, Roosevelt appointed Taussig chairman of a commission with the task 'to study the social and economic conditions in the British West Indies.'[69] When the commission expressed its intention to visit the British West Indies, the British were surprised and somewhat suspicious, as a highly qualified Royal Commission had recently completed a very similar survey. The voluminous report produced had, however, not yet been published to avoid its being used in enemy propaganda. As a result the Americans had not had access to the report, and the British were in any case unable to prohibit the proposed visit. In fact, Taussig's commission reached very similar conclusions to those of the West India Royal Commission of 1938/9.[70] In its report, the American commission acknowledged the sincere attempts of the Colonial Office to deal with social grievances through its 'Colonial Development and Welfare program'.[71] In addition, the report proposed the formation of

69 FDRL, Taussig Papers, Box 35, Report of the Commission to Study Social and Economic Conditions in the British West Indies, appointed by the President of the United States on 13 November 1940. Other members were two military men, Lt-Colonel A.F. Kibler and Lt-Commander W.S. Campbell.

70 Report of the West India Royal Commission, 1945.

71 FDRL, Taussig Papers, Box 35, Report of the Commission ..., p.94.

an American 'Advisory Committee for the Caribbean Area' to co-operate with the relevant British organizations, chiefly the 'Development and Welfare Organisation for the Caribbean' under its comptroller Sir Frank Stockdale. The purpose of this co-operation was to complement military defence strategy for the region, by pre-empting and thus preventing social unrest in the event that colonial development programmes were disrupted by the course of the war.

In October 1941, the 'Caribbean Office' was established in the United States State Department, with Court du Bois at its head. Roosevelt also began implementing the recommendations of the commission, appointing five members to the Advisory Committee for the Caribbean Area, including Taussig and Tugwell, as well as Martin Trasvieso, the Supreme Court Justice of Puerto Rico, and the black Judge William H. Hastie, Civilian Aide to the Secretary of War. In addition, Tugwell, Taussig and du Bois were nominated to serve as experts on a 'Joint Anglo-American Commission', to further institutionalize future co-operation in the Caribbean.

As with earlier discussions on military questions, negotiations leading to the formation of the AACC were characterized by mutual suspicion and prejudice. As a result, the process was lengthy and difficult. The Colonial Office dragged its feet on the matter, once again revealing its deeply rooted suspicions regarding American interference in British colonial policy. It took the real threat of the U-boat war to convince both parties of the necessity for urgent co-operation. The history of the AACC has been well documented,[72] so I will focus attention here on how the problem of supplies in the period of U-boat warfare was solved.

The Emergency Land-Water Highway and the West Indies Schooner Pool

The U-boat warfare in the Caribbean had virtually brought to a standstill the provision of basic supplies to the region. In May 1942, the supply officers of the AACC met in Kingston, Jamaica, to discuss what could be done to reverse the situation. While all governments in the area were requested to do everything in their power to meet domestic food demand, it was agreed that many Caribbean islands could not survive without supplies from outside the area. With the aim of securing transport from the United States of

72 James A. Bough, 1949; Herbert Corkran, 1970; Howard Johnson, 1984a; Frances McReynold Smith, 1958; Annette C. Palmer, 1989, pp.147–84; Bernard C. Poole, 1951; Herward Sieberg, 1985, pp.358–97; Sir Frank Stockdale, 1947; Charles W. Taussig, 1945–6; Rexford Guy Tugwell, 1958; Eric Williams, 1969, pp.81–95.

America to the region, and the exchange of goods within the West Indies, it was decided:

- to develop an integrated programme of control of small vessels (schooners) for service in the Caribbean;
- to establish emergency caches of concentrated foods;
- to provide an emergency land-water supply route from Florida through Cuba, Haiti, the Dominican Republic and Puerto Rico to serve the Eastern Caribbean and a separate route from Cuba to Jamaica.[73]

This land-water highway was opened in October 1942, in the process lopping off 800 miles of hostile territory. The governments of Cuba, Haiti and the Dominican Republic, with the support of several American institutions, acted speedily to construct road and rail networks for efficient overland transport, and to set up stockpiles at strategic points. From Puerto Rico, schooners and other small boats transported the goods to the Eastern Caribbean and the Guianas. The West Indian Schooner Pool was set up for this purpose by the American AACC officer, du Bois. Its members were numerous private ship-owners and traders, working together with the colonial administrations, to control and co-ordinate water traffic between the Leeward and Windward Islands, by prioritizing what freight was most important and ensuring the even distribution of supplies.[74] As many of the schooners came from Bridgetown, Barbados was chosen as the pool's headquarters and main point of exchange of goods. Around 75–80 per cent of all small vessels which operated regularly in this area were involved in the scheme; in July 1943 this amounted to 84 ships with a load capacity of 7,000 tons. A charge was levied for each ton transported, and paid into a special fund which was used to compensate the owners of boats sunk during the war. The pool began operation in August 1943, after the worst of the U-boat campaign was over. The Schooner Pool proved so successful that it outlasted the war in the form of the Schooner Owners Association. Whether the pool as originally conceived fulfilled its function – of regulating the supply of essential foodstuffs to the Leeward and Windward islands during the war period – is a matter of debate, with reports of uneven and infrequent provision in different areas. However it did at least

---

73 FDRL, Taussig Papers, Box 34, Caribbean Commission, US section, Final Reports, Appendix IV, Land-Water Supply Route – The British West Indies Schooner Pool, September 1942, Box 47, Caribbean Land-Water Emergency Route ..., AACC, US Section, 23 January 1943.

74 FDRL, Taussig Papers, Box 47, Operating Plan of the West Indies Schooner Pool.

ensure that the islands survived through the most dangerous months of the war.[75]

Social and economic conditions in the Caribbean during the war

The Colonial Development and Welfare Act

The West India Royal Commission of 1938/9 pointed to severe economic problems and social grievances in the British colonies as responsible for the disturbances of the 1930s.[76] Members of the commission spent several months in the West Indies, researching social and economic conditions and their effects on the local population. They conducted interviews, held public hearings, demanded memoranda and examined the files of the colonial administrations. The commission's mandate was to evaluate current social and economic problems in order to make appropriate recommendations to the British government.[77] The most important conclusion was that a major reorganization of the agricultural sector (nothing less than an 'agrarian revolution'), through a progressive development policy, was essential to solve pressing social problems in the rural areas and to slow down migration from the rural to the urban areas. In an attempt to stimulate self-sufficiency, plantation owners and small farmers were to be encouraged to switch over to mixed farming. The commission criticized existing labour relations, the low wage level, the lack of development of trade unions and hopelessly inadequate industrial health legislation. The main recommendations of the commission concerned the establishment of the West Indies Welfare Fund to be administered from outside the existing colonial administrations.

The Colonial Office had already agreed in principle to invest substantially in a development programme for the troubled region, even before the Royal Commission left London. Malcolm McDonald, Secretary of State for the Colonies, in fact intended to expand this programme to include all the colonies, using the West Indies as a model of the new 'development poli-

75 Alex P. Zeidenfeldt, 1950. See also Herbert Corkran, 1970, pp.25–6; Frances McReynold Smith, 1958, p.279; David John Morgan, 1980, p.171; Annette C. Palmer, 1988, pp. 169–72; Bernard C. Poole, 1951, pp.198–200; Herward Sieberg, 1985, pp.372–3.

76 Report of the West India Royal Commission, 1945; and Claus Füllberg-Stolberg, 1990b. See also chap.2, this volume.

77 The files of the commission are kept at the Public Record Office in London (CO 950). See Howard Johnson, 1978.

cy'. The officials involved in planning were aware that a sum of at least £10 million per annum would be needed if the policy was to amount to more than a symbolic gesture. The outbreak of war seemed to put the brakes on far-reaching initiatives planned in colonial policy. But in a Colonial Office memorandum in 1939, the Head of the Economic Department at the time, Gerard Clauson, argued convincingly that the war had made it more necessary than ever for Britain to make a gesture of goodwill in colonial policy. Clauson was later made Assistant Under-Secretary of State in 1940. In his memorandum he summed up the underlying motives as: 'There have been two motives behind this proposal, the one a desire to avert possible trouble in certain colonies, where disturbances are feared ..., the other a desire to impress this country and the world at large with our consciousness of our duties as a great Colonial Power.'[78] In fact, the outcome of negotiations between the Colonial Office and the Chancellor of the Exchequer on the issue clearly shows that the economic and social needs of the colonies were not the determining factor. McDonald's proposed financial schedule, considered the minimum of what was urgently required, was immediately cut by half: £5 million for Colonial Development and Welfare and £500,000 for Colonial Research.

The West Indies were the only colonies in which the programmes envisioned by the Act were actually set up and running before 1945.[79] The Development and Welfare Organization established there was headed by a comptroller, Sir Frank Stockdale, the former agricultural adviser in the Colonial Office, who was assisted by experts in various fields. In cooperation with the colonial governments, but acting in its own right as an extension of the Colonial Office, the Development and Welfare Organization planned development projects and distributed finance from the Colonial Development and Welfare Fund as it saw fit. But the Development and Welfare Organization was not granted the independence from the Colonial Office that the Royal Commission had recommended in order to ensure a speedy, unbureaucratic distribution of funds. Instead, the comptroller's authority was weakened from the start by the fact that he could only propose, but not approve, the allocation of larger sums. His executive authority was restricted not only by the metropolis, but also by the individual colonial administrations which regarded him as usurping the Governor's rights.

The impact of the Colonial Development and Welfare programme has been overestimated by some historians.[80] Even in the Caribbean, the new policy did not advance much beyond the planning stage during the war.

78 CO 852/250/15606 part 2 Memorandum by Clauson, 7 July 1939.

79 David Gordon M. Rampersad, 1979.

80 See Claus Füllberg-Stolberg, 1989, pp 142–3.

Between 1940 and 1945, financial contributions from the fund amounted to approximately £2,500,000 of which £1,800,000 were spent on the West Indies. The lion's share of this sum, £1,500,000, went to Jamaica, the island with the most unrest.[81] Compared to the war loans and 'gifts' of more than £20 million made by the colonies to Britain, the amount spent by the Colonial Development and Welfare Fund seems insignificant. Sieberg concludes that of the new 'developmental aid', the inhabitants of the West Indies received 14 shillings per capita while all other colonial subjects had to be satisfied with just 5 pennies per capita.[82] The material impact of the Fund on the colonies was, at least during the war, even less than that of its predecessor, the Colonial Development Act of 1929.

Export and food production

The war caused problems in the export of traditional plantation products (mainly sugar and bananas) throughout the Caribbean. While sugar was considered a basic necessity and was bought up by both Britain and the United States, the export of bananas to Britain ceased altogether, and the quantities destined for the United States were drastically reduced due to transport restrictions. In Jamaica, the whole banana harvest was bought up by the government and distributed to the local population.[83]

The entire sugar crop of the West Indies was purchased during the war years by the British government at fixed prices. The USA bought large proportions of the sugar crops of Cuba and Puerto Rico, which made up more than 50 per cent of the region's output. Especially in Cuba, sugar production recovered remarkably after the worldwide depression of the 1930s. Between 1940 and 1944 output increased from 2.7 to 4.2 million tons, its value going up even more from $110 to $251 million owing to favourable purchase arrangements with the United States government. On the other hand the traditional Cuban export of tobacco products lost its lucrative European market during the war, while the fruit and vegetable trade suffered from closed shipping lines and scarce transport space.[84]

Haiti and the Dominican Republic also exported sizeable quantities to the United States and Great Britain. The year 1942 saw massive stockpiling of sugar, with a bumper crop that year, and ongoing transport difficulties due to the U-boat campaign. The surplus, about two-thirds of the export crop, was

81 *Development and Welfare in the West Indies 1945–46*, Report by Sir John MacPherson, Comptroller (London: HMSO), 1947; colonial no. 212. See also Herward Sieberg, 1985, p.238.

82 Herward Sieberg, 1985, p.238.

83 Caribbean Commission, 1943, p.35; Ken Post, 1981, vol.I, p.142, and vol. II, p.370.

84 Louis A. Pérez, 1988, p.282.

only cleared during the years that followed. To relieve the situation, production quotas for different areas were introduced and land earmarked for sugar production was used for food production.[85]

The Caribbean plantation economies were traditionally dependent on the importation of large quantities of food. From the beginning of the war in Europe, food-crop production was encouraged throughout the region. The respective governments employed various incentives to stimulate efforts to improve the self-sufficiency of their territories. Public land was rented at a nominal fee to anyone who was willing to cultivate food crops, and state agencies guaranteed financial support and the purchase of produce at fixed prices. Growers of food were granted priority for the limited supply of fertilizers. Everywhere the plantations had to allocate a certain amount of their land for this purpose. In practice, the 'grow more food' campaign did not prove especially effective.[86] Nevertheless, it was a valuable lesson in self-sufficiency for the population of the Caribbean, and it disproved the notion, held for centuries, that the plantation economy was a law of nature. The cultivation of food crops on plantation land also demonstrated that diversification in agriculture, moving away from monocrop export production, could be achieved by political means.

In Trinidad, 3,000 acres of sugar-estate land were earmarked for food production,[87] 30 food depots were established to purchase the produce of the adjacent districts,[88] and even public parks were used as 'war gardens'.[89] However, work on the American military bases proved to be far more attractive and led to a shrinking of the rural labour force by more than one-third.[90] Barbados, with its sugar monoculture and high population density, was particularly dependent on food imports and so compulsory cultivation of food crops by sugar estates on one-quarter to one-third of their total acreage was introduced. The same measures were enforced in the Windward Islands. It was estimated that 'it would need an acreage equal to three times the total cultivable area of the Colony', just to feed the population of Barbados.[91] In the Leeward Islands, there were also problems with the application of the drive towards self-sufficiency. In Antigua, as in Trinidad, the construction works of the American bases absorbed the bulk of the labour force, and in St Kitts it proved difficult to convert sugar land to food crop cultivation.

---

85 Caribbean Commission, 1943, pp.31–4.

86 *Ibid.*, p.29.

87 FDRL, Taussig Papers, Box 54, 'Possibilities of growing Food Crops in the British Colonies in the Caribbean area in lieu of Sugar'.

88 Caribbean Commission, 1943, p.29.

89 Michael Anthony, 1983, pp.113–16.

90 FDRL, Taussig Papers, Box 54, 'Possibilities of growing Food Crops ...'

91 Caribbean Commission, 1943, p.31.

In the case of Jamaica, the programme proved more successful. In 1943 the Governor announced that more than 20,000 acres of land on the island had been planted with food crops. The production of maize, peas and beans increased substantially; about 75 per cent of its condensed milk and meat requirements were locally produced. The local use of bananas previously exported to the United Kingdom further reduced demand for imported cereals. Funds that had been used to purchase the banana crop, were now used to subsidize the increased production of food crops.[92] But the estates were slow to accept loans from the Food Production Board, and the peasants also seemed unwilling to get into debt.[93]

The United States of America, too, initiated price-support and marketing programmes to stimulate domestic food-crop production in Puerto Rico and the Virgin Islands. In Puerto Rico a far-reaching land reform (the 500 acre law) was enacted in 1940. It was intended to provide the necessary means to limit the control of land by a few corporate enterprises engaged in export agriculture, and give support and incentives to small cultivators to increase production for the local market as well as to get a larger share of cash-crop production. Between 1940 and 1945 a large proportion of corporate land had been purchased by the Land Authority. It was cut up into small plots and given to small peasants and landless farm labourers at no charge but without the right of ownership. The Act was intended to alleviate the worst living conditions of the rural poor by supplying a base of subsistence and simultaneously to increase food production.

The so-called 'proportional profit-farms' were intended to combine the advantages of large-scale production with profit-sharing and co-operative managing and working arrangements for all participants. Again land ownership was transferred to the Land Authority, as the proper government agency, the farm was co-operatively worked by management and labourers, and the profit gained was shared proportionally. The 'proportional profit-farms' kept the plantations intact and continued to be export-oriented single-crop producers. By the end of the war about one-third of the corporate holdings over 500 acres had been purchased by the Puerto Rican government for that purpose. After 1945 these schemes were not expanded because the focus of the government development programme 'Operation Bootstrap' shifted generally from agriculture to industry.[94]

In Cuba and Haiti, laws and decrees were passed making food production compulsory. In Haiti the situation became critical due to the catastrophic failure of a huge agricultural project. The Société Haïtiano-Américaine

92 *Ibid.*, p.31.

93 Ken Post, 1981, vol. I, pp.252–3 and vol. II, pp.371–4.

94 James L. Dietz, 1986, pp.194–201.

de Développement Agricole (SHADA), a joint venture of the American Export-Import Bank and the government of Haiti, was created to cultivate a rubber substitute called 'cryptostegia'. The original plan was to allocate 100,000 acres for the project. This land was to be expropriated from small farm owners in the area of Cap-Haïtien, Les Cayes and Gonaïves. In actual fact more than 50,000 acres were seized by the Haitian state and 35,000 acres were planted with cryptostegia.[95] The intention was to employ about 100,000 male labourers. What this plan did not take into account was the effect on domestic food production, as it was assumed that 'a large proportion of the field work is done by women', who will 'raise food in their own patches.'[96]

One year later, the Americans acknowledged the disastrous effect of this programme of expropriation and forced labour: 'The SHADA cryptostegia program combined with the current drought has seriously reduced food production at the present time.'[97] Despite this, the Americans refused to assist in reversing the plan and returning the land to food production, arguing that 'in view of the cryptostegia failure it was politically and economically unwise for this government to immediately enter upon another development program administered by American agencies and personnel in Haiti.'[98] 'The land will be returned to the owners but SHADA will do nothing to cushion the shock of this termination.'[99]

On the other hand, the damage done to the political and economic relations between Haiti and the United States of America needed to be redressed. President Lescot's image at home had suffered badly through the SHADA affair, and he needed at least symbolic support from the Americans. Nelson A. Rockefeller, Coordinator of Inter-American Affairs, was advised against donating funds to the Haitian government because of corruption among politicians. As one civil servant rather patronizingly advised, it 'should merely be used as a catalytic agent to show them how to help themselves.'[100] Thus the Americans were able to blame the resultant food shortage on the dispossessed Haitian farmers, rather than on the appropriation of their land

95 NAW RG 59/838/5018/6-1744 Confidential Memorandum re Haitian Agricultural Extension Program, 17 June 1944, p.1.

96 NAW RG 59/838. 50/40 US Department of Commerce, Economic Study of Haiti, 21 January 1943, p.9.

97 NAW RG 59/838/5018/6-1744 Confidential Memorandum re Haitian Agricultural Extension Program, 17 June 1944, p.1.

98 NAW RG 59/838/5018/6-844 Food program for Haiti, Confidential Memorandum of conversation, Dept. of State, 14 June 1944, p.1.

99 RG 59/838/5018/6-1744 Confidential Memorandum re Haitian Agricultural Extension Program, 17 June 1944, p.1.

100 NAW RG 59/838.5018/6-1444 W. C. Brister to Nelson A. Rockefeller, 12 June 1944.

for large scale cryprostegia production. United States officials suggested the following:

- training programmes to teach Haitians in Haiti improved techniques of food production;
- Haitians of proven talent could be granted scholarships to the United States to study agricultural methods.[101]

In the context of the above, these suggestions appear like a mockery of the Haitian peasants who had been very well capable of supporting themselves before the introduction of the disastrous cryptostegia policy. The conclusion of the war spelt the end of the rule by 'emergency measure' of President Lescot, and the end of his political career. His government had been too closely associated with the SHADA and the costly cryptostegia program.

The French West Indies were also dependent on food imports, primarily from France. The agreement of neutrality between Admiral Robert and Admiral Greenslade included the provision of basic commodities by the USA. Quarterly 'Plans of Economic Needs of French Antilles and Guiana' were submitted by the American Consulate in Fort-de-France via State Department courier to the United States Government.[102] These basic commodities were partially paid for with sugar, rum and bananas for the United States, so as not to waste valuable cargo space.[103] Temporary food shortages did occur, caused both by the war, and by the United States' manipulation of this dependency in order to enforce the agreement with Vichy France and to ensure that Robert towed the line, politically and militarily.[104] In 1943, the United States used the same methods to destabilize Robert's rule and to replace him with Henry-Etienne Hoppenot.[105]

Corruption and embezzlement of government resources and war subsidies involving military and civil personnel were widespread throughout the Caribbean, with Cuba and the Dominican Republic topping the list. Ambassador Braden suggested in 1942 that the provision of financial assistance to Cuba should be tied to demands putting into effect serious measures

> to eradicate widespread corruption with resulting extravagance, inefficiency and adverse effect on co-operation with us in war effort. …

101 NAW RG 59/838/5018 6-1744 Confidential Memorandum re Haitian Agricultural Extension Program,17 June 1944, p.2.

102 NAW RG 59/851 B. 24/14.

103 Fitzroy André Baptiste, 1988 p.172.

104 *Ibid.*

105 *Ibid.* See also the section 'Political Development' in this chapter (pp. 128–40).

> This situation cannot longer be ignored and unless steps are taken by the Cuban Government to regain the confidence of its own people our efforts to assist Cuba economically ... would be severely handicapped. ... Moreover, these conditions are now so well known everywhere that I question whether as a matter of principle we can afford to utilize public funds for purposes which may later be misinterpreted with consequent embarrassment.[106]

One year later corruption in Cuba had apparently become worse – the Ambassador referring to President Batista as the 'Trujillo of Cuba' – but the United States State Department refused to 'take the Cuban Government to task for its unfortunate domestic corruption' even where United States assistance or money was involved. The same diplomatic code of conduct was applied to the Dominican Republic where the reports showed that graft, corruption and embezzlement by President Trujillo and his family had reached outrageous dimensions, obviously also involving United States military personnel. Trujillo and his satellites controlled virtually the entire economy, financially participating in almost every deal done in that country. The opportunities to further enrich himself increased during the war years which placed a heavy burden on the local population. The newly appointed United States Ambassador to the Dominican Republic apparently uncovered, among other things, the embezzlement of United States funds to encourage food production at the height of the U-boat war in Caribbean waters. He reported to the Secretary of State:

> It may be recalled that during the war emergency our Government has been supporting the economy of the Dominican Republic in various ways ... [in] the case regarding the food purchasing program, the benefits ... are not being extended to producers (i.e., the Dominican people) but are being siphoned off by middlemen headed by the President and other high officials of the Dominican Government, who control original purchases from farmers, as well as processing and distribution. For instance, the Dominican Government has consistently declined to publish the price schedule to be paid by the American Government, notwithstanding its commitment to do so in the purchase agreement, and it deliberately maintains producers in ignorance of such prices, apparently for the purpose of permitting middlemen to buy as cheaply as possible. This results in limiting production of foodstuffs for export, and hence runs counter to the purpose of the program.[107]

106 NAW RG 59/FW 837.50/148 Department of State, Adviser on Political Relations, Memorandum Laurence Duggan, 27 November 1942.

107 NAW RG59/839.00/7-544 Ambassador Briggs to SoS, 5 July 1944, p.3.

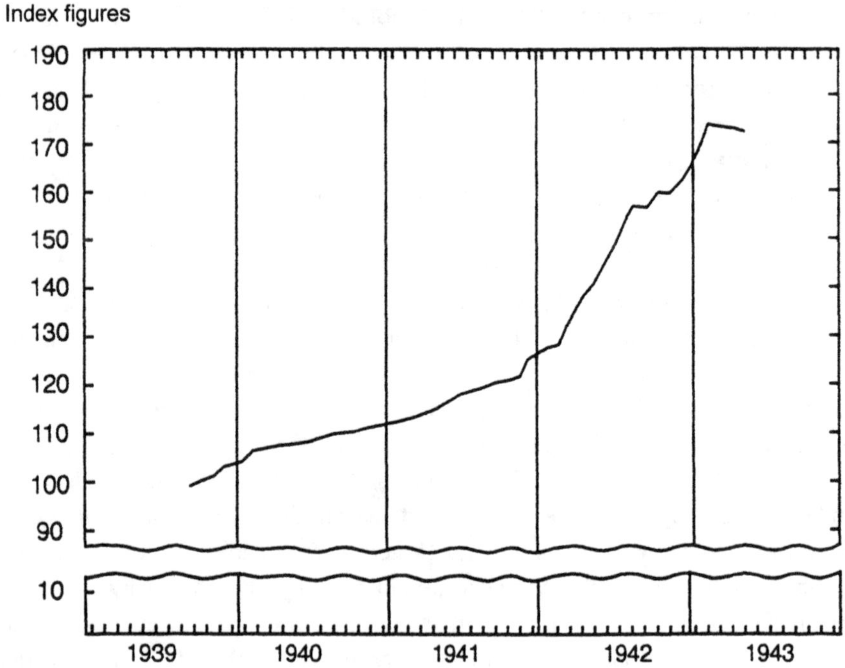

Figure 3.8 Antigua: Cost of living, 1939–43

Source: Governor, Leeward Islands, BWI. Compiled by: British Section, Anglo-American Caribbean Commission. Drawn in the Department of State, Offices of the Geographer, 19 July 1943, 1035-D

Ambassador Briggs suggested serious measures to correct the misuse of war assistance but was discouraged in his efforts by the United States military who 'regard President Trujillo and his Government with great favor' as 'the best possible government in the best of all Caribbean worlds.' The serious rift between the War Department and Ambassador Briggs threatened to grow into a real 'incident' but was finally smoothed out by the State Department.

Unemployment, wages and cost of living

In 1943, the Caribbean Commission published data on the development of wages and consumer prices. These charts, reproduced above, and on pages 121–9 and 131–4, show the increase in the cost of living in various areas of the Caribbean during the war.

I have already dealt with the general impact of the construction work at the United States military bases and the temporary demand for labour this created. As this demand for labour and for certain exports (bananas) reduced, the United States government tried to compensate by introducing a farm

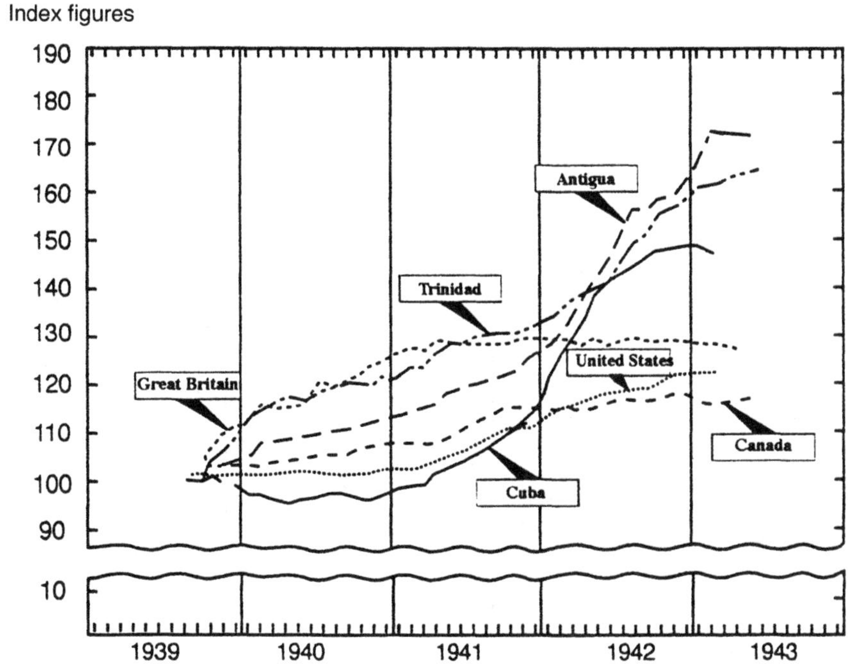

Figure 3.9 United States, Great Britain, Canada, Trinidad, Antigua: Cost of living; Cuba: Food prices, 1939–43

Source: US Bureau of Labor Statistics; Great Britain Bank of England, Statistical Summary; Canada, Department of State and Commerce; Trinidad, Department of Labour, BWI; Antigua, Governor, Leeward Islands, BWI; Cuba, Ministry of Agriculture; Compiled by: Anglo-American Caribbean Commission. Drawn in the Department of State, Offices of the Geographer, 21 July 1943, 1039-D.

labour scheme providing jobs for Jamaican and Bahamian migrant workers on food farms in the United States of America. There was also considerable inter-island migration caused by the construction of the military bases. Puerto Rico and the US Virgin Islands faced a serious unemployment crisis. In 1942, official statistics put the unemployment figure at 12 per cent of the entire work-force. The social effects were so serious that hearings were held in May 1943 before the Committee on Insular Affairs of the House of Representatives.

In Puerto Rico, the two reformers, Luis Muñoz Marín, as head of the local government, and Governor Rexford Tugwell, considered the ongoing land reform as only one measure to relieve unemployment and ameliorate social conditions. Both men shared the view that the government had to play a leading role in planning, initiating, and promoting economic and social development. Accordingly a Central Planning Board, a Development Company and a Development Bank were established to create the infrastructure for a

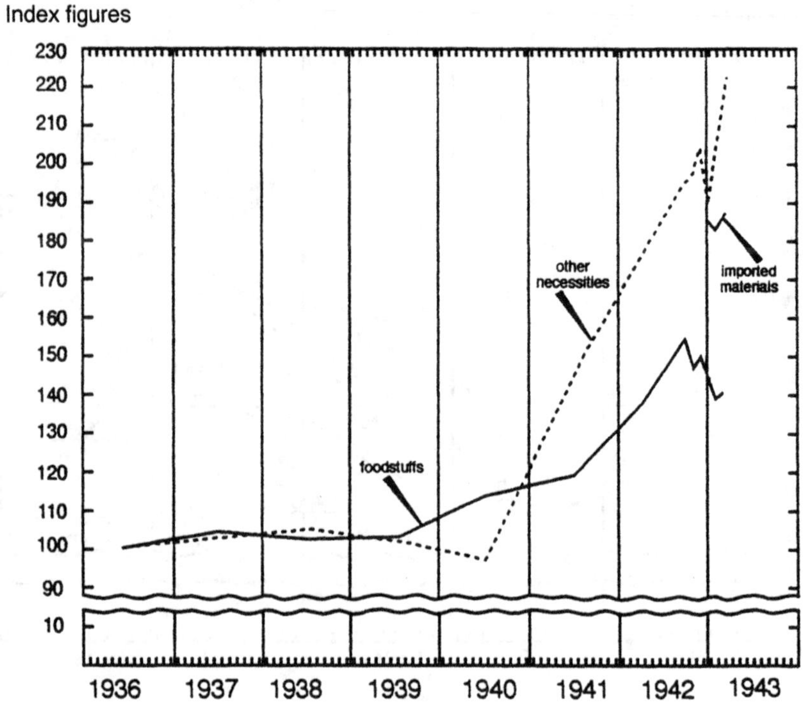

Figure 3.10 Index of retail prices, Dominican Republic, District of Santo Domingo, 1936–43

Source: O.P.A. 'Control of Inflation – Dominican Republic'. Drawn in the Department of State, Offices of the Geographer, 10 July 1943, 1030-D

large-scale development programme, 'Operation Bootstrap', that should completely transform the social and economic structure of the country after the war.

The Development Company was set up to encourage the use of Puerto Rico's natural resources in industrial production, to develop marketing and export of locally produced goods, to establish and operate publicly owned enterprises which should take a leading role in manufacturing and distributing and to promote Puerto Rican entrepreneurship by assisting them with funds and tax incentives. For that purpose the Central Development Bank made loans on easy payment available to local firms that had the potential to contribute to the industrialization strategies set out by the Central Planning Board. Before these operations were introduced in 1942/3, legislation had already enacted a Minimum Wage Board, a Housing and Water Resources Authority, and a Food and Supply Commission.[108]

108 See James L. Dietz, 1986, pp.181–94; Gordon K. Lewis, 1963 (1974), pp.143–66.

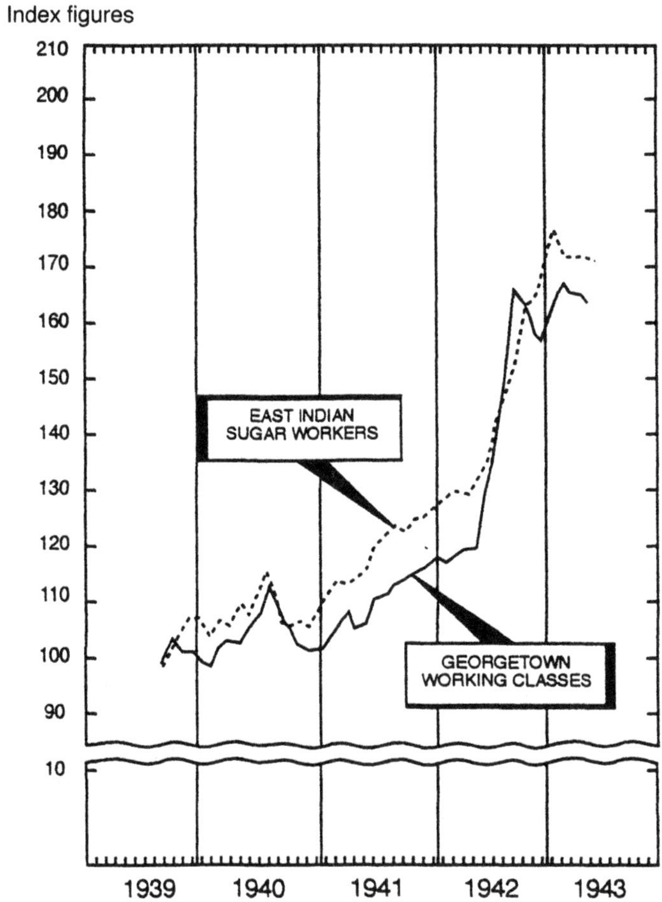

Figure 3.11 British Guiana: Cost of living, 1939–43

Source: Department of Labour, British Guiana. Compiled by British Section, Anglo-American Caribbean Commission. Drawn in the Department of State, Offices of the Geographer, 24 July 1943, 1040-D

Despite these newly introduced measures, social and economic crisis could not be averted during the war.[109] The Administrator of the Federal Work Agency described the situation in the following strong terms:

> The important needlework industry of Puerto Rico is staggering along, many of its shops closed for lack of material from abroad. Industries manufacturing hair nets, hosiery, and similar products have been hard hit

109 *Ibid.*

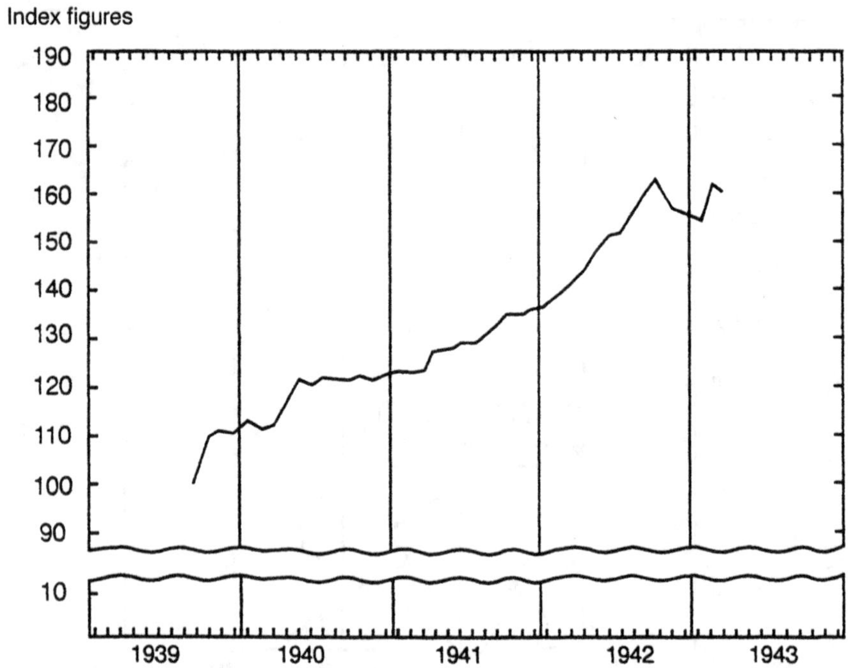

Figure 3.12 Barbados: Cost of living, 1939–43

Source: Department of Labour, BWI. Compiled by British Section, Anglo-American Caribbean Commission. Drawn in the Department of State, Offices of the Geographer, 18 July 1943, 1034-D

> by the recent reduction of 35 per cent in the quota of artificial silk. Thousands of stevedores and transportation workers are without employment. Building and construction work is diminishing, with important Army and Navy contract work now furnishing substantial employment soon to be completed.[110]

During the war, minimum wage levels were introduced and/or raised throughout the Caribbean, which caused a general rise in wages. In most cases, however, the increase in wages was not accompanied by an increase in living standards. On the contrary, the price of consumer goods rocketed sky-high when war restrictions caused shortages. So, for example, in Puerto Rico, while wartime wages shot up an extraordinary 50 per cent, there was a simultaneous increase in food prices of 50 per cent to 210 per cent between 1941 and 1949.[111]

110 Caribbean Commission, 1943, p.8.
111 *Ibid.*, p.203.

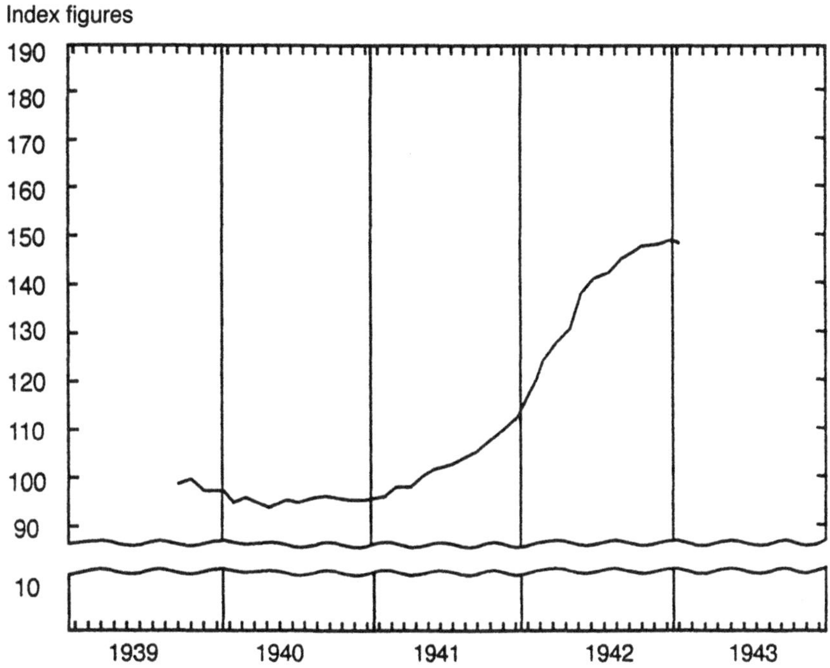

Figure 3.13 Cuba: Food prices, 1939–43

Source: Cuban Ministry of Agriculture. Compiled by US Section, Anglo-American Caribbean Commission. Drawn in the Department of State, Offices of the Geographer, 8 July 1943, 1028-D

In Cuba, President Batista ordered a 50 per cent increase of the minimum wage rate for sugar workers after the price rise in 1942. It was followed by wage increases in other occupations in 1943. On the whole the Cuban economy improved during the war, proving an exception to the trend in the region. This was due to the increased demand for sugar in wartime, and the arrangement whereby the United States bought the entire export crop at a fixed price. Other sectors of the economy also expanded, increasing government revenue substantially. At the same time unemployment rose in industries affected by the interruption of trade. Dockworkers and employees in tourism felt the impact of war most seriously.[112] The expanding economy in Cuba seems to have increased the general standard of living for broad sections of the population, despite the associated increase in consumer prices. It is still controversial how far the economic growth was distributed. A study by the United States Embassy in Cuba came to the following conclusion: 'The effective purchasing power of

112 Louis A. Pérez, 1988, pp.284–6; Julian Alienes Urosa, 1949, pp.13–66.

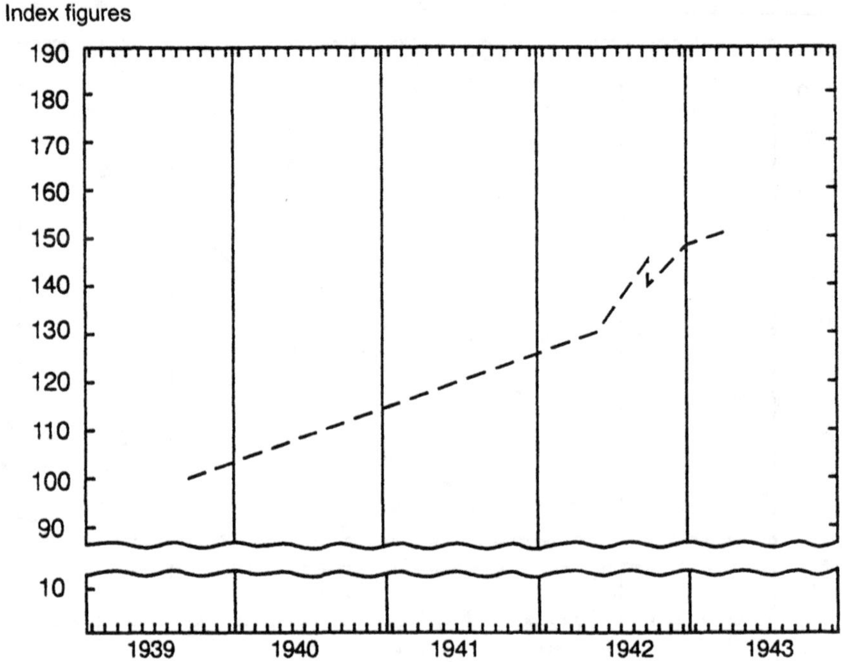

Figure 3.14 Dominica: Cost of living, 1939–43

Source: Administrator of Dominica, Windward Islands, BWI. Compiled by British Section, Anglo-American Caribbean Commission. Drawn in the Department of State, Offices of the Geographer, 20 July 1943, 1037-D

the Cuban working-classes has expanded steadily since the beginning of World War II. In 1943, purchasing power was the greatest since 1929, and in most respects was surpassed only in the exceptional year of 1919 and 1920 during the so called "dance of the millions".'[113] Even if this estimate was, for tactical reasons, slightly exaggerated, Cuba does seem to represent an exception to the otherwise contrary tendencies in the region.[114]

Living conditions in Curaçao and Aruba were only temporarily affected by direct military action, but did not return to normal until early 1945. As far as importation of foodstuffs went, there was a fundamental shift to Latin American products: the import of such products in 1944 was ten times the amount in 1940; the cargo trade in 1944, however, was only 30 per cent of the pre-war level. The balance of trade for 1944 shows that 82 per cent of all trade

113 NAW RG 837. 5017/118 Memorandum comparing Cuban Prosperity in 1943 with Pre-war Year of 1939, 15 March 1944.

114 Data given by Julian Alienes Urosa, 1949, pp.9–66 confirm the trend.

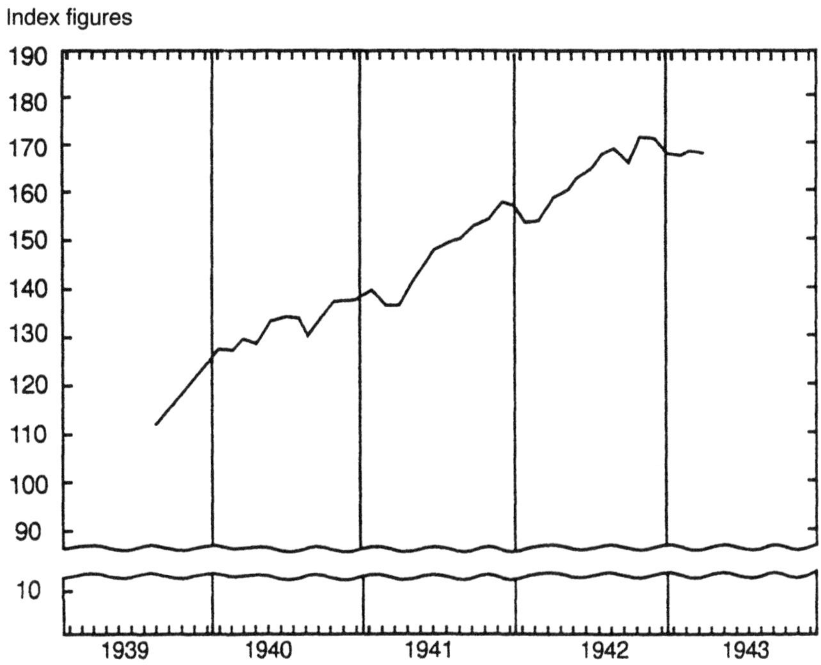

Figure 3.15 Jamaica: Cost of living, 1939–43

Source: Labour Department, Jamaica, BWI. Compiled by British Section, Anglo-American Caribbean Commission. Drawn in the Department of State, Offices of the Geographer, 14 July 1931, 1028-D

consisted of oil products, which is consistent with the important role played by the refineries on Curaçao and Aruba in supplying the Allies with oil.[115]

All governments in the Caribbean imposed measures to regulate exports and imports during the war. The independent republics participated in the decentralized control plan of the United States Office of Economic Warfare. The requirements of Puerto Rico and the US Virgin Islands were worked out by the War Food Administration and the General Supplies Administration of the dependent territories. Imports into the British West Indies from the United States were obtained by government purchases which were arranged by the British Colonies Supply Mission, collaborating with specific War Administration Agencies of the United States with regard to shipping. Inter-regional trade was also monitored by the United States Office of Economic Warfare.[116]

115 I wish to thank Dr R. Römer for providing these data. See also Bernard C. Poole, 1951, p.179.

116 Caribbean Commission, 1943, pp.36–7.

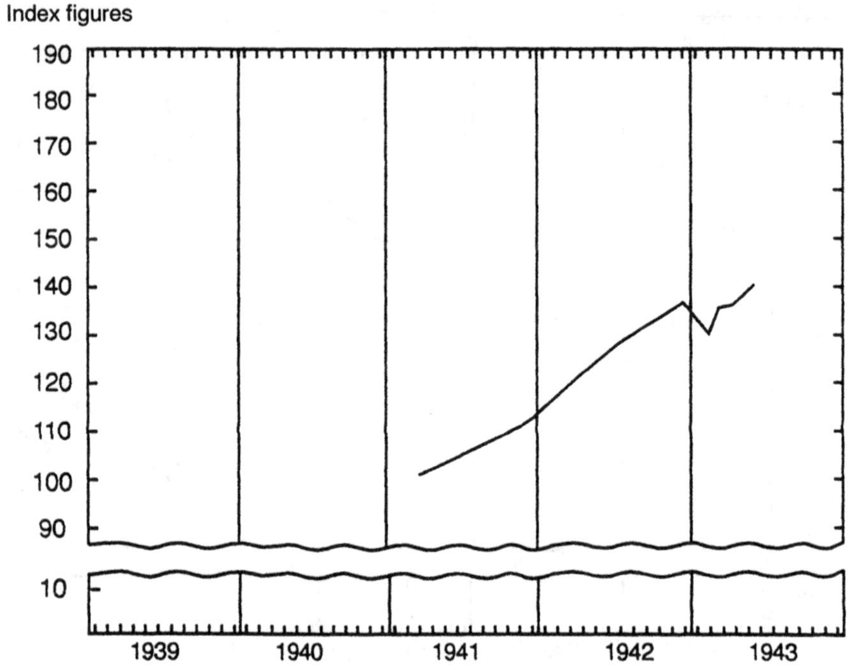

Figure 3.16 Puerto Rico: Cost of living, 1939–43

Source: US Bureau of Labor Statistics. Compiled by US Section, Anglo-American Caribbean Commission. Drawn in the Department of State, Offices of the Geographer, 18 July 1943, 1036-D

Measures to control the consumption of strategic goods were introduced in all territories of the Caribbean. This included the rationing of petroleum products and tyres, and in some countries electricity was also rationed where it depended upon power plants fuelled by diesel oil. Food rationing proved to be more difficult to enforce in most areas, and was limited to the allocation of basic commodities to retailers. Direct consumer rationing occurred in the French West Indies, in some of the British West Indies and in the Virgin Islands. Price controls, combined with subsidies for most basic necessities, were introduced in most of the British West Indian colonies to delay the rapid increase in the cost of living.

Political development

Major political changes in the Caribbean countries – both colonial and independent – emerged towards the end and in the aftermath of the war.

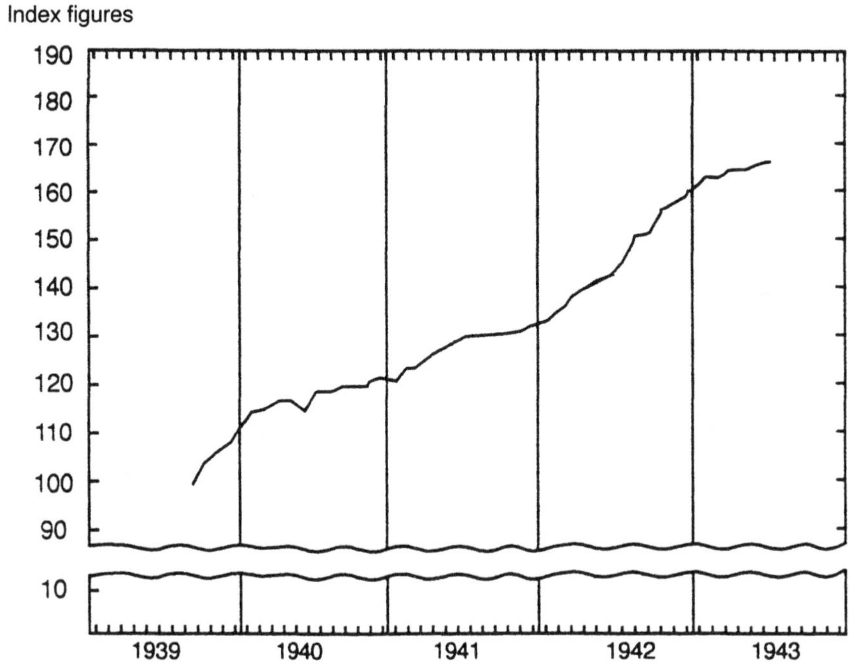

Figure 3.17 Trinidad: Cost of living, 1939–43

Source: Labour Department, Trinidad, BWI. Compiled by British Section, Anglo-American Caribbean Commission. Drawn in the Department of State, Offices of the Geographer, 17 July 1943, 1033-D

The economic and social impact of the war on Haiti, especially the dislocation and expropriation of small peasants by several war production schemes, led to severe social unrest, culminating in the overthrow of the Lescot government in January 1946 by a leftist military junta. The drafting of legislative measures to limit and control personal and corporate holdings by foreigners clearly reflected the war experience of large-scale United States interference.

Politics in Cuba during the first period of Batista's rule, 'formerly divided between Washington and Havana – or rather between the Presidential Palace in Havana and the US embassy – became further divided between the Presidential Palace, the US embassy, and the Cuban military barracks.'[117] The highlights of political development during the war years were marked by the constitution of 1940 and the 1944 election of Ramón Grau San Martín, the exiled political hero of the masses during the early post-Machado period in 1933/4. The drafting of the Cuban constitution of 1940 involved a joint effort

117 Franklin W. Knight, 1989, pp.174–5.

of all major political forces of government and opposition, including old '*machadistas*' and communists.

> The net result was the promulgation of a remarkably progressive constitution. The document provided for universal suffrage, free elections, and referenda, and sanctioned a wide range of political and civil liberties ... maximum hours and minimum wages, pensions, workers' compensation, and the right to strike. For all its enlightened clauses, however, the constitution of 1940 remained substantially a statement of goals, an agenda for future achievement.[118]

Batista won the subsequent free and fairly conducted election in 1940 against Grau San Martín who had just returned from exile. But despite Cuba's relative prosperity during the war years, popular discontent increased because of the uneven distribution of economic growth. The election of Grau San Martín in 1944 raised high hopes among his old working-class followers. The people, however, were quickly disappointed by a government that continued and even aggravated the politics of individual enrichment, embezzlement and corruption. The number of civil servants – most of them party thugs now occupying lucrative government posts – more than doubled during Grau San Martín's term of office. 'Violence and terror became extensions of party politics and the hallmark of Auténtico rule.'[119]

The brutal dictatorship of Rafael Trujillo in the Dominican Republic strengthened during the war. His regime, though obviously resembling the fascist dictatorships of Europe, was tolerated and even encouraged by the United States because he entered the war on the side of the Allies. Trujillo not only concentrated all the political power in his hands and ruthlessly suppressed any opposition, but he also shamelessly profited from government-favoured enterprises on an unprecedented scale. His militantly racist policies – highlighted by a massacre of several thousand Haitian sugar workers in 1937 – were complemented by settling Jewish refugees from Europe at Soshua on the North coast of the island, a scheme cynically promoted as a means of 'whitening' Dominican society.

Simultaneously Trujillo demonstrated sincere support for the Western Allies in their war effort, thereby keeping the USA from interfering with internal politics. These policies remained effective until the arrival in 1944 of a new United States Ambassador in Ciudad Trujillo, as the capital, Santo Domingo, was renamed in honour of the dictator. When Ambassador Ellis E.

118 Louis A. Pérez, 1988, p.281.

119 *Ibid.*, p.284.

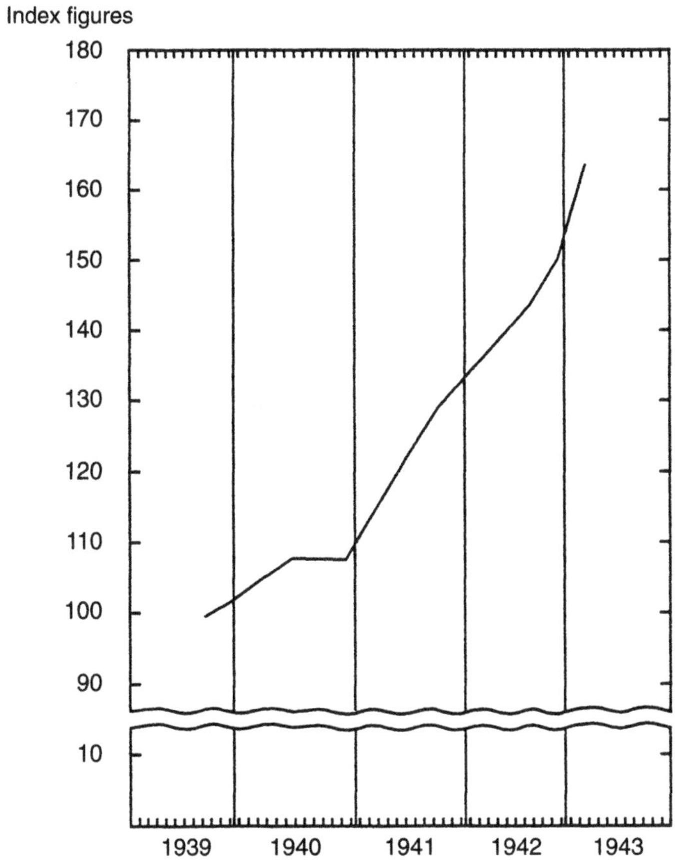

Figure 3.18 Montserrat: Cost of living, 1939–43

Source: Governor, Leeward Islands, BWI. Compiled by British Section, Anglo-American Caribbean Commission. Drawn in the Department of State, Offices of the Geographer, 8 July 1943, 1027-D

Briggs critically reviewed not only Trujillo's political agenda but also the open secret of United States military embroilment in several of the dictator's corrupt schemes involving war resources, relations became tense. The ambivalence of United States policy towards the Trujillo dictatorship in the Dominican Republic is made plain in a detailed report written by the Ambassador four weeks after his arrival:

> Notwithstanding Trujillo's dedication of his Government – internationally – to the principles of liberty, justice and democracy, his administration of the country – domestically – shows a cynical disregard of those principles. His regime is an enterprise operated primarily for the

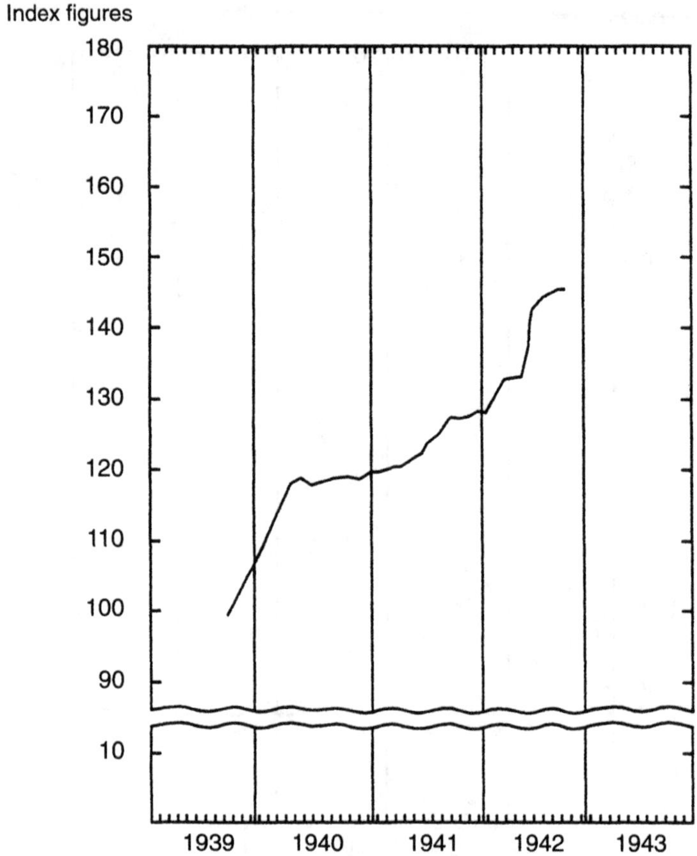

Figure 3.19 St Kitts: Cost of living, 1939–43

Source: Governor, Leeward Islands, BWI. Compiled by British Section, Anglo-American Caribbean Commission. Drawn in the Department of State, Offices of the Geographer, 15 July 1943, 1032-D

> personal enrichment of himself, his relatives and his satellites. His greed results in the impoverishment of the Dominican people, economically and morally. The dictator's vanity, which not infrequently dictates his course of action, is colossal.[120]

Nonetheless Briggs recommended a policy of non-interference. 'Promotion of his overthrow is not the responsibility of the American Government nor would such action be consistent with our present commitments with respect to non-intervention. Trujillo is primarily a Dominican problem, for solution

120 NAW RG59/839.00/7-544 Ambassador Briggs to SoS, 5 July 1944, p.1.

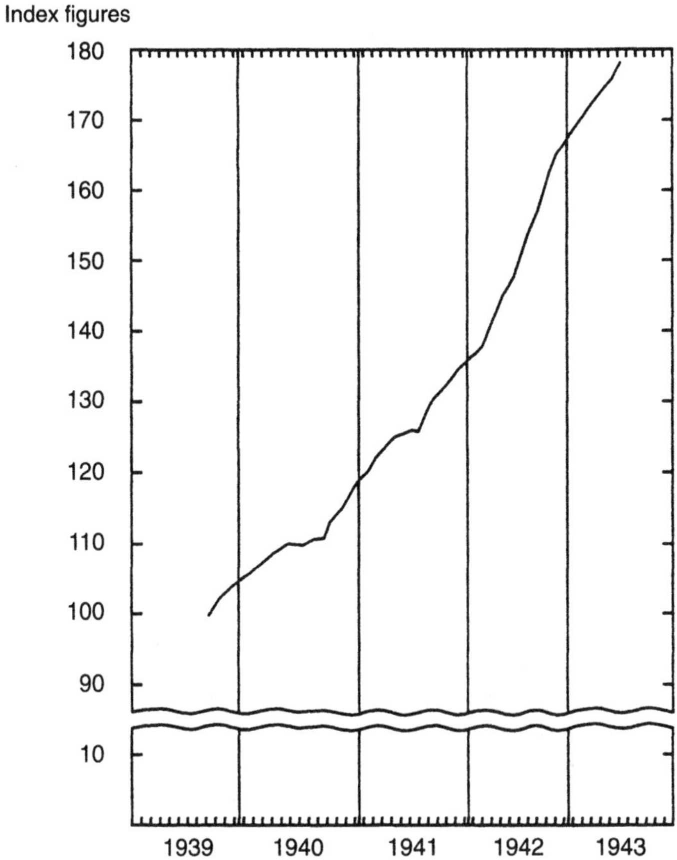

Figure 3.20 St Lucia: Cost of living, 1939–43

Source: Administrator, St Lucia, Windward Islands, BWI. Compiled by British Section, Anglo-American Caribbean Commission. Drawn in the Department of State, Offices of the Geographer, 9 July 1943, 1029-D

by the Dominican people.'[121] Yet, the question of 'favors to dictators', the Ambassador continued, would inevitably arise in regard to other American republics. 'We must be scrupulously honest in all our government dealings with the Dominican Government and people', he concluded idealistically. In practical terms this meant putting an end to the admitted American wartime contributions to the enrichment of the dictator – 'whose personal pocket book might be the first to suffer' – but otherwise doing business as usual.[122]

121 *Ibid.*, p.2.
122 *Ibid.*, p.3.

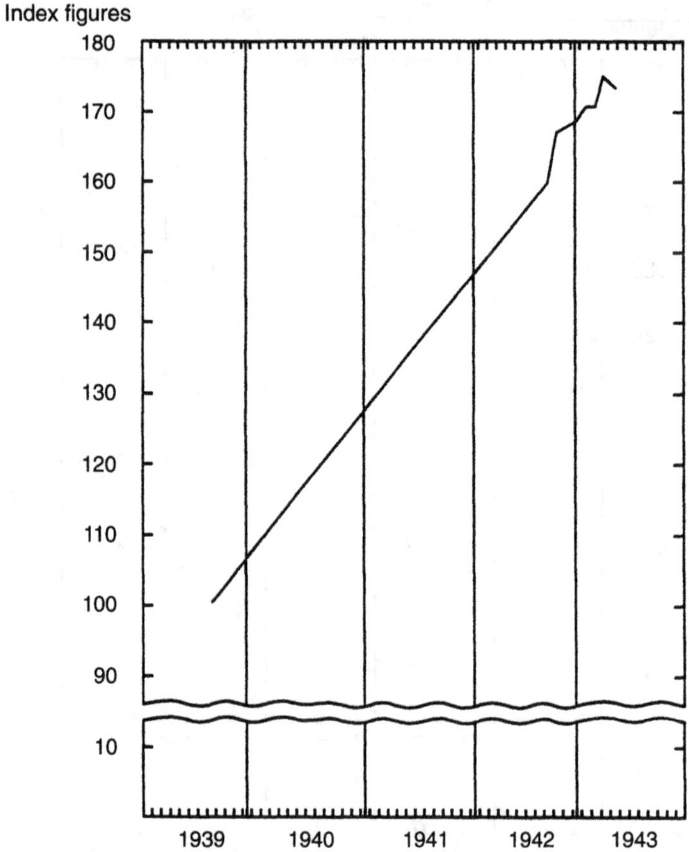

Figure 3.21 St Vincent: Cost of living, 1939–43

Source: Labour Department, St Vincent, BWI. Compiled by British Section, Anglo-American Caribbean Commission. Drawn in the Department of State, Offices of the Geographer, 20 July 1943, 1038-D

The 1940s are quite properly regarded as the real turning point in Puerto Rico's modern history. The island experienced the fortunate co-operation of two eminent politicians, one representing the Puerto Rican people, the other the hegemonic power of the USA, but both of them committed to social reform. Luis Muñoz Marín, a talented bilingual poet and journalist – 'the greatest politician the island produced'[123] – won the 1940 election with his Popular Democratic Party using the symbol (straw-hatted *jíbaro*) and slogan (*pan, tierra y libertad*) of the Zapata movement in the Mexican Revolution and joining forces with Rexford Tugwell, the last United States Governor of Puerto Rico.

123 Franklin W. Knight, 1990, p.269.

Tugwell, a professor of economics and political science from Columbia University, was a member of Roosevelt's original 'brains trust' of the 1930s, but having lost his influence in United States politics was transferred to Puerto Rico. Muñoz Marín, who spent most of his childhood and adolescence in the USA, finally returned to Puerto Rico in 1931 and first joined the Liberal Party. When he was expelled from that party in 1937 he founded the Popular Democratic Party leading it to its first and narrow victory in 1940. 'It was the good fortune of Puerto Rico, in one sense, that the federal New Deal delayed some eight years in appointing a convinced New Dealer to the Puerto Rican office and that, in turn, the local political situation delayed the advent to power of a reformist party about the same period of time.'[124] Both men shared similar political visions and complemented one another in administration, planning and securing popular support. They embarked on a 'Little New Deal' for Puerto Rico that completely transformed the island politically, socially and economically.

The war also accelerated the process of decolonization in the dependent territories of the Caribbean. The wartime coalition of the United States of America and the Soviet Union, the going into exile of the Dutch and French governments, the military operations in the region, and especially the close co-operation of Great Britain and the United States of America in the Western hemisphere, all put pressure on the European colonial powers to abolish, or at least reform, the traditional type of colonialism.

The first push came well before Pearl Harbour and the declaration of war by the United States at the meeting of Roosevelt and Churchill at Placentia Bay, where the famous Atlantic Charter was drafted. Its Article III, to be much disputed later, stated: 'They respect the right of all peoples to choose the form of government under which they will live; and they wish to see sovereign rights and self-government restored to those who have been forcibly deprived of them.'[125]

While Roosevelt and the United States State Department emphasized the Article's principle and global meaning, the British government, startled by telegrams from every corner of the Empire asking for interpretation, played down its general impact, limiting its scope to the fascist occupation of European countries. But the formula assumed a dynamic of its own, and the peoples of the colonial world used the principle to serve their demand for self-government and independence. Churchill was reported to have made several emotional outbursts about the alleged American attack on the British Empire, but was supposed to have been advised by Roosevelt that one could not 'fight a war against fascist slavery, and at the same time not work to free people all

124 Gordon K. Lewis, 1963 (1974), p.158.

125 Quoted in David John Morgan, 1980, vol. 5, p.1.

over the world from a backward colonial policy.'[126] The Colonial Office finally took up the question of decolonization and turned it into a timetable for colonial reform aiming at the 'well-being of the peoples of the Colonial Empire' in accordance with the statement on 'Colonial Development and Welfare' issued in 1940. During further negotiations with the United States on the future status of colonial dependencies and mandated territories within the United Nations, the British government emphasized the different stages of development of the colonies within the Empire: 'It is therefore the duty of the "Parent" or "Trustee" States to guide and develop the social, economic and political institutions of the Colonial peoples until they are able without danger to themselves and others to discharge the responsibilities of government.'[127]

In the British West Indies, Jamaica was chosen as a showcase to demonstrate the British policy of colonial reform. The drafting of a new constitution granting internal self-government and an election based on universal suffrage in 1944 paved the way for constitutional decolonization in the British West Indies. The first demands for self-government in Jamaica had been raised as early as the period of severe social unrest in the 1930s. The Jamaica Progressive League and other organizations forwarded proposals for constitutional reform toward self-government to the West India Royal Commission in 1938. The commission did not elaborate on the question of constitutional reform because this was officially not part of its task. The immediate impact of war had postponed further negotiations. When in 1942 the People's National Party (PNP), founded in 1938 by Norman Manley and others in the Fabian tradition of the British Labour Party, and two other organizations sent another memorandum on constitutional reform to the Secretary of State for the Colonies, this coincided with the Anglo-American discussions on the colonial question and was consequently adopted to show goodwill on colonial reform. Contrary to the expectations of the Jamaican Governor, who played down the new initiative, the Colonial Office warmly welcomed the memorandum as a basis for further negotiations. As one top official put it:

> If we proceed vigorously towards a new constitution we shall proclaim our good faith to the world, and to the American world in particular; ... we shall to some extent avoid the perpetual references to Jamaica in both houses of Parliament, references which are so disturbing to good government in that Island; and we shall at least appear to give some constitutional advance willingly instead of having had it dragged out of us.[128]

---

126 Elliott Roosevelt, 1946, pp.36–7.
127 David John Morgan, 1980, vol. 5, p.8.
128 CO 137/849, 68714/42 Memorandum by Battershill, 16 November 1942. Quoted in Ken Post, 1980, vol. 1, p.289.

The constitution was finally enacted in 1944, and the first electoral struggle under universal suffrage took place in Jamaica even before the war ended. Ironically, Manley and the PNP, the major force pushing for decolonization, lost the first election by a clear margin to the eccentric yet popular and charismatic Alexander Bustamante – who had initially opposed the move towards self-government strongly – and his Jamaica Labour Party (JLP), founded just in time for the election. The so-called Labour Party scored a landslide victory (23 seats); five seats went to independent candidates. For the PNP (four seats) and Manley, who failed to win a seat, the election ended in disaster and humiliation.[129]

In the French West Indian colonies, the Vichy collaboration under United States control ended after the invasion of North Africa by Allied troops in November 1942. The decisive moment came when Admiral Darlan – commander-in-chief of all Vichy forces – changed sides and brought French North Africa under the control of the Allies. Even after his assassination in December 1942, the United States found an acceptable successor in General Giraud, who was preferred by the Americans to General de Gaulle and his Free France movement backed by Great Britain.

Then the USA increased pressure on Admiral Robert, who was still being tolerated as High Commissioner in Martinique, to make way for a takeover of the French West Indies by a Giraud instead of a de Gaulle representative. The transfer of power to Giraud forces in Martinique and Guadeloupe took place when Robert finally left his headquarters in June 1943, forced out of office by a combination of local resistance and outside pressure; in French Guiana, the change was engineered by the United States even before the admiral's departure. Bowing to US pressure, the admiral agreed to hand over power to Henry-Etienne Hoppenot, formerly the head of Giraud's mission in Washington DC. Despite the formal union of Generals de Gaulle and Giraud as leaders of the Committee of National Liberation, the rift between the two men remained, and the majority of the people of French Guiana, Martinique, and especially Guadeloupe showed their support for de Gaulle, regarding Hoppenot as a puppet of the United States.[130]

The post-war perspectives of French colonial policy differed from British plans for colonial reform. Even more than Churchill, de Gaulle hesitated to embark upon decolonization and abolition of the French empire overseas. His vision of the future for the French colonies ranged from association to incorporation. The 'Union Française', a close association of the dependent African and Asian territories with the 'parent' state, and the incorporation of the old plantation colonies in the Caribbean and Algeria as overseas departments,

129 See Ken Post, 1980, vol. 2, pp.481–503.

130 See Fitroy André Baptiste, 1988, pp.191–214.

were intended as substitutes for independence. On the eve of the 1945 United Nations conference in San Francisco, the Free France movement published a statement on the 'Evolution of Colonial Peoples', declaring that the 'people of Martinique, Guadeloupe and Guiana refuse to consider themselves in need of an international guardian' because they 'enjoy political rights precisely like those of the inhabitants of metropolitan France.'[131]

The most stagnant and inflexible colonial power in the Caribbean turned out to be the Netherlands. Paul Blanshard, a well informed contemporary observer and special adviser to the United States government stationed in the Caribbean during the 1940s, characterized the Dutch West Indies as the 'most fundamentally undemocratic' colonies in the region.[132] The last step taken before the war to promote autonomy and participation of the colonial peoples in fact led to nothing more than a concentration of power in the hands of the Governor and his administration.[133] The promise by Queen Wilhelmina from her exile in London to establish 'a solid foundation of complete partnership' between the Netherlands and 'her overseas territories'[134] proved to be empty until long after the war. The so-called 'Kielstra incident' can be taken as an example demonstrating the arrogance and paternalism with which colonial rule was executed.

Governor Kielstra of Dutch Guiana, who had opposed the military takeover by American forces from the beginning, lost the support of the local population as well, including the small minority of franchise holders in that colony, who were allowed to participate in the legislature. His direct opponent was Bos Verschuur, a coloured schoolteacher and elected legislator, who filed and circulated a petition asking Queen Wilhelmina to replace Governor Kielstra, whose autocratic rule had lost him all support and respect from the people. Governor Kielstra, instead of forwarding it to the Queen, withdrew the petition and interned Verschuur, its author, without trial or public hearing, referring to a technical wartime rule that required the Governor's approval of petitions prior to circulation. The Governor, whose manner of proceeding was never disapproved of by the Dutch government, was finally removed from Dutch Guiana, only to become Ambassador to Mexico. After the war he even returned as Dutch representative on the Caribbean Commission and was 'chosen to 'represent' the Dutch colonial people at the San Francisco conference of the United Nations.'[135]

---

131 'Free France' published by the French Press and Information Office, New York, vol. 7, no. 7, 1 April 1945.

132 Paul Blanshard, 1947, p.273.

133 Sir Harold Mitchell, 1972, p.121.

134 Quoted in Caribbean Commission, 1943, p.57.

135 Paul Blanshard, 1947, p.301.

The high hopes Charles Taussig, the chairman of the United States delegation to the Anglo-American Caribbean Commission, had placed on the future role of that regional organization in securing speedy decolonization, faded away after Roosevelt's death on the eve of the first United Nations meeting in San Francisco. The president made sure that Taussig joined the United States delegation to the conference, but the latter's anti-colonial position was shared neither by the Secretary of State, Stettinius, nor the majority of the delegation. Not even Taussig's close contacts with Eleanor Roosevelt helped strengthen his influence on the delegates.[136] The Roosevelt tradition in colonial affairs was sacrificed to a preoccupation with military considerations and the impending split in the war coalition. The United States delegation looked for a compromise with the European colonial powers and close Anglo-American co-operation at the conference. Instead of supporting the claim for unconditional decolonization and independence voiced by Russia, China, the emerging bloc of 'Third World' countries and even the British Dominion, Australia, the United States of America settled on the British formula of 'progressive development toward self-government.'[137]

The Anglo-American Caribbean Commission was expanded after the war to take in France and the Netherlands, but it was *de facto* limited in its political scope 'to be mainly concerned with work in the fields of research, collection of information, consultation and exchange of views with the governments of the area served by it.'[138] The United States Department of Inter-American Affairs initially objected to the expansion of the Commission, because the inclusion of France and the Netherlands might strengthen old colonial ties and reduce the presence and influence of the United States.[139] Instead it was decided to use the enlarged Caribbean Commission to further penetrate the Caribbean economically after the war 'without assuming the financial or administrative burden of formal empire.'[140]

The organization initiated a great deal of research on important issues concerning the region – regional economic planning, markets, industrial and

136 He had a conversation with Mrs Roosevelt arranging 'emergency contacts with the President' for the Conference in San Francisco on the very day of Roosevelt's death, 12 April 1945. FDRL, Taussig Papers, Box 49. Memorandum of conversation at the White House with Mrs. Roosevelt. See Wm. Roger Louis, 1977, pp.493–4.

137 Wm. Roger Louis, 1977, pp.532–47.

138 Eric Williams, 1969, p.120.

139 FDRL, Taussig papers, Box 52. Excerpt from minutes of Secretary Staff Committee re-Expansion of Anglo-American Caribbean Commission, 24 July 1945.

140 Howard Johnson, 1984b, p.198.

trade development, transport, statistical aid, and so on – but lacked the authority to implement practical measures or to promote genuine West Indian representation and participation. Eric Williams, the historian and first prime minister of Trinidad & Tobago, who for several years worked with the Caribbean Commission, at last, as co-chairman of the Caribbean Research Council, reported bitterly on his clashes with metropolitan authorities.[141] Even the enthusiastic pioneer of the Anglo-American beginnings of the Caribbean Commission, Rexford Tugwell, openly admitted: 'Both the Colonial Office and the State Department were looking over our shoulders. And just from the outside, looking in, were the representatives of the people who were a long way from trusting, or being trusted by, the appointed officials.'[142]

Paul Blanshard sums up the experiences of the dependent Caribbean peoples during wartime by concluding:

> They have received spasmodic charity without honor or self-respect. They were not consulted when the Caribbean bases were leased by Britain to the United States, they were not consulted when the Caribbean Commission was formed, and they were not invited to San Francisco for the formation of the United Nations, ... They have helped to fight two wars for freedom, but never been invited to a peace conference.[143]

141 Eric Williams, 1969, pp.105–27.
142 Rexford Guy Tugwell, 1958, p.274.
143 Paul Blanshard, 1947, p.334.

4

Proletarian movements (1940–90)

Patrick Bryan

Introduction

The modern Caribbean proletarian movement emerged out of the historic upheavals of the 1930s. Since then the Caribbean proletarian, and more specifically the trade union, movement has fluctuated in its growth. The political alliances, fragmentation and ideological influences that have shaped the history of the proletarian movement are inseparable from the goals of redistribution of income and services and from the broader and changeable context of national and international capitalism and politics. The first period of consolidation and rapid development can be seen between 1940 and 1947, when Second World War conditions favoured the development of viable trade unions. The second period after 1947 saw a continued growth of trade unions, but it was an epoch significantly influenced by the ideological pressures of the Cold War, and by national developmental policies that responded less favourably to proletarian autonomy. The post-1970 decline in post-war prosperity confirmed the tendency in the earlier period to control unions more rigorously. Simultaneously, proletarian movements have depended less on their earlier political alliances.

Although the Caribbean area consists of a series of territories with varied linguistic, political and constitutional traditions, proletarian movements in this region have complemented each other in a number of ways. One common, indeed overriding, influence was United States capital which, starting from the very end of the nineteenth century, established in the Caribbean plantations of sugar and bananas, constructed railroads, built military bases, constructed a railroad and then a canal across the Isthmus of Panama, and acted as a magnet for Caribbean workers seeking higher wages. Oil refineries in Curaçao, Aruba and Trinidad also attracted migrant workers. Labourers from Curaçao travelled to Cuba to work on sugar estates while British West Indians moved into Curaçao.[1] Not surprisingly, in most Caribbean territories proletarian

1 René A. Römer, 1981a, pp.95–7.

protests emerged from within the ranks of the agro-proletariat of the sugar industry, the single largest employer of labour in most Caribbean countries. Secondly, the return of migrants from the Spanish Caribbean, following the Great Depression, was a factor in the social crisis of the period 1935–8 in the British Caribbean. Spanish Caribbean governments, faced with the severe depression of the 1930s and declining social and economic opportunities for their own labouring classes, barred the entry of migrants from other parts of the Caribbean. British West Indians working on sugar and banana plantations in the Spanish Caribbean and Central America were also sent home during the 1930s. These returning migrants faced deteriorating social and economic conditions in their home territories, and declining opportunities for viable employment.

United States capital, which had augmented the sugar industry in the Spanish Caribbean, had attracted seasonal labourers from other territories in the Caribbean. So too did the construction of military bases by the United States at Chaguaramas and Wallerfield in Trinidad. Trinidad's petroleum industry also contributed to making that island an attractive destination for other British Caribbean islanders. (In 1931, there were 46,391 citizens from other areas of the Caribbean working in Trinidad, of whom 14,949 were from Grenada and 10,425 from St Vincent.) The Vincentian Ebenezer Joshua served as Chairman of Grenadian Uriah Butler's British Empire Workers, Peasants and Ratepayers Union for 13 years before returning from Trinidad to his native St Vincent in 1951. Upon his return he ran on the ticket representing the United Workers, Peasants and Ratepayers Union of St Vincent. He later founded his own People's Political Party linked institutionally with his Federal Agricultural and Industrial Workers Union.[2] In nearby Grenada, work in the oilfields of Trinidad and Aruba, and on the Chaguaramas Base, together with high prices paid for cocoa during the Second World War, provided for Grenadians a material well-being that ceased when Trinidad imposed restrictions on Grenadian labour there after the War. These returning workers, influenced by the growth of trade unions in Trinidad, became less subordinate to the paternalism of the Grenadian estates.[3] The Grenadian Eric Gairy had worked in the Aruba oil refinery, gained experience as a labour organizer there, returned home in 1949, and founded, in 1951, the Grenada United Labour Party (GULP) as the political arm of the Grenada Manual and Mental Workers Union (GMMWU). In October of that year he won seven of eight seats and 71 per cent of the eligible vote in the local legislature.[4]

2 Patrick Lewis, 1974, p.181.
3 Brian Meeks, 1993, p.136.
4 *Ibid.*, p.137.

The return of Jamaicans (including Alexander Bustamante) from the Spanish Caribbean helped to spark the upheavals in 1938 in Jamaica. In fact, several Jamaicans joined the massive proletarian upheavals in Cuba in the 1930s, and some were members of the Communist Party of Cuba.[5] Vere Bird of Antigua had encouraged the formation of trade unions in Montserrat because Antiguan planters, opposed to trade unionism at home, habitually contracted workers from the smaller island to replace Antiguan trade unionists.[6] Uriah Butler was a Grenadian who was active in the formation of the Oilfield Workers Trade Union in Trinidad, and was in fact imprisoned during the War, regaining his freedom only in 1945. British West Indians also provided trade-union leadership in the Dutch Caribbean island of Curaçao. It has been argued, on the other hand, that linguistic and ethnic diversity was a constraining factor in the formation of trade unions in the Dominican Republic, where sugar workers were primarily Haitians and British West Indians. The latter conclusion is not entirely valid, however, in view of the experience of Jamaicans in Cuba, and West Indians in Curaçao; and in light of the particular authoritarian structure of politics in the Dominican Republic, which, as Catherine Conaghan and Rosario Espinal point out, had an 'exclusionary character' right up to the 1980s.[7]

Caribbean proletarian organizations have also been influenced by the complex ethnic make-up of the Caribbean with its European, African and Asian populations. The Partij Nationalistiche Republick (PNR) established in Suriname in 1973 was an offshoot of the Wi Egi Sani (Our Own Business), a Black Nationalist cultural group founded in the 1950s. In Haiti, *négritude,* in association with democracy and socialism, promoted the growth of the Mouvement Ouvrier Paysan and the Fédération des Travailleurs Haïtiens. The history of trade unionism in Guyana, apart from demonstrating the association between national politics and the labour movement, illustrates the importance of ethnicity as Indians and Africans pursued their separate ethnic interests. The tension between Indian and African Guyanese had been evident to the Moyne Commission, before which separate organizations represented one or other major ethnic group. The tide of Indian nationalism, rising with Mahatma Gandhi's campaign against British imperialism in India, promoted Indian cultural nationalism in both Trinidad and Guyana. The socialist orientation of Adrian Cola Rienzi, the Indo-Trinidadian lawyer who was one of the founders of the Oilfield Workers Trade Union (OWTU) and the All Trinidad Sugar Estates and Factory

5 Barry Carr, 1998, p.89.
6 Patrick Lewis, 1974, p.171.
7 Catherine M. Conaghan and Rosario Espinal, 1990, p.558.

Workers Trade Union (ATSEFWU), ensured that at least until 1944, when he retired from labour politics, the Trinidadian proletariat was organized more along class than along ethnic lines.[8] Ethnic divisions emerged more strongly after the war. In Trinidad, Ranjit Kumar's leadership of labour emphasized the welfare of the Indian proletariat. Indian ethnicity also manifested itself in the emergence in 1950 of Bhadase Sagan Maraj, who unified rival Hindu religious organizations into the Sanatan Dharma Maha Sabha Association (the Great Council of the Holy Scriptures). He used 'his wealth and notorious strong-arm tactics to take over the leadership of the sugar workers, who since 1945 were the objects of union rivalry'. With the Maha Sabha and the sugar workers under his control, 'Maraj had a powerful Indian ethnic base to support his political arm, the People's Democratic Party.'[9] A racial division of labour accompanied the ethnic configuration of Trinidad (and Guyana) – an almost equal division of population between Indians and Africans. Indians had a more pronounced presence in the sugar and rice industries, Afro-Trinidadians in oil and urban occupations. Perry Mars has observed the close association between the strongly Indian Guyana Agricultural and General Workers Union (GAWU) and the Marxist Peoples' Progressive Party (PPP) in Guyana.[10]

But even in Trinidad, ethnicity was not exclusively a function of Indian politics and trade unionism. Uriah Butler with his Baptist Church, his potent Old Testament consciousness, his association with the Negro Welfare Social and Cultural Association and his initial ties with the OWTU, seemed to represent the black ethnic stream of Trinidad's unionism. Butler identified himself with Moses the liberator of the Israelites, whom the Egyptians had enslaved. Moses has more than once emerged in black Caribbean history as a metaphor for liberation from slavery and from the thralldom of white plantocratic supremacy. A strong Old Testament consciousness also evoked Joseph, sold into slavery by his brothers, as an instrument of liberation for those who had enslaved him. Butler organized a Moravian Baptist Church – the Moravians and the Baptists being the two Christian denominations in the Caribbean often associated in the popular mind with black welfare. Butler declared that 'he would not sheathe his sword (we assume a sword of righteousness) until the British West Indies enjoyed British rights and British privileges. He was the "Servant of the Living God" and those who followed him were following God.'[11] Butler was also the 'Chief Servant', and 'in interviews

8 Kelvin Singh, 1994, p.218.
9 Patrick Lewis and Kelvin Singh, 1987, p.56.
10 Perry Mars, 1990, p.85.
11 Kelvin Singh, 1994, p.209.

with Butlerites today the sense of awe and worship in which he was held can still be felt.'[12]

The messianic impulse was also present in Antigua, where Vere Bird was called 'Papa Bird' and according to one report 'there was also a certain amount of mysticism about Bird; perhaps this is from his religious training in the Salvation Army. He drew people to him and the workers were prepared to sacrifice anything to follow him.'[13] In Jamaica Bustamante was the 'leader' and 'Chief' (he was also Chief Minister) and his followers were disciples who proclaimed in song: 'We shall follow Bustamante until we die.' St William Grant, one of Bustamante's chief lieutenants, declared Bustamante to be a man of divine attributes. Bustamante, a near-white Jamaican, very cleverly and very successfully tapped the ethnic sentiments of Jamaica's black working class by describing the nationalist People's National Party (PNP) and their Trades Union Advisory Council (TUAC) allies as bearers of 'brown man' government, and their aspirations towards self-government as a return to slavery. Proletarian protests in Jamaica reiterated the view that the black working class was still subject to slave conditions and to racism.[14] Grenada's Eric Gairy, sharing the messianic, personalistic and authoritarian impulses of Uriah Butler and Bustamante, claimed to have a 'historic mission to lead his people out of the wilderness into the Promised Land.'[15] Radicalism was, however, implied rather than intended. Ultimately, messianic leadership of the proletariat proved politically conservative. A. W. Singham has argued that the leaders 'are seldom emancipated enough themselves to really want to see the social structure drastically changed, and particularly the patterns of authoritarianism. They tend to be much more concerned with proving their own capabilities to run the existing system, and hence their right to membership in the elite.'[16] With the institutionalization of trade unions in most Caribbean societies messianic leaders gave way to professional trade unionists, certainly from the 1970s onward.

Ethnicity continued to have an influence on trade-union organization up to the 1970s, which witnessed a re-emergence of radical political thinking in the British Caribbean, influenced by the rise of the Black Power Movement in the United States of America, and renewed flirtations with Marxism. The fact is that Blacks constituted both an oppressed race and an oppressed class. Ethnic-related issues were couched in class terms, and class-related issues in ethnic terms. Class and ethnic liberation were often indistinguishable, in the

12 Rhoda Reddock, 1994, p.141.
13 Novelle Richards, 1963, p.29.
14 Gladys Bustamante, 1997, pp.30, 92–3.
15 A. W. Singham, 1968, p.146.
16 *Ibid.*

British Caribbean at least. There is little doubt that in Jamaica the Inter-Trades Union Advisory Council which, in the 1970s, brought together a number of small unions which opposed 'political unionism', was influenced by the argument that political parties with which trade unions had been allied had not been sufficiently attentive to the interests of black workers. The University and Allied Workers Union (UAWU) grew out of the Black Power *Abeng* movement, and the Marxist Workers' Party of Jamaica (WPJ) came out of the UAWU and *Abeng*. In Dominica, the Dominican Liberation Movement Alliance and its mass base the National Workers Union were also rooted in Black Power. The work of Walter Rodney to establish his Working People's Alliance (WPA) in Guyana represents an effort to bridge the gap between the two main ethnic streams of Guyana, the Indian and African.[17] For despite Cheddi Jagan's Marxism, it was only too evident that his leadership mobilized Indians while Forbes Burnham mobilized the African Guyanese population. The ethnic factor was also present in Cuba's labour history, from a different point of view. Most Afro-Cubans were, at the start of the Revolution, unskilled workers. 'Castro's pointed criticism of such discrimination made his movement attractive to black workers. Indeed, blacks and mulattos became the staunchest supporters of communism in Cuba in hopes that socialism would eliminate racism in the workplace as well as society.'[18]

Thus, the proletarian movement prior to the 1940s encountered resistance from economic and political leadership in the Caribbean. However, the Second World War and its immediate aftermath facilitated the growth and consolidation of trade unions.

The impact of the Second World War

At the heart of the question of the future of proletarian organizations was the issue of the domestic and international distribution of power and wealth. Proletarian movements seek to improve the quality of life of their members through a redistribution of income and the democratization of social benefits – such as minimum wages, health, housing and education. The extent to which such gains are made is a function of the political and legal structure and of the ability of the organized working class to extract benefits from an often-hostile employer class. Worker welfare is also linked with the orientation of the State. As C. Y. Thomas has noted, 'the choice between the

17 See Rupert Lewis, 1998.
18 Michael Conniff and Thomas Davis, 1994, p.246.

authoritarian state and a more parliamentary bourgeois-democratic orientation is a very significant choice in terms of the advance of the working class and peasantry.'[19] Also, the extent to which the working-class leadership sought to achieve social gains in the political and ideological context of 'world revolution', or in the context of more narrow 'economistic' ends, determined where labour movements stood in respect to international ideological conflicts.

The struggle of the Western democracies against fascism promoted proletarian internationalism. The War created an environment that was more sympathetic to social reform, and participatory democracy. Thus the proletarian movements which had emerged as a spontaneous, violent, anti-systemic, and major social and political force in most parts of the Caribbean during the 1930s became beneficiaries, between the late 1930s and 1945, of legislation that allowed for legal representation and collective bargaining by the working class. Domestic political strategies designed to deal with proletarian movements therefore vacillated between repression, incorporation, alliance and control. Those strategies mirrored the fundamental conflict between a mainly white employer class with a political, economic and social interest to protect, and a mainly black or coloured subordinate class that sought to promote its interests precisely against those of the employer class. It is not surprising that Whites in Dominica, for example, opposed the extension of democratic participation to the working classes, who now threatened not only to have a voice against capital at the work-place but a voice in political decision-making through the extension of the franchise.[20]

The history of proletarian organizations in the Caribbean demonstrates the interaction between domestic and international political forces and issues in shaping that history. However, these domestic or national policies were themselves influenced by international circumstances and ideology, for example, the Second World War, the demands of international capital and the Cold War. Simultaneously, domestic or national political traditions and orientations helped to determine the ways in which proletarian organizations were incorporated or repressed.

Proletarian movements, by adopting an internationalist posture in the interests of worker solidarity, are significant as world movements. The alliance between liberal capitalism and socialism against fascism between 1940 and 1945 created the opening for growth and consolidation of proletarian organizations. However, after 1947 intense ideological debates between Cold War warriors both obscured the accompanying struggle between the

19 C. Y. Thomas, 1984, p.98.
20 Patrick L. Baker, 1994, p.161–2.

United States of America and the USSR (Union of Soviet Socialist Republics) over spheres of influence, and contributed to rifts in the international labour movement on the basis of Cold War alliances. Furthermore, the structure of international capitalism partly determined the pattern of growth of Caribbean economies, which in turn helped to shape national policy towards proletarian movements. All the way through to the 1980s and beyond, trade union organizations have grown, decayed, fragmented, undergone ideological shifts, and altered political alignments.

Proletarian movements emerged from the social protest of the working classes of the Caribbean against the abuses of capital. This was a fundamental cause for their emergence, but not for their acceptance by political establishments. Political acceptance and integration of proletarian organizations rested on several considerations. The first was the dominant ideological orientation of the 'Western democracies', and the second was the extent to which political administrations viewed autonomous workers' organizations as a threat to the political, social and economic order. A third factor was the emergence of the middle classes, which often provided leadership of the proletarian movements. The ideological outlook of segments of the middle class partly determined the direction of proletarian movements. But the middle-class orientation was never ideologically cohesive or monolithic. There were really three possible directions for the proletariat on the march. The first and most radical possibility was the establishment of the proletarian state based on the experience of the Soviet Union. The second was to have their dissidence redirected into the channels of 'responsible' unionism. The third was surrender to outright repression. The Caribbean has experienced all three. Middle-class leadership has taken all three orientations.

Caribbean labour 1940–7

By 1940 widespread workers' struggle in the British Caribbean, in Puerto Rico, in Cuba, in the Dominican Republic, and in the Dutch Caribbean had consolidated the concept of trade unionism. The Friendly Society was definitively overtaken by the concept of workers' struggle against capital by the 1930s. St Lucia and Dominica, for instance, though still influenced by the Friendly Society idea, had by the 1950s become part of mainstream developments in proletarian organization. The Second World War itself proved a catalyst for the growth and consolidation of proletarian movements. In fact, the alliance between the USSR and the Western allies against the Axis powers, which can be viewed, as Eric Hobsbawm does, as a 'bizarre alliance' between liberal capitalism and communism, came closest to providing a framework of co-operation between workers in colonial dependent countries, industrialized Europe and the communist USSR. The World Federation of Trade Unions (WFTU), founded in 1945 in Britain, was a product of this alliance. More broadly, democracy and social welfare became intertwined.

The alliance between liberal capitalism and communism laid the foundation for the concept of the popular front (against fascism). It was precisely the popular-front concept which had made it possible for the Communist Party to establish trade unions in Cuba after 1939 with the full co-operation of the dictator, Fulgencio Batista, who until then had routinely butchered trade unionists in the tradition of his predecessor, Gerardo Machado (1925–33). The *abrazos* exchanged between the Communist Party and the Batista government, whose axis was the army, allowed the communists to organize labour rapidly and effectively between 1939 and 1945, ensured peace on the industrial front through no-strike agreements, constitutionally entrenched the rights of labour, and hiked wages. Labour organizations that opposed the arranged peace between labour and capital in Cuba made no headway against the political alliance between Batista and the communist labour organizers until the Cold War.

Since the Western allies also had, in theory at least, fought for democracy and had been militarily victorious in 1945, the concept of democracy was favoured over the totalitarian ideology of fascism. It is for this reason that the dictator Rafael Trujillo of the Dominican Republic (1930–61), who had amply demonstrated his authoritarian outlook by crushing autonomous labour movements in the Dominican Republic in the 1930s, extended an olive branch to labour in the 1940s, in order to establish his democratic credentials. Dominican workers, promptly taking advantage of Trujillo's democratic opening, established several labour federations, resorted to industrial action, and forced major wage concessions from the dictator. By 1946, however, Trujillo, preferring order to the potential disruption of freedom, returned to his more familiar policy of repression. The olive branch wilted. The dictator, having harassed and assassinated the major leaders of the Dominican trade unions, tied the rump of the labour movement to his personalist regime, and paternalistically granted concessions to labour. The labour movement, by its obsequious behaviour, demonstrated its full understanding of Trujillo's Bismarckian message,[21] that labour should look to him rather than to their own organizations for survival and prosperity.

The democratic opening created by the War also provided Haiti in 1946 with a vigorous trade unionism, which, in the words of Mats Lundhal, was to prove 'a parenthesis' in Haitian post-war history.[22] Any hope that the Haitian

21 A. S. Bronstein, 1997, p.8.
22 Mats Lundahl, 1988, p.110.

labour movement would thrive on, or stimulate, democratic tendencies in Haiti received the kiss of death from President François Duvalier (1957–71) who declared that repression of unions would be 'total, inflexible and inexorable.'[23] Duvalier, who had witnessed the role played by organized labour in toppling the regime of Paul Magloire (1950–6) through a general strike, had no intention of allowing the existence of unions to pose a political challenge to his authoritarian regime. For years, Haitian labour organization became an offshore endeavour.

The War stimulated nationalism and anti-imperial sentiment. The curtain came down on the British Empire partly because, from Britain's point of view, reconciling conflicting producer interests in the far-flung empire proved difficult, and partly because of adverse United States sentiment against the British Empire. In addition nationalist movements in India, Africa and the Caribbean nudged Britain into a politics of constitutional decolonization in the Caribbean, which, starting in 1944 in Jamaica, and extending itself through the island chain over the next decade, introduced universal adult suffrage. The latter, by broadening the franchise to include all adults over age 21, allowed, for the first time, mass participation in general elections. As Lawrence Nurse has observed 'The enfranchisement of the (descendants of) the ex-slaves was in its own right critical to the evolution of a system of political democracy and an important step towards decolonization.'[24] This constitutional development facilitated the alliance between proletarian movements and the middle-class agitation for self-government and independence. In turn, nationalist movements, adopting the British approach to socialism, worked in tandem with unions to open the way for national independence. The alliance between political parties and unions created the danger that unions would respond more to the demands of those political parties than to the expectations of the workers themselves. But the opposite was also possible in the 1940s. The strategic alliance of proletarian organizations with middle-class political parties reduced the precarious existence of proletarian organizations. Middle-class political parties, which envisaged an interventionist rather than a *laissez-faire* state, upon achieving power were in a stronger position to legislate in favour of the proletariat where 'legal barriers made union action on the industrial front ineffective or difficult.'[25] In the twilight of empire the British government opted for a gradualist socialism that was to have a pronounced political and ideological impact on the Caribbean colonies. In these colonies, especially following the Moyne Commission (which had been

23 *Ibid.*, p.107.
24 Lawrence Nurse, 1992, p.24.
25 George Eaton, 1987, p.14.,

appointed to examine the roots of the proletarian turbulence in the British Caribbean between 1935 and 1938), the British government gave legal sanction to, and moral support for, the formation of unions. The Moyne Commission's Report emphasized the need for social reform.

Labour was in full process of incorporation as the State endorsed the 'creation of institutionalized channels for the resolution of labour-capital conflict.'[26] The British government, through the leadership of the Trades Union Congress (TUC), advocated 'responsible trade unionism', which was another way of insisting that proletarian movements would not move in the direction of revolution but instead that of harmonization of the interests of labour and capital. The ideological orientation, the financial and legal assistance, as well as the training in principles and practice offered by the TUC to British Caribbean unions, produced a trade-union structure in most of these colonies that mirrored British practice. The consequence was the co-optation of the working class, through the mediation of a Caribbean leadership which was determined to prove to the metropolis that it was politically 'responsible'.

In Jamaica the People's National Party (PNP), founded in 1938 under socialist auspices, linked itself to the Trades Union Advisory Council (TUAC),[27] which also favoured socialism and independence. The leadership of the Oilfield Workers Trade Union (OWTU), and of the Federated Workers Trade Union (FWTU), in Trinidad, had a socialist orientation, calling for nationalization of land and of the petroleum and sugar industry, a 40-hour working week, minimum wages, and a fully elected Legislative Council. The association between reformist political parties, operating from a Fabian socialist principle, and trade unions was also evident in St Kitts, Antigua, Dominica, St Vincent and Barbados. The Barbados Progressive League created the Barbados Labour Party (BLP) and the Barbados Workers Union (BWU) in 1941. In all cases there was either a significant overlap of leadership of unions and political parties, or parties and unions, as in Antigua and St Kitts, shared the identical leadership. Mass-based political parties, then, emerged during the War. In Jamaica, however, it was not the socialist PNP and its TUAC arm that actually dominated the labour scene. That honour belonged to Alexander Bustamante, who founded the island-wide Bustamante Industrial Trade Union (BITU), as a blanket union incorporating sugar, banana and wharf workers. The first elections under universal adult suffrage in Jamaica brought Bustamante's Jamaica Labour Party (JLP) to power in 1944. Unlike elsewhere in the British Caribbean the JLP was not immediately committed to self-government. However exceptional Bustamante may have been in this respect,

26 Ruth Berins Collier, 1994, p.73.

27 Later renamed Trades Union Congress (TUC).

he represented a major tendency in the British Caribbean: to promote an alliance between trade unions and political parties. In Trinidad, however, trade unions evolved independently of political parties. Here, it could be argued that the nationalist movement, identified with the People's National Movement (PNM) of Eric Williams in the mid-1950s, followed the trade union movement. Uriah Butler's efforts in Trinidad to associate his Workers, Peasants and Ratepayers Union with his British Empire Workers and Citizens Home Rule Party failed to achieve political power.

The involvement of the colonial power in the formation of trade unions was not confined to the British Caribbean. The governors of Curaçao in the 1930s also demonstrated a paternalistic interest in labour legislation prompted by the mother country, Holland. The structure of the trade union movement in Curaçao mirrored the Dutch experience of independent and Christian (Catholic) labour unions. The Dutch trade unions, to which Curaçao unions were affiliated, provided training of union leaders and technical assistance. Collaboration with Dutch labour was channeled through the Nederlands Katholiek Vakverbond (Dutch Catholic Trade Congress), and the Nederlands Verbond van Vrije Vakverenigingen (Dutch Free Trade Unions Congress).[28] Trade unions emerging in Martinique and Guadeloupe from 1936 had institutional connections with French labour unions. With the policy of assimilation since 1946 the trade unions of the French islands agitated for the 'same social advantages as the French working class.'[29] Though the unions of Martinique and Guadeloupe had institutional connections with the French labour movement, there was no automatic transfer of legislation across the Atlantic. The gains made by those unions were made possible by proletarian struggle in the Caribbean itself.

While unions in Guadeloupe and Martinique moved closer institutionally to French mainland unions, in Puerto Rico the labour movement, almost synonymous until then with the Federación Libre de los Trabajadores (FLT), in 1940 reduced its association with the US-based labour organization, the American Federation of Labor (AFL). In Puerto Rico, the radical nationalist movement of Pedro Albizu Campos in the 1930s was proof enough that the search for a new and radically different political and social order had preceded the War. However, the perceived failure of the sugar-based union (the FLT), which was affiliated to the American AFL and to the Puerto Rican socialist party of Santiago Iglesias, to focus on the interest of workers created the conditions for the formation of the Confederación General de Trabajadores (CGT) in 1940. The CGT supported the anti-colonial struggle, national libera-

28 René A. Römer, 1981a and 1981b.

29 Cécile Celma, 1987, p.19.

tion, a strong, united proletarian movement, the deepening of proletarian class-consciousness, and greater union democracy. As such it enjoyed an ideological empathy with the populist Partido Popular Democrático (PPD) of Luis Muñoz Marín, who, at least between 1940 and 1945, advocated nationalization, independence and social democracy, denounced economic and political colonialism, challenged the huge United States sugar combines, and addressed issues of cultural nationalism and colonialism. Major strike action by the CGT between 1940 and 1945 in pursuit of improved wages and working conditions was an indication of the new thrust of Puerto Rican labour under the forceful leadership of its Secretary-General, the dedicated and committed Juan Sáez Corales, who had emerged from the ranks of the working class. The CGT not only secured membership in the World Federation of Trade Unions (WFTU) but entered the ranks of the Confederación de Trabajadores de America Latina (CTAL), which advocated class struggle. But the establishment of the CGT, to counter the 'simple anti-hacendado policy (of the FLT) more appropriate to the nineteenth century and perhaps to the early years of US control,'[30] did not mark the beginning of a labour movement necessitating political acceptance of trade unionism. That hurdle had been passed long before, with the foundation of the FLT. The CGT, unlike proletarian organizations in several other Caribbean territories, represented an orientation directing labour organization along a course of autonomy from national politics – without prejudice to a tacit alliance with the PPD. It was dedicated first and foremost to the welfare of labour.

Even without the actions of the CGT, however, significant labour legislation based on United States practice was passed. There were laws increasing the minimum wage in the sugar-cane and home-needlework industries, 'the result of the extension to Puerto Rico of the Fair Labor Standards Act, approved by the US Congress in 1938.'[31]

The Cold War Era

Democracy continued to be a driving force in the growth of trade unions, but after the beginning of the Cold War in 1947, the proletarian movement was influenced by the struggle between Western capitalism and communism, which had succeeded fascism as the new totalitarian challenge to 'the West'.

30 James L. Dietz, 1986, p.222. See also Blanca G. Silvestrini, 1979, pp.121–46 (*passim*).

31 Emilio Pantojas-García, 1989, p.539.

In the mind of Washington, and indeed of the American Federation of Labor-Congress of Industrial Organizations (AFL-CIO), anti-communism and democracy became synonymous terms. Equally important was the post-war hegemonic power of the United States of America, which divided the world into communists and non-communists. The World Federation of Trade Unions (WFTU), which had represented workers without reference (in the interests of international proletarianism) to socialist or capitalist ideologies, weakened considerably following the withdrawal of those countries which identified themselves with the 'democratic West' against the 'totalitarian and communist' USSR. Friends of democracy were expected to follow the banner of the International Confederation of Free Trade Unions (ICFTU), founded in 1949 as an anti-communist alternative to the WFTU by the British TUC and the American AFL-CIO. In the British Caribbean, even unions with strong socialist credentials withdrew from the WFTU and joined the ICFTU. The reluctance of Ebenezer Joshua of St Vincent to leave the WFTU proved politically catastrophic for him. The ICFTU established a hemispheric arm, ORIT (Organización Regional Interamericana de Trabajo), and a Caribbean arm, CADORIT (Caribbean Division of ORIT), in order to ensure a strong voice in 'democratic unionism' which became a synonym for non-communist trade-union organization.

The Cold War, and specifically the formation of CADORIT, to some extent redirected British Caribbean labour organization into the channel of anti-communism. Formerly, British Caribbean labour had grouped itself into the Caribbean Labour Congress, which assumed that the welfare of Caribbean labour would be best accommodated within a broader grouping of independent Caribbean states – in short a Federation of the British West Indies. However, as Caribbean leaders reduced their socialist rhetoric, in rhythm with the new anti-communist dispensation, the Caribbean Labour Congress was allowed to die from inanition.

Other hemispheric labour organizations such as the Mexican-based CTAL, which was committed to proletarian internationalism, and the Peronist ATLAS (Agrupación de Trabajadores Latinoamericanos Sindicalistas), collapsed. Latin Americans' beliefs that they were the best judges of the needs of their proletariat remained largely a sentimental credo in face of the superior financial resources of the ICFTU, and the aggressiveness of AFL-CIO foreign policy.

The Cold War did not necessarily mean, however, that proletarian organizations were constrained in their efforts to better the lot of workers through 'bread and butter' unionism. As the Director-General of the International Labour Organisation (ILO) noted in 1997, 'ideological rivalry upheld a sort of emulation between the countries of both camps to prove their social superiority, including through ratifications (of ILO

Conventions).'[32] For example, in Cuba, the governments of Ramón Grau San Martín (1944–8) and Prio Socarrás (1948–52) underwrote the struggle of the anti-communist wing of the Confederación de Trabajadores Cubanos (CTC) to remove the communist leadership of that organization, so meticulously built up by the communists after 1939 in association with the dictator, Fulgencio Batista. But Cuban unions in the 1950s under the leadership of the *Auténticos* aggressively pursued bread-and-butter unionism.[33] The absence of ideology in workers' ranks has indeed often been noted. 'Strikes multiplied, workers made significant gains, and laws were passed restricting the freedom of action of foreign owners ... Prio (Socarrás) was in a difficult position throughout 1948–52, faced as he was with worker militancy and a labor leadership that was often independent.'[34] The People's National Party (PNP) in Jamaica founded the National Workers Union (NWU) in 1952 as an alternative rank-and-file organization to the TUAC/TUC, which had been dominated by the radical wing of the PNP. The Cold War in Cuba, Jamaica and elsewhere placed some restraint on the communist organization of trade unions, but never prevented proletarian organizations from bargaining with capital.

In the case of the Dominican Republic, the assassination of Rafael Trujillo in 1961 released the pro-democratic and social-reformist political energies of the country, leading to the formation of several labour confederations and political parties that mirrored diverse ideological orientations. In 1961 a general strike, lasting for 12 days, shook the Dominican Republic, now led by Joaquin Balaguer, Trujillo's heir.[35] From then onwards, the proletarian movement effected political alliances, thereby linking their survival with the precarious existence of those political parties. There were communist-inspired unions, unions closely associated with the AFL-CIO, yet others associated with the democratic Left of Venezuela and Costa Rica. Unions, taking advantage of the opportunities opened by the brief democratic-populist regime of Juan Bosch (February to September 1963), allied with anti-Trujillo parties. In the long run, however, the Bosch regime, unable to tame the political forces in the Dominican Republic, succumbed to a conservative *coup d'état* in 1963.

The rise to power of the former lieutenant of Rafael Trujillo, Joaquin Balaguer, who was equally violent in his anti-communist ideology, kept the

32 International Labour Organisation, Director-General, 1997, p.21.

33 The Partido Revolucionario Cubano (PRC), founded in 1934 to pursue the objectives of the failed 1933 Revolution, became widely known as the *Auténticos,* or true revolutionaries. The *Auténticos* gave political support to Grau San Martín and Prio Socarrás in the 1940s.

34 Harold Sims, 1992, p.240.

35 Frank Moya Pons, 1995, p.382.

unions divided and splintered throughout the 1970s. Balaguer was an absolutely faithful ally of the United States during the Cold War, and the terrorism of his anti-communist youth organization, La Banda, helped to ensure that radical proletarian organizations would not threaten the status quo. The reality is that the Cold War provided regimes such as those of Balaguer with the excuse to pursue repressive policies against proletarian organizations on the grounds that they were communist. Balaguer's battle against a strong, autonomous proletarian movement did not rest solely on his negative view of communism; equally important was the need to depress wages in the Dominican Republic in order to attract United States capital. Balaguer, in his single-minded pursuit of programmes for economic development directed by United States capital, differed from the rest of the Caribbean only in style, not in substance. The American Institute for Free Labor Development (AIFLD), originally created in 1962 by the AFL-CIO to combat Castroite communism, actively worked on social programmes – including housing – to lure the Dominican working class into the bosom of the ICFTU and ORIT. The AIFLD, 89 per cent of whose funds came from USAID[36] between 1962 and 1967, financed International Trade Secretariats (ITS – world groupings of national industrial unions in a particular industry or related group of industries), and several of these came to play an important role in the Dominican Republic, and other parts of the Caribbean. Among the ITS to enter the Dominican Republic were the International Transport Workers Federation, and the Postal, Telegraph and Telephone International (PTTI), both of which worked to 'strengthen reformist unions against existing progressive unions in their respective sectors. The government encouraged these efforts by using force against independent labor organizations and leaders.'[37] Labour leaders, during the first half of Balaguer's presidency (1966–78), were assassinated, jailed or fired. Company or 'sweetheart unions' were, however, usually acceptable.

In British Guiana (later Guyana), the AIFLD played a more open political role in 1962 when it maintained anti-Jagan trade-union leaders on its full-time payroll. However, 'after fires and widespread arson resulting in some $40 million damage and CIA engineered strikes and riots in 1963' it proved impossible at that time to remove the Marxist Cheddi Jagan from office.[38] The Cold War dictated that a Marxist party with an important mass following should not be allowed to lead British Guiana into political independence in a United States sphere of influence.

36 Hobart A. Spalding, Jr, 1977, p.260.
37 *Ibid.*, p.270.
38 Jack Woddis, 1976, p.64.

'Developmentalism' in the Cold War era

The hegemony of the United States of America, already evident in the expanding power of the AFL-CIO, was also reflected in its role as the principal source of investment capital in the era of post-war prosperity. The North American bourgeoisie 'saw in the industrial expansion of Latin America opportunities for new investments and for the expansion of capital goods exports.'[39]

The post-war era was marked, then, not only by the start of the Cold War but also by a period of international prosperity that, objectively, facilitated successful bargaining between trade unions and employers in most of the Caribbean. Wage increases, reduced working hours, the principle of the minimum wage, the working week of approximately 40 hours, pension schemes, improved conditions of work and the principle of collective bargaining, widened the field of action of labour unions, which attracted larger sections of the proletariat. In 1938 Jamaica had six unions; in 1947 it had 23, with a membership of 63,000; in 1958 19 with a membership of 63,809; and in 1960 20 unions with 162,100 members.[40] The number of unions in Trinidad grew from 17 in 1938 to 23 in 1947, representing 20,000 workers. By 1958 there were 64 unions with 41,118 workers, and in 1960 36 unions with 53,000 members.[41] By 1965 there were approximately 40 active unions in Trinidad with a total membership of 80,000 or roughly 25 per cent of the work-force.[42] In Cuba, by 1958 some 33 national federations of industries and six provincial federations composed the anti-communist CTC-A.[43] These had a membership of 2,490 unions and a million workers.[44] While the CTC membership was predominantly composed of industrial, commercial and service workers, it actually cut across the whole labour force, including white-collar personnel in banking and other offices, and 500 agricultural unions. Unions represented one of every five Cubans, the average for most of the Caribbean. The CTC, like most of the unions in the Caribbean, had become an umbrella or general union, a structure that had the advantage of greater economy, and reduced duplication of services. The prosperity that followed the War and was to continue until the early 1970s encouraged a harmonization of the interests of

39 Emilio Pantojas-García, 1989, p.553.

40 B. C. Roberts, 1964, p.123.

41 Kelvin Singh, 1994, p.218.

42 Ron Ramdin, 1983, p.203.

43 CTC-A is used to draw a distinction between the CTC as a communist-led organization and the CTC as led by the 'Auténtico' party. After the Revolution it was designated the CTC-R (Revolutionary CTC) to distinguish it from its predecessors.

44 Harold Sims, 1992, p.238.

labour and capital. In other words, labour would forgo the proletarian revolution in exchange for systematic increases in income.

In the United States of America itself the harmonization of the interests of capital and labour had introduced United States workers to a higher standard of living and to the era of mass consumption. However, continued wage increases, by making labour more expensive, encouraged United States firms to seek out cheaper sources of labour outside the mainland. United States unions counter-attacked by co-operating with unions in countries which were hosts to United States capital. Thus the Jamaican NWU, founded as an anti-communist union in 1952, worked very closely with the United Steel Workers of America (USWA), which had a vested interest in maintaining high wage levels in the Jamaican bauxite and alumina industry. The USWA position mirrored a metropolitan orientation that discouraged capital from leaving the United States to invest in areas where labour was cheaper, thereby creating 'unfair competition for job opportunities.' In the case of Puerto Rico, mainland enterprises were attracted by the lower wages in the United States 'commonwealth', and mainland unions operating in Puerto Rico systematically hiked up wages in the direction of mainland rates. This situation created opportunities for small economies to attract capital. Puerto Rico was to take a lead on this road which others were to follow.

The Haitian president, François Duvalier, pronounced that since 'capital (was) fleeing the country for more hospitable shores ... all popular movements will be repressed with utmost rigour.' In Trinidad Albert Gomes, one of the founders of the FWTU, distanced himself from proletarian organizations before the end of the 1940s, when he declared bluntly that he had 'joined battle on labour's behalf' only to live long enough to realize that the 'irresponsibility of labour is today the outstanding threat to that rational ordering of the economic and social forces without which development is impossible.'[45] These two statements demonstrate that the 1940–7 epoch, which had entrenched labour as a legitimate political and social actor in most Caribbean countries, was about to be succeeded by a period dominated by Cold War considerations and by the urge to create ideal conditions to attract capital. High levels of social protection such as trade unions may provide can be perceived as creating 'a competitive disadvantage'.[46]

In the 1950s, in other words, Caribbean leadership dropped the socialist rhetoric of wartime and the immediate post-war years. The substituting rhetoric addressed itself less to social issues and a transforming social policy and more to developmental policies. Economic growth facilitated by the

45 Malcolm Cross, 1988, p.295.

46 International Labour Organisation, Director General, 1997, p.21.

importation of capital on terms which were to its own advantage took precedence over the empowerment of the working class. Not surprisingly the period after 1947 saw a weakening of ties, where they had existed, between unions and governments.

In Puerto Rico, the CGT split as the PPD moved to co-opt it into a new policy orientation minimizing social radicalism in favour of policies that encouraged the creation of a climate friendly to foreign investment. The industrialization programme advocated by Muñoz Marín was intended to be a panacea for Puerto Rico's economic crisis, and a solution to the provision of employment.[47] Muñoz Marín's dictum that 'the worst wage is no wage at all' was a pronouncement of intent to control the demands made by unions. Despite Muñoz Marín's control of organized labour, and the argument that PPD populism had always been determined to entrench 'imperialist capitalism' in Puerto Rico,[48] there is little doubt that he and the PPD were responsible for substantial legislation that benefited labour.[49] Pedro Cabán's comment for Puerto Rico applies almost equally to the entire Caribbean area:

> Popular support for the colonial state as a compassionate force for positive social change was enhanced by progressive social legislation and widespread union approval of the industrial development programme. The legitimacy of the prevailing colonial arrangement was fortified by an ideology of developmentalism that advanced the notion that social equity would be realized under a state-guided programme of foreign-financed industrialization.[50]

However, Caribbean governments found it increasingly difficult, even when they had a pro-labour orientation, to pursue simultaneously a policy of attracting foreign investment and empowering labour, and gradually trade unions recognized that successful bargaining would come to rely more on their agitation than on political alliances. This reorientation was first evident in Puerto Rico, which had led the Caribbean in an economic development programme still generally referred to as 'the Puerto Rican Model.' The CGT of Puerto Rico attempted to maintain its integrity as a strictly pro-worker organization by establishing the CGT *Auténtico*, but the organization was dissolved in 1954. A further effort to establish the Unión General de Trabajadores (UGT) as a new all-embracing autonomous union, free of political links in the

47 Emilio Pantojas-García, 1989, p.551.
48 *Ibid.*, p.557.
49 Gordon K. Lewis, 1963, p.162.
50 Pedro A. Cabán, 1989, p.560.

spirit of the original CGT, weakened rather than strengthened the proletarian movement, however.

The fact is that the generation of employment opportunities for an expanding labour force became central to Caribbean investment policies from at least the 1950s. Governments became less concerned about improving wages and conditions of work for the proletariat than about providing more jobs for the growing number of unemployed. The very social policies of governments that reduced infant mortality and extended the lifespan of the population served to expand the labour force. The economic policies in the larger Caribbean territories had the effect of expanding light manufacturing and services. Therefore, in general, the Caribbean proletariat, which in 1940 had been primarily agricultural, had by the 1960s become mainly employed in light manufacturing industries and in services. In countries such as Guyana and Jamaica a bauxite and alumina industry provided relatively high wages but employed only a small fraction of the labour force. In Trinidad, the petroleum industry continued to provide high-paying employment and between 1973 and 1981 was a beneficiary of the OPEC-generated increase in oil prices. Trinidad's oil production rose from 21.4 million barrels per annum in 1943 to 83 million barrels in 1977.[51] In fact, the oil boom, also facilitated by the discovery of offshore resources, served to postpone tendencies towards confrontation between organized labour and government. In the French Antilles, the primary sector occupied 'no more than 18 per cent of the population as against 48 per cent in 1954 while the tertiary sector has more than doubled, occupying 63 per cent of the population in 1974, compared to 30 per cent in 1954.'[52] The industries introduced, whether in light manufacturing or heavy industry, have been, however, capital rather than labour-intensive, which meant that the size of the industrial working class did not grow significantly in the Caribbean.

Economic policy under Puerto Rican Governor Muñoz Marín led to the complete phasing out of sugar (as in Antigua) which had contributed 48 per cent of total production in 1946. A conscious policy of import substitution created a new industrial base that saw the construction of some 660 factories providing 45,900 new jobs in 1960. In that year Puerto Rico had two oil refineries and a petrochemical complex. Economic change of this nature was not confined to Puerto Rico. In Barbados mechanization and technical changes in reaping and loading sugar-cane reduced factories from 52 in 1946 to eight in 1980. The work-force employed in sugar declined in number from 25,000 in 1946 to 9,000 in 1980. In Jamaica, in 1968, there were 1,382 factories

51 Doddridge Alleyne, 1988, p.22.
52 Raymond Massé, 1980, p.64.

in production and in the 15 years after 1956 the Jamaica Industrial Development Corporation introduced 178 new industries to the island. Despite the expansion of garment production in Jamaica, Barbados, the Dominican Republic and Trinidad, and the significance of tourism in the first three, the sugar industry still remains a significant source of employment in Jamaica, Cuba and the Dominican Republic. In Barbados, information services provided a little less than 3 per cent of jobs. In the larger Caribbean territories, food-processing, beverages, breweries, pharmaceuticals, dairy products, paints and construction have become increasingly important employers of labour. Most of these jobs were less arduous and more prestigious than jobs in the sugar industry, or in domestic service.

In the Dominican Republic Rafael Trujillo's economic policy generated for the first time a proletariat that was not attached to the sugar industry. His regime established factories for the manufacture of flour, cement, bottles, paper, rope and rum. There was a pasteurization plant and the first major hotels were constructed. Trujillo's own tendency to seize arbitrarily the land of smallholders in the countryside swelled the number of Dominicans departing from the countryside for the city. At the same time the introduction of new crops in the countryside intensified *latifundism* and expanded the agro-proletariat. Trujillo's successor, Joaquin Balaguer, oversaw an era (1970–5) which showed one of the most rapid rates of growth in manufacturing in Latin America.[53] In Suriname the mechanization of agriculture, and the expulsion of labour from the agricultural sector – particularly Indians and Maroons – 'produced a new layer of dispossessed farmers in the countryside, who either formed the ranks of the rural proletariat by becoming wage labourers on (large estates) or moved to the city' in search of employment.[54] Rapid urbanization increased the pressure on Caribbean governments to provide employment opportunities.

The weakness of the alliance between manufacturers, sections of the middle class and organized labour was soon to be demonstrated in the determination of political parties to discipline their mass following. As Glen Richards has observed for St Kitts:

> The formation of a trade union government, while seeming to finally establish industrial and political equality between workers and employers, soon led to the transformation of the union itself into an instrument for the disciplining of plantation labour to the needs of the sugar industry. This was possible because the organization of plantation workers, by

53 Catherine Conaghan and Rosario Espinal, 1990, p.560.
54 Sandew Hira, 1983, p.166.

> stifling the independent activity of workers, made them less able to defend their own interests independent of the union leadership... As government ministers, the union leaders now had responsibility for the prosperity of the sugar industry and they sought increasingly to subordinate the special interests of workers to the general needs of the industry.[55]

Economic change in the Caribbean since the 1940s brought more women into the paid labour force. The employment of women in manufacturing, for example, increased from 14.4 per cent in 1946 to 27.1 per cent in 1966 and to 53.0 per cent in 1979 in Barbados.[56] The percentage of female participation in the Barbados labour force has moved from 42.6 per cent in 1950 to 47.4 per cent in 1990. In Jamaica the equivalent figures are 36.4 per cent and 45.7 per cent; in the Dominican Republic 9.0 per cent and 15 per cent and in Guyana 18 per cent and 25 per cent. In all cases the trend was towards increased participation, except for Haiti where there was a decline from 48.8 to 41.6 per cent.[57] The growing integration of women in the labour force has not meant a leadership role for women in trade unions despite the fact that Trinidad had made a start in 1947 with a Women Workers Trade Union – catering 'for all female workers in all trades and industries' – and in 1956 founded a Domestic Workers Trade Union under the auspices of the Caribbean Women's National Assembly.[58]

There is a linear relationship between the structure of Caribbean political regimes and the institutional consolidation of proletarian organizations. In contrast to the efforts of Trujillo to co-opt the Confederación Dominicana del Trabajo (CDT) as an organization expected to look to the dictator rather than to the union for the promotion of workers' interests, in the British Caribbean the pronounced tendency was for proletarian organizations to be linked with political parties. These political links enabled the unions to survive and grow despite the reservations of the employer class. There were few, if any, political parties in the British Caribbean that did not assume a mass base in proletarian organizations. In the case of Cuba, the relationship took the form of an alliance between the Confederación de Trabajadores Cubanos and President Fulgencio Batista. Later, the CTC anti-communist leadership allied with the regimes of Grau San Martín and Prio Socarrás to oust the communists from the leadership of the CTC. After 1959, Fidel Castro and the CTC

55 Glen Richards, 1995, p.294.
56 Roslyn Lynch, 1995, p.29.
57 Franklin W. Knight, 1993, p.37.
58 Rhoda Reddock, 1994, pp.282–3.

1 Water piped to the countryside, St Kitts, early twentieth century

2 Spring Hall windmill and sugar factory, Barbados, early twentieth century

3 Loading sugar cane, Trinidad, c.1930

4 Members of 4H Club, St Kitts

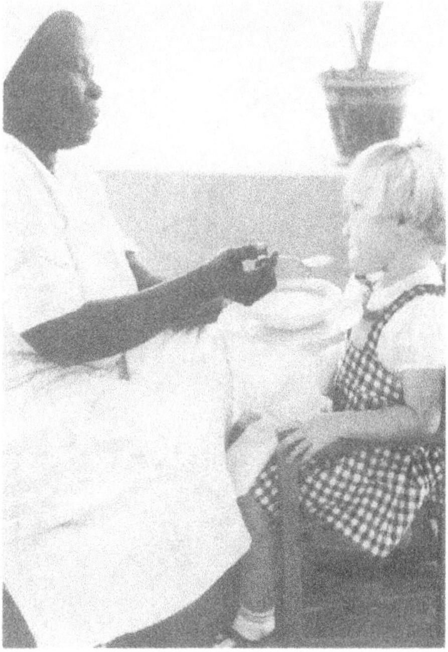

5 Nurse and child, Barbados, c.1950

6 Rural primary school, St Kitts, early twentieth century

7 A. A. Cipriani, Trinidad & Tobago, and T.A.Marryshow, Grenada

8 Tubal Uriah 'Buzz' Butler, Trinidad & Tobago

9 Pedro Albizu Campos, Puerto Rico

10 Norman Washington Manley, Jamaica

11 Alexander Bustamante, Jamaica

12 François Duvalier, Haiti

13 Eric Matthew Gairy, Grenada

14 Presidents Sténio Vincent of Haiti and F.D. Roosevelt of the United States, Union Club, Cap Haïtien, 1934

15 George Padmore (Malcolm Nurse), Trinidad & Tobago

16 Luis Muñoz Marín, Puerto Rico

17 Street demonstration, St Kitts, c.1960

18 Marcus Mosiah Garvey, Jamaica

19 C. L. R. James, Trinidad & Tobago

20 Audrey Jeffers, Trinidad & Tobago

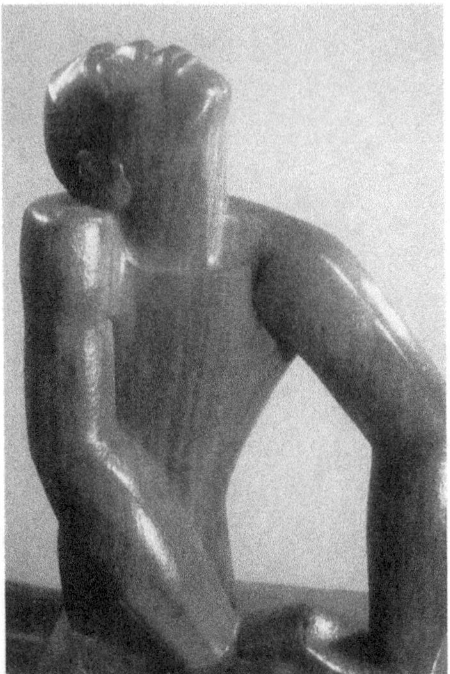

21 'Negro Aroused' sculpture by Edna Manley, Jamaica

22 Immigrant Guadeloupeans after arriving at Ellis Island, New York, 1911

23 West Indian immigrants in the Clapham Common Underground Shelter, London, 1948

24 Drying cocoa beans, Trinidad, early twentieth century

25 Puerto Rican tobacco workers, early twentieth century

26 Jamaican Chinese army volunteers during the Second World War

27 West Indians in the RAF and ATS, London, during the Second World War

28 Eric E.Williams, Trinidad & Tobago

29 George Price, Belize

30 Fulgencio Batista, Cuba

31 Rafael Leonidas Trujillo, Dominican Republic

32 Fidel Castro (centre) and comrades, Cuba, 1957–8

33 Gerardo Machado, Cuba

34 Juan Bosch, Dominican Republic

35 Forbes Burnham, Guyana

36 Cheddi Jagan, Guyana

37 Janet Jagan, Guyana

38 Emperor Haile Selassie of Ethiopia greeted by Prime Minister Errol Barrow, Barbados, 1965

39 Marine oil rig, offshore Trinidad, c.1960

40 Natural Gas plant, Point Lisas, Trinidad & Tobago

41 Piarco International Airport, Trinidad & Tobago, 1950

42 Public Library, Bridgetown, Barbados

worked out an accommodation in which the communist leadership of the CTC was restored and the labour organization became one of the major columns of the socialist revolution. Proletarian organizations were tied into production and policy so that the workers' movement is fundamentally a part of the bureaucratic Cuban socialist state. The socialist revolution could assure the worker of significant social benefits in education, in health and in housing. It could not, however, grant such benefits without a reduction of the autonomy previously enjoyed by the Cuban labour movement. Benefits for labour were now assessed in relation to the broader social and economic objectives of the socialist regime, which insisted that prior to the Revolution the workers' movement had been a selfish beneficiary of Cuba's 'distorted' capitalist economy. Close links between the revolutionary and labour leadership have not meant the end of labour history, as such, in Cuba. However much unions had become weakened in the 1960s they were allowed a stronger voice in the early 1970s, with the Cuban government's commitment to 'rectification' in identifying problems and proposing solutions at the workplace.[59] The highly centralized state apparatus provided openings for workers to negotiate with managers concerning elemental norms of production, and to receive material incentives. In some cases these 'elemental norms' were set so low that workers were able to exceed their quotas in record time and win material bonuses. Not surprisingly, after the mid-1980s material incentives were reduced without a return, however, to the 'moral incentive' period of the Guevarist 1960s.[60]

Allied with the issue of institutional links with political parties is the larger issue of the extent to which proletarian organizations have been victims of middle-class politics. One view is that the proletarian movement was emasculated by middle-class politicians who, determined to prove themselves 'responsible' political leaders, allied with the proletarian movements in order to control and integrate them into the political system. This view is supported by the reality that proletarian movements in the Caribbean hardly ever threatened to blossom into proletarian revolution. Even in Cuba it was Fidel Castro's very adept manipulation that converted the anti-communist CTC into a bastion of support for the socialist regime. A second, and to some extent opposing view is that the alliance between unions and political parties had positive consequences for both unions and parties. This view is supported by the fact that in several Caribbean countries the empathy between marginalized middle-class leaders and the working classes ensured a significant degree of acceptance of the role of proletarian organizations in reducing the

59 Frank T. Fitzgerald, 1989, p.285.
60 *Ibid.*, p.305.

excesses of unbridled capitalism. The view is also supported by the reality that labour unions have enjoyed greatest acceptance and success in an environment of middle-class-led democratic constitutionalism, allowing for broad participation in political decision-making, and have had the most precarious existence where political authoritarianism – for example in the Dominican Republic – has pursued, until recently, a politics of mass exclusion. In that Republic, the military autocracy of Rafael Trujillo, followed by the civilian Bonapartism of Joaquin Balaguer (1966–78 and 1986–96), gave little room for labour to function autonomously from a highly centralized administration. The efforts by Juan Bosch in 1963 to encourage the growth of autonomous unions in the Dominican Republic failed because his regime was caught between the demands of the radical element of his own party which sought proletarian revolution, and the extreme Right which mounted an anti-communist reaction.

The weakness of both interpretations is that they assume a homogeneous middle-class and working-class agenda. In fact, the middle class was divided along ideological lines. In Jamaica, the NWU and the TUC leadership was dominated by members of the professional middle class (including journalists and lawyers), the one segment centrist, the other revolutionary and reformist. In the eastern Caribbean, the labour movement, as it evolved in Antigua, Montserrat and St Kitts, was directed not by members of a professional middle class, but by a leadership recruited from the upper segments of the working class. Equally important, an examination of the political and legislative action of Vere Bird and Robert Bradshaw of Antigua and St Kitts, respectively, demonstrates the same concern for 'developmentalism' that came to characterize all Caribbean leaders. Joaquin Balaguer and Juan Bosch of the Dominican Republic can only be described as of middle-class origin, but their political orientations were very different. Revolutionary credentials belonged to the middle-class lawyer, Fidel Castro, rather than to the working-class leader, Robert Bradshaw. At the same time, in Guyana, the Marxist revolutionary, Cheddi Jagan, was a dentist who was the child of sugar workers, and his political rival, Forbes Burnham, was a middle-class lawyer. The dictates of national development rather than middle-class ideas – if such things exist – determined policy. In the words of Carl Stone, 'as elected party leaders won greater control of the levers of public policy making, their priority concern for labour was pushed into the background as they confronted larger questions of development policy and found they had to reconcile conflicts between a variety of social interests.'[61]

61 Carl Stone, 1986, p.102, quoted in Lawrence Nurse, 1992, p.35.

Proletarian movements since the 1970s

Chronologically, the Second World War epoch and its aftermath together constituted the most successful period for proletarian organizations. Throughout the Caribbean gains were made in new collective wage agreements, and in some cases, pension funds were established. Antigua, for example, passed minimum-wage legislation as early as 1937. Under this law, which was sparingly used, 'the government could appoint a minimum-wage advisory committee to investigate the conditions of employment in any occupation and to make recommendations as to the minimum rates of wages which should be paid.'[62] Jamaica adopted, in 1938, minimum-wage legislation and a national minimum-wage law was passed in 1974. In Martinique and Guadeloupe there was a legal minimum wage, and wages were linked (in theory) to the cost of living. In Puerto Rico, both Puerto Rican and United States 'minimum wage authorities set minima on an industry-by-industry basis and have vigorously pursued a policy of narrowing the gap between wage rates on the island and the standard federal minimum wage rate applied on the mainland.'[63] The closer Puerto Rico moved towards the mainland standard of wages, of course, the less attractive it became as a target for investment. Up to 1956 the government of Curaçao regarded instigation to strike as a threat to law and order. There had been, however, incremental improvements in the legal position of labour unions: the Shop Closing Act (1972), the Sickness Insurance Act (1936), and the regulation of labour contract in the Civil Code in 1941. In 1958 the Act on Collective Labour Agreements was introduced.

A factor weakening the relationship between unions and political parties was that several Caribbean governments often came into possession of the 'commanding heights of the economy'. In 1978, the ILO concluded that in the English-speaking Caribbean 'the facts that these governments are major employers in their own right, fix minimum wages for many workers, and often play an active role in the settlement of labour disputes means that they already are extensively involved in the regulation of labour markets.'[64] What was true of the British Caribbean was even more accurate for the Dominican Republic, where Rafael Trujillo's extensive properties became state property upon his assassination in 1961. The Dominican State, no less than the socialist Cuban State, held the commanding heights of the economy.

The consequences were predictable. Firstly, legislation to restrain labour took precedence over promotion of labour welfare in the interests of industrial

62 Baldwin Spencer, 1978, p.111.

63 T. M. Dickey, 1981 (abstract).

64 International Labour Organisation, 1978, p.22.

peace. Secondly, there was, in some countries at least, growing disillusionment with the association between politics and trade unionism.

Workers, recognizing the distance between them and their political representatives, reverted to the traditional strike weapon, which in Antigua destroyed 2,000 acres of sugar-cane in 1950 and 70,000 tons in 1961.[65] In the latter country, the view that political allies had betrayed the workers was manifested in the decision of George Walter to break with Vere Bird and to establish his own union and party. In Jamaica, the Inter-Trades Union Advisory Council (ITAC) was established in the 1970s precisely to protest against 'political unionism' in the country. In short, the National Workers Union and the Bustamante Industrial Trade Union were viewed as adjuncts to the People's National Party and the Jamaica Labour Party, respectively. In Barbados, the Barbados Workers Union, linked traditionally to the Barbados Labour Party, severed its links with the latter, and entered into a closer relationship with the marginally more radical Barbados Democratic Party. Efforts by the Barbados Labour Party to establish a national rival to the BWU failed.[66] In Curaçao, after a major upheaval in 1969, the association between political parties and unions became even looser. At the same time, in Cuba the socialist revolution hitched the unions ever more closely to the ruling party. In the Dominican Republic unions attached to political parties never seemed happy with the connection since the parties were clearly pursuing their own ideological objectives. The trade-union movement has itself splintered because of competition between rival unions. Whatever the causes of disputes, Caribbean governments pursued the policy of ensuring peace on the industrial front.

Caribbean governments passed legislation to ensure peaceful industrial relations. As early as 1952 the Jamaican government passed the Public Utilities Undertaking and Public Service Arbitration Law. In 1965 and 1972 the Trinidad government passed the Industrial Stabilization Act (ISA) and the Industrial Relations Act (IRA). In 1975 the Jamaican government passed the Labour Relations and Industrial Disputes Act (LRIDA). In 1967 Antigua and Dominica introduced a Trade Disputes Act, and in 1970, the Bahamas passed its own Industrial Relations Act. The Guyana Labour Amendment Act was passed in 1984. In the Dominican Republic President Balaguer conceded the right of unions to organize, but in practice placed multiple constraints on labour. In 1966, the Dominican government froze wages in the public and private sector. A 1969 law made 'collective negotiation possible only when employers and the government decided to do so.' The replace-

65 Glen Richards, 1995, p.294.
66 Hilary Beckles, 1990, pp.197–204.

ment of union boards by means of firing unco-operative labour activists (who did not enjoy job immunity) was another method adopted to emasculate labour.[67] In 1974 the Dominican Republic's Minister of Labour was given greater powers over the internal affairs of unions. Ministers of Labour from Jamaica through to Trinidad and the Dominican Republic were given powers to appeal to 'national interest' in order to abort major strikes. The Dominican Republic is now, however, in its post-Balaguer period. In 1990 the government of the Partido Revolucionario Dominicano conceded the right of free-zone workers (mostly women) to organize unions. In 1992, a new labour code was issued which revised the ceiling on compensation for redundancy, extended the scale of overtime pay rates, 'offered holiday bonuses, repealed rules restricting night work and employment of women in work underground, and offered protection of the principle of freedom of association.'[68]

In Puerto Rico the Governor extended a long hand to control 'every phase of labour relations, even that of arbitration of grievances.'[69] In the 1970s Puerto Rican labour organizations, despite ideological and organizational divisions, reasserted their autonomy and demonstrated a heightened political consciousness and a greater sense of solidarity.[70] There was a corresponding decline in the strength of AFL-CIO affiliated unions. The PPD under Hernández Colón was unable to assert the domination over the Puerto Rican unions that Muñoz Marín had been able to exercise. In the French Caribbean departments of Guadeloupe and Martinique, the institutional links with French political organizations have been reduced. Guadeloupan and Martiniquan sections of the Parti Communiste Français (PCF) have, for example, renamed themselves the PCG and the PCM and adopted the slogan of autonomy. The search for autonomy on the political front has been accompanied by the gradual loosening of the Antillean workers' movement 'from its organizational moorings with French union and political forces.'[71] The times had changed. Unions no longer assumed that the interests of workers were best fostered by political alliances or links with metropolitan unions. The developmental strategies pursued by Caribbean governments had demanded from labour sacrifices that were not producing the expected material rewards. 'Disproportionate income gains for industry relative to labour resulted in a very skewed pattern of income distribution. As the industrialization process gained momentum ever larger amounts of accumulated capital

---

67 Rosario Espinal, 1988, p.187.
68 A. S. Bronstein, 1997, p.11.
69 Miles Galvin, 1979, p.150.
70 Pedro A. Cabán, 1989, p.587.
71 Alain-Philippe Blérald, 1983, p.158.

were repatriated to the United States.'[72] Caribbean governments resorted to compulsory arbitration when they came to the conclusion that free and unrestrained collective bargaining was dysfunctional in relation to their broad economic policies. Unions responded by behaving autonomously. Since 1969, the year in which workers revolted against the conservative labour politics of the Curaçao government, unions have asserted their autonomy of political parties more vigorously.

Labour legislation in the Caribbean became, then, directed towards reducing the power of labour, and placed industrial action increasingly under the umbrella of legislation which provided for arbitration of disputes. Unions were not necessarily happy with this arrangement, since the settlement of labour disputes on the shop floor was generally preferred to settlements by legislative enactment.

Strike action in Caribbean states was not necessarily a consequence of wage disputes. An equally large number of strikes occurred over union representation, unjust dismissals, and perceived violation of contracts and agreements. Firstly, the union leadership was happiest when it could organize either the most highly paid workers or attract workers in an industry (such as sugar) which had large numbers of workers. In Jamaica alone there were 157 such disputes in 1972, 135 in 1974, 201 in 1975 and 158 in 1976 – even though there were statutory provisions for recognition.[73] Secondly, some employers continued to resist union representation and agreements that they construed as unjust. Governments, on the other hand, were not necessarily hostile to labour; but in many cases had to respond to the demands of the class coalitions that constituted the political parties.

Labour legislation did not succeed in reducing labour disputes, partly because the relationship between unions and governments had not only loosened but in many cases had ceased to exist. Puerto Rico experienced wildcat strikes (1968–73), and squatters' movements (1966–72, 1977–83), in addition to riots and social violence. The Dominican Republic experienced 'food riots from 1984 (reflecting) popular anger and frustration with the adjustment policies and the ineffectiveness of existing institutions and organizations in articulating popular demands.'[74] In Jamaica, the pervasiveness of strikes in 1969 was celebrated in the song, 'Everything Crash'. In Jamaica, Guyana and Trinidad disputes increased over the period 1972–6 (see Table 4.1).

72 *Ibid.*, p.157.
73 Compton Bourne, 1978, p.45.
74 Catherine Conaghan and Rosario Espinal, 1990, p.567.

TABLE 4.1 Strikes in the English-speaking Caribbean, 1972–6

Country	*1972*	*1973*	*1974*	*1975*	*1976*
Jamaica	395	371	443	551	471
Trinidad	334	656	800	662	684
Barbados	n.a.	36	36	30	45
Guyana	175	172	136	129	284
Antigua	n.a.	70	102	109	129
St. Kitts	nil	54	6	12	20

Source: Compton Bourne, 1978, Table 1: Labour Disputes, p.45.

Guadeloupe had an average of nine labour disputes per annum between 1970 and 1976, and 134 between 1977 and 1979. Martinique experienced an average of seven disputes per annum for the period 1970 to 1976.[75]

As job security became more of an issue workers resorted to intermediate pressure tactics to have their cases heard. Sick-outs and go-slows became very common in the 1960s and 1970s. The fact is, however, that the union leadership, despite growing professionalism, continued to be faced with the problem of lack of information on the ability or inability of employers to pay. Compton Bourne has also noted that bargaining capabilities are also 'severely limited' by the problem of 'labour productivity and by the macro-economic effects of particular wage settlements. Wage changes lag behind price changes, partly as a consequence of the fixed-term nature of contracts.'[76]

The decline of the post-war 'golden age' since the 1970s, the consequent decline of the harmonization of labour and capital, the devastating impact of 'structural adjustment' in some countries of the Caribbean, have impressed on, or rather reinforced in the collective mind of organized labour, the limitations on the power of national governments to act favourably on behalf of workers. Workers and the unemployed bore the brunt of structural adjustment that dogmatically imposed devaluation. The new metropolitan orthodoxy of 'globalization', free trade, deregulation and 'privatization' that rapidly followed the policies of structural adjustment reduced even further the autonomy of governments of the Caribbean, which have been pressured into surrendering the 'commanding heights' of the economy. Advances in technology, while potentially allowing for maximum efficiency in an enterprise, posed major threats to security of employment, leaving unions to face the

75 International Labour Organisation, 1980, p.635.
76 Compton Bourne, 1978, p.36.

difficulty of agitating in order to maintain their real wages in the context of inflation and a precarious job market. Proletarian agitation can then carry with it the stigma of anti-nationalism. Technological advance in a region that has always had 'surplus labour' has long been an issue, in respect of technical changes in the sugar industry, for example. The challenge for unions was clearly how to look after the welfare of labour while offering opportunities to the unemployed in a world becoming more polarized into very rich and very poor. Almost in the footsteps of socialist Cuba, trade-union leaders, who have become far more professional, envisaged unions as engaging in dialogue on national policy. Trade-union leaders had little choice but to seek a 'balance between defending trade-union rights and promoting the overall development of the country.'[77] Jamaican unions may pragmatically assess 'privatization' case by case, Puerto Rican unions may more generally oppose 'privatization',[78] but in the long run unions have the awesome reality to face that the mobility of contemporary international capital 'will affect economic development policy and labour laws and practice.'[79] Cuba lost the protected market of the post-*glasnost* USSR and COMECON during the 1990s and the English-speaking Caribbean is expected to lose protected markets in Europe early in the twenty-first century. From the point of view of the trade-union leadership, the trends in the global economy posed a fundamental threat to worker well-being not only from the point of view of securing higher wages, but from the point of view of job security. The Director-General of the ILO makes the point very well:

> Although globalization obliges us to re-examine the basic concepts and values of standard setting and specify their meaning or relevance, it also instills, in an insidious and more radical way, doubts as to the pre-eminence of these values. The end of the ideological, social and political confrontation which divided the world, combined with globalization, is ushering in a new *Weltanschaung* with the result that globalization is becoming an end in itself. By a strange irony of history, the 'dawning of a new age' is no longer expected to occur with the end of the class struggle, which finally reaches its fulfilment in the withering away of the State; this time will only come now once the State has been stripped of its social and economic prerogatives and a global civil society emerges which is answerable only to the laws of economic rationality, itself the

77 Dwight Nelson, 1986, p.49.

78 Interview with Mr Lloyd Goodleigh, President of the Caribbean Congress of Labour, Kingston, Jamaica, November 1998.

79 William C. Doherty, 1994, p.53.

> sole guarantee of a future so full of prosperity and promises that people forget the harshness of their present circumstances. This new form of ideology of progress persists in affirming, like all that have preceded it, that human progress is more important than actual human beings; and it might well, as the same causes engender the same effects, result in the same disillusions.[80]

Contemporary labour unions in the Caribbean have negotiated (often with sophisticated legal assistance), resorted to strike action, both affiliated with political parties and reduced that affiliation when necessary, worked closely with the ILO and labour organizations such as the AFL-CIO. However, trade unions in most areas of the formerly British Caribbean have also taken various initiatives to improve the welfare of their membership and now more than ever emphasize 'productivity training'. The often adversarial relationship between capital and labour accompanies efforts to reduce the disadvantages of unions at the bargaining table by education in economics, sociology, politics and international trade.

Unions have always placed emphasis on worker education, a policy that in the contemporary world has become even more essential. In this respect Barbados, always passionate about education, has conducted courses in trade unionism for its members since 1961. The BWU has links with the Commonwealth Trades Union Council, the AIFLD, the Canadian Labour Congress, the Frederich Ebert Stiftung (FES), the Postal Telephone and Telegraph International (PTTI) and the International Union of Food and Agricultural Workers. Worker-based credit unions have expanded from four in 1966 to 24 in 1995 with assets of over $187,000,000.[81] The union also purchased about 98 acres of land for the purposes of a residential Labour College (established in 1969), a housing complex, a shopping centre and recreational facilities. In Jamaica, the Joint Trade Union Research Development Council (JTURDC) was established in 1980, a combined effort of the BITU, NWU, the TUC and the Jamaica Local Government Organization (JALGO). In Puerto Rico in the late 1970s, similarly, workers' unions established organizational linkages in the interests of greater solidarity among workers in face of austerity packages. The Trade Union Education Institute was established at the Mona (Jamaica) campus of the University of the West Indies in the 1970s and a Labour Relations Institute is located at the University of Puerto Rico. Guyana has established the Hubert Critchlow College, Trinidad & Tobago the Cipriani Labour College. Suriname has estab-

80 International Labour Organisation, 1997, pp.5–6.

81 Evelyn Greaves, 1996, p.190. The sum is in local currency.

lished a Labour College and in Curaçao there is the Caribbean Institute for Social Formation (CARISFORM).

The end of the Cold War, for the time being, is causing unions to recognize a community of workers' interests (at home and abroad), which had been partly obscured by the Cold War and by competition between the unions themselves. In Jamaica there is a growing awareness of the need for a united front of labour to combat globalization. In 1992 Jamaica established a Jamaica Confederation of Trade Unions, which, conceived as an umbrella for all unions, already has 14 attached to the organization. All the major unions form part of the new Confederation. Unions recognize that globalization demands a new cross-national co-operation. The Caribbean Congress of Labour, successor to the Caribbean Labour Congress, now embraces unions in the wider Caribbean to include Suriname and Bermuda.[82] Its dialogue with unions in the Spanish Caribbean is an indication that the movement is in closer touch, institutionally, with the states that form part of the new Association of Caribbean States.

Summary

When the Caribbean proletariat took direct action in and after the 1930s to improve social and economic conditions they were challenging the contemporary political, economic and social order, which had been fashioned by the liberal epoch after about 1870 when the sustained expansion of world trade, and even favourable terms of trade for the Caribbean in cacao, tobacco and sugar, had simultaneously created fundamental disparities in the quality of life of the employer and the working classes.

The challenge to that order in the 1930s was sustained by the democratic thrust during and immediately after the Second World War, by the revolutionary myth of a proletarian state in some quarters, and in others by 'economism' – pragmatic day-to-day victories won by negotiation, withdrawal of labour and strategic alliances with sympathetic political parties. The hope of proletarian revolution grew fainter in face of the dominant metropolitan ideology of democracy, anti-communism, the superordinate power of North American capital, and above all by the reality that post-war prosperity and optimism made it possible for proletarian movements to succeed in bringing gains to workers. The hopes of non-revolutionary proletarian organizations were grounded in the misguided belief that the ultimate removal of the social abuses of capitalism would be corrected by sustained negotiation.

82 Interview with Mr Lloyd Goodleigh, President of the Caribbean Congress of Labour, Kingston, Jamaica, November 1998.

Dashed also was the hope that political independence – strongly supported in the post-war epoch even by metropolitan nations – guided by the middle classes in the Caribbean would provide the political tools for the creation of a society marked by social justice, by the mixed economy – neither capitalist nor socialist – and even by the socialist economy, which had converted the USSR from a backward capitalist state into one of two super-powers.

But the middle classes represented every shade of ideology, the working classes were perhaps less committed to proletarian revolution than to material improvement (for the aspirations of the proletariat were not uniform), and post-war prosperity came to an end by the early 1970s. The messianic political leadership in existence at the start of the proletarian surge amounted to little more than a temporary challenge to the prevailing social order whose leaders had more in common with their metropolitan counterparts than with the people. The working classes in countries such as Trinidad & Tobago and Guyana, both divided by ethnicity, gave greater emphasis to their cultural and racial uniqueness than to broad workers' struggle.

Political acceptability was another matter, which varied according to specific national traditions and institutions. Authoritarian regimes such as those in Hispaniola gave little or no scope for proletarian movements to assert themselves without victimization or murder. Pre-revolutionary martyrdom in Cuba helped to create autonomous working-class organizations, which in the 1950s fell under the sway of corrupt leaders and gangsters led by cynics, who, prior to 1959, used the instruments of murder and corruption (along with negotiation) to persuade the Cuban working class of their dedication to worker welfare.

For the most part the more sophisticated leadership of proletarian organizations has become more aware of the international and national issues constraining them. A continuous education process, gaining in sophistication, now enables unions to compromise and bargain between the Scylla of low wages and the Charybdis of unemployment.

5

DECOLONIZATION, POPULIST MOVEMENTS AND THE FORMATION OF NEW NATIONS, 1945–70

James Millette

OF all the major unintended consequences of the Second World War, the decolonization of the European colonies was the most improbable of all. When the War began it seemed at first to be just another white man's war. This is to say that ever since the French Revolutionary and Napoleonic wars, the first of the really major modern conflicts to convulse the globe, it was an article of faith mutually agreed between the major combatants that however fierce the warfare might be between the European powers, it was *their* war: a war between civilized combatants for the realization of civilized objectives in no way altering the general dominant relationship exercised by the European powers and peoples over those they had long colonized. Of course, the pretence was always challenged; in part by the need to recruit the indigenous or other oppressed peoples to help pursue these conflicts, and in part by the fact that the colonized and the oppressed often perceived the schisms and the conflicts among the ruling élite as providing them with unrivalled opportunities for pursuing their own causes. The French Revolution was barely two years old when the slaves revolted in St Domingue. The Civil War in the United States was still in its infancy when Frederick Douglass recognized it as presenting an unrivalled opportunity for promoting the cause of slave emancipation: 'God be praised!', he said. And Wendell Phillips, the abolitionist, expostulated: 'I [now] believe in a sunny future, because God has driven them mad: and in their madness is our hope.'[1] Before the First World War had ended, colonized Arabs, Indians, Africans, and other peoples of African descent in the Caribbean and the United States had developed new notions of self-worth, and in particular a repudiation of the subordinated position to which the European and European-descended peoples had relegated them. As Britain had discovered in Palestine, it was one thing to fan the flames of Arab nationalism against the Turks, it was another thing to cope with the demands of aroused nationalists for an end to the British occupation of Egypt.[2] In fact with so much evidence to the contrary, the greatest improbability was the per-

1 Lerone Bennett, Jr, 1993, p.172.
2 Denis Judd, 1968, p.291.

sistent belief among the major powers that a war of the magnitude of the Second World War, especially given its declared aims, could be pursued without unravelling the whole edifice of colonial rule.

Yet, of all the questions facing the Western European powers at the end of the Second World War none was to prove more persistent than the colonial question. For more than three hundred years the principal colonial powers had enjoyed a relatively undisturbed possession of their colonies in the Caribbean. Then, in the late eighteenth and early nineteenth centuries nationalist revolutions had taken place to the north and to the south of the Caribbean, resulting in independence in the United States and the newly established republics of South and Central America. From these processes the Caribbean islands and associated territories (the Guianas and British Honduras) had been nearly totally exempt. With the sole exception of Haiti and the Dominican Republic, none of the other European possessions had acceded to independence until Cuba did so in 1902. By 1945 nothing else had changed. Yet between 1945 and 1962 the balance was to be tilted, not completely, but significantly, in favour of self-government and independence, especially in the anglophone and, to a much lesser extent, in the Dutch Caribbean.

That this was so had as much to do with international developments as with the march of events taking place in the Caribbean itself. Even before the War an increasingly broad-based anti-colonial nationalism had been breaking out all over the world. In fact, in respect of this development the Second World War merely marked the realization of a trend that had originated in the wake of the First.[3] In the Middle East, in South and South-east Asia, in China, throughout Africa, but particularly in West Africa, and in the Caribbean, the colonized peoples had been showing themselves increasingly capable of challenging and threatening to throw off the yoke of colonialism so long imposed on them. Colonized peoples, commonly regarded as mere factors of labour – producers of raw materials, consumers of imported manufactures and objects of a fierce and unrelenting oppression – were standing up and proclaiming themselves nationals of the countries in which they lived, with a right to be free and a right to be heard.

Until 1917 these views found no real articulation in what passed for serious discourse in international affairs. But in the era of the First World War, anti-colonial views and activism became increasingly popular. Intra-imperialist conflicts in Africa, the upsurge of Arab nationalists against the European powers seeking to take the place of the collapsed Ottoman Empire, and the unintended outcomes of the European civil war that raged between 1914 and 1918, provided fertile ground in which the seeds of colonial nationalism could sprout and grow.

3 Henri Grimal, 1978; also Rudolf von Albertini, 1969.

In addition the new rhetoric of self-determination, weakly expressed in Woodrow Wilson's Fourteen Points, and much more clearly and unequivocally proclaimed by the new Union of Soviet Socialist Republics (USSR), or Soviet Union, became an inseparable part of the struggle to promote a separate and distinctive ideological platform in opposition to capitalist and imperialist world domination. Thenceforward, the struggle for socialism and national liberation became inseparable counterparts. Of course, as time passed, such a linkage complicated the struggle for self-government and independence enormously, but there is no minimizing the role played by the new ideology in consolidating the self-perception of colonized workers as a class, in stiffening their resolve and in dignifying their efforts to improve their material condition and gain social and political agency for themselves. In international affairs, the Soviet Union tilted the balance in favour of the colonized and semi-colonized peoples by specifically recognizing new states struggling to free themselves from the grip of the established imperialist states, and by entering into treaty agreements with them. Afghanistan, Turkey, Mongolia, Iran, China and Yemen were some of the beneficiaries of these policies, as were India, Indonesia and Korea for other reasons.[4] The beginning of the modern, organized challenge to colonial rule in West Africa, resulting in the emergence of the West African National Congress in 1920, was in some part due to the anti-colonial ferment then felt most strongly in Asia and the Middle East. Ethiopia, a very traditionalist African state, responded to the new influences with expected ambivalence. In the mid-1920s, emigré Russians were employed by the young Ras Tafari as skilled workers and technicians, and diplomatic representation was extended to the new revolutionary state.[5] The United States, too, was impacted by the influence of 'Bolshevism'. The 'Industrial Workers of the World', the 'Wobblies', added a new verse to their organization's song:

All hail to the Bolsheviki!
We will fight for our class and be free
A Kaiser, King, or Czar, no matter which you are
You are nothing of interest to me;
If you don't like the red flag of Russia
If you don't like the spirit so true,
Then just be like the cur in the story
And lick the hand that's robbing you…[6]

4 Jack Woddis, 1967, pp.29 ff.
5 Harold G. Marcus, 1995, p.72.
6 Robert K. Murray, 1964, p.39.

In the Caribbean, as well as in the ranks of prominent Caribbean activists abroad, some sort of radical philosophy was nearly always manifest. Abroad, Claude McKay, Hubert Harrison, Cyril Briggs, W. A. Domingo, Otto Huiswood, Eric Walrond, Ferdinand Smith, Joel A. Rogers, Una Marson, A. A. Maloney, Jesús Colón, Arturo Schomburg and others provide evidence of a broad-ranging ideological representation that had one thing in common, namely its Caribbean origins. Many of these individuals were believed to be communist.[7] In the Caribbean it was no coincidence that some of the staunchest supporters of the decolonization movement, destined to play crucial roles in its unfolding, were men and women of action like George Padmore, C. L. R. James, Cheddi Jagan, Richard Hart and Claudia Jones, who were not only anti-colonial advocates but also self-proclaimed Marxists.

Marcus Garvey and the UNIA, as well as the Pan-Africanists, though often at odds,[8] contributed vital new ingredients to the building of an angry and militant anti-colonial consciousness in several sectors of the colonized populations. Taken together, all these factors contributed to the construction of an increasing national consensus that was clear on the need to oppose colonialism, if at the same time unsure about how far to go in opposing it and what precisely to replace it with. By the middle of the second decade of the century factors in the region and outside of it were clearly beginning to influence the course of constitutional development in the region, and to set the stage for changes which would, in due course, result in political independence for the majority of the British West Indian colonies.

At the end of the Second World War, therefore, the West Indies still comprised an amalgam of independent, colonized and semi-colonized territories. Haiti, the Dominican Republic and Cuba were independent in name, but dependent in fact. All of them had experienced the subordination that flowed from a too-intimate historical contact with the 'colossus to the north' and were in different stages of responding to it. Typically they were all ruled by dictators whose origins owed something, if not everything, to the consistently hostile United States attitude to the struggling nationalist movements in each of those countries. The introduction of American-style national guard formations had fostered, and in Haiti had strengthened, the tradition of unpopular dictatorships which ruled with the support of an entrenched military at the

7 See Winston James, 1998, pp.1–3 and chap. 2. As James put it: 'It is no exaggeration to say that the FBI files on 'Negro Activities' in the United States during the 1920s are also very much intelligence reports on *Caribbean* radical activity in America, and especially in New York City'; p.3, his emphasis.

8 See, for example, Garvey's letter of 1 August 1921 to the League of Nations protesting against its recognition of the Pan-African Congress led by W. E. B. DuBois, quoted in Franz Ansprenger, 1989, p.131.

expense of struggling national democratic organizations and their leaderships.[9] The island of Puerto Rico was on the threshold of experiencing a modification of its colonial status, the metamorphosis into a quasi-autonomy which would endure for the rest of the twentieth century and into the twenty-first. Together with St Thomas, St Croix and St John, Puerto Rico comprised the United States colonial complex in the region. In the rest of the Caribbean a patchwork of European colonial systems prevailed, from the Bahamas, Bermuda and the British Virgin Islands in the north, on through the French and British West Indian islands of the eastern archipelago down to the Guianas in the eastern Caribbean, the Dutch islands of Aruba, Curaçao and Bonaire, and British Honduras and Jamaica and its dependencies in the west and north-west.

In the previous decade and a half the world had changed in ways which neither the colonizers nor the colonized had yet fully grasped. Until the early 1930s colonialism and neo-colonialism had remained for the most part virtually unchallenged. But the decade was still young when revolution broke out in Cuba in 1933, thereby marking the beginnings of another phase of revolutionary unrest; largely suppressed in the 1930s and 1940s, it erupted again in 1953 at Moncada six years before the triumph of the Castroite revolution. In Puerto Rico the radical nationalist movement of the late 1930s, led by Pedro Albizu Campos, signalled the growing restiveness of the Puerto Rican people under colonial rule.[10] Thenceforward, until the early 1950s, the constitutional question remained a primary concern for insular and metropolitan political figures.

The larger French- and Spanish-speaking islands of the northern Caribbean were all, to different degrees, under the formal or informal subordination of the United States. As early as 1904 the Roosevelt Corollary to the Monroe Doctrine set out in unmistakable terms the determination of the United States to exercise a 'police power' over the affairs of the independent Caribbean states.[11] Before that the Platt Amendment had grudgingly conceded independence to Cuba on condition that the right of future United States intervention in Cuban affairs be specifically recognized.[12] Under the aegis of the Roosevelt Corollary, Haiti and the Dominican Republic endured long periods of occupation by the United States that had the effect, among other things, of neutralizing the nationalist formations and facilitating the emergence of dictatorships, which ingratiated themselves with United States

9 See, for example, Michel-Rolph Trouillot, 1990.

10 Manuel Maldonado-Denis, 1972, pp.112ff; also Juan Angel Silén, 1970 (1971).

11 Roosevelt's Fourth Annual Message, 6 December 1904, in Louis L. Snyder, 1962, pp.408–13.

12 See Louis A. Pérez, 1986 (1991).

imperialism by ruthlessly suppressing what remained of popular nationalist sentiment in those two states.[13]

The word that best explains the relationship between these countries and the United States is neo-colonialism, except that in its classical form neo-colonialism posits what the United States was loathe to admit, namely, the political independence of the state or states concerned. Driven in part by racist ideology, in part by economic motivation and in part by apprehension over the role of the European nations in the Caribbean, the United States regarded Caribbean independence as an inconvenience to be modified by a unilateral imperialist policy which was consistently implemented by successive United States governments between 1904 and 1934.[14] It was not until the administration of Franklin Delano Roosevelt and the inauguration of the Good Neighbor Policy that a change in form, if not in substance, occurred. As the Cuban crisis of 1933 demonstrated, the United States, though unwilling to intervene militarily, was by no means reluctant to influence the political outcome consequent on the fall of the Machado dictatorship. In doing so it helped to spawn another dictatorship, that of Fulgencio Batista whose excesses triggered the emergence of the Cuban revolution of 1959 and a nationalism much more radical than any that the island had ever known.[15] In this sense it is difficult to speak of the emergence of a truly independent state in Cuba outside of the context of the Cuban revolutionary process.

Additionally, in the period of the First World War the United States embarked on two initiatives which effectively closed the door to national aspirations in the Danish Virgin Islands and Puerto Rico. As elsewhere in the West Indies, popular nationalism had been growing in the Danish islands, significantly under the influence of trade-unionist and working-class agitation. Internally, Danish ineffectiveness and neglect facilitated the development of a broad-based disenchantment with the colonial power, and a growing sentiment in favour of a new, and hopefully, better relationship with the United States.[16] For its part, the United States was also exhibiting a renewed interest in the islands. Ultimately, partly to forestall their transfer to an unfriendly European power, possibly Germany, and partly to promote her strategic interests in the region, she purchased the Virgin Islands from Denmark in 1917. Thus ended a long chapter of negotiations with the Danish Crown dating back to 1867. The treaty documents offered the inhabitants of the islands two options: either to

---

13 Suzy Castor, 1971; Gérard Pierre-Charles, 1975; Georges Michel, 1996; also Felix Servio Du Coudray, 1976 and Julio Gautreau, 1986.

14 Dana G. Munro, 1964, 1974; also Lester D. Langley, 1982.

15 Luis E. Aguilar, 1972; also, David E. Cronon, 1959, pp.538–67.

16 The impact of working-class activism on the decision to sell the islands to the US is well told by Gregory La Motta, 1989, pp.178–95.

become United States citizens, or, providing that they opted to do so within one year of the treaty signing, to retain their Danish citizenship. Even so they were free to renounce their Danish citizenship at any time thereafter and assume the citizenship of the United States. As United States citizens their civil rights and status would be determined by the United States Congress subject to the stipulations contained in the treaty of purchase.[17]

In the case of Puerto Rico, the period 1898 to 1917 witnessed the gradual establishment of United States sovereignty over the island in such a way as to foreclose the realization of a Puerto Rican nation state. Military rule was replaced by a civil administration in 1900, and 17 years later United States citizenship was extended to the island's inhabitants. Rexford Tugwell, one of the more honest and enlightened United States governors of the island, opened a window, in the 1940s, to the self–interested motives that lay behind this escalation of the status of the island's citizens. '[The grant of citizenship] was done in a sudden realization of strategic possibilities', he wrote, 'not as part of a policy, and, significantly enough, in time of war when Puerto Rican loyalty was important.'[18] Plainly stated, the grant of United States citizenship to Puerto Ricans was inspired more by the strategic considerations of the United States, and in particular the interest in expanding the military draft to the island, than by any other factor. To this day, some Puerto Ricans still declare themselves mystified and perplexed by the decision.[19] To an even greater degree than in the case of Cuba, the claims of the nationalist movement were swept aside and the prospects for independence were relegated to the distant future. As such the 'status question', by which is meant the determination of the island's future relationship with the United States, has become a permanent issue in the island's politics.[20] It is indeed a curious anomaly that Puerto Rico, possessed of an autonomous constitution in the waning days of Spanish imperialism and perceived as an inspiration for the English-speaking Caribbean in the 1950s and 1960s in political as well as in economic matters, has remained in the limbo of an undetermined colonial relationship with the United States while the majority of the territories of the anglophone – and Suriname in the Dutch – Caribbean have proceeded to self-determination and independence.[21]

The emergence of new nations in the Caribbean in the twentieth century, therefore, consists largely of the emergence of self-government and independence in the former British West Indies. These territories apart, Suriname alone in the Netherlands Antilles has acceded to independence. The

17 Charles Callan Tansill, 1968.
18 Rexford Guy Tugwell, 1947, p.70.
19 Juan García-Passalacqua, 1984, pp.32–3, and n.3.
20 See Surendra Bhana, 1975.
21 Gordon K. Lewis, 1963 (1974).

other entities in the Netherlands Antillean zone are still, at the time of writing, colonies and semi-colonies of the Dutch, in different stages of affiliation with the metropolitan country. In these territories, the post-war experience witnessed the manifestation of the two distinctive trends replicated in the wider Caribbean. The collapse of the Netherlands in the Second World War and the Allied, essentially British, occupation of Aruba and Curaçao, stimulated the emergence of a metropolitan outlook favourable to the ultimate decolonization of the Dutch colonies as early as 1942.[22] Queen Wilhelmina, then in exile in London, projected the reform of the empire to facilitate the emergence of internal self-government in the colonies.[23] But decolonization did not necessarily connote independence. Only in Suriname did the decolonization process result in independence, in 1975, and that was followed by prolonged revolutionary instability between 1975 and 1989.[24] In the other territories, the trend has been towards a sort of associated statehood which, unlike the development of that process in the English-speaking Caribbean, has stopped short of independence while avoiding the formal political integration which at one time seemed distinctly possible. Some similarity with the British West Indies is suggested by the fate of the federal idea, such as it was, in the Netherlands Antilles.

In the case of the French colonies, the most important development has been the declaration of the French government in 1946 conferring departmental status on the territories concerned.[25] Since then the prospects of nationhood for the French colonies have been submerged by the insistence that the colonies are overseas departments (*départements d'outre-mer*) of France, a declaration that marked the triumph of assimilation over separation. In its early days the initiative was promoted as a peculiarly French approach to the decolonization question, allegedly intended, in due course, to result in independence. The fact that the new doctrine applied to all French colonies alike masked its real implications for the Caribbean colonies. When the African colonies, caught up in the 'winds of change' sweeping the continent, began to abandon assimilation and to opt for independence, departmental status emerged as inimical to independence in the French Antilles. At the same time that the African colonies were becoming independent the French West Indies were becoming locked into a new subordinate relationship with France which has now reached the stage of virtual constitutional ossification.

It was in the British West Indies, therefore, that the most widespread, and consistently militant challenges to colonial rule were made. Between

22 Fitzroy André Baptiste, 1988, chap.3; and Peter C. Verton, 1990a, p.67.
23 Peter C. Verton, 1990b, p.205.
24 Sandew Hira, 1983, pp.166 ff.
25 Guy Lasserre and Albert Mabileau, 1972, pp.82–102.

1934 and 1939, hunger marches, strikes and various forms of labour unrest, often accompanied with violence and the destruction of property, challenged the industrial and political order and laid the basis for the many significant changes that were to come.[26] Alarmed by these developments the British government responded by establishing the Moyne Commission which in due course reported to the effect that there was little hope for social accord in the future without significant trade-union and political reform. Though the implementation of its recommendations was delayed by war, the coming of the peace ushered in a period expectant with the need for change and for social and political progress.

By the end of the War two of the main facilitating concessions had already been made: trade unions had been legalized and, in the political arena, adult suffrage had been introduced, beginning with Jamaica in 1944 and gradually spreading throughout the other colonies thereafter. Where, in the early 1930s, the Crown Colony system in its varied forms was ubiquitous throughout the British West Indies, in the period after 1945 it embarked upon a transformation which, though agonizingly slow in the eyes of some anxious contemporaries would, nonetheless, result by the early 1960s in the coming of political independence to Jamaica and Trinidad & Tobago.

In the wider world, developments were taking place which also provided a favourable backdrop to the events taking place in the region. At the start of the twentieth century, to all appearances, imperial policy was firmly on the side of the maintenance, some thought in perpetuity, of the existing colonial arrangements. It was admitted that from time to time minor changes might be made so as to accommodate the imperial convenience, or to assuage some of the political demands of local inhabitants. But there was no expectation of an early advance to representative government for the majority of colonies, or of the even more dizzying ascent to responsible government status for those already possessed of the representative system. The fortunes of war, if nothing else, had significantly changed that perspective. Of all the major European imperial powers, Great Britain alone had avoided defeat during the war. Belgium, Holland and France had been overcome, with the fate of the metropolitan imperial centres themselves for a long time seriously in doubt. Britain had survived only because of the alliance forged between itself, the United States and the Soviet Union after 1941. Accordingly, a new reality had emerged in the Caribbean and in the world.

In the Caribbean, the European imperial powers were forced to accommodate the interests and the aspirations of the United States in the region;[27]

26 See O. Nigel Bolland, 1995; and chap.2, this volume.
27 See, for example, Richard Hart, 1999, chaps 33–4.

in the world the ascendancy of Western Europe was, for all practical purposes, a thing of the past. It soon became plain that, in colonial affairs as in other spheres of international business, the interests and the dictates of the two new super-powers, the United States of America and the USSR, had to be taken seriously into consideration. A significantly different international environment was in the process of emerging. The United Nations, unlike the League of Nations, embodied an entirely different concept of international relations. Where the latter talked of 'mandates' and 'tutelage', the former was firmly in support of self-government and independence, as its Charter indicated.[28] That commitment provided an international arena in which, between 1945 and at least until the liberation of the Portuguese colonies in the mid-1970s, the independence struggles of the colonies were often second only to the Cold War issues (with which they were often intertwined) in claiming the attention of the United Nations.

Yet, if someone standing on Jamaica's Blue Mountain peak on 1 August 1838 could, by chance, have had a perfect and unrestricted view of the islands and territories of the Caribbean Sea and had dared to surmise that, in about 125 years, the sons and daughters of ex-slaves would be rapidly and aggressively taking their freedom and independence from the European powers by which they were then colonized, such a person would have been declared insane and confined to the nearest lunatic asylum. In 1824, 14 years before emancipation in the British West Indies, a lonely voice crying in the wilderness had proposed immediate independence for the West Indian colonies.[29] The main impediment standing in the way of that objective, argued the author, was 'the deserved hatred of the injured Negroes, and the hypocritical professions of loyalty, the insatiable rapacity, the domineering insolence, of the present race of West Indian proprietors.' John Taylor was, of course, way ahead of his time. And yet, in the main, this is the history of the 25 years between the end of the Second World War and the outburst of youthful rage associated with the Black Power unrest which swept through many of the colonies and ex-colonies of the Caribbean in the years immediately leading up to and including 1970. By that time political independence was a reality in all but a few of the Caribbean territories, and indeed the dominant paradigm was influenced not so much by the realization of political independence as by the perception that what had been achieved had not gone far enough and needed to be complemented by new struggles aimed at achieving economic as well as political independence. The most serious of all the rebellions against economic dependence and neo-colonialism took place in Trinidad & Tobago in

28 United Nations Charter, 1945: Colonies and Trust Territories, Article 73.
29 John Taylor, 1824.

1970, but the whole region was affected by a new spirit of criticism, frustration and rejection of the post-colonial status quo to such an extent that, within a decade of the accession of Jamaica and Trinidad & Tobago to independence, doubts were being expressed in several Caribbean colonies about the supposed superiority of independence over the colonial condition.[30]

Historical hindsight has the unfortunate habit of collapsing periods of time into swiftly disappearing blobs on the chronological scale. Twenty-five years is not an unreasonably long time, but it is an aeon to those condemned to live it out, for the most part, in a fever of unfulfilled expectations, with no certain knowledge of what the future would bring. And so it was in the British West Indies. By 1962 two of the major colonies would be independent, but even they did not know that in 1945. At the close of the War constitutional government was still prescribed by three crucially important factors upon which colonial government had always relied. Its fundamental character was sexist, racist and unrepresentative.

The first important factor had to do with the presumption that colonial government existed for the exclusive purpose of promoting the interest of white males. By custom, white British men were entitled to enjoy constitutional prerogatives in the colonies which they would have enjoyed had they stayed at home. Because the colonies were peopled by non-Whites as well as Whites, the former living under one form or the other of social, economic and political subordination, British males in the colonies frequently enjoyed, in practice, political privileges which many of them, given their social and economic status, would not have enjoyed at home. Nor were these privileges automatically transferable to other white men in the colonial situation, whether or not they were free.[31]

Secondly, participation in colonial government was also withheld from white women, whatever their status. It is difficult to know which probability was more abhorrent to the official colonial mind: the active involvement of black and coloured men, or the active participation of white women in the political system. But the reality was that white women, unlike white men, were not participants in the political process in the Caribbean until the 1920s. And when women were given the vote, it was black women and not their white counterparts who emerged as elected and nominated participants in the

30 A review of the pertinent literature suggests that such was the case in the French and Netherlands Antilles, as well as in several of the remaining British colonies in the region. See, for example, Malcolm Cross and Gad Heuman, 1988.

31 Until at least the early nineteenth century, nationality and religious belief were important factors in determining access to political participation in the British colonies. See *Cambridge History of the British Empire*, 1929–59, vol. II, pp.150–2. Also James Millette, 1985, pp.9–10.

political process. It is a remarkable, but easily understood fact, that the very status that white women possessed as the privileged darlings of the social elite also stood in the way of their participation in the 'dirty game' of colonial politics.

Thirdly, colonial government was minority government. The Crown Colony system, right up until the outbreak of the Second World War, reflected not the triumph of inclusion but the persistence of exclusion of the vast majority of the black and coloured electorate throughout the region. One of the peculiarities of the British West Indian colonies was their unique demographic composition. Unlike the vast majority of slave environments in the Americas, the British and French colonies of the Caribbean were possessed of populations which were initially overwhelmingly made up of slaves. An inverted V-shaped social structure was the norm: large numbers of slaves resided at the bottom, much smaller numbers of free Coloureds and Blacks occupied the middle, and a tiny white minority dominated from above. This was typical for the islands of the first sugar revolution, very atypical for nearly all other slave environments.

In Cuba, the Dominican Republic, Puerto Rico and Brazil, as well as in the United States, however small or however large the slave population might be, it was far from being for most of the time the numerically dominant proportion of the population. At emancipation in 1886 Cuba had about half as many slaves as the whole of the British West Indies had in 1838; but slaves constituted a minority of the Cuban population. In Brazil (1888) and the United States (1863), at emancipation the slave population was accounted in millions, but those millions were far outnumbered by the larger territorial populations of the countries concerned. As unrepresentative, or as undemocratic, as government might have been in those countries, that characteristically derived from causes not exclusively associated with the phenomenon of slavery. As oppressed as the ex-slaves and their descendants were, they were nonetheless oppressed *minorities*. In the smaller Caribbean islands, on the contrary, it was the *majorities* who were oppressed.

In the British West Indies, slavery and its legacies could not therefore be dissociated from the tradition of minority government. What is more, it was in the British West Indies, more than in any other part of the New World, that the racialization of slavery was most developed. Not only did emancipation not purge society of the racial prejudices formulated and spawned in defence of the slave order, but it also marked the beginning of the application of racial prejudice and race-based oppression to a legally free black population. That is why, in the British West Indies, the post-emancipation period did so little to address the question of popular political representation. But it is also why, given the marked demographic imbalance, the prospects for nation-building in the British West Indies were so positive once emancipation had taken place. By a curious inversion of historical determination the Caribbean has become the principal, and arguably the only, environment in the world in which ex-slaves have moved from slavery to political empowerment, save and except for the Mamelukes in Egypt in the pre-modern period.

That those prospects were not immediately realized in the British West Indies is part of the historical record. Elsewhere in the Caribbean as in the case of Haiti, Cuba and the Dominican Republic, emancipation was achieved cheek-by-jowl with some concurrent attempt at resolving the national question, peculiarly and logically formulated (especially after the Haitian and Latin American revolutions) in terms of the constitutional break with the formally existing colonial powers. In these environments the challenge of nation-building was directly addressed in the nineteenth century. Emancipation and self-determination were inseparable. In the British West Indies, on the other hand, the post-emancipation period constituted a transitional stage between slavery and political participation and was at best a distant prelude to nationalist reification. The post-emancipation societies of the British West Indies, again because of their unique demographic structure, simply did not possess the numbers of Whites who could either promote the development of a national consciousness, or boldly strike out on their own to cut the imperial umbilical cord and assert the claims of nationhood. Precisely because they were minorities, racially at odds with the broader population, they struggled to maintain the relationship with the mother country, or sought in times of stress to exchange the colonial relationship for immersion in the United States or Canada, or some other state, where their minority position could be converted into a majority with all the security that such a conversion was thought to bring.

For all of these reasons, the outstanding political lesson of the post-emancipation period was that political privilege could not automatically be inherited by the unrepresented masses merely as a consequence of the emancipation process. And yet, if there was a nationalism to be realized in the British West Indies it could only be realized by the agency of the masses. Martin R. Delany, the black American emigrationist, had returned from visiting the Niger in 1859 with his Jamaican colleague Robert Campbell, convinced that the claims of black people would never be respected 'until they are presented in a national capacity'.[32] For many reasons, the nationalist potential in the British West Indies remained dormant for nearly sixty years after emancipation. Not so in other parts of the region: nation-building in the Caribbean began with the revolution in the French colony of St Domingue. Emancipation and nation-building were, ultimately, parts of an integrated

32 Martin R. Delany, 1859, p.210.

process, as they were to be in the Dominican Republic and Cuba. In the aftermath of the overthrow of the plantocracy in St Domingue, and the successful defence of the revolution from external attack, a new state was born on 1 January 1804. Haiti was the first Caribbean nation-state to emerge at the beginning of a process that witnessed, over roughly the next 160 years, the impact of an uneven but persistent decolonizing movement. In 1865, the Dominican Republic, partly as a result of the impact of the Haitian Revolution, had finally and permanently established its own independence as the second Caribbean nation-state. By the turn of the century in Cuba and Puerto Rico, the slave question was already settled and the national question was firmly on the agenda. As events turned out, they were lost to Spain, but immediately denied nationhood by virtue of the colonial and neo-colonial relationship foisted upon them by a newly emergent United States imperialism.

In the anglophone Caribbean it was not until the years between 1897 and 1937 that the nationalist sentiment began slowly to develop. Within that period it grew in strength as a result of myriad impulses. Emerging full blown at the centre of a process that formally came of age at Montego Bay in 1947,[33] it passed into history, in its political aspects, with the failure of the Jamaican referendum in 1961, and subsequently of the West Indian Federation in 1962.

It is obvious, therefore, that the period embracing the two world wars was significant in the development of West Indian nationalism. The baby that was conceived in the period of the First World War was born by the end of the Second. In 1944, before the war was ended, adult suffrage was introduced in Jamaica, and the two-party hegemony over Jamaican politics represented by the People's National Party (PNP) under the leadership of Norman Manley, and the Jamaica Labour Party (JLP) led by Alexander Bustamante, had begun. For the next two decades the rivalries between these two parties provided an important background to the struggle for self-government and independence in the wider anglophone Caribbean. Elsewhere in the region important modifications of the constitutional status quo prior to 1939 were also made. Adult suffrage was introduced in Trinidad & Tobago in 1946, in Barbados in 1950, in British Guiana in 1953, and generally in the other islands in due course. By the beginning of the 1950s important political organizations, commonly associated with trade unions, had emerged or were in the process of emerging. Typically they were led by individuals claiming to speak on behalf of the increasingly restive masses partially organized in trade-union organizations that spread throughout the region as a whole.

33 Conference on the Closer Association of the British West Indian Colonies, Montego Bay, Jamaica, 11 to 19 September 1947, 1948.

In these new circumstances the acquisition of the vote was enormously influential, but not decisive. As events showed, in Trinidad & Tobago in 1950 and in British Guiana in 1953, the vote facilitated the more effective engagement of the masses in political activity, but political authority still remained in the hands of the colonial government. Thus, while it was impossible to return to business as usual after the war, it was still possible to frustrate and obstruct the swift march of the populist momentum that was developing. History will never know what might have transpired in the British West Indies in the absence of the new, emergent, international political culture favouring decolonization and national independence. But it is reasonably safe to say that, in the absence of such a culture, the emergence of new nations in the anglophone Caribbean would have been either very long delayed or undertaken in circumstances which would have yielded much less autonomy and independence than was eventually achieved.

Even before the War ended important inroads had been made in the prevailing imperialist psychology that had prevailed at its outbreak. The contradiction between imperialism and a war allegedly fought for decency and democracy was constant. Nowhere was the paradox more real than in the principles of the Atlantic Charter, jointly proclaimed by the leaders of the United Kingdom and the United States on 12 August 1941. The Charter was a difficult document: it was very good for propaganda, but not so good for imperialism. In fact, its genesis lay in the contradiction between the United States and Great Britain on the question of colonialism. Roosevelt, in particular, felt that there was a kind of ignominy in helping Britain to win the war, if the outcome would be the simple reinstatement of the old colonial system. Churchill, on the other hand, felt that the British Empire was not Roosevelt's business and that, in any case, (perhaps more to the point) the United States was itself an imperial power, if perhaps less directly so than Britain.[34] Speaking in the House of Commons on 7 September 1941 Churchill sought to reinterpret the Atlantic Charter so as to have it believed that the promise of 'sovereignty, self-government and national life' enshrined in the Charter applied only in respect of their restoration to those European states invaded and occupied by the Nazis. The joint declaration of the two Allied powers had, in his estimation, no direct significance for the 'progressive evolution of self-governing institutions in the regions and peoples which owe allegiance to the British Crown.'[35] Even so, the Empire of his urgent imagination consisted principally of India whose subordination to the British had always been one of history's larger inconsistencies. When the 'midnight hour' arrived in India on 25 August 1947 there was probably not a single British administrator who

34 Wm. Roger Louis, 1978, p.26 and n.48.

35 Great Britain Parliament, 1940–1, vol.374, cols 68–9.

recognized the Indian solution as one that might be logically emulated or automatically applied in other parts of the empire. And while Indian independence led to the concurrent independence of Pakistan and was followed by the decolonization of Ceylon and Burma, it remained very much an anomaly, seen by some as unconnected to the general question of colonial freedom as was the Irish independence that preceded it, or the emergence of an independent Israel from the collapse of the British mandate in Palestine in 1948.

Ten years were to pass before the Gold Coast Revolution, as George Padmore called it, resulted in Ghana's independence in 1957 and the beginnings of a wider movement of decolonization in Africa and the Caribbean. What is also often ignored is the fact that even the British Labour Party, which seemed more likely than the Conservatives to contemplate the liquidation of the British Empire, was an unreliable asset in the fight for colonial self-government. In fact, the Labour Party out of office was always more militantly anti-colonialist than Labour administrations ever were in government; A. A. Cipriani of Trinidad had discovered that to his cost in the crucial period of the 1930s.[36] It might have been that, in opposition, Labour politicians tended to veer to the Left, while in government they cleaved to the Right. Or again it could be that in opposition more attention was paid to what the Fabians were doing or what the acknowledged anti-colonialists such as Fenner Brockway, Labour member of parliament for Eton and Slough, were up to. Whatever the reason, prominent Labour politicians often spoke out against the prospects of colonial liberation.

Herbert Morrison, Home Secretary in the Churchill wartime Cabinet, and a prominent and sometimes revered Labour Party member, publicly expressed his belief in 1943 that '... to talk about grants of full self-government to many of the dependent territories for some time to come ... would be like giving a child of ten a latch key, a bank account and a shot-gun.'[37] Ernest Bevin, Labour Foreign Secretary after the War (sometimes called the Labour Churchill), insisted in the Commons that the British Empire should be maintained since its fall would mean that 'the standard of life of our constituents would fall quite considerably.'[38] It is not

36 Sahadeo Basdeo, 1983, especially chaps. 3 and 4.

37 *Manchester Guardian*, 11 January, 1943.

38 Cheddi Jagan, 1966, pp.172–3. Bevin's view was complemented by that of John Strachey, Minister of Food, who on 20 January 1948 told the Commons: 'Our national position is really too grave to warrant any indulgence in our particular opinion on the methods of overseas development. By one means or another, by hook or by crook, the development of primary production of all sorts in the colonial territories and dependent areas in the Commonwealth in far more abundant quantities than exist today, is, it is hardly too much to say, a matter of life or death for the economy of this country.'

an overstatement to say that, in the first half of the twentieth century, it was economic interest or imperial calculation, not altruism, that inspired even the most liberal-sounding schemes for colonial assistance emanating from London.[39]

In West, East and Central Africa (ignoring for the time being the strange character of secondary colonization in South Africa), between 1947 and at least the late-1960s, Labour and Conservative governments alike showed little real disposition to provide unequivocal support for self-government except on terms and conditions inimical to the long-term interests of the colonized. To be blunt, they often had to be dragged kicking and screaming to the negotiation table, sometimes to meet there with nationalist leaders who had only recently graduated from the British colonial prison system because of their effective mobilization of the thousands and tens of thousands of ordinary people whose interests they represented.

One of the major dilemmas, of course, was social. The colonial leaders were leaders because they stood at the front of the workers and farmers, the unemployed and the dispossessed – in a phrase, the masses. British administrators well understood that these were leaders of a different type, likely under favourable circumstances to be inimical to the long-term well-being of British influence and interest. Educated or uneducated they were, to the British, agitators and malcontents who had to be disciplined and, if possible, frustrated in their search for political power. If only they knew! In retrospect, the agitator and the radical of yesterday was often quickly transformed, by the delights of office, or the prospect of it, into the responsibly conservative statesman or trade unionist, quickly distancing himself from his roots, political and otherwise, except at election time. So Norman Manley had his Bustamante, Butler his Rienzi, Clement Payne his Grantley Adams, Williams his Gomes, and Jagan his Burnham. But, of course, the British did not know. And much time, and ink, was spent spying on 'communists' and other dissidents, writing voluminous reports about their activities, their affiliations and their objectives, and in endless harassment and political manipulation, the end result of which was the hoped-for creation of a reliable political class to which power could be transferred. To a large extent they succeeded, even if at the time they did not know it.

---

39 See Claus Füllberg-Stolberg, 1989, pp.142–63. Füllberg-Stolberg argues that the Colonial Development Act of 1929 was 'primarily intended to mitigate the crisis in England itself.' The 1940 Act, on the other hand, 'in practice only "touched up" the worst eyesores produced by the economic and social deficiencies of British colonialism and then only in areas afflicted with unrest, the West Indies, for the principal audience to which these reforms were directed was the United States, with its anti-colonialist attitudes' (p.141).

Another major dilemma was economic; here success was more difficult to achieve. Everywhere in the colonial world, the closer one came to the post-war period the greater was the frustration and the more desperate the struggle to break out of the cycle of impoverishment and destitution imposed by a wretchedly exploitative Crown Colony system. Colonialism might or might not have endured longer had it been economically efficient. But it was not, and that was its Achilles heel. It was the grinding poverty of the masses that brought them out into the streets and exposed them to the wider discourse about political and ideological change. And it is in the context of this discourse that they came to believe what the new political leaders were telling them, that they had first to seek the political kingdom after which, in the Biblical phrase, 'everything else would be added unto them'. This socialization, however, brought with it an increasing awareness of class as well as race and created a political culture fiercely unforgiving of the Crown Colony system and its inability to deliver economically.

It was not only that the system *could not* deliver; it was not *meant* to deliver. And so in the final analysis, it was the starkly exploitative character of Crown Colony government that was its own undoing. The economic exploitation that the Crown Colony system engendered was devastating in its effects on the working people of the subregion. As with the planters in the slave period, the colonial administrators in the era of the Crown Colony government were their own worst enemies. Between the turn of the century and the 1930s nothing had happened to demonstrate that there was, either in the United Kingdom or in the colonies, a sense of urgency in bringing the system to an end. In fact, as Gordon Lewis has so succinctly argued, the Crown Colony system was perfectly suited to the task of doing nothing slowly.[40] In place of checks and balances it revolved around an unending series of tinkered adjustments. It was like a stick fight: a constant 'carraying' for position with the unstated objective of always frustrating the general will.

The typical colonial state, in its Crown Colony apparition, was founded on the presumption that the less popular the political administration, the better. Participation in government was for the chosen few operating within a virtually closed circle, entry into which was by way of a narrow doorway guarded by Downing Street. The operating principle was exclusion, not inclusion. Included were virtually all adult white males, from among whom, by virtue of either office, social standing or wealth, individuals were chosen to participate in the legislature. Excluded were all non-Whites, except for those few who, by an amalgam of colour, talent and compromise, recommended themselves to the colonial and metropolitan administrations. Black and brown

40 Gordon K. Lewis, 1968.

people had to catch the eye of the Governor and earn his favour, usually by distancing themselves as much as possible from the broader population. That done, they would then be admitted by nomination into the holy of holies, the Legislative Council, thereafter to support openly and faithfully the policies of the colonial administration.

The supreme premise upon which all of this was based was the primacy of the metropolitan economic interest. If mercantilism had been abandoned in the metropolitan country it was alive and well in the colonies, at least in its neo-mercantilist form. Ever since the middle of the nineteenth century this had meant that the colonies were stripped of the old colonial protection on the metropolitan market but saddled with the obligation of adhering to a continuing preference for metropolitan manufactures at home. After 1865 and the expansion of the Crown Colony system, the neo-mercantilist exploitation of the British West Indian colonies entered upon a new phase. The British government became directly involved in providing the environment in which metropolitan capital could prosper, and it became itself a major entrepreneur. Wherever and whenever profitable new industries developed, British capital and the Crown Colony system could be perceived working in tandem for the greater good of the imperial interest.

It is an interesting reflection that many of these industries might well not have developed *without* Crown Colony government. Is it only coincidence that Trinidad, the most prosperous of the British West Indian colonies from at least the last third of the nineteenth century, and an oil producer from as early as the first decade of the twentieth, was also the mother of all the Crown Colonies, pioneering that system in the early nineteenth century and being (but for the complicated case of British Guiana) the last of the major West Indian colonies to leave it in the 1950s? In the case of Jamaica, it has been argued that the 'constitutional change of 1866 was central in accounting for the genesis of the tourist industry' in that island.[41] And there is little doubt that among the factors accounting for the choice of Trinidad and British Guiana as the prime areas for capital investment in the nineteenth century was the fact that they both possessed subordinate political systems.

Colonial government had always been inspired by the desire to promote the economic interest of the mother country. Founded as it was on the mercantilist principles of the closed imperial economy, the primacy of imperial over colonial interests, and the zero-sum competition in trade, commerce and financial strength between rival European countries, colonial government had always

41 Frank Fonda Taylor, 1993.

been concerned with economic gain. As time went on, however, there was always a tension between political control and economic management. On the one hand it suited England, for all the well-known reasons associated with the development of parliamentary government in the seventeenth century, to extend the same principles to the colonies. But, on the other hand, it was a positive embarrassment in practice to try to harmonize those principles with the goals of maximizing imperial benefit from the exploitation of colonies responsible, in large part, for their own internal government. In the British West Indies, in the nineteenth century, perhaps the island of Barbados provided the most important example of this difficulty. There, unlike in Jamaica and the Crown Colonies, the Barbados legislature successfully thwarted the implementation of the Encumbered Estates Act which, after 1854, effectively transferred substantial amounts of plantation property from West Indian to British hands at what today would be called 'fire sale prices'.[42] That transfer of property was the precursor to the penetration of large-scale British metropolitan capital into the sugar industry in Trinidad, British Guiana and St Lucia after 1866.[43]

Crown Colony government resolved the longstanding contradiction between metropolitan and colonial political economy dating back to the end of the mercantilist era and its further aggravation by the arrival of free trade economics. It might have been that its declared origins had to do with issues apparently far removed from economic considerations, issues more closely associated with humanitarianism, trusteeship, good government or even with race.[44] In Trinidad, in 1810, Crown Colony government was posited on race and on the need to reform slavery, and the desirability of using Trinidad as an 'island of experiment' for that purpose.[45] In the case of Jamaica, half a century later, the shift from representative to authoritarian government was posited in part on the need to spare white society the unspeakable horror of possibly having to submit to the emergence of a political system dominated by black and coloured politicians.[46] And standing behind these two watershed developments were two realities: the real and inescapable responsibility of the imperial government for the orderly resolution of colonial problems. Good order meant, as Froude put it, avoiding 'the grosser anomaly' of black people wielding political authority over Whites.[47] In an empire dominated by the racist ideology of pseudo-Darwinism and the Hamitic hypothesis, race alone could explain the drift to authoritarianism in

42 See R. W. Beachey, 1957; also Hilary Beckles, 1990, p.133.
43 James Millette, 1988a, pp.289 ff.
44 James Millette, 1985, pp.264 ff.
45 *Ibid.*
46 Thomas C. Holt, 1992, chaps 7 and 8.
47 Quoted in Waldo Hilary Dunn, 1961–3, vol.2, p.492.

the British West Indian colonies; but there is no doubt that economic interest reinforced the trend.

In other words, by the end of the nineteenth century, if Crown Colony government had not existed, it might well have had to be invented. Representative government, especially in resource-rich colonies of the Empire peopled by a majority of non-Europeans, did not sit well with the global perspectives of the then-existing 'world's only superpower'. That is why, at the very moment when responsible government and Dominion status were becoming commonplace in the colonies of European settlement, the West Indies were slipping down the ladder of constitutional change. And there were many who believed that was where they should stay.

At the end of the War, Crown Colony government was still a barrier to the economic empowerment of the people. In Great Britain the search for profits had been replaced by the post-war drama of the fight for existence; and the fight for existence was grimly dependent on the continuing survival of the Crown Colony system. In the Caribbean after the Second World War there was, in the public mind, a growing association between the absence of economic advancement and the lack of political representation. The many crises of the 1930s and early 1940s were grounded in the increasingly acute perception on the part of working people that the existing colonial system was grinding them into the dust, not from necessity but from choice. Wages were low; but then they had almost always been low. Profits were high, but the stockholders and the proprietors were the beneficiaries, not the workers. The colonies were, in the most brutal interpretation of the phrase, 'colonies of exploitation'. The prevailing concept posited the existence of a well-fed, well-paid, well-housed and prosperous administrative, commercial and managerial sector side by side with a working population bordering on destitution, disease-ridden, poorly paid, scandalously housed, and oppressively taxed. Even in the most prosperous sectors of the economy, petroleum in Trinidad, bauxite in British Guiana and Jamaica, for example, workers earned in one week, if they were lucky, a small fraction of what the managers and supervisors and overseers earned in half a day. In fact, the introduction of such industries was not kindly regarded by the sugar industry, traditionally the largest employer of labour, for fear of the damage they might do to its notorious tradition for paying very low, or starvation wages. Indeed, the fact that these industries came into being was as much a testimony to their ability to inflict a political defeat on the sugar interest as it was to the growing relevance of their products in an increasingly industrialized world.[48]

48 M. Shahabuddeen, 1983, p.250.

Equally, the administrative costs of colonial rule supported an officer class with a level of remuneration which had long given cause for negative comment by interested observers. The lack of economic progress in Trinidad 'was not to be wondered at', wrote Frederick A. Ober at the beginning of the twentieth century,

> with a governor at $25,000 per annum, an attorney-general at $7500, a colonial secretary and a director of public works at $6000 each, and fifteen other public 'servants' with salaries ranging from $3000 to $5000 apiece. Think of a relatively insignificant country like Trinidad, with less than half a million inhabitants ... most of these ... living from hand to mouth, paying their 'governor' a salary half as large as that received by the President of the United States![49]

General advances in the constitutional status of the colonies were few and far between. Until the 1920s colonies possessing fully nominated chambers remained in possession of them until the middle of the decade when the recommendations of the Wood Commission began to take effect.[50] Between the middle of the 1920s and the middle of the 1940s, the arrangements implemented consonant with those recommendations remained in place until the riots and strikes that swept the region in the 1930s. But these changes of themselves did not do more than mildly amend the existing structures. Real power remained in the hands of the Crown, its representatives and its servants. But the groundwork for far more sweeping changes to follow was beginning to fall into place.

Between 1945 and 1970 a bewildering number of options emerged relative to the constitutional development of the colonial territories of the Caribbean. At first, even in the English-speaking colonies there was no clear commitment by the powers concerned to facilitate the development of self-government, still less independence, in the dependent territories of the Caribbean. In fact, even the anti-colonialists were not very optimistic about the prospects for independence of the individual colonies, whence was born the idea of West Indian federation. Curiously enough, it was in Puerto Rico that the first major step toward self-government was taken. Puerto Rican nationalism, suppressed since 1898, embarked upon a political path which, in the post-war period, resulted in some significant, but limited changes. An elected governorship was established in 1948 and *estado libre asociado* was implemented in July 1952. But the triumph of Muñoz

49 Frederick A. Ober, 1907, pp.409–10.
50 Gordon K. Lewis, 1968, *passim*; also Hume Wrong, 1923.

Marín and the *Populares* was in retrospect the beginning of a long period of stalemate, frustration and uncertainty, the result of which is that no serious political development has taken place in the island since the 1950s. If there was a lasting Puerto Rican influence on the rest of the Caribbean it was to be observed in the economic and not in the political sphere. Politically, there is some reason to perceive *estado libre asociado* as a sop to the Puerto Rico nationalists whose bid for independence in 1938, and again in 1950, had been violently suppressed by the United States.[51] Since its establishment, *estado libre asociado*, or Commonwealth status as it is sometimes called, has acted as much as a brake on further constitutional development as it has been a facilitating instrument for allowing Puerto Ricans to participate in the administration of the island's affairs. The new arrangement did not immediately settle the status question. Almost immediately Puerto Rican organizations favouring independence petitioned the US government and effectively placed the question of the island's independence before the Eisenhower administration. Some evidence exists that the case for independence was considered if only because the United States and Puerto Rico were anxious to have the island's constitutional situation removed from the purview of the Fourth Committee of the United Nations, on the grounds that the island was no longer a colony but had attained 'a full measure of self-government'.[52] Also, whatever prospects there might have been for successfully pursuing independence through the medium of the United Nations quickly evaporated in the context of the United States' hegemonic control of the Latin American vote in the United Nations,[53] the violent attack against the United States

51 Juan Antonio Corretjer, 1965, 1950, 1969; Pedro Albizu Campos, 1977; also Gordon K. Lewis, 1963 (1974). A hostile, vitriolic and sensationalist account is provided by Wenzell Brown, 1945.

52 Luis Muñoz Marín, Governor of Puerto Rico to President of the United States, 17 January 1953. See also Bernard M. Shanley, Special Counsel to the President, to Hon. John Foster Dulles, Secretary of State, 16 December 1953 stating that: 'The President indicated that he would fully approve an independent status for Puerto Rico.' Also see, Henry Cabot Lodge, Jr, US representative to the United Nations, to Governor [sic] [Sherman] Adams, on the subject of Puerto Rican Independence, 20 January 1954. 'It is impossible to get anything done in Puerto Rico without the total cooperation of General [sic] Muñoz. I believe that regarding independence, very careful consideration should be given to taking him into our confidence. We could work the thing out, even though it might take years. I understand that in 1948, General [sic] Muñoz proclaimed a program of building up the island to an economic position whereby he could ask the United States for either independence or statehood.' *National Archives*, Washington, DC.

53 Juan M. García-Passalacqua, 1984, pp.124 ff.

Congress in 1954,[54] the successful anti-Batista revolution in Cuba in 1959, the United States invasion of the Dominican Republic in 1965, and Cold War considerations.[55]

Internally, the impact of these influences was further exacerbated by the defeat of the *Populares* in the elections of 1968. Since then, the resurrection of statehood as an alternative to both *estado libre asociado* and independence has further complicated the issue. In addition there is an ever-increasing incremental impact derived from the decades-long existence of the status quo. To this must be added the reinforcement provided by an ever-broadening United States bureaucratic, economic and military presence. Not least, there is the continuing Puerto Rican immigration to the mainland and the gradual absorption of emigré Puerto Ricans into a rapidly developing, dynamic Latino culture in the United States.[56] Taken together all of these factors pose increasingly difficult hurdles in the way of the realization of the Puerto Rican nation-state. Barring the most spectacular political reversal imaginable, the Puerto Rican nationalist aspiration resides for the time being in the diasporic imagination of an increasingly frustrated, and probably declining number of United States citizens and insular residents of Puerto Rican descent.

Economically, however, Puerto Rico's experiences in the 1940s and 1950s formed the basis of an economic model of development which held out the hope of transforming the formerly agricultural and under-developed West Indian islands into modern, industrialized economies. Indeed, if any lesson was learned from the Puerto Rican experience it was that self-government and independence would be a distant dream without a demonstrated capacity for self-sustaining economic growth. The irony is that while, in Puerto Rico, the Puerto Rican model of development was never widely perceived as preparing that island for self-government and independence, in the larger British West Indian colonies the increasingly articulate nationalist leaders

54 Federico Ribes Tovar, 1974; also Earl Parker Hanson, 1960.

55 In the 1970s the Puerto Rican problem achieved an enhanced level of scrutiny in that the issue, often on the initiative of Cuba, engaged the attention of the United Nations on several occasions. Probably as a result, President Ford proposed in early 1977 that the issue should be closed by conferring statehood on the island. See, *Communication from the President of the United States transmitting A Draft of Proposed Legislation to Enable the People of Puerto Rico to Form a Constitution and State Government, to be Admitted into the Union, and for Other purposes,* 17 January 1977. See also, Rubén Berrios Martínez, 1977.

56 Some interesting perspectives on the many-sided problematic posed by Puerto Rican access to the United States are provided by Manuel Maldonado-Denis, 1980.

embraced the model as a prescription for constitutional autonomy which only the foolhardy would dare to deny.[57]

First in Jamaica, and later in Trinidad & Tobago, the old agricultural economy became the butt of fierce and unrelenting criticism by the new nationalist parties and their leaders. In January 1955, after 11 years in opposition, the People's National Party (PNP) came to power under the leadership of Norman Manley. Its declared objectives differed significantly from those of the Jamaica Labour Party (JLP) which had preceded it. It was committed to achieving self-government, and it was committed to the reform of the economy. The Puerto Rican model acted like a magnet on the Jamaican reformers, the more so since its principal propositions echoed the sentiments vigorously espoused by the noted West Indian economist, W. Arthur Lewis. A St Lucian, Lewis had emerged in the 1930s as an informed and sophisticated analyst of the West Indian economic condition. He had briefed the Fabians on the crises of the thirties and had devoted much time and energy in the intervening years to teasing out a theory of economic growth for backward, under-developed, colonial economies such as those abounding in the British West Indies. If Teodoro Moscoso was the economic guru presiding over the reorganization of the Puerto Rican economy, W. Arthur Lewis soon became the dominant economic influence in the reform of the economies of the anglophone Caribbean.[58] As a team they advised the new administration led by Dr Eric Williams after his People's National Movement (PNM) swept to power in Trinidad & Tobago in 1956.[59]

Clearly, however, whatever inspiration Puerto Rico could offer in the economic sphere, it had little or nothing to offer politically. *Estado libre asociado* became a glass ceiling beyond which the aspirations of the Puerto Rican people have not been allowed to rise for more than fifty years. In the search for self-government and independence the British West Indies were on their own. But they were not helpless. Between 1945 and 1962 four factors of overwhelming significance stand out.

The first of these was the growing nationalist preoccupation of the masses, and the increasing rejection of the status quo throughout the region.

---

57 This is not to say that the system has not had its critics. A substantial literature exists, dating from the early 1960s, in the pages of the *New World Quarterly* and its associated, occasional publications. Indeed a generational school of Caribbean economists, historians and political scientists, mainly located in the University of the West Indies and the University of Guyana, has produced some very fine critical and polemical studies in opposition to the main tenets of the Puerto Rican model of development. See, for example, Lloyd Best, 1963; and Havelock Brewster and Clive Thomas, 1967.

58 See W. Arthur Lewis, 1977.

59 Eric Williams, 1969 (1971), p.246.

By whatever measure one chose, the evidence was clear that the Caribbean people were claiming the Caribbean region as their own and were determined to rid themselves of the Crown Colony system, particularly its political aspects. Since the First World War a nationalist spirit had been developing, and it matured quickly in the period after the Second World War. For many reasons that sentiment was most clearly developed in Jamaica. As early as 1938 Norman Manley had noted its existence:

> Anyone looking at the past ten years will realise that we in this country have been more and more concentrating upon our own affairs. We have thought more about Jamaica, spoken more about Jamaica, breathed more of the atmosphere of Jamaica than ever before ... There is a tremendous difference between living in a place and belonging to it and feeling your destiny is irrevocably bound up in the life and destiny of that place.[60]

What Manley said of Jamaica in 1938 could easily have been said of any other part of the anglophone Caribbean in the succeeding period. Under its influence, the masses willingly accepted the views of their leaders that the British West Indian colonies were embryonic nations, possibly possessed of a collective destiny. They were not sure how this destiny was to be realized; but masses usually are dismissive of such minor details. That was for their leaders to decide. But there was no way in which their sentiments could be mis-read.

In Trinidad & Tobago, in 1956, the nationalist sentiment was even more clearly stated in the context of the emergence of the PNM, one of whose founding documents, the People's Charter, described the new party as 'rally, a convention of all and for all, a mobilization of all the forces of the community, cutting across race and religion, class and colour, with emphasis on united action by all the people in the common cause.'[61] The era of elitist affirmation of the right to speak on behalf of the colonial state had ended.

Secondly, the colonized peoples were not standing still. For the vast majority of them the colonial experience was rooted in two factors above all else: economic oppression and racial discrimination. In work-places the ordinary people often confronted both: criminally low wages, abysmal working and living conditions, racial arrogance and racial slight. Even despite the crises of the thirties, conditions remained largely the same especially in the traditional agricultural industries, but the newer sectors such as petroleum, bauxite and tourism were by no means exempt. Mona Macmillan, writing in

60 Quoted in Philip Sherlock and Hazel Bennett, 1998, p.368.

61 Quoted in Eric Williams, 1969 (1971), p.145.

1957, described Whites as dignified and assured when dealing with black and coloured people but given to 'sudden almost brutal bursts of self-assertion born of many generations of being fetched and carried for by hosts of slaves and of exercising unquestioned authority over them'.[62] Race, and the assumption of racial superiority, were the heart of the matter. Colonial racist ideology was founded on the belief that the agricultural and industrial servitude of black people was one of the fundamental rights of Europeans. Even the most liberal of Europeans were committed to that point of view. Sydney Olivier, Governor of Jamaica between 1907 and 1913, is a classic example. Himself the chairman of a commission of enquiry into the West Indian sugar industry in the period of depression which (again) recommended the promotion of peasant proprietorship,[63] he was also the author of a book which, whatever else it might have done, never seriously challenged the sacred principle of colonial government.[64]

This was, indeed, the horns of the dilemma: how to perpetuate the agricultural and industrial servitude of the masses while at the same time embarking on the liberalization of the Crown Colony system? It was a question for which British imperialism had no ready answer. Sir Harry Johnston, a liberal on the Congo question and a supporter of Edmund Dene Morel in exposing it, was outraged by the idea that

> semi-savages should be driving ill-bred sheep, scraggy cattle or ponies hardly fit for polo over plains and mountains that are little else than great treasure-vaults of valuable minerals and chemicals; or that they should roam with their blow-pipes and bows and arrows through forests of inestimable value for their timber, drugs, dyes, latices, gums, oil-seeds, nuts or fruits, be turning this waiting wealth to no use, not allowing it to circulate in the world's markets.[65]

He had very clear views on how Central Africa should be developed: it 'must be ruled by whites, developed by Indians and worked by blacks.'[66] Thirty years earlier he had written that 'the negro race will (not) be competent to rule itself or others for at least another century.'[67] It would be a short century.

Perhaps the most telling indicator of the pernicious racial discrimination prevailing in the islands in the era of the struggles for self-government and

62 Mona Macmillan, 1957, p.42.
63 Great Britain Parliament, 1930 (Lord Olivier).
64 See Sydney Olivier, 1906 (1939).
65 Sir H.H. Johnston, 1920, p.59.
66 Quoted in Eric Stokes, 1966, p.357.
67 A. J. Hanna, 1956, p.227.

independence lies in the unceremonious exclusion of Michael Manley – son of a Jamaican chief minister and himself to be prime minister, 1972–80 – from Doctor's Cave in Montego Bay in the late 1950s. But what was the isolated experience of the middle class was the day-to-day reality of the lower classes.[68] Accordingly, the work-places became the foci of organized rejection of the socio-economic and political system, and the founts from which important political organizations emerged. In the midst of the nationalist fervour low wages, land hunger, deficient social services, poor housing, a narrowly elitist education system, and discrimination – always discrimination – continued to be, as they had been for decades, the principal problems besetting the ordinary people as they struggled for survival.

As a result many peoples' organizations, many workers' groups and many radical and progressive movements emerged in all of the territories, and the list of those who fought and died, unheralded and unsung in the battle for change, grew ever longer. Everybody knows about the prominent figures, the principal political parties, the charismatic leaders; but the mass movements that developed in all the territories could not and would not have been built without the tailor, the sailor, the candlestick-maker, the seamstress, the ironer and the cook. The folk heroes of the labour and political movements are known in the districts in which they were born, in which they lived and died, but they are seldom recognized in the pages of the works written about these periods. Yet they made the movement, they made the victories, they carved the building blocks upon which self-government and independence were ultimately to be erected.[69]

The third factor of importance resided in the British political tradition itself. Every facet of that tradition, until the post-war period, had operated against the extinction of the old political order. But the new international context created a different paradigm within which the principles of the tradition could be ignored only at great expense. Since the mid-nineteenth century British colonial government had allowed for the progressive enhancement of previously subordinate colonial constitutions. Starting with Canada, responsible government had recognized the right of colonial peoples to be governed by their own freely elected representatives from among whom ministers would be chosen. These ministers would be responsible not to the Crown, but to the colonial legislature, however called, and ultimately to the people. Ministers would be removable by the legislature and not by the Crown. The Governor would reign but would not rule. In effect, the

68 See, for example, Arbuthnot John Graham Knox, 1962, pp.284 ff.

69 See, for example, Ken Post, 1978; also Bukka Rennie, 1973; and Ron Ramdin, 2000.

customary supervision of the metropole over colonial politics was withdrawn, even though some affairs, such as foreign relations, defence and the like, remained in the purview of the Crown. In internal matters, the sovereignty of the Crown was recognized on the understanding that it would not be 'actively exercised'. The impact of metropolitan policy outside the reserved areas was curtailed, and in its place the responsibility of the executive to the colonial legislature, and, thereby, to the people, was enshrined.

This model had been in existence since the 1840s. It had been extended to Australia, New Zealand, South Africa and throughout Canada itself in the interim. It had been withheld from the West Indies for reasons already discussed having to do with race and its ramifications, and with economic considerations. But now, more than a century later, history again posed the question: was responsible government applicable to the 'white dominions' alone, or was it for all colonies? The answer to that first question in 1865 was 'yes'; the answer to the same question in the 1950s and 1960s was a resounding 'no'! As events were to show the West Indies would not only attain self-government but move on to independence while Canada, to take one specific example of the dominions, would need to take unusual steps to erase the ambiguity surrounding its status as an independent country by 'patriating' the constitution in 1982.[70]

There was another twist to the economic argument, which marked the degree to which political reality had changed between the wars. Economic self-sufficiency was the petard on which colonial independence had often come to grief. In 1936, in Puerto Rico, the Tydings Bill had offered independence to the island on the clear understanding that thereafter it would be on its own economically. The Puerto Rican élite, as well as their Republican supporters in Congress, balked at the idea and the proposal was lost.[71] In the British colonies financial insufficiency had coincided with the general decline from representative to Crown Colony government. Continuously dependent on loans and grants from the imperial treasury, the islands had become wedded to the belief that independence was unthinkable. Yet, on both sides, the perspectives were beginning to change. The riots of the thirties moved London to take more seriously its economic responsibilities to the colonies, and the Colonial Development and Welfare scheme was born.[72] In the islands

70 Canada Act, 1982, incorporating the Constitution Act, 1982; see also, Canada House of Commons, 1980.

71 Harwood Hull, writing in the *New York Times*, described the Bill as an 'obnoxious choice between an economically ruinous independence and a continuance of the present unsatisfactory colonialism.' Quoted in Roberta Ann Johnson, 1980, p.64, n.99.

72 Great Britain Parliament, 1940. See also Howard Johnson, 1977, pp.53–83.

the general notion of the impracticability of independence for individual impoverished colonies was being replaced by the aspiration to independence within the context of closer association and federation of the anglophone colonies. And in that context, as time was to prove, the question was not 'if' but 'how much?'.

For a brief period in the twentieth-century history of the West Indies, federation came to be everyman's solution to the West Indian problem, British Honduras and British Guiana excepted. From the imperial point of view it was perceived as the ideal solution, one which the Colonial Office had long advocated, mainly for administrative and financial reasons. From the perspectives of the islands, it was perceived as the only enabling formula which would allow them all to meet the test for full self-government and independence, and raise some reasonable expectation for the creation of a viable, self-sufficient West Indian nation-state.

Over a span of 15 years, the idea of a West Indian Federation was born, developed and died. The Montego Bay Conference of 11–17 September 1947 marked the first full engagement of the emerging West Indian political leadership with the federal idea. The loss of the Jamaica referendum by the People's National Party in September 1961 marked its demise. This was quickly followed by the decision of both Jamaica and Trinidad & Tobago to sue for separate independence, which was achieved by 6 August 1962 in the case of the former and 31 August in the case of the latter.

That they were able to do this owed much to the fact that these two colonies had enjoyed a political experience much more consistent with the emerging model of constitutional decolonization than any other of the territories of the British West Indies. Between 1937 and 1962 they had developed on a political and economic trajectory which went much further towards satisfying the formal prerequisites for independence than the Federation itself. Certainly, by the early 1960s the reality was that the Federation would succeed or not succeed to the extent that Jamaica and Trinidad & Tobago maintained their adherence to it. On the other hand, it was becoming increasingly arguable that the Federation might well be acting as a fetter on the future development of the larger, more populous and more prosperous islands. In addition, political and constitutional development in the larger units had vaulted beyond that attained by the Federation, whose political status was, unlike that of Jamaica and Trinidad & Tobago, unrelated to specific constitutional accomplishments attained as a result of specific, political acts. The supposed ascendancy of the Federation was predicated on the fulfilment of an ideal, which was as metropolitan in conception as it was regional. But the real power lay in the larger units. And on every crucial question that faced the Federation in which the interest of the centre was counterpoised to the interest of the larger units, the units won. Whether it was the federal premiership, economic development, freedom of movement, or, ultimately, the survival of the Federation itself, there was no contest between the centre and the essential periphery.

In Jamaica, the crisis that began at the Frome sugar estate in Westmoreland, in April–May 1938, had been followed by numerous strikes and demonstrations in Kingston and elsewhere in the island. By the time the crisis had ended a nationalist movement with a clear though unsettled leadership had emerged. It was clear in that thereafter, and for decades to come, the two individuals thrown up by the crisis, Alexander Bustamante and Norman Manley, would occupy positions of leadership in the nationalist movement. But it was unsettled in that they would not do that together but rather in a rivalry which, exploited by the British government for all it was worth, would result in due course in the establishment of a political momentum that would realize much less than was possible, and much less than the masses deserved for their efforts. So much so, that it is a truism that the ascendancy of Bustamante, in the period 1944 to 1955, significantly retarded the pace of political and constitutional development in Jamaica. By 1955, when the PNP finally came to power in Jamaica, the island had moved from the 'embryonic' or nominal 'ministerial system' which it had obtained in 1945 to a more advanced system of ministerial rule in which Norman Manley was designated chief minister. This was followed by another PNP victory in 1959, the grant of full internal self-government, and, for Manley, the new designation of premier.

In Trinidad & Tobago, as in Jamaica, there was a prolonged hiatus between 1937 and the mid-1950s. Uriah Butler, the popular hero of the riots and strikes of 1937, was completely marginalized by 1950. The imperial government, for its part, embarked upon a campaign that had as its prime objective the complete de-legitimization of Butler and the Butlerites. Perhaps, left to himself, Butler might have accomplished that on his own: he was well-meaning, charismatic, anti-colonial and 'grass-roots' to the core. But he was also politically innocent, deeply religious, conservative and royalist. He epitomized perfectly that ideological commitment of the West Indian peasant to the 'benevolent despotism' of the British monarchy which has been, and continues to be, thoroughly appreciated and exploited by the metropolitan and colonial élite. He had little patience with the political radicalism of the Negro Welfare Cultural and Social Organisation (NWCSA, better known as the NWA) and of its leadership, or they with him. The Oilfields Workers Trade Union, whose founding he had done so much to inspire and facilitate, expelled him from its leadership in August 1939. But the British government did not leave anything to chance; it imprisoned Butler in November and kept him in prison for the duration of the Second World War. After his release he was kept on a very tight leash; his organizational headquarters were frequently raided, and he himself was hounded politically and ultimately sidelined by the machinations that brought the middle classes into politics in the elections of 1946, and the 'Gomes government' to office in 1950 on a constitution framed so as to perpetuate the Crown Colony system with the willing assistance of myriad opportunists dancing on the grave of the mass movement of the 1930s and 1940s.[73]

In effect, the 'Gomes government' was but an interlude between the unfulfilled prospect of a Butler administration and the one led by Dr Eric Williams which took office in September 1956. Williams was everything that Butler was not: intellectual, articulate, urbane, worldly wise, methodical, and very well informed. He had a certain knowledge of what was taking place not only in the region but in the world as a whole. He saw the national situation in the context of Third World development in the post-war period. He had a 'feel' for the possibilities of the moment and he exploited them to the hilt. Before he arrived on the scene, a variety of political groupings and organizations had preceded him; some were revolutionary, some were radical, some were progressive, some were conservative, perhaps even reactionary. But unlike in Jamaica, there was no viable political *party*; and there existed a gap which Williams moved quickly to fill. With Manley and the PNP very much in mind, he had within nine months founded a party, the PNM, launched a mass movement, and taken the reins of government. Under a new constitution, he was designated chief minister. He well understood what that meant. He had a greater initiative in determining the direction of governmental policy than any local politician who had preceded him; but he was not yet in charge. By 1959, however, Cabinet government was introduced; by the end of 1961 full internal self-government was achieved. In reality, not only Jamaica but also Trinidad & Tobago had leapfrogged beyond the traditionally more advanced Barbados, the Bahamas and Bermuda in constitutional terms. Equally, the existence of a federal prime minister since 1958, in the person of Barbadian Grantley Adams, did nothing to diminish the fact that within the period of Federation, it was those two nations, demographically and economically dominant as they were, and not the Federation that had made the most meaningful political and constitutional strides forward. Between December 1959 and early January 1960, Jamaica had indeed discussed with the British government the possibility of 'going it alone'. Specifically the question was raised about 'what might take place... if after the Inter-Governmental Conference (called to take up the question of the federal finances) Jamaica found it impossible to continue within the Federation'.[74] The ensuing discussion was interesting, if

73 See Morley Ayearst, 1960, pp.79 ff; also John Gaffar La Guerre, 1983; and Patrick Solomon, 1981.

74 S. R. Ashton and David Killingray, 1999, Document 119, Colonial note of 19 January 1960; see also Documents 112, 113 and 118.

only because it did not rule out the probability that Jamaica, though a 'marginal' case in terms of size, population and financial and economic resources, might yet attain national sovereignty and membership of the Commonwealth. The failure of the Federation, therefore, was thoroughly intelligible in the face of the different political dynamism that had developed between 1947 and the early 1960s. And so, too, was the consequential accession of Jamaica and Trinidad & Tobago to independence in August 1962.

Until the mid-1960s the idea of a reduced federation continued to engage the attention of Great Britain and the politicians of the smaller islands, but this was not to be. By then, however, Britain was perceived as predominantly concerned, as political wags put it, with 'winning its own independence' from the 'Little Eight' and passing on to Barbados an inadequately supported financial responsibility for the smaller islands which it was itself unwilling to assume. In terms of Barbadian politics, the initiative had also passed from Grantley Adams and the Barbados Labour Party to the Democratic Labour Party, led by Errol Barrow. He had none of Adams's conservatism, none of Adams's distrust of radical constitutional change which had bedevilled him throughout his political career. And so, after an interlude of four years the most viable of the smaller states, Barbados, pressed for and obtained its independence in 1966.

This left the other small island states adrift, and was followed in 1966 by the introduction of a new status, that of 'associated states' for Antigua and Barbuda, St Kitts-Nevis, and the Windwards (at this time meaning Dominica, Grenada, St Lucia and St Vincent & the Grenadines). In effect associated statehood meant an upgrade from the colonial status to something just short of full internal self-government. The larger and more viable of the smaller islands were empowered to legislate for their own internal government, foreign affairs and defence excepted. The new arrangements included clauses reserving to the British Government the right 'to legislate on any matter as might appear necessary to [it] to prevent circumstances arising in a territory which might prejudice the discharge of Britain's responsibilities.'[75] Disputes over the management of the police power, accompanied by the fact that, for a while, British governors or administrators continued to preside over the affairs of the territories, clouded the interpretation of exactly what internal government meant, whether it was unqualified or limited.

Nevertheless, between 1966 and 1974 associated statehood remained in uneasy effect in the erstwhile colonies. The integrity of the system came under serious challenge in Grenada where the new social and political forces

75 S. R. Ashton and David Killingray, 1999, Document 248, pp.702–3. See also Documents 234, 235 and 249.

that would produce the Grenada revolution of 1979–83 fiercely opposed the conversion of associated statehood to independence without the preliminaries of a referendum as promised in the 'associated states' legislation.[76] But Grenada gained its independence, after which several other territories moved to do the same: St Lucia (1977), Dominica (1978), St Vincent & the Grenadines (1979), Antigua & Barbuda (1981) and St Kitts-Nevis (1983).

Of the territories which had remained outside the federal experiment, British Guiana and British Honduras, the former attained its independence (as Guyana) in 1966, the latter (as Belize) in 1981. In several respects, the circumstances of decolonization in Guyana differed markedly from the road taken by the other British West Indian colonies. The circumstances of the delayed achievement of independence in Guyana are explained in part by the impact of Cold War politics in the region, but still more by the profoundly different ideological environment in which decolonization unfolded in Guyana. In fact decolonization is not quite the word that applies. In Guyana, almost from the beginning of the post-war decolonization process, there existed a more fully formulated perspective of what that process should mean and how it was to be achieved. Undoubtedly the inspiration was Marxist, and in that sense the Guyanese process was radically different from that occurring in any other British West Indian colony.

The evolution of this departure from the West Indian norm was principally the work of Dr Cheddi Jagan, who returned to Guyana in 1943 after graduating as a dentist in the United States. Guyana in 1943 was something like Trinidad & Tobago in 1956, at or near the bottom of the regional political scale. The labour unrest in the colony in September and October 1935 had not had an effect comparable to that which took place in Trinidad & Tobago and Jamaica in 1937–8. In addition, the political institutions were moribund, none more so than the Legislative Council. Even though the political traditions deriving from the old Dutch system had facilitated the survival of an elective element side by side with the emergence of the Crown Colony system, an election had not been held for eight years, and would not take place for another four. Local wags called the long-serving Council the 'Long Parliament'. There is no doubt that its existence helped prepare the way for the emergence of Cheddi Jagan on the local political scene. First, it operated against the growth of militant political leadership which might have been encouraged by reasonably frequent general elections. Secondly, given the restricted nature of the franchise, and the high property qualifications for electoral candidacy, it dramatically restricted the personnel from which popular leadership might develop. Of course, this was exactly the point; except that,

76 Sir Fred Phillips, 1985, pp.73–4.

in an ironical unforeseen consequence, an arguably brilliant strategy was foiled by a concatenation of unusual circumstances. A little-known Indo-Guyanese dentist, satisfying all the formal electoral and political qualifications, who soon acquired mass appeal in a colony substantially populated by Indian workers, and who was also possessed of an unexpectedly radical political outlook, emerged within a system accustomed for 12 years to doing nothing!

For a brief period Jagan served an apprenticeship in the political system, winning a seat in the Legislative Council as an independent when elections were at last held in 1947, joining the Labour Party in the same year, and leaving it in March 1948. In the interim some of the members of the Party, organized around the towering presence of Hubert Nathaniel Critchlow, had distinguished themselves by supporting the appointment of Frederick J. Seaford, managing director of Booker Brothers, to the Legislative Council against the recommendation of the party executive, voting for the removal of the export tax on gold and its substitution by a 25 per cent tax on gold purchases within the country, and voting against the introduction of adult suffrage.[77]

From this and other experiences over the next five years, Jagan concluded that:

> [T]he Marxist-Leninist concept of the state was pellucidly clear. The sugar-coated government used every device to serve big business – tax and other concessions to the capitalist class; measures to maintain a cheap and abundant labour force in and around the sugar plantations; pressure on the working people; constitutional reform aimed at preserving the colonial *status quo*.[78]

From this conclusion emerged in due course the People's Progressive Party (PPP), founded in 1950, a new party in Guyana and a spectacularly different party from others in the region.

There had been other parties and movements like the PPP before, and more were to follow. But most of them were small and insignificant, ephemeral and generally ineffective. This is not to say that they were unimportant. The smaller, revolutionary formations played a very important role in maintaining the spirit of militancy and resistance among the working people, and in keeping before the eyes of the larger and more established political organizations the aspirations and objectives of the radicals in their midst. But size was not a

77 Cheddi Jagan, 1966, pp.69 ff.

78 *Ibid.*, p.73.

guarantor of success. Cipriani's Trinidad Labour Party (TLP) inherited a mass following from the Trinidad Workingmen's Association (TWA). Self-styled a socialist party, it was Utopian, visionary and elitist, and eventually collapsed because of the errors which distanced it from the 'barefoot men' it purported to lead. The PPP was different in that alone of all Left parties and organizations, and alone of the all the major political parties formed in the anglophone Caribbean in and after the 1930s, it espoused from its very founding a consistently radical political programme, and acquired and held the support of a committed mass following. Such a party was a force to be reckoned with.

On nearly all the major questions of the day Guyana, in the era of PPP-dominated administrations, had a different point of view. In a very short space of time it distanced itself from those parties whose principal goal was what has been called 'constitutional decolonization'. In all the other colonies, the objectives of the decolonization movement were understated so as to embrace political, but not ideological or economic decolonization. In Guyana, political decolonization was a stage, even if an important first stage, in the radical transformation of society. Even in Trinidad & Tobago where the need for popular education of the electorate was clearly identified by the PNM, the parameters surrounding the search for a more developed political consciousness remained firmly located within the dominant capitalist mode. As for economic transformation, the Puerto Rican model of development represented the acme of regional aspirations. Together with *The Economics of Nationhood*, published by the Trinidad & Tobago government at the height of the intergovernmental polemic over Federation, it comprised the most elaborated theory of economic change emanating from official sources in the decolonization period. Summarized briefly, the crucial ideas emanating from these two sources were industrialization, aggressively promoted with the engine of foreign capital and foreign expertise; and a strong Federation, with the responsibility for economic development in the affiliated territories placed at the centre and not in the periphery.

The Guyana model envisaged political independence as a first stage. Thereafter, as the model was often later elaborated, it was to be followed by a national, anti-imperialist, democratic revolution aimed at shifting the levers of social and economic power from the hands of the metropolitan and colonial bourgeoisie into the hands of the working people and their allies. An essential aspect of the model lay in the nationalization of what was then often called 'the commanding heights of the economy'. Ultimately, this second stage, the period of socialist orientation, would be replaced by one in which the making of the socialist revolution would take pride of place. These ideas, consolidated by other less stringent differences, separated Guyana from the rest and formed one of the important reasons why Guyana remained outside the West Indies Federation during its brief existence.

Within Guyana the PPP was reviled by the plantocracy and other representatives of big and middle-sized business, as it was by the colonial administration. But the party's strength resided in the electorate, the more so after the coming of adult suffrage. It won the elections of 1953 against the expectations of nearly all its opponents. Of the 24 seats in the Legislative Council, it contested 22 and won 18. Thereafter it governed for 133 days after which it was violently forced out of power in 1953, and replaced by an interim administration. It was twice returned to office, in 1957 and 1961, but was again undone by external intervention in 1964. By this time the party had split into two factions, and for a while two PPPs existed. In 1956 a new constitution was agreed on and, in 1957 a general election was called. The battle was not only about electoral seats but also about control of the PPP. The Jagan wing of the party triumphed, winning nine of the 14 seats to the PNC's three, notwithstanding a drastic re-drawing of the constituencies meant to favour the opponents of the PPP. As a result the PPP remained under the control of the Jagans, Cheddi, his wife Janet and other loyalists, and Forbes Burnham became the leader of the newly established People's National Congress (PNC).

In a sense, political normalcy was restored. Of course, political normalcy in Guyana was always relative. Part of the hope was that the emergence of the PNC would spearhead the formation of a grand coalition which could defeat the PPP. That was not to be. In 1961 the PPP again demonstrated that, in electoral terms, it was unassailable in the country. It won the general elections handsomely, gaining 20 of the 35 seats, the PNC winning 10 and the newly established United Force gaining four. The time had come for more decisive measures to break the power of the PPP.

In the logic of events, it had been imagined by the PPP, and perhaps by others too, that the 1961 elections would pave the way for independence. Notwithstanding the suspension of the government in 1953, there had been a steady enhancement of the constitution in Guyana. The Waddington constitution was superior to many of the regional constitutions, and so was the constitution of 1956–7. In addition, the world had changed significantly between 1953 and 1961. Independence for the British colonies was no longer perceived as quite so unthinkable as formerly. Even the status of the leader of government had been improved. Chief minister after 1957, Jagan had been designated premier in 1961. But it was the very prospect of an independent Guyana under PPP leadership that alarmed and angered its opponents. More importantly, granted the geo-political situation that had developed in the region in the aftermath of the Cuban Revolution, and in the general context of the Cold War, the Kennedy administration indicated, in clear and unmistakable terms, its unqualified opposition to the emergence of what it perceived as another Cuba in the Caribbean.

By this time a kind of condominium had emerged in respect of the management of the decolonization process in the former British colonies. Where, in the period during and shortly after the Second World War, the United States had excoriated the British on the issue of colonialism, by 1961 it had embarked on a more considered and self-interested policy, the aim of which was to ensure that independence would only be granted to colonies meeting its own standards of political and ideological reliability.[79] By this standard, Guyana was not ready for independence, certainly not under Jagan's leadership. Consequently, the British government, acting under United States influence, determined that elections should be held not under the first-past-the-post system, as was the tradition in the other Caribbean islands, and in Great Britain itself, but by the proportional voting system.[80] In making this decision the British government had been comforted by the support offered by the governments of Jamaica and Trinidad & Tobago: indeed 'the outcome might have been awkward' had they not done so.[81] In sum, whatever trumpeting the United States might have done about the general principle of self-determination for the European colonies, when it came to the Caribbean it was very comfortable with continuing British imperial hegemony in the West Indies.[82] It was also clear that, however much the regional governments were prepared to criticize the British government for its many sins, they were not prepared to stand up to it in the face of its shameless intervention in Guyana to procure an electoral result more in harmony with the imperial interests of itself and the United States than with the democratic wishes of the people of Guyana.

As for Jamaica and Trinidad & Tobago, old antagonisms still persisted towards the PPP and, in particular, towards Dr Jagan. In Jamaica the PNP had, in March 1952, expelled its own 'Marxist Left' from the party under great and sustained pressure from the British authorities.[83] In 1953, the most prominent West Indian leaders of the time, Alexander Bustamante, Norman Manley and Grantley Adams had personally congratulated the British government on its suspension of the British Guiana constitution, and the colony's refusal to be

79 Cary Fraser, 2000, pp.584–610.

80 S. R. Ashton and David Killingray, 1999, Documents 214, 215, 217, 219, 223 and 224. See Annex to 217, pp.606–8; also record of a conversation between Harold Wilson, UK prime minister and Cheddi Jagan, premier of British Guiana, on 29 October 1964, pp.627–9.

81 S. R. Ashton and David Killingray, 1999, (Colonial Office) record of a discussion in London between Duncan Sandys (Secretary of State for the Colonies), and (Dean) Rusk (US Secretary of State), on the current situation (in British Guiana), 19 December 1963, Document 219, pp.613–15.

82 S. R. Ashton and David Killingray, 1999, Document 220, p.617.

83 Trevor Munroe, 1992.

drawn into the Federation had not helped. With what seemed at times to be an unseemly display of enthusiasm, many of the island governments had either prohibited the Jagans from entering or travelling through their islands, or insisted on a noticeably unfriendly police surveillance when they were allowed to do so. Dr Jagan himself also complained that, on several occasions, his attempts to engage his counterparts in discussion of the Guyanese situation met with indifference or outright rejection. On the specific question of constitutional development in Guyana the British perception was that

> Dr. Williams' public statements...have been extremely helpful to British policy and critical of Dr. Jagan's obduracy, and the Trinidad representative to the United Nations has on instructions taken the same line. Indeed, Trinidad alone of the Afro-Asian States, abstained with Britain on the Ghana motion urging that a date be fixed for Guyana's independence. Trinidad's representative went further and spoke against the motion. Here, again, Dr. Williams' record compares favourably with Jamaica's despite the latter's closeness to the United States.[84]

Bustamante, the Jamaica Prime Minister, quixotic and mercurial as ever, offered to intercede with Britain on Jagan's behalf, with a view to postponing the imposition of proportional representation, but only on condition that he abandoned his 'policies' and probably also his principles, in exchange.[85]

It cannot be discounted that, once the split developed between Jagan and Burnham, the West Indian leaders automatically took sides and acted in accordance with their own prejudices and interests. Jagan was Indian and his political following was overwhelmingly Indian. Racial chauvinism was part of the mindset of the largely Afro-Caribbean regional leadership class. Colonialism had done its job very well, and there was an instinctive inclination on the part of that leadership to see Jagan as an upstart Indian making trouble for the more sophisticated and respectable leaders. Burnham was 'Odo', a member of the post-war generation of educated Blacks, some of whom had served in the British armed forces, been educated in British universities, and were enamoured of the monarchy. Jagan was educated in the United States, at a time when it was fashionable to sneer at its educational institutions and at the

---

84 S. R. Ashton and David Killingray, 1999, Document 218, p.611. Sir Norman Costar, UK High Commissioner to Trinidad & Tobago, 1962–6, to Duncan Sandys, Secretary of State for the Colonies, 18 December 1963. One wonders what Williams's response might have been to Costar's unflattering remark that, 'by British political standards' he (Williams) would have belonged 'to the Middle or Middle Right of the British Labour Party'; *loc.cit.*

85 S. R. Ashton and David Killingray, 1999, Document 225, p.630.

credentials emanating from them. He was married to a white woman – a Rosenberg and a Marxist – whose participation in the country's politics, then and later, was problematical for many traditional participants. An attack on Burnham, therefore, was an attack on a regional class, reinforced by the back-handed criticism of their own policies that Jagan's adoption of socialism seemed to imply. It cannot be discounted either that many of the region's leaders, who had themselves been accused of communist leanings or affiliation, welcomed the opportunity to allay suspicion of such a deadly commitment by proving how anti-communist they were in the case of Guyana.

Suffice it to say that, as a result of the introduction of proportional representation, preceded and accompanied by well-documented and well-financed subversive activity inspired and supported by the British and United States governments, the PPP was at last defeated electorally in the elections of 1964.[86] A coalition government comprising the PNC and the United Force, led by Forbes Burnham, came to power. Ultimately Guyana gained its independence in 1966. In due course, Burnham amended the Guyana constitution, proclaimed Guyana a republic and adopted what he described as co-operative socialism. He also institutionalized electoral rigging as a fact of life, in consequence of which in a series of farcical electoral contests the PNC was time and again returned to political office. It is a scandalous reality that the open corruption on which these victories were based did nothing to sour relations between Guyana under Burnham and the rest of the anglophone Caribbean. Indeed, after 1968 Burnham emerged as one of the principal promoters of the integration that resulted in the launching of the Caribbean Free Trade Area (CARIFTA) and ultimately the Caribbean Community (CARICOM).

But if Guyana under the PPP was a pariah nation to the regional political élite, it was anything but that to the regional political opposition which began to emerge in the years after independence. The honeymoon period for the new national governments was short-lived, largely because the leaders and the masses had entered upon the road to independence with quite different objectives. Decolonization had about it a revolutionary colouring; expectations were high among the people that the establishment of the self-governing nation-state would usher in a period of material, moral and spiritual fulfilment. In this hope they were deeply disappointed. In fact between 1962 and 1970 the opposition to the newly independent governments was not so much to be found inside parliament as outside of it. And it was a radically transformed opposition.

The parties of independence were traditional, very imitative of the British model and anxious to conform to the tenets of the 'Westminster model'. They were much more concerned with the trappings of democratic

86 Cary Fraser, 2000, pp.600 ff.

power than with the exercise of democracy itself. Political office, flag, anthem, a seat in the United Nations, a national airline at whatever cost, a two-party system and elections every five years: these were the prime requisites of the new nationalists. Their support base lay emphatically among those who had either directly benefited from the transition to independence, like the office holders, or who were prepared to lie in waiting for the expected economic largesse promised by the Puerto Rican model of development. Also, the principal parties in opposition had nothing to offer that was really different from what the parties in office were doing, Guyana of course excepted. It is a truism, supportable by an examination of most of the newly independent countries of the decolonization era, that the nationalist parties that had led the struggle for independence were generally superior to the traditional parties that opposed them. Invariably also, they were more progressive, some of them even radical. But they were not revolutionary; and the popular feeling was that the time had come for revolution.

In other words, the views of the PPP, which had made it unpopular with the nationalist, regional and metropolitan élite between 1950 and 1964, were precisely the views which large numbers of people were espousing in the post-independence Caribbean as early as 1965. Political independence alone was clearly not enough; economic independence, based on socialism or socialist orientation, was necessary. Those sentiments were echoing and reverberating from several sources. The Cuban Revolution was one. It had been developing simultaneously with the nationalist ferment in the anglophone Caribbean. Precisely at the point when the Revolution was challenging the hegemony of the United States in Cuban affairs, Jamaica and Trinidad & Tobago were entering upon negotiations for independence from the United Kingdom. But these were two different processes, travelling on two different trajectories, one socialist, the other nationalist. Cuba was formally independent but had been thoroughly neo-colonized by the US and was fighting to put an end to neo-colonialism. The British colonies were dependent, suing for control of their own affairs, and were soon to emerge as independent nation-states. It was their misfortune that, by the time they achieved independence, these two processes were more closely aligned than they had ever been before. The attainment of political independence led to a sharpened perception of the persistence of neo-colonial domination of the regional economies. In this sense, the attainment of constitutional independence had been the initial step in what was to become, in the period between 1962 and 1983 – the year marking the collapse of the Grenada Revolution – nearly a quarter-century of struggle for the deeper and fuller national liberation which the nationalist parties had failed to provide.

If the social basis of the regional independence movement, in its leadership aspect, was the educated black middle class, the social basis of the struggle against neo-colonialism was the working class, the radical or revolutionary intelligentsia, and the very volatile, urban youth which together constituted the most disappointed segments, and the most vocal critics of the post-independence societies. The most important manifestation of this new development, and the phenomenon that signalled the decisive disappearance of the nationalist solidarity that had seemed to exist at independence, was the emergence of the Black Power movements in the Caribbean in the period 1968–70. For nearly two years the region was continuously in the grip of a rolling series of crises, in reality one major crisis, which continued to escalate against the background of the growth of an increasingly revolutionary spirit in the Caribbean and a radicalizing civil-rights and revolutionary commotion in North America.[87]

As early as 1965 fissures had begun to appear in the nationalist structures. In March 1965, the passing of the Industrial Stabilization Act,[88] in an atmosphere of generalized crisis, marked the decisive break between the PNM and the radical trade-union movement, especially in the oil and sugar industries. In August–September 1965 widespread attacks against the Chinese community in Jamaica marked the beginnings of an assault by dispossessed Blacks against a community perceived as largely responsible for their deprivation.[89] But the fissures were opened wide by the Rodney Affair, which occurred in Jamaica in October 1968.[90] At the same time, the repercussions of the Rodney Affair in Jamaica stimulated sympathetic reaction in Trinidad, first of all among the radical academic and student sectors of the University of the West Indies at St Augustine, and subsequently in the capital city and its environs, in the east-west corridor stretching westwards from Port of Spain, southwards to Caroni and San Fernando, and then virtually throughout the whole country. Under the leadership of the National Joint Action Committee, largely comprised of leading figures in the University student movement, and to some extent the progressive trade unions and quickly mushrooming community and other populist groups, a vigorous popular challenge to the Williams regime

87 See Selwyn D. Ryan and Taimoon Stewart, 1995; also, James Millette, 1995, pp.59 ff.

88 Trinidad & Tobago Parliament, 1965. See also, Roy D. Thomas, 1989, chap.IV.

89 See T. Lacey, 1977.

90 The reference is to the widespread unrest that occurred in Kingston, Jamaica, in 1968 when Dr Walter Rodney, a Guyanese Marxist historian then on the faculty of the University of the West Indies, Mona, was prevented from returning to Jamaica where he was domiciled after attending the Black Writers' Conference in Montreal. Rodney had been doing grass-roots work among the Kingston underclass and, in particular, lecturing frequently on African and Caribbean history, and attempting to put the popular discontent of the post-independence years in a radical historical context. See Walter Rodney, 1969.

was mounted. It was the fiercest confrontation between government and people in the anglophone Caribbean until the Grenada Revolution of 1979. Between 26 February 1970, when the rebellion began, and 20 April when it was suppressed, the people marched and marched and marched again, in the process bringing the country to a near-standstill for nearly two months.

The Jamaica and the Trinidad & Tobago crises both had their roots in the deep disillusionment of the black masses with the post-independence realities, and in the manifest indifference of the ruling political establishments to the growing roar of criticism from below. But if the Jamaican crisis of 1968 was essentially social in nature, and limited largely to the ghettoized sections of greater Kingston, the crisis in Trinidad & Tobago was much more profound, much more political and overwhelmingly much more threatening to the continued existence of the status quo. In the latter, the army became involved, first as a consequence of the government's attempt to use it to contain and control, and possibly to put down the growing outrage, and secondly, as a result of the bid made by some young, Sandhurst-trained members of the officer corps to take control of the military and bring it firmly over to the side of the popular movement, as a prelude to replacing the government.[91]

If ever there had been a possibility of closing the breach between the Williams regime and the radical opposition, that possibility was killed in the protracted proceedings that followed the declaration of a state of emergency in April. Several prominent political activists, trade unionists and other individuals caught up in the events were detained; the most prominent open space in downtown Port of Spain, Woodford Square, re-christened by Williams himself in 1956 as 'the University of Woodford Square', was closed to the public; several trials for mutiny against army officers and other personnel were undertaken; and a general clamp-down on virtually all kinds of political activity was, for a while, enforced. The government, for its part, used the moment to engage in a radical reformulation of its economic policies. Taking many pages out of the briefing books of the radical opposition, it embarked on a modified development programme with the State at the centre, and with the nationalization of the oil and sugar industries, and the localization of banks, insurance companies and some other foreign-owned enterprises, as the centrepiece. To some extent, at least, the post-independence regime had moved in the direction of responding to the charge that colonialism had been succeeded by neo-colonialism. It was a claim that was seriously contested in the years that followed.[92]

91 Herman L. Bennett, 1989, chap.6.

92 An insightful interpretation of the significance of these events is provided by Raphael Sebastien, 1981, pp.41–65. See also, José Miguel Sandoval, 1983.

The regional 'Black Power' manifestation was not unique to Trinidad & Tobago and Jamaica, nor to the anglophone territories. In Grenada, the Black Power unrest in Trinidad & Tobago stimulated the beginnings of a political momentum that resulted in the Grenada Revolution in 1979.[93] In the Bahamas, Black Power sentiment augmented the wave of popularity that fortified the Pindling government and set the stage for independence, which was achieved in 1973. Even Bermuda, dominated by the white political establishment since the days of slavery, had to accommodate to the emergence of the Progressive Labour Party, strongly identified with the black masses and the increasingly militant trade union movement.

In the Netherlands Antilles and Suriname, the absence of independence did not render inapplicable the major tenets of Black Power ideology in the wider Caribbean. Obviously, the critique of neo-colonialism could not be applied in its purest form; but the essence of economic exploitation was real. Much critical attention had been focused on the Caribbean bauxite industry in the discussion of regional integration in the anglophone Caribbean in the 1960s. Suriname was, with Jamaica and Guyana, one of three major Caribbean producers. Economic nationalism was fashionable. It also made good sense for countries which produced valuable raw materials while forfeiting the gains to be made from 'value added' strategies because of their inferior location in a structurally disadvantageous production process. And if, in the anglophone Caribbean, neo-colonial exploitation persisted despite independence, in Suriname the perception was that the existing colonial condition underwrote the economic exploitation that was taking place. The absence of a militant trade-union movement was a major deficiency. The attempt by Anton de Kom to build such a movement in the 1930s had been quickly and unceremoniously crushed by the colonial government. De Kom himself was hurriedly shipped off to Holland.[94] Accordingly, it was not until 1966 that the first collective-bargaining agreement was signed with the Aluminium Company of America (ALCOA), the major industrial employer and producer in the country.

Independence had always been a thorny question in Suriname, as were all seriously important political questions given the demographic composition of the country. Suriname was, in a sense, the quintessential plural society of which J. S. Furnivall had written, except that it was even more pluralized than the model he had addressed. Hindustanis (Indians), Creoles (Blacks), Javanese (Indonesian descendants), Maroons, Chinese, Amerindians,

93 Richard Jacobs and Ian Jacobs, 1979, *passim*; also, David E. Lewis, 1984, chap.11.

94 See Anton de Kom, 1934.

Europeans and mixed peoples constituted a racial kaleidoscope in a population of less than 500,000 in 1972,[95] and a society further complicated by serious, religious, cultural and class divisions.

There was no majority population, but there were two pluralities of Indians and Blacks, divided among themselves and insecurely conscious of the existence of other smaller, but not insignificant social groupings. It was a situation made for political complexity; but it also facilitated compromise. In 1955 the National Party of Suriname (NPS), led by Johan Adolf Pengel, and the United Hindu Party (VHP), led by Jaggernath Lachmon, fashioned a coalition which successfully took power in 1958 and held it until 1967. The period of 'elite-cartel democracy' as it was called,[96] was more a union of two dominant individuals than of two parties, or even two peoples. There were major differences on major issues, including adult suffrage and independence; but the leaders calculated that there was greater danger in being separate than in being united. The emergence of the Progressive National Party (PNP), formed by a group of intellectual dissidents within the NPS, the end of the NPS-VHP coalition, its substitution by a PNP-VHP alliance, and the death of Pengel, all signalled the changing contours of Suriname's politics. Since the 1960s the Nationalist Republican Party (PNR) had called for total national independence, an unrealizable prospect in the period of the NPS-VHP coalition. But popular nationalism had been growing. The slogan 'boss in our own house' had been popular for years. The 'Wi egi sani' (Our Own Thing) movement, led by the poet Robin 'Dobru' Ravales, had a powerful cultural resonance among the grass-roots as well as among the nationalist intelligentsia. And then there was the emergence of radical and revolutionary organizations, Marxist in inspiration, such as the Progressive Union of Workers and Peasants (PALU), the Surinamese Socialist Union (SSU), the People's Party (VP), and the Democratic Peoples Front (DVF),[97] some of which were to play very important roles in the struggles for political and economic independence of the 1970s.

But if independence was in the air it was Black Power which lit the fuse that thereafter ignited the torch of liberty. And it was not in Suriname, but in Curaçao, that the Netherlands Antilles' contact with the regional 'contagion' of the late 1960s and 1970s was most deeply experienced. On 29 May 1969, an industrial conflict that had been brewing for some time burst into the open. Negotiations between the oilworkers' union, the Curaçao Workers Federation (CFW) and Werkspoor Caribbean (WESCAR), a large Dutch con-

95 Betty Sedoc-Dahlberg, 1990, p.289 ff; also, Henk E. Chen and Hans Buddingh', 1987.

96 Henk E. Chen and Hans Buddingh', 1987, pp.21ff.

97 *Ibid.*, pp.26ff.

struction and oil services company, broke down, and a strike was called for the following day. WESCAR, as contractor to Royal Dutch Shell, was paying lower wages for the same work performed by employees of Shell on its facilities. The principal issue at stake was equal pay for equal work. The company was clearly disinclined to settle the issue on terms acceptable to the union, and the government showed no disposition to intervene, at least at first. The situation escalated when the broader trade-union movement decided to come out in solidarity with the CFW. What had started as an industrial conflict involving one union and one company soon became a general strike, with workers and their allies ranged against the economic and political élite. A workers' march from the oil refinery at Fort Amsterdam to Willemstad was intercepted by the police. Violence ensued, looting and arson took place, two workers were killed, several were injured and a significant part of the capital city was burned to the ground. What had attained the character of a general strike had now assumed the outlook of a general uprising against the status quo. Dutch citizens were attacked in the streets and there was every sign that the pent-up fury and disgust of the people had overflowed.

As elsewhere in the region and in the United States, Black Power slogans were familiar. Benjamin Fox, generally regarded as the founder of the Black Power movement in the island, had been proselytizing for years about the need for black political, economic and cultural assertiveness in an island overwhelmingly (more than 80 per cent) peopled by Blacks. Also, the People's National Party (PNP), led by Dr Moises Frumencio da Costa Gomez, had pledged itself to fight for the national autonomy of the Netherlands Antilles. In sum, Curaçao was a powder keg, and it was one of the first islands to blow up in the period of Black Power conscientization. Prime minister Ciro Croon, reluctant to intervene at the outset, eventually called on the Dutch for assistance. Troops were flown in, the strikes and demonstrations were crushed, and 'order' was restored.[98]

As brief as the confrontation had been it was a watershed in the modern development of the island, and indeed of the Netherlands Antilles and

98 There is no English language account of these events, and very little analysis in the Dutch language accounts of politics in Curaçao in this period. An official Report, in Dutch, exists, written by A. F. Paula, 1969; see also René A. Römer, 1974. In addition there are the newspaper reports of the time of which three are important: *Beurs en Niuewsberichten*, (*Stock and News Bulletin*), the establishment business daily; *La Prensa*, the conservative, papiamentu language daily; and *Vitó* (the *Overseer*), the radical papiamentu weekly. In all of this research I had the willing assistance and expertise of Eugene Godfried, witness to and participant in the events of 1969, and at present a radio journalist and Caribbean specialist with Radio Havana, Cuba.

Suriname. The Croon government was forced to resign and new elections were called. When they were held, the people voted for change. Ernesto Netto Petrona, leader and founder of the Patriotic Party of Aruba, became the first black prime minister of the Netherlands Antilles. Similarly Ben Leito, born in Curaçao, was appointed Governor of the Netherlands Antilles, the first Black to fill that position. Antilleanization was, at least symbolically, under way, a factor that was effectively exploited for a while by the Movement for a New Antilles (MAN) formed by Dom Martina in 1976. Arising out of the ashes of the conflict was the Workers' Liberation Front of May 30, 1969 (FOL), led by the veteran trade unionist Wilson 'Papa' Godett. Amador Nita, a member of the Front, became Minister of Labour. Radical, revolutionary and other progressive and democratic organizations, drawing support among the young and the politically energized mass movement, also sprang to life. Among these were Hubbentut '70, a movement of militant youth; the Farmers' Co-operative of Curaçao (KOPAK), and the Workers Crusade Party of Curaçao.

Events in Curaçao had a wider impact. In Suriname their influence was felt directly. Workers' strikes in 1969 retired Pengel from political life; he died in 1970. The emergence of the Centrale 47 (C-47) trade-union organization, led by Eddie Bruma, shook up the traditional workers movement, the Moederbond, long dominated by the NPS. As with everything else in Curaçao, times were changing and the Curaçao wind, blowing from the west, made them change faster still. In addition the Dutch government, then in the hands of the socialists and fearful of a repetition of the Curaçao experience in the far more volatile environment of Suriname, committed itself to independence, which became a reality in 1975. In this sense, it may be said that at least one chapter of the struggle for independence in Suriname was fought on the streets of Willemstad.

The separate political process enfolding in Suriname between 1954 and 1975 was the beginning of a continuously disappearing prospect for political integration in the Dutch islands. The integration project depended inordinately on three island territories which, at different stages in the process, all discovered that there were more interesting options to explore. Curaçao and Aruba, the putative leaders of the Leeward Islands group, each had different claims to pre-eminence. In terms of size and population, Curaçao was largest, economically Aruba was strongest, and the contradictions between them could not easily be resolved; so much so that some observers have openly counselled the surrender of autonomy and the return of direct, modified rule by The Hague.[99] In any case Aruba opted for, and received, *status aparte* in 1981.[100] In the Windward Islands the same forces of separation and autono-

99 Robertico Croes and Lucita Moenir Alam, 1990, p.95.
100 *Ibid.*, pp.81ff.

my were at work, complicated by the fact that St Maarten, the natural leader of the group, is itself a small island divided between Dutch and French proprietorship and possessed withal of an economic prosperity apparently securely based on tourism. In none of these islands has there been, and arguably there cannot be, a viable decolonization project. Even Suriname, Curaçao and Aruba are still heavily dependent on Dutch aid; if the probability of such a project is measured by the yardstick of economic self-sufficiency, not much change can be envisaged in respect of the constitutional status of these islands. In a sense the Dutch islands are where the anglophone Caribbean was in the early 1950s, apparently without hope of independence unless merged into a large unit which remains elusive. Whereas the federal experiment in the case of the latter gave rise eventually to the reality of independence, the challenges of independence for all of the Netherlands territories, including Suriname, might one day stimulate another look at the prospect of constructing a unified, independent and viable state out of the bits and pieces that now exist.

In the case of British Honduras the march to independence was impeded by the longstanding, persistent claims by Guatemala to a significant part of the country.[101] In 1981 Belize joined the emerging Caribbean Commonwealth as an independent nation. By then, however, independence was a jaundiced and sometimes maligned objective in the eyes of those who had expected more, and had received less, from its realization. It was not only that a new generation of sometimes severely critical analysts and politicians derided the achievement of self-determination, but also that the feeling was strong that the benefits of independence had been enjoyed largely by those social sectors which had often opposed its realization in the period of decolonization. Indeed, contemporaries in the still-colonized areas of the Caribbean often referred to the ambivalent benefits of the independent states as one of the principal reasons underlying their own uncertainties about the merits of complete secession from the colonial attachment.

In the French and Netherlands Antilles, and in the still-dependent British colonies, the sentiment for independence is at best lukewarm, sometimes even non-existent.[102] In the period 1956–68 departmentalization was stoutly resisted in the Caribbean by a variety of popular political organizations in Martinique, Guadeloupe and Guyane. In the early 1960s, Antillean national-

101 Narda Dobson, 1973, chaps 11 and 12; also, R. A. Humphreys, 1961, and O. Nigel Bolland, 1986.

102 See, for example, Robertico Croes and Lucia Moenir Alam, 1990, p.91. The very mixed blessing of independence in Suriname since 1975 is an additional, and more immediate, disincentive to the Netherlands Antilles. See article by Fabian Badejo, in Betty Sedoc-Dahlberg, 1990, p.141.

ists, led by Aimé Césaire's Parti Progressiste de la Martinique, proposed autonomy as an alternative to assimilation and departmentalization.[103] Even the Parti Communiste Martiniquais (PCM) avoided independence and embraced the option of autonomy. It was left to smaller and less prestigious political, social and intellectual organizations to agitate, with predictable futility, the cause of Martiniquan independence.[104]

So, too, was the case with Guadeloupe. Historically the more radical of the two principal French West Indian colonies, the island lived up to its reputation in the 1960s and 1970s. The Parti Communiste Guadeloupéen, one of whose principal members, Henri Bangou, was Mayor of Pointe-à-Pitre, was at best ambivalent about independence. But a much more spirited and militant nationalist struggle for independence was waged in Guadeloupe. Inspired by the anti-imperialist theories of the period, and undaunted by the unequal prospect of resorting to revolutionary violence against the French State, the Groupe des Organisations Nationales de la Guadeloupe (GONG) emerged in the early 1960s out of a background of social and political discontent, labour agitation and strikes. Notwithstanding the existence of an organized Communist Party, the GONG quickly became the most important anti-colonial formation in the island, and in due course it was joined by the Front for Guadeloupean Autonomy (FGA).[105] Unlike the Communist Party, the strategy of both of these organizations was to work outside the existing political structures and, if possible, to drive the French from the island, in emulation of the achievements of the Vietnamese and Algerian revolutionaries. Cuban revolutionary ideology was also a significant factor. But though these militant organizations caught the imagination of a significant sector of the Guadeloupean masses, their active base remained small and their members paid a high price for their militancy. Many of them were killed or injured in confrontations with the French military, and others were tried and imprisoned for long periods in metropolitan jails. Also, the brothers Felix and Henri Rodes, publishers of the newspaper *Le Contrat Social*, played an important role in popularizing the radical cause and perpetuating the call for independence even after the radical upsurge had passed away.

In French Guiana, Guyane, a small movement aspiring to national independence dated from 1960. The major parties, particularly the Parti Socialiste Guyanais and the Gaullist Rassemblement pour la Republique, the latter more predictably than the former, eschewed the independence option. It was left

103 Aimé Césaire, 1961; see also, Richard D. E. Burton, 1978.

104 See, for example, Armand Nicolas, 1996–1998, vol.3. Nicolas was for a long time the General Secretary of the PCM.

105 L. Farrugia, 1979, pp.136–80.

to Unité Guyanaise, a small Marxist party, to carry the banner of national liberation and independence. As in Guadeloupe, a militant, violent organization, the Front National Libéré de la Guyane, briefly took the stage until it was outlawed and suppressed.[106] All in all, the challenges to continued departmentalization, such as they were, sputtered and died by the end of the 1960s. Since then resistance has been replaced by an apparent resignation with the result that nation building in the French Antilles seems for the moment to be permanently postponed.

Nationalism is sentimentally and culturally Caribbean, but the political activism required to take the final, few steps across the Rubicon in the service of unequivocally breaking the colonial connection is almost completely absent. Quietly, and no doubt to the great satisfaction of the colonial powers, the challenges that decolonization offered to the continuing presence and influence of the imperialist powers seem to have been overcome, at least for now, and a new era of quiet imperialism is slowly consolidating itself in the region.

106 See Pierre Albert Murtil, 1977.

6

African and Indian consciousness

Tony Martin

African consciousness

> I love the [African] race. I am not fighting for the race for my personal benefit, for having obtained the object of my ambition, I could sit down and practice my profession; but I believe that the cause of the people is greater than the cause of the individual, hence I am associated with it.
>
> *Henry Sylvester Williams*
> at the Princes Building, Port of Spain, 1901[1]

The fact of African consciousness is a recurrent and dominant theme in the history of the twentieth-century Caribbean. It has been a major influence on political development and closely intertwined with the history of trade unions and with expressions of popular culture.

The roots of twentieth-century African consciousness naturally stretch back into the nineteenth century and beyond. The end of slavery unleashed a flood of pent-up African interest, which sought to capitalize on the newfound freedom in its efforts at concrete expression. A desire for a physical return to Africa became the preoccupation of many, including Jamaican Maroons who went to Sierra Leone in 1800, even before the abolition of slavery. Mandingoes from Trinidad sought repatriation to the Gambia. Jamaican John Brown Russwurm became Governor of Maryland colony in present-day Liberia. Robert Campbell of Jamaica relocated to Nigeria, where he became a leading citizen of Lagos. Edward Wilmot Blyden of St Thomas became a major intellectual figure from his base in Liberia and Sierra Leone. Congolese from Cuba, in their organized thousands, sought repatriation to the Congo.

1 The *Mirror*, 1901, quoted by James R. Hooker, 1975, p.44.

Missionaries and revolutionaries journeyed to Africa.[2] Liberia's president saw in the immigration of several hundred Barbadians the 'vindication of [God's] goodness and justice. ...'[3]

African consciousness was fed also by a brisk commerce in the other direction. 'Liberated Africans', rescued from slave ships, were brought to the Caribbean. So were indentured workers after slavery. African-born soldiers of the West India Regiment were demobilized in the British Caribbean.[4] African leaders were exiled to the islands – King Behanzin of Dahomey to Martinique, King Jaja of Opobo in Nigeria to St Vincent. King Jaja's widow was still very much alive in Trinidad in 1937.[5] Caribbean-based intellectuals, not surprisingly, evinced a great interest in things Pan-African, through their newspapers, books and private correspondence. African consciousness in the twentieth century therefore rested on deep foundations.

The century opened in a fashion highly symbolic for Afro-Caribbean racial consciousness. A Trinidadian former schoolteacher, Henry Sylvester Williams, convened the world's first Pan-African Conference. He brought together over thirty eminent delegates from Africa, African America and the Caribbean, augmented by people of African origin living in Europe. There had been gatherings with an international flavour among African peoples before, but this was the first self-consciously 'Pan-African' conference.[6]

Caribbean delegates came from Jamaica, Antigua, St Lucia, Dominica, Haiti and Trinidad. Williams and Antiguan delegate Joseph Mason, pastor of a London church, were secretary and president respectively of the African Association, founded in London in 1897. It was under the auspices of this association that the Pan-African Conference was convened. Trinidad delegates R. E. Phipps and A. Pulcherie Pierre, both lawyers, were among the association's earliest members. Other delegates included Professor W. E. B. DuBois, African America's most prominent intellectual of the time; Bishop Alexander Walters of the African Methodist Episcopal Zion Church, a prominent political and church figure in the United States; Benito Sylvain of Haiti, who had

2 Carey Robinson, 1969, p.152; Carl Campbell, 1974b, p.29–38; *idem*, 1974a, pp.129–32; Hollis R. Lynch, 1967, p.34; *idem*, 1971, p.46; Okon E. Uya, 1971, p.46; Robert Campbell's account of his trip to Abeokuta can be found in Martin R. Delany and Robert Campbell, 1969; Benito Sylvain, 1905; Tony Martin, 1984b, p.211–15; C. L. R. James, 1938a (1963), p.265; A. H. Barrow, 1900.

3 Edward Wilmot Blyden to the Gentlemen of Barbados, 10 March 1864, in Hollis R. Lynch, 1978, p.64.

4 See A. B. Ellis, 1885.

5 'African Queen Found in Mayaro', *Sunday Guardian*, 28 February 1937, p.3.

6 For general accounts of the conference see James R. Hooker, 1975; Owen C. Mathurin, 1976; Tony Martin, 1984b, pp.201–16; Bishop Alexander Walters, 1914.

journeyed to Ethiopia to meet the Emperor Menelik II, and who represented both Ethiopia and Haiti at the conference; and T. R. Johnson, former Attorney-General and later Secretary of State of Liberia.

The conference sought to inform delegates of conditions facing the African race world wide. It tried to organize a Pan-African lobby in London and to foster a spirit of common purpose among Africans scattered around the world. It especially sought an amelioration in the conditions facing Africans in South Africa and it petitioned Queen Victoria to this effect. The official conference document, 'To the Nations of the World', of which Williams was one of the signatories, contained the following prophetic and often quoted passage: 'The problem of the twentieth century is the problem of the color line, the question as to how far differences of race … will hereafter be made the basis of denying to over half the world the right of sharing to their utmost ability the opportunities and privileges of modern civilization.'[7]

At least three of the Caribbean delegates later emigrated to Africa. George Christian of Dominica became a successful lawyer and legislator in the Gold Coast (Ghana) where he was a member of the Legislative Council from 1920 to 1940.[8] Richard E. Phipps, the Trinidad barrister, returned home after the conference and emigrated to the Gold Coast in 1911. He remained there until his death around 1926.[9] Williams himself lived in South Africa from 1903 to 1905,[10] and died in Trinidad in 1911.

Williams moved rapidly to implant in the Caribbean the Pan-African Association (PAA) formed at the conference. He toured Trinidad and Jamaica in 1901, lecturing and organizing branches. The quality and enthusiasm of the response in both places attested to the potency of racial consciousness as a mobilizing force among the Caribbean masses. The Trinidad branch of the PAA was formally established during Williams' visit in early July 1901. Attorney Emanuel M'Zumbo Lazare was president of the central executive, with the 'strikingly beautiful school mistress',[11] Mrs Philip John, as secretary. Lazare's rationale for joining the association may be inferred from his motion carried unanimously at Williams' first Port of Spain lecture, to a crowd of over one thousand persons. 'The meeting assembled here,' he moved, 'appreciates the successful efforts made by the Pan-African Association in London to ameliorate the condition of our oppressed brethren in Africa, and is of the

7 Quoted in Tony Martin, 1984b, p.208.
8 Owen C. Mathurin, 1976, p.165.
9 *Ibid.*, p.167.
10 See James R. Hooker, 1975, chap. 7 and Owen C. Mathurin, 1976, chap. 8. Hooker says Williams remained in South Africa until 1904. Mathurin gives the date as 1905.
11 James R. Hooker, 1975, p.39.

opinion that the organization should be strongly supported by members of the race in this island.'[12]

For Lazare, as for his middle-class African-conscious contemporaries, the struggle at home (in this case, Trinidad), was largely indivisible from the struggle for African advancement around the world. Their strong commitment to Africa did not prevent them from playing leading roles in the struggles not only for racial justice, but also for broad political reform at home. Edgar Maresse-Smith, a foundation member, had led the famous campaign in 1888 for a strong Afrocentric observance of the fiftieth anniversary of emancipation.[13] So had Rev. Philip Henry Douglin, head of the Pan-African Association in San Fernando. A Barbadian by birth, Douglin had laboured for 17 years with the West Indian Church Association at the Rio Pongo.[14]

Williams had stopped in Jamaica on his way to Trinidad. There he reported five hundred members enrolled during his visit and a further five hundred by the time he got to Trinidad. The rapid growth in Jamaican PAA membership was facilitated by the affiliation, *en masse*, of the People's Convention, led by Dr J. Robert Love.[15]

African consciousness in the first two decades of the century was further fed by a variety of sources. The quest for democratic government, even where pursued by multi-racial pressure groups, almost inevitably harboured racial undertones. The governments were mostly white, while the disfranchized masses were mostly African.

Many of the older forms of interaction with Africa also continued. Missionaries continued to travel to Africa. A reduced West India Regiment still did service on the continent. The British government recruited policemen, civil servants, and railway employees in the Caribbean for work in Africa,[16]

12 Quoted in *Ibid.*, pp.43–4.

13 *Ibid.*, p.7.

14 Owen C. Mathurin, 1976, p.95.

15 James R. Hooker, 1975, p.48; Owen C. Mathurin, 1976, p.89.

16 The author interviewed a Trinidadian, the late Mrs Irene Cleghorn, who accompanied her husband, a Trinidad Government Railway employee, to Nigeria in the early twentieth century. In 1975 he met a Guyanese lady who was born in the Gold Coast (Ghana), where her father worked as a policeman. His own grandfather, a Trinidad Government Railway station master, is said to have passed up an opportunity to work in Nigeria, for reasons unknown. Trinidadians were offered a free second-class passage to and from Lagos, three-year contracts renewable for a second term and, after one year, free passage to Lagos for their families in lieu of a free return passage home. A copy of the contract is in Enclosure to Trinidad Despatch No. 411 of 14 October 1913, CO 295/484, Colonial Office Records, Public Record Office, London.

just as African soldiers and police had earlier been recruited for service in the Caribbean. Lawyers, doctors, teachers and other professionals qualifying overseas continued to head for Africa after graduation, as they have continued to do to the present day, in larger numbers than is popularly realized. Caribbean seamen settled in African ports. Some of these people returned eventually. Others stayed but maintained contact with friends and relatives in the Caribbean.[17] Out of all this came a complex network of mutual knowledge and cross-fertilization of ideas.

Thus Henry Sylvester Williams could have two Caribbean employees in his Cape Town law practice from 1903 to 1905;[18] Caribbean workers in Kano, Northern Nigeria, could organize a branch of Marcus Garvey's Universal Negro Improvement Association (UNIA) around 1920;[19] and a Vincentian, J. G. Gumbs, could be chairman of South Africa's Industrial and Commercial Workers Union in the 1920s (the executive committee often contained three or four Caribbean members).[20] This cross-fertilization of experience is richly demonstrated in the case of the Jamaican, A. S. W. Shackleford, who emigrated to Nigeria as a railway employee, headed Marcus Garvey's UNIA in Lagos and became an important businessman in Ghana and Nigeria.[21] Some Caribbean emigrants to Africa, such as soldiers and policemen, may have played less than positive roles. But even here, the experience of Africa could have the ultimately positive result of an enhanced racial consciousness.

The most forceful articulators of pride in the African race were often also the leaders of organizations and movements, whether multi-racial or not, for broad political and social change. It may be that early conditioning to a life of struggle for racial justice equipped them with the tools for the wider struggles against colonialism and lack of democracy. Certainly colonialism was at the core of the problem of racial injustice, so that the struggle against colonialism was a natural extension of the struggle for basic human rights for Africans. As members and leaders of multi-racial movements they easily made the transition to representing the welfare of the entire community, though usually not at the cost of denying their own racial pride. Thus Emanuel M'Zumbo Lazare, the son of African-born parents, could be an elected member of the Port of Spain Borough Council, president of the PAA, a leader of

17 African-born demobilized West India Regiment soldiers were the major element in the Trinidad Police Force at some points in the nineteenth century according to Algernon A. Burkett, 1914, p.3. They were called 'Yurabas' (Yorubas), according to this account.

18 James R. Hooker,1975, pp.67–8.

19 *Negro World* (New York), 21 August 1920.

20 Clements Kadalie, 1970, p.220; Tony Martin, 1976 (1986), pp.119–20.

21 Rina Okonkwo, 1985, pp.45–58.

the multi-racial Ratepayers Association and later the second African Trinidadian appointed to the Trinidad & Tobago Legislative Council.[22] These activists regarded the entire society as rightfully theirs. Their strong espousal of African consciousness did not in any way deter them in their quest to capture centre stage in the political and social affairs of the respective territories.

It can be argued that a new African ethnicity developed out of slavery in the Caribbean (and in many other places as well). Due to the intermingling of African ethnicities during and after slavery, the post-emancipation African in the Caribbean owed allegiance to the continent, and not necessarily to any individual polity within it.[23] It was this essentially Pan-African reality and outlook that allowed Africans in the Caribbean and America to pioneer the movement for worldwide African collaboration.

It is nevertheless also true that self-consciously African communities persisted in some areas in the Caribbean into the twentieth century, providing an ongoing source of African remembrance for the population at large. Some, like the Maroon communities of Jamaica and Suriname, evolved during slavery and though associated with a particular geographical area, may well have become essentially part of the new Caribbean African ethnicity.

Others, like the Yoruba, Congo, Hausa and other communities of Trinidad, were influenced by post-emancipation arrivals. Even here, though, the movement towards a new African ethnicity was well advanced by the 1900s. There is no doubt, for example, that the Yoruba communities in Trinidad established their dominance over rival African ethnicities and then absorbed many of them into their religious and cultural milieu.

The early calypsonian, Sam Manning, gave a brief but interesting description of one such Yoruba community in Trinidad around 1910. He identified a fierce racial pride as one of their outstanding characteristics. 'The Yorubas were a proud, independent people. ... Through everything [they] still clung to the beliefs and culture of their tribe' and, it would appear, despised other Africans who resorted to race mixing.[24] Since it has been demonstrated that these Yorubas had a tremendous impact on the culture and outlook of Trinidadians (and noteworthily on the development of calypso),[25] it must be assumed that they also influenced the feelings of racial consciousness that diffused throughout the community. In Dominica the African 'Oku' community in the early twentieth century preserved its own language, settled its own

22 For a biographical sketch of Lazare, see Algernon A. Burkett, 1914, p.95; Brinsley Samaroo, 1971, p.89.

23 For an argument to this effect see Don Robotham, 1988, pp.23–38.

24 Tony Martin, 1984b, p.218.

25 See Maureen Warner-Lewis, 1991, pp.141–57.

internal disputes, practised co-operative work and celebrated 1 August, Emancipation Day, every year.[26]

The practice of journalism was yet another important element fostering racial consciousness. Several of the major proponents of African consciousness and political reform also doubled as owners of newspapers and active journalists. Dr J. Robert Love, the third African to sit on Jamaica's Legislative Council, and 'kingmaker' for the first two, mentor of Marcus Garvey and head of the Jamaican Pan-African Association, published the *Jamaica Advocate.* The slogan 'Africa for the Africans, at home and abroad', popularized later by Garvey, appeared in a Love article as early as 1898.[27]

Theophilus Albert Marryshow, Grenada's 'Father of West Indian Federation,' published the *West Indian* from 1917. He supported Garvey in the 1920s and attended W. E. B. DuBois' 1921 Pan-African Congress in London.[28] Garvey himself, in whom African consciousness reached its apogee, published three newspapers in Jamaica – *Garvey's Watchman* around 1910 or earlier, the *Blackman* from 1929 to 1931, and the *New Jamaican* from 1931 to 1933. He also began *Black Man* magazine in Jamaica in 1933 and continued it in England, and published two papers, *La Nación* and *La Prensa,* among Caribbean emigrants in Costa Rica and Panama respectively, between about 1910 and 1912.

Where Afro-Caribbean newspaper editors were not themselves major political figures, their publications were usually active in the struggle for racial uplift and social change.[29] Somewhat unusual was the case of the *Argos* in Trinidad. There the wealthy Chinese-Trinidadian merchant, George Lee Lum, owned the paper but allowed the editorial staff free rein to play a major role in the propagation of an African consciousness. White community leaders complained to the Colonial Secretary in 1919 that the *Argos* was 'owned by a Chinaman of no particular persuasion and run by four or five "coloured gentlemen" of the most pronounced type of hater of the white man.'[30]

A similar radicalizing role was played by foreign-based publications owned, edited or otherwise influenced by Caribbean emigrants abroad,

---

26 Interview with J. R. Ralph Casimir, Roseau, 1985, cited in Tony Martin, 1988 (1989), p.123.

27 Tony Martin, 1976 (1986), p.111.

28 *Ibid.*, p.96.

29 The following were among nineteenth century examples for Trinidad – the *Trinidad Press*, the *Trinidad Colonist*, the *Telegraph*, *New Era* and *San Fernando Gazette.* See Bridget Brereton, 1993, pp.274–83; and M. Thomas-Bailey, 2001.

30 Messrs George T. Huggins *et al.* to Colonial Secretary, 30 July 1919, Colonial Offices Files, Public Record Office, London, CO 295/522. See also Tony Martin, 1984c, p.49.

especially in North America and Europe. Garvey's *Negro World* (1918–33) occupies pride of place in this category. In the early 1920s its circulation in Dominica exceeded that of the two local papers, one African- and the other European- owned.[31] It was implicated in the rise of African consciousness and accordingly banned (along with other foreign-based publications) by governmental authorities in several Caribbean territories, from Cuba to Guyana.[32]

The *Africa Times and Orient Review,* published in London (1912–14, 1919–20) by the African Dusé Mohammed Ali, circulated in the Caribbean and carried articles pertinent to the area. Garvey worked for and published in this magazine in 1913. From New York after the First World War came the *Crusader,* organ of the African Blood Brotherhood, led by Kittitian Cyril Briggs. Jamaican W. A. Domingo published the *Emancipator* at about the same time, also from New York.

From Hamburg and elsewhere in Europe in the 1930s came the Communist International's *Negro Worker,* edited by Trinidad's George Padmore, head of the Negro Bureau of world communism's Red International of Labour Unions (Profintern). From London in 1937 Padmore launched *International African Opinion,* organ of his newly formed International African Service Bureau, with fellow Trinidadian C. L. R. James as editor.[33]

The general pattern of African consciousness described here was true also for Cuba, the Caribbean's largest island and most populous nation. The fact that Afro-Cubans were not in a clear majority, the reality of United States occupation (1898–1902 and 1906–9) and the grant of universal male adult suffrage in 1902, nevertheless provided Cuba with distinctive features. Cuba formally ended slavery in 1886, the last Caribbean nation to do so, even though most Afro-Cubans had already emancipated themselves by that time. The Afro-Cubans formed themselves into African 'societies', published newspapers, maintained a strong practice of African religion and, for thousands of Congolese in Cuba, tried to return to Africa.[34] Inspired by the Afro-Cuban General Antonio Maceo, they constituted the majority of the Liberation Army in the 1895–8 War of Independence against Spain.

Traditional Spanish racism, which existed even within the Liberation Army, and which not even Maceo, Cuba's most successful general, could avoid, intensified during the United States occupation of 1898–1902. The United States withdrew in 1902 leaving white Cubans and Spaniards firmly in

31 Tony Martin, 1988 (1989), p.134.

32 Tony Martin, 1976 (1986), pp.94–6.

33 James R. Hooker, 1967, p.49.

34 'Benito Sylvain of Haiti on the Pan-African Conference of 1900', in Tony Martin, 1984b, pp.211–5. For a detailed treatment of the broader picture see Aline Helg, 1995. The present discussion of the period relies heavily on Helg.

charge. Afro-Cubans were largely locked out of political power, segregation remained rampant and aspects of African culture, such as the *Santería* religion, were criminalized. In addition, losses in the independence wars of 1868–78 and 1895–8, coupled with a deliberate 'whitening' policy of massive Spanish immigration, together put the Afro-Cuban population into relative decline.

The enduring Cuban (and Latin American) fiction of a racial democracy made the situation more complex and frustrating.[35] By 1907 a rising consciousness had produced several manifestos and proposals to stem the racist tide. There were calls for the recognition of the inordinate sacrifices made by Afro-Cubans in the recent independence war; there were calls to boycott elections until Afro-Cubans were guaranteed the right, not merely to vote, but to be appointed to high office; there were calls for an independent African political party. Evaristo E. Estenoz, a former Liberation Army officer, tried unsuccessfully to establish an Afro-Cuban caucus within the Liberal Party, the party favoured by most Afro-Cubans. Over two hundred people attended a 1907 conference in Camaguey to establish a *Directorio de la Raza de Color* (Coordinating Council for People of Colour). The group promised to unite Africans and mulattos in a self-reliant organization for 'the progress of our race'. It eschewed any intention of forming a race-based political party.[36]

On 7 August 1908 Estenoz formally established the Independent Party of Colour (Partido Independiente de Color), which was legally recognized by the United States occupation. The total absence of Afro-Cuban winners in the local and provincial elections appeared to be the last straw for Estenoz. The new party condemned the exclusion of Afro-Cubans from the judiciary and diplomatic service, proposed a campaign against illiteracy and in favour of expanded elementary education, demanded the admission of Africans into military and naval academies, denounced the death penalty, and advocated prison reform, workmen's compensation and an eight-hour working day. It opposed the ban on African immigration. It also opposed the Platt Amendment, under which the United States reserved the right to intervene in Cuban affairs. All of these proposals spoke directly or indirectly to areas of racial discrimination. The party prematurely contested national elections in 1908 and was heavily defeated.[37]

Correspondents to the party's newspaper, *Previsión* (*Foresight*), meanwhile exhibited the same racial pride and desire for a strong race that were by now commonplace in the Caribbean. 'I am a black dot,' wrote one reader, 'one out of the anonymous mass of my race, who longs to see the

35 Aline Helg, 1995. For a similar fiction of racial democracy in Brazil see Abdias do Nascimento, 1979 (1989).

36 Jorge Castellanos and Isabel Castellanos, 1990, pp.311–12.

37 *Ibid.*, p.317; Aline Helg, 1995, pp.146–7.

advance of my people through our own effort, through the compact union and solidarity of our family.'[38]

The white Cuban power structure repressed the Independent Party of Colour with a ferocity which, while not fundamentally unusual in the context of Caribbean history, nevertheless assumed many of the characteristics of contemporary North American racism. Estenoz was arrested and jailed twice in 1910, as were the top leadership of the party and hundreds of supporters. Many Afro-Cubans were randomly arrested and jailed. US-type stereotypes of Afro-Cubans as rapists and rumours of a Haitian-type revolution were used as a smokescreen to cover the repression. Emulating a common North American tactic, Cuba's white rulers found an Afro-Cuban, Martin Morúa Delgado, the only African in the island's senate, to introduce a law banning racially based and therefore 'racist' political parties. The Morúa Law passed in 1910, by which time Estenoz was claiming 93,000 members. Morúa obligingly died four days afterwards, mercifully spared the carnage soon to be visited upon Afro-Cubans in the name of his law.[39]

With the leadership out of jail in 1911 the party continued to mobilize while trying to appease white racism. In 1912, with the party still banned and presidential elections imminent, a few hundred party members staged an 'armed protest', in the tradition of similar contemporary protests by veterans and other groups. This provided the pretext for their annihilation. The white structure, always united across party lines in its eagerness to extirpate the Afro-Cuban party, unleashed a reign of terror. Thousands of troops were deployed and the white population was armed. Africans were lynched, shot and beheaded. Afro-Cuban corpses were left to litter the streets. An estimated 2,000 to 5,000 Afro-Cubans, many of them people unconnected to the party, were killed by the military and vigilantes. Thousands were arrested. A large number became refugees. Estenoz and other leaders were slaughtered and their bodies desecrated.[40]

The Cuban massacre of 1912 remains one of the worst reverses suffered by African consciousness in Caribbean history. No other race, save for the indigenous people, has suffered this type of carnage primarily on the basis of racial aspiration.

The First World War ushered in a period of intense African consciousness in which the middle classes, though still as race-conscious as before, were frequently upstaged by the masses. Consciousness on a mass level had always been present, often as a normal concomitant of working-class life, not

38 Aline Helg, 1995, p.151.

39 *Ibid.*, pp.165, 172. Jorge Castellanos and Isabel Castellanos, 1990, pp.318–19.

40 Aline Helg, 1995, pp.211–26; Jorge Castellanos and Isabel Castellanos, 1990, pp.322–34.

requiring any special demonstration. In so far as the Afro-Caribbean working class maintained African religious practices, or passed on the art of drumming and other cultural and social expressions, it was a living repository of African consciousness. It often also, on that account, bore the brunt of colonialist repression. Its bass drum was outlawed; its annual carnival celebrations in Trinidad were endemically under attack; various expressions of African religion were criminalized in Cuba; its Spiritual Baptist religion was banned in Trinidad's Shouter Prohibition Ordinance, patterned after a similar law against the Shakers of St Vincent;[41] and it came under police attack in the carnival-related Canboulay Riots of 1881 in Trinidad. Canboulay, the torchlight procession that ushered in carnival, was outlawed.[42] Trinidadian Lewis Osborn Innis, writing in 1910 of the events of previous decades, observed that 'it was found necessary to make special legislation against the beating of the big African drum, to which the *bass people* were fond of dancing *calindas* (a most indecent performance) on account of the noise it made.' The consequence of hostile legislation was that 'the archaic instrument died a natural death, and quatros, bandols, flutes and clarionettes reigned in its stead, to the great comfort of the decent inhabitants.'[43]

The upsurge in mass African consciousness which took place around the First World War was fed by a variety of forces. First, the war itself served as a profound radicalizing influence. The endemic racism at home erupted into startling clarity in the British colonies when local Whites refused to serve in the same military units as non-Whites, except as commissioned officers. The result was that many white volunteers proceeded directly to England or Canada where they enlisted in white units. Those who went through the initial formalities at home did so, in the case of Trinidad, in a Whites-only Merchants and Planters Contingent, organized by the white community for the occasion. C. L. R. James, later one of the region's leading intellectuals, recalls being rudely rejected when he (perhaps inexplicably) attempted to join the white contingent.[44]

The imperial government in London did not help matters by proclaiming the conflict a 'white man's war' and initially rejecting Afro-Caribbean efforts to volunteer. When non-white soldiers were finally accepted they were mustered primarily into the British West Indies Regiment (BWIR), a specially

41 See Edward L. Cox, 1994, pp.208–43.

42 For a pro-establishment account of anti-Canboulay activity see L. O. Innis, 1910, pp.82, 89–91.

43 *Ibid.*, p.97. The Indian 'tom tom' (presumably tassa drum), also a nuisance to authorities, was not banned.

44 C. L. R. James, 1963, p.40.

organized unit. Here the rank and file were mostly African and the officers were white. Though trained as soldiers the former were used for the most part as labourers. The final indignity came at Taranto, Italy, at war's end, when they were required to clean the latrines of Italian labourers. It was at this point that the West Indians mutinied.[45]

During their stay abroad the men of the BWIR experienced racism in its most virulent forms. They were especially incensed at the treatment of continental African troops and came into conflict with white South African and other soldiers on this account.[46] They also came in contact with Garvey's race-uplift ideas. This was an explosive combination and the soldiers returned home in 1919 bitter, radicalized and more race-conscious than before. They were heavily implicated in the political agitation, labour unrest and anti-racist violence that ensued in British Honduras, Trinidad, Jamaica, Grenada and elsewhere.[47] Several veterans emerged as major leaders of the inter-war years, among them S. A. Haynes of British Honduras, the anomalous popular white leader, Captain A. A. Cipriani of Trinidad and Tubal Uriah Buzz Butler of Grenada and Trinidad.

The war years with their increase in prices and allegations of profiteering also gave the Workingmen's Association and similar bodies issues around which to rally. As in earlier periods, the activities of Caribbean emigrants abroad again helped raise consciousness at home. The British-based Society of Peoples of African Origin (SPAO) brought together Africans, Caribbean residents and African Americans in England. Led by a Sierra Leonean, J. Eldred Taylor, its membership included prominent Caribbean residents such as F. E. M. Hercules and Audrey Jeffers.[48] Jeffers would return home to Trinidad in 1920 and found the Coterie of Social Workers (1921), for decades the dominant social service and women's organization in the region.

As a schoolboy at Queen's Royal College in Port of Spain, Hercules founded a Young Men's Coloured Association in 1907. During the British anti-African riots of 1919 he emerged as a major spokesman for his embattled community.[49] Shortly afterwards he toured the Caribbean, like Henry Sylvester Williams 18 years earlier, and established local branches of the SPAO.[50]

45 For the story of the British West Indies Regiment, see C. L. Joseph, 1971, pp.94–124 and Glenford D. Howe, 1994, pp.27–62. On the Taranto mutiny see W. F. Elkins, 1970, pp.99–103.

46 Conversation with Mr Baden Semper, a BWIR veteran, 1968, Ellerslie Park, Trinidad.

47 See, for example, Tony Martin, 1984c, pp.47–58.

48 See, for example, W. F. Elkins, 1972, pp.47–59.

49 *Ibid.*

50 *Ibid.*

The intensified race consciousness of the First World War period and afterwards was part of the worldwide phenomenon known as the New Negro Movement. Emanating from African America, the New Negro ideology embraced pride in race, advocated the strengthening of Pan-African linkages, urged resistance to oppression and encouraged a deeper identification with Africa. It also spawned its literary and artistic counterpart, known in African America as the Harlem Renaissance. The single most important catalyst for the New Negro movement, in the Caribbean, in African America and around the world, was the Jamaican Marcus Garvey.

Garvey's instrument was the UNIA (its full name being the Universal Negro Improvement Association and African Communities League) which he founded in Jamaica in 1914. His perspective was global from the very beginning and the formation of the UNIA came after four years of travel in Central and South America and Europe. In the Americas he had followed the footsteps of Caribbean emigrants to places like Costa Rica and Panama. In England he met with African seamen and intellectuals, the latter at the *Africa Times and Orient Review,* which employed him. His consciousness had already been fed by early reading of Pan-African history, particularly the works of Edward Wilmot Blyden. He was said to have been a protégé of Dr J. Robert Love and corresponded in 1915 with the African American Pan-Africanist and educator, Booker T. Washington.

Like many of the leading race-conscious Caribbean personalities of his and earlier generations, Garvey had passed through the crucible of agitation for political reform. In 1910, the year in which the Independent Party of Colour was banned in Cuba, he was an assistant secretary of the National Club in Jamaica. Legislative Council members were among the club's adherents. Unlike many of the middle-class leaders, however, Garvey also had intimate experience of the labour movement, having led one of the British Caribbean's earliest strikes in 1908.[51]

As a result of his travels and his readings Garvey was struck by the universal suffering of the race, as well as by the possibilities of regeneration inherent in organization. He saw race consciousness in the Caribbean as pivotal to this regeneration and Caribbean people as the instruments of positive change. Writing in London in 1913 he declared:

> As one who knows the people well, I make no apology for prophesying that there will soon be a turning point in the history of the West Indies; and that the people who inhabit that portion of the Western Hemisphere will be the instruments of uniting a scattered race who,

51 I have documented all of this in Tony Martin, 1976 (1986).

> before the close of many centuries, will found an Empire on which the sun shall shine as ceaselessly as it shines on the empire of the North today.[52]

Garvey's grand design envisaged a strong African race, with its African homeland reclaimed from European colonialism, strong enough to protect its scattered members and respected in the world comity of nations. These ideas could be seen in the aims and objects of the UNIA published in 1914.[53] In a word, Garvey's was the philosophy of Black or African nationalism (as he himself described it). Its main tenets were race first, self-reliance and nationhood (political self-determination).

After a year and a half of modest success in Jamaica, Garvey left for the United States, where a projected five-month stay lasted 11 years. There, by dint of relentless effort backed by superb promotional and organizational skills, he was well established by 1918. By 1919 the movement had assumed a solidly international character, with branches in Canada and the Caribbean, among other places, in addition to the United States. The UNIA's major organ, the *Negro World,* begun in New York in 1918, almost immediately appeared in the Caribbean.

One of the earliest British West Indian branches of the new UNIA (the organization having reorganized itself in New York) was in St Vincent, under the leadership of R. E. M. Jack.[54] The St Vincent branch helped in the formation of branches in Dominica and other islands.[55]

In the Caribbean, as in many other places, the Garvey Movement found itself preaching to the converted. But the converted lacked a global organization and they flocked to the UNIA with its immense ability to link up local struggles and provide material and moral support in a systematic way. Even before starting a local UNIA chapter, the nucleus of would-be Dominica Garveyites, under J. R. Ralph Casimir and others, formed a Dominica Brotherhood Union in January 1920. One of their first acts was the drafting of a pledge, 'The Negro to Help the Negro.' It read:

> We hereby sincerely and truly pledge to give our support, and we are quite ready at any moment to shed our blood and to give our very lives to this cause and shall do all what is in our power to help one and all members of the race who [are] for this good and just cause.

---

52 Quoted in Tony Martin, 1983c, p.21.

53 Quoted in *ibid.*, pp.31–2.

54 Tony Martin, 1988 (1989), p.121.

55 *Ibid.*

We vow that we are sincerely and truly New Negroes. So help us Good God.[56]

The impact of Garvey's movement on the Caribbean was immense. His 'race first' ideology found ready acceptance both among the masses and among substantial sections of the middle classes. There were branches of the UNIA throughout the Greater Caribbean area. Next to the United States, this was the region where the UNIA proliferated most. Cuba led the world outside the United States, with at least 52 branches; Panama was next with 48; Trinidad & Tobago was third with 32.[57]

The movement penetrated every level of society and became entrenched among the most influential agencies for political and social change. The regional labour movement of the inter-war years in the British Caribbean was thoroughly Garveyite. D. Hamilton Jackson, leader of the St Croix Labour Union, was a Garvey sympathizer.[58] Hubert Critchlow of the pioneering British Guiana Labour Union reported Garveyite influence within his union.[59] Clement O. Payne of Barbados and Trinidad, founder of the Barbados Workers Union, was a Garveyite.[60] Garvey himself founded a Jamaican Workers and Labourers Association in 1930. In Trinidad the connection between the Trinidad Workingmen's Association, for years the country's major quasi-political body, and the UNIA was especially close. There was considerable overlapping between the leadership of the two organizations, and the Workingmen's Association held its regular meetings at Liberty Hall, the UNIA's Port of Spain headquarters.[61]

The massive UNIA presence in Cuba provided a new source for African consciousness in the wake of the slaughter of 1912. Historians of Cuba have in the past largely ignored it, however, since the UNIA based itself primarily among the Jamaican immigrant population. United States

56 9 January 1920; papers of J. R. Ralph Casimir, Roseau, Dominica, quoted in Tony Martin, 1988 (1989), p.117.

57 These figures are based on surviving records lodged in the UNIA Central Division (New York) files, Schomburg Center for Research into Black Culture, New York. In many instances the figures are actually understatements. For a complete listing and tabulation of branches based on the Central Division files, see Tony Martin, 1976 (1986), pp.361–73.

58 Tony Martin, 1976 (1986), p.99.

59 *Ibid.*, pp.235, 267n.48; Hubert Critchlow, 1945, p.51.

60 *People* (Trinidad), 21 August 1937, p.4. Here Payne is listed along with other Garveyites as a member of the Universal Management Committee planning Garvey's visit to Trinidad.

61 Tony Martin, 1984b, pp.50, 60, 65, 67–70, 78, 79. On the Jamaican Workers and Labourers Association see *Blackman* (Jamaica), 26 April 1930.

corporations (especially in the sugar industry) were able to get around the ban on African immigration by importing Jamaicans and Haitians as contract labourers.[62] (Many thousands were deported in the most deplorable conditions in the 1930s.) There was also a sprinkling of workers brought in from throughout the anglophone and francophone Caribbean and Bermuda, but they tend in historical accounts to be subsumed under the designation Jamaican. Between 1907 and 1929, 102,972 Jamaicans are said to have entered Cuba. Between 1912 and 1929, 183,983 Haitians entered, for a total influx of 304,955 Africans.[63] This was more than the entire 'black' Cuban population of 1907 and about half of the combined 'black' and 'mulatto' populations, to use the census terminology of Cuba's notoriously inaccurate racial statistics.[64]

The immigrants were concentrated in the eastern provinces of Oriente and Camagüey, where the bulk of the Afro-Cuban population resided. While the Haitians were overwhelmingly illiterate, the Jamaicans enjoyed a much higher literacy rate than the Afro-Cubans,[65] and access, however limited, to the diplomatic support of a powerful nation (Great Britain).

The racist Cuban press kept up a hysterical tirade against the newcomers, and especially the Jamaicans. They accused them of corrupting their 'docile' Afro-Cuban kinsmen and of sacrificing white Cuban children for their Obeah rites. At least one Jamaican was lynched in 1919 on a false charge of Obeah.[66]

It was into this tropical version of the southern United States that the Jamaicans injected the most powerful African-conscious organization in the world. A mere eight years after the slaughter of 1912 the officers of Garvey's Black Star Line were entertained to a banquet by President Mario G. Menocal.[67] In 1921 Garvey himself visited Cuba and was treated almost as a head of state. He was received by President Menocal and the Governor of Oriente province. He addressed various Afro-Cuban groups, including Club

62 For details of Cuba's Spanish- and US-inspired anti-African immigration laws see Juan Pérez de la Riva, 1979, pp.28–9.

63 *Ibid.*, tables VI and VII, n.p.

64 For a discussion of the racial flip-flops of Cuban census records see Carlos Moore, 1988b, pp.357–65. The census figures are in Jorge Castellanos and Isabel Castellanos, 1990, p.353.

65 84.4 per cent of the Haitians were illiterate; 92.4 per cent of the Jamaicans were literate; only 30 per cent of Afro-Cubans in Matanzas province in 1919, in the same age range as the immigrants, were literate: Juan Pérez de la Riva, 1979, tables VI and VII, and p.12.

66 Juan Pérez de la Riva, 1979, pp.57, 63–5.

67 *Negro World*, 1 May 1920; Hugh Mulzac, 1972, pp.83–5; Tony Martin, 1976 (1986), p.154.

Atenas, Havana's most prestigious society of colour.[68] So great was the power of the Cuban UNIA by 1923 that the resident British diplomatic representatives agreed to extend it recognition as the quasi-official body representing British Caribbean workers in Cuba. (The Foreign Office in London vetoed the idea after canvassing Caribbean governors.)[69]

The precise impact of the UNIA on Afro-Cubans remains to be definitively studied but it must have been substantial. Immigrants were targets of the same racist hysteria confronting Afro-Cubans and some Jamaicans and Haitians joined the Independent Party of Colour's armed protest in 1912.[70] Cubans are said to have been avid readers of the *Negro World*'s Spanish section. Jamaicans translated the English sections for them.[71]

Of 88 (possibly 89) names of Cuban UNIA presidents and secretaries in the mid-1920s, only three are Spanish and none appear to be Haitian,[72] but this does not necessarily refute the presumption of UNIA influence on the Afro-Cuban population. A Cuban historian has made the plausible but undocumented assertion that '[t]en per cent of the UNIA branches of Oriente and Camagüey included Cubans in their hierarchy.'[73] The sheer size of the Cuban UNIA, the diplomatic courtesies extended to Garvey and the fact that the virulently anti-African Machado dictatorship found it necessary to ban the UNIA for a while in the late 1920s and early 1930s,[74] all suggest an organization of some influence.

The entire political generation between the world wars was profoundly touched by Garvey. His popularity in the Caribbean was still evident in 1937, way past his heyday, when he toured the area for the last time. He was entertained royally and was everywhere the recipient of diplomatic courtesies usually reserved for representatives of a sovereign people. In Port of Spain the Mayor, Alfred Richards, and City Council honoured Garvey with a civic reception.[75] 'This is my second visit to Port of Spain,' Garvey told a Port of Spain audience. 'The first time was in 1914 when I was returning to Jamaica from England. I stopped off here then unknown to those I met.' In Guyana

---

68 Amy Jacques Garvey, 1963, p.58; Tony Martin, 1976 (1986), p.184; Bernardo García Domínguez, 1988, pp.300–2.

69 Tony Martin, 1976 (1986), pp.49–51.

70 Aline Helg, 1995, pp.209–10.

71 Bernardo García Domínguez, 1988, p.303.

72 UNIA Central Division (New York) Files, Schomburg Collection, New York Public Library.

73 Bernardo García Domínguez, 1988, p.303.

74 *Negro World*, 4 August 1928; *Blackman* (Jamaica), 28 June 1930; Tony Martin, 1976 (1986), p.51.

75 *The Caribbee* (Trinidad), Xmas Number, 1936, p.8; Tony Martin, 1984b, p.85.

he was received by the British Governor and feted at the Town Hall in Georgetown.[76]

Garvey's African nationalism was the dominant organizational expression of Pan-Africanism in the inter-war years, but it was not the only expression. Caribbean Africans both at home and abroad continued to be prominent in all variants of Pan-Africanism. The leadership of George Padmore and C. L. R. James, in what may be described as the communist variant of Pan-Africanism, has already been noted. In the Pan-African Congresses of African-American scholar W. E. B. DuBois, Pan-Africanism found its liberal integrationist expression. DuBois convened congresses in 1919, 1921, 1923 and 1927. The first three convened in a variety of European capitals (Paris, London, Brussels and Lisbon). The fourth, largely the work of African American women, convened in New York. Caribbean delegates were sometimes the majority element at DuBois' congresses. E. F. Fredericks of Guyana served on the executive committee of DuBois' first congress in Paris in 1919.[77]

The ascendancy of working-class African nationalism in the Garvey Movement and in trade unions into the 1930s, meanwhile, did not in any way eclipse similar sentiments among the African middle and upper classes. Nationalistic elements everywhere made common cause with Garveyism; and independent expressions of African nationalism continued to arise among those not openly associated with the UNIA.

The African Caribbean middle class was in the ascendant in the 1930s, and a dim light appeared visible at the end of the colonialist tunnel. A superior secondary education awaited the academically gifted. University education abroad followed for the exceptionally brilliant, the wealthy, the fortunate and the ambitious. The result was an African middle class of great erudition, with a confidence tested in successful intellectual competition with the best of Europe and North America and with no reason to be awed by European colonialists, many of whom they regarded as their intellectual inferiors. With Marcus Garvey rising to pre-eminence in the Pan-African movement, George Padmore becoming the major African figure in the Communist International and C. L. R. James occupying a similar position in the Trotskyist Fourth International,[78] African Caribbean people had no need to doubt their abilities.

---

76 *Port of Spain Gazette*, 21 October 1937, p.13; *Daily Argosy* (Georgetown), 23 October 1937.

77 W. E. B. DuBois, 1919, p.271.

78 Three of James' most important books appeared in the 1930s – *A History of Negro Revolt* (1938b [1994]); *The Black Jacobins* (1938a [1963]); *World Revolution* (1937). See also Tony Martin, 1984a, pp.165–78.

Among the middle classes, as among the working class, interaction with African Americans and continental Africans overseas continued to help raise racial consciousness. The role of Trinidad's F. E. M. Hercules in inter-war London has already been noted. At about the same time Audrey Jeffers, later the doyenne of Trinidad's rising African élite and the leader of the anglophone Caribbean women's movement, was an active participant in London-based Pan-African activities. Jeffers was present at the inaugural dinner of the African Progress Union (APU) in London in 1918. The largely West African and Caribbean membership of the APU were 'actuated ... by intense love for their country and race ... .' They felt 'that only Africans or descendants of African blood can rightly and truly interpret the feelings, aspirations and idiosyncrasies of their kith and kin ... .'[79]

Jamaica's Amy Ashwood Garvey, first wife of Marcus Garvey, actually founded a West African organization, the Nigerian Progress Union, in London in 1924.[80] H. O. B. Wooding, later Chief Justice of Trinidad & Tobago, was made an honorary member of WASU, the British-based West African Students' Union. *WASU* magazine commented on this event in 1927:

> Mr. H.O. Beresford Wooding, President of the Union of Students of African Descent of Great Britain, was appointed as honorary member of the WASU ... for though a West Indian by birth, he has shown such widespread interest in general Negro questions – African and other – that most of us have come to regard him as a man of exceptional value – an *agboni agba* – for the whole Negro race.[81]

Wooding took his Pan-Africanism to the ultimate level when he married a Ghanaian. 'It will no doubt interest our readers,' *WASU* commented in 1928, 'to learn of the recent marriage of Mr. Wooding to Miss Coussie, a member of a prominent family on the Gold Coast. Surely this is one of the signs of the times pointing to the ultimate and desired return of our brethren to their motherland.'[82]

People like Jeffers and Wooding, though politically conservative and economically well-to-do, nevertheless maintained a finely-developed sense of racial consciousness. They could be quite outspoken on perceived slights to the race and strove, within the limits of their social orientation, for the uplift of their group.

---

79 *African Telegraph* (London), December 1918, p.89, and January–February 1919, p.111.

80 'Nigerian Progress Union,' *Spokesman*, I, 3, February 1925, p.16.

81 *WASU*, 3 and 4, March and June 1927, pp.6–7.

82 *WASU*, 6 and 7, August 1928, p.4.

The nationalism of this group found an increasingly important outlet through literature, both scholarly and creative. Garvey helped usher in the 'Harlem Renaissance' of the 1920s with an unparalleled promotion of African-conscious literary activity. He defined the aesthetic of his literary offensive in his essay on 'African Fundamentalism' in 1924:

> The time has come for the Negro to forget and cast behind him his hero worship and adoration of other races, and to start out immediately to create and emulate heroes of his own. We must canonize our own saints, create our own martyrs, and elevate to positions of fame and honor black men and women who have made their distinct contributions to our racial history... . We must inspire a literature and promulgate a doctrine of our own without any apologies to the powers that be. The right is ours and God's. Let contrary sentiment and cross opinions go to the winds.[83]

T. Albert Marryshow of Grenada joined Garvey's literary movement with a poem, 'And Yet', published in the UNIA's *Negro World* in 1920:

> Poor rags and all tatters
> My portion might be,
> And yet robed in Manhood
> No slave dwells in me;
> The world's dearest mantle
> Is true Liberty![84]

Dominica's Garveyite poet, J. R. Ralph Casimir, published poems for at least seven decades, sometimes under the pseudonym *Civis Africanus* (Citizen of Africa). His early poems were often penned in praise of prominent literary and political figures of the race. At least one of his poems, 'To the Africans at Home' (1922), was published 'at home' in the *Gold Coast Leader*.[85]

---

83 Tony Martin, 1991, p.4. See also *idem*, 1983a and 1983b.

84 Tony Martin, 1991, p.171.

85 On Casimir's poetry see Tony Martin, 1983a, pp.64-5. On Casimir's career in the UNIA see Tony Martin, 1988 (1989). Casimir's books of poetry include *Poesy: An Anthology of Dominica Verse, Book Four* (1948), *The Negro Speaks* (1969), *Farewell (And Other Poems)* 1971), *Black Man, Listen! And Other Poems*, with an introduction by Phyllis Shand Allfrey (1978), and *Freedom Poems* (1985). Casimir also published the following books, which this author has not seen: *Pater Noster And Other Poems, Africa Arise And Other Poems, A Little Kiss and Other Poems, The Negro Speaks* and *Poesy*, Books I, II and III. Casimir's poems are also to be found in Dominican newspapers and in Tony Martin, 1991, p.234.

H. A. Vaughan of Barbados captured the resurgent celebration of blackness in his poem, 'Revelation':

> Turn sideways now and let them see
> What loveliness escapes the schools,
> Then turn again, and smile, and be
> The perfect answer to those fools
> Who always prate of Greece and Rome,
> 'The face that launched a thousand ships,'
> And such like things, but keep tight lips
> For burnished beauty nearer home.[86]

Vaughan was a leading figure in the Forum Club of Barbados. Their members kept in close touch with the literary developments of the Harlem Renaissance.[87] His reference to the 'loveliness' that 'escapes the schools' reflected another concern of his colleagues, namely the need for a more Afrocentric curriculum. In January 1932 a Forum Club committee of C. W. Wickham, J. C. Hope and Vaughan, together with two members of the Barbados Elementary Teachers Association, met with a Commission of Enquiry into the educational needs of the British West Indies. They requested further Caribbean content and the removal of racially offensive material from the British-imposed textbooks.[88]

Carter G. Woodson, 'Father of African-American History,' considered Caribbean Africans to be ahead of their African-American counterparts in this respect. 'It would hardly seem out of place,' Woodson wrote, 'to remark that while the "highly educated Negroes" of [the United States] oppose the teaching of Negro culture these leaders of the West Indies are boldly demanding it… .'[89] Garvey's 1920 First International Convention of the Negro Peoples of the World had also called for the teaching of black history in schools.[90] Garveyite Hubert H. Harrison of St Croix and Harlem observed in 1920 that 'The educational system in the United States and the West Indies was shaped by white people for white youth, and from their point of view, it fits their purpose well.' The lamentable results of such mis-education he saw in the fact that Caribbean and African American boys and girls 'readily accept the assumption that Negroes have never been anything but slaves and that

86 H. A. Vaughan, 1985, p.1. This collection was first published in 1945. 'Revelation' is undated. Only two items are dated: one 1935 and the other 1944.

87 Interview with H. A. Vaughan, Christ Church, Barbados, 1980.

88 *Forum Quarterly*, March 1932, pp.30, 31.

89 *Negro World*, 18 April 1931.

90 Amy Jacques Garvey, 1923 (1986), p.142.

they never had a glorious past as other fallen peoples like the Greeks and Persians have.'[91]

Garvey's call for Africans to 'inspire a literature and promulgate a doctrine of our own' found a ready echo in the non-anglophone Caribbean as well. The indigenist movement of Haiti was ushered in by the journal *La Revue Indigène* (1927–8). The writers of this movement, among them Jean Price-Mars and Jacques Roumain, rediscovered and treated with a new respect the folkways and religion of their fellow Haitians. They translated and read the works of the Harlem Renaissance.

This trend intensified with the Griot movement, led by François Duvalier and Lorimer Denis, whose *L'Essentiel de la Doctrine des Griots* appeared in 1938. They also published the magazine *Les Griots* in 1938–9. Duvalier and Denis were uncompromising in their advocacy of 'race first'. They urged Haitians to rediscover and respect the African essence of their culture as a means of national regeneration.[92]

The *négritude* movement of francophone Caribbean and African writers, like its Haitian counterpart, took off with the publication of a magazine: *L' Etudiant Noir* was published in Paris in 1934. Its editors were *négritude*'s best-known personalities, the poets Léopold Senghor of Senegal, Léon Damas of French Guiana and Aimé Césaire of Martinique. For over ten years these three oversaw a flourishing movement which combated French cultural imperialism, rejected the European demeaning of African history, sought escape from assimilation into French culture and embraced the Harlem Renaissance. This did not prevent them from adopting some aspects of European radicalism, such as communism and socialism.

In their efforts to reject Europe, however, the *négritude* poets practically fell into the European pseudo-scientific trap of presenting Europe as the embodiment of science and reason while willingly embracing the stereotype of Africa primarily as emotion and rhythm. 'Hurray for those who have never invented anything,' proclaimed Aimé Césaire in his famous *Cahier d'un Retour au Pays Natal*, 'for those who have never explored anything/ for those who have never tamed anything.' The more radical Martiniquan, Frantz Fanon, rejected all of this as 'banal exoticism'.[93]

The most incongruous irony of the *négritude* trap lay in the word itself. Contrary to popular scholarly opinion and doubtless unknown to the movement's founders, the term had been invented over a hundred years earlier by

91 Tony Martin, 1991, p.9.

92 J. Michael Dash, 1975, pp.117–34; G. R. Coulthard, 1962, pp.42, 48; Janheinz Jahn, 1969, p.215.

93 Janheinz Jahn, 1969, p.225.

the 'father of American psychiatry,' Benjamin Rush (1746–1813). 'Negritude', for Rush, connoted the disease allegedly derived from leprosy, of black skin colour.[94] If the African-conscious *négritude* movement almost fell into the trap of its Eurocentric opposite, its *negrista* counterpart of Cuba and Puerto Rico was, from its very conception, a by-product of European pseudo-scientific disdain for the African. *Negrismo* was 'launched' by the white Puerto Rican Luis Palés Matos' poem 'Pueblo Negro' in 1926. Its proponents, almost exclusively white, presumed to speak for the African masses in the Caribbean's two 'whitest' countries. *Negrismo* was perhaps an inevitable development in societies which adhered to the myth of a racial democracy, societies capable of probably the worst purely racial massacre of the post-emancipation Caribbean (the 1912 racial massacre in Cuba),[95] which segregated Africans and kept them illiterate while ruthlessly discouraging any manifestations of independent African political activity, and which simultaneously proclaimed the absence of racism in their countries.

The *negrista* movement, like *négritude*, exoticized African people into sensuous, sinewy, simple-minded, non-ambitious, animalistic, drum-beating, dancing children of nature who had somehow preserved the desirable primitive purity which Europeans had lost through what Palés Matos called their 'dangerous cerebralisation ....'[96] For Palés Matos, Asia dreamed of *nirvana*, America danced to its jazz and Europe theorized, while Africa grunted 'nyam nyam.'[97]

Negrismo was an Antillean derivative of the European 'anti-rationalist' movement personified by Leo Frobenius, André Gide, Pablo Picasso, Oswald Spengler, Sir Harry Johnson, Sigmund Freud and others. Its earliest Antillean luminary was the Cuban ethnologist Fernando Ortiz. *Negrista* poets mostly constructed primitive straw Africans whom they could idealize while oppressing the real Africans all around them.

In the Cuban poet Nicolás Guillén *negrismo* found its only non-white luminary. Guillén wrote his share of naked African women poems, though his

94 Thomas S. Szasz, 1970, pp.153–9.

95 The 1912 Afro-Cuban death toll (two to five thousand) appears greater than fatalities for the Jamaica rebellion of 1865. The Dominican Republic's later massacre of Haitians (1937) may possibly be included in this comparison, depending on whether one classifies it as a purely racial event or not.

96 Quoted in G. R. Coulthard, 1962, p.30.

97 From the Luis Palés Matos poem, 'Nam-Nam' – '*Asia sueña su nirvana./ América baila el jazz/ Europa juega y teoriza./Africa grune: ñam-ñam.*' Quoted in Paul A. Davis, 1979, p.73. Representatives of the 'anti-rationalist' idea were active even around the Harlem Renaissance, where white literary bankroller, Charlotte Osgood Mason, tried to steer her beneficiaries into 'primitive' expression. See David Levering Lewis, 1981 (1989), p.155.

communist affiliation brought him an awareness of the real struggles of Afro-Antilleans. But he was no more able than his white counterparts to write the genuine race-uplift poetry of the Garvey Movement, or the indigenist movement in Haiti, or the other movements more rooted among African-Caribbean intellectuals. *Negrismo* got as far as advocating a 'mulatto' poetry to reflect the reality, as they perceived it, of Caribbean life.[98] It got no further.

All of these literary movements of the 1920s to the 1940s interacted with and were influenced by the Harlem Renaissance. Some of the leading figures of the renaissance, including Jamaican Claude McKay and Barbadian/Guyanese/Panamanian Eric Walrond, were themselves from the Caribbean. But the greatest Harlem influence of all was Langston Hughes. His works were widely praised, reproduced and translated in such places as the *Forum Quarterly* (Barbados), *La Relève* (Haiti) and *Adelante* (Cuba). Léon Damas and Palés Matos read Hughes. Guillén met him in Havana and wrote up a record of their conversation.[99] Amy Jacques Garvey, wife of Marcus Garvey, praised him in 1926 on the publication of his now famous essay on 'The Negro Artist and the Racial Mountain', wherein Hughes had written in terms reminiscent of Garvey's 'African Fundamentalism' – '..."Why should I want to be white?"....We younger Negro artists who create now intend to express our individual dark-skinned selves without fear or shame. If white people are pleased we are glad. If they are not, it doesn't matter.'[100]

The rising African consciousness of the period was reflected throughout the arts. C. L. R. James' 1936 novel, *Minty Alley*, made a statement by setting itself in an impoverished African Trinidadian environment.[101] Boscoe Holder chose African Caribbean subjects for his paintings. In Trinidad, Holder and Beryl McBurnie took African dance from the countryside and the barrack yards onto the stage,[102] as Olive Walke would later retrieve folk songs from village and hamlet. Nicolás Guillén elevated Afro-Cuban music (the 'son') to respectability. To crown it all, working-class Trinidadians would, after years of experimentation, reinvent the banned African drum in the guise of the steelband.

---

98 For more on *negrismo* see Magali Roy Fequiere, 1996, pp.82-7; Dennis Sardinha, 1976; Keith Ellis, 1973; Jorge Castellanos and Isabel Castellanos, 1990, pp.352–89.

99 See, for example, *Forum Quarterly*, Xmas Number 1931, pp.7ff.; J. Michael Dash, 1975, p.122; Dennis Sardinha, 1976, p.11; Jorge Castellanos and Isabel Castellanos, 1990, p.372; G. R. Coulthard, 1962, pp.51, 83; Magali Roy Fequiere, 1996, p.86.

100 Amy Jacques Garvey, 1991, p.84.

101 C. L. R. James, 1936 (1971).

102 See, for example, Molly Ahye, 1983.

The spirit of a blossoming racial consciousness could also be seen in scholarly writings of the period. Despite (perhaps even because of) the Eurocentric education forced on Caribbean children, there was a long tradition of Afrocentric journalism and scholarly writing. In the inter-war years J. A. Rogers of Jamaica and the United States travelled the world in search of obscure information on African history. So for many years did his friend Arturo A. Schomburg of Puerto Rico and New York, African America's most celebrated bibliophile.[103] In 1917 Grenada's T. Albert Marryshow wrote *Cycles of Civilization* wherein he chastised the racist utterances of General Jan Christian Smuts of South Africa and asserted the African origins of civilization.[104] Rogers' books, beginning with *From Superman to Man* in 1917, are still immensely popular. Norman Eustace Cameron of Guyana published *The Evolution of the Negro* in two volumes in 1929 and 1934. He advocated race pride, saw no need for massive (as opposed to selective) emigration to Africa and saw economic advance as the way out for African people. 'As long as Negroes are poor they will be despised,' he wrote. 'When they become wealthy as a people all their faults will be overlooked or spoken of in hushed whispers which will not affect them.'[105]

The foreign-based, among them James, Padmore and Rogers, surpassed those at home in the sheer volume of their output. Most were self-trained as historians. In Eric Williams of Trinidad, however, the Caribbean produced a formally trained historian of great brilliance. With an island scholarship from Queen's Royal College and an Oxford first-class degree behind him, he moved on to a doctorate at Oxford University in 1938. His dissertation, revised and published as *Capitalism and Slavery* in 1944, combined the race consciousness of the age with brilliance of scholarship. The result was a seminal work. Following a thesis advanced by James, Williams meticulously demonstrated the slave trade to be a major source of the capital formation that financed England's Industrial Revolution.[106] His first book, in keeping with the spirit of the period, was *The Negro in the Caribbean* (1942).[107] He surveyed the history of the Caribbean masses, championed their anti-colonial grievances, spoke favourably of Garvey and looked towards a better future for the region.

A discussion of African consciousness in the inter-war years would not be complete without reference to the Rastafarian Movement and the Italian

---

103 On Schomburg see Elinor Des Verney Sinnette, 1989; Winston James, 1996, pp.92–127.

104 T. Albert Marryshow, 1917 (1973).

105 Norman Eustace Cameron, 1929–34 (1970).

106 Eric Williams, 1944.

107 Washington, DC: The Associates in Negro Folk Education, 1942.

fascist invasion of Ethiopia. Rastafarianism emerged in Jamaica in the early 1930s. Many of its initial adherents came out of the Garvey Movement, with its universal African consciousness and its widespread Ethiopian symbolism. The coronation of Emperor Haile Selassie (formerly Ras Tafari) of Ethiopia in 1930 provided a rare opportunity for an internationally disseminated non-pejorative view of Africa. Out of the Garveyite background and with the stimulus of the coronation came the new movement.

The poor and oppressed Africans of Jamaica who initiated the movement ingeniously constructed an Afrocentric theology, world view and lifestyle to replace European cultural imperialism. Haile Selassie, an African, was recognized as God. Africa was the promised land and focal point of repatriation. Africans had been forcibly deposited into exile in the west (Babylon). Africans, as the true Israelites of the Bible, were God's chosen people. The white so-called Jews of Europe, relatively recent converts to Judaism, were a trick to confuse Africans. Like the contemporaneous Nation of Islam in the United States, Rastafarians argued that only Africans, in the universal persecution meted out to them and in their forced dispersal throughout the earth, satisfied the biblical conditions for God's chosen people. The new movement proclaimed a doctrine of black supremacy. Rastafarians embraced Garvey as a prophet, a John the Baptist, second in veneration only to His Imperial Majesty, Haile Selassie.

The movement emerged from intense repression in the colonial and post-colonial Jamaican state to impact fundamentally Jamaican and Pan-African society. Rastafarians practically developed a new language. They gave the world reggae music. They Africanized painting, sculpture, dance, theatre and ceramics in Jamaica. They influenced the culinary arts. They challenged some of the core concepts of Christianity. Their once-persecuted dreadlocks in time became commonplace all over the African world among adherents and non-adherents alike. Non-Africans have become attracted to the movement in recent years.[108]

The Italian fascist invasion of Ethiopia in 1935 was perhaps the most traumatic event to affect the Caribbean and the rest of scattered Africa since the European 'scramble' for the continent in the late nineteenth and early twentieth centuries. Ethiopia became the only African country to repel European aggression militarily when the Emperor Menelik II routed the Italians at the Battle of Adowa in 1896. The coronation of Haile Selassie enhanced this tradition of veneration for Ethiopia. Then in 1935 Benito Mussolini, Italy's dictator,

108 Among the voluminous literature on Rastafarianism the following may be mentioned – M. G. Smith *et al.*, 1960; Leonard E. Barrett, 1968; Horace Campbell, 1985; Joseph Owens, 1976 (1979); Rex Nettleford, 1972; Barry Chevannes, 1994; *idem*, 1995.

invaded Ethiopia, dropped poison gas on its inhabitants, overran the country and forced the Emperor to flee to Europe. The League of Nations declined to come to Ethiopia's aid. In the Caribbean, as elsewhere, the populace was enraged. Young men tried to volunteer for the Ethiopian army; dock workers refused to unload Italian ships; there were protest rallies and demonstrations. Calypsonian Tiger, in Trinidad, sang: 'De gold, de gold, de gold, de gold/De gold in Africa/Mussolini want from the emperor.'[109]

Caribbean emigrants abroad were equally active. In England, James formed the International African Friends of Ethiopia.[110] Garvey, now also resident in England, criticized the Emperor for keeping Ethiopia weak but nevertheless supported the Ethiopian cause. His support often found poetical expression, as witness the following lines from 'The Beast of Rome' (1935):

> The Rome of sin and human hate
> Has plagued the world before,
> But God will serve their awful fate
> On Ethiopia's shore.
> Their guns and gas may threaten all
> As hymns they sing at home
> But ere Adowa's final fall
> The fight shall pass from Rome.[111]

Caribbean emigrants also proliferated in the myriad pro-Ethiopia movements that flourished in the United States. One New Yorker, former Trinidadian Colonel Hubert Fauntleroy Julian, went to Ethiopia to help train Haile Selassie's air force.[112]

The Second World War, like the first, brought more blatant racism, and as a consequence, heightened racial consciousness. A heavy United States military presence in the Caribbean (including African-American units) inevitably brought United States-style race relations closer to home. As in the First World War, the British War Office resisted African-Caribbean troops and non-combatant forces for as long as it could. This included women aspirants to the Auxiliary Territorial Service (ATS), who like their male counterparts were only allowed in late in the war.[113]

---

109 Richard K. Spottswood, 1987; Canboulay Productions, 1991.

110 C. L. R. James, interview with the author, San Fernando, Trinidad, 13 March 1980.

111 Tony Martin, 1983b, p.85.

112 On Caribbean and other African reaction to the Italian invasion, see William R. Scott, 1993; Joseph E. Harris, 1994; Robert G. Weisbord, 1970, pp.34–41; Kevin A. Yelvington, 1999, pp.189–225.

113 Ben Bousquet and Colin Douglas, 1991.

Those who eventually went overseas were rewarded with enhanced opportunities for Pan-African contact, as they mingled with Africans, African Americans and other colonized and oppressed peoples brought together for the war effort. Dudley Thompson, a Jamaican volunteer in the Royal Air Force, described the experience this way: 'One lasting effect on me of this war period was that by 1945, I was coming into contact [in England] for the first time with West Indian, African, and Black American soldiers, and with students, writers and blue-collar workers from the British colonies – all of us meeting in the Mother country ...'[114]

This contact had repercussions for the growth of African consciousness and anti-colonialism all over the African world. Perhaps most symbolic of this was the Fifth Pan-African Congress which met in Manchester, England, in 1945. It was convened by Padmore of Trinidad and Kwame Nkrumah of Ghana, with African America's DuBois as honorary chair and Jamaica's Amy Ashwood Garvey as co-chair of the opening session. Delegates included Jomo Kenyatta of Kenya, a UNIA delegation from Jamaica, workers domiciled in Britain and trade unionists from the Caribbean and Africa. Two of those present, Nkrumah and Kenyatta, returned home shortly afterwards to lead their respective independence struggles; and Caribbean delegates followed them, as it were. Padmore was later to become Nkrumah's adviser on African affairs in independent Ghana. Thompson, who attended the conference, subsequently won a Rhodes scholarship, studied law at Oxford and Gray's Inn, and practised in Tanzania and Kenya. It was he who organized the legal defence for Kenyatta's trial for alleged leadership of the Mau Mau uprising.[115]

Caribbean pre- and post-independence politics in the 1950s, 1960s and 1970s would be leavened by several leaders with a Pan-African experience. Eric Williams returned home from America to become Trinidad's first prime minister. Thompson returned from East Africa to Jamaica to become a Cabinet minister in People's National Party governments. Errol Barrow, son of a Garveyite,[116] and a Royal Air Force officer in the Second World War, became prime minister of Barbados. Forbes Burnham, law student in England and later prime minister and president of Guyana, seems to have picked up some Garveyite sympathies along the way. His People's National Congress adopted Garvey's colours of red, black and green for its flag. *Négritude* founder Aimé Césaire became Mayor of Fort-de-France, Martinique, in 1945.

---

114 Dudley Thompson, 1993, p.31. See also Khafra Kambon, 1988, pp.17–25.

115 Dudley Thompson, 1993, *passim*.

116 Barrow's father was also a bishop in the African Orthodox Church, which had its origins in the Garvey Movement: Bishop Reginald Barrow, interview with the author, Barbados, 1980.

George Weekes, Trinidad's pre-eminent labour leader from the 1960s to the 1980s, replicated the experience of the First World War generation. He served in Africa and Europe with the Second World War Caribbean Regiment and returned home to join the Universal African Nationalist Movement and other neo-Garveyite organizations.[117] As late as 1970 Maurice Bishop, radicalized by the Black Power movement in England, returned home to Grenada to lead a similar struggle and eventually become prime minister.

Many returnees of the 1950s and 1960s in time made the transition from youthful idealism (or even radicalism) to middle-aged pragmatism (or even conservatism). A new generation of race-conscious individuals took their place. Soon some of those who were on the cutting edge of race consciousness in the 1930s and after, would find themselves defending the status quo against Black Power.

The Caribbean Black Power movement spun off from the civil-rights movement in the United States, and became fully conscious of itself in the mid-1960s. Several of its main North American leaders had a Caribbean connection. Malcolm X, the most important theoretician of the movement, despite his early death in 1965, was the son of Garveyite parents and a Grenadian mother. Kwame Touré (formerly Stokely Carmichael), who first popularized the slogan 'Black Power' in 1966, emigrated from Trinidad to New York as a child. Once established in the United States, Black Power quickly spread to the largely Caribbean-African populations of Britain and Canada. Caribbean students demonstrated in London in 1967 against the banning of Carmichael by the Trinidad government.[118]

In the United States, Black Power called for racial pride and empowerment in the face of the traditional denial of human rights to African Americans. In the Caribbean it called for racial pride and empowerment against the multinational corporations that dominated regional economies. Its efforts were also directed against the new local ruling elements who were perceived as conduits for neo-colonial foreign domination.

The historical connections between African consciousness at home and abroad were vividly demonstrated in 1968, when events in Montreal, Canada, triggered what came to be known as the 'Black Power Revolution' in Trinidad. In the aftermath of a Black Writers Conference in Montreal in 1968, Walter Rodney, a Guyanese history professor at the University of the West Indies, was denied re-entry into Jamaica. Rodney was disliked by the government for having made common cause with the poor in general and

117 Khafra Kambon, 1988, pp.20–5.

118 *Trinidad Guardian*, 18 August 1967, p.1; *Morning Star* (London), 18 August 1967, p.3.

Rastafarians in particular. His summary expulsion led to demonstrations, and police repression against the demonstrators and riots. Three people were killed. That same year Caribbean students and their allies at Sir George William University in Montreal occupied some campus property. They had vainly sought redress for years against a white professor who had been shown to discriminate against black students in the awarding of grades. Students at the University of the West Indies in Trinidad expressed solidarity with their colleagues in Montreal and pressured the Trinidad authorities into providing legal and other assistance to the arrested victims. When the Canadian Governor-General visited Trinidad, students blocked the university entrance. The distinguished visitor and Prime Minister Eric Williams were unable to enter. Demonstrations against Canadian targets (including banks and the country's High Commission) ensued. The students, organized in the National Joint Action Committee (NJAC), were joined by workers, the unemployed and broad segments of the general populace. By 1969 the movement had grown to massive proportions. It now operated under the banner of Black Power. As in the United States, leaders adopted African names and styles of dress. Once again, as in earlier historical periods, race consciousness served as catalyst for broad social change. The whole neo-colonial structure of the society came under scrutiny and efforts at African-Indian co-operation were initiated.[119]

Radical elements within Williams' People's National Movement persuaded the 1968 party convention to sanction a commission of enquiry into racism faced by Caribbean residents in Britain, Canada and the United States.[120] In 1969 an aroused public opinion pressured the government into appointing commissions of enquiry into racial discrimination at the Trinidad Country Club and in the private sector, with an emphasis on banks.[121] By April 1970, a state of emergency was declared, an attempted army coup failed and the Williams government barely kept power. In the immediate aftermath the Williams administration heeded the wishes of the people by nationalizing and localizing many of the 'commanding heights' of the economy.

In Grenada, Black Power had its greatest success when demonstrations in sympathy with the Trinidad struggle of 1970 grew in time into the New Jewel Movement (NJM), led by Maurice Bishop. The NJM seized power in 1979 from

---

119 The literature on the Black Power movement is voluminous. See, for example, Khafra Kambon, 1988, chaps 12, 13 *et passim*; Catherine A. Sunshine, 1988, pp.58-64; Selwyn D. Ryan and Taimoon Stewart, 1995.

120 *Report of a Cabinet Appointed Enquiry into Discrimination*, 1969.

121 The Country Club hearings were widely reported in the Trinidad press and overseas during August 1969 and beyond. See also Tony Martin, 1970.

the government of Eric Gairy, in the Commonwealth Caribbean's only successful coup (Trinidad having had unsuccessful attempts in 1970 and 1990).[122]

As in the case of the Garvey Movement in the 1920s and the literary movement of the 1930s, the Black Power radicalism of the late 1960s and the 1970s in the English-speaking states had its counterparts throughout the Caribbean. The May 1969 workers' riots in Curaçao, for example, were alleged to have a Black Power connection, though those allegations rested more on objective similarities than on organizational links. A new party, the Workers' Front, emerged from the agitation and captured three of the 12 available seats in the September 1970 elections, enabling it to enter into a coalition government. In the process the workers challenged the incumbent Democratic Party and what one workers' leader, Stanley C. Brown, called 'the Protestant-Jewish power group' on the island. Brown demanded 'our own culture, reparations from Holland ... just like the Germans gave the Jews' and social services at least to the minimal level enjoyed in Holland.[123] Papiamentu, the local Creole language, was one of the beneficiaries of the riots. Workers insisted on increased status for their language; politicians and the media acceded to these demands. Much later (1986) Papiamentu obtained a foothold in the school curriculum.[124]

Related efforts in Suriname to recognize officially the African-based Sranan Tongo *lingua franca* ran foul of Hindu and Javanese opposition.[125] The Créole language of St Lucia, Dominica and other islands has undergone significant revitalization. In Trinidad, Yoruba classes, once held by Garveyites in the 1940s, have been revived in a small way, partly as a response to the widespread efforts to spread Hindi among the Hindu Trinidadian population.

In Cuba in the 1970s the Castro regime was able to funnel the rising tide of African consciousness into the most ambitious foreign-policy initiatives to come out of the Caribbean. Cuba established a military presence in several

---

122 The following are among the many works on the Grenada Revolution – Didacus Jules and Don Rojas, n.d.; David E. Lewis, 1984; Tony Martin, 1983–5; Chris Searle, 1983.

123 Catherine A. Sunshine, 1988.

124 *New York Times*, 1 March 1970. The Sephardic Jews among the island's élite were said to be looking for an accommodation with the African population. The Ashkenazi Jews were said to view the riots as the work of 'anti-Semitic' Black Power groups financed by Arab money. Such was apparently not the case, since 'the commission which investigated the... riots, which I chaired, didn't find any evidence of Black Power connections. The same goes for Cuban connections. Black Power slogans and Castro caps were used as symbols of protest' (personal communication from René A. Römer, 26 March 1998). See also William A. Anderson and Russell R. Dynes, 1975.

125 Peter Meel, 1990, p.277.

African countries, but none so startling as in Angola, where Cuban military might succeeded in reversing a South African invasion and ultimately hastening the demise of apartheid in Southern Africa.[126]

The 1980s often appeared to be marked by economic recession, a drift away from political radicalism and a trend back towards reinforced non-African economic influence, facilitated by IMF pressures and the global move towards economic privatization. Yet they were also a time of intense consolidation and regrouping among the preservers of African consciousness. After the overtly political activity of the 1970s there was a shift towards the painstaking 'consciousness-raising' work of cultural and academic effort. Grass-roots groups from Bermuda to Guyana initiated a brisk commerce of itinerant Afrocentric lecturers, primarily from the United States, many of Caribbean origin. They spoke to packed houses and helped usher in an era of expanded knowledge of, and pride in, African history. They were part of a tradition that went back at least to Henry Sylvester Williams' tour of 1901 and one that included Garvey and the many emissaries of the UNIA who criss-crossed the region in the 1920s and 1930s. In many ways they played roles similar to those of the more ostensibly religious (but nevertheless political) Indian missionaries who will be discussed later in this chapter.

A resurgence of interest in Garvey contributed to these developments and came to a climax in his centenary celebrations of 1987. Caribbean people at home and abroad joined with Africans everywhere for a year of conferences, building-dedications, pilgrimages, book-launchings and erection of monuments to Garvey's memory.

Middle-class Africans were again swept into the tide of rising consciousness. There were several attempts in Trinidad & Tobago to organize a confederation of African associations. In Barbados a Roman Catholic priest became an important stimulus to these developments. The middle class increasingly rediscovered such predominantly working-class African religions as Winti (Suriname), Orisha or Shango (Trinidad and elsewhere) and Voodoo (Haiti). Decolonization brought the decriminalization of Winti, Obeah (in Guyana) and the Spiritual Shouter Baptists (in Trinidad & Tobago). Caribbean and neighbouring people from Cuba to Brazil played a prominent role in a growing world Orisha movement.

One tangible result of the cultural and academic interest was the movement for reinstating Emancipation Day (1 August) as a time of solemn celebration in the Commonwealth Caribbean. Emancipation Day became a public holiday in Trinidad & Tobago in 1984. As of 1998 it was being officially celebrated in Barbados, Jamaica, Guyana, the Bahamas, Grenada, Montserrat

126 Carlos Moore, 1988a.

and St Lucia. In Trinidad the celebration has assumed massive proportions. A permanently constituted Emancipation Support Committee co-ordinates a lecture series, an Emancipation Village, cultural extravaganzas, an outreach programme into schools and the work-place and an Emancipation Day street parade. As elsewhere in the African dispersion, the wearing of African traditional clothes on important occasions has become widespread, actually exceeding, in some countries, the practice on the African continent itself.

So African consciousness once again gathers momentum outside the structure of government, though this time governments appear less hostile than before, and on occasion they are even supportive.

Indian consciousness

> If the East Indian showed that progressive increase in number which they had shown up to now, and taking into account their natural productivity, it was no mere hyperbolical statement that Indians would people the colony and drive out the rest of the inhabitants. The African was not as productive as the East Indian: and if circumstances did not compel him to leave the colony, he would naturally die out. Such a thing had taken place at Mauritius. And Trinidad would be maintained and owned by the Indian in the field, the office and the shop.
>
> Report of Speech by F. E. M. Hosein,
> Trinidad, 1913.[127]

In Trinidad, Guyana and Suriname, areas of very large Indian population, and to lesser degrees elsewhere, African consciousness has had to co-exist with Indian consciousness. African consciousness, as we have seen, has traditionally wedded itself to the wider national interest and has tended to direct its activity against colonialism and other forms of foreign domination. In so far as foreign influence has emanated from Europe and North America, white people have borne the brunt of whatever racial animosity African consciousness has generated. Until relatively recently, African consciousness has tended either to treat its Indian counterpart with 'benign neglect' (to borrow a North American phrase) or to incorporate it into a presumed common struggle against a common European foe.

Indian racial consciousness, while exhibiting many features in common with African nationalism, and often utilizing the same rhetoric, has tended

127 *Port of Spain Gazette*, 6 May 1913, p.5.

historically to assume a more narrowly communal posture with a resultant focus on the African, more than on the European, as a primary adversary. Yet the interaction between the two groups has been fluid enough to ensure full acceptance for the occasional Indo-Caribbean who chose to operate within African nationalist organizations. This was true even for Garvey's UNIA, the most African-conscious of Caribbean movements. Here, the easy acceptance of Indians (and occasionally others) underscored the broader nationalism of these movements, despite their emphasis on African racial pride. The secretary of the UNIA in Montreal, Canada, was for many years an Indo-Caribbean.[128] Hucheshwar G. Mudgal of India and Trinidad edited Garvey's *Negro World* in the 1930s and was a staunch defender of Garvey's African nationalism.[129]

In the Caribbean itself Africans have occasionally intervened decisively in the promotion of Indian nationalism. The *East Indian Weekly* (1928–32), perhaps Trinidad's most important Indian nationalist newspaper to date, was owned by Leonard Fitzgerald Walcott, an African nationalist and Garveyite.

Indians outside of Trinidad, Guyana and Suriname, for their part, have often been less resistant than in the areas of major Indian population to an accommodation with African culture. In St Lucia in the 1940s, three Indian members of the Garveyite Universal African Nationalist Movement, which had its headquarters in New York, answered 'yes' on their application forms to the question, 'Are you of African blood and descent?'[130]

A half-million indentured Indian labourers were introduced into the Caribbean between 1838 and 1917, in an effort on the part of the European planters to deprive the newly emancipated Africans of the bargaining benefits of free labour.[131] The immigrants came in large numbers to Guyana, Trinidad and Suriname, and in smaller numbers to Guadeloupe, Jamaica, Martinique, St Vincent, Grenada and St Lucia. Africans were forced to help finance Indian immigration through general taxes. In Jamaica additionally, African emigrants to Panama and elsewhere had to pay a 'departure tax' which went towards financing Indian immigration.[132]

---

128 The Montreal UNIA files give his name as Felix A. Mahomed (possibly a misspelling for Mohamed or Mohammed). He joined the branch on 25 October 1920 and became secretary in 1926 – information courtesy of Dr Leo Bertley of Vanier College, Montreal, who is working on a book on the Montreal UNIA.

129 H. G. Mudgal, 1932. See also *Negro World*, 23 September 1922, p.4, 21 October 1922, p.4, 2 August 1930, p.6; Tony Martin, 1984b, p.81; *idem*, 1976 (1986), pp.93, 254, 260-1.

130 Application forms (including photographs of applicants), Unit no. 14, Castries UANM in privately held UANM papers. One hundred forms were perused by the author. The three Indian members were from Forestière.

131 Eric Williams, 1970 (1984), pp.347–60.

132 Winston James, 1998, p.29.

In the territories of significant Indian settlement especially, conditions favoured a communal existence and the consequent maintenance of an Indian consciousness. As in the case of the failed 1806 attempt to settle Chinese in Trinidad,[133] Indians were consciously developed into a buffer by the European rulers in an effort to deflect African agitation away from themselves. 'One thing more,' wrote a committee of white leaders in Trinidad in 1919, when it seemed that the buffer arrangement might have been in danger of breaking down,

> in the years gone by the large East Indian indentured population, numbering many thousands and largely under the control of their respective plantation owners, managers and overseers, was looked upon as a substantial safeguard against trouble with the negroes and *vice versa.* With the abolition of immigration such a counterpoise has ceased to exist and the "creole coolie" will either remain an interested spectator or join the mob.[134]

In 1897 an assistant under-secretary at the British Colonial Office urged increased Indian immigration and its spread to new areas such as Dominica 'not as a means of procuring labour, but with the distinct object of not leaving any of these Islands entirely to the Negro race.' Joseph Chamberlain, Secretary of State for the Colonies, was sympathetic to the idea of immigration 'to maintain and strengthen the leaven of East Indians in the population.'[135] Influential French opinion in Martinique in 1855 saw the buffer value of Indians as the strongest argument for preferring them to other immigrants. Indians, it was argued, would stand aloof from African-fomented strikes and disturbances.[136]

Buffer policies were facilitated by residential separation and differences in race, religion, language and legal status between indentured Indians and Africans. Furthermore, though most Indians remained in the Caribbean, the fact that as many as 25 per cent exercised their option to return to India may long have contributed to a psychology of transience. Two decades after the end of indenture in 1917, specially chartered ships still encountered more Guyanese and Trinidadian Indians wishing to return home than there was space for.[137]

---

133 Barry W. Higman, 1972, p.33.

134 George F. Huggins *et al.* to Colonial Secretary, 30 July 1919, CO 295/522, Colonial Office files, Public Record Office, London.

135 Minute by C. P. Lucas, October 1897, CO 884/5: West Indian no. 79, Colonial Office files, Public Record Office, London, quoted in K. O. Laurence, 1994, p.517.

136 'L'Immigration Indienne,' *Journal Officiel de La Colonie*, 4 February 1855, p.395.

137 *Trinidad Guardian*, 7 August 1936, p.1. Here only 50 of 100 assembled hopefuls were chosen, with more selections promised for the following week. Those selected were sent to a holding station (on Nelson Island) to await the repatriation ship *Ganges*, due in with Guyanese repatriates.

Communalism among the Indians, more developed than for any other Caribbean group, provided the infrastructure for Indian nationalism and quickly found expression in politics. In 1897 Trinidad Indians memorialized a visiting West India Royal Commission for communal representation in the Legislative Council.[138] Indian communalism in politics could on occasion be used as a weapon to frustrate or delay constitutional advance sought by Africans. The case of the Wood Commission of 1921–2 is illustrative of this. The commission was sent to the Caribbean from London in response to the demands, spearheaded by the African population, for democratization of the political process. These demands figured prominently in the primarily African riots of the post-war period in Belize, Trinidad and elsewhere.[139]

Several Trinidad Indians appearing before the commission opposed introduction of the elective principle into Trinidad politics. The East Indian National Congress (EINC) demanded proportional or communal representation 'on the ground', as Wood explained, 'that otherwise there was a danger of their being outvoted.'[140] C. B. Mathura, later editor of the *East Indian Weekly* and one of an Indian minority favouring an elective franchise, saw the position of the EINC and its chief spokesman, Rev. C. D. Lalla, as the introduction into Trinidad of 'a miniature India with class legislation, perhaps caste representation – Brahmin for Brahmin, Hindu for Hindu and so on.'[141]

The East Indian National Association of Princes Town and several prominent Indians preferred to keep undemocratic Crown Colony rule, since they did not think that there were enough qualified Indians to compete successfully in an elective system.[142] Several of the Indian leaders advanced as a further reason for opposing the African quest for democracy what F. E. M. Hosein described as 'the veiled and some times open hostility of the coloured race.'[143]

The positions of the Indian leadership were finely nuanced, however. They were overwhelmingly separatists, and disagreed only on how best to secure this objective. F. E. M. Hosein felt that non-communal elections need not be an obstacle 'to preserve the purity and pride of race'. The entire leadership, he said, was 'at one in its aim; namely, the advancement and prestige of East Indians separate and distinct from the rest of a heterogeneous community.' This, he said, 'is a laudable desire with which the whole [Indian leadership] fully sympathizes ....'[144]

138 Bridget Brereton, 1981, pp.110, 115.

139 See, for example, Tony Martin, 1984c, pp.47–58.

140 *Report by the Hon. E.F.L. Wood*, 1922, p.224 (the Wood Report).

141 Editorial, *East Indian Weekly*, 12 January 1929, p.6.

142 *Ibid.*

143 F. E. M. Hosein, 1929, p.3.

144 *Ibid.*

Major Wood partly acceded to the Indian demands. He denied their request for communal representation while nevertheless retaining a strong non-elective element which made it possible for the government simply to appoint Indians to the Legislative Council, if they should fail to secure adequate representation via elections. His arguments against communalism were nevertheless interesting:

> ... it would accentuate and perpetuate the differences which, in order to produce a homogeneous community it should be the object of statesmanship to remove. The East Indians are an important element in the community, and it would be a great misfortune if they were encouraged to stand aside from the main current of political life instead of sharing in it and assisting to guide its course. Finally, if a concession of this kind were granted to the East Indians, there would be no logical reason for withholding it from persons of French, Spanish or Chinese descent, a situation which would became impossible.[145]

A similar demand from the British Guiana East Indian Association in 1936 elicited a similar official response.[146]

In objecting to Indian communal requests, Trinidad's Legislative Reform Committee 'deprecated differentiation between East Indian and Creole, since they formed one community and the difference between them was one of domestic life only.... In their view any system of communal representation involving preferential treatment to one race would create friction.'[147] This remains a classic statement of the traditional Trinidadian African view of Indian nationalism, with its presumption of a commonality of interest between the two groups, its profound under-estimation of Indian opinions to the contrary and its mild irritation at the recurrence of 'preferential treatment'.

Among the key elements feeding communalism was an intense interaction with emissaries from India. Whether secular or religious, such emissaries encouraged attitudes of separatism and bolstered feelings of racial pride. Long after the end of the indenture system, members of the Indian Civil Service visited the Caribbean periodically. They lobbied on behalf of local Indians, encouraged feelings of closeness to Mother India and arbitrated disputes within the Indo-Caribbean community.[148] (From the late 1940s diplomatic representatives of independent India played a similar role – with the United

145 *Report by the Hon. E. F. L. Wood*, 1922, p.24.
146 Hugh Tinker, 1982, p.38.
147 *Report by the Hon. E. F. L. Wood*, 1922, p.23.
148 For example, Peter Ruhomon, 1938 (1988), p.242.

States State Department being among those evincing an interest in Indian diplomatic activity.)[149]

When in 1938–9 London sent out a West India Royal Commission (once more following rioting, primarily among the African population), the (British) Indian government sent along a special 'officer on deputation' to mobilize Caribbean Indians and help them put their grievances before the commissioners. While full publication of the commission's report was withheld until after the Second World War, the separate *Report on the Condition of Indians in Jamaica, British Guiana and Trinidad* was published straight away in 1939.[150] This represented merely the latest episode in a hundred years of special British solicitude for its Caribbean Indian population, which gave rise, as early as the nineteenth century in British Guiana, to the 'notion of the "pampered coolie"'.[151]

Visits by India-based religious missionaries were even more frequent than those of the Indian Civil Service and equally influential, if not more so. Both Hindu and Muslim missionaries travelled the circuit from Trinidad to Guyana to Suriname, with sometimes a stop in the United States, or other Caribbean destinations. Missionaries commanded great respect among their overseas compatriots. They founded local religious organizations and local branches of Indian ones. They also explicitly preached racial pride and encouraged racial exclusiveness. Their missionary zeal was exemplary. Visiting Vedic missionary to Trinidad, Pundit Mehta Jaimini, visited 38 towns and villages and delivered 79 lectures in less than three months in 1928–9.[152]

The parting advice given by visiting Pandit Ayodha Prasad to the Arya Samaj Association of Trinidad in 1936, was instructive. He was on his way to Suriname, he explained, when he discovered the Indian community of Trinidad. He completed his work in Suriname and retraced his steps to Trinidad, where, despite some local opposition (probably from rival religious groupings), he was welcomed by Indian Hindus, Muslims and Christians. 'I am leaving Trinidad,' he said on his departure, 'but I want Indians to think that they are Indians first and everything else after.' He continued, 'They must maintain their national identity and their language.'[153] His local followers were profuse in their gratitude. '[You have achieved] the redemption of sons of India who had been denationalised and alienated,' they confessed. An

149 Records of the Department of State, National Archives, Washington, DC, RG 59, 844g.00 –'Activities and duties of the Indian Commissioner to the West Indies,' 22 December, 1949, from Port of Spain, Index to Purport Books.

150 J. D. Tyson, 1939 (the Tyson Report).

151 K. O. Laurence, 1994, p.283.

152 *East Indian Weekly*, 16 March 1929, p.6.

153 *Trinidad Guardian*, 11 June 1936, p.14.

address presented to Prasad, Professor Satya Charan and B. T. Shastri showed the close relation between religious proselytization and racial consciousness:

> The introduction of the Arya Samaj Movement in this colony has, indeed, infused new life in Indian Society. It has made us proud of the civilisation of India. It has engendered in our hearts a love for the ancient glory and culture of our Motherland. It has urged upon us the necessity of preserving and maintaining a knowledge of our mother-tongues. It has sponsored the cause of Indian thought and Indian culture. It has saved the Indian community from the perilous plight of being hopelessly absorbed by alien religions and alien culture. The movement has, in short, raised us from a mine of disillusionment and has created for us a bright and prosperous outlook.[154]

While Hinduism and Islam may have seemed natural vehicles for Indian communalism and racial pride, the Christian denomination most closely associated with the Indians in Trinidad played a similar role. The Canadian Mission (Presbyterian Church of Canada) was unique among Christian churches in its single-minded concentration on the Indian community. Its missionaries often trained in India for Caribbean work. They studied Indian religions and spoke Indian languages. Their local catechists and clergy were Indian. The churches and schools (elementary, secondary and teacher-training) they established were overwhelmingly Indian, as were the local teachers they recruited. Classes were taught in Hindi, which was a compulsory subject in their teachers' colleges.[155]

Communalism found further expression in the media. Some major newspapers and periodicals in Trinidad carried special Indian sections in the 1930s.[156] (A Trinidad Garveyite leader noted in 1937 that the major dailies carried Indian, Portuguese, Spanish and Chinese sections, but no African sections.)[157] The 'Indian National Hour', begun in January 1936 on Afro-Guyanese radio station VP3BG, was apparently heard on short-wave radio in Trinidad.[158] By the mid-1930s, movies imported from India had become important missionaries of cultural rejuvenation and racial awareness.[159]

154 *Ibid*, 4 June 1936, p.14.

155 Brinsley Samaroo, 1975, pp.225–9 *et passim.*

156 The *Trinidad Guardian's* Indian section existed for several years from 1934. The *Beacon's* section ran from 1932 to the journal's demise in 1933.

157 *People*, 10 July 1937, pp.9, 10. The Garveyite was P. O. Thompson.

158 *Trinidad Guardian*, 29 October 1936, p.14.

159 Ranjit Kumar, 1981, pp.12, 13; Kumar was a pioneer in this endeavour. Brinsley Samaroo, 1987, pp.43, 44.

The 1930s activity represented a major upsurge in Indian consciousness paralleling (or perhaps competing with) the contemporaneous rise in African consciousness. The 'Indian News and Views' section of the *Trinidad Guardian* in 1936 welcomed the growing popularity of saris among Indian women as a manifestation of this consciousness and commented, 'It is hoped that others will identify themselves in like manner and thus preserve their national characteristics as true and loyal daughters of Mother India.'[160] (Interestingly, the dhoti, the most characteristic form of Indo-Caribbean male attire, was allowed to die a natural death.)

One of the most enduring aspects of Indo-Caribbean nationalism has been the demand for Hindi in schools. The Canadian Mission schools, as we have already seen, accommodated these demands very early on. Schools run by Hindu organizations continued the practice later. By 1938, 49 Guyanese schools were receiving government grants for the teaching of Hindi.[161] Public interest in this subject has remained strong.[162]

The main arguments on both sides of this issue were aired in 1936, in what may be the definitive statements on the question. In the course of the debate differing perspectives on Indian nationalism were ventilated. The anti-African feeling which has informed Indian nationalism from time to time also found frank expression. 'Trinidadian' initiated the exchange with a letter to Trinidad's *Sunday Guardian*. He agreed with Indian missionary P. Kodanda Rao of the Servants of India Society, Poona, and a personal friend of Mahatma Gandhi, that there was no need for the compulsory teaching of Hindi to Indian children in Trinidad schools. (Rao, who also laboured among the Indians of Guyana, was not the last Indian to consider Indo-Caribbean nationalism excessive.) 'Trinidadian' reviewed the pronouncements of 'prominent' Indo-Trinidadians on the issue. One had said that if Hindi were not taught, Indians would lose their culture. Another said that Indians would become denationalized, and no longer true Indians.

It was all right for Indians to learn Hindi, Urdu, Arabic, or any of the multitudinous languages spoken in India, 'Trinidadian' thought. But it was unreasonable to advocate the compulsory teaching of Hindi. Suppose for the moment that the government did indeed grant the Indian request. This

160 *Trinidad Guardian*, 11 June 1936, p.14.

161 Peter Ruhomon, 1938 (1988), p.287.

162 An expatriate Englishman living in Trinidad ignited considerable controversy in 1987 when he gave Hindi equal billing with English as the national languages of Trinidad & Tobago in a publication designed primarily for tourists – *BWIA Sunjet* magazine, 1987, p.84.

would, in 'Trinidadian's' view, open a Pandora's box of inter- and intra-ethnic strife:

> What will be Government's position when the Negroes of Trinidad also demand that one of the languages of Africa must be compulsorily taught to Negro children in our schools ... ? Is it to be expected that Government will begin to reorganize our schools to suit the whims of every national community of Trinidad which has representatives of almost every people under the sun ... ? And if even the Negroes do not agitate because of a broader outlook, is it not a certainty that among the Indians who constitute about one hundred and fifty thousands, you will find one-third approaching Government [for the teaching of Tamil, since Tamils are one-third of the Indian population]?

A demand for Bengali would be next, 'Trinidadian' thought, and the process could potentially be never-ending. He (or she) perceived a misapprehension among Trinidad Indians to the effect that India was a cohesive society with a single 'mother tongue'.[163]

The 'Indian News and Views' section of the *Trinidad Guardian* provided the forum for the Indian response. It came from H. M. Khan of St Joseph. In a minor concession to 'Trinidadian' he urged the teaching of both Hindi and Urdu, the two most popular local Indian languages.

> In advocating the claims of the East Indians I am not unmindful of the claims of the African race ... . Yet the fact that no similar demand is made by the African people [he ascribed not to] their broader outlook, but [to their] apparent, and to me, sad and deplorable loss of national consciousness. Sad it is indeed for the majority of them have merged themselves in custom, culture and language foreign to their own. Their national spirit seems to be almost dead. ... East Indians have not as yet reached that phase of life, but if no cognisance is paid to their languages and culture, their story some day will be like their African neighbours.[164]

Khan's analysis went to the heart of the two communities' differing approaches to racial consciousness and was fairly reflective of attitudes among Indian communal leaders. It ignored the special circumstances of slavery and the legislative proscription of African religion, music and the like. It also ignored the government-sanctioned activities of the Canadian Mission, Indian government emissaries, 'Protectors of Immigrants' and the whole

163 *Trinidad Guardian*, 7 June 1936, p.4.
164 *Ibid.*, 14 June 1936, p.26.

panoply of Indian protection, for which there was no counterpart in the African community. In dismissing the African claim to 'broader outlook', Khan in fact overlooked a great strength of African nationalism. For people like Henry Sylvester Williams, Garvey, F. E. M. Hercules and Padmore had salvaged what they could from their much-repressed African heritage and had built a new racial consciousness, less dependent on the mechanical transference of African cultural forms, but no less potent for that. This may explain why Africans from the Caribbean often played leadership roles in the Pan-African struggle (not infrequently on the African continent itself), while Caribbean Indians were more likely to be *recipients* of cultural largesse from Mother India.

Khan's ideas nevertheless were then, and continue to be now, orthodoxy among some influential segments of Trinidad Indian opinion. In 1988 the small Trinidad Hindu journal *Sandesh* editorialized in similar vein, though with a slightly new twist: 'The Europeans spared no moment in denuding the Africans of their culture and religion and left no stone unturned in trying to do the same to the Indians. But the Indians were made of stener [sic] stuff ...'.[165]

Khan said that the East Indian Educational Board had extracted a promise of part-time Hindi and Urdu teachers in schools where Indians predominated. He acknowledged that Trinidad was now home for its Indian community. But his was a Trinidad where Indians would aggressively 'mould their character from Indian Culture, thereby retaining their national consciousness.'[166]

'Trinidadian' predictably took exception to Khan's disparaging remarks on African racial consciousness. He saw Trinidad Indians' fierce communalism as reflective of the worst of India itself, where communalism and intolerance were responsible for most of the country's problems. 'The Indian mind is probably the most intolerant in the world,' he declared. 'And this communal and caste intolerance has defied even the vastnesses of the Atlantic and Indian Oceans. It scorns the distance of many thousand miles between India and Trinidad. ... And the worst part of it is, they are called Cultures of India, and if you dare to go against them, you are termed denationalised!' 'Trinidadian' finally contrasted the extreme communalism of Trinidad Indians with more progressive elements in India itself. He quoted J. M. Len Gupta of the Indian National Congress, addressing his own people, in terms reminiscent of Karl Marx's essay on 'The British Rule in India': 'If it is found that Hindu Culture means purdah, and Mohammedan Culture means the harem, both [cultures] must go. If Hindu Culture means caste system and marriage

165 *Sandesh*, 1 April 1988, p.1.
166 *Trinidad Guardian*, 14 June 1936, p.26.

before puberty, and Mohammedan culture means polygamy, none of them should have a place in our social reforms.'[167]

Yet African and Indian nationalisms co-existed reasonably peacefully despite mutually negative stereotypes and petty name-calling. Among some intellectual articulators of Indian consciousness, however, there could be found a mature anti-African racism, reinforced with apparent relish from the prevailing notions of European pseudo-scientific intolerance.

F. E. M. Hosein, the leading Trinidad Indian intellectual of his day (a graduate of Canadian Mission schools, Queen's Royal College, Oxford University and Lincoln's Inn), made something of a classic statement along these lines in 1913, when he likened his African compatriots to 'an inferior race'. The occasion was a major address at an 'inaugural' meeting of the East Indian National Congress. Before a multi-racial (but predominantly Indian) audience which included the British administrator of St Vincent, and Governor Sir George R. LeHunte of Trinidad & Tobago, Hosein predicted the demise of the African population and the ultimate control of the country by Indians. In language indistinguishable from the racist rhetoric of Anthony Trollope, James Anthony Froude and other purveyors of European pseudo-scientific racism,[168] Hosein declared that:

> The Indian was full of his racial prejudice. The time was not when he was not civilized. He had heard of the great races of the earth. But among the great sons of the earth Africa was not mentioned, and when mentioned it was in a humble capacity. From him, the son of India had nothing to learn, – unless, perhaps, something to ridicule. ...[169]

Hosein's remarks drew instant reprimands from the administrator of St Vincent and Governor LeHunte. The African Trinidadian writer, Algernon Burkett, responded in the press and the *Argos* editorially blasted this 'tirade of a half baked East Indian collegian against the Afro-Trinidadian and tacitly others. ...'[170]

In 1936 the prominent and not particularly radical African Trinidadian lawyer, Henry Hudson-Phillips, felt similarly compelled to refute publicly a

167 *Ibid.*, 21 June 1936, p.4. In his further response (*Trinidad Guardian*, 28 June 1936, p.4), Khan rather implausibly suggested that the Hindu-Muslim conflict was 'more of a newspaper propaganda for the outside world'. For Marx's essay see Karl Marx and Frederick Engels, 1968, pp.35–41.

168 See, for example, Eric Williams, 1962 (1993), pp.30–4.

169 *Port of Spain Gazette*, 6 May 1913, p.5.

170 *Argos*, 7 May 1913, p.5, and 8 May 1913, p.4. But Burkett's biographical sketch of Hosein published in 1914 did not refer to this incident – Algernon A. Burkett, 1914, p.66.

disparaging allegation, this time by the Rev. J. D. Ramkeesoon, Anglican minister and first regular non-white columnist in the *Trinidad Guardian*. Ramkeesoon blamed the Africans, victims both of slavery and the post-slavery assault on free labour, rather than the European planters, for the 'necessity' of importing Indian labour.[171] Like Hosein, Ramkeesoon was again appropriating the prevailing arguments of European anti-African racism. In fact, four years earlier leaders of the Forum Club and the Elementary Teachers' Association of Barbados had protested about similar passages in British-authored textbooks imposed on Caribbean schoolchildren.[172]

The Indo-Guyanese historian, Dwarka Nath, as late as 1970 was still broadcasting these sentiments almost verbatim: 'But nothing could induce [the Africans] to work regularly,' he lamented. 'The greater number did nothing at all, but lived on such fruits and ground provisions as they could get.'[173] Like Hosein, Ramkeesoon remained unmoved by public criticism. The Colonial Indian Committee, of which he was a member, told the West India Royal Commission in 1939 that 'at a perilous time' in Trinidad's history, Indians had 'saved it from ruin ...'.[174]

The Indian masses often harboured similar feelings of racial superiority towards Africans. This was a contributory factor (together with fear of Christian proselytization) in a widespread early Indian refusal to send their children to school with Africans. The 1869 Keenan Report on Trinidad education noted that the Indian

> is able fully to appreciate the importance and value of education. But he is proud of his ancient lineage, is influenced by the prejudices of caste, and declines to associate intimately, or to bring up his children in

---

171 *Trinidad Guardian*, 12 February 1936, pp.2, 3, 12. The Indian view of Indian immigrants 'rescuing' the Caribbean from ruin induced by 'lazy' Africans remains an enduring and contentious historiographical notion.

172 *Forum Quarterly*, March 1932, p.31, quoting the following racist statements – 'With the abolition of slavery the prosperity of Jamaica declined. The present population consists largely of blacks most of them averse to work as their wants are few and easily satisfied.' (From *Our Empire Overseas*, published by Blackie and Sons). 'Negroes are lazy, and finding that they could make as much money as they wanted by working only two or three days a week they could not be persuaded to work more and most of the West Indian planters were in consequence ruined.' (From Professor Meiklejohn's *Short History of England*). Eric Williams has refuted these arguments – Eric Williams, 1970 (1984), pp.328–60.

173 Dwarka Nath, 1950 (1970), p.6.

174 J. D. Tyson, 1939, p.101. For other similar Indian submissions to the commission see also pp.95 and 96.

> the same school, with creoles of the African race. If, therefore, it be deemed desirable to educate the Coolies, exceptional provisions and arrangements are indispensable.[175]

As late as 1939 Indians in Jamaica and Trinidad were preferring to keep their daughters at home and uneducated rather than letting them attend racially integrated schools. Jamaica's East Indian Association requested a return to the racially exclusive schools of the indenture period, but that island's Director of Education preferred a policy of 'no race discrimination'. In Trinidad an Indian government representative, like Keenan in 1869, endorsed local Indian requests, which included enhanced recognition for Hindu and Muslim schools, 'non-Christian Indian teachers', and a technical institute exclusively for Indians, although the latter never materialized.[176]

Such attitudes were reinforced by the colour-caste system of Hinduism, which held light skin in high regard. While intra-Indian caste distinction tended to diminish in the Caribbean, the Indian community as a whole incorporated Africans into their scheme of things as the blackest and lowest of outcasts.[177] Some associated Africans with 'the demon Rakshasa and Ravan the enemy of the God Rama…'[178]

Indo-Trinidadian nationalist, H. P. Singh, pointed out in 1965 that Hinduism recognized four main castes. 'Outside the pale was a fifth class, the Panchamas, … the "untouchables, the unapproachables and the unlookables."' Below these outcasts came the rest of humankind (but, in this context, Africans specifically). Any advocacy of Indian-African miscegenation would be 'asking Indians to violate their sacred laws'.[179] (The Dalits or Untouchables of India, on the other hand, have in recent years reached out to African Americans for support in their struggle against upper-caste Hindu oppression.)[180]

Indian racial disdain for Africans was also influenced by Indian attitudes towards Europeans. Despite occasional fatal clashes between Indian workers and European plantation managers, there was often a deep Indian posture of admiration and respect for Europeans. Whites had brought the Indians to the Caribbean in conditions of semi-slavery, but they also occupied a special paternalistic and benevolent relationship with Indians. Whites were also the

---

175 Patrick J. Keenan, 1869, p.47.

176 J. D. Tyson, 1939, pp.8, 71–2, 87, 99.

177 Walton Look Lai, 1993, p.255.

178 K. O. Laurence, 1994, p.279.

179 H. P. Singh, 1993, p.97. Singh's ideas were apparently widely held, though not necessarily always expressed so forthrightly. See, for example, Rabindranath R. Maharaj, 1977, p.82.

180 V. T. Rajshekar, 1987, p.4.

power élite in a multi-racial society. By judiciously offering a limited promise of Indian-European racial kinship, the European community could provide the hope of exalted status, at least over the Africans. Some benevolent Europeans even founded and participated in Indian organizations. Suriname's first important Indian organization, the Suriname Immigrants' Association, was founded in 1910 by a Dutch immigration agent-general.[181] An English Methodist missionary organized the Susamachar East Indian Young Men's Society in Guyana in 1919. Other British missionaries followed him as leaders of the organization.[182] At the society's inaugural meeting the acting Governor, Cecil Clementi, delivered an address on 'The Kinship between the Indian and British Races'.[183]

Clementi is sometimes considered one of Guyana's more racist British rulers.[184] Yet his declaration of 'kinship' with Indians suggests a fascinating, though as yet unexplored, further dimension of anti-African feeling among the Indians. The nineteenth and early twentieth centuries saw a flowering of European adulation for the supposed Aryan super-race who had thousands of years ago allegedly subjugated India and enshrined the idea of a master race via the caste system. All-conquering Europe of the modern age became the latest manifestation of Aryan genius. 'Sir William Hunter's *Imperial Gazeteer of India* (1881) referred to the Aryan as "the splendid ... stock from which the Brahman, the Rajput, and the Englishman alike descend."'[185] Indo-Caribbeans could therefore now bask in the glory of a presumed Aryan kinship with the British. A British finance minister in the Government of India in 1862 saw the British presence there as an expression of 'a sacred mission, to stretch out the right hand of aid to our weaker [Indian] brother, who once far outstripped us, but has now fallen behind in the race.'[186] An Indo-Surinamese Marxist historian saw Suriname's 'Indian compradors', even in the post-independence era, as still promoting 'the colonial view according to which Indian culture was more close to the "normal" white culture.'[187]

Many of these racial factors came into play in the success of the Canadian Mission. Indians respected the Canadians in part 'because they were white'.[188] The Canadians in turn championed political causes seen as anti-African by the African community and helped institutionalize Indian

181 Rosemarijn Hoefte, 1990, p.148. The association originally included Indonesians, but it soon became all-Indian.

182 Peter Ruhomon, 1938 (1988), pp.218, 250–1.

183 *Ibid.*, p.249.

184 Francis M. Drakes, 1991, pp.8, 9; Eusi Kwayana, 1988, p.49.

185 V. T. Rajshekar, 1994, p.26.

186 *Ibid.*, p.27, quoting Samuel Laing, 1862. Europe's infatuation with Aryanism culminated in Adolf Hitler.

187 Sandew Hira, 1987, p.205.

188 Brinsley Samaroo, 1975, pp.48.

exclusivism.[189] The occasional white racist statement directed against Indians did not materially affect the relationship discussed here. The resulting paradox saw the African Trinidadian historian Eric Williams much more exercised over European racist treatment of the Indians than is the case among most contemporary Indo-Caribbean historians themselves.[190]

The insistent advocacy of racial nationalism on the part of Indo-Caribbean leaders did not completely stem the tide of acculturation to the larger societies. The twentieth century witnessed a steady increase in Indian participation in such African-dominated cultural expressions as Trinidad carnival and calypso music. Sometimes such acculturation took place in spite of the strident efforts of the Indian leadership.

Newspaper photographs of the 1930s, even on the pages set aside for Indian opinion, already showed the inexorable progress of acculturation. There were scenes of Western-style weddings, and the exceptional photo of the marriage of a prominent Indian businessman to an Afro-Caribbean woman. There was the picture of Ms. Guyadeen's dance class in Trinidad, featuring girls, predominantly but not exclusively Indian, posing in the stylized gestures of European dance. Prominently featured in Ms. Guyadeen's class was Freida McBurnie, sister of Beryl McBurnie, the great figure of Trinidad's Afro-Caribbean dance.[191]

Powerful elements within the Indian leadership cautioned against such signs of acculturation. Attacks on the 'denationalization' of their people and programmes of 're-Indianization' have been the largely successful devices used to whip the Indian masses back into line. 'The process of denationalization of the Indian born in this colony is even now proceeding rapidly apace and unchecked,' F. E. M. Hosein wrote in 1922; and there was 'every indication that the younger generation of East Indians will be completely assimilated with and absorbed by the coloured race' if something were not done soon. He sought to forestall assimilation and 'preserve the purity and pride of race'.[192]

Trinidad's *East Indian Weekly* in 1929 bemoaned the increasingly denationalized young generation which had done nothing to advance the race and was 'day by day, becoming increasingly disrespectful to their women folk.' Missionary Pundit Jaimini had reversed this trend, however, for 'whereas previously there has been [a] sort of losing of ground, now a spirit of renaissance, or of race-determination, or race consciousness has gone forward throughout the whole Indian community.'[193]

189 *Ibid.*, pp.54, 55.
190 For example, Eric Williams, 1962 (1993), pp.109, 110.
191 Interview with Frieda McBurnie-Artmann, Trinidad, 28 January 1987.
192 *East Indian Weekly*, 12 January 1929, p.3.
193 *Ibid.*, 9 February 1929, p.10.

The Indian government's emissary, J. D. Tyson, provided the formula for continued successful re-Indianization in 1939 when he astutely pointed out that while some acculturation was unavoidable, it was not necessarily inconsistent with the laudable goal of Indian nationalism. The correct strategy, he advised, was for 'the Indian, while retaining his purity of race [to] become a Trinidadian in outlook. ...'[194]

Despite the competing nationalisms, there has often been a lingering perception on both sides that this did not amount to serious racial animosity. C. L. R. James ventured the opinion in 1938, perhaps unduly sanguine even for that period, that there was 'no racial ill-feeling' between Indians and Africans in Trinidad.[195] One Muslim and two Hindu organizations informed the visiting British Moyne Commission at about the same time that there was no racial prejudice in Trinidad.[196] In 1966, after the worst racial riots in British Caribbean history, Marxist Cheddi Jagan still argued that '[r]ace has never been a serious problem' in Guyana.[197]

Nor was the African population reluctant to encourage the more benign expressions of Indian nationalism. Such an opportunity was afforded by a celebratory banquet of 1936 for Leslie Grant Dookhie, Trinidad's fifth Indian Island Scholarship winner, and the first to capture the Jerningham Gold Medal in the process. Dookhie, a 'son of India', had distinguished himself, thereby proving 'not only a credit to himself, or his parents, but to the East Indians of the colony'.[198] C. Henry Pierre, a featured speaker for the occasion, considered it 'a natural and laudable' thing for Indians to be proud of one of their own. 'This race-consciousness is a difficult, if not impossible, thing to cast into the Stygian waters of oblivion,' he said. 'In spite of every effort, it proves irrepressible and asserts itself at every odd moment.' But he did not favour the demand, coming from some quarters, for a specially Indian education for Indo-Trinidadian youth. For 'it seems to me,' he argued, 'that for weal or for woe, the present and future of Trinidad Indians are inextricably bound with the destiny of this beautiful and gorgeous island of ours.' He acknowledged, however, that he was treading on sensitive ground – 'I have said enough either to bring down the approval or the ire of many but I do not mind; it is an honest conviction even though it may be erroneous.'[199]

194 J. D. Tyson, 1939, p.26.
195 C. L. R. James, 1938b (1994), p.58.
196 Brinsley Samaroo, 1974, p.95.
197 Cheddi Jagan, 1966, p.289.
198 *Trinidad Guardian*, 2 July 1936, p.4.
199 *Ibid.*, 4 July 1936, p.8. Pierre was of mixed African and Indian ancestry but still well-respected in the Indian community.

Indo-Caribbean nationalism has been supported by a plethora of racially-focused organizations extending into every sphere of life. The East Indian Institute was founded around 1892 as British Guiana's first 'organized attempt to bring Indians together' for social, economic, political and other reasons.[200] This was followed in 1916 by the omnibus British Guiana East Indian Association (BGEIA). The association's constitution was an articulate and representative statement of Indo-Caribbean nationalist aspirations. It promised in part:

> 1. To unite the members of the East Indian race in all parts of the colony for representative purposes …
> 5. To secure representatives of East Indian nationality in the Legislature and in all corporations where the interests of East Indians are concerned or stand to be affected, every candidate selected, to give a pledge, beforehand, to protect and further the interests of the race, as far as it lies in his power …
> 7. To urge the establishment of special Government Schools under East Indian Masters for the teaching of both Hindi and English to children of East Indian parents …
> 11. To advocate and promote, by all possible legitimate means, the intellectual, moral, social, economical, political and general public interest and welfare of the East Indian community at large …[201]

Trinidad's counterparts of the BGEIA were the East Indian National Association (1897) and the East Indian National Congress (1909). Jamaica in 1938 boasted an East Indian National Association and a 'newly formed' East Indian National Union.[202] Throughout the twentieth century exclusively Indian organizations have permeated every sphere of existence. An East Indian Literary and Debating Association was active in Trinidad in 1917. Clubs bearing similar names were still active decades later.[203] There was an East Indian Cricket Club in Guyana in 1914 and both individual clubs and an East Indian Cricket Board of Control in Trinidad. International matches were arranged (e.g. in 1942) between Indian teams from both countries.[204]

200 Peter Ruhomon, 1938 (1988), p.234.

201 *Ibid.*, pp.235, 236.

202 J. D.Tyson, 1939, p.10.

203 For example, *Port of Spain Gazette*, 18 December 1919, p.4 (East Indian Literary Club); *Trinidad Guardian*, 5 July 1936, p.2 (Indian Literary and Debating Club); H. P. Singh, 1993, pp.xvi–xvii (the Minerva Club, 'an Indian Social, Literary and Debating Club' of the 1930s and 1940s).

204 For example, Peter Ruhomon, 1938 (1988), p.256; *Trinidad Guardian*, 2 March 1939, p.5; *Port of Spain Gazette*, 22 November 1942, p.6.

The Balak Sahaita Mandalee (Child Welfare Society) founded in Guyana in 1936 had as its motto, 'Better mothers, better children, better house life and a better Indian community.'[205] Trinidad boasted a Trinidad Girls in Training, 'an organization for East Indian teen age girls in the Canadian Mission.'[206] In an apparent effort to parallel the work of Trinidad's premier social worker, Audrey Jeffers, Indian leaders in 1936 attempted to establish a 'Breakfast Shed for Indian children'. The moving force behind the effort was A. C. B. Singh, president of the Trinidad Indian League and chairman of the East Indian Social Workers of Port of Spain. 'If we have any element of sympathetic and charitable feelings for which our race is so characteristic,' he said, then his committee should 'leave no stone unturned ... to enhance our position in the colony ....'[207]

During the Second World War some Trinidad Indians wished to form a separate Indian contingent.[208] There was a short-lived Indian Teachers Union in Trinidad combining the Canadian Mission Teachers Association, the Sanatan Dharma Maha Sabha (Hindu) Teachers Association and the Muslim Teachers Association.[209] A 1947 editorial in the Trinidad *Observer*, edited by H. P. Singh, referred to recently abortive efforts at an Indian motor insurance company, an Indian Chamber of Commerce and an Indian Welfare Committee.[210]

The India Club (1942–54), an ostensibly social organization in Port of Spain's exclusive Queens Park West, was started by Dr D. P. Pandia, a visiting Indian Congress Party member. 'Clearly,' commented an Indo-Trinidadian historian of this development, 'the Indian community [in Trinidad] viewed itself as a distinct and separate community, one nation living in a common space with other nations.'[211] Pandia also founded several other Indian political, cultural and welfare associations throughout Trinidad.[212] Other social clubs of this period and later carried names such as the West India Club and Himalaya Club. By the 1980s and 1990s, with Indo-Trinidadian nationalism possibly at its most

---

205 Peter Ruhomon, 1938 (1988), pp.251, 252.

206 *Trinidad Guardian*, 14 June 1936, p.26.

207 *Ibid.*, 7 May 1936, p.4. Among the members of Singh's committee were Mrs F. E. M. Hosein of Arima, C. B. Mathura (later a well-known politician) and H. P. Singh, the 'Father of Indian Nationalism in Trinidad' to his followers.

208 *Trinidad Guardian*, 21 February 1942, p.4. There is a reference here to a similar call for a Chinese contingent.

209 H. P. Singh, 1993, p.xlii. No date is given here but it appears to be *circa* the 1940s to early 1950s.

210 *Ibid.*, p.xxiv.

211 *Ibid.* Pagination in this book is erratic. Sometimes more than one page bear the same number.

212 *Ibid.*, p.xxv.

strident ever, the University of the West Indies (Trinidad campus) boasted a Society for the Propagation of Indian Culture (SPIC), which was inevitably followed by the Society for the Propagation of African Nationalism (SPAN).[213] An Indo-Trinidadian nationalist was probably correct when he observed in the 1990s that Indians 'were the most organized community in Trinidad.'[214]

Indian organization has been paralleled over the years by Indian publications. In Trinidad these have included *Koh-i-noor* (1898–99), the *East Indian Herald* (1919), the *East Indian Patriot* (1921–25), *East Indian Weekly* (1928–32), the *Indian Magazine* (1937), the *Sentinel* (1946), the *West Indian Magnet* (1932), the *Statesman* (*c* 1940s), the *Observer* (1941) and *Sandesh* (1980s).[215] Guyana in the 1930s published *Indian Opinion* and the *Guiana Indian*. In politics Indian nationalism has run the gamut from the early efforts at communal representation to open advocacy of Indian parties to calls for secession and the building of an Indian 'homeland' or empire in the West.

In 1944 the communal representation idea was still alive and well when Trinidad's Adrian Cola Rienzi (born Krishna Deonarine) threatened (unsuccessfully) to demand 'special representatives on all elective and representative bodies.'[216] Trinidad's Indian Association sought (also unsuccessfully) to have proportional representation enshrined in the country's 1962 independence constitution. A three-man delegation (H. P. Singh, Lennox Deyalsingh and Kenneth Lalla) was despatched to London for the purpose.[217] In the 1970s Vernon Jamadar, representing one faction of the Indian-dominated Democratic Labour Party, renewed the call for proportional representation.[218] In Guyana, where ethnic animosity led to serious violence, all major political players, including the British government, had by 1964 come around to advocacy of proportional representation (though there was no agreement as to its precise implementation).[219]

The plethora of separatist cultural and social organizations and the early and frequent calls for communal representation did not automatically translate into exclusively Indian political parties. From the limited representative government introduced into Trinidad by the Wood Report of the 1920s, to universal adult suffrage in 1946 (and beyond), Indian politicians often participated in multi-racial parties and groupings. This was true of both major early

213 Keith Smith, 1993, p.7. According to Smith SPIC was 'to many on campus, a racist organization.'

214 H. P. Singh, 1993, p.xxvii.

215 *Ibid.*, pp. xvii–xx for information on most of these.

216 Brinsley Samaroo, 1974, p.95. Rienzi was contesting the Franchise Committee's recommendation of English language tests for voting eligibility.

217 H. P. Singh, 1993, p.xiv, and pp.23–56, text of *idem*, 1962.

218 John Gaffar La Guerre, 1974, p.105.

219 Hamilton Green, 1987, p.90; Cheddi Jagan, 1966, p.314.

parties, the Trinidad Workingmen's Association/Labour Party of A. A. Cipriani and the British Empire Workers and Citizens Home Rule Party of Tubal Uriah 'Buzz' Butler. Timothy Roodal was leader of the southern section of the former in the 1920s; Adrian Cola Rienzi, a veteran of the radical Indian National Party of the 1920s, became a leading Butler collaborator in the 1930s. In Guyana Joseph A. Luckhoo in 1916 became the first Indian to be elected to the legislature. He did so as a candidate for the multi-racial People's Association.[220]

To many, both observers and participants, it was universal adult suffrage (1946 in Trinidad & Tobago, 1948 in Suriname, 1953 in Guyana), with its new potential for appeals to the mass of citizens, that brought race to the forefront of electoral politics. Trinidadian Dr Patrick Solomon, an electoral candidate in 1946 and later deputy prime minister under Eric Williams, blamed Indians for this development.[221] H. P. Singh blamed Africans.[222] From this point on, the Hindi expression meaning 'vote for your own' passed into the political vocabularies of Trinidad (*apan jhaat*), Suriname (*apanjaht*) and Guyana (*appan jaat*). In 1958 chief minister Eric Williams of Trinidad deplored a letter from 'Yours Truly, Indian' to 'My Dear Indian Brothers,' said to have been circulated by partisans of the Indian-dominated Democratic Labour Party. The letter contained 'nothing of taxation or Government policy,' he noted. It was 'sheer race ....'[223] In 1961 Janet Jagan, American-Jewish wife of Indo-Guyanese politician Cheddi Jagan, denied a newspaper allegation that she had openly advocated *appan jaat*.[224] Her husband blamed 'Indian racist leaders' for 'originat[ing]' the term.[225]

Indian nationalism became entrenched in Trinidad politics with the appearance of the People's Democratic Party (PDP) to contest the 1956 elections. Bhadase Sagan Maraj doubled as leader of the major Hindu organization, the Sanatan Dharma Maha Sabha, and the new party. The result was a party that was perhaps closer to Hindu communal association than orthodox political party. It lacked the basic political structures (party groups, a constitution, etc.) and relied instead on pundits, prayer meetings and the like[226] to spread a political message clothed in the authority of religious and racial sanctions.

The PDP's offspring, the Democratic Labour Party (DLP), inherited the mantle of an Indian party, though with an infusion of multi-racial appointees

220 Francis M. Drakes, 1991, p.8.

221 Patrick Solomon, 1981, p.75.

222 H. P. Singh, 1993, p.xliii.

223 *Trinidad Guardian*, 2 April 1958, pp.1, 13. See also Selwyn D. Ryan, 1972, p.191.

224 *Thunder* (Guyana), 13 May 1961, p.3.

225 Cheddi Jagan, 1966, p.114. Hamilton Green blamed Jagan's party – see Hamilton Green, 1987, pp.50, 58.

226 Selwyn D. Ryan, 1972, pp.141, 143.

imposed from the top of its still haphazard party structure. Some Indo-Trinidadian intellectuals were among the critics of the communalization of Trinidad Indian politics. 'It was a great pity,' they wrote of the DLP, 'that the broader, national issues were not emphasized as against the narrow racial problems.' On the PDP/DLP continuum of the 1950s and 1960s they observed:

> The link between the Maha Sabha and the politicians ensured a preoccupation with the cultural concerns of one racial grouping and discouraged the mass of East Indians from looking critically at the society and their leaders.
>
> A leader was judged by his ability to erect temples or chant the rudiments of Hindi. His ability to discuss the problems of an emergent country was hardly even considered.[227]

The communalization of Indian politics in Trinidad was heightened with the rise of Eric Williams and his People's National Movement (PNM) in 1956. Williams was heir to a hundred years of African struggle at the centre of Trinidad politics. Africans inevitably predominated in the PNM's hierarchy and membership. Williams' gifted leadership unleashed the pent-up African nationalist fervour of decades, as British colonialism seemed headed for certain demise. Yet the PNM was never a narrowly communal party, in the manner of the PDP and the DLP. It aspired to be a genuine national party which reflected its multi-racial society.

In the prospect of PNM rule, the more extreme elements of Indian nationalism saw writ large all the fears of their forefathers, who had consistently sought communal representation since the early 1900s. For H. P. Singh in 1956, 'A vote for a PNM candidate [would be] a vote against the Indian community ....' And PNM rule meant, in the words of a Singh disciple, 'racist black fascist neo-colonial domination.'[228] Singh was an executive member of the DLP but chafed at the efforts of its leaders to impose a multi-racial executive on its Hindu base. He insisted on a totally 'Indian organization – call it a political party if you will .... We are conscious of the full implications of the advocacy of such a measure ....'[229] It was to this end that he formed the small Indian Association of Trinidad and Tobago in 1962.[230]

227 John Gaffar La Guerre *et al.*, 1973, pp.5, 6.

228 H. P. Singh, 1993, pp.xlv, xlvi, lxiii.

229 *Ibid.*, p.3.

230 In response to PNM questions raised in parliament the DLP eventually tried to distance themselves from Singh, while resisting pressure to disavow him unequivocally – *Ibid.*, p.lxv.

Criticism of this nature, compounded by a PNM defeat at the federal elections of 1958, caused Williams to call the Hindu-based DLP a '"recalcitrant and hostile minority" ... masquerading as the Indian Nation and prostituting the name of India "for its selfish and reactionary political ends."'[231] In India itself, Williams showed, the (Trinidad) Maha Sabha's namesake had been denounced by leader Jawaharlal Nehru as representing 'small upper class reactionary groups taking advantage of the religious passions of the masses ...'[232] He dismissed the local Maha Sabha types as 'reactionary Indian politicians who see the political leader as a man of racialism ....'[233]

The PDP/DLP group underwent various name changes in later years. In a coalition with African (often ex-PNM) and French Creole elements it shared power in the National Alliance for Reconstruction (NAR) government of 1986–91, only to reconstitute itself as a separate party (this time called the United National Congress), when the NAR coalition unravelled. The UNC finally became the government in 1995, with the help of the Tobago-based remnants of the NAR.

The historic quest for Indian communalism has sometimes led, especially in recent years, to extremist demands for partition and/or secession. In the 1950s there were calls and rumours of calls for a Guyana-Trinidad unification, presumably to constitute 'an East Indian Empire.'[234] Similar sentiments were said to have been expressed in the 1940s.[235] Trinidad's Indian Association in its 1962 pre-independence memorandum to the British government demanded 'parity' (defined as 50 per cent of civil service, police, legislative and other appointments) or 'partition'.[236]

In the 1980s some Indo-Trinidadians sought entry into Canada as 'refugees' from alleged political persecution in Trinidad.[237] Others sought entry into the United States on similar grounds.[238] Such 'refugees' may have been among those who constituted themselves the Indesh Freedom Party in

231 *Trinidad Guardian*, 2 April 1958, p.13.

232 Selwyn D. Ryan, 1972, p.140, quoting Jawaharlal Nehru, *Discovery of India* (no further reference given).

233 Eric Williams, 1959, p.107. Williams thought here that 'little remains of ... African culture ...'

234 H. P. Singh, 1993, p.117; Cheddi Jagan, 1966, p.299, quoting the British Robertson Commission of 1954 in Guyana.

235 H. P. Singh, 1993, p.115.

236 *Ibid.*, p.7.

237 *Ibid.*, p.115. This was also widely discussed in the Trinidad press.

238 The present writer was approached by public defenders in the Boston area who sought historical data to make a case for indigent Indo-Trinidadians facing deportation. The potential deportees were seeking refugee status.

1990. From Canada they claimed a substantial portion of Trinidad for the establishment of an 'Indian homeland'.[239]

A coalition of Trinidad-based Indian groups countered with the more grandiose proposal of a federated homeland of Bharatiyadesh/Industan, comprising Trinidad, Guyana and Suriname. Its 1991 'Declaration on the Question of the Creation in the Americas of an Indian Homeland' announced that 'it is only with the creation of Bharatiyadesh/Industan can the Indian spirit realize its full potential. This vision of Bharatiyadesh/Industan is latent in the very being of every Indian, it has been a persistent and strong desire, a longing, a dream – a vision awaiting realisation.'[240]

Secessionist tendencies in most countries have been accompanied by violence. Indo-Caribbean nationalism has also been characterized by persistent undertones of threatened violence. H. P. Singh saw violence as inevitable where two peoples co-existed in the same space – 'one must as a rule become the HAMMER,' he warned, 'and the other the ANVIL.'[241] His disciples in 1993 saw violence as a viable option for attainment of an Indian homeland. If 'peaceful constitutional means' proved ineffective, they wrote, 'Indians should not hesitate to use militant means for ultimate freedom.'[242] 'Ethnic tensions reached their peak [in pre-independence Suriname of the early 1970s] with stoning, arson, and continued protest demonstrations mounted by Hindustanis and others against the Creole-led [independence] movement.'[243]

As early as 1913, F. E. M. Hosein resorted to ambiguously militaristic metaphors to 'play the prophet' and suggested that the 'invasion from India' would in time 'drive out the rest of the inhabitants' of Trinidad. 'The African was not as productive as the East Indian,' he said, 'and if circumstances did not compel him to leave the colony, he would naturally die out.' Indians would then become 'master of the whole island ...'. Governor G. R. Le Hunte rose from the audience in an unusual gesture to object, *inter alia*, to Hosein's use of the terms 'invasion' and 'master'.[244]

During the election campaign of 1964 in Guyana, People's Progressive Party candidate Brindley H. Benn is said to have urged Indians to 'sharpen your cutlasses'.[245] In Trinidad, DLP leader Rudranath Capildeo in 1961 told an

239 H. P. Singh, 1993, p.117.

240 *Ibid.*, pp.115, 119. The groups were the Indian Review Committee, Equality Editorial Committee and Indian Arrival Day Committee.

241 *Ibid.*, p.48. Singh's thinly veiled threats of violence were expressed as early as 1953 – see p.xliii.

242 *Ibid.*, p.lxvii.

243 Edward Dew, 1990, p.195.

244 *Port of Spain Gazette*, 6 May 1913, p.5.

245 Hamilton Green, 1987, p.102.

election campaign audience variously estimated at between 17,000 and 35,000 people, 'I am asking you to arm yourselves with a weapon in order to take over this country.'[246] The government of Eric Williams later declared a state of emergency in some DLP strongholds.

It was in Guyana, however, that the potential for violence inherent in the co-existing nationalisms became manifest. Guyana received the largest number of Indian immigrants in the region. By 1911 Indians were already officially the largest ethnic group (helped by the separation of 'Coloureds/Mixed' from 'Blacks' in the census).[247]

Africans in Guyana complained longer and more bitterly than their compatriots elsewhere of the British assault on their well-being brought about by Indian immigration. They often demanded equal facilities for African and Caribbean immigration to redress the population imbalance being foisted upon them. A. R. F. Webber raised this question in 1924 in his reply to the Governor's speech, read on behalf of the elected members in the colonial legislature. The electives wanted a more vigorous government pursuit of Caribbean immigration, instead of 'pursuing feverishly our activities in India'. Webber warned of 'a large body of public opinion [which] feels that it is essentially necessary to preserve the balance of the races in the colony, and not allow any one race to become too predominant.'[248]

In 1925 Garveyites were among those appointed to a government-appointed committee looking into the possible importation of 'agricultural families of African race and origin' under the Colonization Scheme of 1919. A year earlier the Negro Progress Convention petitioned the Governor to appoint a committee to visit the Caribbean and Africa in search of immigrants who would come in 'on the same terms and conditions as are being offered to the Indians'. In 1919 a large delegation had asked Lord Milner, Secretary of State for the Colonies, to facilitate African immigration.[249] To add insult to injury, while Indian missionaries and Indian government emissaries were free to foster Indian nationalism, African-American race-uplift publications (including Marcus Garvey's *Negro World*) were banned.[250] Serious conflict between Indians and Africans was nevertheless long avoided because patterns of residential separation, until the 1940s, restricted day-to-day contact.

---

246 *Sunday Guardian*, 15 October 1961, quoted in Selwyn D. Ryan, 1972, p.268.

247 Walton Look Lai, 1993, p.302.

248 *Index to Debates of Combined Court*, 1924, 1925, p.186, at Guyana National Archives, Georgetown. Webber was the Senior Financial Representative.

249 *Negro World*, 9 May 1925, p.6, quoting an article from the *Daily Argosy*, n.d.

250 Officer Administering the Government, C. Clementi to Rt. Hon. Viscount Milner, PC, etc. etc., 2 September 1919, CO 111/624, Public Record Office, London. See also Tony Martin, 1976 (1986) p.95.

Universal adult suffrage in 1953 brought an electoral victory for the People's Progressive Party (PPP), led by the Indian Cheddi Jagan and the African Forbes Burnham. Some see this collaboration as a golden age of inter-racial co-operation, while others see it as an enlightened effort at the top which did not permeate down through the ranks of the PPP. The British ousted Jagan from government after 133 days for his Marxism, followed by a split in 1955 between Jagan and Burnham. Burnham's PPP faction eventually became the People's National Congress (PNC). The now predominantly Indian PPP won elections of 1957 and 1961 with the predominantly African PNC forming the major opposition party. The period 1962–4 saw inter-racial violence on a scale hitherto not known in the anglophone Caribbean. The British government introduced proportional representation in 1964, resulting in a PPP defeat at the polls that year. Some voices could be heard in the period from 1953 to 1964 in favour of partition of the country. It is note-worthy, however, that even in the most perilous times both major parties sought to maintain a least an appearance of inter-racial co-operation in their respective ranks.

The efforts to reconcile political separatism with a racial *modus vivendi* have been at their most pragmatic in Suriname, where the three major political parties unabashedly based themselves on the three largest ethnic groups of Hindustanis (Indians), Creoles (primarily Africans, but not including the majority of African Maroons) and Indonesians. (Creole and Hindustani emigrants in Holland even vote for diferent Dutch parties.)[251] Major efforts at co-existence were directed at building coalition governments rather than forcing integration within each party. At one time in the 1950s and 1960s the Creole and Hindustani parties remained in coalition for 15 years. The military government's effort (1980–7) at what one writer called 'anti-apanjaht Utopianism'[252] gave way eventually to a resumption of coalition politics among separatist elements.

Indo-Caribbean nationalism may eventually co-exist peacefully with its African counterpart in an atmosphere of mutual respect. Escalating conflict cannot, however, be automatically ruled out. Indo-Caribbeans at times see themselves as the Jews of the Caribbean, evoking violent analogies with Nazi Germany and Palestine. 'Hindus are like Jews,' Indo-Trinidadian businessman Motilal Moonan told an interviewer. 'They have an inner drive to do the best they can. Moreover, in Hinduism it is no sin to be wealthy.'[253] For the ex-

251 Wilhelmina van Wetering, 1990, p.295.

252 Edward Dew, 1990, p.194. On Indian hostility to independence see Albert Gastmann, 1971, p.146.

253 Dave Ramsaran, 1993, pp.113, 114.

tremist H. P. Singh the analogy had violent implications: '[Trinidad] is Nazi Germany and the Jews are the Indians.'[254] It was left to the British Moyne Commission in 1938–9 to warn against the potentially disastrous consequences of this analogy: 'We would avoid any system of sectional quotas which would lead to the deplorable system of "government by arithmetic," the adoption of which in Palestine ... if anything exacerbates communal feelings instead of allaying it.'[255]

Compared with many parts of the world, Caribbean ethnic tensions have not been very severe. Yet the challenge remains – how to prevent ethnic nationalism from spilling over into ethnic violence.

254 H. P. Singh, 1993, p.48.
255 Quoted by Hugh Tinker in Bridget Brereton and Winston Dookeran, 1982, p.41.

7

THE CUBAN REVOLUTION AND ITS IMPACT ON THE CARIBBEAN

Marifeli Pérez-Stable

Introduction

'This time the revolution is for real,' Fidel Castro proclaimed on 1 January 1959. Since then, Cuba has charted a course different from the rest of the Caribbean; the revolution effected the island's real independence from the United States and restructured Cuban society in favour of the popular classes. Revolutionary Cuba offered an alternative to dependent capitalism, though one sustained by substantial trade, credit and aid from the Soviet Union until 1989. Socialism registered social advancements (such as health and education) which towered impressively over those of most of the Third World, though it never quite realized stable rates of economic growth and steady improvements in overall living standards. While firmly bound by a single party, the political system also drew on the exceptional leadership of Fidel Castro and at least initially an extraordinary fount of popular support. Thus, Cuban socialism never quite acquired the profile of its erstwhile allies in the Soviet Union and Eastern Europe.

Upon the downfall of the dictator Fulgencio Batista, Cuba experienced a 'real' revolution. During 1959–60, the domestic and international bases of Cuban development changed radically. The old dominant classes lost their power and the United States its presence, while the popular classes became the bulwark of the new government. Had the Soviet Union not existed or had it not become the benefactor of the new Cuba, geo-politics would have, in all likelihood, rendered radical consolidation impossible. Thus the Cold War offered the revolution the security to withstand the unrelenting hostility of the United States. The old Soviet Union also provided an ideological referent for Cuban socialism, its distinctive markings notwithstanding. On the island, one-party politics and centrally planned economics likewise constituted the central institutions of state socialism. In the post-Cold War world, Cuba has therefore confronted a latent political crisis as well as an unprecedented economic collapse – caused, on the face of it, by the disintegration of the Soviet

Union and the annulment of state socialism as a viable alternative to capitalism, but just as importantly if less apparently rooted in the domestic dynamics of Cuban socialism. Having thus far survived the demise of its patron and the escalation of the United States embargo, the Cuban government has defiantly persisted in claiming the right to craft a more just and sovereign alternative to the reigning model of global integration. At the turn of the century, Cuba remains on a course different from the rest of the Caribbean.

Cuba's dogged insistence on forging an alternative path has, in and of itself, made the island a beacon for its neighbours – albeit an enduring, kindred traveller never quite settled in the region. This chapter provides an overview of Cuban development over the past four decades – from the momentous first two years of the revolution, when its radical tempo and nationalist tenor were defined, to the 1990s, when domestic and international circumstances considerably dimmed the long-term prospects of Cuban socialism. At each juncture, it focuses on the political system, economic development and international relations. Understanding the island's history is essential, even if, eventually, current efforts to deflect international trends toward market economics and political democracy falter. Whatever the future holds, Cuba will always have its alternative past as a mark of distinction on the Caribbean imagination.

The Cuban Revolution (1959–61)

The Cuban Revolution brought to power a government without a clear blueprint for the future: the call to restore the constitution of 1940 – the signal banner of the anti-Batista opposition – provided only broad brush-strokes for representative democracy and socio-economic reform.[1] After 1 January 1959, the popular classes unleashed a concatenation of demands (jobs, higher wages, lower rents, land reform), which placed the revolutionary government at the crossroads of responding to them or tempering them for the sake of a broadly based national front. By responding to these demands, the government quickly sidetracked the calls for elections and moderation and accordingly collided with Cuba's dominant classes and the United States. The *fidelistas* never gave an inkling that they had any qualms about up-ending what until then had seemed to be immutable: the submission of the popular classes and of the nation. They dared to dream of a new Cuba, and the overwhelming

1 For an overview of twentieth-century Cuba up to the early 1990s, see Marifeli Pérez-Stable, 1993.

majority of Cubans enthusiastically assented. More important than elections was the creation of a society of equality, full employment, agrarian reform, universal education and real democracy, and these achievements, the leadership argued, would be the gauge of the government's legitimacy. Moreover, many of those calling for immediate elections had been silent during Batista's dictatorship and had the most to lose by the revolution's redistributive policies. '*Politiquería* [politicking] is as odious as tyranny,' Fidel Castro asserted in May 1959.[2] Indeed, the revolution had so aroused the will, energy and passion of the Cuban people that holding elections seemed a meaningless formality.

The new Cuba, nonetheless, faced the challenge of establishing an alternate institutional order, and, in fact, the social revolution brought forth new institutions. The Rebel Army, the National Institute of Agrarian Reform (INRA), and the National Federation of Sugar Workers (FNTA) supervised the transformation of rural Cuba. The Labour Ministry, the Central Organization of Cuban Trade Unions (CTC), and the popular militia directed popular mobilization in the cities. In June 1959, as landowners closed country stores and denied credit to rural workers, the government opened the first *tiendas del pueblo* (people's stores).[3] In October, when a group of citizens cleaned and painted the Havana waterfront in preparation for a convention of travel agents, the practice of volunteer work was born.[4] In February 1960, as relations with the dominant classes deteriorated, the central planning board, Junta Central de Planficación (JUCEPLAN), was formed.[5] In March 1960, the Association of Rebel Youths (AJR) enlisted the considerable energies and enthusiasm of Cuban young people.[6] In September 1960, after the Organization of American States (OAS) rebuked Cuba and United States intervention seemed imminent, Fidel Castro charged the Committees for the Defence of the Revolution (CDR) with neighbourhood vigilance.[7] In August 1960, the Federation of Cuban Women (FMC) also came into being in the midst of the social revolution.

Fidel Castro himself was the most powerful political resource of the revolution. He had an exceptional ability to interpret and address the reality of Cuba as well as an extraordinary capacity to impress upon his followers the magnitude of their mission. Fidel had proved his talents in the opposition to Batista and did so once again in 1959–61 as weather vane to the revolution.

2 *Revolución*, 11 May 1959, p.1.
3 *Revolución*, 6 June 1959, p.16.
4 *Revolución*, 10 October 1959, p.1.
5 *Revolución*, 20 February 1960, p.1.
6 *Revolución*, 22 March 1960, p.4.
7 *Revolución*, 30 September 1960, p.1.

The first few months of 1959 crafted a 'Fidel-*pueblo* binomial' which became the crux of revolutionary politics; Fidel used a clear and new language: he explained, the people understood.[8] The revolution was now the Sierra Maestra, *el pueblo* the Rebel Army, the United States and Cubans without national dignity, the enemy. Just as the dominant classes witnessed the almost instant withering of their strength in early 1959, so did the popular classes sense the birth of a new power – inchoate, amorphous, unstructured, but nonetheless real. And Fidel infused *el pueblo* with the purpose to conclude the task so often frustrated: the constitution of Cuba as a nation.[9]

In May 1960, before a million Cubans in Havana, Fidel Castro officially announced that the government would not hold elections. His audience shouted back that the people had already voted, and they had voted for Fidel.[10] The revolution polarized Cuba and disallowed neutrality. *Con Cuba o contra Cuba* was the battle cry and Fidel the embodiment of Cuba. Had Cuba not been 90 miles from the United States, the revolution might have found more tolerant middle ground. That nearness and the almost immediate enmity of President Dwight Eisenhower's administration moulded the radical nationalism that rendered the revolution so intransigent. During 1950–4, a reformist government in Guatemala had encountered fierce domestic and United States opposition and had failed to take steps to defend itself. Cuba was not Guatemala, Fidel no Jacobo Arbenz, the Rebel Army indivisible.[11] Not as prominent but no less relevant was Bolivia during the period 1952–6 where accommodation to local capitalists and foreign interests compromised a social revolution. So that the Cuban Revolution would not be so compromised, decisive and effective central authority was mandatory. Castro never hesitated to exercise it.

Commitment to remedying the social injustices of the past radicalized the Cuban Revolution. Never before in Cuban history had those in power been so defiant and so insistent: 'Cuba is not a simple geographical reference,' proclaimed an editorial in the daily newspaper *Revolución*.[12] *Con Cuba o contra Cuba* became *con Fidel o contra Fidel*.[13] Indeed, in 1959–61, radicalization, polarization, and centralization consolidated the revolution around Castro. The new Cuba embarked on a quest of historic proportions with

8 *Revolución*, 11 April 1959, pp.1, 14.

9 The Sierra Maestra was the mountain range in eastern Cuba where Fidel Castro and his followers launched guerrilla warfare against Batista's army. *Revolución*, 6 July 1959, pp.2, 19.

10 *Revolución*, 2 May 1960, p.1.

11 *Revolución*, 10 November 1959, p.10.

12 *Revolución*, 1 September 1960, pp.1–2.

13 *Revolución*, 4 March 1960, p.13.

immediate rewards in rising standards of living for the popular classes (no less than 15 per cent of national income shifted from property owners to wage earners during 1959–60), as well as with more ethereal bequests of dignity and honour.[14] In June 1960, Fidel exclaimed:

> The revolution shows that ideals are more powerful than gold! If gold were more powerful than ideals, those large foreign interests would have swept us off the map; if gold had more power than ideals, our *patria* would be lost because our enemies have plenty of gold to buy *conciencia* [our conscience] and yet all our enemies' gold is not enough to buy the *conciencia* of a revolutionary ... Workers, peasants, Cubans of dignity ... will not trade their revolution, their *patria* for gold.[15]

The Cuban Revolution mobilized an overwhelming consensus around a programme of national sovereignty and social justice. By the fall of 1960, the State controlled 'the commanding heights of the economy': United States and most Cuban capital was dispossessed. Before leaving office in January 1961, Eisenhower severed diplomatic relations with the Cuban government; a partial embargo on trade had been enforced since the previous October. On 16 April 1961, on the eve of the United States-sponsored Bay of Pigs invasion, Fidel declared the revolution socialist and thus cleared the way for Cuba's three-decade affiliation with the Soviet Union. That the revolution left no options to its opponents but imprisonment, execution, exile or silence seemed less compelling then to most Cubans than its promise of a new Cuba. Even when, at the height of the Cold War, the revolution sided with the Soviet Union, its nationalist and egalitarian appeals proved stronger to most Cubans than the anticommunism to which they had until recently subscribed. National affirmation against the United States became the overriding consideration, and, therefore, survival subsumed all other concerns. For the sake of *la patria*, iron-handed unity behind Fidel Castro was enforced. Politics acquired a sense of military discipline hostile to political diversity and independent organizations. Political democracy – with its fastidious insistence on checks and balances, separation of powers, and individual rights – had decidedly limited vistas. Instead, the new government relied on an impressive popular consensus, Castro's forceful leadership, and the monopoly of a single party to safeguard national sovereignty and to promote social justice. After the revolutionary forces routed Brigade 2506, a contingent of Cuban exiles, at the Bay of Pigs on 19 April 1961, the Cuban people embraced the quotidian tasks of constructing the new Cuba.

---

14 Felipe Pazos, 1962, p.9.

15 *Revolución*, 9 June 1960, p.1.

The revolution in the 1960s

The new Cuba required the mobilization of *el pueblo cubano* to defend the nation and develop the economy. By 1961, the popular militia numbered more than 300,000, the Committees for the Defence of the Revolution nearly 800,000.[16] The Federation of Cuban Women mobilized housewives for the chores of the revolution. The trade unions sought a more co-operative, less confrontational profile under socialism: wage increases and the right to strike were exchanged for full employment and job security. Born in urban Cuba, volunteer work spread to the countryside. In the battle for economic development, thousands of city dwellers wielded *machetes* (cane knives) and downed the tall stalks of cane. In 1961, the literacy campaign enlisted nearly 300,000 people.[17] The struggle to survive infused these mobilizations with a military mission. Institutionalizing the revolution, however, supposed a civilian understanding of participation, or at least, involvement and consultation. Tensions between military exigencies and civilian imperatives punctuated the new politics.

During the early 1960s, the revolutionary leadership followed the models of socialism then in existence. In 1961, Castro's July 26th Movement, the Revolutionary Student Directorate (DRE), and the Popular Socialist Party (PSP) fused into the Integrated Revolutionary Organizations (ORI).[18] By the end of 1960 the government had taken the first steps toward central planning. Neither the ORI nor the socialized economy – the first incarnations of the central institutions of state socialism on the island – succeeded in con-

16 Jorge I. Domínguez, 1978, pp.208, 262.

17 Richard R. Fagen, 1969, pp.47, 50.

18 Fidel Castro's organization, the July 26th Movement, drew its name from the aborted attack on the Moncada Barracks in Santiago de Cuba on 26 July 1953. It had two wings: urban groupings throughout the island and the guerrilla core in the Sierra Maestra. Founded by José Antonio Echevarría and other university students in Havana, the Revolutionary Student Directorate, like the July 26th Movement, advocated armed struggle against Batista. On 13 March 1957, the DRE assaulted the Presidential Palace but failed to execute its goal: the assassination of Batista. Echevarría and other DRE leaders died in the confrontation. The Popular Socialist Party was the old Communist Party. Though radical in the 1920s and 1930s, the party accommodated to the democratic and redistributionist status quo of the 1940s. A reformist, if militant, organization, the PSP joined the anti-Batista struggle only at the end. The party, however, counted on a much more sophisticated organization and more disciplined cadres than either the July 26th Movement or the DRE; it also had crucial international connections to the Soviet Union which the revolutionary government needed. Sectarian conflicts among these three organizations marred early efforts to build a single ruling party.

solidating leadership unity, maintaining popular support, and promoting economic growth. In 1962, sectarianism threatened to sunder the party: PSP members were manoeuvering to gain control of the ORI at the expense of the July 26th Movement and the DRE. The economy, moreover, did not perform as expected, and the government introduced rationing for most consumer goods. Not surprisingly, popular enthusiasm waned as daily living, even if more equitable, became more austere and the revolution became more a matter of routine. In addition, Cuban leaders were also disillusioned with the Soviet Union: they considered themselves more radical and militant and were mistrustful of new ties of dependence that might constrain their options.

By the mid-1960s, the Cuban Revolution was ebbing. The revolutionary times of 1959–61 had been heady, extraordinary, moving; governing and living through them had demanded quite different skills and energies than the subsequent more 'normal' times. In 1965–6, the *fidelistas* turned away from the then-extant socialist models in politics and economics and launched the radical experiment to put a Cuban face on state socialism. The new Communist Party of Cuba (PCC) was founded in 1965; Castro and his closest associates, particularly in the Revolutionary Armed Forces (FAR) and the Interior Ministry (MININT), claimed control of a refurbished party and sidelined the old communists. The primacy of moral incentives, mass mobilizations and vanguard cadres marked the 'Cuban heresy' of 1966–70. Ernesto 'Ché' Guevara pointedly outlined the heresy's rationale:

> Pursuing the chimera of achieving socialism with the aid of the blunted weapons left to us by capitalism (the commodity as the economic cell, profitability, and individual material incentives as levers, etc.), it is possible to come to a blind alley. And the arrival there comes about after covering a long distance where there are many crossroads and where it is difficult to realize just where the wrong turn was taken. Meanwhile, the adapted economic base has undermined the development of consciousness. To build communism, a new man must be created simultaneously with the material base.[19]

Moreover, larger sugar harvests, culminating in ten million tons in 1970, would accelerate capital accumulation and allow Cuba the resources to strike a more balanced relationship with the Soviet Union. The revolution would, the *fidelistas* hoped, succeed where staid, bureaucratic means had not, and the outcome would be popular participation, economic growth, better living standards, and a more secure sovereignty.

19 Ernesto 'Ché' Guevara, 1971, pp.342–3.

The radical experiment yielded a débâcle. Mass mobilizations, weak or non-existent institutions and economic mismanagement undermined Cuba's heresy. A record-breaking harvest of 8.5 million tons in 1970 did not begin to make up for poor economic performance in most other sectors. After March 1968, when the State nationalized more than 58,000 small businesses and banned self-employment, daily life assumed increasingly baneful qualities as the state sector failed to provide the goods and services which the private sector had.[20] Consumption was at least 5 per cent below the already rationed levels of 1962.[21] In 1969–70, nationwide absenteeism reached 20 per cent of the labour force; some areas in Oriente province registered an astounding 50 per cent rate. A 1968 survey of 200 enterprises indicated that 25 to 50 per cent of the work-day was wasted. Indeed, workers had staged an unco-ordinated strike of sorts: they had no incentive to work for there was little to buy.[22] By 1970, Cuban leaders could no longer maintain their heresy.

In the late 1960s, the revolution also challenged the Soviet-backed communist parties in Latin America by promoting armed struggle to spark other revolutions. In 1967, this strategy was dealt a serious blow when Guevara died in Bolivia; other revolutions would pointedly not join Cuba's in a Latin American front against the United States. Early in 1968, the Soviet Union delayed petroleum shipments to Cuba, an apparent censure of the *fidelista* policies abroad and at home and a painful reminder of the defiant island's dependence. On 23 August 1968, Soviet and Warsaw Pact forces invaded Czechoslovakia. Under the leadership of Alexander Dubcek, the Czech Communist party had initiated a process of socialist renovation through market reforms and political liberalization. Though Czechoslovakia also claimed the right to bestow its own face on contemporary socialism, Cuba extended qualified support to the invasion. On the surface, this support was surprising. Relations between Cuba and the Soviet Union were tense. Czechoslovakia was a small country whose sovereignty was pre-empted by a large and powerful neighbour. But Fidel valued the preservation of socialism over Czech sovereignty and deplored that the Communist Party had deviated from socialist precepts far enough to warrant such an infringement. The Prague Spring had promoted a vision of socialism that ran counter to Cuba's radical experiment. The invasion provided Cuban leaders with the opportunity to assert their opposition to market socialism and extend a conciliatory gesture to the Soviet Union.[23]

By 1970, international failure, economic collapse and popular demoralization left the Cuban leadership no choice but to turn to the Soviet Union and

---

20 Héctor Ayala Castro, 1982, pp.17–20.

21 Carmelo Mesa-Lago, 1981, p.44.

22 Jorge I. Domínguez, 1978, p.276.

23 Jacques Lévesque, 1978; W. Raymond Duncan, 1985.

Eastern Europe. The revolution had miscarried the attempt to generate the economic and political resources to sustain the Cuban heresy. The then-extant models of state socialism were the only other option; there was also no alternative to accepting the new dependence. Precedence had to be given to civilian pursuits and economic development. By the end of the 1960s, the Cuban people had manifested a '*resignación de apoyo*' (resigned support).[24] Indeed, the year 1970 poignantly marked the end of the revolution. Relative institutionalization would follow in the 1970s, imparting a more settled context to charismatic authority, one-party politics and mass mobilizations. The reality of socialism slowly gained ascendance over the effervescence of revolution.

The Cuban government in the 1970s and early 1980s

Drawing upon this 'resigned support' and the disposition to listen to its directives on the part of most Cubans, the Communist Party pursued a process of institutionalization. The citizenry, however, did not have the right to opt out of socialism or challenge the party and the leadership. One of the principal charges of institutionalization was to establish the responsibilities and jurisdictions of the political leadership, the state administration, and popular participation. The PCC was to rule, the State to administer, the popular organizations to involve 'the masses' in the daily routines of socialism. The Armed Forces played a crucial role in the initial period of institutionalization as 'civic soldiers' assumed numerous and varied assignments in civilian life.[25] In 1976, a new constitution sanctioned the socialist order.

The Organs of Popular Power (OPP) embodied the process of institutionalization. Municipal, provincial and national assemblies were constituted to supervise the state administration. Thus, the superintendence of schools, clinics, grocery stores, garbage collection, maintenance shops, movie theatres and small local industries was transferred to municipal assemblies. By the early 1980s, over one-third of the national economy was under local Popular Power administration.[26] Between 1977 and 1983, local industries under OPP supervision tripled their output in value.[27] Although no campaigning was allowed, citizens elected their local delegates via secret ballots and multiple candidacies every two-and-a-half years. Municipal assemblies elected the membership of Provincial Assemblies, which in turn chose the delegates to

24 Interview with Cuban Vice President Carlos Rafael Rodríguez on 6 June 1984.

25 Jorge I. Domínguez, 1978, pp.341–78.

26 Andrew Zimbalist, 1985, p.223.

27 *Bohemia*, 13 July 1984, p.58. Value expanded from 500 million pesos to 1500 million.

the National Assembly. One of the duties of the latter was the confirmation of members of the Councils of State and Ministers submitted by the Politburo (of the PCC). The Councils and Popular Power were under tight party control. Nearly 50 per cent of the Council of State and about 25 per cent of the Council of Ministers were Politburo members. Over 80 per cent of the Council of State and 65 per cent of the Council of Ministers belonged to the Central Committee. More than 90 per cent of National Assembly delegates were members of the Communist Party. About 75 per cent of all local delegates were PCC or Communist Youth militants.[28] The separation of political leadership, popular supervision and state administration was not achieved.

Municipal assemblies and local delegates constituted the most important link between the State and the citizenry. Three times a year, delegates engaged their constituencies in assemblies of *rendición de cuentas* (rendering of accounts). Two years after the establishment of Popular Power, in 1978, the National Assembly heard a report that noted the local meetings had become formalistic 'to such an extreme that at times delegates prepare their presentations beforehand and do not fully express their opinions.'[29] Too often delegates used the same rationale as ministers and managers to justify problems; they were not doing their job, and attendance at *rendición de cuentas* had consequently declined. The National Assembly did not receive the report well. National delegates argued that local delegates were being held responsible for problems originating with state functionaries. Ministries, government agencies and enterprise administrations refused to recognize the authority of local delegates who, in turn, had no power to force compliance with their requests for information.

A 'duality of centralization and decentralization' characterized Popular Power.[30] Too often local meetings were no more than the 'fulfilment of a liturgy'.[31] At their best, they addressed immediate and concrete issues: local Popular Power allowed the citizenry a voice in the conduct of local affairs, a potential arena for self-government. At their worst, local assemblies became rote events which did not empower the citizenry. Moreover, the OPP were inaugurated amid an economic downturn after a period of relative expansion during the early 1970s. Popular expectations had closely associated the promise of democratization with improvements in standards of living. Local assemblies, however, did not have the power nor the resources to enhance their legitimacy by extending material benefits. Between 1976 and 1984,

28 William M. LeoGrande, 1978, pp.1–31; Lourdes Casal and Marifeli Pérez-Stable, 1981, pp.81–103; Jorge I. Domínguez, 1982b, pp.19–70; Archibald R.M. Ritter, 1985, pp.270–90.

29 *Granma*, 30 June 1978, p.4.

30 Carollee Bengelsdorf, 1994.

31 *Granma Weekly Review*, 13 July 1980, p.2.

elections turned over about 50 per cent of the delegates. Between 5 and 10 per cent of incumbents were recalled during their tenure. High turnover rates could well have been an indication of the vitality of Popular Power since more ordinary Cubans were partaking in public responsibilities. Frequent rotation, however, could also have been a signal that many local delegates had declined renomination because their offices carried much frustration and no power.

Meeting briefly twice a year, the National Assembly had more formal and symbolic purposes. While it was not a permanent legislature and carried little weight in the daily governing of Cuba, the Assembly regularly heard reports on the provinces and national ministries, and approved annual budgets, economic plans, and a myriad of laws. Often there was debate among the delegates; the way the agenda was worded, however, revealed the nature of the debate: discussion and approval of the items at hand. Debate could modify but never reject proposals. The Assembly approved most matters unanimously, or nearly so. Yet, the number of delegates participating in discussions increased over time. Invariably, however, once President Castro spoke definitively on an issue, discussion stopped. Nonetheless, the National Assembly provided a forum for widened participation within the leadership and an avenue for regular disclosure of information to the public.

Popular Power exemplified the politics of Cuban socialism. Local assemblies took public opinion into account more systematically than the politics of mobilization had during the 1960s. They did not, however, bestow upon the population the opportunity – let alone the power – to discuss and decide matters of substance. Their mandate was to supervise the State, not, for example, to debate investment policies or resource allocation. Involvement – not substantive participation – was the distinguishing characteristic of Popular Power at the local level. Moreover, involvement was to be as individuals, not organized groups. Local assemblies were, nonetheless, a significant institutional advance over the radical experiment. At the national level, Popular Power allowed a broader spectrum of the leadership to become involved in national discussions. While the Communist Party made all fundamental decisions, the Assembly did discuss issues of substance. Castro's contribution to proceedings was decisive: he always had the final word.

Institutionalization also entailed economic reorganization. In 1975, the PCC congress approved the Economic Management and Planning System (SDPE), which introduced relative decentralization, profitability criteria, material incentives, and self-financed enterprises. During the late 1970s and early 1980s, the economy began to acquire a new face. With more variety, better quality and higher prices, a parallel market regularly supplemented rationing for people with higher incomes and for most Cubans on special occasions. Between 1980 and 1986, peasant markets operated and offered a variety of fruits and vegetables the public had not seen in years. By 1979, over 45 per cent of workers laboured under output norms and quotas.[32] In 1980–1, the State implemented wage and price reforms. Except in the two Havana provinces, enterprises were permitted to contract labour directly. In 1984, a new law allowed the market to regulate the buying and selling of housing. Daily life in socialist Cuba was assuming a less baneful aspect.

The SDPE, however, was in tension with the visions of the 1960s. While in essence the system repudiated them, the revolutionary experience precluded their overt dismissal. Efficiency and rationality had simply not inspired the revolution. Though necessary to motivate a majority of workers, material incentives encouraged self-interest; only moral incentives could promote and sustain a revolutionary *conciencia*. At the 1975 party congress, Castro warned that the new 'mechanisms' were not meant to solve all problems:

> We can[not] do without moral incentives, we would be making a great mistake, because it is absolutely impossible for economic mechanisms and incentives to be as efficient under socialism as they are under capitalism, for the only thing that functions under capitalism is incentive and economic pressure brought to bear with full force, namely, hunger, unemployment, and so on.[33]

Politics and ideology were still paramount, and the economy could not be divorced from the legacy of the revolution.

Institutionalization also brought changes to the mass organizations, which had emerged or become transformed amid the social revolution but had suffered a decline during the radical experiment. The CTC and the FMC, for instance, turned their attention to the specific interests of workers and women under socialism. During the late 1960s, trade unions had become adjuncts of management and the party; grass-roots chapters responded largely to vanguard workers. In 1973, the CTC congress declared '*El sindicato es de todos*' ('the union belongs to all'), evoking a more inclusive theme than the vanguardism of the radical experiment. During the 1970s and early 1980s, unions and workers were more involved in establishing working conditions and in managing the Cuban economy; collective work agreements, labour grievances councils, regular monthly assemblies, and periodic national congresses provided new institutional channels. Workers, however, wielded power vicariously: the PCC was their vanguard political organization, Castro the premier defender of their welfare. Between 1975 and 1986, the PCC, in fact, became more representative of other social sectors: party members

32 Andrew Zimbalist, 1985, p.219.
33 Fidel Castro, 1975, p.136.

accounted for nearly 30 per cent of all professional, technical and administrative workers but a mere 12 per cent of all production workers.[34]

In 1974, the PCC established an affirmative action policy to promote women to leadership positions in the party, the mass organizations, and Popular Power. While in the early 1970s, women held about 6 per cent of these positions, by the mid-1980s they accounted for more than 25 per cent. The FMC 'lobbied' to remove barriers to female employment: a 1976 Labour Ministry resolution limiting women's access to over 300 job categories was eventually whittled down to about 25. Even though their educational profiles were quite similar, women still earned lower wages than men: in the mid-1980s, nearly 63 per cent of male workers laboured in sectors paying wages above the national average; less than 40 per cent of women were so employed. The PCC and the FMC also conducted an educational campaign to attack the 'subjective' factors blocking women's full equality in society.[35] But the political system did not allow for the autonomous articulation of a labour or feminist agenda outside the realm of the Communist Party.

The 1970s proved to be auspicious ones for Cuba's international relations. Although guerrilla movements in Latin America had faltered, the Chilean electorate finally broke Cuban isolation. In 1971, Salvador Allende warmly welcomed Castro on an extended visit to Chile – his first to Latin America in more than a decade. Between 1970 and 1975, eight countries in Latin America and the Caribbean established diplomatic relations with Cuba. The Cuban government also became more active in the Non-Aligned Movement, and Castro promoted the idea of confluent interests between the Soviet Union and the Third World. In 1975, with Soviet logistical support, Cuban and MPLA (Popular Movement for the Liberation of Angola) troops scored an extraordinary victory against the forces of rival Angolan groups and South Africa and secured the independence of Angola. In 1977, with even greater Soviet support, the Cuban Armed Forces came to the aid of Ethiopia when Somalia invaded the Ogaden Desert. In 1979, revolutions came to power in Grenada and Nicaragua. In Maurice Bishop and the Sandinistas, the Cuban government found truly kindred allies in the Western Hemisphere.

After 1968, relations with the Soviet Union and Eastern Europe improved noticeably. Soviet economic aid began to increase; Cuba joined the Soviet and Eastern European trading bloc, COMECON, and thus secured a long-term commitment to Cuban development, even if the island was primarily to supply sugar to its partners. The Soviet Union, moreover, renewed assurances on Cuban defence, increased the supply of armaments, and

34 Marifeli Pérez-Stable, 1993, p.147.
35 *Ibid.*, pp.139–42.

upgraded the quality of military aid. In 1972, all the capitals in Eastern Europe welcomed Castro. Between 1972 and 1975, Castro reciprocated by playing host to his fellow communist leaders. In early 1974, Leonid Brezhnev visited Cuba and addressed a large congregation of citizens in the Plaza of the Revolution. The Soviet leader emphasized the soundness of the new course in Cuban domestic and foreign policies; the Cuban-Soviet rapprochement was complete. In Cuba, the Soviet Union saw a valuable link to Latin America and the Third World. Although under radically different terms than those anticipated during the late 1960s, Cuban economic and security needs were met. The Cuban government accepted new ties of dependence as the price for maintaining socialism 90 miles from the United States.

Sending troops to Angola in support of the MPLA underscored a series of characteristics of post-1959 Cuban politics. Named Operation Carlota after a rebellious slave in the nineteenth century, the Angolan expedition in 1975 was a Cuban initiative made possible only because of Soviet support. To a significant degree, Cuban foreign policy attained this extraordinary triumph because the Vietnam War had left the United States in a relatively weakened international position. Ultimately, Castro and his closest associates made the decision to send troops to Angola. Opposition within the leadership was highly unlikely; popular support was assumed and probably materialized after the fact. After so many setbacks in Latin America, victory in Angola replenished national pride. This pride, moreover, was not just national: in an April 1976 speech on the island's involvement in Africa, Castro referred to Cuba as an 'Afro-Latin' nation, the first ever political affirmation of race and national identity.[36] The Cuban government also enjoyed the prestige that resulted from an activist foreign policy. Involvement in Angola likewise highlighted the primacy of political over economic considerations. The economic costs of Operation Carlota and what turned out

---

36 Race in post-1959 Cuba is a lightly studied subject. On the one hand, the Cuban government claims to have eliminated the material sources of racism; on the other, few would disagree that cultural changes happen at a much slower and uneven rate than structural transformations. By all accounts, non-white Cubans benefited disproportionately from the revolution: they were, after all, over-represented among the poorest sectors of the population. Cuban involvement in Africa, undoubtedly, had a beneficial impact on black racial pride; Castro's statement underscored a reality that no political leader had ever dared to call by its proper name. In the 1990s, there were numerous reports of increased racial tension on the island, in no small part due to non-white Cubans' less privileged access to the hard currency that is indispensable to ease the inordinate burdens of daily life. For an excellent monograph on the history of race relations at the turn of the last century, the inexorable reference moment for most discussions about race and national identity, see Aline Helg, 1995; also David Booth, 1976, pp.129–72; Alejandro de la Fuente, 1995, pp.131–68; and Enrique Patterson, 1996, pp.49–67.

to be a 15-year stay in Angola were secondary to the goals of internationalism and greater manoeuverability for Cuba in world affairs. Similarly, these higher national objectives obscured the major toll that support for the MPLA would take on ordinary citizens. By all accounts, nevertheless, most Cubans who served in Angola did so voluntarily, with great distinction, and notable valour.

The 1980s began less propitiously. The year 1980 tested the Cuban government as no other had done since 1970. In April, 10,000 Cubans flocked to the Peruvian Embassy; between April and September, 125,000 Cubans left Cuba via the Mariel boatlift.[37] The government labelled those leaving as 'scum' who traded the ideals of *la patria* for the lures of consumerism. The PCC organized *mítines de repudio* – meetings of repudiation – in front of the homes of those intending to leave. Two decades after the revolution, there was still no room for dissent: *Con Cuba o contra Cuba* steadfastly defined the intransigent bases of Cuban politics. The Mariel exodus, moreover, dampened the until then slowly improving relations with the United States. The election to the United States presidency of Jimmy Carter in 1976 had created new opportunities for dialogue. In 1977, Interests Sections opened in Havana and Washington, and rapprochement proceeded cautiously; the end of the United States ban on travel to Cuba and the release of 3,000 Cuban political prisoners were among the most notable accomplishments. In 1978, Cuba also initiated a dialogue with members of the Cuban diaspora who favoured the lifting of the United States embargo; for the first time in two decades, Cubans abroad were permitted by the government to visit their families on the island, and more than 100,000 did in 1979. The well-being of Cuban Americans produced a 'demonstration effect', which undoubtedly contributed to the Mariel exodus.

With the 1980 inauguration of President Ronald Reagan, a hostile United States administration again confronted Cuba. While the Interests Sections

---

37 Until 1995, the US government granted Cubans privileged entry into the United States. The Cuban Adjustment Act of 1966 sanctioned automatic political asylum to any Cuban who entered the United States, legally or illegally. At first, US administrations used immigration policy as a means to 'brain drain' revolutionary Cuba; then, they skillfully appealed to the images of fleeing refugees as a powerful indicator of the Cuban government's dwindling support. Over the last decade of the century, Cubans' privileged entry contrasted sharply with the restricted policy toward Haitians: because the line between political exiles and economic refugees was never positively clear in either case, the prejudicial treatment of Haitians by the Immigration and Naturalization Service was particularly glaring. After the 1994 Cuban migration crisis, the US and Cuban governments signed an immigration agreement that guaranteed immigration visas to 20,000 Cubans annually. In May 1995, the Clinton administration ended Cubans' privileged entry: since then, Cubans who enter the United States illegally are deported, unless they can prove political persecution.

remained open, much of the progress made during the Carter presidency withered away. The Reagan administration reinstated the travel ban and thus American citizens were prohibited from travelling to Cuba at a time when tourism was emerging as an important source of hard currency. United States foreign policy-makers often noted the need to 'go to the source' of outside intervention in Central America, an unmistakable reference to Cuba. The United States invasion of Grenada in 1983 dramatically reinforced the Cuban government's renewed sense of vulnerability to a United States military action. In 1984, the United States and Cuba, nonetheless, reached an important immigration agreement; but the Cuban government suspended it a few months later when the Reagan administration began the transmission of Radio Martí.

By the mid-1980s, Cuba faced decidedly mixed prospects at home and abroad. Steady economic growth had eluded dependent socialism: during the 1960s, the economy had registered a slight decline in growth per capita; only during the 1970s had growth reached a respectable 5 per cent per capita; by 1985 per capita growth had declined again, to about 2.5 per cent. In large part, the centrality of sugar accounted for this disappointing record: during the 1980s sugar averaged more than 75 per cent of the value of total exports, only moderately lower than in the 1950s; sugar production per capita was only 0.7 ton, 23 per cent lower than in the 1950s. Sugar continued to be the bulwark of dependence: the Soviet Union accounted for about the same share of Cuba's total trade in the 1980s as the United States had in the 1950s. The State's commitment to social equity, however, had partially protected the popular classes from the consequences of inconsistent growth: since 1959, the share of national income going to the bottom 40 per cent of the population had increased from 6.5 per cent to about 26 per cent.[38]

The modest liberalization of the early 1980s somewhat relaxed the State's control over people's lives. Peasant markets, arts-and-crafts fairs, self-employment and a housing market gave the population opportunities to earn and spend more. Outright corruption, and what the Cuban leadership deemed to be corrupt practices, undoubtedly spread: many functionaries exploited the perquisites of office for personal gain; ordinary citizens took full advantage of the market to make money, and goods and services were sold at often exorbitant profit; workers and managers frequently used factory inventories for private gain. *Conciencia* and revolutionary fervour were everywhere retreating. In the Soviet Union, Mikhail Gorbachev's reform programmes of *perestroika* and *glasnost* were then in their incipient stages. When the process of 'rectification' was launched in 1986, the leadership did not take cues from its mentor; instead, it drew upon Cuba's own past and tried to rekindle the revolutionary spirit.

38 Marifeli Pérez-Stable, 1993, pp.87, 89.

The Cuban government in the late 1980s

Although Cuban rectification and the Soviet reform programme coincided in time, their differences were profound. Whereas the Gorbachev reforms aimed (but ultimately failed) to maintain central planning while gradually implementing far-reaching market reforms and to institute an unprecedented pluralism in the Soviet polity, the rectification evoked the radical experiment of the 1960s. Cuba, however, was no longer in the grip of revolution, and Cuban society manifested many of the same problems afflicting state socialism elsewhere. After 1986, the Cuban government confronted mounting and multiple crises. Competing models of socialism had guided the organization of central planning and one-party politics. More predominant during the 1960s, the first built upon the experience of the social revolution – charismatic authority, popular mobilizations, moral incentives, national independence – to strive for a *sui generis* socialism. Following the débâcle of 1970, the second model turned to the practice of state socialism in the Soviet Union and Eastern Europe. Institutionalization, relatively less centralized planning, material incentives, and dependence on the socialist countries characterized the 1970s and early 1980s. While the first clearly thrived on the popular enthusiasm evident in the early years of the revolution, the second admitted the normalcy – and therefore the different expectations – of daily life. The first's *conciencia* aimed to make history, the second's to put rice and beans on the dinner table.

By the time the third congress of the Communist Party convened in February 1986, the leadership considered the second model to be largely exhausted. Change – though not in the direction of *perestroika* and *glasnost* – was in the offing. Between February and December 1986, Castro introduced the process of rectification.[39] Major policy initiatives were still his prerogative:

39 On the anniversary of Playa Girón (Bay of Pigs), Fidel Castro berated the new wave of mercenaries that threatened *la patria* and called for a renewed struggle against the would-be capitalists. After April, the rectification began to take shape in various fora. At a gathering of co-operative farmers, Castro announced the banning of the free markets (*Granma Weekly Review*, 1 June 1986, pp.3–4). Meeting with enterprise representatives from the two Havana provinces, he assailed the 'liberal-bourgeois' period of 'bitter experiences' and called for a 'strategic counteroffensive' (*Granma*, 27 June 1986, pp.1–3). Throughout July and August, enterprise meetings in the other provinces continued elaborating on the problems of the SDPE (*Granma*, 8 July 1986, p.11; 9 July 1986, pp.1 and 3; 10 July 1986, p.3; 11 August 1986, p.3; and 19 August 1986, p.3). On 26 July Castro railed against the 'generalized stupidities' that money was the principal motivation of people and exalted the value of voluntary work (*Granma Weekly Review*, 2 August 1986, p.3). In December, the party congress closed with a calling to renew moral principles and regenerate *conciencia* (*Granma*, 1 and 2 December 1986; Supplement, 5 December 1986).

the PCC lacked the institutional wherewithal to challenge his authority or the logic of revolution which he sought to perpetuate. Since neither Castro nor this logic was compatible with a political opening and market reforms, retrenchment from the SDPE was the only politically viable option. The rectification process strove to redress long-standing economic problems by using non-market mechanisms and favouring collective over individual incentives. Old forms of labour mobilization were revitalized; micro-brigades, construction contingents and volunteer work exemplified the reinforcement of politics to attain economic results. The new directions aimed to mobilize revolutionary *conciencia* in pursuit of economic objectives and regain the Cuban *imprimatur* on socialism. But the policies of curbing market mechanisms and appealing to *conciencia* raised a serious dilemma: if they had not worked when the effervescence of revolution was palpable, how could they possibly render the desired results nearly thirty years after the fact?

In 1989, a new stage began in the politics of rectification. Domestic developments first underscored the urgency of revising the status quo. The summer of 1989 notoriously highlighted the pitfalls of charismatic authority and the weakness of Cuban institutions, especially the Communist Party. In June, the government arrested Division-General Arnaldo Ochoa, Hero of the Republic of Cuba, veteran of the wars in Ethiopia and Angola and commander-designate of the Western Army, Colonel Antonio de la Guardia of the Interior Ministry, and 12 other high-ranking military and security officers. The 14 – individuals of high prestige, singular valour, and impeccable revolutionary credentials – faced accusations of drug-trafficking and endangering national security. After a military court found them guilty, Ochoa, de la Guardia, and their two top aides were put to death before a firing squad. The others received jail sentences ranging from 10 to 30 years.[40] The party also discharged Interior Minister José Abrantes and the top commanders of the security establishment; Abrantes was eventually arrested, brought to trial, and sentenced to a 20-year prison term for dereliction of duty.[41]

The trials of 1989 might have had a political script. General Ochoa might have been involved in an incipient movement for reform within the armed forces, especially among Angolan veterans. Had that been the case and had the drugs scandal not eliminated him, Ochoa might have been well-positioned to advance the reform cause as the commander-designate of the

40 The Ochoa-de la Guardia public proceedings, their press coverage, and other related documents can be found in *Causa 1/89: Fin de la conexión cubana,* 1989; Andrés Oppenheimer, 1992, pp.17–163, is an insightful analysis of the drug trafficking trials of 1989.

41 *Granma*, 30 August 1989, pp.3–5. In January 1991, Abrantes suffered a fatal heart attack while under confinement.

powerful Western Army. His actions and those of Antonio de la Guardia and the other officers might have been authorized, or at least known and overlooked, at the highest levels of the Cuban government. Whether or not there was conspiracy or high-ranking complicity was, in important ways, secondary. The crisis underscored a crucial dimension of Cuban politics. The exercise of charismatic authority depended on a special relationship with the 'masses' as well as steadfast élite loyalty. Although after 1970 institutions had increasingly mediated between the government and the citizenry and had provided fora interactions within the leadership, they had not overridden the dynamics of charismatic authority.

The case laid bare the central predicament of Castro's leadership. The need for élite allegiance resulted in the tolerance of wide-ranging behaviour among high-ranking officials. The government had long faced the problem that many among the leadership lived well beyond the means of the average citizen.[42] Privileged lives in the face of an ideology of equality and an economy of austerity had undoubtedly eroded state legitimacy. Nonetheless, corruption had to reach truly brazen proportions for action to be taken against the culprits. Whether or not he knew about the Ochoa-de la Guardia undertakings, Castro was ultimately responsible for the events of 1989. The crisis was primarily about the patterns of governance that had failed to monitor such behaviour and about institutions which did not function, or functioned weakly.

Internationally, the year 1989 likewise underscored the imperative of change. Crisis in the Soviet Union and the demise of Eastern European socialism belied the premise of the irreversibility of socialism and signalled the end of the world that had supported Cuba. One-party politics and command economies had run their course: socialist democracy and sustained economic growth had proven to be beyond their means. The people – workers, peasants, the intelligentsia – resoundingly repudiated state socialism. The collapse of communism in Eastern Europe confronted the Cuban government with the international shambles of the political model that had consolidated the revolution. Emphasizing the roots of the revolution and socialism in Cuban history, the rectification aimed to renew the political system and renovate popular adherence to the current leadership.

In September 1989, the party called for an institutional *perfeccionamiento* (improvement), vehemently denying that the recent trials had constituted a political crisis, though obliquely recognizing that the summer of 1989 had strained political legitimacy.[43] 'We must say it clearly: what has just happened has revealed a series of flaws which, in one way or another, involve all the

42 José Luis Llovió-Menéndez, 1988.
43 *Granma Weekly Review*, 10 September 1989, pp.1, 11.

institutions of the Revolution.' The cornerstone of this *perfeccionamiento* was the fourth PCC congress. Cuban leaders claimed pre-congress assemblies yielded unanimous support for 'the Party, the Revolution, and ... comrade Fidel'; at the same time, they underscored the imperative of overcoming the pernicious pitfalls of *la doble moral* (duplicity) and *el afán de unanimidad* (eagerness to achieve unanimity).[44] However, in the early 1990s as in the early 1960s, the political system was bereft of the institutions and guarantees to overcome these pitfalls. Cuban politics was 'absolutist': that is, it allowed no quarter for compromise on the vision of *patria* consecrated by the revolution.[45] Iron-clad unity was the *sine qua non* of national sovereignty; the expression of individual or sectoral interests was regarded as contrary to the national interest; acceptance of *el comandante*'s incontestable primacy was an inviolable imperative. Thus, only *masses*, not *citizens*, were compatible with absolutist politics. To overcome duplicity and conformism, the political system would have needed to promote an integrative politics, supportive of the diversity in Cuban society and respectful of the expression of individualism, values clearly in conflict with charismatic authority, a single party, and mass mobilizations. Yet, Cuban leaders had no other ways of rallying the support, or at least the acquiescence, of the 'masses'. Herein lies the latent political crisis of contemporary Cuba: the leadership governs by re-enacting the revolutionary past, while the Cuban people – most of whom were born or became adults after 1959 and thus have no memories of the social revolution – lack the institutional means to affirm or reject the choices made by their government on their behalf.

The perfeccionamiento and the 'special period': Cuba in the 1990s

In October 1991, less than two months after the failed *coup d'état* against Gorbachev, the Cuban Communist Party held its fourth congress. During the uncertain days of late August, the Cuban government had issued a subdued statement about non-interference in Soviet internal affairs.[46] The prospect of a successful coup had raised hopes for a modest stabilization of trade with the Soviet Union; had the coup succeeded, Cuba would have also recovered

44 For the first quote, see *Granma*, 28 January 1991, p.3; for the pitfalls of *la doble moral* and *el afán de unanimidad*, see *Granma Weekly Review*, 25 March 1990, pp.2–3 and *Granma*, 13 April 1990, p.1.

45 I am using the concepts of 'absolutist' and 'integrative' politics as per Víctor Pérez-Díaz, 1993.

46 *Cuba en el mes*, August 1991, p.65.

a politico-ideological ally. When the PCC congress convened, the Cuban leadership knew that all hopes of reinstating the *status quo ante* in the rapidly decomposing Soviet Union had definitively vanished. Cuba was decidedly alone. The conclave emphasized the historic roots of the revolution and socialism in Cuba and declared the PCC to be 'sole party of the Cuban nation, *martiano*, Marxist, and Leninist'.[47] In his address, Castro unequivocally established the inviolable boundaries of Cuban politics in the 1990s: 'We are the only ones and there is no alternative.'[48] A commitment to reform Popular Power was one of the most significant outcomes of the party congress.[49]

In 1992, the Cuban government modified electoral laws to allow for the direct election of deputies to the national and provincial assemblies of Popular Power. As in the past, however, only official candidates could legally aspire to a seat in the assemblies. In December 1992, delegates for the municipal assemblies were chosen for two-and-a-half-year terms in races featuring at least two candidates. In February 1993, deputies to the National Assembly and delegates to the provincial assemblies were elected to five-year terms. Since there was only one nominee per seat, candidates needed more than 50 per cent of the validly cast ballots in order to be elected. Thus, citizens had a negative choice if they did not wish to vote for the entire slate: they could withhold their vote for particular candidates, register a blank or defaced ballot, or abstain from voting altogether.

The two-step electoral process resulted in distinctively different outcomes. In December, more than 97 per cent of the electorate turned out to vote. Various sources estimated that up to one-third cast invalid ballots (blank or defaced), an act tantamount to an anti-government vote.[50] Initially, the government neither refuted these estimates nor gave its own figure. Two months later, it admitted to less than 15 per cent null or void votes; the final official figure is 10 per cent.[51] Undoubtedly, the much-delayed and amended official reaction lent credibility to the unofficial estimates.

---

47 *Granma*, 13 October 1991, p.7.

48 Foreign Broadcast Information Service, *Latin America – Cuba: Fourth Congress of the Cuban Communist Party*, October 15, 1991, p.25.

49 In the ensuing paragraphs, I focus on the 1992–3 elections, the first in which the electorate voted for national and provincial deputies. In 1995, there were mid-term elections for municipal delegates, a routine matter since 1978. In January 1998, following another round of municipal elections in October 1997, national and provincial deputies were again selected in nationwide elections. The 1992–3 round serves as a useful and revealing gauge of the political context of Cuba's electoral process – a constant underlying the various elections during the 1990s.

50 *CubaFax Update*, 31 December 1992.

51 Spanish News Agency EFE, 23 February 1993 for the 15 per cent figure and *Granma*, 27 February 1993, for the final official figure.

Cuban leaders were obviously surprised: up to one-third of the electorate had sent them a strong and unexpected message. Business could not be allowed to proceed as usual in February, and it did not. The party prepared for the second round as it had not for the first: indeed, like the two-month official silence on the percentage of invalid ballots, the intensity of the February 'campaigning' supported the unofficial estimates of the December outcome. The government's overriding objective was to demonstrate an indisputable popular mandate. First, Castro – Cuban nationalist *par excellence* – made a patriotic appeal to vote in favour of all the candidates: *la patria* demanded a demonstration of unity rather than a selective vote. Conveniently, the tightening of the embargo by the United States in the Cuban Democracy Act of 1992 lent new urgency to Castro's summons to patriotism. Second, the government exerted pressures to bring the stray one-third back into the fold and to dissuade other citizens from invalidating their ballots or voting selectively. It updated voter registration lists, increased the number of polling places, and sent the CDR leadership to visit every home to instruct the citizenry on the allegedly complex voting procedures.

On 24 February 1993, more than 99 per cent of the electorate went to the polls: 88.5 per cent voted the straight ticket and 7.2 per cent cast invalid ballots; in Havana, nullified ballots totalled 14.3 per cent. No deputy received less than 87 per cent of the votes. Unofficial sources placed the proportion of invalid ballots in Havana between 10 and 20 per cent and the percentage of its residents voting selectively at 30 per cent.[52] Officially, then, about 18 per cent of the voters did not do what the government had asked them to do: vote for the entire slate.

What did the 1992–3 elections demonstrate? First, in February, the Cuban government displayed a certain strength in mobilizing the population, which out of conviction, fear or a sense of helplessness complied with its demands for a show of unity. The election also revealed a profound weakness: the outcome was gained on the basis of mobilizational politics, a formula that worked well in the early years of the revolution but that in the 1990s hardly translated into effective, long-term governance. Second, the December outcome was especially telling: when the government did not mount an incessant campaign, up to one-third of the electorate cast a protest vote. Would it not be reasonable to expect that many more citizens would express their opposition in a freely contested election or plebiscite?

The Cuban leadership has long deferred coming to terms with the central contradiction of its governance. From the outset, it faced the daunting chasm between revolutionary ebullience and quotidian exigencies. Though

52 Spanish News Agency EFE, 23 February 1993.

manifested in different ways since 1959, the tension between institutionalization and mobilization has been a constant; at its core lies the question of channeling the 'spirit' of the revolution into the 'flesh' of life. At no time has the political system created the institutions necessary to renovate the upper echelons of leadership and forge a standard of citizenship requiring something less than full mobilization. In its origins, the Cuban government drew support and legitimacy from the reservoir of nationalism and the ideal of egalitarianism. Subsequently, it failed to create the institutional foundations for the Cuban people to renew their commitment to the ideals of 1959. In fact, Cuban politics left no room for the natural cycles of support and disaffection. The absolutist politics of *la patria* penalized or ostracized citizens known to harbour even the most trivial reservations. Cubans still had no options but to support the government unconditionally or to face jail, death or exile, or maintain silence; the political system provided no space for partial or half-hearted support, let alone peaceful opposition. Even if with diminishing returns, *las masas* continued to dominate the political purview of the Cuban government.

At one time Cuban leaders mustered overwhelming active support; later, relative institutionalization combined such support with a more passive disposition to listen to leadership directives; now, at the turn of the century, they are mired in a conundrum. They continue to have a core of adherents, which allows them to resort to their long-standing pattern of governance; at the same time, they have probably lost the acquiescence they once had from a majority of the population, and the longstanding pattern does not afford them the means to renew popular confidence. Indeed, *la doble moral* and *el afãn de unanimidad* are unbridgeable pitfalls within the jagged terrain of Cuban politics. Even without the goodwill, let alone the endorsement, of the majority, the government can survive if the population remains indifferent, fearful, or paralysed by a sense of helplessness. Seen from their vantage point, what Cuban leaders must thwart is the coalescing of discontent into an opposition movement that can jeopardize both their rule and what they understand to be *la patria.* Battered legitimacy is not a lethal threat; the organization of alternatives is.

Maintaining unity within the leadership has been a central element in the political strategy of the 1990s. Inordinately inhospitable circumstances might have provoked a schism in the leadership over which course to follow; that they did not and, moreover, that the government effectively promoted significant leadership rotation are important measures of political adaptability and endurance. Since 1989, the leadership has successfully met the challenge of rotation and unity in at least five instances. First, in 1989, the Ochoa-de la Guardia trials shook the armed forces and, particularly, the Interior Ministry, the two institutions at the medulla of the regime. After the military effectively took over the Interior Ministry, extensive turnover of high- and middle-level state-security officers followed. The armed forces also experienced turnover, though not as widely. Second, the most important outcome of the 1991 PCC congress was the renovation of the Central Committee (CC). More than two-thirds of its members were newly elected or promoted to full membership; the 1991 CC was also more representative of ordinary citizens (as opposed to cadres), the under-fifty generations, and the provinces than previous central committees.[53] Third, the profile of National Assembly deputies elected in 1993 showed a similar trend.[54] Fourth, in 1994, the party replaced seven of the fourteen provincial secretaries with younger cadres; in 1995, three additional provinces received new PCC secretaries.[55] Finally, in January 1995, the Council of State announced a major Cabinet reshuffle, in which seven younger, presumably more reform-oriented individuals assumed the economic ministries.[56] Rotation has also taken place at lower levels of the PCC, the ministries, the mass organizations, and Popular Power.[57] The government has emphasized the routine nature of these changes at all levels. Normalization of staffing alterations has reached the point, in fact, that following the early-1995 Cabinet reshuffle, the ministries introduced 'transition ceremonies' in which the old team passed the torch to the new.[58]

That Cuban leaders have weathered what seemed to be insurmountable difficulties underscores their mettle and bolsters their self-confidence. Nonetheless, they also know they that some day they will face Castro's death or retirement; without him, they may just not prevail. Current insistence on mobilizational politics is not preparing them well for that inescapable day of reckoning. That the Cuban people are not rising in opposition to them (whether it is out of conviction, fear, or a sense of helplessness), however, allows them to continue governing in, more or less, the usual ways.

The Cuban government has mostly focused on the economic dimensions to the crisis of the 1990s. With the collapse of European communism, the cutback of trade with the Soviet Union, and unrelenting United States hostility, it devised an alternative 'special period' strategy for economic survival. Although the new strategy included some structural reforms, mostly in the foreign-trade sector, the heart of it was enshrined in a food-production programme to promote self-sufficiency through state agriculture and labour mobilizations. The strategy also focused on a package of state-propelled, non-market austerity

53 Marifeli Pérez-Stable, 1993, p.172.

54 Marifeli Pérez-Stable, 1995, pp.56–7. In the July 1995 mid-term local elections almost 52 per cent were first-time delegates. *Cuba-L Service*, 14 July 1995.

55 *Cuba en el mes*, July 1994, pp.44–7 and July 1995, p. 47.

56 *El Nuevo Herald*, 25 January 1995, pp.1, 4.

57 *Cuba en el mes*. August and September 1994, pp.20–5 and p.42, respectively.

58 *Ibid*., March 1995, p.51.

measures, such as reducing electricity consumption and oil deliveries, further rationing food products and consumer goods, and cutting back on bureaucratic personnel. While the government accepted decentralization in the economy's external sector, it continued to insist on state-centred and mobilizational responses on the domestic front. At its 1991 congress, the Communist Party resisted the re-opening of the peasant markets and – its decidedly mixed results notwithstanding – persisted with the food plan. Between 1989 and 1993, the economy contracted between 35 and 50 per cent.[59]

Not until 1993 did the government begin to take steps to address the profound economic crisis by implementing some market reforms, i.e., making the dollar legal tender, liberalizing agricultural co-operatives, and legalizing self-employment in a limited number of activities.[60] In 1994, selected price increases, a new tax system, and free markets for agricultural products and light consumer durables were approved. Since then the leadership has stayed the course of reform only within the tenor of mobilizational politics, and Cuba has yet to reach a reform consensus among the leadership to adopt market reforms wholeheartedly. Castro frequently rails against the 'excesses' of the profit motive and extols 'politically correct' reforms so as 'never' to compromise socialism. In the summer of 1995, he noted: 'If there has to be more opening, we will do it, though I do not see an immediate need for that.'[61]

Unlike China and Vietnam, Cuba has not formulated a more comprehensive programme for economic transformation.[62] There are two central conditions for economic recovery: cutting back subsidies for state enterprises and fully liberalizing Cuban entrepreneurship. The former carries two obvious dangers: massive unemployment and a reduced state sector; the latter, which would alleviate unemployment, is an unavoidable complement to the first. While in 1995 the government authorized additional activities for self-employment, it continues to dampen private initiatives by sporadically

59 After three years (1994–6) of modest economic growth, the government anticipated a slowdown in 1997. A mounting trade deficit (from $642 million in 1994 to $2.2 billion in 1996), a growing foreign debt ($9.7 billion in late 1994 to $11 billion in mid-1996), and a ballooning (but not officially specified) internal debt (due to the unprofitable state sector) were threatening to reverse the gains since 1993. Lower sugar prices, higher oil prices, and difficulties in obtaining foreign loans to support the harvest completed the dismal outlook for 1997. *Miami Herald*, 19 December 1996, p.A22.

60 For an overview of the economic reforms, see Carmelo Mesa-Lago, 1994; Manuel Pastor, Jr. and Andrew Zimbalist, 1995, pp.7–12; and Jorge F. Pérez-López, 1995.

61 *Associated Press*, 6 September 1995.

62 For a foreign perspective, see the report of Spain's former finance minister: Carlos Solchaga, 1996–7, pp.43–53. For a Cuban perspective, see: Julio Carranza Valdéz *et al.*, 1995.

confiscating 'illicit gains', harassing 'profiteers' and imposing stiff taxes payable in hard currency. In 1996–7, political priorities clearly overwhelmed the process of economic reforms: Cuban leaders are not ready to relinquish state control over most of the economy, which is ultimately unavoidable if they are serious about long-term economic recovery. Through tax increases and frequent supervision, the government has limited the operation of home-based restaurants (*paladares*) and the rental of rooms in private homes to tourists. In April 1997, Vice President Carlos Lage discounted the legalization of small- and medium-sized, privately owned enterprises any time soon.[63] Although the Cuban leadership remains more open to liberalization in the external sector, the foreign-investment law of 1995 embodies the official ambivalence. On the one hand, it allows for wholly foreign-owned ventures, it sanctions foreign ownership of real estate, and it generally improves the climate for foreign investment. On the other hand, the State retains full control of labour as foreign investors still cannot hire and pay workers directly. Foreign direct investment is, at any rate, quite modest: as of the mid-1990s, the government received commitments of $2.1 billion, which, in effect, probably meant well under $1 billion in actual investments.[64]

During the 1990s, the United States tightened the embargo against Cuba. The Cuban Democracy Act of 1992 and the Cuban Liberty and Democratic Solidarity Act of 1996 (the Helms-Burton law) are attempts to force the rest of the world (most of which maintains normal diplomatic and commercial relations with the island) to abide by the United States embargo.[65] Helms-Burton is particularly objectionable to major United States allies in Europe and the Western Hemisphere: it prescribes a variety of retaliatory measures against foreign corporations and citizens who 'traffic' in property confiscated from

63 *Granma*, 27 March and 15 August 1996; *El Nuevo Herald*, 6 May 1997.

64 *Economist*, 19 October 1996, p.49. In the late 1980s, Cuba's Gross Social Product (GSP) was about 25 billion *pesos* a year. After contracting up to 50 per cent in the early 1990s, the economy resumed modest growth in 1994. Even if $1 billion have been invested, the sum pales next to the estimated $5–6 billion a year Cuba received from the Soviet Union in the form of subsidies, credits and aid.

65 President Clinton signed Helms-Burton into law after the Cuban air force shot down two US civilian planes in February 1996. Though the Cuban government maintains that the two planes, owned by a Cuban-exile organization (Brothers to the Rescue), were shot down in Cuban air space, the United Nations International Civil Aviation Organization (ICAO) concluded in July 1996 that the downing had occurred in international waters. Nonetheless, Brothers to the Rescue planes violated Cuban air space on the day of the shootdown and on no less than two other occasions. Prior to February 1996, the Federal Aviation Administration took no action against the organization, even though its pilots had violated international law.

United States citizens and thus constitutes a flagrant case of extraterritoriality, that is, a demand for universal applicability of a United States law. Though the Clinton administration indefinitely suspended the most objectionable of these measures – the right to bring suit in United States courts against those who do not abide by Helms-Burton's provisions – the European Union lodged a complaint against the United States in the World Trade Organization (WTO). This issue has created a serious rift between the Western powers. While Cuba itself is of almost no significance, the principle of free trade is. Indeed, it is astounding that the United States allowed the island to interfere in the functioning of the WTO – an organization created at the behest of the United States, which has generally ruled favourably to its interests in disputes. On the matter of immigration, however, the United States and Cuban governments are abiding by an agreement of 1994, which has virtually eliminated the flow of Cuban rafters and allows for an annual granting of up to 20,000 visas for Cubans to migrate to the United States.

From a Cuban point of view, Helms-Burton culminates the consummate arrogance of the United States. The law pretends to dictate the criteria by which a regime in Cuba may be considered democratic, the most important being the compensation or restitution of confiscated United States property. It specifically states that no government will be considered one of transition if Fidel and Raúl Castro are at the helm. In early 1997, the Clinton administration released a document (mandated by Helms-Burton) outlining a programme of political and economic change for the island and promising up to $8 billion in aid and investments. However laudable and necessary the transition to democracy and a market economy might be, United States policy, at the time of writing, surely dims its prospects. The influence of the Cuban-American community in crafting Washington's policy toward the Cuban government is especially notable in both acts of the 1990s. The Helms-Burton law in particular incorporates a provision that further embroils the issue of confiscated property: it includes the claims of exiles who were Cuban citizens at the time of the confiscations but subsequently became American citizens. Though a minority of Cuban Americans favour a new United States policy, most are adamantly wedded to the policy of sanctions. In practice, however, the Cuban-American community manifests a different attitude: it annually sends up to $800 million (mostly in cash remittances, family visits and medicines) to relatives on the island, making these contributions (which often violate the embargo) second only to tourism in keeping the Cuban economy afloat. In the absence of an overriding urgency or imperative, the Clinton administration has upheld and reinforced the embargo so as to pacify an important domestic constituency in Florida, the fourth-largest electoral state in the nation. In the 1990s, Cuba largely became a domestic issue and consequently, *pace* the early hopes of the revolution, no more than a simple geographical reference.

Looking forward: Cuba at the turn of the century

Nearly forty years after the revolutionary victory, Cuba is facing the eventual likelihood of a future course more akin to that of the rest of the Caribbean: market economics and political democracy. Until 1989, the Cold War bestowed upon the Cuban government a peculiar mantle of security: while the United States almost relentlessly pursued its overthrow and isolation, the Soviet Union provided it with a safety net of trade, credit and aid that buffered the economy not only from the United States embargo, but also from the uncertainties and competitiveness of the global market. Since the early 1990s, with a vanished safety net and a stricter-than-ever United States embargo, Cuba has confronted extraordinarily precarious conditions. So far, Cuban leaders have defied the odds and survived. They have done so at a price: by reinforcing the politics of mobilization and insisting on the viability of an efficient socialist economy, they are not preparing themselves well for the aftermath of Castro's passing from the scene. Their strength today might well be their weakness tomorrow.

Various scenarios may yield a transition from the status quo of the late 1990s. Though highly unlikely after the enactment of the Helms-Burton law, United States policy toward the Cuban government may yet moderate and render hollow the call for iron-clad unity behind Castro. If he were to die or fall gravely ill, the leadership would quickly have to establish new ways of governing. If the population were at or near a state of rebellion, Cuban leaders would face the decision of how much overt repression to exert, which might indeed strain their unity. While the economy modestly recuperated between 1994 and 1996, stagnation or a new round of decline might prod the leadership into a more coherent and thorough reform programme.

Social scientists (or anyone else for that matter) were not particularly prescient regarding the collapse of Eastern European communism. Even considering what we now know retrospectively, it would be hazardous to predict the timing and nature of change in Cuba. Given the absence of institutions, actors, and interests independent of Castro, many scenarios are possible. However it begins, though, the transition from the present is likely to respond primarily to one of two processes. The first is one of liberalization, by which government and opposition élites negotiate, bargain, and agree to a timetable for open elections and a new constitution. The second is one of collapse and defeat for the government amid a popular explosion and possible United States intervention. Naturally, a scenario of liberalization would be much more propitious to the peaceful and democratic emergence of a new Cuba.

Over the past four decades, Cuba has had a singular impact on the Caribbean. Upon the downfall of Batista's dictatorship in January 1959, colonialism was the region's hallmark. Shortly thereafter, most of the territories gained their independence, and the Cuban Revolution displayed a particular kind of sovereignty. While dependent capitalism and fragile political democracies (if existent at all) limited economic potential and citizen participation in Latin America, Cuba proclaimed socialism as the path to development and true democracy. In the early 1960s, national liberation movements swept Africa and Asia, and in the Western Hemisphere, Cuba embodied the fledgling hopes for equity and emancipation in what had just become known as the Third World. And, in part and for a while, the revolution fulfilled those expectations. In the eyes of the rest of the Caribbean, the Cuban people enjoyed a modest standard of living in a society that struggled against economic, racial and gender inequalities. Though bereft of civil liberties, ordinary Cubans had some degree of involvement at the local levels of government and were not subjected to brutal repression typical of military dictatorships elsewhere in the Western Hemisphere during the 1960s and 1970s. Cuba at that time was a beacon of sorts for a more just society – not one that the rest of the Caribbean necessarily wanted to emulate, but one whose existence rendered the regional political spectrum fully pluralist.

It is one no longer. Though some still look toward the island as an alternative, Cuba – as its economy and political system are presently constituted – is no longer the beacon it once was. The domestic and international resources that allowed the Cuban government to craft a path of socialism and independence from the United States have been depleted: the model simply lacks long-term viability. In fact, the island is rapidly becoming more like the rest of the Caribbean: tourism and immigrant remittances, for example, are two of its most important sources of hard currency. Sooner or later, Cuba will be fully integrated with its neighbours. Given the obstinacy of United States policy and the region's understandable inability to defy Washington by embracing Cuba now, that reintegration will take place under a different Cuban government and a more market-based economy. The prospect raises at least two crucial sets of questions.

The first is more practical. On what terms will this reintegration take place? Will the Cuban economy become the motor for a regional integration that enhances Caribbean interests albeit in the inescapable context of globalization? Is a Mercosur-like integration of the region a realistic prospect? Or is Cuba's full reincorporation into the United States orbit inevitable? How will the Caribbean economies fare against the competition of Cuba's much larger, potentially richer, and more populous market, particularly if a complementary integration does not take place? The second is more symbolic. What will the legacy of the Cuban Revolution actually be? Will subsequent Cuban governments renege on it completely? Will future opposition movements eventually unfurl the banners of justice and sovereignty harking back to the heyday of the 1960s? What will a new Cuba represent within the political spectrum of the Caribbean? How will the demise, or revival, of the revolutionary legacy shape and influence that spectrum? The new century will, undoubtedly, surprise us with its answers and raise as-yet-unanticipated questions in the aftermath of the Cuban Revolution.

8

Political processes in the Caribbean, 1970s to 2000

Anthony P. Maingot

Introduction

By the 1960s, every government in the Caribbean – whether independent or not – faced two crucial questions related to viability and sustainability. First, could the economies of these small nations – and especially the parliamentary democratic ones – handle the social tensions engendered by high rates of unemployment, declining agricultural production, urbanization, the mobilization of demands by both unionized and non-unionized labour and, crucially, the expectations of highly educated but unemployed youths? Second, and directly related to this question of economic viability, was a political question: could the political institutions inherited from the colonial period handle the kinds of ideological change being demanded by an increasingly radicalized youth? To them it was not enough to reform the institutions, they were demanding a complete shift in the social-class and racial composition of the State and the economy.

These general questions elicited general answers. At a general level it was agreed early on that by the 1970s the whole Caribbean was experiencing powerful demographic pressures and high rates of unemployment, especially among the young, only partly relieved by a continuing outflow of migrants. Beyond those general secular features, however, general answers do not explain how and why individual countries in the Caribbean addressed these problems. It is part of the complexity of ex-colonial, multinational archipelagic areas, such as the Caribbean, that the answer to these questions cannot be generalized for the region as a whole. Not all the governmental responses were the same and, certainly, not all the consequences of those individual responses were of a kind. It is a virtual truism, thus, that once the general macro-social and economic regional trends are oulined, the political consequences have to be studied, if not country by country, at least in terms of the major ex-colonial blocs.[1] For instance, such are the differences regarding the admittedly important role of race in the social movements of the Caribbean, that there has to be a methodology for resolving the 'particular versus the general' impasse in the study of the region's political processes. The method applied here is to delineate quite explicitly what one might call the various 'general contours' which characterized the politics of a particular period and, within those contours, analyse what was demonstrably distinct and idiosyncratic in each case. We begin with the general social, political and economic contours as outlined by one extremely prescient analyst of all things Caribbean, the former prime minister of Trinidad & Tobago, the historian Eric Williams.

Writing in the late 1960s, Williams was not in a sanguine mood. In fact, he held a very bleak view of the Caribbean region. He claimed to see everywhere the contrast between rising unemployment and rising per capita incomes. Relatively small pockets of wealth were engendering dangerous and rising levels of expectation, and these expectations were not being addressed much less met anywhere in the region. Most dramatically affected, he noted, were the young, the social sector from which the greatest threat to the existing system would come. Aside from these economic and demographic problems, there was, said Williams, a problem of context: the region had 'no serious indigenous intellectual life' within which to debate these issues. The Caribbean, he concluded, fitted author V. S. Naipaul's 'harsh but true' description of West Indians as being 'mimic men' – imitators of all things foreign.[2]

One of the 'foreign' doctrines Williams feared was Black Power. 'As the Black Power movement makes headway in the United States in its fight for black dignity,' he argued, 'there are the obvious repercussions in the Caribbean.' To Williams, this issue of race conflict expressed itself in different forms, but everywhere in the Caribbean of the late 1960s and early 1970s the signs of racial trouble were ominous:

> Jamaica is seething with racial tension, black versus brown and white. The labour unrest in Antigua and the labour riots in Curaçao were both responses to Black Power propaganda. The large Indian population of

1 It might well be true, as E. H. Carr says, that history and the historian 'thrives on generalizations'. Even Carr, however, cautioned against 'over-generalization'. For that reason he is in agreement with Marx's caution that 'Events strikingly similar, but occurring in different historical milieu, lead to completely dissimilar results.' Marx was especially suspicious of conclusions based on 'feelings of familiarity' which led to false analogies. See Edward Hallett Carr, 1963, pp.80–2.

2 Eric Williams, 1970 (1984), p.502.

> Guyana, Surinam and Trinidad and Tobago adds another dimension to the racial disharmony … . In this bleak picture the only bright spot is the apparent success of Castro's Cuba with the full integration of the black population into his society.[3]

Despite this bow to Cuba, Williams was not about to recommend the Cuban path. 'The real tragedy of Cuba,' he wrote, 'is that she has resorted to the totalitarian framework …'.[4] He had earlier adamantly rejected the 'Castroist organization of the economy' as an authoritarian and inefficient system which had 'turned its back on the Caribbean' to integrate itself into the socialist bloc.[5] In the 1960s and beyond, said Williams, the Caribbean could not escape the Cold War which he defined as the confrontation between the dominant ideologies and points of view that faced the world: capitalism and socialism.

Events would prove Williams only partly right: the political processes of the 1970s to the 1990s were certainly traumatic but the institutions inherited from the colonial past proved to be equal to the task, their resilience a testimony to the ability of ex-colonial populations to make democracy work in ways the colonial masters had not thought to be certain of success.

Williams was undoubtedly correct in his geo-political observations that the Caribbean was experiencing a mixture of racial and ideological conflicts. Yet one could hardly attribute the multiple challenges which confronted these small Caribbean states during the decades of the 1970s and 1980s to either the totalitarianism versus democracy issue, or the racial divide, or even both together. There was more to the evident instability in the region. Virtually every part of the Caribbean was undergoing the kind of structural socio-economic changes which tend to create tension and friction across the board, from demographics to economics to the structure of politics and the role of the State.

The Caribbean was not alone in experiencing these changes. The post-war decolonization process was everywhere characterized by three fundamental tendencies: nationalism (and especially ethno-nationalism), a brand of political populism led by urban élites, and statism, or the comprehensive involvement of the State in economic planning and execution. In addition, contrary to Williams' description of a region bereft of intellectual life, there were some very *engagé* thinkers writing and advising. In fact, political actions at the time, including those of Williams in Trinidad, were undergirded by highly sophisticated intellectual schemes which became ideological road maps.

---

3 *Ibid.*, p.503.
4 *Ibid.*, p.510.
5 Eric Williams, 1963, p.365–7.

TABLE 8.1 Agricultural employment and output: Selected territories, 1960–70

Territory	*1960* Employment (% of total)	Output (% of total)	*1970* Employment (% of total)	Output (% of total)
Barbados	26	28	16	14
Guyana	37	26	29	19
Jamaica	39	12	29	8
Trinidad & Tobago	21	12	16	5
Eastern Caribbean Common Market	46	36	32	22

Source: World Bank, 1978, 119.

In his fundamentally influential 1950 treatise on economic development in the West Indies, W. Arthur Lewis made the assertion that the case for rapid industrialization in the West Indies rested chiefly on over-population. The key sector of the traditional economy, agriculture, would increase its productivity but its employment-absorbing capacity would remain static. Even industrialization and manufacturing, with its acknowledged employing capabilities, was only part of the answer as Lewis understood it: there were what Lewis called 'two other principal opportunities, ... the development of the tourist industry, and emigration.'[6] The real growth, thus, would be in manufacturing, expected to grow by 4.9 per cent, and services, government and tourism, expected to grow by 5 per cent.

The problem was that nowhere in the region, not even in Barbados, one of the few places where fertility rates had been dropping, were things working out the way they were supposed to. Table 8.1 shows that, as Lewis predicted, agriculture was not able to absorb new sources of labour but that, unlike his prediction, its productivity had also been dropping.

Unemployment continued to be the dominant theme in development studies and political analysis. There were fundamental gender and demographic reasons why women and young people constituted the majority of the unemployed. In the early 1980s, the ratio of female to male unemployment, for instance, was 2.25 in Jamaica and only a little less elsewhere.[7] The problem among the young was even more telling, given the threat of social

6 W. Arthur Lewis, 1950a, p.55. Sir Arthur Lewis was awarded the Nobel Prize in Economics in 1980. See also *idem*, 1954.

7 Caribbean Community Secretariat, 1988, p.13.

tension they represented. In Trinidad, by the mid-1980s, the unemployment rate among those aged 15–24 was 62 per cent and in Jamaica, where agriculture still employed many of the young, 47 per cent. Such figures are fundamental to an understanding of the political movements which shook the whole region in the 1970s. Also fundamental is to understand how migration, one of the preferred remedies for unemployment, not only did not succeed in defusing the social tensions but, indeed, may have had an unintended but distinct impact on those tensions.

Even before the Lewis treatise, and certainly after it, the assumption of continued and uninterrupted high rates of migration had become an integral part of general economic thinking about development. To John Kenneth Galbraith, for instance, governments had to pursue education but especially migration if they were to break what he called the 'equilibrium of poverty'.[8] That was the theory, the actual example of the use of mass migration as an instrument of development had been set by Puerto Rico in the 1950s and 1960s.

As the foremost authority on the Puerto Rican case noted at the time, migration was 'the only means, short of widespread death' of reducing the population pressure.[9] Such a reduction, in turn, was essential, he said, if the industrial, agricultural, educational and other reconstruction programmes were going to have a chance to work. The rest of the Caribbean followed the Puerto Rican example, in this as in so many other strategies. Emigration was actively encouraged everywhere in the region. The *Barbados Development Plan, 1979–83*, for instance, made projections for population and employment based on three assumptions: a stable pattern of mortality, a marginal decline in fertility and a continuation of the level of emigration experienced in the post-censal period. Similar demographic calculations were made by the Commonwealth Secretariat with the warning that population pressures, especially from the young and unemployed, were sure to continue the political pressures faced by the region.[10]

Beyond the demographics and other objective conditions, there was the radicalization of ideas. In fact, a fundamental element in many of the political upheavals in the region was the ideological marriage of Marxist revolutionary strategy and black racial consciousness. The latter was especially crucial because, as Norman Girvan put it in 1975, race 'has been a central factor in the political economy of exploitation and for that reason of central importance in the politics and ideology of resistance.'[11] This was a widely

8 John Kenneth Galbraith, 1979, pp.120–39.
9 Clarence Senior, 1953, p.30.
10 Caribbean Community Secretariat, 1988, p.5.
11 Norman Girvan, 1975, p.3.

shared interpretation of political events at the time.[12] Girvan was quick to point out, however, that since the social and political structures 'vary widely from country to country', such variations gave rise to specific variations in the politics of resistance and the ideologies which guided them.

This link between race and revolution held true for much but certainly not all of the Caribbean. Race, for instance, played an insignificant role in the Cuban Revolution of 1959 though it certainly played an important part in the wars of independence and in the 'revolution' of 1933–4.[13] Similarly, while race was a major part of the Dominican Republic's sense of identity, it was based on that country's unique relationship with its neighbour, Haiti, and her occupations and conflicts. Race has not been demonstrated to have been a factor in the 1965 uprising in the Dominican Republic.[14] In Puerto Rico, even as incisive a critic of Caribbean race relations as Gordon K. Lewis had to admit that while race discrimination existed, it had a 'Latin' form and certainly was not important in the island's politics.[15] Where race, or at least skin tone, has historically played a vital role is the island of Haiti. And, yet, as James Leyburn noted quite early on, the element of caste divisions was so much stronger than the element of class as to make Haiti a *sui generis* case.[16] Where race did play a fundamental part in the political processes and social movements, peaceful and violent, was in the English-speaking Caribbean and to a lesser – but still important – degree in the Dutch island of Curaçao.

Post-1968 mass movements

In 1967 the Department of Government at the Mona (Jamaica) campus of the University of the West Indies (UWI) published a book of readings on the region's politics. Four years later, that same department published another reader asserting that the 1967 version was distinctly 'backward'. As the main editor, Trevor Munroe, put it, 'nothing in the [1967] Reader even hinted at the imminence of the October 1968 rebellion [Rodney affair] in Jamaica, the Trinidad revolutionary upheaval of 1970, the radical nationalism in Guyana in 1970–71, and the Black Power emanations in every territory of the archipeago.'[17]

12 Norman Girvan and Owen Jefferson, 1975; Trevor Munroe and Rupert Lewis, 1971.
13 Tomás F. Robaina, 1965.
14 Hugo Tolentino Dipp, 1992.
15 Gordon K. Lewis, 1963 (1974), pp.281–7.
16 James G. Leyburn, 1941.
17 Trevor Munroe and Rupert Lewis, 1971, p.vii.

What the Caribbean was experiencing was what Williams had predicted in 1963: alternatively known as 'Third World revolutions', the 'politics of mass mobilization', or in its more radical form, what Frantz Fanon called the rebellion of the 'wretched of the earth'. Not surprisingly, all these terms and their meanings appear in the 1971 UWI reader. In lieu of what the editor called the 'backward' essays by many of the established political scientists, there now appeared the writings of revolutionary activists: Frantz Fanon, Walter Rodney, the Tricontinental in Havana, excerpts from many radical publications: Jamaica's *Abeng*, Trinidad's *Moko* and proclamations of the Black Power group, the National Joint Action Committee (NJAC) of Trinidad & Tobago.

How well did the 1971 reader represent what was happening? With hindsight it can be said that while the various Black Power movements were high in emotional intensity and revolutionary rhetoric, in terms of duration and enduring social impact they were hardly revolutionary. The Jamaican case is a good place to start since that is where the first movement combining Marxism with Black Power took place.

In October 1966 the government of Jamaica had to declare a state of emergency in order to quell widespread disorders and violence in West Kingston. A combined force of soldiers and police carried out a house-to-house search for arms and a number of persons were taken into custody. Calm was soon restored. However, trouble broke out again in 1968. A rise in the cost of living had followed the devaluation of the Jamaican dollar and this was accompanied with a jump in the already high unemployment rate. There was widespread discontent in urban areas with the grave deterioration in many public utilities such as the telephone service, light and power. Rural Jamaica was also in distress. Two years of drought had reduced the island's water supply and crippled small farmers who produced vegetables, root crops and other staples of the local diet. Invariably, however, tensions are at their highest in urban working-class areas and in the 1960s it was in West Kingston, known as the island's powder-keg, that agitation was at its highest. It was fanned by the teaching of militant Black Power advocates heavily influenced by the Black Power movement in the United States of America, but also, as a University of the West Indies report noted, by the blending of Marxist analysis and what they termed 'the ideology of Rastafari racism'.[18] Although the Rastafari movement would eventually spread to other islands, at this point it was an uniquely Jamaican phenomenon. Other Black Power movements did not have the same religious goals as the Jamaican Rastafari and were to a greater extent blendings of ideas from working-class 'back-to-Africa' movements and Marxism, an essentially European and bourgeois intellectual

18 M. G. Smith *et al.*, 1960. Report reprinted in *Caribbean Quarterly*, 28, 1967.

ideology. It was an explosive mix, but it was not among the working class that the movement started. It started on the usually bucolic campus of the University of the West Indies. Matters came to a head on 8 October 1968, after the Jamaican government ordered the prohibition of entry and exclusion from the island of a Guyanese member of the university staff, Walter Rodney, already a major intellectual force in the nascent Black Power movement in the English-speaking Caribbean. An orderly but illegal march of university students protesting at the exclusion soon degenerated into rioting. Three lives were lost and there was much property damage before the military restored order. What would become known as the 'Rodney Affair' had repercussions in Trinidad, again beginning at that island's campus of the University of the West Indies. Before that, however, events in the Dutch Caribbean showed just how volatile the region was.

In 1969 rioting broke out in Willemstad, the capital of Curaçao, an island that seemed one of the most stable and orderly in the Caribbean. Dutch paratroopers were flown in at the request of the island's government and calm was imposed, but not before much of the heart of the famous shopping centre had been destroyed. The immediate cause was a dispute over wages paid by an independent engineering company which was subcontracted to the Shell Refinery, the island's largest employer. In sympathy with the employees of the subcontractor, other workers joined in a demonstration on the morning of 30 May in front of Shell headquarters. When the marchers moved on towards Willemstad, the police were waiting for them. Several men were shot. By the time the streets were cleared, however, the centre of the capital was ablaze, the streets littered with plate glass, discarded display cases, cameras, and the relics of looting.[19] As is often the case with such unexpected movements, it took the violent action of small groups to highlight the relatively few but nevertheless ignored pockets of unemployment and poverty that existed on the island of well-paying jobs. The oil-refining industry and the invariably crowded duty-free shops and resort hotels had all been sustaining this prosperity. Indeed, Curaçaoan sociologist, René A. Römer, found that by the 1970s the level of education on the island was such that even working-class people aspired to middle-class lifestyles.[20] Curaçao was proof that radical movements are not necessarily a product of generalized poverty for such did not exist in the island. What did exist was a high correlation between race and social status, with all the resentments such racial stratifications engender. Neither did

19 On the immediate events surrounding the Curaçao riots, see the official Government of the Netherlands report, A. F. Paula, 1970. A good sociological interpretation of the racial dimensions of the riots is provided by René A. Römer, 1975, pp.253–63.

20 René A. Römer, 1977, p.181.

extreme poverty exist in the next island to experience a movement mixing race and Marxist revolutionary ideology – Trinidad, twin island of the nation of Trinidad & Tobago, one of the most prosperous countries of the Commonwealth Caribbean.

Early in 1970, Trinidad experienced large-scale mobilizations of people demanding radical changes in society. There were marches of unemployed in Port of Spain, organized and led by militant Black Power leaders, many of them university students; there was also considerable unrest in the small Defence Force. Interestingly enough, the events in Trinidad were sparked by an incident at Sir George Williams University in Canada, an illustration of how increased migration had united these two countries. The importance of this latter event, relates an eyewitness, was that it was 'the catalyst for the raising of consciousness and the consequent political action of the masses,' in Canada and in Trinidad, all heavily influenced by the civil-rights movement in the United States.[21] When a section of the army mutinied and pledged to join the Black Power revolution, it appeared to some that the government of Eric Williams was doomed. Their hopes for power were short-lived. The mass of the populace refused to join the rebellion and the loyal section of the army, the coastguard and the police defended the government and soon squashed the uprising. A state of emergency was declared, a curfew imposed, and most of the mutineers and civilian radicals were placed under arrest.

The disorders in Jamaica, Curaçao and Trinidad served as a hurricane warning to the new states and nations, which, as already outlined above, faced grave difficulties, some of which may be called the dilemmas of development. There was more money in circulation but more unemployment; more jobs for the experienced and skilled, fewer for the increasing number of educated young and the unskilled. In island after island, the gap was widening between those with high incomes and those with little or nothing, and the disparity was displayed for all to see: new American-style residential suburbs with luxury houses within eyesight of the festering slums. Dependence on foreign markets left the agricultural producers of export crops with a feeling of insecurity. Inflation and steep increases in the cost of living wiped out the benefits that might otherwise have come from increases in salaries and wages. The inflow of foreign capital and the grant of special incentives to investors roused suspicions that a country was being sold out, that its capacity to make its own fiscal decisions was being weakened. These were among the most serious causes of social discontent. In addition, race, always latent as a source of conflicts, became openly a dominant factor in

21 Valerie Belgrave, 1995, p.120.

Caribbean politics. This factor deserves special treatment, especially as it reflects on the ties between the islands and the United States and other areas with large Caribbean diasporas.

External forces encouraged the growth of stronger, and at times bitter, racial feeling: the racial policies of South Africa, the assumption of power by a white minority in Rhodesia, Britain's immigration policy, the support given by many people in Britain to Powellism, the discrimination and injustices to which black people were subject in the United States. West Indians also found an increase of racial prejudice in Canada, long a haven and refuge for their students and for those seeking advancement. The militant Black Power movement in the United States, led among others by Trinidad-born Stokely Carmichael (Kwame Touré), encouraged a more articulate and positive assertion of blackness, of black dignity, of the right of black people everywhere to equality before the law and to equal opportunities of employment. The American movement was the protest of a minority group; that in the Caribbean was a claim by the majority group to economic as well as political power. The Black Power militants of the United States were convinced that only self-contempt and discrimination shut them off from a share of the good things in American life that they saw white Americans enjoying. The West Indians had Black Power through universal adult suffrage; almost all who symbolized political authority, whether Governors-General or prime ministers, were black. But what about 'national control of our national resources'? They began to ask whether political independence did not mean financial independence and also a shift away from the essentially authoritarian attitudes of a colonial administration.

The role of Cuba, the Grenada Revolution and Manley's Jamaica

All these factors contributed to a certain level of conflict in the area; but they were not the only ones. Other factors which made politics in the Caribbean in the post-independence era increasingly conflictive were exogenous. West Indian leaders would probably have disagreed among themselves on the particular weight that should have been attached to each foreign influence, but they would have agreed with the Williams statement quoted above that in the post-independence period, geo-politics, and the ideological divide which drove it, was an influential factor in many of the area's political processes. First, there had been a decisive shift from an Eurocentric orientation in most things (education, defence, culture, recreation, commerce) to a United States-centred one. With this shift came, of course, all the perceptions and definitions of the United States, of its vital interests – at home and within its sphere of influence. The latter took on special significance when it came to the role of Cuba in the region. It is obvious that even though the United States's conflict with Cuba, for instance, preceded the independence of all the new Caribbean states, it slowly but surely became an integral part of their concerns during the post-independence era.[22] Even after establishing diplomatic relations with Cuba, Eric Williams would severely criticize the Cuban model and warn Cuba against intervention.

Second, the entry of Cuba as a regional geo-political player was reason enough for the entry of other players, especially the so-called middle powers, Venezuela and Brazil, and the transnational actors representing ideological interests (Marxist-Leninists, Christian Democrats, Social Democrats, trade union federations) as well as transnational corporations.[23] It is important to note, however, that the traditional and historical openness of the area continued so that very often the presence of these actors was more invited than imposed. This certainly included the Cubans whose presence was often used as leverage on the international community, particularly the United States, but also Western Europe, all of whom provided levels of financial assistance which were not insignificant to these economically strapped islands. By the mid-1970s, however, the perception of the role of Cuba began to change.

Cuba, which had always upheld its status as a Latin American or continental country, slowly but surely made its presence felt in the insular Caribbean from the early 1970s. As already noted, the West Indian leadership was initially not excessively concerned, at least not outwardly. Even the suspected role of Cuba in training some of the soldiers who participated in the 1970 Black Power revolutionary attempt in Trinidad[24] had not stopped that country from joining Guyana, Jamaica and Barbados in establishing diplomatic relations with Cuba in 1972. By the end of the decade, however, a series of events made the actions of Cuba a matter of direct concern to the post-independence leadership of the West Indies. In fact, three different Cuban involvements in the Caribbean brought that island centre stage while at the same time revealing the fact that the region had entered a new phase in its international relations.

First was the 1975 airlift, through Barbados initially and Guyana later, of a division of Cuban troops for Angola. Eric Williams of Trinidad was

22 See Anthony P. Maingot, 1994a, pp.113–39.
23 See *idem*, 1984, pp.63–84.
24 Deryck R. Brown, 1995, pp.543–78.

particularly put out by the discovery of what old Cuban hand Herbert L. Matthews called 'this sensational development in hemispheric history'.[25] To Matthews, Angola was as much a part of Moscow's designs as it was of Cuba's. It is this perception of a wider Cold War-related threat which led to the first discussions on mutual security assistance between Trinidad and Barbados.

It should be clear that the objection of some Caribbean leaders was not to Cuban actions against South Africa, whose abhorrent system of *apartheid* had no sympathizers in the islands. The objection was to violations of their sovereignty by an action which demonstrated Cuban audacity and logistical capabilities while at the same time showing how easily these small states could unknowingly be drawn into an East-West tangle. This apprehension was increased by the second dramatic move by the Cubans: their actions in Grenada.

It was in the context of the dramatic actions in Angola by Cuba that West Indian apprehensions escalated in the months after a *coup d'état* toppled the government of Eric Gairy in Grenada in 1979. While the movement against the increasingly eccentric and incompetent Gairy had wide support, it was actually led by a small group of middle-class radicals called The New Jewel Movement.[26] Their leader was a charismatic young lawyer, Maurice Bishop, whose Marxist ideology was not revealed to the Grenadians until after the *coup d'état*, but whose wide appeal and popularity were undisputed. Such was the unpopularity of Gairy in the other West Indian islands that the initial shock at this first violent overthrow of an independent West Indian government changed to a posture of cautious hope on the part of many. The West Indian government leaders, however, with the exception of Forbes Burnham of Guyana who was a strong supporter from the very inception, were not as sanguine. They eventually adopted a stance of silent vigilance and studied neutrality *vis-à-vis* the Grenada People's Revolutionary Government. There was no neutrality on Cuba's part nor on the part of the United States. They quite rapidly made Grenada part of their ongoing conflict in the region. Cuba almost immediately had the only resident ambassador on the island, who soon presided over a growing Cuban presence. It seemed to replicate the situation in Guyana, where the Cuban mission took up nearly half a city block and where Cuba's multiple involvements had long been the talk of Georgetown. Some 15 Cuban doctors arrived; so did fishing trawlers and instructors. On 18 November 1979 prime minister Maurice Bishop told

25 Herbert L. Matthews, 1976, p.31.

26 A good overview can be had from Anthony Payne, *et al.*, 1984, and Jay R. Mandle, 1985.

a rally that he expected 250 Cubans to start building a new international airport.

Eventually there would be 700 Cuban workers. There would also be a full-scale Soviet Embassy staffed by a diplomat whose previous post was ambassador to Argentina, the Soviets' most important trading partner in Latin America. Not since the Second World War and the building of the United States military bases had these small islands of the region seen such activity, and certainly never since the conflict in British Guiana in 1953 had these former British colonies been in the midst of such an East-West conflict. For this, in the final analysis, is what it was, just as Williams had predicted in 1963: as much a supra-national, international-relations conflict as it was a national one. The Caribbean was converted into an arena of Great Power politics as the United States focused on the airport as a major military threat. Whatever private apprehensions West Indian leaders had about the ultimate use of this airport, they kept their counsel, noting publicly that the projected Grenadian runway was no longer than four others already in service in various West Indian islands.

The assassination of prime minister Maurice Bishop and several of his closest advisers, on 19 October 1983, by a small ultra-Leninist clique within the regime brought down the first West Indian attempt at creating a socialist state closely allied to Cuba. It also led to the invasion of Grenada by the United States of America, aided by small units of soldiers from Jamaica and police from the Eastern Caribbean.

It should be evident that Cuba had gone, in a very short space of time, from being an 'outsider' (both politically and culturally) to being virtually the major player in important parts of the West Indies. Jamaica, where the 'democratic socialism' of Michael Manley (1972–80) developed very close ties with Fidel Castro's regime, became the third source of East-West confrontation in the region.

It is only fair to note that minus the geo-political or East-West competition which was already engaged in the region, Manley's effort to restructure the society through a mixed-economy model was not all that radical. In fact, it was in keeping with the trend among a wide spectrum of the political élites of these nations to move towards a state-directed populism through an economically active state, an assigned role for the private sector and an active, non-aligned Third World foreign policy. The evidence now seems to be that this was, in fact, as much as the existing West Indian political cultures were willing to bear. The development of socialism, with all the sacrifices that system of government necessarily entails, appeared in the late 1970s and early 1980s as a very remote possibility.[27]

---

27 See Anthony P. Maingot, 1979, pp.254–89.

TABLE 8.2 Social class and ideological position in Jamaica, 1978

Social Class	*Support for capitalism*[a] %	*Support for demo-socialism*[a] %	*Support for communism*[a] %	*Support for increasing government ownership*[b] %	*Opposition to increasing government ownership*[b] %
Kingston middle class	45	25	3	27	73
Kingston working class	20	38	14	48	52
Small farmers	4	33	2	21	79

Notes

a Support for ideological principles (6 February 1978)

b Views on increasing government ownership (30 January 1978)

Percentages are of those who gave answers to questions on these ideologies.

Sources: Dr Carl Stone: Poll, *Weekly Gleaner*, 6 February 1978, p.1; and Dr Carl Stone: Poll, *Weekly Gleaner*, 30 January 1978, p.1.

In 1984 Carl Stone concluded that 'in Jamaica there is neither a will to achieve the socialist alternative nor the necessary political supports to sustain it even if such a will existed.'[28] It was clear, at least by 1978, that the majority of Jamaicans were in no mood for radical Left experiments in 'scientific socialism', as the data in Table 8.2 indicate. Even among the urban working class, the most radical in Stone's sample, only 19 per cent favoured government expropriation of land and only 12 per cent saw the private sector as 'exploiters' (though 48 per cent saw it as 'selfish'). Hardly surprising, therefore, that fully 63 per cent of the urban working class disliked the leader of the Communist Party, Trevor Munroe, and that 65 per cent disliked D. K. Duncan, the visible radical in Manley's circle. That this radicalism was very much an urban phenomenon is illustrated by Stone's finding that fully 42 per cent of the small farmers could not even identify the radical leaders.

That Jamaican parliamentary democracy survived the hectic 1976–80 period is in itself an accomplishment not to be minimized. It is clear, however, that Jamaicans in 1978 were showing their deep-rooted conservative instincts and having second thoughts about any new 'socialist offensives'.

28 Carl Stone, 1984, p.56.

The conservative reaction

By the early 1980s West Indian leaders appeared to have few doubts about Cuban military capabilities and every incident involving the Cubans contributed to the perception of a threat, even those which were not so intended. A defensive attitude began to develop very rapidly. By the early 1980s, for instance, the nations of the Eastern Caribbean were ready to do something positive about their security. Out of this developed a set of ideas increasingly called the 'Adams doctrine', after Barbados prime minister Tom Adams. This doctrine was premised on the belief that threats to their small democracies would not come from external forces directly but from the critically timed assistance these external forces might give to the small groups at home who would subvert democracy. The need, then, was for a small but mobile force which counted speed as its most effective asset.

The Adams doctrine was as much a product of the thinking of the Ronald Reagan administration in the United States of America as it was of Tom Adams' own geo-political views and of events which unfolded in the area during the late 1970s. It is important to know, therefore, that the first use of the Adams doctrine was not in Grenada, in October 1983, but in Union Island in the St Vincent Grenadines (97 miles due east of Barbados), in early December 1979. An invasion of alleged Rastafarians from the Grenadian island of Carriacou led to a request by St Vincent for assistance. Elements of the Barbadian defence forces intervened to help put down the movement. This was the first intervention in the name of collective security in the young history of Eastern Caribbean sovereignty. It was this incident, and the suspicion that the revolutionary government in Grenada was training others for similar acts, which led eventually to the signing of a formal collective security understanding in September 1982. The 'Memorandum of Understanding' regarding security and military co-operation was signed by Barbados and all the independent states of the Organization of Eastern Caribbean States (OECS), except Grenada. It is one of those ironies of history that it should have been the fear of the ultimate intentions of one of their own which led these islands to shape their first collective security agreement. The Western Hemisphere's collective security treaties, from the Act of Chapultepec (Mexico, 1945) to the Pact of Rio de Janeiro (1947) and finally the charter of the Organization of American States (Bogotá, 1948), had been directed at outside forces – the Axis powers and later Soviet communism. The independent West Indian islands had created what they thought was additional protection to that already granted by these treaties.

By mid-1986 there had been no implementation of this Security Pact. The reasons for this were various, including the death in early 1985 of its major proponent, Tom Adams. More important, however, was the opposition of many leaders of the West Indian democracies. That opposition reflected a built-in distrust of military structures and a belief that the best defence of democracy is social and economic development. In the words of St Kitts-Nevis prime minister Kennedy Simmons, security cannot be won by force of arms. Sir James ('Son') Mitchell, prime minister of St Vincent, was adamant on the subject: 'The age old lesson,' he noted, 'is if you live by the sword, you perish by the sword.'[29] The best defence of democracy was democratic practice itself.

By the mid-1980s, the independent nations of the English-speaking Caribbean had firmly established the basis for their nationhood: parliamentary pluralism, a largely pro-Western foreign policy, the Regional Security System, and close relations, in security and economic matters, with the United States of America. Between themselves, their trade and other economic arrangements were handled through the Secretariat of the Caribbean Community (CARICOM). Through the Caribbean Basin Initiative (CBI) launched by United States president Ronald Reagan to assist the islands to access the United States market, they were more firmly than ever in the 'American camp'. This did not mean, however, that the region had overcome the structural problems which had contributed to the tensions during the period of the Cold War. It merely meant that in the post-Cold War period the geo-political dimension of any particular crisis was absent. The crisis of 27 July 1990 in Trinidad illustrates this.

Claiming intolerable oppression from the State, Abu Bakr, leader of a Black Muslim group called the Jamaat al Muslimeen, attempted a *coup d'état*. Over thirty people died in the events which included storming and blowing up the Port of Spain Central Police Station, taking over the state-owned television station, an assault on parliament and taking as hostages the prime minister, A. N. R. Robinson, and most of his Cabinet. All this was followed by massive looting and burning of city businesses. Thanks to the loyalty of the police and defence forces (with strategic United States assistance in certain key areas) the coup attempt was suppressed and Abu Bakr and his followers arrested, tried and convicted of rebellion. In a strange twist of legal reasoning, Abu Bakr's appeal to the Privy Council of the House of Lords in England (still the court of last resort for the English-speaking islands) was upheld on the grounds that a presidential pardon had been involved in the surrender and was legally binding. By the late 1990s Abu Bakr was back, organizing and sounding quite as menacing as ever. How to explain this phenomenon of rebellion, conviction and subsequent exoneration? Was it *sui*

29 Quoted in Anthony P. Maingot, 1997, p.101.

generis Trinidadian, an aberration in Caribbean history, or was it more generally indicative of Caribbean constitutional practice and political culture? After all, even taking into account all the differences that each case brings with it, there were rather similar outcomes following the rebellions in Trinidad in 1970 and Curaçao in 1969, and the *coup d'état* in Suriname in 1980. What did these rebellions, and the subsequent direct participation in electoral politics of the perpetrators in the cases of Curaçao and Suriname and indirectly in the case of Trinidad, portend?

One sweeping and decidedly pessimistic view is that of Selwyn D. Ryan. He argues that all these crises of the last three decades represented not just a challenge to 'all the paradigms upon which Caribbean societies and state systems rested in the post war era,' but, indeed, 'a general... undermining [of] the integrity of Caribbean island states ...'.[30]

A more positive approach would look at the responses of Caribbean peoples to these various challenges and argue that these responses reflected the strength of democratic institutions, including the independence of the judiciary and a solid popular belief in human rights, not an undermining of the integrity of the systems. Indeed, in virtually all the countries where there had been serious challenges to the existing political systems, whether it be Jamaica, Trinidad, St Lucia, Dominica, Curaçao, Suriname or others, the times of challenge were invariably followed by elections which were models of transparency and accountability, albeit heated and contentious. The December 1997 elections in Guyana were more controversial and disputed but even in that difficult situation of racial polarization, a committee of distinguished West Indians negotiated a peaceful settlement which was generally complied with. The general conclusion is that the parliamentary system appears to work for these small states. If there was a dramatic political failure during those years it was that of the Caribbean Left. As Brian Meeks has noted, given the speed with which erstwhile dominant Left positions and models lost credibility by the end of the 1980s, it is perhaps even more appropriate to talk of a 'paradigm collapse'.[31] The particular historical conditions of decolonization in the Caribbean might explain why.

It is crucial to keep in mind that nowhere in the Caribbean – with the possible exception of Cuba – had there been a national liberation struggle. According to the dominant theory in the 1970s and 1980s, this was the precondition for the creation of the nationalist-socialist state. Decolonization was not resisted by the colonial powers and, indeed, in the French, Dutch and certain British territories, decolonization politics, at least

30 Selwyn D. Ryan, 1991a, p.ix.
31 Brian Meeks, 1993, p.4.

as understood in the Third World, were often rejected outright. The same can be said for Puerto Rico and the US Virgin Islands. This more conservative approach to state and social development has been an unique part of the history of the area and deserves to be analysed in the form of specific case studies.

The French Caribbean

Richard Burton puts the situation of the French Caribbean in no uncertain terms: 'There being no signs whatsoever that France will "abandon" its Caribbean possessions in the short, medium or long term, it seems that political independence, as the formerly independentist Union Populaire pour la Libération de la Guadeloupe put it in the regional elections of 1992, "*n'est pas à l'ordre du jour*".'[32] Burton is correct. Aside from constitutional tinkering by whatever metropolitan government happened to be in power – usually matters of a greater or lesser degree of decentralization of the departmental administration – there has been an impressive stability in France's arrangements and relations with its Départements d'Outre Mer (DOMs).

To French West Indian leaders, the interpretation of what 'decolonization' and 'nationhood' meant was permeated by a national ideology which had at its core the search for identity through *racial identification*. The latter pursuit was much more intense but, interestingly enough, much more peaceful, than it had been, for instance, in the British Caribbean. In the latter, the policy of autonomous cultural development, pursued as much in India as in the West Indies, contrasted dramatically with the French colonial policy of *assimilation*, nothing short of total cultural absorption with language as the dominant cultural symbol and social glue.

It is the colonials' reaction to a policy which amounted to cultural domination which led Martiniquan poet and politician Aimé Césaire and his generation to pursue the idea of *négritude*, a black identity which was believed to transcend any particular social class status. Decolonization for the black colonial, said Césaire, had an unique, because racial, dimension. As such, the racial struggle, he noted in his 1956 letter of resignation from the French Communist Party, was of 'a totally different nature from the struggle of the French workers against French capitalism.'[33] Maurice Thorez, to whom this letter of resignation was addressed, was the Secretary-General of the French

32 Richard D. E. Burton and Fred Reno, 1994, p.18.

33 Aimé Césaire, 1957, p.8.

Communist Party whom Césaire accused of not understanding the particular circumstances of a decolonization process in which race, not class, gave particular form to oppression.

The paradoxical thing about this French West Indian stance on decolonization was that leaders such as Césaire felt that cultural and psychological liberation could well be achieved even as their islands remained, after 1946, integral parts of the metropolitan French political, economic and constitutional system. To these political leaders, the real struggle facing the new DOMs of Martinique, Guadeloupe and Guyane had always been asserting their uniqueness even while finding ways of extracting the greatest number of political and economic advantages from the metropole. The political trick was to achieve this with little or no harm to the ongoing pursuit of a French 'Antillean' identity.

Economically, these Caribbean DOMs continue to be sustained by large transfers of public funds into infrastructural works, guaranteed high salaries as well as a social net covering pensions, education, unemployment compensation and medical services. There are also significant subsidies for agricultural products such as bananas, sugar and rum. Throughout the decades of the 1970s and 1980s, the French state's public welfare expenditure per capita was consistently at least twice as high for the DOMs as for the metropole. Additionally, and crucially in terms of continued Antillean support for the arrangement, public expenditure on the DOMs has been sustained even during periods of economic downturn or budgetary belt-tightening in France itself.[34]

As firm as the political relationship with France is, however, the racial and cultural debate about 'identity' continues in a way not found in the other territories. As the last decade of the twentieth century came to a close, Martiniquans in particular were locked in a debate between the advocates of *négritude* (*á la* Césaire) and *créolité*. The central thesis of the former is that the population of Martinique is fundamentally African/black and the various ethnic minorities and/or racial mixtures are marginal to this 'core' of the nation. The ideology of *négritude* maintains that cultural, and perhaps biological, *métissage*, while tolerated in practice, should be discouraged and condemned in principle. Those who advocate *créolité* on the other hand, believe that the national 'core' and key social dynamic of the nation – both in biological and cultural terms – is mixture and it is this mixture or blending which has created a 'creolized' society. It stands to reason, therefore, that Créole, not French, is the national language and *métissage,* far from being discouraged, should be celebrated.

The fundamental aspect of this debate as far as political processes are concerned is that it is not the stuff of class warfare but of cultural battles

34 See R. Chane-Tune, 1986, *passim.*

played out through literary thrusts and parries. Césaire, who stepped down as Deputy for Fort-de-France, Martinique, in 1993, continued to the end of the century at the centre of this debate. Given the centrality of race in Martinique and the Caribbean, it is a debate which promises not to end any time soon.[35]

The Dutch Caribbean

As is the case with the other ex-colonial territories, the key characteristic of the constitutional arrangements and political systems of these Dutch islands is that they are pluralist democracies which are highly regarded internationally for their human rights records and peaceful transitions of power. But the Dutch islands, much more than is the case with the English-speaking territories which opted for independence and the French ones which opted for integration, have had difficulties responding to the 'dilemma of decolonization'. While they have debated the adoption of various constitutional arrangements, from a DOM-style arrangement to a 'commonwealth' of independent states, nothing has been finalized at the time of writing.

The Dutch Caribbean's new constitutional link with the Netherlands came in 1954 with the signing of the Statute or Charter of the Kingdom. This made Suriname and the Netherlands Antilles autonomous partners in the Kingdom of the Netherlands. It was a truly complex arrangement given the social and cultural variations involved. The so-called ABC islands (Curaçao, Aruba and Bonaire), were all highly stratified by race and religion, but this was ameliorated by the common language, Papiamentu, which provided a common bond. The other three islands, Sint Maarten (shared with French St Martin), St Eustatius and Saba, were English-speaking and shared much in common with their English-speaking neighbours in the Leeward Islands. On the other hand, Suriname, located on the South American mainland, was a truly 'plural society' where the Creoles or Blacks tended to favour independence but the equally numerous Asians (descendants of the indentured labourers from India and Indonesia) did not. The latter believed that they were best protected by an ongoing relationship with the Netherlands.

The 'honeymoon' of this arrangement would not endure. Contrary to the case of France where there has been a metropolitan consensus on the ties with the overseas departments, the majority opinion in the Netherlands

35 Richard D. E. Burton, 1996, pp.135–52.

since the early 1960s was that these territories constituted a liability rather than an asset. Again, as distinct from the French, and more akin to the British case, the Dutch have, at least since the 1960s, tried to persuade their Caribbean partners to opt for independence. It was only in 1975, after much cajoling and a substantial offer of economic assistance (the so-called 'Golden Handshake'), that Suriname opted for independence. It is one of those ironies of the decolonization process that the dismal performance of the Surinamese political leadership after independence became a major contributor to the disenchantment with the independence option among the Dutch islands. As significant as this negative example was as a disincentive to independence, it certainly was not the only one. Global economic recession was another. In 1983 the Netherlands Antilles was hit with what Robertico ('Bettico') Croes calls 'four lightning punches': Venezuela's devaluation of its currency, the *bolivar*, the United States' cancellation of the tax treaty with the Netherlands which had made Curaçao a favourite low-tax haven for United States multinational corporations; the closing of the Exxon refinery in Aruba, and the departure of Shell from its refinery in Curaçao.[36] This led to a desperate search for economic alternatives. Aruba decided that a political move was a prerequisite to its economic turn-around and in 1983 decided to secede from the Netherlands Antilles generally and from Curaçao specifically. It chose to opt, by 1986, to have a distinct and separate position within the kingdom called *Status Aparte*. Defence and international affairs remained the responsibility of the kingdom but in everything else Aruba acted with virtual autonomy. At a minimum, continued ties with the Netherlands guaranteed significant metropolitan financing of development projects as well as the right to migrate to the Netherlands.

In 1986, there was an assumption in the Netherlands that full independence for Aruba would follow in 1996. But no such independence occurred as the 'Arubanos' joined their other Antillean colleagues in promoting what two Dutch scholars have called 'upside-down decolonization': postponing independence indefinitely.[37] A dramatic shift in ideology had taken place among Arubanos: any suggestion that they move towards independence was now to be regarded as a 'colonial imposition'. Only the natives could decide what their constitutional status could be.

As already noted, the case of Suriname since its independence in 1975 was not an encouraging one to Antilleans. During the first 15 years of its independence, the country saw coup after coup, a dramatic flight of educated citizens, a disastrous drop in the economy and a frightening rise in narco-

---

36 Bettico Croes, 1990, B415–B432.

37 See Rosemarijn Hoefte and Gert Oostindie, 1991, pp.71–98.

trafficking. To democrats, the military regime of Desi Bouterse, who governed from 1980 to 1987, and after that behind the scenes, was an especially objectionable, even terrifying, one. Playing an ideological geo-political game with Cuba and Bishop's Grenada, Bouterse presided over the murder of 17 of his most outspoken opponents in 1983 and then fought a war in the backlands against a Bush Negro (Maroon) guerrilla army led by a former military colleague, Ronny Brunswyk.[38] Right to the end of the decade of the 1990s, Suriname appeared caught in a tragic morass of ethnic political divisions, corruption and periodic military meddling.

Clearly, it was not just the negative example of Suriname's performance and the economic recession which brought about the change in the hearts and minds of the Arubanos and Dutch Antilleans. There was also a growing concern with new threats to security coming from organized crime which was feeding on the increasing use of the islands as trans-shipment points for drugs heading towards the United States. The constitutional arrangements with the Netherlands not only ensured security but also allayed the fear that, without the Netherlands, Aruba would be just another cog in the United States' hemispheric security system. These were just some of the reasons why, contrary to 'Third World' ideologies of decolonization and experiences elsewhere, by the end of the 1990s, the Netherlands, far from exercising hegemonic power or disengaging from its Caribbean islands, found itself ever more involved, including providing the highest per capita aid in the world, all, according to one scholar, 'to the dismay of politicians in The Netherlands'.[39]

All in all, the case of the Netherlands Antilles in general, and Aruba in particular, reflected the varied and complex ways in which the 'responsibilities' of a decolonization process were being confronted in the Caribbean. Few cases, however, exemplify this complexity with more poignancy than that of Puerto Rico.

The Puerto Rican case

Despite its *sui generis* political history, the Puerto Rican case can be studied as an interesting combination of the paradoxes and dilemmas of other experiences with decolonization in the region.

In ways strikingly similar to the processes experienced by the French and the Dutch Antilleans, many Puerto Ricans see no contradiction between

38 On this war see Edward Dew, 1989, B415–B432.
39 Rosemarijn Hoefte and Gert Oostindie, 1991, p.81.

the pursuit of an independent culture and identity and continued economic and even political integration into the United States system. Time and time again, through free elections and plebiscites, a majority of Puerto Ricans has demonstrated that they are not keen to take on the economic challenges of independence. This is what their political mind has dictated, but it has not placated their cultural heart. Like the French Antilleans, Puerto Ricans, regardless of political orientation, have always had a profound concern with the preservation of their distinct Latin American culture. In particular they uniformly insist on the retention of the Spanish language and all that implies culturally. As distinct from the French Antilleans who can celebrate both their native Créole and their command of the purest metropolitan French, or the Dutch Antilleans who are content to use their native Papiamentu as the language of emotions while struggling with Dutch for instrumental and pragmatic purposes, the Puerto Ricans have no option *vis-à-vis* the linguistic hegemony of the English-speaking United States. According to José Luis González, this linguistic-cultural issue has played itself out in all four of the historical 'stages' of Puerto Rican history.[40]

The presence of such difficult choices has often led Puerto Rican intellectuals to extremes of romanticism. According to Gordon K. Lewis, what many nationalistic Puerto Ricans wanted to avoid was something that Alexandre de Tocqueville lamented with respect to America: a trend in which the love of the beautiful was increasingly sacrificed to the cultivation of the useful.[41]

This said, the question for Puerto Rico and, indeed, for the rest of the Caribbean, is whether a traditional nationalistic, not to say romantic, definition of the beautiful can survive modernization and globalization – in other words, integration into a metropolitan market and system. An important contemporary Puerto Rican writer articulated the dilemma quite succinctly: 'The majority of Puerto Ricans prize their American citizenship. It represents for us economic stability and the assurance of civil liberties and democracy. On the other hand, we also cherish our language and culture. Thus, Puerto Rico's situation has historically been a paradox.'[42]

Despite Ferré's assertion, the reality is that Puerto Rico's decolonization represents more of a dilemma than a paradox. If paradox is the denial of expectations (as in surprise), dilemma is the absence of optimal choices which means that any option chosen represents a trade-off. Gordon Lewis was undoubtedly sociologically correct when he noted that the belief, in Puerto Rico as elsewhere, that it is possible to change the technological foun-

40 José Luis González, 1989.
41 Gordon K. Lewis, 1963 (1974), p.295.
42 Rosario Ferré, 1998, p.23.

dation of a society and leave untouched its cultural superstructure was naive Utopianism. Yet all societies, from Mexico to China to France, seek to defend their cultural patrimonies in the face of the homogenizing tendencies of modernization. Puerto Ricans have been neither unique nor exaggerated in pursuing and promoting this cultural reflex. And yet, it has to be admitted that it is the very tenacity of Puerto Rican cultural identity which has made quite intractable – at least in the short to medium term – the impasse over status. The maneouvering over the issue of independence is illustrative of this. While it is true, as the non-binding plebiscite of 1993 indicated, that only 4 per cent of the people favoured independence, there has always been a menacing adamance about that minority. As the leader of the Partido Independentista Puertorriqueño (PIP) put it: 'What would the United States do with the hundreds of thousands of Puerto Ricans who adamantly oppose statehood? *Independentistas* have vowed to continue the struggles for independence – indeed for secession – under statehood.'[43]

The threat is hardly disguised in Berrios' query: 'Is the United States willing to risk a Caribbean Quebec or a tropical Northern Ireland?' This adamance is certainly bolstered by the fact that the many who do not share their political aspirations for independence do share their wider cultural aspirations. However, to argue from this that the majority of Puerto Ricans are ready to pick up arms to promote their cultural identity flies in the face of both Puerto Rican and Caribbean history. A brief review of the political history of the island is necessary to place all this in context.

Conquered by the United States of America as part of the Spanish-American-Cuban War, Puerto Rico remained a classical non-self-governing colony right into the 1940s. The paradox lies in the democratic development of internal Puerto Rican politics. In 1938 Luis Muñoz Marín returned to his native island very much influenced by the ideology of the Mexican revolution and the New Deal of Franklin Delano Roosevelt. His party, the Partido Popular Democrático (PPD), adopted the Mexican theme of 'Pan, Tierra y Libertad.' As in Mexico, the appeal was directed to the largely impoverished peasantry and workers on the sugar estates.

Muñoz determined that the divisions over the issue of status were such that the only way to organize a mass party which could eventually determine the future of the island was to make status a non-issue in any particular election. He was enormously successful, at least tactically, as the success of the constitutional and political measures he pushed shows.

In 1950 Congress approved Public Law 600 which provided for a new status for the island. In August 1951, the voters in Puerto Rico approved the

43 Rubén Berrios Martínez, 1997, p.110.

establishment of a constitutional convention to elaborate an island charter based on PL 600. The vote was 387,016 in favour and 119,169 against. Finally, on 3 March 1952, the draft constitution creating the Estado Libre Asociado (later translated as 'Commonwealth') was approved by a vote of 373,594 in favour, 82,877 against.

On 9 July 1952 the new Commonwealth of Puerto Rico was officially proclaimed. While certainly a great political victory for Muñoz and his party, it in fact deepened the island's dilemma, by entrenching the fundamental principle of sovereign consent: there could be no changes in the 'compact' except by mutual – Puerto Rican and American – consent, democratically entered into. In many ways, this was the first Caribbean case of 'upside down' decolonization.

The relationship with the United States remained very stable while the PPD controlled, in virtually hegemonic fashion, the island's politics. But, if politics was to be about leadership and programmes, not status, it was to be expected that the 'normal' processes of democratic politics – personal ambition and intra-party squabbles – would eventually take their toll. This occurred in 1968 when the post-Muñoz PPD split and opened the door to the Governor's mansion to the pro-statehood New Progressive Party (NPP). The PPD recouped enough votes to win the 1972 elections, only to be defeated by the NPP again in 1976.

The PPD, having put the status issue on hold in order to carry out a fully fledged social, political and economic agenda, and having succeeded beyond anyone's most optimistic predictions, had fallen victim to their own successes. By 1980 Puerto Rico had been transformed by two processes: the transition from a basically agricultural economy into a manufacturing and services based one, and a mass migration to the north-east of the United States of America. Both processes tied the island's economy more tightly with that of the metropole and ensured an enormous expansion of federally mandated welfare benefits such as food stamps. Whatever the cultural differences, such programmes certainly reinforce many other types of bonds.

Yet this is where the contemporary dilemma had its origins. Rather than the classical case of hegemonic leadership which tends to be based on a combination of material, political and moral factors, those attributes are split in Puerto Rico. The fastest growing political tendency is the pro-statehood one, but it is forced to justify its political and economic leadership on grounds which differ little from those of the *Independentistas*: the retention of the essential elements of Puerto Rico 'nationality' in all its cultural complexity even as Puerto Ricans retain their United States citizenship. On the other hand, *Independentistas* have to argue, above and beyond the culture and nationality issue, that independence would economically favour not only Puerto Rico but, indeed, the United States and the whole Caribbean.

TABLE 8.3 Statistical picture of Puerto Rico, 1983–99

	1983	*1999*
GNP (in real terms)	$3.8 bn	$6.0 bn
Personal consumption	$4.0 bn	$7.1 bn
Exports	$8.5. bn	$30.3 bn
Employed	703 000	1.5 m
Unemployment rate	23.5%	12.5%
Employment/manufacturing	131 000	159 000
Employment/services	132 000	307 000

Source: Carmen Ana Culpeper, president of the Puerto Rico Chamber of Commerce, Presentation to World Peace Foundation Meeting, 6 May 2000.

All the parties, thus, defend the retention and enhancement of a Puerto Rico nationality with language, religion and a 'community of memories' at its core. If anything, they favour the intensification of what Robert Bellah calls the 'practices of commitment' which define 'the patterns of loyalty and obligation that keep the community alive.'[44]

In the final analysis, therefore, neither the material nor the cultural 'realities' of Puerto Rico are negotiable. This is what has made the constitutional arrangement originally designed by Muñoz Marín so hard to replace. Precisely because the 'Commonwealth' status provided for economic growth along with an authentic autonomous development of Puerto Rican society, including the creation of its own flag, its 'anthem', its own Olympic teams, and the promotion of its culture through state-funded agencies such as the Instituto de Cultura Puertorriqueña, it is a difficult formula to defeat. But it is precisely such 'thick' ethnic identifications and activities which have moved important United States politicians such as Senator Daniel Moynihan of New York to question Puerto Rico's eventual incorporation into the American Union.[45]

Whatever the constitutional-political relationships with the United States might turn out to be, the dire prediction of the radical Caribbean Left that the Puerto Rican 'model' was finished, was true only in terms of its exportability. In fact, as the data in Table 8.3 demonstrate, that model continued to provide significant economic dividends to the island right to the end of the second millennium.

With such a performance, despite increasing disengagement in terms of special conditions and privileges from Washington, it is not clear that statehood is indispensable for continued economic development. This seemed

44 Robert N. Bellah *et al.*, 1985, pp.152–5.

45 See Daniel Patrick Moynihan, 1993, pp.73–4.

to have been one of the messages sent by the results of the 1998 plebiscite. Whatever optimism existed about Puerto Ricans finally making up their minds was dashed by these results. It is not just that statehood was supported by only 46.5 per cent and independence by a mere 2.5 per cent, but rather that there was such controversy over the very wording of the plebiscite. This led to a quasi-boycott by the PPD which asked their members to vote the *quinta columna*, 'None of the Above'. They received 50.2 per cent of the vote.

Not only did Puerto Rico appear to have returned to square one, it appeared to have done so while polarizing attitudes about the mechanism and processes of voting on the particular status they desire. There was no evidence that there was any such disharmony in elections which were not referenda on the relationship with the United States. While this is clearly a difficult balancing act, it is not at all evident that the effort is either futile or, indeed, unproductive. Perhaps the present state of Puerto Rico's democracy is evidence that despite the eternal indecisiveness about status, Puerto Ricans have not laboured in vain. It is widely accepted that the Puerto Rican people have displayed a noteworthy political maturity as characterized by their ability to evolve an essentially sound and balanced development programme in the face of inordinately difficult circumstances and continued uncertainty about their ultimate political status. As such, Puerto Rico was very much part of a much larger Caribbean 'decolonization' process. This was not the case with the two other Greater Antilles, the Dominican Republic and Haiti.

The Dominican Republic and Haiti

In the Dominican Republic, the three-decade rule of Rafael Leonidas Trujillo (1930–61), despite some important structural changes, had left the country divided between a very large working class and a small rich élite. Frank Moya Pons sums it up nicely when he notes that in 1930 Trujillo came to rule over a traditional two-class, provincial, peasant-based, backward and poor society and when he died in 1961, he left a society in transition, 'but still underdeveloped, with a capitalist economy deformed by monopolistic industrial growth.'[46] Since there existed neither democratic accountability, nor freely accessible institutions nor avenues for peaceful dissent, politics during the Trujillo years necessarily became conspiratorial and violent. This propensity of the political culture continued for years after the assassination of the dictator in 1961.

46 Frank Moya Pons, 1995, p.380.

The April 1965 coup against the provisional government unleashed urban civil war in the capital city which led to a United States invasion. The size (42,000 men), the mission (stop the communists) and the mechanism (secure OAS approval) all signalled a new determination on the part of the United States to take a fresh approach to keeping order in the Caribbean. Intervention would no longer be a 'surreptitious' action by the CIA – as in the Bay of Pigs, 1961 – but rather a massive military operation. Grenada, 1983, would be a sequel.

Contrary to what many were predicting, the Dominican people managed to return from the edge of the political precipice and create a dynamic, post-dictatorial political system. It was not without its imperfections and more than once it required pressure from both the United States and the international community to keep the democratization process on an even keel. Above and beyond the political institutionalization into parties and interest groups, political maneouvering has continued to be a function of *personalismo* and did not always respect the democratic and sovereign consent of the people. The inability of the widely popular José Francisco Peña Gómez to become president was not due solely to the fact that he was black and of Haitian descent. Certainly these were disadvantages, but they did not stop significant majorities from voting for him. He was indisputably the single most important leader of the country's largest and best-organized political party, the Partido Revolucionario Dominicano (PRD). It was, rather, the capacity to manipulate even the most sophisticated electoral and voting safeguards which better explain Peña's political fate. No one Dominican caudillo dominated the skills of electoral skulduggery, personal manipulation and strategic alliances with erstwhile enemies more adeptly than Joaquín Balaguer. The enemy of his enemy was invariably a potential ally. Having served dictator Trujillo for decades, Balaguer survived the fall of the strong man and served six elected terms between 1965 and 1996. He headed a party (the Partido Reformista Social Cristiano) but always marched to his own drummer. Such was the idiosyncratic nature of Balaguer's governance that in the election of 1996 he ignored the candidate of his own party and supported the young and relatively inexperienced candidate of a party organized on Leninist lines, Leonel Fernández, of the Partido de Liberación Dominicana (PLD). The alliance reflected Balaguer's historic capacity to make concessions in cases where it was impossible for him to hold power but which allowed him to stop sworn enemies from doing so.

It is too early to evaluate the performance of Leonel Fernández as president. It is however possible to note several aspects of his rise to power which say much about the Dominican Republic and its Caribbean context. First, as a returned immigrant from the United States, Fernández represents the fruits of the enormous migration to the United States which began in the early

1960s. He is a product of the increasingly bi-national and bilingual links between his native country and the perhaps million and a half Dominican immigrants in the United States. This trend towards bi-nationality can only grow and assume more importance both in the island and in the United States. Second, despite his political origins in the radical wing of the PLD, Fernández accelerated the process of economic restructuring which he had inherited. The privatization, decentralization and liberalization of the import-export regimes are the centres of gravity of his economic programme. Third, by opening up full diplomatic relations with Cuba, he gave notice that there is no single geo-political guideline in the Caribbean, that if hegemony still exists, it exists in modified form. Fourth, he forcefully signalled his intention of seeking fuller integration into Caribbean marketing arrangements such as CARICOM and the Central American Common Market. By the end of the 1990s, the Dominican Republic was a member of CARIFORUM and had been sponsored by the English-speaking Caribbean for membership in the Lomé Convention, which governs trade relations between the European Union and the ex-colonial states in Asia, the Caribbean and the Pacific.

In other words, contrary to the isolationism of the Trujillo-Balaguer era, with its exaggerated Hispanic ethno-nationalism, Fernández projected the Dominican Republic as a Caribbean country. Admittedly, not all the implications of that new orientation have yet revealed themselves. For one, the traditional Dominican hostility towards its immediate neighbour, Haiti, was still awaiting resolution as the millennium closed. It is true that the political leadership of Haiti had not made this process easy. Nothing about that state has been easy or uncomplicated.

The conflicts that occurred in Haiti between the end of the American Occupation (1915–33) and the rise of François ('Papa Doc') Duvalier in 1957 were traditional ones between black and mulatto élites and their supporters in the army. Much of this changed in the first years of the Duvalier presidency. Faced with a rebellious officer corps, Duvalier first built two counterforces, a paramilitary guard soon nicknamed the 'Tontons Macoute', and then the much larger National Security Volunteers. Second, he instituted – and systematically carried out – the death penalty for conspiracy, whether actual or even seriously contemplated. Third, he changed the constitution, making himself 'president for life' and, upon his death, having that presidency pass on to his only son, Jean-Claude ('Baby Doc') Duvalier. 'Baby Doc', however, had none of the steel-willed and ruthless determination to exterminate real and potential enemies, had no links to the Voodoo priests (*hougans*), and, because he married a mulatto, could not claim the *noirist* (black) leadership of his father. He was thus less able to resist the pressures from and the emphasis on human rights of the Jimmy Carter administration in the United States. 'Baby Doc' simply did not have the staying power of his father. Faced with widespread rioting, he decided to accept a French offer of exile and an American offer to transport him to that country.

This sketch of Haitian political history highlights the second fundamental operating principle of Haitian politics: it has always been a deadly game in which there are no second prizes; winning is everything – call it holistic intransigence. It characterized the four short-lived military regimes which followed 'Baby Doc's' departure and the final emergence in the late 1980s of a charismatic – some would say messianic – figure. The story from that point is a complex one combining continuities with a violent past, attempted changes by an idealistic movement with a legitimate grass-roots following, and above all, the dramatic figure of Jean-Bertrand Aristide.

National and international revulsion at the attack by armed thugs on Aristide's St Jean Bosco Church on 11 September 1988 – which left 13 dead and 70 wounded – led to the overthrow of General Henri Namphy's military government on 18 September. Another wing of the military was ready to occupy the presidential palace. It was time to put one's hopes on yet another uniformed man, namely General Prosper Avril, who was once a loyal servant of the Duvaliers – a true wolf in sheep's clothing. Hope has to spring eternal among those who follow Haitian events, even though that hope invariably flies in the face of incontrovertible experience. 'Of the four governments to rule Haiti since the departure of Jean-Claude Duvalier,' United States Deputy Assistant Secretary of State for Caribbean Affairs, Richard Melton said after the coup, 'we judge the Avril government as offering the best, and perhaps the last real chance for democratic reform in Haiti for the foreseeable future.'[47]

Melton spoke too soon. Although the bloody attack on Aristide and his parishioners had triggered the coup, that event should have alerted Haiti watchers to the disintegration in the military. A series of purges in the post-Duvalier period had fissured the military hierarchy, and this at a time when the benefits from smuggling (from toothpaste to illegal drugs) were increasing the perquisites of a military career. Indiscipline and greed are fatal to any organized body, and perhaps even more so to one that has a monopoly on force. It is therefore important to note that the coup that brought down Namphy was led by Sergeant Joseph Hébreux and his non-commissioned-officer colleagues. It was the first entry into Haitian politics of the *ti soldats* (little soldiers), a fact that gave the more populist-oriented some hope.

Paralleling the collapse of military discipline was the rise of a series of paramilitary groups, again without any known central command. Haitians

---

47 Quoted in Anthony P. Maingot, 1996a, p.145.

called them variously *grupes sans maman* (groups without mothers), *zenglendo* (bandits), or simply *escadrons de la mort* (death squads).

In March 1990, the pattern of apparently uncontrollable anarchic behaviour – strikes, crime, roving gangs – brought down the Avril regime. This time General Hérard Abraham was the saviour, mainly because he did not take the presidential sash himself but rather bestowed it on Ertha Pascal-Trouillot, a Supreme Court Justice.

Abraham won the respect of a wide array of foreign groups, from the Organization of American States (OAS) to ex-President Jimmy Carter's special electoral observation team. The state machinery, however, was in an advanced state of decomposition. Military units in outlying towns refused to accept the officers assigned by Abraham, Pascal-Trouillot admitted that her government was unable to collect taxes and pay its employees. Even the committee set up by Abraham for the elections he had called was said to be penniless.

Haiti thus held its first truly democratic elections on 16 December 1990, in a state of near anarchy and with a bankrupt government. The elections were carried out with foreign funding (an estimated $40 million), under foreign supervision (civilian and military), and even with foreign management. These were the elections that Aristide swept with a movement called Se Lavalas (we will wash away). He never gave the appearance of being a conventional seeker of formal political office. In fact, he made a distinct point of dismissing constitutional and party politics as irrelevant. Asked as late as May 1990 whether he had political ambitions, he responded, 'I do not suffer from that sickness.' And yet he constantly advocated and called for political change. So sudden and unexpected was Aristide's entry into the 1990 electoral campaign that he was not listed in the handbook prepared for the election of 29 May 1990 by the National Democratic Institute for International Affairs.

His was more a messianic movement than a campaign. 'You see,' Aristide told a veteran Haiti watcher, 'I don't have to campaign. It's the people who will do the campaigning.' He had, he said, 'accepted this rendezvous with history'; he was 'one with the Haitian spirit'.[48] Certainly his status as a priest, even though expelled from the Salesian order, contributed to this nearly ethereal image. There was nothing here of the traditional Haitian-Caribbean macho man. The aura of purity and cleansing the Se Lavalas movement invoked was a winning combination; Aristide won nearly 70 per cent of the vote in an election that attracted 85 per cent of the electorate. He swept every section of the island. It was a national victory.

But Aristide's political problem had been evident from the start. Surrounded by ideologues and idealists, all political amateurs, Aristide never

48 *Ibid.*, p.146.

seemed able to distinguish friend from foe. Worse, he never seemed interested in the profane art of political maneouvering. In fact, he seemed to excel at turning allies into opponents. It need not have been that way. Despite social chaos and the bankruptcy of the State, Aristide had several things going for him in addition to his massive popular support; most importantly, the support of the United States and other contributors of substantial foreign aid. Yet Aristide soon committed his most costly errors: marginalizing, then antagonizing and eventually attacking his own political party and its followers in the legislature, and then the international donors. This behaviour best revealed not only Aristide's *modus operandi* but how soon and completely he had acquired the Haitian habit of 'holistic intolerance' and of emphasizing the presidency as the only significant office: *personalismo* in its purest form.

No one, however, predicted a significant political crisis. The army was thought to have been brought under civilian control. The government had secured a $442-million loan from a consortium led by the World Bank, and the United States Ambassador, Alvin P. Adams, Jr, commented that Aristide 'has gotten off to a very credible start. The process is well begun.' Even the formerly sceptical business community was cheered by what it perceived as a new realism on his part.

In September 1991 Aristide made a triumphal trip to the United Nations, and received keys to the cities of New York and Miami. On 30 September, the day after his return to Haiti, Aristide was overthrown by what was apparently a rabble of soldiers and police. The *ti soldats* brutally suppressed public protests, and the president was courageously freed from detention and escorted to the airport by the French and United States Ambassadors.

The accusation that the Haitian élite and the army overthrew Aristide is certainly unimpeachable. But it does not tell the whole story. After all, no one, certainly not Aristide, ever entertained the illusion that the bourgeoisie was his friend. The same holds true for many of the corrupt bureaucrats and military men. Their interests were direct targets of Aristide's speeches and policies. The task is not to ask who were his class enemies but rather, who were his steadfast friends, and did they – could they – make any difference in the boiling Haitian political cauldron?

Part of the answer to the first part of the question can be approached from the angle of the experienced editor of Haiti's *Le Nouvelliste*, who wrote on 30 August 1991 that the 'fratricidal' struggle for power between Aristide and his *Selavalassien* clique and the members of the other parties with whom they formed the government could 'end in a catastrophe.' The explanation was relatively simple: the former had the mantle of newness, honesty and sincerity, and the latter had the political sagacity and contacts. At the time of writing this chapter, and after a massive American intervention and considerable assistance from the international community, Haitian politics is still stymied, not to say paralysed, by the internecine struggles of the 'democratic' politicians. The four years of President Raoul Préval ended after the presidential elections of December 2000, an election which all the opponents of Aristide's newly-named 'Fami Lavalas' party vowed to boycott and which was won by that party's candidate, Jean-Bertrand Aristide. He controls both the House and the Senate, and can change the constitution at will, appoint all state officers, civilian and police, and do all this with considerable popular support, at least initially.

In his superbly revealing study of Haitian politics, David Nicholls cautions that when Haitians quote the proverb, 'Apré bon dié sé léta' (after God comes the State), 'it is not the goodness or the benevolence of God that people have in mind; it is rather His remoteness, unpredictability, and power.'[49]

If this is true of God, how much truer it must be of the State, which has historically been feared by that mass of dispossessed – and increasingly displaced – peasants. For 200 years the meagre yet amazingly munificent cow called the State has nurtured a small élite and a much larger middle sector. Interestingly enough, the battles in post-dictatorship Haiti are still largely over control of the state-owned corporations and the many jobs, prebends and, let it be said, sinecures they guarantee. As such, Haiti's political trajectory has been very different from that of the rest of the Caribbean. All indications are that, at least over the short to medium term, it will continue to be an object of Caribbean and international concern.

Conclusion

Short of full-scale social and political revolution, which by the end of the 1990s appeared nowhere in the offing, these West Indian societies will probably not soon radically change their political systems. It is also highly unlikely that they will be able to break out of the present pattern of demographic and other structural pressures which have existed for decades. Similarly, the dependence on external markets, capital and investment will probably continue for at least the short to medium term. What has changed dramatically is the way in which élites evaluate and define these problems. The tendency by the end of the millennium was to ask: in the global economy of the late 1990s, what does economic independence mean and which nation has it? The

49 David Nicholls, 1985, p.220.

fact is that everywhere in the Caribbean, even in Cuba, there is an acknowledgment and then a bending to the global exigencies of the times. This sense of realism and pragmatism appears to be a general trait. The lack of dogmatism, flexibility, and the ability to survive the best of times and the worst of times, have always been the greatest strengths of Caribbean peoples. It is interesting that there is no agreement on what the explanation for this collective good sense might be. One explanation has to do with the experiences derived from smallness and vulnerability, the 'be agile and on your toes, and never over-commit yourself' posture. Some see it as a legacy of slavery: the determination never to be enslaved in any form or fashion again. There is plausibility to this latter interpretation which interestingly enough also serves to explain the Caribbean peoples' capacity to explode in protest against injustices of all kinds. A keen capacity for moral indignation is an ongoing Caribbean characteristic. Another explanation is the live-and-let-live attitudes characteristic of societies where everyone was 'transported' from elsewhere. Pretensions of all types are invariably levelled, sometimes by the biting humour and ridicule of popular music, often by open, though civil, resistance, and occasionally by outright retaliation. Whatever the explanations, the fact is that in this post-Cold War era, the Caribbean will need all its good and democratic instincts to tackle not just the enduring and intractable problems described in this chapter but also some of the new challenges which were revealing themselves as the new century began.

9

THE FORCES OF REGIONAL CO-OPERATION, 1942–97

Antonio Gaztambide-Géigel

VARIOUS and often contradictory forces have shaped the discourse and practice of regional co-operation in the Caribbean since the Second World War. Many of these forces – such as cultural heritages and international identities – have been simultaneously internal and external to the region. Some have been only external, such as imperial policies and the evolution of capitalism, while others can be considered internal to the region, as is the case with national identities and leaders, and diverse social groups. Most of these have stimulated as much as they have deterred efforts and projects of co-operation. At least until the 1970s, however, nothing galvanized cooperation in the Caribbean as much as the ideas and projects of economic development.

Antecedents, forces and levels of co-operation

Ideas and projects of regional co-operation and integration have been propagated in the region since the nineteenth century. The birth of some Latin American republics bathed by Caribbean waters was of a federative nature; as was the case with Central America, and Colombia, Ecuador and Venezuela. In the rest of the Hispanic Caribbean, Cuban, Dominican and Puerto Rican revolutionaries proposed the idea of the 'Antillean Federation' (or 'Confederation of the Antilles'). More significantly, Dominicans and Puerto Ricans fought in the Cuban war of independence and they all conspired for Puerto Rican independence.

In the territories of the other European powers, the continuation of colonialism itself provided attempts at joint administration. Such was the case when Great Britain, the empire with the greatest number of Caribbean colonies, set up a joint regime for the Leeward Islands. Several 'Royal Commissions' proposed – particularly after the abolition of slavery – a number of federative formulas that would make the government of the colonies more efficient and less costly. The Dutch Empire attempted the same, governing their Leeward Islands, the 'Curaçao islands' and Suriname jointly from Paramaribo between 1828 and 1845.[1]

Before that, both smuggling and varied forms of legal trade had created communication networks between the territories of the various European powers. After 1791, slave resistance made Haiti a mythical promised land that should be emulated or, in some cases, fled to. The abolitionist struggles also created communication and co-operation networks, particularly in the British colonies.[2]

Ironically, the Antillean identity weakened in the Hispanic Caribbean, somewhat distancing itself from the rest of the region after the Cuban-Spanish-American War. The 'search for identity' that loomed among Spanish-speakers on the arrival of United States imperialism in 1898 adopted Hispanic and Latin American, rather than Antillean, expressions. In the territories of the European powers, however, federative ideas began to take on a new resonance among local élites. Furthermore, the imperialist partition of Africa after 1885 renewed Afro-American and Afro-Antillean identities that would have an outstanding expression in the movement known as *négritude.*[3]

In that sense, the oldest forces in inter-Caribbean relations are those diverse cultural heritages which, beyond their linguistic dimensions, have ethno-racial roots. On the one hand, ethno-cultural perceptions distanced the Hispanic from the non-Hispanic part of the region. On the other hand, Afro-Antillean identity became central to the strongest of the various international identities labelled 'Caribbean': the one that makes it the same as 'West Indian' and 'Antillean'.[4]

A second, more recent influence was advanced capitalist imperialism. The transformations in the sugar industry, as well as in transportation and communications, during the last third of the nineteenth century, slowly weakened centuries-old identities and communication links.[5] This 'new' imperialism thus fragmented a region which, ironically, had been integrated between the seventeenth and nineteenth centuries by the slave-labour plantations and the rivalries of mercantilist imperialism.

---

1 Gordon K. Lewis, 1968, particularly chaps 5 and 6; Cornelis Ch. Goslinga, 1979, chaps 18 and 25.

2 Gordon K. Lewis, 1983, chap.4.

3 For an interpretation of both searches for identity as part of the same phenomenon, see René Depestre, 1987, pp.337–62.

4 On the subject of the ethno-racial dimension, see *Diversidad cultural y tensión regional: América Latina y el Caribe*, 1993, pp.11–17. About Caribbean identities, see Antonio Gaztambide, 1996a, pp.74–96.

5 About these transformations, although focused on the sugar industry, see Manuel Moreno Fraginals, 1983b, pp.56–117.

Both forces continue to influence the international dynamics of the region. It has been said, and rightly so, that co-operation within the Caribbean has come about as a result of imperial initiatives, or in the course of opposing them, but never detached from the hegemonic powers. At the same time, the rise of decolonization and nationalism – originally favourable to co-operation – ended up generating a centrifugal effect of national projects and identities wary of any 'alien' influences.[6]

This approach, however, gives too much weight to government forces, tending to overlook the multiple communications between human beings who in the process cultivate or erode the co-operation schemes reached between governments. These non-governmental forces, ranging all the way from foreign corporations to sporting events, have increasingly helped to mould the future of international relations in the Caribbean, which were mostly – as in the rest of the world up until the Second World War – relations between nation-states.

One of the significant changes of our own time is precisely that peoples have more openly taken possession of their histories, including their relations. Imperialism itself has evolved into what some have christened 'hegemonism', moving away from classic colonialism and acknowledging – at least formally – a community of peoples with the same collective and individual rights.[7] Although we have been talking about their importance for some time now, we continue to study mainly the governments.

The first impact of the War can thus be visualized in terms of self-determination of the peoples, mass democracy and economic development. The contemporaneity of the idea of development needs to be underscored in order to understand better one of the peculiarities of our time and the most notable force in regional co-operation. This chapter adopts as a point of departure the transformation and ever more central role of economic development in this process. Unleashed as a questioning of the capitalist countries' economic hegemony, the ideas and discourses about development have moved and shaped the greater part of regional co-operation.

Self-determination, democracy and development: The impact of the Second World War, 1942–58

The Second World War was, perhaps, the first truly worldwide war. Allied governments promoted through the Atlantic Charter the idea that they were

6 Francine Jácome, 1994, pp.243–50.

7 See, for example, Antonio Gaztambide, 1991 (1993), pp.29–55.

fighting for democracy, development (which did not yet have that name) and the self-determination of all peoples. These objectives aroused great expectations, especially for colonial peoples.

Latin America and the colonial Caribbean reflected this phenomenon in a particularly dramatic way. The formal renunciation of both unilateral military and open political intervention was the most coherent and consistent aspect of an initial stage of the Good Neighbor Policy of the United States government. During the War, the priority of 'anti-Axis hemispheric solidarity' generated a flexible and often contradictory diplomacy in favour of economic co-operation.[8]

The establishment of the Anglo-American Caribbean Commission in 1942 was the main counterpart of this second stage of the Good Neighbor Policy for the colonial territories. In their case, the initiative came from Charles W. Taussig, President of the American Molasses Company of New York, but the motivation stemmed equally from the geo-political interests dictated by the War. First, the British Caribbean became especially important to the USA because of the air and naval bases acquired in 1940 in exchange for old destroyers. Second, the whole area turned into an object of concern because of the threat to the Panama Canal and to the flow of strategic products, particularly bauxite and petroleum, by German submarines and discontented populations.[9]

By forming a bilateral commission, presided over by Taussig and the British Sir Frank Stockdale, Franklin D. Roosevelt's government decided against the alternative of occupying the British Caribbean, as proposed by the Governor of Puerto Rico, Rexford G. Tugwell.[10] Indeed, the War imposed upon the United States and Great Britain the liberalization of their colonial regimes and opened up a space for a variety of populist alternatives. There was a mutual influence between the reformist project and experience in Puerto Rico and the framing of a project for the British possessions.

The British, indeed, were pioneers in referring to the 'economic development of underdeveloped countries' when they approved the Colonial Development and Welfare Act in 1940. As a result of the 'Moyne Report' of 1938–9, Stockdale had been appointed the first Comptroller for Development and Welfare in the West Indies and his successors would continue to represent Great Britain in the Commission.[11] As we shall see, the success of this

---

8 For a more detailed discussion, see chap.3 of this volume.

9 On the colonial Caribbean in this section, see Antonio Gaztambide, 1989, pp.109–21, and Humberto García Muñíz, 1988, chaps 1 and 2.

10 Howard Johnson, 1984a, pp.26–47.

11 Great Britain, Colonial Office, 1947, p.1. On the British and development, see, for example, the participation of British and colonial economists in the seminal works included in A. N. Agarwala and S. P. Singh, 1958.

formula would lead – after the War – to its expansion to the whole colonial Caribbean.

Very diverse forces in the Caribbean republics, although touched less directly by the War, took advantage of this juncture to call for new human relations. In Latin America, the Great Depression of the 1930s had generated a challenge to the traditional oligarchies and imperialism that has been characterized as populism. Accelerated by the War, these changes – and the discourses that validated 'economic planning' – spread throughout the region. The Antillean republics thus participated in the efforts made by Latin American governments between 1947 and 1948, to replace the unilateral Pan-Americanism of the Monroe Doctrine with multilateral inter-American relations.[12]

As a concession to these efforts, and within the context of the Cold War, the Inter-American Treaty for Reciprocal Assistance was approved and the Organization of American States (OAS) was created. On the other hand, while an economic agreement at the OAS was impossible, the region obtained at the United Nations an Economic Commission for Latin America (ECLA). Contesting Washington's protests and maneouvres, the region opted for ECLA as a better forum for their interests than the OAS's Economic and Social Council.

Partly as a reaction to the ideas and tendencies represented by ECLA, United States president Harry S. Truman announced in his 1949 inaugural address an international technical co-operation programme that would come to be known as 'Point Four'. The following year, Truman started to articulate a new policy towards Latin America, baptized in 1954 by his successor, Dwight D. Eisenhower, as the Good Partner Policy. As with the second stage of the Good Neighbor, United States policies towards the rest of the colonial Caribbean and Puerto Rico followed parallel courses.

In March 1946, the Anglo-American Commission became the Caribbean Commission, incorporating representatives from France and the Netherlands. The Commission continued to be a colonial institution, but since 1945 delegations had been expanded to four members in order to give 'natives' some representation. The second West Indian Conference – until then the only forum accessible to Antilleans – met simultaneously with representatives from the 15 territories under the four colonial powers.[13]

Economic development remained the greatest interest of colonial representatives, who in turn used other fora to promote their respective political rights, until around 1950 when conflicts began to arise between the forces represented in the Commission. The 'natives' spoke in the name of govern-

12 About the United States and Latin America in the rest of this section, see Antonio Gaztambide, 1986.

13 'An Agreement for the Establishment of the Caribbean Commission', in Herbert Corkran, 1970, pp.213–19.

ments increasingly representative and autonomous. The imperial powers, in turn, devised diverse ways of responding to their claims for greater self-government and economic development, coinciding in their resistance to a greater participation by Antilleans in the Commission.

The forces that would bring the Commission to its demise, however, would be more complex. Puerto Ricans would move towards a more Antillean and Latin Americanist identity within the context of Point Four and general support for democratic movements. Others, however, did not share the same enthusiasm for closer relations with the United States. British colonies, in particular, put more emphasis on the dissolution of colonial ties while at the same time maintaining a prudent distance from the new metropolis.

While the colonial Caribbean worked in co-operation towards development and self-determination, the rest of the region was besieged by a chain of dictatorships in the Antillean, Central American and continental republics. A fluid 'Caribbean Legion' had gained prestige since 1948 as a result of the anti-dictatorial struggle – led by José Figueres – in Costa Rica, also stimulated by the democratic governments of Cuba, Guatemala and Venezuela.[14] In the middle of the next decade, on the contrary, Costa Rica would find itself isolated within a sea of dictators, to such an extreme that there was also talk of an 'International of the Swords'.

Within that context, Puerto Rico projected itself in various ways as a democratic and developmentalist oasis. On the one hand, the government received the exiled Venezuelan leader, Rómulo Betancourt, who had been forced out of Figueres' Costa Rica by the United States, and Muñoz Marín cultivated the friendship of both in what would later be known as the 'Democratic Left'. At the same time, its new élite hardly dissimulated their lack of sympathy for the governments of Fulgencio Batista in Cuba and Rafael Leonidas Trujillo in the Dominican Republic, and supported those in exile who were fighting to overthrow them. On the other hand, the outstanding role of government and economic planning in Puerto Rican projects and in Point Four also seemed to go against the grain of metropolitan policy.

Rise and fall of the imperial initiatives: The enduring impact of the Federation of the West Indies and decolonization, 1958–67

The project for a Federation of the West Indies was developed parallel to and stimulated by the Caribbean Commission. Its genesis combined British and

14 Charles D. Ameringer, 1974.

Antillean forces, these coming mainly from the Lesser Antilles. These were the leaders and groups that, since the 1930s, had identified the federative project with the feasibility of greater self-government (meaning both democratization and increasing independence), and who in turn had emerged as powerful actors with the expansion of suffrage after the War. The unequal advance of both aspects of self-determination in the various territories, however, would end up undermining the project itself.[15]

Although short-lived, the Federation shaped the most consistent force in regional co-operation – the English-speaking territories. It was created in the course of a decade, during three conferences called by the metropolis: the first in Montego Bay, Jamaica, in 1947, and the other two in London, in 1953 and 1956. The Bahamas and Bermuda were not invited in 1947. The continental territories of British Guiana (now Guyana) and British Honduras (now Belize) – as well as the British Virgin Islands – excluded themselves in 1951. So the long, complex, and often bitter negotiations were developed with and between the representatives of the British islands minus the Virgins.

On July 1957 London approved – without formally granting the condition of Dominion Status (equivalent to independence within the British Commonwealth) – the Constitution of the West Indies.[16] The West Indies federal government was inaugurated on 3 January 1958 with the arrival of the Governor-General, Lord Hailes, in the federal capital in Trinidad, established after long discussions. The Federal House of Representatives was elected shortly thereafter and the government formally inaugurated – with great celebrations – on 22 April. Sir Grantley Adams, majority leader in Barbados, was elected prime minister.

The government was completed by a 19-member Senate, appointed by the Governor-General in consultation with the territories, a modest Supreme Court, and a Council of State (Cabinet) with no less than three members to be chosen from the Senate and the remainder from the House. The Federation included 13 islands organized into ten local and two subregional governments, thus:

- *Local governments:* Barbados, Jamaica, Trinidad & Tobago, Antigua, Montserrat, St Kitts-Nevis-Anguilla, Dominica, Grenada, St Lucia and St Vincent;
- *Subregional governments:* Leewards Group (Antigua, Montserrat and St Kitts-Nevis-Anguilla), and Windwards Group (Dominica, Grenada, St Lucia and St Vincent).

15 About the Federation, see especially John Mordecai, 1968.

16 Great Britain, Parliament, 1960. Subsequent references are taken from this version.

The government that they inaugurated with such pomp, however, was extremely weak, in terms of composition as well as resources and areas of jurisdiction. The constitution prohibited simultaneous membership in the federal and insular parliaments, so most of the unit leaders chose the local sphere. The decision, above all, by Norman Manley – Jamaica's prime minister and leader of the People's National Party (PNP) – not to run for the prime minister's position in the Federation, anticipated the forces that would bring the Federation to its demise. As a result, the elections left the West Indies Federal Labour Party holding a plurality of 22 out of 45 seats in the House against 20 for the opposition.

Inadequately financed by a mandatory levy from the units, the federal government could do little more than to manage its own operations plus the West India Regiment (in charge of defence), the University College of the West Indies and the Federal Shipping Service. In his first 'Address from the Throne', the Governor-General complained about these three institutions absorbing 60 per cent of the budget.[17] The Federation further assumed the responsibilities of the Development and Welfare Organization and of the Regional Economic Committee (established in May 1951), also managing the respective transfers.[18] It is worth noting that most of these bodies existed prior to 1958 – and would survive the end of the Federation in 1962.

In September 1961 a plurality of the Jamaican electorate voted against remaining in the Federation, in a referendum held as a result of a public proposal by Sir Alexander Bustamante and his Jamaica Labour Party (JLP). Immediate British acceptance led to Jamaica's independence and the end of the federative project the following year. Eric Williams, prime minister of Trinidad & Tobago, maintained his position – in spite of multiple efforts, particularly by the leaders of the smaller islands – that Jamaican secession implied the end, dramatized by the phrase: 'Ten minus one equals zero.'

Most authors point to the differences between Jamaica and Trinidad, or to the former's wariness of the Federation, as the decisive factor in the project's demise. Federal economic weakness certainly had its roots in Jamaica's preference for an internal free trade system – as opposed to a customs union from the rest of the world – as something more compatible with its plans for development. Trinidad, in turn, only accepted the immigration that would come with the 'free movement of people' if it came hand in hand with the customs union. What proved fatal was the combination of these disagreements with the acceleration of independence, Jamaican internal politics and the deterioration of relations between the three main federalist leaders: Adams, Manley and Williams.

17 Quoted by John Mordecai, 1968, p.97.

18 Great Britain, Colonial Office, 1958, pp.5–12.

These three factors exemplify the centrifugal effect of the formation of national projects and identities wary of any 'alien' influences. One should not underestimate, for example, the weight of Williams' preference for a strong federative scheme in contrast to 'federalist' Manley's minimalist inclinations. According to a participant who later became one of its principal scholars: 'Thus when the Federation was created in 1958, it was for the Eastern Caribbean the fulfilment of the political ambitions of forty years, backed by much sentiment and propaganda, whereas in Jamaica it was still a recent and strange idea, hardly a dozen years old, which had not yet sunk into the popular subconscious.'[19]

Meanwhile, it took the imperial powers over three years to move towards transforming the Caribbean Commission into a less colonial institution. The new Caribbean Organization would start off haunted by this indifference from the metropoles, the Federation's unwillingness to assume the British economic contribution, and the refusal by Williams' government to pay for the expenses of the Commission's headquarters in Port of Spain. Williams had publicly expressed his hostility ever since he had been dismissed, in 1955, from the third-ranking position in the Commission's hierarchy, in charge of research.

Ironically, the transformation of the Commission into the Organization came about under an agreement between the metropoles, signed in Washington in June 1960, and put into effect in San Juan, Puerto Rico in September 1961.[20] With its headquarters at that capital city, but keeping Martinique's Clovis F. Beauregard as Secretary-General, the Organization's Caribbean Council convened, with representatives from the French Departments of Guadeloupe, Guyane, and Martinique, the Netherlands Antilles, Suriname, Guyana (still British), the British and US Virgin Islands, the West Indies (the Federation) and Puerto Rico.

With the Federation's disappearance in 1962, and the subsequent absence of Jamaica and Trinidad & Tobago, the endeavour was doomed to fail. By 1964, the ten smaller islands of the former Federation were listed as 'special observers', while the Bahamas and British Honduras were listed as 'prospective members'.[21] Having received notice of withdrawal from Guyana, Suriname and – above all – Puerto Rico, the fifth meeting, held in Curaçao at the end of that year, finally decided on its dissolution. The Caribbean Organization – as Herbert Corkran concludes – 'finally floundered on the twin

19 John Mordecai, 1968, p.30.

20 'Agreement for the Establishment of the Caribbean Organization and Annexed Statute of the Caribbean Organization, signed at Washington, 21st June 1960, and into force September 1961' in Herbert Corkran, 1970, Appendices C and D, pp.224–34.

21 Caribbean Organization, 1964, p.29.

43 Wedding party, St Kitts, c. 1940

44 and 45 West Indian emigrants in Cuba, c. 1920

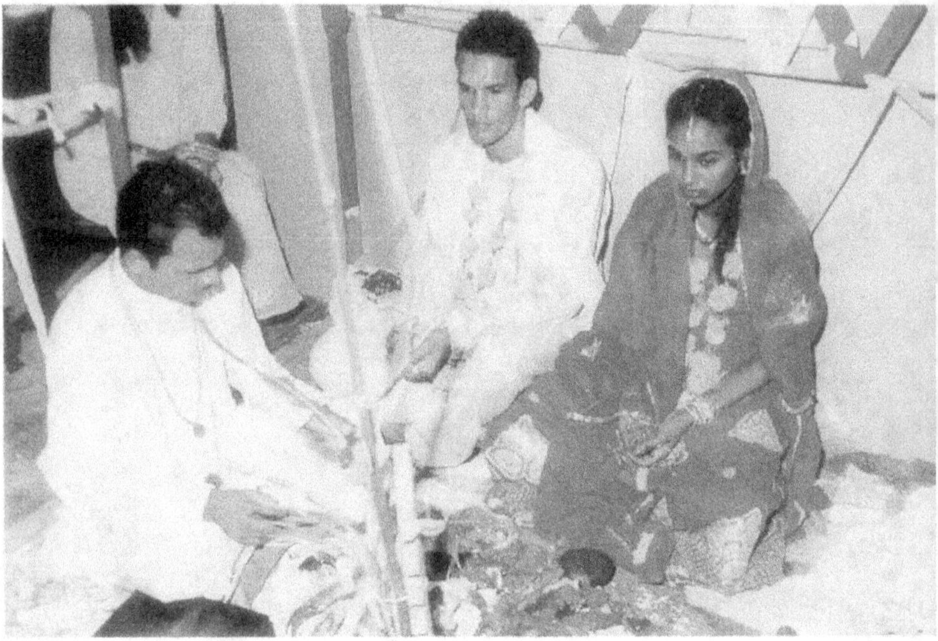

46 Hindu wedding, Guyana

47 Hindu pundits, Trinidad, early twentieth century

48 Muslim gathering, Guyana, c.1950

49 Jordanites, Guyana

50 Queen's College netball team, Barbados, 1951

51 'Pan around the neck' steelband, Trinidad & Tobago

52 Women in traditional dress, Dominica

53 West Indian emigrant priest, St Thomas Apostolic Church, Cuba, c.1920

54 Grandchildren of West Indian emigrants dancing the Maypole, Baragua, Cuba

55 West Indies cricket team, 1928

56 Rastafarian, Jamaica

57 African consciousness expressed in dress, Jamaica

58 British Caribbean politicians discussing Federation at Lancaster House, London, 1956; from left: N. W. Manley and E. L. Allen (Jamaica), V. C. Bird (Antigua), and Robert Bradshaw (St Kitts)

59 Advisory Council to the Governor-General of the Federation of the West Indies, Port of Spain, 1958

60 Lady Springer, Prime Minister Bernard St John, Queen Elizabeth II, Governor-General Sir Hugh Springer, Mrs St John, Prince Philip, Barbados, 1985

61 Grantley Adams, Barbados

62 Rosan Girard, Guadeloupe

63 Maurice Bishop, Grenada

64 Eugenia Charles, Dominica

65 United States troops patrol St George's, Grenada, 1983

66 Celia Cruz, Cuba

67 Mutabaruka, Jamaica

68 Nicolás Guillén, Cuba

69 University of Puerto Rico tower at Rio Piedras, San Juan

70 Imperial College of Tropical Agriculture, now the Administration Building of the University of the West Indies, St Augustine, Trinidad & Tobago

71 University of Havana, Cuba

72 Université des Antilles et Guyane, Fouillole, Guadeloupe

73 Preparing to ship bananas, mid-twentieth century

74 Alumina plant, Clarendon, Jamaica, 1970

75 Work floor, clothing factory, Barbados

76 Titchfield Hotel, Port Antonio, Jamaica, 1905

77 Modern beach hotel, Boscobel, Jamaica

78 Caribbean vernacular architecture, Port of Spain, Trinidad & Tobago

79 Los Wild Indians, Dominican Republic

80 Ernie Ranglin, Jamaica

81 Louise Bennett, 'Miss Lou', Jamaica

82 Robert Nesta 'Bob' Marley, Jamaica

rocks of the ever-growing formal autonomy of many of the territories in the region, side by side with the stubbornly persisting economic and even political dependency of most of them on the metropolitan powers.'[22]

The government of Puerto Rico had announced its intention, since the Curaçao meeting, to continue with its efforts through the Caribbean Economic Development Corporation (CODECA), created by law on June 1965, together with a 'Plan for Informal Co-operation', meaning without metropolitan participation.[23] With Puerto Rico's Luis A. Passalacqua Christian as its Executive Director, CODECA physically occupied the Organization's offices and took custody of its library on behalf of the government of Puerto Rico. CODECA collapsed after the election in Puerto Rico in 1968 of a government uninterested in the region, but the library and documentation accumulated since the Anglo-American Commission are still at the Caribbean Regional Library of the University of Puerto Rico at Río Piedras.

In contrast with the Commission, however, co-operation efforts also continued in the Commonwealth Caribbean, where the Federation had an impact that would last to the present. Paradoxically, its most enduring legacy was perhaps the consolidation of a West Indian identity – nearly non-existent at the beginning of this period – which in turn adopted the Caribbean identity as its own. The institutions of co-operation that survived, such as the Caribbean Meteorological Service and the West Indies Shipping Corporation (WISCO), contributed to this process. The most important – given its implications in the formation of intellectual and professional élites – is the University of the West Indies (UWI), which in 1962 consolidated the programmes located in Mona, Jamaica, with those in St Augustine, Trinidad and later added another main campus at Cave Hill, Barbados.

The contradictory effect of the Cuban and the cultural revolutions, 1959–79

The 1959 Cuban Revolution restored the Caribbean to the leading role in the international scene it had lost for nearly two hundred years. Ironically, although it related intensely and later on consistently to part of the region, the revolution adopted and fostered Latin American and so-called Third World

22 Herbert Corkran, 1970, p.151.

23 'Act Creating the Caribbean Development Corporation, 1965', and 'Plan for Informal Cooperation in the Caribbean, submitted by the Government of Puerto Rico to the Conference on Economic Coordination in the Caribbean, Puerto Rico, May 1965', in Roy Preiswerk, 1970, pp.253–60.

identities above any variation of Caribbean identities. In this and other ways, its impact would not only be centrifugal but also polarizing in the region's international relations. Yet Cuba established and promoted new types and principles of regional co-operation.

Just like the 1961 Alliance for Progress, the revolution would be an expression as well as a result of a crisis in the Latin American policies of the United States. Coinciding with – and perhaps intensifying – the end of the first co-operation initiatives, both would end up cancelling out the OAS's potential for co-operation. Additionally, the region would be the principal stage for both, since they were precipitated by the fall of two dictators supported by Washington: Marcos Pérez Jiménez of Venezuela, in January 1958, and Fulgencio Batista of Cuba, in January 1959.

The Caribbean's Democratic Left, on the contrary, was strengthened by the dictators' poor socio-economic performance and the support of burgeoning bourgeoisies. ECLA's prestige also grew, since its most systematic support came from the populist and democratic regimes of South America and it seemed to diagnose precisely what was happening. The process that followed would complete the transition into the second phase, the developmentalist period of the Good Partner Policy, now under the name of Alliance for Progress.

In this first developmentalist pact, the United States foreign policy élite would identify with industrialization supported both by the individual states and multilateral efforts. In return, Latin American bourgeoisies would accept a greater participation of United States private capital in the process. Washington, however, would still try to sell the 'Puerto Rican model' of unrestricted expansion of its economy.[24]

Another Caribbean element of the Alliance, then, was the leading role played by Puerto Rico with the appointment of Teodoro Moscoso, first as United States Ambassador to Venezuela and then as Alliance co-ordinator, as well as Arturo Morales Carrión's appointment as Deputy Assistant Secretary of State for Inter-American Affairs. This excessive 'Puerto Ricanness' of the project revealed the limited extent of United States concessions, thus restricting its impact beyond the Caribbean Basin.[25]

Finally, the role of the Dominican Republic, in the development and conclusion of this very brief chapter of inter-American co-operation for democracy and development, rounds off the picture of the region's protagonist role. The isolation of Trujillo's dictatorship and the subsequent support for the elected government of Juan Bosch symbolized the Alliance's commitment to democracy. The rapid overthrow of Bosch's government and the sub-

24 Jerome Levinson and Juan de Onís, 1970.

25 Walter R. Bonilla Carlo, 1998.

sequent co-operation of the OAS with the United States invasion of Santo Domingo in 1965 marked the end of the episode and also of the OAS as an effective co-operation mechanism.[26]

The consolidation of another dictatorial regime, François Duvalier's in Haiti, completed the centrifugal effect of the Cuban Revolution over the Antillean republics, and for decades made co-operation between their governments impossible. More so since, during its first decade, Cuba's international policy emphasized support to guerrilla movements and other groups contesting the dominant élites. Paradoxically, that same policy fostered co-operation between non-governmental forces.

Other initiatives by revolutionary Cuba also encouraged non-governmental co-operation in areas such as culture, health, and sports, in which Cuba maintained and even broadened its co-operation with other Antillean societies. This occurred especially after 1968, when the worldwide cultural revolution and the relative weakening of United States hegemony coincided with the 'institutionalization' period in Cuba, and a more Third World – and along the way Caribbean – rather than revolutionary international policy.[27]

The earliest and most symptomatic of these initiatives was the Casa de las Américas, engaged in literary and cultural co-operation since 1959. During the 1970s, for example, the annual literary contest sponsored by the Casa added alternate categories of English, French and Creole language literatures. Regional-identity institutions were also multiplied, such as the Casa del Caribe in Santiago de Cuba, and its Caribbean cultural festivals which have been held since 1981.

In the area of sports, Havana had been the venue for the first Central American and Caribbean Games in 1930. Upon the creation of the Central American and Caribbean Sports Organization (ODECABE) in 1960 and the ninth games, held in Jamaica in 1962, Cuba became a power in this area, reducing its polarizing effect. More noticeable was Cuba's absence from co-operation in professional baseball, since 1949, through the 'Caribbean Series'. It is worth noting that in both cases an international identity was adopted far beyond the insular identity, although only in the second instance was it exclusively *Caribbean*.

During the 1970s, Cuba's government set up scholarships and other sport collaborations, even with Puerto Rico, and collaboration in the fields of science and health with some of the independent countries. An important influence in this moderation and Caribbeanization of Cuba was the establishment of diplomatic relations with the new states. The governments of Barbados, Guyana, Jamaica and Trinidad & Tobago – acting in concert – established

26 Piero Gleijeses, 1978; Gérard Pierre-Charles, 1981, parts 3 and 4, pp.141–251; Alonso Aguilar Monteverde, 1965 (1968), chaps 9 to 11.

27 There is a vast bibliography on Cuban international relations; see especially Gerardo González Nuñez, 1991.

diplomatic relations with Cuba towards the end of 1972, followed by the Bahamas in 1974, and Suriname and St Lucia in 1979. Although their actual co-operation with Cuba varied, the first four also contributed to the end of the OAS's prohibition of relations between its members and Cuba, allowing for a renewal in diplomatic relations with several American states.

Throughout this process, Cuba maintained the principle of solidarity in international relations, including the continuation of its relations with nationalists in the colonies and opposition groups in the independent states. Another expression of this principle was support to various countries, regardless of their political regimes, which are facing natural disasters such as earthquakes and hurricanes.

This Cuban Third World approach was, in turn, a reflection of a wider international process, as mentioned above, of which revolutionary Cuba was part and symbol: the global cultural revolution. During the last quarter of a century, common understandings about the most important human relations have been transformed. In other words, the predominant discourse concerning the relations between men and women, parents and children, the State and the individual, in short, the powerful and the weak, has changed radically. Even more important, the vision about the relationship between human beings and the rest of nature has been transforming.[28]

By 'common understanding' I mean the way in which at least a decisive sector, if not the majority, of the population thinks. It is embodied in the discourses, the social imagery, the world vision eventually adopted by the communication media and international organizations, as well as most governments and their educational systems, and – above all – the creative people of the arts world. As a Puerto Rican writer, Ana Lydia Vega, put it: 'The seventies ... mark a true ideological revolution in the world. ... The Vietnam War, feminism, student protests, revolts in the Black ghettos of the United States, African countries' independence, and the Cuban Revolution are only a few of the hecatombic events that transformed the intellectual scene of the Island.'[29]

The forces of change, the protagonists of the catastrophic events mentioned by Vega, were women, urban youths, ethno-culturally subordinated groups and societies, and dissidents and persecuted from all walks of life. They rebelled against the emptiness – for most of humanity – of the promises of capitalist and patriarchal 'Progress', and against the modern power élites that in practice denied their foundational principles, even in some of the socialist countries.

---

28 Antonio Gaztambide, 1996b, pp.198–203. See also Eric Hobsbawm, 1994 (1996), chap.11.

29 Ana Lydia Vega, 1989, p.22.

In summary, multiple identities – now called 'transnational' – were created and recreated, among them the ethno-cultural (including racial), sexual, generational and class identities.[30] International identities were also stimulated – in our case Antillean, Caribbean, Latin American, Third World, and so on. On the other hand, the large component of anti-imperialist and anti-Western sentiment in the global cultural revolution reinforced 'national identities' through the leftist revolutionary nationalism of which Cuba is still the standard-bearer, particularly in the Americas.

Simultaneously, and also stimulated by the United Nations' support to non-governmental organizations (NGOs), new forces of regional co-operation sprang up during the 1970s. Movements for peace, environmental protection, and the preservation of natural resources began to be organized on a regional basis.[31] Women, youth and students came into contact and formed organizations, while at the same time new cultural forces – such as the *salsa* of the Spanish-speaking or the reggae of the English-speaking cultural worlds – became unleashed.[32] It is also worth highlighting the professional and intellectual organizations that came about under a Caribbean identity, such as the Association of Caribbean Historians (ACH) and the Caribbean Studies Association (CSA), both founded in Puerto Rico in 1974 and 1968 respectively.

Religions and churches, with their longstanding traditions, took on a particularly strong role among the NGOs. One of their scholars summarizes the spirit of the times:

> The decade of the 1970s was for the Caribbean a period of rapid social change. A number of Caribbean regional institutions, including the Caribbean Conference of Churches (CCC), were [sic] developed during this decade and with them came the promise of fruitful, though unfamiliar, co-operation among Caribbean societies. A growing sense of self-worth among newly independent Caribbean people after centuries of colonial domination was fueled by widespread international preoccupation with the issues of justice and human rights. A new awareness of a common destiny for Caribbean people determined largely by geography and culture began to dawn on Caribbean politicians .... The revolution that had taken place in the communication media, most aptly symbolized by the portable transistor radio, resulted in the masses of the Caribbean people being better informed and more politicized than ever before.[33]

30 Daniel Mato, 1994a, pp.251–61.
31 Francine Jácome, 1993a, pp.69–87.
32 About women, for example, see Fredericka M. Deare, 1995, pp.30–75, and other articles in *Caribbean Studies* 28, 1, 1995.
33 Robert W. M. Cuthbert, 1986, p.1.

New regional initiatives: From CARIFTA to CARICOM, 1968–75

All the forces outlined in the previous section – particularly decolonization and the rise of the Third World movement – gave impetus to ideas and discourses on economic development. This led, for example, to the United Nations' proclamation of the 1960s as the Decade of Development, and the empowerment of the international institutions involved in its promotion. With the success of the European Common Market – and its potential threats to former colonial territories – integrationist schemes also acquired great prestige, which in the Americas translated into the Latin American Free Trade Area, and the Central American Common Market.

The forces that led the Commonwealth Caribbean down the integrationist road were also internal to the region, which explains their success and continuity. Perhaps the most notable of all was Eric E. Williams' leadership. One of the first to adopt a Caribbean rather than West Indian identity, Williams had proposed back in 1942 – commenting on the Anglo-American Commission – 'an economic federation of all the Caribbean areas', referring to what we call today the insular Caribbean.[34] Combined with his defence of a stronger English-speaking Federation – and in the face of its failure – he reiterated in 1962 the idea of a Caribbean Economic Community.[35]

As one of several initiatives, Williams convened the first Conference of Heads of Government in Port of Spain in July 1963. The meeting included the four countries that had already achieved independence or self-government (Barbados, Guyana, Jamaica and Trinidad & Tobago), which were already referred to as the 'Big Four', as opposed to the Federation's 'Little Eight'. That first conference and the two that followed – in Jamaica in 1964 and Guyana in 1965 – did not go far beyond maintaining the existing co-operation spaces, partially due to Guyana's turbulent transit to independence in 1966.

Around 1967, on the contrary, all sorts of forces contributed to the integrationist impetus. First, ECLA-inspired import-substituting industrialization had become far more attractive and acceptable. Second, the idea of a 'regional substitutive industrialization' acquired intellectual prestige with the proposals of Trinidadian economist William G. Demas,[36] and several studies by UWI economists commissioned by the governments of Jamaica

34 Eric Williams, 1942a, p.104.

35 See also Eric Williams, 1969 (1971), pp.286–8.

36 William G. Demas, 1965.

and Trinidad. Third, Forbes Burnham – who emerged as the predominant leader at Guyana's independence – adopted an aggressive integrationist policy.

In July 1965 – even before Barbados and Guyana gained full independence (1966) – Burnham agreed with Barbados' prime minister, Errol Barrow, and Antigua's Vere Bird, on the creation of a Caribbean Free Trade Association (CARIFTA). The initiative was not implemented until a mission from the Incorporated Chamber of Industry and Commerce of the Caribbean which went all over the region between September and October 1966 'had a catalytic effect upon the various governments.'[37] Preceded by a meeting of experts in Guyana in August 1967, the Fourth Heads of Government Conference – which had met in Barbados that same year – adopted the CARIFTA agreement as the basis for free trade within the region to be established the following year.[38]

By 1 August 1968 the ten Federation territories and Guyana embarked on economic integration through CARIFTA. The three original proponents plus Trinidad & Tobago started in May. The now-associated states of Dominica, Grenada, St Lucia, St Vincent and St Kitts-Nevis-Anguilla – favoured by the agreement as Less Developed Countries (LDCs) – joined in July after having created in June, with Antigua and Montserrat, an East Caribbean Common Market (ECCM).[39] Montserrat, which was still a British colony, and the ever-reluctant Jamaica, completed the 11.

Jamaica's reluctance is ironic, since CARIFTA seemed to vindicate the position they had taken during the Federation era: a free-trade zone rather than a customs union or common market and – as the government itself took pains to point out – co-operation but not integration. The Association consisted basically of eliminating the tariffs between signatory governments, except for a list of products which would be reduced throughout a five-year period in the More Developed Countries (MDCs) and ten years for the LDCs. A Council of Ministers would overlook the enforcement of these and many other provisions and exceptions.

Jamaica objected, however, to the location in Barbados of one of the two institutions created along with CARIFTA: the Caribbean Development Bank. The Bank was located there with the primary objective of financing

37 Anthony Payne, 1980, p.70.

38 'The Caribbean Free Trade Association (CARIFTA) Agreement and Related Documents, 1968', in Roy Preiswerk, 1970, pp.412–45; see Appendix 'A': Resolution adopted by Fourth Heads of Government Conference on Regional Integration, pp.430–1. Subsequent references to the agreement are taken from this version.

39 'Agreement for the Establishment of an East Caribbean Common Market, 11th June 1968', in *ibid.*, pp.463–80.

projects in the LDCs with the support of Canada, the United States and Great Britain. Initially abstaining from joining, Jamaica was able to postpone its establishment until February 1970.

The second institution – the Commonwealth Caribbean Regional Secretariat – seemed more promising. Established in Georgetown, Guyana, with William Demas at the helm since 1970, the Secretariat would serve the 'policies of regional integration and co-operation' of the Heads of Government Conferences. To this end, it was to work with two divisions: one to assist the Council of Ministers in the administration of free trade and integration, another one to co-ordinate all the other areas of 'functional collaboration'.[40]

Four years after its establishment, CARIFTA was a complete success from the point of view of an increase in trade between the participating territories. The former British Honduras, now Belize, had joined in May 1971. The MDCs benefited the most, however, causing great discontent among the LDCs. This dissatisfaction, coupled with Jamaica's consistent reluctance, blocked any attempt towards greater integration. Divisions grew sharper with differing approaches to Great Britain's imminent integration into the European Economic Community.

This last circumstance, combined with the benefits of free trade and the upsurge of Third World movements since 1970, nourished the force that would push regional integration forward: a dramatic turn-around by Jamaica. This turn-around was driven by a PNP return to government – after a broad electoral victory – now under the leadership of Michael Manley. Having adopted a strong Third World discourse, Manley's government embraced the integrationist cause.

The leadership of Demas and the Regional Secretariat, expressed in a pamphlet entitled *From CARIFTA to Caribbean Community*,[41] also contributed to a statement by the Seventh Conference of Heads of Government, gathered in Trinidad in October 1972, in favour of a common market and regional community that would incorporate, by May of the following year, the co-ordination of foreign policies and greater functional co-operation. In the face of multiple objections from the LDCs, however, the Eighth Conference of Heads of Government, assembled in Guyana in April 1973, approved the Georgetown Accord which – among other concessions – postponed the start for the MDCs until August, and until May 1974 for the

40 'The Regional Secretariat: Agreed Memorandum, Georgetown Conference, January 1968', in *ibid.*, 1970, pp.457–60.

41 Published in Georgetown by the Commonwealth Caribbean Regional Secretariat, in 1972.

LDCs.[42] Even so, the governments of Antigua and Montserrat postponed their decisions.

On 4 July 1973, four of the leading actors in this process – Errol Barrow from Barbados, Forbes Burnham from Guyana, Michael Manley from Jamaica, and Eric Williams from Trinidad & Tobago – signed the 'Treaty of Chaguaramas' in Trinidad, establishing the Caribbean Community and Common Market (CARICOM). The principal text established the Community, including the common market in an annex.[43] All the LDCs joined the following year.

CARICOM would maintain the Conference of Heads of Government as the maximum organ, the Secretariat (now of the Community) and the Council of Ministers (now of the Common Market). The latter's principal task would be to continue with the liberalization of trade and to progressively establish a common external duty. The Council's mission, however, was dramatically broadened to include the 'coordination of economic policies and development planning', seeking to harmonize, for example, tax incentives for industrialization and the free flow of capital.

CARICOM also intensified functional co-operation through a series of ministerial committees defined as 'community institutions', initially in health, education, labour, foreign affairs, finance, agriculture and mines. Already-existing co-operative institutions were now called 'associated institutions'. Among these appeared a new one, created at the same time as the Community, to foster industrialization in the LDCs: the Caribbean Investment Corporation (CIC).

The most innovative aspect of the Community was the co-ordination of foreign policies. Since the Seventh Conference in 1972, the heads of government of the independent countries had decided to establish diplomatic relations with Cuba. As of 1973 they also negotiated with the European Economic Community (EEC) on behalf of all of the Community, culminating in February 1975 in the Lomé Convention between the EEC and the former African, Caribbean and Pacific territories.

Ironically, the forces that revitalized co-operation and sent the region down the integrationist path responded, in part, to a strengthening of a West Indian identity, but assumed then the broader Caribbean distinction. As before, however, those same forces that at a given point in time were centripetal, would now become centrifugal. By the mid-1970s, old and new

42 The Georgetown Accord, 12 April 1973, mimeograph; also reproduced in Caribbean Community Secretariat, 1973, pp.93–7.

43 *Treaty Establishing the Caribbean Community,* 1973. Subsequent references are taken from this version.

influences would lead to a redefinition of the Caribbean and – therefore – of what constituted regional co-operation.

Epilogue: The forces leading towards a redefinition of the region, 1975–97

The heyday of the Third World movement, which had its clearest expression in the movement of Non-Aligned Countries, contributed to the ground lost by regional identities and projects as they had been defined until then. Cuba's leadership and Guyana's activism in the Non-Aligned Movement, as well as the former's role in Africa, weakened their respective commitments to the region. At the same time, the trade negotiations of several member countries with Venezuela, as well as Jamaica's approach to Mexico, weakened CARICOM.

The governments agreed that the scope of co-operation should be expanded, but they started to define themselves with regard to two tendencies: favouring ties with the rest of the insular Caribbean, or seeking links also with the rest of the countries around the Caribbean Sea basin. In the latter direction, CARICOM established official representation with the Central American Common Market and the Andean Pact and increased its trade with Latin America. Nevertheless, the first tendency – stimulated by Eric Williams' government – initially prevailed, with the support of those who tended to exclude the Commonwealth Caribbean from the rest of Latin America.

Although ECLA included the Antillean states and colonial powers from the very beginning, it had maintained since 1966 a sub-regional office in Port of Spain to tend to the new English-speaking states and CARIFTA. In May 1975, ECLA established – with the opposition of the United States and qualified approval from the rest of the colonial powers – the Caribbean Development and Co-operation Committee (CDCC). The Committee was composed by the economic ministers from the governments 'of the countries within the sphere of action of the ECLA office in Port of Spain and the Governments of Cuba, Haiti and the Dominican Republic and other Caribbean countries as they achieve independence…'.[44]

In the following decade, the CDCC incorporated several non-independent territories as 'associate members': the Netherlands Antilles,

44 Resolution 358 (XVI): 'Establishment of a Caribbean Development and Co-operation Committee', 13 May 1975, 1974–5, pp.156–7, 247–8. United Nations E/ECLA/989/Rev. 1, pp.156–7, 247–8.

the British Virgin Islands, and the US Virgin Islands. By that time, ECLA had ratified the tendency by changing its name to Economic Commission for Latin America *and the Caribbean*. In 1991, Puerto Rico joined the CDCC, but by then multiple forces had moved the region in the opposite direction.

During the 1980s, Latin America adopted the role of the American portion of the Third World. In the region as a whole, the foreign debt crisis had the contradictory effect of putting an end to the optimism of substitutive industrialization, while ratifying the 'underdeveloped' condition of the region. At the same time, although the economic achievements of Chile's military government fertilized the subsequent surge of neo-liberalism, the thunderous failures of the rest of the military governments re-established the link between democracy and development.

In the Caribbean, the United States reassertion of hegemony fostered the idea of the region as a somewhat Meso-American part of the Latin American Third World. The United States counter-offensive focused on the Antilles and Central America, specifically on Grenada, Nicaragua and El Salvador. Although thus aimed at what has been called the geo-political Caribbean – revealingly the definition of the region that prevails in the United States – the government of President Ronald Reagan christened its positive face, in 1983, the Caribbean Basin Initiative (CBI).[45]

Ironically, regional reactions, more than United States actions, constituted the redefining forces towards what has also been called the Wider Caribbean or *Gran Caribe*. During the Central American crisis, the so-called 'regional powers' (Colombia, Mexico, and Venezuela) activated – together with Panama – their respective 'Caribbean vocations' through the Contadora Group, named after the Panamanian island where it first met.[46] They later became a 'support group' for Central American countries seeking their own solutions under the name of Esquipulas, also after the place of origin – this time in Guatemala. They evolved by 1989 into the Group of Three (G-3), co-ordinating their regional policies and pursuing a free-trade area.[47]

Around the turn of the decade, CARICOM also moved towards both a greater integration among themselves and a widening of regional integration beyond the Commonwealth Caribbean. The Tenth Meeting of the Conference of Heads of Government adopted, in Grenada in July 1989, the 'Grand Anse Declaration and Work Programme for the Advance of the Integration

45 For the view of a US scholar and participant, see Robert A. Pastor, 1992; for a critique from this side, see Carmen Gautier Mayoral *et al*., 1990. See also chap.10 of this volume.

46 Marisol de Gonzalo, 1987.

47 José Briceño-Ruiz, 1997, 152–68.

Movement', calling for the establishment of a common market by July 1993 and recognizing 'the primary importance of Human Resource Development'. Its most momentous decision, however, turned out to be the establishment of an 'Independent West Indian Commission for Advancing the Goals of the Treaty of Chaguaramas'.[48]

Chaired by the internationally prestigious Chancellor of the UWI, Guyanese Sir Shridath Ramphal, a group of 16 business, government, intellectual, labour and religious leaders worked for two years – from April 1990 to May 1992 – meeting throughout the Commonwealth Caribbean, most of the West Indian diaspora and part of the rest of the basin. Besides focusing its numerous recommendations on the 'deepening' of CARICOM integration, the West Indian Commission included – among various proposals for 'an increasingly "Caribbean Basin" approach to international negotiations and development issues' – the establishment of an Association of Caribbean States.[49]

When a Special Meeting of the Conference of Heads of Government – though lukewarm towards deeper integration – adopted the latter proposal in October 1992, many more forces were moving the whole region in that direction. On the one hand, the geo-political scenario had completed a dramatic transfiguration, beginning with the end of the Cold War – which culminated in 1991 with the demise of the Soviet Union – and followed by the unleashing of multiple transformations now identified with the terms 'globalization' and 'neo-liberalism'. Of particular concern was the dual trend towards trade liberalization and the consolidation of economic blocs, especially a broader and more integrated European Union slated for 1992 and the new North American Free Trade Agreement (NAFTA) between Canada, Mexico and the United States, proposed for 1993.[50]

On the other hand, regional interaction had intensified. Mexico, Puerto Rico and Venezuela were admitted in 1990 as observers in some of CARICOM's institutions and ministerial committees; Anguilla, Bermuda, the Cayman Islands and Colombia joined later. Of the previous observers (along with Aruba, the Dominican Republic and the Netherlands Antilles), Suriname became the first non-English-speaking full member in 1995 and Haiti was admitted to provisional full membership in 1997. The British Virgin Islands and the Turks & Caicos Islands had become associated members in 1991.[51]

48 West Indian Commission, 1992 (1993), Appendix 'A', pp.525–8.

49 *Ibid.*, chap.1 and Appendices 'A' to'D'; chap.11, quote p.457.

50 Andrés Serbín, 1996, pp.61–82.

51 *Ibid.*, pp.87-91; *El Mundo* (San Juan), 1990, p.12; and http:// www.caricom.org/ expframes.htm.

The Central American countries, having achieved a regional solution to their crisis, also moved towards greater integration. In the additional context of the 1992 Columbus Quincentennial, efforts multiplied to reintegrate Cuba further into the regional fold.[52]

Finally, after formal discussions with the Central American governments in 1992 and 1993 and bilateral negotiations with the rest, the CARICOM governments and those of the G-3 and Suriname agreed in Port of Spain, in October 1993, to the constitution of the Association of Caribbean States (ACS). The Association was founded at Cartagena de Indias, Colombia, on 24 July 1994, 'recognising the importance of the Caribbean Sea which constitutes the common patrimony of the peoples of the Caribbean, and recalling the role it has played in their history and the potential it has to operate as a unifying element in their development'. It was defined as 'an organization for consultation, co-operation and concerted action', and further innovated by including in its activities 'the preservation of the environment and conservation of the natural resources of the region and especially of the Caribbean Sea'.[53]

The ACS was formed by 25 sovereign states: the G-3, the five Central American republics, the 12 CARICOM independent governments, Cuba, the Dominican Republic, Haiti, Panama and Suriname, and by 11 additional associate members: Anguilla, Aruba and the Netherlands Antilles, Bermuda, the British Virgin Islands, the Cayman Islands, the French Departments (Guadeloupe, Guyane and Martinique), Montserrat, and the Turks & Caicos Islands. Venezuelan Simón Molina Duarte was elected as its first Secretary-General.

Thus, most of the states and territories of the basin adopted the Caribbean identity as at least one of their own. Ironically, only Puerto Rico and the US Virgin Islands – both of which had participated in the earliest contemporary co-operation schemes – were absent from the ACS, presumably because Washington disagreed with the participation of Cuba. Puerto Rico's absence ran counter to a very determined effort by the government headed by Rafael Hernández Colón, from 1985 to 1992, to resume the Caribbean vocation abandoned in 1968. The inauguration in 1993 of a new government – again uninterested – only compounded US reticence.

Interestingly, perhaps the single most important positive force – the West Indian Commission – also represented the consolidation of that

52 *El Nuevo Día* (San Juan), 13 December 1992, p.53. See also, Andrés Serbín and Joseph Tulchin, 1994.

53 'Convention Establishing the Association of Caribbean States', http://www.acs-aec/major documents, Article III.; see chap.10, this volume.

identity, from its controversial name to its chairman's words: 'Historical forces and the Caribbean Sea have divided us; yet unfolding history and the same Sea, through long centuries of struggle against uneven odds, have been steadily making us one. Now West Indians have emerged with an identity clearly recognizable not only to ourselves and our wider Caribbean but also in the world beyond the Caribbean Sea.'[54] The various forces mentioned at the beginning of this chapter – all of which came into play in these later developments – may eventually do the same for the broader, 'Meso-American' identity of the *Gran Caribe.*

54 West Indian Commission, 1992 (1993), p.xxi.

10

CARIBBEAN INTERNATIONAL RELATIONS AT THE TURN OF THE CENTURY

Anthony T. Bryan

Introduction

The contemporary context of Caribbean international relations is determined to a large extent by the historical heritage of the region. Slavery, colonial rule, economic dependence and monoculture left a legacy of hegemony by European powers, and also induced the region's political and economic fragmentation. Militarily, during the sixteenth century, England challenged Spanish power in the Caribbean, and France then contended with Britain's power until the Napoleonic Wars. In the seventeenth century the Dutch also played a part in colonizing the Caribbean. They occupied St Martin in 1630 and Curaçao and Bonaire in 1634. At the end of the nineteenth century, after the brief Spanish-American-Cuban War of 1898, the United States occupied Cuba and Puerto Rico and in 1917 purchased the Virgin Islands from Denmark in order to gain harbour facilities. In the twentieth century, Germany and then the Soviet Union challenged the dominance of the United States, which had emerged as a major regional power during the late nineteenth century. Politically, Haiti, the Dominican Republic, Cuba and the colonies of Spain on the Caribbean littoral won their independence from their European colonizers during the nineteenth and early twentieth centuries, only to fall under the massive economic, political and military influence of the United States. Economically, the Caribbean remained linked to Europe and the United States.

For the first half of the twentieth century, the international relations of the wider Caribbean region can be characterized as circumstances of limited complexity in a predictable world environment. The key elements in these relations were the historical links with Europe, and the region's geo-political and economic dominance by the United States, the pre-eminent military power in the Americas. During the period of the Cold War (1945–89), characterized by the military-ideological confrontation of the two superpowers, the United States (although challenged by the Soviet Union) took a major role in shaping the international relations of the Caribbean. The US sponsored the overthrow of governments (Guatemala 1954), financed invasion by political exiles (Bay of Pigs, Cuba 1961), undertook successful military intervention (the Dominican Republic 1965 and Grenada 1983) and implemented concerted efforts to destabilize governments which were perceived as unfriendly, or sympathetic to communism or the Soviet Union. Only the Cuban Revolution led by Fidel Castro survived US opposition.

During this era the most compelling change in the post-Second World War Caribbean was the move towards political independence of most of the English-speaking Caribbean countries and Suriname, as well as the granting of various degrees of internal autonomy for other British and Dutch possessions. During the 1970s, 1980s and early 1990s the countries of the Caribbean belonged to regional and international subsystems whose norms were slowly, though constantly, evolving. Caribbean diplomacy had successes in multilateral fora such as the United Nations and the Non-Aligned Movement, and in demonstrating a capacity successfully to negotiate preferential trade and aid agreements with Europe, the United States and Canada. Cuba's economy was supported heavily by the Soviet Union in the face of economic pressure from the United States. During the 1980s the member states of the Caribbean Community and Common Market (CARICOM) expanded trade, economic and functional co-operation with their Latin American neighbours, in particular, Venezuela, Colombia, Brazil, Mexico and the countries of Central America. As ultra-Caribbean relations developed, the Caribbean integration process slowly began to widen beyond the political, linguistic and cultural demarcations which had been the historical legacy of colonialism. By the end of the twentieth century, CARICOM had expanded to include Suriname and Haiti; and the Association of Caribbean States (ACS), comprising 25 full-member and 12 associate member-states of the wider Caribbean, had been established.

The international relations of the Caribbean have never been limited to relations among states. Since the sixteenth century various actors, international, regional, local, state and non-state, have interacted on issues and have sought in various ways to shape the conduct and norms of the region's international affairs. However, by the beginning of the 1990s, radical changes taking place outside the Caribbean had changed the comfortable and predictable world in which Caribbean international relations had been set and to which Caribbean diplomacy had become accustomed. The bipolar political structure of world politics that arose after the War has now collapsed. The old assumptions, the seemingly immutable structures and intellectual constructs that underpinned the functioning of the international system since the end of the Second World War, have been swept away by the tidal wave of far-reaching post-Cold War changes, political and economic, taking place in many areas of the globe.

As the world enters the new millennium, trade liberalization, the globalization of economic production, and the use of cyberspace for business transactions, have destroyed barriers to commerce between nations and ushered in a new global community dominated by the explosive revolution in information technology. The trends and characteristics of the emerging international order suggest a disturbing fluidity and uncertainty about the future, brought about by rapid and often unpredictable changes. Regional conflicts now have their origins in purely local conditions and their resolution is less amenable to the coaxing of major powers; economic issues are now preeminent over international political matters; and objectives such as democracy, good governance, economic integration and free trade, sustainable development, preservation of the environment, global climate change, drug trafficking, money laundering, and cyberspace crimes, have risen to the top of the global agenda. The Caribbean region, like much of the developing world, is caught up in the tide of these profound transformations that are indicative of the replacement of one international system by another.

The past and the present

Despite the rapid global changes, some features in the Caribbean's international relations remain constant. Today, as in the past, both the United States and Europe claim the right to mould the international and the domestic circumstances of the region. This time the battles are economic and are being waged in the World Trade Organization (WTO) over the future of preferences for Caribbean bananas, sugar and rum in the expanded markets of the European Union (EU); and with the Organisation of Economic Cooperation and Development (OECD) over the future of offshore financial services in the Caribbean. The economic survival of Cuba is also caught up in the battle between the United States and the world over the extra-territoriality of the US in enforcing its embargo against the largest Caribbean island. Today, as in the past, non-state actors such as international drug traffickers, and offshore money launderers (modern-day pirates), use their financial, political and military power to advance their illegal cross-border activities. Today, as in the past, many non-Caribbean countries such as France, the Netherlands, Russia and Japan have significant political and economic interests in the region. However, today, unlike in the past, relatively autonomous multinational institutions such as the International Monetary Fund (IMF), the World Bank, and the Inter-American Development Bank, provide considerable economic assistance to the region and exercise sometimes disproportionate political and economic influence on governments.

Although threats to the sovereignty and security of Caribbean states have been constant, in the last decades of the twentieth century global television and cyberspace have broken free of the constraints of national boundaries and challenged the *sine qua non* of governments, namely their ability to govern decisively within their own borders. There are unprecedented clashes both internationally and within states over the governance of virtually every human activity from free speech to press freedom, crime and punishment, privacy and investment regulation. In essence, the international environment in the Caribbean is polycentric, as various external state and non-state actors pursue their own competitive interests. Much like 'the powers and the pirates' of centuries past, today's actors are contributing to changes in the international environment of the lands and peoples of the Caribbean Sea.[1]

Mainstream theoretical perspectives on realism and pluralism, as well as the literature on democracy, socialism, non-alignment, fragmentation, multilateralism, unilateralism, bilateralism and regionalism, have served as mantras at various times since the 1960s to explain in part the ideologies, practices and customs associated with Caribbean international relations, and foreign-policy behaviour. However, the dominant international-relations perspective that has been shared by all Caribbean countries is their vulnerability as small states in the international system.[2]

Asymmetry remains central to the region's relations with its Latin American neighbours, North America, Europe and Asia. As these small states try to overcome their vulnerabilities and take responsibility for their future in the emerging global system, an array of rapid changes during the 1990s has opened up a new range of issues, rules and activities in the international arena. The traditional paradigms and theoretical analyses of international relations from both global and regional perspectives are being brought into question.

The major political and economic challenges facing the Caribbean at the dawn of the twenty-first century have been discussed in several recent general studies and a productive dialogue among scholars and policy makers has ensued. Similarly, discussions on the state of security, always a major concern for the Caribbean region, have gone through an interesting evolution in the post-Cold War period: namely, the new emphasis on the strong links between the range of development and security concerns.[3] The vulnerability of Caribbean states has increased; and the challenges to domestic economic secu-

1 For a detailed discussion of change and continuity in the architecture of Caribbean international relations, see Jorge I. Domínguez, 1997, pp.3–19.

2 See the seminal work, Commonwealth Secretariat, 1985. There have been subsequent reports on this topic.

3 See for example, Andrés Serbín, 1998; Georges A. Fauriol and G. Philip Hughes, 1995; Jorge I. Domínguez, 1995; Anthony T. Bryan, 1995; Anthony P. Maingot, 1994b, p.533; Hilbourne A. Watson, 1994; H. Michael Erisman, 1992; Andrés Serbín and Anthony T. Bryan, 1991.

rity, as well as its political consequences, are receiving additional emphasis in the effort to define the architecture of the region's international relations at century's end. In exploring the current dynamic, this chapter looks at the political economy, governance, and the security dimensions of the contemporary international relations of the Caribbean. It identifies some of the tangible and intangible elements of the new regionalism and the diplomacy of those relations, as well as some trends that will contribute to an agenda for action in the early years of the twenty-first century. Its main focus is the CARICOM subregion.

Trends in the political economy of the Caribbean

At the turn of the century, most Caribbean countries have been able to cope with rapid changes in the global system. The English-speaking Caribbean countries, in particular, have been exemplary in their practice of democracy and political stability. Others such as Suriname and Haiti are trying to nurture new democratic regimes. Economically, the region has followed the neoliberal reform rule book and implemented policies mandated by the International Monetary Fund, the World Bank, and regional funding agencies. States have trimmed fiscal deficits, privatized state-owned commercial enterprises that were losing money and liberalized their trading regimes. Only Cuba continues to labour under a deliberate ideological model that does not encourage political democracy, while its economy mirrors some version of '*à la carte* capitalism' in the face of a persistent US embargo. Recent economic reforms have encouraged direct foreign investment in certain sectors of the Cuban economy and permitted the evolution of a small merchant class within the margins of the state-managed economy.[4]

The structural adjustment policies and reforms carried out by several Caribbean countries since the mid-1980s were not willingly implemented nor sustained by domestic political constituencies. For the most part, such changes in the macro-economic environment were mandated by international financial or donor institutions and implemented by reform-minded governments or by governments who saw no alternative. Such adjustment has been a challenge for small open Caribbean economies which are vulnerable to large external shocks and find it difficult to carry sufficient reserves, maintain adequate borrowing capacity, and encourage proper exchange-rate policies.

In general, the present transition in the political economy of the Caribbean region is full of uncertainties. Some politicians have portrayed liberalization and privatization policies as growth-inducing policies when in

4 On Cuba's regional relations see Joseph Tulchin *et al.*, 1997.

effect they are not. Undertaking such reforms encounters resistance and attracts costs. Also, individual countries are starting to question the immediate costs of the hemispheric and global momentum toward free trade because in some countries trade liberalization, far from leading to greater exports, is provoking macro-economic disequilibrium and jobless growth. Global economic turmoil in various regions since 1995 has raised questions about the capacity of most countries in the region to achieve long-term growth in the face of recurrent crises. Inequality in the distribution of income and wealth is of deep concern to the region's planners.

Concerns for alleviating poverty and income inequality caused by the reforms have not been fully integrated into proposals for growth. Many of the Caribbean's smaller economies are heavily dependent upon one (or a few) traditional export commodities for which world prices are not likely to rise. Increased crime, diminishing social support services, and dramatic increases in the poverty index (visible even in relatively prosperous societies such as Trinidad & Tobago, the Dominican Republic and Barbados) constitute major negative impacts of the reforms. In many Caribbean countries, the much-heralded free-market economic reforms have produced their own immediate Waterloo – benefits for a few, uncertainty for the many, and the further impoverishment of the masses through the fiscal inability of governments to maintain essential social services and infrastructure. Much more has to be done domestically and at the international donor level to compensate the losers.

Caribbean democracy and governance

Certain issues of governance have emerged with the changes in political economy. Strengthening democracy is one of the major items on the immediate agenda. There is widespread official and public perception in the region that economic vulnerability is at the core of Caribbean insecurity. Instability will increase if the economic pillars that support democratic regimes are eroded. Similarly, Caribbean democracy and internal security are also vulnerable to the illegal drug trade, the corruption of law enforcement officials, and domestic insurrection. In some states, such as Trinidad & Tobago, Guyana, Jamaica and Haiti, ethnic and class tensions may worsen if economic circumstances deteriorate and political factions further exploit delicate situations. While the countries of the Commonwealth Caribbean maintain some of the hemisphere's strongest traditions of parliamentary democracy, even the much-trumpeted Westminster model of parliamentary government is susceptible to authoritarian dispensation in the deliberate weakening of traditional safeguards and rules.

It is difficult to be complacent about the future of democracy even in the English-speaking Caribbean countries. Troubling trends apparent since the

1980s, namely, declining voter turnout particularly among the youth, and sharp declines in public interest in parliamentary proceedings, could eventually strengthen the emergence of Cabinet dictatorships and single-party rule, or perpetuate the financial and organizational advantages of dominant parties. Similarly, failure to invest consistently (because of budgetary constraints or lack of foreign assistance) in institutions such as the legal systems and mechanisms for public security is placing severe strains on democratic governance.[5]

A concurrent trend is the inability of the State (during circumstances of considerable downsizing and economic liberalization) to deliver levels of welfare and social services similar to those of the period from the 1960s to the mid-1990s. There is pressure upon governments to provide economic support and to deliver social services more rapidly and efficiently even while their capacity to do so is severely diminished. The managerial capacity of the State in some countries needs to be rebuilt in order to deliver public services and to confront the challenges created by a competitive market economy. Public tolerance for further sacrifice is also diminishing as the tasks of dismantling or restructuring state enterprises and financial systems continue. While inflation rates and fiscal deficits are being contained in most Caribbean countries, and growth rates are respectable, the economic foundations are shaky. Revenues from privatization sales and reductions in basic government services are not formulas for sustainable growth. Given the domestic costs, both political and economic, preparing for global enterprise competitiveness is a real challenge for most countries of the Caribbean.

Within the political fabric, declining access to scarce economic largesse, the spectacle of corruption in government abuses of political power, and the use of declining public funds to reward the ruling party faithful have severely weakened traditional political parties in the Caribbean. Many have also lost their historical and ideological differences. But Caribbean electorates are demanding more accountability and clearer economic programmes from their leaders. There is public anger at economic inequalities, rising social ills, and rampant corruption.[6]

In sum, trends in Caribbean governance and the democratic tradition – namely, dramatic shifts in social and class structure; declining political participation; frustration with the parliamentary system of politics; changes in leadership; conversion to neo-liberal economic policies by political parties which have traditionally represented labour; and changing relationships between labour, business and government – will all have an impact on the political economy of the region in the twenty-first century.

5 See Patrick Emmanuel, 1993; Selwyn D. Ryan, 1997; Clifford E. Griffin, 1997.

6 See Ivelaw L. Griffith and Betty N. Sedoc-Dahlberg, 1997; Trevor Munroe, 1995.

Globalization

The fundamental shifts in the international system since the Cold War ended at the beginning of the 1990s have highlighted a series of trends that were already developing before that time. 'Globalization' is the term most often used to describe these trends of the growing integration of economies world wide through increases in trade, investment flows and technology transfer. This process has been facilitated by rapid advances in communications and information technology, as well as by an international policy environment which emphasizes trade liberalization, privatization and deregulation of financial markets. In general terms, its main elements are the spread of economic activities at a global level, and the political and cultural adjustments that accompany that expansion. The economic activities relate to the freer movement of goods, capital, services, people, skills and knowledge across geographic borders. Fostered by rapid technological change, and characterized by a dilution of the control of national governments, globalization has earned ideological connotations.

The present period of globalization received strong impetus from the Bretton Woods institutions created in the early post-war period, in particular the General Agreement on Tariffs and Trade (GATT). The various rounds of GATT – culminating with the Uruguay Round, which ended in 1994 – have accomplished a vast reduction in tariff rates, particularly in manufacturing. Finally, while advances in communications and information technology have facilitated the globalization process, the demise of most socialist economic models and the failure of inward-looking economic policies in the developing world have also contributed to the globalization process by discrediting alternative world views.

Supporters of globalization emphasize the welfare benefits associated with increased specialization and trade, such as lower import prices and increased flow of capital and technology across countries. Also cited are the more efficient allocation of savings and the structural changes in economies, both of which permit faster growth. Critics of globalization argue that unrestricted trade and capital mobility result in low-wage regions attracting industries away from high-wage areas, thus lowering living standards in the latter. Some also argue that global financial markets undermine the ability of sovereign nations to carry out an independent economic policy, while poor nations are further marginalized from the more positive aspects of the globalization process. The political implications of this process for the Caribbean are important.[7]

7 For contemporary insights on the globalization phenomenon see the essays in Thomas Klak, 1998, and Felipe Aguero and Jeffery Stark, 1998.

Globalization of the Caribbean's political economy is not a late-twentieth-century phenomenon; it always has been a companion of production specialization, from the sugar plantations of the past to the tourist enclaves of today. Since the sixteenth century, the Caribbean has been integrated into the world economy through trade and investment. Throughout its history, the Caribbean as a region has had to respond to cyclical fluctuations in the international economy and to adjust its political and economic relationships to challenges in the international economic environment. More often than not, these have involved strategies to compensate the region for the disadvantages of small size and the legacies of exploitation in the colonial past. In this historical process, the economic systems of Caribbean countries have benefited from a series of special preferential trade and financial arrangements designed to underwrite their survival and viability.

What was different at century's end was the 'special relationships' coming to a close, and the development assistance policies of the former colonial powers becoming based on their assessments of the real needs of developing countries rather than on geo-political, cultural, emotional or traditional ties. Most Caribbean countries are highly dependent on North America and Europe as markets for their exports and have reason to be concerned about general changes that will make nonsense of the existing system of preferences and significantly alter their access to these markets. The Caribbean is once again the arena for political battles over international trade, with the outcome to be decided in Washington, Brussels, and at the WTO in Geneva.

FREE TRADE AND ECONOMIC INTEGRATION

At the turn of the century, the trade challenges facing the Caribbean region are diverse, including the problem of finding ways for small, fragmented economies in the Western Hemisphere to survive in an increasingly competitive, global trading environment. It is still not clear whether the international trade environment will be global and driven by international rules and by a body such as the World Trade Organization; or if it will be dominated by trade within economic 'blocs' such as the North American Free Trade Agreement (NAFTA) or the Free Trade Area of the Americas (FTAA). There is still uncertainty regarding the trading regime of the Caribbean in relation to North America and Europe, specifically Caribbean membership in the FTAA and in a new European Union partnership with the African, Caribbean and Pacific (ACP) group of countries. Also, the integration of Cuba into the regional and global economy, on terms acceptable to its people, remains as one of the more problematic items facing its neighbours, as well as Europe and North America.

The rules governing international trade are undergoing continual change. The WTO requires countries to dismantle non-tariff barriers, progressively liberalize trade in goods and services, and eliminate all discriminatory practices and tariffs in favour of those of domestic origin. By the year 2004 the Caribbean countries will be expected to adhere to the new trading arrangements. So at the dawn of a new millennium, the challenges confronting the Caribbean with respect to trade with Europe and the Americas are essentially similar: the future of existing regimes of significant preferences, the need to plan for the long term without such preferences, and the development of a strategy to meet the transition. In addition, given the possible division of the world into a number of large trading blocs, growth in the economies of the Caribbean will depend to a large extent on participation in or access to these trade arrangements. A Caribbean strategy for participation is evolving which anticipates regional negotiation for simultaneous access to as many global, regional and bilateral trade pacts as possible, rather than having to choose between them.

The trade policy commitments and challenges faced by the Caribbean countries are numerous and stem from multilateral, regional, and hemispheric trade liberalization initiatives, as well as national policy differences among this group of states that are diverse in size, population and resources. The process of integration has advanced most rapidly in CARICOM since its formation in 1975. The theories and strategies for Caribbean integration have evolved over time. But within the context of second generation regional integration theories and smaller economies' agendas, new integration prerogatives and prescriptions for wider Caribbean regionalism have emerged.

The history of the regional integration movement in the Caribbean has been cyclical. Each attempt at regional integration has met with surges of excitement and optimism, sobriety, a sense of failure, disenchantment, then renewed optimism, and another cycle. The cycles have been characterized by periodic querying of the concept of integration itself. The fundamental premise for the idea of regional integration in the Caribbean has been the promotion of economic development. Integration has been advanced primarily as a means of accelerating the industrialization of the countries' primary-product economies and societies and achieving then-desired goals of economic development. The nature of the relationship between integration and economic development has been altered over the years, as thinking has changed on the processes of economic development and integration (today's concept of 'open regionalism' is an example), but the relationship itself has never strayed far from the fundamental premise. The key institutions in the development of Caribbean integration, the Federation of the West Indies (1958–62), the Caribbean Free Trade Area (CARIFTA) (1965–73), and more recently CARICOM, reflect this process.

Historically, Caribbean theories about integration have moved through several phases since the 1950s: from industrialization by invitation, to regional import substitution, through structuralism and dependency, centre-periphery models, and the neo-functionalist theory of 'integration by stealth'. In their early works on regional economic integration, the thinking of Caribbean social scientists corresponds to that of the Latin Americans, although the former developed fairly independently out of economic circumstances similar to those in Latin America. Subsequently, the influence of the Latin American schools of thought on Caribbean economic theory became more visible.[8] By the time governments in the Caribbean were ready to establish the proposed free trade institution CARIFTA in December 1965 (despite warnings from university economists regarding the inadequacy of its institutional structure), substantial pride was felt in the fact that the strongest impetus for regional co-operation had come from economic theorists, social scientists, politicians and business people representative of several Caribbean countries. Moreover, the academic thrust and accompanying theoretical constructs had been directed mainly from the Institute of Social and Economic Research at the University of the West Indies. This Caribbean ethos must be viewed as an important stage in a region very much concerned with exercising autonomy of thought and action. This time there were no exogenous institutional or governmental actors openly directing the establishment of CARIFTA, as had been the case with the Federation. By the time CARICOM was established most Caribbean leaders and bureaucrats were persuaded that deliberate and incremental progress toward regional integration was a practical course.[9] In the history of CARICOM, this added intellectual understanding of the superior bargaining strength that comes from regional co-operation, and the benefits of participating as a bloc in the global economy, has emerged as a strong pivot in the movement for Caribbean regional integration, and in the region's conduct of its international relations.

Collectively, while the contributions of Caribbean theorists were remarkable, the matching of theory and practice in the CARICOM integration experience has been less than distinguished. By the end of the century, CARICOM's membership comprised 13 English-speaking countries of the Commonwealth Caribbean, plus Suriname and Haiti.[10] Unlike the Federation,

8 For discussion of the symbiosis between the Caribbean and Latin American schools of thought, see Norman Girvan, 1973; Anthony T. Bryan, 1984.

9 A detailed discussion of the contributions of Caribbean scholars and practitioners to integration theory is found in Anthony T. Bryan and Roget V. Bryan, 1999.

10 Suriname and Haiti are the only new members accepted in the recent history of the Community. The Bahamas was not one of the original members of CARICOM. It first had observer status and finally became a member of the Community in July 1983. The organization was established in July 1973 with four signatories: Trinidad & Tobago, Jamaica, Barbados and Guyana. By May 1974 the remaining members of CARIFTA had joined.

CARICOM has been able to survive. However, like the Federation and CARIFTA, ongoing national rivalries and regional economic difficulties have characterized CARICOM and have threatened the viability of the regional integration movement since its inception.

Generally, CARICOM has done well with respect to both foreign-policy co-ordination and functional co-operation. No other regional integration group in the Western Hemisphere has demonstrated such a vocal commitment to co-ordination of foreign policy, despite some notable fragmentation (as in the varied national responses to the US intervention in Grenada in 1983 and the signing of separate bilateral 'Shiprider Agreements' with the United States in 1997 and 1998). Functional collaboration efforts have also resulted in a number of very successful regional institutions of CARICOM.[11] However, progress toward true regional economic integration has been slow. The success stories in the area of functional co-operation have not been repeated in the area of economic integration. From a broad perspective, the CARICOM economic integration strategy has not advanced dramatically because it was always a second-best solution and the process has been a means to an end but not an end in itself. Individual states have always been ready to defect, in deed if not in word, from second-best arrangements, while the reality of uneven costs and benefits has served to inhibit the deepening and widening of the integration mechanism.

At the turn of the century, in order to accelerate the integration process and establish the CARICOM Single Market and Economy (CSM&E), the organization is undergoing a comprehensive reform process. The establishment of the CSM&E will entail the removal of all remaining tariff and non-tariff barriers for regional goods and services, require free movement of capital and people, and confer on citizens the right to establish companies in any Caribbean nation. It will mean that taxation and incentives will be harmonized, and a regional transportation policy governing the provision of air and sea transport will be developed. Members will agree to rules ensuring free and fair competition within the region, along with new mechanisms for settling economic disputes. Finally, members will move in concert to develop a common money and capital market, and may in future consider the operation of a common currency. Preparations for the CSM&E have involved the planned implementation of nine protocols that revise the founding Treaty of Chaguaramas and create a new CARICOM legal framework. Protocols dealing with institutional reforms, service sector liberalization, industrial

11 These institutions include the Caribbean Examinations Council (CXC), Caribbean Meteorological Organization (CMO), Council of Legal Education, Caribbean Development Bank (CDB), and the University of the West Indies (UWI).

policy, agricultural policy and trade policy, as well as protocols on disadvantaged countries, regions and sectors; transportation and competition policies; and dispute settlement were scheduled for ratification during the year 2000. Given that by 2004 Caribbean nations must accede to WTO rules, and given the history of slow implementation of the earlier CARICOM integration process, it is likely that the regional arrangements will largely coincide with those under FTAA and WTO.

Regional integration in its present form in CARICOM still has severe limitations because conglomeration of small economies yields a mass that, in many respects, is inadequate to ensure development and transformation. While size constraints are important, it is clear that the declared ambitious integration goals have not always been followed up by timely or practical action. Many factors are responsible: waning political will, changes in integration strategy, failure to implement national adjustment programmes, and technical obstacles to the implementation and enforcement of common policies. With respect to institutional infrastructure, as long as regional governments see advantage in collaborating, a Secretariat will be needed to prepare for, co-ordinate, and implement decisions of the Heads of Governments. As the range of issues for international negotiation increases in the new global environment, international negotiations have become an area of region-wide import for the Secretariat. What is needed is a rationalization of the various ad hoc mechanisms that have been assigned functions by the Heads of Governments. This is necessary in order to reduce overlapping and unnecessary competition and to ensure that matters are not neglected where jurisdiction is unclear. Similarly, the current phenomenon of globalization, with both its benefits and its ominous downside for small nations, strengthens the need to widen the scope and membership of the Caribbean Community and to move toward a more outward-looking integration agenda.

Across the Caribbean region, there is genuine concern about the challenges and opportunities presented by the FTAA and the new Lomé partnership agreement (successor to Lomé IV) between the EU and the ACP. The consensus is that some of these small, fragile economies will not be able to compete internationally or to survive the wave of globalization.[12] But while the regional market is too small, fragile and vulnerable, in global terms, it is still a base that could be improved upon with strategic global repositioning. The prevailing argument among the region's economists is that 'widening' the regional integration movement would be more in line with current integration

12 For recent discussions of the small-state trading dilemma in the Caribbean, see Anthony T. Bryan, 1998; Richard L. Bernal, 1998; Henry S. Gill, 1997; Norman Girvan and Miguel Ceara Hatton, 1998; Richard L. Bernal, 1996.

realities in the global economy. Consequently, traditional, narrow definitions of the Caribbean are being abandoned and replaced by a 'wider' Caribbean vision, and 'second-generation' regional integration theories are starting to be formulated for the Caribbean. What is the nature of the new Caribbean regionalism? In the early twenty-first century how broadly will the Caribbean be defined?

Redefining the Caribbean

On 24 July 1994, a major step toward implementing a wider Caribbean vision was taken when the convention establishing the Association of Caribbean States was signed in Cartegena, Colombia. The proposal for the creation of the ACS had been put forward by the heads of government of CARICOM in October 1992. The idea had its origins in the document, *Time for Action: The Report of the West Indian Commission,* which recommended that CARICOM 'bridge the divide between its Member States and the rest of the Caribbean and Latin America' through functional co-operation and economic integration.[13] The ACS vision encompasses countries with different geographic, demographic and economic ideals and development levels and also different historical, cultural and linguistic backgrounds. It offers a new regional configuration that provides a framework for closer political, economic and functional co-operation in the wider Caribbean. There are 37 signatories to the convention. Twenty-five of them are independent states eligible for full membership, and the other 12 are non-independent states eligible for associate status. The ACS membership includes all countries in the Caribbean Sea (regardless of their constitutional status), the rimland countries of Central America, as well as Colombia, Venezuela and Mexico. By the end of 1999, all of the countries eligible for full membership had ratified the convention.

The broad objectives of the ACS as enshrined in the convention are:

1) strengthening the regional co-operation and integration process, with a view to creating an enhanced economic space in the region;
2) preserving the environmental integrity of the Caribbean Sea, which is regarded as the common patrimony of the peoples of the region; and
3) promoting the sustainable development of the Caribbean region.

---

13 See West Indian Commission, 1992 (1993). The report (592 printed pages) was the result of a three-year consultation with Commonwealth Caribbean people (including governments, the private sector, NGOs and civil society in general) in the region, the United Kingdom and North America.

The ACS is seen primarily as an 'integration grouping' and a consensus-building political entity, with a role in the advancement of trade liberalization and regional integration. Yet the ACS has the potential to become the world's fourth-largest regional grouping (three-quarters the size of South America's MERCOSUR). The ACS countries currently have a population of 216 million, an accumulated GDP of US$506 billion, and approximately US$180 billion in merchandise trade.[14] Clearly, the prospect of increased ultra-regional trade and investment is a strong catalyst for the ACS and one of the motives for a renewed look at regional integration as a means of facilitating broader Caribbean insertion into the global economy.

Not surprisingly, many regional policy-makers regard the ACS as a very ambitious attempt to integrate a region that has been characterized by its heterogeneity. But the ACS represents an important space both for consolidating a complex web of bilateral and subregional processes and for the smaller economies of the Caribbean region to forge alliances, unify their policies, and build negotiating power in the wider hemispheric free trade process. More important, in the context of regional integration theory in the Caribbean, the ACS represents a 'second-generation' approach to the integration prerogative. Its objective is multi-faceted, and its approach to regional integration is hybrid. Its agenda is pragmatic. The most intensive efforts of the ACS Secretariat are directed toward the issues of regional transportation and sustainable tourism, as well as science, technology, health, education and culture, where success is likely. In essence, the ACS is not an integration process *per se,* but an 'attempt to strengthen the region's negotiating position in regional diplomacy.'[15]

While the potential of the ACS is apparent, there is concern as to whether it can define, seize and effectively occupy its own policy space. This pertains in particular to CARICOM and other regional groupings such as the Central American Common Market (CACM). Possible overlap with the ACS, and the full implications of membership in the ACS for the CARICOM states and other regional groupings, will need to be monitored and studied with a view to rationalizing relations between these integration schemes. In sum, the challenge for the ACS is to become an effective vehicle for regionalism and not merely another piece of idle machinery.

---

14 Miguel Ceara Hatton, 1998, 'The Role of the Association of Caribbean States in Promoting Economic Integration within the Greater Caribbean,' ACS Secretariat, unpublished manuscript; Henry S. Gill, 1995.

15 See Winston C. Dookeran, 1996b; and Riyad Insanally, 1998.

TRADE: THE CARIBBEAN AND THE FTAA

Caribbean countries face a steep adjustment curve in preparation for the FTAA. Decades of protectionist policies must be eliminated in order to mitigate the shocks that opening up domestic markets will have on their economies, and benefit from the opportunities that global market opening will eventually confer. Consequently, several factors will affect the participation of Caribbean countries in the FTAA.

The FTAA would give Caribbean countries greater access to Latin American markets. Apart from Trinidad & Tobago, CARICOM countries conduct very little business in Latin America. The FTAA would also provide greater and more stable and predictable access to the US market for small Caribbean countries, who have a greater need for secure market access and stable and transparent trade rules in order to trade effectively. Membership of the FTAA is also likely to reduce uncertainty in the regulations governing the trade in goods and services and produce clearly defined mechanisms for dispute settlement.[16] Further, for a small country facing the risk of domestic policy reversals, establishing regional economic policy in the framework of a multilateral arrangement can have the benefit of increasing domestic policy consistency. Trade liberalization, which has been resisted in some Caribbean countries, could, therefore, be reinforced or accelerated as a result of participation in the FTAA. So, for the medium to long term, the FTAA holds the potential for promoting increased economic growth in the Caribbean region.

Conversely, both political and economic fears have been expressed by smaller less-developed economies in the hemisphere, concerning their integration into larger economic areas. On the political side, nations fear the loss of sovereignty implied by any international commitment would have domestic repercussions. Smaller nations fear this the most because they are acutely conscious of their weak bargaining power. However, realistically, in light of the changing global dynamics and the increasing globalization of the world economy, such short-term losses would occur anyway for all countries participating in the hemispheric integration process. On the economic side, small countries are mainly concerned about the exposure of their domestic industries to foreign competition and about the costs of adjustment to the widened market. For CARICOM countries and many of the small economies of Latin America, the costs of transition to a wider, more open and reciprocal hemispheric market are a serious concern. While FTAA membership will probably

16 See 'Factors Affecting the Participation of Caribbean Countries in the Free Trade Area of the Americas', 1995.

accentuate these trends, the real issue facing the smaller economies of the Caribbean is how to secure sufficient bargaining power to influence the provision of transitional arrangements which would provide some protection from the deep shocks of the FTAA process. So far, the trade dynamic in the Western Hemisphere has not been very accommodating to the smaller economies.

In a scenario where NAFTA membership and NAFTA parity remain elusive, and any possibility of securing special concessions for small economies within the FTAA is subject to negotiation on a case-by-case basis prior to 2005, the challenges for Caribbean states appear overwhelming. CARICOM's response to the specific concern about limited bargaining power is the decision to conduct its member country negotiations on the basis of a regional group approach, even though the strategy involves some loss of sovereignty for individual countries. CARICOM has turned over its own external trade relations to the Regional Negotiating Machinery (RNM) established in February 1997 in order to enhance the co-ordination and execution of its own external relations with the FTAA and the EU. The RNM works with the CARICOM Secretariat and other organs and member-states of the Community to develop a co-ordinated and cohesive strategy to prepare CARICOM countries for their entry into the FTAA.[17] However, the relationship of the CARICOM Secretariat to the RNM, as well as the division of powers, is still unclear and will have to be re-examined. Perhaps the eventual inclusion of the RNM within the Secretariat would strengthen CARICOM and clarify its role in the new era of widespread trade re-negotiations.[18] For CARICOM, clearly the main issue is the identification of concrete measures to meet the needs of its small, fragile economies, given the level of adjustment needed and the great disparities in size and development of the economies participating in the FTAA process.

As formal negotiations for the establishment of the FTAA by January 2005 progress, the Central American and Caribbean countries are accelerating their trade relations with each other. The proposed creation of a Caribbean-Central American Free Trade Area is consistent with the FTAA process and part of a trend where principal subregional groupings are also establishing trade agreements among themselves in order to strengthen their bargaining positions during the negotiations. In the long term, however, the 'new

17 The RNM consists of CARICOM members and the Dominican Republic for the EU-ACP negotiations. However, the Dominican Republic has elected to be a part of the Central American group, rather than the RNM, with respect to the FTAA negotiations.

18 See Gladstone Bonnick, 2000.

regionalism' paradigm for the Caribbean will also depend on implementing other, very challenging regional objectives. These will include the liberalization and harmonization of investment regimes, the convergence of regulatory frameworks to match global best practices, the promotion of free trade in goods and services throughout the region, the fostering of competition in the transport and telecommunications sectors, the enhancement of convergence in macro-economic policies, the promotion of continued institutional reforms in order to face the hemispheric integration challenge, and the preparation for effective participation in trade negotiations and the capacity to implement resulting agreements.

The FTAA initiative is already testing the economic diplomacy of the Caribbean region, and its limited human, financial and technical resources, by placing heavy demands on its trading regimes and negotiating capabilities. In the early years of the twenty-first century, the region is participating in complex negotiations in parallel but different time frames, with each impacting on the other.

TRADE: THE CARIBBEAN AND EUROPE

In June 2000, the EU and the ACP signed a partnership agreement to replace the existing Lomé IV Convention. The principle of partnership through a series of Lomé Conventions is one of the distinguishing features of EU co-operation with the ACP grouping as it has evolved since 1975. The Lomé Conventions comprised a succession of comprehensive agreements covering aid and trade, based on the principle of non-reciprocity. Since the inception of Lomé I in 1975, the European Community has been enlarged, with consequent effects on the shape of Lomé policy. After the negotiation of Lomé IV in 1989, the Lomé partnership came under increasing pressure as a result of several factors. The new GATT arrangement as finalized in the Uruguay Round ushered in a climate of trade liberalization spearheaded by the WTO. At the same time, there was a widespread sense of 'aid fatigue', due in part to disillusionment proceeding from a recognition that the aid had not achieved the desired result. Those opposed to further aid pointed to the development successes concentrated in Asia despite a lack of European assistance to that region. In addition, the demise of both the Eastern European bloc and the Soviet Union caused a change of focus and perspective in Europe.

An expanded post-Cold War EU is starting to favour its new partners in Eastern Europe and the Mediterranean. The EU's move toward a more global development co-operation policy has placed significant pressure on Lomé's present exclusive membership structure of ACP countries, which is seen to be inconsistent with the new directions in EU development co-operation policy.

The EU has not abandoned its ACP partners, but the geo-political and historical justification for EU-ACP relations since 1975 has disappeared.

The new EU-ACP partnership agreement sets the broad lines for future co-operation. There is a commitment by the EU to employ stricter conditionalities in an effort to foster trade and investment so that sustainable development is achieved without substantial European aid. The broad framework of co-operation after 2000 includes an emphasis on decentralized co-operation with the identification of new private sector partners, efficiency in the use of aid resources, the incorporation of respect for human rights, and demands for the consolidation of good governance and democratic principles as essential elements of co-operation.

Europe is a major trading area for Caribbean countries and the EU-ACP partnership is vital for the 12 independent CARICOM countries, the Dominican Republic, Haiti and Suriname. The regional co-operation programme functions through a special body, CARIFORUM (comprising the Caribbean members of the Lomé Convention), which maintains a formal relationship with the EU. The Caribbean countries that were beneficiaries of the Lomé Conventions have grown accustomed to a strongly concessionary trade environment for the region's sugar, bananas and rum, guaranteed by treaty obligation.

In retrospect, although the various Lomé agreements served to protect traditional exports, the trade results have been uninspiring. They did not benefit the Caribbean countries in terms of stimulating export expansion or export diversification by sector or by product. At century's end, trade with the European Union accounted for some 17 per cent of all CARICOM trade and the EU has been running a trade surplus with the Caribbean in recent years. Protection of traditional export staples, such as bananas, sugar and rum, was central to the Caribbean region's motives for entering into the Lomé agreements. The arrangements guaranteed the region reasonable market access for these products. The sugar and banana protocols also allowed ACP countries to benefit from a relatively generous EU price for their exports because of the Common Agricultural Policy. Yet trade liberalization has put the benefits of higher prices and the guaranteed access of the protocols at risk, while the pressure of the WTO and major trading partners (both within and outside Europe) also threatens their very existence.

The preferential access of the commodities produced by the ACP countries to the EU is to be restructured, primarily because of the WTO rulings. However, particular commodity issues have not yet been resolved. For example, the bulk of CARICOM sugar is currently traded under the ACP/EU Sugar Protocol at a price negotiated annually, which, at present, is about three times the world market price. This contrasts with the situation in 1975 when the Protocol was first negotiated and the world price of sugar was considerably higher. The EU and the ACP countries are looking to complete a new agreement on sugar by 2002. Similarly, the dispute between the US and the EU over bananas is caught up in their long-term battle over agriculture. Eventually, the EU will be forced to put a regime in place which will no longer be able to insulate the Windward Islands from the competition of low-cost Latin American banana producers. The Caribbean countries may have the moral high ground in the dispute, but in the new century they will have to face the possible demise of a non-viable or non-competitive industry.[19] As Europe restructures from many trading partners into one, and as EU-ACP co-operation becomes but one of a varied group of relationships maintained by the EU with developing and other countries, more fundamental shifts with significant implications for the Caribbean are likely.

THE NEW REGIONALISM

In general, at the beginning of the twenty-first century, the countries of the Caribbean are struggling toward greater progress on economic and trade policy reform. But any regional strategy must take into account the specific economic characteristics of its member countries. They are small economies in terms of territory, population size and GDP. They are also open economies: their external transactions are large relative to their total economic output. Openness renders them extremely vulnerable to external shocks, such as fluctuations in international commodity prices or policy changes abroad. Vulnerability is compounded by the region's narrow export base, and most countries depend for their export earnings on a small number of natural-resource products or tourism. The generous preferential market access for their exports to the EU and North America is in danger of being eroded or phased out in the coming years. Export diversification has been limited and insufficient for generating satisfactory growth rates. Dependence on trade taxes for government revenue is also common among the majority of CARICOM countries; thus, particularly in the Organization of Eastern Caribbean States (OECS) economies, the pursuit of any trade liberalization initiatives affects national fiscal accounts disproportionately.

On the positive side, Caribbean countries share location advantages, such as proximity to the US market and strategic location on the main trading routes between the Americas and Europe. Geographic location brings advantages for the further development of tourism services but also is a disadvantage to the island members in terms of high infrastructure and transportation costs. Such characteristics have important implications for the design

19 For a detailed history of the banana issue, see Paul Sutton, 1997, pp.5–36.

of a regional strategy for the Caribbean. The lack of a sizeable regional market, for example, indicates that the Caribbean approach to integration must, by definition, differ from that of MERCOSUR or other large integration areas. But the region's high level of trade openness also dictates that successful interaction with the world economy and the promotion of long-term, sustainable, export-led growth should be key elements in the development strategy.

Despite a number of common features, Caribbean economies are also different in terms of natural endowment, economic output, and relative wealth. In the case of CARICOM, three countries, Trinidad & Tobago, Jamaica and Barbados, together account for almost 80 per cent of the Common Market's total GDP and more than two-thirds of its merchandise exports. At the other extreme are the six small island states of the OECS, which together account for just one-tenth of CARICOM's total GDP and only 7 per cent of its exports. Realistically, integration of the Caribbean economies is hampered by great deficiencies in infra-regional transport infrastructure, with high costs and low reliability of delivery being the major impediments to the development of intra-and extra-regional trade.

Similarly, while the Caribbean Community has a long tradition of regional co-operation and integration, the results have not always matched its ambitious goals. Avowed co-operation, combined with lack of institutional capacity, has often sown the seeds of potential conflict. Disparities in resources and capabilities, as well as the compulsion of the leadership, particularly in the smallest or least powerful members of the group, to guard jealously the political sovereignty of the national entities, have often undermined multilateral initiatives. As new attempts are made to widen the Caribbean or to craft a new regionalism with an increase in the number of states, policy-makers will have to create formal and informal mechanisms to compensate for differing capabilities and resolve conflicts prompted by sovereign national interests.

The structuralism, neo-structuralism and dependency theories that provided the intellectual foundations for the Caribbean integration movement and the region's political economy are no longer relevant. The theories and strategies may have been accurate for the times, but at the turn of the century there is still a gap between the intellectual paradigm and political and economic realities. Pleading for the luxury of hemispheric uniqueness because of smaller-economy status is no longer a realistic option for the Caribbean. The assumption that small Caribbean economies cannot compete in international markets is no longer valid. Some small economies can dominate specific niche markets (tourism in the case of many Caribbean countries and certain energy-based or petrochemical industries in the case of Trinidad & Tobago). Highly educated and skilled labour resources in the region can compete with many other areas of the world. However, strategic alliances and collaboration with government, business and civil society in other countries in the wider Caribbean are necessary in order to realize the region's full potential. The new regionalism in the Caribbean also highlights a more profound process. The countries are now more willing to explore the options of multiple integration schemes simultaneously, as they approach the consolidation of hemispheric integration by the year 2005.[20]

In the Caribbean, integration emerged as a response to overcoming the development constraints of small size. The new regionalism is an accelerated response to the new dynamics of globalization. The missing element in the new regionalism is the corporate integration of national companies, which outgrow their markets and accelerate the flow of goods and services, capital, and finance throughout the region. Corporate integration is the stimulus that will push Caribbean regionalism into the new age.[21] In essence, the acceptance of globalization, corporate integration and the hemispheric trade momentum requires a management process and a strategy by small countries to reassess the dynamics of regionalism and international economic relations in a much broader context than was originally conceived by many Caribbean theorists. In the Caribbean context of political economy, the colonial past is no longer the emotional road map for the integration of the region.

The new regionalism in the Caribbean is also one that reflects a paradigm shift in integration theory and practice, from a vertical perspective (North America and Europe) toward a horizontal relationship between the countries of the wider Caribbean and Latin America. This is an important sea change because of historical circumstances that resulted in the cultivation of different international relations trajectories for the Spanish-speaking and English-speaking islands of the Caribbean. In this context, the roles of Puerto Rico, the Dominican Republic and Cuba are instructive. Traditionally, Puerto Rico's relations with the CARICOM region have been limited because of its constitutional status as a Commonwealth of the United States. From 1985 to 1992 the administration by Puerto Rico of the 936 Caribbean Development Program, and its corollary Caribbean Basin Technical Advisory Group (CBTAG), placed that country at the centre-stage of regional economic development and the transfer of technology and resources to the Caribbean. Under subsequent administrations, Puerto Rico has turned its attention away from regional initiatives and towards preoccupation with its constitutional status.

20 Miguel Ceara Hatton suggests that there is need for a 'new integrationist culture' (see Miguel Ceara Hatton 'Hacia la integración del gran caribe: Una respuesta a la globalización', unpublished manuscript, 1998).

21 This dynamic between globalization and corporate integration is analysed by Richard L. Bernal, 1997.

The issues of Puerto Rico's overall commitment to and identity with the rest of the Caribbean remain unclear.

In contrast, the Dominican Republic has a strategy that seeks to improve on those decades when, because of a history of US interventions and an overwhelming dependence on trade with the United States, it was excluded from the broader international arena. Today it is a committed member of both the ACS and CARIFORUM, participates fully in regional trade diplomacy, has signed a bilateral agreement with CARICOM, and has found a regional diplomatic niche by serving as a link between CARICOM and Central American countries in the formation of a strategic trade alliance between the two regions.

Similarly Cuba, which suffered a diplomatic setback in the region after the US intervention in Grenada in 1983, has re-emerged as a strong actor in regional diplomacy. It is a founding member of the ACS, has re-established diplomatic relations with most Caribbean countries, and has cultivated strong economic links with several CARICOM countries. The members of CARIFORUM have also sponsored its membership of the ACP. For Cuba, the ACS, CARICOM and CARIFORUM are mechanisms to break its regional isolation and to reincorporate itself into the hemispheric community. However, Cuba is on the horns of a dilemma with respect to the expansion of hemispheric trade. It is not a member of the FTAA process and has been largely isolated from the hemispheric economic movement because of US pressure.[22]

In sum, in the early years of the twenty-first century the degree of action or inaction at various levels by both the English-speaking and Spanish-speaking Caribbean states will of necessity influence the prospects for long-term regional co-operation and integration efforts.

Caribbean security

The topic of small-state security was one of the major concerns of Caribbean scholars during the 1970s and 1980s while the Cold War was still germane. The topic had both domestic and international facets. Its major themes (geopolitics, militarization, external intervention, subregional imperialism, domestic

---

22 For a discussion of the many dimensions of Caribbean-Latin American relations see Anthony T. Bryan and Andrés Serbín, 1996. On the initiatives of Puerto Rico, the Dominican Republic and Cuba see David E. Lewis, 1996, pp.41–61; Norman Girvan and Miguel Ceara Hatton, 1998.

and regional instability, peace and development) were eventually categorized under the broader designation of 'vulnerability.'[23]

The threats to economic security, identified during the Cold War era, involved 'action that can have the effect of undermining a state's economic welfare and which, additionally, can also be used as an instrument of political interference.'[24] The argument was framed in the prevailing economic and development models of the period (which included protected domestic and regional markets, bilateral and multilateral concessionary aid, and commodity price stabilization) and did not foresee the challenges which would emerge as a result of the completion of structural adjustment, the process of liberalization of the global economy, and the implementation of new trading blocs. While the liberalization of economies and the evolving financial markets in the Caribbean may be a welcome and legitimate development, there is an enormous 'downside' to the process of trade and financial liberalization. Without effective controls and safeguards the economies of small states are susceptible to a range of new vulnerabilities.

TRANSNATIONAL CRIME AND MIGRATION

A major concern is the spread of transnational crime in the Caribbean. The globalization process coupled with the communications/technology revolution has made the international system more 'interactive, integrated, interrelated, and inter-connected'. This dynamic has unlocked doors and opened windows of opportunity, enabling the underworld to widen and deepen its reach, become more sophisticated in its operations, and intensify its level and pace of transactions. In many instances fortified by a command of the power of technology and disregard for human life and humane values, coupled with indiscriminate ruthlessness, transnational criminals are able to corrupt societies with little regard for national boundaries, state sovereignty or levels of political and economic development. National policies, decision-making, the content of diplomacy, interdependence, redistribution of power – even the diplomatic temperament among nations – are impinged on, or in some instances crafted to suit. As transnational criminal activity continues to escalate and increasingly undermine the activity of legitimate enterprises, the conduct of global politics will necessarily change. Such is the power that transnational criminals exert, and with which nations small and large have to

23 See Anthony T. Bryan *et al.*, 1990; Colin Clarke and Anthony Payne, 1987; Humberto García-Muñiz, 1986; Sheila Harden, 1985; Commonwealth Secretariat, 1985. For a review of the scholarship see Ivelaw Lloyd Griffith, 1995a.

24 Commonwealth Secretariat, 1985, p.23 and pp.112–13.

contend. Increasingly also, the major contributor to corruption and criminality in the region is the illegal drug-trafficking trade. Some Eastern Caribbean countries, the Bahamas and Haiti became key trans-shipment routes for South American cocaine into US and European markets.[25] There is a number of theories to explain the resurgence of drug-trafficking along Caribbean routes: Colombian cartels have had to divert from an exclusive Mexican path because of increasing expenses and have found eager outlets in the Caribbean; the United States has fortified its border patrol and surveillance of Mexico, and even though the latter is certainly not impregnable, traffickers have found the Caribbean more amenable; and Brazilian and Venezuelan cartels are exploiting their criminal associations in the Caribbean, developed in the 1970s and 1980s.[26] This substantial 'transit traffic', while destined for North America and Europe, has also increased the availability of cocaine within the Caribbean and cocaine abuse is now widespread in a number of countries.

While most Caribbean countries co-operate with the United States in counter-narcotics efforts, some US anti-drug action appears to push extra-territorial jurisdiction too far. This perception has provoked government and public hostility in some Caribbean countries where the US is criticized for having little regard for national sovereignty. A case in point is the United States Maritime and Overflight (Shiprider) Agreement intended to stem the intra-regional flow of drugs. The agreement permits land and sea patrols by US coastguard and navy vessels, maritime searches, and seizures and arrests by US law-enforcement authorities within the national boundaries of Caribbean countries. It also allows US aircraft to overfly Caribbean countries and order suspect aircraft to land there. By the end of 1998 most Caribbean countries had signed some version of the agreement, but its impact yet remains to be seen.

In sum, the narcotics-trafficking phenomenon in the Caribbean generates and aggravates ordinary crime, promotes substance dependency, diverts national funds, and creates serious controversy in the relations between states. The transnational nature of the drug trade is difficult to combat. Narcotics trafficking is unlikely to stop in the short term, given the demand in the developed countries, the ease of electronic money laundering, onshore bank secrecy, a network of official protection enjoyed by traffickers, and the 'corporate' structure of the drug trade. A new policy is emerging – one that chases the money rather than the drugs and is more focused on reducing demand in North America and Europe.

25 The scope of the drug-trafficking trade in the Caribbean is discussed in the following: Ivelaw L. Griffith, 1997; David A. Andelman, 1995, pp.42–9; Cathy Booth, 1996; Klaus de Albuquerque, 1996.

26 Anthony P. Maingot, 1999.

Stimulated by the drug trade, corruption at all levels in the Caribbean is a very disturbing trend. In this context, offshore financial centres (OFCs) in the Caribbean occupy a precarious position in the flow of laundered money throughout the region. Given the globalization of finance and investment, the importance of these centres for the economies of small island states is understandable. Though international financial services and the OFCs are potentially rich sources of national revenue, governments have to accelerate their efforts to prevent the use of these institutions as safe havens for laundering the proceeds of drug trafficking and organized crime. Such use has dangerous implications for Caribbean countries. Powerful countries with extraterritorial reach in such matters have the potential to attack the financial sector of small countries that permit such activities.

In mid-1999 the Organization of Economic Cooperation and Development (OECD), a conglomeration of the world's wealthiest states, unilaterally devised international standards to combat 'harmful tax competition' directed against 47 countries (15 of them from the Caribbean) with offshore financial services and nominal corporation taxes, which it claims are causing capital flight and injury to the tax regimes in OECD countries. The establishment of such criteria and threats to 'blacklist' certain Caribbean OFCs have moved the governments of the Caribbean to open a dialogue with the OECD. Such co-operation is intended to formulate joint approaches to maintain acceptable international regulatory standards, implement international best standards and practices, and to eliminate opportunities for money laundering using onshore financial institutions.[27] As the Caribbean moves toward free trade and common markets, anti-laundering measures become more necessary. There are terrible costs to society, polity and economy associated with inaction in these circumstances. The developed countries can make a distinct contribution to small economies by providing institution-building and training for competent regulation of the offshore financial centres.

Migration and international economic interdependence, as well as the economic, trade and foreign-investment consequences of migration (for both the sending and receiving societies), have also emerged as major security issues in the international relations of the Caribbean. The flood of Haitian and Cuban refugees to the US in the 1980s and 1990s illustrates the extent of the problem. Haiti and Cuba (for other reasons) may be extreme scenarios of migration and refugees propelled by combinations of political and economic

---

27 For a discussion of the OECD measures see Bruce Zagaris, 1998. On money-laundering counter-measures see Ivelaw L. Griffith, 1995b; Anthony P. Maingot, 1996b, pp.32–7.

circumstances. However, migration, legal or illegal, will continue as a safety valve for economic dislocation in the Caribbean. The resulting movement of human talent does not necessarily present a doomsday scenario for either the Caribbean or receiving countries such as the United States. The remittances and investments sent by productive Caribbean emigrants should be regarded as part of a larger trans-border contribution to long-term economic growth, peace and security in the hemisphere. In spite of frequent anti-immigration fervour, the United States, and other developed receiving nations, stand to benefit economically from the immigration flows.[28]

It is not clear how changes in migration patterns to North America and Europe will affect the levels of remittances that now constitute an important aspect of many Caribbean economies. However, should immigration from the Caribbean be limited to those who are highly skilled and educated, the countries will lose on two counts: the investment made in educating them and the forgone returns of their education. The challenge for Caribbean countries is to create the economic opportunities to retain their skilled labour force.

Environment and sustainable development

The environment and sustainable development are also important security issues for the Caribbean. They are in fact critical to the economic survival of many countries. The environment is at the centre of the tourism industry, the principal source of revenue for many countries, and co-ordination in the tourism sector inevitably implies co-ordination in the area of the environment. The urgency for effective disaster emergency-response, storm hazard assessment and impact monitoring, disaster preparedness and prevention, relevant insurance, environmental health and population relocation are some of the urgent matters which dictate consensus and collaboration at the regional and international levels.[29] Political issues aside, Haiti is an extreme example of a crisis in Caribbean environmental demographics. Under current conditions, the land can no longer support its population adequately. Many of Haiti's economic problems stem largely from the degradation of natural resources, the uncertainty of politics and development planning, and inadequate distribution and delivery systems. The depletion of the country's resources is a fundamental cause of conflict and human misery and national and regional policies must make sustainable development a priority.

At another level, the rapid industrialization of Trinidad & Tobago provides a case study in the inherent risk for environmental disaster in a small

28 On the various dimensions of this topic, see Max J. Castro, 1999.

29 See Erik Blommestein *et al.*, 1996.

country. Trinidad & Tobago has a hydrocarbon-based economy and by 1999 it had become the major energy-based economy in the island Caribbean with large new investments in heavy manufacturing activities including sugar refining, oil refining, the production of ammonia, methanol, urea, direct reduced iron, steel and cement. The industrialization of Trinidad & Tobago's economy is due primarily to its vast resources of relatively cheap natural gas. The necessary associated environmental planning for industrialization of this magnitude still lags. A lack of environmental awareness and regulatory inaction has resulted in a large majority of industries discharging unmonitored, untreated quantities of wastes into the land environment and into the Caribbean Sea.

In the twenty-first century, whether it is natural-resource depletion (Haiti) or rapid industrial growth (Trinidad & Tobago), Caribbean governments need to overcome their ambivalence towards environmental issues. Governments, in collaboration with the private sector, international donor agencies, and NGOs as advocates, must develop regional strategies and set up effective mechanisms and infrastructure to regulate and enforce appropriate policies.

The new diplomacy

The Caribbean can be described as the only region in the world, with a relatively small population, which harbours such a diversity of political, as well as administrative and institutional systems in a small geographical space. Historical fragmentation into Spanish, English, French, Dutch, and more recently American systems of politics and governance testifies to the plurality of possible constraints placed on collaboration in the multilateral arena. But difficult situations do not necessarily mean a lack of solutions. Indeed, if local or regional imperatives for collaboration do not prevail, international and hemispheric circumstances will dictate other responses.

Multilateral intervention by United States and United Nations forces in October 1994 to restore political freedoms in Haiti serves as an example of how the internal abuse of democracy and justice in one country can impact on, not only its own economic and entire developmental ethos, but also the stability and security of the region. The concerted and measured diplomatic and military response of CARICOM and other Caribbean nations to these events subsequently had an impact on both the hemispheric body, the Organization of American States (OAS), and on the United Nations. The situation was sufficiently serious to solicit widespread international collaboration. But it was only as a 'regional' collective that the Caribbean could play its part in any significant way.

A new international role for Caribbean nations will take into account their participation in multilateral missions. Caribbean people have participated in election-observer missions, and the region's police and defence forces have been involved in international monitoring and security missions. CARICOM countries, with their traditions of parliamentary democracy and well-established professionalism in civil services and police and military forces, are poised to play active roles as trainers and observers in the international promotion of democracy world wide. Such roles are subject to the economic limitations placed on small states. But with financial support from the UN or the OAS, Caribbean nations could become more actively involved in addressing international problems. A multilateral Caribbean impact on the promotion and enhancement of good governance, democracy, human rights and justice in the region would seem to be a requisite for the twenty-first century.

In the course of the twentieth century, diplomacy underwent enormous changes. But even more profound transformations began during the last decades of the century. The diplomatic sanctuary of sovereignty, which protected countries against interference in their internal affairs by other states or international bodies, began to be eroded. Information technology and cyberspace overcame distance and facilitated continuous contact with all segments of a country's own diplomatic establishment as well as with international institutions. At the same time the flow of communication over the Internet largely defeated national, regional and even global efforts to exercise sovereign control.

Today, the major political factor influencing diplomacy is the relative decline of the role of national governments. They face severe competition in diplomatic activities from other actors: private sectors, religious groups, immigrants, media, NGOs and other elements of civil society. The other actors demand that their interests be taken into account and that they have some voice in the making of foreign policy. Similarly, legislative branches of countries are themselves contributing to this evolution in diplomacy. The parliamentarians of the world have set up a structure of global and international interaction and are claiming a role in diplomatic meetings, which was traditionally reserved for the executive arm of government. Involvement of the media – and through them the ordinary people – in international affairs has led to strong displays of public diplomacy. Public pressure groups or vested interests can influence governments to follow or abandon certain courses of action, often in disregard of international commitments or true national interests. In many instances, the appropriateness of external policies of the government is publicly questioned in the media. Non-governmental organizations, pressure groups and lobbies of all kind now surround bilateral as well as multilateral events and insist on being heard and consulted. External involvement in internal issues and conflicts also increasingly relies on specialized, mainly non-governmental institutions. Delegates of the International Red Cross and others in the humanitarian field are playing important roles as intermediaries and even negotiators in conflict resolution. In essence, individual countries, however big and powerful, can no longer handle global problems by themselves. They have to be tackled by the international community as a whole.

Professional diplomacy itself is undergoing considerable change with respect to methodology and mechanisms. In several Caribbean countries, the need to maintain costly diplomatic missions and consular posts has been questioned, even though the element of personal diplomacy would be difficult to replace as a mechanism for bilateral relations. In the multilateral field fruitless ideological and political confrontations are giving way to co-operative interaction aimed at actually dealing with the problems at hand. Neither individual countries nor international institutions can afford the endless conferences and meetings of the past. This has led to an increasingly informal approach to discussions, with fewer formal meetings. The preparatory role of international secretariats and the importance of interaction with them through permanent missions (or over the Internet) are constantly growing, and it is now possible to expedite complex issues in less time.

At the level of foreign ministries new communications technology allows the diplomat to have continuous contact with the home base. Information technology also contributes to networking by missions and posts abroad, and between them and the databases of the foreign ministry, other ministries, and government agencies that conduct or influence foreign policy both at preparatory and decision-making levels. The administrative work, accounts and consular matters of most missions can be handled at the foreign ministry itself. In the future such networks may well be extended to include the private sector and non-governmental bodies which have a stake in external relations. Similarly, networking will go beyond national establishments to include members of regional groups such as CARICOM with resulting enhancement of their capacity and efficiency.

During the twenty-first century the new diplomacy will become even more important, and it will evolve further in ways that cannot yet be imagined. Consequently, it is important that those involved in the study, teaching and practice of diplomacy in small countries should fully exploit the potential provided by the new tools of diplomacy. The Caribbean must be a part of this momentum.

Conclusion

The global economic environment is in a state of rapid transition. The new dispensation in both the developing and developed world is the opening up of national and regional economies to market forces. Profound transformations in the relations between State, civil society and the economy are accompanying the process. In this vaguely Darwinian scenario, concepts of nationhood are being challenged by international integration, and national governments and politicians are hard pressed to demonstrate proper administrative capacity over this implicit surrender of sovereignty. The Caribbean countries have to cope with these new dynamics. There are no precise road maps, no easy solutions – only operational principles.

Integration into the global economy is the best route for Caribbean countries. Free trade is inevitable; economic marginalization would represent one of the major security threats. While larger countries are not tolerant of exceptions to the new trading rules being made for smaller countries, a weaning period to adjust to new arrangements can be negotiated. In addition, Caribbean countries have to turn their attention to forging economic development strategies that go well beyond the current global euphoria with liberalization and privatization. In undertaking this task, CARICOM countries in particular have an advantage in respect of human capital. High literacy rates and excellent records of primary and secondary school enrolment must now be bolstered by policies to raise educational quality in technologies, management and finance which are crucial ingredients for competition in the emerging global economy.[30]

The challenges are complex but they all lead eventually to global interaction. Caribbean countries need to reposition their economies to take advantage of the transitions in the global economy. Preliminary studies suggest that many Caribbean countries could have a comparative advantage in the services sector: primarily the provision of health care, biotechnology, tourism, education, and the financial, retirement and information-processing industry. But they need to move quickly to develop niches and proceed beyond the stage of simply exporting manufactured goods. Services are increasing more rapidly as a component of international trade than is the export of manufactured goods. This repositioning should not mean the abandonment of traditional sectors of the economy, such as manufacturing or agriculture. Rather it should include, if possible, the reform and strengthening of these sectors for global competitiveness.

The public and private sectors in the Caribbean will have to work in harness to secure capital, technology and marketing through joint ventures, and strategic corporate alliances. Similarly, every effort will have to be made to repatriate or engage the talent of Caribbean human resources resident outside the region. The forward-looking planners should already anticipate that the

30 World Bank, 1994, p.1281; Gladstone Bonnick, 2000.

Caribbean's demography has expanded to include significant financial, intellectual and market sectors among Caribbean peoples in Florida, New York, Toronto, London and many other European and Latin American capitals.

In general, many of the trends outlined in this chapter have important implications for the security of the Caribbean region. Similarly, political polarization, ethnic and class tensions, environmental degradation (including oil spills and hazardous waste dumping), and food security are also 'grey area' concerns for the future of Caribbean security. They are as much a part of the agenda for discussion as security mechanisms, regional international regimes, or notions of co-operative security. Caribbean nations must be responsible for their own security. Some issues can be addressed on a national or regional basis, others will have to be tackled through bilateral mechanisms, and yet others will require a global approach. Caribbean security issues for the twenty-first century will be complex and in most cases interrelated.

Finally, small states of the Caribbean must find ways to position themselves on the international stage and claim some of the diplomatic spotlight for themselves. The pre-requisite for such 'niche diplomacy' is a precise correlation of basic national and international interests. The active involvement of civil society, NGOs and public opinion is important to ensure that a national or regional 'brand name' diplomacy has intellectual substance, and provide continuity from one political administration to another. Some precise areas for niche diplomacy for the Caribbean are in the areas of tourism, the environment, ocean policy, energy diplomacy, financial services, regulatory diplomacy, and emphasis on a rules-based international order. These are areas in which Caribbean countries have a large stake. In niche diplomacy a country's (or region's) foreign policy can be proactive, and occupy secure and influential places on the international scene, by emphasizing national or regional distinctiveness and by concentrating limited resources on certain specific objectives.[31] Caribbean international relations of the twenty-first century will also demand new proactive strategies, hard reciprocal bargaining and a rejection of the siege mentality of the past.

As this chapter has tried to point out, there is a strong link between political economy, development concerns and security issues in Caribbean international relations. Successful policies are those that enhance economic development, show distributive justice, encourage the rule of law, protect fundamental human rights and security, and foster the growth of democratic institutions. The Caribbean's pursuit of creative diplomacy, and successful international relations, will require partnership between government, civil society and the private sector in the context of a liberalized economic system.

---

31 On niche diplomacy see Alan K. Henrikson, 1998; Andrew F. Cooper, 1997.

Demographic and social structural changes in the contemporary Caribbean

Fe Iglesias García

Introduction

'The Caribbean' has been defined in differing ways depending on the purposes of the research involved. Geographically, the term is often used to refer to all the continental and insular territories within, or bordered by, the Caribbean Sea. In more general terms, the Caribbean is considered to be the insular area plus those continental nations in which, under the control of the European colonial powers and with the use of a slave and semi-slave labour force imported from Africa, India, China and other parts of the world, the plantation economy was developed. The most conventional definition includes the islands from the Bahamas to Trinidad & Tobago and the continental enclaves of Belize, Guyana, Suriname and French Guyana.

Understood in this way, the Caribbean can be seen to have a certain unity that distinguishes it from other 'regions', since in it an unusual group of societies has been produced. The composition of its population is different from any other area in the world; the intermingling of races, languages, customs, cultures and religions which characterize the various groups of people that inhabit the Caribbean has made it one of the most heterogeneous regions on the planet.[1]

There is no question but that this unity, simultaneously diverse and similar, is the distinguishing mark of a region which is, from every angle, exceedingly complex. Its complexity may be seen in the mosaic of ethno-cultural configurations, linguistic and religious expressions, forms of social organization, and modalities of daily conduct that characterize the region – a mosaic whose complexity and diversity are, almost paradoxically, the region's unifying trait.[2]

1 Franklin W. Knight and Colin A. Palmer, 1989, pp.1–2.
2 Franklin W. Knight, 1990.

It is a commonplace observation that the racial composition of the Caribbean is the product of its history, a history in which modern slavery played a determining role,[3] though other factors such as the type of colonization and migratory movements subsequent to the abolition of slave labour also played some part.

As the autochthonous population virtually disappeared, the Caribbean communities began to re-form with the arrival of people from diverse places, and of many different ethnic backgrounds and races. The traits which distinguish these societies are the product of the social relations established between the various human groups that settled in the particular place, and those of their descendants, in a centuries-long exchange and renewal of elements.

The complex social organism of modern slavery is the common basis of the forms that mark the region, and the root of the structural processes that acted upon it. It is slavery that impressed its economic, social, and cultural mark upon the region. But slavery had its particular characteristics in each individual country of the Caribbean, and those conditions internal to each country have manifested themselves as variants of a single social structure.

Largely determined by economic needs, demographic events played an important role in the region and exercised great influence on the resulting whole. Many and varied migratory movements occurred, in an almost regular pattern, triggered by the need for labour in the various subregions, and they had a profound effect on social processes.

It is not easy to study the ethnic and social structure of such a diverse unity. Within the region, we find communities whose racial make-up is largely African, others in which most of the inhabitants are of specific types of mixed blood (with various strains involved in the mix), communities with a predominantly white population, and some in which all or almost all races are present. It is for this reason that we must analyse this problem in the context that characterizes the differing groups of nations.

I am not talking about formulating a classification on the basis of skin pigmentation, but rather on the basis of the differences associated with the

---

3 '...[But] we are not in the presence of a question of races; rather, [we are talking about] a system of land exploitation that divides the populace into two groups: a small number of people serving capitalism who direct and administer the sugar cane crops and the manufacture and shipping of the sugar, and a mass of salaried workers of a race which, depending upon the circumstances of the place, is forced most peremptorily by need to accept a minimum wage and tolerate a lower standard of living: blacks in Jamaica and Barbados, blacks and Indians in Trinidad-Tobago and British Guiana, blacks and whites in Cuba and Puerto Rico'. Ramiro Guerra y Sánchez, 1970 (1976), pp.5–6.

cultural elements and social relationships that determined the way those groups were linked and the way they were sited within the social structure, which almost always directly corresponds to the weighting of the various races. This means that one can hardly generalize for the entire region, because, as Franklin W. Knight has pointed out, the region

> ... is like a prism with light passing through – whatever enters is transformed. This leads to enormous imprecision in self-definition or even in how others may choose to view them – and a veritable nightmare for statisticians, demographers, and especially those obsessed with color and race. Nothing in the Caribbean is simple. Bipolar contrasts rarely exist. Things tend to be placed along a fluid spectrum, and the local speech richly reflects this graduated variety.[4]

The author of this chapter has been through this 'nightmare', has been the victim of the lack of uniformity in classification, not to mention the many gaps in the data on some aspects or countries.

Despite many similarities with the countries of Latin America, the characteristics of the Caribbean states manifestly differentiate them from those countries. Two tendencies that can be seen in the countries of the Caribbean colonized by Spain are a predominance of a population of European descent and greater segregation than elsewhere. Consequently, race relations are much more complex in these countries than in others, although in those in which the population is very diverse, one can also find serious inter-ethnic conflicts.[5]

It is well known that before the abolition of slavery, in most of the Caribbean the white population, 'reduced on each island to the number strictly essential for administering the plantations, governing the colony, collecting the taxes and tariffs, and keeping the slaves in hand, did not increase, because on those islands there was neither room nor incentive of any kind for new European settlers. For two hundred years, their history was limited to the mere relieving or monotonous succession of plantation administrators and employees.'[6]

This meant that in countries such as Haiti, Jamaica and most of the smaller Caribbean islands, the white population was a minority. In others, such as Guyana, Suriname and Trinidad & Tobago, the need for labourers after the abolition of slavery led to a massive transport of contract labourers

4 Franklin W. Knight, 1990, pp.308–9.

5 Bridget Brereton, 1981.

6 Ramiro Guerra y Sánchez, 1970 (1976), p.24.

from Asia,[7] which means that today in those nations, the population is multi-racial and multi-ethnic, with only a tiny presence of Whites.

In Cuba, the Spanish presence never ceased being renewed; many Peninsular Spaniards and Canary Islanders were also victims of contract labour,[8] but others enjoyed the possibility of rising in the social structure. In Puerto Rico, there was also a relatively large immigration of Whites around 1815, and this group was incorporated into the dominant stratum, thereby strengthening it.[9] At any rate, after the abolition of slavery, important transformations can be observed in the racial composition of the various sectors and classes, especially in those countries in which Blacks had not been repressed by a white majority, whose numbers might have been kept high or even increased by an immigration policy aimed at 'whitening' *(blanquear)* the country, as in the case of Cuba.

There can simply be no doubt that the abolition of slavery brought about radical transformations in the make-up of those societies, and that the simple division by classes – which virtually coincided with the races – underwent profound mutations. In most of the Caribbean states, Blacks were never a minority, and so never displayed the classic psychology of the minority group, the highly oppressive sense of being black. Their overwhelming numerical superiority gave them greater economic, political and social security, and therefore greater opportunity to rise through the various social strata.

In recent years, the region has experienced important economic and social changes which have entailed transformations in its occupational and social structure, but the ethnic composition has not demonstrated any notable change. In my view, the most notable feature of the region is the stability shown over the course of the twentieth century by the racial composition inherited from the plantation society.

It is significant that the proportions of the various races and ethnic groups have not shown any radical changes as a consequence of the

7 Bridget Brereton, 1981, pp.96–115.

8 Fe Iglesias García, 1994, p.93.

9 'The Real Cédula de Gracias of 1815 served to open the Island's doors to all white foreigners who were able to bring in capital, technical knowledge in sugar production, or slaves. It was in this way that a considerable number of Englishmen, Frenchmen, Dutchmen, Germans, and Spaniards, plus Creoles fleeing the Wars of Independence in Spain's South American colonies, came to Puerto Rico.... [What] we are dealing with, then, is a qualitative "whitening" or "bleaching out", that is, a re-Europeanization of the white elite whose relative weakness in the face of the rising energies of the mulatto sector had to be alarming for the colonial regime' (José Luis González, 1981, pp.47–8 and 50).

economic and social transformations attendant on the Second World War. This fact reflects a separation between racial and ethnic groups on the basis of cultural barriers and racial prejudices. One objective measure of this is the index of *mestizaje,* which reflects the tendency toward (ethnic and racial) endogamy that characterizes the evolution of the Caribbean population, although it must be noted that there are differing points of view with respect to this point.[10]

But the truth is, statistics give evidence of considerable stability in the proportions in which the ethnic groups are represented. Some communities have undoubtedly remained closed due to racial prejudices, as in the case of the 'poor whites' of Barbados[11] and some sectors of the élites, such as the 'French Creoles' in Trinidad or the *béqués* of Martinique,[12] and there have also been exclusions for religious reasons, as in the case of Jews and Hindus. Nonetheless, from the point of view of culture and society in general, the encounter between such dissimilar identities and the slow acculturation of the transplanted populations and their Creole descendants produced a fertile genesis which gave way to a new, and constantly re-enriching, culture, and this is one of the distinguishing marks of the world of the Caribbean.

The close correlation between class and colour in these societies is a reality, but there is no rigid system of castes. Skin colour does have an influence on the possibilities of upward social mobility, but it is not an exclusive determinant. The real division of society is horizontal, into social classes; it is not based exclusively on identification by skin colour or ethnic identity. In the Caribbean there is a complex range of *parallel* hierarchies within the various social estates – Blacks, Mixed-race, Indians, Chinese, Whites – each with its own classes. Cross alliances occur when links between the classes

---

10 Gordon K. Lewis has the following to say on this matter, writing in the 1960s: 'Generally, however, racial purity is at a minimum. Thus, the last handful of pure Caribs are dying out; the Chinese in Trinidad are already nearly half mixed; and where racial endogamy is consciously pursued it tends to characterize marginal small groups like the Grenada and Barbados "poor whites" or the French "Cha-Chas" of St Thomas, whose anomalous position as lower class economically but upper class in race and culture drove them, understandably, into their present-day closed communities, and whose members exhibit, as the price for their attitude, a high degree of consanguine degeneracy. The East Indian elements in Guyana and Trinidad, it is true, may appear to belie this general argument. Yet their members exhibit more racial admixture than they sometimes care to admit; the practice of familially-arranged early marriage, itself a device to ensure a "pure" union, is gradually breaking down as Indian youth revolts against it, and the Indian norms of feminine submissiveness and filial obedience thus are being constantly violated… .' Gordon K. Lewis, 1968, p.19.

11 F. A. Hoyos, 1978, p.96.

12 Bridget Brereton, 1989, pp.93–4.

emerge which are based on economic interests, political affiliation, social bonds, religious practices and family relationships. Still, both in White-majority communities and in others, we find a marginalized sector made up of the poorest persons of colour.

As the twentieth century advanced, the relationships and organization of production associated with capitalism came to have a greater and greater presence. Little by little, all spheres of social life were determined or recreated and reproduced under the demands of the political and economic relationships of capitalism. The bourgeois society accelerated the social division of labour, the expansion of production, urbanization and industrialization, and the growth of the trade, transport and service sectors. This in turn modified, more or less profoundly and to a greater or lesser degree depending on the country, the dynamics of social and consequently race relations.

Ethnic and racial structure

The most significant contrasts occur with respect to the 'whitest' islands, though it is quite difficult to precisely determine the issue of race in discriminatory societies. Censuses classify this population characteristic on the basis of skin colour and the 'personal observation' of the census-takers,[13] which implies that the white group will always be over-counted. In Puerto Rico, the percentage of Whites increased from 72.9 per cent in 1920 to 76.2 per cent in 1935,[14] and by 1950 stood at 80 per cent.[15]

In subsequent years, this differentiation is lost, since the Puerto Rican statistics consider almost everyone 'Hispanic'.[16] This classification is implicitly discriminatory on the basis of ethnic identification, since in the United States, Hispanics are differentiated from persons considered 'Whites'. In addition, the imprecision of the categories makes it difficult to study the percentage of *mestizaje* in a society in which most people desire to 'rise' into the white estate. The 'whitening' of Puerto Rico seems more a product of racial mixing than of an immigration of Whites or emigration of Blacks.

13 Cuba, Oficina General de los Censos (OGC), 1955, p.xv.

14 Reconstruction Administration of Puerto Rico, 1938, p.18.

15 United Nations, 1956, p.261. I should note that population statistics almost always have a category designated as 'unclassified' or 'unknown'. I have attempted to exclude this category whenever possible, but it has not always been feasible to do so; therefore, not all cases add to 100 per cent.

16 United States Central Intelligence Agency (USCIA), 1991, p.256.

TABLE 11.1 Population of Cuba by skin colour (percentage of total)

	1899	*1907*	*1919*	*1931*	*1943*	*1953*	*1981*
Asian	1.0	0.6	0.5	0.7	0.4	0.3	0.1
White	66.9	69.7	72.3	72.1	74.3	72.8	66.0
Mestizo (mixed)	17.2	16.3	16.0	16.2	15.6	14.5	21.9
Black	14.9	13.4	11.2	11.0	9.7	12.4	12.0

Sources: Memorias inéditas del censo de 1931, 1978; Cuba, 1945; Cuba, Oficina General de los Censos, 1955; Junta Central de Planificación de Cuba, 1971; Cuba, Oficina Nacional del Censo, 1983.

In the case of Cuba, information is more detailed, and the 'whitening' that is observed through mid-century can be seen to be largely due to a considerable immigration of Spaniards.[17] The changes since the late nineteenth century are presented here (in Table 11.1).

The subjective element is clearly evident in the differentiation between 'Blacks' and 'mestizos', and this subjectivity may explain the decline in the number of persons classified as Blacks in 1943. That is, this is not a change brought about by the immigration of Haitians and Jamaicans because immigration had been almost entirely eliminated since the previous decade, and the effects of the whitening due to Spanish immigration occurred prior to this census. Whatever the case, we can clearly see a lower percentage of non-white population.[18] The most significant change is a decline in the proportion of Whites from 73 per cent in 1953 to 66 per cent in 1981, almost the same percentage as in 1899, and an increase of almost 8 per cent in the number of 'mestizos' over the same period, though in earlier years this number had been declining. Undoubtedly these transformations are due to the fact that since 1959, racial prejudice has decreased appreciably and there has been a greater mixing of the races. The reduction of the percentage of Whites may also have been affected by the fact that Spanish immigration had come to an end, plus the fact that emigrants from Cuba during recent years have been largely

17 Fe Iglesias García, 1993.

18 'The immigration of Haitians, the second largest after that of Spanish, had also declined considerably. After an influx of 35,971 into the country in 1920, the number fell to 18,750 in 1925 and at the end of the next five-year period, i.e., 1930, had fallen further, to 5,126. A similar decline may be seen in the number of Jamaicans between the period from 1921 to 1925, which totaled 32,601, and the period from 1926 to 1930, which totaled 6,111. In 1931, only 52 Jamaicans and 22 Haitians immigrated to Cuba. This current appears to have been suspended due to provisions adopted to avoid undesirable immigration' (*Memorias inéditas del censo de 1931*, 1978, p.59).

white. Unfortunately for our purposes, the 1970 census did not address the question of race; this would have made it possible to gauge more precisely the change over the last three decades.

As the Dominican Republic had another type of settlement pattern, its population is predominantly mixed-race, in which almost every person is a descendant of both Europeans and Africans. According to the 1935 census, Whites constituted between 13 per cent and 14 per cent of the population, with Blacks between 15 per cent and 16 per cent, while 'mulattos', or mixed-race persons, made up the overwhelming majority, between 70 per cent and 71 per cent. In the 1950s, a certain 'whitening' seems to have occurred, since the proportion of Whites now increased to 28.1 per cent, that of Blacks fell to 11.5 per cent, and the number of 'mulattos' also fell, to 60.4 per cent.[19] These percentages continued, with slight variations, during the following two decades.[20] In the 1980s, the number of mestizos rose to 73 per cent and 'pure' Whites and Blacks fell to 16 per cent and 11 per cent respectively,[21] almost exactly their current numbers.[22]

Jamaica and Haiti are the two largest Caribbean nations with an overwhelming majority of Blacks. Table 11.2 presents the ethnic composition of Jamaica in the second half of the century. In Haiti, 'pure' Blacks totalled 95 per cent of the population in 1960, with '*mulâtres*' about 4 per cent and Whites constituting a tiny minority.[23] These percentages have not changed appreciably since then;[24] Blacks continue to be the predominant group, with a very small number of Whites. Haiti is the Caribbean's pre-eminent 'black' nation.[25]

TABLE 11.2 Composition of Jamaican population (By percentage of total)

Ethnicity	*1943*	*1960*	*1980*	*1991*
Black	77.7	76.8	76.3	76.3
'Mulatto'	17.7	14.5	15.1	15.1
Indian	2.12	3.36	3.4	3.0
White	1.29	0.07	3.2	3.2
Chinese	0.99	1.22	1.2	1.2
Other	0.16	3.9	0.9	1.2

Sources: Countries of the World and their Leaders, Yearbook, 1984, vol. 1, p.590; USCIA, 1991, p.158.

19 United Nations, 1956, pp.259–61.
20 *Libro de nuestro siglo,* 1970, pp.1833–4; New Encyclopaedia Britannica, vol. II, 1975, p.615.
21 *Countries of the World and their Leaders, Yearbook,* 1984, p.450.
22 USCIA, 1991, p.85.
23 New Encyclopaedia Britannica, vol. IV, 1975, p.843.
24 *Countries of the World and their Leaders, Yearbook,* 1984, p.123.

The arc of the Antilles presents a unique gamut of skin tones: in the French Antilles, Martinique is unquestionably more mixed-race and lighter-skinned than Guadeloupe. The centre of civil and military administration, Fort-de-France, was settled mostly by soldiers, administrators, magistrates and businessmen engaged with France. But the greatest diversity is seen in the islands of the Guadeloupe archipelago: Marie Galante was more suited for growing sugar-cane, and so from the beginning its population was predominantly black, while the small dependencies such as Îles des Saintes and La Désirade were characterized by a very light-skinned settlement group. It is in St Barthélemy that one encounters the greatest contrast with Guadeloupe. The 'St Barts' are descendants of Normans, Bretons or the Charentais who settled on the island. The small Dutch island of Saba also has the hallmarks of a white enclave in the tropics.[26]

In the anglophone islands of the Lesser Antilles, one also finds great contrasts: from the indigenous people of Dominica who mostly live in a small reserve of several hundred citizens, among whom not a few are of mixed race, one passes to the Leeward Islands, in which more than 80 per cent of the population is black, while in the Windwards the percentage of mixed-race people is greater (35.4 per cent). There is also some Indian and Chinese presence in these islands. The Bahamas and Barbados each have a population that is largely black; in both, mixed-race people account for more than 10 per cent of the population, although the ethnic composition of Barbados is more varied.[27] In Trinidad & Tobago, the population is multi-racial and multi-ethnic (see Table 11.3).

This ethnic complexity is mirrored in the diversity of religions: the 1946 census recorded 35 per cent Roman Catholic, 24 per cent Anglican, 22 per cent Hindu, 6 per cent Muslim, and 7 per cent other non-Christian. The rest of the population was made up of Protestant Christians of various denominations: Adventists, Baptists, Moravians, Methodists, etc.[28] More recent data show Muslims at 6 per cent, Hindus at 24 per cent, and Christians at 60 per cent, of whom 29 per cent are Catholic.[29]

The most significant datum here is that the various ethnic groups have remained relatively stable, indicating a tendency to endogamy, which is almost certainly influenced by the factor of religion. The mixed-race population has shown little change, though the Indian population increased

25 Guy Lasserre, 1974, p.57.

26 *Ibid.*

27 *Memorias inéditas del censo de 1931,* 1978; United Nations, 1956; New Encyclopaedia Britannica, vol. IV, 1975.

28 Lloyd Braithwaite, 1975, p.59.

29 *Europa Yearbook*, 1995.

TABLE 11.3 Composition of population of Trinidad & Tobago (percentage of total)

Race/ethnic group	*1946*	*1970*	*1990*
Black	46.9	43.0	39.6
Indian	35.1	40.0	40.3
Mixed	14.1	14.0	18.5
White	2.7	1.0	0.6
Chinese	1.0	1.0	0.4
Syrian	0.2	—	0.1
Other	0.02	—	0.2

Sources: United Nations, 1956, p.261; *Countries of the World and their Leaders, Yearbook,* vol. 1, pp.1131; *South America, Central America and the Caribbean,* 1995, p.603.

between 1946 and 1970, Blacks and Whites fell slightly, and the Hindu population remained stable.

In the continental enclaves of the Caribbean, the population structure is more complex. In 1946, 16.9 per cent of Belize's population were descendants of the ancient Maya, 6.9 per cent descended from the Caribs, with 38.3 per cent Blacks or Creoles, 31.1 per cent of mixed race, and the rest Syrians, Indians and Chinese, with only 4 per cent Whites. That composition has not changed a great deal, as we see by the fact that in 1991 there were reported to be 39.7 per cent Creoles, 33.1 per cent of mixed race, and 9.5 per cent Maya.[30]

Guyana presents similar characteristics: in 1946, Indians represented 43.5 per cent of the population, with Blacks and mixed-race persons together totalling near 50 per cent, 4.3 per cent Amerindians, 0.9 per cent Chinese, and the only Whites mentioned being the 2.3 per cent Portuguese population. By the 1980s, Indians had increased to 51 per cent of the population, with Blacks and mixed-race persons falling to 43 per cent, Amerindians comprising 4 per cent, and Whites and Chinese at 2 per cent; identical percentages were reported in 1991. In French Guiana the population is very similar to that of the Lesser Antilles, as it is in the Dutch insular possessions.

The most complex racial and ethnic mix is found in Suriname. In 1970, Indians comprised 30 per cent of the population, with Javanese at 16 per cent, 'Creoles' (Blacks and mixed-race) at 37 per cent, and Amerindians and Maroons making up 12 per cent. There were no more than 5,000 Europeans (1.4 per cent), not many more than Chinese.[31] In 1991, the population was reported to be 37 per cent Indian, 31 per cent Creoles, 15.3 per cent Javanese,

30 United Nations, 1956.

31 Guy Lasserre, 1974, p.287.

2.6 per cent Amerindians, 10.3 per cent Maroons, 1.7 per cent Chinese, and only 1 per cent Whites.[32]

When the Caribbean is seen as a region, the non-white component is clearly in the majority: In 83.5 per cent of the countries, it is over 90 per cent of the population,[33] although this does not necessarily imply any absence of racial conflict or prejudice, which persist as legacies of the slave society. Even in Cuba, where as state policy since 1959 obstacles to racial integration have been eliminated and discrimination eradicated, it can still be reported that 'the elimination of institutionalized racism and the removal of judicial barriers that stood in the way of [citizens'] enjoyment of equal rights independent of skin color have not meant the eradication of racism in all its expressions, as some dared think would happen.'[34]

Demographic changes

The Caribbean is also characterized by the great contrasts presented by the spatial distribution of the population. The population densities of the region's countries range from the highest to the lowest to be found anywhere on the planet. Generally speaking, high population densities are typical of the small islands, with the exception of the archipelago of the Bahamas, which includes many tiny uninhabited islands, although even here the density has risen from 6.9 inhabitants per square kilometre in 1950 to 23.3 in 1995. This is one element that has not undergone great variation over time, since even in 1950 Barbados was a densely populated island with concentrations approaching 500 inhabitants per square kilometre, while today there may be more than 600 persons in the same area.[35] In 1962, it was calculated that there were 2.2 individuals per acre of cultivable land in Barbados.[36]

While the continental territories are sparsely populated, as in the case of Belize, even there the densities have risen considerably in recent years. In 1950 Belize had three inhabitants per square kilometre, rising to 9.3 in 1995; Guyana had 1.9 in 1950, rising to 3.8 in 1995. Except for Puerto Rico, which had a population density in 1980 of 350.3 persons per square kilometre, the Greater Antilles generally present lower densities than the smaller islands. In

32 USCIA, 1991, p.296.

33 Franklin W. Knight, 1990, p.372.

34 Juan Antonio Alvarado Ramos, 1996, p.37.

35 Densities are calculated on the basis of population data contained in Cuba, Centro Latinoaméricano de Demografía (CLD), 1995, p.17.

36 E. Gordon Ericksen, 1962, p.29.

the 1950s, Cuba had fewer than 60 inhabitants per square kilometre, and in 1995 the figure had still not reached 100, while the population density of the Dominican Republic jumped from 47 per square kilometre in 1950 to more than 156 in 1995, and Haiti experienced an even sharper increase, from 49 inhabitants per square kilometre in 1950 to 258 in 1995.[37]

With regard to the rate of population growth, one finds a recent tendency toward a slowdown in the rate of growth, a logical consequence of the modernization achieved by these societies. Some small islands show no growth or even a decline in the growth rate; this is undoubtedly due to emigration, which, as we know, is a widespread and constant phenomenon within the demographic evolution of the region. The mean rate of growth for every hundred inhabitants has fallen from an average of 2.5 in 1950–5 to 1.3 between 1980 and 1985 and 0.8 in the five-year period 1990–5.[38]

The French overseas departments in the Antilles experienced an extraordinary spurt of growth after the Second World War. Maintenance of the birth rate at high levels and a rapid drop in the death rate kept the natural growth rate at 3 per cent per year (3.1 per cent between 1954 and 1961), though a campaign aimed at birth control (offset somewhat by rising life expectancy) reduced this rate to just over 2 per cent in 1970. Organized emigration to France reduced population growth to 1.3 per cent per year during the 1970s.[39]

The much-discussed case of Puerto Rico reflects birth rates that are still quite high (21.8 births per thousand inhabitants in 1982) and a relatively low death rate (6.5 per 1,000 in the same year), which keeps the population growth rate at a high level; the escape valve for this population growth is also emigration.[40]

In Cuba, one finds a downward trend in both mortality and births: In the first years of the century, both rates were high (30 and 47 per 1,000, respectively, in 1907). These numbers fell moderately until the 1930s. In the 1950s, the birth rate was in the order of 28 per thousand inhabitants, though this rate skyrocketed after 1959, reaching 36.3 in 1964. The birth rate began to fall in 1967, and by the late 1980s averaged about 17 births per 1,000 inhabitants; during the 1990s, it dropped to 14 births per 1,000. The death rate began to fall in the 1930s, reaching 6.3 per 1,000 inhabitants in 1953; after that, it fluctuated between 5 and 6 deaths per 1,000,[41] though between 1990 and 1996 the average rose to 7 deaths per 1,000 inhabitants.[42]

37 Cuba, CLD, 1995.
38 United Nations, Comisión Económica para América Latina (CEPAL), 1992, p.6.
39 Guy Lasserre, 1974, p.320.
40 James L. Dietz, 1986, p.284.
41 Cuba, Centro de Estudios Demográficos (CED), 1976, pp.30, 53.
42 Cuba, Oficina Nacional de Estadísticas (ONE), 1997, p.63.

In Barbados, the birth rate fell from 20.8 per 1,000 in 1970–5 to 15.7 in 1990–5, while the death rate has held steady between 8 and 9 per 1,000. In Trinidad & Tobago, births averaged between 10 and 14 per 1,000 between 1987 and 1996, and since the 1990s, deaths have been at about 7 per 1,000; in Jamaica, the trend is similar.[43]

The only countries in which the growth rate has shown little change are Haiti and the Dominican Republic; in both, the rate is high (about 2 per cent for the five-year period 1990–5), indicating high birth rates. Still, the general trend in the region is toward a decline in the rates of both birth and death, as is to be expected from the modernization that the region has been experiencing. Over the latest five-year period, Haiti is the country with the highest rates of birth and death (35.5 per 1,000 and 11.9 per 1,000, respectively). In birth rates it is followed by the Dominican Republic (28.3 per 1,000), where the death rate is considerably lower (5.6 per 1,000).[44]

It is well known that the settlement of the Caribbean was the result of immigration, forced or voluntary, but during the present century the inhabitants of the Caribbean have initiated a process of outmigration, emigration, in search of better job opportunities; the diaspora has extended to many countries. Initially, specific economic conditions or situations spurred intra-Caribbean migrations. Thus Cuba, the Dominican Republic, and Trinidad & Tobago have been the recipients of immigrants from other countries in the region. This movement reversed, however, as a result of the worldwide economic crisis of the thirties, and people began to emigrate toward the economic or political centres of empire; this trend strengthened after the Second World War.[45]

In the case of Puerto Rico, the basic emigatory current began flowing toward the United States at the beginning of this century, and from the 18,000 people who emigrated in 1930–9 the number rose dramatically to 151,000 in the following decade. The peak was reached between 1950 and 1959, when emigrations reached 430,000; the exodus slowed in the 1960s, and since then there has been some indication of a return to the island. Still, there is a large Puerto Rican community in the United States, mainly based in New York City.[46]

With regard to Cuba, one notes a slight movement toward the United States in the 1950s, turning sporadically massive and of another nature since 1959, with the triumph of the Revolution. In 1959, there was a first wave of emigration for political reasons, raising the emigration totals considerably.

43 United Nations, CEPAL, 1992, p.13.

44 *Ibid.*

45 Bonham C. Richardson, 1989, p.203; see also chap.12, this volume.

46 Blanca G. Silvestrini and Maria D. Luque de Sánchez, 1987 (1992), pp.582–4; see also James L. Dietz, 1986, pp.284–6.

Cuban emigration rates fluctuate appreciably, reflecting the changing possibilities of leaving the island, political factors, and also economic reasons. The period of greatest sustained emigration was from 1959 to 1962, when the average rate rose to 12.5 persons per 1,000 inhabitants, although this rate was counteracted by the return of exiles.

In late 1962, due to a decision made by the United States, the regular lines of communication between the two countries were interrupted; this caused a temporary drop in emigration. It began to rise again in 1966, and was maintained at over 55,000 emigrants per year until 1972, when it began to decline, and then experienced a sharp drop-off after 1973. The Mariel exodus in 1980 brought the rate to more than 140,000 emigrants, the greatest number for any single year.[47] Within the framework of the immigration agreements between Cuba and the United States, until 1980 emigrants averaged about 9,000 per year, though after 1980 the number dropped to an average of about 5,000. The so-called 'raft-people *(balsero)* crisis' caused emigration figures to rise to an estimated 40–45 thousand in 1994.[48] According to official figures, emigration between 1990 and 1996 averaged 120,040, or about 1.6 per 1,000 inhabitants.[49]

In general terms, Cuban emigration has depended on the government's policy on leaving the island with no intention of returning. The Cuban diaspora is distinguished from the more general Caribbean diaspora in that the decision to leave the country implies that one renounces the possibility of coming back, although in recent years regulations have been made somewhat more flexible. Currently, emigration is governed by the immigration accords between Cuba and the United States, which is the preferred destination country, although Cubans also migrate to other countries, among which Spain and other Latin American countries are the most important.[50] The proportions of emigrants by sex, age and profession corroborate our view that this is an atypical migration.[51]

Although the United States is also an important destination for the inhabitants of the English-speaking Caribbean, emigration to Great Britain has been considerable. In 1980, the number of Caribbeans residing in Great Britain was calculated to be approximately 650,000. The movement from the French and Dutch Antilles toward France and the Netherlands is more modest in comparison.[52]

47 Cuba, Comité Estatal de Estadísticas, 1982, pp.60–2; *ibid.*, 1985, p.81.
48 Enrique Juan de Díos Fernández Figueroa, 1995, p.316.
49 Cuba, ONE, 1997, p.71.
50 Antonio Aja Diaz, 1996, pp.11–48.
51 Cuba, Comité Estatal de Estadísticas, 1982, pp.63–8.
52 Bonham C. Richardson, 1989, p.217.

The emigration rate from the Dominican Republic began to rise in the 1960s, and continues to hold at between two and three persons per 1,000 inhabitants. Haiti's rate has always been high, though it experienced an increase between 1970 and 1975 and reached its maximum between 1975 and 1980.[53] The flow of Haitian and Dominican emigrants is generally toward the United States, although recently Spain has begun to be an important destination for Dominicans.

In the 1990s, all the islands, with the exception of the archipelago of the Bahamas, present a negative migration rate; the island with the greatest relative exodus is Grenada, with 32 emigrants per thousand inhabitants. The continental enclaves have also been affected by emigration, Guyana perhaps the most, with 20 per 1,000 inhabitants; in Suriname the figure is six while Belize shows no emigratory movement.[54] Some sources point out that low population density has been the cause of a series of waves of immigration from neighbouring countries.[55]

But emigration is not the only movement from place to place that the Caribbean population has experienced in recent years. In recent decades the Caribbean as a whole has undergone an intense process of urbanization, as has all of Latin America. But this does not mean that all the nations of the Caribbean have achieved a uniform degree of urbanization. Generally speaking, one finds a phenomenon similar to that of continental Latin American countries, which has been described as the 'hypertrophy of cities in terms of population due to non-industrial causes.'[56]

This shift from the countryside to the city does not always correspond to the economic and financial functions of urban centres; in some cases it has been subordinated to the dependency that exists between the Caribbean nations and their respective centres of empire outside the region, although most of the changes do coincide with important transformations of the countries' financial structures.

The parameters for distinguishing between the urban and rural populations vary from country to country. If only the population residing in large cities is to be considered urban, then the percentage of urbanization would be reduced, although in almost every case, high rates of urban growth are noted. Seen as a whole, the urban population has grown in recent years. In Barbados it rose from 37.2 per cent in 1970 to 44.8 per cent in 1990; in Cuba, from 60.2 per cent to 74.9 per cent over the same period; in Jamaica it rose

53 Cuba, CLD, 1995.
54 USCIA, 1991; Cuba, CLD, 1995.
55 *Europa Yearbook*, 1995, p.105.
56 José E. Iturraga, 1951, p.5.

by 26 per cent; and in Guyana and Trinidad & Tobago, by 17 per cent. Haiti and the Dominican Republic show the greatest increase in the population residing in cities, with increases of 53 per cent and 49 per cent, respectively. But the great difference is that in Haiti, the majority of the population continued to be rural, though the percentage fell from 80 per cent in 1970 to 70 per cent in the 1990s, while in the Dominican Republic, there was an appreciable reduction in the population residing in rural areas.[57]

Puerto Rico has experienced rapid de-ruralization. The rural population fell from 66.6 per cent in 1940 to 23 per cent in 1960.[58] Salaried agricultural workers fell by 83 per cent between 1940 and 1984, while manufacturing workers rose by 154 per cent and employees in other sectors, including trade and government, rose by 146 per cent.[59]

If one takes the population living in cities of approximately 20,000 or more inhabitants, the country where the most rapid urbanization process has taken place (of the seven for which information is available: Barbados, Cuba, Guyana, Haiti, Jamaica, the Dominican Republic, and Trinidad & Tobago) is the Dominican Republic. In 1950, 11.1 per cent of its population lived in cities of that size, while by 1970 this number had risen to 30.2 per cent. If one takes cities of 100,000 or more inhabitants, residents in that same country rose from 8.5 per cent in 1950 to 20.7 per cent in 1970. In Cuba no great leaps have been observed in these numbers; in Haiti the figures for the first type of population rose from 5.1 per cent in 1950 to 12.7 per cent in 1970 and from 4.3 per cent in 1950 to 20.7 per cent in 1970 for the second.[60] Nevertheless, an increase in tourist activities combined with the recent establishment of process industries backed with American capital, which take advantage of the particularly low labour costs, have also contributed to an intensification of the population shift to the cities.[61]

This is not a mere repetition of the phenomenon of urbanization seen in Europe in the nineteenth century, in which industrialization played a fundamental role. The size of the urban population of the Caribbean is not always directly related to the urban areas' level of production. The percentage of the economically active population employed in the secondary (manufacturing) sector has not changed in any appreciable way during recent years in any country in the region, although in most cases its structure has changed considerably: the active population employed in crafts and semi-skilled labour has fallen dramatically, while that in the modern industrial

57 United Nations, CEPAL, 1992, p.6.

58 Blanca G. Silvestrini and Maria D. Luque de Sánchez, 1992, p.527.

59 Fernando Picó, 1988, p.262.

60 United Nations, CEPAL, 1980, pp.57–8.

61 Academia de Ciencias de Cuba, 1979, p.90.

sector has proportionately risen. This means that there has been industrial progress brought about by the manufacturing sector and by an increase in productivity, but that it has been virtually unaccompanied by any proportional increase in industrial employment.

Population and economic sectors

I will not attempt to discuss here whether the growth in the tertiary sector of the economy is or is not an indicator of underdevelopment.[62] In my view, models valid for other communities cannot be applied to the analysis of Caribbean societies. In the study of social organizations as complex as these, one must use extreme flexibility and pay special attention to their particularities.

It is obvious that the rapid expansion of the service sector is not in every case an indicator of economic development. Nor have those countries in the Caribbean, in which relatively rapid growth has been achieved, always arrived at the stage of post-industrial society, although this does not in every case imply a deepening of underdevelopment, either. One must not forget that the Caribbean is under the direct influence of societies which have achieved a high level of progress and that many models have been transplanted to the region; the effects may be positive or negative, as the case may be, and so careful analysis is called for.

It is clear that the classic industrial revolution did not occur in the region – that is, a revolution that triggered accelerated growth in the secondary sector. Cuba might possibly be considered the exception, even taking into account the limited scope of that process during the last quarter of the nineteenth century. Its two basic industries have depended on agricultural raw materials, however, so industrialization in Cuba rested on the growth of agriculture.

In general terms, statistics on the distribution of the population employed in the various sectors of the economy in recent years reflect a clear decline in the agricultural sector, a slight increase in the industrial sector, and significant growth in services. The explanation for these shifts is to be found in the rapid increase of tourism in most of the countries and the introduction of industries employing advanced technologies which reduced the need for labour.

For a more in-depth analysis, it would be necessary to study in detail the percentage of each sector within the Gross National Product (GNP), and that would require digressing from the central objectives of this chapter. But one cannot deny that in most of the countries under consideration, extremely

62 Jorge Ibarra, 1995, p.97.

important changes have taken place, nor that these changes have entailed transformations in the social structure. Most societies have ceased to be predominantly agrarian and have joined the development of international capitalism, albeit, naturally, at something of a disadvantage.

The worldwide financial crisis of the 1930s aggravated the economic situation in every Caribbean nation; the way in which they confronted it varied, and the political and economic consequences led development down various paths. Made even worse in Puerto Rico by the collapse of the sugar market and the ravages of a hurricane in 1932, the crisis placed the island in a tense situation which obliged the United States government to take urgent measures to save the economy. A system of economic reforms aimed at transforming the economic structure was implemented, and the policy of expansion was strengthened by the effects of the War and the post-war period. During the 1940s, agriculture continued to be the element of the country's economic activity that contributed most to the GNP, with 31 per cent of the total, but that percentage quickly began to decline. The number of sugar-processing factories fell by some 30 per cent between 1940 and 1960, and in 1981 only one-tenth of the sugar produced in 1952 was recorded.[63]

Changes in the working population by sector of the economy clearly reflect the transformations experienced by Puerto Rico during the last 60 years, as we can see in Table 11.4.

The accelerated process of de-ruralization can be seen in the fact that in 1979, agriculture contributed only 3.4 per cent to the GNP, while industry contributed 19 per cent and the services sector, 45 per cent.[64] This demonstrates that it was not industry that caused the change. In fact, the rapid rise in the tertiary sector over recent years is taking place at the expense of industrial production, which corroborates the trend toward increased tourism. Tourists registered in Puerto Rican hotels increased from 57,721 in 1950 to 637,944, while at the same time the number of families included in the Nutritional Assistance Plan (or PAN, its abbreviation in Spanish) rose from

TABLE 11.4 Employment by sector, Puerto Rico, 1930–96 (percentage of employed)

Sector	*1930*	*1960*	*1980*	*1990*	*1996*
Agriculture	52.2	23.0	3.5	3.6	3.0
Manufacturing	21.8	17.2	19.1	17.0	15.0
Services	20.0	58.1	71.3	79.5	82.3

Sources: ILO,1990, pp.230–2; ILO, 1992, p.40; ILO, 1997, p.193.

63 Blanca G. Silvestrini and Maria D. Luque de Sánchez, 1992, p.571.
64 EFE News Agency, 1986, p.1222.

397,133 in 1977–8 to 412,645 in 1983–4.[65] Thus, the rapid development experienced by Puerto Rico did not eliminate unemployment and poverty. In 1973, Luis Muñoz Marín said the following:

> Because of its economic progress, Puerto Rico has taken its place among the foremost countries of the world; [but] with respect to what we have done with that economic progress, we are bogged down at the level of the unjust, perplexed world that surrounds us .... We multiply the production of wealth by more than twenty times .... but improvement in the injustice with which that production is distributed among Puerto Ricans has not been as marked as it should be. We might say that the change has been from poverty aggravated by the unjust way in which scarcity is distributed to prosperity that is a challenge to us because of the unjust way in which its wealth is distributed.[66]

Another nation that has achieved notable advance is Trinidad & Tobago, whose economic structure has also experienced profound changes (see Table 11.5). Although tourism has increased in recent years, oil refining – part of the crude oil being local and part imported – is the country's leading industry, representing 80 per cent of its export value, though due to technological advances it employs only some 3 per cent of the active work-force. This explains the drop in the industrial sector since 1946, which should not be seen as an indicator that the country is moving backward, and in part explains the great difference between the secondary and tertiary sectors.

Despite the fact that Cuba represents a unique case from the point of view of class structure, the division by sector of the employed population has not experienced any radical change. Although between 1931 and 1953, there was a reduction in the primary sector of more than 10 per cent (from

TABLE 11.5 Employment by sector, Trinidad & Tobago, 1946–95 (percentage of employed)

Sector	*1946*	*1960*	*1970*	*1980*	*1995*
Agriculture	27.0	19.9	12.5	9.1	10.6
Manufacturing (includes mining)	20.5	19.3	15.0	15.0	14.0
Services	46.8	55.1	72.5	75.2	75.6

Sources: ILO, 1990, pp.235; ILO, 1992, p.158; ILO, 1997, p.194.

65 Fernando Picó, 1988, p.287.

66 Quoted in *ibid.*, p.287.

52.8 per cent to 42.2 per cent), the number of those employed in industry and manufacturing did not increase appreciably, leading one to infer that the drop in the primary sector was to the benefit of the tertiary sector, which grew by the same percentage (from 30.9 per cent in 1931 to 41.1 per cent in 1953).[67] It is not possible to quantify the changes that have occurred in Cuba since 1959 because there is no information available closer to that date than the data relating to the 1953 census, nor are there enough censuses from the period of the Revolution, the last being in 1981. But it can be safely said, for example, that the primary sector has continued to have an important place in the economy, at 30.6 per cent in 1970, 22.6 per cent in 1981, and 23.2 per cent in 1996, the last year for which figures have been published. The secondary sector did not make any great leaps, growing from 16.7 per cent in 1953 to 19.4 per cent in 1970 and 20.4 per cent of the labour force in 1981, though in recent years it has dropped to 17.7 per cent. Meanwhile, the tertiary sector continued to grow: in 1970 it employed 50 per cent of the active population, growing to 57 per cent in 1981, and 58.4 per cent in 1996.[68]

Although the growth in Cuba's industrial sector is based on an increase in agricultural raw materials, the employment structure shows that no major changes have occurred in the country's economic structure, and that agriculture continues to be a large part of the economy. One important element in the growth in the tertiary sector is the rise in jobs in health services and education from 1959 onward, though recent years have seen a rapid growth in tourism, as part of a reorientation of the economy.

In the Caribbean as a whole, there has been an appreciable shift to the tertiary (service) sector. This shift is general throughout the region, but is most pronounced in certain countries, such as the French overseas departments (see Table 11.6).

TABLE 11.6 Employment by sector: Guadeloupe/Martinique/Guyane (percentage of employed)

	Guadeloupe			*Martinique*			*Guyane*		
Sectors	*1964*	*1974*	*1982*	*1961*	*1974*	*1982*	*1967*	*1974*	*1982*
Agriculture	32.4	17.2	13.1	38.1	14.7	7.5	18.4	15.5	11.4
Manufacturing	10.3	7.7	2.8	12.1	6.4	3.0	6.0	8.0	4.1
Services	57.2	52.9	58.7	46.8	67.7	60.5	73.1	65.4	59.3

Sources: ILO, 1992, pp.202–4, 206–8, 214–16.

67 Cuba, OGC, 1955; *Memorias inéditas 1931,* 1978; Cuba, 1945.

68 Cuba, Oficina Nacional del Censo (ONC), 1983; Junta Central de Planificación de Cuba, 1971; Cuba, ONE, 1997.

It is interesting that in these communities, both production sectors fell, although manufacturing suffered a sharper drop than agriculture. One must bear in mind that as in the case of Puerto Rico, part of the working population receives subsidies, which are indirectly reflected in the two last years of the table, where the figures do not add up to 100 per cent.

Most of the small islands have ceased to be agricultural communities and have become important tourist centres. The most significant case is perhaps that of Barbados, which was the world's most important sugar plantation centre in the seventeenth century. By 1946, agricultural activity had fallen to the point that it employed only one-third of the active population, while almost 40 per cent worked in services; in the 1960s, agriculture fell to 23 per cent, while services continued to climb, reaching 53 per cent. There is also a large number of persons employed in the secondary sector (which grew from 14 per cent in 1960 to 16 per cent in 1970), apparently due to the assembly industry.[69]

The 1970s saw a continued decline in employment in agriculture and in the 1990s agricultural employment hovered between 4 per cent and 5 per cent. This was accompanied by an increase in employment in services, from 64 per cent in 1970 to more than 75 per cent at the current time. The secondary sector fell from 16 per cent to around 10 per cent between 1970 and the present time.[70] The island's economy is currently centred on light manufacturing and tourism, in which most of the work-force now is employed.

Because of their geographical position and conditions, in the Bahamas agriculture was never developed on a large scale. Since the 1960s, most workers have been employed in the tertiary sector, with 42.5 per cent in 1960, increasing to 76.9 per cent of the work-force in 1980, and to 79.3 per cent in 1989, almost all associated with tourism.[71] Agriculture and fishing continued to lose ground, and employment in those industries fell from 38 per cent in 1963 to 5 per cent in 1980, standing today at approximately 3 per cent. A similar phenomenon has occurred in the secondary sector.[72]

In Jamaica, agriculture was the fundamental activity in the 1970s, when 60 per cent of the island's inhabitants depended on agricultural employment for their livelihood. Because of the island's mountainous terrain, cultivable land measures less than 15 per cent of the surface. One of the particular features of Jamaica is the importance of small agricultural plots. In the 1970s, the 140,000 peasants who owned fewer than five acres represented more than

69 International Labour Organisation (ILO), 1990, pp.168–9.
70 ILO, 1997, p.104.
71 USCIA, 1991, p.26.
72 ILO, 1990, p.56.

70 per cent of the total number of landowners, though they owned less than 13 per cent of the land in cultivation. The other side of the coin is that 350 landowners whose holdings measured more than 500 acres represented no more than 0.2 per cent of the total landowners but controlled 37 per cent of all agricultural land.

In 1950, sugar and bananas represented 65 per cent of the country's exports; the population employed in the agricultural sector totalled 36 per cent of the work-force, with only 13 per cent of all workers employed in industry. That situation continued into the 1960s. But by 1970, sugar and bananas represented no more than 18 per cent of the value of total exports while the production of bauxite rose 79 per cent between 1963 and 1973 and that of aluminium 227 per cent over the same period; metals' share of total exports rose from 11 per cent in 1953 to 63 per cent in 1972, and foreign investment in these two sectors rose from 31 per cent in 1953 to 45 per cent of the total in 1972.[73]

Between 1960 and 1980, no great changes took place. Jobs in industry did not increase but the sector sustained a growth rate averaging 3.2 per cent between 1980 and 1991.[74] Nor was there any sharp reduction in jobs in the agricultural sector (although they fell from 36 per cent of the total work-force in 1970 to 18 per cent in 1980). The primary sector's share in the GNP averaged 8.4 per cent between 1980 and 1986 and 7.6 per cent between 1987 and 1991.[75] Growth in jobs in the service sector rose, as tourism on the north coast increased the number of visitors and diversified the economy.[76]

It is characteristic of Jamaica that an abrupt decline in the number of jobs in agriculture has not occurred, but in the 1990s, the percentage of workers in manufacturing and industry fell to 11 per cent and that in the service sector rose to 61 per cent, with a slight decrease in the number of agricultural workers (to 27 per cent).[77] Still, with respect to industry and mining's share in the GNP, Jamaica was second in the region, with 52 per cent, behind only Trinidad & Tobago with 56 per cent.[78]

In 1960, 67 per cent of the population of the Dominican Republic still lived in rural areas, and 60 per cent of the work-force was employed in agriculture. Due to the importance of large estates and ownership of land by large agricultural enterprises, the agricultural structure in this country was diametrically opposed to that of Haiti and Jamaica. Large estates *(latifundios)* are a

73 Michael Manley, 1987, pp.38, 273.
74 ILO, 1990, pp.212–14.
75 CEPAL, 1992, p.89.
76 ILO, 1990, pp.212–14.
77 ILO, 1997, p.114.
78 United Nations, 1970–6.

legacy of Spanish colonization; the introduction of the big sugar plantation in the late nineteenth century and the policies of the dictator Rafael Trujillo (1930–61) helped to strengthen their predominance. Estates of more than 1,200 acres (500 hectares) controlled 43.7 per cent of the land in cultivation, though no more than 0.7 per cent of the properties. On the other hand, small farms of fewer than 5 hectares (about 12 acres), which constituted 75 per cent of the number of rural properties, covered only 13.7 per cent of the land in cultivation. The medium-sized property (farms of from 10 to 100 hectares, 25 to 250 acres) is more common than in the other islands of the Antilles: 11 per cent of rural property, 33 per cent of all cultivated land comes into this category.

The existence of these large rural domains has engendered a very serious agricultural problem: many Dominican rural workers do not live on the land. Of those who worked in agriculture, 22.3 per cent were agricultural workers, while only 17.7 per cent farmed land they owned. After the expulsion of the Trujillo clan, sugar-cane land which had been in large estates was redistributed. In the early 1970s, the primary sector still produced only 23 per cent of the GNP.[79]

Trends in employment by sector in recent years can be seen in Table 11.7. In 1981, the primary sector still employed 22 per cent of the working population, while the secondary sector had fallen slightly. What differentiates the Dominican Republic from the other Caribbean countries that experienced rapid growth in the area of tourism – leading to an accelerated growth in the service sector at the expense of agriculture – is that in the Dominican Republic agriculture continues to be a fundamental sector of the economy, contributing 20.4 per cent to the GNP between 1980 and 1986 and 18.1 per cent between 1987 and 1991.[80] The creation of duty-free zones has allowed the development of light industry, and tourism is beginning to increase in importance.[81]

TABLE 11.7 Employment by sector, Dominican Republic, 1960–96 (percentage of employed)

Sector	*1960*	*1970*	*1981*	*1996*
Agriculture	61.4	44.3	22.0	14.4
Manufacturing	8.4	8.2	11.7	17.5
Services	23.3	26.0	59.2	67.3
Unspecified	6.5	19.0	22.0	0.2

Sources: ILO, 1990, pp.186–8; ILO, 1997, p.111.

79 Guy Lasserre, 1974, pp.248–57, 340.
80 United Nations, CEPAL, 1992, p.89.
81 USCIA, 1991, p.85.

Haiti represents the extreme of dispersion in the agrarian structure. In 1970, 90 per cent of agricultural properties were of fewer than five hectares, with 50 per cent being less than one hectare.[82] Small-scale agriculture on subsistence farms has produced such a level of under-development that 85 per cent of the population lives in extreme poverty.[83]

With respect to the distribution of the working population by sectors, agriculture still employs 60 per cent of the population, although the number of those who work in services grew from 7 per cent in 1950 to 21 per cent in 1990, while manufacturing and industry grew only from 3.7 per cent to 5.7 per cent (see Table 11.8).[84] But Haiti is a special case, in which all the socio-economic indicators for the country indicate a very pronounced level of under-development. It should be noted that most of its economically active population are concentrated in the primary sector. A considerable part of that rural population live, in practice, outside the monetary circuits in a subsistence economy.

Of the continental enclaves, Belize continues to be a country whose population is employed mainly in agriculture. In 1946, 40 per cent of those employed were concentrated in the primary sector, and even as late as 1980 that sector represented 31.2 per cent; by 1994, the number had fallen to 23 per cent. As in Haiti and the Dominican Republic, part of the employed population was classified as working in 'unspecified activities', which is typical of backward economies. The tertiary sector has little relative importance.[85] In Suriname, the number of workers in the primary sector fell from 25 per cent of the total work-force in 1964 to 9.2 per cent in 1980; those employed in the secondary sector were unchanged between 1968 and 1994, while the numbers working in services increased from 49 per cent in 1964 to 75 per cent in 1980. In the 1990s, there has been a rapid decline in agriculture, to

TABLE 11.8 Employment by sector, Haiti, 1950–90 (percentage)

Sector	*1950*	*1971*	*1981*	*1990*
Agriculture	83.2	61.4	57.4	57.3
Manufacturing	4.9	5.1	5.7	5.7
Services	9.5	16.6	21.1	21.1
Unspecified	2.4	16.8	12.2	12.2

Sources: ILO, 1990, pp.208–10; ILO, 1992, p.70.

82 Guy Lasserre, 1974, p.257.
83 USCIA, 1991, p.132.
84 ILO, 1990, pp.208–10; ILO, 1992, p.70.
85 ILO, 1990, pp.169–70; ILO, 1997, p.105.

5.6 per cent, and in the manufacturing sector, to 8 per cent, while the service sector has now reached 77 per cent.[86]

In 1946, Guyana was an agrarian society, with 45.9 per cent of its active population working in the fields and 34 per cent in the service sector.[87] Even in 1980 about 20 per cent of the working population was employed in extractive jobs, which represented 26 per cent of the GNP between 1980 and 1986; meanwhile, the service sector had grown to 39.9 per cent. In the 1990s, Guyana continued to decline in the secondary sector, while agriculture still contributed 26.8 per cent to the GNP.[88]

The general trends with respect to the distribution of workers in the Caribbean manifest themselves in a decline of the population working in the primary sector, a slight increase in the number of workers in industry and manufacturing, and rapid growth in service jobs. The causes are not identical in all cases, nor does the growth of the service sector have the same significance; sometimes it may be the result of the spread of small business, or it may simply reflect a lack of available jobs in other sectors. Nor is this trend attributable to the same causes as in societies which have achieved a high level of development. It is well known that the tendency to increase employment in the tertiary sector is a characteristic typical of post-industrial societies.

In the case of the Caribbean region, this tendency has a number of causes, among which we might single out the rapid development of tourism and the fact that some countries have artificially imposed the models of their colonial centres. But there are still some countries in the region which have not initiated the process of transformation to be seen in the most outstanding cases.

Social structure

It would be foolhardy to attempt a study of the class structure of the many and diverse countries of the region, both because of the limited state of the historiography and because of the kind of information that is available at the current time; it would be more difficult still to analyse the classes on the basis of differentiation by race. Nevertheless, the statistics on employment by occupational categories available for some countries make it possible to enter into

86 ILO, 1990, pp.236–8; ILO, 1997, p.120.
87 ILO, 1990, pp.204–6.
88 United Nations, CEPAL, 1992, p.89.

an examination of the changes in the social structure, which is a first step towards investigating the problem.

During this century, transformations have occurred in the Caribbean which have produced important changes in its social and class structure. Even those countries which have maintained their essential characteristics have been influenced by the incorporation of international capital into the region. There have been great disparities, both between countries and internally within specific societies. In almost all, there exist tourist enclaves which contrast greatly with the country's traditional agrarian communities. In some countries, industrial elements with advanced technology have been introduced, or assembly-industries have been established; these are elements imported from more advanced societies. Similar phenomena have occurred in the financial area.

All these elements have caused changes in the social structure which it is possible to document if one utilizes the internationally accepted classifications used to categorize the working population. A self-employed person is considered to be that person who works in his/her own business, professional services, or owned or leased farm. Salaried workers are those who work for hire as the employee of another person, entity, institution or government, and non-remunerated family employees are those who work without pay in tasks that contribute to the operation of a family farm, or business, or profession.[89]

These categories have been refined and diversified in recent years, but unfortunately, not all countries include them in their censuses; therefore we must work with the data available. Fortunately, there are figures for most of the probable cases, so they are valid for making at least some generalizations. I have based my analysis of the working population on statistics published by the International Labour Organisation, since this body has observed these categories throughout the years. Other sources, such as the yearly reports of the Economic Commission for Latin America and the Caribbean, tend to process and organize information on the basis of other criteria; thus, it is not possible to fill in gaps by using other sources.[90]

As a society develops, the number of self-employed and non-remunerated family workers declines. Two basic tendencies are at work in this phenomenon: first, an appreciable part of those who are self-employed engage in this type of work as a means of subsisting in the face of a lack of stable employment; second, there is a concentration of the means of production. These two causes act inversely with respect to the consolidation of capitalist relations and the increase in the salaried working class.

---

89 Cuba, OGC, 1953, p.xix.

90 United Nations, CEPAL, 1995, p.43.

Unfortunately, there is no information detailed and precise enough to allow us to measure the changes. Statistics for Jamaica demonstrate the very limited advance of the proletarianization of that society, when one would have expected that the incorporation of the island into international capitalism and the production of aluminium and bauxite would have stimulated the growth of the salaried class. The figures actually reflect an increase of self-employment from 26.5 per cent in 1946 to 34 per cent in 1960 and 40 per cent in 1980, although the percentage of non-remunerated family members fell from 5.8 per cent in 1946 to 3.6 per cent in 1980. Unfortunately, this classification category has not been used in the 1990s.

In the category of occupations we note that numbers for those classified as farmers and fishermen did not appreciably decline between 1960 and 1992 (averaging around 37–8 per cent); and we know that Jamaican agriculture is characterized by a predominance of small independent country-people, which increases the importance of this category in the region (whose extreme case is Haiti). Meanwhile, those classified as businessmen/businesswomen and salespersons, a group which is composed basically of small merchants and street pedlars, grew from 10 per cent to 16.7 per cent over the same period and the salaried working class remained virtually static, growing only from 27.5 per cent in 1960 to 28.1 per cent in 1992. One might, then, infer that the independent country-person still has an important place in Jamaica's social structure, and that the working class is growing slowly, while the number of small-business persons has grown modestly.

It is important to note here that the middle class has been strengthened by a rise in the number of professionals, from 4 per cent to 7.4 per cent, and a growth in administrators, managers and office workers from 6.3 per cent to 12.7 per cent, doubling since 1960.[91] This coincides with the trend toward an increase in the middle sectors referred to by most authors who have studied the transformations occurring in the region.[92] From the racial point of view,

---

91 ILO, 1990.

92 'The old middle class – the doctors and lawyers and small merchants of the old small towns – has practically disappeared. Its successor, the new middle class, consists of the motorized salariat of both government service and private firms, high-fee lawyers and doctors, and new technocrats, who are anxiously on their way up, materialistic, full of social fear of those beneath them, often trying to hide their own recent lowly social origins' (Gordon K. Lewis, 1985, p.17). With respect to the racial position of this sector, we are told that '... little by little an incipient middle class was formed that was situated in a position midway between the dominant white stratum and the broad black working masses.... [Although] it is characterized as "mulatto," in every territory this sector presented different racial characteristics, depending upon particularities in the racial composition of the country' (Andrés Serbín, 1987, p.163).

in the early 1960s it was noted that 'what is commonly called the middle class is chiefly composed of colored people of mixed African and British stock with a mixture of other races, while the "working class" is principally Negro with some Indians. Small business is largely Chinese and Indian; big business is Syrian and Jewish'.[93] Still, it is clear that the majority of Jamaicans, 'probably as high as 90 per cent of them, can make claim to an African ancestry. Yet many of these persons, particularly those who constitute the middle classes, or the more privileged sectors of society, find it difficult to come to terms with their possession of a black skin.'[94]

Trinidad & Tobago experienced a drop in the number of self-employed from 27.3 per cent in 1946 to 12 per cent in 1980, though over the last decade of the century it has grown again, to an average of about 17 per cent. Probably the basic cause of this turn-around is that jobs declined. Nevertheless, the percentage of salaried workers remained high, more than 70 per cent in 1946 and reaching a high of 86.7 per cent of all working persons in 1980, while at the end of the century the figure was over 70 per cent.[95] In the statistics categorizing employees by profession, one notes an increase in the proportion of non-agricultural workers during the 1980s and 1990s; between 1960 and 1990, farmers and agricultural workers grew from 8.4 per cent to 11 per cent, businesspersons and salespersons rose from 8 per cent to 10 per cent, and professionals and technical workers grew from 8 per cent to 10 per cent.[96]

All of these changes coincide with the general trends associated with the progress of a society, and so do not explain the increase in the number of self-employed. Nonetheless, one sees here a social structure that is reasonably well balanced, especially when compared with the extreme cases of the region. The influence of race on the class structure manifests itself in the fact that those categorized as 'French Creoles' still form a largely closed élite that generally practises endogamy.[97]

The case of the Bahamas is illustrative of the importance of agriculture in the relationship between independent work and salaried labour. It is well known that large-scale exploitation of the land did not develop in these islands. The number of self-employed persons fell from 22 per cent in the 1960s to 10 per cent in 1980, while salaried workers increased from 77 per cent to 88 per cent. Non-remunerated family member workers have remained few. Numbers of agricultural workers remained at about 6 per cent between

93 E. Gordon Ericksen, 1962, p.37.
94 Colin A. Palmer, 1989, p.111.
95 ILO, 1990, p.538; ILO, 1997, p.194.
96 ILO, 1997, p.120.
97 Bridget Brereton, 1989, p.94.

1970 and 1980, while those of salaried workers in other sectors have fallen and those working in business and services grew.[98]

In the case of Barbados, we have already seen the sharp drop in agriculture. Data for 1980 show a large percentage of salaried labour, some 91.3 per cent of the work-force, while 8.5 per cent were independent and 0.2 per cent worked for some relative. In 1993, 23 per cent of all employees were non-agricultural labourers, while 18.1 per cent were in the service sector, 7.5 per cent in the professions and technical work, and 13.5 per cent in management. With the drop in the importance of agriculture in the economy of Barbados, agricultural workers totalled only 3.3 per cent of the work-force.[99]

The de-ruralization of Puerto Rico is evidenced in the decline in the proportion of agricultural workers, from 3.6 per cent in 1980 to 3.4 per cent in 1996; non-agricultural wage workers grew in number from 34.5 per cent of the work-force to 38.9 per cent in 1992, but fell to 33.9 per cent in 1995. Puerto Rico is one of the countries with the largest percentage of professionals and technical workers: 12.5 per cent in 1980 growing to 15.6 per cent in 1992, 15.1 per cent in 1995, and 16.5 per cent in 1996. It also has the highest percentages of employees in managerial and administrative positions of all Caribbean countries studied, the percentages growing from 21.4 per cent in 1980 to 25 per cent in 1992 and 26 per cent in 1995.[100] On the basis of these data, one can infer that a large percentage of the population belongs to the so-called middle class, that a class of country-people hardly exists, and that the salaried workers in other sectors, not always blue-collar workers, have lost ground in the social structure.

In the French overseas departments, salaried workers have made up a large percentage of the labour force since the 1960s. Data for 1967 indicate that in Guadeloupe they made up 68.57 per cent of the whole, in Martinique 79.7 per cent, and in Guyane 72.6 per cent. The basic source we have used for these figures gives no information of this kind for later years.[101]

In analysing the distribution of the working population by economic sector, the particular situation of Haiti is unusual; distribution by type of work and the trends in that category corroborate these results. In 1950, self-employed workers made up 45.1 per cent of the work-force, with their family members comprising another 42 per cent, while salaried workers totalled only 12.6 per cent. In 1971, 17.8 per cent of the working population was classified as salaried, rising to 19.2 per cent in 1982 and showing the same

98 ILO, 1990, pp.168–9; ILO, 1992, p.56.
99 ILO, 1990, p.458; ILO, 1997, p.181.
100 ILO, 1990, pp.530–2; ILO, 1997, p.119.
101 ILO, 1990, pp.200–1, 206–7, 214–16.

numbers in 1992. Self-employment rose to 68.7 per cent, while the numbers of non-remunerated family members fell to 12 per cent. In this case, data are available for employment activity by occupation, and the results are extremely interesting. Professionals and technical workers represented 0.5 per cent of the working population in 1950; this figure rose to only 0.6 per cent in 1982 and to 2.8 per cent in 1992. Workers in manufacturing and industry rose only from 5.7 per cent of the work-force in 1950 to 9.5 per cent in 1982, decreasing to 9.4 per cent in 1992. Agricultural workers numbered 85.6 per cent of the economically active population in 1950, 70.2 per cent in 1982, and 70.4 per cent in 1992, in keeping with the under-developed economic structure that characterizes this nation.[102] From the point of view of race, we are told the following:

> In the Haitian context... the terms *noir* and *mulâtre* do not refer to ethnic type exclusively. They also carry social and political connotations. Social, because while the illegitimate child of a Black working woman and a White sailor on shore leave might be described as *mulâtre* in appearance, he would certainly not be considered as belonging to the *mulâtre* (i.e., upper) class. Conversely, a Black high government official or successful businessman would make certain he was by marrying into a *mulâtre* family. Political, because Haitian political factions have traditionally formed along class – and therefore color – lines.[103]

The Dominican Republic presents indicators which reflect a considerable backwardness. In 1960, the number of self-employed stood at 44.8 per cent of the working population, non-remunerated family members at 11.2 per cent; the level of self-employment rose to 45 per cent in 1971 and fell again to 40 per cent in 1981, while non-remunerated family members fell to 9 per cent of the work-force in 1971 and again to 3.6 per cent in 1981. Although the increase is slow, one sees a rise in salaried workers from 44.1 per cent in 1960 to 46 per cent in 1971, 56.3 per cent in 1981, and 59.4 per cent in 1996. With respect to the distribution by professions, technical workers and professionals rose from 1.8 per cent of the working population in 1950 to 3.2 per cent in 1971 and 11 per cent in 1996; the proportion of agricultural workers fell from 56 per cent in 1950 to 44 per cent in 1970, 22 per cent in the 1980s, and 16.9 per cent in the 1990s; and workers in the manufacturing and industry sector rose from 12.0 per cent to 31 per cent over the same period.[104]

---

102 *Ibid.*, pp.208–10; ILO, 1992, p.70.

103 Léon-François Hoffman quoted in H. Hoetink, '"Race" and Color in the Caribbean', in Sidney Mintz and Sally Price, 1985, p.63.

104 ILO, 1990, pp.190–2; ILO, 1997, pp.187, 233.

Cuba presents a unique case. It is the 'oddball' of the region in many ways. Even before 1959 one could note certain peculiarities in its social structure. The changes that occurred between 1943 and 1953 show the accelerated advance of capitalist relationships of production. In 1943 almost 50 per cent of the working population was self-employed, with salaried persons representing 42.2 per cent and 8 per cent categorized as 'owners'.[105] In the classification by occupation, 3.7 per cent were professionals, 8.6 per cent 'managers, landowners, and higher employees', with non-agricultural workers representing 30 per cent. With respect to agriculture, 38 per cent were categorized as 'farmers and farm administrators', while farm workers *per se* comprised only 3 per cent of the total; as a percentage of only agricultural employees, these totalled 92.6 per cent and 6.9 per cent, respectively. This means that most farmers still worked more or less independently, although we should note that this census was taken during the *tiempo muerto,* or off-season; in 1953, during the harvest, when a second census was taken, job opportunities were of course greater and the differences are considerable.

Salaried workers during the ten years between the censuses of 1943 and 1953 rose to 72.6 per cent of the work-force, with the self-employed falling to 24 per cent and non-remunerated family workers holding steady at 3.9 per cent. In the classification by occupations, we can detect a slight increase in the professionals, to 4.4 per cent, while non-agricultural workers fell to 27 per cent. The most significant change is found in agriculture, where 41 per cent of those counted were categorized as farmers and fishermen. But within the group of 807,514 workers in this category, 568,779 (70 per cent) were agricultural workers, while only 27.5 per cent were 'owners'. This indicates a rapid proletarianization of the peasant class.[106]

It is well known that in 1959 a new period of Cuban history began, introducing radical changes in the social structure. Unfortunately, there is no census information for the 1960s, so it is very difficult to follow the course of the changes brought on by the implementation of the socialist character of the Revolution and the elimination of private property.

In the 1970 census, 108 persons were classified as 'employers', representing 0.004 per cent of those recorded, 1.3 per cent worked in the private sector, 1.1 per cent were self-employed, and 1.3 per cent worked for a family member. There was a total of 230,525 small independent farmers,[107] representing 8.8 per cent of the whole, while state workers totalled 2,288,406 – 87.4 per cent

105 Cuba, 1945, pp.1070–1.

106 Cuba, OGC, 1955, pp.200–4.

107 This includes those persons who worked land of which they were legal holders, whether as 'owners' or in usufruct. Cuba, Comité Estatal de Estadísticas, 1985, p.181.

of the 2,618,616 people classified.[108] This implies a radical change in the employment structure of the country, since in 1953 63.3 per cent of all employees worked in the private sector, and only 8.8 per cent worked for the government.[109] From the point of view of classification by occupation, the most significant changes are that the number of professionals and technical workers grew to 8 per cent and of non-agricultural workers to 41.5 per cent. According to international classifications, through 1981 the number of professionals rose to 24.5 per cent, farmers, fishermen and miners fell from 27.5 per cent to 18.2 per cent, and non-agricultural workers also fell, from 42.1 per cent in 1970 to 33.3 per cent in 1981.[110]

The classification for 1984 indicates that for the 3,364,300 persons employed in the civil sector, there was an increase to 92.8 per cent of state employees, salaried workers in the private sector totalled 0.4 per cent, and the self-employed made up 1.2 per cent. Changes in agricultural policy led to what was called 'co-operativization', which in 1984 employed 71,300 co-operativists[111] representing 2.1 per cent of all workers. The number of small farmers fell to 118,000, for 3.5 per cent; the 5.6 per cent of non-state agricultural workers break down into 62.2 per cent small independent farmers and 37.8 per cent co-operativists, which implies a considerable reduction in the private sector. Between 1970 and 1984, landowners and usufructuaries fell by 146,900, that is, by 55.5 per cent. If we except co-operativists, one can deduce that the private sector in agriculture – the only private sector in the country's economy – underwent an absolute reduction of 74,600.[112]

Statistics relating to the distribution of the labour force in the state civil sector reflect no great changes between 1980 and 1985 (see Table 11.9). Although the number of labourers fell in relative terms, it rose in absolute terms: the proportion of directors/leaders (*dirigentes*) grew by 6.8 per cent and of technical workers, by more than 35 per cent. Both the increase in state workers and the process of co-operativization and consequent reduction in the number of independent farmers indicate the strengthening of the socialist relationships of production during the 1980s, while the changes that occurred due to the dissolution of the socialist bloc have brought about inverse transformations in the Cuban economy. Table 11.10 shows a small drop in state workers and a sharp decline in the national private sector, which is composed basically of small farmers. What one notices is the appearance

108 Junta Central de Planificación de Cuba (JUCEPLAN), 1971.

109 Cuba, OGC, 1955, pp.1070–1.

110 ILO, 1990, p.478.

111 This includes persons grouped in agricultural or fishing co-operatives. Cuba, Comité Estatal de Estadísticas, 1985, p.181.

112 *Ibid.*, p.187.

TABLE 11.9 Labour force by occupational category, Cuba, 1980–5 (in thousands and by per cent of total)

Category	*1980*	*%*	*1985*	*%*
Labourers	1354.3	52.1	1627.9	50.5
Technical	484.5	18.6	657.6	20.4
Administrative	180.3	6.9	251.4	7.7
Service	348.0	14.8	438.4	13.6
Directors/leaders	232.8	8.9	248.2	7.7

Source: Cuba, Comité Estatal de Estadísticas, 1985, p.193.

TABLE 11.10 Percentage employed by type of property, Cuba, 1970–96

	Category	*1970*	*1981*	*1994*	*1995*	*1996*
1	Total	100.0	100.0	100.0	100.0	100.0
2	State entities	86.3	91.8	81.6	77.9	77.7
3	Co-operatives	—	1.1	8.4	9.7	9.6
4	Mixed businesses and corporations	—	—	2.2	2.4	3.0
5	Political, social and mass organizations	—	—	0.9	0.9	1.1
6	National private business	12.5	5.5	3.7	5.2	5.3
7	Self-employed	12.	1.6	3.2	3.9	3.3

Source: Cuba, Oficina Nacional de Estadísticas, 1996, p.109.

of two new categories of employment, 'self-employment' and workers in 'mixed businesses'. These are the result of economic reforms which have been slowly introduced over the last few years.

With the sole exception of Cuba, in recent years the Caribbean has experienced a strengthening of capitalism which is reflected in its social structure. The region's incorporation into the contemporary trend toward globalization has naturally proceeded in varying degrees from country to country, and social changes have also varied from country to country, depending on specific conditions.

12

The migration experience

Bonham C. Richardson

At 3:30 p.m. on Sunday, 1 August 1970, the M. V. *Christena* cast off from the Treasury Pier at Basseterre, St Kitts, in the north-eastern corner of the Caribbean Sea. The vessel was bound for the smaller sister island of Nevis, a routine 75-minute trip for the twin-engined boat, which was the conventional means of inter-island travel for residents of the two islands. The *Christena* was fatally overcrowded on that afternoon. About halfway to Nevis the vessel began to take on water. At 4:10 p.m. the *Christena* rolled sharply to starboard, apparently capsized, and then sank in a very few minutes. A total of 227 died from drowning, and 92 survived, thanks mainly to an heroic Nevisian fishing crew aboard the sloop *Sea Hunter*.

The Commission of Inquiry that investigated the sinking of the *Christena* reconstructed the events of the voyage and also brought to light shortcomings that had led to the tragedy. The laws governing inter-island travel were found to be anachronistic and focused more on the prevention of smuggling than on passenger safety, and regulations concerning vessel safety and crew training were sharply questioned.[1] Beyond the immediate aftermath of the sinking of the *Christena* was the enduring sorrow that the event brought to every village community on both islands. Three decades later, especially in Nevis where the great majority of those who died on the *Christena* resided, memories of the event continue to evoke sadness and reflection.

The sinking of the *Christena* with its associated loss of life is among the more dramatic sea accidents in the eastern Caribbean during the latter half of the twentieth century, especially because it involved a regularly scheduled means of public conveyance. Residents of every island along the arc of the Lesser Antilles from Puerto Rico to Trinidad are familiar with the region's brisk and often informal inter-island sea traffic; local crews and local vessels fish daily in coastal waters, and they continuously transport agricultural produce, manufactured goods and people from one island to the next.[2] Owing to the

1 *Report on the Circumstances* ..., 1970.
2 Douglas C. Pyle, 1981.

hazards involved in sea travel on rickety, ageing vessels amidst tricky winds and occasionally stormy conditions, mishaps and accidents are not uncommon. Nearly every coastal village of the eastern Caribbean has its own sad memories of friends and loved ones who have 'gone bottom'.[3] In recent years the illegal narcotics traffic across the Caribbean from northern South America to the United States has intensified the dangers of inter-island travel.

The risks and dangers of sea travel are not confined to the eastern Caribbean but are common to the entire region. Nor have these risks been undertaken only during the twentieth century. Since British slave emancipation in 1834, men and women of the region have travelled away – usually to return to those remaining behind – on journeys lasting for days, months and lifetimes. The reasons for travel are innumerable, although many are related to the Caribbean's fragmented insularity, the associated small size of many of the islands, and the resultant lack of local resources and opportunities. Human movement away from and back to the Caribbean has sustained those remaining in many ways. At the end of the twentieth century travels by Caribbean peoples are much more extensive than in the past, and most of this human movement is accomplished by aircraft rather than by ocean-going vessels.

These human movements usually are labelled, of course, as 'migrations', and the Caribbean is well known, even to the most indifferent observers, as a region from which thousands of peoples have emigrated in the very recent past. The Mariel boatlift brought 120,000 Cuban political and economic refugees to southern Florida during the summer of 1980. American policies toward Haitian immigration are discussed in United States presidential campaigns. The presence of crack-dealing Jamaican drug 'posses' has been publicized from the east coast of the United States to Kansas City and Dallas in the American heartland. And the estimated three million Puerto Ricans in New York City and elsewhere are hardly worth mentioning, not because Puerto Ricans are unimportant, but because they have become so well established in the eastern United States that 'migrants' seems a curiously inappropriate term to describe them.

Europeans also identify the Caribbean region as a source area of many of the people who have migrated there in the latter half of the twentieth century. Black (West Indian) Britons who emigrated to the United Kingdom in the 1950s now have British-born grandsons and granddaughters. Thousands from France's overseas departments of Guadeloupe, Martinique and French Guiana reside in Paris and other French cities. The Netherlands has had its population density increased even further by the Surinamese

3 H. Beck, 1976.

escaping political rupture at home as well as residents of the Netherlands Antilles fleeing unemployment in their home islands.

One might even argue that the Caribbean, owing to its turbulent and continuous movement of peoples, now finds itself, of all things, prototypical. 'Third World' no longer inspires images of a rustic mud-hut peasantry, villagers who toil for a lifetime within sight of their birthplaces. Rather, the stereotypical picture of human populations in less-developed regions of the world is that of people on the move to regional centres, capital cities, work-places overseas, and, more and more, to Europe and North America. The traits that Caribbean migrants have developed over the decades – adaptability, a matter-of-factness in dealing with continuous change, ready acceptance of different ways of doing things, abilities to cope without recourse to tradition, and a host of similar cultural traits familiar to those who study the peoples of the Caribbean – are suddenly becoming recognized as crucial by those attempting to capture the essence of what 'globalization' is all about. As Sidney Mintz argues in pointing out the relevance of the Caribbean experience to perceived contemporary worldwide change: 'Words such as diaspora, transnational, ecumene (*oikoumenê*) and hybridity are increasingly employed in a lexicon created in large measure to deal with what is thought to be a qualitatively new epoch in world cultural history.'[4]

Globalization aside, the Caribbean's unique history saw a coerced labour force imported as a 'native' populace. Since then there never has been congruency between the region's populations and the resources they have either consumed or produced. So as soon as Caribbean peoples have been free to leave, they have done so in large numbers, tapping outside sources of opportunity for themselves and for those staying behind. These outside possibilities have, of course, changed greatly over time as have the home islands of Caribbean peoples themselves, changes influenced by decisions usually made outside the region. Accordingly, Caribbean peoples' migration destinations, and the routes taken to reach them, have changed continuously. Each generation of Caribbean migrants has located different destinations and in so doing they have developed a tradition of remarkable adaptation. To emphasize the importance of the history of Caribbean migration is thus not simply to appeal for an appreciation of background information. Rather, it underlines concrete historical experiences that inform the present and continue to provide meaning and significance for the people who inhabit the region at the end of the twentieth century.[5]

4 Sidney W. Mintz, 1996, p.300.
5 Rosemary Brana-Shute, 1983.

The evolution of a Caribbean migration tradition

Despite Columbus's initial contact and the subsequent demise of the Caribbean's aboriginal populations, the region itself was not fully harnessed to the European-centred world economy until early in the seventeenth century; this enduring link was forged because of the region's relative proximity and accessibility to Europe and because tropical staples – mainly sugar-cane – could be produced in the Caribbean but not in Europe's mid-latitudes.[6] The inclusion of the Caribbean region into Europe's economic orbit was accompanied by remarkable local and regional ecological transformations in the islands themselves. Introduced African slaves stripped the native vegetation from insular landscapes, changing heterogeneous island ecosystems into mono-crop economic units. These ecological changes led to soil erosion and also intensified drought, calamities no longer reduced by protective forest covers. Local environmental corrective actions, further, were rare because European planters' decisions were directed by metropolitan market demand for cane sugar rather than the environmental attributes of Caribbean islands themselves.[7]

Just as tropical staple crops produced on Caribbean islands were sent to Europe, the character of the insular plantation colonies themselves reinforced the necessity of a continuous flow of goods and peoples into the region. Locally produced food crops for slaves were usually relegated to marginal hillsides, so foodstuffs from eastern North America supplemented slave diets. These food imports were expensive, unreliable, and subject to sea blockades, warfare and weather events. The tragically high infant and child mortality rates and even periodic famine among Caribbean slaves on nearly every plantation island[8] called for replenishment, through migration, of their ranks by continuous shipments of 'salt water Negroes' from Africa.

Human mobility was, of course, a principal means by which Caribbean slaves resisted these conditions. And it seems unsurprising that birds and boats, images connoting flight or movement, were important symbols in Caribbean slave societies.[9] The realization of freedom among Caribbean slaves involved running away, or marronage, and Maroon societies of varying character and size existed as by-products of Caribbean slave plantations in the mountains, forests and other generally inaccessible zones throughout the region.[10] Escape from slavery by actually emigrating to other Caribbean

6 Philip D. Curtin, 1990; Immanuel Wallerstein, 1980, pp.166–7.
7 Bonham C. Richardson, 1992, pp.13–37.
8 Kenneth F. Kiple, 1984.
9 Orlando Patterson, 1978, pp.126–9.
10 Richard Price, 1996.

islands was extremely rare but not unknown.[11] A folk tale from the Grenadines, for example, tells of a rebellious slave from Grenada who swam to Carriacou in order to escape planter reprisal for an abortive rebellion;[12] and the forced deportation of the Black Caribs from St Vincent to Central America in 1797 marked the origin, during the era of slavery, of a migration tradition still practised by the Garifuna who live in the far western Caribbean today.[13]

Formal emancipation in the British Caribbean in 1834 was followed by a four-year apprenticeship period everywhere except in Antigua, where full emancipation was granted in 1834. In many of the smaller British islands prior to full freedom on 1 August 1838, planters passed a series of vagrancy and trespassing laws designed to immobilize newly emancipated slaves. The plantocracy, further, nearly monopolized the land in the Leeward Islands of St Kitts, Nevis and Montserrat as well as Barbados. In these small places where land was unavailable to sustain landed peasantries such as emerged in Jamaica and British Guiana, human migration – not a village adaptation – was the fundamental response to formal emancipation.[14]

Within a decade after emancipation, men and women from these small British islands sailed away to the newly emerging plantation colonies of Trinidad and British Guiana where sugar planters were offering double the wages they could earn by staying at home. The voyages themselves were accomplished on the decks of small sailing schooners and sloops, vessels whose crews probably had been slaves themselves and who were thereby extending a sailing tradition that reached back for decades.[15] By 1845, less than a decade after full emancipation, over 10,000 migrants from the Leewards and Barbados had travelled to Trinidad; another 8,000 had sailed eastward from Trinidad, against the equatorial currents and prevailing winds, to arrive safely in British Guiana.[16]

Embarking on such a journey was often illegal, the plantocracies of the Leewards (from which so many were leaving) having passed a series of quarantine and family support laws designed further to immobilize potential migrants. The voyages themselves traversed unmarked rocks and shoals, probably went far out to sea to avoid apprehension and re-enslavement (up to 1848) by the French in Guadeloupe and Martinique, and thereby involved constant risks of death by drowning. Then the return voyages underwent the same hazards. By 1848, thousands from the 'old islands' north of Trinidad (the

11 For example, Neville A. T. Hall, 1985.
12 Donald R. Hill, 1977, p.206.
13 Nancie L. Gonzalez, 1988.
14 Woodville K. Marshall, 1968, p.254.
15 J. S. Scott, 1986.
16 Bonham C. Richardson, 1983, p.88.

Leewards as well as the Windwards) had returned home, many of them bringing money and purchased goods home with them, just as they do in the late twentieth century. The returners had successfully resisted local planter oppression, resistance associated precisely with migration and return, and they had thereby begun the migration traditions that have characterized these islands to the present day.[17]

The British Colonial Office approved bringing indentured workers to the Caribbean from India under labour contracts starting in 1838, a labour system set in motion to address the labour 'shortage' bemoaned by local planters whose workers were beginning to ask for higher wages. From then until 1917 more than 400,000 men and women were shipped from recruiting terminals in Calcutta and Madras to work on British Caribbean plantations; their destinations were mainly British Guiana (240,000), Trinidad (144,000) and Jamaica (33,000), with smaller numbers sprinkled throughout the other islands. The French and the Dutch imported workers from India into the Caribbean as well. Between 1852 and 1885, France brought nearly 100,000 Indians to Guadeloupe, Martinique and French Guiana, some from the French Indian enclave at Pondicherry and many aboard British ships. Roughly 35,000 Indians came to Dutch Suriname between 1872 and 1917; when the importation of Indians ended in Suriname, some 22,000 Javanese were contracted for labour there, an immigration into that South American colony that lasted until 1939.[18]

Other world regions, tropical as well as non-tropical, supplied labourers to the Caribbean realm in the latter decades of the 1800s, further diversifying the region's human population. Contingents of free Africans 'liberated' from Spanish and Portuguese slave ships were brought to the British islands after 1834. A variety of Europeans, notably Portuguese Madeirans, came in the middle decades of the nineteenth century. Yucatecan Indians were deported to Cuba after the Caste Wars between the Maya and Mexicans at mid-nineteenth century. In the last decades of the century, tens of thousands of sugar-cane workers from Spain, mainly from Galicia and also from the Canary Islands, augmented the Cuban plantation labour force. Between 1848 and 1878, 125,000 Chinese were brought to Cuba: 'Once landed, they were offered for sale as though they were slaves, although technically it was their contracts that were sold.'[19] Chinese contract workers toiled alongside black slaves in Cuban sugar-cane fields, and their treatment and housing hardly distinguished them from their enslaved co-workers.

17 Elizabeth M. Thomas-Hope, 1995.
18 Hugh Tinker, 1974.
19 Rebecca J. Scott, 1985, p.29.

By the last two decades of the nineteenth century, human movements within the *circum*-Caribbean realm were being inspired by international capital investments and global economic trends more than ever. The French effort in trying to construct a canal across the Isthmus of Panama from 1881 to 1888 attracted thousands of workers from throughout the region; by late 1884, nearly 35,000 men are said to have emigrated for canal work to Panama from Jamaica, and 15,000 already had returned. As early as 1888 some 2,000 Jamaicans had emigrated to Costa Rica. There they established themselves as woodsmen, railroad workers and general labourers as the eastern rim of Central America opened up to American-financed banana production.[20]

But nineteenth-century Caribbean migration trajectories were not simply directed toward economically bright destinations. Economic dislocations and shifts that created opportunities in some places produced, as often as not, downturns in others. A severe, externally influenced economic depression in the 1880s and 1890s in the French and British Caribbean sugar colonies meant lowered wages and grim conditions at home that sent local residents to seek work elsewhere.[21] So work opportunities in Central America, although they necessitated extended family separations and arduous travel experiences, were doubly attractive to working peoples from the smaller islands during the depression years. Although Jamaicans comprised the bulk of the Antillean labour force for the French canal project in Panama, for example, Créole-speaking St Lucians were especially welcome. But when the canal effort was abandoned in 1888, hundreds of black St Lucians and others were stranded in Central America.[22]

Twentieth-century Caribbean migrations

The geo-political ascendance of the United States at the opening of the twentieth century was felt no more strongly than in the Caribbean, and it was perhaps inevitable that United States domination of the region would influence immediately the volume and directions of Caribbean migrations. From 1900 to 1913 an estimated 20,000 Jamaicans and others migrated to Costa Rica's Limón district to work for the United Fruit Company. They carved a banana enclave from the rainforests of the area, settling there with their families and with the support of transplanted Jamaican churches, lodges and other social groups. In

20 Malcolm Jarvis Proudfoot, 1950, pp.14–15.
21 Bonham C. Richardson, 1997.
22 C. Washington Eves, 1893, p.243.

1910 they struck for higher wages as the Artisans' and Labourers' Union. United Fruit officials countered by importing hundreds of men from St Kitts as strike-breakers. That tactic was less than successful because the workers from Jamaica and St Kitts found much in common and developed a sense of solidarity.[23] In a broad regional sense, Caribbean migrants to Costa Rica and elsewhere developed socio-political skills at their migration destinations that they subsequently – in probably more cases than are realized – took back to their home islands.

Some of the Jamaicans who had gone to Limón later travelled on to work on the Panama Canal and vice versa. When the Americans decided to renew, and eventually to complete, the construction of a canal across the Isthmus of Panama, the question of a labour source arose almost immediately. And during 1903 American officials conducted a survey of sorts throughout the region with an eye to establishing possible labour-recruiting stations. Jamaica wanted no part of it, American representatives insulted Danish and French colonial officials, and the various British Crown Colonies (in the Leewards and Windwards) were considered by the Americans to be too closely controlled by the British Colonial Office. Eventually the Americans settled on Barbados as their principal recruiting terminal because of the receptivity of the local (and somewhat autonomous) legislature and the willingness of shipping lines to haul deckloads of black workers from that outermost island of the eastern Caribbean to the Panamanian port of Colón.[24]

From 1905 to 1913 officials at the American labour-recruiting terminus at Bridgetown sent 20,000 (all male) contract workers to Panama from Barbados. But men with formal contracts were in the minority of those heading for Panama from Barbados and from other Caribbean locales. Until the canal's completion in 1914, when the majority of black islanders were sent back home, tens of thousands went to Panama for relatively high wages (US 10 cents per hour!) and to avoid limited, seasonal employment on their own depression-stricken plantation islands. Not all Caribbean peoples travelling to Panama in that decade worked as earth shovellers or on dynamite crews. There also were labouring niches for vegetable traffickers, laundresses, carpenters, seamstresses and a great variety of others. Perhaps as many as 40,000 Barbadian men and women (for a total of 60,000 from an island population of only about 180,000) went without contracts. Maybe as many as 80,000 Jamaican men and women went as well. Black migrants from the French, Dutch and Danish islands went too, but in fewer numbers than those from the British Caribbean colonies.[25]

---

23 Aviva Chomsky, 1996, pp.34, 147–72.

24 Bonham C. Richardson, 1985, pp.111–15.

25 Velma Newton, 1984; Michael L. Conniff, 1985.

The exodus to Panama was in many ways an extension of the past; men and women from the small islands had been travelling about for decades, of course, and in 1904 there was even a residual Antillean population in Panama left over from the French construction project to pave the way for cousins, sons, daughters and fellow islanders coming to work for the Americans. But the magnitude of Caribbean migration to Central America – like the immensity of the Panama Canal project itself – was unprecedented, and it thereby created demographic and economic tremors throughout the region that would irrevocably transform the character of Caribbean migration. Perhaps 15,000 British West Indians died in Panama before 1920; and the great majority of those who lived through the period probably stayed away forever, many moving on to the banana lands of Central America and even emigrating to New York after the project was finished.[26] Those who did return home often did so for brief periods before travelling away again.

The similarly unprecedented volume of money flowing back to the islands from those working in Panama in the first two decades of the twentieth century ameliorated the effects of economic depression in the Antilles. Returnees often bought small plots of land with their earnings, thereby realizing a measure of independence and self-respect at home with what they had earned abroad. It was perhaps the first time black West Indian working peoples envisaged the economic possibility of sustaining a resident populace at home by working abroad. The earliest migrations after slavery had been important symbolically. On the other hand, American wages earned by migrating islanders in the early twentieth century were economically crucial, underpinning livelihood strategies that involved, paradoxically, people leaving in order to stay at home.[27]

After Panama, thousands moved on to the Greater Antilles to earn money in the sugar-cane fields of Cuba and the Dominican Republic where American capital was transforming landscapes just as it had financed the canal project. Direct American military involvement in the Greater Antilles[28] had been accompanied by massive United States financial investments in the sugar industries there. United States interests had greatly influenced Cuban sugar since the late nineteenth century, but by the early twentieth American money was building and improving sugar refineries, extending railroads, clearing forests, and expanding sugar-cane acreage into sprawling agro-industries.[29] For example, by 1911 the La Romana sugar estate, a branch of

26 Irma Watkins-Owens, 1996.
27 Bernard Nietschmann, 1979.
28 B. J. Calder, 1984; Louis A. Pérez, 1986.
29 Manuel Moreno Fraginals, 1985.

the American-owned South Porto Rico Sugar Company, had been created in the forests and scrublands of the southern part of the Dominican Republic and covered an incredible 144,000 acres.[30]

The seasonal cane harvests in the Greater Antilles, from January until June or July, required thousands of cane-cutters, a periodic need for labour that could not always be supplied by the host countries. So thousands of men from nearby islands – many of whom were veterans of the Panama Canal – routinely travelled to Cuba and the Dominican Republic each year and then returned at the end of the season. Young men from the Leewards – Anguilla, Antigua, St Kitts, Nevis, Montserrat – headed to San Pedro de Macorís in the Dominican Republic via sailing schooners and aboard steamers each January. They were foreigners (and thereby somewhat easily controlled) in the large, Spanish-speaking territory and often derided as dark-skinned *cocolos* by the native Dominicans. Officials of the Dominican Republic insisted that the migrant workers performed jobs that locals should have filled, although American estate owners countered that the Dominicans were lacking in both numbers and motivation to constitute a reliable harvesting work-force.[31] Cuban officials levelled the same complaints against itinerant Jamaican cane-cutters. In 1919 and again in 1920, as many as 24,000 Jamaicans emigrated officially to Cuba, the majority as seasonal plantation workers.[32]

Haiti also emerged as an important source of migrant labour for the sugar-cane industries of the Greater Antilles early in the twentieth century. The common border with the Dominican Republic increased informal as well as officially-monitored back and forth movements of Haitian cane-cutters. By 1920, nearly as many Haitians as immigrants from the smaller British islands were working in the Dominican Republic. Haitian cane workers had already begun to head for Cuba as well, migrations facilitated by steamer travel; between 1915 and 1930 as many as 600,000 Haitians went to Cuba for work, a figure that may be inflated because some were counted more than once. By 1930, Haitians had come to outnumber by far all other foreign workers in the cane fields of the Dominican Republic.[33] Men from throughout the rest of the Caribbean came to the Greater Antilles as well. Migrants from the Danish islands (before the territories were sold to the United States) came to Cuba, and some estimate that one-fifth of the male working population of the Dutch Antilles had gone to Cuba by 1920.

30 Melvin M. Knight, 1928, p.139.
31 Patrick Bryan, 1985, pp.236–8.
32 Franklin W. Knight, 1985, p.101.
33 Samuel Martínez, 1995, pp.40–1.

The effects of these seasonal labour movements were obvious in the migrants' home islands as well. Especially in the small Leeward Islands of the British Caribbean, the first six months of each year saw mothers, wives and children waiting for the arrival of postal money orders sent from Hispaniola. When the men finally reappeared after the crop had been harvested in the Dominican Republic, they overtaxed the labour requirements of the sugar estates on their home islands. The resulting local unemployment, always a problem in the Leewards during the latter half of the year, rose markedly when local migrant labourers returned. So did incidents of petty crime, civil disturbances and crop theft. Men who habitually travelled away and returned each year preferred one another's company to those who did not. Such men congregated in rum shops, scuffled with one another, complained loudly about injustices at home, and were predictably branded 'troublemakers' by colonial officials. The fluctuating demographic patterns, economic opportunities, and even the social character of the tiny Leewards in the early twentieth century, were thus influenced far less by local events than by the tempo of the seasonal cane harvests in the Greater Antilles.[34]

Steamer routes at the end of the nineteenth century had taken a very few West Indians to the eastern seaboard of the United States. But during the first quarter of the twentieth century – until the United States established a strict 'national origins' quota on immigrants on 1 July 1924 – 102,000 black West Indians came to the United States. United States authorities did not collect data as to islands of origin; the immigrants came from the Dutch, Danish, French and Spanish-speaking islands, although the great majority were British West Indians.[35] Evidence is even sketchier concerning the relative social statuses of those who travelled to the United States versus those emigrating seasonally to the Greater Antilles. Newspaper reports and old people's recollections nevertheless suggest that those travelling to North America usually were economically better off; apparently those who were among the better-educated, lighter-skinned, and more able to purchase steamer tickets left the islands for the United States in disproportionately large numbers.[36]

The destination for the overwhelming majority of black West Indians emigrating to the United States was the New York City area. The first stop for many was Ellis Island – better known in American lore as the staging area for European immigrants to the United States – where they were checked for diseases and parasites, and given literacy tests. Once they were admitted to take up residence in the city, they soon learned the realities of the United States

34 Bonham C. Richardson, 1983, pp.129–30.
35 Ira D. A. Reid, 1939.
36 Bonham C. Richardson, 1983, pp.131–5.

colour caste system. In the islands they had been artisans, shopkeepers, estate overseers, positions significantly elevated socially from the field labourers who now were travelling annually by the thousands to the Greater Antilles. Yet in New York they were undifferentiated 'coloured', and the positions open to them as porters, janitors, maids and general labourers were the same sorts of menial low-paid positions accorded to recently arrived blacks from the United States south, positions they never would have considered had they stayed at home. West Indians interacted of necessity with their black peers who had recently come to the New York City area from the southern states of the United States. Yet these interactions were uneasy, the two groups often seeing each other as rivals, even if the white power-holders in the city did not.[37]

The West Indian presence in New York in the early twentieth century was important not only as an element in the history of Caribbean migration but also in the overall context of black history in the United States. In many cases the recent arrivals refused to accept the American colour caste system, not through overt civil disobedience but through their expression, presence and capacity to organize. While many black Americans continued to belong to the Republican Party, 'Caribbean Americans' first footholds in politics began in the Democratic Party,'[38] the beginnings of a political tradition that later came to encompass the vast majority of black Americans, of both southern and Caribbean origins.

Caribbean writers and artists contributed disproportionately to Harlem's black renaissance, mixing their artistic talents with black causes. Writers such as Claude McKay from Jamaica[39] and Eric Walrond of British Guiana contributed significantly to a literature emphasizing black pride, and labour organizers Ashley Totten and Frank Crosswaith of the Virgin Islands sought better conditions for all black workers, not only those of West Indian parentage.[40] Jamaican Marcus Garvey, having served brief labouring stints in both Costa Rica and the Canal Zone, arrived in New York in 1916. He had already established the Universal Negro Improvement Association (UNIA), then he transferred it to New York, and distributed from there his influential international newspaper *Negro World*, which stressed black pride and the importance of ties between African-Americans and Africa itself. Copies of *Negro World* found their way back to every island in the British Caribbean, were often branded as seditious by colonial administrators, and helped to sustain UNIA chapters

37 Irma Watkins-Owens, 1996.

38 *Ibid*, p.170.

39 Tyrone Tillery, 1992.

40 Jervis Anderson, 1982.

throughout the region. Garvey's influence, West Indian in origin but affecting African-Americans everywhere, especially in the United States, was of fundamental importance in the evolution of black consciousness in the early twentieth century.[41]

New York was not the sole metropolis of the eastern United States to become home for migrants from the Caribbean. A sizeable West Indian enclave in Boston was established before the turn of the century. Economic downturns in the Bahamas sent many labouring men, especially from the Bahamian out-islands, to Miami for seasonal wage labour. 'In Miami and the communities beyond it Bahamians were employed as domestic servants, farmers, cooks, hotel waiters, bellmen, hackmen, draymen, carpenters, painters, masons, bakers and workers in laundries.'[42] Some of the Bahamian middle class also headed for Miami where they became prosperous in a relative sense, although they never were able to rise above the city's strict colour lines.

Interrelationships among Caribbean migrations, extra-regional cultural contacts, and black assertiveness were also evident in the impact that the British West Indies Regiment had throughout the region during the First World War and immediately thereafter. The unit was composed of white officers and black enlisted personnel from throughout the British Caribbean. Involved in road-building projects in France and combat in the Levant during the war, the more than 15,000 soldiers of the regiment suffered nearly 900 battle casualties, and another 1,000 died of disease. At war's end the unit was relegated to demeaning clean-up duty in Sicily. Black, mainly Jamaican, non-commissioned officers of the regiment, fed up with the racism they had suffered during the War, formed the revolutionary Caribbean League while in Sicily. They vowed that Blacks should govern themselves upon their return to the British Caribbean, using force if necessary. The British War Office and Colonial Office, both alarmed by the rhetoric (which the sergeants thought had been secret) and the obvious potential that combat-trained personnel had for revolution, had two destroyers standing by in the Caribbean region when the regiment was mustered out early in 1919.

The only place where subsequent rioting was attributed directly to returned soldiers was in British Honduras in July 1919, but the absence of widespread disturbances elsewhere in the region only slightly diminished the fear that colonial officials had of the returned soldiers who felt they had earned equality by fighting alongside Europeans. Migration, incidentally, may have played a doubly important role in the experiences of the returning members of the British West Indies Regiment. Many of the most troublesome

41 Tony Martin, 1976 (1986). See also chap.6, this volume.
42 Howard Johnson, 1988, p.95.

of the soldiers, Jamaican members of the unit's Ninth Battalion, earlier had been labourers on the Panama Canal.[43]

The First World War also indirectly improved economic prospects for estate labourers throughout the Caribbean, those staying at home as well as those who had come to migrate for a living. The war had heightened an international demand for sugar, and much of rural Europe – its beet-sugar fields cratered from artillery salvos and its labour force depleted – lagged briefly in production. The international price for sugar soared, quickening the pace of migrations of small islanders to the Greater Antilles and also inspiring planters on those same small islands to extend cane acreages by planting in marginal areas and trying to keep their workers at home with increased wages. Opportunities for migrants from English-speaking islands also appeared in the region's growing petroleum industry whose bosses and managers usually were white (English-speaking) Americans; black labourers – mainly from Trinidad, Grenada and St Vincent – travelled to northern Venezuela to construct oil derricks in the Lake Maracaibo estuary. Then they went to Curaçao, where they were joined by other migrants, who had come from as far afield as Portuguese Madeira, to build the Royal Dutch Shell oil refinery so that Maracaibo oil might be refined in a safe, placid offshore Dutch colony rather than in politically volatile Venezuela. A similar refinery, this one constructed by the Standard Oil Company of New Jersey, was built in Dutch Aruba beginning in 1929. The refinery complexes of the Netherlands Antilles and their associated construction, maintenance and service-oriented jobs occupied thousands of migrating men and women – again, mainly from the English-speaking Caribbean – for three decades thereafter.

The world market price for sugar plummeted in 1921, to 18 shillings per hundred lbs on the London market, from 58 the year before; then the price crept upward in the next few years only to fall to nine shillings per hundred lbs on the London market in 1929.[44] These dramatic economic events were a preview of the depression decade of the 1930s, and the general economic downturn curtailed greatly the volume of inter-island labour migration that had occupied an entire generation of working men and women of the Caribbean. The few published migration data from the period show that the flows of itinerant labour into Cuba[45] and the Dominican Republic[46] were both reduced sharply after 1920. In both places – where grass-roots sentiment had

43 C. L. Joseph, 1971.
44 Noel Deerr, 1949–50, vol. II, p.531.
45 Franklin W. Knight, 1985, p.101.
46 Bonham C. Richardson, 1983, p.126.

long opposed the presence of seasonal immigrants from the British Caribbean – laws were passed at the beginning of the depression decade to curtail the entry of foreign workers, although underpaid Haitians continued to come to both places in some numbers.[47]

These external decisions that directly affected the livelihood aspirations of small-island Caribbean migrants were new only in that they had been imposed by the Dominican and Cuban authorities. The recent closure of the United States in 1924 as a possible emigration destination, further, had by no means been the first such experience for travelling West Indians. Panama had been shut off as a wage source by the Americans in 1914 (and earlier by the French in 1889), and before that an ephemeral dock construction project in Bermuda had closed down in 1906. Even in the nineteenth century, when sugar prices had fallen in Trinidad, small-island migrants had been driven back to their home islands. These were the downsides of the volatile 'boom-and-bust' economic cycles that had been so much a part of the Caribbean past, would become so much a part of the region's future, and already had inspired resilience and adaptation among emigrating peoples of the Caribbean, teaching them never to devote themselves fully to fickle and short-lived wage destinations.

Despite the valuable lessons learned by migrating men and women from the islands, the closure of emigration destinations nonetheless created socio-economic despair among the region's working people. A pent-up work-force with few emigration outlets could hardly turn inward to perform non-existent wage tasks in their own home islands that had been similarly affected by economic depression. Economic misery prevailed in the eastern Caribbean in the depression decade of the 1930s, and symptoms of unrest – threats to planters, cane fires, minor civil disturbances – were commonplace. On 28 January 1935 an angry crowd of estate workers assembled at a sugar factory west of Basseterre, St Kitts, demanding bonus pay for that year's crop such as they had received in the past. When their demands were denied, the 'St Kitts Riots' followed with associated vandalism in both town and country districts. News of the riots spread quickly through the neighbouring islands of the British Caribbean where depression had brought social conditions to their kindling points. Roughly similar riots extended in the next few years through most of the islands. During the explosive period of the late 1930s in the British Caribbean '(e)very British Governor called for warships, marines and aeroplanes; total casualties in the British colonies amounted to 29 dead, 115 wounded.'[48]

47 Samuel Martínez, 1995, pp.40–1.

48 Eric Williams, 1970 (1984), pp.473–4. See chap.2, this volume.

Information and editorials about these related disturbances had been published in all of the islands by increasingly articulate working-class newspapers. And the riots were in many ways expressions of political dissatisfaction among brown middle classes and black labouring classes of the British Caribbean. Reports and commissions marking the aftermath of the riots, moreover, recommended less harsh measures of political control in each of the insular colonies, a relaxation that inevitably increased elements of self-rule. Older informants throughout the region invariably point to the riots of the 1930s as providing the first glimmers of self-determination and political independence. And it is important that many of the rioters themselves – as noted in the several published reports that followed the disturbances – were erstwhile labour migrants whose migration possibilities had been all but eliminated by general economic depression abroad.[49]

The laws passed by Dominican and Cuban authorities reduced much of the inter-island migration to their countries, but they did not effectively evict all unwanted migrants. And during the depression decade of the 1930s foreign ethnic groups were targeted by host populations in the Caribbean as sources of crime and impropriety in general just as similar migrant groups have been persecuted at other times and in other places. The tragic 'Trujillo massacre' in the Dominican Republic in 1937 saw the slaughter of between 15,000 and 25,000 itinerant Haitians who lived in the western parts of the country. The massacre apparently was directed by the Dominican dictator, Rafael Trujillo, and accomplished by those who resented the Haitian presence, resentment that Dominicans had felt for many decades against the pulses of Haitian individuals and armies across the international boundary that bisects Hispaniola. Exactly what Trujillo expected to accomplish from this atrocity is still being debated; he apparently meant to spare those Haitians working on sugar estates, thereby delivering the chilling message that Haitians would be welcome in the Dominican Republic only if they were inhabitants of the dank, unsanitary barracks on the estates.[50]

Similarly horrifying reprisals were not forthcoming against itinerant minorities elsewhere in the region during the 1930s, although economic conditions were grim in all of the islands. In both the British and French Caribbean colonies 'the consequences of poverty were squalid living conditions, ill health, and misery.'[51] Conditions were little better during the following decade when the Second World War engulfed the region. Short-lived jobs became available on island bases that the United States secured from Britain

49 Bonham C. Richardson, 1989, p.215.

50 Samuel Martínez, 1995, p.45.

51 Bridget Brereton, 1989, p.102.

in exchange for a number of near-obsolete naval destroyers. Men and women of the English-speaking islands found employment as construction labourers and domestics in Trinidad, Antigua, British Guiana, New Providence and also St Thomas, jobs that involved inter-island travel by sailing vessels and the attendant threats from German submarines. In many ways, the Second World War period tied the region even closer to the United States. This shift was most noticeable at a grass-roots level in the small colonies controlled by Britain, France and the Netherlands because the people there – formerly accustomed to receiving pounds, francs and guilders for their work – found themselves more and more working for the 'Yankee dollar'.[52]

The sudden devaluation of the British pound in 1949 increased the costs of non-British imports into the British islands by 50 per cent, literally overnight. But the emigration outlet that would compensate for the ever-worsening conditions in the British Caribbean had its beginnings the year before. In June 1948, the S.S. *Empire Windrush* had arrived in Britain carrying 492 passengers from the English-speaking Caribbean, mostly Jamaicans but also other islanders.[53] The arrival of the *Windrush* is the generally acknowledged beginning of the massive exodus to Britain of tens of thousands of British West Indians during the 1950s in order to provide manpower to help rebuild post-war Britain, whose local labour force had been seriously depleted in the war. The black West Indians travelled using newly minted British passports, so that accurate records as to how many left specific islands were never kept, yet island residents still recall the excitement among those leaving for England whose anticipation rivalled that in the days of the Panama Canal. Estimates of total Caribbean migration to Britain from 1951 to 1961 – travel that took place on board ships as well as via trans-Atlantic airplane charters – range from 230,000 to 280,000.[54]

Tiny Montserrat is estimated to have lost over 30 per cent of its population to emigration to Britain in the 1950s.[55] Percentages were lower in the other, larger islands, although the entire Caribbean lost many of its more capable and technically skilled personnel; a local malaise, therefore, became noticeable in parts of the region as many of the more active and industrious departed.[56] Those young West Indian families who had left home were busy establishing themselves in Britain in unfamiliar surroundings amidst an indifferent-to-hostile white society. They settled in London and the industrial Midlands, performing jobs that in some cases put them in competition against

52 Alan Richmond Prest, 1948.

53 M. Banton, 1953.

54 Ceri Peach, 1968.

55 Stuart B. Philpott, 1973.

56 David Lowenthal and Lambros Comitas, 1962.

working-class Britons. Although many of the West Indians had actually been recruited by British agencies such as London Transport, British Railways and the National Health Service, some of these organizations establishing recruiting stations in the islands themselves, the welcome for black immigrants to the 'mother country' was far from warm. Anti-black riots broke out in west London in 1958,[57] the most dramatic event in an era of racial tensions and increasing animosity toward the recent migrants to the United Kingdom. In 1962 Parliament passed the controversial Commonwealth Immigrants Act that thereafter barred resident West Indians from bringing in any but their closest relatives.

Late in the 1990s, an estimated 0.9 per cent of the United Kingdom's 59 million people had 'Caribbean' birthplaces. Add to that their children and, increasingly, their grandchildren who live in the United Kingdom, and an estimate of 750,000 to one million 'West Indian Britons' seems reasonable. The British census of 1971 was the first to identify Caribbean peoples residing there by island or country of birth: 172,000 at that time were from Jamaica, 27,000 from Barbados, 21,000 from Guyana, 17,000 from Trinidad & Tobago, and smaller numbers from the Leeward and Windward Islands. The numbers for most of these places – except for Trinidad & Tobago which showed a slight increase – had declined by the time of the 1991 census.[58] Although these census data are silent as to ethnic identity, many Caribbean peoples are of (indentured) Indian ancestry. Yet far more numerous are Afro-Caribbean peoples. They reside mostly in Britain's industrial slums and suffer high rates of unemployment; the voluminous academic literature concerning them, moreover, usually has focused on their impoverishment and lack of economic opportunities, and the ill-feeling that exists between them and many of the country's Whites.[59]

Yet the permanence of the Caribbean presence in the United Kingdom recently has awakened a more contemplative kind of migration research, an approach different from the earlier demographic descriptions or race-relations frameworks whose conclusions usually could be determined before the research itself was carried out. Elizabeth Thomas-Hope, for example, has urged that those studying Caribbean migration to Britain eschew a routine cataloguing of movements of people as labour units and instead consider a more meaningful interpretation that 'at the level of societal meaning and personal consciousness has scarcely been touched upon.'[60] Such an approach involves

57 Edward Pilkington, 1988.
58 Mary Chamberlain, 1995, p.254.
59 For example, S. Patterson, 1969.
60 Elizabeth M. Thomas-Hope, 1992, p.8.

a knowledge of the historical circumstances of these migrations and invariably calls for intense interviews with individuals as family members.[61] The geographer John Western has interviewed roughly forty Barbadians who reside in the London area, learning, among many other things, that they continue to differentiate themselves from other West Indians and that most are generally positive about their experiences in Britain.[62] Western's study explores the migration at the individual level while never losing sight of the big picture and questions of identity and migration. The anthropologist George Gmelch used similar interviewing techniques in determining the conditions, prospects and anxieties for Barbadians who have ventured abroad and also those who have returned home.[63]

Those from French and Dutch Caribbean territories inhabiting their respective metropoles are more recent European arrivals and are numerically fewer than in Britain. They are nonetheless noticeable because of their predominantly urban residential preferences. A French government-sponsored travel agency (known in France by its acronym BUMIDOM) began to send workers from the French Caribbean to France in 1963, at about the same time Britain was closing its doors to Caribbean peoples. The transportation of both men and women by this immigration agency to metropolitan France placed the newly-arrived either directly into jobs or vocational training centres. The 1990 French census enumerated roughly 105,000 persons of Caribbean origin residing in France, a figure that has fluctuated over the past two decades because of an active population circulation between Paris and the Caribbean; these movements, often of relatively young working people, doubtless reflect the islands' departmental status and relative ease with which people can come and go.[64] An estimated 30,000 from the Netherlands Antilles and 200,000 Surinamese resided in the Netherlands late in the 1990s. A high percentage of the latter are Surinamese of Asian origin, those who fled the country in the mid-1970s fearing possible discrimination under a predominantly black government in an independent Suriname.

Whereas hundreds of thousands of Caribbean migrants and their children live in Western Europe, Caribbean peoples now residing in North America (mainly the United States) can be counted in the millions. And in the same way that metropolitan labour needs drew tens of thousands of black West Indians to Britain in the 1950s, a growth in the supply of low-wage jobs in the eastern part of the United States – part of the 'restructuring of economic

61 For example, Mary Chamberlain, 1995.
62 John Western, 1992, p.267.
63 George Gmelch, 1992.
64 M. Byron and S. Condon, 1996, pp.91–104.

activity in the U.S.'[65] during the 1960s and 1970s – has led to an influx of Caribbean peoples into the United States. This influx has been facilitated by the United States Immigration Act of 1965 that modified the national origins quotas previously favouring Europeans.

Population estimates of Caribbean peoples in the United States are confounded by the differences between legal and illegal migrations, distinctions interpreted very differently depending upon whether or not the interpretation is provided by a native-born (white) citizen of the United States. Strictly speaking, the United States formally admits 600,000 persons from abroad each year, but some estimates suggest that as many as 500,000 illegal immigrants enter the United States annually. The 'legal' and 'illegal' categories are viewed by Caribbean peoples mainly as bureaucratic hurdles to circumvent rather than immutable law. They are aware of a West Indian presence in the United States since early in the twentieth century, so that many people in the Caribbean see the changes in the 1965 United States immigration law as representing continuity rather than change.[66]

Late in the 1990s perhaps six million people of Caribbean origin resided in the United States, an estimate that is necessarily vague because of the legal-illegal differences and other complications. As an example of the difficulties in arriving at these population estimates, Larson and Sullivan have pointed out,[67] in attempting to estimate the number of Dominicans from the Dominican Republic residing in the United States, that estimates can vary from 300,000 to 1,000,000 (!) depending on the sources used and the author's emphasis. Particular characteristics of each sending area and its relationships with the mainland, furthermore, must be taken into account when arriving at these estimates. In the case of the Dominican Republic, researchers must consider the undetermined number of 'illegals' who have travelled clandestinely to Puerto Rico by boat and then on to the United States, where in the past they have been seen as virtually indistinguishable from Puerto Ricans as far as immigration authorities are concerned. Like Puerto Ricans, most Dominicans live in the New York City area.

Similar considerations must be made when attempting to estimate the number of Caribbean peoples from other places who have come to the United States. Three-quarters of the roughly one million Cubans are in southern Florida,[68] their numbers augmented by more than 100,000 who came during the Mariel boatlift in 1980. The 700,000 British West Indians reside

65 Saskia Sassen, 1988, p.56.
66 Charles V. Carnegie, 1983.
67 E. M. Larson and T. A. Sullivan, 1987.
68 G. J. Grenier and A. Stepick III, 1992.

mainly in the New York City area;[69] Jamaicans are a large plurality in this group which includes residential enclaves from every island in the greater New York area (e.g., Nevisians in New Haven, Connecticut, and Anguillans in Perth Amboy, New Jersey). The perhaps 800,000 Haitians are also mainly in New York, but in the region of 70,000 of them live in southern Florida, many coming by way of the Bahamas.[70] The 1990 United States census enumerated 900,000 of Puerto Rican descent in New York,[71] although most estimates range considerably higher. Puerto Ricans living in the United States are, of course, not 'foreign' migrants, although they have often been treated in the same rough way by employers as have undocumented migrants from other Latin American states, in part because of their skin colour.[72]

Puerto Ricans in both their home island and in the United States realize, even if others do not, that their longevity in the New York area has made them an integral part of the United States. New York was an exile destination as early as the 1870s and 1880s for influential Puerto Ricans seeking political independence from Spain. At the turn of the century Arturo Alfonso Schomburg, a scholar and activist from Puerto Rico, later a political leader in Harlem, established his residence in the aptly-named 'San Juan Hill' area of Manhattan.[73] The great surge of migrants from Puerto Rico to New York came after the Second World War, the majority being poor and thereby filling working-class positions. Later migrants have included representatives from all segments of Puerto Rican society. The island's Commonwealth status means that travel back and forth from one place to another is by now so common and routine that 'migration' is a questionable term when attempting to describe the Puerto Rican experience in the United States. In New York one can dine in a growing number of Puerto Rican restaurants, read (in either English or Spanish) books describing the American-Puerto Rican experience, and vote for ever-enlarging slates of political candidates of Puerto Rican origin. Yet Puerto Ricans do not necessarily see themselves as 'assimilated' into American culture and recognize the need to assert themselves politically, seeking power within a political geographic context that often turns on the enduring dilemma as to 'whether Puerto Ricans are a national minority or a nation'.[74]

The size and locational concentration associated with the recent movements of Puerto Ricans and others coming north, combined with an earlier presence of Caribbean peoples in the United States, have strongly imprinted

69 Philip Kasinitz, 1992.
70 Michel S. Laguerre, 1984, pp.24–5; Dawn I. Marshall, 1979.
71 G. Haslip-Viera, 1996, p.14.
72 R. Weisskoff, 1985, p.79.
73 G. Haslip-Viera, 1996, p.6.
74 J. R. Sánchez, 1996, p.296.

American culture. This imprint is of course obvious in the New York City area where music, cuisine, fashion, residential patterns, educational expectations, race relations and much more have been influenced greatly by recent migrants from the Caribbean.[75] Despite prejudice against them, Haitian vodun ceremonies are now routinely carried out in Brooklyn apartments. These ceremonies celebrate African/Haitian ethnicity, seek spiritual identity with Africa itself, and thereby attract not only Haitians who reside in New York but other African-Caribbean peoples who live there, and even African-Americans from the United States.[76] Every Labor Day in the New York City borough of Brooklyn, tens of thousands of Caribbean New Yorkers join together in a carnival celebration reminiscent of Trinidad's pre-Lenten Mardi Gras festival and provide a pan-Caribbean identity for participants unlike any they could have achieved by staying in the home islands.[77]

If New York could be described as the centre of gravity for Puerto Ricans, Jamaicans and Haitians who have migrated to the United States, Miami has become – extending the metaphor – weighted down by Cubans. An estimated one-third of Miami's residents are foreign-born, a larger fraction than for any city of the United States. The concentration of banks, commercial outlets and transportation facilities in Miami has made it, according to some, the most important city of Latin America and the Caribbean. Indeed, tens of thousands of Miami's residents come from the Caribbean, Central America and South America. But if the corpus of the city itself is Latin American, its heart is certainly Cuban. Nearly three-quarters of Miami's Hispanic population are now Cuban. The Cuban American sociologist Lisandro Pérez points out that Spanish is not simply a language that Miami Cubans speak at home; rather Spanish has become a 'public language' in the city.[78] Pérez also identifies an 'exile ideology' that underpins Cuban life in Miami, an ideology focused precisely upon the Cuban homeland and an uncompromisingly hostile attitude toward Fidel Castro's political regime.

Beyond New York and Miami, the presence of Caribbean peoples in the United States has influenced the culture of the entire country. Some trace the rhythms of rap music – a principal voice of urban Black America – to Trinidad. No college campus or university town is without its local reggae ensemble, some of the members being from Jamaica! Baseball, America's so-called 'national pastime', has become so thoroughly infused with Caribbean players that it seems a different game from the one it was only a few decades ago. Every American schoolboy knows of San Pedro de Macorís, the

75 Nancy Foner, 1987, pp.17–30.
76 Karen M. Brown, 1991.
77 Donald R. Hill and R. Abramson, 1979.
78 Lisandro Pérez, 1992, p.93.

Dominican Republic's 'home of shortstops'.[79] During the 1996 United States major-league baseball season, the most common player's surname was Martínez, the second most common, Pérez!

But culture and institutions are abstractions that are ultimately dependent upon individual people who introduce, create and change. Most Americans express surprise when they learn of the Caribbean identities of people who are influential throughout America. Most are aware of Sidney Poitier and Harry Belafonte, and the baseball players. Colin Powell's Jamaican background has been similarly well publicized. Yet few are aware that Louis Farrakhan (the erstwhile Louis Walcott), perhaps the best known (and certainly most feared) black political figure in America today, is originally from Boston's Caribbean enclave.[80] Shirley Chisholm, the black congresswoman who made a brief run at the United States presidency in 1972, was of Barbadian parentage, as was Robert Maynard, the late newspaper publisher from Oakland, California. Malcom X's mother was Grenadian. And the reputations of Princeton University and Boston University have been enhanced by the accomplishments of the Nobel Laureates Arthur Lewis and Derek Walcott, both originally from St Lucia.

Yet the influence and creativity of the recent arrivals from the Caribbean to the United States have not transformed the fundamentally menial jobs that most of them take when they first arrive. Strikingly similar to the experiences of black and brown West Indian women who arrived in New York early in the twentieth century, for instance, many – maybe most – Caribbean women become maids, caretakers to the elderly, or babysitters when they come to New York now, a tendency that involves for many of them 'stepping down the occupational hierarchy' from jobs they had at home as teachers, clerks or government workers.[81] In the same vein, some of the hardest manual work done anywhere in North America – cutting sugar-cane in southern Florida on peaty soil unsuited for mechanical harvesters – is the near-exclusive domain of itinerant West Indian men, mainly Jamaicans, brought north each year for the work. It is exceedingly strenuous labour involving risks to health, questionable payment procedures and semi-isolation from the local populace, reminiscent of conditions in the Greater Antilles in the early twentieth century. The contemporary exploitation of the migrant workers from the Caribbean in the Florida cane-lands, not incidentally, is in many ways an extension of the exploitation of United States Blacks who were brought to southern Florida from Alabama and Tennessee to do the same work in the 1930s and 1940s.[82]

79 Rob Ruck, 1993.
80 M. Gladwell, 1996.
81 S. Colen, 1989, pp.173–4.
82 Alec Wilkinson, 1989.

Canadian population statistics for 1991 enumerated 233,000 residing there whose birthplace was either 'Caribbean or Bermuda'. Add to that the births of children and also illegal migration, and one can understand how some informal estimates range as high as 500,000 Caribbean people in Canada. Presenting further complications, thousands of black Britons have migrated to Canada in the recent past and are thereby reported for census purposes as 'British' in origin. The 1981 Canadian census reported 211,000 Caribbean people in Canada, 55 per cent of whom were female; at that time the largest Caribbean places represented among this group were Jamaica (78,000) and Haiti (27,000).[83] Estimates one decade later have Jamaica (150,000) and Guyana (80,000) sending the most from the Caribbean to Canada.

Changes in Canadian immigration regulations in 1967 eliminated the racial bias therein. Afterwards, Caribbeans – mainly from the former British colonies of the region and exploiting the longstanding economic and social ties between Canada and the Caribbean – began to come to Canada within a somewhat complicated immigration 'points system' based on education, job skills and employment needs. The decade of the 1970s was a major period of Caribbean migration to Canada – those coming before 1974 possessing, in the aggregate, higher levels of education than those who came thereafter.[84] Illegal immigration has since swelled the numbers. During the 1980s thousands of Indo-Caribbean people from Guyana and Trinidad entered Canada, in part because of the downturn in world oil prices leading to unemployment in Trinidad. Many Indo-Guyanese have come to Canada claiming 'refugee' status because of Guyana's troubled political climate, taking advantage of a provision in Canada's immigration policy that remains 'complicated and complex'.[85] A few Indo-Trinidadians have also made the same claim, responding to perceived discrimination by black-dominated governments there before 1995.

The Caribbean 1 per cent of all people living in Canada is heavily concentrated in the country's urban south-east, perhaps 60 per cent of all Canadian Caribbeans in the Toronto area and another 20 per cent in Montreal, the latter including a sizeable number of French-speaking Haitians. Caribbean peoples represent a highly visible minority within Canada's largely European population, adding cultural zest and flair far beyond their numbers. The Caribana celebration each summer in Toronto resembles Labor Day in Brooklyn and is now ingrained in Canadian culture. Several Dominicans are stars on the city's popular major-league baseball team. Jamaican-born sprinters

83 A. H. Richmond, 1989, p.5.

84 *Ibid.*

85 Wolseley W. Anderson, 1993, p.48.

Ben Johnson and Donovan Bailey have won Olympic gold for their adopted country. Whereas a number of Caribbean-Canadians have achieved success in business and the professions, a disturbingly high number of young Afro-Caribbean men is said to suffer discrimination in the Toronto area, and publicized assertions about racism there have led to varying levels of government concern.[86]

Although long-distance human migrations from the Caribbean to North Atlantic metropoles have been noticeable and well-publicized, intra-regional movements of peoples within the Caribbean continue as they have for more than one and one-half centuries. But now they involve an immense volume of people. Especially in the smaller islands, where tiny island size and associated limited economic opportunities send people away, men and women travel about to sell fruit, find jobs, fish, transport goods, seek specialized medical attention, escape local authorities, vacation and for many other reasons. Consequently, there are few islands of any size or importance in the region without their own itinerant 'foreign' minorities. The presence of these groups, the local functions they serve, and the reasons for their presence vary greatly. Trinidad, an emigration destination of small islanders for many decades, now hosts a sizeable number of Guyanese who fled political and economic problems in their own country in the 1970s and 1980s; thousands of Guyanese also reside across the border in Suriname for the same reasons. 'Down islanders' from the Leewards – mainly St Kitts and Nevis – inhabit the United States Virgin Islands and are considered rustic and ill-mannered by the native Blacks there.[87] The more than 30,000 Cubans living in Puerto Rico were mainly from the Cuban economic élite of pre-Castro Cuba. Now they represent a so-called 'middleman minority' in greater San Juan, a role similar to that played by the Portuguese in Guyana and the Chinese in several other Caribbean locales.[88]

The most distressing case of intra-regional migration in the Caribbean awakens memories of the past. Each year thousands of Haitian men and some women still emigrate to work in the cane-lands of the Dominican Republic. Estimates range from just over 100,000 to half a million annually, numbers that – as in earlier decades – are only vaguely known because of ever-changing labour demands, exploitative non-contract hiring, and changing immigration rules that defy accurate body counts. Haitian cane workers in the Dominican Republic work 12-hour days, are pitifully underpaid and receive little or no medical attention; and some may be actually locked inside barracks at night. The term *neo-slavery* has been applied to these conditions

86 *Ibid.*, pp.123—32; Frances Henry, 1994.

87 R. Dirks, 1975.

88 Jorge Duany, 1989.

by more than one observer, and the plight of the Haitians working in the Dominican Republic was the subject of several international human-rights investigations during the 1980s.[89]

The Haitian labour migrations across the border (informal movements are known locally as going 'under the wire') have been occurring for decades. Second- and third-generation cane-cutters from Haiti thus travel to jobs across the border which, taken altogether, may be the largest source of wages for Haiti as a whole. The sugar-estate jobs they perform underpin the Dominican Republic's sugar industry and are related to migrations of another kind; part of the labour shortage in the eastern half of Hispaniola arose because so many Dominicans have headed to the United States and Puerto Rico. The ultimate interpretation of the circulations of Haitian people to cut Dominican sugar-cane, however, lies in their deep impoverishment. As anthropologist Samuel Martínez reports, 'thousands of Haitians ... have so few other economic alternatives at home that they cross the border of their own volition, knowing it likely that they will be taken to a sugar estate, where mistreatment and exploitation await them.'[90]

What Caribbean migration means

The several generations of Caribbean migration and return have helped to create local societies that reflect continuous movements of peoples. Especially in the Caribbean's smaller places and rural zones, the preponderance of the very old and very young in the local populations is noticeable to even the most casual observers. In the past, beginning with the earliest movements away from the small British islands in the 1830s, migration was the province of young and middle-aged adult males. Island census reports throughout the British Caribbean in the nineteenth and early twentieth centuries all reflected an absence of men. When so many young men went to Panama from Barbados early in this century, women at home were called upon to be police constables, cane-cutters and field labourers.[91] A high incidence of lesbianism in Carriacou at mid-twentieth century was attributed to the relative absence of men.[92] Somewhat similarly, Jamaican men who toil seasonally in the Florida cane-lands today speak of 'Joe Grind' as the generic fellow back

89 Roger Plant, 1987.
90 Samuel Martínez, 1995, p.14.
91 Bonham C. Richardson, 1985, p.132.
92 M. G. Smith, 1962a, pp.199–201.

home who 'takes over' among the Jamaican women when the men are away working.[93]

But at the turn of the century Caribbean women now emigrate in roughly the same numbers as men, often taking jobs as domestics in larger, nearby islands or in metropolitan areas.[94] Recent data show that young women from Grenada in fact tend to emigrate earlier than do men.[95] When young parents emigrate for brief or extended periods, the burden of local child care falls to siblings, cousins, aunts, and very often to grandparents. Few school administrators in the region are unfamiliar with the problems of small children who misbehave owing to a lack of parental control and because 'their grandparents cannot keep up with them.'

The principal compensation for the absence of so many young adults in the region is the immense volume of cash remittances that flows back to the predominantly very old and very young who stay behind. In the larger islands, the estimated aggregate totals of money sent home are enormous; in 1994 Jamaican workers abroad sent back an estimated US$327 million dollars, and those from the Dominican Republic abroad remitted the equivalent of US$420 million to families and friends at home.[96] In earlier days migrants abroad sent money home via postal money orders, but in recent decades they have more often sent home cheques through the commercial banking system; this latter remittance strategy allows migrants to avoid unrealistic currency exchange rates, and it also confounds the attempts of researchers to determine remittance totals. It is near impossible, furthermore, to estimate the amount of cash carried home in pockets and purses by either returning migrants or their friends and agents.

If the larger aggregate volumes of remittances come to the larger places, it is nonetheless certain that they are really more important in the smaller islands. Ever since the quantification of insular Caribbean remittance totals became academically fashionable,[97] researchers have endeavoured to determine the sums of money coming from outside. These scholarly efforts are fraught with difficulty – owing in part to informants' obvious reluctance to divulge very personal information – although it generally is conceded that, in the tiny Caribbean islands, money remittances from external sources often exceed internal sources. Canadian anthropologist Hymie Rubenstein offers a provocative thesis based upon his work in St Vincent, suggesting that remittances contribute little to real local development but instead reinforce

93 Alec Wilkinson, 1989, p.170.
94 Elsa M. Chaney and M. G. Castro, 1989.
95 G. R. Pool, 1989, p.251.
96 World Development Report, 1996, pp.218–19.
97 For example, R. A. Manners, 1965.

externally linked dependency.[98] In any event, remittances are fundamental to every small Caribbean society; as Donald Hill remarked for Carriacou in the early 1970s: 'if several thousand Carriacouans returned home and if money stopped coming in from abroad, the entire economic structure of the island would collapse.'[99]

It should not be surprising that, in these circumstances, elements of cultural behaviour can be explained by the continuous sending and receipt of money remittances in small Caribbean societies. Suspicious villagers suggest that postmen often steal envelopes and letters destined for local recipients because they hope to pocket the cash therein; sending money home to one's parents via a neighbour or using an odd return address are thus countervailing methods by which senders of cash attempt to decoy Caribbean postmen. Every small Caribbean island, moreover, has its stock of anecdotes about faithful return migrants who have hidden money from Customs and Treasury agents at either end of their trip in order to bring it home safely to friends and relatives; these stories, of course, tend to reinforce similar behaviour now and in the future. In a somewhat broader sense, the outside world in general might be said to represent a source of money to small islanders of the region; this suggestion is supported by numerous incidents involving the hope for objects washed ashore, money left behind by outsiders, or even buried treasure. This notion, incidentally, has been reinforced by recent experiences in the Bahamas; because of the massive drug traffic in the 1980s between the many Bahamian islands and the cays of southern Florida, a traffic featuring clandestine reloadings of illicit cargoes and high-speed boat chases, residents of the Bahamas 'commonly hope that some lost duffle bag (filled with drugs) will wash ashore and make them rich.'[100]

Those islanders who faithfully send money and also gifts (everything from postage stamps to clothing to refrigerators) to those remaining behind invariably receive warmer welcomes upon their return than those who do not; some island informants insist that those who emigrate in the first place are 'more intelligent' than those who stay. The associated pomp and puffery of some returners – bedecked with clothing from New York, Paris or London – are commonplace throughout the region. And these displays by returners to small Caribbean islands are strikingly similar to those of the past. The strutting self-confidence of the 'Panama men' who returned to Barbados from Colón in the early twentieth century wearing tweed suits and felt hats is still

98 H. Rubenstein, 1983.
99 Donald R. Hill, 1977, p.238.
100 P. T. White, 1989, pp.39–40.

recalled by old Barbadian informants.[101] Decades earlier, during the first pulses of emigration away from the Leewards after emancipation, returners to Nevis are reported to have adorned themselves in 'fashionable array, with a gawdy display of tinsel ornaments' which they had purchased in Trinidad so that those back home would know that they travelled far and successfully.[102]

The admiration of return migrants is not universal in Caribbean societies. Free-spending returners can be abrasive and provoke jealous reaction. The term Nuyorican in Puerto Rico, for example, carries with it as much a connotation of pretence and selfishness as it does awe and admiration (or even suggests someone who never 'made it' at home and had to leave.) For the region as a whole, the many complexities and varying local attitudes about migration and return are said to be part of a wider psychic malaise in Caribbean cultures that attributes a lack of locally based self-confidence and self-reliance in the region to a slavish dependency on the outside: '[A] vicious circle has been set up: psychological dependence leads to an ever-growing economic and cultural dependence on the outside world. Fragmentation is intensified in the process. And the greater degree of dependence and fragmentation further reduces local self-confidence.'[103]

These laments are however not of compelling importance in reducing human movements from and within the region in light of the obvious material and social benefits that – in the eyes of Caribbean beholders – are derived from migration. Throughout this century and even earlier, the most attractive and lavish houses in the smaller islands have been financed from sojourns abroad and even named for migration destinations, such as the 'Aruba houses' in the Grenadines,[104] or the 'Curaçao houses' in Montserrat.[105] Land, automobiles, taxis, rum shops, fishing vessels and livestock similarly have been purchased with money brought or sent home. Education – from blue-collar experience on tractors and oil rigs to data-processing and clerical experience to formal training in law and medicine – is often obtained away from home. Local improvements, from installing screened windows and drainage trenches around the house to sophisticated means of settling local labour disputes, often come from Caribbean migrants' experiences elsewhere. Those who have travelled away and returned often dispense wisdom and advice at the village level that they have learned abroad, counsel often sought by local youngsters. And all of these tangible and intangible benefits obtained by

101 Bonham C. Richardson, 1985, p.149.
102 Bonham C. Richardson, 1983, p.90.
103 Eric Williams, 1970 (1984), p.502.
104 Donald R. Hill, 1977.
105 Stuart B. Philpott, 1973.

those travelling abroad, both now and in the past, are daily reinforced by images of the good (external) life on local television and cinema screens.

Caribbean peoples are acutely aware of the world outside, not simply because of increasing communications technology, but, more important, because of the reservoir of local human experience associated with migration and return. The outside world has offered a variety of hazards and rewards which have changed continuously over the past century and a half. Caribbean men and women travelling away have thus depended on their acuity and adaptability in coping with ever-changing conditions in a variety of places. At migration destinations they often have been insulted, have performed the most menial kinds of labour, and have inhabited the worst housing available, eschewing local standards of propriety in favour of earning short-term wages. From these experiences, a Caribbean migration personality of picaresque resilience has emerged, with flexibility, keen wit, and a broad understanding as the principal elements. And because the only personal support a Caribbean migrant knows often resides in his or her immediate family, to return home is the only enduring directional commitment that he or she has on the journey.

Today, at the turn of the century, old men and women of the region tell each other, their children and grandchildren, and occasional visiting academic researchers about their travels and experiences abroad. Their personal recollections of travel and return rarely extend further back than the depression decade of the 1930s, although some of them recollect hazy images of returning 'Panama men' – with gold teeth, floppy hats, and sweets for the children – from very early in the last century. These old people recount fascinating stories, embellished to be sure but easy enough to corroborate with conventional archival sources. They remember working for Americans during the Second World War in Trinidad and on the oil refineries in the Netherlands Antilles before plant automation drove them home in the 1950s. Many older men and women have retired to the Caribbean after a working lifetime spent in the eastern United States or the British Midlands. Researchers from either of these countries listening to old Caribbean men and women learn much about the under-sides of their own countries. They hear of changing immigration restrictions, passport regulations and green cards. They are told about dismal working conditions for itinerant farm labourers who harvest peas in Wisconsin, tobacco in the Connecticut valley, or the autumn apple crop in western Virginia. They learn that some Caribbean coins work in British vending machines and others in the New York subway system. Throughout, they listen to anecdotes about endemic racism in metropolitan countries. The researcher from those countries is humbled and has the feeling of having come full circle, having travelled away in order to learn about one's own nation.

It seems appropriate that such a search for the meaning of Caribbean migration should lead a visitor to the villages and sugar-cane fields of the islands and rimlands where the migration started in the first place. The physical fragmentation of the region helped to attract outsiders to conquer and then to transform the region physically. Then an introduced over-large population, perhaps inevitably, has had to seek individual and collective livelihoods since then based in part on extraordinary movements away followed often by coming back. Yet migration's continuity in the Caribbean region is sustained, indeed anchored, by those staying behind, those who have never stopped waiting for the migrants' return.

13

THE CHANGING STATUS OF WOMEN IN THE CONTEMPORARY CARIBBEAN

Alice Colón and Rhoda Reddock

Introduction

It is indeed a challenge to attempt a general overview of the changing status of women in the Caribbean, given the many differences in colonial experience, language, cultural traditions, political/economic systems and regimes, relationships with diverse metropolitan powers, and their particular location in the international economic order. Additionally, the differing levels of social and economic development, the ethnic/racial, cultural, religious and class differences, as well as the diversity in sexual orientation and other social dimensions among women, within and among countries, all contribute to the various ways in which women's activism and achievements have occurred. Contacts have also historically been greater within linguistic subregions and with the countries that were their own metropoles, while non-independent nations, of which the Caribbean has a fair number, have been even more isolated from regional developments.[1]

In this context, it is understandable that the absence of comparable data for the entire region complicates our analyses of changes in the status of women.[2] This chapter reflects the authors' greater access to data on the anglophone and hispanophone Caribbean, although efforts were made to incorporate material from the Dutch-speaking and francophone territories. In spite of the regional diversity, it highlights some broad trends regarding changes in women's status: the social and economic transformations due to

1 Among the articles describing and analysing the region's diversity are Patricia Mohammed, 1998a, pp.6–33; Cynthia J. Mesh, 1997, pp.18–38; Marcia Rivera, 1993, pp.11–58.

2 Among the few works including articles on countries of the different linguistic areas are Patricia Mohammed, 1998b; Consuelo López Springfield, 1997; Janet H. Momsen, 1993a; Idsa Alegría Ortega and Alice Colón Warren, 1995; Jean Stubbs, 1999, pp.95–135.

the changing location of Caribbean societies within the capitalist international economic order in the twentieth century, their incorporation into projects of national and social development after the Second World War, and the re-igniting of women's struggles linked to what has been labelled second-wave feminism since the 1960s and also to the globalizing tendencies of the new international division of labour.

Social transformation and women's organizing up to the Second World War

The Caribbean in the international economic context – A gendered analysis

The early twentieth century can be characterized in most territories by the transition from an agrarian, usually plantation-based economy, to one based more on agro-industry, the export of primary products and commerce based on the generalization of wage labour, although in some territories, such as Aruba and Curaçao, plantation agriculture was never the norm. Particularly in the hispanophone Caribbean and Haiti, the intensification of plantation production came later than in other islands and was part of the United States expansion into Latin America and the Caribbean. Begun since the nineteenth century, this was facilitated by the Cuban-Spanish-American War which left Puerto Rico a colony and Cuba under US tutelage, and which justified US interventions into Haiti and the Dominican Republic. The plantation-based economy was more significant in Puerto Rico, Cuba and the Dominican Republic where the sugar industry was already established. It was less so in Haiti where there was little or no infrastructure.[3]

Although it is not the focus of this chapter, it is important to note that major differences existed between what had been the predominantly slave-based societies of the anglophone and francophone Caribbean, where plantations had become dominant earlier, and the settler- and slave-based economies of the hispanophone Caribbean, which intensified their plantation economies later. In the former, plantation economies had led to a fundamentally bipolar social structure with a minority of white landowners or their representatives, and a majority African or African-descended population, mainly slaves and a growing 'mixed' group, many of whom were 'free'. In the hispanophone Caribbean, the later emergence of plantation economies did not change the dominant social structure of a greater proportion of white and

3 Suzy Castor, 1971.

'mixed' settlers and peasants, who were involved in hacienda production and small-scale farming.[4]

In spite of the absence of truly comparative data, it is clear that in the predominantly slave-based economies, women's work in social production and commerce outside of the home was much more significant than in the more settler-based economies.[5] Their relative economic autonomy has been attributed, among other factors, to the reduction of direct patriarchal control by men over women during slavery; the discouragement of the nuclear family among slaves, especially during the period of the sugar revolution; the scarcity of European settler families; the sub-Saharan African tradition of women's productive work outside the home; the greater incorporation of women into alternative forms of production after slavery such as marketing, domestic work, plantation and small-scale agriculture which, although oppressive and less well paid than men's work, provided sources of independent income; and post-emancipation male migration. These trends were reflected in the diversity of family forms which emerged. With a high proportion of female heads of households, women of different ages and stages in the life cycle developed formal and informal networks of support in order to fulfil their responsibilities as the backbone of family and community stability.[6]

Emerging studies on nineteenth-century urban women in Puerto Rico suggest that slave, free coloured and even middle- and upper-strata women were active as wage labourers and in commercial endeavours and that significant numbers of female-headed households depended on this economic activity.[7] Although unquantified, there is also mention of women's work in haciendas, small farms and subsistence agriculture. Nevertheless, women's

4 Sidney W. Mintz, 1971.

5 Problems of measurement of women's economic activity are particularly evident where the formal, modern sector is less prevalent, as it tends to be undercounted in the informal and domestic sectors. Differences in measuring economic participation among countries and over time also pose problems of comparability and make it difficult to assess trends in women's work. Among the references addressing this issue and the recognition of Caribbean women's economic activity see, for example: Henry S. Shryock and Jacob Siegel, 1975, pp.350–5; Clara Báez, 1988, pp.5–14; Mireille Neptune Anglade, 1986, pp.49–53; Gemma Tang Nain, 1995, pp.56–7; Madeleine Sylvain Boucheraeau, 1957, pp.75, 157–67; Sonia Cuales, 1993, p.294.

6 Among the many references see, for example: Janet H. Momsen, 1993b, pp.5, 8; *idem*, 1993c, p.232; Mihelic Lydia Pulsipher, 1993, pp.50–64; Karen Fog Olwig, 1993b, pp.150–66; Sonia Cuales, 1984, p.165; Carolle Charles, 1994, pp.49–53; Gemma Tang Nain, 1995, p.62; Marietta Morissey, 1989; Teresita Martínez-Vergne, 1994, pp.1–36.

7 See Félix V. Matos Rodríguez, 1999.

work outside the home was less visible in the Spanish-speaking Caribbean, where economic activity was more diversified and governed by patriarchal laws and customs regarding land and property holding which reinforced the family as an economic unit under the father's control. There was also a greater predominance of male-headed households, even when there were also high proportions of common-law unions.[8]

The intensification of agro-industry and the export of other primary products throughout the Caribbean at the turn of the century accelerated both the region's immersion into the modern capitalist world system and socio-economic changes that would impact the status of women and gender relations. Where plantation-based slavery had been predominant, the post-emancipation period saw efforts by religious and state institutions to remove what were perceived as aberrations of the slave period regarding the sexual division of labour, women's work and men's place.[9] These were facilitated by the transformations in agricultural and craft production and the movement towards wage labour. The emerging wage-labour opportunities, however, were not equal to those lost through the destruction of the agrarian and craft-based alternatives, as became most evident during the economic depression of the 1930s and its attendant poverty and unemployment. Not surprisingly, women were central to the labour disturbances which characterized this period.[10] These trends led to increased men's employment and a division of labour in which men occupied the modern, dominant sectors, and women an increasingly limited space for economic activity. Their work was concentrated in services, small-scale production and commerce, as seamstresses, hat makers and other crafts, and as vendors, laundresses, cooks and domestic workers.[11] This was particularly felt in the British, French and Dutch Caribbean, where women's work had earlier been more visible. As many as two-thirds of women were recorded as being involved in 'gainful work', including work in agricultural production, at the beginning of the twentieth

8 Jorge Ibarra, 1998, pp.29–30; Marcia Rivera, 1986, pp.31–2; Janet H. Momsen, 1993b, p.5; Jean Stubbs, 1993, pp.222; Helen I. Safa, 1998, pp.204–6; Staff, Social Science Research Center, College of Social Sciences, University of Puerto Rico, 1956 (1972), p.474; Mayone Stycos, 1955, pp.113–4, 150; Helen I. Safa, 1995, p.180.

9 During most of the slave period, women and men both worked in the fields and women's reproductive capacity often took second place to their social production on plantations and in urban economies. Families and marriage were also discouraged. For more on this see Rhoda Reddock, 1985, pp.63–80.

10 See, for example, James L. Dietz, 1986, chap.2; Eugenia Georges, 1990, pp.26–7; Suzy Castor, 1971.

11 Jorge Ibarra, 1998, pp.129–30; Lois Smith and Alfred Padula, 1996, pp.13–14; Isabel Picó, 1986, p.48; Marcia Rivera, 1986, pp.38–40; Sonia Cuales, 1998, p.89; Carolle Charles, 1994, p.62; Janet H. Momsen, 1993c, pp.234–5.

century; this declined to a half or less in many of the countries throughout the first decades of the century.[12] Nonetheless, tobacco, home/small-shop needle trades and some other industries provided some openings for women's entrance into the emerging job market. This was especially so in the Spanish-speaking islands, where their labour force participation had hovered around 10 per cent at the beginning of the century. In Puerto Rico labour-force participation increased to 30 per cent by the 1930s, the result mainly of tobacco and small needlework production. Depending on their level of development, the modernizing economies also offered increasing, although still limited, positions in commercial and office activity, such as in retail trade establishments or as typists, stenographers and telephone operators.[13]

More noticeable also in the hispanophone Caribbean, and to a lesser extent in Haiti, the changes were accompanied by improvements in the country's health and education in order to provide for better-qualified workers and for social support of the poor. The depression of the 1920s and 1930s intensified the suffering and poverty due to unemployment and low wages and made the need for these services more noticeable. Although still in a limited way and to varying degrees, educated women became part of a slowly but steadily increasing number of teachers, nurses, social workers and other professionals who filled state or private educational, health and social welfare services. The emergence of this first identifiable cohort of professional women included not only those in feminine-defined careers, but a few in male-dominated professions such as law and medicine.[14]

The constraints on the employment of professional women appear to have been more forceful in the anglophone Caribbean, where, in addition to colour and racial discrimination in commercial establishments, little attention

---

12 In Barbados, for example, where women's labour-force participation had been similar or higher than men's at around 60 per cent up to the 1920s, it fell to around 40 per cent, much lower than men's, over the 1940s. The same was true of other countries, including Jamaica and the Leeward Islands, where the proportion of gainfully employed women declined from over 70 per cent in the 1910s to around 50 per cent by the 1940s (Janet H. Momsen, 1993c, p.235; Rhoda Reddock, 1993, p.250).

13 Jorge Ibarra, 1998, pp.30–2; Lois Smith and Alfred Padula, 1996, pp.13–14; Marcia Rivera, 1986, pp.30–45; *idem*, 1993, p.21; Magaly Pineda, 1988, p.60; Francisco Cáceres Ureña, 1994, p.13; Madeleine Sylvain Boucheraeau, 1957, pp.160–4; Rhoda Reddock, 1993, pp.250–4; Myriam Cottias and Annie Fitte-Duval, 1995, pp.85–6.

14 Sonia Cuales, 1984, p.166; Madeleine Sylvain Boucheraeau, 1957, pp.157–60; Rhoda Reddock, 1998a, p.3; María de F. Barceló Miller, 1997, pp.20–39; Alice Colón *et al.*, 1986, chap.3; K. Lynn Stoner, 1991, pp.35–8, 141–2; Luz Dalis Acosta de Pérez, 1993, pp.16–19.

was paid to social services by the colonial authorities until the post-war period. Among the middle classes, efforts to institute acceptable notions of women's place meant that there was much resistance to women's employment in the professions, including teaching and government service. In some instances women had to be unmarried, and marriage meant unemployment or temporary employment. Similarly, opportunities for promotion were usually limited in most of the British colonies at this time and women's wages were always lower than those of men.[15]

Women's activism in social and political movements

During the early twentieth century, a differentiation can be made between working-class women's organizing in labour and political bodies and middle-class activism for women's rights, although there is evidence of women of both classes who combined the two interests. From the late nineteenth century, upper- and middle-class women, usually white or mixed-race, had organized in philanthropic groups that supported or established health centres, hostels for working girls, children's homes, shelters, homes for the poor and the elderly, and other social welfare institutions offering food, clothing, education and services that responded to the plight of working-class, poor women.

An early example of this was the Lady Musgrave Women's Self Help Society, formed in Jamaica in 1879, and similar societies such as the Trinidad Home Industries and Women's Self Help Society in Trinidad (1901) with Mrs Hugh Clifford, wife of the Colonial Secretary, as first president, and the British Guiana United Home Industries and Self Help Association, started in 1913 on the encouragement of Lady Egerton, the Governor's wife. Similar examples were the Junta de Damas de Honor de la Sociedad Económica de Amigos del País and El Ropero de Niños Pobres in Puerto Rico and the Société des Femmes Schoelchéristes in the

15 In Trinidad & Tobago for example, the 1935 Education Code prohibited the employment of married women teachers 'except where the services of a suitable unmarried female teacher cannot be obtained' (Education Code, p.15, cited in Rhoda Reddock, 1994, p.49). Similarly writing on Jamaica, Linnette Vassell had this to say: 'There were other gender-based limitations that affected women's participation in the labour force and within the state structure itself. Women had to meet higher entry requirements than men and were restricted to lower positions in the service. The civil service examination required that in addition to the general subjects (bookkeeping, English, and general knowledge), women were generally restricted to lower levels of appointment, lower levels of remuneration and an unstable tenure of service, hence undermining possibilities for social advancement' (1998, p.193).

French Antilles.[16] Although charity, not solidarity, was a main concern of these groups, and they clearly aimed to establish an industrious social order and Western, Christian morals and family standards, they also presented women with opportunities for intervening in public life on a limited scale as well as for income-earning, which was not at the time seen as suitable activity for upper-class, white and 'highly coloured' (i.e. light-complexioned) women.

Women's rights to education and to social protection became central demands of their organizations during the first decades of the century. They promoted and established schools not only for privileged, but also for poor girls and working-class women. In Jamaica for example, a housecraft training centre was established by the middle-class Women's Liberal Club, to train working-class girls for domestic service. In the Spanish-speaking Caribbean and in Haiti, teacher training, commercial institutes and vocational training schools, as well as night schools for working-class women, increased throughout the first decades of the century. In many ways these institutions provided the educated work-force now required for the emerging economic structures by redefining engendered social functions in line with modern visions and changing societies,[17] at the same time as they maintained and in some ways strengthened the sexual division of labour.

Traditional definitions of gender roles were reinforced by diverse religious views and throughout the different ethnic groups in the region. Many of the earlier women's charitable organizations had been established through Christian denominations, for example, the Catholics in the French, Dutch, and Spanish-speaking Caribbean, and Anglican, Presbyterian, Methodist, Moravian and other Christian denominations in the rest of the region. Central to these church women's organizations was the institution of Euro-Christian ideals and standards of family life and the sexual division of labour.[18] Small but significant non-Christian communities were also present, like the Sephardic Jews of Curaçao, who also shared clear notions of women's

---

16 Also, the Asilo San Vicente de Paul in Cuba and the Association des Dames de St François de Sales in Haiti. See Alice Colón *et al.*, 1986, pp.8, 34; K. Lynn Stoner, 1991, p.139; Madeleine Sylvain Boucheraeau, 1957, pp.87, 150, 152; Myriam Cottias and Annie Fitte-Duval, 1995, p.84.

17 Rhoda Reddock, 1998a, pp.2–4; Sonia Cuales, 1998, p.96; Luz Dalis Acosta de Pérez, 1993, pp.16–9; Alice Colón *et al.*, 1986, p.8, chap.3; Jorge Ibarra, 1998, pp.137–8; K. Lynn Stoner, 1991, p.171; Madeleine Sylvain Boucheraeau, 1957, pp.75–9; Myriam Cottias and Annie Fitte-Duval, 1995, pp.83–4.

18 Rhoda Reddock, 1998b, pp.57–8; Alice Colón *et al.*, 1986, p.34; Myriam Cottias and Annie Fitte-Duval, 1995, pp.83–4; Sonia Cuales, 1998, p.97; Madeleine Sylvain Boucheraeau, 1957, pp.75–9; K. Lynn Stoner, 1991, pp.39–41.

place.[19] Sizeable proportions of Indians, more recent immigrants – mainly Hindus and Muslims – were resident in Suriname, British Guiana and Trinidad, as well as other Asians – Javanese in Suriname and Chinese in other parts of the region. Although less evident in the women's civic and labour organizations of the time, they too were influenced by Christian and non-Christian religious ideologies on women's place. These were standards that ran counter to the remembered traditions of the populations of African descent and to the practised reality of the majority of the popular sectors throughout the region, among whom common-law and other forms of unions and women's economic activity were highly prevalent. Nonetheless, they were set as the ideal and norm.[20]

These modernizing civic organizations operated within the parameters of the prevailing class structures, and did not challenge the sexual division of labour in the home, nor traditional ideas on women's purity and nurturing capacities that made them society's moral guardians. At the same time, they worked towards a redefinition of womanhood which incorporated secularizing, modernistic thinking which encouraged the development of their intellectual capacities in order, among other things, to educate future citizens better. Their roles as mothers and carers were redefined to be not ones of servitude or natural instinct, but important social functions necessary for the development of modern society. Women's improved education and social participation were thus defended as a means to ensure the fulfilment of their moral responsibilities to society.[21]

First in Puerto Rico and Cuba, later in the Dominican Republic and Haiti, feminist organizations were in evidence by the 1920s and 1930s, incorporating demands for social reform into those of women's rights. Albeit within the parameters of their class definitions, these women were important in bringing to public discussion issues such as maternal and child health, girls' right to education and its modernization, women's employment, child abandonment, illegitimacy, juvenile delinquency and the need for juvenile courts. In so doing they established 'the social' as a domain of action, which, for these women of higher status, involved a challenge to their domestic cloistering, bringing issues of the domestic sphere to public debate and action. As suggested by K. Lynn Stoner, it also provided a basis for their demands derived from their own roles and capacities and not from their relation to

19 For more on women in the Sephardic Jewish community of Curaçao, see Eva Abraham-van der Mark, 1993, pp.38–49.

20 Rhoda Reddock, 1998b, p.58.

21 K. Lynn Stoner, 1991, pp.39–41; María de F. Barceló Miller, 1997, pp.60–5; Myriam Cottias and Annie Fitte-Duval, 1995, p.89; Petronila Angélica Gómez, 1952, pp.3–5, 12–25.

men.[22] In the English-speaking Caribbean, Martinique and Guadeloupe, this redefinition took place alongside the changing arrangements of race and class, as middle-class, mixed-race, black and, to a lesser extent, Indian women became more educated and better represented in social and economic institutions.[23]

In the Spanish-speaking Caribbean and Haiti, middle- and upper-class women's organizations also moved from purely philanthropic approaches to social welfare definitions that demanded economic and social protection as a public responsibility through government policies and programmes. By the 1930s and 1940s these states had already begun to establish some of these laws and programmes and women were incorporated into their monitoring and implementation. These included, among others, improvements in literacy, schooling and health services, Women and Children's Bureaux, home economics and sanitary programmes, school breakfasts, legislation establishing the rights of children born out of wedlock, maternity leave, and the recognition of civil rights for married women, such as disposing of the products of their work and property.

Many of the programmes, like those of maternal and child health and home economics education, were established earlier and most extensively in Puerto Rico, linked to hygienic and educational plans promoted by United States intervention since the beginning of the century and its New Deal legislation during the Depression. Cuba appeared the most advanced in legislation on the rights of children out of wedlock, adultery, and protection of women workers.[24] Most of these reforms, some modelled on the New Deal, would only be implemented in the British colonies and other parts of the Caribbean after the Second World War. Further research is required on the development of these organizations and programmes in many countries, and on intra-regional linkages and co-operation. It is interesting to note, for example, the similarity of issues and programmes in Haiti and the hispanophone countries. Possible reasons for this could be the similar historical and cultural heritages and contacts which may have existed among these geographically close, Catholic, 'Latin' societies since the period of French and Spanish

22 Most advanced and exhaustive in Cuba, according to Stoner, the discussion on the protection of children out of wedlock, for example, showed how this based women's rights on motherhood rather than on their relation to men in formal marriage, or on the 'respectable behaviour' characteristic of dominant sexual norms. (K. Lynne Stoner, 1991, pp.67–70, 8–10, 34–5, 58–9, 138–42, 240–8; for modernizing views in Puerto Rico see María de F. Barceló Miller, 1997, pp.50–1, 80–3).

23 Rhoda Reddock, 1998a, p.3; Myriam Cottias and Annie Fitte-Duval, 1995, p.84.

24 K. Lynn Stoner, 1991, pp.9, 126–35, 141–7, 162, 177–9, 181–4; Idsa Alegría Ortega and Alice Colón Warren, 1995, pp.34–5; Madeleine Sylvain Boucheraeau, 1957, pp.84–93; Carmen Lara Fernández, 1946, pp.5–17, 153–80.

colonial domination. More importantly, the influence of United States hygenic and social welfare policies and programmes during periods of intervention and through interaction among women at the Pan-American meetings and other international networks, may also be a factor.

Many of the issues discussed by these sectors of Caribbean women were characteristic of a particular strand of feminism, now usually referred to as 'social feminism', which accepted differences in responsibilities between the sexes, but stressed the incorporation of women's capabilities, as well as their particular contribution to politics and society, alongside men. The different strands were the basis of debate among women's organizations, particularly after the enfranchisement of United States women in the 1920s, when this country's Women's Party brought to international fora the discussion of declarations of equal rights for women, while this was opposed by social feminists who had defended protective legislation as a barrier to the super-exploitation of women.[25]

In the Caribbean this 'social feminism' was always combined with a concern for national and racial progress and identity, for example, liberation from traditional cultural legacies and colonial ties, and the then prevalent United States control in Haiti and the Spanish-speaking islands. In the case of the English-speaking countries, it was African, and to a lesser extent Indian nationalism, and the improvement of the status of the race, that was invoked in women's mobilization. In the Spanish-speaking Caribbean many women distanced themselves from what they identified as North American and European feminism, which was interpreted in its more radical strand as more concerned with women's individual rights and hostile to men.[26]

Although much of the activist efforts of social reform were directed at working-class women as beneficiaries, they seldom aimed to transform the prevailing inequitable class structures. Rarely, if at all, were women of working-class sectors incorporated into the middle- and upper-class women's organizations, or involved in the design and implementation of the emerging programmes. This was true even among the more politically radical Marxist-oriented feminist sector in Cuba, which nonetheless maintained closer ties with the labour movement.[27]

---

25 Naomi Black, 1989; Nancy F. Cott, 1987; Madeleine Sylvain Boucheraeau, 1957, pp.89, 94; Petronila Angélica Gómez, 1952, pp.17–20; Carmen Lara Fernández, 1946, pp.147–50; María de F. Barceló Miller, 1997, pp.60–5; Judith Sealander, 1983.

26 K. Lynn Stoner, 1991, pp.10, 23, 29, 35, 55–7; Rhoda Reddock, 1998a, pp.4–5; Petronila Angélica Gómez, 1952, pp.6, 17, 35, 44–6; Carolle Charles, 1994, p.146; Mercedes Solá, 1922, pp.28–30.

27 K. Lynn Stoner, 1991, pp.75, 129–30, 145, 175–6; Vivian Mota, 1980, pp.266–9; María de F. Barceló Miller, 1997, pp.96–113; Rhoda Reddock, 1998a, p.4.

Working-class women did, however, organize themselves socially in self-help groups, lodges, friendly societies, church groups and clubs as documented in the English-speaking Caribbean and Suriname. But they were also among the most militant members of African-nationalist organizations, workingmen's (sic) associations, emerging trade unions, and workers' organizations, based mainly in tobacco and needlework industries in the Spanish-speaking, and the agricultural and emerging industrial sectors in the English-speaking Caribbean. They participated actively in strikes and demonstrations over working and economic conditions which intensified throughout the region in the 1930s, the decade of the Depression,[28] and against repressive regimes such as those of Cuba and Haiti in the 1930s and 1940s.[29]

In these struggles, however, their main focus was not gender inequality, although they included demands for equal pay and child care. While there were examples of working-class feminism in organizations in the English-speaking Caribbean, Puerto Rico appears as the main exception, where there was a recognized strand of workers' feminism, linked to anarcho-syndicalism and the Puerto Rico Socialist Party, which maintained uneven relations with the middle- and upper-class feminist groups.[30]

The most widely recognized and debated issue in advancing women's status throughout the period was, nonetheless, the recognition of their right to vote. Since the 1910s and 1920s there were feminist groups such as the Liga Femínea Puertorriqueña (Puerto Rican Feminine League) and Liga Social Sufragista (Social Suffragist League) in Puerto Rico, Club Femenino de Cuba, the Women's Congresses, and diverse strands of feminist groups in Cuba, the group Fémina (Woman) and the Club Nosotras (We Women) – later Acción Feminista Dominicana (Dominican Feminist Action), in the Dominican Republic, and by the 1930s, Haiti's Ligue Fémenine de Action Sociale (Feminine League for Social Action) and the Jamaica Women's Liberal Club, all of which sought women's suffrage. These debated their ideas in congresses, conferences, literary and debating societies, meetings, through the media, and by publishing their own journals and mobilizing to pressure legislators and administrators within their particular political

---

28 This was especially between 1934–8 with labour unrest in St Kitts, St Lucia, St Vincent, Trinidad & Tobago and Jamaica. Women were very much involved in all of these. See Rhoda Reddock, 1994 and W. Arthur Lewis, 1977.

29 Rhoda Reddock, 1998a, p.4; *idem*, 1993, p.251, 254; Alice Colón *et al.*, 1986, pp. 31–5; Myriam Cottias and Annie Fitte-Duval, 1995, pp.85–6; K. Lynn Stoner, 1991, pp.58, 120–2; Madeleine Sylvain Boucheraeau, 1957, p.94.

30 Alice Colón *et al.*, 1986, pp.10, 11; María de F. Barceló Miller, 1997, pp.84–9; Sandra McGee Deutsch, 1989, p.134; Yamila Azize, 1985; María de F. Barceló Miller, 1998, pp.143–70.

contexts.[31] In Suriname, the change in the colonial constitution of 1936 gave women the right to vote and to be elected. Similarly, although universal suffrage and feminist ideas were discussed by some men and women in the French Antilles throughout this period, particularly related to socialist political projects, it was with their assimilation as French Departments (1946) and with French women's suffrage (1945) that women came to vote in Martinique, Guadeloupe and Guyane.[32] The vote for all women was recognized by the 1930s in Puerto Rico and Cuba, later in the rest of the region, in some like Haiti and St Vincent as late as the 1950s, and in the Bahamas not until 1962, although a restricted female franchise existed earlier than universal suffrage in most territories.

In their struggle women had to face different forms of manipulation and resistance, such as unattainable voting requirements, test votes in the Dominican Republic, and pressures against their registration in Haiti, even after their enfranchisement for the 1957 elections.[33] In Suriname in 1949, a women's political party, the Damescommittee (Ladies Committee), comprising middle-class women who argued that women's interests were not safe in men's hands, contested the first elections with Tine Puscher, a dentist, as a candidate.[34] In Trinidad & Tobago, struggles for women's eligibility as candidates

31 Within the context of colonial ties to the United States and with the enfranchisement of North American women in 1919 as an additional lever in their mobilization, literate Puerto Rican women were granted the right to vote in 1929 and, pushed by the labour movement and more liberal social feminists, universal suffrage was recognized in 1935. In Cuba, women's suffrage became a symbol of the return to a constitutional order, after President Machado had established a dictatorial regime postponing elections and the recognition of women's right to vote, so that after his overthrow this was included in the 1934 interim constitution. In the Dominican Republic, they became involved in Trujillo's consolidation of power, but still had to go through two test votes in the elections of the 1930s before they were officially enfranchised in 1942. Haitian women's demand for the vote had initially to be played down by the Ligue Fémenine de Action Sociale in order to become acceptable, and resistance to its enactment was enmeshed with the *coup d'états* and political changes up to the 1950s. Even after the recognition of their political rights, it was established that women would not be able to vote until three years after they first participated in municipal elections, and they still had to demonstrate so the legislature would pass the enacting law and allow their registration, before they finally voted in national elections in 1957. (Alice Colón *et al.*, 1986, chap.5; María de F. Barceló Miller, 1997, chap.4; K. Lynn Stoner, 1991, pp.58, 72–5, 111–24; Petronila Angélica Gómez, 1952, pp.59, 95, 96; Madeleine Sylvain Boucheraeau, 1957, pp.88–97, 145, 241–6).

32 Myriam Cottias and Annie Fitte-Duval, 1995, p.87; Twie Tjoa, 1995, p.28.

33 See notes 27 and 28; Rhoda Reddock, 1998a, p.6; Vivian Mota, 1980, p.270; Margarita Cordero, 1991, pp.113–7; Madeleine Sylvain Boucheraeau, 1957, pp. 88–97, 145, 241–6.

34 Twie Tjoa, 1995, p.29.

at municipal and national elections were also important battles which had to be fought. By the mid-1930s in Jamaica and Trinidad & Tobago, the first women – Mary Morris Knibb and Audrey Jeffers – were successful in municipal elections, but the majority of women and men still did not have the vote.[35]

In these endeavours, the feminist groups developed networks throughout the region, and with international women's organizations in Europe and the United States such as the Women's International League for Peace and Freedom. Through letters, visits, participation in international meetings and other forms of communication, they supported each others' struggles, operating within the scope of what was an international movement. At the centre of discussions regarding United States-Latin American relations and debates both among United States and international feminist organizations, women of the Spanish-speaking Caribbean and Haiti established links with the Pan-American Conferences which had discussed women's rights since the 1920s, giving way to the formation of the Inter-American Commission of Women (CIM) in Havana in 1928. By the end of the period, Caribbean feminists such as Minerva Bernardino of the Dominican Republic were also active in the development of the United Nations, and the later United Nations Commission on the Status of Women.[36] In the British Caribbean links with Caribbean-born feminists in the North such as Amy Ashwood Garvey, as well as with British feminist and socialist Sylvia Pankhurst, were important. In 1936, the first Conference of British West Indian and British Guianese Women Social Workers, a feminist-oriented gathering, was hosted in Trinidad & Tobago by Audrey Jeffers and her Coterie of Social Workers.[37]

The post-war period up to the 1960s: Between suffrage and 'the Second Wave'

The changing regional context in an international perspective: A gender analysis

The post-war period saw broad political, economic and social changes which sought to re-establish high employment, economic growth and stability after the turmoil of the Second World War and the Depression. These signalled the

35 Rhoda Reddock, 1990b, pp.169–74.

36 Rhoda Reddock, 1998a, p.5; Madeleine Sylvain Boucheraeau, 1957, p.88; Carmen Lara Fernández, 1946, pp.147–51; Petronila Angélica Gómez, 1952, pp.14–21; K. Lynn Stoner, 1991, pp.187–8; María de F. Barceló Miller, 1997, pp.172–4; United Nations, 1995a, pp.11–18; Asociación Dominicana de Mujeres Votantes, Inc. (Recop.) 1992, pp.16–7.

37 Rhoda Reddock, 1994, pp.169–74.

limits of labour-intensive economies based on agro-industries and the beginning of a new phase of internationalization of production and marketing that included the transfer of labour-intensive production to developing countries. While agricultural export production continued to be the main economic sector in many of the Latin American and Caribbean countries at least up to the 1960s, there was also in some islands the beginning of a strategy of export-led industrialization. It can also be characterized as a period of intensified United States influence in the region as the war effort facilitated a shift in responsibility from other colonial powers to the United States. The new export-oriented industrialization, proposed by St Lucian economist W. Arthur Lewis for the British colonies, was based on the industrialization model of tax and other incentives for capital investment introduced in Puerto Rico in the late 1940s.[38]

Additionally, although many development projects, recognized as important prior to the War, had to be postponed or slowed due to wartime exigencies, the State emerged as a major mediating economic actor, facilitating infrastructural and human capital development in health, housing, education and social welfare, required for the renewed industrial structures as well as for social legitimacy. To a great extent this was a response to the new political actors: a militant labour movement and the recently enfranchised and politicized women in some parts of the region.[39] In the English-speaking Caribbean, the labour disturbances of the mid- to late 1930s had caused a rethinking of British colonial policy and a move towards greater state responsibility for the socially and economically vulnerable.[40]

In this new industrialization, in the anglophone and the French Caribbean, the reduction in women's paid employment due to the decline in agriculture was a major justification for the introduction of new industries which would be largely based on women's labour.[41] Women became central to the new labour-intensive production such as garment and textile industries. Nevertheless, the continuing decline in agricultural employment either by the shift from agrarian capitalism, as in Puerto Rico, or by its intensification to provide for incipient industrialization, destroyed economic alternatives for men as well, although their labour-force participation always remained higher than that of women.[42]

---

38 Janet H. Momsen, 1993c, pp.234–5, 236–8; Rhoda Reddock, 1993, pp.255–60; Gemma Tang Nain, 1995, pp.55–6; A. Lynn Bolles, 1986, pp.66–7; Ruth Pearson, 1986, p.287; Luz del Alba Acevedo, 1987, pp.40, 48–9, 52–3, 57, 69.

39 Among the many analyses of the emerging monopoly capitalism see, for example, Ernest Mandel, 1978.

40 Rhoda Reddock, 1994, pp.182–212.

41 See W. Arthur Lewis, 1950b as well as the discussion in Rhoda Reddock, 1994, pp.195–6.

42 *Ibid.*

The expansion of state involvement in the provision of social services, health, education, housing, industrial promotion, commerce, tourism and other personal services provided further openings for women with higher education. As had begun earlier in the Spanish-speaking islands, the establishment of more sophisticated social welfare systems in the British colonies opened up new professional areas for middle-class women working as social welfare officers, for them a prestigious occupation. Opportunities for training in social welfare were introduced and scholarships for overseas study were provided. Based on the Report of the West India Royal Commission, the colonial governments after 1945 were encouraged to provide increased opportunities for women doctors, nurses and teachers in the region.[43]

The demand for female labour in the growing modern economic sectors – manufacturing, civil and other services – made their work more visible although their actual labour-force participation in the anglophone and francophone Caribbean never came close to the levels earlier in the century. Expelled from agricultural production as competition for land intensified and inheritance laws and customs favoured men's access to this and other resources, women in Haiti and some countries in the English-speaking Caribbean increased their concentration in the commercial sector, in markets and as street vendors.[44]

New spaces for women's participation in public and political life

The post-war period was marked by a new vision of economic development. States took over the promotion of 'development' as part of the transition to greater internal self-government in most of the anglophone and Dutch Caribbean and Puerto Rico, and to the status of French overseas departments in Martinique, Guadeloupe and Guyane. Crises in the dictatorial regimes of Cuba and the Dominican Republic, and the establishment of the Duvalier regime in Haiti, also characterized this period. Through their mobilization for suffrage and their more visible role in modernizing economic structures, women had shown their acumen and leadership, which were sometimes rewarded with political office. Audrey Jeffers, for example, was nominated to

43 See W. Arthur Lewis, 1950b; also the discussion in Rhoda Reddock, 1994, pp.213–37.

44 Not even in Puerto Rico – where they were most actively promoted – were the incoming factories able to make up for the loss of needle trades that had flourished in shops and homes during the Depression. Alice Colón *et al.*, 1988; Janet H. Momsen, 1993c, p.235; Rhoda Reddock, 1993, pp.256–7; Mireille Neptune Anglade, 1986, pp.48–53, 101–6, 129; Huguette Dagenais, 1993, pp.91–2; Margaret Gill, 1982, p.15; Isis Duarte *et al.*, 1982, p.16.

the Legislative Council in 1946 as a result of her service in social work and to women's causes. Work in women's organizations intensified and continued. In the British colonies, efforts at forming regional networks, first begun in 1936 with Audrey Jeffers and the Coterie in Trinidad, continued with the formation of the Caribbean Women's Association in 1956 in anticipation of the planned Federation of the British West Indies.[45] Women of the Spanish-speaking areas met at Latin American regional congresses, the Inter-American Commission of Women and the United Nations Commission on the Status of Women.

Most of women's political organizing, however, was channelled through women's arms of the new national political parties, auxiliary structures that operated as solid blocks of loyal support for the diverse political movements. In Suriname, for example, Rosemary Brana-Shute records the work of the *kernen*, community women's clubs in the neighbourhoods of Paramaribo which provided solid support to the Creole-based political party, the Nationale Partij Suriname (NPS).[46] These *kernen*, she noted, were central to the successful mobilization of the party, yet they could not be said to have had power in the organization. She noted:

> ...They agreed that more women need to be in positions of power. In the end, however, the party leadership argued for patience, saying that a vote for a women's party would divide the Creole vote and possibly pass the government over to another ethnic group. The women backed off. It was ethnic solidarity that was accepted as the first necessary step to Surinamese development. Issues of class and gender were played down in the face of the perceived threat to the Creole group as a whole.[47]

Women's common interests and definitions that, at least in Puerto Rico, had for a time united them beyond political differences, were de-emphasized as they organized within parties, and issues of gender inequality tended to give way to those of national development.[48] In the English-speaking Caribbean, for example, women were mobilized on the basis of nationalist ideas in the transition to self-government, in organizations such as the Jamaica Women's Liberal Club, Trinidad & Tobago's People's National Movement Women's League and the Women's Progressive Organization in Guyana. In the French Departments, sections of the Union des Femmes Françaises responded to the mobilization of the Communist Party after Department status brought

45 Rhoda Reddock, 1994, p.239.

46 See Rosemary Brana-Shute, 1993, pp.132–49.

47 *Ibid*., p.139. For a similar discussion on Trinidad, see Rhoda Reddock, 1998c.

48 For some other references about women in parties see Rhoda Reddock, 1998a, pp.5–6; Myriam Cottias and Annie Fitte-Duval, 1995, p.88; María de F. Barceló Miller, 1997, chap.3.

women's suffrage. Trujillo had since the 1930s courted women's support in the Dominican Republic, and, after suffrage, most of the organized feminists established the Feminine Branch of the Trujillo Party, later the Dominican Party, responding to the social welfare and aid programmes that, as a dual strategy, accompanied the government's more dictatorial measures. Also involved in its populist programmes, many women were important in the organization and development of the dominant Popular Democratic Party in Puerto Rico as well as in other political organizations.[49]

Women's mobilization was particularly urgent under repressive regimes in Haiti, Cuba and the Dominican Republic, where they joined struggles for these nations' return to constitutional governments. Ironically, in a cruel twist of equality, the Duvalierist regime broke in some distorted way with traditional notions of femininity. There were relatively more women in parliamentary positions and even as female paramilitary forces in a regime that did not protect women from the most brutal forms of torture and repression.

Women in these countries joined struggles against repressive governments. In Cuba, they were part of the revolutionary student movement, the July 26th Movement; some were even in combat in the Sierra Maestra, and after the triumph of the Revolution, diverse groups formed the Federación de Mujeres Cubanas (Federation of Cuban Women) (FMC), a mass organization linked to the State's social transformations.[50] In Haiti, they joined organizations that denounced and struggled against Duvalier's regime on the island and in the diaspora.[51] In the Dominican Republic, women were also part of organizations such as Juventud Revolucionaria and the clandestine June 14th Movement which had opposed Trujillo since the 1950s, and after his downfall, of the leftist-oriented Federación de Mujeres Dominicanas, which, following the coup against duly-elected President Bosch, in 1965 became a mobilizing force against the United States and international intervention, and for the reinstatement of a constitutional government.[52] Kidnapped, beaten, raped, or murdered, women opposing the regimes, such as Lydia Doce in Cuba, Patria, Minerva and María Teresa Mirabal in the Dominican Republic, and Yvonne Hakime Rimpel in Haiti, became symbols of resistance.[53]

---

49 Rhoda Reddock, 1998b, p.59; Myriam Cottias and Annie Fitte-Duval, 1995, pp.86–8; Carmen Lara Fernández, 1946, p.167; Vivian Mota, 1980, p.271; Mary Frances Gallart, 1997, pp.59–79; Isabel Picó, 1983a, pp.41–64.

50 See, for example: Laurette Séjouneé, 1980.

51 Carolle Charles, 1994, pp.137–41.

52 Magaly Pineda, 1993, pp.313–14; Margarita Cordero, 1985.

53 Carolle Charles, 1994, pp.137–41; Clorinde Zéphir, 1995, pp.15–28. See also notes 46 and 47. 25 November, Day Against Violence to Women in Latin America and the Caribbean, marks the day when the Mirabal sisters were allegedly tortured and murdered.

SOCIAL REFORM AND EXPANSION OF STATE CONTROL, AND RESPONSIBILITY FOR SOCIAL WELFARE

At the same time, the post-war, post-suffrage period can also be considered one of enactment of the first feminist wave's agenda in many of the countries. The improvements in education and social development accompanied by the State's expanded sphere of action in most countries were linked in many ways to what had been the women's groups' demands for social advancement. This is reflected in the 1955 meeting of the Inter-American Commission of Women in Puerto Rico, in which they were touted as a feminist model.[54] It was certainly a feminization of public services, with upper- and middle-class women working as elected officials, state administrators and employees, or as volunteers in private institutions, in the promotion, establishment and monitoring of programmes. Literacy, education, public health, free food and sanitary programmes, public and subsidized housing, juvenile reform and mothers' clubs, all put working-class women and children among the main beneficiaries.[55]

In the anglophone Caribbean, the Women's Work Programme of the Social Welfare departments paid special attention to rural women, organizing them in groups or institutes, all affiliated to national federations such as the Jamaica Federation of Women, and ultimately to the Associated Countrywomen of the World with headquarters in Britain. These institutes encouraged women in productive agriculture and agro-processing activities, craft and community work.[56] As part of a socialist project addressing social inequality, by the 1960s the FMC in Cuba had established programmes which would create the conditions necessary for women's broader social and political participation. These included the great literacy campaign, schools for domestics, prostitutes, peasant girls and women, day-care centres, student internships and other measures of support for domestic work, sanitary brigades and public health promotion, including contraception, breast feeding, and PAP smear tests for cervical cancer.[57]

Most countries for which we have information showed advances in social indicators such as life expectancy, infant mortality and illiteracy. The improvements in education throughout the region were particularly beneficial for women who, although still with higher illiteracy rates than men, were coming

---

54 *El Mundo*, 1 June 1955, p.14; 4 June 1955, p.9; 6 June 1955, p.15; 15 June 1955, p.9.

55 Marcia Rivera, 1987, pp.187–9; *idem*, 1986, p.42; Nilsa Burgos Ortíz, 1997; K. Lynn Stoner, 1991, pp.138–41; Carmen Lara Fernández, 1946, pp.117–22, 155–77; Rhoda Reddock, 1998a, pp.3–4; Madeleine Sylvain Boucheraeau, 1957, pp.140–62; Myriam Cottias and Annie Fitte-Duval, 1995, pp.92–5.

56 Rhoda Reddock, 1994, pp.217–22; 240–2.

57 Among the many references see, for example, Vilma Espín Guillois, 1999; Margaret Randall, 1981; Lois Smith and Alfred Padula, 1996, p.39; Marifeli Pérez-Stable, 1993 (1999), pp.91–4, 107–8; Teresa Valdéz, *et al.*, 1992, pp.51–3, 67, 103–5.

closer to parity. Puerto Rico showed dramatic changes as part of industrializing strategies, including increasing university education, while Cuba, which by the 1950s already had higher indicators, showed more extensive improvements, covering all regions and the lower classes of the island, after the Revolution and in the 1960s. For the English-speaking countries, the social programmes, and improvements in social indicators, established a tradition of British social welfare in a period of movement toward national sovereignty. Martinique, Guadeloupe and French Guiana, on the other hand, were part of the extension of French programmes as they became overseas departments. Without these social or political changes, advances were more limited in the Dominican Republic, despite Trujillo's enactment of social and maternalist programmes, and almost non-existent under the Duvalier regime in Haiti.[58]

58 Again, while advising caution in terms of the comparability of the data, sources show that where in the 1950s life expectancy in most countries for which we have information hovered from 55 to 60 years – 65 for Puerto Rico – by the 1970s it was over 70 years in both Cuba and Puerto Rico, and between 66 and 69 years in most other countries. Infant mortality, already lower in Puerto Rico and in the French departments – at above 60 per 1,000 births by the 1950s – by the 1970s had declined to between 20 and 30 in Puerto Rico, and from more than 80 in most countries, hovered between 40 and 50 in the others. Cuba's progress over the period was most noticeable in terms of illiteracy, which from around 20 per cent in the 1940s and 1950s declined to negligible levels (around 4 per cent) by the 1960s, after the great literacy campaign during the first years of the Revolution. Puerto Rico, which had shown higher illiteracy rates in the 1940s (around 30 per cent), remained with rates closer to 20 per cent in the 1960s, while the French departments and most English-speaking countries ranged from 10 to 15 per cent of illiteracy by the end of the period.

Despite relative improvements, social development indicators were more restrained in the Dominican Republic and reflected the particularly difficult living conditions in Haiti. The Dominican Republic improved its life expectancy from 40 to 60 years, and reduced its infant mortality from the 140s to 75–90 per 1,000 between the 1950s and 1970s, while illiteracy declined from around 60 to the mid-thirties in terms of illiteracy rates over the 1950s. Haiti's life expectancy, 38 years in the 1950s, was still lower than 50 in the 1970s; its illiteracy remained around 70 per cent; and its infant mortality, although declining from over 200 over this period, was still around 135 per 1,000 by the end of the period.

For information regarding these processes of social development see: Blanca G. Silvestrini and María D. Luque de Sánchez, 1987 (1988), pp.521–33; Marifeli Pérez-Stable, 1993 (1999), pp.27–33; Vilma Espín Guillois, 1999, pp.5–40; Huguette Dagenais, 1993, p.85; Joan Neil, 1990, p.15; Vivian Mota, 1980, pp.266–71; Francisco Cáceres Ureña, 1994, p.13; Gisela Quiterio Benítez, 1993, p.67; Suzy Castor, 1994, p.45; United Nations, 1993, pp.26, 135, 136; Jorge Ibarra, 1998, p.132; *La mujer en Cuba socialista*, 1977, p.20; United Nations, 1991b, pp.50–1; United Nations. Department of Economic and Social Affairs, 1975, pp.126–7; José L. Vázquez Calzada, 1988, p.73; Helen I. Safa and Peggy Antrobus, 1992, p.59.

Women also became an important focus of political attention as the limits to employment of the industrial strategies became apparent, and population control became a particularly gendered sub-strategy for development.[59] Birth-control programmes, which had been experimented with in Puerto Rico since the 1930s, by the 1950s and 1960s were denounced as state-imposed population-control policies and as an imperialist attempt to ameliorate the social conflicts and economic inequalities in the region. They were also opposed by the Catholic Church where it was strong, as in Haiti and the Spanish-speaking Caribbean.[60]

By the late 1960s, such programmes had nonetheless been pushed forward throughout the region both by private institutions and governments, not only as a state imposition, but increasingly being accepted by women who faced changing economic and social conditions and new options of regulating their number of children. Impelled by the demand for female labour, requirements of children's higher education, and seeking avenues for further self-development, women in countries like Guadeloupe had begun to reduce the number of their children even before the introduction of these programmes.[61] Only in the Dominican Republic, where Trujillo's pro-natalist measures precluded birth-control programmes until late in the decade, and in Haiti, where these remained weak, did total fertility remain high, at seven and six children per woman of childbearing ages, respectively.[62]

Even as conditions for women's broader economic and political participation were established, what had been the 'maternalist', social feminist agenda of the earlier period continued with its own contradictions. Not only did it establish reformist, middle-class solutions to structural problems of poverty and inequality in most countries, but it left unchallenged the sexual division of labour within the family and in the public sphere. Women's political activity in the countries' party structures was still subordinate and legal restraints maintained gender inequality within family relations, particularly in

---

59 Gemma Tang Nain, 1995, p.56.

60 Alice Colón *et al.*, 1999, chap.4; Bonnie Mass, 1977, pp.66–82; Teresa Arreola, n.d.; Lois Smith and Alfred Padula, 1996, p.71; Carmen Lara Fernández, 1946, pp.140–2; Mireille Neptune Anglade, 1986, pp.35, 49, 66; Cacos La Gonaive, 1993, p.311; Huguette Dagenais, 1993, p.98.

61 United Nations, Department of Economic and Social Affairs, 1975, pp.75–6; Huguette Dagenais, 1993, pp.96–8; Janet H. Momsen, 1993c, p.239; Sonia Cuales, 1984, pp.167–8; Clara Báez and Ginny Taulé, 1993, p.98; Robin Morgan, 1993a, p.292; Mariví Arregui, 1994, pp.1–44; Alice Colón *et al.*, 1999, chap.4.

62 By the end of the 1960s, total fertility rates had declined to around three children in Puerto Rico, Trinidad & Tobago, Barbados and Bahamas, down from 4 and 5 in the 1950s. Carmen Lara Fernández, 1946, pp.140–2; Mireille Neptune Anglade, 1986, pp.49, 66; United Nations, 1993, p.133.

the Spanish-speaking Caribbean and Haiti, where the Napoleonic tradition maintained men as protectors of married women and children.[63] Women's sexual subordination was not directly recognized and challenged, but merely ameliorated by claims for child support, or social services, which were related to their domestic and child-rearing responsibilities and did not question the division of labour. Maintaining the ideal of the 'male breadwinner', the programmes showed themselves to be more 'feminine' than feminist,[64] ignoring the challenging edge that had been implied in the defence of motherhood as a social function. This represented what has been called a move to 'public patriarchy', immersing 'social' programmes in the modernizing political agenda but without a particular focus on women's unequal status.[65] Even projects incorporating women in wage work in the anglophone Caribbean emphasized women's role as mothers and wives and never challenged the sexual division of labour.

The new international division of labour, the new women's movement and transformations in gender relations – 1960s to the present

THE RE-EMERGENCE OF THE WOMEN'S MOVEMENT IN ALL ITS DIVERSITY

There were instances of continuity in Caribbean women's networking and action against discriminatory practices at national, regional and international levels since the early years of the century. Still, movements for peace, national liberation, workers' rights, 'Black Power', racial equality, civil rights and students' rights, among others emerging by the 1960s, opened up new democratic spaces within which the women's struggles could be located.[66] Impelled in different ways by the intensifying international and United States' feminist

63 Margarita Cordero, 1991, pp.113–18; Isabel Picó, 1983a, pp.41–64; Myriam Cottias and Annie Fitte-Duval, 1995, pp.86–8; Gisela Quiterio Benítez, 1993, pp.84–6; Monique Brisson, 1988, pp.30–9; Comisión de Derechos Civiles, ELA de Puerto Rico, 1972, pp.185–94.

64 The term 'feminism' is a contentious one but it continues to be used in the Caribbean. We define it simply as: the awareness of the subordination of women and the conscious action to change this. By this definition, feminists may differ as to the causes of this subordination and the changes necessary to remove or transform it.

65 K. Lynn Stoner, 1991, pp.145–6; Helen I. Safa, 1995, pp.40, 46.

66 Rhoda Reddock, 1998b, p.61; Magaly Pineda, 1993, p.315; Alice Colón Warren, 1995, p.164.

movements, there was the emergence of new organizations in the early 1970s, such as Puerto Rico's Mujer Integrate Ahora (Women Join Now) and Federación de Mujeres Puertorriqueñas (Federation of Puerto Rican Women), the later Dominican Republic's Promoción de la Mujer (Women's Promotion), the Jamaica Association for the Repeal of Abortion Laws (JARA), and the Centre Haïtien de Recherche pour la Promotion de la Femme (Haitian Research Centre for the Promotion of Women), which was established in Haiti with government and international support.[67] Although mobilizing on women's issues in the region pre-dated the United Nations' Declaration of the International Women's Year in 1975 and the following Women's Decade 1976–85, this was also a major stimulus to a new generation of activists, many coming from leftist groups and orientations. Additionally it served to reawaken the older activists, many of whom were now affiliated to national political parties.

This second wave of feminist mobilization expanded during the 1970s with greater strength in Puerto Rico, the English- and Dutch-speaking Caribbean, and throughout the 1980s in the Dominican Republic and Haiti, after the coming-to-power of the Dominican Revolutionary Party in 1978 and the downfall of Duvalier in 1986 opened possibilities for more democratic organization.[68] Feminist organizing and research along gender lines has apparently been more limited in the French departments, where, in spite of efforts on both sides, there appears to have been limited contact both with French and Caribbean feminism.[69]

From the inception of the Cuban Revolution to the mid-1970s, women's unequal status was addressed following the socialist paradigm of promoting their incorporation into social production, although without a greater recognition of the specificity of gendered power structures or a further opening to feminism. Cuban and socialist-oriented women region-wide have networked with women's organizations in socialist countries and become leading members of the FDIM/WIDF (Women's International Democratic Federation) since the 1960s.[70] By the 1970s, however, the FMC played an increasingly complex

67 Comisión de Derechos Civiles, ELA de Puerto Rico, 1972, pp.26–31; Magaly Pineda, 1984, p.46; Idsa Alegría Ortega and Alice Colón Warren, 1995, p.107; Rhoda Reddock, 1998b, pp.59–60; Carolle Charles, 1995, p.68.

68 Rhoda Reddock, 1998a, pp.7–8; Idsa Alegría Ortega and Alice Colón Warren, 1995, pp.107–8; Gisela Quiterio Benítez, 1993, pp.110–11; Carolle Charles, 1994, pp.153–5.

69 Cynthia J. Mesh, 1997, pp.19, 27–30; Huguette Dagenais, 1993, p.84.

70 Monique Brisson, 1988, pp.32–7; Madeleine Sylvain Boucheraeau, 1957, pp.94, 97, 144; Asociación Dominicana de Mujeres Votantes, Inc. (Recop.), 1992, p.17; Vilma Espín Guillois, 1999, pp.38–43; Rhoda Reddock, 1998a, p.5.

mediating role with the State, while later in the 1980s and 1990s, Cuban women also began participating in feminist regional actions and institutions, establishing academic programmes in women's studies, and organizing meetings and congresses with Latin American, Caribbean and other feminists.[71]

At the state level, in the 1970s and 1980s, the liberal women-and-development paradigm, favoured by international development institutions, was paramount. It argued that given conditions of poverty and inequality, issues of income and employment generation and development should be the most important in the region. Moving beyond these and earlier liberal concerns for the right to education and political participation, many of the late-twentieth-century feminist groups sought to challenge all structures of inequality – social, ethnic/racial, economic, political, cultural, sexual – and the exploitative economic systems and development policies that sustained them.[72] The feminist critique of economic neo-liberalism, for example, was important in the 1980s and 1990s.

Feminist work has been broad-based but also addressed the specificity of gender issues, including, for example, not only access to schooling and training at all levels, but sex typing in careers and vocational training, sex stereotypes in educational materials and practices and the media, equal pay and employment opportunities, and remaining inequalities in legislation. Since the 1980s there has also been a greater emphasis on women's health, on sexual and reproductive rights, and particularly on the issue of violence against women. This has been a central issue for the women's movement in the entire region, acting as a unifying force bringing solidarity among women of all countries, classes, ethnicities and political persuasions.

In the 1990s there was a heightened discussion and interest in women's participation in relation to power structures, the diversity of family types and the particular plight of female heads of household in the region. The ever present racial/ethnic diversity characteristic of the Caribbean was also addressed during this period. Black women, for example, began to organize in the Spanish-speaking Caribbean and Hindu women in Trinidad & Tobago.[73] With the exception of the Netherlands Antilles and Suriname, issues of

71 In 1997, the FMC of Cuba hosted the Third Regional Meeting of CAFRA. Among the many references see, for example: Vilma Espín Guillois, 1990; Teresa Valdéz, Enrique Gomarez, Esther Veliz and Carolina Aguilar, 1992, pp.105–8; Luisa Campuzano, 1996, pp.4–10; Amelia Suárez Oquendo and Carmen Mora Hernández, 1995, pp.147–62; Lois Smith and Alfred Padula, 1996, p.55; Sheryl L. Lutjens, 1995, pp.100–24; Jean Weissman, 1995, p.20; 'Feminismo y la ideología cubana', 1993, pp.11, 16.

72 Rhoda Reddock, 1998b, pp.61–71.

73 *Fempress*, 1995; Rhoda Reddock, 1998b, p.63.

sexual rights and orientation continue to be less open to public discussion and organization.[74]

While the movement has grown in strength and its influence can be felt throughout the region, it faces a number of threats and concerns, and there is increasing evidence of a backlash against it. These are evident not only through the continued escalation in violence against women in spite of the legal and social measures instituted, but also in the emerging arguments regarding male marginalization, especially in the education systems of the anglophone Caribbean. Beyond this backlash, a genuine concern with masculinity and the analysis of manhood has also inevitably emerged in the region. In 1998, the Caribbean Network for Masculinity Studies was established at the University of Puerto Rico, Río Piedras, with a regional membership, and men's groups have emerged tentatively in the region since the early 1990s with the formation of Fathers Incorporated in Jamaica and Men Against Violence against Women in Trinidad later in the decade.[75]

The women's movement in the Caribbean has been formed by a variety of organizations which do not necessarily label themselves feminist, although they may have a feminist orientation, as well as feminist leaders and members. A feminist identification is not shared by most women in the region,[76] although many women and men have been influenced by feminist ideas. Women's mobilization thus ranges from the reactivated civic and professional organizations; income-generating projects; community-based and popular-sector women's organizations; non-governmental organizations; women's sections of political and labour organizations; and service institutions, to autonomous feminist groups. These have developed work ranging from popular education and

74 Alice Colón Warren, 1995, p.182; M. Jacqui Alexander, 1994, pp.5–23; see also Gloria Wekker, 1993, pp.11–24; *idem*, 1998, pp.105–29.

75 In general, feminist research and action in Puerto Rico only later began to emphasize issues of development, race, family headship and masculinity, and there were fewer linkages with income-generating and community-development projects. But work was done related to sexism in education and the media, women's health, sexual and reproductive rights, and violence against women. Other countries, on the other hand, have been more advanced in their work related to issues of poverty and income generation, and have later addressed other specific gender issues. Activism on men and masculinity has been most developed in the English-speaking Caribbean.

76 For example, influenced by leftist-socialist, nationalist, Black Power and anti-war orientations, feminism was (and continues to be in some instances) regarded with suspicion by many who considered that it has not responded to the interests of Third World, working-class, poor women, or it is interpreted as anti-men and equated with homosexual and other stereotypes. (Magaly Pineda, 1984, p.46; Suzy Castor, 1994, pp.30–1, 52–3).

consciousness-raising, lobbying and organization, to more specialized research, legal, health and anti-violence mobilization and services.[77]

This feminist and women's activism has also included the development of academic programmes and research on women and gender at universities

---

77 Among the examples in the English-speaking Caribbean, from the 1970s to the 1990s, we can mention Sistren (Women's Theatre Collective in Jamaica), BOWAND (Belize Organization for Women and Development), Concerned Women for Progress in Trinidad – which spawned two daughter organizations, the Group and Women Working for Social Progress (Workingwomen); CDW (Committee for the Development of Women in St Vincent and the Grenadines), Sisi No Dada in St Kitts, Belize Rural Women's Association, Red Thread in Guyana, and the Women's Forum in Barbados. Although race issues have been more related to the situation of populations of African descent, in Trinidad & Tobago where there is also a large proportion of people of Indian descent, ethnic diversity has begun to be considered, leading to groups like the Hindu Women's Association (Gemma Tang Nain, 1995, pp.60–1; Rhoda Reddock, 1998b, pp.59–62).

In the Dutch Caribbean, the Union of Antillean Women became the first organization with a clearly feminist orientation in Curaçao, joined in the 1980s by other groups such as the Women's Centre (SEDA), working on human resource development and training and INFESE, a research and education project. (Sonia Cuales, 1998, pp.96–7). Among the many groups emerging in Haiti after the downfall of Duvalier have been Fanm D'Ayiti, Comité Féminin, SOFA (Worker Solidarity with Haitian Women), Kay Fanm (Women's House), Ligue des Femmes Rurales, CPFPO (Center for the Promotion of Working Women), ENFOFANM (Centre National et International de Documentation et d'Information des Femmes en Haïti), and the feminist-identified Mouvement Fémenine Haïtien, and Mouvement Haïtien de Libération de la Femme. The return of a military dictatorial regime after 1991 renewed repression against Haitian women and women's organizations, hindering their further development (Carolle Charles, 1994, pp.153–5; Suzy Castor, 1994, pp.26–35; Monique Brisson, 1988, p.39).

In the Spanish-speaking Caribbean, among the Puerto Rican groups with a more continuous presence, following earlier organizations, are Organización Puertorriqueña de la Mujer Trabajadora (OPMT – Puerto Rican Organization of Working Women), Feministas en Marcha, Taller Salud, Casa Pensamiento, which have been joined by others such as Encuentro de Mujeres (no longer working), women's sections of worker's and political organizations, and service institutions like Pro Familia and the women's shelter Casa Protegida Julia de Burgos. Groups such as the Coalición Puertorriqueña de Lesbianas y Homosexuales have organized around gay and lesbian rights since the 1980s, while issues of race were being recognized only in the 1990s with organizations such as the Unión de la Mujer Puertorriqueña Negra. Efforts at co-ordination among different organizations around particular issues include the Coordinadora Paz para la Mujer, dealing with violence against women, and Grupo pro Derechos Reproductivos (Reproductive Rights Coalition) (Idsa Alegría Ortega and Alice Colón Warren, 1995, pp.107–8, 110).

in Puerto Rico, the Dominican Republic, Cuba and the English-speaking Caribbean, incorporating a political commitment to women's equity and equality and a participatory methodology in education and research projects.[78] It has led, as well, to the establishment of state machineries dealing with women's/gender issues in most countries, some beginning even before International Women's Year, as in Jamaica and Puerto Rico.[79]

Efforts at regional co-ordination and collaboration have been most developed in the English-speaking Caribbean, where, since 1970, CARIWA (Caribbean Women's Association) has become an umbrella for various councils within that subregion. A meeting in 1977 with the participation of governments, the University of the West Indies, United Nations institutions,

---

In the Dominican Republic, we find the broader based movement of groups with the most continuous effort at co-ordination in the Coordinadora de ONG's en el Area de la Mujer, working since the early 1980s. Among the many groups we find the pioneering CIPAF (Centro de Investigación para la Acción Femenina), the Centro de Servicios Legales para la Mujer, Esclavas del Fogón, Asociación de Mujeres Dominicanas, MUDE (Mujeres en Desarrollo), Ce-Mujer (Centro de Solidaridad para el Desarrollo de la Mujer), Centro de Apoyo Aquelarre, Collectives 'Mujer y Salud', joined by working-class groups such as Asociación de Trabajadoras del Hogar, and by service institutions such as Pro Familia. Dominican women were pioneers in the Spanish-speaking Caribbean organizing around race in the Movimiento por la Identidad de la Mujer Negra (Clara Báez and Ginny Taulé, 1993, p.26; Gisela Quiterio Benítez, 1993, pp.106–11).

78 In Puerto Rico, there have been projects on sexism in education in the University of Puerto Rico and the Interamerican University since the early 1970s, which became more institutionalized by the 1980s into centres like CERES (Center for Research, Resources and Services for Women) in the Social Science Research Center at the Río Piedras campus and Pro-Mujer at the Mayagüez campus of the University of Puerto Rico, and in more recent groups and projects working on gender in other institutions of higher education. In the Dominican Republic, CIPAF organized the Cátedra Libre sobre la Mujer at the Universidad Autónoma de Santo Domingo, and gender programmes have been established at the Instituto Tecnológico de Santo Domingo and the Catholic University Madre y Maestra. The University of Havana in Cuba has also established an interdisciplinary programme on women and has organized congresses on women's and feminist studies. In the English-speaking Caribbean, the Women and Development Unit (WAND) was established in the Extra Mural Department of the University of the West Indies since 1978, followed in 1982 by Women and Development Studies Groups that by 1993 evolved into the Centre for Gender and Development Studies on three different campuses. (Alice Colón Warren, 1995, p.166; Luisa Campuzano, 1996, 8–9; Marcia Rivera, 1993, pp.50–1; Rhoda Reddock, 1998a, p.8.)

79 Rhoda Reddock, 1998b, pp.61–2; Idsa Alegría Ortega and Alice Colón Warren, 1995, p.110; United Nations. ECLAC, CARICOM, UNIFEM, 1994, p.44; Gemma Tang Nain, 1995, p.61.

CARIWA, national and regional women's organizations, and international development agencies gave rise to a Regional Plan of Action for Caribbean Women which included the establishment of the Women and Development Unit at the University of the West Indies (WAND), the Women's Desk of the Caribbean Community (CARICOM) Secretariat, and the Women and Development Programme of the United Nations Economic Commission for Latin America and the Caribbean (UN/ECLAC).[80]

The location of INSTRAW (United Nations International Research and Training Institute for the Advancement of Women) in the Dominican Republic, as well as other United Nations activities, including its international conferences, provided spaces for exchange and discussion among women of the various subregions. ECLAC also held regular meetings of follow-up and regional planning for the entire Latin American and Caribbean region. Contacts were still limited between countries of the different linguistic subregions, and particularly with non-independent countries, which do not have official representation in these bodies. Regional women's organizations at the 1995 Fourth World Conference on Women in Beijing, and in other events, highlighted the need for representatives of non-independent nations at international fora.[81]

The regional non-governmental organization that has gone the furthest as a space of exchange for women's groups throughout the region has been the Caribbean Association for Feminist Research and Action (CAFRA). Promoting regional actions, campaigns, research projects, cooperation and collaboration, and establishing a base of support, CAFRA defined a Caribbean feminism linking women's subordination with other systems of hierarchy – race, class and nation – and has sought to go beyond boundaries of language and culture characterizing the region. Although based in the English-speaking Caribbean (Trinidad & Tobago), CAFRA's membership spanned all the linguistic areas, and by the 1990s, published its newsletter both in Spanish and English.[82] Among other efforts, the Encuentros Feministas Latinoamericanos y del Caribe, Latin American and Caribbean networks on women's health, violence against women and other issues, and black-women networks, have provided spaces where Spanish-speaking feminists have been more active, but more recently have proposed the promotion of the participation of women from other linguistic

80 Rhoda Reddock, 1998b, p.60.

81 See, for example, United Nations, ECLAC, CARICOM, UNIFEM, 1994, pp.17–8; Idsa E. Alegría Ortega, 1995, pp.19–20; Peggy Antrobus, 1995, pp.21–9; United Nations, CEPAL, 1984.

82 Rhoda Reddock, 1998a, p.7; *idem*, 1998b, p.63; Gemma Tang Nain, 1995, pp.62–3; Fredericka M. Deare, 1995, pp.30–60.

areas.[83] Despite efforts on all sides, membership and participation in regional initiatives from the francophone Caribbean have been inconsistent and limited.

Legal and institutional reforms

Feminist activism since the 1970s has addressed family and labour legislation as well as new areas such as sexual and domestic violence, and child support. The constitutional recognition of women's equal rights, advanced at international fora and established in Cuba and Puerto Rico since mid-century, was established in many of the Caribbean countries by the 1990s. Additionally, most independent countries are signatories to the Convention on the Elimination of all Forms of Discrimination Against Women (CEDAW).[84]

Enactments and improvements in provisions for maternity leave were also in place in a great number of countries by the 1990s, having been an important mobilizing issue for Jamaican women as early as the late 1970s.[85] Protective laws which were found to be discriminatory were repealed by the mid-1970s in Puerto Rico, although less extensively in other countries such as Cuba and the Dominican Republic.[86] Even when it may be implied in other statutes, laws on equal pay were only explicit in some countries such as Jamaica, St Vincent & the Grenadines, Cuba, the Dominican Republic and Puerto Rico.[87] Other labour legislation was less generalized. Only in Cuba has

83 Highlighting issues of race, a Network of Black Afro-Latinamerican and Afro-Caribbean Women was formed after the first Latin American and Caribbean Encounter of Black Women held in the Dominican Republic in 1992. Other Caribbean regional projects and organizations have included the socialist-oriented Women for Caribbean Liberation in 1987, no longer in existence, and the Iniciativa Caribeña de Género, a research initiative. The location of the DAWN (Development Alternatives with Women for a New Era – a well known international organization of feminist researchers and activists) in WAND in the 1990s, also enriched linkages among Caribbean researchers and activists, and with those of other regions in the South. (Rhoda Reddock, 1998b, p.63; Sandra McGee Deutsch, 1989, pp.140–3; *CAFRA News*, vol. II, 1997, nos. 1–2, p.6; *Fempress*, 1995; Peggy Antrobus, 1995, p.27).

84 K. Lynn Stoner, 1991, p.183; Comisión de Derechos Civiles, ELA de Puerto Rico, 1972, p.16; United Nations, 1995a, pp.11–6; United Nations, ECLAC, CARICOM, UNIFEM, 1994, p.53.

85 United Nations, ECLAC, CARICOM, UNIFEM, 1994; Rhoda Reddock, 1998b, p.62.

86 Esther Vicente, 1987, p.175; Vilma Espín Guillois, 1990, pp.84–6; Gisela Quiterio Benítez, 1993, p.82, 90–1.

87 United Nations, ECLAC, CARICOM, UNIFEM, 1994, p.57; Luz Dalis Acosta de Pérez, 1993, pp.78–9; Alice Colón Warren, 1995, p.167.

there been a number of preferential posts identified to promote employment for women.[88] Customary laws in Haiti and agrarian reform regulations in the Dominican Republic, on the other hand, continued to give preference to men in access to land.[89]

Family law was reformed in various countries to establish a greater equality between marital partners in issues such as administration of common property, maintenance, child custody and joint households, in Cuba considering even the sharing of domestic work.[90] Yet only laws in Haiti, Cuba, Barbados and Trinidad & Tobago have offered greater recognition to common law unions.[91] Additionally, only a few countries, including Cuba, Barbados, Puerto Rico, Guyana and the French departments, have decriminalized abortion. This remains a difficult issue especially in predominantly Catholic countries, although haemorrhaging due to unsafe abortions continues to be one of the leading causes of maternal mortality.[92]

As noted earlier, since the 1980s, violence against women became an intensely unifying factor throughout the region, leading to the public discussion of women's subordinate status as a social, public, political problem. Beginning in Puerto Rico, Trinidad & Tobago, and St Vincent & the Grenadines, mobilization has led to the enactment of laws and decrees to eradicate rape and other sexual offences, domestic violence, sexual harassment and other forms of violence against women in at least ten countries.[93] The continued escalation of violence, however, has brought the recognition that legislative change is a necessary but not sufficient measure to solve this intractable problem.

---

88 Vilma Espín Guillois, 1990, p.86.

89 United Nations, 1991a, p.24; Mireille Neptune Anglade, 1986, p.15.

90 Miguel Guillermo Wasmer, 1977, pp.282–339; Esther Vicente, 1987, pp.182–4; Monique Brisson, 1988, pp.33–6; Gisela Quiterio Benítez, 1993, pp.81–5; Maritza Severiya, 1982, p.34.

91 Miguel Guillermo Wasmer, 1977, pp.292–3; Monique Brisson, 1988, pp.33–6; United Nations, CEPALAC, Fondo Naciones Unidas para la Mujer, 1995, p.53; United Nations, CEPALAC, 1986, pp.120–2; United Nations, 1991a, pp.20–4; United Nations, ECOSOC, ECLAC, 1984, p.6; Clara Báez and Ginny Taulé, 1993, p.62; Helen I. Safa, 1998, p.206.

92 Dinnys Luciano, 1997, pp.20, 30; United Nations, CEPALAC, CELADE, 1995, p.167; United Nations, 1991b, pp.67–9; Huguette Dagenais, 1993, p.98; United Nations, 1993, pp.58–9, 65; United Nations, 1995b, p.15; Alice Colón *et al.*, 1999, chap.4; United Nations, Department of Economic and Social Development, 1992, vol. 1, p.132; Frederick E. Nunes and Yvonne M. Delph, 1977.

93 United Nations, ECLAC, CARICOM, UNIFEM, 1994, pp.30, 60; Rhoda Reddock, 1998b, p.62; Idsa Alegría Ortega and Alice Colón Warren, 1995, pp.108–9; United Nations, 1995b, p.176; United Nations, Fondo de Población…, 1997.

THE CHANGING INTERNATIONAL DIVISION OF LABOUR – A GENDER ANALYSIS

Programmes of economic restructuring (structural adjustment) since the 1980s, on the other hand, have had a major negative effect on women's economic and social status. The United Nations Women's Decade had begun at the end of a period of economic expansion and favourable terms of trade for less industrialized countries which had spurred optimism regarding the integration of women into the ongoing process of development. Expansion into new economic areas such as financial and producer services, advanced electronic technology, professional instruments and pharmaceutical products, and even data-processing accompanied expanding labour-intensive manufacturing, as well as a move to tourism and other personal services in different countries.[94]

These industrial trends were continued after the prolonged economic and fiscal crisis had clearly taken hold by the end of the 1970s, and by the 1980s they were restructured to include the imposition of neo-liberal policies of stabilization and structural adjustment, with their globalizing economic tendencies and declining public employment and services. If Puerto Rico was protected from the most intense impacts of the crises by its access to United States public benefits, it still suffered from chronic, increasing joblessness and from trends of privatization and labour deregulation that intensified by the 1990s. In Cuba, where policies had pushed towards full employment for both sexes and the expansion of social services, these were critically curtailed by the fall of the European and Soviet socialist governments and the intensification of the United States' anti-Castro policies since the early 1990s.[95]

Although still limited compared to its supply, the demand for female labour in the modern economic sectors continued to make women's employment more central to economic strategies. By the 1970s, therefore, Momsen and others argue that after a 50-year decline, increases in women's employment were evident. Women's economic activity in the Spanish-speaking Antilles, although remaining lower, tended to move closer to that in the rest of the Caribbean, where it represented a shift in industrial sectors more than an expansion. Nonetheless, the displacement of men's and women's employment with the decline of agriculture and primary indus-

94 United Nations, Department for Policy Coordination and Sustainable Development, 1995; Helen I. Safa, 1995, pp.6–13; Rhoda Reddock, 1998b, pp.64–5; Janet H. Momsen, 1993c, pp.232–4; Ruth Pearson, 1986, pp.287–90; Alice Colón Warren, 1997, pp.141–5; Nancy Fernández, 1993.

95 María de la Luz Havel, 1993; Carolina Aguilar *et al.*, 1996, p.12.

tries, more than the increase in women's jobs, appeared to be the dominant tendency.[96]

With advances in education in all countries except Haiti, the numbers of female Caribbean professional and technical workers increased, especially in areas required by dominant economic strategies. More detailed analyses in various countries, however, show that even with advances like those in Cuba and Puerto Rico, there was still a gender-based labour segregation that concentrated women in the health, educational and social services, as well as in the less technically developed specializations. Most importantly, in few countries did women surpass one-quarter of the administrative and managerial occupations, and most of these not in the highest-ranked positions.[97] Moreover, still facing employment limitations, women's increasing economic activity also meant growing vulnerability to a more precarious labour market of unstable jobs. Women's increasing labour-force participation was also associated with increasing unemployment, which in most countries remained higher than men's.[98]

In practically all countries agriculture continued its tendencies of decline and of defeminization, remaining an important, albeit diminishing, source of work for women only in Haiti. The establishment of export-processing zones since the 1980s, and the expansion of female-dominated labour-intensive

96 Huguette Dagenais, 1993, pp.87–92; Janet H. Momsen, 1993c, pp.235–8; Helen I. Safa, 1995, pp.15, 23, 26; United Nations, CEPALAC, 1986, p.31; United Nations, 1991b, pp.105–6; United Nations, 1995b, pp.153–4; United Nations, 1991a, pp.5–6; Alice Colón Warren, 1997, pp.145–50; Clara Báez, 1998, pp.46–50; Mireille Neptune Anglade, 1986, 77–8, 111; Joan Neil, 1990, pp.3–11.

97 United Nations, 1995b, pp.164, 153, 154; United Nations, 1991b, pp.105–6; Alice Colón Warren, 1997, pp.142, 153; Kevin A. Yelvington, 1993, p.268; Janet H. Momsen, 1993c, pp.236–40; Huguette Dagenais, 1993, pp.90–2; Mireille Neptune Anglade, 1986, pp.106–10; Clara Báez, 1998, p.52, 55; Gisela Quiterio Benítez, 1993, pp.43, 47; Teresa Valdéz *et al.*, 1992, pp.43–5; Helen I. Safa and Peggy Antrobus, 1992, p.52.

98 Only in Puerto Rico (where labour-force participation remained more limited) and St Kitts were some measures of women's unemployment lower than among men. The tendency was particularly dramatic in the Dominican Republic, where female labour-force activity had climbed to over 70 per cent by the 1990s, but half of these women were unemployed. What is noteworthy here is that more women defined themselves as workers, even if unemployed. In Cuba, the special period also brought about a decline in employment, affecting men more than women, but still offering them more opportunities than women (United Nations, Department for Policy Co-ordination and Sustainable Development, 1995d, pp.55–6; Huguette Dagenais, 1993, pp.92–3; Alice Colón Warren, 1997, pp.144, 155; United Nations, 1995c, pp.63–4; Clara Báez, 1998, pp.52–3; Carolina Aguilar *et al.*, 1996, p.12; United Nations, 1995b, p.53; Joan Neil, 1990, pp.4–5.)

TABLE 13.1 Social benefits, women's economic activity and participation in agriculture, 1980

Territory	*% Women over 15 & economically active*	*Women as % of agricultural workers*	*% Women professional/ administrative*	*% Women in clerical/ sales/ services*	*% Women in production/ transport/ labourers*	*Government social benefits as % of GDP*
Antigua & Barbuda	36.3	25.3	50.40	62.70	8.44	n/a
Bahamas	34.0	n/a	46.69	61.71	11.17	0.5
Barbados	60.4	41.7	48.96	60.55	26.65	0.9
Belize	n/a	n/a	53.63	46.30	9.65	n/a
Cuba	33.8	13.1	n/a	n/a	n/a	7.1
Dominican Republic	13.5	2.1	47.37	37.26	21.54	0.5
Guyana	27.7	10.3	n/a	n/a	n/a	0.8
Haiti	58.1	36.7	40.13	47.56	14.22	0.1
Jamaica	66.1	36.4	n/a	n/a	n/a	0.3
Martinique	50.0	27.8	57.68	72.95	10.26	n/a
Montserrat	47.7	22.0	49.20	65.79	14.28	n/a
Netherlands Antilles	n/a	n/a	42.84	52.13	10.41	n/a
Puerto Rico	26.2	2.6	52.70	52.98	20.95	n/a
St. Vincent & The Grenadines	41.2	41.0	n/a	n/a	n/a	n/a
Suriname	28.9	28.6	n/a	n/a	n/a	0.6
Trinidad & Tobago	33.4	17.5	49.61	53.49	11.74	0.3

Source: Janet H. Momsen, 1993c, p.233.

industries continued to offer employment to women in various countries. Nevertheless, as earlier on in Puerto Rico, Curaçao and Jamaica, capital flight in search of lower production costs left thousands of women jobless in areas with higher wage levels or rising demands. This dispersion of industries within and out of the region limited employment opportunities even in countries with the most dramatic growth in export-processing manufacturing such as the Dominican Republic.[99]

With the limits to employment in other sectors, the region has undergone a process of expansion of the services sector in which women have had the most dramatic participation, surpassing men in this job sphere practically everywhere. This trend has expanded with the displacement of workers from formal employment, which led to an increase in self-employment and the informal economy. Throughout the region, and particularly in the French- and English-speaking countries, women have dominated domestic and other personal services, trade and commerce, including street vendors, *madan saras*, or higglers, who market goods within and among the islands and to Central America.[100]

These developments, along with consequent economic, social and political linkages established by globalization, have favoured migration, in particular female migration, as a means of expanding family income. Remittances, monetary and material, impacted not only on household levels and patterns of consumption, but on the different countries' balance of payments. As such, Báez has suggested that migration has been not only a form of individual resistance but an axis sustaining the prevailing economic models.[101] New ways of life have been developed linking transnationalized Caribbean communities with their countries of origin.

Although island hopping – Haitians to the Dominican Republic, Guadeloupe and other islands, Dominicans to Puerto Rico, movements

---

99 United Nations, ECLAC, CARICOM, UNIFEM, 1994, p.46; United Nations, 1991b, pp.105–6; United Nations, 1991a, pp.5–6; Joan Neil, 1990, pp.7–9; Sonia Cuales, 1993, pp.295–6; Sonia Cuales, 1984, p.166; Huguette Dagenais, 1993, p.92; A. Lynn Bolles, 1986, pp.66–8; Teresa Valdés *et al.*, 1992, pp.41, 44; Clara Báez, 1998, pp.52–4.

100 United Nations, ECLAC, CARICOM, UNIFEM, 1994, pp.26, 46; United Nations, 1991b, pp.105–6; United Nations, 1991a, pp.5–6; Joan Neil, 1990, pp.6–7; Sonia Cuales, 1984, p.166; A. Lynn Bolles, 1986, pp.64–5; Clara Báez, 1998, pp.54–5; Ximena Aranda, 1988, pp.20–1; Helen I. Safa and Peggy Antrobus, 1992, pp.64–5; Mireille Neptune Anglade, 1986, pp.62, 106; Lesley McKay, 1993, p.278; Carolle Charles, 1994, pp.50–2.

101 Saskia Sassen, 1988; Helen I. Safa and Peggy Antrobus, 1992, pp.69–72; Clara Báez, 1998, 56–7; Karen Fog Olwig, 1993b, pp.150–67; United Nations, ECLAC, CARICOM, UNIFEM, 1994, pp.11–12; Isis Duarte *et al.*, 1982, pp.77–86.

among the Dutch- and English-speaking countries – and migration to the respective European metropoles have historically been common journeys for women of the different linguistic areas, other countries such as Spain (for Dominicans), Canada (for Haitians), and increasingly the United States (for everyone) have attracted growing numbers of Caribbean migrants. Although migration was earlier dominated by men, women became a majority of migrants to the United States from some countries such as Jamaica as early as the 1960s, and comparative data for New York City showed their continuing predominance in streams from most islands by the 1990s.[102]

Data on migration outflows to New York City and the United States Middle Atlantic Region for the 1980s and 1990s showed how women of different racial/ethnic and class groups responded to the labour demand of the changing job spheres in receiving countries. Sectors of higher-educated Caribbean women – nurses, teachers, academics and others – have responded to a metropolitan demand for professional, technical, clerical and administrative support services, in what has been considered a drain on their nations' investment in education.

Beginning with the earlier Puerto Rican outflow, the majority of the migrants, however, provided the backbone of textile and other labour-intensive manufacturing and were displaced as the industries fled the core cities. As they became concentrated in the growing lower-level service jobs, conditions of peripheral employment and marginality, compounded for many by the vulnerability of undocumented status, were reproduced in the metropoles.[103] The vulnerability and exploitation appears even more starkly among the growing number of women migrating as domestics within the Caribbean, to Europe, North America and other countries, or as sex workers in a (by its nature, less firmly documented) transnational industry that profits from women's sexual and social subordination.[104]

---

102 Massive among Puerto Ricans – given colonial ties – since the 1950s, and facilitated for the other islands by changes in US immigration policy after 1965, Caribbean migration was impelled since then by political, as well as economic conditions in some of the islands, becoming more generalized with the economic crisis and the increasing linkages of that nation with the region throughout the 1980s. New York (City), Department of City Planning, 1992, pp.14–25, 74, 149; *idem*, 1996, pp.10–12, 20, 232–7; Altagracia Ortíz, 1996.

103 New York (City), Department of City Planning, 1996, pp.29–30; *idem*, 1992, p.254; United Nations, ECLAC, CARICOM, UNIFEM, 1994, pp.11–2; Alice Colón Warren, 1998, pp.272–4.

104 Clara Báez, 1998, pp.58–61; United Nations, ECLAC, CARICOM, UNIFEM, 1994, p.14; 'Tourism and the sex-trade project', *CAFRA News*, 1997, pp.16–7. It has also been recognized although as a local problem in Cuba (María Isabel Domínguez, 1996, p.36).

Transformations in gender relations

The relative economic autonomy and continuing improvements in social status still placed Caribbean women in a more favourable situation than that found in other regions. By the 1990s the Dominican Republic had come closer to the rest of the region, and only Haiti remained at significantly lower levels in all of the social indicators considered. Life expectancy in most countries hovered around 75 years (with a five- to seven-year female–male differential), official literacy was around 90 per cent, and education had been approaching gender parity not only at primary, but at secondary and tertiary levels since the 1980s. Fertility continued declining, many countries achieving close to two children per woman of child-bearing ages, or – like Barbados and Cuba – even lower, although it remained closer to three children in Trinidad & Tobago and some other Eastern Caribbean countries.[105]

Studies of Spanish-speaking Caribbean populations suggest some questioning of male domination and established gender roles, including the expectation that women contribute to the household's income. In the rest of the Caribbean there is evidence of shared economic responsibility, social networking and decision-making in family and community affairs.[106] Contrary to the thesis of male marginalization, however, these improvements in women's education contrasted with their continued subordinate status and the sexual division of labour in both the public and domestic sphere.

In most of the region, women's economic pressures and responsibilities were exacerbated by the combination of social and economic crises and the challenges to dominant gender relations, leading to increased gender-based conflict, separation, divorce and female-headed households in relation to

105 The Dominican Republic followed more closely with a 70-year life expectancy and 80-per cent literacy rate and a total fertility rate slightly higher than three children per woman. Female enrolment at higher educational levels actually reached over 60 per cent in some countries such as Cuba and Puerto Rico, and Jamaica, Bahamas, Trinidad & Tobago and other English-speaking countries. Despite some setbacks there was no turning back on these trends as a result of the crises and cutbacks of the 1980s. Only Haiti continued with the most difficult health and education conditions, improving their rates only from 50 to 58 in life expectancy between the 1970s and 1990s, maintaining literacy rates of around 40 per cent and fertility rates around five children or higher. (United Nations, 1993, pp.26, 133–5; United Nations, 1991b, pp.51, 52, 68, 69; United Nations, ECLAC, CARICOM, UNIFEM, 1994, pp.43, 45, 47; United Nations, 1995b, pp.68–70, 93, 119; United Nations, CEPALAC, 1986, pp.42, 91, 106.)

106 See, for example, Helen I. Safa, 1995, pp.84–7, 110–20, 136–43; Marya Muñoz-Vázquez and Edwin Fernández, 1988, pp.49–70, 81; Riva Berleant-Schiller and William M. Maurer, 1993, pp.65–79; Mihelic Lydia Pulsipher, 1993, pp.50–64.

dual-earner households.[107] Most importantly, women's responsibility for the family and children remained practically unchallenged. Family support in the work-place and the public sphere has been limited, even in Cuba, where there have been more concerted efforts to address this issue, restricting women's opportunities for advancement.[108] On the other hand, informal female support networks, common in different forms throughout the region, have also come under great pressure by community dispersion through migration, declining relations with the extended families, and even with the increasing economic constraints which reduced the possibilities of sharing services and resources.[109]

Additionally, despite openings at all levels, there is evidence that professional, technical and vocational education remained segregated and sexist stereotypes were reproduced in the media, school texts, curriculum contents and teachers' attitudes and practices.[110] Moreover, studies in the Spanish- and French-speaking Caribbean show that even if male dominance has been questioned, there has been much less questioning of the sexual double standard – that men have sexual freedom/control and access to multiple partners, while women remain restricted by codes of faithfulness when they are in a relationship. If these codes take on a stricter appearance in the Spanish-speaking islands, they are nonetheless present in the rest of the region.[111] Challenges to established gendered power relations may lead to conflict as

---

107 Haiti, Jamaica and some of the English-speaking countries showed the highest proportions (over 40 per cent) of female family headship, but in the Spanish-speaking Caribbean, Puerto Rico approached the moderate levels of female family headship (20–9 per cent) common among some of the islands like Trinidad & Tobago, while the Dominican Republic and Cuba reached the higher levels (30–9 per cent) prevailing in most of the others. (Isis Duarte and Ramón Tejada Holguín, 1995, p.48; United Nations, 1991b, pp.27–8; Helen I. Safa, 1998, pp.207–8; Alice Colón Warren, 1997, p.161; United Nations, ECLAC, CARICOM, UNIFEM, 1994, p.40; Gisela Quiterio Benítez, 1993, p.31; Marya Muñoz-Vázquez and Edwin Fernández, 1988, p.20; Teresa Valdés *et al.*, 1992, p.50.)

108 Huguette Dagenais, 1993, p.98; Carolle Charles, 1994, p.47; Janet H. Momsen, 1993c, p.243; Karen Fog Olwig, 1993b, pp.150–1; Carolina Aguilar *et al.*, 1996, p.13; Helen I. Safa, 1995, pp.74, 150–1, 172, 181–2.

109 Janet H. Momsen, 1993b, p.2; Karen Fog Olwig, 1993b, pp.150–66; Helen I. Safa, 1995, p.117; Anne R. Roschelle, 1997, p.107–25.

110 Zoraida Santiago, 1987, pp.244–6; Isabel Picó, 1983b; Clara Báez and Ginny Taulé, 1993, pp.29–30; Gisela Quiterio Benítez, 1993, pp.64–5; Teresa Valdéz *et al.*, 1992, p.65; Margarita Paiewonsky, 1993, pp.30–59.

111 María del C. Santos Ortíz and Marya Muñoz, 1989; Denise Paiewonsky, 1994, pp.118–33; Ginny Taulé, 1993, pp.74–5; Rebeca Cutié, 1997, pp.22–4; Karen Fog Olwig, 1993b, p.153; Kevin Yelvington, 1993, p.271; Lesley McKay, 1993, p.282; Huguette Dagenais, 1993, p.101; Carolle Charles, 1994, pp.46–7.

men resist and continue to exert their control through these and other means, including the increasingly visible gender violence.[112]

Women and political participation

In the prevailing context of economic crisis and gender subordination, women's paid and unpaid work was key in reproducing the dominant strategies of development, becoming a palliative to the declining social services and joblessness resulting from the states' fiscal policies. Suffering the most from economic restructuring, personally and through their families, they took over the health and well-being of households and social sectors left unattended through neo-liberal economic initiatives. These conditions also catalysed women's social and political mobilization.

Throughout the 1970s and 1980s, women from the rural and urban popular sectors organized and struggled for better living conditions – for access to food, land, housing, health, education, social services, environmental protection, and other basic needs – in what have been called the new social movements. Riots, revolts, demonstrations and other forms of pressure against states that were imposing land evictions, excessive taxes, cutbacks in social spending and other suffocating policies intensified. These became massive by the 1980s in countries like Jamaica, the Dominican Republic and Haiti, where women's demonstrations in 1986 signalled the downfall of Jean-Claude Duvalier. Compared to the earlier mobilizations of the 1930s, which had led to social welfare programmes, these contested issues of reproduction in a more politicized, counter-hegemonic way, as they identified adequate living conditions not as assistance but as an entitlement and a social right. Such mobilizations also tended to become less hierarchical, more flexible, and more focused on the solution of people's immediate problems than traditional political activism. In this way they proffered a movement toward a redefinition of politics, political styles and objectives according to their own social needs and spheres.[113]

Women's unequal sharing in power nonetheless continued, evident in their exclusion from higher decision-making positions in party and electoral politics. In some Dutch- and English-speaking countries such as Curaçao, the Bahamas, Barbados and Dominica, the structures were open enough to allow

---

112 M. Jacqui Alexander, 1994, p.18; Idsa Alegría Ortega and Alice Colón Warren, 1995, p.105; Helen I. Safa, 1995, p.183.

113 Suzy Castor, 1994, pp.16–46; Carolle Charles, 1994, pp.153–6; Clara Báez, 1993, pp.1–20; Margarita Cordero, 1994, pp.13–23; Gemma Tang Nain, 1995, pp.60–9; Rhoda Reddock, 1998b, pp.64–9; Sonia Cuales, 1998, p.97; Marya Muñoz-Vázquez, 1996, pp.161–83.

women to be heads of government or deputy prime ministers, or to hold enough positions to have political influence. Most countries showed increases in women's parliamentary representation over the 1980s (surpassing that in Latin America which rarely exceeded 10 per cent), in about half of the Caribbean region, at some point in the 1990s. The highest was found in Montserrat, where it reached 31 per cent in 1992, and in Cuba, where it was still 23 per cent at this date, although this figure represented a decline from 34 per cent in 1985.

Still, increases have not been totally consistent and in other countries women's representation in parliament remained much lower or non-existent. The Dominican Republic, for example, showed an increase from 8 per cent to 12 per cent for women in parliament between 1985 and 1992, while in Puerto Rico, although doubling compared to the previous elections, representation of women in the legislature was only 18 per cent in 1996.[114]

Although in some countries levels of political representation were greater than those of Latin America and other regions in the South, generally, women still tended to be excluded from the positions and institutions of

TABLE 13.2 Percentage of women in Commonwealth (English-speaking) Caribbean parliaments, 1995–2000

Country	*1995*	*2000*
Antigua & Barbuda	11.1	8.8
The Bahamas	10.8	19.6
Barbados	18.4	20.4
Dominica	9.4	9.7
Grenada	17.9	17.9
Guyana	20.0	1.5
Jamaica	12.3	16.0
St Kitts & Nevis	0	13.3
St Lucia	14.3	13.8
St Vincent & the Grenadines	9.5	14.3
Trinidad & Tobago	20.6	20.9
Belize	10.3	18.4

Source: Commonwealth Parliamentary Union, *Women in Commonwealth Parliaments*, prepared for Commonwealth Workshop on Gender and Democracy, Windhoek, February 2000.

114 United Nations, ECLAC, CARICOM, UNIFEM, 1994, p.31; Idsa Alegría Ortega and Alice Colón Warren, 1995, p.107.

TABLE 13.3 Participation of women in parliamentary assemblies in selected Caribbean countries, 1980, 1985, 1992 (per cent)

Country	*1980*	*1985*	*1992*
Anguilla	15	8	0
Antigua & Barbuda			0
The Bahamas	5	7	13
Barbados	9	10	13
Belize	12	8	11
British Virgin Islands	0	0	8
Cuba	23	34	23
Dominica	13	13	16
Dominican Republic	7	8	12
Grenada		29	7
Guyana	14	22	17
Haiti	8		
Jamaica	8	5	12
Montserrat	8	15	31
Netherlands Antilles			18
Puerto Rico	5	8	10
St Kitts & Nevis	7	7	7
St Lucia	7	13	14
St Vincent & the Grenadines	8	0	17
Trinidad & Tobago	13	15	18
Turks & Caicos	0	11	19

Sources: United Nations, ECLAC, CARICOM, UNIFEM, 1994; for Puerto Rico: Isabel Picó, 1983a, pp.58–61; Idsa Alegría Ortega, 1989, p.4.

greatest influence and decision-making.[115] Women's activism has nonetheless led to increasing attention to their concerns in party platforms. Feminists in Puerto Rico, the Dominican Republic and Haiti have elaborated critical analyses of these platforms suggesting that most remained vague and did not question gendered power inequalities in the allocation of social functions and responsibilities. At a broader level there has been a call to redefine politics

115 Over the period between the 1980s and 1992, there were no women parliamentarians in Anguilla, Antigua & Barbuda and Martinique and in other islands, including Puerto Rico, Dominican Republic, Guadeloupe and some of the English-speaking countries, they ranged from 7 to 12 per cent. Participation in local electoral bodies tended to be higher than this only in some countries. (United Nations, 1991b, pp.31–2, 40–2; United Nations, 1995b, pp.186–7; United Nations, ECLAC, CARICOM, UNIFEM, 1994, p.31; Idsa Alegría Ortega, 1996, p.5; Magalys Arocha *et al.*, 1995; Gisela Quiterio Benítez, 1993, pp.98, 99.)

away from extreme partisanship and place people's needs at the centre of policies, recognizing women's social and economic contributions, the inter-relations of production and reproduction, and the indivisibility of the social, economic and political dimensions of development.[116]

Organizations have proposed agendas such as CIPAF's Programa Mínimo Feminista and the 1995 Primer Plan de Igualdad de Oportunidades para las Mujeres del Ayuntamiento del D.N. in the Dominican Republic, which posed the need for proactive mechanisms to ensure women's full political participation. This included the demand for their participation in the elaboration, monitoring and evaluation of state measures and programmes which would move them towards the redefinition of politics and development. Similarly in 1995, the collective document *Twelve Points to Power*, in Trinidad & Tobago, put forward to all political parties some common demands of women in that country.[117]

Conclusions

The transformations in Caribbean women's status over the twentieth century were substantial although not homogenous. Along with similar changes in other parts of the world, this can be described as one of the great revolutions of the twentieth century. In this context the mobilizations, organization and struggles of feminism, nationalism, workers' rights and other social movements have to be located within the persistence and innovativeness of the international capitalist economic order and its accompanying modernizing visions within this region.

Caribbean countries went through an uneven process of social and economic 'development', educational expansion and changing demands for female labour that supported women's claims to increased political rights and a redefinition of social relations. Pushed forward by a 'first wave' of feminist organizing, women were gradually recognized as an important political constituency, and in subsequent decades geared their newly acquired activism and political recognition towards broad political, economic and social changes in their societies.

Greater focus on the still-prevalent gender inequalities became heightened with the re-emergence of feminist activism in the 1970s and 1980s.

116 Idsa Alegría Ortega, 1995, p.5; Suzy Castor, 1994, pp.58–97, 160; Margarita Cordero, 1991, pp.98–104; Margarita Ostolaza Bey, 1989, chaps 4, 5; *Mujeres en Marcha*, 1996.

117 For more on this see Diana Wells, 1998.

Although small, these feminist-oriented groups, usually more radicalized than other women, promoted public discussion and action on issues relevant to and supported by a broader base of women. They had an impact that transcended their actual numbers. At the same time, state mechanisms created to work on gender issues may have been limited in budget, training, leadership or outlook, but in many cases have been important in providing a climate of support and promoting co-ordination among women's organizations. In a context of great resistance, increasing, though still limited numbers of pro-feminist men in the region also recognize the importance of these transformations to human society.

By the end of the century, Caribbean women had, to varying degrees, experienced improvements in educational levels and labour-force participation in leading economic sectors, moved to higher-level occupations, and pushed for more egalitarian legislation. The century ended, however, without the full acceptance of the equal value of women and men or the redefinition of social spheres that would provide for the unleashing of the full human potential of both women and men. Gender inequality in domestic responsibilities, in sexual control, and in power and decision-making at the highest economic and political levels, remains particularly resistant.

Women's organizations continued to question the neo-liberal political and economic policies that exacerbated gender conflict and inequality and reproduced women's subordinate status, thus redefining politics and development with demands emerging from their own needs and spheres. With a recognition of the unequal incorporation of women into prevailing institutions and structures, Caribbean and other feminists emphasized the gendered and hierarchical nature of development strategies and of definitions of politics and power, as they continued to challenge not only gender, but all other, not unrelated social inequities, including those based on race/ethnicity, class and sexual orientation in our societies.

14

THE CARIBBEAN FAMILY: CONTINUITY AND TRANSFORMATION

Raymond T. Smith

Introduction

The Caribbean family, assuming that one can generalize across such a diverse region, has proven exceedingly difficult to describe. High rates of teenage pregnancy, illegitimacy and unstable marriage are as characteristic today as they were in the early nineteenth century, but what those rates mean is not self-evident. Most writers have assumed that they reflect loose morals, family disorganization, and inadequate child care. But Caribbean people are family people, embedded in extensive networks of kin and practising such institutions as 'family land', the fostering of children and ritual godparenthood. This contradiction – negative images of family life imposed upon a reality of complex, supportive and extensive kinship ties – has been present throughout Caribbean history. Although it complicates the understanding of Caribbean family life, it affords insight into class and racial ideologies.

Different sections of the population of Caribbean societies appear to differ in their family practices, with higher status groups seeming to marry more frequently and to live in nuclear families of husband, wife and legitimate children. Are these apparent differences the result of lower-class deviation from a 'normal' pattern, or do different sections of the population practise different family institutions? The most widely accepted explanation of variation in family form is that high rates of illegitimacy, unstable sexual unions, a low marriage rate, and the occurrence of female-headed households, are patterns of behaviour forced upon the lower classes by the economic conditions under which they live. The implication is that the more privileged classes lead a 'normal', 'natural' family life with stable monogamous marriage as the basis for raising children in two-parent families. This explanation flows from the premises of the positivistic social science of the 1940s and 1950s that is still dominant in much of the region, and from the general bourgeois assumption that economics is the driving force of social life.[1] It has the advantage of seemingly universal application; it can be deployed as readily in Cuba as in Guyana, in Haiti as in Aruba, and it seems to apply regardless of race. Although the legacy of slavery is often invoked to explain supposed family disorganization, that legacy can also be viewed as continuing economic deprivation.

Another explanation, attracting more attention in recent years, is that variations in family structure derive from the varied cultural traditions of the different population segments of Caribbean societies. Thus, it has been argued that the apparently deviant family behaviour of lower-class African Americans is really the transformed and adapted expression of a basically African pattern of kinship, comparable to the similarly persistent patterns of European or Indian family life. The earliest and most-quoted proponent of this point of view was Melville J. Herskovits, an American anthropologist. With the recent upsurge in studies of the African diaspora it has attracted renewed interest. Plural society theory similarly insists upon the existence of discrete 'cultural sections', each with its own kinship system.[2] While avoiding the issue of African survivals, this theory also assumes that an essential culture is embodied in each section of the population.

The family and kinship systems of the Caribbean are much more complex than is suggested by the theories outlined above. Immigrants to the Caribbean region did indeed bring with them varied customs and kinship practices, many of which remained incorporated in the conscious and unconscious ideas and behaviour of the immigrants, and some of which were passed on to their descendants. It is also true that the harshly exploitative labour systems of slavery, indenture and the modern plantation system have affected population dynamics and family activities alike. However, several hundred years of complex social history have seen the development of a new way of life and new cultural practices, particular to this region. That history must be studied in its local details as well as in its broad general sweep.

This new way of life, created in the Caribbean, has been referred to as Creole society.[3] Creole society is a new, locally developed system of social

---

1 An extensive body of research material on the family has come from the Women in the Caribbean Project; this project reported on studies in Barbados, Antigua, St Vincent, Jamaica and Guyana (1986, vol. 35, nos. 2 and 3). The research scholars collected both 'objective' survey data and 'subjective' case material, but the theoretical orientation of most of the papers is still generally positivist, assuming that human behaviour is determined by functional requirements or by the need to survive, or adapt to material conditions. Other recent work stimulated by feminist concerns also focuses primarily on the economic aspects of domestic life.

2 M. G. Smith, 1962b; *idem*, 1966.

3 See Raymond T. Smith, 1967 and Edward Brathwaite, 1971 for discussions of this concept.

relations, embodied in Creole cultural forms – of language, law, economic relations, religiosity, political concepts, and familial forms. Creole culture contains within itself a complicating factor that has bedevilled social research: an ideology of difference, a shared conviction that Caribbean societies are made up of fundamentally discrete groups – variously termed 'races', 'colour-classes', or even 'social or cultural segments' that coincide with race. These culturally constituted groups are sometimes seen as the bearers of ancestral cultural traditions derived from Africa, India, China, Europe or aboriginal America, traditions that are believed to be resistant to the solvent effects of local nationalism. Or they may be thought to differ in intelligence, aptitudes or other qualities. This ideology of difference is an intrinsic part of the development of colonial systems in which power was deployed through a complex of institutions and practices that served to maintain and reproduce a hierarchical social order itself based on racial domination.[4]

Belief in profound differences is one thing and the reality of daily life is another. The inevitable consequence of living in small communities requiring intense interaction was a convergence upon common understandings and common modes of interaction. Europeans were the dominant element in this region, but they were not able to impose an imported culture and imported standards upon passively receptive 'others'. An avalanche of recent literature has focused on the resistance offered by subordinated (or 'subaltern') groups to the domination exercised by colonizing groups.[5] However, that resistance was not merely reactive; in language, in kinship patterns and in political organization, new Creole systems were developed through which the various elements in these societies – dominating and dominated – constituted each other. To refer to this as a 'common culture' is misleading if that term implies uniform beliefs and ways of behaviour; the distinctive feature of Creole society was the hierarchical differentiation of the population, and the continual reproduction of differences among the groups so differentiated. If aboriginal cultural differences tend to disappear, then it becomes necessary, in a system of this kind, to create, or recreate, them in the form of invented traditions.[6] Notwithstanding these ideologies (which have found their way into social theory as the concept of 'pluralism'), the most important observation for understanding the dynamics of

4 Virtually all present-day Caribbean societies profess democratic and egalitarian ideals that are embodied in laws and written constitutions. However, the actual practice of social relations continues to be strongly authoritarian, hierarchical, gender-based and inflected by a consciousness of race.

5 Some better-known examples of that literature include James C. Scott, 1985, and for the Caribbean, Barbara Bush, 1990; Jean Besson, 1987.

6 See Eric Hobsbawm and Terence Ranger, 1983.

Caribbean kinship is precisely the interaction of individuals of different social categories within a hierarchically structured system of class or status relations.[7] Indeed, it is the interaction that produces, reproduces and modifies the differences themselves.

That interaction has produced, and continues to produce, a system of kinship and marriage in which different types of conjugal union – legal marriage, non-legal co-residential unions, and visiting unions – are practised at all levels of the social hierarchy, producing differentially valued patterns of domestic life. The essential component of this system of kinship and marriage is the general subordination of women, a gender subordination that is essential to the reproduction of the societal status hierarchy with its strong racial component. The participation of the upper and middle classes in this complex system of kinship and marriage is concealed behind a façade of respectability. However, the reality is that men of higher social status have had privileged sexual access to women of lower status, as well as exercising authority over their own wives and daughters, and in the process have actually created the dual marriage system that is characteristic of these societies. The term 'higher social status' is used deliberately to indicate relative status, for we are dealing here with a very general phenomenon and not a practice confined to a small group of élite men. The institution of the 'outside woman' or 'the deputy', as Trinidadians call it, is extremely widespread.

It is against this general background that the family in the contemporary Caribbean must be understood.

Discourse on the family as an integral part of social structure

European colonizers viewed any kinship and family practice different from their own as uncivilized; in the Caribbean those attitudes were quickly applied to aboriginal Indians, to enslaved Africans, and – to a lesser degree – to indentured labourers from India and China. In the late nineteenth century anthropology established a more tolerant, and professedly objective, view of kinship variation, but this tolerance has been strangely absent from writing on Caribbean family forms, which have generally continued to be viewed as distorted and disorganized versions of the supposedly natural pattern of stable nuclear families. The monogamous nuclear families considered ideal by the dominant Europeans (though not necessarily practised by them)

7 See Verena Martínez Alier, 1974 (1989); Raymond T. Smith, 1988.

were no more 'natural' than any other form, but elaborate theories have been devised that argue the functional necessity of nuclear families for producing normal human beings.[8]

Although the discussion of family problems has now been taken up by social scientists and social workers, the elements of their discourse are quite familiar from the eighteenth and early nineteenth centuries onwards. In 1774 Edward Long reported that the Creole Blacks of Jamaica

> are all married (*in their way*) to a husband, or wife, *pro tempore*, or have other family connexions, in almost every parish throughout the island; so that one of them, perhaps, has six or more husbands or wives, in several different places ... In their care for their children, some are remarkably exemplary. A Negroe has been known so earnest and sincere in the tuition of his child, as to pay money out of his own pocket for smith's work ... They ... seem[ing] to hold filial obedience in much higher estimation than conjugal fidelity; perhaps, because of the whole number of wives or husbands, one only is the object of particular steady attachment... They laugh at the idea of marriage, which ties two persons together indissolubly. Their notions of love are, that it is free and transitory.[9]

Long is best known for his racism, but he was also a well-informed planter and a close student of the customs of his workers. This statement encapsulates the contradictory views that continue to pervade discussions of Caribbean kinship. In spite of his irony ('married *in their way*') he cannot deny the strength of kinship ties even in the absence of stable, monogamous conjugal unions. Writing in the eighteenth century, his rhetoric typically contrasts the supposedly loose, disordered and uncivilized behaviour of Africans and Creoles with the (equally hypothetical) 'civilized' customs of Europeans.[10] After slavery was abolished in 1838 the rhetoric changed but the contrast remained.

By the mid-nineteenth century Christian missionaries, whose task it was to convert the heathen, contrasted the disorder and backwardness of slaves with the enlightened order of the lives of Christian converts. James M. Phillippo, a Baptist missionary, writing in 1843, described the state of slavery

8 See, for example, Talcott Parsons, 1955.

9 Edward Long, 1774 (1972), vol. 2, pp.414–15.

10 Elsewhere in his two-volume work Long deplores the fact that many white women are unable to find husbands while white men, infatuated with women of colour, are living in non-legal unions.

in much the same terms as Long described the inferiority of Africans, and went on to say:

> The sanctities of marriage were almost unknown; there was no such thing, indeed, as legitimate marriage among the slaves. This sacred institute was ridiculed by the negroes, and regarded as inimical to their happiness ... Licentiousness the most degraded and unrestrained was the order of the day. Every estate on the island – every negro hut was a common brothel: every female a prostitute, and every man a libertine ... hundreds were known to have become mothers before they had even entered upon their teens.[11]

Phillippo the Christian was less tolerant than Long the racist; in his missionary zeal he completely discounted the strengths of the family and kinship practices developed under slavery, supposing that Christianity would, if it had not already, transform uncivilized African slaves into faithful copies of European Christians.

> From this revolting picture we turn with pleasure to the contrast as exhibited in the progress of the last twenty years ... everywhere marriage is now the rule, and concubinage the exception .... Their ideas of the marriage state are entirely changed. It is now associated with everything virtuous and honourable in human conduct ... Mutual harmony and tenderness, every mild virtue and soft endearment, which gives home its solace and its charm, is now to be seen in lovely exercise in many a negro family.[12]

Phillippo's intimation of a massive change in the kinship behaviour of African Jamaicans was premature; Long's description remained more accurate even for the nineteenth century, and commentators continued to deplore the freedom with which unions were made and broken.

Whatever their intention regarding slavery and the fate of African Americans, European commentators have *always* drawn contrasts between themselves and black people; have set up a contrast between the marital and kinship behaviour of black and white, a contrast that pervades all narratives and discourse, be they popular or scholarly. The only way in which Blacks could be deemed 'civilized' was by adopting the ideal behaviour of the Whites; by becoming what Horace Russell has termed 'the Christian Black',[13]

---

11 James M. Phillippo, 1843 (1971), p.218.
12 *Ibid.*, pp.220–33.
13 Horace O. Russell, 1983.

an image that converged with that of a 'stable peasantry'. The tendency to think in these contrasted terms is with us still. Slavery, blackness, poverty and sinful sexual relations are fused in a stubbornly persistent conception of sexual imperfection.[14]

Of course, the contrast between black and white does not exhaust the patterns of perceived diversity in societies that have seen the immigration of Spanish peasants, Portuguese plantation workers, indentured immigrants from India and China, and smaller groups from the Middle East, but in the discussion of family life, race is a major theme.[15] In Cuba, for example, with a much larger white population than Jamaica, and with a Catholic regime that had always advocated the conversion of African slaves, race continued to be a major line of cleavage in society, conflict over inter-racial marriage was endemic, and illegitimacy rates among slaves and free coloureds remained high throughout the nineteenth century.[16] In the early 1970s, 51.7 per cent of 'married' women in the Dominican Republic lived in consensual rather than legal unions.[17] It is clear that whatever the actual state of domestic and kinship relations in Caribbean societies, discussion of family problems has a much wider social, and even political, significance.

The family in a changing socio-economic environment

In a volume on the contemporary Caribbean it is not feasible to examine the extensive literature on slavery, nor is it necessary. The idea that present-day patterns of black family life have their origin in slavery is a persistent folk tradition, but even if it were true it would be necessary to understand how such patterns could be reproduced in each generation and what social practices accounted for their persistence. For our purposes it is sufficient to note the enormous ideological significance of the *belief* in the slavery origins of the family system, to consider briefly the late-nineteenth-century developments in the economy of the region, and to deal more specifically with the changes that have taken place, or not taken place, during the period of rapid population growth, economic development and political reform, since the late 1940s.

14 For a penetrating study of the religious dimension of these conceptions see Diane J. Austin-Broos, 1997.

15 See Sidney W. Mintz, 1974 (1989), chap.1, for a brief but comprehensive discussion of this diversity.

16 See Verena Martínez Alier, 1974 (1989), pp.57–70.

17 José Miguel Guzmán, 1980, p.19.

The first transformation consequent on the abolition of slavery

The abolition of slavery, and the collapse of the eighteenth-century mercantilist system, resulted in the establishment throughout the region of colonial states based upon large-scale plantation agriculture. A few of the islands maintained an approximation to the eighteenth-century pattern of small estates with a highly paternalistic system of labour relations, and Haiti – an independent state with a generally ruined plantation sector and a large 'reconstituted peasantry' – was an exception.[18] But most Caribbean territories had taken on the characteristic pattern of large rural populations providing seasonal labour for sugar plantations, or for smaller farms growing tropical produce such as coffee, banana and tobacco. Societies throughout the region (with the exception of Haiti) continued to be dominated by small populations of Europeans or Creole Whites, while the mass of rural labour was of African or mixed African-European descent, or imported directly from India, China or Indonesia. A new 'intelligentsia', of lawyers, doctors, teachers, journalists and government bureaucrats, constituted a racially heterogeneous middle layer. Urban economies were undeveloped and the cities were usually ports for the export of crops and the import of manufactures, military garrisons and – as seats of colonial government – centres of administration.

Several different patterns of family life have been identified as belonging to various social segments within these late-nineteenth-century colonial Caribbean societies. High-status Europeans, be they British, Dutch, French or Spanish, were assumed (incorrectly) to live in typically bourgeois European domesticity, marrying status equals and raising children who would either return to Europe or succeed to positions of domination in the colonial hierarchy. The family life of these strata has received little scholarly attention, though a certain number of family histories of seventeenth- and eighteenth-century planter dynasties have been studied.[19]

Beneath these élite strata the middle class of bureaucrats, professionals and tradesmen was firmly established by the late nineteenth century, living in comfortable urban residences serviced by an abundant supply of cheap domestic labour, and struggling to consolidate their status position by educating their children in the highly restricted secondary education system. Throughout the region this small 'middle class' tended to be predominantly 'coloured' or 'mulatto'; that is, of mixed racial origin and oriented toward the cultural standards of the dominant European élites. However, there is some difference in this regard between the Hispanic Caribbean and the rest.

18 See Sidney W. Mintz, 1989, chap.10.

19 See for example, Richard Pares, 1950; Michael Craton and James Walvin, 1971; Michael Craton, 1978.

Cuba, Puerto Rico and the Dominican Republic continued to be settled and farmed by Spanish immigrants long after the non-Hispanic Caribbean had become almost exclusively plantation colonies operated by slave labour. In the Hispanic Caribbean the large-scale plantation intruded into countries where small farms and moderate-sized *haciendas* predominated; during the nineteenth century large plantations drew labour from these peasant populations as well as importing African slaves. Consequently, the intermediate classes in these territories were predominantly white rather than mulatto, and a populist tradition of descent from the *jíbaro*, or peasant farmer class has continued to be important. In the non-Hispanic Caribbean, a tradition of small-scale farming grew in *opposition* to an already established plantation regime, and when slavery was abolished African ex-slaves established themselves as small landowners wherever that was possible.

These developments are important to the understanding of family structure since it has been supposed that forms of family organization are closely associated with – or even determined by – occupation and landholding. The most crudely deterministic theories assert that it is the seasonal, uncertain, and exploitative labour market of large-scale plantation agriculture that creates the conditions making for unstable family life. This instability, it is argued, spreads outwards from the plantation into the communities from which migrant labour is drawn. Underlying such theories there is a not-so-hidden assumption that a 'normal' and 'stable' family life is easily understood; it is the 'natural' family of man, wife and their children. A series of influential studies, based on research carried out in the 1940s and 1950s, presented analyses that generally linked apparent variations in family structure to the historically derived economic or class position of the groups involved.[20] For example, Edith Clarke in Jamaica compared the family life of a prosperous citrus-farming community with a sugar plantation area, and a poor area of small-scale cultivators providing seasonal labour for the plantations. Based on her assumption that 'the paternal relationship can only develop satisfactorily where the child shares a home with his mother and father during infancy and childhood,' she argues that Sugartown (the plantation community) displays the highest level of familial disorganization, while Orange Grove (the citrus area) has the most stable family life.[21] Mocca (the poor farming area) is somewhere in between; legal marriage was less prevalent than in Orange Grove, but the stability of 'faithful concubinage' rooted in a family-based agriculture kept men close to home for

20 Among such studies were T. S. Simey, 1946; Madeline Kerr, 1952; Lloyd Braithwaite, 1953; Raymond T. Smith, 1956; Julian H. Steward *et al.*, 1956; Edith Clarke, 1957; George E. Cumper, 1958; Hyman Rodman, 1971; William Davenport, 1961; Sidney Greenfield, 1961.

21 Edith Clarke, 1957.

much of the time, providing a more suitable family environment for child development.[22] This myth of the indispensability of the nuclear family persists in the face of a huge anthropological literature documenting the wide variation in arrangements for successful child-rearing in human societies.

A variation on the theme of economic determinism is provided in the summary discussion of marriage and the family in Puerto Rico in the late 1940s, though here the authors assume a variation between 'patrilineal families in some groups and matrilineal families in others' depending upon the nature and amount of property controlled by various family members.[23] Non-legal 'common-law' marriages are said to occur because institutionally sanctioned unions are irrelevant where inheritance is unimportant and status does not depend on marriage.[24] Many other studies of the period presented similar functionalist analyses, and although most of them were based on anthropological field studies (some explicitly synchronic and historical), they had the effect of typifying a Caribbean society that had not changed appreciably since the creation of a post-slavery social order. The Puerto Rico study was much more explicitly historical, but it too typified various communities in terms of sequentially emergent 'sub-cultures', rooted in various modes of economic activity, so that the present array of types represented historical as well as modern conditions.

The period since the Second World War

The Second World War was a turning-point in modern Caribbean history. It not only marked the beginning of the end of European colonialism and the extension of United States hegemony, but since then almost all Caribbean societies have experienced increases in levels of living and undergone internal transformations in class structure that have impacted upon family life. These changes in the social and economic context of family life were gradual and are easily overlooked. For example, writing in the late 1980s Mintz refers to 'The peoples of the Caribbean, predominantly poor, rural, agricultural, and illiterate'.[25] It is not clear what period he is referring to, but profound changes have affected

22 Brodber notes that Clarke's reference to the 'looseness of conjugal ties' among the lower-class African Jamaican population was a characterization which had become commonplace in Jamaica after a similar pronouncement in 1937 by the Board of Supervision. Erna Brodber, 1986, p.47, n.1.

23 Julian H. Steward *et al.*, 1956, pp.474–5.

24 *Ibid.*, 1956, p.475.

25 Sidney W. Mintz, 1989, p.32.

even rural agricultural populations, changes that are well documented in the studies resulting from the Women in the Caribbean Project.[26] For many territories they involve a shift away from the plantation-dominated economies of the nineteenth and early twentieth centuries, with their huge rural agricultural labour forces, to economies with much larger urban populations engaged in manufacturing, mineral extraction, tourism and other service industries. This has been accompanied by higher educational levels, improved medical care, greater expectations of upward social mobility, the increased importance of cash income, and enhanced levels of expectation of consumption of material goods such as refrigerators, cooking stoves, radios, televisions, and electric or gas power to operate them. In Guyana the mechanization of the rice industry had, by the 1970s, completely transformed the patterns of family labour, effectively removing women from the arduous tasks of transplanting and reaping rice, while the electrification of rural areas (erratic though the supply might be) profoundly altered the patterns of everyday life. In Puerto Rico, Cuba, Jamaica, the Dominican Republic and Trinidad vigorous programmes of economic development through industrialization were instituted and agriculture has everywhere declined as the major employer of labour. If the crude determinism of some of the functionalist theories were correct there should have been marked changes in family structure. In fact, relatively few changes flowed directly from higher levels of living, throwing considerable doubt on the assumption that Caribbean forms of family are caused by poverty. Roberts and Sinclair state flatly that 'no fundamental change in family forms has taken place since emancipation' in Jamaica, though as demographers they are well aware of such important things as declining fertility.[27]

Much of the most recent research on Caribbean family life has been inspired by feminist concerns, and particularly with the plight of women heads of households who are obliged to raise children without adequate means. The situation is nicely exemplified by the cases discussed by Helen I. Safa in her study of 157 female garment workers in Puerto Rico.[28] Puerto Rico was the leader among Caribbean societies in developing export-driven industrialization beginning in the 1940s, and its pattern of development became known throughout the region as 'the Puerto Rican model'. Safa begins by sketching in the effects of these developments as agricultural employment declined, displacing mainly male workers, and the demand for low-paid industrial workers, mainly women, increased. The garment industry, the focus of her study, is the largest industrial employer in Puerto Rico; she studied

26 See note 1 above, page 507.

27 George Roberts and Sonja Sinclair, 1978, p.9.

28 Helen I. Safa, 1986.

three factories – one in the city of Mayagüez and two newer plants situated in rural towns several miles from Mayagüez. The patterns of displacement of male labour and the preference for younger women workers discussed by Safa are clearly reminiscent of the early stages of development of the textile industry in Britain or in New England.[29] She shows clearly that in the rural towns young women workers are generally part of large households with multiple wage-earners, so that low wages and the presence of older dependent kin are offset by the relatively high aggregate household income consisting of several wages plus transfer payments such as food stamps and welfare. Although it was easier for women than men to find work in factories, and many men became dependent on the earnings of female household members, this had not affected male familial authority. 'These rural peasant households are still strongly patriarchal, despite the man's loss of earning potential. As they marry, rural women transfer patriarchal authority to their husbands, who are still considered the boss in most households. Husbands often pay the bills, and the wife may turn her pay-cheque over to her husband.'[30] Furthermore, these rural households remain embedded in extensive networks of kin, along which help of various kinds is transmitted.

In the urban area of Mayagüez the women factory workers are older and many of them are married, contributing a considerable share of the expenses of relatively small households, or they are separated or widowed and carrying the whole burden of maintaining a small and relatively kin-isolated household. Under these circumstances, argues Safa, there is a breakdown of patriarchal authority and this is reflected in labour relations. Whereas the younger rural women workers are deferential to managers, 'among these older women, work has contributed to their sense of self-worth and independence and to a breakdown of the patriarchal tradition still prevalent in the rural area. Thus they are more likely to question management's authority and to argue for their rights than younger, rural women.'[31] It appears from her figures that almost one-third of these older women workers are 'formerly married', that is, either divorced or separated, and although this clearly contributes to their sharply reduced economic circumstances the causes of the separation or divorce are not stated.

In the same volume, Bolles discusses the household and family situation of 127 female factory workers in Kingston, Jamaica, in 1978–9.[32] Bolles refers to these households as 'working class' and their members seem to span a fairly wide band of the new urban occupations produced

29 See, for example, Neil J. Smelser, 1959; Tamara K. Hareven and Randolph Langenbach, 1978.

30 Helen I. Safa, 1986, p.91.

31 *Ibid.*, p.95.

32 A. Lynn Bolles, 1986.

by the post-war economic changes referred to above. She is particularly concerned with the worldwide increase in the proportion of households reported to be headed by women, and regards this study as throwing light on the relation between this phenomenon and the existence of 'an insecure and inadequate wage economy based on international monopoly capital,'[33] as well as the greater dependence of female-headed urban households on informal-sector economic activities. Her case materials are interesting for the information they provide about the sheer diversity of economic activity and sources of income, even in households that are clearly a part of the upwardly mobile lower middle class. The case she cites of the widowed Mrs Gordon, whose income as a factory worker is supplemented by the incomes of her two daughters who are secretaries, enabling her to live in her own house in a middle-class area and support her son in secondary school and her deceased husband's brother's daughter in teacher-training college, is quite familiar in modern Jamaica. However, she is surely correct when she points out that female-headed households are generally less fortunate than this one, especially in periods of high unemployment, even when the woman is in a fairly steady visiting union with a man who contributes to the household income. Less certain is the suggestion that the high incidence of female-headed households and unstable conjugal unions can be attributed to the peculiar combination of international capitalism and informal-sector economic activity. Looking back on a supposed golden age of high employment and relatively high wages in the late 1950s and 1960s, she says:

> Fifteen to twenty years of essentially steady working-class wage labour offered those men the kind of financial security and opportunities available to their female counterparts ... During that period, these women and the men made commitments to one another, strengthened by their economic circumstances. They married or established long-term companionships, i.e., stable unions.[34]

The generalization implied in this passage is consistent with the assumptions pointed out at the beginning of this chapter; that these patterns of family life and conjugal union are forced upon the lower and working classes by the economic conditions under which they live. In that respect Bolles' article is typical of most of the work produced under the stimulus of a feminism that lays emphasis upon the undue burdens placed upon women who raise families without the active support of a male conjugal partner.

---

33 *Ibid.*, p.65.
34 *Ibid.*, p.77.

The evidence is conclusive that urban households containing a couple who are married, or in some kind of co-residential conjugal union, are generally economically better off than are female-headed households without a male partner. However, it cannot then be concluded that economic factors cause the unstable unions that leave women struggling to raise children outside wedlock. In spite of the economic declines of the 1980s discussed by both Safa and Bolles, the general trend throughout the Caribbean (with the possible exceptions of Haiti and Guyana) has been toward higher levels of living, increased social mobility, and a considerable expansion of the urban middle class, while at the same time patterns of household composition and family formation have not changed accordingly, as is made clear by Roberts and Sinclair, cited above (page 516).

Further interesting evidence is provided by Karen Fog Olwig, based on the study of 45 households on the island of St John in the American Virgin Islands, carried out in 1974–5. By the time of her study the economy of the island had been completely transformed from the semi-subsistence agriculture co-existing with large cattle farms that had succeeded the original plantation economy after slavery was abolished in 1848. In the mid-1950s Robert Manners reported that the inhabitants had largely abandoned agriculture and were subsisting on remittances from relatives abroad. This has been succeeded by the transformation of St John into what Olwig calls a large tourist park; almost half of the island's acreage was bought up by Laurence Rockefeller and presented to the United States government for conversion into a national park administered by the Park Service. This park, along with the Caneel Bay Resort, attracts thousands of tourists and a large number of North American part-time residents who have built houses there, providing wage work that sustains the 2,500 inhabitants. As she says, this wage employment 'allows many of them to live in modern housing and own cars. Affluence finally seems to have come to St John. On the surface, the establishment of the park and the growth of tourism have been of great benefit to the island society... many new economic opportunities brought by tourism have carried the peasants into the mainstream of modern Western life.'[35] Along with increased economic prosperity couples have generally substituted legal marriage for the common-law unions that were previously common as a prelude to marriage, but this has not altered patterns of conjugal instability, since there is a commensurate increase in divorce, separation and remarriage that closely matches the developmental cycles of the earlier periods in St John history.[36]

35 Karen Fog Olwig, 1985, p.163.

36 *Ibid.*, p.186.

It could be argued that rising levels of living in the Caribbean have taken place without any change in overall patterns of class inequality, so that relative deprivation remains essentially unchanged.[37] Indeed, some would argue that the gap between rich and poor has widened, thus exaggerating the relative poverty of the lower classes. Furthermore, the economies of the region, dependent on volatile markets for agricultural produce, bauxite, oil and tourism, sustain highly unstable labour markets and are characterized by large-scale and fluctuating unemployment. Some relief has been provided through massive migration to Europe and North America, though it is often the most skilled who emigrate. In Jamaica, the capital city of Kingston now contains more than one-third of the population, including large numbers concentrated in impoverished areas and living on uncertain incomes from 'informal' economic activities. Under those circumstances it is indeed difficult to maintain any kind of stable domestic life, but it would be a mistake to assume that the characteristic shape of Caribbean family life is produced solely through lack of steady incomes. In her discussion of the recent economic changes in St John, US Virgin Islands, Olwig makes the important point that residents do not maintain semi-subsistence activities in fishing and gardening because of any economic imperative; rather, their desire is to maintain some important elements of the culturally constituted exchange system that links kin together. As she perceptively concludes, the St Johnian notion of the family has remained remarkably stable over time, but that 'family' has never been the nuclear family. It has always been rooted in wider kinship solidarities and it is those solidarities which seemingly irrational economic exchanges are designed to preserve in the new conditions of the modern Caribbean.[38]

The family as a socio-cultural system: Some theoretical issues

Although the economic base of contemporary class structure is a crucial datum in the understanding of kinship patterns it is not in any sense a simple determinant of those patterns. Familial and kinship behaviour is partially constituted by unstated and usually unseen assumptions and expectations which are a part of the fabric of society itself, and not just a reflex of economic resources. How is that social fabric to be understood?

37 See Derek Gordon, 1987.

38 See Karen Fog Olwig, 1985, chap.8.

In spite of several decades of criticism of structural-functional theory, Caribbean society is often described in terms of cultural norms and roles transmitted through socialization. These concepts do have limited heuristic value, but they are easily reified into imaginary conformities and deviancies enacted by supposedly rule-governed social actors whose failure to obey the rules must be accounted for by forces external to the social-cultural system – forces such as the economy, the world system of capitalism, or adaptation to a material environment. Such theories have produced widely differing interpretations. The most common is that lower-class family life is disorganized and pathological because of inadequate resources available to maintain a normal pattern of family roles – especially in the case of men who supposedly lack the material basis for playing the role of husband/father. Some scholars have turned this explanation on its head (without altering the fundamental logic of the functional theory), and argued that in a context of extreme economic hardship the lower-class family, especially the lower-class African American, has displayed extraordinary adaptability, and far from being pathological should be regarded as a highly successful institution.[39]

Widespread recognition of the limitations of such mechanistic, functional models in recent social science has encouraged students to pay much closer attention to the processes through which actors construct, reproduce and transform social arrangements, with a consequent displacement of method from broad surveys of household composition, mating typologies and such like, to detailed studies of social practice. In the field of kinship studies this has meant, initially at least, the collection of case studies. The importance of this method of data collection was clearly recognized by the research scholars involved in the Women in the Caribbean Project. Unfortunately, most of the studies in that project used case materials within a continuing structural-functional framework, modified only to include network analysis.

A prerequisite for comprehending changes in patterns of Caribbean family life is to understand the changes that have taken place in the way in which we study and understand kinship. Highly abstract models which measure the relationship of variables derived from aggregate statistics are of little significance unless complemented and corrected by studies that take into account the structures of meaning that infuse and motivate social action, as well as studies of the structured social space within which that action occurs. Scholars who specialize in survey research and demographic analysis have been among the first to realize the need for subjective understanding. Thus,

39 See, for example, Andrew Billingsley, 1968; Joyce A. Ladner, 1971; Robert Hill, 1971, and to some extent Joyce Bennett Justus, 1981, though she places more stress on socialization into a particular pattern of gender identity.

Roberts and Sinclair explain that 'reliance on questionnaires calling for precoded answers of the Yes/No type are wholly inadequate, and at times misleading, when applied to certain forms of information', and they advocate the use of tape recordings to convey 'the attitudes, feelings and values of the respondent in a way which no other approach could capture.'[40] Similarly, J. Massiah, also a demographer, discussing the Women in the Caribbean Project, explains that 'The major object of the project was therefore to identify the subjective meaning of the social realities which women face.'[41] However, it is not surprising that the most intensive studies using such methods have been carried out by anthropologists, and that it is in the discipline of anthropology that the most far-reaching theoretical reconsiderations have been made.

Household, family and kinship

For hundreds of years it has seemed natural to collect information on families by listing the inhabitants of 'households' and recording their relationship to each other. There were moments in the history of Caribbean plantation societies when populations were tallied on other bases. Slaves, and the indentured workers who replaced them after emancipation, were sometimes housed in barracks. Planters frequently listed their slaves without reference to location or relationship, just as they listed their draught animals. But whenever family relations were at issue, the household was the unit of study. Unfortunately the concept of household is singularly inappropriate for capturing the complexities of Caribbean kinship and family life.

Households are both real and important, of course. As in most societies Caribbean peoples build houses in which they cook, eat, sleep and raise their children. Some of those houses are remarkably attractive and have been celebrated in print.[42] However, the European assumption – incorporated uncritically into much social science – that the normal, natural core of a household group is a married couple with their own children, is a source of confusion. Although many, perhaps most, domestic groups do consist of such a collection of individuals, many do not, and family relationships often stretch beyond the bounds of any one domestic group. This was already recognized by Long, in the passage quoted earlier, when he says of eighteenth-century slaves that they 'are all married (*in their way*) to a husband, or wife,

40 George Roberts and Sonja Sinclair, 1978, p.252.
41 Joycelin Massiah, 1986, p.1.
42 See Pamela Gosner, 1982.

pro tempore, or have other family connexions, in almost every parish throughout the island; so that one of them, perhaps, has six or more husbands or wives, in several different places.'[43] The households of eighteenth-century planters, with their extensive complements of servants, and collections of 'outside' children, also deviated sharply from the imagined norm. Detailed genealogical studies carried out in Jamaica and Guyana show that it is still common for adults to enter into multiple unions, for women to have several 'sets' of children, and for children to be moved from house to house in a complex pattern of fostering.[44] Although at any one moment it may be the case that a majority of households appear to be simple nuclear family households consisting of a man and a woman in some kind of conjugal union, along with their children, this does not justify the conclusion that the normal Caribbean family is nuclear and any other pattern is deviant, abnormal or disorganized.

Gary Brana-Shute's study of a group of men who regularly frequented a neighbourhood bar in the Suriname capital city of Paramaribo provides some vivid examples of the way in which men are both marginal to, and yet an integral part of, households.[45] Although the sample is small, and Suriname cannot be taken to represent the Caribbean as a whole, the patterns of interaction between men and the women with whom they have children are easily recognizable in other countries. The men who frequent the *winkel* (the equivalent of the English-speaking Caribbean's rum shop) are neither poor nor middle class. They are working men with enough money to enable them to participate in the reciprocity system of the regular patrons of the bar, and have enough left over to maintain relationships with – usually – several women.

The case of Marcell, a skilled blue-collar worker, is remarkably similar to cases collected in Jamaica,[46] and could be duplicated in almost any Caribbean society. In his early twenties, Marcell earns a relatively large amount of money by local standards.[47] Brana-Shute reports that in one month Marcell earned Sf435 (the equivalent at the time of the fieldwork of about $250 US).[48] A week after receiving his pay-cheque he had only Sf25 left. The first Sf102 went to pay off his two-week bar bill at the *winkel* (Brana-Shute notes that some women manage to support themselves and their children on less than Sf60 per month). The next largest amount, Sf100, went to his present partner with whom he

43 Edward Long, 1774 (1972), vol. 2, pp.414–15.

44 See Raymond T. Smith, 1988; Averille White, 1986; Erna Brodber, 1986; and Jean Jackson, 1982.

45 Gary Brana-Shute, 1979; see also Willem F. L. Buschkens, 1974, for material on Suriname Creole family life.

46 See Raymond T. Smith, 1982, p.132.

47 Gary Brana-Shute, 1979, pp.24–7, 75–9, 82–107.

48 In 1974 one Suriname florin (Sf) was equal to approximately 57 US cents.

shares a small house (and some of that money found its way to her family). Since he had lived for much of his life with his paternal aunt, he continues to give her financial support; this month he gave her Sf50, and another Sf30 went to her daughter, his cousin, for the care of her children. Two women with whom he maintains visiting relationships received Sf25 and Sf10, while his sister was given Sf10, and another Sf14 was used to pay rent for the house where he spends most of his time. Whatever prevents Marcell from settling down into a stable marriage, it is not poverty. Brana-Shute is careful to point out that middle-class men, who are generally established in stable marriages, do not frequent the *winkel* on a regular basis, nor are the very poor able to do so. Nonetheless, it would be a mistake to assume that the pattern of extra-residential relations exemplified by Marcell is confined to a narrow segment of the population. Visiting unions are common at all levels of the social hierarchy.

This case, and the many others like it, are crucial for understanding that the patterns of domesticity, and of conjugal unions, are not coerced by poverty. In a paper dealing with a small sample of working women in Montserrat, Yolande T. Moses lays a great deal of stress on the inability of men to live up to the ideals of male gender roles, but she quite rightly points to the nature of the roles themselves and the manner in which male children are socialized into particular patterns of behaviour such that they are not taught 'responsibility, independence and flexibility'.[49] Money is profoundly significant for Marcell, but not because he is short of it. Money is the instrument through which he establishes the very meaning of his identity and personality, at least within the confines of his class and social ambience. Brana-Shute discusses with considerable sensitivity the way in which Marcell's apparently spendthrift habits locate him within a meaningful social world. Feminists may not be so tolerant of actions that appear irresponsible to them, but these patterns have developed over a long period of time in societies with a combination of rigid class hierarchies and male dominance over women.

In order to understand the way in which these factors structure patterns of family relationship it is necessary to examine the system of marriage and mating.

Marriage and the social hierarchy

The Europeans who settled the Caribbean, driving out or killing off the aboriginal inhabitants, and importing bound labour of various kinds, established

49 Yolande T. Moses, 1981, p.511.

laws regulating marriage and family relations based upon those of their respective European homelands. They were never exactly the same laws because they had to reflect the social conditions of the colonies, and especially they had to take account of slavery and the racial regimes that derived from it.

Martínez Alier[50] demonstrated the importance of the legal regulation and restriction of marriage between Whites and free persons of colour in Cuba, and it is evident that the contradictions within colonial Spanish laws in respect of race were pervasive throughout the Spanish New World colonies. Ramón A. Gutiérrez provides detailed evidence of the way in which Catholic doctrine and Spanish laws were distorted in order to accommodate slavery and sexual domination in New Mexico.[51] In both cases restrictions on marriage were accompanied by the widespread practice of concubinage of high-status men with lower-status women, and the proliferation of 'outside', or illegitimate, children.

These practices were not peculiar to the Spanish colonies. Lazarus-Black shows in detail the manner in which the British colonists in Antigua reshaped English law to meet the requirements of a slave regime. However, the slave regime was not just divided into slave and free, black and white. Antiguan colonial society 'differentiated individuals on the basis of their property, position within the division of labour, religious affiliation, and race, and discouraged alliances between men and women of different categories.'[52] The hierarchical distinctions among Whites affected marriage laws even before slavery was fully established; late-seventeenth-century Antiguan laws controlled sexual relations between free persons and indentured servants, and these *preceded* laws concerned with slaves.[53] As in England, Antiguan laws placed power in the hands of legitimate males. Women and bastards had no power over either property or persons, but in Antigua (as in other parts of the West Indies) the laws were also shaped to maintain the particular hierarchy of free persons, indentured servants and slaves. Although Antigua did not enact specific laws against racial intermarriage on the Cuba pattern, it imposed differential penalties according to status upon persons found guilty of 'Carnall Coppulation between Christian and Heathen.'[54] By the end of the eighteenth century, when slavery was under attack and amelioration laws were passed, Antiguan law-makers sharply altered the meaning of 'marriage' as it was to apply to slaves; they 'preserved the idea of a faithful union

50 Verena Martínez Alier, 1974 (1989).

51 Ramón A. Gutiérrez, 1991.

52 Mindie Lazarus-Black, 1990, p.67.

53 *Ibid.*, p.77.

54 *Ibid.*, p.74.

between one man and one woman, but without the element of contract. … As a result, the meaning of marriage had been changed.'[55] This special kind of marriage among slaves was encouraged by planters to the extent of making public displays, rewarding couples who stayed together, and recording these 'marriages' in the plantation records. It differed from English law in totally reversing the principle of inheritance of status and property through the father; here slave status was transmitted to offspring through the mother, and paternity remained devoid of legal significance. This principle was general throughout the Caribbean.

Emancipation radically altered the legal environment in which kinship was defined and operated, but practice was much more resistant to change since it was, and is, embedded in a markedly hierarchical social order. Caribbean societies are still obsessed with the question of illegitimacy and the instability of conjugal unions, but the obverse of that preoccupation with illegitimacy and informal sexual unions is the crucial part played by marriage in the maintenance and reproduction of the hierarchical nature of Caribbean societies. As I have argued elsewhere,[56] marriage, co-residential non-legal unions, and visiting unions are all institutionalized throughout Caribbean societies, though they occur with varying frequencies in different classes and in different territories. They are themselves ranked in value just as they are assumed to be appropriate for different social circumstances. Although it continues to be assumed that the family forms and marital institutions of the higher status groups are 'European', that assumption derives its significance only by contrast to the supposedly 'disorganized' (and therefore inferior) forms of the generality of the population. The limited research on higher-status groups has shown a continuing preoccupation with marriage as a device for preserving property, status (particularly the racial component), and family honour through female sexual purity. Verena Martínez-Alier demonstrated the importance of these elements in the value system of nineteenth-century Cuba by focusing on cases involving their violation,[57] but recent research in Jamaica has shown similar patterns among socially dominant families.[58]

Douglass' work also demonstrates that behind the apparent dominance of nuclear-family forms revealed by household surveys, the actual structure of familial relations among the socially prominent is extensive, social life is intensely kinship-dominated, and household boundaries are highly permeable. One finds, too, the marked gender hierarchy that is one of the

55 *Ibid.*, p.78.
56 Raymond T. Smith, 1988.
57 Verena Martínez Alier, 1974 (1989).
58 Lisa Douglass, 1992.

dominant characteristics of all Caribbean societies, and is pervasive throughout the class system.[59]

The class elements most preoccupied with the problem of lower-class family disorganization are those with a deep interest in marking their own higher status and separating themselves from a tainted past. The so-called 'coloured middle class' emerged as a privileged section of slave society as the favoured, but illegitimate, offspring of white men and black or coloured women. Variously termed *mulattoes, gens du couleur*, or *Free Coloured*, these groups were the very embodiment of the concept of racial hierarchy at the same time as they fervently embraced ideals of equality and achievement. With a historical origin in concubinage they became the most ardent proponents of legal, respectable, status-enhancing marriage, and an important component of status continued to be race or colour. At the same time, the men of this group continued to practise the dual-marriage system which enjoined legal marriage to a status equal while permitting non-legal unions with status inferiors.[60]

In spite of the changes of the past forty or fifty years these structural principles continue to inform behaviour. Gender inequality demands that married women observe the rule of sexual fidelity while males are permitted, even expected, to have outside affairs. Women of lower social status recognize that non-legal, visiting unions with men of higher status confer various kinds of social advantage ranging from enhanced employment prospects to better life-chances for 'outside' children. Such advantages do not always materialize, of course, but in hierarchically structured societies they are an important consideration.

In Caribbean societies marriage has always meant higher status and been associated with the consolidation of power and property. The efforts of the churches to infuse into it a set of religious meanings have been only partially successful. In Latin America the Catholic Church has often been the champion of individual rights against parental or societal restrictions, but has never been able to overcome them.[61] In the Protestant Caribbean religion has been an enormously powerful influence but has never been able to establish the indispensability of marriage as a prerequisite for sexual relations; it remains a part of the status system. For the poor, marriage may be a distant goal, to be achieved perhaps late in life, but having little to do with the mundane tasks of raising children and maintaining domestic life.

---

59 See Larissa Adler Lomnitz and Marisol Pérez-Lizaur, 1987, for interesting comparative material on Mexico.

60 See Verena Martínez Alier, 1974 (1989); Raymond T. Smith, 1988; Jack Alexander, 1984.

61 See Verena Martínez Alier, 1974 (1989), pp.48–56; Ramón A. Gutiérrez, 1984.

Caribbean societies display distinctive forms of family life that derive from the manner in which marital patterns, status hierarchies and gender differentiations interact with domestic relations. Kinship is neither weak nor disorganized, contrary to much writing on this subject, and should not be measured by comparison with inappropriate models. This does not mean that social problems, including problems of family relations and child care, do not exist, for they do. Those problems are often exacerbated by poverty, and the disruptions consequent on urbanization and migration also contribute to their prevalence. But these factors do not cause Caribbean peoples to shape their family life in the ways that they do.

The importance of feminist studies

Beginning in the 1970s the feminist movement began to have an impact on the conduct of research in the Caribbean, and this movement was itself an indicator of the growing influence of egalitarian individualism. As explained by Massiah, in her overview of the Women in the Caribbean Project, 'Like women researchers in many regions of the world, WICP researchers were faced with the situation that knowledge of women's experiences in their region has been filtered through studies and methodological tools designed, conducted and interpreted by males.'[62] Many similar statements are to be found prefacing papers coming out of this particular project, some quite sweeping in their condemnation of previous work, though frequently without specific reference. For example:

> Ethnographers, male and female, are themselves products of a dominant system of perception and derive their models of society from male informants whom they find to be more 'articulate'. The alternative views women hold of themselves and the world they live in are submerged and revealed only in so far as they 'fit' and can be expressed through the idiom of the dominant ideology.[63]

Unfortunately this kind of indiscriminate condemnation lacks theoretical articulation, consisting merely of general statements about the bias in observation, as though gathering data exclusively from women would, in itself, solve the problem of conceptualizing gender. It would be unfortunate if

62 Joycelin Massiah, 1986, p.1.
63 Christine Barrow, 1986, p.132.

Caribbean ethnography were to degenerate into a battle over 'perspectives'. Consider the following male perspective on these issues: 'A methodological and analytical concentration on women and children biased almost all prior studies of West Indian society. A relative neglect in the study of males resulted in portraits of Afro-Caribbean society populated almost solely by women and children.'[64] The shift during the 1970s toward studies stressing the female point of view was occasioned less by academic interest than by developments in the societies of the Caribbean, some of them stimulated by the growth of the women's movement in North America.

In 1975 the United Nations launched the International Decade of the Woman, and this set off a burst of activity that included the introduction of new legislation, as well as many new research projects devoted to feminist issues. Cuba was one of the first countries to introduce comprehensive legal reform in the shape of a new Family Code based on several years of public discussion. The Federation of Cuban Women, formed in August 1960, was instrumental in stimulating public discussion of the early drafts of the Code, which was finally enacted on 14 February 1975, to become effective on International Women's Day, 8 March 1975. It is, of course, significant that family legislation should be considered primarily a 'women's issue'. The Cuban Code was prefaced by a statement by the president to the effect that 'obsolete judicial norms from the bourgeois past which are contrary to equality and discriminatory with regard to women and children born out of wedlock...must be replaced.'[65] In spite of the references to the bourgeois past the Code itself seeks to strengthen the institutions of marriage and the family, and goes on to lay out most of the ideals incorporated in the legislation of other Caribbean states, stressing the equal rights of men and women, their mutual obligations in respect of child care, and the obligations of both partners to share in housework and child care. A key element in most new codes is the equal rights of inheritance of children born in and out of wedlock. In Cuba this important right was actually written into the constitution as Article 36, which states: 'All children enjoy equal rights, whether they be conceived inside or outside marriage. All labels indicating illegitimacy are abolished.'[66] While these ideals have been widely disseminated through Caribbean societies over the past 15 or 20 years, it is not yet possible to say what effect they have had, if any, in changing real relationships.[67]

64 Gary Brana-Shute, 1979, p.vii.

65 Cuba, Ministry of Justice, 1975, p.5.

66 Cited in Margaret Randall, 1981, p.44.

67 See Gloria Cumper and Stephanie Daly, 1979, for material on the English-speaking Caribbean.

Attempts to change social behaviour through legal enactment are extremely interesting for the light they throw on emergent ideologies and values, but they also reveal societal contradictions. For example, the laudable desire not to discriminate against children who are born illegitimate would logically reduce the value of marriage, even though marriage and marital stability are proclaimed as the goals of family policy. However, it seems unlikely that these laws will, in themselves, disturb the hierarchical association between marriage and social class. Since the law clearly requires that the paternity of illegitimate children (the status itself is hardly affected by most of the legal reforms, in spite of the brave words of the Cuban Constitution) be established before the rights of the child *vis-â-vis* the father can be enjoyed, many ways of evading paternal responsibility remain. The main effect of these legal reforms will be felt among those sections of the population where visiting unions, non-legal co-residential unions, and legal marriage are of minimal status significance – namely the lower and lower middle classes – though it is precisely here that women will feel most acutely the diminishing of the relative status of the legal wife and her 'inside' children.

Gender

Feminist studies have certainly been important in drawing attention to certain neglected dimensions of the Caribbean social order, but they have also pointed to the importance of gender *as an analytical concept* without, as yet, fully exploiting it. No amount of 'letting women speak for themselves', as Barrow puts it,[68] will facilitate an understanding of the way in which gender – masculinity *and* femininity – are socially and culturally constructed in and through the practices of everyday life, unless such speaking is understood as an integral part of the structure in place. This is the importance of the feminist turn in social theory; it focuses attention on a neglected dimension of social action, a dimension that is general throughout the society and not confined to the actions, thoughts or utterances of women. Therefore, feminism is important to an understanding of contemporary family life and to the recent history of the Caribbean family, not because it has induced women to take a more equal part in social life (there is some doubt as to the extent of actual changes in this regard, as is noted by Anderson),[69] but because it draws attention to a powerful set of mechanisms through which the society as a whole reproduces itself.

68 Christine Barrow, 1986, p.133.
69 Patricia Anderson, 1986, pp.295–6.

Social science followed common sense in assuming that the family of man, woman and their children is a *natural* phenomenon through which biological and social reproduction is achieved. This assumption is deeply rooted and embodied in the frequent assertions about the damage inflicted on children by being separated from one or both their parents.[70] Integral to this image of the family as a natural unit is the related assumption that males and females are specialized in both biological and social reproduction. Women, it is believed, are naturally suited for bearing and caring for children, while men are naturally suited to provide for and protect the mother-child unit, so that a complex pattern of personal and social characteristics derives from this natural division of labour. Upon this foundation is built a complex pattern of what used to be called sex-role differentiation.

The term *gender* gained currency in order to stress that such patterns of sex-role differentiation do not derive from natural differences between men and women, but are culturally constructed and socially institutionalized patterns that are ideologically justified by reference to assumed natural differences. Male domination of women and complex structures of exploitation go far beyond any conceivable requirement of the bearing and suckling of infant children, and this is true even in societies that espouse values of individualism and equality. Furthermore, gender constructions do not confine themselves to the processes associated with biological reproduction. They effloresce into complex differentiations in work patterns, notions of legal and religious competence, assumptions about mental ability and moral adequacy. There is good reason to believe that these cultural constructions of gender are not merely secondary rationalizations of 'real' sexual differences, but that sex itself is largely a cultural construction in the sense that physical differences are a very small part of the culturally constructed perception of those differences.[71]

The mechanisms of societal reproduction of which gender is such an important part begin at the top. In every Caribbean territory there is a section of the population that is, significantly, designated 'the prominent *families*'. The 1956 study of Puerto Rico by Julian Steward and his students contained a chapter by Raymond L. Scheele on 'The prominent families of Puerto Rico'.[72] Scheele establishes first the importance of race as a component of this group's identity. Although persons with some African or Indian ancestry may belong to what is sometimes described as one large family, the group was essentially constituted as being white. Much is made of 'the double standard'

70 For example, 'residential separation of children from either or both their parents probably inflicts as much damage on Jamaicans as the poverty with which it is linked.' M. G. Smith, 1989, p.101.

71 See Thomas Laqueur, 1990, for a persuasive exposition of this idea.

72 Raymond L. Scheele, 1956, pp.418–62.

in sexual relations, a complex cultural and social construction that begins with the differential socialization of boys and girls which becomes most significant from about the age of 14 or 15.

> Boys now have considerable freedom, and men expect them to become involved in affairs with lower-class girls, often with the household maid.... Their relationship with girls of their own class, however, should be romantic. The upper-class girl is chaperoned whenever she goes out with a boy.[73] ... The double standard, although not limited to the prominent families, is a crucial feature among this group. According to this standard, men are fairly free to have premarital affairs and extramarital sexual relations, whereas complete chastity is expected of the women...virility in the male is highly esteemed and ... is largely measured by the number of his amorous adventures ..... The girl, on the other had, traditionally is sheltered, protected, chaperoned, and taught to believe that sex for her should be procreational rather than pleasurable.[74]

All this was related to the system of marriage through which the prominent families reproduced themselves by the judicious selection of family alliances. As Scheele puts it, 'approval of a marriage partner depends upon the prospective husband's potential earning power and the spouse's social position, wealth, and racial background.'[75] The subordination of women within this class was quite evident, as was their culturally defined role of bearing children and reproducing the class system itself.

Less evident is the way in which outside unions – the 'amorous adventures' referred to above – embodied the structural principles of the social order. Lower-status women entered these unions (consciously or unconsciously) precisely because they conferred upon them, and any offspring that resulted, an advantageous prestige that they would not otherwise experience. Scheele argues that the system was changing because 'American influences' were leading to the emancipation of young Puerto Rican wives, but there is ample evidence in his account that such a process was not very far advanced. Eduardo Seda, reporting on field research carried out between 1959 and 1961 in a rural Puerto Rican community, describes in vivid terms the way in which the same pattern of gender hierarchy, operating in reduced economic circumstances, produced unstable marriages and casual sexual encounters rather

73 *Ibid.*, p.437.
74 *Ibid.*, p.441.
75 *Ibid.*, p.442.

than the stable dual-marriage system more common in the past and among the more affluent.[76]

A more recent study of the prominent families of Jamaica has revealed a picture not unlike that of Puerto Rico.[77] However, this study was carried out some 40 years after Scheele's work, and in the wake of a feminist movement that has certainly affected younger women of the Jamaican élite and tempered the sexual adventuring of élite men. Yet, Douglass is still able to write that

> Lower-class men frequently are irregular and irresponsible participants in the role of a father and husband. This may be a means of asserting autonomy from women, but it also entails less authority for these men within the family. Among the middle-class and the family elite, men assert their freedom by their personal autonomy and their outside relations, but they more consistently maintain authority at home and in the family. This male dominated order of things is preserved not only through male initiative, but also by the family women (ladies) who thrust power upon men.[78]

This remarkably perceptive observation cuts to the very heart of the matter, laying bare the largely unstated assumptions about gender that combine with class and racial factors to establish the hierarchical structure of Caribbean societies. As Brana-Shute shows for Paramaribo, power resides in masculinity and for a reasonably well-off working-class man like Marcell the power is made manifest in his support of a multiplicity of partners rather than in a stable marriage (though such a union is by no means precluded for lower-class men). Just why there should be a class difference in the configuration of behaviour is undoubtedly related to the way in which class, gender and race are combined, and here is where it is important to remember that gender is a relational category. As Douglass shows, there is a preoccupation in West Indian societies with the question of what constitutes ladylike behaviour, but such behaviour is not expected of lower-class women.

The failure to distinguish adequately between gender roles and economically inflected familial behaviour is brought out by Quiñones-Arocho in an article reviewing a number of works dealing with recent changes in women's status in Caribbean societies.[79] She shows how diametrically opposed conclusions are drawn from virtually the same data; are women

76 Eduardo Seda, 1973, pp.68–73.

77 Lisa Douglass, 1992.

78 *Ibid.*, p.22.

79 María Isabel Quiñones-Arocho, 1992.

reaping the benefits of recent changes in the direction of more egalitarian gender relations, or is their situation deteriorating? As she perceptively demonstrates, most studies assume that it is changing economic circumstances that produce changes in gender relations, but what is needed is careful study of 'the specificities of gender ideologies and practices' if one is to 'understand the articulation between political and economic circumstances and the particularities of family and kinship forms in the Caribbean.'[80]

Conclusion

In April 1922 Jean Price-Mars, the renowned Haitian diplomat and scholar, gave a talk on the peasant family which he later incorporated as an Appendix in his book on Haitian folklore, *Ainsi Parla L'Oncle.*[81] Concerned to explain the remarkably high rates of illegitimacy in rural Haiti, he wonders whether his audience will not consider 'peasant family' a contradiction in terms. But with a dexterity that one can only envy some seventy years later, he suggests that the Haitian rural family is, at one and the same time, a survival of ancient African forms that also bear a strong resemblance to those of ancient Greece and Rome, a dynamic cultural growth in local Haitian conditions, and perhaps an evolutionary stage in a transition to a full Christian life. He describes a courtship and traditional non-Christian marriage ceremony, complete with formal letter of request and payment of bride-price (called dowry by Price-Mars), observed in Kenscoff in rural Haiti. Anticipating much of the subsequent debate over cultural origins he asks whether these customs are 'daughters of our soil or rather do they come to us from across the sea'. Although he asserts that Africa is the origin of most of them, he judiciously argues that 'None of them are entirely local creations, yet none have reached us without alteration. They exist in our personality itself, the whole charged with reminiscences and stamped by successive mutations which mark the complexity of our ethnic origins.'[82] As if sensing that this idyllic picture of a patriarchal family regime derived ultimately from Africa is less than the whole story, Price-Mars suddenly shifts his attention from the protective male who is the head of the African family group to the much-remarked veneration of the African for his mother. In yet another turn he points out that in 'Saint Domingue the godmother has almost replaced the mother in the affection of

80 *Ibid.*, p.93.
81 Jean Price-Mars, 1928 (1983).
82 *Ibid.*, p.203.

her child; it is because the child, hardly nubile, is torn from his mother whose service is required for exploitation.'[83] Thus the white race, through slavery, 'during two centuries of outrageous promiscuity, of corruption, and of degeneration... sullied the age-old chastity of the black woman imposing upon her the brutal rule of concubinage.'[84]

I have cited Price-Mars at some length because he draws together a number of conflicting explanatory threads that were to be singled out for separate treatment in subsequent writing on the Caribbean family. There is much to be said for his attempt to hold them all together in what might now be regarded as a post-modernist discourse. But the world has moved on and one would be hard pressed to find today the courtly practice of seeking written permission from kin before establishing a consensual union. Nor is there any evidence that the Caribbean family is slowly evolving toward some abstract Christian ideal. Price-Mars, for all his invocation of Africa, does not consider the full range of variation in family arrangements to be found in that continent, much less in the world at large. Had he done so he would have strengthened his case for tolerance.

Once one abandons the idea that the contemporary Caribbean family is some distorted version of a 'natural' nuclear type, it becomes possible to consider its strengths and weaknesses more realistically. As Edward Long perceived in the eighteenth century, unstable marriage and a pattern of multiple unions were not incompatible with careful and effective child-rearing. In the rural Caribbean of past generations, and in some places today, extensive networks of kin facilitated the distribution of resources in such a way that child-rearing was not an intolerable burden on women without husbands. Although gender hierarchies clearly placed men in a dominant position, from which they exploited women, those same women had a secure place in the wider kinship system as mothers and sisters. The changes of the past forty years have transformed the social, economic and political context within which kinship, marital and family relations exist. Massive urbanization has left many women cut off from the support of kin, even though there is a remarkable resilience in the strength of kinship ties that stretch from city to the countryside, and even across the seas. The patterns of multiple unions that were set in small communities where men accepted a broad range of responsibilities for the support of kin, have often been replaced by similar behaviour in a much more fragmented urban social milieu where women are quickly abandoned.

As the twenty-first century begins there have been marked changes in the patterns of family life in the industrialized countries of Europe and North

83 *Ibid.*, pp.216–17.
84 *Ibid.*, p.217.

America. Shrinkage in the size of households, a more widespread acceptance of non-legal co-residential unions, a decline in the stigma attached to illegitimacy, and a continuing increase in the frequency of divorce, have all been interpreted as signalling the decline of the family. It is tempting to assume that there is a basic similarity between these developments and the patterns of Caribbean family life discussed in this chapter. The temptation must be resisted. The changes in Europe and North America represent a continuation of trends long apparent in those societies, and reflect a growing individualism and egalitarianism. Those trends have some resonance in the Caribbean, but the structural features of this region are fundamentally different, so that apparent similarities in family life must be treated with extreme caution.

The family in the contemporary Caribbean continues to be shaped by, and an integral part of, the hierarchical structure of society as a whole. Considerable headway has been made in dismantling the legacy of colonialism, and there is a general acceptance of ideals of equality, opportunity and freedom. As in the metropolitan countries, those ideals frequently serve as vehicles for the institutionalization of inequalities justified by 'achievement'. But here in the Caribbean egalitarianism (conceived as equality of opportunity to become unequal) has fewer opportunities for embodiment, and the remnants of an older system of inequalities are everywhere evident. The family, as the locus of generation of the classes themselves, has been slow to change. The dual-marriage system, in which women are the tokens in male strategies of power, continues to flourish. As we saw in the case of Marcell of Paramaribo, it is not poverty which shapes the patterns of family relations, but the striving of men to establish a sense of valued being; a striving in which women are, for most of the time and for whatever reason, active accomplices.

15

Ideology, identity, culture

Rex Nettleford

Introduction

The Caribbean is the crossroads where different civilizations have met, criss-crossed and interacted for five centuries. In light of the region's historical experience and existential reality, it remains a rich and vibrant laboratory in the quest for definition(s) about self and society.

The region continues to be described in sundry ways in that quest. Ideological designations have found their way from the North Atlantic into the political vocabulary of the Caribbean's struggles out of the colonialism and client-statehood consequent on persistent designs for control of or influence over the region by external forces.

So, in response, nationalism has been common to the 'progressive forces' in the region's nation-states that have emerged from the time when Haiti emancipated itself from chattel slavery by armed resistance and Simón Bolívar conducted liberationist assaults against Spanish rule in the nineteenth century, to the twentieth-century post-war self-government movements leading to the establishment of a number of independent nation-states stretching from the Bahamas in the north to Guyana in the south.

Since then, individual territories have identified themselves or have been identified in whole or in part as democratic socialist (Jamaica under Michael Manley and the People's National Party in the 1970s); as communist (Cuba under Fidel Castro and the Cuban Communist Party since the early 1960s and Grenada under Maurice Bishop and his People's Revolutionary Government between 1979 and 1983); as democratic capitalist (the Dominican Republic since the 1960s and Jamaica under Edward Seaga and the Jamaican Labour Party throughout the 1980s); or as co-operative republican (Guyana under Forbes Burnham and his People's National Congress throughout the 1960s, 1970s and 1980s). The 'mixed economy' label provided safe haven for most West Indian polities which oscillated pragmatically between the bipolarity of the Cold War's opposing extremities of communism and liberal democracy, between the late 1940s and the late 1980s. All the West Indian nations laid claim to the ideological pedigree of 'anti-imperialist', 'populist', 'progressive' politics. Within this framework, a certain pluralism was simultaneously invoked, in the name of sovereignty and justice. In the matter of ideology, as in identity, the Caribbean retained its character as a place of options.

The plurality of the region's linguistic inheritance had a similar effect. So the region comprises and has been described severally as:

(1) the Spanish-speaking Caribbean (covering the Hispanic or Ibero-Caribbean countries of the Dominican Republic, Cuba and Puerto Rico – despite its Anglo-Saxon United States connection – as well as those Latin American countries washed by the Caribbean Sea, Nicaragua, Costa Rica, Panama, Colombia and Venezuela);
(2) the anglophone Caribbean (the islands of the former British West Indies, Guyana and Belize as well as the US Virgin Islands acquired by purchase from Denmark early in the twentieth century);
(3) the francophone Caribbean (Haiti, Guadeloupe, Martinique, Guyane, St Martin); and
(4) the Dutch-speaking Caribbean (comprising Curaçao, Bonaire, Aruba, Suriname, Saba, St Eustatius and St Maarten, though the three last-named speak English for daily social intercourse).

But there also exist other Caribbeans, linguistically speaking. There also exist 'Creole' languages ranging from the *srnan tonga* of Suriname, through *kweyol* in the French-speaking countries cited above as well as in former French colonies later ceded to the British (e.g., St Lucia, Dominica and Grenada), to *papiamentu* in Curaçao and *Jamaica Talk*, the Twi-based 'nation-language' of Jamaica.

In the matter of ethnicity the region has by and large tried to escape explicit racial identification. Widespread miscegenation over time has everywhere defied claims to ethnic purity in any case. Yet different groups of West Indians continue to describe themselves either as 'Africans' (especially in Guyana where such a categorization has carried political significance, and among Jamaican Rastafarians in their objection to being severed from ancestral hearths) or as 'Afro-Caribbean' or 'African Caribbean' (usually in celebration of the African presence in Caribbean history and development). The term 'Indo-Caribbean' identifies the descendants of indentured labourers brought to the region from India after the abolition of slavery in the nineteenth century while 'Indios', a designation peculiar to the Dominican Republic, carries currency reportedly among many Dominicans not anxious to identify with the African legacy. 'Mulatto', 'people of colour', and 'Creole' are terms associated with the celebration of the mixed-blood ideal (*mestizaje*) and in the case of 'Creole' sometimes especially with the pedigree of French European stock (as in Trinidad). The category 'white' refers to persons of pure Caucasian stock or, as in the case of 'Jamaica Whites', to persons who have been genetically deblackened by generations of conscious 'upward' mobility via cross-breeding. The matter of racial identity is indeed historically and culturally determined by a plurality of factors driving some people to a hyphenated persona resulting as much in self-doubt and psychic confusion as in sophisticated and painless acceptance of heterogeneity as a valid basis for human existence.

Religious pluralism is no less a feature of the multi-sourced Caribbean. Christian orthodoxy evidenced in Roman Catholicism and Anglicanism as imperial denominations as well as Protestantism in all its varied forms has had to share ecumenical space with Hinduism, Islam, the Baha'i faith and Buddhism; and inter-faith exercises have been known to be a feature of special occasions in Trinidad or on separate campuses of the regional University of the West Indies.

But native-born and native-bred religious expressions among the mass of the population have found dynamic and cogent force in such creolized forms as the voodoo in Haiti, Santería of Cuba, Mita in Puerto Rico and Palo in the Dominican Republic, Winti in Suriname, Pukkumina (Pocamania) of Jamaica, Zion Revivalism and its variants evident all over, Orisha (Shango) of Trinidad, and the later Rastafarianism which has spread since the 1960s from its native Jamaica not only to the rest of the region but into the Caribbean diaspora throughout North America and Western Europe – thanks to the pervasive influence of reggae, the urban Jamaican musical form made popular by a galaxy of superstars led by Robert Nesta (Bob) Marley who became a Rastafarian.

For all the region's diversity and threatened continuing fragmentation, all the above may be said to speak to a process of formation of a Caribbean identity rooted in a culture shared by all who inhabit the communities of the region, in terms of a history of valiant effort to forge out of an unruly diversity integrated 'wholes' that serve to foster and facilitate survival and beyond.

I

Caribbean culture, in so far as it is conceded to exist, is at once the cause, occasion and result of evolved and evolving paradoxes. The psychic inheritance of dynamic response to disparate elements interacting to find form and purpose within set geographical boundaries over time could not have produced otherwise.

Derek Walcott, poet and Nobel laureate, had long ago described the cultural dialectic of his region's historical experience and contemporary reality in the following way: '[b]ut the tribe in bondage learned to fortify itself by cunning *assimilation of the religion of the Old World.* What seemed to be *surrender was redemption.* What seemed the *loss* of tradition was its renewal. What seemed *the death* of faith was its *rebirth.*'[1] Caribbean existential reality is here portrayed as a creature of paradox. Surface appearances may well be masks for their opposites. What one sees is not likely to be what one gets. Edward Kamau Brathwaite, the poet-historian, summed up the contradictions in his seminal essay *Contradictory Omens,* a profound statement on cultural diversity and integration in the Caribbean.[2] Fragmentation is visible, the unity is 'submarine'.

My own conclusions on the anguished urgency of Caribbean cultural identity find focus in the agony of choice encountered in the process of becoming in a world caught in dynamic interaction, and in quest of inner logic and consistency.[3] Antonio Benítez-Rojo, the Cuban novelist and social commentator, echoed this in his engaging essay 'The Caribbean and the Post-Modern Era' with:

> ... every Caribbean person knows, intuitively at least, that the Caribbean is much more than a system of binary oppositions. It can also be seen as a cultural sea without frontiers ... how shall we articulate consistently the magical alongside the scientific, the metaphysical with the epistemological, the mythological with the historiographical, Oshun or Shango with Karl Marx, Mackandal with Michael Foucault?[4]

Turbulence and chaos are ready handmaidens to creativity and renewal. The entire Caribbean, and indeed all of the modern Americas of which the Caribbean, like the United States, is only one part, are the creatures of the awesome process of cross-fertilization following on the encounters between the old civilizations of Europe, Africa and Asia on foreign soil and those which they, in turn, had with the old Native American civilizations developed on American soil long before Christopher Columbus set foot on it. It is a development that has helped to shape the history and modern condition of the world for some half a millennium and one that has resulted in distinctive culture-spheres in the Western Hemisphere, each claiming its own inner logic and consistency. The Caribbean, at the core of which are a number of island nations, themselves in subregional groupings, is conscious of the dynamics of

1 Derek Walcott, 1974, p.7, my emphasis.
2 Edward Brathwaite, 1974.
3 Rex Nettleford, 1978.
4 Antonio Benítez-Rojo, 1995, p.256.

its development. For it rests firmly on the agonizing and challenging process 'actualized in simultaneous acts of negating and affirming, demolishing and constructing, rejecting and reshaping'.[5]

Nowhere is this more evident than in the creative arts, themselves a strong index of a people's cultural distinctiveness and identity. Admittedly, other indices of culture such as linguistic communication, which underpins the oral and indigenous scribal literatures of the region, religion and kinship patterns, reveal the texture and internal diversity that are the result of cross-fertilization of differing elements.

The result is an emerging lifestyle, world-view, and nascent ontology and epistemology that all speak to Caribbean historical experience and existential reality, in some cases struggling to gain currency and legitimacy world wide (and even among some of its own people) for being native-born and native-bred. For this is the original meaning of 'Creole'. Whites born in the American colonies were regarded as 'Creoles' by their metropolitan cousins. And the Jamaican-born slaves were similarly differentiated from their 'salt-water Negro' colleagues freshly brought in from West Africa. The term was soon to be hijacked by or attributed to the mulatto (half-caste) who defiantly claimed certified rootedness in the colonies – a status not as easily claimed by the person of African or European descent whose ancestry lay elsewhere, it was felt, other than in the Caribbean or the Americas.

To this day genuine Caribbean expressions are regarded as those that have been 'creolized' into indigenous form and purpose distinctively different from the original elements from which those expressions first sprang. With some of those original elements, especially those from a European source, themselves reinforcing their claims on the region whether through politics, economic control or cultural penetration, the Caribbean is becoming even more conscious not only of its own unique expressions but also of the dynamism and nature of the process underlying these expressions. These in turn constitute the basis for the claims made for a *Caribbean* identity.

II

In the Commonwealth Caribbean such identity and expressions invariably bring to ready consciousness the resonant sounds of 'cheng' and 'ping' of the reggae in electronic flight and the steelpan backing calypso singers or accompanying road marchers in carnival. These follow on a time when the

5 Rex Nettleford, 1978, p.181.

mambo, merengue, chachacha and the *son* bore surface testimony to the aesthetic energy and artistic vigour of the mass of the wider Caribbean population, the real sources and determiners of a Caribbean ethos which is the hallmark of any true 'identity'.

For it was to their hounfors, Santería rituals, Shango yards and Pocomania tables that one turned for those treasures of creativity which followed on the early encounters between civilizations from the Old World of western Europe and western Africa on foreign soil.[6] This soil stretches from Nova Scotia along the eastern seaboard of what became the United States of America, bulging out into the Caribbean Sea linked by an archipelago of limestone rocks which foreign tourists are encouraged to call 'pearls' and 'paradise', and projecting down the South American coast to northern Uruguay. That tract of real estate became distinctive not simply for the institutions of slavery and the colonial system that supported and all but extended western Europe's sustained experiment in human degradation and labour exploitation. It became distinctive because of the internal process of adaptation, adjustment, change and dynamic creativity dictated by survival needs and sustained by the invincibility of the human spirit. Caribbean civilization is indeed a creature of paradox, a model of contradictions, and textured diversity.

In so far as 'survival' meant 'identity', and identity in turn became a function of survival, the suffering, severed hordes of humanity demonstrated from very early on their deep grasp of the fact that 'the material base of Caribbean existence must always be supported and informed by a native cultural vision which has absolute confidence in its human worth', as George Lamming, the Caribbean writer, once stated.[7] It is this piece of knowledge and the commitment to its dynamic application that has guided the efforts at articulating a Caribbean identity – more aptly, a Caribbean civilization (or the germ of it) now that power has been transferred to most of those limestone rocks (by negotiation, granted) following on the more

---

6 From a vast literature, see (among much else) on voodoo: Harold Courlander, 1960; Michel S. Laguerre, 1989; Leslie G. Desmangles, 1992. On Santería: William Bascom, 1950, pp.4–68; George Brandon, 1993. On the Orisha movement (Shango): George Eaton Simpson, 1965; William Bascom, 1972; Maureen Warner-Lewis, 1991; James Houk, 1995. On Kumina/Pocomania: Edward Seaga, 1969, pp.3–13; Maureen Warner-Lewis, 1977. On Rastafarianism: M. G. Smith *et al.*, 1960; Joseph Owens, 1976; Leonard E. Barrett, 1968 (1977); Barry Chevannes, 1994; *idem*, 1995. For a good general survey, including chapters on voodoo, *candomblé* (Brazil), Santería and Revivalism, see Joseph Murphy, 1994. See also chap.16, this volume.

7 See George Lamming, 1985.

epic independence of Haiti and Cuba, gained by force of arms, in 1804 and 1902 respectively.

Such a history of severance, suffering and survival is supposed to be a thing of the past and many Caribbean inhabitants would wish to be well rid of it even by way of historical amnesia. But the region is not likely to promise any such escape since the processes set in place by slavery, colonialism and the plantation economy continue apace, replete with paradoxes. These are not likely to disappear in light of yet unrealized efforts at integration as in the case of significant post-Federation attempts at greater and more effective functional co-operation between a set of countries in the region.[8] 'Integration' efforts are also evident within individual societies where the 'white bias' persists in the face of black majorities as in Jamaica and arguably in post-revolutionary Cuba, or where the claims of a Euro-African posture defy a numerically strong Asian (i.e., Indian) presence as in the case of Trinidad and Guyana.[9] There is, as well, the clear evidence of designs for intensified cultural penetration via satellite and continuing economic control from outside via the International Monetary Fund (IMF). Political independence, which has been regarded as a positive and ennobling response to the systemic denial of freedom and self-expression for the mass of the population, is now seen as having failed, not having delivered all that it promised. The decade of the nineties witnessed the retention on the Caribbean political landscape of 'dependencies' of Britain,

---

8 Since the break-up of the Federation of the West Indies (1958–62), the Commonwealth Caribbean has made several attempts to maintain strong economic social and cultural links. The Treaty of Chaguaramas (1973) led to the establishment of a Caribbean Community and a Caribbean Common Market (Caricom). The regional University of the West Indies was allowed to survive the federation; a Caribbean Development Bank has been in operation since October 1969, when it was established; it came into force on 26 January 1970. Collaboration in the fields of sports (cricket), the arts (Caribbean Festival of Arts, or Carifesta, the spread of carnival and calypso throughout the region and of reggae from Jamaica to the Eastern Caribbean) and the media (Caribbean Broadcasting Union, a Caribbean News Agency – CANA, etc.) has been encouraged and flourishes. In 1989 the Heads of Caricom Governments Meeting in Grenada decided to set up the West Indies Commission 'to formulate proposals for advancing the goals of the Treaty of Chaguaramus.' The Commission reported in 1992, calling for 'action' (see West Indian Commission, 1992).

9 See David Dabydeen and Brinsley Samaroo, 1987; also John Gaffar LaGuerre, 1974; and Leo Despres, 1964. In 1980 there were 231,330 persons identified as 'Negro/Black' and 389,760 as 'East Indian' in Guyana (*Population Census of Guyana*, 1980, vol. 2, p.476, Table 7.2.1.) In 1990, 'Indians' were 40.3 per cent and 'Africans' 39.6 per cent of the population of Trinidad & Tobago (*Population and Housing Census of Trinidad & Tobago*, 1990, vol.II, p.100, Chart 2).

the Netherlands, the United States and France scattered all over the region. To many of the inhabitants of the US Virgin Islands, the Netherlands Antilles, Montserrat, the British Virgin Islands, the Cayman Islands, the Turks & Caicos Islands, Martinique, Guadeloupe and Guyane, political independence is not a clear option. For them such a status may well mean penury.[10] They came to this conclusion looking at the economic fate of Jamaica, Guyana and Trinidad & Tobago, which were all part of the vanguard in the fight for self-government and the latest to join the earlier independent Haiti, Cuba and the Dominican Republic; and the last named three could none of them be considered 'economic miracles' of the Caribbean in the twentieth century.

Yet even while such reservations are expressed, these dependencies seek greater cultural bonds with the newly independent countries which are generally felt to have achieved greater cultural certitude as part of their liberation process. It is possible to regard the Caribbean as a 'cultural unit' without its having to be politically independent. This is indeed yet another paradox to those Caribbean men and women who recall that the triumph of colonialism had a great deal to do with the control of the minds and aesthetic vision of the colonized and that the self-government movement advocated the unlocking of the creative potential (collectively and individually) of the tribe(s) in bondage as much as it fought for the acquisition of symbols of statehood.

Back in the independent nations of the regions, the notion of identity and the expressions of it must, in the post-colonial era, take into account such variables as the administration, distribution and location of power, economic viability and sovereignty with respect to how the region relates to the rest of the world geo-politically, economically and culturally. The clear and established 'Caribbean expressions', which have been the subject of anthropological investigation and tourist curiosity and have served as mild entertainments for an outside world that expects minstrelsy from exotic climes, must now be seriously put into perspective. For in contemporary life, identity goes beyond jump-up and calypso, beyond reggae, and beyond exteriorities of dreadlock, red-green-and-gold woollen cap and the smoking of marijuana as a sacrament, regarded by many as the essence of *exotica Caribbeana.*

It goes, in fact, into the interiorities of self-determination, sovereignty (both territorial and cultural) and independence for individuals and nations

---

10 See World Bank, 1993, pp.51–72. These consist of papers prepared for the June 1992 meetings for the Caribbean Group for Cooperation in Economic Development (CGCE), dealing with human-resource development and poverty.

alike. And it is precisely for this reason that the centuries of popular cultural expression by the mass of the population, who were always central to the process of creolization or indigenization, must be taken into account. After all, it is that historical experience which now informs existential reality, giving to the Caribbean well-articulated parameters of concern in building nations and shaping societies as part of a still-emerging civilization.

Contemporary identity in Caribbean terms must therefore take into consideration not only the notions or theories that have been employed to articulate, explain and comprehend the phenomenon itself, but also the divisive forces of geography, colonization and the distinctive 'culture-spheres' resulting from the geo-politics of superpower rivalry over centuries of plantation slavery and mercantilist greed.

The realities of the latter half of the twentieth century, when the notion of the region being an 'American Mediterranean' followed on its proven strategic importance during the Second World War and the ensuing Cold War, forced the region back to its history of resistance and efforts at self-determination, as well as the deep social forces which long gave it ideal, form and purpose.

Yet, in February 1982, President Reagan of the United States of America unveiled a plan to promote economic development and fight communism in the Caribbean Basin.[11] This was long in coming and it did not disappoint many who had long entertained fears that the strategic importance of the Caribbean to a neighbouring superpower would finally determine the initiatives by that superpower to have control over the region's mind as well as its matter, or at least to have it 'develop' in directions compatible with the geo-political needs of that superpower. For Reagan's Basin Initiative did take a position of far-reaching cultural significance in the scheme of Caribbean development.

The notion that the region should be a satellite of this or that superpower is itself a denial of the Caribbean having its own inner logic and consistency, its own sense of direction, its own vision independent, in significant ways, of external factors, and possessing a history and set of experiences that are peculiar to itself, unique and discrete. The view of the Caribbean as the fourth border of the United States, as an extension of both Europe and its cultural extension (the United States), or as a neo-colonial outpost still to be captured, tamed and controlled by this or that ideological system, fits into the

11 See Carmen D. Deere *et al.*, 1990, chap.6. The Caribbean Basin Initiative was a proposed plan of trade and investment incentives designed 'to improve the economic well being of the Caribbean area' and enacted into a law known as the Caribbean Basin Economic Recovery Act (CBERA). See also Kathy McAfee, 1991, chap.3, for an account of the 'failure of the Initiative'.

picture of a region without its own inner dynamic and perhaps without its own identity. George H. Bush's Enterprise of the Americas Initiative (EAI), which came later, was conceived in the same vein.[12]

The fractious, fragile nature of the region aids and abets the perpetuation of such monstrosities of perception; and the continuing economic dependency of the region on the North Atlantic nations reinforces among persons living within the region the notion that nothing that they have created by themselves can possibly be of value. Such a 'castrated metaphor' is the bane of the region's existence, not only in its relations with the external world but also in the relations between classes (and some would add, racial groups) living within the different territorial units of the region.

The relative international success of some seemingly 'harmless' artistic expressions emerging from Caribbean sensibilities and creative energies has served to obscure the continuing intellectual dependence of the region on Europe and, in the more modern and sometimes simplistic modes, on the United States of America. For those who see culture as 'mind', this phenomenon overtaking the Caribbean region in its post-colonial state must be one of the most fateful challenges to cultural identity and political independence and a poignant paradox at end of century. It is supposedly natural for the United States to require of the economically dependent Caribbean undivided loyalty to the intellectual traditions inherited and consolidated by the richest and the most powerful country in the liberal-corporate community of nations. The minds of those who might have managed to escape the colonial ravages of mental slavery in the Caribbean are therefore challenged not to function except within predetermined parameters set by a superpower which may have need for countries in its backyard for strategic purposes. Some would say that this is against the logic of Caribbean history which has always manifested an active struggle against domination.

The Cold War may have ended and ideological affinities supposedly no longer dictate the capacity of this or that country to attain eligibility for technical assistance or trade, but a Cuba presided over by Fidel Castro determined to stay loyal to revolutionary socialism is still treated as a pariah by a triumphant capitalist United States. Even if the European Union is far less paranoid about the ghosts of fellow-Europeans Marx and Lenin, the global economy in its late-twentieth-century dispensation serves to reinforce the unbroken dependency and congenital vulnerability of the 'two-thirds world'

---

12 The United States Enterprise of the Americas Initiative (EAI) of 1990 was the brainchild of US president George H. Bush. It proposed to 'write off a portion of the outstanding debts of Caribbean and Latin American countries to the US Government, but with stringent conditions that would include tightened schedules for repayment of their foreign debts' according to Kathy McAfee, 1991, p.29.

83 Saint-John Perse (Alexis Léger), Guadeloupe

84 Arthur Lewis, St Lucia

85 Derek Walcott, St Lucia

86 V. S. Naipaul, Trinidad & Tobago

87 Alejo Carpentier, Cuba

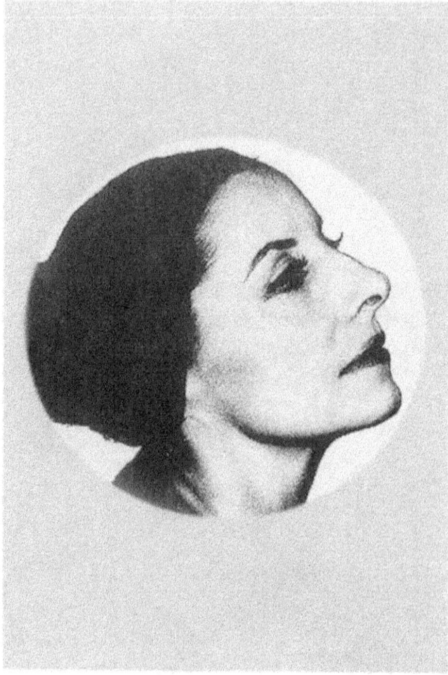

88 Alicia Alonso, Cuba

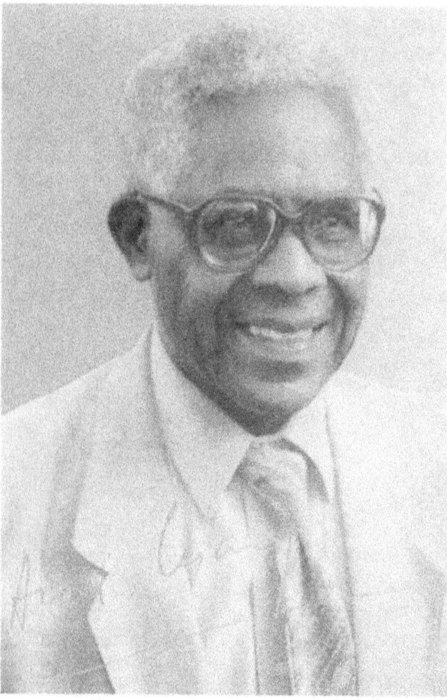

89 Aimé Césaire, Martinique

90 Patrick Chamoiseau, Martinique

91 Garfield Sobers, Barbados

92 Sammy Sosa, Dominican Republic

93 Nita Barrow, Barbados

94 Joaquín Balaguer, Dominican Republic

95 Women march for peace, Puerto Rico, 2000

96 Caribbean dance pioneers: Beryl McBurnie (Trinidad & Tobago), Ivy Baxter (Jamaica), Lavinia Williams (Haiti), Rex Nettleford (Jamaica)

97 Justice Kay Beckford inspecting guard of honour, Jamaica

98 Sila Maria Calderón, Puerto Rico

99 Suburban development, Portmore, Jamaica

100 La Rose King and Queen in traditional costume, St Lucia

101 Jonkonnu costume, The Bahamas

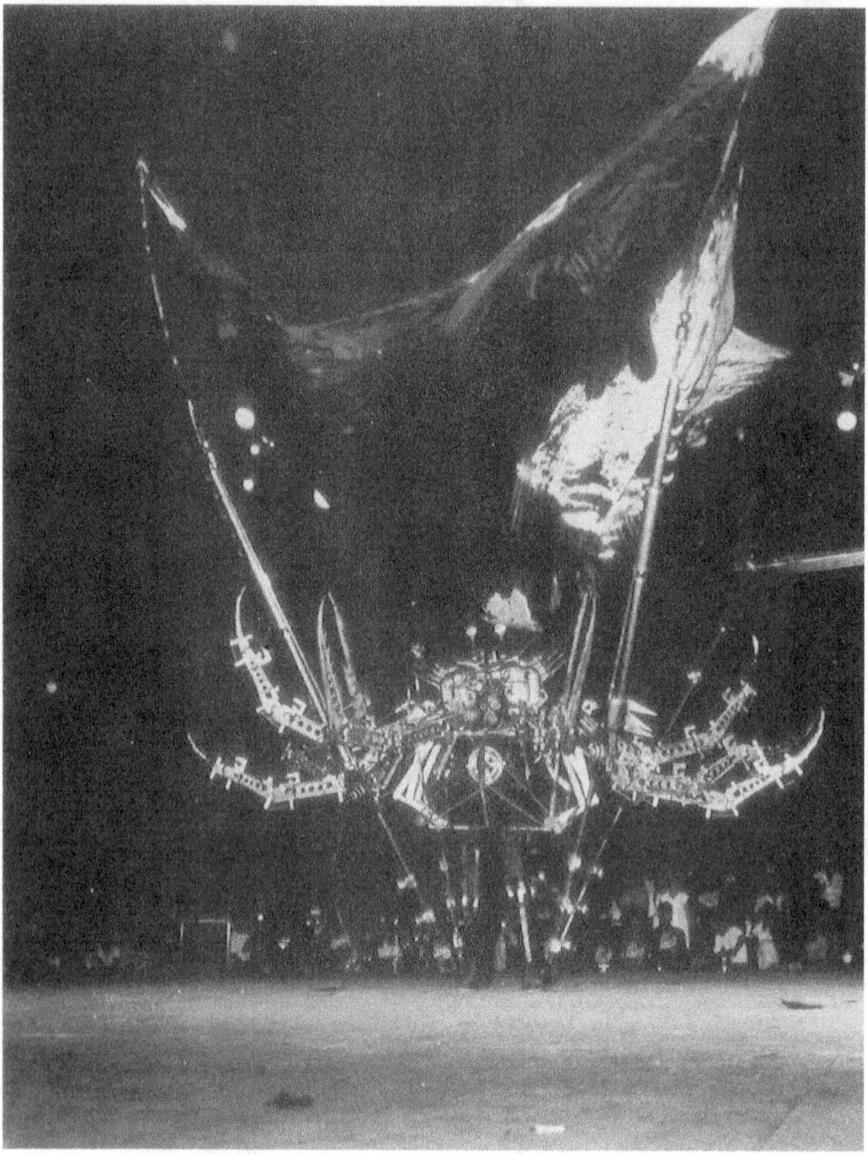

102 'Mancrab', king of the carnival band 'River', by Peter Minshall, Trinidad & Tobago, 1983

of which the Caribbean is unmistakably an integral part. So the old questions of sovereignty and self-determination (in short, of identity) are bound to persist with paradoxical tenacity into the twenty-first century.

The entitlement of a North American Free Trade Area (NAFTA), with its threats of exclusion of Caribbean countries in matters of trade, investment and labour exchange, the inauguration of the European Common Market which changed the scenario for traditional exports like banana and sugar in once-preferential markets, and the vigorous pursuit of the cultural penetration of the minds tenanting the region via satellite communication, maintain the old areas of concern for survival and introduce new ones for a region that has known struggle and resistance for most of its first 500 years.

Many of the strategies of survival employed over time have been enshrined in the repertoire of cultural values which describes and governs Caribbean social and political life to this day. I refer to such phenomena as armed conflict in liberation struggle; maronnage (evident in physical flight from loci of oppression whether plantation, work-place and country, or psychic withdrawal and calculated duplicity in dealing with the dominant ethos); cultural assertion, especially through the exercise of the creative imagination in the production of uniquely Caribbean works and expressions of art (music, dance, theatre, plastic arts and crafts, language and literature); the appeal to religion giving rise to Caribbean religious expressions with implications for the durability of a Eurocentric political legitimacy; the appeal to ethnicity, with assertion of racial pride and dignity without degeneration into racism; the appeal to nationalism drawing on the inheritance of the territorial impulse of mankind, and the related claim to the right to self-determination which informs all efforts for freedom which characterize Caribbean history.

III

Yet such underlying unities of Caribbean history and existence do not rule out the fact of differences, deeply entrenched and active enough to present the region with contradictions. As I have said elsewhere:

> [the] common history of domination and the struggle for political freedom, economic viability, cultural identity and, within that framework, the common process of creolisation offer a logical basis for ease of communication between the different communities of the insular Caribbean and the mainland Latin American areas. Yet there are divisive forces rooted in the realities of geography … which separate community from

> community. The dominant European colonising forces have also bequeathed imprints of language, religion and other cultural forms to their different spheres of influence, placing Caracas nearer to Madrid than to Port-of-Spain and Kingston nearer to London than to Havana.[13]

Despite continuing efforts to address these concerns, the tyranny of psychic distance between geographical neighbours persists with all that implies. Change in this regard may indeed come in the forseeable future, but only incrementally. 'The fact is underscored by the poignant presence of distinctive culture-spheres known severally as Plantation America ... Meso-America ... and Euro-America'.[14]

But that is not the end of the story: the peculiar and unique circumstances of the encounters at different points of Caribbean history of in-coming migratory hordes of humanity into the different geographical areas of the Americas resulted in further variations within and across the different culture-spheres, spawning contradictions and stubborn difficulties not only for the concept and reality of cultural identity but for practical programmes in inter-cultural relations, as relations within the Organization of American States (with its anglophone Caribbean membership of recent vintage)[15] would affirm. It is such contradictions (the source of creative tension as much as of debilitating confusion) that are not always fully appreciated by those outside the region who devise 'Basin Initiatives' or EAIs *for* 'the Basin', and are likely to defeat the objectives of any plan concocted in Washington DC, however well-meaning.

Still, the possibility of the European Union in Brussels 'planning' the redefinition of 'the Caribbean' for purposes of administering Lomé IV is clearly evident in the shift of focus from the Caricom Caribbean to the Dominican

---

13 Rex Nettleford, 1978, p.149.

14 *Ibid.* The full text reads: 'The fact is underscored by the poignant presence of distinctive culture spheres known severally as (i) Plantation America, brutalised and ravaged and for that reason endemically rebellious (ii) Meso-America, valiantly resistant to the onslaughts of European 'discovery' and correspondingly majestic in its ancestral certitude and (iii) Euro-America, still the active and often assertive purveyor of the ideas and technology of the Conqueror forebears and therefore reflective of the ambivalence with which any thrust towards regional co-operation must contend'. The last is an evolved paradox that will keep evolving as long as the world is ordered into the superordinate Eurocentric North Atlantic and the developing 'Other' covering places like the islands of the Caribbean, largely peopled by non-Caucasians.

15 The newly independent countries of the Commonwealth Caribbean first sought membership in the Organization of American States and some were accepted in 1969.

Republic.[16] Some would argue that such enforced forging of links between the Hispanic and the Commonwealth Caribbean may well be the best thing for meaningful Caribbean integration which is long overdue. The paradox is that the persistence of outside direction in a region which sets such great store by its historical claim to independence is as strong today as it was a hundred years ago. What is more, the denial of an underlying unity (through historical experience and socio-economic realities) *must* be borne in mind if one is to understand the ideological alignments which sometimes transcend geopolitical, geo-cultural spheres.

So for all the unease that is evident in the relations between the United States and the Commonwealth Caribbean in the burden borne by the latter under structural adjustment, that part of the Caribbean shares more of values, meanings and belief-systems with the United States than either shares with the Latin (Franco- and Ibero-) section of the region. This is so because both the United States (at least its ancestrally significant parts) and the Commonwealth Caribbean, as ex-colonies of Great Britain, are the common inheritors of Anglo-Saxon notions of freedom, rights at common law, Lockean ideas of political obligation or accountability and even views about artistic cultural autonomy, with the mediation of state power being kept either to a minimum or qualitatively as passive as possible, and facilitatory at best. These are cultural values cherished by anglophone Caribbean peoples and should be easily understood by Americans of the United States of America who are no less insistent in their advocacy of a right to these values.

Yet problems of misunderstandings and ignorance persist. Washington gratuitously insists on holding tutorials on democracy for the Commonwealth Caribbean which houses in Barbados the oldest elected legislature of unbroken history in all of the Americas. Admittedly, within the Caribbean itself there are questions rooted in the perceived and actual difference of cultural values and identity among the communities themselves. One question that comes to mind is whether Euro-America, which takes in large geographical spaces and assumes commanding psychological postures in both North and Latin America, is able to nurture sensibilities that are compatible

16 The Lomé Agreement which came into operation in 1973 linked the Caribbean countries and other former European dependencies in Africa and Asia (the ACP countries) with the EEC in the hope of providing the developing world with partners in the linkage with significant economic benefits by way of grants, soft-loans, technical assistance and the like. Lomé IV began in 1994. This Agreement is seen by some as the European counterpart to the US Initiatives (CBI & EAI) described above and CARIBCAN, the Agreement which linked the region with Canada for similar purposes.

with the other two dominant culture-spheres. While Euro-America makes claims to ethnic purity (or *cultural* purity for that matter), Plantation America thrives on miscegenation (even if with some ambivalence) and cultural pluralism.[17]

If Caribbean Latins see themselves as 'Europeans overseas', then it is reasonable to suggest that their commitment to the Americas in any deep cultural sense is bound to be seriously flawed – especially in terms of a Latin American development path based on the utilization of indigenous resources. For the notion of Caribbean solutions for Caribbean problems is as rooted in cultural impulses as it is in political ones.

A sense of cultural unity will help in no small way to achieve closer co-operation between nations of the wider Caribbean as was envisaged by the West Indian Commission in its recommendation, later implemented, of an 'Association of Caribbean States'[18] which carries with it the pedigree of endorsement by the likes of Eric Williams, founding father of Trinidad & Tobago, and José Martí, patron saint of nineteenth-century Cuban revolutionism.

Problems are not mitigated by the fact that many Caribbean countries would regard themselves as having within their borders all the 'culture-spheres' indicated above. What cannot be denied is that they are all part of 'the Americas', itself the creature of the past five hundred years of myriad encounters between immigrants themselves, and between immigrants and the indigenous peoples, representing age-long contradictions that will not disappear overnight.

A commitment to *American* civilization (of which Caribbean civilization is but a variant) is a culture value of strategic importance in the living of life in the Western Hemisphere and a factor in any discourse on identity. The right to one's identity-determination is a value about which Caribbean peoples generally feel intensely, since most of what they have created out of the belly of this Caribbean/American experience (whether it be in language/literature, religion, kinship patterns, artistic expressions or politico-economic organizations) is the victim of Eurocentrism.

The Euro-American's entrapment in the ancestral heritage of Mediterranean and Northern European philosophies and systems of knowledge merely makes him/her ripe for the thought-systems of Europe – whether of the Right or the Left. Indeed, the great intellectual struggles of eighteenth- and nineteenth-century Europe continue to find new and welcoming arenas in those parts of the 'New' World that are clearly satisfied with merely preserving the cultural legacies of the Old.

---

17 M. G. Smith, 1965; *idem*, 1991.

18 West Indian Commission, 1992, pp.446–52.

IV

The habit is of course all-pervasive and infectious. For Afro-Americans in all parts of Plantation America have attempted to replicate Africa, or what is believed to be Africa, in the 'New' World. The true strength of the Plantation America culture-sphere is, however, paradoxically what it shares with Meso-America, viz the consciousness of a 'Creole' (native-born and native-bred) reality in the Americas. While the latter is posited on a mestizo equilibrium of forces between indigenous Amerindian and invading or settler European cultures, the former (Plantation America), though posited on similar notions of a cross-fertilization ideal, carries with it an overt and dominant 'white bias' reinforced in class categories in the cultural apparatus of the sphere. It is the endemic revolt against this phenomenon by a numerical majority forced to operate as a cultural minority that culturally marks off much of the Commonwealth Caribbean and parts of Meso-America from Euro-America, though *mestizaje* is itself reported not to be free of racial preferences tilting to the 'white bias'. The assertion of the 'African presence' for centrality in a nascent Caribbean civilization informs the Plantation American cultural sensibility and presents some psychic problems, not only for the United States, which has still to answer this question, but also for Latin American communities where that presence is either denied or has long been submerged. For the politics of this cultural phenomenon turns on a possible raising of consciousness among the underclass which may want recognition far beyond that given to them when they are made to surface for folklore displays before foreign dignitaries on official visits to those lands.

Many Caribbean people are becoming increasingly weary of being engaged as minstrels or being treated as specimens for anthropological research. They regard neither opportunity for display of their talents as a cultural value worth taking seriously, and they devise secret weapons to fight the tendency both within their territories and outside them. Within the Caribbean Basin, Latin American countries such as Costa Rica, Panama, Honduras, Mexico, Colombia and Venezuela admit to having spreading 'Caribbean segments' in terms of the African presence.

There is of course more than the African presence now seeking a centrality of place and purpose in Commonwealth Caribbean life. There are large populations of Indians in Guyana and Trinidad, numerically strong enough to question what is their seeming marginalization in a polity officially committed to majority rule. Fancy franchises involving proportional representation are said to have kept the Indians out of political power for a long time in Guyana; and cries of racism were heard to come from a mainly Indian opposition unable to dislodge a largely Euro-African ethnic aggregation forming the government of Trinidad & Tobago. They were later to come also from a largely Indian government unable to influence the Euro-African ethos out of its narrow commitments. The Muslim Hosay festival[19] and the Hindu Divali festival are 'national' events in Trinidad but it is the strongly Euro-African pre-Lenten carnival which is all-embracing as a truly national expression, spreading to the rest of the Commonwealth Caribbean and to the Caribbean diaspora in North America and the United Kingdom.[20] The Afro-Indian or Indo-Trinidadian 'chutney' is still in relative infancy.

The creolization process must now spread to embrace the Indian variable as it did Europe and Africa for two centuries before the arrival of India after emancipation. It is clearly a matter of time but it is also a matter of commitment on the part of the 'Creole' population in Trinidad as well as of the 'African' in Guyana to allow the process to run its course. At the same time, Indians will themselves have to exhibit a similar commitment to their own transformation into 'West Indians' through inter-culturation without resorting to exaggerated claims on 'Mother India' just as corresponding claims by Blacks on 'Africa' or by Whites on 'Europe' have had to be greatly modified or discreetly abandoned over time. The 'problem' in Trinidad at the turn of the century is that Blacks are restating claims to Africa, in response to Indo-Trinidadians' new claims to be 'Indian' *and* 'Creole/Trinidadian', which partly respond to the assumption of the centrality of the Afrocentric struggle. The myth of relations must take precedence over the myth of origins. None of this will be possible without the guarantee of a level playing field for all who are involved, and who crave for ease of access not only to political and economic power but also to a sense of social place and purpose, and to an equitable share in the cultural certitude of the Caribbean.

V

It is clear from the above that the issue of identity is yet to find consensus in Plantation America-Caribbean itself. Perceptions of what constitutes the cultural ethos of that part of the region vary. They have ranged from imperialist notions of that part of the Caribbean being still an extension of Europe, to neo-Marxist interpretations about the cultural consciousness being determined by the material base and rooted in the experience of a Caribbean proletariat – both urban

19 John Nunley and Judith Bettelheim, 1988.

20 Errol Hill, 1972 (1997), especially Introduction to the paperback edition; see also John Nunley and Judith Bettelheim, 1988.

and rural. The paradox of the Eurocentric orientation of Caribbean colonization and the Creole or Afrocentric struggle against it would be regarded by some as the dialectics of Caribbean existence and therefore a cultural value to be treasured. To others the bourgeois synthesis of nineteenth-century Europe is all but dead and claims are therefore made on behalf of an urban proletariat who are seen as the true creators of a unique 'roots culture', especially in Jamaica with its reggae artists and Rastafarian brethren and sistren, and in Trinidad with its steelband men and women and its calypso kings and queens traditionally drawn from the lower socio-economic groups.

Between these two points there is the melting-pot theory, which claims inter-racial bliss at its most idealistic and concentrates, at its most analytical, on the phenomenon of syncretism or on the more dynamic process of creolization, which now carries its own signature. There is, as well, the pluralist view with its emphasis on segmentation and the institutional differentiation between racial/cultural groups, and this has invited the counter-theory of stratification. Then there is black nationalism which sees the African heritage as the engine of cultural dynamics, presenting identity problems for the massive Indian populations of Trinidad and Guyana as well as for the numerically small but affluent and economically influential Syrian/Lebanese and Chinese groups all over the region. It also creates unease in some Latin American territories where Blacks are traditionally marginal to the ethos. None of these notions can be regarded as mutually exclusive, for there are elements of most of them in the postures taken by this or that protagonist of Caribbean cultural identity.

The Caribbean migrant carries with him/her all this textured, if contradictory, view of self, society and the world and presents to many a host society particular problems of understanding, decoding of behaviour, and identity, since the Caribbean person is likely to operate on several levels simultaneously or may exhibit tremendous flexibility in adapting to changing situations as circumstances demand. Where unpredictability is of tactical advantage such a person may very well think of several identities instead of one. This paradox is likely to intensify in the interest of survival, and against the background of a globalization not only of what one eats or wears but of how one thinks of self and society.

The quest for a Caribbean cultural identity has of course been a vigorous and consistent one within the Caribbean for a long time. And the efforts of such Caribbean writers as Alejo Carpentier and Nicolás Guillén, both of Cuba, to defy the imperialist view of Caribbean culture have been continued by others who are firmly against the suggestion that we should be but a distorted echo of what occurs elsewhere.[21] Of course Jean Price-Mars of Haiti,

21 Roberto Retamar, 1974, quoted in Rex Nettleford, 1978, p.179.

George Padmore of Trinidad, Marcus Garvey of Jamaica, and Aimé Césaire and Frantz Fanon of Martinique were in the vanguard of a conscious counter-offensive to the dying, but still gasping, view that things Caribbean (especially if laced with African ingredients) are subordinate to European expressions of artistic and intellectual achievement.

There has been no shortage of commitment to the cause of putting right a misguided perception that has long outstayed its earlier welcome into would-be civilized society. This has been an underlying theme, indeed a central theme, in copious outpourings in the region's literature, music, dance and plastic arts, all giving the African presence an elemental cogency in the Caribbean cultural reality since, according to some, the African heritage has been the crucible in which a definitive Caribbean has been forged – a claim which understandably presents a serious problem for Indians in Guyana and Trinidad. For the Hispanic Caribbean the crucible may well be something else – the Iberian heritage, perhaps. But there is historic significance in the fact that the Cuban leadership of the revolutionary era should declare the Cuban heritage an Afro-Latin one,[22] no doubt because it is *Caribbean*. This makes modern Cuba a horse of a different colour from the pre-revolutionary days of overt racial discrimination and the purity-of-blood preoccupations of the mating game. It is also different if looked at in terms of the orientation of nationalists such as José Martí and even of Alejo Carpentier himself, whose literary concerns were more focused on the dialectical relationships between America and Europe.

The Haitian Revolution had of course long presented the entire region with an appropriate, if awesome, icon for its political and cultural struggles. But Latin America, despite the acknowledged insights of Simón Bolívar into the region's cultural realities, seemingly took much longer to make the journey away from that vision of the African presence as an offering of raw sensuality and minstrelsy to a perception of that presence as an expression of cultural dynamism and elemental power. The Cuban Revolution admittedly comes a distant second behind the Haitian in this essential detail but it has carried for many in the Caribbean the burden of that wider-ranging aspiration for freedom, self-determination and economic deliverance through self-help.

This in good measure explains the ease with which anti-imperialist Caribbean leaders such as Eric Williams of Trinidad & Tobago, Michael Manley of Jamaica, Errol Barrow of Barbados and Forbes Burham of Guyana

22 Fidel Castro declared Cuba's 'Afro-Latinity' in a marathon speech he delivered at a mass rally in Sam Sharpe Square, Montego Bay, on 16 October 1977, during a state visit to Jamaica.

established full diplomatic relations with Cuba,[23] despite the disapproval of the Oval Office which had long sought to banish Castro and his errant supporters from the international community, much as the fledgling United States did to Haiti in the early nineteenth century after a combination of slaves and their free coloured descendants dared to liberate themselves by force of arms and set up an independent state at the time.

VI

An understanding of this shared human thirst for freedom in terms of its cultural significance is critical. For the impulses that drive the Caribbean people (like people anywhere) to freedom within nation-states, to the right to choose their own friends and political systems, and to independent paths to development are the same impulses which drive them to the creation of their own music, their own languages and literature, their own gods and religious belief-systems, their own kinship patterns, modes of socialization and self-perceptions. All plans made for them from outside must take this fact into account, whatever may be the dictates of military and strategic interests or the statistical logic of tabulated growth rates and gross national products.

The Caribbean people, faced as they are with the post-colonial imperative of shaping civil society and building nations, expect to be taken seriously in terms of their proven capacities to act creatively in co-ordinated social interaction over centuries in the Americas. They feel passionately that their history and experience are worthy of theory and explanation and expect others to understand and appreciate this fact. They are unique, paradoxically because they are like everybody else. The Caribbean has been engaged in freedom struggles; its inhabitants have been at the job of creating their own languages, and designing their own appropriate lifestyles for as long as and, in some cases, longer than most parts of what became the United States of America. Recognition of this and the according of the status due to such achievement is a prized wish of all Caribbean people – black, white, brown, mestizo, Indian (indigenous and transplanted), Chinese and Syrian/Lebanese.

The great value placed on racial dignity and racial pride by Caribbean people of African ancestry should not be seen as an epidermal indulgence. It

23 In 1973, Jamaica, Barbados, Trinidad & Tobago and Guyana established full diplomatic relations with Cuba.

merely reflects the determination and resolve of a set of people who understand that their survival depends on the final disappearance from human consciousness of that view of the world which denigrates things African-derived and regards as superior all things European, and that sensibility which violates their sense of person, place and purpose wherever Western values rooted in the Graeco-Christian heritage and reinforced by fantastic achievements in science and technology prevail. None of this necessarily leads to racism despite the high profile of black nationalism and Black Power in the recent social history of the Americas. The Caribbean Black is too sophisticated to be racist but intelligent enough to be race-conscious. On that delicate balancing of sensibilities one lives and has one's being. Such a paradox will continue to inform Caribbean reality as long as racism and its related iniquities continue to rear their ugly heads.

The Caribbean person who is aware of his/her condition sets great store by the escape from colonial dependency. The search for greener pastures by migration to lands which can provide jobs, educational opportunities and a better material life does not necessarily rob the Caribbean migrant of the thirst for independence. So the Hispanics will invoke an impassioned Hispanicism (language, customs, etc.) to ward off the impositions of Anglo-Saxon United States of America. Yet the Caribbean Latin Americans, like their Afro-West Indian counterparts, treasure the products of their years of symbiotic interaction with the Caribbean environment they leave behind and regard themselves as uniquely 'Caribbean'. The anglophone-Caribbean person will indulge Anglo-Saxon postures when in New York if only to lord it over a United States black counterpart. But this is frequently a tactical tool from the armoury of weapons utilized to face the firing line of institutionalized racism against Blacks, if not to combat the growing satellization (by the Eurocentric United States) of the region. The anglophone-Caribbean person also knows that although the sun has set on the British Empire which once colonized and conditioned people of his ilk, it has not set on the English language – as a consequence of the extensive global power of the anglophone United States. Language here becomes an important instrument of survival in hostile climes and a means of asserting identity.

The cultural value of self-definition, through the exercise of one's creative imagination, however, remains the political imperative of territorial integrity and ideological independence. The calypso and the reggae are not merely artistic vehicles for social comment and social protest: they become the actual weapons of war against dependency and a threatening denigration within Caribbean society itself. Alejo Carpentier, Nicolás Guillén and Alicia Alonso created within the Cuban Revolution; and the Caribbeanism of Louise Bennett, George Lamming, Derek Walcott, Vic Reid, Kamau Brathwaite, Samuel Selvon, Vidia Naipaul, Wilson Harris, Martin Carter *et al.* represents the voice of liberation itself. To understand the Caribbean, one must understand these people.

VII

In fact, long before *perestroika, glasnost*, the disintegration of the Soviet Empire and, with it, the decline of communist Stalinist ideology, a certain paradox began to evolve within several countries of the region. There was a clear shift of authority and ethical authenticity from the bureaucratic and formally legitimated centres to a broader social base. One began to recognize deeper dimensions of change and cultural expression in the region. As a United States intellectual once observed, one began to discern more clearly a world that could no longer be defined by artists, novelists and social scientists, much less by politicians and publicists, who construe the forces of history from private, academic or 'managerial' positions. The region was coming to be defined less by its traditional administrative regimes, Spanish, English, French or Dutch – and more 'by the quality of the popular cultures and the messages they transmit to the official realm'.[24]

For there is increasing belief within the Caribbean of the capacity of the mass of the population in the region to take decisions in their own interest. The people who inhabit it are in many ways insisting on their right to do this. Many who give leadership to the mass of the populations in the region are very aware of the disintegration of a number of the old certitudes which propped up Western civilization, with the impact of science and technology and clear indications that the new mass society world wide is not without distinctive forms and expressions of its own. They do not (or they no longer) conceive of a 'mainstream culture' outside of what they themselves have to offer to human civilization. They see themselves as part-determiners of that mainstream and not as outsiders to be let in. It is a far cry from the days when they dutifully accepted their sibling status and held on to the apron-strings of mother-countries. The new posture is disruptive, admittedly, for it questions in fundamental ways the old relationships which bred the ghastly cliché that places like the Caribbean have achieved nothing because they have created nothing. The region has long been disproving this, of course, not only in its political but also its cultural action.

---

24 The quote is attributed to Richard Morse in an unpublished paper for discussion when he was head of the Latin American and Caribbean Center, Woodrow Wilson Program, Smithsonian Institution, Washington DC.

More and more the 'tribes' on Planet Earth, in the face of a threatened homogenization, perceive themselves to be in global bondage. They will therefore want to fall back on reserves of energy generated out of the specificity of their own experience and encapsulated in manifestations of the languages they have created, the gods they have come to worship, the kinship patterns they have devised for their own survival, the structures of thought and the artistic products emerging from their intellectual and collective imagination. What is now seen as 'surrender' may well be the 'redemption' of humankind, and what seems the 'death of faith' may well be its 'rebirth', as the Caribbean has long known in its protracted struggle for self and cultural certitude over the half of a millennium dating from 1492.

Religion, myths and beliefs: Their socio-political roles

Robert J. Stewart

Introduction

The Caribbean is a religious region as distinctly as it is a region in geographical, historical, linguistic, literary and musical terms. It is a place where world religions have flowed together, and where European distinctions of secular and sacred, Church and State, and human society and divine community have been defied. After slave emancipation – as early as the 1790s with the revolution in Haiti and as late as 1886 in Cuba – the close relationship between religion and socio-political issues established in the era of slavery was manifest. The most dramatic example of this in the anglophone Caribbean was the 1865 Morant Bay Rebellion in Jamaica, 31 years after British slave emancipation. It was a movement of political protest among black Jamaicans that would have been unlikely outside of a religious matrix – in this case, the native Baptists – that provided motivation and leadership. It was a relationship that could not be dissolved, and was ill-explained, by modern Western distinctions between religion and politics.

The already varied religious traditions in the West Indies were further diversified in the second half of the nineteenth century by the immigration of indentured labourers from Asia and Africa. African immigration into the British West Indies was not on the scale of African arrivals in Cuba, which continued to be a slave society for most of the nineteenth century, and where the symbiosis of Roman Catholicism and African traditions produced forms of Afro-Cuban religion generically known as Santería. Nevertheless, comparable religious forms were either started or revivified in the anglophone Caribbean with the Africans who arrived as emancipated slaves or indentured migrants. Kele in St Lucia, Orisha worship in Trinidad, Big Drum in Carriacou, and Kumina in Jamaica, for example, are religions that relate to the spirit world in traditional African ways, although they may include in their pantheons spirits which originated in other cosmologies, such as Hinduism, Native-American belief, or the Catholic cult of the saints.

Although Chinese immigrants were among the Asians who were indentured to provide a steady supply of labour after slave emancipation, they had little impact on the history of religion in the Caribbean. They were readily assimilated by the mainstream Christian churches. In Jamaica, for example, the descendants of Chinese immigrants became stalwart members of Roman Catholic congregations in the twentieth century. Middle Eastern immigrants in the early twentieth century, mainly from what is now Lebanon, are generically called 'Syrians' in the West Indies. They brought Arabic surnames with them but the majority of them were already Christians, and they were absorbed largely into traditional churches, especially the Roman Catholic Church. Immigrants from the Indian subcontinent, however, introduced major variations in the Caribbean religious scene. Where they now constitute an ethnic majority, such as in Trinidad and Guyana, forms of Hinduism have become defining features of the religious landscape. Although many Indians converted in response to missionary activity, especially by Canadian Presbyterians from the 1860s, Hinduism remains a more important element than Christianity in Indian cultural identity in Guyana's and Trinidad's cosmopolitan society.

Immigrants from India also brought Islam with them. They were not the first Muslims in the Caribbean; there was a Mandingo Muslim community of ex-slaves in Port of Spain, Trinidad, for example, from the early nineteenth century. But while many African Muslims were brought to other parts of the Caribbean during the centuries of the slave trade, their inability as slaves to reproduce an Islamic community meant that their beliefs and practices either withered or became so diffused in Creole society that it is difficult to document a Muslim tradition in the West Indies as a whole before the beginning of Indian immigration in the 1830s. Hinduism and Indian Islam had less discernible influence in societies such as Jamaica where the overwhelming majority of the population continued to be of African ancestry, and where the most viable religious forms had been preserved in Afro-Christian syntheses. But African-Caribbean conversions to Islam are evident throughout the second half of the twentieth century. In Trinidad especially, where manifestations of African spirit-belief traditions are just as strong as in other parts of the Caribbean, many people of African ancestry have adopted Islam to the extent that it has discernibly influenced community values as well as politics.

Perhaps the most dramatic challenge in the twentieth-century Caribbean to the religious and secular status quo was the development of the Rastafari in Jamaica in the 1930s. The Rastafari have become a phenomenon throughout the Caribbean and, indeed, throughout the entire worldwide black diaspora. They are now commonplace to the extent that their dreadlocks, their wearing of the Ethiopian colours of red, gold and green, their influence on reggae music, and their linguistic innovations have made them easily identifiable. But their world view, which can be called a kind of African Zionism, has been deceptively oversimplified in popular understanding. Rastafari consciousness owes much to the world view that was also fundamental to the more consciously socio-political movement of Garveyism, which was based on a black theology that overturned the negative valuations attached by colonialism to the word 'African'. Marcus Garvey's pan-Africanism and his theology of a black God proved to have universal appeal throughout the African diaspora, foreshadowing the appeal that Rastafari style and consciousness would have later in the twentieth century. Rastafari is not only a legacy of Garveyism, however, but has roots in the Revival tradition that preceded it.[1] The Rastafari theme of liberation from Babylonian captivity in the West and return to Africa also echoes a long established mythology in Afro-Caribbean folk consciousness in which motifs of spirit return are expressed in story, song and religious metaphor.[2] The African consciousness of Rastafari goes deep in the Jamaican and West Indian past, and is an example of the processes of continuity and change, of rooted consciousness and startling innovation, that are characteristic of Caribbean history.

The mainstream Christian churches, such as the Anglicans, Roman Catholics, Presbyterians, Methodists, Baptists, Moravians and Congregationalists, remained important in the twentieth-century Caribbean. Their priests, pastors and missionaries relied on Europe and, increasingly, on North America to replenish their ranks, although as the century progressed most of these churches gradually moved toward indigenization of leadership. They tended to maintain spiritual rationalizations for the socio-political status quo, propping up the colonial hierarchies of class and colour, retaining patriotic links with the metropole, and becoming tentatively progressive when Creole nationalism led to movements for local leadership, autonomy and, in the 1960s and 1970s, independence. Even then their alliance was mainly with local oligarchies against mass movements for popular democracy or revolution. The mainstream churches in the twentieth century were not universally conservative or oligarchic, however. There have been individuals and groups within the churches who have promoted a version of the social gospel or a West Indian formulation of liberation theology. Contrasting with this development is the growth of evangelical fundamentalism, and a key role in the history of religion in the twentieth-century Caribbean has been played by Pentecostal churches originating in North America which have gained strength in conditions of post-colonial dependence and economic instability.

---

1 Barry Chevannes, 1994, pp.21, 120. For Garveyism, see chap.6, this volume.

2 Lorna McDaniel, 1990.

This chapter surveys the major ways in which religious beliefs, practices and organization were integral to issues of society, economy, politics and culture in the twentieth-century Caribbean. It looks at the diversity of Christianity, examines world views derived from African traditions, and discusses the importance of Islam and Hinduism. This overview does not mention every nation and colony in the region, and it does not give due notice to every variety of religious experience and innovation that imperialism and creolization have produced. Nor does it include a section on Judaism.[3] Judaism in the Caribbean has been secularized to the extent that it figures little in the interface of society and belief, though it remains fairly significant in Cuba. In spite of these lacunae, however, the general patterns, variations and iterations that together give a fair view of the socio-political importance of religion are delineated here. The overview suggests that the unseverable link between religion – whether viewed as institution, movement or cosmology – and Caribbean socio-political history was continued in the twentieth century.

Afro-Caribbean world views

Two general types of religious groups emerged from the African chrysalis. One comprised those which incorporated biblical symbolism and Christian eschatology in a symbiotic manner.[4] This type was manifested in various forms of Revivalism, such as that seen among the Spiritual Baptists and the Shakers in the Lesser Antilles, the practitioners of Pukumina and Myal-derived Revivalism in Jamaica,[5] and the Rastafari. These forms of Afro-Christian religion were particularly vexatious for colonial authorities and local Eurocentric elites, for they spoke to the socio-political world with a voice that joined militant black affirmation with the apocalyptic judgement of New Testament eschatology. The other type comprised those which were more traditionally African in cosmology, pantheon, practice and reverence for ancestors, such as Maroon religion, Kumina, Kele, Shango, Big Drum, Santería and Vodou.

Scholars differ in their definitions of 'world view'. A clear and succinct definition is given by the Jamaican sociologist Barry Chevannes. In his formulation, world view consists of cosmology, ethics and symbol system. He

3 Readers can refer to Carol S. Holzberg, 1987, and Tony Martin, 1994, for aspects of the Jewish presence in the twentieth-century Caribbean.
4 Leslie G. Desmangles, 1992, p.8.
5 Barry Chevannes, 1994, pp.17–21.

defines cosmology as 'systematic beliefs about the nature and origins of the world, the ordering of its constituent parts, and theory of causation.'[6]

Afro-Caribbean world views, as they developed during the centuries of slavery and after emancipation in the nineteenth century, were neither pure relics of African civilization nor corrupted versions of European Christianity. There was change and development according to an internal rhythm, responding simultaneously to external metropolitan pressure and to local class, colour and political relationships. Within an African matrix, Christian forms of worship, symbol and vocabulary were appropriated to a different grammar and syntax. Before the twentieth century, the functions of traditional African religion – explanation, remedy and control of natural phenomena and human events – had been modified to make sense of the traumas of the Middle Passage and the dispersal of African peoples throughout the plantation societies of the Caribbean. The same functions were needed to make sense of the continuities and changes brought by the twentieth century: migration of labour within the Caribbean and toward the metropole and North America; the further industrialization of agriculture; the unionization of labour; continuation of colonial rule or the consolidation of authoritarian regimes in independent states; the increasing military, political and cultural influence of North America; and movements toward nationalism and independence in the British and Dutch Caribbean.

One group of Afro-Trinidadians who managed to preserve African religious forms well into the twentieth century were the Radas, whose religious culture had originated in Dahomey. Colonial authorities included their religious practices under the general term 'Obeah', which Europeans tended to use indiscriminately to name all forms of African or Afro-Creole religion. The practice of Obeah was made punishable by law in 1868 in Trinidad, as it had been throughout the rest of the British West Indies before emancipation because of its perceived connection with slave rebellion and resistance, especially the use of poisons. As a result of the 1868 legislation in Trinidad, the Radas were occasionally convicted, jailed and flogged for their religious practices.[7]

More numerous in Trinidad and in other islands of the southern Caribbean were the Spiritual Baptists, also known as the Shakers, or Shouters, who originated from a symbiosis of fundamentalist Baptist worship, maintained by Blacks from the United States South who settled in Trinidad in the nineteenth century, and the practices of African immigrants such as the Radas. The origins were external, but the creole fusion was indigenous.[8]

---

6 Barry Chevannes, 1995, p.xvi.

7 Bridget Brereton, 1981, p.134.

8 *Ibid.*, pp.134–5.

The Spiritual Baptists, still active today, are non-doctrinaire and heterodox in relation to dominant Christian orthodoxies (as are the Shakers of St Vincent). Their world view is reflective of colonial Creole society. It is hierarchical and complex. Relationships of authority are important but not clearly defined. They believe in a pantheon of spirits who have human qualities, powerful but not omnipotent. Their efforts to help humans can lead to unpredictable consequences which might not necessarily be beneficial.[9]

Similar to other Afro-Christian religions in the Caribbean, the Spiritual Baptists have not become peripheral in island society. Their faith is of the here-and-now. Physical and social as well as spiritual benefits are expected from membership and participation. In Trinidad & Tobago, the more than 10,000 Spiritual Baptists, while mostly of African descent, are increasingly inter-class, and there are also increasing numbers of Indian and white creole participants. The spiritualities of Islam, Hinduism and Buddhism have influenced Spiritual Baptist belief.[10] This quality of being permeable, of openness to a variety of religious influences, is characteristic of African and Afro-Caribbean religions. It contrasts with the tendency of European churches to be hermetic and to value purity of doctrine and practice.

Throughout the twentieth-century Caribbean, politics and economics have had to contend with traditionally conflicting Euro-Creole and Afro-Creole world views. They differ in the way they organize and prioritize ideas of work and progress. 'Technology and modernisation are invading all quarters of the human mind and destroying links to Africa,' writes the linguist and cultural historian Mervyn Alleyne. But, he continues, the African collectivist principle 'enters the city, the factory, and the office where it sows chaos.'[11] He could have added the place of religious worship to his list. Alleyne's generalization of the European/African polarities in the Caribbean is perhaps too stark. But religion has always been a factor in the Creole conflicts which prompted his assertion. An example and a test case is provided by historian Edward Cox in a recent study of the Shakers of St Vincent. Cox documents the failed campaign of colonial authorities to eradicate Shakerism.

'Shakerism' and 'Shakers' were terms used by outsiders, such as colonial officials and mainstream church leaders. The Shakers identified themselves as members of the United Penitential Faith, and called themselves the Converted. Shakerism was seen as a breakaway movement from Methodism. But as an Afro-Creole development, it was more than just an independent

9 Stephen D. Glazier, 1983, p.24.
10 *Ibid.*, pp.3, 9, 32.
11 Mervyn Alleyne, 1989, p.165.

movement in the traditional Protestant mode; it had more in common with forms of Afro-Christian Revivalism that had taken hold throughout the post-emancipation British Caribbean, and was one of the sources of the Spiritual Baptist practice through Vincentian migrants to Trinidad. The Converted leaders and members were mostly rural labourers, and they tended to maintain simultaneous membership in the mainstream churches.

From the opening of the twentieth century, colonial government authorities, mainstream church leaders and medical officers conspired to eliminate Shakerism from St Vincent. Their problem was to devise legislation that did not appear to infringe religious freedom. The dilemma for the authorities was how to define Shakerism not as a religion but as a public nuisance. The Governor of the Windward Islands defined Shakerism as not a religion but 'a degrading practice followed at Meetings which are more or less disorderly and in that account a Public Nuisance.'[12] Contradicting their strategy to eliminate any spiritual aspect from their portrayal of Shakerism, colonial officials in St Vincent also claimed that Shaker leaders were Obeah practitioners who had an undue influence over the minds of black Vincentians. Perhaps the most revealing complaint of Shakerism's dysfunctionality in colonial society was that of sugar-estate owners and managers who were disturbed when participation by workers in Shaker ceremonies interfered with plantation labour routine.

An anti-Shaker ordinance was passed in 1912. It allowed the raiding of Shaker premises without warrant and the prosecution of the Converted on the grounds of reasonable suspicion rather than probable cause. Fines of £50 and six months' imprisonment with hard labour were allowed.[13] The law was in effect for 53 years (1912–65). Shaker leaders were repeatedly fined and jailed, yet there was no time between 1912 and 1965 that Shakerism did not thrive in St Vincent, and the law was utterly ineffective. At the end of the twentieth century, Shakerism was considered a stable religion in St Vincent.

The black church in the Caribbean continued its role as both an organizing principle and a source of identity in social and political movements. A clear example of this can be seen in the career of T. U. B. Butler in Trinidad. Butler was a Grenadian who migrated to Trinidad in 1921 to work in the oilfields. After a disabling work accident in 1929, he could no longer work, but would emerge as an influential labour leader in a 1935 oil-workers strike. Before then, however, Butler built his power base within a religious congregation. After his accident, he became deeply involved in the Baptist church, but soon founded his own Butlerite Moravian Baptist church. The Butlerite

12 Edward L. Cox, 1994, p.212.
13 *Ibid.*, pp.222, 231.

church became a centre for political motivation and labour organization. Butler's leadership style was intensely Baptist – Biblical in imagery, messianic in vision – and his church proved the prelude to his founding of his own political party in 1936. He became the chief oil-worker organizer in 1935–7.[14]

Butler's style was rooted in a religio-political world view. It was not the only ideology in the twentieth-century Caribbean, but it was traditionally the most influential in Afro-Caribbean societies. It was, however, Jamaica that provided the most dramatic example of traditional Afro-Christian political prophetism in the early twentieth century.

Nineteenth-century Jamaican Revivalism was bridged into the twentieth century by Bedwardism. Alexander Bedward, born in 1859, began his ministry in 1891. He was a healer in the Jamaican Native Baptist and Revivalist traditions, but he also became a charismatic leader as Marcus Garvey did later, on a grander scale. Like any black religious mobilizer in the colonial West Indies, Bedward was considered a threat by government authorities. Bedward's followers responded militantly to the threat of suppression. Leaders dressed in white military uniforms and led processions of Bedwardites who marched with a distinctive strut. At his ascension, predicted for the final day of December 1920, Jamaica and the world, he prophesied, would be apocalyptically renewed and Whites would be destroyed. Whites in Jamaica, of course, feared an uprising, and remembered slave and post-slave rebellions that were characteristic of Jamaican history.

None of the apocalyptic events Bedward predicted occurred. He was arrested and confined in an insane asylum until his death. From the viewpoint of the socially and politically dominant Whites, Bedward was truly insane. But the anthropologist Martha Beckwith, in her 1929 study of Jamaican folklore, *Black Roadways*, noted a less literalist non-white view in Jamaica at the time that Bedward was a 'prophet who was to the wise foolishness but whom the common people heard gladly ....'[15]

Jamaica contributed two Afrocentric politico-religious movements that far exceeded in influence all similar movements in the Caribbean: Garveyism and Rastafarianism. Marcus Garvey (1887–1946) believed that he spoke and wrote 'with a mission from the High God'. That mission was the education of black people to appreciate each other and to love the race.[16] For Garvey, the people of the African diaspora were children of captivity. Africa was the 'new, yet ever old, land of our fathers, the land of God's crowning glory.' Blacks in exile were like the children of Israel who, by God's command, turned toward

14 Bridget Brereton, 1981, p.180.
15 Martha Beckwith, 1929, p.169.
16 David Lowenthal and Lambros Comitas, 1973, p.87; chap.6, this volume.

the promised land.[17] Garvey's movement, organized in the United Negro Improvement Association (UNIA), was both spiritual and political, similar to Butler's organization in Trinidad. Garvey's leadership was charismatic and messianic. In the UNIA, he blended high-church formality and Baptist evangelicalism with an African sense of festival.[18]

Garvey's movement inspired and was succeeded in popular consciousness by the Rastafari movement. While Garveyism had almost immediate appeal outside of Jamaica throughout the African diaspora in the Caribbean, North, Central and South America, and Europe, Rastafarianism remained a local Jamaican development for decades before migration and Rastafari-inspired reggae music carried it throughout the world.

The Rastafari emerged among the unenfranchised masses in twentieth century Jamaica, which was typical of Britain's post-emancipation colonies in its oligarchy, metropolitan control, and strict class and colour hierarchical patterns in all its institutions, including government, education and the churches.[19] Colonial society was defined by the Rastafari as Babylon, and their condition as one of Biblical captivity, estranged from an Ethiopian Zion.[20] The founders of the movement were greatly inspired by Garvey's politico-religious preaching, such as his description of the yearning of Blacks in the diaspora to 'lay down our burden and rest our weary backs and feet by the Niger, and sing our songs and chant our hymns to the God of Ethiopia'. The Rastafari chose Ethiopian Emperor Haile Selassie as the symbol and reality of a black God, accepting as absolute the emperor's biblical identity as the direct descendant of King David and the 225th in a line of Ethiopian kings in an unbroken succession from the Queen of Sheba.[21]

On all the major issues that enter into their doctrine – interpreting scripture, repatriation, the meaning of death, the sacrament of *ganja* (marijuana), the role of women, hair style, language, diet, and so on – the Rastafari have disagreed, and there is not likely to be a unified resolution or an orthodoxy in a religion that is decentralized and has relied greatly on the prophetism of local leaders.[22] But one of the significant points of agreement among the Rastafari is their discernment of an unholy alliance between the leaders of Church and State. Powerful and wealthy leaders of State and society looked to the churches to rationalize their injustices toward the black poor, according to

17 Leonard E. Barrett, 1974, p.130.
18 *Ibid.*, p.142.
19 *Ibid.*, p.157.
20 Joseph Owens, 1976, p.70.
21 Leonard E. Barrett, 1974, pp.145, 158.
22 The best current source on the complex development and diversity of the Rastafari is Barry Chevannes, 1994.

the Rastafari critique. Churchmen in return received benefits from their wealthy secular clients. And the church that most represented for them accommodation with Babylon was the Roman Catholic Church.[23]

While the Rastafari celebrate their African roots, they do not identify with those Caribbean religions that are closest in practice to traditional West and West Central African religions. Among Caribbean world views, the most African are those that maintain devotions to ancestral spirits and a pantheon of deities, within which hierarchically there is a high god who is indifferent to the quotidian concerns of devotees. It is more the spirits who are involved with the daily affairs of health, wealth and interpersonal relationships. The Rastafari, influenced as they are by Hebrew monotheism and Christian incarnationalism, reject African spiritism as it has been creolized in Jamaica, in such religions as Convince, Kumina, Pukumina and Revival. Spirit belief, essential to African traditions, is especially strong in the countries with francophone and hispanophone histories, those which have inherited the Roman Catholic tradition of the saints.

Several anglophone islands which were at one time in the empires of France and/or Spain have religions that revolve around ancestral spirits and African deities. In Grenada and Carriacou, there is Big Drum, also known as the Nation Dance. Ceremonies are organized for significant occasions by families or by groups that represent a single occupation. A funeral, a serious illness, a marriage, and economic misfortune are examples of reasons for practising the Nation Dance, during which the ancestors are summoned by dancing and drumming, their pardon is asked if they have been offended, and they are requested to intervene for the benefit of the parties for whom the ceremony has been organized. Kele in St Lucia is similar to Big Drum, but is more intricately African and incorporates ancient Amerindian elements. As with Big Drum, Kele ceremonies are performed at important life junctures or crises. Drums and work tools, as well as Amerindian stone axes, are ceremonial implements. The axes derive from a synthesis of Amerindian and African belief, and they are called 'Changó', or Shango, named after the Yoruba deity of thunder and lightning. Kele invokes the spirits through dancing, drumming and the sacrifice of a goat. The ancestors are fed, and they may possess participants in the ceremony. The deity Shango is central in Orisha, or the devotion to powerful spirits, in Trinidad and Grenada. The spirits are mainly Yoruba deities, although a few Creole spirits have entered the pantheon. An Orisha ceremony can last for days. It is similar to Haitian Vodou in that it begins with Roman Catholic devotions, then transitions into communication with the Orishas through drumming, dancing, singing and possession. As in

23 *Ibid.*, p.161.

Kele, animal sacrifice is essential for proper feeding of the spirits. The goal of Orisha devotion is individual well-being and communal equilibrium.[24]

Perhaps the best-known forms of Afro-Caribbean religion are Haitian Vodou and Cuban Santería. The Vodou cosmology is intricate and its pantheon is richly and colourfully populated. It is a symbiosis of the Catholicism of the slave masters and the spirit beliefs of slaves from Nigeria, Dahomey, Senegal and Kongo. The spirits or *loa*, best rendered as '*lwa*' to capture Créole pronunciation, are mainly Dahomean deities in what is known in Haiti as the Rada pantheon, after the Dahomean kingdom of Arada. There are also Taino and Creole deities who, reflecting Haiti's harsh history, tend to be more volatile. They inhabit the Petro pantheon. The *lwa* are associated with Catholic saints; saints' names and printed icons acted as masks for the African deities when devotion to them was suppressed at various times in the past.[25]

Vodou has had political implications ever since slave rebels invoked the *lwa* for strength and protection in the struggle that led to an independent Haiti. The power of Vodou as a source of political resistance was demonstrated in the twentieth century. During the United States occupation of Haiti from 1915 to 1934, about five thousand armed peasants, called Cacos, carried out a sustained guerrilla resistance. They were inspired by the angry Petro *lwa*, and they were supported by the mass of ordinary Haitians who demonstrated against what they saw as the return of the white domination against which their slave ancestors had fought.[26]

During and after the occupation, Roman Catholicism strengthened its institutional presence in Haiti, and provided a means of contact with the wider world which had been denied Haiti by the country's international isolation since its independence. The Catholic Church had to contend with Vodou, and was at various times both suppressive and tolerant of Haiti's Afro-Creole ancestral traditions. The result of the Church's periodic attempts to suppress Vodou was invariably the reaffirmation of the Petro *lwa* among Catholics who also served the *lwa*.[27] In 1970, towards the end of the administration of François Duvalier, the government officially acknowledged Vodou and promised protection to its adherents. The policy was continued during the 1971–86 administration of Jean-Claude Duvalier. Ironically, it was an allied anti-government resistance of radical Catholic priests and Vodouisants in the service of the Petro *lwa* that led to the resignation and exile of Jean-Claude

---

24 See George Eaton Simpson, 1978, pp.73–9, 83–6 for Shango (Orisha) in Trinidad and Grenada; pp.102–3 for Big Drum; and pp.103–6 for Kele.

25 Leslie G. Desmangles, 1992, pp.36, 114, 121–2, 123, 130, 138, 144–5, 158–9, 173.

26 *Ibid.*, pp.48–9.

27 *Ibid.*, pp.52–3.

Duvalier in 1986.[28] The socio-political influence of Vodouism needs to be understood as complementary to Catholicism in Haiti, as will be seen below.

Santería resembles Vodou in its spirit devotion, ceremony and incorporation of the Roman Catholic cult of the saints. Whereas Dahomean deities are hegemonic in Vodou, Yoruba deities predominate in Santería. Santería is also called Lucumí, a term of Yoruba ethnic identity in Cuba. Afro-Cuban religion is actually more varied than the use of the name Santería indicates, and is a palimpsest of Kongo, Yoruba, Calibar, Dahomean-Fon, Taino and Spanish Catholic influence. Santería actually names only one of the four major Afro-Cuban religions, Regla de Ocha. There is also Ñañiguismo (la Sociedad Secreta Abakuá), Palo Monte or Mayombe (Kongo), and Cuban Vodou (la Regla Arará).[29]

Afro-Cuban religion and Vodou link monotheism and polytheism, in that the Orishas and *lwa* are emanations of a high god. This supreme being is distant, and communication with the deities below him is the main purpose of ceremony. In Afro-Cuban belief, a supernatural power pervades the cosmos. It is called '*achê* or '*ashê* in Lucumí, and it can be focused and contained in certain material objects. The invested object takes on a personality that identifies it with the deity that is the font of its *ashé.* Sacred stones in particular are objects of power, and they are washed and fed as not only representations but as actual embodiments of the Orishas. Afro-Cuban and Vodou rituals are comparable in their complex ceremonies, within which are mediated the relationships between humans and the deities. Music and dance are essential in these ceremonies, and in the twentieth century Afro-Cuban rhythms have defined Latin American music as well as greatly influenced world music. Revelation of divine purpose is sought by Afro-Cuban diviners at important life junctures, and magic, or the manipulation of divine power for a specific effect, is common. The effects sought are practical and inter-personal, and can be beneficial or harmful, such as gaining or repelling another's affection, causing harm toward an enemy, achieving success in business or causing a rival to be unsuccessful, or curing an illness.[30] This is similar to Obeah in the anglophone Caribbean.

Santería and the other forms of Afro-Cuban religion function as social and economic networks. The healing practices of their diviners and herbalists constitute a health system complementary to that of the State. Both in the

---

28 *Ibid.*, pp.56–7.

29 Eugenio Matibag, 1996, pp.7, 10. George Brandon, 1993, describes throughout the complexities of the Afro-Cuban religious 'intersystem;' see especially pp.163–75.

30 Eugenio Matibag, 1996, pp.11–16; George Brandon, 1993, p.16; Migene González-Wippler, 1995, pp.100–3, 181.

Caribbean and abroad, among the large Latino immigrant communities in North America, believers and their *santeros* or leaders constitute fictive extended families.[31] They are not congregations in the ecclesiastical sense, nor do they have a hierarchy or centralized authority.

The attitudes of Cuba's governments and middle and upper classes toward Afro-Cuban religion have been ambivalent from the late nineteenth century, and have vacillated between tolerance and repression. African ethnicity and religion had been cultivated in Cuba in the institution of the '*cabildos*' from before independence. Cuban *cabildos* were patterned on Spanish religious confraternities. In Cuba as in Spain, they functioned importantly not only as religious societies but as mutual aid and funeral associations as well. In Cuba, the *cabildos* were originally under the direction of diocesan priests, who carried out a kind of 'guided syncretism',[32] accommodating African customs as a temporary strategy toward eventual full assimilation of Africans into Spanish Catholicism. The strategy failed and the *cabildos* became little nations of African ethnic identity and Afro-Cuban religious innovation.

Throughout the twentieth century, the place of African culture in Cuban identity has been a constant issue of debate among the middle class and government leaders, both before and after the Castro revolution. Three general viewpoints emerged, according to George Brandon: 'an anti-Africanist tendency, a syncretist tendency promoting the blending of spiritism and the African religions, and an avant-garde tendency among some Cuban intellectuals that promoted the African religions as sources of artistic inspiration and national culture.'[33] Governmental fears of the *cabildos* as sources of political mobilization and resistance drove them underground in the twentieth century, but they continued in the form of the Afro-Cuban nation religions or 'reglas.'

By the mid-1970s, the Cuban government had come officially to accept Afro-Cuban religion as part of the national culture. During the first 15 years after Fidel Castro's revolution, however, State policy was one of suppression. The Marxist government did not attempt to wipe out private religious belief as such, but sanctions were imposed on any religious group that was seen to be an economic, political or ideological obstacle to socialist reconstruction.[34] The Afro-Cuban religious subculture was suspect for a number of reasons. It was accused of maintaining an alternative economy in conflict with the centralized planned economy of the State. Believers maintained forms of mutual

31 George Brandon, 1993, pp.106, 149.
32 *Ibid.*, pp.70–1.
33 *Ibid.*, p.82.
34 *Ibid.*, p.102.

aid, of savings and insurance, that had been developed in the *cabildos*. They established networks among themselves for obtaining materials, including sacrificial animals, needed in their ceremonies. The potential of religious societies for mobilizing workers and obstructing government policy was shown in 1970 when the Abakuá society organized a strike of black dock-workers that paralysed the port of Havana for a day. Previously, in the late 1960s, the military had had to suppress armed guerrillas led by anti-revolutionary *santeros*. Ideological conflict resulted from the lack of any distinction between the secular and sacred in Afro-Cuban cosmology, a world view that countered Marxist doctrine. In addition, Santería was associated with odious pre-revolutionary regimes. Both Gerardo Machado, president from 1925 to 1933, and Fulgencio Batista, constitutional president in 1940–4 and dictator from 1952 to his overthrow in 1958, were said to invoke the power of the spirits for power and protection. Both were particularly associated with self-aggrandizement, political repression and the strengthening of United States control over Cuban affairs.[35]

The revolutionary government's propaganda against religious groups and practices of African origin included charges that they led to juvenile delinquency, criminality, mental backwardness and educational retardation. But the campaign did not result in the eradication of African beliefs and practices. Repression simply forced the religious societies to go deeper underground and to increase in membership.[36]

The revolutionary government's acceptance of Afro-Cuban religion in the 1970s may have been part of a strategy to depoliticize it through folklorization. The Cuban National Institute of Ethnology and Folklore had been studying African religious sects from the 1960s. The result of the Institute's study was the decision to accept African religious expression as a cultural artifact, a colourful relic in a materialist society from a time of ignorance and underdevelopment. African religious dances and music were performed for entertainment by the National Folklore Ensemble.[37]

But a series of events in the 1970s and 1980s resulted in circumstances that would cause the government to retreat from its former attitudes toward Afro-Cuban religion. Cuban involvement in African wars of liberation led to greater tolerance of African traditions. Economic setbacks in Cuba caused many in the population to turn increasingly to the power of the Orishas for refuge and strength. Growing popular discontent in the island perhaps moved the government to back away from systematic stigmatization of deeply held beliefs.

---

35 Eugenio Matibag, 1996, pp.227, 229–30.

36 *Ibid.*, pp.230–1.

37 George Brandon, 1993, p.102.

And as Cuba opened gradually to tourism, demonstrations of Santería, not simply choreographed folkloric productions, proved of interest to foreigners.[38]

The African roots of Cuban culture seemed to receive official recognition in 1987 when the Oni of Ife, the spiritual leader of the Nigerian Yoruba, visited Cuba. After the Oni met with Castro and members of the Politburo, it was arranged for the Fourth International Congress on Orisha Tradition and Culture to meet in Cuba in 1988, bypassing the originally planned site in Haiti. In exchange, Cuba established a José Martí Cultural Center in Ife. At the end of the twentieth century, Santería continued in Cuba to honour the ancestors, worship the Orishas, and order daily life. In 1985, the Catholic Church in Cuba acknowledged that 85 per cent of Cubans practised some form of Afro-Cuban religion.[39]

Compared with Cuba, Puerto Rico's Yoruba tradition in religion is weaker, yet nevertheless traceable. Shango, the deity of thunder, lightning and fire, has been identified in local groups such as that of Santiago Matamoros (St James the Apostle) on the north-eastern coast.[40] Traditionally, the term *santeros* in Puerto Rico referred to craftsmen who made wood carvings of the saints. This is similar to the tradition in the Dominican Republic of making wood (*palo*) saints.[41] In the Dominican Republic's popular religion, as in Puerto Rico's synthesis of Taino, Catholic, and African influences, the divine is approached through the saints who mask a pantheon of spirits. This communication is mediated by specialists such as the *brujos*, who control possessing spirits, and the *curanderos*, who communicate with the spirits to gain knowledge of curing herbs and roots.[42]

The major differences between the Cuban and Puerto Rican manifestations of Santería have been the larger influence in Puerto Rico of Spiritism, originating in the nineteenth-century French theosophy of Allan Kardec, and the feedback from the North American experience of Puerto Ricans. The island's peculiar 'commonwealth' relationship with the United States allowed Puerto Ricans to be the pioneers of Latino identity along the United States' Atlantic coast. The tensions caused by their minority ethnicity and anomalous condition of quasi-citizenry, as well as their urban proximity to later hispanic immigrant communities, especially Cubans and Dominicans, have resulted in their engrafting of new Santería branches onto Puerto Rican popular religion in North America and in the island.[43]

38 Eugenio Matibag, 1996, p.231.
39 *Ibid.*, p.232.
40 Migene González-Wippler, 1995, pp.104–6.
41 Andrés I. Pérez y Mena, 1995, p.144.
42 'Dominican Republic: Religion', 1989, p.1.
43 Andrés I. Pérez y Mena, 1995, pp.149–51, 152.

Throughout the greater Caribbean, wherever imperialism brought together Amerindians, Europeans and Africans, common orientations toward the spirit world are observable, in spite of linguistic differences and geographical contrasts. At the far south-eastern rim of the region, Suriname, formerly Dutch Guiana, has a religious culture whose dynamics are comparable to those found in Vodou, Santería, and the various forms of Afro-Christian syntheses throughout the anglophone West Indies. Suriname's Maroon traditions, based on kinship, ancestral spirits, local deities and a protecting high god, continued in the twentieth century to be vital among the Ndjukas, Saramakas and other Maroon groups, even when perturbed by innovations such as the vindictive and puritanical *Gaan Gadu* anti-witchcraft cult at the turn of the century.[44] Among Suriname's Creole majority, who speak the lingua franca Sranan Tongo, traditional religion is termed *Winti,* or the colonial pejorative *Afkodre* (idolatry). Winti denotes 'winds', or invading spirits. In the Winti cosmology, physical, mental or economic misfortune is attributable to mischievous spirits called *Bakru.* A complex theory of personality can be extrapolated from Winti's veneration of the soul, the *akra* or *yeye.* An individual's soul does not so much isolate the personality as link it to a wider community. The soul is believed to contain a number of guiding spirits, identical to the gods of the pantheon. Each person harbours at least a trinity consisting of a female earth deity, a male African or Amerindian deity, and one of a group of lesser, and less trusted, deities. Winti practice includes ritual libations, herbal baths and the interpretation of dreams. Its adherents are Christian believers as well, and especially identify with the evangelical Moravian Church, implanted by missionaries in Dutch Guiana. The Moravian Church is so rooted that any definition of Surinamese ethnic culture must include it.[45]

Winti has become especially significant as a focus of cultural identity since Suriname's independence in 1975. It is a protean system, open to multiple influences, and has served as a unifier of apparently disparate members of the middle and lower classes and urban and rural communities.[46] Similar to the reverse influence of the North American experience of Puerto Ricans on their island's culture, the quest for identity among young Surinamese growing up in the Netherlands has led them to authenticate Winti in a way that has rebounded to strengthen the post-independence identity of the home country.[47]

---

44 H. U. E. Thoden van Velzen, 1995, pp.197–8, 204–5.
45 Wilhelmina van Wetering, 1995, pp.213, 215, 216–17.
46 Ineke van Wetering, 1999, p.81.
47 Wilhelmina van Wetering, 1995, p.215.

Roman Catholicism in the francophone and hispanophone Caribbean

In the anglophone Caribbean, the Church of England was the predominant religious institution in the colonial State. Even after disestablishment throughout most of the British West Indies in the late nineteenth century, it continued to hold the prestige that had accrued to it throughout the centuries of imperial establishmentarianism. A similar prestige was held by the Roman Catholic Church in the francophone and hispanophone Caribbean. The centrality of the Catholic Church – as a symbol of Spanish and French culture, as an institutional force, and as a system of beliefs – was inherited in the twentieth century by islands such as Puerto Rico, Cuba and Hispaniola.

In Puerto Rico, this inheritance was one of failure. It was a failure to respond humanely to the social questions of class, race, education and indigenous culture.[48] Under the hegemony of the United States, the Puerto Rican Church had little opportunity to adopt progressive policies on these issues. Roman Catholic indifference to social issues was replaced by Protestant colonial condescension.

As a bulwark of Spanish culture, the Catholic Church had taken no initiative in colonial Puerto Rico toward fostering an indigenous clergy. Such a move, the hierarchy feared, might lead to anti-Spanish nationalism. The aristocratic peninsularism of the Spanish church prevented it from identifying with the rural and urban poor. In the twentieth century, that vacuum would be filled by evangelical Protestant churches. Traditional Roman Catholicism lost its influence in Puerto Rico for three main reasons: its aristocratic identification, its indifference to the socio-economic problems of the poor, and its opposition to a liberal education that would lead to rational discourse on issues of faith.[49]

Paradoxically, American colonialism delayed the decline of Catholicism in Puerto Rico. The implementation of the policy of separation of Church and State, the arrival of a North American clergy, more pragmatic, liberal and congregational than the Spanish clergy, and the timid yet certain encouragement of an indigenous clergy, all led to a renewal of the Catholic Church that prevented it from becoming merely a colonial relic.[50]

'It is surprising,' wrote Caribbeanist Gordon Lewis, 'that the relationship between religion and politics has not been closer than it is' in Puerto Rico.[51]

48 Gordon K. Lewis, 1963 (1974), p.271.

49 *Ibid.*, p.273.

50 *Ibid.*, pp.273–4.

51 *Ibid.*, p.275.

No religiously based cultural nationalism has developed on the island. The Church and autonomy have not been historically linked. The possibility of a linkage developed and quickly faded during a brief period after 1898. There was a resurgence of the Catholic Church as a symbol of Puerto Rican tradition threatened by Protestant America. But this brief assertion of hispanic religious culture declined when the Spanish hierarchy was replaced by a North American one.

Twentieth-century Puerto Rico, then, has not been the scene of a continuing conflict between Catholic culture and a colonizing American Protestant culture. The process has been a more complex one of an Americanization of Catholicism and the Puertoricanization of Protestantism. The issue of language provides an example. A prevailing Catholic policy under United States colonialism was to discourage the speaking of Spanish and to promote English, not only in the schools but also in homes. The Church thus became a symbol of alienation from local cultural patterns, of which the vernacular is a primary preserver and transmitter. Protestants, however, for purposes of evangelization, have been much more sensitive to the use of Spanish. Consequently, and in spite of a fundamentalist ideology that rejects both Catholicism and forms of popular spiritism, Protestants have become more identified with local culture.[52]

A consequence of these paradoxes and of North American secularization is that Puerto Rican politicians in the twentieth century have not given priority to religious questions. They have perceived that religious divisions have little correspondence with economic and political ones. The Puerto Rican State in the twentieth century came to recognize the Church not as a symbol of culture so much as an adjunct provider of social services. The Catholic Church's major intervention in politics – the 1960 attempt to create a Christian Action Party – served merely to weaken further its credibility in a secularized colony, and was seen by politicians as the last gasp of an antiquated clericalism.[53]

A comparison of the Catholic Church in Puerto Rico with its situation in other parts of the hispanophone Caribbean indicates similarities and contrasts. Cubans have been nominally Catholic, as have Puerto Ricans. And similar to the Puerto Rican Church, the Church in Cuba has not been a major political force, even before Fidel Castro's enforcement of Marxist ideology effectively defused the Church as both a reactive and innovational social institution within the island. Before Castro, the two major obstacles to the Church's sociopolitical influence were the scarcity of priests in rural areas and the inability

52 *Ibid.*, pp.276–7.
53 *Ibid.*, pp.279–80.

of a predominantly pro-Franco Spanish clergy to respond to contemporary socio-political issues. After Cuban independence in 1902, the Spanish clergy were faced with the challenge of making the Church an authentically Cuban one. Similar to the situation in Puerto Rico, any creative response which might have been forthcoming to this challenge was effectively prevented by the separation of Church and State under United States hegemony. The United States deliberately diminished the role of the Catholic Church in its effort to dehispanicize the island. Catholic parades were banned, for example, and marriage was made a civil matter.[54]

In 1942, the Catholic Church attempted to inject the principles defined in pontifical social encyclicals into Cuban life. The 'Democracia Social Cristiana' movement condemned economic individualism and the supremacy of capital over labour. It was also critical of Marxism, which it defined as the domination of labour over capital.[55] It was with this mindset that the Church welcomed the possibility of limited change at the beginning of Castro's revolution. Catholic priests as well as mainstream Protestant and Jewish leaders expected a renewal in politics and government, but were opposed to the radical changes that soon took place, such as land reform, nationalization of foreign-owned corporations and private-sector Cuban businesses, and the creation of a single-party Marxist State. The Catholic, Protestant and Jewish leaderships were each linked to foreign sources of funding and personnel. The United States-led embargo of Cuba and the flight of Church leaders and members in the 1960s left only a marginalized Roman Catholic remnant on the island.[56]

To this remnant fell the task of initiating a rapprochement with the communist government. It began in 1969 with two pastoral letters. One condemned the United States economic blockade of Cuba and called on Catholics to support government programmes that were in the interests of the common good. The second assured Catholics that co-operation with Marxists in projects with humane ends was morally acceptable. Militantly anti-Castro Catholics considered the letters a capitulation to the Marxist government, while leftist Catholics thought them not sufficiently revolutionary. But the letters, supported by statements from the Protestant Cuban Council of Evangelical Churches, were first steps toward a Marxist-Christian dialogue that would lead to a pragmatic resolution by the end of the century.[57]

Progress toward reconciliation was tentative in the 1970s. In the spirit of the 1969 pastoral letters, the Catholic remnant attempted to become more relevant in the new Cuban social order by showing a willingness to engage in

54 Richard Pattee, 1966, p.109; Geoff Simons, 1996, p.206.
55 Richard Pattee, 1966, p.109.
56 Margaret E. Crahan, 1989, p.212.
57 *Ibid.*

progressive theological discussion on how to contribute positively within the socialist system. They were inspired greatly by the emergence of liberation theology throughout Latin America. Not all Christians in Cuba went along with this trend, and conservative Protestants criticized what they saw as the increasing identification of the Council of Evangelical Churches with the Revolution. Among both Catholics and Protestants, progressive statements from religious leaders did not always reflect the pro-socialist and anti-Castro frictions in the congregations. But the openness toward dialogue expressed by the leaders allowed the Marxist government in the 1970s to become in turn more open to religion, while nevertheless always ready to condemn religion when it became a source of anti-Castro resistance. The government had no positive opinion, for example, of Jehovah's Witnesses and Seventh Day Adventists, considered to be recalcitrantly counter-revolutionary.[58]

The government clarified its official policy on religion in 1976 in Article 54 of the new Cuban constitution. The article was little different from what was contained in pre-revolutionary constitutions. It guaranteed freedom of conscience and religious conviction, as long as religion was not used in opposition to the government, education, and the duties of work, national defence and reverence for national symbols. Nevertheless, church leaders were gratified by the clarification. They were even more pleased with the 1978 platform of the Communist Party, which went beyond the constitution by adopting an acceptance of religious believers as participants in a revolutionary society. The platform considered believers and non-believers to be equal in terms of social rights and responsibilities. In 1980, the Second Party Congress went as far as noting the possibility of strategic Marxist-Christian alliances toward a just society.[59]

By 1980, the position of Christians committed to living and working in Castro's Cuba was one of ideological compromise. They could be revolutionaries in their acceptance of socialism as an economic solution to past injustices, but did not have to accept Marxist atheism. Certain barriers continued into the final decade of the century. Active Christians as well as religious Jews were excluded from membership in the Communist Party and the Union of Communist Youth, restrictions which limited the institutional influence of believers. Restrictions also continued against public evangelization and the use of public places for religious meetings. Yet by the end of the century, religious leaders in Cuba interpreted their situation positively. They represent a faith that has been strengthened by the cauterization of the revolutionary process.[60]

58 *Ibid.*, pp.214–15.
59 *Ibid.*, p.215.
60 *Ibid.*, pp.216–17.

The visit of Pope John Paul II to Cuba in 1998 gave the Cuban government the opportunity to proclaim its end-of-the-century policy on the relationship between Church and State. Castro's view was that the Pope's visit represented the mutual respect that had come to exist between the Revolution and Catholics in particular, and between the Revolution and all communities of belief and non-belief in general. The theme of reconciliation was furthered by Ricardo Alarcón, National Assembly president, in his statement that the papal visit signified 'the ever more normalized and adjusted relations' between communities of belief and the rest of Cuban society.[61]

In the Dominican Republic, the Catholic Church was a central religious and social institution much in the same way it was in Puerto Rico and Cuba – by virtue of its historical link with Spanish colonialism. The vast majority of Dominicans identified themselves as Catholic, even if their allegiance was only nominal. The Church's historical pride stems from the time of Columbus, and is a result not only of the triumphalism of conquest but also of an awareness of Spanish missionaries' defence of the indigenous Tainos from the depredations of the colonists' exploitation of native labour. The Church's link with the colonial State, however, preserved an ethos of aristocratic power and muted its protest tradition. In the twentieth century, the hierarchy demonstrated its conservatism and its unwillingness to address issues of social injustice and political repression. Thus during the two most critical phases of twentieth-century Dominican history – the long-lasting Trujillo dictatorship of 1930–61 and the short-lived 1965 revolution – the Church was supportive of authoritarianism and passive in the face of mass suffering.[62] The Church joined other élites in opposition to the presidency of Juan Bosch, elected in 1963 on promises of a democratic social revolution.

Outside of its support of political authoritarianism, the Dominican Church's major role has been that of a provider of education and health services. But even in these areas, its priorities have been conservative. It has been most vocal in preaching against divorce and in counselling against artificial birth control. Poverty in the Dominican Republic affected the Church's ability to provide social services. Shortage of funds, together with a lack of systematic social programmes and personnel, dulled the Church's impact on the daily life of the Dominican peasantry and working class.[63]

In a similar way to Puerto Rico and Cuba, the Dominican Republic in the latter third of the twentieth century became more secularized. The separation of Church and State in practical politics has meant that the Church is

61 'An expression of respect,' *Granma* online, 23 January 1998.
62 Howard J. Wiarda and Michael J. Kryzanek, 1982, p.18.
63 *Ibid.*, pp.18, 64.

no longer automatically identified with the status quo, mainly because the Church has lost a privileged voice. It is no longer accepted that the Church can influence political policy and impose its dogma with respect to issues of family and reproductive morality.[64]

The unique history of Haiti offers the third major configuration of religious beliefs and political power after those in the hispanophone and anglophone Caribbean. The disappearance of a white francophone planter class and the uneasy coexistence of Afro-Haitian masses and mixed-race élites after the struggle for independence defined a troubled yet continuing role for the Catholic Church. Francophone culture was preserved in Haiti mainly by the mixed-race élite, and this culture by definition included Catholicism. Although the Créole-speaking majority were nominally Catholic, in practical reality their lives were more influenced by Vodou. Before the twentieth century, the influence of Vodou priests as community leaders, with more authority than the Catholic priests, was well established. Nothing in Haiti's tumultuous twentieth century has uprooted that inherited influence, and a consideration of Haiti's politics cannot ignore Vodou's power.

For the rural Haitian, three facts of existence are of equal and paramount importance because they are organically linked: community, land and the *lwa*. Vodou maintains an equilibrium among these three aspects of Creole culture, and is thus a method of social control. Rural persons of relative wealth and power – the 'gros neg' or 'gros habitant' – are kept in check as well as maintain their influence through Vodou.

In contrast with the Dominican Republic, Haiti's neighbouring country on the island of Hispaniola, twentieth-century Haiti did not inherit the Catholic Church as a powerful or wealthy institution, despite the 1860 concordat with the Vatican. Catholicism was primarily a symbol of identity for Haitian élites, a mask of representation for the world outside and a fence of separation from the Creole peasantry within. The peasantry, however, inherited an African openness to religious power whatever the source. They served the *lwa* and also participated in Catholic rites when they were available. Religion for them was more a link between cultures and classes rather than a symbol of separation as it was for the francophone élite.[65] Catholicism in Haiti, then, can hardly be discussed without reference to Vodou.

Periods of Catholic toleration of Vodou alternated with episodes of attempted repression, such as the Anti-Superstitions Campaigns of 1913 and 1941. In 1941, the Church was given police support in its Operation Cleanup. But repression only strengthened Vodou among Haitian peasants, who resist-

64 *Ibid.*, p.64.
65 Thomas E. Weil, 1982, p.50.

ed violently, forcing President Elie Lescot in 1942 to order an end to the anti-Vodou campaign.

Vodou and Catholicism came into further opposition in the second half of the century with the confluence of cultural nationalism and political power. Afro-Haitian nationalist opposition to the Catholic Church can be defined initially as an opposition to cultural imperialism. European priests were seen as teachers of anti-Haitian values and culture. The hierarchy was criticized as conservative and paternalistic, and the Catholic hierarchical structure was seen as a potential form of political organization ready to counter aspirations of Creole democracy. François Duvalier – Papa Doc – was perhaps the most notorious representative of the cultural nationalist viewpoint in twentieth-century Haitian politics. As president from 1957 to 1971, he demonstrated his opposition to the Catholic Church. He expelled several provincial bishops and the French archbishop of Port-au-Prince in 1960. The Jesuits, accused of conspiring in political resistance, were expelled in 1964. By the end of the 1960s, most foreign priests and teachers had left the country and had been replaced by Haitians. Duvalier succeeded in allying the army and paramilitary forces with means of social control derived from Vodou, all under the aegis of the presidency. Haitian élites, backed by the Vatican, opposed the regime that Duvalier created and maintained partly by means of Vodou.

Although a Vodouist, Duvalier nevertheless effectively used the symbols of the Catholic Church to bolster his image. He used its trappings when face to face with traditional mixed-race élites and with leaders of other governments. In his relationship with the majority of Haitians, however, Duvalier cultivated the image of and identification with the Vodou deity Baron Samedi, the keeper of the tombs. In effect, Vodou became a State establishment. Duvalier organized the loose rural network of Vodou priests under centralized presidential control. For the first time a Catholic idea of hierarchy was imposed on Vodou leaders, who were forced to acknowledge Duvalier's superior authority among them. Their power over their communities was now, in a sense, delegated to them by the Duvalierist State.[66]

After the expulsions of expatriate clergy, the indigenized Haitian clergy was more tolerant of Vodou. Since 1970, Vodou has been officially acknowledged by successive governments. Those who serve the *lwa*, and their '*oungans*' and '*mambos*' – male and female priests – are promised immunity from the persecution that earlier in the century was initiated by State and Church.[67]

---

66 *Ibid.*, p.116.

67 Leslie G. Desmangles, 1992, p.55.

In response to Duvalierism, the Catholic Church did indeed become a source of opposition and protest, but not, as the cultural nationalists originally thought, from a paternalistic and conservative ideology. The strongest opposition to the Duvalierist State was realized in the efforts of liberationist priests, most notably Jean-Bertrand Aristide, to rally discontent among the urban poor. Tellingly, Duvalier deported the French archbishop in 1960 on charges not that he was a neo-colonial reactionary but that he was supporting communist opposition to the regime. Yet it was from among the Haitian priests who replaced the expatriates that a true leftist challenge would arise. The last major Vodou-inspired political resistance in the twentieth century occurred in 1986, this time against the regime of Jean-Claude Duvalier, Papa Doc's son. It was actually a two-pronged movement of radical priests and Vodouists who served the Petro *lwa.*

Aristide, elected president of Haiti in 1990, linked his religiously based resistance to the Duvalierist dictatorship with the country's tradition of slave resistance. He contextualized liberationist theology in terms of Creole history and culture. Vodou became 'a way of applying religious belief to social reality'. Christianity and Vodou, he asserted, are connected in Afro-Haitian consciousness. The connection was established during slavery, and Aristide pointed in support to the tendency of rebelling slaves to undergo multiple baptisms.[68]

According to Aristide, the Catholic Church continued to represent State authority, even after Duvalierism began to challenge the Church. True opposition to the State did not occur until priests who were close to the people began to speak on behalf of the poor. After the departure of Jean-Claude Duvalier from Haiti in 1986, the hierarchy called for national reconciliation, but did not insist on social justice as the price of reconciliation. At a Youth Congress in Les Cayes in August 1986, liberationist sentiment was voiced in the slogan, 'Legliz se nou tout; nou tout se Legliz' (the Church is all of us; all of us are the Church).[69] The conflict within the Church was adjunct to the post-Duvalier national conflict of the time. And in reaction to the challenge of the Youth Congress, the hierarchy took steps to stifle popular radicalism, and Aristide himself was ordered to resign as a priest.

Faith and politics coincide, argued Aristide, in that both are searches for the common good. A prophetic church is one that supports the cause of the oppressed to bring them into a commonality with other social classes in the pursuit of a society characterized by love, justice and freedom. Such a church should not compromise with oppressive political power, nor should it enjoy

68 Jean-Bertrand Aristide, 1991, p.109.

69 *Ibid.*, 1991, p.111.

élite privileges. Political power, Aristide was careful to point out, does not necessarily imply oppression, but should be part of the process of searching for a common good.[70]

At the end of the century, Catholicism and Vodou were in equilibrium in the world view of most Haitians. Catholicism is identified with heaven but Vodou has to do with the earth. Both have distinct but complementary functions. Participation in Catholic ritual is a link with official culture. The administration of the sacraments provides opportunities for social interaction. And the Church is a symbol of contact with a world outside of Haiti. Vodou, through the power of the *lwa*, offers healing and assistance in coping with persistent poverty and famine. *Oungans* and *mambos*, as local leaders, provide services that are beyond the Church's power.[71]

Mainstream Protestant churches

The key issue regarding the traditional or mainstream Protestant churches in the Caribbean is the extent to which they remained dependent on metropolitan control and finances. The issue is relevant to society, culture and politics in that the extent to which the churches were able to indigenize affected the orientation of church members toward self-sufficiency and local authenticity. In general, attitudes of dependence prevailed throughout most of the twentieth century.

In the British West Indies, the Protestant denominations generally accepted Crown Colony government as the best way of providing some measure of justice, solutions to social problems and education. Church leaders were socially comfortable with colonial officials and approving of foreign-owned businesses. A new factor in church dependence in the twentieth century was United States influence. The reliance of some of the churches on North American finances and controlling boards brought about a renewed dependency as well as a diversification of churches and personnel. The pattern of dependence and of accommodation between the Church and colonial society prevailed until the 1960s, the decade when the British West Indian islands began to gain independence. Trained leaders then were still largely expatriates.[72]

The churches in the West Indies began as missions. The Church of England, Baptists, Methodists, Congregationalists, Presbyterians, Moravians,

70 *Ibid.*, p.112.
71 Leslie G. Desmangles, 1992, p.178.
72 Arthur Charles Dayfoot, 1999, p.189.

Quakers and Lutherans had all been a part of West Indian history from the era of slavery. After emancipation in 1834, North American-based Congregationalists, Disciples of Christ, Presbyterians, African Methodist Episcopalians, Lutherans and the Salvation Army entered the Caribbean, and by the twentieth century were in the mainstream together with the older churches. The Seventh Day Adventists bridge the time between these churches and the new twentieth-century congregations derived from other North American movements and denominations.

To what extent did these churches attempt to indigenize in the twentieth century? The Church of England, which was disestablished throughout most of the British Caribbean in the latter third of the nineteenth century, maintained a British connection through its bishops and clergy, mainly English, and by its general cultural orientation.[73] The early twentieth century saw the Methodists falter in their earlier attempt to become a West Indian church. Western and Eastern Methodist Caribbean Conferences had been formed in 1884. But in 1903 both conferences pleaded to be taken back as missions of the Methodist Church in Britain, and this reconnection with the British Methodists took place in 1904. It was not until 1967, after most of the British West Indies had become independent, that an autonomous Methodist Church of the Caribbean and the Americas was formed.[74]

Other older denominations in the Caribbean became dependent in the twentieth century on overseas missions after a period of relative independence. The Lutherans in Guyana, for example, became affiliated as a mission of the United Lutheran Church of America. And the Baptist Missionary Society in England, after withdrawing from the Caribbean in 1896, resumed a financial connection with the Baptists in Trinidad in 1946.[75]

Circumstances that made church independence difficult were generally the same that frustrated any metropolitan-based or originated institution's efforts to indigenize: economic depression in the West Indies, poverty, debt, shortage of staff, the expense of maintaining schools and natural disasters such as hurricane and earthquake. Good intentions were limited by these contingencies. But historical circumstance could also turn into impetus for autonomy. The Moravians, for example, were forced to lessen their dependence on Herrnhut when Germany became involved in two world wars.

The localization of the Presbyterian Church in the West Indies is difficult to describe in general terms, both because of two distinct historical origins and because of Presbyterian identification with Indian ethnicity in the south-

73 *Ibid.*, p.209.
74 *Ibid.*, pp.210–11.
75 *Ibid.*, pp.214–15.

ern Caribbean. In the mid-nineteenth century, both the Church of Scotland and independent Scottish presbyteries merged in one synod in Jamaica. Presbyterianism in Trinidad had two distinct roots: Scottish Presbyterians who began their work in the island in the 1830s, and missionaries of the Canadian Presbyterian Church, active since the 1860s. In Guyana, where the Church of Scotland had existed since 1816, two Presbyterian churches developed, one from the Scottish Church and the other from the Canadian mission. A local presbytery was created in the 1920s in Trinidad and in the 1940s in Guyana, and independence was achieved in the 1970s. Presbyterianism in Grenada grew from a combination of an older Scots Kirk presence and a twentieth-century missionary outreach from Trinidad.

The second half of the century saw significant local initiatives among the Christian churches to become West Indian-focused rather than metropolitan. The focus included social, political and cultural issues as well as theological and liturgical ones. While denominationalism had helped preserve ecclesiastical dependence, ecumenism would serve as the mechanism that would help the churches indigenize. In 1952, Jamaican Congregationalists, Methodists, Moravians and Presbyterians combined in a Church Union Commission. In 1965, Presbyterians and Congregationalists merged in the United Church of Jamaica and Grand Cayman. A significant combination of ecumenism and social action was accomplished with the formation of the CADEC group – Christian Action for Development in the Eastern Caribbean. Lay and clerical representatives of the major churches, including Roman Catholics, from throughout the Caribbean attended the Caribbean Ecumenical Consultation for Development at Chaguaramas in Trinidad in 1971. And in 1973, the regional Caribbean Conference of Churches (CCC) was formed. The CCC was the first such council in the world in which the Catholic Church was an integral member.[76]

The significance of these ecumenical initiatives went beyond institutional co-operation among church leaders. Several conferences and publications within the ecumenical movement took the issue of Caribbean identity under critical consideration. Two 1973 Conferences on Creative Theological Reflection, one in Jamaica and the other in Trinidad, generated a collection of essays published as *Troubling of the Waters.*

In his foreword to that collection, the Roman Catholic Archbishop of Kingston, Samuel Carter, wrote, 'A Caribbean theology is part of the Caribbean identity for which our people are searching in these latter decades of the Twentieth Century.' He went on to assert that the essays in the book were indicative of a process of intellectual decolonization.[77] Carter himself

76 *Ibid.*, p.221.
77 Idris Hamid, 1973, p.4.

was a symbol of ecclesiastical decolonization, in that he was the first native Jamaican to become a Catholic bishop. His statement was all the more remarkable coming from a leader of a church that had long been both a symbol and a mechanism of metropolitan control.

The participants in the Jamaican and Trinidadian conferences and the authors of the essays in *Troubling of the Waters* were not only church representatives but included specialists in Caribbean history and literary criticism. They wrote of theological decolonization, of Black Power, of West Indian values and of education. The writers presented a sophisticated and radical critique of the Christian churches and theology in Caribbean history, and proposed a new theology based on the symbol of Christ incarnate in Caribbean culture and society.

The commitment of the Caribbean Conference of Churches to this critique can be seen in the Conference's attempt to make it available on a popular level throughout the Caribbean through its newspaper, *Caribbean Contact*, published monthly from 1972 to 1994. *Contact*'s articles were brief and focused, and each issue included French and Spanish versions of its major stories and editorials. The paper reported regularly on topics such as education, economic regionalism, labour, politics and sports, especially cricket. It regularly reviewed new books, fiction and non-fiction. Its editorials scrutinized issues such as political corruption and United States involvement in the Caribbean. It maintained a consistent focus on gender issues. And its view was always of the wider Caribbean beyond the anglophone West Indies. *Caribbean Contact* reported throughout its 22-year existence the progressive grounding of the European-derived churches in Caribbean reality.

Did this renewal lead to increased influence in Caribbean society? To a large extent, the pronouncements of progressive and culturally aware Christians within the churches remained an intellectual venture, a discussion among educated specialists on what they wanted a socially committed church to be. That their ability to connect with the aspirations of the population at large was limited is suggested by the fact that the fastest-growing congregations were not among the mainstream churches but among Pentecostal churches and sects originating in North America.

Pentecostalism

By the end of the nineteenth century, several 'Holiness' churches had formed out of movements in American Methodist revivalism. In the early twentieth century, some of them began sending missionaries to the Caribbean. The Church of God, the Church of the Nazarene, and the Pilgrim Holiness

Churches were prominent among them. One of the key ideas in these groups was non-sectarianism, a rejection of the concept of denominationalism within Christianity and a restoration of primitive New Testament holiness. In 1906 the Church of God appeared in Trinidad, and in 1908 in Jamaica. Through a system of missionaries and local evangelists, they eventually spread throughout the West Indies. Church of God Bible institutes were established in Trinidad and Jamaica to train local leaders. The Church of the Nazarene began work in Barbados and Trinidad in 1926, and opened a training college in Trinidad in 1931. The Pilgrim Holiness Church and Holiness Wesleyans also took root in the West Indies, and subsequently merged as the Wesleyan Holiness Church.[78]

Several streams continued to flow into the Pentecostal movement in the West Indies. The Pentecostal Assemblies of Canada started work in Trinidad in 1924. The Assemblies of God of the United States organized several Pentecostal churches in Jamaica in the 1930s. The Church of the Open Bible began working in Trinidad in the 1950s. At the end of the nineteenth century, the campaigns of Dwight L. Moody and Ira Sankey had spread gospel hymns and methods of evangelism which were readily adopted by West Indian Revivalists. Their methods of organized mass campaigns were continued in the twentieth century by evangelists such as Billy Sunday and Billy Graham.[79]

United States hegemony in the region, and its involvement in the affairs of Cuba, Puerto Rico and Haiti, provided opportunities for American Pentecostal churches to send missionaries also to the Créole- and Spanish-speaking Caribbean. Pentecostal congregations were formed among the urban poor in Haiti, giving fundamentalist Protestant Christianity an influence decades before liberationist Catholic priests such as Aristide began to give priority to the same sector of the population. Pentecostals, and fundamentalist evangelical missionaries in some of the more traditional American denominations such as Methodists, Baptists and Presbyterians, rooted themselves among poor Haitians. They became effectively indigenized by training local leaders. The growth of these groups in Haiti was especially rapid in the last quarter of the century, as their ministers and missionaries contributed to the practical improvement of life among the poor through schools, clinics and co-operatives. In a nation starved for education, they offered free schooling. They lived in areas where Catholic priests had traditionally been reluctant to locate. They learned and used Créole in communicating with their congregations, thereby validating a key element in non-francophone Haitian culture.

78 Arthur Charles Dayfoot, 1999, p.205.
79 *Ibid.*, p.206.

They are strongly anti-Vodou, however, and have resisted vigorously the kind of Catholic/Vodou symbiosis that developed in Haitian history. Anti-Vodou sentiment is encouraged as one element of general upward mobility fostered in their congregations.[80]

In Puerto Rico, Pentecostalism appealed to the rural and urban poor more than Catholicism or traditional Protestantism. As Gordon Lewis put it, Pentecostalism provided 'a democratic congregationalist experience for the socially disinherited'.[81] As in Haiti, Pentecostal Protestants in Puerto Rico were more sensitive to the use of the indigenous language as a vehicle for religious instruction, and in this sense became more identified with local culture than either the Catholic or mainstream Protestant churches. The same can be said of Pentecostalism in Cuba, where it was flourishing before Castro's revolution.[82]

Pentecostalism can be identified by a distinct complex of beliefs and practices, a complex that constitutes its appeal to a large segment of the Caribbean population. Worship is simple when compared with the liturgical requirements of more traditional churches. All members of the congregation participate physically and vocally. Preaching is emotional and leads to a call to the altar to acknowledge one's conversion and reception of the Spirit. Holiness and baptism by the Holy Spirit are goals for all members. Evidence of this baptism is given by speaking in tongues. Pentecostalists practise adult baptism by immersion. Fasting is a common practice, as is faith-healing during worship. Separation from the world by simple living identifies Pentecostals, who eschew smoking, drinking, dancing, card playing, movies and the wearing of jewelry. They tend to be openly critical of traditional churches as 'cold' and doctrinally in error. Pentecostals have a fundamentalist view of the Bible's inerrancy, and they accept that Christ's second coming is imminent.[83]

By the 1930s, Pentecostal churches were not peripheral but firmly rooted in Caribbean religious life. They continued to grow vigorously for the rest of the century. There have been splits among them over leadership and belief, which allowed numerous local churches to form. These tended not to be totally independent, however, and often relied on North American missions for organizational and financial guidance.

Interpretations vary of the significance of Pentecostalism in Caribbean societies. The fact that it took hold and began to grow during the final decades of British colonialism in the West Indies is seen as a desire for

80 Thomas E. Weil, 1982, p.54.
81 Gordon K. Lewis, 1963 (1974), p.272.
82 Richard Pattee, 1966, p.109.
83 Arthur Charles Dayfoot, 1999, p.207.

democratic expression among subject peoples. It has been seen also as a form of resistance against British colonialism by its rejection and critique of mainstream churches, most of which had historical British connections.[84] The participatory nature of its worship recalled earlier forms of Afro-Caribbean Revivalism which had always been considered threatening by the colonial State. Pentecostalism continued to make headway in conditions of post-colonial economic dependence and instability. Rather than resistance to a colonial State, post-independent Pentecostals in the anglophone West Indies have emphasized individualism and in-group ideas of self-help, and they have been politically quietistic. In this sense, Pentecostalism can be seen as representing a reaction against the frustrating pace of cultural autonomy and economic self-sufficiency in the Caribbean.

West Indian thinkers who espouse a social gospel or an application of liberation theology to West Indian conditions have been careful to acknowledge Pentecostalism's importance in the lives of Caribbean peoples, but have criticized its apparent indifference to wider socio-political forces. Jamaican Garnet Roper, an evangelical minister and theology lecturer, put forth a cogent critique at a 1990 conference on liberation theology at the University of the West Indies in Jamaica. By commitment and religious experience, Roper understood thoroughly the appeal of Pentecostalism. His critique, then, while representative of the views of non-Pentecostals, could not be dismissed as secular or materialistic, inherently unsympathetic to the religious experience of ordinary people.

Roper recognized that, historically, evangelical Christianity, of which Pentecostalism is the latest manifestation, was primarily a movement among the West Indian 'underclass'. The evangelical consciousness, which first took hold among slaves, included anti-slavery sentiment. Evangelical ministers exercised what in the twentieth century has been called a preferential option for the poor. Thus the Caribbean poor, those who struggle as labourers, domestic workers, small artisans and peasant farmers, have traditionally been the majority members in evangelical and Pentecostal congregations.

The oral and spontaneous aspects of evangelical worship enabled Pentecostalism to take hold as had pre-twentieth-century evangelical Christianity. Pentecostal rituals of prayer, testimony, fasting and ecstatic experience are all within the range of expression of those who participate, rendering a professional clergy and an expensive bureaucracy unnecessary. Pentecostalism provides an experience of empowerment for those who otherwise would be powerless.[85]

---

84 *Ibid.*

85 Garnet Roper, 1991, p.37.

According to Roper, three assumptions inform the attitude of Pentecostals toward politics and the problems of the wider society: the use of material resources is subject to God's will; personal sinfulness is the cause of worldly evil, and social ills can only be redressed through the transformation of individuals; and the credibility and integrity of social change depend upon the personal holiness of those seeking the changes. Structural evils in society are thus inherently linked to personal evil.[86] In the view of critics such as Roper, these assumptions limit the ability of Pentecostalism to deal with fundamental social and political questions. Pentecostals do not understand the corporate or systemic character of evil beyond personal sinfulness. They are unable to extend the implications of the gospel to society, economy and politics. Issues of poverty and political powerlessness are peripheral in the Pentecostal view of salvation history. Similarly, Pentecostals postpone issues of race and cultural identity in favour of an adventism that renders these issues irrelevant. Satisfied in their personal charismatic experience and confident of a heavenly destination, they are so certain about the outcome of history that they see no need for a collective response to here-and-now problems of social injustice.[87] Only by the conversion of individual souls to Jesus Christ will the problems of the world be solved. Roper sums up his critique by observing that Pentecostalism is of the poor without being for the poor. 'The profound issues of poverty, oppression and disenfranchisement', he asserts, 'have hardly engaged its theological formation.'[88]

Diane Austin-Broos, a scholar who writes on Pentecostalism and gender issues, has analysed the significance of Pentecostalism in the Caribbean, specifically Jamaica. She has demonstrated that the Pentecostal organizational reliance on North America maintains a neo-colonial situation of dependency. Yet she has also shown that certain aspects of Pentecostalism developed indigenously, and that the Afro-Creole world view, with its openness to a spiritual cosmology and its presumption that the real is whole and not split between the secular and the sacred, has begun to absorb Pentecostalism into a process of Creole transformation. Austin-Broos's main argument is that in Pentecostalism, biblical poetics combined with the practice of healing allow Afro-West Indians to imagine a community beyond racial hierarchy. For many Jamaicans, these poetics are more real than the discourses of secular history and political and economic progress.[89]

Jamaican evangelists embraced Pentecostalism early in the century, and indigenous preachers gave it a variety and a dynamism that it might have lacked if it had remained purely a North American missionary enterprise. By

86 *Ibid.*, p.38.
87 *Ibid.*, p.40.
88 *Ibid.*, p.43.
89 Diane J. Austin-Broos, 1999, p.217.

the 1980s, Pentecostals constituted about a quarter of the Jamaican population and a third of all Jamaicans who acknowledged a religious affiliation.[90]

The Pentecostal world view contrasts in certain ways with that of Revivalism, which has a longer history and is more traditionally African in the Jamaican religious spectrum. For Revivalists, evil results from malign forces in the world; they can be countered by the power of opposing forces for good, under the control of specialists who can direct them. These cosmological forces do not exist for Pentecostals, for whom evil derives internally and individually through personal sin. Redemption from sin is the only way that evil can be countered. This cleansing can be signified only by Holy Ghost possession and speaking in tongues, experiences not decisive or central in Revivalism. Revivalists counter that Pentecostals are enthralled in a commodified 'church business' issuing from North America. Revivalist healing is open to anyone, and does not require membership, tithing or a confirming baptism in the Holy Spirit.[91]

In spite of these conflicts, the Revivalist and Pentecostalist world views are not entirely antithetical. They are rather distinguishable against a common background of Afro-Caribbean religious consciousness. Personal transformation, healing, possession either by the Holy Ghost or angels or spirits, eudemonic hope in the present, and a millenial expectation for the future are shared by Revivalists and Pentecostals.[92]

Pentecostals view 'life' as a whole in which personal, social and historical aspects are subsumed in a biblical mythology, according to which their status as saints is the 'really real' within the world. They see the history of slavery and emancipation as an analogue of the more real passage from sin to redemption.[93] And all current politics are assessed in terms of that passage. When they are cleansed and healed, 'Jamaican Pentecostals', Austin-Broos observes, 'do not reconstitute their whole social world but rather enter a heaven on earth sustained only in saintly practice.' The possibility of being released from suffering is extended only to the saved, not to the larger society. And the only way for non-Pentecostal sufferers to find healing is conversion in response to Pentecostal evangelization.[94]

Similar to the Rastafari, Pentecostals synthesize Biblical mythology and Caribbean history. In both views, African origin plays a part. For the Rastafari, Africa is central in the mythology of Babylonian captivity. For the Pentecostal, African origin is a phase that is transcended in salvation history. To seek one's

90 *Ibid.*, p.219.
91 *Ibid.*, pp.221–2.
92 *Ibid.*, p.222.
93 *Ibid.*, pp.222–3.
94 *Ibid.*, p.224.

roots in a specific African time and place would be in vain, for one's true roots are in the Adam of Genesis. African sin as well as European exploitation led to slavery. But slavery created in Afro-Caribbean people, in the Pentecostal view, a capacity and readiness for redemption unique among all the races and ethnicities in the Caribbean.[95] Pentecostals affirm African identity in their passage from slavery to freedom, even though African identity is not the beginning and end of their history, as it can be seen to be among the Rastafari. And it is important to note that being Pentecostal does not thoroughly alienate the West Indian saint from his or her culture and history. Austin-Broos quotes a Jamaican Pentecostal pastor in this regard:

> Jamaicans accepted Pentecostalism because they already lived in a Spirit-filled world. They were African themselves. They were emotional. They liked rhythm in their worship, pipe and drum, and they knew what it was to be Spirit-filled from the days of the Great Revival [1860–1]. The whole world of Jamaica was busy with spirits, so the message of the Holy Spirit was welcome. Americans didn't need to tell Jamaicans that.

Even though there is no racial hierarchy in heaven, those who have already suffered as Africans have fewer hurdles in acquiring holiness.[96]

Throughout the Caribbean, the Pentecostal world view is comparable to its Jamaican manifestation. In Haiti, Pentecostals have adopted military imagery to define their presence in the world. This is so because they have had to contend vigorously with two religious powers which are fundamentally a part of Haitian history and culture – Roman Catholicism and Vodou. Pentecostal congregations in Haiti typically have called themselves 'the Army', seeing themselves in alliance with platoons of angels in combat with the *lwa* or spirits of Vodou. The confrontation is similar to but more marked than that between Pentecostals and Revivalists in Jamaica. The Vodou *lwa* are amoral spirits who may be benevolent or malign. Haitian Pentecostal converts continue to accept the reality of the *lwa*, but they are reinterpreted as evil spirits in league with Satan. Indeed, many Pentecostals believe that converts who backslide into Vodou may be punished by the wrathful *lwa* for having previously abandoned them. And Pentecostals are wary that the *lwa* can invade their services, which can resemble Vodou ceremonies by their use of drumming and the experience of possession; a wicked *lwa* can imitate the Holy Spirit, whose possession alone can lead to holiness.[97]

95 *Ibid.*, pp.227, 237.
96 *Ibid.*, pp.229.
97 Frederick Conway, 1980, pp.12–13, 14.

In spite of this conflict, however, both Pentecostalism and Vodou are part of an Afro-Haitian belief system, in the way that Pentecostalism and Revivalism are in Jamaica. When a member of a Haitian family converts to Pentecostalism, this does not interfere with that family's cult of the *lwa*. A family may encourage a sick member to convert for the healing benefits that they could receive. For them, Pentecostalism is more an innovation within a tradition than a wholly new religious choice.

As in Jamaica, Haitian preachers have effectively indigenized Pentecostal belief and practice. Yet they have had to rely materially on a North American organizational hierarchy that maintains a sense of dependency and inferiority. Pentecostalism has fostered images of an enlightened and generous United States and of a devalued Haitian culture. The belief exists that Haitians are backward and poor because of personal sins. The Eurocentric message from North America is that their sins derive from their continuation of African superstitions and forms of family life.[98]

In Puerto Rico, Pentecostalism grew remarkably in the 1950s and 1960s, corresponding with the promise of prosperity resulting from the island's commonwealth relationship with the United States. Converts were not newly rich, however; they were mainly poor and members of the lower middle class who saw the possibility of upward mobility in the post-war decades. One study of Puerto Rican Pentecostalism points to its accommodating propensity, its adaptibility to changing socio-economic conditions. It is generally supportive of the current political economy. Thus Pentecostals are consistently in favour of continuing commonwealth status and would accept statehood as the only alternative. Pentecostals are generally against independence, and Pentecostalism can be seen as a function of the Americanization of the island. The tension between indigenization and dependency that can be seen in the independent nations of the Caribbean, then, is comparably absent in Puerto Rico, where Pentecostalism is unambiguously a satellite of the movement in the United States, as the Puerto Rican government is satellite to that of Washington.[99]

In the southern Caribbean's twin-island nation of Trinidad & Tobago, Pentecostalism took root rather later than it did in other parts of the region. Its significant growth occurred in the final quarter of the century, and the 1990 census showed it to be the fourth largest religious group after Roman Catholics, Hindus and Anglicans.[100] As in Jamaica and Haiti, Pentecostalism in Trinidad needs to be seen in its relationship with traditional African belief systems, which are manifested in Trinidad & Tobago in a continuum that includes Obeah, Rada,

98 *Ibid.*, pp.23–5.
99 Anthony L. LaRuffa, 1980, p.60.
100 Garth L. Green, 1999, p.192.

Shango and the Spiritual Baptists. Pentecostals preach against those beliefs and practices as they do against Vodou in Haiti and Revivalism in Jamaica. But the antagonism involves a kind of symbiosis. Trinidadians continue to engage in the manipulation of forces for revenge or personal gain by consulting Obeah specialists, but have at the same time embraced Pentecostal rites of exorcism as the most popular counter to Obeah.[101] In this sense, Pentecostalism has become part of the indigenous warp and woof of traditional beliefs. Yet Pentecostalism among all the Christian churches in Trinidad has proceeded to reinforce North American institutional and financial ties when other denominations have attempted to become independently West Indian.[102]

As Trinidadian Pentecostals are pulled outward by their links with North America, they are oriented upward by the values espoused in their pastors' sermons. These values are adjunct to the desire for social and economic mobility, and define the personal and family disciplines that are a twentieth-century iteration of the ideals of respectability that evangelical missionaries in the post-emancipation West Indies emphasized as the keys to entry into a new middle class of freed yeomen, artisans and entrepreneurs. Sobriety, cleanliness, thrift, monogamy and the nuclear family are preached as values that support economic success.[103]

As an Utopic heaven on earth, the Pentecostal world is tangent to the secular socio-political order. The two touch, however, on certain issues that Pentecostals have made moral priorities. They have taken public stands against alcohol and drug consumption, pornography and abortion – in other words, against those social problems that most obviously involve personal sins. They were particularly vocal against communism in the second half of the century when Cuba and Grenada, and the existence of several national political parties throughout the Caribbean which espoused some form of socialism, made it seem that it was a real 'threat'. Pentecostals did not counter communism with an articulated political ideology, except that which they absorbed from their ties with the United States. Their most urgent objection to communism was that they would lose their freedom to preach the gospel under an atheistic regime.[104]

As their numbers increased, Pentecostals in the Caribbean strove for the respectability accorded the traditional mainstream churches, and the Hindu and Muslim communities where Indians are a significant sector of the population. A somewhat dramatic example is afforded in the 1995 Hallelujah controversy in Trinidad. In November 1994, one of the masquerade bands

101 Stephen D. Glazier, 1980, p.70.
102 *Ibid.*, pp.70–1.
103 *Ibid.*, pp.71–2.
104 Garnet Roper, 1991, p.42.

preparing to participate in the 1995 pre-Lenten Carnival announced that it would be called 'Hallelujah'. This drew an immediate protest from a group of Pentecostal pastors. They attacked the band's designer, Peter Minshall, for desecrating the religious word 'hallelujah' by including it in the devil-glorifying festival of Carnival. Over two hundred pastors, combined under the leadership of Pastor Winston Cuffie of the Miracle Ministries in Couva, petitioned the government to intervene against Minshall's band. They invoked a law, the Public Holidays and Festivals Act, to argue that the band broke a prohibition against any carnival representation that brought a religion into disrepute. The government refused to intervene, the band did not change its name, and it went on to win the Band of the Year title.[105]

Many issues surfaced during the controversy, but the main one was that Pentecostals did not want Christianity as they defined it to be associated with the cultural form, Carnival, that is the most public annual expression of national identity in Trinidad & Tobago. For two centuries, Carnival has been a means by which various social groups, whether identified by class, religion or ethnicity, have symbolically claimed inclusion in Trinidadian society and culture. During the colonial era, governmental and ecclesiastical authorities attacked Carnival in terms similar to those they used in their condemnations of Afro-Creole forms of religion, such as Myal, Revival and Shakerism. Carnival resulted in the disturbance of public order, lewdness, criminality and disloyalty to the Empire. The festival was not free from official attempts to suppress it until after independence in 1962, when it became the cultural symbol of a new nation. From that time, it has been embraced by whatever political party happens to be in power as a symbol of the ruling group's legitimacy.[106]

Pastor Cuffie called Minshall a 'false prophet' who manipulated 'spirit powers' to blind people to his blasphemy against the 'true and living God'. In Cuffie's view, Carnival was a symbol of abomination. Minshall, however, saw Carnival as a symbol of national equality, unity and redemption if performed as a festival of celebration and not of debauchery.[107] The religious controversies over Carnival were symptomatic of post-colonial uncertainties about the meanings of culture and society. Minshall was defended against the Pentecostals by Catholic and Anglican priests, who argued against what to them appeared to be a sectarian attempt to impose, as one priest put it, 'their own definition of self, God and country on the whole society in the name of religion.'[108] Further countering the Pentecostals was the Afrocentric viewpoint

105 Garth L. Green, 1999, pp.189–90.
106 *Ibid.*, p.191.
107 *Ibid.*, pp.198, 201.
108 *Ibid.*, p.206.

articulated by Hollis Liverpool, a scholar and calypsonian known as Chalkdust. He explained that Carnival was an African way of praising God for all He has given, especially life itself. In his view, the lack of an historical understanding of the African aspect of Trinidadian culture was behind much of the controversy over Carnival.[109]

The Pentecostal contention came to be not simply against the use of the expression 'hallelujah' but for recognition of Pentecostal pastors as representatives of a religious and social group and for that group to be accorded the same respect as others in Trinidad & Tobago – Hindus, Muslims, Roman Catholics and the traditional Protestant churches. When the prime minister refused to intervene in the dispute, Cuffie construed it as evidence of anti-Pentecostal discrimination.[110] By mounting their protest over Carnival in general and the name of a band in particular, Pentecostals indirectly acknowledged the yearly festival as a key symbol of nationhood. But by claiming a kind of proprietorship over a biblical praise word used as the name of a band, they signalled the absolutism inherent in their world view.

The paradox of Pentecostalism is that it seems both alien and native. Its tendency to absolutize and its organizational and financial ties with North America open it to criticism as a subversion of the twentieth-century endeavour to construct a West Indian cultural identity and to achieve institutional and psychological independence from metropolitan control. At the same time, Pentecostalism has become indelibly a defining way of life and a world view for masses of Caribbean people whose priorities are eking out a living and finding the validation of holiness in the Pentecostal family. The paradox is extended by the emigration of huge numbers of West Indians in the second half of the last century to the cities of Canada, the United States and the United Kingdom. They brought with them a Caribbean brand of Pentecostalism that has enabled them to negotiate their relationship with the wider metropolitan world. Pentecostalism among ethnic minorities and immigrants has been interpreted as compensation for marginalization and modernization. Newer studies, however, reinterpret it as a forum for the construction of new identities with which immigrants counter the dominant and often racist representations made about Caribbean people. West Indian Pentecostal immigrants deal with the problems of the socio-political order not by trying to change it but by changing themselves within – by adopting a Christian identity and forming fictive family relationships that transcend ethnic and racial identities imposed externally.[111]

---

109 *Ibid.*, pp.207–8.
110 *Ibid.*, p.209.
111 Nicole Rodríquez Toulis, 1997, pp.2, 268–70.

Islam and Hinduism in the southern Caribbean

Between 1838 and 1917, roughly half-a-million indentured workers from the Indian subcontinent were brought into the British West Indies and Suriname. Their labour was desired mainly to compete with or replace that of emancipated slaves. Most of these Indians were indentured in Trinidad and Guyana. The third highest concentration in the British Caribbean was in Jamaica. By the end of the twentieth century, however, only slightly more than 1 per cent of Jamaicans were Indians, while in Trinidad and Guyana they were about 40 per cent and 54 per cent respectively. In Suriname they are 37 per cent of the population.

In the view of Creole colonial society, which considered itself Christian, Islam and Hinduism were signs of low status. Mainstream Christianity was considered the bulwark of civilization, and non-Christian traditions were judged accordingly. The churches, the government and the press together maintained contemptuous views of Islam and Hinduism (especially the latter) as 'heathen' and unworthy of institutional recognition, and as sinister religions with a degraded sense of morality. But the majority of Indians did not abandon their traditional religions in the interests of respectability. Though targeted for evangelization by Anglicans, Roman Catholics and, from the 1860s, by the Canadian Presbyterian Mission, only a small minority converted. Most continued to follow their Muslim imams and Hindu pandits, and the strength of their adherence to their world views provided a shield against the contempt of colonial Christian society.[112] It is mainly because of their perseverance that the religions of Islam and Hinduism have become part of the cultural legacy of the southern Caribbean.

The challenge of Islam

Islam came to the Caribbean with Muslim African slaves. In the sixteenth century, the Spanish noted the problem of Wolof and Mande slaves attempting to convert Amerindians.[113] Generally, the Islam of slaves was modified and absorbed in the process of creolization to the extent that there has been no continuous link with an Islamic past among current Afro-West Indians.

Trinidad has perhaps the most discernible African Muslim history. A community of Mandingo Muslim freed slaves existed in Port of Spain prior to emancipation. They saved and pooled money to purchase the freedom

112 Bridget Brereton, 1981, p.112.
113 Clyde-Ahamad Winters, 1978, pp.41–2.

of other Mandingo slaves, and extended their activities into trade, money lending, planting, and the purchase of property, including slaves. They also continued to petition for repatriation to Africa, but were denied assistance by the colonial government. Under a succession of patriarchs, this community maintained an Islamic identity for some time after emancipation. By the 1860s, however, they were no longer a distinguishable community in Trinidad.[114] It would be more than a hundred years later, in the 1970s, that an Afro-Trinidadian Muslim movement would emerge again, this time as a serious challenge to the post-colonial State.

In the meantime, Muslim Indians kept Islam alive in Trinidad and Guyana. Although a minority among the indentured immigrants (13 per cent in Trinidad, 17 per cent in Guyana), Muslims ensured that Islam became a part of the pluralism that has made some commentators see Trinidad's society as the most cosmopolitan in the Caribbean. For example, 'Hosay', a creolized festival of the Shi'ite commemoration of the murder of Hosein, Muhammed's grandson, has become a major annual national celebration, an Indian working-class fête in which Sunnis and Hindus (and non-Indians) participate as well as Shi'ites.[115] Indeed, Islam's influence on affairs in Trinidad has been greater than the numbers might suggest. As a guide it has had a dual role; it has been a source of both reconciliation and challenge.

Indians in the southern Caribbean have interpreted the problem of identity largely in racial and religious terms.[116] Since the end of indentureship in the early twentieth century, they have relied on the mythology of the 'brotherhood of the boat' to maintain a sense of unity that transcended the divisions of caste, language and religion in India. Older Indo-Trinidadians today still accept the myth but lament a widening gap between Hindu and Muslim group identities, and they are nostalgic for a time when it was sufficient only to be Indian. They liken the gap to that between Indian and Creole, or Afro-Trinidadian – a gap that has been politically exploited from mid-century.[117]

Oral tradition has it that the first generation of Indian Muslims after the expiration of indentureship kept their religion alive in quiet and humble ways. Imams were not trained specialists but simply individuals with leadership qualities who happened to know Islam a little better. The religion was displayed in village and neighbourhood observances. Throughout the century, however, especially from the 1940s, increasingly larger *masjids*, or mosques, were built, and observances became large-scale, island-wide, and

114 Bridget Brereton, 1981, pp.67–8.
115 *Ibid.*, p.104.
116 Aisha Khan, 1997, p.129.
117 *Ibid.*, pp.132–3.

carefully organized. Imams became more important as administrators of *jamaats*, or congregations.[118]

This institutionalization has made Islam a very visible part of national life in both Trinidad and Guyana. Certain aspects of religious memory and practice, however, have ensured that Islam has not been creolized to the extent that Christianity and traditional African beliefs have been. Oral history keeps alive a memory of how Muslim imams and their informal *jamaats* in the villages and on the plantations early in the century struggled to keep an Islamic Indian identity intact in an alien environment. Focus on the subcontinent has also been maintained by customary visits of Muslim missionaries and teachers from India and later Pakistan. They have served as arbiters of theological interpretation, and contact with them has conferred credibility on local imams in the Caribbean.[119]

Events on the subcontinent, especially those with religious significance, can be of as much immediate concern as Caribbean events to Indian Muslims as well as Hindus in the West Indies. The Ahmadiyya movement, for example, which developed in India in 1889, stimulated debates over theology and tradition among Indo-Trinidadian Muslims. The Ahmadiyyas were reformists who claimed that their founder, Mirza Ghulam Ahmad, was the last prophet after Muhammed. Ahmadiyya missionaries were active in Trinidad in the first half of the century, and today they have a few imams, *masjids* and *jamaats* on the island. They are a minority, yet they have stimulated debate on issues of orthodoxy among the majority Sunni Muslims, a debate that is not over local identity but which links Muslims in the Caribbean with Islam as a world-wide community.[120]

Such debates are part of a tension between exterior ideal (issues of religious truth) and local reality (issues of West Indian identity). This tension often translates into conflict between generations. Younger Indo-Caribbean Muslims are more likely than older ones to have the means and the freedom to travel and study Islam abroad, which often leads them to seek a universal Islamic identity. Older imams in the Caribbean, however, tend to be more concerned with ideas that have an historical or Creole context, such as evaluating Muslim identity in terms of an immigrant past or of the demands of 'living good with people' in a plural society.[121]

That ideal has been put to the test by post-war politics in Trinidad and Guyana, where race-based political parties carried the two nations into independence from Britain. Afro-Creoles have been pitted against Indians in

118 *Ibid.*, pp.133–4.
119 *Ibid.*, pp.134–5.
120 *Ibid.*, pp.135–6.
121 *Ibid.*, p.136.

bitter political rancour that has been the source of both political patronage and bloodshed in the second half of the century. Muslim Indians have been affected by this divisiveness. When the party of Indian nationalism, the People's Democratic Party (PDP), was organized in the 1950s, the party's head, Bhadase Sagan Maraj, called on all Indo-Trinidadians to vote together, whether Hindu or Muslim. But the head of the rival Afro-Trinidadian People's National Movement (PNM), Eric Williams, attempted to exploit the religious diversity of the Indian population, who were divided among orthodox Hindus, reformist Hindus, Muslims and Christians. Williams gave key party positions to Muslim and Christian Indians, and portrayed the PDP as an exclusivist brahmin party, not progressive enough for a post-colonial cosmopolitan society like Trinidad.[122]

It was during the 1956–62 period of political mobilization that a number of new Muslim religio-cultural associations was created, such as the Anjuman Sunnat-ul-Jamaat. They were mainly Sunni, but were distinguished by varying theological emphases. These organizations are not functions of one or more political party, and are analogous to the linkages of churches and congregations one might find among Christians. But they are politically important in two ways. One is that they rely on State patronage as well as private donations. Another is that the larger associations, by networking a large number of people through member *masjids* and *jamaats*, and by providing their halls for secular meetings, have great potential for mobilizing their members in particular political directions.[123] Younger imams in these associations, for example, have the power to turn Caribbean Muslims either toward a deracialized Islamic universalism or to reinforce the racial divisions magnified by politicians in their exploitation of religious and ethnic diversity. Indian Muslims have had to navigate the channels between other, Hindu or Christian Indians and Afro-West Indians, and can steer either toward alliances or continuing animosities. The peculiar choices offered in the Caribbean are between a 'pure' Islam and a 'primitive' Indian identity, or between 'culture' as ethno-religious purity as opposed to 'Creole'.[124]

In the final three decades of the century, a number of predominantly Afro-Trinidadian *jamaats* came into existence. Their imams were inspired by notions of Black Power and by the thrust of militant Islam throughout the world, but especially in Libya and the Middle East. These organizations recall to mind the nineteenth-century Mandingo Muslim community in Port of Spain, although they were not a renewal of the older African Muslim tradi-

122 *Ibid.*, p.137.
123 *Ibid.*, p.138.
124 *Ibid.*, pp.139, 140.

tion. The best-known name among these new imams was Yasin Abu Bakr, leader of the Jamaat-al-Muslimeen.

Abu Bakr's *jamaat* consisted mainly of Afro-Trinidadians, but included a small number of Indians. The Muslimeen became known throughout the Caribbean and the world in the summer of 1990. Led by Abu Bakr, on 27 July they carried out an armed takeover of parliament and the Trinidad & Tobago television station, and fire-bombed police headquarters in Port of Spain. They held prime minister A. N. R. Robinson and several members of parliament and the Cabinet hostage, forcing Robinson to sign a letter of resignation. Robinson was bound, beaten and shot in the leg. More than twenty deaths resulted from the coup attempt. The Muslimeen surrendered on 1 August and were charged with treason, murder, kidnapping, possession of arms and ammunition, and shooting with intent to kill. Abu Bakr was a former policeman named Lennox Phillip, and the Muslimeen included a number of ex-policemen and soldiers. Their attempted coup recalled the 1970 Black Power revolt in Trinidad, which involved an army mutiny and a similar state of emergency.

Abu Bakr's revolt was ostensibly against government corruption, including what he perceived as the corruption of Muslim members of government. As an imam building a *jamaat* in which he sought to teach a 'purer' form of Islam, and which consisted of many underemployed and unemployed young men from the poorer areas of Port of Spain, Abu Bakr perceived himself to be a threat to the primarily Indo-Trinidadian Muslim establishment. As he explained it, 'certain members of the Indian community had what they viewed as a hegemony on Islam and they felt themselves threatened by the emergence of a defiant group of African Muslims who were really practicing (Islam's) true tenets.' He also distinguished his followers from the ordinary run of Afro-Trinidadians who were mentally dependent and lacking in the ideals of self-sufficiency that he taught and practised in his *jamaat*. The Muslimeen coup was based, he claimed, on a morality of justice mandated by the Koran. As witnesses of God, Abu Bakr maintained, they had to stand out firmly for justice. The injustices and contradictions of Trinidad demanded a militant response. The court system guaranteed the oppression of the weak by the strong. Economic differences, the very visible gap between rich and poor, demanded enforcement of the Koran's teaching of justice.[125] While it is debatable whether or not Abu Bakr's coup had much to do with religion, his activism and his militant conception of Islam are symptomatic of unresolved conflict among Caribbean Muslims, the conflict between the desire for a pure and universal Islam and the need to live the religion among the social, political and cultural compromises that define daily life in the Caribbean.

125 *Trinidad Under Siege,* 1990, pp.9–10, 11–12.

Hinduism and pluralism in the southern Caribbean

Similar conflicts are reflected among Hindu Indians in Trinidad and Guyana, between an ideal Hinduism and one defined mainly by the specifics of place. Oral tradition maintains the myth that in the beginning – that is, during the era of indentureship – there were no significant differences between Muslim and Hindu, that all were Indian, defined more by common customs of food and dress than religious difference. Part of the truth in the myth is that Indian identity was not so much brought on the boat from the subcontinent as it was formed in the rural-proletariat and peasant-farmer culture of plantation society.[126] There is also the fact that the distinctions between Hindu and Muslim were sharpened after the era of indentureship, and that Hinduism as experienced in the Caribbean involves innovations in response to specific West Indian challenges.

Hinduism by the end of the twentieth century could no longer be associated exclusively with India. To the extent that there has been a worldwide diaspora of Indians over the last century and a half – first as contracted labour, later as free migrants – to that extent has Hinduism become a global religion. This fact allows comparison with Islam. Indian communities throughout the world are touched by movements toward a resurgent and militant Hinduism that their emigrant ancestors might not have recognized in the localized devotions of their villages in India. The Hinduism that has developed both on the subcontinent and among Indo-Caribbean people is to a large extent a function of the colonialism under which it has had to survive. As Vinay Lal, a scholar of the Hindu diaspora, writes:

> Indeed, the very notion of 'Hinduism' appears to be the handiwork of British scholar-administrator types and Indian nationalists, and it is the cumulative effect of the codification of Hindu law, the creation of the census, and other features of the enumerative modality of the colonial state, that appear to give birth to the 'Hindu'.[127]

From the last quarter of the nineteenth century, the tide of events in India has influenced the development of a Hindu world view in the Caribbean. Pandits from reformist organizations, resulting from the kind of Hinduism Lal describes as taking shape under British colonial administration, travelled periodically to overseas Indian communities. An example of one such organization that has influenced Hindu thinking in the Caribbean is the Arya Samaj. It was founded in 1875 as a movement toward abolition of caste and the

126 Aisha Khan, 1997, p.132.
127 Vinay Lal, 1996, p.10.

acceptance of equality among all Hindus. It promoted a Vedic-based monotheism, devaluing the village-based deities and devotions that were characteristic of Hinduism when the era of indentureship began. The first Arya Samaj pandit arrived in the Caribbean in 1910. These emissaries helped to stir Indian nationalism in the southern Caribbean, and at the same time contended with the influence of local pandits who had established themselves as leaders with links to the time of indentureship. The long-term significance of organizations such as the Arya Samaj is that a continuing debate is carried on within Indo-Caribbean communities over issues of orthodoxy, literacy, familiarity with Sanskrit, monotheism versus 'idol worship', and so on. And in spite of the emphasis of the Arya Samaj on a clearly defined pan-Indian Hinduism, the movement has enlisted mainly élite Indians in the Caribbean class system. Economic leaders who identify with modernity and Western values have become the main followers of Hindu universalism while the Indian lower classes of workers and farmers are more inclined to maintain older provincial traditions.[128]

Yet even if there had been no influences from the subcontinent on Indo-Caribbean communities in the twentieth century, Caribbean Hinduism would have developed its own style – its own kind of creolization. Indian indentured workers experienced discontinuities similar to those forced upon African slaves earlier in Caribbean history. The colonial plantation strategy of 'divide in order to control' resulted in the mixture of mutually unintelligible subcontinental languages on the estates, and Indians gradually developed their own patois, in Trinidad and Guyana based mainly on the Bhojpuri dialect of Hindi, and in Suriname on Awadhi.[129]

The mix of castes on the plantations, and the inability to maintain sanitary rituals and the rules of occupational specialization, led to a decline in traditional markers of social status. In the mix of languages and castes, the little traditions of village and vernacular devotions gave way to a tendency to a more homogenized Hinduism, a trend that ensured welcome to, if not total agreement with, missionaries from organizations such as the Arya Samaj. And the contempt that Hindu immigrants had to endure from the official arbiters of Christian civilization, for whom Hinduism was merely heathen idolatry, resulted in a defensive commonality of belief and a congregational display of devotional practice that were innovations not inherent in an ancestral Hinduism.[130]

Hinduism has not declined in the Caribbean but has been transformed into a statement of identity within a pluralism represented by the religious traditions of African spirit belief, Afro-Christian syntheses, Islam, Roman Catholicism, Anglicanism, mainstream Protestantism and Pentecostalism.

---

128 Aisha Khan, 1997, p.135.
129 Vinay Lal, 1996, p.11.
130 *Ibid.*, p.13.

While Hindu identity tends not to be as militant when compared with the recent impact of Islam in the southern Caribbean, it was nevertheless vigorously asserted in the final decades of the twentieth century. In Trinidad, for example, the Hindu Maha Sabha movement resolved to construct a temple in every village. And in Guyana, there was a revival of the worship of Kali from the 1970s.[131]

For Indo-West Indians, the twentieth century consisted of conflict and compromise between what historian Kelvin Singh has called modernizing and traditional élites. The modernizing élite emerged from Christianized Indians who, by 1921, were about 10 per cent of Indo-Trinidadians. Most of them were Presbyterians, with smaller numbers of Anglicans and Roman Catholics. By religious conversion, they came closer to acculturation to colonial Christian society.[132]

In terms of politics, the modernizing viewpoint was expressed by the journalist and trade unionist C. B. Mathura in the late 1920s in his columns in the *East Indian Weekly*. In a community such as colonial Trinidad, Mathura argued, all races were interdependent. Indians had much to learn from the other races, and the progress of one race was inextricably bound up with the progress of the others. Representation in government should not be sought on the basis of a racial constituency. Each member of what was then the Legislative Council should represent all races, colours and creeds.[133]

After 1930, the modernizing voice was muted as increasing numbers of Hindu missionaries and Indian nationalist speakers visited the Caribbean, giving support to traditional leaders critical of what they saw as the secularizing tendency of the modernizing élite. Both Hindu and Muslim organizations were formed to counter the viewpoint espoused by activists such as Mathura. 'The establishment of the Anjuman Sunnat-Ul-Jamaat to represent orthodox (Sunni) Muslims,' observes Singh, 'and the Sanatan Dharma Board of Control to represent orthodox (Sanatanist) Hindus in the early 1930s represented the most powerful potential challenges to the modernizing élite.'[134]

This helped set the stage for the consolidation of Indians against Africans as competitive political blocs from the 1950s onward. But at the start of the twenty-first century, the fervour of religious traditionalism lives amongst other forces that challenge ethnic identity defined in religious terms. The control of the traditional élite over mass-level community organization and of the public image of the Indian community through cultural activities alienates not only non-Indians but also increasing numbers of young and urbanized

131 *Ibid.*, p.18.
132 Kelvin Singh, 1996, pp.230–1.
133 *Ibid.*, pp.234–5.
134 *Ibid.*, pp.238–9.

Indians.[135] It is possible that during this century, Indian identity in the southern Caribbean will continue to oscillate between the tides of religio-ethnic continuity and Creole redefinition.

Conclusion

In the twentieth-century Caribbean, people continued to pour libations for their ancestors. They drummed and danced, invoking deities that had travelled across the Atlantic or spirits who had struggled and died as local heroes and family elders. Many opened their lives to Jesus as well as Shango, and daily endeavoured to prepare the earth for the in-breaking Kingdom. They formed their own churches, or were baptized into older ones, and in many cases belonged to more than one, not wanting to close off any divine possibilities. The face of God appeared to believers as a cloudy remoteness, a loving father, a demanding patriarch, an African emperor, or a prismatic diffusion of divine light into a pantheon of lively, kind, mischievous, vain or malign spirits. They read the holy texts – canonical, apocryphal, obscure, ancient as the Vedas, innovative as Rastafari versions. Some saw all people around them as a godly body to be celebrated. Others saw only themselves as holy and all others as fractured by sin.

Religion was also the basis of social identities. Groupings according to race, ethnicity or class were almost always validated by religious mythology. At the same time, however, Creole innovation in religion and progressive ecumenism among churches furthered the as yet unfinished business of defining Caribbean identities which transcend African, European or Asian origins.

Governments and political leaders knew that they had to address religious worlds as well as secular needs. Whether colonial administrations, authoritarian dictatorships, parliamentary democracies, or Marxist socialisms, Caribbean states have had to respond to the power of religious world views and institutions. The responses varied: suppression, co-optation, respectful co-operation, folklorization. Whatever the response, governments could not ignore religion. A definition of religion can also serve as a definition of the modern secular State. Both religion and the State are a set of rituals, rationalized by certain myths, which mobilize power to achieve transformations in society and the natural environment. But whereas the power of the State comes from either force or contractual consent, the power of the religious world is its daily immediacy, its acceptance by believers as the really real world in the midst of partial worlds such as government, political party and geographical place.

135 *Ibid.*, p.246.

17

Education in the Caribbean, 1930–90

Carl Campbell

Introduction: United States influences and the Greater Antilles, 1898–1930

In the twentieth century the United States was the new imperial state in the Caribbean. Its educational power was felt directly in a few Caribbean territories for the first time. American educational ideas and models followed the flag into Cuba (1898–1902 and again 1906–9), Puerto Rico (after 1898), and later the Danish Virgin Islands (after 1917), Haiti (1915–34) and the Dominican Republic (1916–24). Their influence was not felt directly elsewhere in the Caribbean in the early twentieth century as there was no political vacuum in the French, Dutch or British empires. Naturally, the United States could only 'Americanize' in education, and this process was carried furthest where territories were acquired permanently as in the case of Puerto Rico and the Virgin Islands. Cuba escaped into a qualified independence, and so recovered from the shock of having an American military regime establish a public system of elementary education between 1898 and 1902. Haiti and the Dominican Republic, especially Haiti, the two longest-established independent nations in the Caribbean, had very unpleasant experiences with the Americans as educators and military occupants simultaneously. These nations, however, had the cultural capacity to resist immediately and throw off American influence gradually, after the soldiers left.[1]

In prostrate Cuba after 1898 a vast task lay before the United States military government, and it took the bull by the horns. Nothing is as salient in the literature as praise for the energy and foresight of the military governors, especially General Wood, in attempting to build a new education structure in Cuba between 1898 and 1902.[2] The Americans really believed that a public

---

1 Isaac Dookhan, 1994, chap.15; Aida Negrón de Montilla, 1975, pp.235–66; Léon Pamphile, 1985, pp.99–108; Erwin Epstein, 1987, pp.1–23; Donald Clarkson, 1990, pp.32–59; Laurie Johnson, 1995, pp.26–30; Emanuel Hurwitz *et al.*, 1987; Katherine Cook, 1934, pp.1–52.

2 Erwin Epstein, 1987; Edward Fitchen, 1972, pp.123–49.

system of elementary schools and widespread popular education would develop democracy and other American virtues in Cuba which would make the island safe for democracy and even independence. Like all imperialists they had to employ the systems they knew best, and that was the American model of education. They had to Americanize; but unlike in contemporary Puerto Rico, they did not appear to be Americanizing as part of a process of conscious appropriation of Cuba. An independent Cuba with American values, indoctrinated to worship the United States as the greatest and most successful republic, would be a better friend and neighbour than Cuba with Spanish values;[3] but Wood was not trying to take over the island. The power of the army was used to achieve new buildings, trained teachers, higher enrolments; it was an amazing work done in a short time, but it was held together by the force of the military.

No theme or aspect of education in Puerto Rico in the first half of the twentieth century is as pervasive as the Americanization of public schooling. Centralization of the education system, indeed the construction of a system using the English language and patriotic exercises in favour of United States heroes and political culture, under an authoritative American Commissioner of Education, was a powerful vehicle of Americanization.[4] The arguments which compelled or fuelled the process were political or economic. If Puerto Rico was to remain an area of United States political and economic conquest, then the language of the conqueror should become widespread among the conquered. It follows that education policy was highly politicized in Puerto Rico: the Republican party, in favour of statehood, supported the pro-English interest; the Unionist party, not to mention the Independence party, or those politicians on the 'Left', supported the pro-Spanish stakeholders. Over time the sway of battle was something like this: victory for the pro-English interest, 1900–34; a stronger showing for the pro-Spanish party from the mid-1930s, and victory for the pro-Spanish party after 1948.[5] But throughout the whole period the English language stayed in the system, if not as the language of instruction, as a subject; and in the private schools (to which the struggle turned after 1948) English was triumphant.

If Americanization was a larger issue in Puerto Rico than in the Virgin Islands, it was because Puerto Rico was a bigger and more distinctive society than the Virgin Islands. Puerto Rico was valued not merely as a military outpost, but as an arena of economic investment and political control. The administration of the Virgin Islands' education system by naval officers,

3 Laurie Johnson, 1995, pp.26-30; Louis A. Pérez, 1982, pp.3–17.
4 Katherine Cook, 1934, pp.15–33 ; Donald Clarkson, 1990, pp.32–59.
5 Erwin Epstein, 1970, pp.26–43 and 143–75.

putting aside non-existent secondary education, is accounted a great success. As in Puerto Rico, United States authorities speedily brought military efficiency to bear on the school system. Schools were erected, teachers given more training; enrolment and attendance were enforced; teachers' salaries were improved.[6] These types of infrastructural upgrading, whether in health or social welfare, could show results from diligent policy-making and implementation. They stood in contrast to the economic revival of bankrupt plantation enterprises or under-financed small farming, which could not be similarly improved in the short run.

There was no language problem in the Virgin Islands, since English was the popular language even before 1917; nor did this problem exist in the Dominican Republic or Haiti, for a different reason. In the 1920s the Americans shook the Haitian education system out of its traditional pattern by establishing a separate, large-scale, well financed technical/vocational input of schools and training centres, under their own control. The greater part of the pre-1915 system remained in the hands of the Haitians, however, and there was no policy of changing Haiti's culture by imposing English on the country.[7] But whatever the objective merits of vocational education, the United States-founded schools were misconceived because the Americans erected them, and because the entire American occupation was imperialistic. Yet, even if it was for racist reasons that the Americans thought that Haitians needed to learn trades and farm skills more than French literature and classical languages, they still had a strong case, pedagogically, for this policy.[8]

In Haiti the Americans made a bigger impact on education than in the Dominican Republic, where their stay was relatively short and not characterized by any strong effort to vocationalize the curriculum. But between 1916 and 1924 the United States military, as in Puerto Rico and Cuba, did improve the infrastructure of education there. As usual United States military energy, plus the strong revenue position of the country arising from high sugar prices in wartime, caused schools to be built, teachers to be trained, enrolments to swell magically in a short time. The Americans, however, misunderstood the Dominican wisdom of financing education from municipal taxes and unwisely linked it to funds from the general revenues; hence when they suffered a disastrous decline after the 'Dance of the Millions', schools had to be closed. Even if some were reopened before the final departure of the Americans, the

6 Isaac Dookhan, 1994, p.268; Emanuel Hurwitz *et al.*,1987; Katherine Cook, 1934, pp.15–52.

7 Léon Pamphile, 1985.

8 Rayford Logan, 1930, pp.440–9.

fact was that United States education policy in the Dominican Republic, unlike in Cuba or Puerto Rico, was associated with closures of schools, setbacks, indecision and failures.[9]

Left to themselves, the Americans would have steered Caribbean education strongly towards technical/vocational education, with emphasis on agricultural and trade training. This was more central to their traditions than to those of the European nations which had colonies in the Caribbean. At any rate, technical/vocational schooling was the preferred education, as far as United States authorities were concerned, for American Blacks on the mainland, and there was an easy transference of these ideas to the Caribbean islands. But the Americans were not alone, among the imperial rulers of Caribbean territories, in thinking that a strong input of technical/vocational education was necessary at the start of the twentieth century. This was also the opinion of the British and the French governments. The ruling classes in the French Antilles and the British colonies generally agreed, but dithered on or under-financed, rather than supported powerfully, such an object. It might be said that the Americans succeeded in giving Puerto Rico the strongest technical/vocational profile in the entire Caribbean, while apprenticeship schemes, trade training (mostly outside the schools), many school gardens attached to elementary schools, and the odd technical school became the order of the day in other Caribbean territories.[10] In 1930 the education industries of the Caribbean territories showed the marks of practical training, especially at the level of elementary schools, far more than a century or even fifty years previously. This was a notable development, as it signalled a thrust which was to continue accelerating throughout the remainder of the century. But the problems of matching technical/vocational education to the perceived needs of the economies, or of the major stakeholders, were enormous, and never overcome. By 1930 the classic opposition between parents who wished for personal and social mobility of their children, and did not see it coming through technical/vocational education, and governments and ruling classes with a different agenda, was entrenched in the different territories. Everybody not already in the 'modern' sector of the Caribbean economies wished to use education to cross over to it from the traditional, or peasant, or least developed sectors, and this could most assuredly be done by mastering the classical educational legacies of the European ruling classes.[11]

9 Bruce J. Calder, 1984, pp.32–40.

10 Trevor Turner, 1979a, pp.76–83; *idem*, 1979b; Antoine Abou, 1986, pp.75–92 ; Carl Campbell, 1996, pp.72–86; J. C. Dorsainville, 1922, chap.VIII.

11 Kazim Bacchus, 1976, pp.109–23; also *idem*, 1979, pp.83–91.

Depression, war and delayed developmental plans, 1934–45

The depression of the mid- and late 1930s, followed by the Second World War, naturally had an unfavourable effect on schooling in the Caribbean. The chief direct effect was upon government revenues, and thus upon school grants, then upon the availability of male teachers for secondary schools and lycées. Unless metropolitan aid was available as in the case of Puerto Rico, or the value of a local resource was actually enhanced by the War, as in the case of the oil industry in Trinidad, the outlook for schools could be bleak. Yet taking the islands as a whole, the figures indicate that school places only stagnated, and sometimes actually increased, in this period, though perhaps the latter was not as true of the quality of elementary schooling. The schools just managed on fewer resources; everything imported became less available, including schoolbooks and school supplies.[12] The rural schools never had much of these commodities anyway, even in peacetime or boom-time; and since populations were growing, and the major stakeholders in education – governments, churches and parents – still saw the value of school attendance, the pressure for school places actually grew during these years, and urban schools were often overcrowded.[13]

The demand for schooling ran ahead of the supply, in the towns, and among the middle and upper classes of the islands. Governments had long accepted the obligation to educate their citizens, even ambitiously writing compulsory education into constitutions, for example those of Haiti and Cuba.[14] The political rhetoric of compulsory elementary education was commonplace, but no island could put it into effect. The impulse to provide more school places was often independent of the uncertainties of peasant or plantation economies. Where territories were still colonies under metropolitan powers, as in the case of the Dutch, French or British territories, the metropoles and their local authorities still felt the need to control these societies, through spreading European values, and heading off social dissatisfaction by providing means whereby some of the suppressed groups could rise into junior civil-service positions and the professions.[15] Perhaps the strongest direct transmissions of European values were to be found in the rare instances in which schools were founded mostly or exclusively for the children of skilled

12 P. A. E. Collège Tartenson, 1990, p.230.

13 Carl Campbell, 1996, p.215.

14 Laurie Johnson, 1995, p.30.

15 For this sort of analysis applied to the British Caribbean, see Kazim Bacchus, 1994, chap. 12; Charles Tardieu, 1990, pp.172–3.

European workers or oil-company officials. In the independent republics of Cuba and Haiti, unprogressive, corrupt dictatorial governments provided minimum education services for their neglected masses, while allowing the élites, by light taxation, to access private schooling for their own children.[16] The variation in the Dominican Republic was that Rafael Trujillo built primary schools even if he did not encourage modern teaching methods.[17] Education was widely understood to be a main lever of upward social mobility, and thus had support from a wide cross-section of the publics, including better-off small farmers seeking to have their children cross over into the more lucrative modern sectors of the island economies. The basis therefore existed for the Caribbean to join the Western world in the remarkable expansion of formal schooling as a leading industry of the twentieth century.

In the nineteenth century the colonies, under pressure from metropolitan governments and European churches, managed to establish networks of schools crafted from the bottom up, while the territories which reached independence early, namely Haiti and the Dominican Republic, showed a preference for providing education from the top down.[18] The effect of United States intervention in the education systems of some of these Caribbean territories between 1898 and 1930 was to redirect educational efforts, not always for the best motives, to the bottom of the system; in this way their impact might be said to display a democratic impulse. For these reasons the best provision of elementary education in the mid- and late 1930s was to be found in the British and French colonies, while higher institutions of learning were better represented in Haiti, Cuba and the Dominican Republic. The latter was the country with the oldest university in the Caribbean, though it was not always functional or of solid reputation;[19] Haiti had long established a School of Law and a School of Medicine, which were combined into a university in 1944. If the United States contribution to the birth of the University of Puerto Rico seems an outstanding example of concern for education at the top, it should not be forgotten that this university was originally conceived as a training school for teachers, and that its practical bent took it outside the classical ambit of institutions of higher learning in Haiti, the Dominican Republic and Cuba.[20] The University of Havana was probably the finest institution of higher

16 The career of Maurice Dartigue in Haiti seems at variance with this judgement, but he was only one man. See Ester Dartigue, 1994; see also Charles Tardieu, 1990, pp.161–70.

17 Jacobo Moquete, 1986, pp.39–43.

18 Rayford Logan, 1930, pp.401–60, 440–9; Roberto Santos Hernández, 1993; Kazim Bacchus, 1990; also *idem*, 1994.

19 Ian Bell, 1981, pp.174–5; Hariet Bunn and Ellen Gut, 1946, pp.49–51.

20 Luis Nieves Falcón, 1965, pp.50–7.

learning in the Caribbean in the late 1930s and early 1940s; Fidel Castro, son of a privileged family, entered it to study law in 1945.

Whether resources tended to flow from the top to the bottom or the bottom to the top of the education networks, there was a remarkable uniformity in the lack of articulation within these networks. The origins of this characteristic absence of a unified system of education within each territory go back to the experience of slavery and its legacy. Elementary schooling on the one hand, and secondary education on the other, in terms of curricula and clients, were very different and very separate. The absence or narrowness of the passage from elementary to secondary schools or colleges could be seen everywhere, and constituted the chief pressure point which broke education into separate compartments in the islands. Private schools for the élites, not public schools for the masses, were linked socially and academically with the secondary schools and the lycées. And perhaps few features of schooling in the Caribbean were as strongly marked as the profusion of private schools, often run by churches. Private schooling was an extremely vibrant institution in Puerto Rico, the United States Virgin Islands (St Croix) and the independent republics;[21] it was less so in the colonies, where either the Roman Catholic Church was weaker, the élites less powerful, or the public provision more ample. But in both private and public schooling, the role and status of European-derived churches were outstanding; if they created the chaos of the education networks, they also provided the stimulus to expansion.

The religious motivation to convert to Christianity, especially in the presence of large non-Christian minorities such as the Hindus and Muslims in Guyana or Trinidad, and the desire to enlarge church membership while satisfying the aspirations of co-religionists for social mobility of their children, still provided, as they had in the nineteenth century, the rationale for community action by the churches; and rivalries among them, far from being negative, fuelled the expansion of the school networks. Increasingly the State also exerted more power, and rivalries between churches and State also promoted expansion, although Trujillo's Dominican Republic chose to work with the Roman Catholic Church, and Haiti's government was so relatively weak in education that the Church was as yet unchallenged.[22]

In the vicissitudes of formal schooling the enormous prestige of secondary schools and lycées should not be missed. In the British colonies, which had no institutions of higher learning except for odd establishments

21 World Bank, 1987, p.88; Emanuel Hurwitz *et al.*, 1987; Alfonso López Yustos, 1985, pp.181–5; Ian Bell, 1981, pp.168–82.

22 Carl Campbell, 1996, chap. 2; Jacobo Moquete, 1986, pp.52–6; Mercer Cook, 1948; Maurice Dartigue, 1941, pp.30–8.

such as Codrington College in Barbados or the Imperial College of Tropical Agriculture (ICTA) in Trinidad, secondary schools were the apex of the educational ladder, and the best of them evoked enormous respect from their urban publics. The same point could be made with even greater force in the French Antilles, where the lycées were so selective and the curriculum so metropolitan that their graduates became distinctive creatures, the quintessential black Frenchmen and Frenchwomen, ready for entry into higher institutions in France.[23] Perhaps not many poor, black boys attending a French Antillean lycée could resist engulfment by metropolitan culture as disrespectfully as was apparently done by Joseph Zobel in his autobiographical novel.[24] The best products of the secondary schools and lycées of the Caribbean, especially those who won overseas scholarships, the highest accolades of local pre-university education, formed a pool of potential migrants to the metropoles. Since no territory could satisfy the demand for professional and university education, each became the victim of a 'brain drain' to its metropole. Sons, and increasingly daughters in the 1930s and 1940s, went away to study in the United States, England or Europe, some never to return as productive adults to the societies which paid for their basic education.

If there were many similarities in the networks of education across the region, there appears to have been a stronger bifurcation of experience with respect to the politicization of education. In the French Antilles and the Dutch and British colonies, student and teacher strikes, or participation in confrontational politics at the national level, were almost unheard of; while in the independent republics, and to some extent in Puerto Rico, they were not uncommon. Despite United States control, Puerto Rico brought into the twentieth century Spanish colonial traditions of governmental manipulation of schools and teachers for political purposes. Whether through Crown Colony government in the British islands, or by the politics of assimilation in the French Antilles, the British and French governments managed to achieve a high level of political stability in their colonies, and the rule was that teachers and students should keep out of politics. Since change was more gradual and conservative in these tightly governed colonies, the opportunities for student and teacher embroilment in political crises, even those of the 1930s, were reduced. The revolutionary traditions of Haiti, the Dominican Republic and Cuba, however, and their failures to establish stable democracies, created the conditions for the greater politicization of teachers and the educational networks.

---

23 Antoine Abou, 1988, pp.185–227; Alain-Philippe Blérald, 1988, pp.88–93.
24 See Joseph Zobel, 1980, Part III.

Political nationalism was most strident in the independent republics and in Puerto Rico. In the Cuban Revolution of 1933, university and secondary school students helped to create the radical government of Ramón Grau San Martín from September 1933 to January 1934; and student strikes against General Machado before 1933, and against Fulgencio Batista after, marked a level of student involvement in politics unprecedented in any other Caribbean territory. The agenda of 'Cuba Libre' propagated so brilliantly by José Martí called for the highest show of national pride and active patriotism in the schools.[25] In the University of Havana students not only read politics, they routinely took part in national upheavals. To control the political potential of teachers and students, Batista not only appointed teachers, dismissed others, and closed and reopened schools at will; he also undertook a most original experiment for ten years: he sent his sergeants to teach in rural schools, especially in regions suspected to be under communist influence.[26] But it was not only in Cuba that political feelings ran high in educational circles. In all the disturbances of the 1930s in the British colonies, nothing as outrageous happened in the schools as the running-up of a Puerto Rican nationalist flag on the top of a schoolhouse in Ponce, Puerto Rico, in 1936.[27]

Caribbean dictators either wanted to bring schools tightly under their control, as in the case of Batista in Cuba or Trujillo in the Dominican Republic when they felt threatened by elements from these institutions, or they chose to leave schools to their own devices in cases where political threats emanated from other quarters. This latter situation obtained in post-occupation Haiti. Although a particular Minister of Education (Maurice Dartigue) under Presidents Vincent and Lescot was extraordinarily active in the education system, the army, the political parties or the trade unions seemed more dangerous to these presidents than students or teachers.[28] Yet it should be noted that students did strike against Lescot. Trujillo in the Dominican Republic was not especially interested in the schools, but worked to bring them (like everything else) under his control. Like François Duvalier later in Haiti, Trujillo felt that his safety demanded the establishment of a cult of hero worship – he being the sole hero – in the schools, and therefore propaganda to this effect was introduced.[29]

With respect to education the politics of the opposition threw up the most radical attempts to redefine it in the mid-1930s and early 1940s. The radicals identified the enemy either as entrenched local élites or the Americans,

---

25 Laurie Johnson, 1995, pp.26–30; Renate Marsiske, 1989, pp.46–58.
26 Laurie Johnson, 1995.
27 José Solis, 1994, pp.64–5.
28 Ester Dartigue, 1994, pp.7–99.
29 Jacobo Moquete,1986, pp.39–41, 48–9.

or better still both acting in combination. In Cuba students' attempts to establish a people's university (significantly named after their hero Martí), as an alternative to the élitist University of Havana, soon failed. In the ideology of the Cuban opposition movements the schools ought to be patriotic, populist and anti-American. The 'cubanidad' they hankered after apparently had nothing explicitly black or African in its Creole cultural constituents, though more Blacks than ever were in the elementary schools.[30] Neither did the fierce cultural resistance of many Puerto Ricans against the 'Americanization' of the school system involve any cultural redirection in favour of blackness or Africanness; all the Spanish-speaking territories of the Caribbean, which had experienced massive white immigration in the nineteenth and early twentieth centuries, had identified themselves either as white or coloured Creole societies, in which their citizens of African descent had no official cultural existence apart from the mainstream.

However, in the Caribbean societies with black majorities there were attempts to rethink education in the direction of blackness and Africanness, ranging from the feeble incipient strivings of the Forum Club in Barbados or anti-Cutteridge rhetoric in Trinidad & Tobago, through internationalist Garveyism in Jamaica and elsewhere, to full-blown *noirisme* in Haiti.[31] In all these places, except Haiti, the discourse and rethinking left the general ascendancy of metropolitan culture still intact; in the French Antilles there was as yet no serious challenge to francophone assimilationist ideology. But in Haiti a significant cultural redefinition of the society occurred in which the authentic culture of the country was acknowledged to be black and African. Paradoxically, however, the 'Frenchness' of the schools defied all attempts to displace it in favour of the Créole language, or of American or Anglo-Saxon educational models. The 'Griots' (intellectuals and writers inclined to the *noiriste* position) talked about a new kind of education geared towards the Haitian man as a black person, with a distinctly black personality, and there were discourses about the beauty of putting black literature into the schools, but the challenge did not amount to a replacement. And in the end the culture of the country was reoriented, but the schools were not.[32]

If the critique of the school systems from pro-Black Power elements was a sort of thunder from the Left, there was also criticism from the Right. Those who felt that popular education was basically too bookish still had plenty to

---

30 See Laurie Johnson, 1995; Harry Swan, 1978, pp.275–88; Ana Dally, 1994, pp.164–9.

31 For reference to Cutteridge and the Forum Club, see Carl Campbell, 1996 pp.95–104, 202–11; David Nicholls, 1979, chaps 6–7.

32 David Nicholls, 1979, pp.165–72; Léon-François Hoffmann, 1984, pp.57–77.

complain about; and food scarcity during the Second World War as well as the presence of an oil industry in Trinidad and Curaçao strengthened their case that schools should promote agriculture, crafts and trades. In fact island after island had to devise schemes to increase domestic food production during the War. A notable advocate for more technical/vocational education was the Colonial Development and Welfare Organisation in the British West Indies, an aid agency set up by the British government during the War. Its educational policy was that the systems adopted in the colonies were too expensive, that more practical education was needed, that schools should teach the correct use of the land, and that adults, as much as children, should be involved in the work of the schools.[33] When the proposed university for the British colonies was being discussed during the War, some critics felt that it needed a practical bent; perhaps it should be more like the University of Puerto Rico than traditional British universities. At this time, in fact, the University of Puerto Rico was engaged, under Chancellor Jaime Benítez, in a fundamental rethinking of its role, and it had not yet become a first-class institution;[34] hence it was not regarded by officials in the British Caribbean as a proper model, at the same time that the economic programme of industrialization being planned in Puerto Rico was emerging as the correct route for the British islands to follow.

Popular disturbances had a tendency to stir up discourse about the need for more practical or technical/vocational education; and so it was after the riots in the British islands in the late 1930s. The emergence, apparently in greater numbers, of the educated unemployed from secondary schools seemed to increase the urgency for reforms. More 'aid' for education was forthcoming from the United States and the European colonial powers, severally to their own dependencies, and conjointly through the newly formed Caribbean Commission, and practical programmes were favoured. It should be noted that through the Caribbean Commission and through unilateral aid the United States continued to come more and more to the fore as the premier metropolitan power in the region.[35] It was a case of the continuation of United States influence by other means, not this time by occupations or naked 'Americanization', but by dollar diplomacy and military obligations. The political stability of the region, to be achieved partly through the success of reformed educational programmes, was a policy objective of the United States.

It should also not be missed that the years just before and during the Second World War saw greater emphasis on new ideas about social planning,

33 Carl Campbell, 1997, pp.19–22; S. A. Hammond, 1941; *idem*, 1943a; *idem*, 1943b; *idem*, 1943c.

34 Luis Nieves Falcón, 1965, pp.54–72.

35 Ken Post, 1981, pp.168–71.

including the notion that education was more a means of 'development' than something to be consumed for the social gratification of individuals. However restricted metropolitan ideas about development were (whether it was more social development than economic development, whether it was development with or without political independence), whatever the balance of contributions to the ideas from within by locals or from without by metropolitans, the concept that these colonies should be 'developed' came to life in these years.[36] Schools were to become the keys to the human-resource theory of development after the War.

The promise and failure of economic development, 1945–75

The idea of development was eventually underpinned by economic and educational planning. By the 1960s integrated educational planning was in vogue, internationalized by UNESCO and other aid agencies. It was believed that education could contribute to economic development by supplying the manpower deficits of the Caribbean territories, especially for craftsmen, technicians and engineers, and for teachers and middle-level management personnel. Since economic growth and development were to come primarily through industrialization, and industries were located in the modern sector, the main contribution of education would also have to be in that sector. It was at the level of secondary and tertiary education that the greatest investment was expected to yield the highest social returns; and so the 1950s, 1960s and 1970s were marked by huge investment in secondary and university education.[37] The official adulation of technical/vocational education reached a new level, despite warnings from some metropolitan educationalists that a too-facile connection between it and economic development was dangerously deceptive. Puerto Rico got off to the most dramatic and early start in industrialization through 'foreign' (United States) investment, and all Caribbean territories were looking to emulate her, when Cuba, through the Castro Revolution, suddenly jumped out of the pack, and crafted a new oppositional socialist model of economic development which required new approaches to education.

The 1960s was a very hopeful decade in the Caribbean, on the whole. Whether through dependent socialism in Cuba or dependent capitalism elsewhere, there were many signs of progress, new factories, jobs, improved

36 Kazim Bacchus, 1967, pp.221–31; Howard Johnson, 1977.
37 Kazim Bacchus, 1981, pp.215–46.

Gross Domestic Products or some other indicator; but there were also signs of stagnation, massive outward migration and brain-drain – in essence, signs of failure. The intricacies of matching technical/vocational education to economic needs, job requirements and parental aspirations, proved insoluble. Suffice it to say that by the late 1960s, and more so in the 1970s, confidence in economic and educational planning was on the wane; and government after government struggled to find new formulas and new balances between the public and private sectors, between continuing with integrated educational planning and abandoning it for sector-by-sector educational reforms.

Cuba felt that it had discovered the way forward, and since it was then the only Caribbean territory to revolutionize its social, political and economic structures, it had to revolutionize its educational infrastructure too. Cuba abolished church and private schools, and put in new programmes from the bottom to the top, from the mass literacy campaign of the early 1960s to the reorganization of the universities in the 1970s. Work-study programmes appeared in almost all schools; secondary schools were taken to the countryside and made to produce goods and services; the universities were made to concentrate on science and technology.[38] It was hoped partly through education to produce a new socialist person. Education was free for all, with additional opportunities for those who surrendered to the political ideology of the Revolution. As Castro warned the intellectuals, inside the Revolution there were abundant opportunities for advancement; outside the Revolution, nothing.[39]

Without a revolution the Caribbean colonies which became independent nations in the 1960s, chiefly the British territories, had to build on the educational foundations they had inherited from their imperial masters; but they too sought a measure of decolonization in education. Unable to replicate the Cuban model, they adopted features which resembled it, in attenuated forms, and without conscious copying. They strove for a unified, single education system controlled by the State and not by the churches. Inevitably a challenge to the churches developed wherever they showed a capacity or willingness to resist state power; this happened in Trinidad and in Guyana.[40] Secondary education was taken to the countryside and democratized; equality of access to secondary schools was arrived at partly though the infamous Common Entrance Examination; free secondary schooling and even free university education were pronounced in some English-speaking territories; schoolbooks and curricula were redone to reflect local themes and interests;

38 See Marvin Leiner, 1981; Abel Prieto, 1981; Martin Carnoy, 1990.

39 Jorge Domínguez, 1978, p.392.

40 Carl Campbell, 1997, pp.81–96; Kazim Bacchus, 1974, pp.141–62.

traditional classical secondary education was de-emphasized up to a point to make way for technical/vocational subjects; the entire educational industry was expanded by greater expenditure on schools. All these changes left the educational model in the British Caribbean well within the colonial framework of the past, but at least partially decolonized.[41]

Haiti was singularly left out of the massive expansion of the education industry in the Caribbean from the 1950s through to the 1970s. The conviction that education could promote economic development provided the stimulus; so too did the emergence of parliamentary democracies in the former British colonies. Elected politicians either in reformed Crown Colonies or in independent nations had to satisfy voters who had a voracious appetite for secondary education, the level where the highest aspirations of the greatest number coalesced. But new tertiary institutions and universities also sprang into existence. In the British colonies the University (College) of the West Indies opened its doors in Jamaica as a single-campus institution in 1948, but trifurcated into additional regional colleges in Trinidad and Barbados in the early 1960s; the University of Puerto Rico also developed regional colleges at about the same time; the Centre d'Enseignement Supérieur attached to the University of Bordeaux came to life in the French Antilles in the 1960s; so too did the College of the Virgin Islands and the University of Guyana. The Law School in the Netherlands Antilles (later to be enlarged into the University of the Netherlands Antilles) and the College of the Bahamas followed in the early 1970s.[42] In the Dominican Republic after the fall of Trujillo, so many private schools, colleges and even universities came into existence that this country became the Caribbean territory with the most tertiary-level institutions.[43] It followed that training colleges and facilities for teachers, not to mention emergency courses and shortened training in some instances, had to be brought on stream. If primary education was not the focus, that was because such high levels of provision and enrolment existed everywhere, except Haiti, that this sector was not then regarded as the problem.

Dictatorships in the capitalist Caribbean were unkind to education. In the case of Trujillo in the Dominican Republic, it was not that growth did not occur in the education system; it did eventually. But the suppression of the opinions of other stakeholders in education, and the indoctrination of children and teachers to sing the praises of the 'Great Benefactor', rankled. In

41 Carl Campbell, 1997, pp.89–129; Errol Miller, 1989, pp.226–7.

42 Carlos Dip, 1976, pp.431–45; René A. Römer, 1976, pp.47–51; Ethel Ríos de Betancourt, 1972, pp.40–9; Isaac Dookhan, 1981, pp.15–25. See Anthony Payne, 1988, pp.33–53.

43 Ian Bell, 1981, pp.175–82; José del Castillo, 1981, pp.134–5.

these ways Trujillo anticipated Castro and François 'Papa Doc' Duvalier. The difference was that Duvalier did not manage to expand the education system in Haiti, though a literacy programme was mounted, with dubious success.[44] Trujillo and Castro at least were working to modernize their countries, but Duvalier just buried Haiti in a sort of *noiriste* cocoon. Haiti's poverty, its profound problems (not that they were unique), provided an improbable matrix for the solution of its education dilemmas. The social structure was lop-sided; the economy was lop-sided; politics were lop-sided; how could the education system be anything else? Haiti illustrated in the extreme the prior necessity for social and economic reforms, for the settling of laudable national objectives and performance, before education policies could contribute to economic development or social stability.

The continuing struggles of sections of Caribbean societies to discover or reclaim their national identity in and through the schools recorded some new peaks after the Second World War, through the 1960s and into the 1970s. At first the people of the French Antilles seemed to have surrendered complacently to the lure of assimilation and departmentalization (1946), hoping to receive the same social and economic benefits as Frenchmen in France. Then serious opposition to departmentalization began in the 1950s, and became violent in the 1960s; invariably, part of the argument was that the French school robbed Martinicans, Guadeloupeans and Guyanese of their very soul, no less than their language (Créole).[45] A sturdy blow was struck for the Spanish language and Puerto Rican culture in 1949, when, following constitutional changes giving Puerto Rico control of education, the decision was taken by the Popular Democratic Party to make Spanish unequivocally the language of instruction in the schools.[46] If 'Americanization' was not turned back, it was creolized. Almost everywhere in the Caribbean, with the exception of Cuba and the Dominican Republic, the language policy for schools was a troublesome matter which implicitly or explicitly had something to do with the creation or re-creation of national identity. In most instances the language imbroglios were so complex that the best option was simply to leave matters as they stood. In the Dutch Antilles, for instance, a solution for the Dutch Windward islands (where Papiamentu is the Creole language) would not be a solution for the Dutch Leeward Islands (where English is the popu-

44 David Nicholls, 1979, pp.221–38; Ian Bell, 1981, pp.166–7; Jacobo Moquete, 1986, pp.39–41. For a concise statement of Trujillo educational reforms, see Miriam Díaz Santana, 1980, pp.11–12.

45 Dany Bebel-Gisler, 1976, pp.l61–89; Richard D. E. Burton, 1992, vol. 11, pp.169–207; Andre Lucrece, 1981, pp.147–60, 158; Marie-Marthe, 1978, pp.21–42; '"Notre Combat": Extraits de '*Patriote Guadeloupéen et d'autres publications* (1968-76)', pp.73–5.

46 José Solis, 1994, p.111.

lar tongue).[47] The Creole languages of the Caribbean are still outside the formal education systems of the islands and fierce disputes have occurred in Haiti and the Dutch Antilles.

In the British Caribbean, before and after independence, the role of Creole languages in schools as a factor in national identity has been underplayed, and discussed mostly by university intellectuals in limited circles. In Trinidad or Guyana where substantial Indian minorities or near-majorities existed, the construction of a new language policy for schools was even more daunting, as the Creole language (and culture) was not necessarily seen as the heritage of the Indians. Ostensibly to create an acceptable national identity, and without the co-operation of most Indians, young Blacks in Trinidad in the late 1960s, and in 1970, attempted to subvert the government by means of a Black Power movement. Some of its leaders were students at the local university campus; many of its followers were students at the secondary level of the education system. The movement wanted to put black culture into the schools; at one secondary school in the capital, students called for African drumming to be a part of the curriculum.[48] In 1968 the university campus in Jamaica had been rocked by student disturbances arising partly from the expulsion of Walter Rodney, a Guyanese lecturer in African history, who had taken a message of socialism and African pride outside the campus, and had fallen foul of the Jamaican government. For the first time in the history of education in the English-speaking islands student participation in politics had become a significant factor; but the revolutionary predispositions of the Black Power movements in Trinidad and Jamaica were contained by concessions and repression, and the movements transformed themselves into recessive, cultural interest groups, at best talking conventional politics.

The era of contradictions, 1975–90

From the mid-1970s to 1990, expansion of the education industries continued, though at a less rapid rate than in the years after the Second World War. The emphasis of governments was still on the secondary and tertiary levels; it was still believed that education was a vital factor in economic development, even when there was sufficient evidence that development plans had largely failed. Technical/vocational education lost little of its cogency, despite metropolitan misgivings that serious structural reforms had to be made before it could deliver

47 Francine Frank, 1974, pp.111–7; Roberto Martis, 1983, pp.313–67.
48 Carl Campbell, 1997, pp.74–5.

its potential. In fact the argument of some experts abroad that new social and economic objectives had to be set for most Caribbean societies before educational policies could be devised which could contribute to development went unheeded.[49] The countries which had fundamentally reformed their societies frightened the rest of the Caribbean rather than offering any credible models.

Grenada shocked the Caribbean in 1979 by going into a revolutionary mode of government and development which looked like a replication on a mini-scale of the Cuban socialist enterprise. The lines of Grenada's reforms in education resembled those in Castro's Cuba: emphasis on mass literacy and community involvement; an attempt to secure mass mobilization; egalitarian measures, work-study programmes and education for production; new curricula and new books to get rid of colonialism in the schools; teachers exposed to the ordeal of gentle political re-education. Grenada too was looking for the new Caribbean person from the schools.[50] But the revolution committed suicide before anything tremendous could be achieved, and after 1983 the education system returned to its previous course. In the meantime Cuba's educational reforms continued, the emphasis shifting to reform of the universities. Amazingly, Cuba now overproduced professionals and para-professionals, and could use this trained human surplus as part of its foreign policy in the Caribbean and Africa.[51] There was no other Caribbean country where the symmetry between educational plans and wider social objectives was so exact. The Cuban regime consistently committed large revenues to education and training, even when the economy was not growing. The oversupply of trained and well-educated persons, in an economy and society not admitted universally to be 'developed' or even economically independent, reminds us of the complexity of development.

While Caribbean eyes were fixed on Grenada, an unexpected thrust in education was made on the other side of the Caribbean, in Haiti. While most Caribbean countries were attempting to expand the top levels of their education system, Haiti had to begin again from the bottom; and largely through UNESCO and other international agencies, the Jean-Claude 'Baby Doc' Duvalier regime gathered the energy to expand elementary education in large measure, and took the historic decision, not without public resistance, to make Créole of equal importance with French in elementary education.[52] As

49 Kazim Bacchus, 1981.

50 Anthony Payne *et al.*, 1984, pp.26–8. For an unsympathetic account, see Gregory Sandford and Richard Vigilante, 1984, pp.70–4.

51 Mark Richmond, 1990; Martin Carnoy, 1990.

52 Jacomina de Regt, 1984, pp.119–41; Charles Tardieu, 1990, pp.186–93; Errol Miller, 1992, chap.7; for a statement of the case for Créole see Georges Mathelier, 1976.

usual in Haiti, there was a large gap between plans and implementation, but it has been said that the country had not experienced such a massive input of funds and energy into elementary schooling since the creation of the republic. These efforts still left Haiti with an incredibly large percentage of illiterate persons. But illiteracy rates in several other Caribbean territories, though not approaching the Haitian dimension, were surprisingly high even as the 1980s ended. The expansion of the education systems had left large segments of the populations behind, and in the trade-off between quantity and quality, quality seemed to have been the loser in several Caribbean countries. High examination failure rates, high drop-out rates from schools, a high incidence of illiteracy after years of schooling, all marked the inefficiencies of systems. These features can be found at present from Jamaica in the western Caribbean through Haiti and the Dominican Republic, as well as Puerto Rico, down the curve of the islands to Trinidad & Tobago and Guyana. The honourable exceptions only prove the rule. The bewildered education planners began to turn their attention back to the neglected elementary level of the systems.

While the internal efficiency of education systems was more or less always below the desired level, sudden shifts of global macro-economic conditions could and did send education systems into unexpected twists and turns in some islands. The oil boom in Trinidad in the 1970s and very early 1980s gave the government undreamt-of revenues, large amounts of which were put into education; hefty funds were set up for different projects; new structures were erected; and various education subsidies provided by the government. It was the largest expenditure of funds ever on the education system, and it gave Trinidad & Tobago a modern education infrastructure superior to anything in the rest of the English-speaking Caribbean.[53] Simultaneously other parts of the subregion, notably Jamaica, got into debt and came under pressure to finance the educational industries constructed in the post-war years. Jamaica was obliged to constrain its educational services in the late 1970s and 1980s, reducing the output of teachers, raising pupil/teacher ratios, reintroducing fees in secondary schools, and reversing the policy of free university education.[54] With better management and less rhetoric, smaller English-speaking islands, notably Barbados, have managed the oil crisis and structural adjustments with less damage to their education system.

Despite the expansion of educational facilities in all territories, and high enrolments almost everywhere at the level of elementary schools, the public systems of education, faced with population increases, have not been able to

53 Carl Campbell, 1997, pp.194–7.
54 Errol Miller, 1989, pp.214–17.

provide sufficient school places. This has left the field open in several Caribbean countries to private schools which have had a long and successful history in the region. Whether in the form of schools run by individuals or secular groups as a form of business enterprise, or by churches as a fee-paying community service, private schools are currently strongly represented in Puerto Rico, the Dominican Republic and Haiti.[55] In the latter country they actually enrol more children than public schools, leaving ambitious parents with meagre incomes in the desperate situation of financing their children's elementary education.[56] In the French Antilles the secularization of education from the later nineteenth century blocked the flowering of private schools, a large proportion of which were conducted by the Roman Catholic Church.[57] In the English-speaking Caribbean, private schools, especially at the secondary level, have retreated since the 1960s before the advance of public provision. Of course the Cuban Revolution abolished private schools. In the present economic climate favouring privatization, it is not improbable that ever-larger slices of the education provision might fall to private enterprise.

One function historically of private schools in the Caribbean, especially at the level of secondary education, has been to bring girls out from the shade of domesticity into the glare of academic competition. European-derived gender ideology dictated that the lion's share of public schooling above the elementary level was first appropriated by boys, who alone had public, political and professional careers to follow. A virtual revolution in female participation and success in the school systems has occurred in the twentieth century, especially from the 1920s, and its dynamics have not been thoroughly explained as yet by scholarly inquiry. Explanations range from alleged imperial and Crown Colony governmental conspiracy in Jamaica to keep down black men, to psychological hypotheses about the greater adaptability of girls, through repressive gender-related socialization, to cope with the discipline of school life.[58] Conscious policy decisions to secure the place of girls and women in the systems have been taken consistently only in Cuba since the Revolution. The rising participation of girls and women predated the Caribbean feminist movements, but might have been stimulated by them. Ironically girls and women first flooded into the systems on the now-disgraced, old-fashioned gender ideology of inferiority to men, and as the best practitioners of care-giving functions, one of which became school teaching. It is not uncommon now, right across the Caribbean, to find girls and women better represented than males in educational institutions, from sec-

55 Emmanuel Jiménez and Marlaine Lockheed, 1995; Jacobo Moquete, 1986, p.64.
56 Robert Landry, 1988, p.10.
57 Antoine Abou, 1988, pp.76–92.
58 Errol Miller, 1986.

ondary schools, through teacher training colleges, to universities,[59] and this includes special groups such as Indian girls in Trinidad and Guyana who previously had been kept out of school by tradition-bound parents. More alarming perhaps to Caribbean male professionals has been the great success of girls and women in the schools and universities, and their entry into occupations and levels of management hitherto the preserve of men. It is now being said in a few places that men are somehow at risk,[60] while women complain of a lack of empowerment.

Conclusion

It has been shown in this chapter that a strong input of 'American' education was made in the education systems of Cuba, Haiti, the Dominican Republic and Puerto Rico in the first thirty years of the twentieth century, but that this 'Americanization' was resisted and checked by Creole influences. This did not mean the end of the spread of United States influence in Caribbean education; if not imposed by the military, it has been negotiated in aid agreements, or voluntarily adopted by Caribbean leaders who studied in the United States or simply admired American civilization. The University of the West Indies is currently organizing itself increasingly on United States models of higher education. The former British colonies which have passed into independence have only managed incomplete decolonization in their educational systems, while Cuba has evinced the highest level of anti-imperialism (or anti-Americanism) and nationalism. In Puerto Rico national identity has been sought through stout resistance to the use of the English language as the major vehicle of instruction. In the French Antilles departmentalization has denied success to the movements for Antillean identity through education. Though since the mid-1980s greater control over the schools has passed to the local elected authorities, the system remains essentially French.[61]

If the Caribbean black and coloured middle classes have grown tremendously on the backs of the schools in the twentieth century, it is still reasonable to maintain that the African ancestral culture of these beneficiaries, as well as the heritage of Indo-Caribbean people, remain largely outside the mainstream culture of formal, public schooling, even in the territories where Blacks or Indians form a majority. Education in the twentieth century has

59 Isis Duarte, Clara Báez *et al.*, 1989, pp.63–8; Antione Abou, 1987, pp.24–7.

60 See Errol Miller, 1991.

61 *L'Education en Guadeloupe*, 1986; Scott MacDonald and Albert Gastmann, 1984, pp.19–21.

worked relentlessly in the direction of the Europeanization or Americanization of the Caribbean societies, and their separation culturally from ancestral roots in Africa or Asia, although nobody would seriously propose that the Caribbean populations with black majorities learn African languages, although a higher percentage of Blacks live there than in South Africa. Apart from the extraordinary Cuban experience, the most revolutionary development in Caribbean education from 1930 to 1990 has been the tremendous growth of the education industries. In this way the Caribbean joined the Western world in one of the most remarkable movements of the twentieth century, the institutionalization of education for the masses.

18

The quality of life in the twentieth-century Caribbean

Bonham C. Richardson and Joseph L. Scarpaci

Introduction

It is 1950 in Barbados. Visitors arrive at Seawell Airfield (now being extended by a Colonial Development and Welfare Grant) on the propeller airplanes of British West Indian Airways. Most tourists stay at one of the several hotels south-east of Bridgetown in Hastings, among them the Marine Hotel which is 'up to date and with more than 120 bedrooms'.[1] The accommodations there defy comparison with the abject poverty of most black Barbadians. Their tiny wooden houses in the rural tenantries and urban slums often have dirt floors and thoroughly unsanitary conditions; it is therefore little wonder that the 1946 population census of the British Caribbean has shown Barbados's infant mortality rate at 176 per 1,000 live births, by far the highest among the British Caribbean colonies. The journey to and from Bridgetown for rural Blacks is still often accomplished on foot or donkey cart but in recent years by motorbus. British planners attribute Barbados's poverty to its chronic overpopulation (192,800 in the 1946 census) and suggest – as they have for decades – that the 'surplus' people might better be sent to British Honduras or British Guiana. Despite the general impoverishment, all Barbadians revel in the results of the recent test cricket match in London where, for the first time on British soil, the West Indies, powered by the fabled Barbadian batsmen Walcott, Weekes and Worrell, have defeated England.[2] The few Barbadians who own radio sets have heard the news over Radio Distribution, the island's sole radio station. Others have savoured the headlines of the *Barbados Advocate*, the only newspaper. An extra-mural tutor has just come to Barbados representing the University College of the West Indies in Jamaica, which received its Royal Charter one year ago in 1949.

1 W. Adolphe Roberts, 1948, p.148.
2 S. M. Wilson, 1995.

Fast forward (a term unknown in 1950) to Barbados at the end of the twentieth century. Visitors now arrive, often via non-stop jet aircraft (including Concorde) from London, Toronto or New York. The ultra-modern Grantley Adams International Airport (adjacent to old Seawell Field) receives the tourists who next proceed to one of dozens of upscale hotels around the island, in the south but also along the 'Platinum Coast' north of Bridgetown. For over thirty years the island nation of roughly 265,000 people has been politically independent, and it has just hosted its second visit by a United States president since 1982. More than 40,000 private automobiles on the island and over 8,000 trucks and buses are accommodated by new highway construction that has seen a controlled-access high-speed road appear behind Bridgetown to relieve traffic congestion. Barbadians converse with each other, often on one of the country's 111,000 telephones, about friends and relatives not only in Bridgetown but just as often in Brooklyn or Brixton. Barbados's life expectancy and infant mortality are the same as in the United States, and its literacy rate (98 per cent) is higher. Two artificial waterfalls grace the newest indoor shopping mall on Broad Street, projecting an 'oceanscape' atmosphere intended to please the many tourists who collectively spend over US$500 million annually there. Barbadians enjoy seeing (on the country's 70,000 television sets) the documentary/travelogue features about their home island on CNN news from Atlanta, programmes that portray Barbados as fun, sexy, hip and eminently appealing. The island's allure is, however, muted by a growing narcotics traffic which is inevitably accompanied by accelerating local crime rates, prostitution, and a widespread use of firearms – local problems that stem from forces beyond the island, and which were unheard of a few years ago.

The Barbadian transformations in the last half-century are astounding, even in the context of the jaded academic conversations that now deal routinely with 'globalization', and even within the Caribbean itself. In so far as these remarkable Barbadian changes are Caribbean-wide, two points stand out; they are, furthermore, points that have always helped in explaining the region's history and cultures. First, insularity and smallness, the same geographical characteristics that rendered the region so appealing and accessible to earliest European colonists and planters, continue to be crucial. Small islands are easier to transform, whether one is initiating literacy drives, yellow-fever eradication campaigns, road pavement schemes, or drug dealing, than are large places. Smallness also means a connectivity of ideas, trends and material changes so that social scientists' categories of 'culture', 'politics', 'economics', and so forth are even more restrictive in small places than elsewhere.

A second point is that continuous change is the essence of the Caribbean. The region's geographical and economic proximity to Europe and

North America makes individual places within the Caribbean subject to an endless succession of externally instigated (conscious and otherwise) schemes, experiments, plans and projects; so the region's peoples – nearly all of whose ancestors have been exported from elsewhere at one time or another, often as ingredients in these unending transformations – have always had to cope with novelty, difference and reinvention. These key points help to explain why the global change, reconfiguration and hyperactivity that some suggest is without precedent, seem startlingly familiar to Caribbean peoples.[3] Put another way, in the traditional categorizing of various world regions as to the degree of 'contact' they have had with modern ways of doing things, 'the Caribbean is nothing but contact.'[4]

This chapter assesses the broad condition of the quality of life in the Caribbean in the latter half of the twentieth century, a fifty-year period in which the region has progressed from a situation mainly consisting of colonies to one where there is mainly political autonomy. The first section assays aspects of landscape and environment, elements that define the physical attributes of the Caribbean but which also, as always, pose challenges. The second deals with tourism, drugs and crime, the most important externally influenced determinants of change and potential harm. Subsequent sections address politics and the media, carnival, music and sport, and human health. Acknowledging the somewhat arbitrary grouping of the elements within these subtopics reinforces the Caribbean's interconnectedness (thus, tourism, very obviously, has much to do with politics and the media within the region.) The final section of the chapter highlights the legendary creativity and adaptability of the peoples of the Caribbean in the face of the region's current constellation of external influences.

Living in the environment

Fiction and reality both shape outsiders' views of the Caribbean. Gabriel García Márquez conjures up a whimsical view of the region's tropical colour and myriad peoples. His 'Macondo', located on Colombia's Caribbean coast, captures the essence of the ruinous history of the region. The power of microcosmic Macondo is that its extremes of good and bad, evil and beauty, and real and unreal embody nearly all the possibilities of what the Caribbean might be, both to outsiders and residents alike. To be sure, few geographical

3 Sidney W. Mintz, 1996.
4 Michel-Rolph Trouillot, 1992, p.22.

areas in the world remain as diverse and geographically complex as that between Florida, Central America and northern South America. Its archipelago consists of hundreds of islands, two dozen political entities, and direct cultural influences not just from the Western Hemisphere, but from Europe, Africa and Asia.

About 32 million people now inhabit the islands and rimlands that comprise the Caribbean region.[5] Differences in populations and land areas continue to produce great disparities; tiny Saba contains just over 1,000 residents on 11 square kilometres while Cuba has more than 11 million on the largest island in the West Indies. Eastern Caribbean islands are mostly micro-states with populations of fewer than 300,000. Trinidad remains far and away the largest island in this eastern region with a population of 1.4 million (including that of its sister island, Tobago). Distances among differing islands vary from short spans of water which can be traversed in rowing boats to vast expanses of ocean. The 3,000-mile distance from French Guiana (Guyane) in the east to Belize in the west is roughly the same as that separating New York from Los Angeles. Long-distance super-jets have bridged these distances since the 1960s, yet conventional modes of travel from most Caribbean locales, as in the past, usually lead to places outside the region rather than to one another.

The ecological incongruency between the Caribbean's local environments and their historically introduced human populations has led to, among many other things, recurring local food deficits as well as environmental stresses and complexities. Too little rain (such as during the 1997–8 El Niño aridity) decreases local agricultural production, and too much creates damaging hillside soil erosion. At the end of the twentieth century, Caribbean peoples continued to maintain uneasy, ambivalent and complex attitudes toward their physical surroundings. This point is not intended to support the facile pronouncements by planners and others that these peoples, owing to a mystically collective memory of slavery, maintain an illogical reluctance to till the soil. An eminently practical explanation for such an attitude is that the people of the region understand – better than most outsiders – that, for example, external marketing constraints or so-called free-trade arrangements often work against full-time commitments to local agricultural activities.

Nor are Caribbean peoples' attitudes about their environments based strictly upon utilitarian motives. By now a body of academic observations reinforces the point that Caribbean peoples often have sentimental feelings about land, feelings based upon a combination of resistance, family identity and economic value.[6] The idealized character of Caribbean environments as

5 Bonham C. Richardson, 1992.

6 Jean Besson and Janet H. Momsen, 1987; D. Lowenthal, 1961.

former homelands is further reinforced by the memories, embellished and otherwise, held by the millions who have emigrated to Europe and North America in recent decades.[7] A commonly held sentiment among members of the Cuban populations in Miami and the metropolitan New York area, for example, is the idealization of the émigrés' former homeland itself,[8] an attitude also evident among Caribbean peoples who have left to live elsewhere. Fictional accounts of the Caribbean homeland underscore this idealization, by both natives[9] and foreigners[10] alike.

Left unprotected, the beauty and allure of Caribbean environments (as appealing to locals as to vacationing Europeans and North Americans) have ways of sowing their own seeds of ecological destruction. Tiny St Martin (Sint Maarten) in the north-eastern Caribbean provides an example. Owing to the near-unbelievable growth in its tourist industry in the latter half of the century, St Martin has undergone a dramatic transformation, mainly on the Dutch half of the island. In 1980, 300,000 tourists arrived in St Martin, a figure which more than tripled by 1990. Rapid (and therefore shoddy) construction of high-rise condominiums to accommodate the visitors attracted thousands of labour migrants, many from both sides of Hispaniola. A lack of planning or control then spawned a depressing landscape of fast-food franchise outlets. St Martin's landscape is now littered with handbills, refuse and the rusting shells of automobiles, and traffic congestion and power-cuts are routine. The resulting social malaise, accented by growing crime rates, chain-link fences, and 24-hour security guards, is paralleled by an infrastructural breakdown and an airport with 'toilets that do not flush and badly discoloured water flowing through the taps'.[11]

Beach damage and associated deterioration almost always follow the shoreline construction inspired by tourism and population increases. The thermal effluent from the Barbados Light and Power Company plant north of Bridgetown, for example, has led to 'a virtually dead reef directly offshore … near the edge of the thermal plume'.[12] Further activities of the power plant are now being monitored and controlled. Yet rules and regulations intended to protect Caribbean shoreline environments do not themselves guarantee success. Puerto Rican law requires anyone intending to move beach sand to obtain a permit from Obras Públicas beforehand. But once such a permit is

7 For example, John Western, 1992.
8 Lisandro Pérez, 1992.
9 G. García Márquez, 1994; Paule Marshall, 1972.
10 J. Sayles, 1991.
11 Klaus de Albuquerque and J. L. McElroy, 1995, p.83.
12 L. A. Nurse *et al.*, 1995, p.33.

granted 'extraction limits are often exceeded or ignored ... and illegal removal of sand for construction aggregate continues'.[13]

The region's traditional soil-erosion problems continue. Jamaican deforestation for new and ongoing cultivation plots in the island's hills and mountains limit agricultural yields, lead to slope deterioration, and foul small river basins.[14] But nothing matches the remarkable soil erosion which continues as Haiti's geographical hallmark and is closely interrelated with the nation's endemic poverty. Haitian agricultural plots are still subdivided into ever-smaller land parcels to accommodate a combination of cash and subsistence cropping. The forest is essentially gone, and trees not cleared for agriculture end up as charcoal in sacks that yield as little as US 60 cents.[15] In south-western Haiti 20 per cent of the 'soil' is down to bedrock, and every year hillside farmers abandon an estimated 15,000 more acres because of soil erosion.[16]

In southern Haiti the grim erosion that is part of daily life was magnified when hurricane Gilbert struck on 12 September 1988. Eight years earlier, Allen laid waste to much of St Lucia, ruining the entire standing banana crop by snapping off 90 per cent of the banana trees.[17] The hurricanes that rake the region annually are now tracked with sophisticated satellite imagery and the results instantly relayed so that radio and television warnings can be transmitted throughout communities and islands under threat. Although communication innovations have saved lives and help immeasurably in disaster-preparedness programmes, in themselves they provide no protection from a hurricane's wrath; nor do they grant immunity against other storms following close behind in a steady east-west trajectory. In September 1995, Luis – an unusually large and unconsolidated hurricane – hit Barbuda and northern Antigua, destroying 70 per cent of the dwellings and causing severe beach erosion on the former island. Luis proceeded westward, wreaking havoc in St Barthelémy, St Martin, St Kitts and Nevis, leaving altogether 16 dead and causing an estimated US$2.5 billion in damage. Ten days later, hurricane Marilyn crossed the same area, wrecking ships and dwellings in the US Virgin Islands. In St Thomas three-fourths of the island's homes and businesses were damaged or destroyed and an estimated 10,000 left homeless.

Montserrat suffered high winds and rains from both 1995 hurricanes when Montserratians had hardly caught their collective breath from Hugo's passage in September 1989. That storm is perhaps better known for having

13 D. M. Bush *et al.*, 1995, p.52.
14 D. Barker and D. F. M. McGregor, 1988.
15 M. Kurlansky, 1992, pp.167–8.
16 C. J. Paskett and C. E. Philoctete, 1990.
17 M. C. Williams, 1988.

scored direct hits on St Croix, north-eastern Puerto Rico, and the southern United States. In comparative terms, however, Hugo was most damaging to Montserrat; essentially all of the island's 12,000 people were left homeless by Hugo.[18] But the geo-physical hazard for which tiny Montserrat has become world famous is its volcanic activity. The island's crater vented ash and steam on 18 July 1995, a precursor to a series of subsequent eruptions.

Seismologists noted rumblings on Montserrat as early as 1989, and subterranean 'swarms' were recorded in 1992 and 1994. On 12 May 1996, a Mother's Day outburst saw lava flows reaching the sea for the first time. In mid-September a series of dome collapses was accompanied by a volcanic dust plume rising 40,000 feet and thousands of tons of volcanic ash dropping onto the southern half of the island. Two-thirds of Montserrat's human populace was displaced, some twenty lives were lost, and the capital town of Plymouth was abandoned. As the Montserratians moved away (about 3,000 to Antigua and 1,000 to England as well as to North America and other nearby islands) vulcanologists and a few reporters descended on the island. Their scientific curiosity was compounded by the fascination that accompanies imminent danger because Montserrat's internal lava contains a great deal of gas, creating a subterranean build-up or compression that could lead to catastrophe.[19]

Whereas outsiders are appropriately fascinated by the igneous events on Montserrat, West Indians who live along the arc of the Lesser Antilles – which marks the intersection of two of the earth's crustal plates – are familiar with the jolts and tremors that are parts of daily life on the seismically active islands. Trinidadians in early 1997 were startled by an offshore earthquake that measured over 6 on the Richter scale. A better-known volcanic eruption in St Vincent in 1979 caused 15,000 people to be evacuated from the danger area, some to nearby islands.[20] All residents of the Lesser Antilles are, furthermore, at least vaguely familiar with the volcanic cataclysm of Martinique's Mt Pelée in 1902, and most realize that recurrences are inevitable (although the particular places and times are unknown) given the geological underpinning of the region.

Caribbean peoples' relationships with their immediate environments have weakened since mid-century as improvements in intra-island transportation have facilitated personal travel to capital cities and towns, thereby intensifying urban activities. Varying types of motorized vehicles now convey millions of people daily throughout the region to urban jobs, markets, schools, medical appointments, meetings and sources of entertainment.

18 J. B. Campbell and Bonham C. Richardson, 1992, p.408.
19 W. Graham, 1997.
20 H. Sigurdsson, 1982.

Animal-powered modes of travel in the islands are far less common – though by no means absent – than they were at mid-century, but walking for an hour or more to reach one's destination is still routine in the poorer and smaller places. Despite modernization elsewhere, the poorest Haitians walk many miles after going 'under the wire' into the Dominican Republic to work as cane cutters there.[21] Horse-drawn carriages and bicycle-taxis (the former are practically obsolete and the latter never common) now circulate in post-USSR Havana at a time when oil is no longer subsidized. Bicycles in the Cuban capital, estimated at 70,000 in 1990, now exceed 1 million. This Antillean city now has a slightly Asian feel because of this 'new' mode of transport.[22] Variations in types and character of motorized conveyances reflect economic and cultural differences from place to place in the region. Where standards of living are high or fuel prices cheap, as in San Juan, Pointe-à-Pitre, or Port of Spain, rush-hour traffic jams rival those in Europe and North America. Throughout the region, crowded minibuses provide alternatives to more conventional, but often less reliable, means of public bus transportation and are testimonies to the adaptability of small-scale entrepreneurs as in Kingston, Jamaica.[23] The ubiquity of taxis in Barbados and Antigua, where tourism dominates local economies, is not found in banana-oriented St Vincent, although highways in the latter island have been improved through agricultural development grants. In British Guiana in the early 1960s, government subsidies for fuel for local rice farmers led to unusually high rates of tractor traffic along the coastal highway. Late in the 1990s in Cuba, the presence of 40-year-old American automobiles is testimony to the long-standing rupture in United States-Cuba ties, and Havana's high bicycle density reflects the impact of the United States economic embargo.

Whereas intra-island travel for individuals has become mainly motorized in the latter half of the twentieth century, movements beyond one's home island are usually by airplane. And although inter-island movements and travels beyond the Caribbean are normally categorized as 'migration' and discussed at length elsewhere in this volume, it is important to note that air travel in some places is an integral part of local cultures. Alberto Sandoval Sánchez asserts, for example, that the ' … essentialist Puerto Rican identity … (is) … guaranteed in a round-trip ticket ….'[24] And air travel of course brings Caribbean peoples into daily contact with tourists, whose ephemeral contacts with the region invariably include ship or air travel.

21 Samuel Martínez, 1995, p.8.
22 R. Segre *et al.*, 1997.
23 Patricia Anderson, 1987.
24 Alberto S. Sandoval Sánchez, 1997, p.192.

Tourism, drugs and crime

St Martin is only one among many Caribbean locales utterly transformed by jet-age tourism in the past generation. That industry stands far and away as the region's 'engine of growth', carrying with it images of acceleration, movement and prosperity, along with (often illusory) promises to lift Caribbean peoples out of their poverty.[25] From the tourist's point of view, travel to the Caribbean has changed greatly since mid-twentieth century, from extended tours to overnight getaways. During the 1950s, except for the locational proximity that brought thousands of Americans to Cuba, tourism elsewhere in the region was usually characterized by travellers from Britain, France and the Netherlands heading for holidays in family-owned hotels in their particular Caribbean colonies. By the end of the century, however, Americans had come to dominate Caribbean tourism.[26] These sojourners have left their mark everywhere, from the reefs and cays of Belize, where eco-tourism is all the rage, to the time-share condominiums of Aruba, the Grand Caymans and St Martin that accommodate tourists who can afford to pay the US$300 per night (meals extra) for lodging.

Americanization also has meant homogenization, as shown by the Caribbean's mass-market cruise industry. If 'globalization' has a region-wide symbol in the Caribbean, it is the behemoth mega-ship that travels from Miami to one small Caribbean port after another. Each ship carries over 3,000 passengers, heading out each week with the same number. After these 'floating cities' (which pay wharfage charges of up to US$25,000 for a call to a single place) arrive in cash-hungry islands and disgorge their visitors, each passenger spends on average $124 per call, according to a 1995 survey by the Florida-Caribbean Cruise Association.[27] Caribbean cruise ships carried an estimated 300,000 passengers in 1970, a figure that climbed to just under 2.5 million in 1996. This eight-fold increase helps explain why islands and ports are under severe environmental and social pressures. Witness, for instance, the 600-foot climb up Dunn's River Falls near Ocho Rios, Jamaica. This premier destination has been transformed from a quiet nature walk to a busy thoroughfare traversed by some 300,000 cruise ship passengers a year. Souvenir shops, paved walkways, and street vendors now cater to this traffic, detracting from whatever natural amenities the falls might have once had.

The thousands of middle-class American families seeking foreign experiences also shape shipboard and port entertainment, as if passengers never left home. Carnival Cruise Line's *Destiny* calls at Cozumel, Grand Cayman and

---

25 Polly Patullo, 1996.

26 C. Y. Thomas, 1988, p.151.

27 Laura Bly, 1996a.

Jamaica. Billed as the world's largest cruise ship, the 100,000-ton vessel carries 4,400 passengers and crew. This mega-ship naturally demands familiar mega-experiences to accompany it. Locally owned shops cannot possibly accommodate the surge in passenger traffic. In the words of a Norwegian Cruise Line executive, 'You can't take 3,000 people (to an island) and put them into a little bistro … . You need something like a Planet Hollywood.'[28] The replication of chainstore operations featuring North American brand names and advertising logos in one port after another follows these trends. Local handicrafts – if they even are available – are no match for Chicago Bulls T-shirts that become 'foreign' purchases because they were bought in St Thomas or Cozumel. The technology that facilitates tourist traffic to remote corners of the Caribbean, in turn, imposes uniformity on the cultural, built and even physical environments.

It is no secret that the fickle and seasonal tourist trade in the Caribbean galls many local observers. It despoils and cheapens insular landscapes, disrupts local wage scales, emphasizes subservience, and perhaps represents the worst in North American hedonism and vapidity, values that are in turn emulated or encouraged by (especially) young people in the Caribbean. But there are few viable economic alternatives to tourism that earn hard currency, even for some of the larger places in the region. Even Cuba, incredibly, now courts tourism. Although Fidel Castro has fought hard to prevent his island from becoming another Caribbean nation of waiters and room attendants, what was once discouraged is now a growth industry. In 1996 about one million tourists descended on Cuba. At the end of the century, Cuba's gradually opened economy means more tourists and an attendant increase in, among other negative consequences, prostitution. Parts of Havana and Varadero (90 minutes east of Havana) as well as some of the nearby beaches cater mainly to tourists, in some cases even denying access to Cubans. The Cuban leadership begrudgingly accepts this as a trade-off with guarded market liberalization.[29]

The Caribbean's turn-of-the-century version of the naughty weekend escape to Havana of forty years ago often involves young North Americans (and Europeans) being offered, and sometimes sampling, illegal narcotics during their stays in the Caribbean. Police in Jamaica and elsewhere are suspected of turning a blind eye to vacationing (and free-spending) university students from North America who purchase and use marijuana and other drugs during their stays in the islands. But drug use in Jamaica and elsewhere in the Caribbean can be ultimately harmful to the local tourist trade as well as to human health; in the first three months of 1994, 13 tourist visitors to Jamaica died there of cocaine overdoses.[30] Their deaths, tragic as they were

---

28 *Ibid.*

29 R. Segre *et al.*, 1997.

30 Ivelaw Lloyd Griffith, 1997, p.51.

to friends, families and the Jamaican tourist industry, are only a small piece of the most pressing socio-economic issue facing the Caribbean region at the end of the twentieth century.

Illegal narcotics trafficking involves similarly illegal transfers of enormous sums of money within the territories of tiny, politically autonomous states, an imbalance posing direct threats to many of the latter. And the frank opinions of nearly all political leaders of the region – that its drug problem is ultimately one of United States market demand for illegal narcotics – do nothing to discourage American officials from placing collective blame on Caribbean politicians and law-enforcement officials. Certainly, bribes and payoffs from the agents of South American drug lords are difficult to resist, and Caribbean officials have been so accused for at least 15 years, the case of the Bahamas being probably the best known.[31] But the transformations generated by the drug traffic affect everyone else in the region as well. As recently as the mid-1970s, the smuggling of free-port whisky throughout the Lesser Antilles involved informal and somewhat romantic sailing voyages on rickety vessels accomplished by local sailors.[32] Late in the 1990s the illicit traffic in narcotics in high-speed motorboats manned by crews armed with machine guns had all but ended the smuggling that was so much a part of life in the smallest islands of the region. Drugs and increasing crime rates throughout the region, moreover, are intimately linked. Puerto Rico Governor Pedro Rossello estimated in 1997 that eight of ten murders there were related to drugs and the drug trade.[33]

The (illegal) cultivation of marijuana in parts of the Caribbean represents responses to market opportunity as well as to a combination of external constraints against conventional agriculture. Despite government campaigns against the growing of marijuana in Jamaica, the major island zones where the crop is grown are so well-known as to be portrayed in published maps![34] And the 'free trade' sanctions against a protected British market on behalf of Windward banana producers have led to a shift toward narcotics. Late in 1997 it was openly estimated that St Vincent, which has been forced by these sanctions into virtually abandoning bananas, 'can now count marijuana as its principal export crop.'[35]

Yet the Caribbean is far more important as a trans-shipment zone than as a source of illegal drugs. These shipments' trajectories and volumes,

31 P. Eddy *et al.*, 1988.

32 H. Beck, 1976.

33 'Enemy proves elusive in Caribbean drug war. Tightly organized drug rings and the myriad governments in the islands hamper US efforts against smugglers'. Reuters, *Orlando Sentinel*, 2 February 1997.

34 For example, Ivelaw Lloyd Griffith, 1997, p.35.

35 'Expelled from Eden', *Economist*, 30 December 1997, p.37; see also J. Wiley, 1997.

furthermore, vary. When United States authorities impose tight security along its border with Mexico, shipments increase through the Caribbean. In any given month perhaps 40 per cent 'of the cocaine and heroin sold in America comes through the Caribbean.'[36] The region also has convenient air connections for drug exports to Europe. In attempting to curb this traffic, Washington pushes for 'hot pursuit' or 'Shiprider' Agreements that call for United States Coast Guard vessels to enter Caribbean territorial waters in order to intercept contraband drugs bound for American territory. Trinidad & Tobago allows United States aircraft to fly over its territory and intercept aircraft.[37] In Nassau, United States Customs officials have established a pre-clearance facility for all United States-bound planes. Although some nations have agreed to this policy, others are uncertain. Mostly because of concerns about sovereignty, France (in the shape of Martinique and Guadeloupe), Haiti, Jamaica and Barbados have resisted such agreements. The 1989 execution of General Ochoa in Cuba raised the spectre of the Castro government's complicity in using the island as a transfer zone for northern-bound shipments of Colombian narcotics.

Islands whose physical characteristics provide myriad trans-shipment points to the North American mainland host a network of international banks that have proliferated in the Caribbean in the past half-century. In many cases these financial institutions represent global financial restructuring rather than local business outlets.[38] The notoriety of the Caribbean as a zone of 'off-shore banking', furthermore, is closely interrelated with money laundering for the region's narcotics traffic. The 1989 overthrow of Manuel Noriega, as an example, is said to have shifted many millions in Colombian drug money from Panama to Aruba, underscoring the isthmus's century-long history of facilitating more than ships through its territory.[39] The latter island (which has fewer than 70,000 residents) had US$1.4 billion pass through its financial institutions between 1991 and 1995. United States officials, in attempting to expose the sources of these funds, encountered a bewildering web of banking jurisdiction and family businesses cloaked by Dutch banking secrecy.[40] Even the Russians were rumoured to have questionable funds among the 'sixty off-shore banks...said to be operating in Antigua-Barbuda at the end of 1996'.[41]

The inundation of the Caribbean by tourists, money and international brand names always has influenced local tastes and behaviour. Late in the 1990s

---

36 'Expelled from Eden', *op. cit.*, p.37.

37 'Pact opens foreign waters to US drug enforcement', *New York Times*, 20 July 1996.

38 C. Y. Thomas, 1988, p.169.

39 Bonham C. Richardson, 1985.

40 L. Komisar, 1997.

41 Ivelaw Lloyd Griffith, 1997, p.99.

a universal lament in the region was of young persons' preferences for clothing of foreign manufacture and American fast food, trends inspiring parental scolding and a backlash of cultural events celebrating 'traditional' foods and dress as is held in Nevis each August.[42] Modes and types of personal appearances and attire – from dreadlocks to bank uniforms –send many signals about social status, sexual availability and political stances. One's clothing also often betrays nationality; British Virgin Islanders claim that the 'look' of one's apparel indicates whether or not someone is foreign or a (dowdy, behind-the-times) local.[43]

Caribbean landscapes also reflect – not always for the better – changes in shopping behaviour and increased consumerism. The franchise signs of the tourist trade are only the most obvious indicators. Refuse from supermarket packaging litters alleyways of Caribbean cities and, increasingly, rusted hulls of old automobiles and discarded farm machinery are scattered through the countryside. The ubiquity of store-bought foods throughout the region is obvious from the omnipresent plastic shopping bags strewn across fields which are particularly unsightly after sugar-cane harvests.

It would be a mistake to dismiss an increase in Caribbean consumerism as simply one more instance of cultural homogeneity dictated by metropolitan forces. Arlene Dávila points out that North American beer and cigarette advertisements in Puerto Rico tap into both conservative and changing attitudes toward cultural trends in the island.[44] Somewhat similarly, British anthropologist Daniel Miller explains that the marketing and consumption of Coca-Cola in Trinidad simply cannot be understood without an appreciation of local identities and rivalries which help to make a coke 'an intensely local nationalist drink'.[45]

The far-flung, scattered reality of consumer locations throughout the region means that shopping-mall-oriented marketing techniques are rarely applicable in the Caribbean. The traditional higglers, or market women, of Haiti, Jamaica, and other islands have responded in remarkable, yet – to those who have witnessed their adaptability – unsurprising, ways to recent market forces. Whereas in earlier days they may have sold a variety of vegetables and other local food items from stationary retailing locations, some have extended their marketing expertise in extraordinary, transnational efforts. Some higglers now include New York and Miami within their commercial circuits while continuing to extend themselves into village-level retailing niches within the Caribbean itself.[46]

42 Karen Fog Olwig, 1993a, pp.188–9.
43 B. Maurer, 1997b, p.129.
44 Arlene Dávila, 1997.
45 Daniel Miller, 1998a, p.172.
46 M. Kurlansky, 1992, pp.137–42.

Drugs and a growing commercialism, combined with a paucity of local conventional economic opportunities, help to explain a depressing climb in crime statistics[47] throughout the Caribbean in the last two decades of the twentieth century. As these statistics have increased, so have night watchmen, guard dogs, burglar alarms, iron grills, and chain-link fences. There is overwhelming evidence that narcotics are much of the reason. Some Caribbean leaders, while acknowledging the primacy of the illicit drug traffic, blame outside forces. Charges that the developed northern Atlantic countries corrupt local mores are not new. Puerto Rico, for instance, has long been plagued by the cultural quandary imposed by frequent travel to and from the United States mainland. But 'Nuyorican' now carries with it a much more negative connotation than it once did, since it often identifies those responsible for a disproportionate number of crimes on the island.

Statistics on criminals deported to the Caribbean may eventually support these analyses. In 1995, just 1,225 criminals were deported from the United States to the Caribbean, while in 1996 the figure quadrupled to 5,000. Most deportees were serving out drug-related sentences. From Guyana to the Bahamas, local security officials consider the deportees (also from Canada and Europe) a major source of the increase in sophisticated crime in the region. Caribbean officials recognize the right of these nations to deport criminals, yet they are concerned when they receive little or no warning of the returns or the deportees' backgrounds. One scholar at Florida International University, a native Guyanese, has remarked: 'These guys don't go back and plant tomatoes or oranges. They go back and reinvest in what they know best.'[48] These 'reinvestments' in time and equipment have led to alarming increases in the possession of submachine guns, armed robberies, bank heists of unusual sophistication, and even drug-gang slayings. As a merchant from Santo Domingo recently told one of us: 'finding "gainful employment" in the United States carries a high price that no one wants to talk about.'

Politics and the media

The remarkable social and economic changes in the Caribbean region as a whole since mid-century have been paralleled by regionally unprecedented political change. In 1950, only Cuba, the Dominican Republic and Haiti were

47 For example, Ivelaw Lloyd Griffith, 1997, pp.120–1.

48 'Deportees spur Caribbean crime' (an Associated Press report), 3 May 1997, *Tampa Tribune.*

independent Caribbean states. Now there are 12 more politically independent countries (Suriname and most of the former British colonies.) And those places still politically affiliated with metropolitan rulers – a few remaining British dependencies, the Netherlands Antilles, Aruba, the US Virgin Islands and Puerto Rico, and the three French *départements* of Guyane, Martinique and Guadeloupe plus its outliers – all exercise considerable internal political autonomy.

Even though political sovereignty in the region now is widespread, Caribbean locales remain tightly linked to the outside. Puerto Rico, of course, has long been a stepping stone to the United States. Dominicans have been known to cross the 100-mile stretch of the Mona Passage to gain access to points north. Since 1994, would-be illegal immigrants from the Dominican Republic have replaced Haitians and Cubans as the chief concern of the United States Coast Guard. The United States Immigration and Naturalization Service believes that about 20,000 Dominicans a year reach Puerto Rico illegally, all too many crammed into small boats.[49]

Geo-politically speaking, the Caribbean in the latter decades of the twentieth century has been dominated by the rise and longevity of revolutionary Cuba and the growing regional domination of the United States. These interrelated polarities and developments, in turn, spill over into trends and changes that indirectly help to explain much about daily life in the region. Fidel Castro has ruled Cuba since 1959, holding power during the terms of nine of the 42 United States presidents. His presence has helped to inspire direct United States military intervention in the region, not only at the Bay of Pigs in 1961, but also in the Dominican Republic (1965), Grenada (1983), Panama (1989) and Haiti (1995). A genuine fear of the threat of Cuban encroachment by some of the English-speaking states of the region probably pushed them closer to the United States.[50] Similarly, the brief war between Argentina and Britain over the Falkland Islands in 1982 reminded the mini-states of the Caribbean of their potential vulnerability to the historically inspired designs of their larger neighbours, causing a reawakened wariness toward overtures from places like Venezuela and Guatemala (toward Guyana and Belize). The collapse of the Soviet Union in 1989 and the well-publicized preoccupation of Cuba with its internal economic problems have diminished the perceived regional Cuban threat in the last decade of the century.

The unrivalled presence of the United States as the Caribbean's sole geo-political power also has followed naturally from the relative withdrawal,

49 'US push curbs Dominican flow to Puerto Rico'. Reuters, *Florida Sun-Sentinel,* 31 January 1997.

50 Anthony P. Maingot, 1989, pp.279–82.

formal and otherwise, of the European countries as important political players in the region, despite its enduring economic, cultural and family ties with Europe. According to the late Gordon K. Lewis, the defining moment signalling the shift toward the United States for the anglophone Caribbean was the Grenada invasion in October 1983, in which United States troops were accompanied by soldiers of several former British colonies: 'For the previous West Indian generation the final accolade of recognition was an invitation to a Buckingham Palace garden party; for the post-Grenada generation it will be an invitation to a social event at the White House.'[51] European countries have by no means withdrawn from the Caribbean altogether; the Dutch, French and British, and the European Union in general maintain development aid programmes for the region, and all collaborate in some ways with United States authorities to try to help curb the narcotics traffic.

The regional trend toward political independence, along with an economic shift away from a reliance on plantation staple crops, has created internal political changes, eliminating the basis for the adversarial stances maintained by the region's traditional political parties. The labour union parties of the British Caribbean that brought the islands to political independence, starting with the short-lived West Indies Federation (1958–62) and into the 1980s, no longer have a well-defined planter class or cadre of European colonial officials as targets. Caribbean political success is now more a matter of demonstrating skill in negotiating favourable arrangements with multinational corporations or helping in other ways to create local economic opportunity. The passage of time, furthermore, inevitably marks the passing of earlier political leaders along with the zeal and fire that they personified. On 6 March 1997, the deaths of both Michael Manley of Jamaica and Cheddi Jagan of Guyana demarcated a dramatic finish to a turbulent era in West Indian politics. Both were fierce and articulate leaders of their countries' working peoples, taking stances and voicing opinions that extended well beyond the Caribbean.[52]

American political domination of the Caribbean has not, however, reduced the region's impoverishment, complexity or capacity to change. About one-quarter of French Caribbean adults remain unemployed, although they are not poor by regional standards. Guyane experienced riots, looting and arson in 1996 over educational policies. Some residents of French St Martin dislike Guadeloupe's administrative rule over them (and the large island-small island rivalries within multi-island states continue elsewhere). Although Puerto Rico, with its status as a Free Associated State (*Estado Libre Asociado*), has under-

51 Gordon K. Lewis, 1987, p.145.
52 'Michael Manley', *Economist*, 15 March 1997.

gone profound economic improvement and social change since the 1940s, Puerto Ricans voted again in 1998 as to whether they wished to remain a commonwealth, opt for statehood, or seek political independence (although the latter option never garners more than about 5 per cent of the vote). Their two-day general strike in July 1998, provoked by the privatization of a public utility, rekindled independence sentiment throughout the island.

The coupling of United States political-economic hegemony with the onslaught of American-dominated television perhaps presents the severest challenge yet to the survival of local culture. During the 1980s most of the region went from limited television exposure – local programming combined with (often-dated) American offerings – to a full-colour, 24-hour, multichannel cacophony late in the 1990s. Caribbean church leaders lament that lifestyles portrayed on television screens bear little resemblance to those in the Caribbean, raising false expectations, glorifying hedonism, and influencing everything from outlandish dress to poor school performances. Jamaica's Rex Nettleford, in castigating the omnipresence of American television, objects strongly to 'the hijacking of the region's media, the invasion of the Caribbean people's intellectual space and the cultural bombardment of the entire region by every means possible.'[53] Even the region's ultimate social critics, the Trinidadian calypsonians, have weighed in to remark on the influence of American TV; the singer Commentator points out that Trinidad & Tobago has been formally independent 'since '62', but, speaking on behalf of the American 'cultural robber', Commentator continues that 'It is I who control you.'[54]

American TV's impact is of course strongest in the English-speaking areas and Puerto Rico. Its influence has led, naturally enough, to academic studies about its nature and extent. One study of the image of Puerto Rico as portrayed in major United States newspapers during the 1970s found that articles on terrorism and natural disasters far exceeded accounts on cultural events, economic analyses or sports.[55] In surveying the preferences of Jamaican schoolchildren, Hilary Brown learned that, despite the high cost in developing local programmes, there is widespread local popularity for some of the regional productions, such as Jamaica's *Oliver at Large* and Trinidad's *No Boundaries*.[56] Cheryl Renee Gooch, in assessing possible neo-colonial attitudes in Barbadian television programming, suggests that the scrutiny of locally produced shows might be more intense than for those imported.[57]

53 Rex Nettleford, 1993, p.29.
54 M. Kurlansky, 1992, pp.104–5.
55 Joseph L. Scarpaci, 1991.
56 Hilary Brown, 1995, p.78.
57 Cheryl Renee Gooch, 1995, p.115.

Lynette Lashley surveyed a geographical cross-section of television-viewing habits and preferences among youth in Trinidad & Tobago and discovered a clear preference for American television programmes.[58]

Those concerned with the preservation of a distinct French Antillean cultural identity in Guyane, Guadeloupe and Martinique express similar concerns about the domination by metropolitan French television. Local TV features French (not Créole) outlets of the French state-financed stations referred to as RFO (Société Nationale de Radio-télévision Française d'Outre-mer.) The (minimal) RFO programming that deals with the Caribbean emphasizes the French territories' relative affluence (by dwelling often on Haiti's poverty, for example), but the French Antillean stations' main emphases are on metropolitan France and its internal concerns and events. These offerings are interspersed with dubbed American programmes and local news segments to fill in around the main programmes. RFO commercials have a more local flavour because they employ Antillean actors and actresses.[59]

The television era in the Caribbean, as in other places, has meant more staying in at night, as even the poorest usually have TV at home. All around the region (except in Cuba where American movies are shown, but rarely does the state-run network show sitcoms), families and friends stay at home to watch the latest instalment of 'The Bold and the Beautiful' or 'Dynasty'. Television has also led to different social groupings or configurations for commonly-observed media events. Test cricket in the English-speaking islands was a public, pedestrian affair in the recent days of transistor radios, island residents going about their business with radios pressed to their ears and commenting, cheering or gasping – sometimes in consort with total strangers – at particularly crucial moments. Televised cricket continues to be a public event, but now with knots of stationary onlookers crowded into the doorways of restaurants or in front of the windows of retail outlets. The televised cricket image has also reduced the game to a human scale, different from the radio broadcasts that invited imagination and doubtless helped in the building of legendary cricket personalities. American baseball is not shown on Cuban television, although the medium has nonetheless profoundly influenced the country. Cubans were so enamoured with one Brazilian *telenovela* that they decided to name one of the fastest growing private enterprises since 1993 – the home restaurant or *paladar* – after a similar operation portrayed in the Brazilian show.[60]

It would be wrong to suggest that television has extinguished radio in the Caribbean. The latter continues its important regional role, in part because

58 Lynette Lashley, 1995, pp.93–4.

59 J. A. Lent, 1990b, p.178.

60 Joseph L. Scarpaci, 1995.

of the Caribbean's fragmented physical geography. Radio was introduced to Cuba in 1922, to Hispaniola in 1926, and to the rest of the region generally during the 1920s or 1930s. Generations of West Indians in the latter half of the twentieth century have subsequently grown accustomed to their daily routines being punctuated by the radio signals preceding the BBC news, hurricane warnings, or the musical jingles of bank advertisements. And no one in the Lesser Antilles has missed the booming signal from Radio Antilles in Montserrat (now extinguished by the volcano), American pop music from the US Virgin Islands, or the distinctive radio exhortations by American evangelical broadcasters.

Radio Rebelde contributed in no small way to the overthrow of the Batista regime in the late 1950s. Begun by Ernesto 'Ché' Guevara in the Sierra Maestra in February 1958, Rebelde was at first only faintly audible because of its weak transmitter, yet its messages were monitored by the United States government as well as the Cuban citizenry. Rebelde soon became the symbolic rival of the official Cuban government news, carrying rebel slogans, manifestos, and some of Castro's earliest lengthy oratories. It also fulfilled a utilitarian need, appealing to doctors to deliver medical aid to the mountains. During battles, Rebelde employed loudspeakers intended to demoralize Batista's troops.[61] The station also sent personal messages to families and friends from individual rebel soldiers. Cuban radio today broadcasts news, government ideology, and the educational programmes which were especially important in rural areas during the literacy campaigns of the 1960s. In the 1990s the United States-financed Radio Martí presents counter-viewpoints.

Radio's role in disseminating information among families and friends remains important in the smaller islands. Throughout the Eastern Caribbean and in the Bahamas, broadcast death announcements are a principal means of informing family members strung out across far-flung archipelagos – which defy easy or cheap means of daily communication – of the deaths of mothers, fathers and grandparents.[62] Immigrants to the US Virgin Islands from St Kitts and Nevis routinely monitor the (faintly audible) death announcements emanating from Radio ZIZ in Basseterre, St Kitts, and then inform their fellow migrants on either St Thomas or St Croix by telephone if one of their family members has passed away.[63]

Radio's versatility is exemplified no better than in Guadeloupe. The island has a number of different stations which broadcast for different periods each day, in both French and Créole, and toward different audiences. The RFO

61 J. A. Lent, 1990b, pp.123–5.
62 *Ibid.*, pp.263–4.
63 Bonham C. Richardson, 1983, p.52.

station broadcasts news from France (to include French weather and even traffic reports!) as well as from the Caribbean region. Radio Tanbou, one among several small-budget, public service stations on Guadeloupe, operates with limited personnel and some volunteer help and specializes in local culture, Guadeloupean music, and news analysis. The island also has religious (Catholic as well as fundamentalist Protestant) stations and also several small unauthorized stations that are almost village-level media outlets. The exclusive use of Créole (as on Radio Tanbou) underscores a post-colonial and anti-French sentiment. Curaçao also has a proliferation of media outlets for such a small place. With scarcely 150,000 people, the island has nine radio stations, one television station, and nine daily newspapers (six in Papiamentu, three in Dutch)!

The widespread use of radio combined with the omnipresence of television has by no means eclipsed local newspapers, especially in the several places where literacy is essentially universal. Originally intended for the region's élite and middle class, newspapers with working-class or progressive middle-class views emerged even before the early and mid-twentieth century to provide articulate, published challenges to continued colonialism. In this way they acted as both mirror and mould of the region's steady progress toward political independence. Caribbean peoples continue to depend on their newspapers – which they tend to view as more 'theirs' than they do the exotic outpourings of metropolitan news broadcasts – to provide intensely local, opinionated, and colourful coverage of islandwide events.

The first newspaper published in Papiamentu in the Netherlands Antilles was in 1973, an innovation possibly linked with the civil disturbances in Curaçao in May 1969.[64] Papiamentu suffers – even more than Créole – from its small constituency and the associated expensive translation costs for radio and print media. The language is nonetheless spoken by all social classes and in all branches of government in the ABC (Aruba, Bonaire, Curaçao) islands. In 1997 Papiamentu was declared an official language of Aruba, Bonaire and Curaçao and English an official language of St Martin, Saba and St Eustatius (along with Dutch). The lengthy battle against European linguistic domination in the ABC islands is by no means over as Dutch was the only official language there until very recently, and televised English and Spanish soap operas are extremely popular, the latter because three Venezuelan TV stations are in reach of the islands.

Despotic Caribbean political regimes, including earlier colonial governments, have recognized the power of local newspapers and other media outlets. During the Trujillo dictatorship in the Dominican Republic, newspaper, radio and television commentaries were uniformly sycophantic and fawning

64 J. A. Lent, 1990b, pp.198–230.

about the island's political leadership so as to defy credibility.[65] The Burnham government in Guyana from the late 1960s into the 1980s focused less on personality and more on the pre-eminence of 'the (Peoples' National Congress) party' and the country's socialist co-operative imperatives in attempting to thwart published and broadcast dissent from both internal and external sources. The government monopolized and taxed newsprint, declared the (neo-colonial) BBC news irrelevant to the Guyanese experience, and tyrannized those speaking out in opposition. A low watermark in Guyanese political repression was reached in 1979 when a Catholic priest was stabbed to death in Georgetown, probably for his part in supplying photographs to an opposition newspaper, or because he was mistaken for the editor of the anti-government *Catholic Standard*.[66]

In Cuba, official government interpretations of the news as well as government positions on national and international events appear in the daily *Granma*. Human interest and workplace features are carried by *Bohemia* and *Trabajador*, respectively. Cuba's 'Special Period in a Time of Peace' (Cuba's term for domestic austerity measures triggered by the collapse of the socialist countries in Eastern Europe and the former USSR) reduced the number of newspapers circulating. Havana (2.2 million population) received only 7,000 daily copies of *Granma* in the mid-1990s. And although electronic dissemination of news via facsimile and the World Wide Web is tightly controlled, Pope John Paul II's visit to the island in January 1998 allowed hundreds of journalists unprecedented access to Cuba and rare live broadcasts on the state television networks. However, shortly after the Pope's visit all foreigners were forbidden from taking photographs in the nation's public schools unless special permission was given ahead of time.

Late in the 1990s the nearly universal availability of modern telephone service in the region provides easy (though expensive) direct-dial access overseas, very different from the faintly audible operator-assisted calls that once involved one- or two-hour waits. The first direct telephone circuits between New York and Puerto Rico in 1943 were improved by the laying of the first submarine cable between Puerto Rico and the North American mainland in 1959. Then the establishment of the Cayey satellite earth station ten years later has been followed by continuous telephone improvements in all areas of the region. Even cellular phones are now common throughout the Caribbean; local cell antennas were built there during the 1990s, modifying even further the regional landscape.

The global communication revolution also allows displaced West Indians to stay in touch with their home islands in other ways. Digitized

65 *Ibid.*, p.160.

66 *Ibid.*, p.87.

versions of local newspapers from Guyana, Jamaica, Barbados and Trinidad & Tobago are available on international computer web networks. The tens of thousands of West Indian migrants from those and nearby places (the Trinidad papers also carry regional news, mainly from the Windwards) now living in North America and England routinely read articles and editorials and see pictorial news from their homelands. International communication networks, although containing the potential to obliterate regional distinctions in favour of a metropole-dominated homogenization, have, in these cases, helped individuals to maintain their cultural identities, even though they are far from home.[67]

Despite the enormous potential that communications innovations have for increasing the world's knowledge about the Caribbean, metropolitan self-absorption persists. The Pope's 1998 visit to Cuba, advertised by some as one of the most important media events of the year, was completely upstaged on American television by the allegations of President Clinton's sexual improprieties. The adage that Americans will do anything but read about Latin America and the Caribbean might now be modified as 'anything but watch TV about Latin America and the Caribbean'. The reverse is not true because new communications and media possibilities are avidly used throughout the Caribbean to learn about events elsewhere in the world.

Carnival, music and sport

While the atomizing social tendencies engendered by modernization and mass-media technologies move onward, the Caribbean continues as a region of public gatherings and group participation. In the 1950s, public meetings and rallies were the region's cultural hallmarks in its final push toward political autonomy; the massive protests and stadium rallies in Havana before and after the revolution also were conducted on a smaller scale in the British colonies, notably in Grenada and St Kitts, over local political issues. Public protests, buttressed by the power and collective emotion that moving crowds generate, have played formative roles in the region's political past.[68] Furthermore, insularity, especially in the smallest islands where everyone knows everyone else and all of the faces in a given crowd are familiar, doubtless helps explain the ongoing importance of public gatherings. Yet civic outpourings, marches and social coalescence, such as the massive funeral

67 Daniel Miller and Don Slater, 2000.
68 O. Nigel Bolland, 1995.

procession in Guyana that followed Walter Rodney's murder in 1980,[69] remain recognizable elements in Caribbean cultures, regardless of the particular society's scale.

The Caribbean carnival exemplifies the region's tendency toward public gatherings and cultural displays. Carnival varies from place to place as to season, size and lavishness, but it occurs in essentially all Caribbean (and some important non-Caribbean) locales as a street celebration in honour of particular holidays. The result on each island is 'a folk drama in which performers and audience are one and the same'.[70] Caribbean carnivals occur at Christmas, Mardi Gras, the end of the sugar-cane harvest, or at other times depending upon the particular locale. And while costumes, singing and instrumentation vary widely throughout the region, carnivals all rely on a blend of elements from local and external sources and are thereby recognizably Caribbean.

The best known is Trinidad's unrivalled pre-Lenten celebration, a colossal regional and international event that has attracted much academic attention.[71] Carnival in Trinidad is rooted in the island's past in which European and African elements have been forged – often in a crucible of resistance and social inequity accented by drumming, steelbands and ritual stickfighting – into a distinctive contemporary celebration. The Trinidad Carnival is famous for its calypso tents, costumes and the annual climactic road march. So many tourists now descend each year on Port of Spain for Carnival that the celebration's essential attraction, derived from local colour and flair, has become truly international and commercially crucial for Trinidad & Tobago. Grassroots activities of the 1950s that were performed for fun have therefore become lavish displays with sizeable budgets and ever-larger economic payoffs. Accordingly, Trinidad Carnival's tone has changed, in the eyes of some, to an erotic display exemplified by, among other things, the changes in women participants' costumes: 'Voluminous skirts that once offered the illusion of subtlety have been shed and have been replaced by high cut bikinis, a triangular flap and some feathers ....'[72]

No other Caribbean carnival has the discernible and well-documented historic roots that go back as far as Trinidad's, and some can hardly be called 'historic'. The summer carnival in Antigua, for example, was begun in 1957. The St Thomas Carnival, with origins in the early twentieth century, was revived in 1952 as a Labor Day celebration. The recent and increasing

69 George Lamming, 1981.
70 Kenneth M. Bilby, 1995, p.197.
71 For example, Errol Hill, 1972 (1997); Donald R. Hill, 1993.
72 Molly Ahye, 1991, p.410.

commercialization and garishness of these now-annual celebrations in the small islands have inspired sour analyses that they are 'mostly tourist gimmickry.'[73] Yet a closer look suggests that, in important ways, they have evolved differently from the directions that would please local tourist boards. Black Power slogans and motifs – perhaps inspired by publicity from the United States, but given local meanings – are commonly evident in Caribbean carnivals.[74] And racial violence at the 1986 carnival in St Thomas was apparently a reaction to the local (white) commercial control of the celebrations, a situation countered by the slogan of black Thomians, 'Is we carnival!'[75]

Late in the 1990s, many North American and British observers were aware of Caribbean carnivals not because of events in the islands but because these celebrations have been imported into major metropolitan locales. Since 1969 the hundreds of thousands of Caribbean peoples residing in New York have celebrated Labor Day with music, floats and steelbands in the city's now-annual parade which winds along Eastern Parkway in Brooklyn.[76] The late summer Notting Hill Caribbean Carnival in west London annually pits transplanted West Indian exuberance versus the sober control tactics of the London police force, yet it is now sufficiently established that leading British politicians appear for photo opportunities. Toronto's Caribbean carnival, begun in 1967 and featuring distinctive masquerade bands, is not tucked away in one of the city's residential neighbourhoods as in London or New York; rather, it proceeds through the economic and political heart of the city and 'receives massive coverage in the mainstream press.'[77] Peter Minshall, Trinidad's premier carnival-band designer, helped produce the opening ceremonies for both the 1992 and 1996 Olympic Games, and he has also helped to orchestrate France's Bastille Day celebrations. Yet students of cultural globalization would be mistaken to interpret the North Atlantic presence of Caribbean carnivals and their leaders as evidence that these cultural activities had somehow been co-opted by metropolitan powers. Owing to the frequency of travel and the reliability and speed of international communications, the exchanges of ideas in costuming, sound projection and choreography in both the Caribbean and the newly-adopted residential areas for Caribbean migrants now blur the differences between these innovations' sending and receiving areas.

'Global' is indeed an appropriate term to describe the late-twentieth century impact of Caribbean music. Most important on a world scale is the

73 Gordon K. Lewis, 1968, p.30.
74 F. E. Manning, 1978, pp.198–99.
75 Klaus de Albuquerque, 1990.
76 Donald R. Hill and R. Abramson, 1979.
77 F. E. Manning, 1990, p.26.

Jamaican sound generally known as 'reggae', whose universal appeal transcends continents and cultures. Emerging from the Jamaican 'rock steady' and 'ska' style, which itself was influenced by North American soul music, reggae may be dated to the late 1960s. In the following decade, reggae became identified with the Kingston slums and the Rastafarian movement there, and it owed much of its appeal to the sound-track accompanying the internationally popular Jimmy Cliff film, *The Harder They Come*. But reggae soon catapulted the far more famous Bob Marley and the Wailers to international stardom and became closely associated with such names as Burning Spear, Peter Tosh and Bunny Wailer. Reggae in Jamaica has evolved into so-called dance-hall music late in the 1980s and subsequently into 'ragga' (short for 'raggamuffin') music that confirms its roots in the culture of the island's urban poor while drawing on traditional African-based Jamaican music. The astoundingly popular Jamaican reggae music sound has been adopted not only by university students world wide but by groups as disparate as Arizona Indians, urban youth of sub-Saharan Africa, and aboriginal peoples in New Zealand and Australia.[78]

Claims are also made that the extraordinarily popular 'zouk' music originating in the French Antilles in the early 1980s has had a worldwide impact.[79] Zouk's engaging dance rhythms are, like all new Caribbean sounds, based on traditional Antillean roots. And although this new music is recorded and packaged in studios in Guadeloupe and Martinique, zouk has broadly regional origins. It owes much of its rhythm to the popular 'biguine' music played by dance orchestras in the French Antilles in the early twentieth century, but its antecedents may also be traced to the United States, Haiti and the local dance music from Dominica known as 'cadence'.[80] Probably more than reggae, zouk has a growing number of female performers. In comparing zouk and reggae as to their relative popularity world wide, it appears that the former has been limited so far to a francophone base. Zouk music is exceptionally popular in France, in large part because of the European performances of the Antillean band Kassav, although its appeal is confined in North America to Haitian and French Antillean ethnic enclaves. Zouk is also widely popular among young people in the French-speaking areas of Africa.[81]

Cuba's musical imprint internationally has met with commercial and political success. The lyrics of the 'troubadours' Pablo Milanés and Silvio Rodríguez frequently laud the accomplishments of the revolution. Cuban singer Albita Rodríguez, well known in Cuba as a singer of the folkloric

78 Kenneth M. Bilby, 1995.
79 J. Guilbaut *et al.*, 1993.
80 M. Largey, 1995, pp.140–1.
81 Kenneth M. Bilby, 1997, p.71.

guajira songs until she defected to Miami, where she has become a successful Sony recording artist, has brought a dimension of Cuban *son* to a larger North American and European audience. Perhaps the best-known and most commercially successful crossover Latin-to-Pop artist is Cuban-born Gloria Estéfan and the Miami Sound Machine.

The Caribbean's interrelated oral and musical traditions – marked by keen observation, inspired social commentary, and biting satire – converge in the region's calypso music.[82] Centred in Trinidad & Tobago and the adjacent Windwards, calypso in the 1990s has transcended insularity and is immensely popular in the entire region and among the transplanted West Indian communities in North America and the United Kingdom. Early in the century, live Trinidadian calypso could be roughly divided between the 'tents' and the music of the streets, each with distinctive sounds and characteristics.[83] In the years before political independence Trinidadian radiowaves were filled with the music from such luminaries as Kitchener, Spoiler, and the Mighty Sparrow. In all these cases, past and present, 'Calypso lyrics are a bible of Creole thought'.[84] But calypso lyrics are no longer a Trinidadian monopoly.[85] In the 1980s the Barbadian calypsonian Gabby mocked political opportunists and local social proprieties to the point that his music was banned locally, the most sensational event in 'the Bajan calypso boom (that) is the most exciting development in Caribbean popular culture.'[86] Whereas calypso usually is associated with the English-speaking islands of the Eastern Caribbean, song as social commentary is so widespread in the region as a whole that 'one must consider this a pan-Caribbean phenomenon'.[87]

Taken altogether, Caribbean music reflects the essence of the region as well or better than any other element of culture. Its inspiration comes from the traditional sounds and rhythms of the region's ubiquitous village bands and, more and more, from the desperation of the Caribbean's urban slums. Its syncretic character, based heavily on an African base, is identified by musicologists whether one is describing Puerto Rican or Cuban *salsa*, Dominican *merengue*, the *rara* processional bands of Haitian Easter carnivals, the steelband and *soca* music of Trinidad, or the percussion-heavy *tambu* music of the Dutch ABC islands. Even some of the Asian music imported by indentured Indians and Javanese into the southern Caribbean shows signs of blending or creolization; the best example is *chutney* in Trinidad, a kind of calypso sung

82 Gordon Rohlehr, 1990.
83 John Cowley, 1996.
84 Donald R. Hill, 1993, p.1.
85 F. E. Manning, 1985.
86 *Ibid.*, p.15.
87 Kenneth M. Bilby, 1985, p.201.

to Indian musical accompaniment and partly in Hindi. Adapted locally from imported musical traditions both now and in the past, relying heavily on improvization and change, and capable of appealing in a timely fashion to a broad range of listeners, Caribbean music at the turn of the century is one of the region's most distinctive cultural achievements.[88]

Musical events and other cultural activities are combined uniquely within each island culture. In Puerto Rico, as in other places, religious holidays and national political anniversaries converge and are blended into local cultural activities. Although Puerto Rico observes most United States holidays, it too has a host of events unique to the island. These include the Festival Casals, a classical-music concert held in mid-June, as well as year-round performances by the Puerto Rico Symphony Orchestra at the Music Conservatory. Other sources of national heritage are available year-round, such as displays at the Botanical Garden and Museum of Anthropology, Art, and History at the University of Puerto Rico. In San Juan, programmes at the Institute of Puerto Rican Culture and the Dominican Convent complement the many popular festivals held throughout the island. In many ways these activities and institutions serve as a cultural backstop against increasing Americanization, a defensive posture arising from Puerto Rico's political association with the United States as well as a reaction to rampant consumerism.

If music represents the leading edge of the region's cultural achievements in the latter half of the twentieth century, sport cannot be far behind. Even the most casual visitors to the Caribbean notice the ubiquity of baseball diamonds in the San Juan area on an evening flight to Puerto Rico or the impromptu cricket matches in every Barbadian schoolyard on a drive around the island. But the nature of organized sport – while still carrying with it its elementary competitive character and test of physical skills – is ever changing in the Caribbean region. Furthermore, the interrelationships between group passion and metaphorical significance for sport among Caribbean peoples are the subjects of a growing literature produced by popular writers and academics.

Cuban sport is of national significance and along with health care and education is a badge of honour for the nation. The island's commitment to the 1991 Pan American Games, at once a symbol of pride and a national showcase, was made well before the onset of the Special Period. Millions of dollars in infrastructure helped to make Havana a sporting centre with modern stadiums, swimming pools, gymnasiums and living quarters for visiting athletes. Cuban microbrigades built the 'Pan American Village' (Villa Panamericana) at the eastern edge of metropolitan Havana. The very costly

88 P. Manuel *et al.*, 1995.

project has not attracted many subsequent sporting events, although it produced – in Cuban terms – fine housing.[89] The government nonetheless remains committed to sport as a key component of the socialist movement. And Cuban teams continue to travel widely, even when they risk embarrassing the government with high-profile defections as in 1997 when the baseball-playing Hernández brothers left for the United States, one starring for the Florida Marlins in their 1997 championship season.[90]

Cubans and other Caribbean peoples have won a disproportionately high number of Olympic Games medals relative to the region's total population in the second half of the twentieth century. At mid-century, all followers of world athletics (track and field) knew of Jamaican sprinting prowess. In more recent decades, Cuba's remarkable Olympic successes – co-ordinated by the National Institute of Sports, Physical Education and Recreation – have included world-dominating performances in boxing and women's volleyball. A stunning Caribbean Olympic moment came in the 1976 games in Montreal where Hasely Crawford of Trinidad & Tobago won the men's 100-metre sprint, Donald Quarrie of Jamaica captured the gold medal in the 200-metre sprint, and Alberto Juantorena of Cuba (the country's top sports official late in the 1990s) won the men's 400- and 800-metre events. Cuban officials have interpreted their Olympic successes in political-revolutionary terms, and their teams' boycotts of the 1984 (Los Angeles) and 1988 (Seoul) games undoubtedly detracted from the overall quality of the events. West Indian migrants and their descendants in Canada and Great Britain, not incidentally, have won a number of Olympic medals for their adopted homelands, and these athletes' Caribbean origins are widely recognized and publicized.

The acknowledged pre-eminence of West Indian cricket in the British Commonwealth in the last third of the century parallels Cuban Olympic prowess. Some have likened this success to an exotic plant (introduced from England) that has flowered and matured in the personages of the Eastern Caribbean's feared batsmen and fast bowlers who have, in turn, come to dominate international test cricket. West Indian cricket achievements also have been interpreted as individual and team triumph in a fair competitive arena devoid of institutional inequalities. These interpretations have emerged through serious studies by, among others, some of the leading scholars/statesmen in the English-speaking Caribbean. C. L. R. James[91] saw West Indian cricket victories over erstwhile colonial rulers as fostering unity and political dignity. Michael Manley

89 R. Segre *et al.*, 1997.
90 Louis A. Pérez, 1998b.
91 C. L. R. James, 1963.

stressed the collaborative character of Caribbean cricket victories and found in them one of the few concrete examples of genuine regional co-operation.[92]

Although Cuba's athletic triumphs are well-known internationally, its self-acknowledged national sport (and national passion) is baseball. In the late 1990s telephone callers to evening baseball talk shows on Havana's Radio Rebelde went so far as to criticize the Cuban government for allowing the departure of Cuban baseball stars to other Latin American countries and even to Japan. (The defection of Cuban players to the United States, although well-known, is taboo on Rebelde.) Cuban baseball has produced some of the finest active players, such as Omar Linares, in the game today, and the national team – unbeaten since 1991 – won in the Olympics in both Barcelona (1992) and Atlanta (1996). The possibility of an eventual Cuban-United States contest, involving America's best professional players, is a source of endless speculation and conversation on Havana street corners and park benches.[93] From a United States perspective, Cuban baseball is a novel curiosity. More important to most Americans is that, since the early 1980s, the Dominican Republic has supplied dozens of (United States) major-league baseball stars each year. Every American schoolboy knows San Pedro de Macorís as the 'home of shortstops' and several books analyse, among other dimensions of the Dominican-United States baseball connection, the chasm between Dominican poverty and the astounding salaries paid to its players who have become successes in North America.[94]

Baseball's and cricket's immense popularity in the Caribbean notwithstanding, basketball has made phenomenal inroads throughout the region since the 1980s, becoming even more popular than baseball in some parts of the Greater Antilles.[95] Puerto Rico's national basketball team played the so-called 'dream team' from the United States in the 1980s; although they were beaten soundly, Puerto Ricans cherished the confrontation for months. Basketball's popularity in Puerto Rico, given the close connections with New York, is easy to explain. Yet the game has made equally strong progress in the English-speaking islands. Much of basketball's regional appeal may be traced to television and the obvious African-American domination of the game that is watched in Caribbean households during North America's winter basketball season. Mounted basketball hoops are now as common as cricket pitches in Trinidad and in some of the small islands of the Eastern Caribbean where inter-island, island-wide, and local village games played by

92 Michael Manley, 1996; see also Hilary Beckles, 1998.
93 T. Wendel and M. Jamail, 1997.
94 For example, A. M. Klein, 1991.
95 Rob Ruck, 1993, pp.187–8.

both men and women 'basketballers' provide opportunities for social gatherings, much as village markets or election days have in earlier decades.[96]

Human health

The remarkable social and economic changes in the Caribbean in the latter half of the twentieth century have their parallels in an overall regional improvement in health and longevity. With the notable exception of Haiti, the region's human population may be said to have passed through what public health officials commonly refer to as the 'epidemiological transition', a level of human health in which death is brought on less frequently by infectious diseases than by degenerative ones.[97] Fifty years ago, outbreaks of schistosomiasis, Chagas' disease, and even leprosy in particular islands were reasonably common causes of death. Today, at the turn of the century, these diseases, although not yet eradicated altogether, have usually given way to cardiovascular, pulmonary and cancer-related diseases as leading causes of Caribbean mortality, as is common in the rest of the developed world.

A key reason for these changes is an overall improvement in human nutrition.[98] Along with modernization, higher average incomes and side effects from increasing tourism, more food is imported to the Caribbean than ever before. But dietary and health improvements do not invariably come about because more calories per person are now consumed than in the past. In St Vincent, for example, traditional food crops grown in village gardens are now augmented with imported flour, vegetable oils and animal protein so that, ironically on an island where people have traditionally been woefully malnourished, a common nutritional problem is that people eat too much.[99] A somewhat similar situation exists for Puerto Rico where a nutritional combination of old and new has both its positive and negative consequences: 'Within the new epidemiological profile, acute infectious tropical diseases coexist alongside chronic degenerative diseases ... Alcohol abuse and smoking are common, the population is sedentary, the diet contains too much fat and protein, and drug consumption is on the increase.'[100]

Alcohol consumption in the Caribbean continues as an integral element in local cultures, ranging from imported whisky as status symbol for the

96 Jay R. Mandle and J. D. Mandle, 1994.
97 D. P. Sinha, 1995, pp.7–13.
98 *Ibid.*
99 L. S. Grossman, 1998.
100 Pan American Health Organization, 1998.

prosperous down to 'bush rum' in the poorer communities. But greater prosperity has also led to an increase in cigarette smoking, the marketing and sale of cigarettes in the region being one of the more dubious benefits of globalization. A recent report by the United States Surgeon General, in collaboration with the Pan American Health Organization, found that in some Caribbean cities more than half of the young people now smoke. Smoking, furthermore, appears to increase as a function of increasing local prosperity. The economic downturn in the Caribbean in the 1980s (referred to by some as the 'lost decade' because of the erosion of standards of living) saw a decline in tobacco consumption,[101] then economic recovery a decade later saw an increase in tobacco consumption. The smoking prevalence in the Caribbean as a whole in the early 1990s was 37 per cent for men and 20 per cent for women.[102] And although Caribbean health authorities at both a local and regional level publish health warnings against smoking as a serious health risk,[103] smoking's attractiveness, especially among the young, is its association with prosperity and the good life exemplified by both media representations and the omnipresent tourists.

Despite the double-edged character of economic improvement and associated nutritional change, increased longevity in most of the Caribbean region (again, with the painful exception of Haiti) marks a dramatic shift for the better from conditions that existed in the 1950s. The vast majority of Caribbean people can now expect to live into their seventies. Even in places as small as Montserrat which have a very limited number of trained medical personnel, the average age of death for men in the (pre-eruption) early 1990s was 73 and for women 80, mortality statistics comparable to life expectancies in France.

Another fundamental measure of human well-being, that of infant mortality, is arrayed for selected Caribbean countries in Figure 18.1. The means by which the statistic is derived (the number of deaths of infants of less than one year divided by total births and the result multiplied by a constant) is less important than noting that infant mortality is a conventional surrogate measure of general human well-being. Those emphasizing the importance of the infant mortality index point out that infants' health often depends upon, among other factors, nutrition of both infants and mothers, family and community literacy, and family income. Infant mortality rates also indicate the quality of medical care, to include prenatal intervention and post-delivery

101 C. Weil and Joseph L. Scarpaci, 1992.

102 'Public Health Programs and Practices. Surgeon General's Report Focuses on Smoking in Latin America', 1993.

103 For example, D. P. Sinha, 1995, pp.26–7.

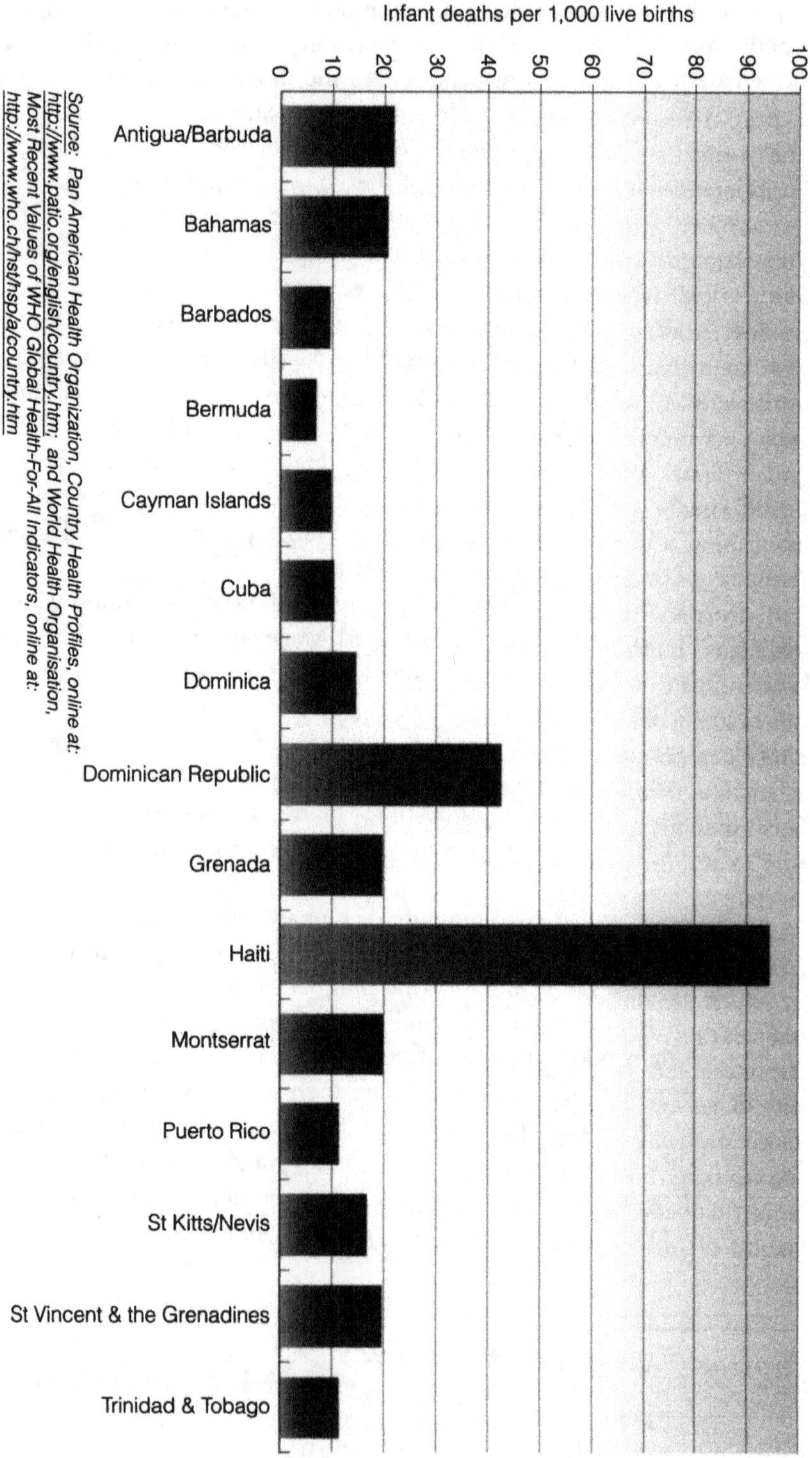

Source: *Pan American Health Organization, Country Health Profiles, online at: http://www.patio.org/english/country.htm; and World Health Organisation, Most Recent Values of WHO Global Health-For-All Indicators, online at: http://www.who.ch/hst/hsp/a/country.htm*

Figure 18.1 Infant mortality rates, selected Caribbean nations, *c.* 1993

check-ups. In Cuba, with one of the lowest infant mortality rates, an estimated 97 per cent of all births are attended by a physician, and a doctor's presence allows not only for high survival rates but also assumes postnatal care should the need arise. Haiti's very high infant mortality figure throws light on the country's poor nutrition, inadequate medical care and general impoverishment; 10 per cent of Haitian babies never reach their first birthday.

Whereas comparative health or quality-of-life data are useful in highlighting similarities and differences among contemporary Caribbean societies, it still is inappropriate to discuss national 'health care systems' in the smallest places. As in the past, doctors are few and specialists rare on islands with less than 100,000 residents. Anguilla, as one example, has only ten physicians, a number that probably would be even lower except for the island's remunerative tourist industry whose very high prices are affordable only by (usually ageing) North Americans and Europeans. In the smaller islands much of the primary health care is still carried out by parents and relatives, and a doctor is sought only under extreme, even near-death, circumstances. In the larger places such as Cuba, Puerto Rico, Jamaica and Barbados, there are well-developed health-care systems composed of a combination of public and private physicians and nurses. Another reason that 'national' health care is a somewhat misleading comparative term for the region as a whole is that specialty health care is often sought away from one's island of residence, in larger neighbouring islands or – if families can afford the travel and medical expenses – in North America or Europe.

Data representing human health and well-being also represent indirectly living conditions and sanitation. Despite the general improvements in Caribbean housing in the past fifty years, shanty towns and slums – some of quite long standing – remain in the larger urban areas as unsightly testaments to post-agricultural societies where no real labour-absorbing industries have replaced fading plantation regimes. One of the most celebrated literary achievements by a Caribbean writer in recent years, Patrick Chamoiseau's *Texaco*,[104] is the saga of a squatter settlement in Fort-de-France. The Martinican author contrasts the geometric, ordered, white, staid character of most of the colonial city with the ill-defined, unplanned, black exuberance of 'Texaco' as a metaphor for his home island in general.

Chamoiseau's theme could be extended across much of the rest of the Caribbean in order to portray urban housing conditions that local governments attempt to improve. Sub-standard housing in the capital towns of the Windwards, for example, often consists of aggregates of small, movable, frame dwellings whose (changing) locations follow paths of least resistance

104 Patrick Chamoiseau, 1997.

to uncontested urban zones. The British geographer Robert Potter has assessed the varied quality of dwellings in this region as well as recent planning and financial initiatives pursued by local governments in attempting to improve urban living conditions, to include the construction of multi-family 'apartment' housing units.[105]

General improvements in housing conditions in the Caribbean may be attributed to a variety of reasons. In the French islands, *départementalisation* (since 1946) was followed by substantial improvements in housing quality in terms of living space, improved sanitation, durability of construction material, and a general use of air-conditioning.[106] The oil boom of the late 1970s in Trinidad & Tobago led to the development of 'residential areas' that were distinctly middle class or to the replacement of older wooden frame houses 'with substantial brick or concrete two-storey houses, often with terrazzo floors and a front yard enclosed by large iron gates. The new houses were replete with electrical appliances and a high standard of plumbing.'[107] Similar upscale housing improvements elsewhere in the region can be traced, more often than not, to money earned abroad as well as to the long-standing practice of self-help housing.[108]

Cuba's socialist government began an aggressive campaign with a series of housing and urban reform laws and policies from the late 1950s designed to help the poor and to phase out free-market prices for housing and land. Castro's well-known anti-urban policies, furthermore, gave preference to rural areas of the country. Havana's grand houses and mansions, left by a fleeing bourgeoisie, housed students and workers travelling to the city for schooling, job training, and political activities in the first decades of the revolution.[109] Although problems of food supply in Cuba probably are more acute than are those of housing at the turn of the century, the latter are nonetheless serious.[110] An ignored and now decrepit housing stock in Havana is both costly and impractical to rehabilitate. The black market is often the only source for tiles, wiring, concrete blocks and other building materials, and an estimated 50 per cent of the city's piped water is lost in old water mains or building cisterns. Most new Cuban construction is now dedicated to earning hard currency, either to attract tourists or a growing foreign business community seeking to establish headquarters in the once 'posh' neighbourhood of Miramar in Havana's western suburbs.[111]

---

105 Robert B. Potter, 1994.
106 S. A. Condon and P. E. Ogden, 1997.
107 Daniel Miller, 1994, p.32.
108 Robert B. Potter and D. Conway, 1997.
109 R. Segre *et al.*, 1997.
110 Joseph L. Scarpaci, 1995.
111 Joseph L. Scarpaci, 1996.

Pockets of traditional water and waste removal still dot the Caribbean region. In Antigua & Barbuda, there is no sewerage system to speak of; 60 per cent of the dwellings in the two islands use septic tanks and soak-aways, and 30 per cent continue to rely on pit latrines. Disease incidence data also throw light on national problems and issues such as food distribution systems and malnutrition. An outbreak of epidemic optic neuropathy appeared in Cuba's western province of Pinar del Río in mid-1992, and it appeared elsewhere in Cuba the following year. The problem, attributable to deteriorating diet, was arrested in some cases with vitamin supplements.

Cuba's similarly direct way of dealing with victims of the AIDS virus has drawn criticism from human-rights groups outside the island. When the first cases of HIV-AIDS infection appeared in Cuba in the early 1980s, it was traced to returning veterans who had fought in Angola and Mozambique. AIDS has since spread throughout the island, helped along, not incidentally, by the acceleration in tourism in the 1990s. In any case, when local public-health officials identify HIV-positive Cubans, they often are relegated to quarantine compounds where they receive direct medical attention and diets superior to those of the average Cuban. Despite external protests against these seemingly radical disease-containment measures, such aggressive tactics seem successful because Cuba has one of the lowest HIV rates in the Western Hemisphere.[112] Curiously, near by, the Bahamas had one of the highest rates of infection in the early 1990s.[113] National policies, therefore, lead to markedly different outcomes.

The recent impact of AIDS throughout the Caribbean has directly affected families and villages because individual victims usually are without the urban anonymity that cloaks so many of the AIDS-sufferers in North America and Europe. Antigua & Barbuda now screens all blood donors for AIDS. In the Bahamas, the leading health problem among pre-school children is AIDS and its related diseases that, tragically, are transmitted to infants during pregnancy and birth. The rate of AIDS infection in Haiti is estimated to be an astounding 10 per cent of sexually active people in Port-au-Prince and 5 per cent in the countryside. Under-reporting and the indifference of Haiti's former military government toward gathering disease statistics may have led, however, to a serious understating of the problem of AIDS there. On top of the other woes Haiti faces, conventional wisdom includes the country within the much-repeated but hardly accurate phrase: 'The four H's of HIV infection: hæmophilia, homosexuals, heroin and Haitians.' Yet the association between high incidences of AIDS and Haitians is not simply another misperception

112 C. Burr, 1997.
113 Marvin Leiner, 1994.

about the country provided by outsiders. Haitian *boungans* or 'bush doctors' have become involved in attempting to combat AIDS both by prescribing particular remedies and also by advising against sexual promiscuity.[114]

The frightening prevalence of AIDS in the region naturally leads to a necessary if uncomfortable reassessment of sexual promiscuity throughout the Caribbean at the end of the twentieth century. The region has long been known by outsiders for its free-and-easy attitude toward sex, from Havana's reputation as a naughty, mid-century playground for visiting American sailors to the bawdy lyrics of so many calypsos in the English-speaking islands. In a far less abstract way, the Caribbean's sexual attractiveness is intimately bound up with the region's tourist industry – a fact whose unpleasantness makes it no less real. The marvels of the computer age provide lurid, online details of sex tours to the Dominican Republic and its famous 'dusky beauties', for example, not only for middle-aged men in Europe and North America but also for schoolchildren everywhere innocently seeking term-paper information about the Caribbean in general. Indeed, prostitution (even among children) in the resort areas along the north coast of the Dominican Republic is well known and, it is claimed by some, even encouraged by a local government hungry for hard currency. Nor does the region's sexual glamour appeal only to visiting men; the number of so-called 'beach boys' of Montego Bay, the Barbadian beaches, and other tourist zones of the English-speaking islands would be far fewer if it were not for the business they conduct with single tourist women.[115]

The obvious dilemma for Caribbean peoples and their governments is how to eliminate the unsavoury and demeaning character of the sex trade, now even more threatening because of the widespread incidence of AIDS, without damaging one of the region's economic staples. The problem is acute in Cuba, whose resurgent tourism is noted for the ubiquity of the teen-age *jineteras* in Havana hotel lobbies and other tourist haunts (although these young women are said to have temporarily halted their trade out of respect for the papal visit of John Paul II in January 1998). The Cuban government seeks to control this traffic by confining prostitutes to certain hotels, and by periodically arresting them in large round-ups. The government also attempts to reduce the spread of AIDS by testing regularly those in contact with foreigners (the obvious source of the infection according to Cuban officials) such as hotel waiters and taxi drivers.[116]

Other data dealing with human health from the region reflect economic and social changes consistent with modernization and urbanization. In

114 M. Kurlansky, 1992, pp.193–4.
115 Polly Pattullo, 1996, pp.86–91.
116 M. Kurlansky, 1992, pp.196–7.

Barbados, two-thirds of all deaths in the 15–44 year age group are from accidents and homicides. A similar 60 per cent of deaths of Bahamian men between 15 and 44 are from accidents and violence. Some of the human costs in providing cheap labour, especially by women in the finishing industries and light-manufacturing enclaves throughout the region, are coming to light in regional health figures. Recent surveys among women working in some of the free-trade districts of the Dominican Republic show a disturbing increase in reproductive problems. And a five-year survey among a sample of Dominican women in some of these 'maquiladora' areas showed alarmingly high incidences of poisoning by heavy metals, lumbago caused by exertion, dermatoses, respiratory problems and hypertension.[117]

The Caribbean and the millenium

At the turn of the century the Caribbean's global role and overall regional identity are usually discussed, labelled and determined – as in the past – more by outsiders than by those in the Caribbean itself. Anthony Maingot expands on this idea with his term 'the Offshore Caribbean'.[118] Noting the similarities between the activities that occur in Britain's Channel Islands and the Caribbean, Maingot points out the truism that 'being offshore is not the same as being onshore.'[119] In its broadest sense, 'offshore' connotes an easy atmosphere and an absence of convention encompassing a range of activities, not all of them financial and not all necessarily bad. Yet 'offshore' is an outsider's term; 'getting away from it all' can be accomplished in the relaxed offshore Caribbean by a middle-class European or North American, not by a Guyanese ditchdigger or a Dominican factory seamstress.

A relaxed regulatory environment can in fact mean quite the opposite for those who supply the labour for new 'offshore' manufacturing operations which mark globalization in the region. Sociologists Alejandro Portes and José Itzigsohn note important responses to these activities that are beginning to take hold in the Caribbean. In the political realm, their survey data in several of the region's cities show that the number of community organizations that respond either favourably or negatively towards this type of production has been relatively few. Although many non-profit and grass-roots organizations oppose offshore production, 'when the moment comes to convert those feelings

117 Pan American Health Organization, 1998.
118 Anthony P. Maingot, 1993; *idem*, 1994a, pp.163–82.
119 Anthony P. Maingot, 1993, p.274.

into actions, it is the traditional political parties' that have spoken out.[120] In this regard, globalization evokes modest local opposition, but the 'new social movements' have not spearheaded this charge.

In its narrower meaning, 'offshore' is of course routinely associated with financial activities that prosper in more relaxed regulatory environments than 'onshore', where those same dealings are subject to burdensome legal constraints and official scrutiny. Much is made of the Caribbean's international importance as an offshore banking area, a zone offering a spectrum of financial services that are comprehensible, not necessarily in a Caribbean context, but 'only...as adjuncts to the North American bloc and to the financial centers of the United States and Canada ....'[121] The region's financial role is often portrayed as flexible and accommodating, providing a place – at least in the accounting ledgers of cyberspace – where business can be conducted readily and discreetly outside the strictures imposed by onshore proprieties. Journalists have pointed out the historical similarities between these current regional activities and piracy or smuggling, describing Caribbean quasi-legal financial practices with such colourful passages as 'buccaneer forays into banking.'[122] Yet these whimsical descriptions should not mislead as to the genuine global impact of Caribbean banking: 'In the 'real' and 'shadow' economies of international finance, the Caribbean has been anything but marginal.'[123]

Just as mid-winter television advertisements beamed into North American households portray the Caribbean as sunny, safe and populated by smiling and relatively light-skinned peoples, so the region's offshore banks emphasize a conservative, colonial heritage. Brochures distributed by banks in the Cayman Islands and the British Virgin Islands, for example, underline political stability, racial harmony and law and order.[124] But the happy combination of conservative European colonial heritages and the absence of intrusive banking regulations imposed by Britain could possibly change, if projected policy changes to establish 'overseas territories' (with associated bank regulation stringencies) in lieu of colonies come about.[125]

Regardless of the particular outcome of British (or Dutch) Caribbean financial developments, the arm's-length 'offshore' attractiveness of the region has a familiar ring to historically oriented scholars of the Caribbean; that is because the region's accessibility, places and resources – rather than its peoples – always have been valued by outsiders. Ever since West African

120 A. Portes and J. Itzigisohn, 1996, p.258.
121 S. M. Roberts, 1995, p.252.
122 Anthony P. Maingot, 1993, p.269.
123 B. Maurer, 1997a, p.254.
124 B. Maurer 1997a; S. M. Roberts, 1995.
125 'Goodbye', *Economist*, 7 February 1998, p.38.

slaves were imported to produce tropical staple crops for metropolitan markets, the socio-historical development of the Caribbean might be interpreted as one long attempt by outside powerholders to bring the region's lands, but not its peoples, into the modern world. And the ingenuity and drive of Western entrepreneurs in developing the region's lands have of course been paralleled by the resistance displayed by the region's working peoples who have pushed as hard as possible in an opposite direction, in attempting to establish physical refuges and personal identity on lands that others have viewed in different, more calculating ways.

The struggle continues. The legacy of this curious historical incongruity between Caribbean lands and the region's peoples – an incongruity produced by outsiders' demands that have in turn been met by internal resistance – is noted by many. Perhaps the most elegant term describing how this regional characteristic has affected its human populace is Orlando Patterson's 'creative nonadaptation'.[126] And it may not be inappropriate to suggest that the profusion of writers, poets, scholars and artists from the region is somehow related to this incongruity. In any case, 'offshore' perceptions of and designs on Caribbean lands are lamented throughout the islands, a collective concern echoed in St Lucian Derek Walcott's 1992 Nobel lecture:

> The Caribbean is not an idyll, not to its natives. They draw their working strength from it organically, like trees, like the sea almond or the spice laurel of the heights. Its peasantry and its fishermen are not there to be loved or even photographed; they are trees who sweat, and whose bark is filmed with salt, but every day on some island, rootless trees in suits are signing favourable tax breaks with entrepreneurs, poisoning the sea almond and the spice laurel of the mountains to their roots. A morning could come in which governments might ask what happened not merely to the forests and the bays but to a whole people.[127]

We are standing today on Varadero Beach, east of Havana. A strolling Canadian couple hears live music coming from the new Jamaican-run Super Club hotel and resort. As they approach the back gate from the beach, a guard intercedes and denies them access as they are not registered guests. The Canadians explain that they wish only to buy a few drinks, hear the music, and spend a few dollars. Undeterred, the guard insists that they not enter the premises. Frustrated, the Canadians stroll elsewhere along the increasingly crowded ocean-front properties at Varadero.

---

126 Orlando Patterson, 1978, p.139.

127 Derek Walcott, 1993, pp.34–5.

Fast rewind back four decades to 1958. A local couple from nearby Matanzas is walking along Varadero Beach. The peninsula has few hotels and is anchored at the end by the well-known Dupont mansion, owned by the family of the United States petrochemical empire. The Matanzas couple hears music and sees a pig-roast on the beach. They walk towards the festivities for a closer look. A guard intercedes and tells them that they cannot trespass. The couple argues in vain that they will simply walk past the house, staying close to the water. Alas, the property is private and Cubans – especially uninvited ones – are not permitted along this section of the waterfront.

In the latter scenario, all began to change within one year. Private property was gradually phased out under the Castro revolution. Cubans of all classes and colours were granted access to many hotels previously reserved for foreigners. The Havana Hilton would be renamed the Havana Libre. Now, as the new century and millenium dawn, foreigners are once again mounting a presence in socialist Cuba. Accordingly, new forms of segregation are appearing in Havana and elsewhere on the island. Dollars, not doctrine, again determine access.

This fictitious episode – based upon real events which are occurring at the beginning of the twenty-first century – portrays a place and a region that have in many ways come full circle despite remarkable change. The Caribbean's diminutive and open characteristics invite, as always, the decisions and whims of outsiders. Those who inhabit the region resist, accommodate and cope as best they can. At the turn of the century, external initiatives directed toward the region are lamented, analysed and discussed in terms of 'globalization'.[128] Having suffered 'discovery', colonization and gunboat diplomacy during the past half millenium, Caribbean peoples can be forgiven if they find the term and the scenario somehow familiar.

Poised at the start of a new millenium, the Caribbean continues to resist the homogenization of its cultures while striving to enhance its quality of life. And, as always, any attempt in considering the region's future must inevitably contemplate its past. In dealing with unpredictable changes introduced or mandated from afar, Caribbean peoples have developed (from their 'creative nonadaptation') remarkable coping skills. As the twenty-first century begins, in the Caribbean and elsewhere, 'global' is now the term universally applied in hopes of capturing the new and unprecedented changes and geographical dislocations that seem to be occurring everywhere. In light of their past, the message that new and unpredictable changes are headed their way is hardly news to the peoples of the Caribbean.

128 Thomas Klak, 1997.

Bibliography

Abou, Antoine (1986) 'L'enseignement technique à la Guadeloupe jusqu'en 1956', *Bulletin de la Société d'histoire de la Guadeloupe,* 67–8, pp.75–92.

——, (1987) 'Portraits statistiques des instituteurs de la Guadeloupe', *Antiane Eco,* 2, pp.24–7.

——, (1988) *L'école dans la Guadeloupe coloniale,* Paris: Éditions Caribéennes.

Abraham-Van der Mark, Eva (1993) 'Marriage and Concubinage among the Sephardic Merchant Elite of Curaçao' in Janet H.Momsen (ed.) *Women and Change in the Caribbean,* Kingston: Ian Randle.

Academia de Ciencias de Cuba (1979), Instituto de geografía. Departamento de geografía económica. *Premisas geográficas de la integración socioeconómica del Caribe,* Havana: Editorial Académica.

Acosta-Belén, Edna (ed.) (1986) *The Puerto Rican Woman,* New York: Praeger.

Acosta de Pérez, Luz Dalis (1993) *Los derechos de las mujeres,* Santo Domingo: Editora Universitaria.

Agar, Herbert (1942) 'The Quest for Equality', *Survey Graphic,* 31 (Color: The Unfinished Business of Democracy), New York: Survey Associates.

Agarwala, A. N. and S. P. Singh (eds) (1958) *The Economics of Underdevelopment: A Series of Articles and Papers,* New York: Oxford University Press.

Aguero, Felipe and Jeffrey Stark (eds) (1998) *Fault Lines of Democracy in Post-Transition Latin America,* Coral Gardens, Florida: North-South Center Press, University of Miami.

Aguilar, Carolina *et al.* (1996) 'Mujer, periodo especial y vida cotidiana', *Temas,* 5.

Aguilar, Luis E. (1972) *Cuba, 1933: Prologue to Revolution,* Ithaca: Cornell University Press.

Aguilar Monteverde, Alonso (1965) *El Panamericanismo: De la Doctrina Monroe a la Doctrina Johnson,* Mexico: Cuadernos Americanos; rev. ed., English translation by A. Zatz, New York: Monthly Review Press, 1968.

Ahye, Molly (1983) *Cradle of Caribbean Dance: Beryl McBurnie and the Little Carib Theatre,* Petit Valley, Trinidad: Heritage Cultures.

——, (1991) 'Carnival, the Manipulative Polymorph: An Interplay of Social Stratification' in Selwyn D. Ryan (ed.) *Social and Occupational Stratification in Contemporary Trinidad and Tobago,* St Augustine: Institute of Social and Economic Research, UWI.

Alba, Victor (1968) *Politics and the Labor Movement in Latin America,* Stanford: Stanford University Press.

Albizu Campos, Pedro (1977) *La conciencia nacional puertorriqueña,* selected, with an introduction and notes by Manuel Maldonado-Denis, Mexico City: Siglo Vientiuno.

Albury, Paul (1975) *The Story of the Bahamas.* London: Macmillan Caribbean.

ALEGRÍA ORTEGA, IDSA (1989) 'Mujeres y elecciones, 1988', *Diálogo* (February).

——, (1995) 'Agenda política de las mujeres caribeñas', *Caribbean Studies,* 28, no.1.

____, (1996) 'Género y política en Puerto Rico', *Puerto Rico Cooperativista,* March–April.

ALEGRÍA ORTEGA, IDSA and ALICE COLÓN WARREN (eds) (1995) 'Feminist Research and Action in the Caribbean', *Caribbean Studies,* 28, no.1 (special issue).

ALEXANDER, JACK (1984) 'Love, Race, Slavery, and Sexuality in Jamaican Images of the Family' in Raymond T. Smith (ed.) *Kinship, Ideology and Practice in Latin America,* Chapel Hill: University of North Carolina Press.

ALEXANDER, M. JACQUI (1994) 'Not Just (Any) Body Can Be a Citizen: The Politics of Law, Sexuality and Postcoloniality in Trinidad & Tobago and the Bahamas', *Feminist Review,* no.48, pp.5–23.

ALEXANDER, ROBERT J. (1967) *El movimiento obrero en América Latina,* Mexico City: Editorial Roble.

ALIENES UROSA, JULIAN (1949) 'Economía de post-guerra y desempleo', *Publicaciones de la Junta Nacional de Economía,* 3.

ALLEYNE, DODDRIDGE (1988) 'Petroleum and Development' in Selwyn D. Ryan (ed.) *Trinidad: The Independence Experience, 1962–87,* St Augustine: Institute of Social and Economic Research, UWI.

ALLEYNE, MERVYN (1989) *Roots of Jamaican Culture,* London: Pluto Press.

ALVARADO RAMOS, JUAN ANTONIO (1996) 'Relaciones raciales en Cuba: notas de investigación', *Temas,* 7, Nueva Epoca.

ALVAREZ CURBELO, SILVIA, MARY FRANCES GALLART and CARMEN I. RAFFUCCI (eds) (1998) *Los arcos de la memoria: el '98 de los pueblos puertorriqueños,* San Juan: Asociación de Historiadores de Puerto Rico.

ALVAREZ ESTÉVEZ, ROLANDO (1988) *Azúcar e inmigración 1900–40,* Havana: Editorial de Ciencias Sociales.

AMBURSLEY, FITZROY and ROBIN COHEN (eds) (1983) *Crisis in the Caribbean,* New York: Monthly Review Press.

AMERINGER, CHARLES D. (1974) *The Democratic Left in Exile: The Anti-Dictatorial Struggle in the Caribbean, 1945–1959,* Coral Gables, Florida: University of Miami Press.

ANDELMAN, DAVID A. (1995) 'The Economics of the Drug Trade', *U.S./Latin Trade: The Magazine of Trade and Investment in the Americas* 3, no.9, pp.42–9.

ANDERSON, CHARNEL (1998) 'The American Presence in Puerto Rico in the 19th Century', Working Paper 77, Caribbean Institute and Study Center for Latin America, Inter-American University of Puerto Rico, San Germán.

ANDERSON, JERVIS (1982) *This Was Harlem: A Cultural Portrait, 1900–50,* New York: Farrar, Straus, Giroux.

ANDERSON, PATRICIA (1986) 'Conclusion: Women in the Caribbean', *Social and Economic Studies,* 35, no.2, pp.291–324.

——, (1987) *Mini Bus Ride: A Journey through the Informal Sector of Kingston's Mass Transportation System,* Mona: Institute of Social and Economic Research, UWI.

ANDERSON, WILLIAM A. and RUSSELL R. DYNES (1975) *Social Movements, Violence and Change,* Columbus, Ohio: Ohio State University Press.

ANDERSON, WOLSELEY W. (1993) *Caribbean Immigrants: A Socio-Demographic Profile*, Toronto: Canadian Scholars' Press.

ANGUSTIAS GUERRERO, MARÍA (1991) *Tras las huellas: la mujer dominicana en el mundo del trabajo, 1900–50*, Santo Domingo: Centro de Investigación para la Acción Feminina.

ANSPRENGER, FRANZ (1989) *The Dissolution of the Colonial Empires*, London: Routledge.

ANTHONY, Michael (1978) *The Making of Port of Spain, vol. 1, 1757–1939*, Port of Spain: National Cultural Council.

——, (1983) *Port of Spain in a World at War, 1939–45*, Port of Spain: National Cultural Council.

ANTROBUS, PEGGY (1995) 'United Nations Conferences: A Framework for Feminist Research and Action', *Caribbean Studies*, 28, no.1, pp.21–9.

ARANDA, XIMENA (1988) 'Women as Social Protagonists in the 1980s', ECLAC, Fourth Regional Conference on the Integration of Women into Economic and Social Development of Latin America and the Caribbean, 27–30 September.

ARISTIDE, JEAN-BERTRAND (1991) 'The Church in Haiti', *Caribbean Quarterly*, 37, no.1, pp.108–13.

AROCHA, MAGALYS, MAYDA ALVAREZ SUÁREZ *et al.* (1995) 'Mujer y poder: las cubanas en el gobierno', Havana.

ARREGUI, MARIVÍ (1994) 'Una doctrina de papel? El incumplimiento por parte de las mujeres católicas de la doctrina sobre el control de nacimientos', *Género y Sociedad*, 1, no.3, pp.1–44.

ARREOLA, TERESA (n.d.) 'Programas de control natal: arma del imperialismo', New York: WIRE Service.

ASHTON, S. R. and DAVID KILLINGRAY (eds) (1999) *The West Indies*, British Documents on the End of Empire, series B, vol. 6, London: HMSO.

ASLAM, ABID (1997) 'Latin America-Caribbean: Crime Stunts Growth, World Bank Says,' Inter Press Service, Global Information Network, 28 February.

Asociación Dominicana de Mujeres Votantes, Inc. (Recop.) (1992) *Perfil de la mujer dominicana ayer y hoy*, Santo Domingo: Universidad Autónoma de Santo Domingo y ADOMUVI, Editora Universitaria.

Association of Caribbean States, Trade, Transport and Tourism (1998) 4th Ministerial Meeting, December, Port of Spain: Association of Caribbean States.

AUSTIN-BROOS, DIANE J. (1996) 'Politics and the Redeemer: State and Religion as Ways of Being in Jamaica', *Nieuwe West-Indische Gids/New West Indian Guide*, 70, nos.1&2, pp.59–90.

——, (1997) *Jamaica Genesis: Religion and the Politics of Moral Orders*, Kingston: Ian Randle.

——, (1999) 'Pentecostal Community and Jamaican Hierarchy' in John W. Pulis (ed.) *Religion, Diaspora, and Cultural Identity: A Reader in the Anglophone Caribbean*, Amsterdam: Gordon and Breach.

AYALA CASTRO, HÉCTOR (1982) 'Transformación de la propiedad en el período 1964–1980', *Economía y Desarrollo*, 68, pp.17–20.

AYEARST, MORLEY (1960) *The British West Indies*, New York: New York University Press.

AZIZE, YAMILA (1985) *La mujer en la lucha*, Río Piedras: Editorial Cultural.

BACCHUS, KAZIM (1967) 'The Development of Educational Planning with Special Reference to the West Indies', *Teacher Education,* 7, no.3, pp.221–31.

——, (1974) 'A Study of Change in a "Plural Society": The Influence of Political Development on Church Control of Schools', *Caribbean Studies,* 13, no.3, pp.141–62.

——, (1976) 'Some Observations on Social Structure and Craft Training in Economically Less Developed Countries', *Canadian and International Education,* 5, no.1, pp.109–23.

——, (1979) 'Structural Transformation as a Pre-Requisite for the Success of Non-Formal Education Programmes in Economically Less Developed Countries', *Canadian and International Education,* 8, no.2, pp.83–91.

——, (1981) 'Education for Development in Underdeveloped Countries', *Comparative Education,* 17, no.2, pp.215–46.

——, (1990) *The Utilisation, Misuse and Development of Human Resources in the Early West Indian Colonies,* Waterloo, Ontario: Wilfrid Laurier University Press.

——, (1994) *Education as and for Legitimacy: Developments in West Indian Education between 1846 and 1895,* Waterloo, Ontario: Wilfrid Laurier University Press.

BAERGA, MARÍA DEL CARMEN (ed.) (1993) *Género y trabajo: la industria de la aguja en Puerto Rico y el Caribe hispánico,* San Juan: Universidad.

BÁEZ, CLARA (1988) '¿Hasta dónde la economía dominicana descansa en le trabajo de las mujeres?' *Población y desarrollo,* 7, no.23, pp.5–14.

——, (1993) 'Democracia y movimiento de mujeres: Hacia una redefinición de los espacios políticos', *Género y Sociedad,* 1, no.1, pp.1–20.

——, (1998) 'Participación laboral y migración de las mujeres dominicanas en un mundo global' in *Las mujeres del Caribe en el umbral del 2000,* Madrid: Dirección General de la Mujer, Comunidad de Madrid.

BÁEZ, CLARA and GINNY TAULÉ (1993) 'Posición socio-cultural y económica de la mujer en la República Dominicana', *Género y Sociedad,* 1, no.2.

BÁEZ EVERTSZ, FRANC (1978) *Azúcar y dependencia en la República Dominica,* Santo Domingo: Editora de la Universidad Autónoma de Santo Domingo.

——, (1986) *La formación del sistema agroexportador en el Caribe,* Santo Domingo: Editora de la Universidad Autónoma de Santo Domingo.

BAKAN, ABIGAIL (1990) *Ideology and Class Conflict in Jamaica: The Politics of Rebellion,* Montreal and Kingston: McGill-Queen's University Press.

BAKER, PATRICK L. (1994) *Centring the Periphery: Chaos, Order and the Ethnohistory of Dominica,* Mona: The Press, UWI.

BANTON, MICHAEL P. (1953) 'Recent Migration from West Africa and the West Indies to the United Kingdom', *Population Studies,* 7, pp.2–13.

BAPTISTE, FITZROY ANDRÉ (1976) 'The British Grant of Air and Naval Facilities to the United States in Trinidad, St Lucia and Bermuda in June–December 1939', *Caribbean Studies,* 16, pp.5–43.

——, (1978) *The United States and the West Indian Unrest, 1918–39,* Mona: Institute of Social and Economic Research, UWI.

——, (1988) *War, Cooperation and Conflict: The European Possessions in the Caribean, 1939–45,* New York: Greenwood Press.

BARCELÓ MILLER, MARÍA DE F. (1997) *La lucha por el sufragio femenino en Puerto Rico 1896–1933*, Río Piedras: CIS/Huracán.

——, (1998) 'Halfhearted Solidarity: Women Workers and the Women's Suffrage Movement in Puerto Rico during the 1920s' in Félix V. Matos Rodríguez and Linda Delgado (eds) *Puerto Rican Women's History: New Perspectives*, Armonk, New York: M.E. Sharpe.

BARCIA, MARÍA DEL CARMEN (1987) *Burguesía esclavista y abolición*, Havana: Editorial de Ciencias Sociales.

BARKER, D. and D. F. M. MCGREGOR (1988) 'Land Degradation in the Yallahs Basin, Jamaica: Historical Notes and Contemporary Observations', *Geography*, 73, pp.116–24.

——, (eds) (1995) *Environment and Development in the Caribbean: Geographical Perspectives*, Mona: The Press, UWI.

BARRETT, LEONARD E. (1968) *The Rastafarians: A Study in Messianic Cultism in Jamaica*, Río Piedras: Institute of Caribbean Studies, University of Puerto Rico; reprinted London: Heinemann, 1977.

——, (1974) *Soul Force: African Heritage in Afro-American Religion*, Garden City, NY: Anchor.

BARROW, A. H. (1900) *Fifty Years in Western Africa*, London: SPCK.

BARROW, CHRISTINE (1986) 'Finding the Support: Strategies for survival', *Social and Economic Studies*, 35, no.2, pp.131–76.

BARTRA, ROGER (1980) *El poder despótico burgués*, Mexico City: Editorial Era.

BASCOM, WILLIAM (1950) 'A Focus on Cuban Santería', *South Western Journal of Anthropology*, 6, no.1, pp.4–68.

——, (1966) 'The African Heritage and Its Religious Manifestations' in Robert Freeman Smith (ed.) *Background to Revolution: The Development of Modern Cuba*, New York: Alfred A. Knopf.

——, (1972) *Shango in the New World*, Austin: University of Texas Press.

BASDEO, SAHADEO (1983) *Labour Organization and Labour Reform in Trinidad, 1919–39*, St Augustine: Institute of Social and Economic Research, UWI.

BAUD, MICHIEL (1994) *Historia de un sueño: Los ferrocarriles públicos en la República Dominicana, 1880–1930*, Santo Domingo: Fundación Cultural Dominicana.

——, (1995) *Peasants and Tobacco in the Dominican Republic, 1870–1930*, Knoxville: University of Tennessee Press.

——, (1996) 'El surgimiento de un campesinado criollo. La producción de tabaco en La Española (1500–1870)', *Ecos* IV, 5, pp.9–40.

BEACHEY, R. W. (1957) *The British West Indian Sugar Industry in the Late Nineteenth Century*, Oxford: Basil Blackwell.

BEAUVAIR, JEAN-PIERRE (1983) 'Achievements and Contradictions of the Cuban Workers' State' in Fitzroy Ambursley and Robin Cohen (eds) *Crisis in the Caribbean*, New York: Monthly Review Press.

BEBEL-GISLER, DANY (1976) *Les enfants de la Guadeloupe*, Paris: Éditions L'Harmattan.

BECK, H. (1976) 'The Bubble Trade', *Natural History*, 85, pp.38–47.

BECKLES, HILARY (1990) *A History of Barbados from Amerindian Settlement to Nation-State*, Cambridge: Cambridge University Press.

——, (1998) *The Development of West Indies Cricket,* 2 vols, Mona: The Press, UWI.

BECKLES, HILARY and VERENE SHEPHERD (eds) (1993) *Caribbean Freedom: Society and Economy from Emancipation to the Present,* Kingston: Ian Randle. Also published as *Caribbean Freedom: Economy and Society from Emancipation to the Present,* 1996.

BECKWITH, MARTHA (1929) *Black Roadways: A Study of Jamaican Folk Life,* Chapel Hill: University of North Carolina Press.

BELGRAVE, VALERIE (1995) 'The Sir George Williams Affair' in Selwyn D. Ryan and Taimoon Stewart (eds), *The Black Power Revolution, 1970,* St Augustine: Institute of Social and Economic Research, UWI.

BELKE, T. J. (1983) '"Roll of the Drums": German Submarines and American Shipping, 1942', *Proceedings of the U S Naval Institute,* 109, pp.58–64.

BELL, IAN (1981) *The Dominican Republic,* London: Westview Press.

BELLAH, ROBERT N. *et al.* (1985) *Habits of the Heart: Individualism and Commitment in American Life,* New York: Harper & Row.

BENERÍA, LOURDES and SHELLEY FELDMAN (eds) (1992) *Unequal Burden: Economic Crises, Persistent Poverty, and Women's Work,* Boulder: Westview Press.

BENGELSDORF, CAROLLEE (1994) *The Problem of Democracy in Cuba: Between Vision and Reality,* New York: Oxford University Press.

BENÍTEZ-ROJO, ANTONIO (1995) 'The Caribbean and the Post-Modern Era' in Vera Lawrence Hyatt and Rex Nettleford (eds) *Race, Discourse and the Origin of the Americas,* Washington, DC: Smithsonian Institute.

'Benito Sylvain of Haiti on the Pan-African Conference of 1900' (1983) in Tony Martin, *The Pan-African Connection,* Dover, Massachusetts: Majority Press, 1984.

BENNETT, HERMAN L. (1989) 'The Challenge to the Post-Colonial State: A Case Study of the February Revolution in Trinidad' in Franklin W. Knight and Colin A. Palmer (eds), *The Modern Caribbean,* Chapel Hill: University of North Carolina Press.

BENNETT, JOHN (ed.) (1975) *New Ethnicity: Perspectives from Ethnology,* St Paul, Minnesota: West Publishing.

BENNETT, LERONE JR (1993) *The Shaping of Black America: The Struggles and Triumphs of African-Americans, 1619 to the 1990s,* New York: Penguin Books; first published, Johnson Publishing Company, 1969.

BENSON, W. (1944) *Social Policy in Independent Territories,* Montreal: International Labour Organisation.

BERGAD, LAIRD (1983) *Coffee and the Growth of Agrarian Capitalism in Nineteenth-Century Puerto Rico,* Princeton: Princeton University Press.

BERGQUIST, C. W. (1986) *Labor in Latin America,* Stanford: Stanford University Press.

BERLEANT-SCHILLER, RIVA and WILLIAM M. MAURER (1993) 'Women's Place is Every Place: Merging Domains and Women's Roles in Barbuda and Dominica' in Janet H. Momsen (ed.) *Women and Change in the Caribbean,* Kingston: Ian Randle.

BERNAL, RICHARD L. (1996) *Strategic Global Repositioning and Future Economic Development in Jamaica,* North South Agenda Paper 18, Coral Gables, Florida: North-South Center Press, University of Miami.

——, (1997) *Trade Blocs: A Regionally Specific Phenomenon or a Global Trend?* National Policy Association Report no.287, Washington, DC: National Policy Association.

——, (1998) 'The Integration of Small Economies in the Free Trade Area of the Americas', *Policy Papers on the Americas,* 9, 1.

BERNSTEIN, MICHAEL (1987) *The Great Depression: Delayed Recovery and Economic Change in America, 1929–39,* Cambridge: Cambridge University Press.

BERRIOS MARTÍNEZ, RUBÉN (1977) 'Independence for Puerto Rico: The Only Solution', *Foreign Affairs,* 55, April.

——, (1997) 'Puerto Rico's Decolonization', *Foreign Affairs* (November–December).

BERTHELOT, JACK and MARTINE GUAMÉ (1982) *Kaz Antiyé Jan Moun Ka Rété/Caribbean Popular Dwelling,* Guadeloupe: Éditions Caribéennes.

BESSON, JEAN (1987) 'Family Land as a Model for Martha Brae's New History: Culture Building in an Afro-Caribbean Village' in Charles V. Carnegie (ed.) *Afro-Caribbean Villages in Historical Perspective,* Kingston: African-Caribbean Institute of Jamaica.

BESSON, JEAN and BARRY CHEVANNES (1996) 'The Continuity-Creativity Debate: The Case of Revival', *Nieuwe West-Indische Gids/New West Indian Guide,* 70, nos.3 & 4, pp.209–28.

BESSON, JEAN and JANET MOMSEN (eds) (1987) *Land and Development in the Caribbean,* London: Macmillan Caribbean.

BEST, LLOYD (1963) 'Chaguaramas to Slavery?', *New World Quarterly,* 1, no.1.

BETANCES, EMILIO (1995) *State and Society in the Dominican Republic,* Boulder: Westview Press.

BETHELL, LESLIE and IAN ROXBOROUGH (eds) (1992) *Latin America between the Second World War and the Cold War, 1944–8,* Cambridge: Cambridge University Press.

BHANA, SURENDRA (1975) *The United States and the Development of the Puerto Rican Status Question, 1936–68,* Lawrence, Kansas: University of Kansas Press.

BILBY, KENNETH M. (1985) 'The Caribbean as a Musical Region' in Sidney W. Mintz and Sally Price (eds) *Caribbean Contours,* Baltimore: Johns Hopkins University Press.

——, (1995) 'Jamaica' in P. Manuel *et al., Caribbean Currents: Caribbean Music from Rumba to Reggae,* Philadelphia: Temple University Press.

——, (1997) 'Tracking the Caribbean Sound: Three Current Hits', *Nieuwe West-Indische Gids/New West Indian Guide,* 71, nos.1 and 2, pp.69–77.

BILLINGSLEY, ANDREW (1968) *Black Families in White America,* Englewood Cliffs: Prentice Hall.

BLACK, CLINTON V. (1983) *History of Jamaica,* London: Collins.

BLACK, NAOMI (1989) *Social Feminism,* Ithaca: Cornell University Press.

BLANSHARD, PAUL (1947) *Democracy and Empire in the Caribbean: A Contemporary Review,* New York: Macmillan.

BLÉRALD, ALAIN-PHILIPPE (1983) 'Guadeloupe-Martinique: A System of Colonial Domination in Crisis' in Fitzroy Ambursley and Robin Cohen (eds) *Crisis in the Caribbean,* New York: Monthly Review Press.

——, (1986) *Histoire économique de la Guadeloupe et de la Martinique du XVIIe siècle à nos jours,* Paris: Kartala.

——, (1988) *La question nationale en Guadeloupe et en Martinique: essai sur l'histoire politique,* Paris: Éditions L'Harmattan.

BLEY, HELMUT (ed.) (1990) *Die Weltwirtschaftskrise der 30er Jahre in der Dritten Welt. Sonderfall oder Einstieg in die Strukturkrise der Gegenwart,* Hannover.

BLOMMESTEIN, ERIK, BARBARA BOLAND, TREVOR HARKER, SWINBURNE LESTRADE and JUDITH TOWLE (1996) 'Sustainable Development and Small Island States of the Caribbean' in George A. Maul (ed.) *Small Islands: Marine Science and Sustainable Development,* Washington, DC: American Geophysical Union.

BLUME, H. (1974) *The Caribbean Islands,* London: Longman.

BLY, LAURA (1996a) 'Cozumel's Ships are Coming in but is Paradise Lost with Cruise Traffic?' *USA Today,* 25 October.

——, (1996b) 'Shootings May Hurt Tourism', *USA Today (Life),* 2 February, Time Multimedia Almanac.

BOLLAND, O. NIGEL (1986) *Belize, A New Nation in Central America,* Boulder: Westview Press.

——, (1995) *On the March: Labour Rebellions in the British Caribbean, 1934–39,* Kingston: Ian Randle.

——, (1996) 'Systems of Domination after Slavery: The Control of Land and Labour in the British West Indies after 1838' in Hilary Beckles and Verene Shepherd (eds) *Caribbean Freedom: Economy and Society from Emancipation to the Present,* Kingston: Ian Randle.

——, (1997) *Struggles for Freedom: Essays on Colonialism and Culture in the Caribbean and Central America,* Belize City: Angelus Press.

BOLLES, A. LYNN (1986) 'Economic Crisis and Female-Headed Households in Urban Jamaica' in June Nash and Helen Safa (eds) *Women and Change in Latin America,* South Hadley, Massachusetts: Bergin and Garvey.

BOND, GEORGE CLEMENT and ANGELA GILLIAM (eds) (1994) *Social Construction of the Past: Representation as Power,* London: Routledge.

BONILLA CARLO, WALTER R. (1998) 'Hacia una experiencia en las relaciones interamericanas: La participación del "Grupo de Puerto Rico" en la crisis de Santo Domingo de 1965', MA thesis, University of Puerto Rico.

BONNICK, GLADSTONE (2000) *Toward a Caribbean Vision 2020: A Regional Perspective on Development Challenges, Opportunities and Strategies for the Next Two Decades,* Washington, DC: Caribbean Group for Cooperation in Economic Development.

BOOTH, CATHY (1996) 'Caribbean Blizzard', *Time,* 26 February.

BOOTH, CATHY and T. LONG (1993) 'The New Face of America, Miami: The Capital of Latin America', *Time,* 2 December (special issue).

BOOTH, DAVID (1976) 'Cuba, Color and the Revolution', *Science & Society,* XL, pp.129–72.

BOSCH, JUAN (1986) *La pequeña burguesía en la historia de la República Dominicana,* 2nd edn, Santo Domingo: Alfa y Omega.

BOUGH, JAMES A. (1949) 'The Caribbean Commission', *International Organization,* 3, pp.643–55.

BOURNE, COMPTON (1978) 'Wage Determination in the Caribbean Countries: Trends and Issues' in International Labour Organisation, *Record of Proceedings of, and Documents Submitted to ILO/DANDRA Regional Seminar: Wage Determination in English Speaking Countries,* Jamaica.

BOUSQUET, BEN and COLIN DOUGLAS (1991) *West Indian Women at War: British Racism in World War II,* London: Lawrence & Wishart.

BRAITHWAITE, LLOYD (1953) 'Social Stratification in Trinidad', *Social and Economic Studies,* 2, nos.3 & 4, pp.5–175.

——, (1975) *Social Stratification in Trinidad: A Preliminary Analysis,* Mona: Institute of Social and Economic Research, UWI.

BRANA-SHUTE, GARY (1979) *On the Corner: Male Social life in a Paramaribo, Creole Neighborhood,* Assen, the Netherlands: Van Gorcum.

——, (ed.) (1990) *Resistance and Rebellion in Suriname,* Williamsburg, Virginia: College of William and Mary.

BRANA-SHUTE, ROSEMARY (1983) *A Bibliography of Caribbean Migration and Caribbean Immigrant Communities,* Gainesville: Center for Latin American Studies, University of Florida.

——, (1993) 'Neighbourhood Networks and National Politics among Working-Class Afro-Surinamese women' in Janet H. Momsen (ed.) *Women and Change in the Caribbean,* Kingston: Ian Randle.

BRANDON, GEORGE (1993) *Santería from Africa to the New World: The Dead Sell Memories,* Bloomington: Indiana University Press.

BRATHWAITE, EDWARD (1971) *The Development of Creole Society in Jamaica, 1770–1820,* Oxford: Clarendon Press.

——, (1974) *Contradictory Omens: Cultural Diversity and Integration in the Caribbean,* Mona: Savacou Publications.

BRENNER, PHILIP, WILLIAM M. LEOGRANDE, DONNA RICH and DANIEL SIEGEL (eds) (1989) *The Cuba Reader: The Making of a Revolutionary Society,* New York: Grove Press.

BRERETON, BRIDGET (1981) *A History of Modern Trinidad, 1783–1962,* London: Heinemann.

——, (1989) 'Society and Culture in the Caribbean: The British and French West Indies, 1870–1980' in F. W. Knight and C. A. Palmer (eds) *The Modern Caribbean,* Chapel Hill: University of North Carolina Press.

——, (1993) 'The Development of an Identity: The Black Middle Class in Trinidad in the Later 19th Century' in Hilary Beckles and Verene Shepherd (eds) *Caribbean Freedom: Society and Economy from Emancipation to the Present,* Kingston: Ian Randle.

BRERETON, BRIDGET and WINSTON DOOKERAN (eds) (1982) *East Indians in the Caribbean,* Millwood, New York: Kraus.

BRERETON, BRIDGET and KEVIN YELVINGTON (eds) (1999) *The Colonial Caribbean in Transition,* Mona: The Press, UWI.

BREWSTER, HAVELOCK and CLIVE THOMAS (1967) *The Dynamics of West Indian Economic Integration,* Mona: UWI.

BRICEÑO-RUIZ, JOSÉ (1997) 'Venezuela y la cuenca del Caribe en la segunda ola de la integración latinoamericana', *Revista Mexicana del Caribe,* II, 3.

BRIGGS, HERBERT W. (1940) 'Neglected Aspects of the Destroyers Deal', *American Journal of International Law,* 34, pp.569–87.

BRISSON, MONIQUE (1988) 'Situation juridique et constitutionalle de la femme haïtienne' in Adeline Chancy and Suzy Castor (eds) *Théories et pratiques de la lutte des femmes,* Port-au-Prince: CRESFED.

BROCK, COLIN and DONALD CLARKSON (eds) (1990) *Education in Central America and the Caribbean,* New York: Routledge.

BRODBER, ERNA (1986) 'Afro-Jamaican Women at the Turn of the Century', *Social and Economic Studies,* 35 no.3, pp.23–50.

BRONSTEIN, A. S. (1997) 'Labour Law Reform in Latin America. Between State Protection and Flexibility', *International Labour Review,* 136, no.1.

BROWN, DERYCK R. (1995) 'The Coup That Failed: The Jamesian Connection' in Selwyn D. Ryan and Taimoon Stewart (eds) *The Black Power Revolution, 1970,* St Augustine: Institute of Social and Economic Research, UWI.

BROWN, HILARY (1995) 'American Media Impact on Jamaican Youth' in H. S. Dunn (ed.) *Globalization, Communications and Caribbean Identity,* New York: St Martin's Press.

BROWN, KAREN M. (1991) *Mama Lola: A Vodon Priestess in Brooklyn,* Berkeley: University of California Press.

BROWN, WENZELL (1945) *Dynamite on Our Doorstep: Puerto Rican Paradox,* New York: Greenberg.

BRYAN, ANTHONY T. (1984) 'The CARICOM and Latin American Integration Experiences: Observations on Theoretical Origins and Comparative Performance' in *Ten Years of Caricom,* Washington, DC: Inter-American Development Bank.

——, (ed.) (1995) *The Caribbean: New Dynamics in Trade and Political Economy,* New Brunswick: Transaction Publishers/North-South Center.

——, (1998) 'Toward 2000: The Caribbean Confronts Changing Trends in International Trade', *Caribbean Affairs,* 8, no.1.

BRYAN, ANTHONY T. and ROGET V. BRYAN (1999) *The New Face of Regionalism in the Caribbean: The Western Hemisphere Dynamic,* North South Agenda Paper 35, Coral Gables, Florida: North-South Center Press, University of Miami.

BRYAN, ANTHONY T. and ANDRÉS SERBÍN (eds) (1996) *Distant Cousins: The Caribbean-Latin American Relationship,* Coral Gables, Florida: North-South Center Press, University of Miami.

BRYAN, ANTHONY T., J. EDWARD GREENE and TIMOTHY M. SHAW (eds) (1990) *Peace, Development and Security in the Caribbean,* London: Macmillan.

BRYAN, PATRICK (1979) 'La producción campesina en la República Dominicana a principio del siglo veinte', *Eme-Eme,* VII, no.22, pp.29–62.

——, (1985) 'The Question of Labor in the Sugar Industry of the Dominican Republic in the Late Nineteenth and Early Twentieth Centuries' in M. Moreno Fraginals, F. Moya Pons and S. L. Engerman (eds) *Between Slavery and Free Labor: The Spanish-speaking Caribbean in the Nineteenth Century,* Baltimore: Johns Hopkins University Press.

——, (1991) *The Jamaican People 1880–1902: Race, Class and Social Control,* London: Macmillan Caribbean.

BUNN, HARIET and ELLEN GUT (1946) *The Universities of Cuba, the Dominican Republic and Haiti,* Washington, DC: Division of Intellectual Cooperation, Pan American Union.

BURGOS ORTÍZ, NILSA (1997) *Pioneras de la profesión de trabajo social en Puerto Rico,* San Juan: Publicaciones Puertorriqueñas.

BURKETT, ALGERNON A. (1914) *Trinidad: A Jewel of the West,* or, *100 Years of British Rule,* London: Francis.

BURR, C. (1997) 'Cuba and AIDS', *National Review,* 49, no.18, 29 September.

BURTON, RICHARD D. E. (1978) *Assimilation or Independence: Prospects for Martinique,* Occasional Monograph Series, no.13, Montreal: McGill University.

——, (1992) 'Between the Particular and the Universal: Dilemmas of the Martinican Intellectual' in A. Hennessy (ed.) *Intellectuals in the Twentieth-Century Caribbean,* vol. II, Basingstoke: Macmillan Caribbean.

——, (1996) 'Two Views of Césaire: Négritude and Créolité', *Dalhousie French Studies,* 35, pp.135–52.

BURTON, RICHARD D. E. and FRED RENO (eds) (1994) *French and West Indian: Martinique, Guadeloupe and French Guiana Today,* London: Macmillan.

BUSCHKENS, WILLEM F. L. (1974) *The Family System of the Paramaribo Creoles,* The Hague: Martinus Nijhoff.

BUSH, BARBARA (1990) *Slave Women in Caribbean Society, 1650–1838,* Bloomington: Indiana University Press.

BUSH, D. M. *et al.* (1995) *Living with the Puerto Rico Shore,* Durham: Duke University Press.

BUSTAMANTE, GLADYS (1997) *The Memoirs of Lady Bustamante,* Kingston: Kingston Publishers.

BYRON, MARGARET and S. CONDON (1996) 'A Comparative Study of Caribbean Return Migration from Britain and France: Towards a Context-Dependent Explanation', *Transactions of the Institute of British Geographers,* 21, pp.91–104.

CABÁN, PEDRO A. (1989) 'Industrial Transformation and Labour Relations in Puerto Rico', *Journal of Latin American Studies,* 21, 3.

——, (1999) *Constructing a Colonial People: Puerto Rico and the United States, 1898–1932,* Boulder: Westview Press.

CÁCERES UREÑA, FRANCISCO (1994) 'Quiénes son las mujeres de hoy', *Hoy,* p.13.

CALDER, BRUCE J. (1984) *The Impact of Intervention: The Dominican Republic During the U.S. Occupation of 1916–24,* Austin: University of Texas Press.

——, (1989) *El impacto de la intervención,* Santo Domingo: Fundación Cultural Dominicana.

Cambridge History of the British Empire (1929–59), 8 vols, Cambridge: Cambridge University Press.

CAMERON, NORMAN EUSTACE (1929–34) *The Evolution of the Negro,* 2 vols, British Guiana: Argosy; reprinted Westport: Negro Universities Press, 1970.

CAMPBELL, CARL (1974a) 'Jonas Mohammed Bath and the Free Mandingoes in Trinidad', *Pan-African Journal,* VII, 2, pp.129–52.

——, (1974b) 'Mohammedu Sisei of Gambia and Trinidad, ca, 1788–1838', *African Studies Association of the West Indies Bulletin,* 7, pp.29–38.

——, (1996) *The Young Colonials: A Social History of Education in Trinidad and Tobago 1834–1939,* Mona: The Press, UWI.

——, (1997) *Endless Education: Main Currents in the Education System of Modern Trinidad and Tobago, 1939–86,* Mona: The Press, UWI.

CAMPBELL, HORACE (1985) *Rasta and Resistance,* London: Hansib.

——, (1994) 'Progressive Politics and the Jamaican Society at Home and Abroad', *Social and Economic Studies,* 43, 3.

CAMPBELL, J. B. and BONHAM C. RICHARDSON (1992) 'Hurricane Hugo's Trajectory' in D. G. Janelle (ed.) *Geographical Snapshots of North America,* New York: Guilford Press.

CAMPBELL, ROBERT (1969) 'A Pilgrimage to My Motherland: An Account of a Journey Among the Egbas and Yorubas of Central Africa in 1859–60' in Martin R. Delany and Robert Campbell, *Search for a Place,* Ann Arbor: University of Michigan Press.

CAMPUZANO, LUISA (1996) 'Ser cubanas y no morir en el intento', *Temas,* 5, pp.4–10.

Canada Act (1982) incorporating the *Constitution Act,* 1982.

Canada, House of Commons (1980) *A Statement of Principles for a New Constitution,* 10 June.

Canboulay Productions (1991) *Sing de Chorus: Calypsoes of Trinidad and Tobago,* Curepe, Trinidad: Sanch.

CANCEL, MARIO R. (ed.) (1997) *Historia y género: Vidas y relatos de mujeres en el Caribe,* San Juan: Asociación Puertorriqueña de Historiadores y Postdata.

CANTON NAVARRO, JOSÉ, OSCAR ZANETTI LECUONA, PEDRO ALVAREZ-TABIO LONGA, FEDERICO CHANG PON and ALEJANDRO GARCÍA ALVAREZ (eds) (1998) *Historia de Cuba: La neocolonia: Organización y crisis, desde 1899 hasta 1940,* Havana: Editora Política, Instituto de Historia de Cuba.

CARDOSO, CIRO F. S. and B. HÉCTOR PÉREZ (1983) *Centro América y la economía occidental, 1520–1930,* San José: Editorial Universidad de Costa Rica.

CARDOSO, FERNANDO HENRIQUE and ENZO FALLETO (1969) *Dependencia y desarrollo en América Latina,* Mexico City: Editorial Siglo XXI.

CAREY, KATHLEEN (1992) 'Optimal Hotel Capacity: The Case of Barbados', *Social and Economic Studies,* 41, no.2.

Caribbean Commission (1943) *The Caribbean Islands and the War: A Record of Progress in Facing Stern Realities.* Washington, DC: Anglo-American Caribbean Commission.

Caribbean Community Secretariat (1973) *The Caribbean Community: A Guide,* Georgetown: CARICOM Secretariat.

——, (1988) *Caribbean Development to the Year 2000,* Georgetown: CARICOM Secretariat.

Caribbean Organization (1964) *The Caribbean Organization – The First Three Years: 1961–4,* Hato Rey, Puerto Rico: Caribbean Organization Secretariat.

Caribbean Subregional Preparatory Conference to the Fourth World Conference on Women (1995) Curaçao, 27–9 June.

CARL, JOACHIM (1957) *Das amerikanische Leih-und Pachtgesetz (Lend-Lease Act)*, Frankfurt: Entstehung und Bedeutung für den Ausgang des Zweiten Weltkrieges.

CARMEJO, M. J. (1990) *Harvesting Oppression: Forced Haitian Labor in the Dominican Sugar Industry*, New York: American Watch.

——, (1991) *Half-Measures: Reform, Forced Labor and the Dominican Sugar Industry*, New York: American Watch.

CARMICHAEL, TREVOR (ed.) (1996) *Barbados: Thirty Years of Independence*, Kingston: Ian Randle.

CARNEGIE, CHARLES V. (1983) '"If You Lose the Dog, Grab the Cat"', *Natural History*, 92, pp.28, 30–4.

——, (ed.) (1987) *Afro-Caribbean Villages in Historical Perspective*, Kingston: African-Caribbean Institute of Jamaica.

CARNOY, MARTIN (1990) 'Educational reform and social transformation in Cuba, 1959–89' in Martin Carnoy and Joel Samoff, *Education and Social Transition in the Third World*, Princeton: Princeton University Press.

CARNOY, MARTIN and JOEL SAMOFF (1990) *Education and Social Transition in the Third World*, Princeton: Princeton University Press.

CARR, BARRY (1998) 'Identity, Class, and Nation: Black Immigrant Workers, Cuban Communism and the Sugar Insurgency, 1925–34', *Hispanic American Historical Review*, 78, no.1.

CARR, EDWARD HALLETT (1963) *What is History?* New York: Alfred A. Knopf.

CASAL, LOURDES and MARIFELI PÉREZ-STABLE (1981) 'Party and State in Post-1970 Cuba' in Leslie Holmes (ed.) *The Withering Away of The State? Party and State under Communism*, London: Sage.

CASIMIR, J. R. RALPH (1988) Interview with J. R. Ralph Casimir, Roseau, 1985. Cited in Tony Martin, 'A Pan-Africanist in Dominica, J. R. Ralph Casimir and the Garvey Movement, 1919–23', *Journal of Caribbean History* 21, 2, 1988, p.123; reprinted in John P. Henderson and Harry A. Reed (eds) *Studies in the African Diaspora*, Dover, Massachusetts: Majority Press.

CASSÁ, ROBERTO (1978–80) *Historia social y económica de la República Dominicana*, 2 vols, Santo Domingo: Editora Alfa y Omega.

——, (1982) *Capitalismo y dictadura*, Santo Domingo: Universidad Autónoma de Santo Domingo.

——, (1986) *Los Doce Años: Contrarrevolución y Desarrollismo*, vol. 1, Santo Domingo: Editora Alfa y Omega.

CASTELLANOS, JORGE and ISABEL CASTELLANOS (1990) *El Negro en Cuba*, Miami: Ediciones Universal.

CASTOR, SUZY (1971) *La ocupación norteamericana de Haití y sus consecuencias*, Mexico City: Editorial Siglo XXI.

——, (1994) *Les femmes haïtiennes aux élections de 1990*, Port-au-Prince: CRESFED.

CASTRO, FIDEL (1975) 'Report of the Central Committee of the Communist Party of Cuba to the First Congress', Cuba.

CASTRO, MAX J. (ed.) (1999) *Free Markets, Open Societies, Closed Borders? Trends in International Migration and Immigration Policies in the Americas*, Coral Gables, Florida: North-South Center Press, University of Miami.

Causa 1/89: Fin de la conexión cubana (1989) Havana: Editorial José Martí.

CELMA, CÉCILE (1987) 'L'Emergence de la classe ouvrière à la Martinique 1880 à 1940: quelques aspects'. Paper presented at the Nineteenth Annual Conference of Association of Caribbean Historians.

CERQUEIRA, M. (1996) 'Health Promoting Schools in the Americas', *World Health*, 49, 4, pp.12–3.

CÉSAIRE, AIMÉ (1957) 'Lettre à Maurice Thorez', *Presence Africaine* (English version).

——, (1961) 'Crise dans les DOM ou crise de la départmentalization', *Présence Africaine*, 36.

CHAMBERLAIN, MARY (1995) 'Family Narratives and Migration Dynamics: Barbadians to Britain', *Nieuwe West-Indische Gids/New West Indian Guide*, 69, 3 & 4, pp.253–75.

CHAMOISEAU, PATRICK (1997) *Texaco*, trans. R.-M. Réjouis and V. Vinokurov, New York: Pantheon.

CHANCY, ADELINE and SUZY CASTOR (eds) (1988) *Théories et pratiques de la lutte des femmes*, Port-au-Prince: CRESFED.

CHANE-TUNE, R. (1986) 'Des niveaux de vie assez éléves', *Les Dossiers de l'Outre Mer*, 83.

CHANEY, ELSA M. and M. G. CASTRO (eds) (1989) *Muchachas No More: Household Workers in Latin America and the Caribbean*, Philadelphia: Temple University Press.

CHARLES, CAROLLE (1994) 'Sexual Politics and the Mediation of Class, Gender and Race in Former Slave Plantation Societies: The Case of Haiti' in George Clement Bond and Angela Gilliam (eds) *Social Construction of the Past: Representation as Power*, London: Routledge.

——, (1995) 'Feminist Action and Research in Haiti', *Caribbean Studies*, 28, no.1.

CHASE, A. (1964) *A History of Trade Unionism in Guyana, 1900–61*, Guyana: published by the author.

CHATELAIN, FRANÇOIS (1954) *La Banque Nationale*, Port-au-Prince.

CHEN, HENK E. and HANS BUDDINGH' (1987) *Suriname: Politics, Economics and Society*, London: Frances Pinter.

CHEVANNES, BARRY (1994) *Rastafari: Roots and Ideology*, Syracuse, NY: Syracuse University Press.

——, (ed.) (1995) *Rastafari and Other African-Caribbean Worldviews*, Oxford: Macmillan Caribbean.

CHOMSKY, AVIVA (1996) *West Indian Workers and the United Fruit Company in Costa Rica, 1870–1940*, Baton Rouge: Louisiana State University Press.

City University of New York (1979), Centro de Estudios Puertorriqueños (History Task Force), *Labor Migration Under Capitalism: The Puerto Rican Experience*, New York: Monthly Review Press.

CLARK, VICTOR S., CHARLES L. DEARING, JAMES A. DICKEY, FREDERICK H. NEWELL *et al.* (1930) *Porto Rico and its Problems*, Washington, DC: Brookings Institution.

CLARKE, COLIN and ANTHONY PAYNE (eds) (1987) *Politics, Security and Development in Small States*, London: Allen & Unwin.

CLARKE, EDITH (1957) *My Mother Who Fathered Me: A Study of the Family in Three Selected Communities in Jamaica,* London: Allen & Unwin; 2nd edn, 1966; reprinted Mona: The Press, UWI, 1999.

CLARKSON, DONALD (1990) 'Formative Influences in Puerto Rican Education' in Colin Brock and Donald Clarkson (eds) *Education in Central America and the Caribbean,* New York: Routledge.

COHN, DAVID L. (1943) 'Lend-Lease Saved the Bacon', *Atlantic Monthly,* pp.68–71.

COLE, C. D. (1953) *An Introduction to Trade Unionism,* London: Allen & Unwin.

COLEN, S. (1989) 'Just a Little Respect: West Indian Domestic Workers in New York City' in E. M. Chaney and M. G. Castro (eds) *Muchachas No More: Household Workers in Latin America and the Caribbean,* Philadelphia: Temple University Press.

COLLIER, RUTH BERINS (1994) 'Labor Politics and Regime Change: Internal Trajectories versus External Influences' in David Rock (ed.) *Latin America in the 1940s: War and Post War Transition,* Berkeley: University of California Press.

COLÓN, ALICE, ANA L. DÁVILA, MARÍA D. FERNÓS and ESTHER VICENTE (1999) *Políticas, visiones y voces en torno al aborto en Puerto Rico,* Río Piedras: Centro de Investigaciones Sociales, Universidad de Puerto Rico.

COLÓN, ALICE and ANA M. FABIÁN (eds) (1995) *Mujeres en el Caribe: Desarrollo, paz y movimientos comunitarios,* Río Piedras: Instituto de Estudios del Caribe and CERES, Centro de Investigaciones Sociales, Universidad de Puerto Rico.

COLÓN, ALICE, MARGARITA MERGAL and NILSA TORRES (1986) *La participación de la mujer en la historia de Puerto Rico (las primeras décadas del siglo XX),* Río Piedras: Centro de Investigaciones Sociales, Universidad de Puerto Rico and Rutgers University.

COLÓN, ALICE, MARYA MUÑOZ, NEFTALÍ GARCÍA and IDSA ALEGRÍA (1988) 'Trayectoria de la participación laboral de las mujeres en Puerto Rico de los años 1950 a 1985: estudio sobre la calidad de vida y la crisis económica en Puerto Rico' in *Crísis, sociedad y mujer: estudio comparativo entre países de América (1950–85),* Havana: Editorial de la Mujer, FMC.

COLÓN WARREN, ALICE (1995) 'Investigación y acción feminista en el Puerto Rico contemporáneo: notas desde un punto en su intersección y movimiento temático', *Caribbean Studies,* 28, no.1.

——, (1997) 'Reestructuración industrial, empleo y pobreza en Puerto Rico y el Atlántico Medio: la situación de las mujeres puertorriqueñas', *Revista de Ciencias Sociales* (Nueva Epoca), 3.

——, (1998) 'The Feminization of Poverty among Women in Puerto Rico and Puerto Rican Women in the Middle Atlantic Region of the United States', *Brown Journal of World Affairs,* V, Issue 2.

Comisión de Derechos Civiles, Ela de Puerto Rico (1972) *La igualdad de derechos y oportunidades de la mujer puertorriqueña,* 9 September, San Juan.

Commonwealth Caribbean Regional Secretariat (1973) *The Georgetown Accord,* mimeograph.

Commonwealth Parliamentary Union (2000) 'Women in Commonwealth Parliaments'. Prepared for Commonwealth Workshop on Gender and Democracy, Windhoek.

Commonwealth Secretariat (1985) *Vulnerability: Small States in the Global Society*, London: Commonwealth Secretariat.

——, (1997) *A Future for Small States: Overcoming Vulnerability*, London: Commonwealth Secretariat.

Commonwealth Secretariat/World Bank Joint Task Force (2000) *Interim Report on Small States: Meeting Challenges in the Global Economy*, London: Commonwealth Secretariat.

CONAGHAN, CATHERINE and ROSARIO ESPINAL (1990) 'Unlikely Transitions to Uncertain Regimes? Democracy without Compromise in the Dominican Republic and Ecuador', *Journal of Latin American Studies*, 22, no.3.

CONDON, S. A. and P. E. OGDEN (1997) 'Housing and the State in the French Caribbean' in R. B. Potter and D. Conway (eds) *Self-Help Housing, the Poor, and the State in the Caribbean*, Mona: The Press, UWI.

Conference on the Closer Association of the British West Indian Colonies, Montego Bay, Jamaica, 11 to 19 September 1947 (1948), Colonial no.218, *Report* and *Proceedings*, London: HMSO.

CONN, STETSON and BRIAN FAIRCHILD (1960) *The Western Hemisphere: The Framework of Hemisphere Defense*, Washington, DC: Office of the Chief of Military History, Department of the Army.

CONNIFF, MICHAEL L. (1985) *Black Labor on a White Canal: Panama, 1904–81*, Pittsburgh: University of Pittsburgh Press.

CONNIFF, MICHAEL L. and THOMAS DAVIS (1994) *Africans in the Americas: A History of the Black Diaspora*, New York: St Martin's Press.

CONWAY, FREDERICK (1980) 'Pentecostalism in Haiti: Healing and Hierarchy' in Stephen D. Glazier (ed.) *Perspectives on Pentecostalism: Case Studies from the Caribbean and Latin America*, Washington, DC: University Press of America.

COOK, KATHERINE (1934) *Public Education in the Virgin Islands*, Washington, DC: US Government Printing Office.

COOK, MERCER (1948) 'Education in Haiti', *U.S. Office of Education Bulletin*, 1.

COOMBS, ORDE (ed.) (1974) *Is Massa Day Dead? Black Moods in the Caribbean*, Garden City, NY: New Anchor Press.

COOPER, ANDREW F. (ed.) (1997) *Niche Diplomacy: Middle Powers After the Cold War*, Basingstoke: Macmillan Press.

CORDERO, MARGARITA (1985) *Mujeres de abril*. Santo Domingo: CIPAF.

——, (1991) *Mujer, participación política y procesos electorales (1986–90)*, Santo Domingo: CIPAF.

——, (1994) 'Representación política y espacios públicos', *Género y Sociedad*, 2, no.2, pp.13–23.

CÓRDOVA, E. (1977) *Fidel Castro and the Cuban Labor Movement*, Ann Arbor: University of Michigan Press.

CORKRAN, HERBERT (1970) *Patterns of International Cooperation in the Caribbean*, Dallas: Southern Methodist University Press.

CORRETJER, JUAN ANTONIO (1950) *La lucha por la independencia de Puerto Rico,* San Juan: Unión del Pueblo Pro Constituyente.

——, (1965) *Albizu Campos and the Ponce Massacre,* New York: World View Publishers.

——, (1969) *Albizu Campos,* Montevideo: Editorial El Siglo Ilustrado.

COTT, NANCY F. (1987) *The Groundings of Modern Feminism,* New Haven: Yale University Press.

COTTIAS, MYRIAM and ANNIE FITTE-DUVAL (1995) 'Femme, famille et politique dans les Antilles Françaises de 1828 à nos jours', *Caribbean Studies,* 28, no.1, pp.85–6.

Countries of the World and Their Leaders: Yearbook (1984) Detroit: Gale Research.

COWELL, NOEL M. (1992) *A Summary of Test Cases in Jamaican Labour Law,* Kingston: Joint Trade Unions Research Development Centre.

COULTHARD, G. R. (1962) *Race and Colour in Caribbean Literature,* Oxford: Oxford University Press.

COURLANDER, HAROLD (1960) *The Drum and the Hoe: Life and Lore of the Haitian People,* Berkeley: University of California Press.

COWLEY, JOHN (1996) *Carnival, Canboulay and Calypso: Traditions in the Making,* Cambridge: Cambridge University Press.

COX, EDWARD L. (1994) 'Religious Intolerance and Persecution: The Shakers of St Vincent, 1900–34', *Journal of Caribbean History,* 28, no.2, pp.208–43.

CRAHAN, MARGARET E. (1989) 'Freedom of Worship in Revolutionary Cuba' in Philip Brenner, William M. LeoGrande, Donna Rich, and Daniel Siegel (eds) *The Cuba Reader: The Making of a Revolutionary Society.* New York: Grove Press.

CRATON, MICHAEL (1978) *Searching for the Invisible Man: Slaves and Plantation Life in Jamaica,* Cambridge, Massachusetts: Harvard University Press.

——, (1986) *A History of the Bahamas,* 3rd edn, Waterloo, Ontario: San Salvador Press.

CRATON, MICHAEL and GAIL SAUNDERS (1998) *Islanders in the Stream: A History of the Bahamian People,* vol. 2, Athens, Georgia: University of Georgia Press.

CRATON, MICHAEL and JAMES WALVIN (1970) *A Jamaican Plantation: The History of Worthy Park, 1670–1970,* London: W. H. Allen.

CREECH-JONES, A. (1945) 'The Conditions of Social Policy and its Cost' in Rita Hinden (ed.) *Fabian Colonial Essays,* London: Allen & Unwin, pp.67–84.

CRITCHLOW, HUBERT (1945) 'History of the Trade Union Movement in British Guiana' in George Padmore (ed.) *Voice of Coloured Labour,* Manchester: PANAF Services.

CROES, BETTICO (1990) 'The Dutch Caribbean Islands' in James M. Malloy and Eduardo A. Gamarra (eds) *Latin America and Caribbean Contemporary Record,* vol. VII, New York: Holmes and Meier.

CROES, ROBERTICO and LUCITA MOENIR ALAM (1990) 'Decolonization of Aruba within the Netherlands Antilles' in Betty Sedoc-Dahlberg (ed.) *The Dutch Caribbean: Prospects for Democracy,* New York: Gordon and Breach.

CRONON, DAVID E. (1959) 'Interpreting the New Good Neighbor Policy: The Cuban Crisis of 1933', *Hispanic American Historical Review,* 39, pp.538–67.

CROSS, MALCOLM (1972) *The East Indians of Guyana and Trinidad,* London: Minority Rights Group.

——, (1988) 'The Political Representation of Organized Labour in Trinidad and Guyana: A Comparative Puzzle' in Malcolm Cross and Gad Heuman (eds) *Labour in the Caribbean*, London: Macmillan Caribbean.

CROSS, MALCOLM and GAD HEUMAN (eds) (1988) *Labour in the Caribbean: From Emancipation to Independence*, London: Macmillan Caribbean.

CUALES, SONIA (1984) 'Mujer, reproducción y capital extranjero: el caso de una empresa multinacional en Curazao', en *La mujer en el sector popular urbano: América Latina y el Caribe*, Santiago: United Nations, Comisión Económica para América Latina y el Caribe.

——, (1993) 'El Caribe de habla holandesa: Luchar hasta el final' in Robin Morgan (ed.) *Mujeres del mundo*, Barcelona: Editorial Hacer.

——, (1998) 'In Search of Our Memory: Gender in the Netherlands Antilles', *Feminist Review*, 59, p.89.

Cuba (1945) *Informe general del censo de 1943*, Havana: P. Fernández y Cia.

Cuba, Centro de Estudios de Alternativas Políticas (1996) *Emigración cubana*, Havana: Universidad de Havana.

Cuba, Centro de Estudios Demográficos (1976) *La población de Cuba*, Havana: Editorial de Ciencias Sociales.

Cuba, Centro Latinoaméricano de Demografía (1995) *Boletin Demográfico*, XXVIII, no.56, Santiago .

Cuba, Comité Estatal de Estadísticas (1985) *Anuario estadístico de Cuba*, Havana.

——, (1982) *Estadísticas de migraciones externas y turismo*, Havana: Editorial Orbe.

Cuba, Ministry of Justice (1975) *Family Code*, Law no.1289 of 14 February 1975, Havana: Editorial Orbe.

Cuba, Oficina General de los Censos (1955) *Censo de población, viviendas y electoral, 1953*, Havana: P. Fernández y Cia.

Cuba, Oficina Nacional de Estadísticas (1997) *Anuario estadístico de Cuba 1996*, Havana.

Cuba, Oficina Nacional del Censo (1983) *Censo de población y viviendas de 1981*, Havana.

Cuba en la mano: Encyclopedia popular ilustrada (1940) Havana: Ucar, García y Cia; reprinted Miami: Mnemosyne, 1969.

CUBANO, ASTRID (1981) 'Economía y sociedad en Arecibo en el siglo XIX: los grandes productores y la inmigración de comerciantes' in Francisco Scarano (ed.), *Inmigración y clases sociales*, Río Piedras: Editorial Universitaria.

CUDJOE, SELWYN (ed.) (1990) *Caribbean Women Writers: Essays from the First International Conference*, Wellesley, Massachusetts: Callaloux Publications.

CUMPER, GEORGE E. (1958) 'The Jamaican Family: Village and Estate', *Social and Economic Studies*, 7, no.1, 76–108.

CUMPER, GLORIA and STEPHANIE DALY (1979) *Family Law in the Commonwealth Caribbean*, Mona: Department of Extra-Mural Studies, UWI.

CURTIN, PHILIP D. (1990) *The Rise and Fall of the Plantation Complex: Essays in Atlantic History*, Cambridge: Cambridge University Press.

CUTHBERT, ROBERT W. M. (1986) *Ecumenism and Development: A Socio-Historical Analysis of the Caribbean Conference of Churches*, Bridgetown: Caribbean Conference of Churches.

CUTIÉ, REBECA (1997) 'Factors influencing teenage pregnancy in Cuba', *CAFRA News*, vol. 11, 1–2, pp.22–4.

DABYDEEN, DAVID and BRINSLEY SAMAROO (eds) (1987) *India in the Caribbean*, London: Hansib.

DAGENAIS, HUGUETTE (1993) 'Women in Guadeloupe: The Paradoxes of Reality' in Janet H. Momsen (ed.) *Women and Change in the Caribbean*, Kingston: Ian Randle.

DALLEK, ROBERT (1979) *Franklin D. Roosevelt and American Foreign Policy, 1932–45*, New York: Oxford University Press.

DALLY, ANA (1994) 'Cuba: educación y racismo durante el periodo de 1792–1959', *Revista Cubana de Ciencias Sociales*, 2–8, pp.164–9.

DALY, VERE (1975) *A Short History of the Guyanese People*, London: Macmillan Caribbean.

D'ANS, ANDRÉ-MARCEL (1987) *Haïti: paysage et societé*, Paris: Kartala.

DARTIGUE, ESTER (1994) *An Outstanding Haitian, Maurice Dartigue: The Contribution of Maurice Dartigue in the Field of Education in Haiti, the United Nations and UNESCO*, New York: Vantage Press.

DARTIGUE, MAURICE (1941) 'Rural Life and Education in Haiti', *Inter-American Quarterly*, 3, no.2.

DASH, J. MICHAEL (1975) 'The Way Through Africa: A Study of Africanism in Haiti', *Bim*, XV, 58, 1975, pp.117–34.

——, (1981) *Literature and Ideology in Haiti, 1915–61*, Totowa, NJ: Barnes and Noble Books.

DAVENPORT, WILLIAM (1961) 'The Family System of Jamaica', *Social and Economic Studies*, 10, no.4, 420–54.

DÁVILA, ARLENE (1997) 'Contending Nationalisms: Culture, Politics, and Corporate Sponsoring in Puerto Rico' in F. Negrón-Muntaner and R. Grosfoguel, eds, *Puerto Rican Jam: Essays on Culture and Politics*, Minneapolis: University of Minnesota Press.

DAVIS, KINGSLEY (1950–1) 'Population and Progress in Puerto Rico, 1938–51', *Foreign Affairs*, 29, pp.625–36.

DAVIS, PAUL A. (1979) 'The Black Man and the Caribbean as Seen by Nicolás Guillén and Luis Palés Matos', *Caribbean Quarterly*, 25, 1 and 2.

DAVIS, W. (1994) 'Entering Haiti; Can we Build Democracy in this Complex, Tortured Land?', *Washington Post*, 18 September, sec. 1.

DAYFOOT, ARTHUR CHARLES (1999) *The Shaping of the West Indian Church, 1492–1962*, Kingston: The Press, UWI; Gainesville: University Press of Florida.

DE ALBUQUERQUE, KLAUS (1990) '"Is We Carnival": Cultural Traditions Under Stress in the U.S. Virgin Islands' in J. A. Lent (ed.) *Caribbean Popular Culture*, Bowling Green, Ohio: Bowling Green State University Popular Press.

——, (1996) 'Drugs in the Caribbean: A Five Part Series', *Caribbean Week* (Barbados), various issues, January–March.

De Albuquerque, Klaus and J. L. McElroy (1995) 'Tourism Development in Small Islands: St Maarten/St Martin and Bermuda' in D. Barker and D. F. M. McGregor (eds) *Environment and Development in the Caribbean: Geographical Perspectives*, Mona: The Press, UWI.

De Barros, Juanita (1998) 'Contested Territories: Public Space in Colonial Georgetown, 1889–1924', Ph.D. dissertation,York University, Canada.

De Betancourt, Ethel Ríos (1972) 'The Rise of the Regional College Movement within the University of Puerto Ríco', *Revista Interamericana,* 2, no.1, pp.40–9.

De Gonzalo, Marisol (1987) 'La significación del grupo Contadora como actor internacional' in Andrés Serbín (ed.) *Venezuela y las relaciones internacionales en la cuenca del Caribe*, Caracas: Inst. Lat. de Invs. Soc.[ILDIS] & Asoc. Vene. de Ests. del Caribe [AVECA].

De Kadt, Emanuel (ed.) (1972) *Patterns of Foreign Influence in the Caribbean*, Oxford: Oxford University Press.

De Kom, Anton (1934) *Wij slaven van Suriname*, Amsterdam, trans. as *We Slaves of Surinam*, London: Zed Press, 1987.

De La Fuente, Alejandro (1995) 'Race and Inequality in Cuba, 1899–1981', *Journal of Contemporary History*, 30, pp.131–68.

De Regt, Jacomina (1984) 'Basic Education in Haiti' in Charles R. Foster and Albert Valdman (eds) *Haiti – Today and Tomorrow*, Lanham, Maryland: University Press of America.

Deare, Fredericka M. (1995) 'Feminist Research and Action Methodology: The Experiences of the Caribbean Association for Feminist Research and Action', *Caribbean Studies,* 28, 1.

Deere, Carmen D., Peggy Antrobus *et al.* (1990) *In the Shadows of the Sun: Caribbean Development Alternatives and US Policy,* Boulder: Westview Press.

Deerr, Noel (1949–50) *The History of Sugar,* 2 vols, London: Chapman and Hall.

Del Alba Acevedo, Luz (1987) 'Política de industrialización y cambios en el empleo femenino en Puerto Rico', *Homines*, special issue 4, pp.40, 48–9, 52–3, 57, 69.

Del Castillo, José (1981) *Ensayos de sociología Dominicana*, Santo Domingo: Ediciones Siboney.

Del Cueto, Mario G. (1982) *Historia, economía, sociedad en los pueblos de habla inglesa del Caribe,* Havana: Editorial de Ciencias Sociales.

Del Toro González, Carlos (1974) *Algunos aspectos económicos, sociales y políticos del movimiento obrero cubano, 1933–58*, Havana: Editorial Arte y Literatura.

Delany, Martin R. (1859) *The Condition of the Colored People of the United States*, Philadelphia, published by the author.

Delany, Martin R. and Robert Campbell (1969) *Search for a Place*, Ann Arbor: University of Michigan Press.

Demas, William G. (1965) *The Economics of Development in Small Countries with Special Reference to the Caribbean*, Montreal: McGill University Press.

Depestre, René (1987) 'Saludo y despedida a la negritud' in Manuel Moreno Fraginals (ed.) *Africa en América Latina*, 2nd edn, Mexico City: Editorial Siglo XXI.

Desmangles, Leslie G. (1992) *The Faces of the Gods: Vodou and Roman Catholicism in Haiti*, Chapel Hill: University of North Carolina Press.

DESPRES, LEO (1964) *Cultural Pluralism and Nationalist Politics in Guyana*, Chicago: Rand McNally.

DEW, EDWARD (1989) 'Suriname' in Abraham F. Lowenthal (ed.) *Latin America and Caribbean Contemporary Record*, vol. VI, New York: Holmes and Meier.

——, (1990) 'Suriname: Transcending Ethnic Politics the Hard Way' in Gary Brana-Shute (ed.) *Resistance and Rebellion in Suriname*, Williamsburg: College of William and Mary.

DHARAM, GHAI (1988) *Labour and Development in Rural Cuba*, London: Macmillan Caribbean.

DÍAZ, ANTONIO AJA (1996) 'El proceso migratorio externo de Cuba: un balance de los años noventa' in *Emigración cubana*, Centro de Estudios de Alternativas Políticas, Havana: Universidad de Havana.

DÍAZ-BRIQUETS, SERGIO (1983) *The Health Revolution in Cuba*, Austin: University of Texas Press.

DÍAZ SANTANA, MIRIAM (1980) *Población y educación en la República Dominicana*, Estudio no.7, Santo Domingo: Instituto de Estudios de Problemas y Desarollo.

DICKEY, T. M. (1981) 'The Puerto Rican Wage Rate Subsidy for Agricultural Labor', Ann Arbor: University of Michigan Microfilms.

DIETZ, JAMES L. (1986) *Economic History of Puerto Rico: Institutional Change and Capitalist Development*, Princeton: Princeton University Press.

DIP, CARLOS (1976) 'Tirso Sprockel and Higher Education in the Netherlands Antilles', *Caribbean Education Bulletin*, 3, no.3, pp.431–45.

Dirección Política de las Fuerzas Armadas Revolucionarias (1983) *Historia de Cuba*, Havana.

DIRKS, R. (1975) 'Ethnicity and Ethnic Group Relations in the British Virgin Islands' in *The New Ethnicity: Perspectives from Ethnology*, St Paul, Minnesota: West Publishing.

Diversidad cultural y tensión regional: América Latina y el Caribe (1993) Co-ord., Francine Jácome, Caracas: INVESP/Ed. Nueva Sociedad.

DO NASCIMENTO, ABDIAS (1989) *Brazil: Mixture or Massacre?* Dover, Massachusetts: Majority Press; first published 1979.

DOBSON, NARDA (1973) *A History of Belize*, London: Longman Caribbean.

DOENITZ, KARL (1959) *Memoirs: Ten Years and Twenty Days*, London: Weidenfeld.

DOHERTY, WILLIAM C. (1994) 'NAFTA and the Caribbean Worker' in JTURDC (Joint Trade Union Research and Development Council), *Gatt and Nafta: The Implication for the Caribbean*, Kingston: JTURDC.

DOMÍNGUEZ, JAIME DE JESÚS (1986) *La dictadura de Heureaux*, Santo Domingo: Editora de la Universidad Autónoma de Santo Domingo.

DOMÍNGUEZ, JORGE I. (1978) *Cuba: Order and Revolution*, Cambridge, Massachusetts: Harvard University Press.

——, (1982a) *Cuba: Internal and International Affairs*, Beverly Hills: Sage.

——, (1982b) 'Revolutionary Politics: The New Demands for Orderliness' in Jorge I. Domínguez, *Cuba: Internal and International Affairs*, Beverly Hills: Sage.

——, (1995) 'The Caribbean in a New International Context: Are Freedom and Peace a Threat to its Security?' in Anthony T. Bryan (ed.) *The Caribbean: New*

Dynamics in Trade and Political Economy, New Brunswick, NJ: Transaction Publishers/ North South Center.

——, (1997) 'The Powers, the Pirates, and International Norms and Institutions in the American Mediterranean' in Joseph Tulchin, Andrés Serbín and Rafael Hernández (eds) *Cuba and the Caribbean: Regional Issues in the Post-Cold War Era*, Wilmington: Scholarly Books.

DOMÍNGUEZ, JORGE I. and ABRAHAM LOWENTHAL (eds) (1996) *Constructing Democratic Governance*, Baltimore: Johns Hopkins University Press.

DOMÍNGUEZ, JORGE I. *et al.* (eds) (1993) *Democracy in the Caribbean: Political Economic and Social Perspectives*, Baltimore: Johns Hopkins University Press.

DOMÍNGUEZ, MARÍA ISABEL (1996) 'La mujer jóven en los 90', *Temas* 5, Nueva Epoca.

'Dominican Republic: Religion.' (1989) Library of Congress online at http://lcweb2.loc.gov/cgi-bin/query/r?frd/cstdy:@field(DOCID+do0045).

DOOKERAN, WINSTON C. (ed.) (1996a) *Choices and Change: Reflections on the Caribbean*, Washington, DC: Inter-American Development Bank.

——, (1996b) 'Crosscurrents in Caribbean Policy Analysis' in Winston C. Dookeran (ed.) *Choices and Change: Reflections on the Caribbean*, Washington, DC: Inter-American Development Bank.

DOOKHAN, ISAAC (1981) 'The Expansion of Higher Educational Opportunities in the United States Virgin Islands', *Journal of Negro Education*, 50, no.1, pp.15–25.

——, (1994) *A History of the Virgin Islands of the United States*. Mona: Canoe Press.

DORSAINVILLE, J. C. (1922) *Le problème de l'enseignement primaire en Haïti*, Port-au-Prince: Imprimerie Centrale.

DOUGLASS, LISA (1992) *The Power of Sentiment: Love, Hierarchy, and the Jamaican Family Elite*, Boulder: Westview Press.

D'OYLEY, VINCENT and REGINALD MURRAY (eds) (1979) *Development and Disillusion in Third World Education, with Emphasis on Jamaica*, Toronto: Ontario Institute of Studies in Education.

DRAKES, FRANCIS M. (1991) 'The People's Association, 1903–21', *History Gazette*, 36.

DU COUDRAY, FELIX SERVIO (1976) *Los 'Gavilleros' del Este: Una Epopeya Calumniada*, Santo Domingo: Universidad Autónoma de Santo Domingo.

Du Sort des Indigènes dans les Colonies d'Exploitation (1905) Paris: L. Boyer.

DUANY, JORGE (1989) 'The Cuban Community in Puerto Rico', *Ethnic and Racial Studies*, 12, 1, pp.36–46.

DUARTE, ISIS *et al.* (1982) *Women and Social Production in the Caribbean*, Seminar sponsored by Institute of Development Studies, University of Sussex, and CEREP, University of Puerto Rico, Río Piedras, Puerto Rico.

DUARTE, ISIS, CLARA BÁEZ *et al.* (1989) *Población y condición de la mujer en República Dominicana*, Santo Domingo: Instituto de Estudios de Población y Desarollo, Estudio 6.

DUARTE, ISIS and RAMÓN TEJADA HOLGUÍN (1995) *Los hogares dominicanos: el mito de la familia ideal y los tipos de jefatura de familia*, Santo Domingo: Institututo de Estudios de Población y Desarrollo, PROFAMILIA.

DuBois, W. E. B. (1919) 'The Pan-African Congress', *Crisis*, XVII, 6.

Duncan, W. Raymond (1985) *The Soviet Union and Cuba: Interests and Influences*, New York: Praeger.

Dunn, H. S. (ed.) (1995) *Globalization, Communications and Caribbean Identity*, New York: St Martins Press.

Dunn, L. L. (1991) *Women Organizing for Change in Caribbean Free Zones*, The Hague: Institute of Social Studies.

Dunn, Waldo Hilary (1961–63) *James Anthony Froude: A Biography*, 2 vols, Oxford: Oxford University Press.

Eaton, George (1987) *Concept and Model of Political Unionism*, Caribbean Labour Series, 13, Curaçao: CARISFORM.

——, (n.d.) *Three Decades of Unionism in Jamaica*, mimeograph, Mona: Main Library, UWI.

Eddy, P. H. Sabogal and S. Walden (1988) *The Cocaine Wars*, New York: Norton.

L'Education en Guadeloupe (1986), Conseil General de la Guadeloupe.

Eisner, Gisela (1974) *Jamaica, 1830–1930: A Study of Economic Growth*, Westport: Greenwood Press.

Elkins, W. F. (1970) 'A Source of Black Nationalism in the Caribbean: The Revolt of the British West Indies Regiment at Taranto, Italy', *Science and Society*, XXXIII, 2, pp.99–103.

——, (1972) 'Hercules and the Society of Peoples of African Origin', *Caribbean Studies*, XI, 4, pp.47–59.

Elliot, A. Randle (1940) 'European Colonies in the Western Hemisphere', *Foreign Policy Reports*, 16, pp.138–48.

Ellis, A. B. (1885) *The History of the First West India Regiment*, London: Chapman and Hall.

Ellis, Keith (1973) 'Nicolás Guillén at Seventy', *Caribbean Quarterly*, 19, 1.

Ely, Roland (1963) *Cuando reinaba su majestad el azúcar*, Buenos Aires: Editorial Sudamericana.

Emmanuel, Patrick (1993) *Governance and Democracy in the Commonwealth Caribbean: An Introduction*, Cave Hill: Institute for Social and Economic Research, UWI.

Epstein, Erwin (ed.) (1970) *Politics and Education in Puerto Rico: A Documentary Survey of the Language Issue*, New Jersey: Scarecrow Press.

——, (1987) 'The Perils of Paternalism: The Imposition of Education on Cuba by the United States', *American Journal of Education*, 96, no.1, pp.1–23.

Ericksen, E. Gordon (1962) *The West Indies Population Problem: Dimensions for Action*, Lawrence, Kansas: University of Kansas Press.

Erisman, H. Michael (1992) *Pursuing Post-dependency Politics: South-South Relations in the Caribbean*, Boulder: Lynne Rienner.

Espín Guillois, Vilma (1990) *La mujer en Cuba, familia y sociedad*, Havana: Imprenta Central de la FAR.

——, (1999) *Informes Centrales de los Congresos de la Federación de Mujeres Cubanas*, Havana: Imprenta Central de la FAR.

ESPINAL, ROSARIO (1988) 'The Dominican Working Class: Labour Control under Trujillo and After' in Malcolm Cross and Gad Heuman (eds) *Labour in the Caribbean: From Emancipation to Independence*, London: Macmillan Caribbean.

'Establishment of a Caribbean Development and Co-operation Committee', 13 May 1975 (1974–5) in *Economic Commission for Latin America. Annual Report* (10 March 1974–6 May 1975), United Nations E/ECLA/989/Rev. 1, pp.156–7, 247–8.

Europa Yearbook (1995) London: Europa Publications.

EVES, C. WASHINGTON (1893) *The West Indies*, 3rd edn, London: Sampson Low, Marston.

'Factors Affecting the Participation of Caribbean Countries in the Free Trade Area of the Americas' (1995) LC/CAR/G.459, Port of Spain, Trinidad: UN/ECLAC Sub-Regional Office.

FAGEN, RICHARD R. (1969) *The Transformation of Political Culture in Cuba*, Stanford: Stanford University Press.

——, (ed.) (1979) *Capitalism and the State in U.S.-Latin American Relations*, Stanford: Stanford University Press.

FALCÓN, LUIS NIEVES (1965) *Recruitment to Higher Education in Puerto Rico, 1940–1960*, Río Piedras: Editorial Universitaria de Puerto Rico.

FARER, TOM (ed.) (1999) *Transnational Crime in the Americas*, New York: Routledge.

FARRUGIA, L. (1979) 'Luttes politiques et ouvrières en Guadeloupe de 1946 à 1978', *L'Historial Antillais/Société Dajani*, 6, pp.136–80.

FAURIOL, GEORGES A. and G. PHILIP HUGHES (eds) (1995) *U.S.-Caribbean Relations into the 21st Century*, policy paper on the Americas, vol. VI, Study 4, Washington, DC: CSIS Americas Program.

'Feminismo y la ideología cubana', (1993) *Novedades CAFRA*, 1–2, pp.11, 16.

Fempress (1995) 'Especial Mujeres Negras', Santiago (special issue).

FEQUIERE, MAGALI ROY (1996) 'Luis Palés Matos, Margot Arce and the Black Poetry Debate', *Centro* VIII, I and 2.

FERGUS, HOWARD A. (1994) *Montserrat: History of a Colony*, London: Macmillan Caribbean.

FERNÁNDEZ, CARMEN LARA (1946) *Historia del feminismo en la República Dominicana*, Ciudad Trujillo: Imprenta Arte y Cine.

FERNÁNDEZ, NANCY (1993) 'La ciencia y la técnica en la batalla por el desarrollo económico y social', mimeograph, in *Encuentro continental: la mujer cubana en los noventa. Realidades y desafíos, un encuentro solidario*, Havana.

FERNÁNDEZ FIGUEROA, ENRIQUE JUAN DE DÍOS (1995) *La historia como condicionante del territorio: el caso de Cuba*, Madrid: Grafinat.

FERRÉ, ROSARIO (1998) 'Puerto Rico, USA', *New York Times*, 19 March.

FITCHEN, EDWARD (1972) 'Alex E. Fraye and Cuban Education 1898–1906', *Revista Interamericana* 2 no.1, pp.123–49.

FITZGERALD, FRANK T. (1989) 'The Reform of the Cuban Economy, 1976–86', *Journal of Latin American Studies*, 21, no.2.

FONER, NANCY (1987) *New Immigrants in New York*, New York: Columbia University Press.

Foreign Broadcast Information Service (1991) *Latin America – Cuba: Fourth Congress of the Cuban Communist Party*, 15 October.

Foreign Policy Association (1935) *Problemas de la nueva Cuba*, New York: Foreign Policy Association.

Forum Quarterly, March 1932.

FOSTER, CHARLES R. and ALBERT VALDMAN (eds) (1984) *Haiti – Today and Tomorrow: An Interdisciplinary Study*, Lanham: University Press of America.

FRANK, FRANCINE (1974) 'Language and Education in the Leeward Netherlands Antilles', *Caribbean Studies*, 13, no.4, pp.111–17.

FRASER, CARY (2000) 'The "New Frontier" of Empire in the Caribbean: The Transfer of Power in British Guiana, 1961–1964', *The International History Review*, XXII, 3, pp.584–610.

FRIEDLANDER, H. E. (1944) *Historia económica de Cuba*, Havana: Jesús Montero.

FRUCHT, RICHARD (1967) 'A Caribbean Social Type: Neither "Peasant" nor "Proletarian"', *Social and Economic Studies*, 16, no.3, pp.295–301.

FÜLLBERG-STOLBERG, CLAUS (1988) '"The Slums of the Empire", Die soziale Lage der ländlichen und städtischen Unterschichten Jamaikas während der 1930er Jahre', *Uni. Zeitschrift der Universität Hannover. Mitteilungsblatt der Hannoverschen Hochschulgemeinschaft* 1, pp.32–8.

——, (1989) 'British Colonial Policy and the Great Depression: The Case of Jamaica', *Journal of Caribbean History*, 23, no.2, pp.142–62.

——, (ed.) (1990a) *Jamaica 1938: The Living Conditions of the Urban and Rural Poor: Social Surveys*, Mona: UWI.

——, (1990b) 'Britische Kolonialpolitik und Weltwirtschaftskrise. Das Beispiel Jamaika 1929–1945' in Helmut Bley (ed.) *Die Weltwirtschaftskrise der 30er Jahre in der Dritten Welt. Sonderfall oder Einstieg in die Strukturkrise der Gegenwart*, Hannover, pp.170–92.

——, (1992) 'Plantation Economy, Peasantry and the Land Settlement Schemes of the 1930s and 1940s in Jamaica' in Claus Füllberg-Stolberg and Swithin Wilmot (eds) *Plantation Economy, Land Reform and the Peasantry in a Historical Perspective: Jamaica 1838–1980*, Kingston: Friedrich Ebert Stiftung.

FÜLLBERG-STOLBERG, CLAUS and SWITHIN WILMOT (eds) (1992) *Plantation Economy, Land Reform and the Peasantry in a Historical Perspective: Jamaica 1838–1980*, Kingston: Friedrich Ebert Stiftung.

FURNIS, EDGAR S. (1950) 'American Wartime Objectives in Latin America', *World Politics*, 2, pp.373–89.

GABRIEL, JÜRG MARTIN (1988) *The American Conception of Neutrality after 1941*, Basingstoke: Macmillan Press.

GAILLARD, ROGER (1981) *Premier écrasement de cacoisme*, Port-au-Prince: Imprimerie Le Natal and Les Presses Nationales.

GALBRAITH, JOHN KENNETH (1979) *The Nature of Mass Poverty*, Cambridge, Massachusetts: Harvard University Press.

GALÍNDEZ, JESÚS (1973) *The Era of Trujillo: Dominican Dictator*, Russell Fitzgibbon (ed.), Arizona: University of Arizona Press.

GALLART, MARY FRANCES (1997) 'Las primarias de la Alcaldesa: apoderamiento femenino en Guayama, 1952' in Mario R. Cancel (ed.) *Historia y género: Vidas y relatos de mujeres en el Caribe*, San Juan: Asociación Puertorriqueña de Historiadores y Postdata.

GALVIN, MILES (1979) *The Organized Labour Movement in Puerto Rico*, London: Associated University Press.

GANNON, MICHAEL (1990) *Operation Drumbeat: The Dramatic True Story of Germany's First U-boat Attacks Along the American Coast in World War II*, New York: Harper.

GARCÍA, GERVASIO and ÁNGEL QUINTERO RIVERA (1982) *Desafío y solidaridad: breve historia del movimiento obrero puertorriqueño*, Río Piedras: Ediciones Huracán.

GARCÍA COLL, CYNTHIA and MARÍA LOURDES MATTEI (eds) (1989) *The Psychosocial Development of Puerto Rican Women*, New York: Praeger.

GARCÍA DOMÍNGUEZ, BERNARDO (1988) 'Garvey and Cuba' in Rupert Lewis and Patrick Bryan, (eds) *Garvey: His Work and Impact*, Mona: Institute of Social and Economic Research, UWI.

GARCÍA MÁRQUEZ, G. (1994) *Collected Stories*, New York: Harper Perennial.

GARCÍA MUÑIZ, HUMBERTO (1986) *Boots, Boots, Boots: Intervention, Regional Security and Militarization in the Eastern Caribbean*, Río Piedras: University of Puerto Rico.

——, (1988) *La estrategia de Estados Unidos y la militarización del Caribe*, Río Piedras: Instituto de Estudios del Caribe, Universidad de Puerto Rico.

——, (1996) 'The South Porto Rico Sugar Company: The History of a U.S. Multinational Corporation in Puerto Rico and the Dominican Republic, 1900–1921', Ph.D. dissertation, Columbia University.

GARCÍA-PASSALACQUA, JUAN M. (1984) *Puerto Rico: Equality and Freedom At Issue*, New York: Praeger.

GARRATY, JOHN A. (1986) *The Great Depression: An Inquiry into the Causes, Course and Consequences of the Worldwide Depression of the Nineteen-Thirties, As Seen By Contemporaries and in the Light of History*, New York: Harcourt Brace Jovanovich.

GARVEY, AMY JACQUES (ed.) (1923) *The Philosophy and Opinions of Marcus Garvey, or, Africa for the Africans*, II, Dover, Massachusetts: Majority Press; reprinted 1986.

——, (1963) *Garvey and Garveyism*, Kingston: A. J. Garvey.

——, (1991) 'On Langston Hughes: I Am a Negro – and Beautiful' in Tony Martin (ed.) *African Fundamentalism: A Literary and Cultural Anthology of Garvey's Harlem Renaissance*, Dover, Massachusetts: Majority Press.

GARVEY, MARCUS (1991) 'African Fundamentalism' in Tony Martin (ed.) *African Fundamentalism: A Literary and Cultural Anthology of Garvey's Harlem Renaissance*, Dover, Massachusetts: Majority Press.

GASTMANN, ALBERT (1971) 'The Politics of Surinam' in T. G. Mathews and F. M. Andic (eds) *Politics and Economics in the Caribbean*, Río Piedras: Institute of Caribbean Studies, University of Puerto Rico.

GAUTIER MAYORAL, CARMEN, ÁNGEL I. RIVERA ORTÍZ and IDSA ALEGRÍA ORTEGA (eds) (1990) *Puerto Rico en la economía política del Caribe*, Río Piedras: Centro de Investigaciones Sociales, Universidad de Puerto Rico & Huracán.

GAUTREAU, JULIO (1986) *Vicentico: Heroe y martir dos veces*, Santo Domingo: Biblioteca Nacional.

GAZTAMBIDE, ANTONIO (1986) 'The Road to Developmentalism: The Transition from the Good Neighbor to the Good Partner in U.S.–Latin American Policy, 1946 –54', Ph.D. dissertation, Princeton University.

——, (1989) 'Camino al desarrollismo: Puerto Rico y la Comisión del Caribe, 1946–1953', *Cuadernos de CENDES*, 12, 109–21.

——, (1991) 'Hacia una historia social de las relaciones interamericanas: el camino al desarrollismo: 1946–1960', *Revista de Ciencias Sociales*, XXX, 1,1 [1993], pp.29–55.

——, (1996a) 'La invención del Caribe en el siglo XX (Las definiciones del Caribe como problema histórico y metodológico)', *Revista Mexicana del Caribe*, I, 1, pp.74–96.

——, (1996b) 'La revolución cultural mundial' in Antonio Gaztambide Géigel and Silvia Alvarez Curbelo (eds) *Historias vivas: Historiografía puertorriqueña contemporánea*, San Juan: Asociación de Historiadores de Puerto Rico.

GAZTAMBIDE GÉIGEL, ANTONIO and SILVIA ALVAREZ CURBELO (eds) (1996) *Historias vivas: Historiografía puertorriqueña contemporánea*, San Juan: Asociación de Historiadores de Puerto Rico.

GELLMAN, IRWIN F. (1979) *Good Neighbor Diplomacy*, Baltimore: Johns Hopkins University Press.

GEORGES, EUGENIA (1990) *The Making of a Transnational Community: Migration, Development and Cultural Change in the Dominican Republic*, New York: Columbia University Press.

GILL, HENRY S. (1995) *The Association of Caribbean States: Prospects for a Quantum Leap?* North-South Agenda Paper 11, Coral Gables, Florida: North-South Center, University of Miami.

——, (1997) 'CARICOM and Hemispheric Trade Liberalization' in Ana Julia Jatar and Sidney Weintraub (eds) *Integrating the Hemisphere: Perspectives from Latin America and the Caribbean*, Washington, DC: Inter-American Dialogue.

GILL, MARGARET (1982) 'Women, Work and Development in Barbados, 1946–1970' in *Women and Social Production in the Caribbean*, Final Report of Seminar sponsored by the Institute of Development Studies, University of Sussex, and CEREP, Río Piedras.

GILMORE, JOHN (1995) *Glimpses of Our Past: A Social History of the Caribbean in Postcards*, Kingston: Ian Randle.

GIRVAN, NORMAN (1973) 'The Development of Dependency Economics in the Caribbean and Latin America: Review and Comparison', *Social and Economic Studies*, 22, no.1.

——, (1975) *Aspects of the Political Economy of Race in the Caribbean and in the Americas*, Working Paper, 7, Mona: Institute of Social and Economic Research, UWI.

GIRVAN, NORMAN and MIGUEL CEARA HATTON (1998) *Caricom, Central America and the Free Trade Agreement of the Americas*, Kingston: Friedrich Ebert Stiftung.

GIRVAN, NORMAN and OWEN JEFFERSON (eds) (1975) *Readings in the Political Economy of the Caribbean*, Kingston: New World Group.

GLADWELL, M. (1996) 'Louis Farrakhan's journey', *Washington Post*, National Weekly Edition, 22–28 January, pp.6–8.

GLAZIER, STEPHEN D. (1980) 'Pentecostal Exorcism and Modernization in Trinidad' in Stephen D. Glazier, ed., *Perspectives on Pentecostalism: Case Studies from the Caribbean and Latin America*, Washington, DC: University Press of America.

——, (1983) *Marchin' the Pilgrims Home: Leadership and Decision-Making in an Afro-Caribbean Faith*, Westport: Greenwood Press.

GLEIJESES, PIERO (1978) *The Dominican Crisis: The 1965 Constitutional Revolt and American Intervention*, Baltimore: Johns Hopkins University Press.

GMELCH, GEORGE (1992) *Double Passage: The Lives of Caribbean Migrants Abroad and Back Home*, Ann Arbor: University of Michigan Press.

GOBIN, S. (ed.) (1992) *The Canadian-Caribbean Connection*, Halifax: Carindo Cultural Association.

GOFF, FRED and MICHAEL LOCKER (1969) 'The Violence of Domination: U.S. Power and the Dominican Republic' in I. L. Horowitz *et al.*, *Latin American Radicalism*, New York: Vintage Books.

GÓMEZ, PETRONILA ANGÉLICA (1952) *Contribución para la historia del feminismo dominicano*, Ciudad Trujillo: Editorial Librería Dominicana.

GONZÁLEZ, JOSÉ LUIS (1981) 'Literatura e identidad nacional en Puerto Rico' in *Puerto Rico: Identidad nacional y clases sociales*, Río Piedras: Ediciones Huracán.

——, (1989) *El país de cuatro pisos*, Río Piedras: Ediciones Huracán.

GONZALEZ, NANCIE L. (1988) *Sojourners of the Caribbean: Ethnogenesis and Ethnohistory of the Garifuna*, Urbana: University of Illinois Press.

GONZÁLEZ NUÑEZ, GERARDO (1991) *El Caribe en la política exterior de Cuba (Balance de 30 años: 1959–1989)* Santo Domingo: Centro de Investigación y Promoción Social.

GONZÁLEZ VALES, LUIS E. (1998) 'The Puerto Rican Campaign Revisited: A Splendid Little War', Working Paper #85, San Germán: Caribbean Institute and Study Center for Latin America, Inter-American University of Puerto Rico.

GONZÁLES-WHIPPLER, MIGENE (1995) 'Santería: Its Dynamics and Multiple Roots' in Anthony M. Stevens-Arroyo and Andres I. Pérez y Mena (eds), *Enigmatic Powers: Syncretism with African and Indigenous Peoples' Religions among Latinos*, New York: Bildner Center for Western Hemisphere Studies.

GOOCH, CHERYL RENEE (1995) 'Loitering on Colonial Premises after Closing Time: An Analysis of Television Programming Policy in Barbados', in H. S. Dunn (ed.) *Globalization, Communications and Caribbean Identity*, New York: St Martins Press.

GOODHART, PHILIP (1965) *50 Ships that Saved the World: The Foundations of the Anglo-American Alliance*, New York: Doubleday.

GORDON, DEREK (1987) *Class, Status and Social Mobility in Jamaica*, Mona: Institute of Social and Economic Research, UWI.

GORDON, ERNLE P. (1988) 'Garvey and Black Liberation Theology' in Rupert Lewis and Patrick Bryan (eds) *Garvey: His Work and Impact*, Mona: Institute of Social and Economic Research and Extra-Mural Studies, UWI.

GOSLINGA, CORNELIS CH. (1979) *A Short History of the Netherlands Antilles and Surinam*, The Hague: Martinus Nijhoff.

——, (1990) *The Dutch in the Caribbean and Surinam 1791–1942*, Assen: Gorcum.

GOSNER, PAMELA (1982) *Caribbean Georgian: The Great and Small Houses of the Caribbean*, Washington, DC: Three Continents Press.

Governance and Democratic Development in Latin America and the Caribbean (1997), New York: United Nations Development Programme.

GRAHAM, W. (1997) 'Getting to Know the Volcano', *New Yorker*, 17 February, pp.43–6.

Great Britain, Colonial Office (1947) *Development and Welfare in the West Indies, 1945–46: Report by Sir John McPherson, Comptroller …*, London: HMSO.

——, (1958) *Development and Welfare in the West Indies, 1957: Report by Sir Stephen Luke, Comptroller …*, London: HMSO.

Great Britain, Parliament (1930) *Report of Sugar Commission* (Lord Olivier) Cmd. 3517, London: HMSO.

——, (1938) *Report of the Commission on Trinidad and Tobago Disturbances 1937*, Cmd. 5641, London: HMSO.

——, (1939) *Report by Major C. St J. Orde Browne on Labour Conditions in the West Indies*, Cmd. 6070, London: HMSO.

——, (1940) *Statement of Policy on Colonial Development and Welfare*, Cmd. 6175, London: HMSO.

——, (1940–1) *Parliamentary Debates*, Hansard Commons vol. 374, cols. 68–9, London: HMSO.

——, (1941) *United Kingdom–United States of America Agreement to Lease Bases*, Cmd. 6259, 27 March 1941, London: HMSO.

——, (1960) *The West Indies (Federation) Order in Council*, 1957, Statutory Instruments 1957 no.1364, London: HMSO.

GREAVES, EVELYN (1996) 'Labour in Independence' in Trevor Carmichael (ed.) *Barbados: 30 Years of Independence*, Kingston: Ian Randle.

GREEN, GARTH L. (1999) 'Blasphemy, Sacrilege, and Moral Degradation in the Trinidad Carnival: The Hallelujah Controversy of 1995' in John W. Pulis (ed.) *Religion, Diaspora, and Cultural Identity: A Reader in the Anglophone Caribbean*, Amsterdam: Gordon and Breach.

GREEN, HAMILTON (1987) *From Pain to Peace: Guyana 1953–64: A Series of Lectures Delivered at the Cyril Potter College of Education Between January and March 1986*. Georgetown: Tropical Airways.

GREEN, WILLIAM (1991) *British Slave Emancipation*, Oxford: Clarendon Press.

GREENBERG, DONALD S. (1962) 'US Destroyers for British Bases', *Proceedings of the U.S. Naval Institute*, 88, pp.70–83.

GREENE, ANNE. (1993) *The Catholic Church in Haiti: Political and Social Change*, East Lansing: Michigan State University Press.

GREENFIELD, SIDNEY (1961) 'Socioeconomic Factors and Family Form: A Barbadian Case Study', *Social and Economic Studies*, 10, no.1, pp.72–85.

GRELLIER, ROCHE (1891) *Etudes économiques sur Haïti*, Paris: A. Rousseau.

GRENIER, G. J. and A. STEPICK III (eds) (1992) *Miami Now! Immigration, Ethnicity, and Social Change*, Gainesville: University Presses of Florida.

GRIFFIN, CLIFFORD E. (1997) *Democracy and Neoliberalism in the Developing World: Lessons from the Anglophone Caribbean*, Aldershot: Ashgat.

GRIFFITH, IVELAW LLOYD (1995a) 'Caribbean Security: Retrospect and Prospect', *Latin American Research Review*, 30, no.2, pp.3–32.

——, (1995b) 'The Money Laundering Dilemma in the Caribbean', *Cuaderno de Trabajo*, 4.

——, (1997) *Drugs and Security in the Caribbean: Sovereignty under Siege*, University Park, Philadelphia: Penn State University Press.

GRIFFITH, IVELAW L. and BETTY N. SEDOC-DAHLBERG (eds) (1997) *Democracy and Human Rights in the Caribbean*, New York: Westview Press.

GRIMAL, HENRI (1978) *Decolonization: the British, French, Dutch and Belgian Empires*, London: Routledge and Kegan Paul.

GROSSMAN, L. S. (1998) 'Diet, Income and Agriculture in an Eastern Caribbean Village', *Human Ecology*, 26, no.1, p.21–42.

Grupo Cubano De Investigaciones Económicas (1963) *Labor Conditions in Communist Cuba*, Miami: University of Miami Press.

GUERRA Y SÁNCHEZ, RAMIRO (1970) *Azúcar y población en las Antillas*, Havana: Havana Imprenta Nacional; reprinted Havana: Editorial de Ciencias Sociales, 1976.

GUERRA Y SÁNCHEZ, RAMIRO *et al.*, (1952) *Historia de la nación cubana*, 10 vols, Havana: Editorial de la Nación Cubana.

GUERRANT, EDWARD O. (1950) *Roosevelt's Good Neighbor Policy*, Albuquerque: University of New Mexico.

GUEVARA, ERNESTO 'CHÉ' (1971) 'Man and Socialism in Cuba' in Bertram Silverman (ed.) *Man and Socialism in Cuba: The Great Debate*, New York: Athenaeum Press.

Guía de población de la República Dominicana (1988) Santo Domingo: PROFAMILIA.

GUILBERT, J. with G. AVERILL, E. BENOIT AND G. RABESS (1993) *Zouk: World Music in the West Indies*, Chicago: University of Chicago Press.

GUILLÉN, NICOLÁS (1972) *Obra Poética*, 2 vols, Havana: Unión de Escritores y Artistas de Cuba.

GUTIÉRREZ, CARLOS MARÍA (1992) *The Dominican Republic: Rebellion and Repression*. Translated by Richard Edwards, New York: Monthly Review Press.

GUTIÉRREZ, RAMÓN A. (1984) 'From Honor to Love: Transformations of the Meaning of Sexuality in Colonial Mexico' in Raymond T. Smith (ed.) *Kinship Ideology and Practice in Latin America*, Chapel Hill: University of North Carolina Press.

——, (1991) *When Jesus Came the Corn Mothers Went Away: Marriage, Sexuality and Power in New Mexico, 1500–1846*, Stanford: Stanford University Press.

GUZMÁN, JOSÉ MIGUEL (1980) *Evaluation of the Dominican Republic National Fertility Survey 1975*, WFS Scientific Reports, no.14. Vooburg, the Netherlands: International Statistical Institute.

HAGGERTY, RICHARD (ed.) (1991) *Dominican Republic and Haiti: Country Studies*, Washington, DC: Library of Congress.

HAILEY, MALCOLM (LORD) (1943) *Britain and her Dependencies*, London: Longman.

——, (1944) *The Future of Colonial Peoples*, 2nd edn, London: Royal Institute of International Affairs.

HAINES, GERALD K. (1977) 'Under the Eagle's Wing: The Franklin Roosevelt Administration Forges an American Hemisphere', *Diplomatic History*, 1, pp.373–88.

Haitian Women between Repression and Democracy (1995) Port-au-Prince: ENFOFANM Editions.

HALEBSKY, SANDOR and JOHN M. KIRK (eds) (1985) *Cuba: Twenty-Five Years of Revolution*, New York: Praeger.

HALL, NEVILLE A. T. (1985) 'Maritime maroons: *Grand marronage* from the Danish West Indies', *William and Mary Quarterly*, 3rd series, 42, 4, pp.476–98.

HALL, THOMAS E. and J. DAVID FERGUSON (1998) *The Great Depression: An International Disaster of Perverse Economic Policies*, Ann Arbor: University of Michigan Press.

HAMID, IDRIS (ed.) (1973) *Troubling of the Waters*, San Fernando, Trinidad: I. Hamid.

HAMMOND, S. A. (1941) *Education in Jamaica*, Kingston: Government Printing Office.

——, (1943a) *The Cost of Education*, Barbados: Advocate.

——, (1943b) *Education in Grenada*, St Georges: Government Printing Office.

——, (1943c) *Education in St Vincent*, Kingstown: Government Printing Office.

HAMSHERE, CYRIL (1972) *The British in the Caribbean*, Cambridge, Massachusetts: Harvard University Press.

Handbook of Jamaica (1931) Kingston: Government Printing Office.

Handbook of Jamaica (1938) Kingston: Government Printing Office.

Handbook of Trinidad and Tobago (1924) Port of Spain: Government Printing Office.

HANDLER, J. S. (1971) 'The History of Arrowroot and the Origin of Peasantries in the British West Indies', *Journal of Caribbean History*, 2, pp.46–93.

HANNA, A. J. (1956) *The Beginnings of Nyasaland and North-Eastern Rhodesia, 1859–1895*, Oxford: Oxford University Press.

HANSON, EARL PARKER (1955) *Transformation: The Story of Modern Puerto Rico*, New York: Simon and Schuster.

——, (1960) *Puerto Rico: Land of Wonders*, New York: Alfred A. Knopf.

HARDEN, SHEILA (ed.) (1985) *Small is Dangerous: Micro-States in a Macro World*, New York: St Martin's Press.

HAREVEN, TAMARA K. and RANDOLPH LANGENBACH (1978) *Amoskeag: Life and Work in an American Factory City*, New York: Pantheon Books.

HARRIS, JOSEPH E. (1994) *African-American Reactions to War in Ethiopia, 1936–1941*, Baton Rouge: Louisiana State University Press.

HARROD, JEFFREY (1972) *Trade Union Foreign Policy: A Study of British and American Trade Union Activities in Jamaica*, London: Macmillan.

HART, RICHARD (1998) *From Occupation to Independence: A Short History of the Peoples of the English-Speaking Caribbean Region*, London: Pluto Press.

——, (1999) *Towards Decolonisation*, Mona: Canoe Press.

HARTLYN, JONATHAN, (1993) 'The Dominican Republic: Contemporary Problems and Challenges' in Jorge I. Domínguez *et al.* (eds) *Democracy in the Caribbean: Political, Economic and Social Perspectives*, Baltimore: Johns Hopkins University Press.

HASLIP-VIERA, G. (1996) 'The Evolution of the Latino Community in New York City: Early Nineteenth Century to the Present' in G. Haslip-Viera and S. L. Baver (eds)

Latinos in New York: Communities in Transition, Notre Dame: University of Notre Dame Press.

HASLIP-VIERA, G. and S. L. BAVER (eds) (1996) *Latinos in New York: Communities in Transition*, Notre Dame: University of Notre Dame Press.

HAVEL, MARÍA DE LA LUZ (1993) 'El bloqueo de Estados Unidos a Cuba y sus efectos en la esfera del comercio exterior', mimeograph in *Encuentro continental: la mujer cubana en los noventa. Realidades y desafíos, un encuentro solidario*, Havana.

HEINL, ROBERT DEBS and NANCY GORDON HEINL (1978) *Written in Blood: The Story of the Haitian People, 1492–1971*, Boston: Houghton Mifflin.

——, (1996) *Written in Blood: The Story of the Haitian People, 1492–1995*, New York: University Press of America.

HELG, ALINE (1995) *Our Rightful Share: The Afro-Cuban Struggle for Equality, 1886–1912*, Chapel Hill: University of North Carolina Press.

HENDERSON, JOHN P. and HARRY A. REED (eds) (1989) *Studies in the African Diaspora*, Dover, Massachusetts: Majority Press.

HENDERSON, JULIA (1945) 'Foreign Labour in the United States during the War', *International Labour Review*, 52, pp.609–31.

HENNESSY, A (eds) (1992) *Intellectuals in the Twentieth-Century Caribbean*, 2 vols, London: Macmillan Caribbean.

HENRIKSON, ALAN K. (1998) 'Diplomacy and Small States in Today's World', the Dr. Eric Williams Memorial Lecture Series, 12th Lecture, Central Bank of Trinidad & Tobago.

HENRIQUES, FERNANDO (1953) *Family and Colour in Jamaica*, London: Eyre & Spottiswoode.

HENRY, FRANCES (1994) *The Caribbean Diaspora in Toronto: Learning to Live with Racism*, Toronto: University of Toronto Press.

HENRY, PAGET (1985) *Peripheral Capitalism and Underdevelopment in Antigua*, New Brunswick: Transaction Books.

HERNÁNDEZ RUEDA, LUPO (1983) 'La situatión laboral en la República Dominicana', *Forum 8*, ed. Frank Moya Pons, Santo Domingo.

HERRERA, CÉSAR (1955) *Las finanzas de la República Dominicana*, 2 vols, Ciudad Trujillo: Impresora Dominicana.

HIGMAN, BARRY W. (1972) 'The Chinese in Trinidad, 1806–1838', *Caribbean Studies*, 12, 3.

——, (1999) 'Reinventing the Wheel: The Jamaican Handcart from Roger Mais to *Cool Runnings*', Keynote address: Australian Association for Caribbean Studies, Third Biennial Conference, La Trobe University, Bundoora, Melbourne, Australia, July 5–7.

HILL, DONALD R. (1977) *The Impact of Migration on the Metropolitan and Folk Society of Carriacou, Grenada*, New York: Anthropological Papers of the American Museum of Natural History.

——, (1993) *Calypso Calaloo: Early Carnival Music in Trinidad*, Gainesville: University Press of Florida.

HILL, DONALD R. and R. ABRAMSON (1979) 'West Indian Carnival in Brooklyn', *Natural History*, (August–September), pp.72–85.

HILL, ERROL (1972) *The Trinidad Carnival: Mandate for a National Theatre*, Austin: University of Texas Press; reprinted London: New Beacon Books, 1997.

HILL, KIM QUAILE (1988) *Democracies in Crisis: Public Policy Responses to the Great Depression*, Boulder: Westview Press.

HILL, ROBERT (1971) *The Strengths of Black Families*, New York: Emerson Hall.

HINDEN, RITA (ed.) (1945) *Fabian Colonial Essays*, London: G. Allen & Unwin.

HINES, CALVIN (1968) 'The U.S. Diplomacy in the Caribbean during World War II', Ph.D. Diss., University of Texas, Austin.

HIRA, SANDEW (1983) 'Class Formation and Class Struggle in Suriname: Background and Development of the Coup D'etat' in Fitzroy Ambursley and Robin Cohen (eds) *Crisis in the Caribbean*, New York: Monthly Review Press.

——, (1987) 'The Evolution of the Social, Economic and Political Position of the East Indians of Suriname, 1873–1980' in David Dabydeen and Brinsley Samaroo (eds) *India in the Caribbean*, London: Hansib.

HOBSBAWN, ERIC (1987) *The Age of Empire, 1875–1914*, New York: Vintage Books.

——, (1994) *The Age of Extremes: A History of the World, 1914–91*; New York: Vintage Books, 2nd edn, 1996.

——, (1997) *The Age of Extremes: The Short Twentieth Century, 1914–91*, London: Abacus.

HOBSBAWM, ERIC and TERENCE RANGER (eds) (1983) *The Invention of Tradition*, Cambridge: Cambridge University Press.

HOEFTE, ROSEMARIJN (1990) 'The Usual Barbarity of the Asians?' in Gary Brana-Shute (ed.) *Resistance and Rebellion in Suriname*, Williamsburg: College of William and Mary.

HOEFTE, ROSEMARIJN and GERT OOSTINDIE (1991) 'The Netherlands and the Dutch Caribbean: Dilemmas of Decolonization' in Paul Sutton (ed.) *Europe and the Caribbean*, London: Macmillan.

HOETINK, H. (1972) *El pueblo dominicano, 1850–1900*, Santiago: Universidad Católica Madre y Maestra.

HOFFMANN, LÉON-FRANÇOIS (1984) 'Francophilia and Cultural Nationalism in Haiti' in Charles R. Foster and Albert Valdman (eds) *Haiti – Today and Tomorrow*, Lanham, Maryland: University Press of America.

——, (1985) 'Slavery and Race in Haitian Letters', *Caribbean Review*, 9, 2, pp.28–32, quoted in H. Hoetink, '"Race" and Color in the Caribbean' in Sidney W. Mintz and Sally Price (eds) *Caribbean Contours*, Baltimore: Johns Hopkins University Press.

HOLMES, LESLIE (ed.) (1981) *The Withering Away of The State? Party and State under Communism*, London: Sage.

HOLT, THOMAS C. (1992) *The Problem of Freedom: Race, Labor and Politics in Jamaica and Britain, 1832–1938*, Baltimore: Johns Hopkins University Press.

HOLZBERG, CAROL S. (1987) *Minorities and Power in a Black Society: The Jewish Community of Jamaica*, Baltimore: North-South Publishing Company.

HONYCHURCH, LENNOX (1986) *The Dominica Story: A History of the Island*, Roseau: The Dominica Institute.

HOOKER, JAMES R. (1967) *Black Revolutionary: George Padmore's Path from Communism to Pan Africanism*. London: Pall Mall Press.

——, (1975) *Henry Sylvester Williams: Imperial Pan-Africanist*, London: Collins.

HOROWITZ, MICHAEL (ed.) (1971) *Peoples and Cultures of the Caribbean*, Garden City, NY: Natural History Press.

HOSEIN, F. E. M. (1929) 'East Indians and Representative Government', *East Indian Weekly*, 12 January 1929.

HOUK, JAMES (1995) *Spirits, Blood and Drums: The Orisha Religion in Trinidad*, Philadelphia: Temple University Press.

HOWE, GLENFORD D. (1994) 'West Indian Blacks and the Struggle for Participation in the First World War', *Journal of Caribbean History*, 28, 1, pp.27–62.

HOYOS, F. A. (1978) *Barbados: A History from the Amerindians to Independence*, London: Macmillan.

——, (1988) *Grantley Adams and the Social Revolution*, London: Macmillan Caribbean.

HUMPHREYS, R. A. (1961) *The Diplomatic History of British Honduras*, Oxford: Oxford University Press.

HURWITZ, EMANUEL, JULIUS MENACKER and WARD WELDON (1987) *Educational Imperialism: American School Policy and the U. S. Virgin Islands*, New York: University Press of America.

HYATT, VERA LAWRENCE and REX NETTLEFORD (eds) (1995) *Race, Discourse and the Origin of the Americas*, Washington, DC: Smithsonian Institute.

IBARRA, JORGE (1995) *Cuba: 1898—1958: estructura* y *procesos sociales*, Havana: Editorial de Ciencias Sociales.

——, (1998) *Prologue to Revolution, Cuba, 1898–1958*, Boulder: Lynne Reinner.

IGLESIAS GARCÍA, FE (1993) 'Características de la inmigración espanola en Cuba' in Nicolás Sánchez Albornoz (ed.) *Españoles hacia América: La emigración en masa, 1880–1930*, Madrid: Alianza Editorial.

——, (1994) 'Contratados peninsulares para Cuba', *Anuario de Estudios Americanos*, 50, 2.

'L'Immigration Indienne', (1996) 'Journal Officiel de La Colonie, February 4, 1855', in Juliette Smeralda-Amon, *La question de l'immigration indienne dans son environment socio-economique Martiniquais, 1848–1900*, Paris: L'Harmattan.

INNIS, L. O. (1910) *Trinidad and Trinidadians*, Port of Spain: published by the author.

INSANALLY, RIYAD (1998) 'The ACS and the Regional Integration Process' in Association of Caribbean States, Trade, Transport and Tourism: 4th Ministerial Meeting, December 1998, Port of Spain, Trinidad: Association of Caribbean States.

Instituto de Ciencias Históricas, Academia de Ciencias de Cuba (1986) *La esclavitud en Cuba*, Havana: Editorial Academia de Ciencias.

International Labour Organisation (ILO) (1952), *Labour Policies in the West Indies*, Geneva: ILO.

——, (1978) *Record of Proceedings of, and Documents Submitted to ILO/DANDRA Regional Seminar: Wage Determination in English Speaking Countries*, ILO Labour Management Relations Series no.57, Geneva: ILO.

——, (1980) *Yearbook of Labour Statistics*, Geneva: ILO.

——, (1990) *Anuario de estadísticas del trabajo 1945–1989*, Geneva: ILO.

——, (1992) *Anuario 1992*, Geneva: ILO.

——, (1997) *Anuario 1997*, Geneva: ILO.

International Labour Organisation, Director-General (1997) *Report: The ILO, Standard Setting and Globalization*, International Labour Conference, 85th Session 1997, Geneva: ILO.

Iturraga, José E. (1951) *La estructura social y cultural de México*, Mexico City: Fondo de Cultura Económica.

Jackson, Jean (1982) 'Stresses affecting women and their families' in Joycelin Massiah (ed.) *Women and the Family*, Volume 2 of Phase 1 Research Papers, *Women in the Caribbean Project*, Cave Hill: Institute of Social and Economic Research, UWI.

Jacobs, Richard and Ian Jacobs (1979) *Grenada: The Route to Revolution*, Havana: Casa de las Américas.

Jácome, Francine (1993) 'Movimientos ambientales y cooperación en el Caribe' in Francine Jácome, Coord., *Retos de la cooperación ambiental: el caso del Caribe*, Caracas: INVESP/Ed. Nueva Sociedad.

——, (1994) 'Identidades nacionales y cooperación en la región del Caribe' in Daniel Mato, Coord., *Teoría y política de la construcción de identidades y diferencias en América Latina y el Caribe*, Caracas: UNESCO/Ed. Nueva Sociedad.

Jagan, Cheddi (1966) *The West on Trial: The Fight for Guyana's Freedom*, New York: International Publishers.

Jahn, Janheinz (1969) *Neo-African Literature: A History of Black Writing*, New York: Grove Press.

James, C. L. R. (1936) *Minty Alley*, London: New Beacon Books; reprinted 1971.

——, (1937) *World Revolution*, London: Secker and Warburg.

——, (1938a) *The Black Jacobins*, New York: Random House; reprinted 1963.

——, (1938b) *A History of Negro Revolt*, Chicago: Research Associates School Times; reprinted 1994.

——, (1963) *Beyond a Boundary*, London: Hutchinson.

James, Winston (1996) 'Afro-Puerto Rican Radicalism in the United States: Reflections on the Political Trajectories of Arturo Schomburg and Jesús Colón', *Centro*, VIII, 1 and 2, pp.92–127.

——, (1998) *Holding Aloft the Banner of Ethiopia*, New York: Verso.

Janelle, D. G. (ed.) (1992) *Geographical Snapshots of North America*, New York: Guilford Press.

Jatar, Ana Julia (1997) 'The Cuban Self-Employed: Emerging Capitalists or Land Rafters.' Paper presented to the Association for the Study of the Cuban Economy, Miami, 8 August.

Jatar, Ana Julia and Sidney Weintraub (eds) (1997) *Integrating the Hemisphere: Perspectives from Latin America and the Caribbean*, Washington, DC: Inter-American Dialogue.

Jeffries, Sir Charles (1956) *The Colonial Office*, New Whitehall Series, London: G. Allen and Unwin.

Jenks, Leland H. (1966) *Nuestra colonia de Cuba*, Havana: Edición Revolucionaria.

JIMÉNEZ, EMMANUEL and MARLAINE LOCKHEED (1995) 'Public and Private Secondary Education in Developing Countries', World Bank Discussion Paper, Washington, DC: World Bank.

JOACHIM, BENOIT (n.d.) *Les racines du sous-développement en Haïti*, Port-au-Prince: Imprimirie H. Deschamps.

JOHNSON, HOWARD (1977) 'The West Indies and the Conversion of the British Official Classes to the Development Idea', *Journal of Commonwealth and Comparative Politics*, 15, no.l.

——, (1978) 'The Political Uses of Commissions of Enquiry: The Imperial-Colonial West Indies Context – The Forster and Moyne Commissions', *Social and Economic Studies*, 27, no.3.

——, (1984a) 'The United States and the Establishment of the Anglo-American Caribbean Commission', *Journal of Caribbean History*, 19, 1, pp.26–47.

——, (1984b) 'The Anglo-American Commission and the Extension of American Influence in the British Caribbean, 1942–5', *Journal of Commonwealth and Comparative Politics*, 22, pp.180–203.

——, (1988) 'Bahamian Labor Migration to Florida in the Late Nineteenth and Early Twentieth Centuries', *International Migration Review*, 22, pp.84–103.

——, (1996) *The Bahamas: From Slavery to Servitude, 1783–1933*, Gainesville: University Presses of Florida.

JOHNSON, LAURIE (1995) 'Education and Cuba Libre 1898–1958', *History Today*, 45 no.8, pp.26–30.

JOHNSON, ROBERTA ANN (1980) *Puerto Rico: Commonwealth or Colony?* New York: Praeger.

JOHNSTON, H. H. (1920) *The Backward Peoples and our Relations With Them*, London: Oxford University Press.

JONES, JOSEPH M. (1944) 'Caribbean Laboratory: There We Can Learn the Potentials of U.S. Influence on World Colonial Policy', *Fortune*, 29, pp.124–8.

JOPLING, CAROL F. (1988) *Puerto Rican Houses in Sociohistorical Perspective*, Knoxville: University of Tennessee Press.

JOSEPH, C. L. (1971) 'The British West Indies Regiment, 1914–8', *Journal of Caribbean History*, 2, pp.94–124.

JUDD, DENIS (1968) *Balfour and the British Empire: A Study in Imperial Evolution*, London: Macmillan.

JULES, DIDACUS and DON ROJAS (eds) (n.d.) *Maurice Bishop: Selected Speeches, 1979–1981*, Havana: Casa de las Américas.

Junta Central de Planificación de Cuba (1971) *Censo, 1970*, Havana.

JUSTUS, JOYCE BENNETT (1981) 'Women's Role in West Indian Society' in Filomena Chioma Steady (ed.) *The Black Woman Cross-Culturally*, Cambridge, Massachusetts: Schenkman.

KADALIE, CLEMENTS (1970) *My Life and the ICU*, New York: Humanities Press.

KAMBON, KHAFRA (1988) *For Bread, Justice and Freedom: A Political Biography of George Weekes*, London: New Beacon.

KASINITZ, PHILIP (1992) *Caribbean New York: Black Immigrants and the Politics of Race*, Ithaca: Cornell University Press.

KEENAN, PATRICK J. (1869) *Report upon the State of Education in the Island of Trinidad*, Dublin: HMSO.

KELSHALL, G. T. M. (1988) *The U-Boat War in the Caribbean*, Port of Spain: Paria Publishing.

KERR, MADELINE (1952) *Personality and Conflict in Jamaica*, Liverpool: Liverpool University Press.

KETCHUM, RICHARD M. (1989) *The Borrowed Years: America on its Way to War, 1938–1941*, New York: Random House.

KHAN, AISHA (1997) 'Migration Narratives and Moral Imperatives: Local and Global in the Muslim Caribbean', *Comparative Studies of South Asia, Africa and the Middle East*, 17, no.1, pp.127–44.

KIMBALL, WARREN F. (1971) 'Lend-Lease and the Open Door: The Temptation of British Opulence, 1937–42', *Political Science Quarterly*, 86, pp.232–59.

KINDELBERGER, CHARLES P. (1973) *The World in Depression 1929–39*, Berkeley: University of California Press.

KIPLE, KENNETH F. (1984) *The Caribbean Slave: A Biological History*, Cambridge: Cambridge University Press.

KLAK, THOMAS (ed.) (1997) *Globalization and Neoliberalism: The Caribbean Context*, Lanham, Maryland: Rowman and Littlefield.

KLEIN, A. M. (1991) *Sugarball: The American Game, the Dominican Dream*, New Haven: Yale University Press.

KNIGHT, ALAN (1987) 'The Working Classes' in Eduardo Achetti *et al.* (eds) *Sociology of Development in Latin America*, New York: Monthly Review Press.

KNIGHT, FRANKLIN W. (1985) 'Jamaican Migrants and the Cuban Sugar Industry, 1900–1934' in M. Moreno Fraginals, F. Moya Pons, and S. L. Engerman (eds) *Between Slavery and Free Labor: The Spanish-Speaking Caribbean in the Nineteenth Century*, Baltimore: Johns Hopkins University Press.

——, (1989) 'Cuba: Politics and Society, 1898–1985' in Franklin W. Knight and Colin A. Palmer (eds) *The Modern Caribbean*, Chapel Hill: University of North Carolina Press.

——, (1990) *The Caribbean: The Genesis of a Fragmented Nationalism*, 2nd edn, New York: Oxford University Press.

——, (1993) 'Societies of the Caribbean' in Jorge I. Domínguez *et al.* (eds) *Democracy in the Caribbean: Political, Economic and Social Perspectives*, Baltimore: Johns Hopkins University Press.

——, (1995) *Race, Ethnicity, and Class: Forging the Plural Society in Latin America and the Caribbean*, Waco: Baylor University.

KNIGHT, FRANKLIN W. and COLIN A. PALMER (eds) (1989) *The Modern Caribbean*, Chapel Hill: University of North Carolina Press.

KNIGHT, MELVIN M. (1928) *The Americans in Santo Domingo*, New York: Vanguard Press.

——, (1939) *Los americanos en Santo Domingo*, Ciudad Trujillo: Ediciones de la Universidad de Santo Domingo.

KNOX, ARBUTHNOT JOHN GRAHAM (1962) 'Race Relations in Jamaica, 1833–1958: With

Special Reference to British Colonial Policy', Ph.D. dissertation, University of Florida.

KOMISAR, L. (1997) 'Drug Smugglers' Dutch Treat', *Wall Street Journal*, 29 May, A-18.

KUCZYNSKI, R. R. (1953) *Demographic Survey of the British Colonial Empire, vol.3, West Indian and American Territories*, London: Royal Institute of International Affairs.

KUMAR, RANJIT (1981) *Thoughts and Memories of Ranjit Kumar*, Port of Spain: Inprint Caribbean.

KURLANSKY, M. (1992) *A Continent of Islands: Searching for the Caribbean Destiny*, Reading, Massachusetts: Addison-Wesley.

KWAYANA, EUSI (1988) 'More than Survival: Afro-Guyanese and the Nation', Paper presented at the International Conference, Genesis of a Nation, II, Guyana, 1988.

LA GONAIVE, CACOS (1993) 'Haití: Una vacación en el paraíso del infierno' in Robin Morgan (ed.) *Mujeres del mundo*, Barcelona: Hacer.

LA GUERRE, JOHN GAFFAR (1971) 'The Moyne Commission and the West Indian Intelligentsia, 1938–1939', *Journal of Commonwealth Political Studies*, 9, pp.134–57.

——, (ed.) (1974) *Calcutta to Caroni: The East Indians of Trinidad*, Port of Spain: Longman.

——, (1983) *The Politics of Communalism: the Agony of the Left in Trinidad and Tobago, 1930–55*, St Augustine: Extra-Mural Studies Unit, UWI.

LA GUERRE, JOHN GAFFAR, BRINSLEY SAMAROO and GEORGE SAMMY (1973) *East Indians and the Present Crisis*, St Augustine: published by the authors.

LA MOTTA, GREGORY (1989) 'Working People and the Transfer of the Danish West Indies to the United States, 1916–7', *Journal of Caribbean History*, 23, no.2, pp.178–95.

LABROUSSE, E. (1962) *Fluctuaciones económicas e historia social*, Madrid: Editora Universitaria.

LACEY, T. (1977) *Violence and Politics in Jamaica, 1960–70*, Manchester: Manchester University Press.

LADNER, JOYCE A. (1971) *Tomorrow's Tomorrow: The Black Woman*, Garden City, NY: Doubleday.

LAGUERRE, MICHEL S. (1984) *American Odyssey: Haitians in New York City*, Ithaca: Cornell University Press.

——, (1989) *Voodoo and Politics in Haiti*, New York: St Martin's Press.

LAING, SAMUEL (1862) *Lecture on the Indo-European Languages and Races*, Calcutta.

LAL, VINAY (1996) 'The Limits of Pluralism, Fuzziness, and the Reification of Hinduism in a Diasporic Civilization: The Case of Trinidad and Guyana.' Paper presented at the Conference on Caribbean Culture, UWI, Mona, 3–6 March.

LAMMING, GEORGE (1981) Foreword to W. Rodney, *A History of the Guyanese Working People*, Baltimore: Johns Hopkins University Press.

——, (1985) Review of *Dance Jamaica: Cultural Definition and Artistic Discovery*, by Rex Nettleford, *Caribbean Contact*, September.

LANDRY, ROBERT (1988) *Haiti's elusive dream*, IDRC Reports, 17, no.1.

LANGER, WILLIAM L. (1947–8) 'Turning Point of the War: Political Problems of a Coalition', *Foreign Affairs*, 26, pp.73–89.

LANGER, WILLIAM L. and S. EVERETT GLEASON (1953) *The Undeclared War*, New York: Council on Foreign Relations.

LANGLEY, LESTER D. (1982) *The United States and the Caribbean in the Twentieth Century*, Athens, Georgia: University of Georgia Press.

LAQUEUR, THOMAS (1990) *Making Sex: Body and Gender from the Greeks to Freud*, Cambridge, Massachusetts: Harvard University Press.

LARGEY, M. (1995) 'Haiti and the French Caribbean' in P. Manuel *et al.* (eds) *Caribbean Currents: Caribbean Music from Rumba to Reggae*, Philadelphia: Temple University Press.

LARSON, E. M. and T. A. SULLIVAN (1987) 'Conventional Numbers in Immigration Research: The Case of the Missing Dominicans', *International Migration Review*, 21,4, pp.1474–97.

LARUFFA, ANTHONY L. (1980) 'Pentecostalism in Puerto Rican Society' in Stephen D. Glazier (ed.) *Perspectives on Pentecostalism: Case Studies from the Caribbean and Latin America*, Washington: University Press of America.

LASHLEY, LYNETTE (1995) 'Television and the Americanization of Trinbagonian Youth: A Study of Six Secondary Schools', in H. S. Dunn (ed.) *Globalization, Communications, and Caribbean Identity*. New York: St Martin's Press.

LASSERRE, GUY (1974) *Les Amériques du Centre: Méxique, Amérique centrale, Antilles, Guyanes*, Paris: Presses Universitaires de France.

LASSERRE, GUY and ALBERT MABILEAU (1972) 'The French Antilles and their Status as Overseas Departments' in Emanuel de Kadt (ed.) *Patterns of Foreign Influence in the Caribbean*, Oxford: Oxford University Press.

LAURENCE, K. O. (1994) *A Question of Labour: Indentured Immigration into Trinidad and British Guiana, 1875–1917*, Kingston: Ian Randle.

LAZARUS-BLACK, MINDIE (1990) 'Legitimate Acts and Illegitimate Encounters: the Development of Family Ideology and Structure in Antigua and Barbuda, West Indies', Ph.D. dissertation, University of Chicago. Published as *Legitimate Acts and Illegal Encounters: Law and Society in Barbuda and Antigua*, 1994, Washington, DC: Smithsonian Institution.

LE GRAND, CATHERINE C. (1995) 'Informal Resistance on a Dominican Sugar Plantation during the Trujillo Dictatorship', *Hispanic American Historical Review*, 75, 4.

LE RIVEREND, JULIO (1965) *Historia económica de Cuba*, Havana: Editora Universitaria.

LEE, J. M. and MARTIN PETTER (1982) *The Colonial Office, War and Development Policy: Organization and the Planning of a Metropolitan Initiative, 1939–1945*, London: published for the Institute of Commonwealth Studies.

LEIBOWITZ, ARNOLD H. (1989) *Defining Status: A Comprehensive Analysis of United States Territorial Relations*, Dordrecht: Kluwer Academic.

LEINER, MARVIN (1981) 'Two decades of educational change in Cuba', *Journal of Reading*, 25, 3, pp.202–14.

——, (1994) *Sexual Politics in Cuba*, Boulder: Westview Press.

LENT, J. A. (ed.) (1990a) *Caribbean Popular Culture*, Bowling Green, Ohio: Bowling Green State University Popular Press.

——, (1990b) *Mass Communications in the Caribbean*, Ames: Iowa State University Press.

LEOGRANDE, WILLIAM M. (1978) 'Continuity and Change in the Cuban Political Elite', *Cuban Studies/Estudios Cubanos*, 8, pp.1–31.

LEUTZE, JAMES R. (1977) *Bargaining for Supremacy: Anglo-American Naval Cooperation, 1937–41*, Chapel Hill: University of North Carolina Press.

LÉVESQUE, JACQUES (1978) *The USSR and the Cuban Revolution: Soviet Ideological and Strategical Perspectives, 1959–77*, New York: Praeger.

LEVINSON, JEROME and JUAN DE ONÍS (1970) *The Alliance that Lost Its Way*, Chicago: Quadrangle Books.

LEWIS, DAVID E. (1984) *Reform and Revolution in Grenada, 1950 to 1981*, Havana: Casa de las Américas.

——, (1996) 'Caribbean Regional Cooperation and Strategic Alliances' in Winston C. Dookeran (ed.) *Choices and Change: Reflections on the Caribbean*, Washington, DC: Inter-American Development Bank.

LEWIS, DAVID LEVERING (1981) *When Harlem Was in Vogue*, New York: Oxford University Press; reprinted 1989.

LEWIS, GORDON K. (1963) *Puerto Rico: Freedom and Power in the Caribbean*, New York: Monthly Review Press; reprinted 1974.

——, (1968) *The Growth of the Modern West Indies*, New York: Monthly Review Press.

——, (1983) *Main Currents in Caribbean Thought*, Baltimore: Johns Hopkins University Press.

——, (1985) *The Contemporary Caribbean: A General Overview*, Washington, DC: Wilson Center.

——, (1987) *Grenada: The Jewel Despoiled*, Baltimore: Johns Hopkins University Press.

LEWIS, PATRICK (1974) 'A Historical Analysis of the Development of the Union-Party System in the Commonwealth Caribbean, 1935-68', Ann Arbor: University of Michigan Microfilms.

LEWIS, PATRICK and KELVIN SINGH (1987) *Caribbean Labour History*, Curaçao: CARISFORM.

LEWIS, RUPERT (1998) *Walter Rodney's Intellectual and Political Thought*, Mona: The Press, UWI.

LEWIS, RUPERT and PATRICK BRYAN (eds) (1988) *Garvey: His Work and Impact*, Mona: Institute of Social and Economic Research and Extra-Mural Studies, UWI.

LEWIS, SYBIL and THOMAS G. MATHEWS (eds) (1967) *Caribbean Integration: Papers on Social, Political and Economic Integration*, Río Piedras: Institute of Caribbean Studies, University of Puerto Rico.

LEWIS, TORRENCE (1980) 'Compulsory Arbitration in Jamaica, 1975–79: The Development of Statutory Legislation and the Effects on Labour and Industrial Relations and the Jamaica Society', Caribbean Studies paper, Mona: UWI.

LEWIS, W. ARTHUR (1950a) 'The Industrialization of the British West Indies', *Caribbean Economic Review*, II.

——, (1950b) *Industrial Development in the Caribbean*, Port of Spain: Caribbean Commission.

——, (1954) *Economic Development with Unlimited Supplies of Labour*, Manchester School of Economics and Social Studies, no.22, University of Manchester.

——, (1977) *Labour in the West Indies: The Birth of a Workers' Movement*, with an Afterword by Susan Craig, London: New Beacon Books; first published London: Gollancz, 1939.

LEYBURN, JAMES G. (1941) *The Haitian People*, New Haven: Yale University Press.

Libro de nuestro siglo (1970) Barcelona: Montaner y Simon.

LLOVIÓ-MENÉNDEZ, JOSÉ LUIS (1988) *Insider: My Hidden Life as a Revolutionary in Cuba*, Toronto and New York: Bantam Books.

——, (1982) *A Third World Proletariat?* London: Allen & Unwin.

LOGAN, RAYFORD (1930) 'Education in Haiti', *Journal of Negro History*, 15, 4, pp.401–60.

LOMNITZ, LARISSA ADLER and MARISOL PÉREZ-LIZAUR (1987) *A Mexican Elite Family, 1820–1980*, Princeton: Princeton University Press.

LONG, EDWARD (1774) *The History of Jamaica*, 3 vols, London: T. Lowndes; reprinted New York: Arno Press, 1972.

LOOK LAI, WALTON (1993) *Indentured Labor, Caribbean Sugar*, Baltimore: Johns Hopkins University Press.

LÓPEZ SEGRERA, FRANCISCO (1979a) 'Algunos aspectos de la industria azucarera cubana, (1925–37)' in Juan Pérez de la Riva *et al.* (eds) *La república neocolonial*, vol. 2, Havana: Editorial de Ciencias Sociales.

——, (1979b) 'La economía y la política en la república neocolonial' in Juan Pérez de la Riva *et al.* (eds) *La república neocolonial*, vol. 2, Havana: Editorial de Ciencias Sociales.

LÓPEZ SPRINGFIELD, CONSUELO (ed.) (1997) *Daughters of Caliban: Caribbean Women in the Twentieth Century*, Bloomington: Indiana University Press.

LÓPEZ YUSTOS, ALFONSO (1985) *Historia documental de la educación en Puerto Rico, 1503–1970*, Puerto Rico: Sandemann.

LOUIS, WM. ROGER (1977) *Imperialism at Bay: The United States and the Decolonization of the British Empire, 1941–5*, London: Oxford University Press.

LOWENTHAL, ABRAHAM F. (ed.) (1989) *Latin America and Caribbean Contemporary Record*, vol. VI, New York: Holmes and Meier.

LOWENTHAL, DAVID (1961) 'Caribbean Views of Caribbean Land', *Canadian Geographer*, 5, pp.1–9.

LOWENTHAL, DAVID and LAMBROS COMITAS (1962) 'Emigration and Depopulation: Some Neglected Aspects of Population Geography', *Geographical Review*, 52, pp.195–210.

——, (eds) (1973) *Consequences of Class and Color: West Indian Perspectives*, Garden City, NY: Anchor.

LUCIANO, DINNYS (1997) 'Sexual and Reproductive Health of Women in the Caribbean', *CAFRA News*, 11, nos.1–2, pp.20; 30.

LUCRECE, ANDRÉ (1981) *Civilises et Energumenes*, Paris: Éditions Caribéenes.

LUNDAHL, MATS (1988) 'The Rise and Fall of the Haitian Labour Movement' in Malcolm Cross and Gad Heuman (eds) *Labour in the Caribbean: From Emancipation to Independence*, London: Macmillan Caribbean.

LUTJENS, SHERYL L. (1995) 'Reading between the Lines: Women, the State and Rectification in Cuba', *Latin American Perspectives*, 22, 2, pp.100–24.

LYNCH, HOLLIS R. (1967) *Edward Wilmot Blyden*, New York: Oxford University Press.

——, (1971) 'Pan-Negro Nationalism in the New World, Before 1862' in Okon E. Uya (ed.) *Black Brotherhood: Afro-Americans and Africa*, Lexington: D. C. Heath.

——, (ed.) (1978) *Selected Letters of Edward Wilmot Blyden*, Millwood, NY: KTO Press.

LYNCH, ROSLYN (1995) *Gender Segregation in the Barbados Labour Market, 1946–1980*, Mona: Consortium Graduate School, UWI.

MCAFEE, KATHY (1991) *Storm Signals: Structural Adjustment and Development Alternatives in the Caribbean*, London: Zed Books.

MCCOOL, G. (1996) 'Labor Group, Children's Letters Question Disney Practices. Manufacturing: Working Conditions in the Company's Overseas Subcontracting are Debated', 7 December, *Orange County Register*, A–1.

MCDANIEL, LORNA (1990) 'The Flying Africans: Extent and Strength of the Myth in the Americas', *Nieuwe West-Indische Gids/New West Indian Guide*, 64, 1 & 2, pp.28–40.

MACDONALD, SCOTT and ALBERT GASTMANN (1984) 'Mitterrand's Headache: The French Antilles in the 1980s', *Caribbean Review*, 13, 2, pp.19–21.

MCELVAINE, ROBERT S. (1984) *The Great Depression: America, 1929–39*, New York: Time Books.

MCGEE DEUTSCH, SANDRA (1989) 'Feminist Studies' in K. Lynn Stoner (ed.) *Latinas of the Americas*, New York: Garland.

MCKAY, LESLEY (1993) 'Women's Contribution to Tourism in Negril, Jamaica' in Janet H. Momsen (ed.) *Women and Change in the Caribbean*, Kingston: Ian Randle.

MCREYNOLD SMITH, FRANCES (1958) 'The Caribbean Commission: Prototype of Regional Cooperation' in A. Curtis Wilgus (ed.) *The Caribbean: British, Dutch, French, United States*, Gainesville: University of Florida Press.

MACMILLAN, MONA (1957) *The Land of Look Behind: A Study of Jamaica*, London: Faber & Faber.

MAHARAJ, RABINDRANATH R. (1977) *Death of a Guru*, London: Hodder & Stoughton.

MAINGOT, ANTHONY P. (1979) 'The Difficult Road to Socialism in the English-Speaking Caribbean' in Richard R. Fagen (ed.) *Capitalism and the State in U.S.-Latin American Relations*, Stanford: Stanford University Press.

——, (1984) 'Perceptions as Realities: The United States, Venezuela and Cuba in the Caribbean' in Heraldo Muñoz and Joseph Tulchin (eds) *Latin American Nations in World Politics*, Boulder: Westview Press.

——, (1989) 'Caribbean International Relations' in Franklin W. Knight and C. A. Palmer (eds) *The Modern Caribbean*, Chapel Hill: University of North Carolina Press.

——, (1993) 'The Offshore Caribbean' in A. Payne and P. Sutton (eds) *Modern Caribbean Politics*, Baltimore: Johns Hopkins University Press.

——, (1994a) *The United States and the Caribbean: Challenges of an Asymetrical Relationship*, London: Macmillan.

——, (1994b) 'Trends in U.S.-Caribbean Relations', *Annals of the American Academy of Political and Social Science*, 533.

——, (1996a) 'Haiti: Four Old and Two New Hypotheses' in Jorge I. Domínguez and Abraham Lowenthal (eds) *Constructing Democratic Governance*, Baltimore: Johns Hopkins University Press.

——, (1996b) 'Bucking the Trend: Offshore Secrecy Centres and the Role of Government', *Caricom PERSPECTIVES*, 66, pp.32–7.

——, (1997) 'The Sovereignty versus Security Paradox in the Caribbean' in Joseph Tulchin *et al.* (eds) *Cuba and the Caribbean*, Wilmington: SR Books.

——, (1999) 'The Decentralization Imperative and Caribbean Criminal Enterprises' in Tom Farer (ed.) *Transnational Crime in the Americas*, New York: Routledge.

MALDONADO-DENIS, MANUEL (1972) *Puerto Rico: A Socio-Historic Interpretation*, New York: Vintage Books.

——, (1980) *The Emigration Dialectic: Puerto Rico and the USA*, New York: International Publishers.

MALLOY, JAMES M. and EDUARDO A. GAMARRA (eds) (1990) *Latin America and Caribbean Contemporary Record*, vol. VII, New York: Holmes and Meier.

MALUQUER DE MOTES, JORDI (1992) *Nación e inmigración: los españoles en Cuba (ss.XIX y XX)*, Oviedo: Ediciones Jucar.

MAM-LAM-FOUCK, SERGE (1996) *Histoire générale de la Guyane Francaise: des débuts de la colonisation à l'aube de Cayenne*, Fort-de-France: Presses Universitaires Créoles/ GEREC.

MANDEL, ERNEST (1978) *Late Capitalism*, London: New Left Books.

MANDLE, JAY R. (1985) *Big Revolution, Small Country: The Rise and Fall of the Grenada Revolution*, Lanham, Maryland: North-South Publishing.

MANDLE, JAY R. and J. D. MANDLE (1994) *Caribbean Hoops: The Development of West Indian Basketball*, Langhorne, Pennsylvania: Gordon and Breach.

MANIGAT, LESLIE (1967) 'Substitution de la prépondérance américaine à la prépondérance française en Haïti au début du xxe siècle: la conjoncture de 1910–1911', *Revue d'Histoire Moderne et Contemporaine*, XIV, 4, pp.326–55.

MANLEY, MICHAEL (1975) *A Voice at the Workplace: Reflections on Colonialism and the Jamaican Worker*, London: André Deutsch.

——, (1987) *Up the Down Escalator: Development and the International Economy: A Jamaica Case Study*, London: André Deutsch.

——, (1996) *History of West Indies Cricket*, London: André Deutsch.

MANLEY, NORMAN (1971) *Manley and the New Jamaica: Selected Speeches and Writings 1938–68*, ed. Rex Nettleford, Kingston: Longman Caribbean.

MANNERS, R. A. (1965) 'Remittances and the Unit of Analysis in Anthropological Research', *Southwestern Journal of Anthropology*, 21, pp.179–95.

MANNING, F. E. (1978) 'Carnival in Antigua: An Indigenous Festival in a Tourist Economy', *Anthropos*, 73, pp.191–204.

——, (1985) 'Calypso and Politics in Barbados', *The Caribbean & West Indies Chronicle*, April/May, pp.14–15.

——, (1990) 'The Art and Politics of a Transnational Celebration' in J. A. Lent (ed.) *Caribbean Popular Culture*, Bowling Green, Ohio: Bowling Green State University Popular Press.

MANSERGH, NICHOLAS (1968) *Survey of British Commonwealth Affairs: Problems of Wartime Co-operation and Post-War Change, 1939–52*, London: F. Cass.

MANUEL, P., K. BILBY and M. LARGEY (1995) *Caribbean Currents: Caribbean Music from Rumba to Reggae*, Philadelphia: Temple University Press.

MARCUS, HAROLD G. (1995) *Haile Selassie I: The Formative Years, 1892–1936*, New Jersey: Red Sea Press; first published Berkeley: University of California Press, 1987.

MARIE-MARTHE (1978) *École et personalité aux Antilles Françaises*, Paris: La Pensée Universelle.

MARIÑEZ, PABLO (1984) *Resistencia campesina, imperialismo y reforma agraria en la República Dominicana, 1899–1978*, Santo Domingo: CEPAE.

MÁRQUEZ, ROBERTO (1989) 'Nationalism, Nation, and Ideology: Trends in the Emergence of a Caribbean Literature' in Franklin W. Knight and Colin A. Palmer (eds) *The Modern Caribbean*. Chapel Hill: University of North Carolina Press.

MARRYSHOW, T. ALBERT (1917) *Cycles of Civilisation*, Patchogue, New York: Pathway Publishers; reprinted 1973.

MARS, PERRY (1990) 'Ethnic Conflict and Political Control: The Guyana Case', *Social and Economic Studies*, 39, no.3.

MARSHALL, ARTHUR CALDER (1938) 'Colonial Overtures: Trinidad Wants to be American', *Living Age*, December, pp.322–5, 355–9.

MARSHALL, DAWN I. (1979) *The Haitian problem: Illegal migration to the Bahamas*, Mona: Institute of Social and Economic Research, UWI.

MARSHALL, OLIVER (ed.) (1992) *The Caribbean at War: British West Indians in World War II*, North Kensington, UK: Notting Hill Urban Studies Centre.

MARSHALL, PAULE (1972) *Brown Girl, Brownstones*, Chatham, New Jersey: Chatham Bookseller.

MARSHALL, WOODVILLE K. (1965) 'Metayage in the Sugar Industry of the British Windward Islands, 1838-65', *Jamaican Historical Review*, no.5 pp.28–55.

——, (1968) 'Peasant Development in the West Indies since 1838', *Social and Economic Studies*, 17, pp.252–63.

——, (1996) 'Peasant Development in the West Indies since 1838' in Hilary Beckles and Verene Shepherd (eds), *Caribbean Freedom: Economy and Society from Emancipation to the Present*, Kingston: Ian Randle.

MARSISKE, RENATE (1989) *Movimientos estudiantiles en América Latina: Argentina, Peru, Cuba y México, 1918–29*, Mexico City: Universidad Nacional Autónoma de México.

MARTIN, LAWRENCE and SILVIA MARTIN (1941) 'Outpost No. 2: The West Indies: Our New Stake in the Caribbean', *Harper's Magazine*, March, pp.359–68.

MARTIN, TONY (1970) 'Black Alice in a South African Wonderland', *Bumbo* 2, London: West Indian Students Union.

——, (1976) *Race First: The Ideological and Organizational Struggles of Marcus Garvey and the Universal Negro Improvement Association*, Westport: Greenwood Press; reprinted Dover, Massachusetts: Majority Press, 1986.

——, (1983a) *Literary Garveyism: Garvey, Black Arts and the Harlem Renaissance*, Dover, Massachusetts: Majority Press.

——, (ed.) (1983b) *The Poetical Works of Marcus Garvey*, Dover, Massachusetts: Majority Press.

——, (1983c) *Marcus Garvey, Hero*, Dover, Massachusetts: Majority Press.

——, (ed.) (1983–5) *In Nobody's Backyard: The Grenada Revolution in its Own Words, vol. I: The Revolution at Home, vol. II: Facing the World*, Dover, Massachusetts: Majority Press.

——, (1984a) 'C. L. R. James and the Race/Class Question' in *The Pan-African Connection*, Dover, Massachusetts: Majority Press.

——, (1984b) *The Pan-African Connection*, Dover, Massachusetts: Majority Press.

——, (1984c) 'Revolutionary Upheaval in Trinidad, 1919' in Tony Martin, *The Pan-African Connection*, Dover, Massachusetts: Majority Press.

——, (1988) 'A Pan-Africanist in Dominica: J. R. Ralph Casimir and the Garvey Movement, 1919–23', *Journal of Caribbean History*, 21, 2, reprinted in John P. Henderson and Harry A. Reed (eds) *Studies in the African Diaspora*, Dover, Massachusetts: Majority Press, 1989.

——, (ed.) (1991) *African Fundamentalism: A Literary and Cultural Anthology of Garvey's Harlem Renaissance*, Dover, Massachusetts: Majority Press.

——, (1994) 'Jews to Trinidad', *Journal of Caribbean History*, 28, no.2, pp. 244–57.

MARTÍNEZ, SAMUEL (1995) *Peripheral Migrants: Haitians and Dominican Republic Sugar Plantations*, Knoxville: University of Tennessee Press.

MARTÍNEZ ALIER, VERENA (1974) *Marriage, Class and Colour in Nineteenth Century Cuba: A Study of Racial Attitudes and Sexual Values in a Slave Society*, London: Cambridge University Press; reprinted Ann Arbor: University of Michigan Press, 1989.

MARTÍNEZ-VERGNE, TERESITA (1992) *Capitalism in Colonial Puerto Rico*, Gainesville: University Presses of Florida.

——, (1994) 'The Liberation of Women in the Caribbean: Research Perspectives for the Study of Gender Relations in the Post-Emancipation Period', *Caribbean Studies*, 27, nos.1–2, pp.1–36.

MARTIS, ROBERTO (1983) 'Education in Aruba: Teachers' Perception of Learning Problems of First and Second Graders', Ph.D. dissertation, University of Michigan.

MARX, KARL (1973) *El Capital*, 3 vols, Mexico City: Fondo de Cultura Económica.

MARX, KARL and FREDERICK ENGELS (1968) *On Colonialism*, Moscow: Progress Publishers.

MASS, BONNIE (1977) 'Puerto Rico: A Case Study of Population Control', *Latin American Perspectives*, IV, no.4, pp.66–82.

MASSÉ, RAYMOND (1980) *La fin des plantations? Evolution des formes de soumission de travail dans deux sociétés neo-coloniales: Martinique et Guadeloupe*, Martinique: Centre de Recherches Caraïbes.

MASSIAH, JOYCELIN (1986) 'Women in the Caribbean Project: An Overview', *Social and Economic Studies*, 35, 2, pp.1–29.

MATHELIER, GEORGES (1976) *Pedagogie et bilinguisme en Haïti*, Port-au-Prince: Université d'Etat d'Haïti.

MATHEWS, THOMAS G. (1976) *Puerto Rican Politics and the New Deal*, Gainsville: University of Florida Press.

MATHEWS, THOMAS G. and F. M. ANDIC (eds) (1971) *Politics and Economics in the Caribbean*, Río Piedras: Institute of Caribbean Studies, University of Puerto Rico.

MATHURIN, OWEN C. (1976) *Henry Sylvester Williams and the Origins of the Pan-African Movement, 1869–1911*, Westport: Greenwood Press.

MATIBAG, EUGENIO (1996) *Afro-Cuban Religious Experience: Cultural Reflections in Narrative*, Gainesville: University Press of Florida.

MATO, DANIEL (1994a) 'Procesos de construcción de identidades transnacionales en América Latina en tiempos de globalización' in Daniel Mato (ed.) *Teoría y política de la construcción de identidades y diferencias en América Latina y el Caribe*, Caracas: UNESCO/Ed. Nueva Sociedad.

——, (ed.) (1994b) *Teoría y política de la construcción de identidades y diferencias en América Latina y el Caribe*, Caracas: UNESCO/Ed. Nueva Sociedad.

MATOS RODRÍGUEZ, FÉLIX V. (1999) *Women and Urban Change in San Juan, Puerto Rico, 1820–1868*, Gainesville: University Presses of Florida.

MATOS RODRÍGUEZ, FÉLIX V. and LINDA DELGADO (eds) (1998) *Puerto Rican Women's History: New Perspectives*, Armonk, NY: M.E. Sharpe.

MATTHEWS, HERBERT L. (1976) *New York Times*, 4 March, p.31.

MAUL, GEORGE A. (ed.) (1996) *Small Islands: Marine Science and Sustainable Development*, Washington, DC: American Geophysical Union.

MAURER, B. (1997a) 'Creolization Redux: The Plural Society Thesis and Offshore Financial Services in the British Caribbean', *Nieuwe West-Indische Gids/New West Indian Guide*, 71, 3 & 4, pp.249–64.

——, (1997b) *Recharting the Caribbean: Land, Law, and Citizenship in the British Virgin Islands*, Ann Arbor: University of Michigan Press.

MECHAM, J. LLOYD (1961) *The United States and Inter-American Security, 1889–1960*, Austin: University of Texas Press.

MEEKS, BRIAN (1993) *Caribbean Revolutions and Revolutionary Theory: An Assessment of Cuba, Nicaragua and Grenada*, London: Macmillan Caribbean.

MEEL, PETER (1990) 'A Reluctant Embrace' in Gary Brana-Shute (ed.) *Resistance and Rebellion in Suriname*, Williamsburg: College of William and Mary.

Memorias inéditas del censo de 1931 (1978) Havana: Editorial de Ciencias Sociales.

MESA-LAGO, CARMELO (1981) *The Economy of Socialist Cuba: A Two Decade Appraisal*, Albuquerque: University of New Mexico Press.

——, (1994) *Are Economic Reforms Propelling Cuba to the Market?*, Miami: North-South Center, University of Miami.

MESH, CYNTHIA J. (1997) 'Empowering the Mother Tongue: The Creole Movement in Guadeloupe' in Consuelo López Springfield (ed.) *Daughters of Caliban: Caribbean Women in the Twentieth Century*, Bloomington: Indiana University Press.

MICHEL, GEORGES (1985) *Les chemins de fer de l'Ile d'Haïti*, Port-au-Prince; reprinted New York: Haitiana Publications, 1989.

——, (1996) *Charlemagne Péralte and the First American Occupation of Haiti*, Dubuque, Iowa: Kendall/Hunt.

'Migration Flows and the Effect on Class Formation and Family Structure in the Caribbean' (1982) in *Women and Social Production in the Caribbean*, Final Report of Seminar sponsored by the Institute of Development Studies, University of Sussex, and CEREP, Río Piedras.

MILLER, DANIEL (1994) *Modernity, an Ethnographic Approach: Dualism and Mass Consumption in Trinidad*, Oxford: Berg.

——, (1998a) 'Coca-Cola: A Black Sweet Drink from Trinidad' in Daniel Miller (ed.) *Material Culture: Why Some Things Matter*, Chicago: University of Chicago Press.

——, (ed.) (1998b) *Material Culture: Why Some Things Matter*, Chicago: University of Chicago Press.

MILLER, DANIEL and DON SLATER (2000) *The Internet: An Ethnographic Approach*, Oxford: Berg.

MILLER, ERROL (1986) *Marginalisation of the Black Male*, Mona: Insitute of Social and Economic Research, UWI.

——, (1989) 'Educational Development in Independent Jamaica' in Rex Nettleford (ed.) *Jamaica in Independence: Essays on the Early Years*, Kingston: Heinemann Caribbean.

——, (1991) *Men at Risk*, Kingston: Jamaica Publishing House.

——, (1992) *Education for All: Caribbean Perspectives and Imperatives*, Washington, DC: Inter-American Development Bank.

MILLETTE, JAMES (1985) *Society and Politics in Colonial Trinidad*, London: Zed Press; first published as *The Genesis of Crown Colony Government: Trinidad, 1783–1810*, Curepe, Trinidad: Moko Enterprises,1970.

——, (1988a) 'Labour vs Capital after Emancipation, 1838–97' in James Millette (ed.) *Freedom Road*, Havana: José Martí Publishing House.

——, (ed.) (1988b) *Freedom Road*, Havana: José Martí Publishing House.

——, (1995) 'Towards the Black Power Revolt of 1970' in Selwyn D. Ryan and Taimoon Stewart (eds) *The Black Power Revolution, 1970: A Retrospective*, St Augustine: Institute of Social and Economic Research, UWI.

MINTZ, SIDNEY W. (1971) 'The Caribbean as a Socio-cultural Area' in Michael Horowitz (ed.) *Peoples and Cultures of the Caribbean*, Garden City, NY: Natural History Press.

——, (1974) *Caribbean Transformations*, Baltimore: Johns Hopkins University Press; reprinted New York: Columbia University Press, 1989.

——, (1996) 'Enduring Substances, Trying Theories: The Caribbean Region as *Oikoumenê*', *Journal of the Royal Anthropological Institute*, 2, pp.289–311.

MINTZ, SIDNEY W. and SALLY PRICE (eds) (1985) *Caribbean Contours*, Baltimore: Johns Hopkins University Press.

MITCHELL, SIR HAROLD (1972) *Caribbean Patterns: A Political and Economic Study of the Contemporary Caribbean*, Edinburgh: W. and R. Chambers.

MOHAMMED, PATRICIA (1998a) 'Towards Indigenous Feminist Theorizing in the Caribbean', *Feminist Review*, 59, pp.6–33.

——, (ed.) (1998b) 'Rethinking Caribbean Difference', *Feminist Review*, 59, special issue.

MOMSEN, JANET H. (ed.) (1993a) *Women and Change in the Caribbean*, Kingston: Ian Randle.

——, (1993b) 'Introduction' in Janet H. Momsen (ed.) *Women and Change in the Caribbean*, Kingston: Ian Randle.

——, (1993c) 'Development and Gender Divisions of Labour in the Rural Eastern Caribbean',in Janet H. Momsen (ed.) *Women and Change in the Caribbean*, Kingston: Ian Randle.

MOORE, BRIAN L. (1987) *Race, Power and Social Segmentation in Colonial Society*, New York: Gordon and Breach.

MOORE, BRIAN L. and SWITHIN R. WILMOT (eds) (1998) *Before and After 1865*, Kingston: Ian Randle.

MOORE, CARLOS (1988a) *Castro, the Blacks and Africa*, Los Angeles: Center for Afro-American Studies, UCLA.

——, (1988b) 'Is Cuba a Black or White Country?' in Carlos Moore, *Castro, the Blacks and Africa*, Los Angeles: Center for Afro-American Studies, UCLA.

MOQUETE, JACÓBO (1986) *Filosofía y política de la educatión dominicana*, Santo Domingo: Universidad Autónoma de Santo Domingo.

MORAL, PAUL (1978) *Le paysan haïtien*, 2nd edn, Port-au-Prince: Éditions Fardin.

MORALES CARRIÓN, ARTURO (1983) *Puerto Rico: A Cultural History*, New York: Norton.

MORDECAI, SIR JOHN (1968) *The Federation of the West Indies*, Evanston: Northwestern University Press.

MORENO FRAGINALS, MANUEL (1983a) *La historia como arma y otros estudios sobre esclavos, ingenios y plantaciones*, Barcelona: Editorial Crítica.

——, (1983b) 'Plantaciones en el Caribe: El caso Cuba-Puerto Rico-Santo Domingo (1860–1940)' in Manuel Moreno Fraginals, *La historia como arma y otros estudios sobre esclavos, ingenios y plantaciones*, Barcelona: Editorial Crítica.

——, (1985) 'Plantations in the Caribbean: Cuba, Puerto Rico, and the Dominican Republic in the Late Nineteenth Century' in Manuel Moreno Fraginals, F. Moyo Pons and S. L. Engerman (eds) *Between Slavery and Free Labor: The Spanish-Speaking Caribbean in the Nineteenth Century*, Baltimore: Johns Hopkins University Press.

——, (ed.) (1987) *Africa en América Latina*, 2nd edn, Mexico City: Editorial Siglo XXI.

MORENO FRAGINALS, MANUEL, F. MOYA PONS, and S. L. ENGERMAN (eds) (1985) *Between Slavery and Free Labor: The Spanish-Speaking Caribbean in the Nineteenth Century*. Baltimore: Johns Hopkins University Press.

MORGAN, DAVID JOHN (1980) *The Official History of Colonial Development*, 5 vols, Atlantic Highland, New Jersey: Humanities Press.

MORGAN, ROBIN (ed.) (1993a) *Mujeres del mundo*, Barcelona: Hacer.

——, (1993b) 'El Caribe: Efecto laboratorio' in Robin Morgan (ed.) *Mujeres del mundo*, Barcelona: Hacer.

MORRISSEY, MARIETTA (1989) *Slave Women in the New World: Gender Stratification in the Caribbean*, Lawrence: University Press of Kansas.

Moses, Yolande T. (1981) 'Female Status, the Family, and Male Dominance in the West Indian Community' in Filomena Chioma Steady (ed.) *The Black Woman Cross-Culturally*, Cambridge, Massachusetts: Schenkman.

Mota, Vivian (1980) 'Politics and Feminism in the Dominican Republic, 1931–45 and 1966–74' in June Nash and Helen I. Safa (eds) *Sex and Class in the Caribbean*, South Hadley, Massachusetts: J. F. Bergin.

Moya Pons, Frank (ed.) (1983) 'La Situación Laboral en la República Dominicana', *Forum 8*, special issue, Santo Domingo.

——, (1995) *The Dominican Republic: A National History*, New Rochelle, New York: Hispaniola Books.

Moyne, Lord (1940) 'The West Indies in 1939', *Geographical Journal*, 26, pp.65–92.

Moynihan, Daniel Patrick (1993) *Pandemonium: Ethnicity in International Politics*, New York: Oxford University Press.

Mudgal, H. G. (1932) *Marcus Garvey: Is He the True Redeemer of the Negro?*, New York: H. G. Mudgal.

La mujer en Cuba socialista (1977), Publicación Oficial del Ministerio de Justicia de Cuba, Havana: Empresa Editorial Orbe.

La mujer en el sector popular urbano en América Latina y el Caribe (1984), Santiago: United Nations, CEPALAC.

Mujeres en Marcha, Year XIII, 3, 1996.

Mulzac, Hugh (1972) *A Star to Steer By*, New York: International Publishers.

Munck, Ronald (1988) *The New International Labour Studies: An Introduction*, London: Zed Books.

Muñoz, Heraldo and Joseph Tulchin, (eds) (1984) *Latin American Nations in World Politics*, Boulder: Westview Press.

Muñoz-Vázquez, Marya (1996) 'Gender and Politics: Grassroots and Leadership among Puerto Rican Women in a Health Struggle' in Altagracia Ortíz (ed.) *Bridges in Transnational Labor*, Philadelphia: Temple University Press.

Muñoz-Vázquez, Marya and Edwin Fernández (1988) *El divorcio en la sociedad puertorriqueña*, Río Piedras: Ediciones Huracán.

Munro, Dana G. (1964) *Intervention and Dollar Diplomacy in the Caribbean, 1900–21* Princeton: Princeton University Press.

——, (1974) *The United States and the Caribbean Republics, 1921–33* Princeton: Princeton University Press.

Munroe, Trevor (1972) *The Politics of Constitutional Decolonisation: Jamaica, 1944–62*, Mona: Institute of Social and Economic Research, UWI.

——, (1992) *The Cold War and the Jamaican Left: Re-Opening the Files*, Kingston: Kingston Publishers.

——, (1995) 'Democracy and Drugs in the Caribbean: Some Policy Perspectives', paper presented at the Conference on International Narco-Trafficking and the Economy of Caribbean States, Institute of International Relations, UWI, Trinidad, 19–21 January.

Munroe, Trevor and Rupert Lewis (eds) (1971) *Readings in Government and Politics of the West Indies*, Mona: Department of Government, UWI.

MURPHY, JOSEPH (1994) *Working the Spirit Ceremonies of the African Diaspora*, Boston: Beacon Press.

MURRAY, ROBERT K. (1964) *Red Scare: A Study in National Hysteria, 1919–20*, New York: McGraw Hill.

MURTIL, PIERRE ALBERT (1977) *Indépendance pour la Guyane*, Paris: La Pensée Universelle.

NASH, JUNE and HELEN SAFA (eds) (1986) *Women at Work and Change in Latin America*, South Hadley, Massachusetts: Bergin and Garvey.

NATH, DWARKA (1950) *A History of Indians in Guyana*, London: published by the author; 2nd revised edn, 1970.

NEGRÓN DE MONTILLA, AIDA (1975) *Americanization in Puerto Rico and the Public School System, 1900–30*, Río Piedras: Editorial Universitaria.

NEGRÓN-MUNTANER, F. and R. GROSFOGUEL (eds) (1997) *Puerto Rican Jam: Essays on Culture and Politics*, Minneapolis: University of Minnesota Press.

NEIL, JOAN (1990) 'Adjustment, Transition, Transformation and the Social Sector: A Framework for Continuing Analysis and Policy Reformulation', ECLAC, Subregional Headquarters for the Caribbean, 20 November.

NELSON, DWIGHT (1986) 'Comments by Senator Dwight Nelson' in Bustamante Institute of Public and International Affairs, *Trade Unions and Democracy: A Seminar held in Kingston*, Kingston: The Institute.

NELSON, LOWRY (1950) *Rural Cuba*, Minneapolis: University of Minnesota Press.

NEPTUNE ANGLADE, MIREILLE (1986) *L'autre moitié du développement: à propos du travail des femmes en Haïti*, Paris: Éditions des Alizés, Difusion Kaitala, Montreal: ERCE.

NETTLEFORD, REX (1972) *Identity, Race and Protest in Jamaica*, New York: William Morrow.

——, (1978) *Caribbean Cultural Identity – The Case of Jamaica: An Essay in Cultural Dynamics*, Kingston: Institute of Jamaica.

——, (1985) *Dance Jamaica: Cultural Definition and Artistic Discovery*, New York: Grove Press.

——, (1989) (ed.) *Jamaica in Independence: Essays on the Early Years*, Kingston: Heinemann Caribbean.

——, (1993) *Inward Stretch, Outward Reach: A Voice from the Caribbean*, London: Macmillan.

New Encyclopaedia Britannica (1975) Chicago: Encyclopaedia Britannica.

New York (City), Department of City Planning (1992) *The Newest New Yorkers: An Analysis of Immigration into New York City during the 1980s*, New York: Dept of City Planning.

——, (1996) *The Newest New Yorkers, 1990–94: An Analysis of Immigration into New York City in the Early 1990s*, New York: Dept of City Planning.

NEWTON, VELMA (1984) *The Silver Men: West Indian Labour Migration to Panama, 1850–1914*, Mona: Institute of Social and Economic Research, UWI.

NICHOLLS, DAVID (1979) *From Dessalines to Duvalier – Race, Colour and National Independence in Haiti*, London: Macmillan Caribbean.

——, (1981) 'No Hawkers and Pedlars: Levantines in the Caribbean', *Ethnic and Racial Studies,* IV, 4, pp.415–31.

——, (1985) *Haiti in the Caribbean Context,* New York: St Martin's Press.

NICOLAS, ARMAND (1996) *Histoire économique de la Martinique,* 2 vols, Paris and Montreal.

——, (1996–8) *Histoire de la Martinique,* 3 vols, Paris: Éditions L'Harmattan.

NICOLESCU, BARBU (1958) *Colonial Planning: A Comparative Study,* London: G. Allen & Unwin.

NIETSCHMANN, BERNARD (1979) 'Ecological Change, Inflation, and Migration in the Far Western Caribbean', *Geographical Review,* 69, pp.1–24.

'"Notre Combat": Extraits de *Patriote Guadeloupéen et d'autres publications* (1968–76)', Guadeloupe: Association Générale des Etudiants Guadeloupéens.

NUNES, FREDERICK E. and YVONNE M. DELPH (1977) 'Making Abortion Reform Work: Steps and Slips in Guyana' *Reproductive Health Matters,* 9.

NUNLEY, JOHN and JUDITH BETTELHEIM (1988) *Caribbean Festival Arts: Each and Every Bit of Difference,* Seattle: University of Washington Press.

NURSE, L. A., K. A. ATHERLEY and L. A. BREWSTER (1995) 'The Impact of Thermal Effluent Discharge on the Barbados Southern West Coast' in D. Barker and D. F. M. McGregor (eds) *Environment and Development in the Caribbean: Geographical Perspectives,* Mona: The Press, UWI.

NURSE, LAWRENCE (1992) *Trade Unionism and Industrial Relations in the Commonwealth Caribbean,* Westport: Greenwood Press.

OBER, FREDERICK A. (1907) *Our West Indian Neighbors: The Islands of the Caribbean Sea,* New York: James Pott.

OFFNER, JOHN L. (1992) *An Unwanted War: The Diplomacy of the United States and Spain over Cuba, 1895–8,* Chapel Hill: University of North Carolina Press.

OKONKWO, RINA (1985) *Heroes of West African Nationalism,* Enugu, Nigeria: Delta.

OLIVIER, SYDNEY (1906) *White Capital and Coloured Labour,* London; republished, London, Hogarth Press, 1933, 1939.

——, (1933) *Jamaica: The Blessed Land,* London: Faber & Faber.

OLWIG, KAREN FOG (1985) *Cultural Adaptation and Resistance on St John: Three Centuries of Afro-Caribbean Life,* Gainesville: University Presses of Florida.

——, (1993a) *Global Culture, Island Identity: Continuity and Change in the Afro-Caribbean Community of Nevis,* Chur, Switzerland: Harwood Academic Publishers.

——, (1993b) 'The Migration Experience: Nevisian Women at Home and Abroad' in Janet H. Momsen (ed.) *Women and Change in the Caribbean,* Kingston: Ian Randle.

——, (ed.) (1995) *Small Islands, Large Questions: Society, Culture and Resistance in the Post-Emancipation Caribbean,* London: Frank Cass.

OPPENHEIMER, ANDRÉS (1992) *Castro's Final Hour: The Secret Story Behind the Coming Downfall of Communist Cuba,* New York: Simon & Schuster.

ORTÍZ, ALTAGRACIA (ed.) (1996) *Bridges in Transnational Labor,* Philadelphia: Temple University Press.

OSTOLAZA BEY, MARGARITA (1989) *Política sexual en Puerto Rico*, Río Piedras: Ediciones Huracán.

OWENS, JOSEPH (1976) *Dread: The Rastafarians of Jamaica*, Kingston: Sangster; reprinted London: Heinemann, 1979.

P. A. E. Collège Tartenson (1990) *L' École d'hier à la Martinique*, Martinique: CRDP, Antilles Guyane.

PADMORE, GEORGE (ed.) (1945) *Voice of Coloured Labour*, Manchester: PANAF Services.

PAIEWONSKY, DENISE (1994) 'De crisis personales y políticas', *Género y Sociedad*, 1, 3, pp.118–33.

PAIEWONSKY, MARGARITA (1993) 'Imágen de la mujer en los textos de historia dominicana', *Género y Sociedad*, 1, 1, pp.30–59.

PALLISTER, JANIS L. (1991) *Aimé Césaire*, New York: Twayne.

PALMER, ANNETTE C. (1983) 'The Politics of Race and War: Black American Soldiers in the Caribbean Theater during the Second World War', *Military Affairs*, XLVII, pp.59–62.

——, (1985) 'Black American Soldiers in Trinidad, 1942–4: Wartime Politics in a Colonial Society', *Journal of Imperial and Commonwealth History*, 9, pp.203–18.

——, (1989) 'The United States and the Commonwealth Caribbean, 1940–5', Ph.D. dissertation, Howard University.

PALMER, COLIN A. (1989) 'Identity, Race and Black Power in Independent Jamaica' in Franklin W. Knight and Colin A. Palmer (eds) *The Modern Caribbean*, Chapel Hill: University of North Carolina Press.

PAMPHILE, LÉON (1985) 'America's Policy Making in Haitian Education, 1915–34' *Journal of Negro Education*, 54, 1, pp.99–108.

Pan American Health Organization (PAHO) (1998) *Country Profiles*, online at http://www.paho.org.

PANTOJAS-GARCÍA, EMILIO (1989) 'Puerto Rican Populism Revisited: the PPD during the 1940s', *Journal of Latin American Studies*, 21, 3.

PAQUETTE, ROBERT L. (1988) *Sugar Is Made with Blood*, Middletown, Connecticut: Wesleyan University Press.

PARES, RICHARD (1950) *A West-India Fortune*, London: Longmans, Green.

PARRIS, CARL (1976) 'Chaguaramas Revisited' in Leslie Manigat (ed.) *The Caribbean Yearbook of International Relations*, Leyden: A. W. Sijthoff; St Augustine: Institute of International Relations, UWI.

PARRY, J. H. and P. M. SHERLOCK (1971) *A Short History of the West Indies*, 3rd edn, London: Macmillan Caribbean.

PARSONS, TALCOTT (1955) 'The American Family: Its Relations to Personality and to the Social Structure' in T. Parsons and R. F. Bales, *Family, Socialization and Interaction Process*, Glencoe, Illinois: Free Press.

PASKETT, C. J. and C. E. PHILOCTETE (1990) 'Soil Conservation in Haiti', *Journal of Soil and Water Conservation*, 45, 4, pp.457–9.

PASTOR, MANUEL, JR. and ANDREW ZIMBALIST (1995) 'Cuba's Economic Conundrum', *NACLA: Report on the Americas*, XXIX, pp.7–12.

PASTOR, ROBERT A. (ed.) (1985) *Migration and Development in the Caribbean: The Unexplored Connection*, Boulder: Westview Press.

——, (1992) *Whirlpool: US Foreign Policy toward Latin America and the Caribbean*, Princeton: Princeton University Press.

PATTEE, RICHARD (1966) 'The Role of the Roman Catholic Church' in Robert Freeman Smith (ed.) *Background to Revolution: The Development of Modern Cuba*, New York: Alfred A. Knopf.

PATTERSON, ENRIQUE (1996) 'Cuba: Discursos sobre la identidad', *Encuentro de la cultura cubana*, 2, pp.49–67.

PATTERSON, ORLANDO (1978) 'Migration in Caribbean Societies: Socioeconomic and Symbolic Resource' in W. H. McNeill and R. S. Adams (eds) *Human Migration: Patterns and Policies*, Bloomington: Indiana University Press.

PATTERSON, S. (1969) *Immigration and Race Relations in Britain*, London: Oxford University Press.

PATTULLO, POLLY (1996) *Last Resorts: The Cost of Tourism in the Caribbean*, Kingston: Ian Randle.

PAULA, A. F. (1970) *De meidagen van Curaçao: het volledige en ongewijzigde rapport dat de Commissie tot onderzoek van de achtergronden en oorzaken van de onlusten welke op 30 mei 1969 op Curaçao plaatsvonden, in mei 1970, bij de Antilliaanse regering indiende* (The May Days of Curaçao: The Complete and Unedited Report of the Commission Appointed to Investigate the Background and Causes of the Disturbances which Took Place on 30 May 1969, as presented to the Government of the Netherlands Antilles in May 1970), Willemstad, Curaçao.

PAYNE, ANTHONY (1980) *The Politics of the Caribbean Community, 1961–79: Regional Integration among New States*, New York: St Martin's Press.

——, (1988) 'One University, Many Governments: Regional Integration, Politics and the University of the West Indies', *Jamaican Historical Review*, 16, pp.33–53.

PAYNE, ANTHONY and PAUL SUTTON (eds) (1993) *Modern Caribbean Politics*, Baltimore: Johns Hopkins University Press.

PAYNE, ANTHONY, PAUL SUTTON and TONY THORNDIKE (1984) *Grenada, Revolution and Invasion*, New York: St Martin's Press.

PAZOS, FELIPE (1962) 'Comentarios a dos artículos sobre la revolución cubana', *El Trimestre Económico*, 29.

PEACH, CERI (1968) *West Indian Migration to Britain: A Social Geography*, London: Oxford University Press.

PEARCE, JENNY (1984) *Under the Eagle: U.S. Intervention in Central America and the Caribbean*, Boston: Southend Press.

PEARSON, RUTH (1986) 'Gender and New Technology in the Caribbean: New Work for Women?' in June Nash and Helen Safa (eds) *Women and Change in Latin America*, South Hadley, Massachusetts: Bergin and Garvey.

PÉREZ, LISANDRO (1992) 'Cuban Miami' in G. J. Grenier and A. Stepick III (eds) *Miami Now! Immigration, Ethnicity, and Social Change*, Gainesville: University Presses of Florida, pp.83–108.

PÉREZ, LOUIS, A. (1982) 'The Imperial Design', *Cuban Studies*, 12, 2, pp.3–17.

——, (1983) *Cuba Between Empires, 1878–1902,* Pittsburgh: University of Pittsburgh Press.

——, (1986) *Cuba under the Platt Amendment 1902–34,* Pittsburgh: University of Pittsburgh Press; reprinted 1991.

——, (1988) *Cuba between Reform and Revolution,* New York: Oxford University Press.

——, (1990) *Cuba and the United States: Ties of Singular Intimacy,* Athens, Georgia: University of Georgia Press.

——, (1998a) *The War of 1898: The United States and Cuba in History and Historiography,* Chapel Hill: University of North Carolina Press.

——, (1998b) *Cuba and Cuban Americans: An Irreconcilable Relationship,* Cuba Briefing Paper, Washington, DC: Georgetown University.

PÉREZ DE LA RIVA, JUAN (1979) 'Cuba y la migración antillana, 1900–31' in Juan Pérez de la Riva *et al., La república neocolonial,* vol. 2, Havana: Editorial de Ciencias Sociales.

PÉREZ DE LA RIVA, JUAN *et al.* (1975–9) *La república neocolonial,* 2 vols, Havana: Editorial de Ciencias Sociales.

PÉREZ-DÍAZ, VÍCTOR (1993) *The Return of Civil Society: The Emergence of Democratic Spain,* Cambridge, Massachusetts: Harvard University Press.

PÉREZ-LÓPEZ, JORGE F. (1995) *Cuba's Second Economy: From Behind the Scenes to Center Stage,* New Brunswick: Transaction.

PÉREZ-STABLE, MARIFELI (1993) *The Cuban Revolution: Origins, Course, and Legacy,* New York: Oxford University Press; 2nd edn, 1999.

——, (1995) 'Legislative and Electoral Dynamics: Reforms and Options' in 'Transition in Cuba: New Challenges for U.S. Policy', pp.39–65, unpublished report, A project of the Cuban Research Institute and the Latin American and Caribbean Center, Miami: Florida International University.

PÉREZ Y MENA, ANDRÉS I. (1995) 'Puerto Rican Spiritism as a Transfeature of Afro-Latin Religion' in Anthony M. Stevens-Arroyo and Andrés I. Pérez y Mena (eds), *Enigmatic Powers: Syncretism with African and Indigenous Peoples' Religions among Latinos,* New York: Bildner Center for Western Hemisphere Studies.

PHILLIPPO, JAMES M. (1843) *Jamaica: Its Past and Present State,* London: John Snow; reprinted Freeport, NY: Books for Libraries Press, 1971.

PHILLIPS, ANGHELEN A. and GEOFFREY DE SOLA PINTO (1982) *Jamaican Houses: A Vanishing Legacy,* Kingston: Stephenson's Litho Press.

PHILLIPS, C. (1997) 'Unmarooned', *New Republic,* 28 April, pp.45–9.

PHILLIPS, SIR FRED (1985) *West Indian Constitutions: Post Independence Reform,* New York: Oceana Publications.

PHILLIPS, PETER (1988) 'Race, Class, Nationalism: A Perspective on Twentieth Century Social Movements in Jamaica', *Social and Economic Studies,* 37, 3.

PHILPOTT, STUART B. (1973). *West Indian Migration: The Montserrat Case,* London: Athlone Press.

PICÓ, FERNANDO (1981) *Amargo café,* Río Piedras: Ediciones Huracán.

——, (1987) *La guerra después de la guerra,* Río Piedras: Ediciones Huracán.

——, (1988) *Historia general de Puerto Rico,* Río Piedras: Ediciones Huracán.

Picó, Isabel (1983a) *La mujer y la política puertorriqueña,* Río Piedras: Centro de Investigaciones Sociales, Universidad de Puerto Rico.

——, (1983b) *Machismo y educación,* Río Piedras: Centro de Investigaciones Sociales, Universidad de Puerto Rico.

——, (1986) 'The History of Women's Struggle for Equality in Puerto Rico' in Edna Acosta-Belén (ed.) *The Puerto Rican Woman,* New York: Praeger.

Pierre-Charles, Gérard (1967) *L'économie haïtienne et sa voie de développement,* Paris: G. P. Maisonneuve et Larose.

——, (1975) *Haití: la crisis interrumpida, 1930–75,* Havana: Casa de las Américas.

——, (1981) *El Caribe Contemporáneo,* Mexico City: Editorial Siglo XXI.

Pilkington, Edward (1988) *Beyond the Mother Country: West Indians and the Notting Hill White Riots,* London: I. B. Tauris.

Pineda, Magaly (1984) 'La fuerza laboral femenina en la República Dominicana: un proyecto de educación y acción con obreras industriales', in *La mujer en el sector popular urbano en América Latina y el Caribe,* Santiago: United Nations, CEPALAC.

——, (1988) 'Pour un feminisme de base populaire, un projet de recherche éducation-action avec des ouvrières industrielles' in Adeline Chancy and Suzy Castor (eds), *Théories et pratiques de la lutte des femmes,* Port-au-Prince: CRESFED.

——, (1993) 'El Caribe de habla española: Nosotras no somos ovejas' in Robin Morgan (ed.) *Mujeres del mundo,* Barcelona: Hacer.

Pino Santos, Oscar (1973) *El asalto de Cuba por la oligarquía financiera yanqui,* Havana: Casa de las Américas.

Plant, Roger (1987) *Sugar and Modern Slavery: A Tale of Two Countries.* London: Zed Books.

Platt, Raye Robert, J. K. Wright, J. C. Weaver and J. K. Fairchild (1941) *The European Possessions in the Caribbean Area: A Compilation of Facts Concerning Their Population, Physical Geography, Resources, Industries, Trade, Government, and Strategic Importance.* New York: American Geographical Society.

Plummer, Brenda Gayle (1988) *Haiti and the Great Powers, 1902–15,* Baton Rouge: Louisiana State University Press.

——, (1992) *Haiti and the United States: The Psychological Moment,* Athens, Georgia: University of Georgia Press.

Pool, Gail R. (1989) 'Shifts in Grenadian Migration: An Historical Perspective', *International Migration Review,* 23, pp.238–66.

Poole, Bernard C. (1951) *The Caribbean Commission: Background of Cooperation in the West Indies, 1946–51,* Columbia: University of South Carolina Press.

Population Census of Guyana (1980), vol. 2, Georgetown: Government of Guyana.

Population and Housing Census of Trinidad and Tobago (1990), vol. II, Port of Spain: Central Statistical Office, Government of Trinidad & Tobago.

Portes, A. and J. Itzigsohn (1996) *Las Ciudades del Caribe,* Santo Domingo and Baltimore: Facultad Latinoamericana de Ciencias Sociales and Johns Hopkins University Press.

POST, KEN (1978) *Arise Ye Starvelings: The Jamaica Labour Rebellion of 1938 and its Aftermath,* The Hague: Martinus Nijhoff.

——, (1981) *Strike the Iron: A Colony at War, Jamaica 1939–45,* 2 vols, Atlantic Highland, New Jersey and The Hague: Humanities Press and Institute of Social Studies.

POTTER, ROBERT B. (1994) *Low-Income Housing and the State in the Eastern Caribbean,* Mona: The Press, UWI.

POTTER, ROBERT B. and D. CONWAY, (eds) (1997) *Self-Help Housing, the Poor, and the State in the Caribbean,* Mona: The Press, UWI.

PRATT, JULIUS W. (1950) *America's Colonial Experiment: How the United States Gained, Governed, and in Part Gave Away a Colonial Empire,* New York: Prentice Hall.

PREISWERK, ROY (ed.) (1970) *Documents on International Relations in the Caribbean,* Río Piedras and St Augustine: Institute of Caribbean Studies, University of Puerto Rico; Institute of International Relations, UWI.

PREST, ALAN R. (1948) *War Economics of Primary Producing Countries,* Cambridge: Cambridge University Press.

PRICE, RICHARD (1966) 'Caribbean Fishing and Fishermen: A Historical Sketch', *American Anthropologist,* 68, pp.1363–83.

——, (ed.) (1996) *Maroon Societies: Rebel Slave Communities in the Americas,* 3rd edn, Baltimore: Johns Hopkins University Press.

PRICE-MARS, JEAN (1928) *Ainsi parla l'oncle,* Paris: Imprimerie de Compiègne. Translated into English as *So Spoke the Uncle* by Magdaline W. Shannon, Washington, DC: Three Continents Press, 1983.

PRIETO, ABEL (1981) 'Cuba's National Literacy Campaign', *Journal of Reading,* 25, 3, pp.215–21.

PROUDFOOT, MALCOLM J. (1950) *Population Movements in the Caribbean,* Port of Spain: Caribbean Commission.

PROUDFOOT, MARY (MACDONALD) (1954) *Britain and the United States in the Caribbean: A Comparative Study in Methods of Development,* New York: Faber.

'Public Health Programs and Practices. Surgeon General's Report Focuses on Smoking in Latin America' (1993) *Public Health Reports,* 108, 1, Jan.–Feb. pp.141–2.

'Puerto Rico, USA', (1998) 'Tradition, Democracy, Vitality', online at http://www.pr.eda.com/vitality.html.

PULIS, JOHN W. (ed.) (1999) *Religion, Diaspora, and Cultural Identity: A Reader in the Anglophone Caribbean,* Amsterdam: Gordon and Breach.

PULSIPHER, MIHELIC LYDIA (1993) 'Changing Roles in the Life Cycles of Women in Traditional West Indian Houseyards' in Janet H. Momsen (ed.) *Women and Change in the Caribbean,* Kingston: Ian Randle.

PUMARADA O'NEILL, LUIS (1990) *La industria cafetalera de Puerto Rico, 1736–1969,* 2nd edn, Mayagüez: Oficina Estatal de Preservación Histórica.

PYLE, DOUGLAS C. (1981) *Clean Sweet Wind: Sailing Craft of the Lesser Antilles.* Preston, Maryland: Easy Reach Press.

QUAMINA, ODIDA T. (1987) *Mineworkers of Guyana,* London: Zed Books.

QUIÑONES-AROCHO, MARÍA ISABEL (1992) 'Caribbean Women: Changes in the Works', *Nieuwe West-Indische Gids/New West Indian Guide,* 66, 1 & 2, 89–94.

QUINTERO RIVERA, ANGEL G. (1988) *Patricios y plebeyos: burgueses, hacendados, artesanos y obreros: las relaciones de clase en el Puerto Rico de cambio de siglo,* Río Piedras: Ediciones Huracán.

QUITERIO BENÍTEZ, GISELA (1993) *Mujeres Latinoamericanas en Cifras, República Dominicana,* Santiago: Instituto de la Mujer, Ministerio de Asuntos Sociales de España y FLACSO.

RAJSHEKAR, V. T. (1987) *Dalit: The Black Untouchables of India,* Atlanta: Clarity Press.

——, (1994) *Brahminism,* Bangalore: Dalit Sahitya Akademy.

RAMDIN, RON (1983) *From Chattel Slave to Wage Earner: A History of Trade Unionism in Trinidad and Tobago,* London: Martin Brian and O'Keefe.

——, (2000) *Arising From Bondage: A History of the Indo-Caribbean People,* New York: New York University Press.

RAMÍREZ MORILLO, BELARMINO (1991) *El populismo en la República Dominicana,* Santo Domingo: Editora Cumbre.

RAMPERSAD, DAVID GORDON M. (1979) 'Colonial Economic Development and Social Welfare: The Case of the British West Indies, 1929–47', D. Phil. dissertation, Oxford University.

RAMSARAN, DAVE (1993) *Breaking the Bonds of Indentureship: Indo-Trinidadians in Business,* St Augustine: Institute of Social and Economic Research, UWI.

RANDALL, MARGARET (1981) *Women in Cuba: Twenty Years Later,* Brooklyn: Smyrna Press.

RATTNER, BEATE and GERHARD SANDNER (eds) (1993) *Territorialkonflikte im Karibischen Meeresraum,* Hamburg.

Reconstruction Administration of Puerto Rico (1938) *Census of Puerto Rico, 1935,* Washington DC: Government Printing Office.

REDDOCK, RHODA (1985) 'Women and Slavery in the Caribbean: A Feminist Perspective', *Latin American Perspectives,* Issue 44, 12, 1, pp.63–80.

——, (1990a) 'Women and Garment Production in Trinidad and Tobago, 1900–60', *Social and Economic Studies,* 31, 1.

——, (1990b) 'Feminism, Nationalism and the Early Women's Movement in the English-Speaking Caribbean, (with Special Reference to Jamaica and Trinidad and Tobago)' in Selwyn Cudjoe (ed.) *Caribbean Women Writers: Essays from the First International Conference,* Wellesley, Massachusetts: Callaloux Publications.

——, (1993) 'Transformation in the Needle Trades: Women in the Garment and Textile Production in Early Twentieth-Century Trinidad' in Janet H. Momsen (ed.) *Women and Change in the Caribbean,* Kingston: Ian Randle.

——, (1994) *Women, Labour and Politics in Trinidad and Tobago: A History,* Kingston: Ian Randle.

——, (1998a) 'Address to the Planning Meeting of the First Caribbean Feminist Encounter', Port of Spain, 12–3 December.

——, (1998b) 'Women's Organizations and Movements in the Commonwealth Caribbean: The Response to Global Economic Crisis in the 1980s', *Feminist Review,* 59.

——, (1998c) 'Women, the Creole Nationalist Movement and the Rise of Eric Williams and the PNM in mid 20th Century Trinidad and Tobago', *Caribbean Issues*, 8, 1.

REID, IRA D. A. (1939) *The Negro Immigrant: His Background, Characteristics and Social Adjustment, 1899–1937*, New York: Columbia University Press.

RENNIE, BUKKA (1973) *The History of the Working Class in the Twentieth Century (1919–56): The Trinidad and Tobago Experience*, Trinidad: New Beginning Movement.

Report of a Cabinet Appointed Enquiry into Discrimination against Nationals of Trinidad and Tobago in the United Kingdom, Canada and the United States of America, by Clive Spencer, President, Trinidad and Tobago Labour Congress, (1969) Senate Paper No. 7 of 1969, Port of Spain: Government Printery.

Report on the Circumstances Surrounding the Sinking of the M.V. 'Christena' (1970), St Kitts: Government Printery.

Report by the Hon. E. F. L. Wood, MP, on his Visit to the West Indies and British Guiana, (1922) London: HMSO.

RETAMAR, ROBERTO (1974) 'Caliban', *Massachusetts Review,* Winter–Spring, pp.7–72. Quoted in Rex Nettleford, *Caribbean Cultural Identity – The Case of Jamaica: An Essay in Cultural Dynamics,* Kingston: Institute of Jamaica.

Retos de la cooperación ambiental: el caso del Caribe (1993) Francine Jácome (co-ord.) Caracas: INVESP/Ed. Nueva Sociedad.

REYNOLDS, DAVID (1981) *The Creation of the Anglo-American Alliance, 1937–41: A Study in Competitive Co-operation,* London: Europa Publications.

RIBES TOVAR, FEDERICO (1974) *Lolita Lebrón, La Prisionera,* New York: Plus Ultra Educational Publishers.

RICHARDS, GLEN (1995) 'Higher Wages and Perfect Personal Freedom: StKitts/Nevis, 1836–1956' in Mary Turner (ed.) *From Chattel Slaves to Wage Slaves,* Kingston: Ian Randle.

RICHARDS, NOVELLE H. (1963) *The Struggle and the Conquest: Twenty-five Years of Social Democracy in Antigua,* Antigua: published by the author.

RICHARDSON, BONHAM C. (1983) *Caribbean Migrants: Environment and Human Survival on St Kitts and Nevis,* Knoxville: University of Tennessee Press.

——, (1985) *Panama Money in Barbados, 1900–20,* Knoxville: University of Tennessee Press.

——, (1989) 'Caribbean migrations, 1838–1985' in Franklin W. Knight and Colin A. Palmer (ed.) *The Modern Caribbean,* Chapel Hill: University of North Carolina Press.

——, (1992) *The Caribbean in the Wider World, 1492–1992: A Regional Geography,* Cambridge: Cambridge University Press.

——, (1997) *Economy and Environment in the Caribbean: Barbados and the Windwards in the Late 1800s,* Mona: The Press, UWI.

RICHMOND, A. H. (1989) *Caribbean Immigrants: A Demo-economic Analysis.* Ottawa: Ministry of Supply and Services.

RICHMOND, MARK (1990) 'The Cuban Educational Model and its Influence in the Caribbean Region' in Colin Brock and Donald Clarkson (eds) *Education in Central America,* New York: Routledge.

RIESGO, RODOLFO (1985) *Cuba: El Movimiento Obrero y su Entorno Sociopolítico, 1865–1983,* Miami and Caracas: Saeta Ediciones.

RITTER, ARCHIBALD R. M. (1985) 'The Organs of People's Power and the Communist Party: The Nature of Cuban Democracy' in Sandor Halebsky and John M. Kirk (eds) *Cuba: Twenty-five Years of Revolution,* New York: Praeger.

RIVERA, MARCIA (1986) 'The Development of Capitalism in Puerto Rico and the Incorporation of Women in the Labor Force' in Edna Acosta-Belen (ed.) *The Puerto Rican Woman,* New York: Praeger.

——, (1987) 'La mujer y el contexto social de los años cuarenta', *Homines,* special issue 4, pp.187–9.

——, (1993) 'El Caribe: los movimientos de mujeres y los estudios de género' in Claudia Serrano (co-ord.) *La investigación sobre la mujer en América Latina,* Santo Domingo: INSTRAW/CIPAF.

ROBAINA, TOMÁS F. (comp.) (1965) *Bibliografía sobre estudios afro-americanos,* Havana: Biblioteca Nacional José Martí.

ROBERTS, B. C. (1964) *Labour in the Tropical Territories of the Commonwealth,* London: London School of Economics.

ROBERTS, GEORGE and SONJA SINCLAIR (1978) *Women in Jamaica: Patterns of Reproduction and Family,* New York: KTO Press.

ROBERTS, S. M. (1995) 'Small Place, Big Money: The Cayman Islands and the International Financial System', *Economic Geography* 71, no.3, pp.237–56.

ROBERTS, W. ADOLPHE (1941) 'Future of the British Caribbean', *Survey Graphic,* 30, pp.228–33.

——, (1948) *Lands of the Inner Sea: The West Indies and Bermuda,* New York: Coward-McCann.

ROBINSON, CAREY (1969) *The Fighting Maroons of Jamaica,* Kingston: Collins and Sangster.

ROBOTHAM, DON (1988) 'The Development of a Black Ethnicity in Jamaica' in Rupert Lewis and Patrick Bryan (eds) *Garvey: His Work and Impact,* Mona: Institute of Social and Economic Research and Department of Extra Mural Studies, UWI.

ROCK, DAVID (1994) *Latin America in the 1940s: War and Postwar Transitions,* Berkeley: University of California Press.

RODMAN, HYMAN (1971) *Lower-class Families: The Culture of Poverty in Trinidad,* New York: Oxford University Press.

RODMAN, SELDON (1954) *Haiti: The Black Republic,* New York: Devin-Adair.

RODNEY, WALTER (1969) *The Groundings with my Brothers,* London: Bogle-L'Ouverture Publications.

——, (1981) *A History of the Guyanese Working People, 1881–1905,* Baltimore: Johns Hopkins University Press.

RODRÍGUEZ DEMORIZI, EMILIO (1964) *Papeles de Pedro Fco. Bonó,* Santo Domingo: Academia Dominicana de la Historia.

ROHLEHR, GORDON (1990) *Calypso and Society in Pre-Independence Trinidad,* Port of Spain: G. Rohlehr.

RÖMER, RENÉ A. (1974) *Naar de voltooiing van de emancipatie:beschouwingen naar aanleiding van het verschijnsel 30 mei,* (Toward the Completion of Emancipation: Views Regarding the Phenomenon of 30 May), Willemstad, Curaçao.

——, (1975) 'Race and Class in Political Perspective', *Kristof,* 2, 6.

——, (1976) 'Education in Caribbean Perspective: The Sprockel Period', *Caribbean Education Bulletin,* 3, 3, pp.47–51.

——, (1977) 'Un pueblo na kaminda: Een sociologisch historische studie van de Curacaose samenleving', Ph.D. dissertation, University of Leiden.

——, (1981a) *Curaçao,* Curaçao: Association of Caribbean Universities and Research Institutes.

——, (1981b) 'Labour Unions and Labour Conflict in Curaçao', *Nieuwe West-Indische Gids/New West Indian Guide,* 55, 3 & 4.

ROORDA, ERIC P. (1998) *The Dictator Next Door: The Good Neighbor Policy and the Trujillo Regime in the Dominican Republic, 1930–45,* Durham: Duke University Press.

ROOSEVELT, ELLIOTT (1946) *As He Saw It,* New York: Duell, Sloan and Pearce.

ROPER, GARNET (1991) 'The Impact of Evangelical and Pentecostal Religion', *Caribbean Quarterly,* 37, 1, pp.35–44.

ROSCHELLE, ANNE R. (1997) 'Declining Networks of Care: Ethnicity, Migration, and Poverty in a Puerto Rican Community', *Race, Gender and Class,* 4, 2, pp.107–25.

RUBENSTEIN, H. (1983) 'Remittances and Rural Underdevelopment in the English-Speaking Caribbean', *Human Organization,* 42, pp.295–306.

RUCK, ROB (1993) *The Tropic of Baseball: Baseball in the Dominican Republic,* New York: Carroll & Graf.

RUHOMON, PETER (1938) *Centenary History of the East Indians of British Guiana, 1838–1938,* Georgetown: East Indians 150th Anniversary Committee; reprinted 1988.

RUSSELL, HORACE O. (1983) 'The Emergence of the Christian Black: The Making of a Stereotype', *Jamaica Journal,* 16, pp.51–8.

RYAN, SELWYN D. (1972) *Race and Nationalism in Trinidad and Tobago: A Study of Decolonization in a Multiracial Society,* Toronto: University of Toronto Press.

——, (ed.) (1988) *Trinidad: The Independence Experience, 1962–87,* St Augustine: Institute of Social and Economic Research, UWI.

——, (1991a) *The Muslimeen Grab for Power,* Port of Spain: Imprint Caribbean.

——, (ed.) (1991b) *Social and Occupational Stratification in Contemporary Trinidad and Tobago,* St Augustine: Institute of Social and Economic Research, UWI.

——, (1997) 'Democratic Governance and the Social Condition in the Anglophone Caribbean' in *Governance and Democratic Development in Latin America and the Caribbean,* New York: United Nations Development Programme.

RYAN, SELWYN D. and TAIMOON STEWART (eds) (1995) *The Black Power Revolution, 1970: A Retrospective,* St Augustine: Institute of Social and Eeconomic Research, UWI.

SAAKANA, AMON SABA (1987) *The Colonial Legacy in the Caribbean,* London: Karnak House.

SAFA, HELEN I. (1986) 'Female Employment in the Puerto Rican Working Class' in June Nash and Helen Safa (eds) *Women and Change in Latin America,* South Hadley, Massachusetts: Bergin and Garvey.

——, (1995) *The Myth of the Male Breadwinner,* Boulder: Westview Press.

——, (1998) 'Female Headed Households in the Caribbean: Sign of Pathology or Alternative Form of Family Organization?' *The Brown Journal of World Affairs* V, 2, pp.204–6.

SAFA, HELEN I. and PEGGY ANTROBUS (1992) 'Women and the Economic Crises in the Caribbean' in Lourdes Benería and Shelley Feldman (eds) *Unequal Burden: Economic Crises, Persistent Poverty, and Women*'s *Work,* Boulder: Westview Press.

SAINT JOHN, SPENSER (1889) *Hayti: or the Black Republic,* London: Smith Elder.

SAMAROO, BRINSLEY (1971) 'Cyrus Prudhomme David', *Journal of Caribbean History,* 3.

——, (1974) 'Politics and Afro-Indian Relations in Trinidad' in John LaGuerre (ed.) *Calcutta to Caroni,* Port of Spain: Longman.

——, (1975) 'The Presbyterian Canadian Mission as an Agent of Integration in Trinidad during the Nineteenth and Early Twentieth Centuries', *Caribbean Studies,* 14, 4.

——, (1987) 'The Indian Connection: the Influence of Indian Thought and Ideas on East Indians in the Caribbean' in David Dabydeen and Brinsley Samaroo, eds, *India in the Caribbean,* London: Hansib.

SAN MIGUEL, PEDRO (1992) 'Las sociedades campesinas antillanas: perspectivas comparativas sobre Puerto Rico y Santo Domingo', paper presented at the II Seminario sobre Identidad, Cultura y Sociedad en las Antillas Hispanoparlantes.

——, (1993) 'Exacción estatal y resistencias campesinas en el Cibao durante la ocupación norteamericana de 1916–24', *Ecos* I, 2, pp.77–100.

——, (1996) *Los campesinos del Cibao, 1880–1963,* Río Piedras: Editorial Universitaria.

SÁNCHEZ, J. R. (1996) 'Puerto Rican Politics in New York: Beyond "Secondhand" Theory' in G. Haslip-Viera and S. L. Baver (eds) *Latinos in New York,* Notre Dame: University of Notre Dame Press.

SÁNCHEZ ALBORNOZ, NICOLÁS (1988) *Españoles hacia América: la emigración en masa, 1880–1930,* Madrid: Alianza Editorial.

SÁNCHEZ TAYLOR, J. (1997) 'Selling Difference: The Gendered and Racialised Nature of Sex Tourism in the Hispanic Caribbean.' Paper presented for the Society for Caribbean Studies, Panel: Gender Issues in the Caribbean, Hull, UK, July 2.

SANDFORD, GREGORY and RICHARD VIGILANTE (1984) *Grenada: The Untold Story,* Lanham, Maryland: Madison Books.

SANDNER, GERHARD (1993) 'U-Boot Krieg in der Karibik. Anmerkungen und Ergänzungen zum gleichnamigen Buch von G. T. M. Kelshall' in Beate Rattner and Gerhard Sandner (eds) *Territorialkonflikte im Karibischen Meeresraum,* Hamburg.

SANDOVAL, JOSÉ MIGUEL (1983) 'State Capitalism in a Petroleum-Based Economy: the Case of Trinidad and Tobago' in Fitzroy Ambursley and Robin Cohen (eds) *Crisis in the Caribbean,* New York: Monthly Review Press.

SANDOVAL SÁNCHEZ, ALBERTO S. (1997) 'Puerto Rican Identity up in the Air' in F. Negrón-Muntaner and R. Grosfoguel (eds) *Puerto Rican Jam: Essays on Culture and Politics*, Minneapolis: University of Minnesota Press.

SANTIAGO, ZORAIDA (1987) 'Los estereotipos sexuales en la selección de carreras', *Homines*, special issue 4, pp.244–6.

SANTOS HERNÁNDEZ, ROBERTO (1993) *La educación desde el antiguo oriente al plan decenal en República Dominicana*, Santo Domingo: Editora Alfa y Omega.

SANTOS ORTÍZ, MARÍA DEL C. and MARYA MUÑOZ (1989) 'An Exploratory Study of the Expression of Female Sexuality: The Experience of Two Groups of Puerto Rican Women from Different Social Backgrounds' in Cynthia García Coll and María Lourdes Mattei (eds) *The Psyochosocial Development of Puerto Rican Women*, New York: Praeger.

SARDINHA, DENNIS (1976) *The Poetry of Nicolás Guillén: An Introduction*, London: New Beacon Books.

SASSEN, SASKIA (1988) *The Mobility of Labor and Capital: A Study in International Investment and Labor Flows*, Cambridge: Cambridge University Press.

SAUNDERS, GAIL (1990) *Bahamian Society after Emancipation*, Nassau: the Author.

SAYLES, J. (1991) *Los Gusanos: A Novel*, New York: HarperCollins.

SCARANO, FRANCISCO (ed.) (1981) *Inmigración y clases sociales*, Río Piedras: Editorial Universitaria.

——, (1993) *Puerto Rico: cinco siglos de historia*, San Juan: McGraw Hill.

SCARPACI, JOSEPH L. (1991) 'The Image of Puerto Rico in the United States' Press: 1970–80'. Paper presented at the Caribbean Studies Association Meeting, Havana, Cuba, June.

——, (1995) 'On the New Economic Geography of Havana's Food and Paladar Market'. Paper presented to the Association for the Study of the Cuban Economy, Miami, 9 August.

——, (1996) 'Industrial Analysis: Miramar's (Havana) Real Estate Market, *Cuba News*, 9 December, Miami: Miami Herald Publishing.

SCHEELE, RAYMOND L. (1956) 'The Prominent Families of Puerto Rico' in Julian H. Steward *et al.*, *The People of Puerto Rico: A Study in Social Anthropology*, Urbana: University of Illinois Press.

SCHMIDT, HANS (1971) *The United States Occupation of Haiti, 1915–34*, New Brunswick: Rutgers University Press.

SCHWARTZ, ROSALIE (1997) *Pleasure Island: Tourism and Temptation in Cuba*, Lincoln: University of Nebraska Press.

SCOTT, J. S. (1986) 'The Common Wind: Currents of Afro-American Communication in the Era of the Haitian Revolution', Ph.D. dissertation, Duke University.

SCOTT, JAMES C. (1985) *Weapons of the Weak: Everyday Forms of Peasant Resistance*, New Haven: Yale University Press.

SCOTT, REBECCA J. (1985) *Slave Emancipation in Cuba: The Transition to Free Labor, 1860–99*, Princeton: Princeton University Press.

SCOTT, WILLIAM R. (1993) *The Sons of Sheba's Race: African-Americans and the Italo-Ethiopian War, 1935–41*, Bloomington: Indiana University Press.

SEAGA, EDWARD (1969) 'Revival Cults in Jamaica', *Jamaica Journal*, 3, 2, pp.3–13.

SEALANDER, JUDITH (1983) *As Minority Becomes Majority: Federal Reaction to the Phenomenon of Women in the Work Force, 1920–63*, Westport: Greenwood Press.

SEARLE, CHRIS (1983) *Grenada: The Struggle Against Destabilization*, London: Writers and Readers Publishing.

SEBASTIEN, RAPHAEL (1981) 'The Political Economy of Capitalism of Trinidad and Tobago: An Overview', *Tribune: A Journal of Socialist Thought*, 1, 1, pp.41–65.

SEDA, EDUARDO (1973) *Social Change and Personality in a Puerto Rican Agrarian Reform Community*, Evanston: Northwestern University Press.

SEDOC-DAHLBERG, BETTY (ed.) (1990) *The Dutch Caribbean: Prospects for Democracy*, New York: Gordon and Breach.

SEGRE, R., M. COYULA, and J. SCARPACI (1997) *Havana: Two Faces of the Antillean Metropolis*, New York and London: Wiley.

SÉJOUNEÉ, LAURETTE (1980) *La mujer Cubana en el Quehacer de la Historia*, Mexico City: Editorial Siglo XXI.

SENIOR, CLARENCE (1953) 'Migration and Puerto Rico: Population Problems', *Annals of the American Academy of Political and Social Science*, 285.

SERBÍN, ANDRÉS (ed.) (n.d.) *Venezuela y las relaciones internacionales en la cuenca del Caribe*, Caracas: Inst. Lat. de Invs. Soc.[ILDIS] & Asoc. Vene. de Ests. del Caribe [AVECA].

——, (1987) *Etnicidad, clase y nación en la cultura política del Caribe e habla inglesa*, Caracas: Biblioteca de la Academia Naciońal de la Historia.

——, (1996) *El ocaso de las islas: El Gran Caribe frente a los desafíos globales y regionales*, Caracas: Editorial Nueva Sociedad.

——, (1998) *Sunset Over the Islands: The Caribbean in an Age of Global and Regional Challenges*, New York: St Martin's Press.

SERBÍN, ANDRÉS and ANTHONY T. BRYAN (eds) (1991) *El Caribe Hacia el 2000*, Caracas: Editorial Nueva Sociedad.

SERBÍN, ANDRÉS and JOSEPH TULCHIN (eds) (1994) *El Caribe y Cuba en la posguerra fría*, Caracas: INVESP/Ed. Nueva Sociedad.

SEVERIYA, MARITZA (1982) 'The Problem of Unmarried Women in the Netherlands Antilles' in *Women and Social Production in the Caribbean*, Final Report of Seminar sponsored by the Institute of Development Studies, University of Sussex, and CEREP, Río Pedras.

SHAHABUDDEEN, M. (1983) *From Plantocracy to Nationalisation: A Profile of Sugar in Guyana*, Georgetown: University of Guyana; reprinted 1984.

SHERLOCK, PHILIP (1980) *Norman Manley*, London: Macmillan.

SHERLOCK, PHILIP and HAZEL BENNETT (1998) *The Story of the Jamaican People*, Kingston: Ian Randle.

SHRYOCK, HENRY S. and JACOB SIEGEL (1975) *The Methods and Materials of Demography*, Washington, DC: Government Printing Office.

SIEBERG, HERWARD (1985) *Colonial Development: Die Grundlegung moderner Entwicklungspolitik durch Großbritannien, 1919–49*, Stuttgart: Beiträge zur Kolonial- und Überseegeschichte, Bd. 31.

SIGURDSSON, H. (1982) 'In the Volcano', *Natural History*, 91, no.3, pp.60–6, 68.

Silén, Juan Angel (1970) *Hacia una visión positiva del Puertorriqeño*, Río Piedras, trans. Cedric Belfrage and republished as *We, the Puerto Rican People,* New York: Monthly Review Press, 1971.

Silverman, Bertram (ed.) (1971) *Man and Socialism in Cuba: The Great Debate,* New York: Athenaeum Press.

Silvestrini, Blanca G. (1979) *Los trabajadores puertorriqueños y el Partido Socialista, 1932–40,* Río Piedras: Editorial Universitaria.

——, (1983a) 'La política de salud pública de los Estados Unidos en Puerto Rico, 1898–1913: Consecuencias en el proceso de americanización' in Blanca G. Silvestrini (ed.) *Politics, Society and Culture in the Caribbean,* Río Piedras: Universidad de Puerto Rico.

——, (ed.) (1983b) *Politics, Society and Culture in the Caribbean: Selected Papers of the XIV Conference of Caribbean Historians,* Río Piedras: Universidad of Puerto Rico.

Silvestrini, Blanca G. and María D. Luque de Sánchez (1987) *Historia de Puerto Rico: trayectoria de un pueblo,* San Juan: Cultura Puertorriqueña; reprinted San Juan: Editorial La Biblioteca, 1988; San Juan: Ediciones Cultural Panamericana, 1992.

Simey, T. S. (1946) *Welfare and Planning in the West Indies*, Oxford: Clarendon Press.

Simnett, W. E. (1940–1) 'Britain's Colonies in the War', *Foreign Affairs,* 19, pp.655–64.

Simons, Geoff (1996) *Cuba: From Conquistador to Castro*, New York: St. Martin's Press.

Simpson, George Eaton (1965) *Cults in Trinidad*, Río Piedras: Institute of Caribbean Studies, University of Puerto Rico.

——, (1978) *Black Religions in the New World*, New York: Columbia University Press.

Sims, Harold (1992) 'Cuba' in Leslie Bethell and Ian Roxborough (eds) *Latin America between the Second World War and the Cold War, 1944–8*, Cambridge: Cambridge University Press.

Singh, H. P. (1962) 'The Hammer and the Anvil: The Indian Case for Proportional Representation in Trinidad and Tobago'; reprinted in H. P. Singh, *The Indian Struggle for Justice and Equality Against Black Racism in Trinidad and Tobago (1956–62)* Couva, Trinidad: Indian Review Press.

——, (1993) *The Indian Struggle for Justice and Equality Against Black Racism in Trinidad and Tobago (1956–62)* Couva, Trinidad: Indian Review Press.

Singh, Kelvin (1994) *Race and Class Struggles in a Colonial State: Trinidad 1917–45,* Mona: The Press, UWI.

——, (1996) 'Conflict and Collaboration: Tradition and Modernizing Indo-Trinidadian Elites (1917–56)', *Nieuwe West-Indische Gids/New West Indian Guide,* 70, 3 & 4, pp.229–53.

Singh, Susheela (1984) *Guyana, Jamaica and Trinidad and Tobago: Socio-Economic Differentials in Cumulative Fertility,* WFS Scientific Reports, no.57, Voorburg, the Netherlands: International Statistical Institute.

Singham, A. W. (1968) *The Hero and the Crowd in a Colonial Polity,* New Haven: Yale University Press.

SINHA, D. P. (1995) *Food, Nutrition and Health in the Caribbean,* Kingston: Caribbean Food and Nutrition Institute.

SINNETTE, ELINOR DESVERNEY (1989) *Arthur Alfonso Schomburg: Black Bibliophile and Collector, A Biography,* New York: New York Public Library and Wayne State University Press.

SIRES, RONALD (1957) 'Government in the British West Indies: An Outline', *Social and Economic Studies,* 6, pp.109–32.

SMELSER, NEIL J. (1959) *Social Change in the Industrial Revolution: an Application of Theory to the Lancashire Cotton Industry, 1770–1840,* London: Routledge and Kegan Paul.

SMERALDA-AMON, JULIETTE (1996) *La question de l'immigration Indienne dans son environment socio-economique Martiniquais, 1848–1900,* Paris: Éditions L'Harmattan.

SMITH, KEITH (1993) 'Ah, That Hulsie [Bhaggan]', *Trinidad Express,* 24 November 1993.

SMITH, LOIS and ALFRED PADULA (1996) *Sex and Revolution: Women in Socialist Cuba,* New York: Oxford University Press.

SMITH, M. G. (1962a) *Kinship and Community in Carriacou,* New Haven: Yale University Press.

——, (1962b) *West Indian Family Structure,* Seattle: University of Washington Press.

——, (1965) *The Plural Society in the British West Indies,* Berkeley, University of California Press.

——, (1966) 'Introduction' in Edith Clarke, *My Mother Who Fathered Me: A Study of the Family in Three Selected Communities in Jamaica;* 2nd edn, London: G. Allen & Unwin.

——, (1989) *Poverty in Jamaica,* Mona: Institute of Social and Economic Research, UWI.

——, (1991) *Pluralism, Politics and Ideology in the Creole Caribbean,* New York: Research Institute for the Study of Man.

SMITH, M. G., ROY AUGIER and REX NETTLEFORD (1960) *The Rastafari Movement in Kingston,* Mona: Institute of Social and Economic Research, UWI.

SMITH, RAYMOND T. (1956) *The Negro Family in British Guiana: Family Structure and Social Status in the Villages,* London: Routledge & Kegan Paul.

——, (1967) 'Social Stratification, Cultural Pluralism and Integration in West Indian Societies' in Sybil Lewis and Thomas G. Mathews (eds) *Caribbean Integration: Papers on Social, Political and Economic Integration,* Río Piedras: Institute of Caribbean Studies, University of Puerto Rico.

——, (1982) 'Family, Social Change and Social Policy in the West Indies', *Nieuwe West-Indische Gids/New West Indian Guide,* 56, nos. 3/4, pp.111–42.

——, (ed.) (1984) *Kinship Ideology and Practice in Latin America,* Chapel Hill: University of North Carolina Press.

——, (1988) *Kinship and Class in the West Indies: A Genealogical Study of Jamaica and Guyana,* Cambridge: Cambridge University Press.

SMITH, ROBERT FREEMAN (ed.) (1966) *Background to Revolution: The Development of Modern Cuba,* New York: Alfred A. Knopf.

SNYDER, LOUIS L. (1962) *The Imperialism Reader,* New York: Van Nostrand.

SOLÁ, MERCEDES (1922) *Feminismo*, San Juan: Cantero, Fernández.

SOLCHAGA, CARLOS (1996–7) 'Cuba: perspectivas económicas', *Encuentro de la cultura cubana*, 3, pp.43–53.

SOLIS, JOSÉ (1994) *Public School Reform in Puerto Rico*, London: Greenwood Press.

SOLOMON, PATRICK (1981) *Solomon: An Autobiography*, Port of Spain: Imprint Caribbean.

South America, Central America and the Caribbean (1995), 5th edn, London: Europa Publications.

SPALDING, HOBART A., JR. (1977) *Organized Labor in Latin America: Historical Case Studies of Workers in Dependent Societies*, New York: New York University Press.

SPENCER, BALDWIN (1978) 'Wage Differentiation in Antigua' in International Labour Organisation, *Record of Proceedings of, and Documents Submitted to ILO/DANDRA Regional Seminar: Wage Differentiation in English-Speaking Countries*, Geneva: ILO.

SPOTTSWOOD, RICHARD K. (ed.) (1987) *Where Was Butler? A Calypso Documentary from Trinidad*, El Cerrito, California: Folklyric Records.

SQUITIERI, T. (1993) 'Time for Praying, Packing. Fear Rules Haiti Once Again', *USA Today*, 18 October, p.1–A.

Staff, Social Sciences Research Center, College of Social Sciences, University of Puerto Rico (1956) 'Comparative Analysis of Regional Subcultures' in Julian H. Steward *et al.*, *The People of Puerto Rico: A Study in Social Anthropology*, Urbana: University of Illinois Press; reprinted Ithaca: Cornell University Press, 1972.

STANNARD, HAROLD (1945) 'The British West Indies', in Rita Hinden (ed.) *Fabian Colonial Essays*, London: G. Allen and Unwin.

STARKEY, OTIS P. (1939) *The Economic Geography of Barbados*, New York: Columbia University Press.

STEADY, FILOMENA CHIOMA (ed.) (1981) *The Black Woman Cross-Culturally*, Cambridge, Massachusetts: Schenkman.

STEVENS-ARROYO, ANTHONY M. and ANDRES I. PÉREZ Y MENA (1995) *Enigmatic Powers: Syncretism with African and Indigenous Peoples' Religions among Latinos*, New York: Bildner Center for Western Hemisphere Studies.

STEWARD, JULIAN H. *et al.* (1956) *The People of Puerto Rico: A Study in Social Anthropology*, Urbana: University of Illinois Press; reprinted Ithaca: Cornell University Press, 1972.

STINNER, WILLIAM F., KLAUS DE ALBUQUERQUE and ROY S. BRYCE-LAPORTE (eds) (1982) *Return Migration and Remittances: Developing a Caribbean Perspective*, Washington, DC: Smithsonian Institution.

STOCKDALE, SIR FRANK (1946) *The Work of the Caribbean Commission: Report of the AACC for the Year 1945*, Washington, DC: Caribbean Commission.

——, (1947) 'The Work of the Caribbean Commission', *International Affairs*, 23, pp.213–21.

STOKES, ERIC (1966) 'Malawi Political Systems and the Introduction of Colonial Rule, 1891–96' in E. Stokes and R. Brown (eds) *The Zambesian Past: Studies in Central African History*, Manchester: Manchester University Press.

STOKES, ERIC and R. BROWN (eds) (1966) *The Zambesian Past: Studies in Central African History*, Manchester: Manchester University Press.

STONE, CARL (1984) *Electoral Behaviour and Public Opinion in Jamaica*, Mona: Institute of Social and Economic Research, UWI.

——, (1986) *Class, State, and Democracy in Jamaica*, New York: Praeger.

STONER, K. LYNN (1991) *From the House to the Streets: The Cuban Woman's Movement for Legal Reform*, Durham, North Carolina: Duke University Press.

STUBBS, JEAN (1989a) *Tabaco en la periferia*, Havana: Casa de las Américas.

——, (1989b) *Cuba: The Test of Time*, London: Latin American Bureau.

——, (1993) 'Women and Cuban Smallholder Agriculture in Transition' in Janet H. Momsen (ed.) *Women and Change in the Caribbean*, Kingston: Ian Randle.

——, (1999) 'Gender in Caribbean History' in B. W. Higman (ed.) *General History of the Caribbean*, vol. VI, Oxford: UNESCO Publishing/Macmillan Caribbean.

STYCOS, MAYONE (1955) *Family and Fertility in Puerto Rico: A Study of the Lower Income Groups*, New York: Columbia University Press.

SUÁREZ OQUENDO, AMELIA and CARMEN MORA HERNÁNDEZ (1995) 'La participación de la mujer en Cuba: balance y perspectivas', *Caribbean Studies*, 28, 1, pp.147–62.

SUNKEL, OSVALDO and PEDRO PAZ (1970) *El subdesarrollo latinoamericano y la teoría del desarrollo*, Mexico City: Editorial Siglo XXI.

SUNSHINE, CATHERINE A. (1988) *The Caribbean: Survival, Struggle and Sovereignty*, Washington, DC: EPICA.

SUTTON, CONSTANCE R. and ELSA M. CHANEY (eds) (1987) *Caribbean Life in New York City: Sociocultural Dimensions*, New York: Center for Migration Studies.

SUTTON, CONSTANCE R. and SUSAN MAKIESKY-BARROW (1981) 'Social Inequality and Sexual Status in Barbados' in Filomena Chioma Steady (ed.) *The Black Woman Cross-Culturally*, Cambridge, Massachusetts: Schenkman

SUTTON, PAUL (ed.) (1991) *Europe and the Caribbean*, London: Macmillan.

——, (1997) 'The Banana Regime of the European Union, the Caribbean, and Latin America', *Journal of Interamerican Studies and World Affairs*, 39, 25–36.

SWAN, HARRY (1978) 'The Nineteen Twenties: A Decade of Intellectual Change in Cuba', *Revista Interamericana*, 8, 2, pp.275–88.

SYLVAIN, BENITO (1905) 'The Pan-African Conference' in *Du Sort des Indigènes dans les Colonies d'Exploitation*, Paris: L. Boyer, 1905, trans.Tony Martin, in Tony Martin, *The Pan-African Connection*, Dover, Massachusetts: Majority Press, 1984.

SYLVAIN BOUCHERAEAU, MADELEINE (1957) *Haïti et ses femmes*, Port-au-Prince: Les Presses Libres; Chapel Hill: University of North Carolina Press.

SZASZ, THOMAS S. (1970) *The Manufacture of Madness*, New York: Harper & Row.

TANG NAIN, GEMMA (1995) 'The Impact of Prevalent Economic Strategies on Women's Lives in the English-Speaking Caribbean: Women's Responses and Community Projects of Economic Development' in Alice Colón and Ana M. Fabián (eds) *Mujeres en el Caribe: Desarrollo, paz y movimientos comunitarios*, Río Piedras: Instituto de Estudios del Caribe and CERES, Centro de Investigaciones Sociales, Universidad de Puerto Rico.

TANSILL, CHARLES CALLAN (1968) *The Purchase of the Danish West Indies,* New York: Greenwood Press; first published by Johns Hopkins University Press, 1932.

TARDIEU, CHARLES (1990) *L'Éducation en Haïti, de la période coloniale à nos jours,* Port-au-Prince: Henri Deschamps.

TAULÉ, GINNY (1993) 'Análisis genérico del trabajo secretarial en Santo Domingo', *Género y Sociedad,* 1, 1, pp.74–5.

TAUSSIG, CHARLES W. (1945–6) 'A Four Power Program in the Caribbean', *Foreign Affairs,* 24, pp.699–710.

TAYLOR, FRANK FONDA (1993) *To Hell with Paradise: A History of the Jamaica Tourist Industry,* Pittsburgh: University of Pittsburgh Press.

TAYLOR, JOHN (1824) *Negro Emancipation and West Indian Independence: The True Interest of Great Britain,* Liverpool: Printed by R. Rockliff.

TAYLOR, PHILIP B. (1969) 'Hemisphere Defense in World War II', *Current History,* 56, pp.333–9.

Ten Years of Caricom (1984) Washington, DC: Inter-American Development Bank.

THÉBAUD, SCHILLER (1967) 'L'évolution de la structure agraire d'Haïti de 1804 à nos jours', thesis for the licenciature, University of Paris.

THOMAS, C. Y. (1984) *The Rise of the Authoritarian State in Peripheral Societies,* New York: Monthly Review Press.

——, (1988) *The Poor and the Powerless: Economic Policy and Change in the Caribbean,* New York: Monthly Review Press.

THOMAS, HUGH (1971) *Cuba: The Pursuit of Freedom,* New York: Harper & Row.

THOMAS, ROY D. (ed.) (1987) *The Trinidad Labour Riots of 1937,* St Augustine: Extra-Mural Studies Unit, UWI.

——, (1989) *The Development of Labour Law in Trinidad and Tobago,* Wellesley, Massachusetts: Calaloux Publications.

THOMAS-BAILEY, M. (2001) 'The Black Press in Trinidad 1850–1955', M. Phil. thesis, UWI, St Augustine.

THOMAS-HOPE, ELIZABETH M. (1992) *Explanation in Caribbean Migration: Perception and the Image: Jamaica, Barbados, St Vincent,* London: Macmillan Caribbean.

——, (1995) 'Island Systems and the Paradox of Freedom: Migration in the Post-Emancipation Leeward Islands' in K. F. Olwig, (ed.) *Small Islands, Large Questions: Society, Culture and Resistance in the Post-Emancipation Caribbean,* London: Frank Cass.

THOMPSON, DUDLEY (1993) *From Kingston to Kenya: The Making of a Pan-Africanist Lawyer,* Dover, Massachusetts: Majority Press.

TILLERY, TYRONE (1992) *Claude McKay: A Black Poet's Struggle for Identity,* Amherst: University of Massachusetts Press.

TINKER, HUGH (1974) *A New System of Slavery: The Export of Indian Labour Overseas, 1830–1920,* London: Oxford University Press.

——, (1982) 'British Policy Towards Indian Identity' in Bridget Brereton and Winston Dookeran (eds) *East Indians in the Caribbean,* Millwood, NY: Kraus.

TJOA, TWIE (1995) 'The Political Participation of Women in Suriname from a Herstorical Perspective', *Tijdsschrift voor Maatschappijwetenschappen,* 2, 2.

TOLENTINO DIPP, HUGO (1992) *Raza e historia en Santo Domingo,* Santo Domingo: Fondo de Cultura Dominicana.

TOULIS, NICOLE RODRIQUEZ (1997) *Believing Identity: Pentecostalism and the Mediation of Jamaican Ethnicity and Gender in England,* Oxford: Berg.

'Tourism and the sex-trade project' (1997) *CAFRA News,* 11, 1–2, pp.16–7.

TRASK, DAVID F. (1981) *The War with Spain in 1898,* New York: Macmillan.

Treaty Establishing the Caribbean Community (1973) Georgetown: Caribbean Community Secretariat.

Trinidad & Tobago, Parliament (1965) *Act No. 8 of 1965.*

Trinidad Under Siege: The Muslimeen Uprising (1990) Port of Spain: Trinidad Express Newspapers.

TROUILLOT, MICHEL-ROLPH (1988) *Peasants and Capital: Dominica in the World Economy,* Baltimore: Johns Hopkins University Press.

——, (1990) *Haiti, State Against Nation: The Origins and Legacy of Duvalierism,* New York: Monthly Review Press.

——, (1992) 'The Caribbean Region: An Open Frontier in Anthropological Theory', *Annual Reviews in Anthropology,* 21, pp.19–42.

TUGWELL, REXFORD GUY (1947) *The Stricken Land: The Story of Puerto Rico,* New York: Doubleday; reprinted New York: Greenwood, 1977.

——, (1958) 'The Caribbean Commission: Notes on its Beginnings' in A. Curtis Wilgus (ed.) *The Caribbean: British, Dutch, French, United States,* Gainesville: University of Florida Press.

TULCHIN, JOSEPH, ANDRÉS SERBÍN and RAFAEL HERNÁNDEZ (eds) (1997) *Cuba and the Caribbean: Regional Issues and Trends in the Post-Cold War Era,* Wilmington: Scholarly Books.

TUMIN, MELVIN (1961) *Social Class and Social Change in Puerto Rico,* Princeton: Princeton University Press.

TURNER, MARY (ed.) (1995) *From Chattel Slaves to Wage Slaves,* Kingston: Ian Randle.

TURNER, TREVOR (1979a) 'Objectives and Provisions for Agricultural Education: The Case of Colonial Jamaica 1867–1920' in Vincent D'Oyley and Reginald Murray (eds), *Development and Disillusion in Third World Education, with Emphasis on Jamaica,* Toronto: Ontario Institute of Studies in Education.

——, (1979b) 'Objectives and Provisions for Trade and Technical Training: The Case of Colonial Jamaica 1867–1920' in Vincent D'Oyley and Reginald Murray (eds), *Development and Disillusion in Third World Education, with Emphasis on Jamaica,* Toronto: Ontario Institute of Studies in Education.

TURNIER, ALAIN (1955) *Les États Unis et le marché haïtien,* Washington, DC.

United Fruit Co: Un caso de dominio imperialista en Cuba (various authors, 1976), Havana: Editorial de Ciencias Sociales.

United Nations (1956) *Demographic Yearbook, 1956,* New York: United Nations Publications.

——, (1970–6) *Statistical Yearbooks,* New York: United Nations Publications.

——, (1991a) 'Situación comparativa de la mujer en algunos paises del Caribe según determinados parámetros sociales, económicos, demográficos y legales', New York: United Nations, 29 April.

——, (1991b) *The World's Women 1970–1990: Trends and Statistics*, New York: United Nations.

——, (1993) *Population, Social Equity and Changing Production Patterns*, Santiago: ECLAC and Latin American Demography Center.

——, (1995a) *The United Nations and the Advancement of Women, 1945–96*, The UN Blue Book Series, vol. II, New York: United Nations Department of Public Information.

——, (1995b) *Situación de las mujeres en el mundo, 1995: Tendencias y estadísticas*, New York: United Nations.

——, (1995c) *Las mujeres en una economía mundial en evolución*, New York: United Nations.

——, (1995d) *Women in a Changing Global Economy*, New York: United Nations Department for Policy Coordination and Sustainable Development.

United Nations, Comisión Económica Para America Latina (CEPAL) (1980) *Anuario Estadístico de America Latina y el Caribe*, Santiago: United Nations.

——, (1984) 'Informe de la reunión regional de América Latina y el Caribe preparatoria para la Conferencia Mundial para el Examen y la Evaluación de los logros del Decenio de las Naciones Unidas para la Mujer: Igualdad, Desarrollo y Paz', Havana, Cuba, 19–23 November.

——, (1986) *El Decenio de la Mujer en el escenario Latinoamericano: realidades y perspectivas*, Santiago: United Nations.

——, (1992) *Anuario Estadístico de America Latina y el Caribe*, Santiago: United Nations.

——, (1994) *Anuario Estadístico de America Latina y el Caribe*, Santiago: United Nations.

——, (1995) *Patrones reproductivos, estructura familiar y trabajo feminino en América Latina y el Caribe*, Santiago: United Nations.

United Nations, Cepalac, Fondo Naciones Unidas Para La Mujer (1995) 'Programa de Acción Regional para las Mujeres de América Latina y el Caribe 1995–2001', Santiago: United Nations.

United Nations Charter (1945) Colonies and Trust Territories, 'Declaration Regarding Non-self-governing Territories'. New York: United Nations.

United Nations, Department of Economic and Social Affairs (1975) *Status of Women and Family Planning*, Report of the Special Rapporteur appointed by the Economic and Social Council under Resolution 1326 (XLIV), New York: United Nations.

United Nations, Department of Economic and Social Development (1992) *Abortion Policies: A Global Review*, 1, New York: United Nations.

United Nations, ECLAC, CARICOM, UNIFEM (1994) 'Achieving Social Justice, Equity and Development: a Review of the Status of Women of the Caribbean Subregion in Preparation for the Fourth World Conference on Women, 1995', Working Document, Subregional Conference Preparatory to the Fourth World Conference on Women, Curaçao, Netherlands Antilles, 28–9 June.

United Nations, ECLAC, UNIFEM (1994) 'Platform for Action Presented by the NGOs of the Caribbean Subregion' in Caribbean Subregional Preparatory Conference to the Fourth World Conference on Women, 1995, Curaçao, 27–9 June.

United Nations, ECOSOC, ECLAC (1984) 'Report of the Group of Experts on Operational Strategies for the Advancement of Women up to the Year 2000'.

United Nations. Fondo de Población de las Naciones Unidas, Dirección General de Promoción de la Mujer, Asociación Dominicana pro Bienestar de la Familia (1997) *Ley 24–97 Contra la violencia intrafamiliar, 1997.*

United States Central Intelligence Agency (USCIA) (1991) *World Fact Book,* Washington, DC: CIA.

UYA, OKON E. (ed.). (1971) *Black Brotherhood: Afro-Americans and Africa,* Lexington: D. C. Heath.

VALDÉZ, JULIO CARRANZA, LUIS GUITIÉRREZ URDANETA and PEDRO MONREAL GONZÁLEZ (1995) *Cuba: la restructuración de la economía: una propuesta para el debate,* Havana: Editorial de Ciencias Sociales.

VALDEZ, TERESA, ENRIQUE GOMAREZ, ESTHER VELIZ and CAROLINA AGUILAR (eds) (1992) *Mujeres Latinoamericanas en Cifras, Cuba,* Santiago: Instituto de la Mujer, Ministerio de Asuntos Sociales de España y Facultad Latinoanericana de Ciencias Sociales.

VAN ALSTYNE, RICHARD W. (1952) *American Crisis Diplomacy: The Quest for Collective Security, 1918–52,* Stanford: Stanford University Press.

VAN VELZEN, H. U. E. THODEN (1995), 'African-American Worldviews in the Caribbean' in Barry Chevannes (ed.), *Rastafari and Other African-Caribbean Worldviews,* Oxford: Macmillan Caribbean.

VAN WETERING, INEKE (1999) 'Cultural Encounters in the Diaspora: Suriname Creole Religion in the New World' in John W. Pulis (ed.), *Religion, Diaspora, and Cultural Identity: A Reader in the Anglophone Caribbean*, Amsterdam: Gordon and Breach.

VAN WETERING, WILHELMINA (1990) 'Dissonance in Discourse: The Politics of Afro-Surinamese Culture in the Netherlands' in Gary Brana-Shute (ed.) *Resistance and Rebellion in Suriname,* Williamsburg, Virginia: College of William and Mary.

——, (1995) 'Demon in a Garbage Chute: Surinamese Creole Women's Discourse on Possession and Therapy' in Barry Chevannes (ed.), *Rastafari and Other African-Caribbean Worldviews,* Oxford: Macmillan Caribbean.

VASSELL, LINNETTE (1998) 'Colonial Gender Policy in Jamaica, 1865–1945' in Brian L. Moore and Swithin R. Wilmot (eds) *Before and After 1865,* Kingston: Ian Randle.

VAUGHAN, H. A. (1985) *Sandy Lane and Other Poems,* Bridgetown: Bim Magazine.

VÁZQUEZ CALZADA, JOSÉ L. (1988) *La población de Puerto Rico y su trayectoria histórica,* Río Piedras: Raga Offset Printing Service.

VEESER, CYRUS (1996) 'Remapping the Caribbean: Private Investment in the United States Intervention in the Dominican Republic, 1890–1908', Ph.D. dissertation, Columbia University.

VEGA, ANA LYDIA (1989) 'De cómo fue descubierto el Caribe y no precisamente por Cristobal Colón', *Diálogo,* mayo.

VELIZ, CLAUDIO (ed.) (1968) *Latin America and the Caribbean: A Handbook,* London: Blond.

VERTON, PETER C. (1990a) 'Politics and Government in Curaçao' in Betty Sedoc-Dahlberg (ed.) *The Dutch Caribbean: Prospects for Democracy,* New York: Gordon and Breach.

——, (1990b) 'The Dutch Decolonization: Independence for the Netherlands Antilles?' in Betty Sedoc-Dahlberg (ed.) *The Dutch Caribbean: Prospects for Democracy,* New York: Gordon and Breach.

VERTOVEC, STEVEN (1992) *Hindu Trinidad: Religion, Ethnicity and Socio-Economic Change,* London: Macmillan Caribbean.

VIBERT, PAUL (1895) *La république d'Haïti: son présent, son avenir économique,* Paris: Berger-Leverault.

VICENTE, ESTHER (1987) 'Las mujeres y el cambio en la norma jurídica' in Yamila Azize (ed.) *La mujer en Puerto Rico,* Río Piedras: Ediciones Huracán.

VON ALBERTINI, RUDOLF (1965) 'Die USA und die Kolonialfrage, 1917–45', *Vierteljahreshefte für Zeitgeschichte,* 13, pp.1–13.

——, (1969) 'The Impact of the Two World Wars on the Decline of Colonialism', *Journal of Contemporary History,* 4, no.1.

WAGENHEIM, KAL (ed.) (1988) *The Puerto Ricans: A Documentary History,* 2nd edn, Princeton, New Jersey: Marcus Wiener.

WALCOTT, DEREK (1974) 'The Muse of History – An Essay' in Orde Coombs (ed.) *Is Massa Day Dead? Black Moods in the Caribbean,* Garden City, NY: New Anchor Press.

——, (1993) *The Antilles: Fragments of Epic Memory,* Nobel Lecture, New York: Farrar, Straus and Giroux.

WALLACE, ELISABETH (1977) *The British Caribbean: From the Decline of Colonialism to the End of Federation,* Toronto: University of Toronto Press.

WALLERSTEIN, IMMANUEL (1980) *The Modern World-System II: Mercantilism and the Consolidation of the European World-Economy, 1600–1750,* New York: Academic Press.

WALTERS, BISHOP ALEXANDER (1914) *My Life and Work,* New York.

WARNER-LEWIS, MAUREEN (1977) *The Nkuya: Spirit Messengers of the Kumina,* Mona: Savacou Publications.

——, (1991) *Guinea's Other Suns,* Dover, Massachusetts: Majority Press.

WASMER, MIGUEL GUILLERMO (ed.) (1977) *La mujer en Cuba socialista,* Publicación Oficial del Ministerio de Justicia de Cuba, Havana: Empresa Editorial Orbe.

WATKINS, TOM H. (1993) *The Great Depression: America in the 1930s,* Boston: Little Brown.

WATKINS-OWENS, IRMA (1996) *Blood Relations: Caribbean Immigrants and the Harlem Community, 1900–30,* Bloomington: Indiana University Press.

WATSON, HILBOURNE A. (ed.) (1994) *The Caribbean in the Global Political Economy,* Boulder and London: Lynne Rienner.

WATT, D. C. (1963) 'American Strategic Interest and Anxieties in the West Indies: An Historical Examination', *Journal of Royal United Service Institution,* 108, pp.224–32.

WATTS, DAVID (1987) *The West Indies: Patterns of Development, Culture, and Environmental Change since 1492,* Cambridge: Cambridge University Press.

WEBB, BARBARA J. (1992) *Myth and History in Caribbean Fiction: Alejo Carpentier, Wilson Harris, and Edouard Glissant,* Amherst: University of Massachusetts Press.

WEIL, C. and J. SCARPACI (eds) (1992) *Health and Health Care in Latin America and the Caribbean During the Lost Decade,* Minneapolis: University of Minnesota, Prisma Institute.

WEIL, THOMAS E. (1982) *Haiti,* Washington, DC: The American University.

WEISBORD, ROBERT G. (1970) 'British West Indian Reaction to the Italian-Ethiopian War: An Episode in Pan-Africanism', *Caribbean Studies,* X, 1, 1970, pp.34–41.

WEISSKOFF, RICHARD (1985) *Factories and Food Stamps: The Puerto Rico Model of Development,* Baltimore: Johns Hopkins University Press.

WEISSMAN, JEAN (1995) 'Transformations in the Lives of Former Domestic Workers in Cuba'. Paper presented at the XIX LASA Congress, Washington DC.

WEKKER, GLORIA (1993) 'Mati-ism and Black Lesbianism: Two Idealtypical Expressions of Female Homosexuality in Black Communities of the Diaspora' *Journal of Homosexuality,* 24, 3 & 4, pp.11–24.

——, (1998) 'Of Sex and Silences: Methodological Considerations on Sex Research in Paramaribo, Suriname', *Thamyris,* 5, 1, pp.105–29.

WELLES, SUMNER (1944) *The Time for Decision,* New York: Harper.

——, (1947–8) 'Intervention and Interventions', *Foreign Affairs,* 26, pp.116–33.

——, (1928) *Naboth's Vineyard: The Dominican Republic, 1844–1924,* 2 vols, New York: Savile Books; reprinted 1966.

WELLS, DIANA (1998) 'Re-Dying the Cloth: The Women's Political Platform and Trinidad and Tobago's General Election of 1995', *Identities,* 5, 4.

WENDEL, T. and M. JAMAIL (1997) 'Baseball in Castro's Cuba', *USA Today Baseball Weekly,* 29 January–4 February, pp.20–4.

West India Royal Commission Report (1945) ([1938–9]; Chairman: Lord Moyne), London: HMSO.

——, (1940) *Recommendations,* Chairman: Lord Moyne, London: HMSO.

West Indian Commission (1992) *Time For Action: Report of the West Indian Commission,* 2nd edn, 1993, Mona: The Press, UWI.

WESTERN, JOHN (1992) *A Passage to England: Barbadian Londoners Speak of Home,* Minneapolis: University of Minnesota Press.

WHITE, AVERILLE (1986) 'Profiles: Women in the Caribbean Project', *Social and Economic Studies,* 35, no.2, pp.59–81.

WHITE, P. T. (1989) 'Coca', *National Geographic Magazine,* 175 (January), pp.3–47.

WIARDA, HOWARD J. and MICHAEL J. KRYZANEK (1982) *The Dominican Republic: A Caribbean Crucible,* Boulder: Westview Press.

WICKER, E. R. (1958) 'Colonial Development and Welfare, 1929–57: The Evolution of a Policy', *Social and Economic Studies* 7, pp.170–92.

WILEY, J. (1997) 'Dominica's Economic Diversification: Microstates in a Neoliberal Era?' in T. Klak (ed.) *Globalization and Neoliberalism: The Caribbean Context*, Lanham, Maryland: Rowman and Littlefield.

WILGUS, A. C. (ed.) (1958) *The Caribbean: British, Dutch, French, United States*, Gainesville: University of Florida Press.

WILKINSON, ALEC (1989) *Big Sugar: Seasons in the Cane Fields of Florida*, New York: Alfred A. Knopf.

WILKINSON, BERT (1997) 'Caribbean-Crime: Don't Blame Deportees Says Human Rights Body', Inter Press Service, Global Information Network, 12 June.

WILLIAMS, ERIC (1942a) *The Negro in the Caribbean*, Washington, DC: Associates in Negro Folk Education; reprinted Westport: Negro Universities Press, 1969.

——, (1942b) 'Crossways of the Caribbean', *Survey Graphic*, 31 (Color: The unfinished business of democracy), New York: Survey Associates.

——, (1944) *Capitalism and Slavery*, Chapel Hill: University of North Carolina Press.

——, (1959) 'The Political Leader Considered as a Man of Culture', *Présence Africaine* (English edition), 24–5.

——, (1962) *History of the People of Trinidad and Tobago*, London: A. Deutsch; reprinted 1964, 1993.

——, (1963) 'International Perspectives for Trinidad and Tobago', *Le Monde Diplomatique*, August, 1963; reprinted in *Forged From the Love of Liberty: Selected Speeches of Dr. Eric Williams*, Port of Spain: Longman Caribbean, 1981.

——, (1969) *Inward Hunger: The Education of a Prime Minister*, Chicago: University of Chicago Press; reprinted Chicago: University of Chicago Press, 1971.

——, (1970) *From Columbus to Castro: The History of the Caribbean, 1492–1969*, New York: Harper & Row; reprinted 1971, 1984.

——, (1975) *The Threat to the Caribbean Community*, Port of Spain: People's National Movement.

——, (1981) *Forged From the Love of Liberty: Selected Speeches of Dr. Eric Williams*, Port of Spain: Longman Caribbean.

WILLIAMS, M. C. (1988) 'The Impact of 'Hurricane Allen' on the St Lucian Banana Industry', *Caribbean Geography*, 2, pp.164–72.

WILLIAMSON, CHILTON (1952) 'Britain's New Colonial Policy, 1940–51', *South Atlantic Quarterly*, 51, pp.399–473.

WILSON, S. M. (1995) 'Cricket in the Blood', *Natural History*, 104, 5, pp.58–65.

WINTERS, CLYDE-AHAMAD (1978) 'Muslims in Pluralistic Societies: The Case of the West Indies', *Al-Ittihad*,15, 3, pp.39–55.

WODDIS, JACK (1967) *Introduction to Neo-Colonialism: The New Imperialism in Asia, Africa and Latin America*, New York: International Publishers.

WOLF, ERIC (1966) *Peasants*, Englewood Cliffs, New Jersey: Prentice-Hall.

Women in the Caribbean Project (1986) *Social and Economic Studies*, vol. 35, 2 & 3 (special issue).

World Bank (1978) *The Commonwealth Caribbean*, Baltimore: Johns Hopkins University Press.

——, (1987) *Haiti: Public Expenditure Review*, A World Bank Country Study, Washington, DC: The World Bank.

——, (1993) *Caribbean Region – Current Economic Situation, Regional Issues, and Capital Flows 1992*, Washington, DC: World Bank.

——, (1994) 'Caribbean Region: Coping with Changes in the External Environment,' *LAC* 1281, April.

——, (1996) World Development Report, *From Plan to Market*, Oxford: Oxford University Press.

World Fact Book (1991) Washington, DC: Central Intelligence Agency.

WRONG, HUME (1923) *Government of the West Indies*, Oxford: Oxford University Press.

YELVINGTON, KEVIN A. (1993) 'Gender and Ethnicity at Work in a Trinidadian Factory' in Janet H. Momsen (ed.) *Women and Change in the Caribbean*, Kingston: Ian Randle.

——, (1999) 'The War in Ethiopia and Trinidad 1935–6' in Bridget Brereton and Kevin A. Yelvington (eds) *The Colonial Caribbean in Transition*, Mona: The Press, UWI.

YERXA, DONALD ALLEN (1984) *The United States Navy and the Caribbean Sea, 1914–41*, Ann Arbor: University of Michigan Press.

——, (1991) *Admirals and Empire: The United States Navy and the Caribbean, 1898–1945*, Columbia: University of South Carolina Press.

YOUNG, LOWELL L. (1973) 'Franklin D. Roosevelt and America's Islets: Acquisition of Territory in the Caribbean and the Pacific', *Historian* 35, pp.205–20.

ZAGARIS, BRUCE (1998) 'OECD Report on Harmful Tax Competition: Strategic Implications for Caribbean Offshore Jurisdictions', *Tax Notes International*, November.

ZANETTI, OSCAR and ALEJANDRO GARCÍA (1987) *Caminos para el azúcar*, Havana: Editorial de Ciencias Sociales.

——, (1998) *Sugar and Railroads: A Cuban History, 1837–1959*, Chapel Hill: University of North Carolina Press.

ZEIDENFELDT, ALEX P. (1950) 'Transportation in the Caribbean During World War II', *Interamerican Economic Affairs*, 4, pp.75–96.

ZELEZA, PAUL (1987) 'Trade Union Imperialism: American Labour, the ICFTU, and the Kenyan Labour Movement', *Social and Economic Studies*, 36, 2.

ZÉPHIR, CLORINDE (1995) 'Dictator Duvalier Orders the Torture of Journalist Yvonne Hakime Rimpel' in *Haitian Women between Repression and Democracy*, Port-au-Prince: ENFOFANM Editions.

ZIMBALIST, ANDREW (1985) 'Cuban Economic Planning: Organization and Performance' in Sandor Halebsky and John M. Kirk (eds) *Cuba: Twenty-Five Years of Revolution*, New York: Praeger.

ZOBEL, JOSEPH (1980) *Black Shack Alley*, trans. Keith Warner, London: Heinemann; originally published as *La rue cases-nègres*, 1950.

INDEX

www.ingramcontent.com/pod-product-compliance
Lightning Source LLC
LaVergne TN
LVHW010337220926
848484LV00004BB/918
9781403975935